Fodor's 2002

P9-AQC-817

Caribbean

Fodor's Travel Publications • New York, Toronto, London, Sydney, Auckland
www.fodors.com

CONTENTS

Destination Caribbean 5
Fodor's Choice 28

1 ANGUILLA 33

2 ANTIGUA 55

3 ARUBA 83

4 BARBADOS 111

5 BONAIRE 149

6 BRITISH VIRGIN ISLANDS 174
Tortola 178
Virgin Gorda 194
Jost Van Dyke 203
Peter Island 205
Anegada 206
Other British Virgin Islands 208

7 CAYMAN ISLANDS 216
Grand Cayman 217
Cayman Brac 232
Little Cayman 234

8 CURAÇAO 243

9 DOMINICA 270

10 DOMINICAN REPUBLIC 297

11 GRENADA 336

12 GUADELOUPE 368

13 JAMAICA 398

14 MARTINIQUE 439

15 PUERTO RICO 470

16 SABA 512

17 ST. BARTHÉLEMY 526

18 ST. EUSTATIUS 548

19 ST. KITTS AND NEVIS 560

20 ST. LUCIA 598

21 ST. MAARTEN/
   ST. MARTIN 633

22 ST. VINCENT AND
   THE GRENADINES 662

23 TRINIDAD AND
   TOBAGO 702

24 TURKS AND
   CAICOS ISLANDS 736

25 UNITED STATES
   VIRGIN ISLANDS 761
   St. Thomas 766
   St. Croix 796
   St. John 815

26 BACKGROUND AND
   ESSENTIALS 843
   Island Finder Chart 846–847
   Portrait of the Caribbean 848
   Smart Travel Tips A to Z 851

   INDEX 876

MAPS

ANGUILLA 36–37

ANTIGUA
AND BARBUDA 58–59

ARUBA 86–87

BARBADOS 114–115
Bridgetown 137

BONAIRE 152–153

BRITISH VIRGIN
ISLANDS 176–177
Tortola 180–181
Virgin Gorda 196–197

GRAND CAYMAN 218
Cayman Brac and
Little Cayman 219

CURAÇAO 246–247
Willemstad 259

DOMINICA 272–273

DOMINICAN
REPUBLIC 300–301
Santo Domingo 322

GRENADA
AND CARRIACOU
338–339

GUADELOUPE 370–371

JAMAICA 402–403
Montego Bay Lodging
and Dining 410

MARTINIQUE 442–443

PUERTO RICO
San Juan Lodging,
Dining, and Exploring 472
Puerto Rico 476–477
Old San Juan Exploring 497

SABA 514–515

ST. BARTHÉLEMY
530–531

ST. EUSTATIUS 550–551

ST. KITTS AND NEVIS
St. Kitts 562–563
Nevis 578–579

ST. LUCIA 600–601

ST. MAARTEN/
ST. MARTIN 636–637

ST. VINCENT AND
THE GRENADINES
St. Vincent 666–667
The Grenadines 678–679

TRINIDAD
AND TOBAGO
Trinidad 704–705
Tobago 718–719

TURKS AND
CAICOS ISLANDS
738–739

UNITED STATES
VIRGIN ISLANDS
762–763
St. Thomas 768–769
Charlotte Amalie 790
St. Croix 798–799
St. John 818–819

THE CARIBBEAN
844–845

Circled letters in text correspond to letters on the photographs.
For more information on the sights pictured, turn to the
indicated page number ⓐ⃗ on each image.

DESTINATION CARIBBEAN

Feel the soft sand beneath your feet on a perfect slip of a beach and you'll soon encounter all the wonderful Caribbean trappings that you may only dream about the rest of the year: a palm tree, a peak cloaked in rain forest, a fishing boat drifting on a multihued sea, a whiff of romance. Experience them again and again, and your heart is likely to skip a beat or two each time.

Paradisiacal beaches—366 of them, all lapped by deep blue water—suggest that this island  has never busied itself with anything more pressing than the pursuit of pleasure. But for much of the 18th and 19th centuries, Ⓐ**English Harbour** sheltered Britain's Caribbean fleet. From here such seamen as Lord Horatio Nelson and soon-to-be-king William III routed pirates and fended off other European colonists. These days, pleasure yachts bob where galleons anchored, and once-productive

ANTIGUA

sugar mills litter the interior hills with romantic ruins. History is among the many pleasures of Antigua.

ARUBA

Aruba is the island of the trade winds. The winds filled the sails of schooners that brought the island's Dutch settlers, whose European-style houses, imbued with Caribbean pastels, still grace the waterfront in the capital city of Ⓑ**Oranjestad.** On the west coast the steady breezes attract windsurfers to the shallow, richly colored waters. Winds are fiercer, even savage, on the north coast. Here, amid a landscape of cacti, rocky desert, and wind-bent divi-divi trees, they churn up the surf and over time create weird formations, such as the Ⓐ**Natural Bridge,** one of the island's most famous landmarks. Of course, those breezes also keep you pleasantly cool instead of equatorially hot.

Ⓐ▷ 138

Ⓑ▷ 121

In the center of this sunny sliver of land, densely planted sugarcane fields crowd the byways like a jungle. As you learn at the Ⓐ**Mount Gay Rum Visitors Centre,** it's the sweet sap inside each stalk that forms the rich, dark liquor for which the island is known.

BARBADOS

What pulls most vacationers this far south, though, is the warm Bajan hospitality, the British heritage, welcoming hotels like Ⓑ**Treasure Beach,** and the varied beaches: You'll find warm Caribbean strands with white sand and gentle surf, as well as magnificent Atlantic-pounded, cliff-edged shoreline. Most visitors experience Britain's legacy over tea, at dinnertime (when many a restaurant likes to see gentlemen in jackets and ladies in dresses), and on the playing field. Polo, soccer, horse racing, and rugby are national pastimes: See a cricket match at the Ⓒ**Kensington Oval** and you'll never forget it.

Ⓒ▷ 132

BONAIRE

A market in Ⓐ**Kralendijk** attracts hagglers who vie for produce brought in by boat from lusher islands. But nature holds sway over human pursuits on this scrubby, cactus-covered landfall. Divers come here from all over the world to swim among some of the most prized undersea treasures in the Caribbean: Knobby brain, giant brain, and other varieties of coral flourish in one of the world's largest reef systems. Above the water more than 15,000 flamingos—the biggest flock in the Western Hemisphere—wade in Ⓑ**Goto Meer** and other saltwater lagoons and flats. From afar you can admire the shy birds, rendered brightest pink by their diet of brine shrimp.

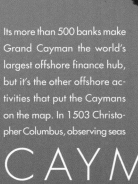

Its more than 500 banks make Grand Cayman the world's largest offshore finance hub, but it's the other offshore activities that put the Caymans on the map. In 1503 Christopher Columbus, observing seas

CAYMAN ISLANDS

teeming with turtles, endowed the islands with the Spanish name for the creatures, Las Tortugas. Pristine waters, breathtaking coral formations, and plentiful and exotic marine creatures (their well-being ensured by aggressive conservation efforts) beckon divers from around the world. Windsurfers, golfers, diners, and shoppers join them, drawn by the islands' mellow civility.

CURAÇAO

Determining that the glare of white houses aggravated his migraines, 19th-century Dutch governor-general "Froggie" Kikker ordered all the houses in Ⓐ**Willemstad,** Curaçao's capital, to be painted bright colors. Today the fancifully hued, strikingly gabled structures glimmering across Ⓑ**Santa Anna Bay** house shops purveying discounted luxury goods. Take in the Floating Market, where vendors sell tropical fruit from their schooners, or stroll along the waterfront, still crowded with fishing boats. Curaçao is known for its diversity, and its population mixes Latin, European, and African ancestries. Religious tolerance is another hallmark; the Western Hemisphere's oldest synagogue in use stands in the center of town. All people are welcome in Curaçao, and even tourists feel the warmth.

Ⓐ❯**258**

Ⓑ❯**259**

DOMINICA

Dominica is far removed from the concerns of the rest of the world. Wedged between Guadeloupe and Martinique, the Caribbean's Nature Island rewards those who discover it with such simple but awe-inspiring pleasures as a walk through elfin forests. The sound of a conch shell being blown as the fishermen come in and the sight of the crisp uniforms on children en route to school in the coastal village of La Plaine hint at the traditional, polite ways of the 70,000 islanders, some of whom are the last remaining Carib Indians. Surrounded by all the mountains, greenery, and waterfalls, you'll find out for yourself why the island's first inhabitants made this their refuge.

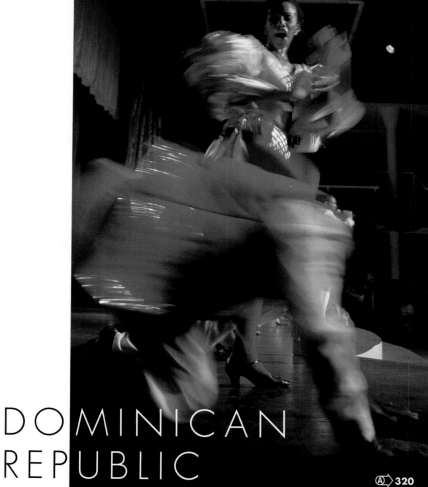

DOMINICAN REPUBLIC

Ⓐ 320

Ⓑ 309

Like the merengue seen on all the dance floors in Ⓐ**Santo Domingo,** the Dominican Republic is charismatic yet sensuous, pulsing with energy yet elegant. The charm of the people adds a special warmth: a gracious wave of greeting here, a hand-rolled cigar tapped with a flourish there, and the dazzling smiles just about everywhere will quickly beguile you. At Ⓑ**El Conuco** restaurant, your waiter might serve you a creation inspired by *nueva cocina Dominicana* and then, a minute later, break into rhythmic drumming in time to background music. And all the while the scent of frangipani surrounds you.

GRENADA

Vestiges of its turbulent past have all but disappeared from Grenada. These days the "Isle of Spice" busies itself cultivating nutmeg, cinnamon, cocoa, cloves, mace, and other spices. The only sounds in the fragrant air are the occasional abrupt call of a cuckoo in the lush rain forests, the crash of surf in the secluded coves, and the slow beat of a big drum dance, which accompanies the launch of a new craft on the boatbuilding islet of Ⓐ **Carriacou.** When the hand of man intrudes on the beach-ringed coast, it's with a gentle touch: resorts tend to be small and charming. In the capital of Ⓑ **St. George's,** a picturesque port of West Indian–style houses often called the most beautiful city in the Caribbean, no building can rise higher than one of the ubiquitous coconut palms. Stop here to buy some deliciously pungent spices to stock your pantry at home. Take a drive to the island's tiny villages, or go for a hike into the rain forest to a secluded waterfall.

Ⓐ▷ 359

Ⓑ▷ 357

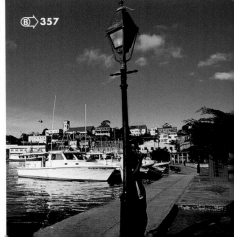

GUADELOUPE

A heady blend of French style
and tropical delights, butterfly-
shaped Guadeloupe is *actuelle-
ment* two islands divided by a
narrow channel: smaller, flatter,
and drier Grand-Terre (Large Land) and wetter and more mountainous Basse-Terre (Low Land). Sheltered by palms, the beaches
on both islands would be beguiling even without the presence
of a woman selling bananas and mangoes to hedonists who
come from afar to escape their cares. The creole fare at mealtimes and the scent of cigarette smoke at beachside cafés makes
Guadeloupe sometimes feel oddly like France itself.

JAMAICA

Chances are you will never fully understand Jamaica in all its delightful complexity, but you will probably have a good time trying. In the resort town of Ⓐ**Port Antonio** you will be greeted with a smile, told where to find spicy jerk pork, and maybe directed to one of the town's watering holes. The potent fruit concoctions served in the local boîtes are laced with local rum and have eased the way to unlikely bonding among an eclectic lot of trav-

elers—among them J.P. Morgan and, later, Errol Flynn— who once shipped in by banana boat. The swash- buckling actor found adven- tures worthy of his celluloid exploits on the nearby Ⓑ**Rio Grande,** where a boatman with a bamboo raft can still provide a ride on the wild side.

MARTINIQUE

Ⓐ 454

Off Martinique, a *gommier*, brightly colored and replete with multihued sails and a crew of oarsmen, is the surest way to tackle the choppy Atlantic; the going is easier at Ⓐ**Les Salines,** an idyllic cove on the gentler Caribbean side of the island. In fact, *la vie en rose* is de rigueur in this stylish French enclave, which is often characterized as a Caribbean suburb of Paris. Exotic fruit grows on the volcanoes' forested flanks amid a profusion of wild orchids and hibiscus. The sheer lushness of it all inspired the tropical paintings of onetime resident Paul Gauguin. He would later say that to truly understand him and his art, one had to understand his Martinique period.

PUERTO RICO

Mother Spain is always a presence here—on a sun-dappled cobblestone street, in the shade of a colonial cathedral or fort. Yet multifaceted Puerto Rico pulses with New World energy.

Coquis (frogs) chant vigorously as only Caribbean creatures can. The rhythms of the streets are of Afro-Latin salsa and *bomba;* the costumes and *vejigantes* (masks) you see in local festivals are bright and colorful. And the U.S. flag flaps in the salty breezes wherever you go.

SABA &
ST. EUSTATIUS

Mountainous Saba shoots straight out of the sea like one of the volcanoes that formed it, and in its precipitous terrain visitors set their sights on either the highlands or the depths. The Bottom, the island's capital, is actually atop a mountain but nestles in a crater, and from there a trail of 900 rough-hewn steps drops to the sea. Divers and snorkelers take a different plunge and end up eye to eye with denizens of the deep. Nearby St. Eustatius, a.k.a. Statia, is another quiet haven for scuba divers and hikers. Still scrappily elegant, the Doncker House, now the Ⓐ**Historical Foundation Museum,** attests to the island's 18th-century heyday. Then it was called the Emporium of the Western World: warehouses stretched for a

Ⓐ⟩ **556**

mile along the quays, and 200 boats could anchor at its docks. These days it's the day-trippers from St. Martin who pull up to the shore.

Chic travelers adore French-speaking St. Barths. But although they come at least partly to see and be seen, all put aside their cell phones long enough to enjoy the lovely beaches—long, surf-pounded strands; idyllic crescents crowded by cliffs or forests; glass-smooth lagoons perfect for windsurfing. After dark the pace picks up in

ST. BARTHS

Ⓐ▷ 542

island restaurants, where talented chefs transform local ingredients into culinary marvels. The French connection doesn't stop there: The harbor in tiny ⒶGustavia even feels like the Riviera. Rent a minimoke, the open-sided beach buggy that's the local vehicle of choice, and explore the hilly roads squiggling to Corossol and Lorient before returning to bustling St. Jean Beach and the ⒷEden Rock. Nothing on St. Barths comes cheap. But while you're sipping Pouilly-Fumé on this hotel's awning-shaded terrace, St. Barths' civilized ways seem worth every penny.

Ⓑ▷ 528

ST. KITTS & NEVIS

A yucca cactus keeps watch over Ⓑ**North Friar's Bay** on St. Kitts' narrow peninsula as the island trails off to Nevis, its diminutive companion just 2 miles distant. And with good reason. St. Kitts and Nevis are locked in a friendly contest to see who can render a more satisfying version of paradise. On both islands, brilliant green fields of sugar-cane run to the sea, once-magnificent plantation houses are now luxurious inns, and lovely stretches of uncrowded beach, like the snowy-white Ⓐ**Pinney's Beach** on Nevis and black-sand Dieppe Bay on St. Kitts, stretch out into the deep blue of the Caribbean and the Atlantic. It's a close call. Both islands attract upscale visitors in search of a low-key vacation. To fill your days, you can learn about local culture and history, meet the friendly islanders, or go hiking, swimming, horse-back riding, or snorkeling. Of course, you can always hop on the ferry, make the 45-minute crossing, and compare for yourself.

Ⓐ 585

Ⓑ 571

Explorers, pirates, soldiers, sugar planters, and coal miners have made their mark on this lovely landfall, and the lush, tropical peaks known as the Ⓐ**Pitons** (Gros and

ST. LUCIA

Ⓐ▷ 623

Ⓑ▷ 621

Petit) have witnessed them all. Today's visitors come to snorkel and scuba dive in the calm, cobalt-blue waters, to sun themselves on the scores of multi-hued beaches, or to go for a sail off tiny Ⓑ**Pigeon Island,** which juts off St. Lucia's northwest coast. You can also spend your days hiking on the trails that lace the presiding peaks, or take to the tortuous road that snakes along the coastline, cutting through forests and plunging and climbing around the island's perimeter. Your reward for meeting these challenges comes in the form of the splendid vistas en route and, at day's end, an alfresco meal at a seaside resort like Ⓒ**Anse Chastanet.**

Ⓒ▷ 606

ST. MAARTEN & ANGUILLA

Anguilla and St. Martin/St. Maarten are only a 15-minute ferry ride away, but they could not be farther apart. In tiny Anguilla, where fishermen have been heading out to sea for centuries in handmade boats, the beaches are some of the Caribbean's best and least crowded. Heavy development has not spoiled the island's atmospheric corners, and Ⓑ**Johnno's Beach Stop,** which pulses on Sunday afternoon, is one of the few gathering places. St. Martin/St. Maarten, a half-French, half-Dutch island, is worldly by comparison. Gastronomy flourishes, most resorts are large rather than small, casinos draw gamblers, sporting opportunities are plentiful, and the sunning, as on Ⓐ**Cupecoy Beach,** is often clothing-optional.

Ⓐ➤ 646

Ⓑ➤ 42

ST. VINCENT & THE GRENADINES

Ⓑ 685

The perfect realization of anyone's dream of heaven could well be Ⓐ**Palm Island,** but it's just one of 32 similarly endowed Grenadine islands and cays in the archipelago. When the largest of them, Bequia, gets down to business, chances are it has to do with boats—whether it's crafting a handsome replica at Sargeant's Model Boat Shop in the town of Ⓑ**Port Elizabeth** or outfitting the real thing at some of the Caribbean's best anchorages. On land, a sense of privilege prevails. Wildlife trusts protect rare species of flora and fauna, and villa walls ensure privacy for the islands' rich and famous human visitors.

TRINIDAD
& TOBAGO

The most southerly of the Caribbean islands, Trinidad is also the most colorful. Cosmopolitan islanders trace their roots to India, China, and Madeira; they practice Hinduism, Islam, and Christianity; and they speak English, Spanish, and French Patois. This heady mix comes to a boil at Ⓐ**Carnival** ("De Mas," as islanders call it). Calypso and steel bands play in Port-of-Spain and elsewhere around the island. The whirl of sensuous fêtes and festivities culminates when costumed revelers parade through the streets from sunrise on the Monday before Ash Wednesday until midnight the following day. On much quieter Tobago nearby, motmot birds put on a show of their own when it comes time to mate—the males clear a patch on the floor of the forest that cloaks the island and do an elaborate song and dance. Another spectacle is always close at hand—the timeless one of palm trees swaying high above a gentle arc of a beach.

TURKS & CAICOS

Ⓐ⟩750

This archipelago of 40 low-lying islands floats between the Bahamas and Haiti, with the Atlantic to one side and the Caribbean to the other. One of the eight that are inhabited, Grand Turk, claims to be the first spot on which Christopher Columbus set foot in the New World. Despite ongoing attempts to cultivate the land, nature still prevails on these islands. Snorkelers and scuba divers explore one of the world's longest coral reefs, not to mention the Wall, a subterranean cliff of coral. The glass-clear Turks and Caicos waters are also the winter home of migrating humpback whales and a year-round playground for turtles, colorful parrot fish, and even dolphins. In fact sea creatures far outnumber humans here: the islands' total population is a mere 25,000. Land-based pursuits don't get much more taxing than teeing off at Providenciales's Ⓐ**Provo Golf Club,** or sunset-watching from the seaside terrace of a laid-back resort.

ⓐ⟩ 814

Stand in the right place on any Virgin Island and you'll spot other islands across the serene waters, seemingly just a swim away. The proximity explains in part the close ties of these 120

U.S. & BRITISH VIRGIN ISLANDS

or so landfalls, despite the fact that some fly the Stars and Stripes and others the Union Jack. What the Virgins share is a volcanic topography that shelters a remarkable variety of creatures and a history of domination by European masters, who ruled sugarcane plantations, worked by slaves, from gracious manor houses such as St. Croix's ⓐ**Whim Plantation,** now a museum. Hundreds of idyllic coves with splendid beaches scallop the islands' shorelines—those on

ⓑ⟩ 200

Virgin Gorda at ⓑ**Spring Bay** and on St. John at ⓒ**Maho Bay** stand out.

ⓒ⟩ 824

FODOR'S
CHOICE

Even with so many special places in the Caribbean, Fodor's writers and editors have their favorites. Here are a few that stand out.

BEACHES

Anse du Gouverneur, St. Barthélemy. This beautiful, secluded spot offers good snorkeling and views of St. Kitts, Saba, and St. Eustatius. ☞ p 542

Baie Orientale, St. Martin. This lively strand with lots of beach bars is best known as the Caribbean's premier clothing-optional beach. The sight of cruise-ship passengers gawking is alone worth a visit. ☞ p 647

Ⓙ Grand Anse Beach, Grenada. Gentle surf laps the gleaming sand of this 2-mi beach. To the north you can see the narrow mouth of St. George's Harbour and the pastel houses in the hills. ☞ p 349

Macaroni Beach, Mustique, St. Vincent and the Grenadines. Surfy swimming, powdery white sand, a few palm huts and picnic tables, and very few people are the draws. ☞ p 690

Marie-Galante Island, Guadeloupe. Virtually untouched by tourism, Marie-Galante has some of Guadeloupe's best beaches. Anse de Vieux Fort is for lovers, Plage de Folle Anse is for sunset walks, and Petite-Anse is for weekend socializing. ☞ p 391

Negril Beach, Jamaica. Although no longer untouched by development, Negril's stretch of sand (a remarkable 7 mi) is still a beachcomber's Eden. ☞ p 420

Seven Mile Beach, Grand Cayman, Cayman Islands. It's actually 5½ mi of white sand, litter- and peddler-free, and headquarters for water sports outfitters. ☞ p 227

Shoal Bay, Anguilla. This L-shape beach of talcum-powder-soft white sand may get crowded, but that's only because it's one of the prettiest in the Caribbean. ☞ p 45

Ⓒ Trunk Bay, St. John, USVI. You'll find sensational snorkeling on this perfect scimitar, one of many such stretches on an island that's 66% protected national park. ☞ p 825

CARIBBEAN CLASSICS

An Aruban casino. The casinos all along L. G. Smith and J. E. Irausquin boulevards have something for the high roller, the curious novice, and those who simply want to see a show. ☞ p 101

Andromeda Gardens, Barbados. Set on rocky outcroppings overlooking the sea, this 6-acre garden contains unique, beautiful plants from all over the world. ☞ p 140

Ⓖ Bonaire Marine Park. The current is mild, the reefs often begin just offshore, visibility is generally 60 ft–100 ft, and the marine life is magnificent. ☞ p 161

Barhopping on Jost Van Dyke, BVI. You can't go wrong at any bar on this island, which does its best to entertain the charter-yacht crowd. ☞ p 203

Hiking on Dominica. The island's lush forests are scored by ancient footpaths (some made by escaped slaves and Carib Indians). ☞ p 283

Ⓑ Santo Domingo's Colonial Zone, Dominican Republic. Wandering the narrow cobbled streets it's easy to imagine what the city was like in the days of Columbus, Cortés, and Ponce de León. ☞ p 320

Ⓗ Golf on Puerto Rico. Puerto Rico has acres and acres of golf greens. Check out Palmas del Mar's Flamboyan course—with its 18 elegant, Rees Jones–designed holes and a Gary Player course as well. ☞ p 490

Ⓔ Shopping for Lace on Saba. On weekdays Saban ladies sell their lace creations—collars, tea towels, napkins, tablecloths—at the community center in Hell's Gate. Many also sell their wares from their homes; just follow the signs. ☞ p 520

Looking for Blue-Glass Beads, St. Eustatius. Made by the Dutch West Indies Company in the 17th century, these beads were traded for rum, slaves, cotton, and tobacco. Look for them on the beaches, especially after heavy rain. ☞ p 554

Duty-Free Shopping, St. Maarten/St. Martin. More than 500 duty-free shops make for great bargain-hunting. ☞ p 651

Ⓕ Bird-Watching, Trinidad and Tobago. You might spot blue-backed manakin, yellow oriole, scarlet ibis, or another of the more than 200 varieties of bird. ☞ p 711

HOTELS

Anse Chastanet Beach Hotel, St. Lucia. Rooms were designed to hug the mountainside; louvered wooden walls open to stunning Piton and Caribbean vistas or to the deep-green forest. $$$$ ☞ p 606

Biras Creek, Virgin Gorda, BVI. Bought by a former guest, this resort is a spectacular hideaway. $$$$ ☞ p 194

Ⓓ Caneel Bay Resort, St. John, USVI. Seven beaches, numerous tennis courts, myriad water sports, and good restaurants make it hard to stir from this luxury property. $$$$ ☞ p 817

Ⓐ Cap Juluca, Anguilla. This 179-acre resort wraps around the sugary white sands at the edge of Maunday's Bay. The children's program includes such activities as visits with local boatbuilders. $$$$ ☞ p 34

Carl Gustaf, St. Barthélemy. Every suite in this hillside gem has a spectacular view of Gustavia's harbor and the coast—and a pool of its own. $$$$ ☞ p 528

"Veni Mangé"

Ⓙ

Ⓚ

Ⓛ

FODOR'S CHOICE

Ⓜ

Ⓝ

Ⓞ

Ⓟ

Ⓠ

Ⓡ

Ⓢ

® **Cotton House, Mustique, St. Vincent and the Grenadines.** Whoever coined the term "lap of luxury" must have had this private-island playground in mind. $$$$ ☞ p 689

Ⓠ **Curtain Bluff, Antigua.** The setting is breathtaking—high on a bluff regally overseeing the calm Caribbean. Country-club elegance prevails. $$$$ ☞ p 57

Franklyn D. Resort (FDR), Jamaica. ☞ Families love this place for its chockablock kids' miniclub complete with arts and crafts classes, children's slides and pools— and mother's helpers as-signed to each family on arrival. $$$$ ☞ p 407

Ⓝ **Grand Lido Sans Souci, Jamaica.** As if the decorative luxury of this pastel cliff-side palace weren't enough, a free spa session is included in the rates. $$$$ ☞ p 405

Ⓛ **Horned Dorset Primavera, Puerto Rico.** The pounding of the surf and the squawk of the resident parrot are the only sounds you'll hear as you lounge on the beach. $$$$ ☞ p 478

Ottley's Plantation Inn, St. Kitts. This great house inn with ravishing gardens epitomizes low-key, worldly sophistication and down-home Caribbean hospitality. $$$$ ☞ p 564

Parrot Cay Resort, Provo, Turks and Caicos. Natural beauty and tranquillity attract jet setters to this resort. $$$$ ☞ p 752

Ⓢ **Ritz-Carlton, St. Thomas, USVI.** This hotel is built like an Italian villa, with elegance everywhere, from the marble-floor reception area to the pool, which seems to flow right into the sea. $$$$ ☞ p 772

Ⓜ **Spice Island Beach Resort, Grenada.** The spacious suites, private plunge pools, and in-room whirlpools are great, but it's the location on beauti-ful Grand Anse Beach that steals the show. $$$$ ☞ p 341

Turtle Beach Resort, Barba-dos. This elegant, all-suite property gives "all-inclusive"

a luxurious new meaning. $$$$ ☞ p 113

Ⓚ **Young Island Resort, St. Vincent and the Grenadines.** This unique island resort is a cross between Swiss Family Robinson's tree house and the Ritz. $$$$ ☞ p 665

Deep Blue View Bed & Breakfast, Bonaire. Down-to-earth and luxury are concepts that blend blissfully at this villa tucked away in the hills. $$$ ☞ p 154

Hotel 1829, St. Thomas, USVI. It's all romance and classic elegance at this historic Spanish-style inn. $$$ ☞ p 770

Avila Beach Hotel, Curaçao. Dutch royals and government VIPs have given this 200-year-old mansion the nod for the peace, privacy, and service it offers. Still, you don't need a royal bank account to stay here. $$ ☞ p 245

Ⓟ **Le Plein Soleil, Martinique.** This small resort is chic, contemporary Creole at its unexpected best. $$ ☞ p 445

Papillote Wilderness Retreat, Dominica. The owners and staff have infused this moun-tain getaway with their charm and warmth—from the gorgeous botanical gardens to the homey rooms. $ ☞ p 277

RESTAURANTS

Casa del Río, Dominican Republic. At this re-creation of a 16th-century castle, the chefs fuse culinary ideas from the Caribbean, France, and Asia to create exquisite dishes. $$$$ ☞ p 312

Anacaona, Providenciales, Turks and Caicos. Caribbean fruits, vegetables, and spices lift traditional French recipes to exotic heights. And the staff is as delightful as the flavors. $$$ ☞ p 749

Auberge de la Vielle Tour, Guadeloupe. The gourmet room at this resort, within a historic sugar mill, serves some of the island's best, most contemporary food. $$$ ☞ p 378

Chez Pascal, Antigua. Perched on a cliff overlooking the ocean, this restaurant is

an authentic piece of sunny, southern France transplanted to Antigua. Melt-in-your-mouth seafood specialties particu-larly shine, as do the silken sauces. $$$ ☞ p 67

Ⓞ **Hemingway's, Grand Cayman, Cayman Islands.** Enjoy Seven Mile Beach breezes while sipping a tropical drink and savoring lemongrass-crusted grouper with *udon* noodles and Portobello mushrooms. $$$ ☞ p 224

Rijsttafel Indonesia Restau-rant, Curaçao. Walls hung with batik, handwoven baskets, and shadow puppets set the stage for a traditional Indonesian rijsttafel banquet, with as many as 25 dishes served buffet-style. $$$ ☞ p 251

Top Hat, St. Croix, USVI. The wonderful Danish menu and the Danish owners are reminders of St. Croix's colonial past. Try the *frikadeller* (meatballs in a tangy sauce) and fried Camembert with lingonber-ries. $$$ ☞ p 803

Virgilio's, St. Thomas, USVI. Come for some of the best northern Italian cuisine in the islands, and don't miss Virgilio's cappuccino, a chocolate-and-coffee drink as rich as dessert. $$$ ☞ p 776

Fatzo, Martinique. This grande dame has it all: contemporary cuisine, ambi-ence, service, history, and an interesting crowd from fun locals to yachtsmen. $$ ☞ p 449

Gasparito Restaurant and Art Gallery, Aruba. Tasty local cuisine is served in the gallery of an authentic country house. $$ ☞ p 92

Ⓙ **Veni Mangé, Trinidad.** Cordon Bleu–trained Allyson Hennessy cooks up the best creole lunches in town. $$ ☞ p 709

1 ANGUILLA

Updated by
Karl Luntta

"But I arranged for lobster in advance," snarled the man at the beachfront table. "That was the whole point of coming here." The waitress tried to soothe him: "I'm sorry; we ran out of lobsters, but it's really no problem—I've talked to the manager." But her gracious assurances and charming West Indian accent had no effect. The man's face reddened until it seemed he would explode. Just then, a handsome, wiry Anguillan man approached from the beach, a bag over his shoulder. "Ah, yes. Here's the manager with fresh lobster now," said the waitress with a smile. "I told you it was no problem."

Peace, pampering, fine dining, and beaches are among the star attractions on Anguilla (pronounced ang-*gwill*-a). If you're a beach lover, you may become giddy when you first spot the island from the air; its blindingly white sand and lustrous blue and aquamarine waters are intoxicating sights. If you like shopping and late-night action, you won't find a lot to do here. There are no glittering casinos or nightclubs, no duty-free shops stuffed with irresistible buys (although you're only about 30 watery minutes from St. Martin/St. Maarten's bustling resorts and casinos). However, if you like sophisticated cuisine served in stunning open-air settings, this may be your culinary heaven. Despite being one of the smaller Caribbean islands, Anguilla has nearly 70 restaurants. Some serve up the latest culinary trends in atmospheres that range from casual to fancy, and others stick to the simple fare you'd expect to find at a barefoot-friendly, beachfront bar.

This dry, limestone isle is the most northerly of the Leeward Islands, lying between the Caribbean Sea and the Atlantic Ocean. It stretches, from northeast to southwest, about 16 mi (26 km) and is only 3 mi (5 km) across at its widest point. The highest spot is 213 ft (65 m) above sea level, and there are neither streams nor rivers, only saline ponds used for salt production. The island's name, a reflection of its shape, is most likely a derivative of *anguille*, which is French for "eel." (French explorer Pierre Laudonnaire is credited with having given the island this name when he sailed past it in 1556.)

In 1631 the Dutch built a fort here, but no one has been able to locate its site. English settlers from St. Kitts colonized the island in 1650, and except for a brief period of independence with St. Kitts–Nevis in the 1960s, Anguilla has remained a British colony ever since.

From the early 1800s various island units and federations were formed and disbanded, with Anguilla all the while simmering over its subordinate status and enforced union with St. Kitts. Anguillans twice petitioned for direct rule from Britain and twice were ignored. In 1967, when St. Kitts, Nevis, and Anguilla became an associated state, the mouse roared; citizens kicked out St. Kitts' policemen, held a self-rule referendum, and for two years conducted their own affairs. A British "peacekeeping force" then parachuted down onto the island, squelching Anguilla's designs for autonomy but helping a team of royal engineers stationed there to improve the port and build roads and schools. Today Anguilla elects a House of Assembly and its own leader to handle internal affairs, while a British governor is responsible for public service, the police, judiciary, and external affairs.

The territory of Anguilla includes a few islets (or cays), such as Scrub Island, Dog Island, Prickly Pear Cays, Sandy Island, and Sombrero Island. The 10,000 or so residents are predominantly of African descent, but there are also many of Irish background, whose ancestors came over from St. Kitts in the 1600s. Historically, because the limestone land was hardly fit for agriculture, attempts at enslavement and colonization never lasted long; consequently, Anguilla doesn't bear the scars of slavery found on so many other Caribbean islands. Because the island couldn't be farmed successfully (although cotton was produced here for a while), Anguillans became experts at making a living from the sea and are known for their boatbuilding and fishing skills. Tourism is the growth industry of the island's stable economy, but the government is determined to keep expansion at a slow and cautious pace to protect the island's natural resources and beauty. New hotels are built small, select, and definitely casino free. The island has chosen to emphasize its high-quality service, serene surroundings, and friendly people.

Lodging

Anguilla accommodations range from grand, sumptuous resorts to apartments and villas—deluxe or simple—to small, locally owned guest houses. Because the island has so many beautiful and uncrowded beaches, it's not necessary (the way it is on some other islands) for beach lovers to choose a particular property because of its beach. If calling to reserve a room in a resort, inquire about special packages and meal plans.

CATEGORY	COST*
$$$$	over $400
$$$	$275–$400
$$	$150–$275
$	under $150

All prices are for a standard double room, excluding 10% tax and 10% service charge and meal plan.

Hotels

$$$$ ⊠ **Cap Juluca.** This 179-acre resort wraps around the edge of Maunday's Bay on a 2-mi (3-km) stretch of sugary sand. The white, Moorish-style, two-story villas are luxurious; the stylish, comfortable rooms feature Moroccan fabrics, Brazilian hardwood, and built-in seating areas. Many of the immense bathrooms have two-person soaking tubs that overlook gardens. Casual George's on the Beach serves grilled fish, steaks, and Spanish-Mediterranean cuisine (except during the Monday-evening West Indian buffet and Friday-evening barbecue beach party). Dinner is also served at the elegant Pimms restaurant, where you'll find Kemia, a tapas bar. An appealing activity program—with water sports, crafts,

lessons on island culture, and visits to local boatbuilders—is in July and August. A garden and a self-guided nature trail provide nonbeach activities for all ages. However, variable standards of service and a sometimes boisterous atmosphere make this a resort more for those who can go with the flow of life on the island. ⊠ *Maunday's Bay (Box 240)*, ☎ *264/497–6666 or 888/858–5822*, FAX *264/497–6617*, WEB *www.capjuluca.com. 98 rooms, 18 private villas. 3 restaurants, bar, room service, pool, spa, 3 tennis courts, croquet, health club, beach, snorkeling, windsurfing, boating, shops, library, baby-sitting, children's programs, laundry service. AE, MC, V. EP, FAP, MAP.*

$$$$ 🏨 **Cuisinart Resort & Spa.** The stark white architecture of the Greek
★ island of Mykonos is the inspiration for this luxurious beachfront resort. Rooms, suites, and penthouses, in a cluster of stucco villas on stunning Rendezvous Bay, are white inside and out. Units are decorated in Haitian cottons, and all have marble bathrooms. The resort is a development of the Cuisinart food-processor company and features a demonstration kitchen with complimentary cooking classes. The open kitchen in the dining room has a clear view of the chefs preparing their magic. The spa offers massages and body treatments, a state-of-the-art, 24-hr fitness center, and an art gallery designed for relaxation and meditation. ⊠ *Rendezvous Bay (Box 2000)*, ☎ *264/498–2000 or 800/943–3210*, FAX *264/498–2010*, WEB *www.cuisinart-resort.com. 93 rooms, 2 penthouses. 3 restaurants, 2 bars, pool, hot tub, 3 tennis courts, health club, beach, snorkeling, windsurfing, boating, shops, billiards, baby-sitting, laundry service. AE, MC, V. EP, MAP.*

$$$$ 🏨 **Malliouhana.** Anguilla's classiest resort—with a remarkable 70%
★ rate of repeat guests—sits on 25 tropical acres along a promontory between two exquisite beaches. The lobby, boutique, restaurants, and bar are in a grand, multitiered open-air structure with tile floors and mahogany walls. Some rooms are in this main building; others are in white Moorish-style buildings set along a bluff and in gardens. The units have white walls and tile floors, Caribbean prints, and rattan furniture with fat, white Haitian cotton-covered cushions; marble bathrooms have oversize tubs. The Malliouhana restaurant is the most elegant on the island. Children will like the small beachfront playground with handsome wooden slides, swings, and games. A villa with three suites and its own pool is perfect for families. ⊠ *Meads Bay (Box 173)*, ☎ *264/497–6111 or 800/835–0796 (direct to hotel)*, FAX *264/497–6011*, WEB *www.malliouhana.com. 34 rooms, 19 suites. Restaurant, bar, 3 pools, hot tub, beauty salon, massage, 4 tennis courts, gym, beach, snorkeling, windsurfing, boating, waterskiing, playground. No credit cards. EP, MAP.*

$$$$ 🏨 **Sonesta Beach Resort & Villas Anguilla.** This pink-and-green Moorish fantasia is right on the beach, and many rooms have grand views of St. Martin. Everywhere you look, lush tropical plants peek through arches and surround fountains. The route to reception, the restaurants, and the pool may take your breath away: you pass through a long, open-air arcade with authentic Moroccan mosaics and by a long reflecting pool. The exterior color scheme is mirrored in the rooms, painted pink and decorated with pastel green-and-pink prints and green accessories. Bold prints hang on the walls and Moroccan throw rugs are scattered hither and yon. Marble bathrooms have spacious tubs. The four-bedroom Oleander villa has Italian marble floors, mahogany furniture and accents, luxury kitchen appliances, ceiling fans, and spacious baths with whirlpool tubs. The Tangier villa has three bedrooms. The resort's two restaurants, Casablanca and Restaurant Ici, are well worth the visits. ⊠ *Rendezvous Bay West (Box 444)*, ☎ *264/497–6999 or 800/766–3782*, FAX *264/497–6899*, WEB *www.sonesta.com. 76 rooms, 8 suites, 3 villas. 2 restaurants, bar, piano bar, pool, beauty salon, 2 tennis courts,*

Anguilla

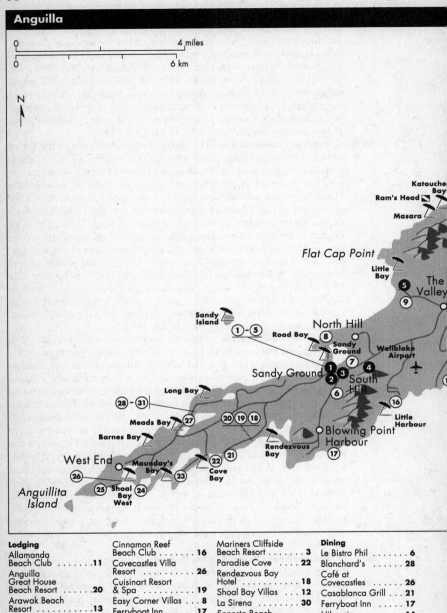

0   4 miles

0   6 km

N

Katouche Bay

Ram's Head

Masara

Flat Cap Point

Little Bay

The Valley

5

9

Sandy Island

1 – 5

Road Bay

North Hill

8

Sandy Ground

Wallblake Airport

7

Sandy Ground

1

3

4

2

South Hill

6

Long Bay

28 – 31

Meads Bay

27

Barnes Bay

20 19 18

16

Little Harbour

Rendezvous Bay

Blowing Point Harbour

West End

Maunday's Bay

23

22 21

Cove Bay

17

26

25 24

Shoal Bay West

Anguillita Island

Lodging

Allamanda Beach Club **11**

Anguilla Great House Beach Resort **20**

Arawak Beach Resort **13**

Blue Waters **24**

Cap Juluca **23**

Carimar Beach Club **29**

Cinnamon Reef Beach Club **16**

Covecastles Villa Resort **26**

Cuisinart Resort & Spa **19**

Easy Corner Villas . .**8**

Ferryboat Inn **17**

Frangipani Beach Club **27**

Malliouhana **31**

Mariners Cliffside Beach Resort **3**

Paradise Cove . . .**22**

Rendezvous Bay Hotel **18**

Shoal Bay Villas . . .**12**

La Sirena **30**

Sonesta Beach Resort & Villas Anguilla **21**

Syd-An's **4**

Dining

Le Bistro Phil **6**

Blanchard's **28**

Café at Covecastles **26**

Casablanca Grill . . .**21**

Ferryboat Inn **17**

Hibernia **14**

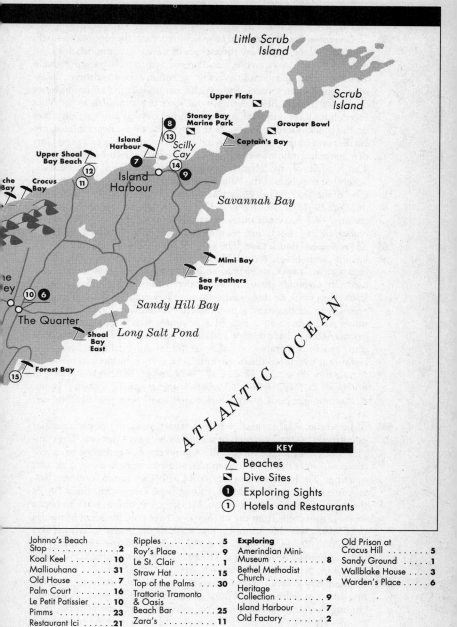

Little Scrub
Island

Upper Flats

Scrub
Island

Stoney Bay
Marine Park

Grouper Bowl

Island
Harbour

Captain's Bay

Upper Shoal
Bay Beach

Scilly
Cay

che
Bay

Crocus
Bay

Island
Harbour

Savannah Bay

Mimi Bay

Sea Feathers
Bay

ne
ey

The Quarter

Sandy Hill Bay

Long Salt Pond

Shoal
Bay
East

Forest Bay

ATLANTIC OCEAN

KEY

Beaches
Dive Sites
Exploring Sights
Hotels and Restaurants

Johnno's Beach
Stop 2
Koal Keel 10
Malliouhana 31
Old House 7
Palm Court 16
Le Petit Patissier 10
Pimms 23
Restaurant Ici 21

Ripples 5
Roy's Place 9
Le St. Clair 1
Straw Hat 15
Top of the Palms . . . 30
Trattoria Tramonto
& Oasis
Beach Bar 25
Zara's 11

Exploring
Amerindian Mini-
Museum 8
Bethel Methodist
Church 4
Heritage
Collection 9
Island Harbour . . . 7
Old Factory 2

Old Prison at
Crocus Hill 5
Sandy Ground 1
Wallblake House . . . 3
Warden's Place 6

exercise room, beach, snorkeling, windsurfing, bicycles, shops, library. AE, D, MC, V. CP, EP, MAP.

$$$ ▦ **Cinnamon Reef Beach Club.** Low-key luxury sets the tone at this small, appealing place. There are three types of casual accommodations, all decorated with Mexican tile, floral prints, and colorful paintings. Villa Suites are unattached and have a living room, raised bedroom, dressing room, sunken shower, patio with a hammock, and stunning views of the Caribbean. Beach Suites, which are the same size as the Villa Suites but all on one level, are in buildings nestled among palm trees on the beach. Garden Suites, on the back side of the Beach Suites, are smaller and have a combined living-bedroom area (you can get a Garden Suite that adjoins a Beach Suite if you need a two-bedroom unit). This is a friendly place with a gracious staff and lots of repeat guests. Several of the chefs at the Palm Court restaurant have won Anguilla's Chef of the Year award. ✉ *Little Harbour (Box 141),* ☎ *264/497–2727 or 800/223–1108,* ℻ *264/497–3727,* WEB *www.cinnamon-reef.com. 8 studios, 14 1-bedroom suites. Restaurant, bar, pool, hot tub, 2 tennis courts, beach, snorkeling, windsurfing. AE, MC, V. CP, EP, MAP.*

$$$ ▦ **Frangipani Beach Club.** The splashy, inviting hotel sits on 1 mi (1½
★ km) of sandy beach and has pink Spanish Mediterranean-style buildings with archways, stone balustrades, wrought-iron railings, and red-tile roofs. Grounds are lushly landscaped with colorful tropical flowers. Each one-, two-, or three-bedroom suite has arched windows and exposed beam ceilings and is tastefully decorated with blond rattan furniture and fabrics in a mix of blue-and-white stripes and colorful prints. All units have marble and tiled bathrooms and doors that open onto spacious terraces or balconies; many have full kitchens. The restaurant overlooks the ocean and has a French-influenced menu. ✉ *Meads Bay (Box 328),* ☎ *264/497–6442 or 800/892–4564 (direct to hotel),* ℻ *264/497–6440,* WEB *www.frangipani.ai. 17 rooms, 8 suites. Restaurant, bar, pool, tennis court, beach, snorkeling, windsurfing. AE, MC, V. EP.*

$$$ ▦ **La Sirena.** At this small, well-run resort, you can opt for a regular guest room, a spacious villa, or a suite with its own hot tub. The complex's white-stucco buildings, all set amid tropical greenery, have red-tile roofs, lots of balconies and terraces, and interesting angles and circular openings. The interior decor is typical Caribbean: rattan furniture, pastel-print fabrics, and, of course, ceiling fans. The second-floor Top of the Palms restaurant serves Italian, Mexican, vegetarian, and Caribbean items; if the smells from the kitchen don't get you, the scent of the sea on a breeze will. It's a four-minute walk to the beach. ✉ *Meads Bay (Box 200),* ☎ *264/497–6827 or 800/223–9815,* ℻ *264/497–6829,* WEB *www.la-sirena.com. 20 rooms, 3 suites, 5 villas. Restaurant, bar, 2 pools, dive shop, bicycles, car rental. AE, MC, V. CP, EP, MAP.*

$$$ ▦ **Shoal Bay Villas.** This small two-story condominium hotel is tucked in a grove of palm trees on 2 mi (3 km) of splendid sand. Units—including two studios, two with two bedrooms, and nine with one bedroom—are brightly decorated in pink and blue, with painted rattan furniture and fully equipped kitchens. All have patios or porches that open to the beach or the courtyard pool. All rooms have ceiling fans; you'll pay a little extra for air-conditioning. Le Beach Restaurant and Bar is an informal open-air, thatched-roof spot that serves breakfast, lunch, and dinner. All water sports can be arranged. ✉ *Shoal Bay (Box 81),* ☎ *264/497–2051,* ℻ *264/497–3631,* WEB *www.sbvillas.ai. 2 studios, 2 2-bedroom units, 9 1-bedroom units, 2 doubles. Restaurant, bar, pool, beach, snorkeling. AE, D, MC, V. EP.*

$$ ▦ **Anguilla Great House Beach Resort.** Rooms here are in white West Indian–style bungalows strung along the bay and one of Anguilla's longest 2½ mi (4 km) beaches. From a chaise on your charming veranda,

the view of the ocean is framed by vine-covered trellises and ginger-bread trim. Most bungalows have five rooms, and each room has ma-hogany furnishings, tropical-print fabrics, a huge tile shower, and ceiling fans. Most rooms have air-conditioning. The restaurant serves a mix of West Indian, French, and Continental cuisines. ⊠ *Rendezvous Bay (Box 157),* ☎ *264/497–6061 or 800/583–9247 (direct to hotel),* FAX *264/497–6019. 27 rooms. Restaurant, pool, exercise room, beach, snorkeling, windsurfing. AE, D, MC, V. EP.*

$$ 🏨 **Arawak Beach Resort.** Built on the site of an ancient Arawak village, this resort recently underwent a much-needed face-lift. Studios and one-bedroom suites are in breezy, hexagonal two-story villas set along a narrow curve of beach overlooking Island Harbour, at the east end of the island. Rooms are painted white and decorated with colorful floral prints. The Restaurant Caribe's menu is Continental but incorporates Caribbean ingredients and fresh local fish. The casual Arawak Beach Bar and Cafe features barbecues and live music on weekends. A small museum displays artifacts uncovered during construction. Canoeing is available. Scilly Cay and its beautiful beaches are just a minute away by launch. ⊠ *Island Harbour (Box 114),* ☎ *264/497–4888,* FAX *264/497–4889,* WEB *www.arawakresort.com. 13 rooms, 4 suites. 2 restaurants, bar, pool, beach, snorkeling, windsurfing, shops. AE, MC, V. EP.*

$$ 🏨 **Ferryboat Inn.** The spacious one-bedroom apartments at this small family-run complex are a bargain. Each is simply decorated with white or pastel fabrics and has a full kitchen, dining area, cable TV, and ceiling fans (two have air-conditioning). It's on a small beach and just a short walk from the ferry dock. The two-bedroom beach house is air-conditioned. All rooms and the open-air restaurant look out across the water toward hilly, more-populated St. Martin—a gorgeous view at night. The restaurant, Ferryboat Inn, is a romantic spot open to the ocean breezes. ⊠ *Blowing Point (Box 189),* ☎ *264/497–6613,* FAX *264/497–6713,* WEB *www.ai/ferryboatinn. 6 apartments, 1 beach house. Restaurant, bar, beach, snorkeling, windsurfing. AE, MC, V. EP.*

$$ 🏨 **Mariners Cliffside Beach Resort.** This popular, casual resort is set between a papaya orchard and the beach. Charming red-roofed, gingerbread-trimmed cottages are clustered together and face the beach or tropical gardens. Accommodations vary considerably in size, from deluxe two-bedroom, two-bath cottages with full kitchens to small rooms with twin beds, minibars, and shower baths. All are decorated with bright Caribbean fabrics and have balconies or patios. West Indian cuisine is the specialty at the open-air restaurant. A stay here puts you at the far end of Anguilla's busiest stretch of sand and just a short stroll from many popular beach bars and restaurants. Charter the resort's Boston whaler for picnics, snorkeling, and fishing trips. ⊠ *Sandy Ground (Box 139),* ☎ *264/497–2671,* FAX *264/497–2901,* WEB *www.mariners.ai. 32 1-bedroom suites, 35 studios. Restaurant, bar, pool, hot tub, tennis court, beach, snorkeling, windsurfing, boating, shops, laundry service. D, MC, V. CP, EP, MAP.*

$$ 🏨 **Rendezvous Bay Hotel.** Opened in 1972, Anguilla's first resort sits amid 60 acres of coconut groves on the fine white sand of Rendezvous Bay, just 1 mi (1½ km) from the ferry dock. The original guest rooms are 100 yards (91 m) from the beach and are quite spare, with one double and one single bed, a private shower-bath, Haitian art on the walls, and ceiling fans. Much newer, connected, two-story villas along the shore have spacious, air-conditioned one-bedroom suites with refrigerators or kitchenettes. These are decorated with natural wicker and pastel prints and can be joined to form suites. For larger groups, entire villas can be rented as well. There's a wide beach and a rocky stretch of coast that's great for snorkeling. ⊠ *Rendezvous Bay (Box 31),* ☎ *264/497–*

6549, 732/738–0246, or 800/274–4893 in the U.S.; FAX 264/497–6026, WEB www.rendezvousbay.com. 20 rooms, 16 1-bedroom villa suites, 8 studios. Restaurant, lounge, 2 tennis courts, windsurfing, recreation room, car rental. AE, D, MC, V. EP, MAP.

$ ⊞ **Syd-An's.** These very basic efficiencies are a true bargain. Eight of the nine rooms have kitchenettes, and all come with shower-bath, air-conditioning, cable TV, and comfortable furnishings. There's no restaurant, but Road Bay, with all its bustling activity, is just across the street. ⊠ Sandy Ground, ☎ 264/497–3180, FAX 264/497–5381, WEB www.inns.ai/sydans. 9 studios. Kitchenettes, shops. AE, MC, V.

Villas and Condominiums

The tourist office has a complete listing of the plentiful vacation apartment rentals. You can contact the **Anguilla Connection** (⊠ Island Harbour, ☎ 264/497–4403, FAX 264/497–4402) for condo and villa listings. **Sunshine Villas** (⊠ Box 142, Blowing Point, ☎ 264/497–6149, FAX 264/497–6021) offers a wide range of island properties.

$$$$ ⊞ **Covecastles Villa Resort.** What look like glistening white pieces of
★ modern sculpture are actually elegant, comfortable, and very private apartments—eight with two bedrooms and four with three bedrooms. Each is decorated with custom-made wicker furniture, raw-silk cushions, and hand-embroidered linens. Balconies are wide and secluded, kitchens are state of the art, and you can't beat the location on one of Anguilla's prettiest beaches. The four-bedroom "supervilla" is super-luxurious, with a grand atrium entrance, a contemporary kitchen, and a 75-ft (23-m) veranda overlooking the ocean. The Café at Covecastles is an elegant, intimate eatery. ⊠ Shoal Bay West (Box 248), ☎ 264/497–6801 or 800/348–4716 (direct to hotel), FAX 264/497–6051, WEB www.covecastles.com. 13 apartments. Restaurant, tennis court, beach, snorkeling, shops. AE, MC, V.

$$$ ⊞ **Blue Waters.** These Moorish-style buildings sit at one end of a spec-
★ tacular ½-mi (1-km) beach and are within walking distance of excellent restaurants. Sunny one- and two-bedroom units are decorated with pastel fabrics and have white-tile floors, separate dining areas, full kitchens, and comfortable balconies or terraces. ⊠ Shoal Bay West (Box 69), ☎ 264/497–6292, FAX 264/497–3309. 9 apartments. Beach, snorkeling. AE, MC, V.

$$$ ⊞ **Carimar Beach Club.** This horseshoe-shape complex on the beach at beautiful Mead's Bay has seven two-story buildings capped by orange-tile roofs. Although only two are on the water's edge, all have ocean views from balconies or patios. Bright white apartments have one or two bedrooms, a living-dining area, and fully equipped kitchens. There's no restaurant, but several are within walking distance. ⊠ Meads Bay (Box 327), ☎ 264/497–6881 or 800/235–8667 (direct to hotel), FAX 264/497–6071, WEB www.carimar.com. 24 apartments. 2 tennis courts, beach, snorkeling. AE, D, MC, V.

$$$ ⊞ **Paradise Cove.** Renovations in 2001 doubled the size of this pretty complex. The luxury one- and two-bedroom apartments and efficiencies are set in four two-story buildings rimmed with balconies and patios and set amid beautiful tropical landscaping. Most of the spacious units overlook the courtyard, which has two whirlpools and a large pool. White rattan and wicker furniture, colorful tropical-print fabrics, fully equipped kitchens (the efficiencies come with kitchenettes), and private laundry facilities are standard. Second-floor units have high ceilings. Maid service and private cooks are available. Cove Beach is just a short walk away. ⊠ Cove Beach (Box 135), ☎ 264/497–6959 or 364/497–6603, FAX 264/497–6927, WEB www.paradise.ai. 12 efficiencies, 14 apartments, 3 suites. Restaurant, bar, pool, croquet, shops, playground, laundry service. AE, MC, V.

$$ 🏠 **Easy Corner Villas.** The location, on a bluff overlooking Road Bay, is a five-minute walk to the beach, but it offers spectacular hilltop views of Salt Pond and the ocean beyond. The price is right at these modest two- and three-bedroom villas, which can be broken down to accommodate couples in one-bedroom units or studios. All are adequately furnished and have well-equipped kitchens with microwaves. ✉ *South Hill (Box 65),* ☎ *264/497–6433 or 264/497–6541,* FAX *264/497–6410. 10 villas. Air-conditioning, kitchenettes, car rental. AE, MC, V.*

$ 🏠 **Allamanda Beach Club.** Enjoy an ocean view from your balcony at this casual resort. One-bedroom suites and studios fill the three-story, white-stucco building just off the beach. Views are better from the higher floors. All units have tile floors, full kitchens, and tropical-print decor. The restaurant, Zara's, is a popular draw. ✉ *Upper Shoal Bay Beach (Box 662),* ☎ *264/497–5217,* FAX *264/497–5216,* WEB *www.allamanda.ai. 16 units. Restaurant, pool, gym, dive shop. AE, D, MC, V.*

Dining

Anguilla has an extraordinary number of excellent restaurants—from elegant establishments to down-home seaside shacks. Most restaurants are open to the breezes, and many have terraces where you can dine under the stars. Call ahead—in winter to make a reservation and in late summer and fall to confirm if the place you've chosen is open. Restaurants not affiliated with a hotel often tack on an additional 5% to the service charge if you pay by credit card.

What to Wear

During the day, casual clothes are widely accepted: shorts will be fine, but don't wear bathing suits and cover-ups unless you're at a beach bar. In the evening, shorts are okay at the extremely casual eateries. Elsewhere, women should wear sundresses or nice casual slacks; men will be fine in shirt sleeves and casual pants. Some hotel restaurants are more formal and may have a jacket requirement in high season; ask when you make your reservation.

CATEGORY	COST*
$$$$	over $35
$$$	$25–$35
$$	$15–$25
$	under $15

*per person for a main course at dinner

West End

CONTEMPORARY

$$$$ ✕ **Pimms.** Local chef George Reid oversees this elegant restaurant at the Cap Juluca resort, and he's receiving accolades for his culinary magic. The innovative menu is Caribbean at heart but globally inspired. The menu features fresh local ingredients but hints at Asian and European influences. Look for pan-seared tuna with risotto, grilled Anguillan lobster, mustard-encrusted grouper, and filet mignon. The setting at the water's edge on a half-moon bay is open to soft evening breezes, and some tables are so close to the water that you can actually look down and see fish swimming about. ✉ *Maunday's Bay,* ☎ *264/497–6666. Reservations essential. AE, MC, V.*

ECLECTIC

$$$$ ✕ **Malliouhana.** Sparkling crystal and fine china, exquisite service,
★ and a spectacularly romantic candlelit, open-air setting complement exceptional haute French cuisine at this restaurant in the Malliouhana resort. Consulting chef Michel Rostang, renowned for his Paris boîte, and chef Alain Laurent create a new menu each season. Past choices

have included conch chowder with fennel, lobster and crab pancake, crayfish brochette, braised mahimahi with sweet-potato puree, and grilled snapper with pumpkin. Don't pass up dessert, which might include a creamy raspberry cheescake. The wine cellar has nearly 25,000 bottles. ⊠ *Meads Bay,* ☎ *264/497–6111. Reservations essential. AE, MC, V. Closed Sept.–Oct.*

$$$ ✕ **Blanchard's.** Bob and Melinda Blanchard's popular waterfront spot
★   has floor-to-ceiling doors that fold back to let in the breezes. The menu has Cajun, Caribbean, and Asian dishes: green-chili corn cakes, wild-mushroom ragout, and Indonesian beef satay for starters; swordfish stuffed with leeks and fontina cheese or red snapper brushed with a balsamic mango glaze for entrées. Fish is the specialty, but if you hanker for more straightforward fare, you can order a Black Angus handcut steak, a free-range chicken, or one of the daily pastas. Desserts are tempting, especially the cappuccino brownies and the remarkable gingerbread box filled with warm bananas and cinnamon cream. There's also a 2,000-bottle wine cellar and a selection of fine Armagnacs and cognacs. ⊠ *Meads Bay,* ☎ *264/497–6100. Reservations essential. AE, MC, V. Closed Sun. and Aug.–Sept. No lunch.*

$$$ ✕ **Café at Covecastles.** Elegant, intimate dinners are served here in a garden overlooking beautiful Shoal Bay. Each season a new menu of excellent dishes combines the best of Caribbean and French cooking. Past favorites include West Indian chicken stew, lobster medallions with ginger sauce, roasted vegetable lasagna, balsamic-marinated tuna with sautéed spinach, and veal chops in truffle cream sauce. There are only seven tables here, and Covecastles Villa Resort guests have priority, so call for reservations well in advance. ⊠ *Shoal Bay West,* ☎ *264/497–6801. Reservations essential. AE. Closed Sept.–Nov. No lunch.*

$$ ✕ **Top of the Palms.** The atmosphere may be casual at this indoor-outdoor eatery overlooking the pool on the second floor of La Sirena hotel, but the chefs are definitely on their toes. Anguillan fish soup or crispy conch fritters are good starters. Then move on to seafood quesadillas, tagliatelle with fresh garden vegetables, steamed grouper on a bed of lemongrass, or thyme-crusted fillet of snapper. ⊠ *Mead's Bay,* ☎ *264/ 497–6827. AE, MC, V.*

ITALIAN

$$$$ ✕ **Trattoria Tramonto & Oasis Beach Bar.** Listen to the waves lapping softly in the distance and feel the soft ocean breezes as you dine by candlelight here. Authentic Northern Italian cuisine is the specialty. Try the shrimp with porcini mushrooms and saffron or the lobster ravioli in a truffle sauce, and for dessert don't miss the tiramisu. Come between 5 and 6 for Bellinis, Michelangelos, Puccinis, and Leonardos— champagne drinks mixed with various fruits. Although you might wander in here for lunch after a swim, when casual dress is accepted, you'll still be treated to the same impressive menu. ⊠ *Shoal Bay West,* ☎ *264/497–8819. MC, V. Closed Mon. and Sept.–Oct.*

Sandy Ground, South Hill, and Rendezvous Bay

CARIBBEAN

$ ✕ **Johnno's Beach Stop.** Performances by the island band Dumpa and the AnVibes make this *the* place to be on Sunday afternoon, but the grilled or barbecued lobster, kingfish, snapper (all caught by Johnno himself), and chicken are good any time. This is a classic Caribbean beach bar, attracting a funky eclectic mix, from locals to movie stars. ⊠ *Sandy Ground,* ☎ *264/497–2728. MC, V.*

CONTEMPORARY

$$$ ✕ **Restaurant Ici.** Tables right at the edge of the beach show off a romantic night sky at this popular eatery at the Sonesta Beach Resort &

Villas Anguilla. Specialties are grilled lobster with lemon butter and firecracker sauce, beef tenderloin with roasted-garlic potato pillows, and tomato gnocchi. The lunch menu has salads, sandwiches, pizzas, and burgers. ✉ *Rendezvous Bay,* ☎ *264/497–6999. AE, MC, V.*

ECLECTIC

$$$$ ✕ **Casablanca Grill.** Multiarched ceilings with Moroccan mosaics and evening views of St. Martin/St. Maarten's twinkling lights lend a dramatic air to this favored dining spot in the Sonesta Beach Resort & Villas Anguilla. The menu offers light selections that are frequently grilled, such as local lobster, skewered shrimp, free-range chicken, filet mignon, and fresh grouper. ✉ *Rendezvous Bay,* ☎ *264/497–6999. AE, MC, V.*

$$$ ✕ **Le St. Clair.** People flock to sample chef Franck Duval's eclectic blend of French favorites and Vietnamese specialties. Menu standouts include homemade pâté and pastas, steaks, seafood, fresh spring rolls, local tuna sashimi, and sushi. If you want Vietnamese, call Franck the day before dining to ensure fresh ingredients and adequate preparation time. The beachside setting is informal, and tables are on a huge deck overlooking the water. There's a happy hour every Thursday and Friday from 5 to 7, featuring a tapas bar of Asian savories. Live bands play on Friday nights in season. Le St. Clair serves breakfast, lunch, and dinner Mon.–Sat., brunch only on Sunday. ✉ *Sandy Ground,* ☎ *264/497–2833. AE, MC, V.*

$$ ✕ **Ferryboat Inn.** This charming waterside restaurant at the Ferryboat
★ Inn is a short walk from the Blowing Point ferry dock. Tables are open to the breezes, and the twinkling lights of St. Martin make it even more romantic. The French onion and black-bean soups, grilled lobster, lobster thermidor (the specialty), and entrecôte *du vin au poivre* (a version of steak au poivre with a red wine sauce) are all delicious. There are also veal and chicken dishes, hamburgers, and omelets. ✉ *Cul de Sac Rd., Blowing Point,* ☎ *264/497–6613. AE, MC, V. No lunch Sun.*

$$ ✕ **Ripples.** There's something for everyone at this casual beachfront eatery, where the menu features Mexican, West Indian, Asian, Italian, and vegetarian items. Try the coconut fried shrimp, quesadillas, or veggie sandwiches. ✉ *Sandy Ground,* ☎ *264/497–3380. MC, V.*

FRENCH

$$$ ✕ **Le Bistro Phil.** Owner Phillipe Kim converted his restaurant, formerly Arlo's, to this Parisian-style bistro. The setting is casual and busy, and the menu now emphasizes Kim's roots with an eclectic array of French-influenced and creole-style seafood, pastas, and creative dishes such as the pan-seared tuna steak in an herb reduction, or sautéed medallions of lobster in a crayfish sauce. There are always nightly specials, as well. ✉ *South Hill,* ☎ *264/497–6810. MC, V. Closed Sun. and Sept.–Oct. No lunch.*

The Valley, George Hill, and the Forest

CAFÉ

$ ✕ **Le Petit Patissier.** This café, above the well-known Koal Keel restaurant, was closed at press time, but the owners plan to reopen it. Teas, espresso, and cappuccino plus just-baked pastries, breads, and cakes are served from morning to night indoors or on the small balcony. ✉ *The Valley,* ☎ *264/497–2930. AE, MC, V. Closed Sun. and Sept.– mid-Oct.*

CARIBBEAN

$$ ✕ **Old House.** Guests enjoy the relaxing atmosphere and the local cui-
★ sine at this lovely restaurant on a hill near the airport. Tables are decorated with fresh flowers, even at breakfast, when regulars know to order the island fruit pancakes. For lunch or dinner try the conch sim-

mered in lime juice and wine, curried local lamb with pigeon peas and rice, or Anguillan pot fish cooked in a sauce of limes, garlic, and tomatoes. The daily happy hour, 5–7, is popular and features hot appetizers. ⊠ *George Hill,* ☎ *264/497–2228. MC, V.*

CONTEMPORARY

$$$ ✕ **Palm Court.** This stylish eatery in the Cinnamon Reef Beach Club
★ is a long, palm-lined, open-air corridor with terra-cotta tile floors, Haitian furniture, a beautiful mural of local fish, and arches that frame the twinkling lights of St. Martin. Anguillan chef Vernon Hughes's exciting nouvelle Caribbean menu includes specialties of creamless spiny lobster, pumpkin, and corn bisque, pan-seared tuna in a sweet-potato wrap, Anguillan rock grouper with cracked lemon-pepper, diced lobster and fresh vegetables served on saffron rice, and Caribbean jerk veal chop. The mango puffs in caramel sauce are famous. ⊠ *Little Harbour,* ☎ *264/497–2727. AE, MC, V. Closed mid-Sept.–mid-Oct.*

ECLECTIC

$$$ ✕ **Koal Keel.** This restaurant, in a restored 18th-century great house
★ that was once part of a sugar and cotton plantation, is a nice alternative to the island's beachfront eateries. The dining room has period furniture, and the original stone walls are broken up by window-size spaces open to the breezes. A replica rock oven is used to bake fresh breads and to roast chickens and racks of lamb. The cuisine here is "Euro-Carib," and Chef Smoke makes abundant use of local ingredients. Try the outstanding pea soup, a smooth blend of pigeon peas and Caribbean sweet potatoes, then move on to the succulent goatfish with snow peas and ginger, the fish ravioli with garlic and rosemary, or the roasted rack of lamb in a berry sauce. Save room for the chocolate fondant. More than 20,000 bottles of wine are stored in the wine cellar here. ⊠ *The Valley,* ☎ *264/497–2930. Reservations essential. AE, MC, V. Closed Sept.–mid-Oct.*

$$$ ✕ **Straw Hat.** If you pick a table along the edge of this remarkable restaurant, you can peer right into the sea: the open-air structure is built over the water and gentle waves roll in beneath it. The menu combines French and Caribbean ingredients and cooking styles. For appetizers, start with Caribbean fish chowder, pork with chestnut dumplings, or sautéed shrimp. Grilled New York strip steak, conch cakes, Jamaican jerk pork or chicken, and grouper with citrus sauce are specialties. ⊠ *Forest Bay,* ☎ *264/497–8300. AE, MC, V. No lunch.*

ENGLISH

$ ✕ **Roy's Place.** The dainty pink-and-white-covered deck belies the rowdy reputation of Roy and Mandy Bosson's pub, an Anguillan mainstay with some of the island's best buys. The menu's most popular items are Roy's fish-and-chips, cold English beer, pork fricassee, and a wonderful chocolate rum cake. Sunday's lunch special is roast beef and Yorkshire pudding. A faithful clientele gathers in the lively bar. ⊠ *Crocus Bay,* ☎ *264/497–2470. MC, V. Closed Mon. No lunch Sat.*

East End

ECLECTIC

$$$ ✕ **Hibernia.** Some of the island's most creative dishes are served in this wood-beamed cottage restaurant with water views. Unorthodox yet delectable culinary pairings—inspired by the chef's continued travels from France to the Far East—include Peking chicken pancakes, duck breast with grilled almonds and passion-fruit sauce, fricassee of lobster in mustard-cinnamon sauce, spicy lobster soufflé, and an unusual Thai-inspired bouillabaisse of assorted local seafood. For dessert try the prunes in Armagnac chocolate sauce with homemade chestnut ice cream. ⊠ *Island Harbour,* ☎ *264/497–4290. AE, MC, V. Closed Mon.*

$$ ✕ **Zara's.** Award-winning island chef Shamash presides at this cozy indoor restaurant at the Allamanda Beach Club, where the cuisine is a mix of Italian and Caribbean. Try the lobster pasta in a white-wine sauce, the garlic-crusted snapper, or the very popular seafood platter, which has a bit of everything from conch to calamari. Grilled chicken, steaks, and veal are also available. ⊠ *Upper Shoal Bay,* ☎ *264/497–3229. AE, MC, V.*

Beaches

Renowned for their beauty, the dazzling white-sand beaches are the best reason to come to Anguilla, and each one is different. You'll find deserted sands, long stretches that are great for walking, and beaches lined with bars and restaurants—all accompanied by surf that ranges from wild to super calm.

NORTHEAST COAST

If you make the grueling four-wheel-drive-only trip along the inhospitable dirt road that leads to the northeastern end of the island toward Junk's Hole, **Captain's Bay** will reward you with peaceful isolation. The surf here slaps the sands with a vengeance, and the undertow is strong—wading is the safest water sport.

The mostly calm waters of **Island Harbour** are surrounded by a slender beach. For centuries Anguillans have ventured from these sands in colorful handmade fishing boats. There are several bars and restaurants, and this is the departure point for the three-minute boat ride to **Scilly Cay,** where a beach bar serves seafood.

NORTHWEST COAST

Barnes Bay is superb for windsurfing and snorkeling. In high season this beach can get a bit crowded with day-trippers from St. Martin/St. Maarten.

At **Little Bay** sheer cliffs embroidered with agave and creeping vines rise behind a small gray-sand beach, usually accessible only by water (it's a favored spot for snorkeling and night dives). The hale and hearty can also clamber down the cliffs by rope to explore the caves and surrounding reef.

The clear blue waters of **Road Bay** beach are usually dotted with yachts. Several restaurants, a water-sports center, and lots of windsurfing and waterskiing activity make this area (often called Sandy Ground) a commercial one. The snorkeling isn't very good here, but the sunset vistas are glorious.

From a distance, **Sandy Island,** nestled in coral reefs about 2 mi (3 km) from Road Bay, seems no more than a tiny speck of sand and a few spindly palm trees. Still, it has the modern-day comforts of a beach boutique, a bar, and a restaurant. Use of snorkeling gear and underwater cameras is free. A ferry heads here every hour from Sandy Ground.

Shoal Bay West is a 1-mi-long (1½-km-long) sweep of sand rimmed with mangroves; there are coral reefs not too far from shore. It can be crowded with day-trippers from St. Martin/St. Maarten.

SOUTHEAST COAST

Mimi Bay is a ½-mi (1-km) isolated, difficult-to-reach beach east of Sea Feathers Bay. The trip is worth it. When the surf is down, the reef makes for great snorkeling.

Not far from Sea Feathers Bay is **Sandy Hill,** a base for fishermen. Here you can buy fish and lobster right off the boats and snorkel in the warm waters. Don't plan to sunbathe—the beach is narrow.

Unfortunately, it's no longer a secret that **Shoal Bay East**—Shoal Bay, via Shoal Bay Road—is one of the Caribbean's prettiest beaches. There are beach chairs, umbrellas, and a backdrop of sea-grape and coconut trees. Restaurants offer seafood and tropical drinks, shops sell T-shirts and sunscreen, and the water-sports center arranges diving, sailing, and fishing trips.

SOUTHWEST COAST

Cove Bay, lined with coconut palms, is quiet. There's a little bar and a place where you can rent floats, umbrellas, and mats.

The popular, wide, 1-mi-long (1½-km-long) **Maunday's Bay** is known for good swimming and snorkeling. You can also rent water-sports gear.

Rendezvous Bay is 1½ mi (2½ km) of pearl-white sand. The water is calm, and there's a great view of St. Martin. The open-air bar of the Anguilla Great House Beach Resort is handy for snacks and frosty island drinks.

Adjacent to Maunday's Bay is **Shoal Bay West,** a dazzling beach with several striking villa complexes. Beachcombers may find lovely conch shells here.

Outdoor Activities and Sports

BOATING AND SAILING

Anguilla is the perfect place to try all kinds of boating and sailing activities. The major resorts offer complimentary Windsurfers, paddleboats, and water skis to their guests. If your hotel has no water-sports facilities, you can get in gear at the **Dive Shop** (⊠ Sandy Ground, ☎ 264/497–2020) or charter its *Sundancer,* a 30-ft powerboat. **Tropical Watersports** (⊠ Sandy Ground, ☎ 264/497–6666) rents Sunfish and Hobie Cats. You can rent sailboats and speedboats from **Sandy Island Enterprises** (⊠ Sandy Ground, ☎ 264/497–5643).

FISHING

Albacore and kingfish are among the sea creatures angled after off Anguilla's shores. **Johnno's** in Sandy Ground (☎ 264/497–2728) can help you plan a trip. **Sandy Island Enterprises,** in Sandy Ground (☎ 264/497–5643) offers a wide range of services, including power boat rentals and day trips on sailboats.

HORSEBACK RIDING

Scenic nature trails and miles of beaches are the perfect places to ride, even if you're a novice. Ride English or Western at **El Rancho Del Blues** (☎ 264/497–6164). Prices start at $25 per hour.

SCUBA DIVING

Sunken wrecks, a long barrier reef, and exceptionally clear water offer excellent diving opportunities. The new **Stoney Bay Marine Park,** off the northeast end of Anguilla, showcases the late-18th-century *El Buen Consejo,* a Spanish vessel that sank here in 1772. Other good dive sites include **Grouper Bowl,** with exceptional hard-coral formations; **Ram's Head,** with caves, chutes, and tunnels; and **Upper Flats,** where you are sure to see stingrays. The **Dive Shop** (☎ 264/497–2020) is a full-service dive operator with a PADI Five-Star Training Center. Two guided dives are offered daily; a single tank dive costs $60. At Shoal Bay, contact **Shoal Bay Scuba and Watersports** (☎ 264/497–4371).

SEA EXCURSIONS

Anguilla Sails Ltd. (⊠ Sandy Ground, ☎ 264/497–2253) offers day sails, sunset sails, and moonlight cruises. *Chocolat* (⊠ Sandy Ground, ☎ 264/497–3394) is a 35-ft catamaran available for private charter or scheduled excursions to nearby cays. Rates for day sails start at $30 per person. For a look at what goes on underwater without getting wet, catch a ride ($15 per person) on **Junior's Glass Bottom Boat** (✉ Sandy Ground, ☎ 264/497–4456). Snorkel trips and instruction are available, too.

Picnic, swimming, and diving excursions to Prickly Pear, Sandy Island, and Scilly Cay are available through **Sandy Island Enterprises** (☎ 264/497–5643).

TENNIS
You'll find tennis courts (some lighted) at several resorts. Simply call ahead and make a reservation. Fees range $15–$20 per hour. **Carimar Beach Club** (☎ 264/497–6881) has two hard courts. **Rendezvous Bay Hotel** (☎ 264/497–6549) has two hard courts. The **Mariners Cliffside Beach Resort** (☎ 264/497–2671) has one hard court. **Ronald Webster Park** (✉ The Valley, ☎ no phone) has a hard court open to the public.

Shopping

The free *Anguilla Life* and *What We Do in Anguilla,* available at the airport and in shops and hotel lobbies, have shopping tips. Outstanding local artists sell their work in galleries. For upscale designer sportswear, check out the little shops (most are branches of larger stores in Marigot on St. Martin). For a better selection catch the ferry to St. Martin and spend a day browsing in chic boutiques that carry the latest European fashions.

CLOTHES
Azemmour Boutique (✉ Cap Juluca resort, Maunday's Bay, ☎ 264/497–6666) specializes in European swimwear and also carries fine jewelry. **Beach Stuff** (✉ Back St., South Hill, ☎ 264/497–6814), in its brightly painted building, attracts the younger crowd looking for bathing suits, sunglasses, T-shirts, and other sportswear. **Boutique at Malliouhana** (✉ Meads Bay, ☎ 264/497–6111) is the most upscale shop on Anguilla, selling such designer specialties as jewelry by Oro De Sol, Gottex swimwear, and Robert LaRoche sunglasses. **Caribbean Fancy** (✉ George Hill Rd., ☎ 264/497–3133) features Ta-Tee's line of crinkle-cotton resort wear, plus books, spices, and gift items. **Caribbean Silkscreen** (✉ South Hill, ☎ 264/497–2272) creates designs and prints them on golf shirts, hats, sweatshirts, and jackets. **Java Wraps** (✉ George Hill Rd., ☎ 264/497–5497) has superb batik clothing for the whole family. **La Romana** (✉ Meads Bay, ☎ 264/497–6181), an international specialty boutique, is the place to go for swimwear, Fendi fashions, and fine luggage. **Objets D'Art Collectibles** (✉ Warden's Place, The Valley, ☎ 264/497–2787) sells "wearable art" as well as sandals and jewelry. **Oluwakemi's Afrocentric Boutique** (✉ Lansome Rd.,The Valley, ☎ 264/497–5411) sells books, sandals, umbrellas, jewelry, T-shirts, and hats. You can also choose from an array of fabrics or have apparel custom-made. **Sunshine Shop** (✉ South Hill, ☎ 264/497–6964) stocks cotton *pareos* (saronglike beach cover-ups), silkscreen items, cotton resort wear, and hand-painted Haitian wood items. **Tradewinds Boutique** (✉ Sonesta Beach Resort & Villas Anguilla, Meads Bay, ☎ 264/497–6999) carries Tommy Bahama, Anne Cole, Sloop Jones, and other designer fashions. **Whispers** (✉ Cap Juluca, ☎ 264/497–6666) has Caribbean handicrafts and stylish resort wear for men and women.

FOODSTUFFS
Fat Cat Gourmet. Try this place for escargots to go plus take-out quiche, soups, chili, chicken, and conch dishes. ✉ *George Hill,* ☎ 264/497–2307

HANDICRAFTS

Alicea's Place (⊠ The Quarter, ☎ 264/497–3540) sells locally made ceramics and pottery and Balinese wooden flowers. **Anguilla Arts & Crafts Center** (⊠ The Valley, ☎ 264/497–2200) carries island crafts. **Cheddie's Carving Studios** (⊠ The Cove, ☎ 264/497–6027) showcases Cheddie's creations crafted out of mahogany, walnut, and driftwood. **Devonish Art Gallery** (⊠ George Hill Landing, ☎ 264/497–2949) purveys the wood, stone, and clay creations of Courtney Devonish, an internationally known potter and sculptor, as well as works by other local artists. **Michele R. Lavalette Art Studio** (⊠ North Hill, ☎ 264/497–5668) displays the appealing watercolors and oil paintings of French artist Michele Lavalette, an Anguilla resident since 1985. **Mother Weme** (⊠ The Valley, ☎ 264/497–4504) paints charming montages of Anguillan and general Caribbean life, incorporating homes, churches, marketplaces, and people. Call for an appointment. **New World Gallery** (⊠ The Valley, ☎ 264/407–5950) exhibits local art and sells jewelry, textiles, and antiquities. **Savannah Gallery** (⊠ Lower Valley, ☎ 264/497–2263) specializes in Caribbean art, including watercolors, oil paintings, and brightly painted metal work. **Scruples Gift Shop** (⊠ Social Security Bldg., The Valley, ☎ 264/497–2800) offers simple gift items, such as shells, handmade baskets, wooden dolls, and hand-crocheted mats and bedspreads.

Nightlife and the Arts

Nightlife

A Calypso combo plays most nights in season at **Cinnamon Reef Beach Club** (⊠ Little Harbour, ☎ 264/497–2727).

The **Dune Preserve** (⊠ Rendezvous Bay, ☎ 264/497–2660) is the home of Bankie Banx, Anguilla's famous recording star, who performs here weekends and during the full moon.

Things are lively at **Johnno's Beach Stop** (⊠ Sandy Ground, ☎ 264/497–2728), with live music and alfresco dancing nightly and also on Sunday afternoons, when just about everybody drops by.

There's live music nightly in season at the **Malliouhana** (⊠ Meads Bay, ☎ 264/497–6111) during cocktail hours.

During high season, **Pimms** (⊠ Cap Juluca, ☎ 264/497–6666) entertains with live music at dinner.

At the **Pumphouse** (⊠ Sandy Ground, ☎ 264/497–5154), in the old Rock Salt factory, you'll find live music on weekends and a minimuseum displaying artifacts and equipment from salt factories of the 19th century.

Rafe's Back Street (⊠ Sandy Ground, ☎ 264/497–3918) is the spot to go for late-night—even all-night on weekends—food, music, and dance.

At the **Red Dragon Disco** (⊠ The Valley, ☎ 264/497–2687) a DJ plays music Friday, Saturday, and Sunday nights.

Uncle Ernie's (⊠ Shoal Bay, ☎ 264/497–3907) often has live music, and a spirited crowd heads here almost every night.

The Arts

The **Mayoumba Folkloric Theater** performs song-and-dance skits depicting Antillean and Caribbean culture with African drums and a string band. They appear every Thursday night at **La Sirena Hotel** (⊠ Meads Bay, ☎ 264/497–6827).

Exploring Anguilla

Exploring on Anguilla is mostly about checking out the spectacular beaches and classy resorts. Though the island has only a few roads, some are in bad condition and unmarked. Locals are happy to provide directions, but having a good map—and using it—is the best strategy. Get one at the airport, the ferry dock, your hotel, or the tourist office in The Valley.

Numbers in the margin correspond to points of interest on the Anguilla map.

SIGHTS TO SEE

❽ Amerindian Mini-Museum. A small display of Arawak Indian objects is showcased here. There's also a 4-by-8-ft oil painting that shows what Big Springs, a nearby ceremonial ground, might have looked like when Amerindians lived there. ⊠ *Arawak Beach Resort, Island Harbour,* ☎ *264/497–4888,* WEB *www.arawakresort.com.* 🗐 *Free.* ⊙ *Daily 10–4.*

❹ Bethel Methodist Church. Not far from Sandy Ground, this charming little church is an excellent example of skillful island stonework. It also has some colorful stained-glass windows. ⊠ *South Hill,* ☎ *No phone.*

❾ Heritage Collection. Anguillan artifacts, old photographs, and records trace the island's history from the days of the Arawaks to the present at this inviting museum. You can see examples of ancient pottery shards and stone tools along with fascinating photographs of the island in the early 20th century, including many photos that depict the heaping and exporting of salt and the christening of schooners. Also on display is a complete set of beautiful postage stamps issued by Anguilla since 1967. ⊠ *East End at Pond Ground,* ☎ *264/497–4440,* WEB *www.offshore.com.ai/heritage.* 🗐 *$5.* ⊙ *Mon.–Sat. 9–5.*

❼ Island Harbour. Anguillans have been fishing for centuries in the brightly painted, simple handcrafted fishing boats that line the shore of the harbor. It's hard to believe, but skillful pilots take these little boats out to sea as far as 50 or 60 mi (80 or 100 km). Late afternoon is the best time to see the day's catch. ⊠ *Island Harbour, at northwest end of island, facing Island Harbour Bay.*

❷ Old Factory. For many years the cotton that was grown on Anguilla and imported to England was ginned in this beautiful historic building. Some of the original ginning machinery is intact and on display here, and this is also the home of the **Anguilla Tourist Office.** ⊠ *The Valley,* ☎ *264/497–2759.* 🗐 *Free.* ⊙ *Weekdays 10–noon, 1–4.*

❺ Old Prison at Crocus Hill. On the highest point in Anguilla—213 ft (65 m) above sea level—the historic prison is pretty much in ruin, but the view is outstanding. ⊠ *Valley Rd. at Crocus Hill.*

❶ Sandy Ground. This is by far the most active and most developed of the island's beaches, and almost everyone who comes to Anguilla stops by here at least once. Little open-air bars and restaurants line the shore, and there are several boutiques, a dive shop, and a small commercial pier. This is where you catch the ferry for tiny **Sandy Island,** just 2 mi (3 km) offshore.

❸ Wallblake House. On Wallblake Road, just north of the traffic circle, is a plantation house with spacious rooms and handsome woodwork that was built in 1787 by Will Blake (Wallblake is probably a corruption of his name). The place is associated with many a tale involving murder, high living, and the French invasion in 1796. Its days of debauchery are over, though; today it's owned and actively used by the Catholic Church. On the grounds are an ancient vaulted stone cistern and an outbuilding called the Bakery (which wasn't used for making bread at all but for baking turkeys and hams). Call Father John to make an appointment to tour the plantation. ⊠ *Wallblake Rd., The Valley,* ☎ 264/497–2405.

❻ Warden's Place. This former sugar-plantation great house was built in the 1790s and is a fine example of island stonework. It's now the site of the Koal Keel restaurant, but for many years it served as the residence of the island's chief administrator, who also doubled as the only medical practitioner. ⊠ *The Valley.*

ANGUILLA A TO Z

To research prices, get advice from other travelers, and book travel arrangements, visit www.fodors.com.

AIR TRAVEL

American Airlines is the major airline, with nonstop flights from the continental United States to its hub in San Juan, from which the airline's American Eagle flies three times daily (twice daily off-season) to Anguilla's Wallblake Airport. Windward Islands Airways wings in daily from St. Thomas and at least three times a day from St. Maarten's Juliana Airport. LIAT comes in from Antigua, Nevis, St. Kitts, St. Martin, St. Thomas, and Tortola. Air Anguilla offers several flights daily from St. Martin and the U.S. Virgin Islands and provides air-taxi service on request from neighboring islands. Tyden Air has scheduled daily flights from St. Maarten and several weekly flights to and from St. Kitts and St. Thomas. The airline also offers charter day trips to many neighboring islands.
➤ AIRLINES AND CONTACTS: **Air Anguilla** (☎ 264/497–3643); **American Airlines** (☎ 264/497–3131); **LIAT** (☎ 264/497–2748 or 264/497–5002); **Tyden Air** (☎ 264/497–2719 or 800/842–0261); **Windward Islands Airways** (☎ 264/497–2238).

AIRPORTS

Taxis line up at Wallblake Airport to meet the planes. A trip to Sandy Ground is about $10; to West End resorts it's $16–$22.
➤ AIRPORT INFORMATION: **Wallblake Airport** (☎ 264/497–2719).

BIKE AND MOPED TRAVEL

Motorcycles and scooters run about $30 per day from Boo's Cycle Rental.
➤ CONTACTS: **Boo's Cycle Rental** (⊠ Water Swamp, ☎ 264/497–2323).

BOAT AND FERRY TRAVEL
FARES AND SCHEDULES

Ferries run frequently between Anguilla and St. Martin. Boats leave from Blowing Point on Anguilla every half hour from 7:30 to 5 and from Marigot on St. Martin every half hour from 8 to 5:30. Evening ferries leave Blowing Point at 6 and 9:15 and Marigot at 7 and 10:45. You pay a $4 departure tax before boarding and the $15 one-way fare ($17 evenings) on board. Don't buy a round-trip ticket because it restricts you to the boat for which it is purchased. On very windy days the 20-minute trip can be bouncy, and if you suffer from motion sickness, you may want medication. An information booth outside the customs shed in Blowing Point is usually open daily from 8:30 to 5, but sometimes the attendant wanders off. It's also possible to travel directly by ferry from Julianna Airport on St. Maarten to Anguilla. For schedule information, and info on special boat charters, contact Link

Ferries.

➤ BOAT AND FERRY INFORMATION: **Link Ferries** (☎ 264/497–2231, WEB www.link.ai).

BUSINESS HOURS
BANKS
Banks are open Monday–Thursday 8–3 and Friday 8–5.

POST OFFICES
The post office is open weekdays 10–noon and 1–4. ·

SHOPS
Most shops are open 10–4 on weekdays, but call first, or ask the tourist office for opening and closing times. Or adopt the island way of doing things: If it's not open when you stop by, try again.

CAR RENTALS
This is your best bet for maximum mobility if you're comfortable driving on the left and don't mind some jostling. To rent a car, you'll need a temporary local license, which you can obtain for $21 at any of the car-rental agencies; you'll need your valid driver's license from home.

Apex (Avis) rents sedans and four-wheel-drive vehicles. Budget has four-wheel-drive vehicles and sedans. Connors (National) rents four-wheel-drive vehicles and sedans. Head to Triple K Car Rental for car rentals, including four-wheel-drive vehicles. Rates are $45 to $55 per day, plus insurance.

➤ MAJOR AGENCIES: **Apex (Avis)** (✉ Airport Rd., ☎ 264/497–2642); **Budget** (✉ Airport Rd., ☎ 264/497–5871); **Connors (National)** (✉ Blowing Point, ☎ 264/497–6433); **Triple K Car Rental** (✉ Airport Rd., ☎ 264/497–5934).

CAR TRAVEL
GASOLINE
There are several gas stations on the island, and they are generally open from 7 AM to 11 PM. Gasoline is expensive; expect to pay about EC$7.55 per gallon (about US$2.82 per gallon).

ROAD CONDITIONS
Anguilla's roads are generally paved, but those that are not can be incredibly rutted.

RULES OF THE ROAD
Driving is on the left. Observe the 30-mph speed limit and watch out for livestock that amble across the road.

ELECTRICITY
The current is 110 volts, the same as in North America; standard two-prong plugs will work just fine.

EMERGENCIES
➤ AMBULANCE AND FIRE: Dial ☎ 264/497–2551 for the ambulance. Dial ☎ 911 for fire.
➤ HOSPITALS: **Princess Alexandra Hospital** (✉ Stoney Ground, ☎ 264/497–2551).
➤ PHARMACIES: **Government Pharmacy** (✉ The Valley, ☎ 264/497–2551), in Princess Alexandra Hospital, is open daily 8:30–4; **Paramount Pharmacy** (✉ Water Swamp, ☎ 264/497–2366) is open Monday–Saturday 8:30–7 and has a 24-hour emergency service.
➤ POLICE: Dial ☎ 911 or ☎ 264/497–2333 for nonemergencies.

ETIQUETTE AND BEHAVIOR

It's an Anguillan custom to greet people and exchange polite comments about the day or the weather before getting down to business. It's considered quite rude to skip this step, so join in, even if you're in a hurry.

FESTIVALS AND SEASONAL EVENTS

In February the National Cultural & Educational Festival celebrates Anguilla's traditional cultures with a variety of dance, storytelling, games, and music programs. March brings Moonsplash, a three-day music festival that showcases local talent and begins on the night of the full moon. The Anguilla Culinary Competition is held the last week of May. At the end of July is the International Arts Festival, which hosts artists from around the world. The first two weeks of August is Carnival, which includes parades, street dancing, boat racing, and lots of general merrymaking.

HOLIDAYS

Public holidays for 2002 are: New Year's Day, Easter (Apr. 15), Easter Monday (Apr. 16), Labour Day (May 7), Anguilla Day (May 28), Whit Monday (June 4), Queen's Birthday (June 11), August Monday (Aug. 6), Constitution Day (Aug. 8), Separation Day (Dec. 19), Christmas, Boxing Day (Dec. 26).

LANGUAGE

English, with a strong West Indian lilt, is spoken here.

MAIL AND SHIPPING

Airmail postcards and letters cost $1.50 (for the first ½ ounce) to the United States and Canada, $1.90 to the United Kingdom, and $2.50 to Australia and New Zealand. The only post office is in The Valley; it's open weekdays 8–3:30. When writing to the island, you don't need a postal code; just include the name of the establishment, address (location or post-office box), and Anguilla, British West Indies.

➤ CONTACTS: **Post Office** (⊠ Wallblake Rd., ☎ 264/497–2528).

MONEY MATTERS

Prices quoted throughout this chapter are in U.S. dollars unless otherwise indicated.

ATMS

Don't count on ATMs, which are often on the blink. Remember, ATMs will dispense money in EC dollars.

CREDIT CARDS

Credit cards are not always accepted; some resorts will only settle in cash, but a few accept personal checks. Some restaurants add a charge if you pay with a credit card.

CURRENCY

Though the legal tender here is the Eastern Caribbean (EC) dollar, U.S. dollars are widely accepted. (You'll often get change in EC dollars.) The EC dollar is fairly stable, hovering at EC$2.60–$2.70 to the U.S. dollar. Be sure to carry lots of small bills; change for a $20 is often difficult to obtain.

➤ CONTACTS: **Scotiabank** (☎ 264/497–3333, WEB www.scotiabank.ca).

PASSPORTS AND VISAS

U.S. and Canadian citizens need proof of identity. A passport is preferred (even one that has expired within the past five years). Also acceptable is a government-issued photo ID, such as a driver's license, *along with* a birth certificate (with raised seal) or naturalization papers. Citizens of the United Kingdom, Australia, and New Zealand must have passports. All visitors must also have a return or ongoing ticket. Visitor's passes are valid for stays of up to three months.

SAFETY

The manchineel tree, which resembles an apple tree, bears poisonous fruit, and the sap from the tree causes painful blisters. Avoid sitting beneath the tree because even dew or raindrops falling from the leaves can blister your skin. Be *sure* to take along insect repellent—mosquitoes can be pesky in the late afternoon.

Anguilla is a quiet, relatively safe island, but there's no point in tempting fate by leaving your valuables unattended in your hotel room, on the beach, or in your car.

SIGHTSEEING TOURS

A round-the-island tour by taxi takes about 2½ hours and costs $40 for one or two people, $5 for each additional passenger.

Bennie's Tours is one of the island's more reliable tour operators. Malliouhana Travel and Tours create personalized package tours of the island.
➤ CONTACTS: **Bennie's Tours** (✉ Blowing Point, ☎ 264/497–2788); **Malliouhana Travel and Tours** (✉ The Valley, ☎ 264/497–2431).

TAXES

DEPARTURE TAX
The departure tax is $15 at the airport, $4 if you leave by boat.

SALES TAX
A 10% accommodations tax and a 10% restaurant service charge are added to most bills.

TAXIS

Taxi rates are regulated by the government, and there are fixed fares from point to point (listed in brochures the drivers should have). Posted rates are for one or two people; each additional passenger adds $3 to the total.

Taxis are always waiting to pick up passengers at the Blowing Point landing docks. It costs $14 to get to Malliouhana, $17 to Cap Juluca, and $20 to most hotels farther afield.

TELEPHONES

Cable & Wireless is open weekdays 8–6, Saturday 9–1, and Sunday 10–2; it sells Caribbean phone cards for use in specially marked phone booths. The cards can be used for local calls, calls to other islands, and calls to the United States. Inside the departure lounge at the Blowing Point ferry dock and at the airport there's an AT&T USADirect access phone for collect or credit-card calls to the United States.
➤ CONTACTS: **Cable & Wireless** (✉ Wallblake Rd., ☎ 264/497–3100).

COUNTRY AND AREA CODES
To call Anguilla from the United States, dial 1 plus the area code 264, then the local seven-digit number. From the United Kingdom dial 001 and then the area code and the number. From Australia and New Zealand dial 0011, then 1, then the area code and the number.

INTERNATIONAL CALLS
International direct dial is available on the island. To call internationally, dial 1, the area code, and the seven-digit number to reach the United States and Canada; dial 011, 44, and the local number for the United Kingdom; dial 011, 61, and the local number for Australia; and dial 011, 64, and the local number for New Zealand. Although you can

dial direct from your hotel room, it's cheaper to dial 800/877–8000 and charge your call to a major credit card.

LOCAL CALLS

To make a local call, dial the seven-digit number.

TIPPING

A 10% service charge is added to all hotel bills; sometimes it covers all staff members, sometimes not. If you're unsure whether to tip hotel staff, ask the hotel management. Tip taxi drivers 10% of the fare.

VISITOR INFORMATION

➤ BEFORE YOU LEAVE: **Anguilla Tourist Office/River Communications** (✉ Box 2119 Woodford Green, London, 1G8 0GC, ☎ 0208/505–6614, FAX 0208/505–8974); **Anguilla Tourist Office/Sergat Deutschland** (✉ IM Gulden Wingert 8-C, D-64342, Seeheim, ☎ 6257/962920, FAX 6257/962919.

➤ IN ANGUILLA: **Anguilla Tourist Office** (✉ Old Factory Plaza, The Valley, ☎ 264/497–2759 or ☎ 800/553–4939, FAX 264/497–2710, WEB www.anguilla-vacation.com).

2 ANTIGUA

Updated by
Jordan Simon

It's Antigua Sailing Week, the island's version of the Henley Regatta. Seasoned sea salts claim prized seats on the flagstone terrace of the 18th-century Admiral's Inn in English Harbour. Some boats are docked so close that you can almost eavesdrop from shore. Competitors trade stories (tall and otherwise) of sailing—and drinking—two sheets to the wind, while eyeing the yachts. Blazered bluebloods mingle with lobster-hue tourists; it's Cannes in the Caribbean.

Antigua (an-*tee*-ga), which at 108 square mi (280 square km) is the largest of the British Leeward Islands, is renowned among sailors for its incomparable air of nautical history. For Anglophiles and history buffs, English Harbour and the surrounding villages and sites are also immensely rewarding. And Antigua seduces landlubbers and sailors alike with its sensuous beaches, 366 in all—one for every day of the year and one left over, as locals like to boast. All are public, some are absolutely deserted, and others are lined with resorts that offer sailing, diving, windsurfing, and snorkeling.

The original inhabitants of Antigua were the Ciboney. They lived here 4,000 years ago and disappeared mysteriously, leaving the island unpopulated for about 1,000 years. When Columbus arrived in 1493, the Arawaks had set up housekeeping. The English took up residence in 1632. After 30-odd years of bloody battles involving the Caribs, the Dutch, the French, and the English, the French ceded Antigua to the English in 1667. Antigua remained under English control until achieving full independence on November 1, 1981, along with its sister island, Barbuda, 26 mi (42 km) to the north.

Those in search of beaches, nightlife, shopping, and restaurants should head to the island's northwestern end, where resorts and hotels are scattered from Five Islands Harbour to Dickenson Bay and points north. One of the least developed areas is the southwest, in the shadow of Antigua's highest mountain, Boggy Peak. Friar's Bay and Darkwood Beach hold long, unspoiled scimitars of sand.

Tourism is the leading industry here, and building (and, after several hurricanes in the late 1990s, rebuilding) has been widespread in the last decade. But Antigua maintains a strong sense of national identity to match its rich historic inheritance. Its cricketers, like the legendary Viv Richards (arguably the greatest batsman the game has ever seen), are famous throughout the world. Its people are known for their sharp commercial spirit (a typically revealing—and disarming—sign reads

DIANE'S BOUTIQUE AND CAR PARTS); their wit; and unfortunately, at the government level, their corruption.

Lodging

Scattered along Antigua's beaches and hillsides are exclusive, elegant hideaways; romantic restored inns; go-barefoot-everywhere places; and, increasingly, all-inclusive hot spots for couples. Choose accommodations near St. John's—anywhere between Dickenson Bay and Five Islands Peninsula—if you want to be close to the action. English Harbour, far from St. John's, has the best inns and several excellent restaurants; it's also the hangout for the yachting crowd. Elsewhere on the island, resorts cater more to guests who want to stay put or are seeking seclusion. Be sure to ask about specials: the larger properties often host tour groups who are paying as little as ⅓ the rack rate usually quoted. Many of the smaller establishments have become all-inclusive to survive the fierce competition; some are so remote that trying to arrange an EP rate makes no sense unless you have a car. Another similar trend: restaurants adding a clutch of charming, affordable cottages.

The big news is redevelopment. After the devastation of two hurricanes in 1999, Club Antigua, on the west coast, has reopened as the 462-room all-inclusive Jolly Beach Hotel. Though splashed with color and remarkably cheap, many of the original rooms remain the size of monks' cells and at press time, the venture's success was still undetermined. The Jolly Harbour Villa Resort has been taken over by the people behind the St. James Club, Galley Bay, and Royal Antiguan Resort. The 500-acre complex includes an 18-hole golf course and marina. New villas are being constructed, old ones renovated and modernized, facilities added, and retail dining and shopping spaces created. The project was expected to be fully operational by late 2001, with meal options for rental units ranging from EP to all-inclusive.

CATEGORY	COST*
$$$$	over $450
$$$	$300–$450
$$	$150–$300
$	under $150

*All prices are for a standard double room, excluding 8½% tax and 10% service charge.

$$$$ 🏨 **Allegro Resort Pineapple Beach.** A broad stone walk leads from the reception area to the beach of this bustling all-inclusive. Buildings and staircases are painted in fun gumball colors while public spaces and facilities, including a pool with two bridges and waterfall, have character and charm. The newest units (built in 1999) crawl up a hill and are stylish, with marble tables, natural-wicker armoires and beds, and terra-cotta floors. The buffet-style main restaurant and the more intimate Pineapple Grill serve above-average Caribbean and Continental dishes. The latter, a split-level riot of lime, mango, and peach, is transformed into a late-night disco. The Outhouse Bar is a classic Caribbean hangout and the perfect sunset perch. The Little Village Club offers fully supervised activities, many island-oriented, for kids. You'll also find a full array of sports and nightly entertainment. ⊠ *Long Bay (Box 2000, St. John's),* ☎ *268/463–2006 or 800/858–2258,* FAX *268/463–2452,* WEB *www.allegroresorts.com. 135 rooms. 3 restaurants, 4 bars, air-conditioning, fans, 2 pools, 4 tennis courts, croquet, exercise room, horseshoes, volleyball, beach, snorkeling, windsurfing, boating, waterskiing, fishing, shops, nightclub, children's programs. AE, MC, V. All-inclusive.*

$$$$ 🏨 **Blue Waters Hotel.** Although the twin beaches here are on the small side, the hotel's location on Boon Point—amid 14 acres of tropical gardens—is splendid. The colonnaded lobby has sweeping sea views, a virtual jungle of greenery, and such elegant touches as mosaic tile lamps and peacock wicker chairs. A series of fountains leads to a pool and the beach bar. The rooms are less impressive: stark but sparkling in white with rattan and wicker furnishings, jungle fabrics, and bas-relief, glazed tile bathrooms. Deluxe rooms have sitting areas with built-in sun seats and patios with bougainvillea planters. The four villas and two enormous suites are exquisite, with leaf tracery, tropical fabrics, glass-top wrought-iron tables, and hardwood furnishings. Those on a splurge might consider the hedonistic, fully equipped two-bedroom Rock Cottage: it features glorious decor, inspiring views from every room, and even its own boat (to reach an otherwise inaccessible private beach). Afternoon tea and one sauna per week are included. The casual Palm Restaurant features Italian and international cuisine, while the gourmet Vyvien's has a Continental menu that changes daily. ✉ *Boon Point (Box 256, St. John's),* ☎ *268/462–0290 or 800/557–6536,* FAX *268/462–0293,* WEB *www.bluewaters.net. 73 rooms, 4 villas, 1 2-bedroom cottage. 2 restaurants, 2 bars, air-conditioning, fans, in-room safes, minibars, 2 pools, hair salon, spa, tennis court, gym, 2 beaches, snorkeling, windsurfing, boating, shops. AE, D, DC, MC, V. All-inclusive, EP.*

$$$$ 🏨 **Curtain Bluff.** Howard Hulford built this resort, on a bluff bordered
★ by two exquisite stretches of sand, 40 years ago, and he's still active in its management. You may see him puttering around his beloved gardens (Antigua's lushest and as impeccably manicured as the clientele) or tasting a new wine for his legendary 25,000-bottle cellar. Standard rooms with stylish and soothing fabrics, wicker furnishings, and terraces or balconies are in two-story beachfront buildings that face the Caribbean. A new wing with 18 spacious junior suites replaced one of the original buildings in 2000, and it's stunning, with marble bathrooms, coffered raw wood ceilings, sisal rugs, Mexican earthenware, and elegantly simple lines. Huge split-level one-bedroom apartment suites—each with two balconies, a large living room, and a spacious bedroom—zigzag up the bluff. As for dining, Swiss chef Reudi Portmann has ruled the sterling kitchen of the open-air restaurant since the resort opened. Jackets are required (except Sunday, Wednesday, and in the off-season) for a dinner of classic Continental cuisine. A personal trainer and ATP tennis pros are available, and bar drinks, afternoon tea, and water sports including deep-sea fishing and scuba diving are free. The resort's exceptional service and country-club ambience appeal to a more mature crowd, but honeymooners come here, too (weddings can be arranged and held at Howard's own home for no additional charge). Given its unparalleled setting, quietly posh atmosphere, and numerous extras, Curtain Bluff is that rarity: a world-class resort that's a bargain in its class. ✉ *Morris Bay (Box 288), St. John's,* ☎ *268/462–8400, 212/289–8888, or 888/289–9898 outside NY;* FAX *268/462–8409,* WEB *www.curtainbluff.com. 63 rooms, 7 suites. 2 restaurants, bar, in-room safes, pool, hair salon, putting green, 4 tennis courts, croquet, gym, squash, 2 beaches, dive shop, snorkeling, windsurfing, boating, fishing, shops. AE. FAP. Closed mid-May–mid-Oct.*

$$$$ 🏨 **Galley Bay.** This tony all-inclusive appeals to a lively corporate crowd, as well as to long-time regulars, who find it splashier but even more deluxe than in its previous incarnation. Showy features include a waterfall and man-made pool grotto and a bleached-wood boardwalk along the beach. Ravishing champagne-color sand, a blue lagoon, manicured gardens, and a bird sanctuary with trails surround the enclave. Thatch-roof public spaces are filled with African carvings and Caribbean art naïf, and the wattle-and-daub cottages of Gauguin Village have sin-

Antigua and Barbuda

Lodging

Admiral's Inn 12
Allegro Resort
Pineapple
Beach 17
Blue Waters
Hotel 21
CocoBay 5
Curtain Bluff 7
Dickenson Bay
Cottages 25
Galley Bay 30
Hawksbill Beach
Hotel 31
Inn at English
Harbour 9
Jumby Bay 19
K Club 18
Ocean Inn 14
Rex Blue Heron 6
Rex Halcyon
Cove Beach
Resort 26
Royal Antiguan
Resort 28
St. James's Club 15
Sandals Antigua
Resort and Spa 24
Siboney Beach
Club 23
Sunsail Club
Colonna 22

Dining

Abracadabra 10
Admiral's Inn 12
Alberto's 16
Averill's 8
Bay House 27
Big Banana–
Pizzas on
the Quay 1
Le Bistro 20
Catherine's Cafe 11
Chez Pascal 29
Coco's 4
Coconut Grove 23
Commissioner's
Grill 2
HQ 13
Redcliffe Tavern 3

TO
BARBUDA

ANTIGUA

Boon Pt.
Hodges Bay
Pric

Cedar Grove

21 22

20

23 – 26

27

Dickenson Bay
Runaway Beach

Andes

28

29 30

31

Hawksbill's Beaches

Five Islands

Deepwater Harbour

St. John's

1

1 3

Potters

Parham

Fullerton Pt.

Pearns Pt.

Jennings

2

Jolly Harbour

N

5

4

Bolans

Boggy Peak

All Saints

Darkwood Beach

6

Johnson's Pt.

Urlings

Fig Tree Drive

Johnson's Point

Cades Reef

Old Road

7

8

Carlisle Bay

Rendezvous Bay

Pigeon

Caribbean Sea

0   5 miles
0   5 km

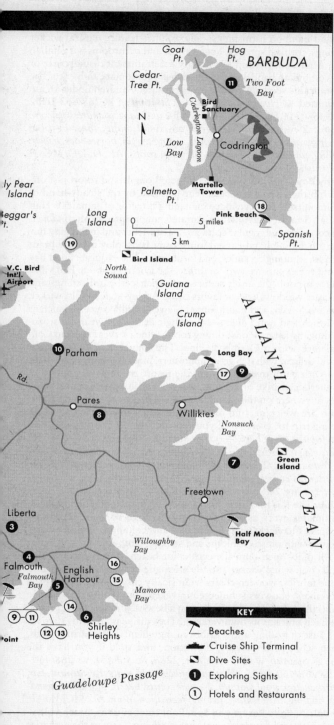

Exploring

Barbuda 11
Betty's Hope 8
Devil's Bridge 9
English Harbour 5
Falmouth 4
Ft. George 3
Harmony Hall 7
Megaliths of
Greencastle Hill 2
Parham 10
St. John's 1
Shirley Heights 6

KEY

⚓ Beaches

🚢 Cruise Ship Terminal

◥ Dive Sites

1 Exploring Sights

① Hotels and Restaurants

uous stucco walls and colorful Haitian artwork. The airy beachfront rooms have terra-cotta tiles, local and Haitian art, and custom-made rattan and bamboo furnishings; deluxe suites feature natural wicker furnishings, tropical spreads, huge patios, and bathrooms with Italian marble. Afternoon tea and live nightly entertainment (usually jazz or lilting West Indian bands) add to the stylish yet intimate ambience. The two restaurants serve invariably excellent fare. Children under 16 are not permitted. ⊠ *Five Islands (Box 305, St. John's),* ☎ *268/462–0302 or 800/345–0356,* FAX *268/462–4551,* WEB *www.classicislandresorts.com. 70 rooms. 2 restaurants, bar, grill, air-conditioning, fans, in-room safes, refrigerators, pool, tennis court, croquet, gym, horseshoes, beach, snorkeling, windsurfing, boating, bicycles, shops. AE, D, DC, MC, V. All-inclusive.*

$$$$ ⊞ **Jumby Bay.** This ultra-swank 330-acre Long Island resort just off-
★   shore from the airport has been reinvigorated by the steady hand of Hans Simonitsch, the legendary managing director of Jamaica's Half Moon Bay. Sizable, individually decorated junior suites are in *rondavels* (round cottages) and regular cottages. Dark wicker and mahogany furnishings, including hand-carved four-poster beds, play up the vibrant throw rugs, stunning ceramics, and local crafts. The exquisite Pond Bay villas and the expansive two- and three-bedroom Harbour Hill villas each have a pool (the latter seduce with their cathedral ceilings and huge picture windows); decor favors Laura Ashley–style florals, wicker, bibelots from Asia, and handpainted tilework. Villa owners—such as Robin Leach and Ken Follett—still mingle at the 250-year-old stone-and-mahogany Estate House dining room, which serves excellent Continental fare with a Caribbean flair. The lounge is a sybaritic yet whimsical delight, with rich green upholstery, pineapple lamps, and walls painted with palm trees. Although the resort encompasses only 88½ acres, guests can bike along nature trails and luxuriate on secluded beaches anywhere on the island. A spa is slated to open in late 2001. Children are welcome, and airport transfers, ferry service, and one snorkeling trip for every week you stay are free. ⊠ *Long Island (Box 243, St. John's),* ☎ *268/462–6000 or 800/237–3237;* FAX *268/462–6020,* WEB *www.elegantresorts.com or www.jumby-bay.com. 38 rooms, 13 villas. 2 restaurants, 2 bars, air-conditioning, fans, minibars, putting green, 3 tennis courts, croquet, gym, 3 beaches, snorkeling, windsurfing, waterskiing, bicycles, shops. AE, MC, V. All-inclusive.*

$$$$ ⊞ **K Club.** The *K* is for Krizia, the famed Italian designer; her dramatic
★   style animates every aspect of this superdeluxe Barbuda hideaway. Public spaces have gleaming white tiles and columns, natural-wicker furnishings with plush cushions, and striking cloth-and-bronze sculptures. All units open onto the ecru-color beach. Room decor is also chic and cool: white wicker and tile are made lively by turquoise- and mint-hue fabrics, wooden chairs whimsically carved with pineapples, bamboo mats, showers submerged in vegetation, wittily provocative paintings (blood red stilettos sitting on a beach), and speckled ceramic lamps. Each unit has its own veranda. The cuisine is an innovative fusion of Tuscan grilling and Caribbean ingredients. The tariff is high, but then what price privacy, discretion, and style if you have the ducats? ⊠ *Spanish Wells Point (Box 2288, St. John's),* ☎ *268/460–0300,* FAX *268/460–0305,* WEB *www.lhw.com. 35 units. Restaurant, bar, grill, kitchenettes, pool, hot tub, 2 tennis courts, beach, snorkeling, windsurfing, boating, waterskiing, fishing, recreation room. AE, MC, V. FAP.*

$$$$ ⊞ **Sandals Antigua Resort and Spa.** Pool competitions, beach volleyball, aerobics, and evening social events are but a few of the activities at this superior resort exclusively for male-female couples. Almost everything—including tennis coaching and scuba diving—is included in the price (spa treatments and weddings are extra). The reception area

opens onto a courtyard with painted tile stairways and an unimpeded sea view. The beachfront restaurant is striking, with its yellow-and-white awnings and painted ceiling. The spacious guest quarters include ocean- or garden-view rooms, beachfront suites, and rondavels that face the beach. All units are fresh and light and have coffeemakers, TVs, patios, and hair dryers. Many have four-poster beds. Four restaurants prepare Continental, Italian, Japanese, and southwestern fare. There's a three-night minimum. ✉ *Dickenson Bay (Box 147, St. John's),* ☎ *268/462–0267 or 888/726–3257,* ℻ *268/462–4135,* WEB *www.sandals. com. 100 rooms, 77 suites, 16 rondavels. 4 restaurants, 4 bars, grill, air-conditioning, fans, in-room safes, 5 pools, 5 hot tubs, hair salon, spa, 2 tennis courts, gym, beach, dive shop, snorkeling, windsurfing, boating, waterskiing, shops, nightclub. AE, D, DC, MC, V. All-inclusive.*

$$$ **CocoBay.** This restful hillside retreat occupies 10 secluded acres on the west coast. Twenty-one individual Creole-style cottages in luscious pastels (powder blue, lilac, coral) with corrugated iron roofs are staggered amid fragrant tropical gardens. Each has a patio with a marvelous bay view and handsome modified planter's chairs. The decor is understated, with the accent on natural beauty: bleached wood louvers, stained pine floors, mosquito netting, and sisal rugs. The blue-and-white tiled bathrooms open onto the terrace (wattle-and-daub walls ensure privacy between adjoining units). A "wellness center" offers massages, facials, scrubs, and aromatherapy. Complimentary cell phones are available, though you pay for the calls you make, and a computer is reserved in the tasteful reception area so you can access the Internet for no extra charge. "It eliminates worries, knowing the option is there," one staffer notes. ✉ *Valley Church (Box 431 St. John's),* ☎ *268/562–2400,* ℻ *268/562–2424,* WEB *www.cocobay.com. 42 rooms, 4 2-bedroom houses. Restaurant, bar, fans, in-room safes, pool, spa, gym, 2 beaches, snorkeling, shops. AE, MC, V. All-inclusive.*

$$$ 🏨 **Hawksbill Beach Hotel.** Thirty-seven acres, including five beaches (one of them clothing-optional), on the bucolic Five Islands Peninsula make up this resort's lavishly landscaped grounds. The main building, the reception area, and the dining room rest on a small bluff with a panoramic view over the restored ruins of a sugar mill, the sea and Montserrat beyond. The classiest accommodations are in the three-bedroom West Indian great house. The 14 secluded Club rooms, which have tile floors, light rattan furnishings, hand-painted bathroom tiles, and vaulted ceilings, also have spectacular views; numbers 138–142 are the best. Deluxe rooms are in gingerbread-trim cottages surrounded by lawns and facing the sea. Less expensive rooms are in garden-view cottages, most with restricted beach views and are the same size as the pricier beachfront units. Still, rooms are on the small side, and though they now have phones and mini-refrigerators, they lack air-conditioning and TVs. Most water sports are free. Hawksbill primarily attracts a mix of mature couples and honeymooners. Men are requested to wear long-sleeved shirts in the dining room after 7 PM. ✉ *Five Islands (Box 108, St. John's),* ☎ *268/462–0301, 416/622–8813 in Canada, or 800/223–6510;* ℻ *268/462–1515,* WEB *www.hawksbill.com. 111 rooms, 1 3-bedroom villa. 2 restaurants, 2 bars, fans, refrigerators, pool, tennis court, 5 beaches, snorkeling, windsurfing, boating, shops, meeting rooms. AE, DC, MC, V. EP, FAP, MAP.*

$$$ 🏨 **Inn at English Harbour.** Generation after generation of families return to this genteel, unpretentious inn. The reception area, a bar-dining room, and six guest rooms are atop a hill with views of English Harbour. Hilltop rooms are in cottage-style units amid English gardens. Down on the beach, 22 rooms are in two-story wooden buildings surrounded by hibiscus and bougainvillea (a Mercedes runs you up and

down the hill). New ownership plans to tear down all but four units and erect two new buildings farther back from the water, which may alter the feel. Rooms are attractively decorated with rattan furniture, tropical- or floral-print fabrics, and the occasional African mask or locally crafted ceramic. The bar, with its green leather chairs, wooden floors, stone walls, and maritime prints, is one of the island's most pleasant. The flagstone-terrace dining room offers an unparalleled romantic ambience and dependable Continental fare. The beach here isn't great, but water taxis to anywhere in the harbor are free, as are nonmotorized water sports. ⊠ *English Harbour (Box 187, St. John's),* ☎ *268/460–1014, 800/223–6510, or 800/424–5500 in Canada;* FAX *268/460–1603,* WEB *www.theinn.ag. 28 rooms. Restaurant, 2 bars, grill, fans, in-room safes, refrigerators, beach, snorkeling, windsurfing, boating. AE, D, DC, MC, V. EP, MAP. Closed mid-Aug.–Oct.*

$$$ 🏨 **St. James's Club.** This out-of-the-way hotel is on a 100-acre spit of land at Mamora Bay. Good-sized rooms, in buildings at the water's edge, have fresh, vibrant color schemes, though years of neglect (and the hotel's origins as a Holiday Inn) still show in the discolored concrete terraces. A tight cluster of two-bedroom villas is atop hills, which spill down toward the main buildings. The new, oceanfront Beach Club caters to tour groups and flight crews, but offers the best value on property: larger, more distinctive rooms at a lower price. The Rainbow Garden restaurant is an elegant spot for a seafood dinner; the more casual, alfresco Docksider Cafe serves island cuisine. The accommodations, lovely setting, and extensive facilities (including a helicopter that you can charter for sightseeing, and a full-scale marina) make this a fine, if overpriced, resort; about 90% of the clientele opts for the all-inclusive package. ⊠ *Mamora Bay (Box 54, St. John's),* ☎ *268/463–2006 or 800/345–0356,* FAX *268/463–2452,* WEB *antigua-resorts.com. 187 rooms, 72 villas. 3 restaurants, 4 bars, deli, air-conditioning, fans, room service, 3 pools, hair salon, hot tub, massage, spa, 7 tennis courts, croquet, gym, 2 beaches, dive shop, dock, snorkeling, windsurfing, boating, casino, nightclub, helipad. AE, D, DC, MC, V. All-inclusive, EP.*

$$ 🏨 **Dickenson Bay Cottages.** There are only 13 units at this small development on Marble Hill, just above Dickenson Bay. The two-story villa-style buildings are surrounded by gardens and are done up with high-quality painted rattan furnishings, blond woods, and vivid abstract and floral fabrics. A well-equipped kitchen and a large living room area with a TV are on the first floor; the bedroom and bathroom are up a flight of stairs. Larger units have two bedrooms upstairs and large verandas overlooking the ocean. Guests have privileges at the excellent but busy beach at Halcyon Cove, a five-minute walk; you can also use the tennis and water-sports facilities there at a 20% discount. Entertainment and restaurants are available at nearby resorts. Though the complex is quite appealing, it's often inexplicably deserted, so ask about last-minute discounts. ⊠ *Marble Hill (Box 1379, St. John's),* ☎ *268/462–4940,* FAX *268/462–4941,* WEB *www.nikegroup.co.uk/antigua/cottages.htm. 13 units. Air-conditioning, kitchenettes, pool. AE, DC, MC, V. EP.*

$$ 🏨 **Rex Blue Heron.** This charming resort sits on a magnificent sweep of sand that is returning after the devastation of Hurricane Lenny. Other than the seemingly endless reception area, everything is cozy and welcoming. Don't be misled by the mousy faux-stucco buildings; each room has hardwood or gleaming white tile floors, powder-blue and tropical-print fabrics, stylish ceramic lamps, and a patio or terrace. All but the standard rooms have air-conditioning, satellite TV, and dazzling ocean views. It's extremely difficult to get a reservation here, because discerning European tour operators keep it booked. The reasonable prices, the intimacy, and the secluded location lure a young, hip clien-

tele. ✉ *Johnson's Point (Box 1715, St. John's),* ☎ *268/462–8565 or 800/255–5859,* FAX *268/462–8005,* WEB *www.rexresorts.com. 64 rooms. Restaurant, bar, air-conditioning, pool, beach, snorkeling, windsurfing, boating, shops. AE, D, MC, V. All-inclusive.*

$$ 🏨 **Rex Halcyon Cove Beach Resort.** Because so many European and American tour groups patronize this large, somewhat impersonal hotel on beautiful Dickenson Bay, it's typically crowded. Two- and three-story flat-roof institutional concrete buildings are set around the courtyard or along the beach. Rooms are generally decorated with white tile, blond woods, and mint-color or floral fabrics, though some have mismatched items—like madras lounges—that give the decor a garage-sale feel. Most have been brightened with fresh coats of paint and new drapes, linens, and upholstery. There's a huge variation in size, decor, and amenities. Beachfront rooms inexplicably lack balconies and only higher-grade rooms have bathtubs (the rest have showers), TVs, and refrigerators. A water-sports center on the busy beach offers windsurfing and waterskiing. The Warri Pier restaurant, perched dramatically on stilts over the ocean, serves seafood dishes and grilled items all day long. ✉ *Dickenson Bay (Box 251, St. John's),* ☎ *268/462–0256 or 800/255–5859,* FAX *268/462–0271,* WEB *www.rexcaribbean.com. 193 rooms, 17 suites. 2 restaurants, 4 bars, grill, ice-cream parlor, air-conditioning, in-room safes, pool, hair salon, massage, 4 tennis courts, beach, dive shop, windsurfing, boating, waterskiing, shops, children's programs, business services, car rental. AE, D, DC, MC, V. All-inclusive, EP, MAP.*

$$ 🏨 **Royal Antiguan Resort.** This nine-story hotel, possibly the island's ugliest, caters to groups and conventions. Though sterile, it has all the amenities and facilities of a moderate American chain. Fortunately, it was given more island flair in 2000, including spectacular large murals painted in the restaurants and local pottery or Carnival costume displays in the lobby. Unusual extras range from dialect classes to palm readings. Rooms and suites have minifridges and TVs; some also have VCRs and marble vanities. Among the facilities are a ballroom, a shopping arcade, a free-form pool with a swim-up bar, three restaurants that serve everything from Italian to Caribbean cuisine, and 150 slot and video poker machines. Royal-blue awnings shade the terraces, the gardens are immaculately tended, and the lobby is enlivened by fountains and hand-painted columns. There are hiking trails and guided nature walks to Ft. Barrington with its stunning views of St. John's Harbour. This resort is popular with young singles, honeymooners, and families on a budget. ✉ *Deep Bay (Box 1322, St. John's),* ☎ *268/462–3733 or 800/345–0356,* FAX *268/462–3732,* WEB *www. antigua-resorts.com. 266 rooms, 12 suites. 3 restaurants, 4 bars, air-conditioning, refrigerators, pool, hair salon, golf, 8 tennis courts, croquet, gym, horseshoes, beach, dive shop, snorkeling, windsurfing, boating, waterskiing, fishing, shops. AE, D, MC, V. All-inclusive, EP.*

$$ 🏨 **Siboney Beach Club.** When Tony Johnson arrived in Antigua in the
★ late 1950s, he planned to stay just a few weeks. He ended up building or refurbishing some of the island's finest resorts and eventually opening his own small gem on Dickenson Bay. Each suite has a small bedroom, a cleverly designed Pullman-style kitchen, a modestly furnished living room, and a small patio or balcony overlooking the garden. Decor varies slightly throughout, but all rooms have rattan furnishings and knickknacks from Tony's travels. The charmingly rustic "tree-house" unit is the only one without air-conditioning. Room 9 is for those who revel in sea views, but the soothing surf of the surf permeates even those with partial views. A few yards away is an excellent, although often busy, calm-water beach and the Coconut Grove restaurant, where you can enjoy meals at the water's edge. ✉ *Dickenson Bay (Box 222, St. John's),* ☎ *268/462–0806 or 800/533–0234 (direct to hotel),* FAX

268/462–3356, WEB *www.turq.com/siboney. 12 suites. Restaurant, bar, pool, air-conditioning, in-room safes, kitchenettes, beach. AE, MC, V. EP, MAP.*

$$ 🏨 **Sunsail Club Colonna.** The British Sunsail outfit is renowned worldwide for its superior, affordable sailing and windsurfing schools, and they're particularly well known for their attentiveness to families. An appealing blend of Caribbean and Mediterranean traits define the property, where red-tile and stucco buildings connected by terra-cotta floors surround a faux sugar mill. The most magnificent touch is the free-form pool, said to be the largest in the Lesser Antilles (a good thing—the property's man-made beaches are smallish). Public areas are a tad dilapidated, but the well-maintained rooms have immaculate tile floors and wicker and rattan furnishings. Units—all with TVs, hair dryers, and patios or balconies—run the gamut from standard hotel rooms to two- and three-bedroom villas (some are poorly designed and don't catch a cross breeze). Use of the superb state-of-the-art sailing and windsurfing equipment and group instruction are free (private lessons are available for a nominal fee). Most meals, usually buffet or barbecue, are also included. Avid sailors should inquire about weekly discounts and the variety of land/sail packages. ✉ *Hodges Bay (Box 591, St. John's),* ☎ *268/462–6263 or 800/327–2276,* FAX *268/462–6430,* WEB *www.sunsail.com. 102 rooms, 15 villas. 2 restaurants, 3 bars, air-conditioning, in-room safes, minibars, pool, 3 beaches, snorkeling, windsurfing, boating, shops, children's programs. AE, D, MC, V. MAP.*

$ 🏨 **Admiral's Inn.** This lovingly restored 18th-century inn is the cen-
★ terpiece of Nelson's Dockyard. Once the engineers' office and warehouse (its bricks were originally used as ballast for ships), the Ad (as yachtspeople call it) reverberates with history. Its best rooms, upstairs in the main building, have the original timbered ceilings—complete with iron braces—hardwood floors, and massive whitewashed brick walls. Straw floor mats from Dominica, four-poster beds in most rooms, and views through wispy Australian pines to the sunny harbor beyond complete the effect. Rooms in the garden annex are smaller and somewhat airless. The Loft (once the dockyard's joinery) has two big bedrooms, an enormous kitchen, and a magnificent harbor view from its timbered living room. This inn sits smack in the middle of a tourist attraction that bustles by day, so you may feel the need to get away; take advantage of the complimentary beach shuttle and the water-sports privileges at its sister property, Falmouth Beach Apartments. The Admiral's Inn restaurant is very popular with locals. ✉ *English Harbour (Box 713, St. John's),* ☎ *268/460–1027 or 800/223–5695,* FAX *268/460–1534,* WEB *www.antiguanice.com. 14 rooms, 1 2-bedroom apartment. Restaurant, pub, air-conditioning, fans. AE, MC, V. EP, MAP.*

$ **Ocean Inn.** At this charming property you can opt to stay in a private home that's been converted into six guest rooms, or in one of five individual cottages, each with a tiny deck overlooking the water. Decor is simple and a tad frilly, favoring florals and pink fabrics. All units have ceiling fans and TVs. But it's the convivial atmosphere fostered by owner-managers Eustace and Sandra Potter that makes this inn special. Informal parties are often thrown by the small, mural-adorned pool, while Thursday Steak Nights lure local characters, yachties, and eccentric expats to the Tree Trunk Bar. There's also a four-bedroom house, replete with kitchen, hot tub, washer-dryer, and private jetty that rents for an astounding $700/night in high season. If a group doesn't take over the joint, the individual rooms are rented—and lucky guests have use of the house's facilities. ✉ *English Harbour (Box 838, St. John's),* ☎ FAX *268/463–7950,* WEB *www.theoceaninn.com. 6 rooms, 5 cottages, 1 4-bedroom house. Bar, grill, air-conditioning, fans, pool. AE, MC, V. CP.*

HOW TO
USE THIS GUIDE

Great trips begin with great planning, and this guide makes planning easy. It's packed with everything you need—insider advice on hotels and restaurants, cool tools, practical tips, essential maps, and much more.

COOL TOOLS

Fodor's Choice Top picks are marked throughout with a star.

Great Itineraries These tours, planned by Fodor's experts, give you the skinny on what you can see and do in the time you have.

Smart Travel Tips A to Z This special section is packed with important contacts and advice on everything from how to get around to what to pack.

Good Walks You won't miss a thing if you follow the numbered bullets on our maps.

Need a Break? Looking for a quick bite to eat or a spot to rest? These sure bets are along the way.

Off the Beaten Path Some lesser-known sights are worth a detour. We've marked those you should make time for.

POST-IT® FLAGS
Dog-ear no more!

"Post-it" is a registered trademark of 3M.

Favorite restaurants • Essential maps • Frequently used numbers • Walking tours • Can't-miss sights • Smart Travel Tips • Web sites • Top shops • Hot nightclubs • Addresses • Smart contacts • Events • Off-the-beaten-path spots • Favorite restaurants • Essential maps • Frequently used numbers • Walking tours • Can't-miss sights • Smart Travel Tips • Web sites • Top shops • Hot nightclubs • Addresses • Smart contacts • Events • Off-the-beaten-path spots • Favorite restaurants • Essential maps • Frequently used numbers • Walking tours •

ICONS AND SYMBOLS

Watch for these symbols throughout:

★	Our special recommendations
✕	Restaurant
🏠	Lodging establishment
✕🏠	Lodging establishment whose restaurant warrants a special trip
☹	Good for kids
☞	Sends you to another section of the guide for more information
✉	Address
☎	Telephone number
FAX	Fax number
WEB	Web site
🎫	Admission price
☺	Opening hours
$-$$$$	Lodging and dining price categories, keyed to strategically sited price charts. Check the index for locations.
① ❶	Numbers in white and black circles on the maps, in the margins, and within tours correspond to one another.

ON THE WEB

Continue your planning with these useful tools found at **www.fodors.com**, the Web's best source for travel information.

"Rich with resources." —*New York Times*

"Navigation is a cinch." —*Forbes* "Best of the Web" list

"Put together by people bursting with know-how."
—*Sunday Times* (London)

Create a Miniguide Pinpoint hotels, restaurants, and attractions that have what you want at the price you want to pay.

Rants and Raves Find out what readers say about Fodor's picks—or write your own reviews of hotels and restaurants you've just visited.

Travel Talk Post your questions and get answers from fellow travelers, or share your own experiences.

On-Line Booking Find the best prices on airline tickets, rental cars, cruises, or vacations, and book them on the spot.

About our Books Learn about other Fodor's guides to your destination and many others.

Expert Advice and Trip Ideas From what to tip to how to take great photos, from the national parks to Nepal, Fodors.com has suggestions that'll make your trip a breeze. Log on and get informed and inspired.

Smart Resources Check the weather in your destination or convert your currency. Learn the local language or link to the latest event listings. Or consult hundreds of detailed maps—all in one place.

Dining

Antigua's restaurants prepare a range of cuisines, and you can find excellent food whether you feel like dressing up or dressing down. It's impossible not to find fresh seafood, and virtually every chef incorporates local ingredients and elements of West Indian and creole cuisine.

Most menus list prices in EC dollars, but you should verify in which currency the prices are listed. It's also a good idea to ask if credit cards are accepted. Dinner reservations are needed during high season.

What to Wear

Perhaps because of the island's British heritage, Antiguans tend to dress more formally for dinner than is the custom on many of the other Caribbean islands. A few places require a jacket. Wraps and shorts (no beach attire) are de rigueur for lunch, except at local hangouts.

CATEGORY	COST*
$$$$	over $35
$$$	$25–$35
$$	$15–$25
$	under $15

*per person for a main course at dinner

CARIBBEAN

$$ ✕ **Commissioner's Grill.** The gaudy raspberry, mango, and blueberry exterior of this 19th-century tamarind warehouse seems edible itself. The interior is more restrained, with white tile floors, powder-blue chairs, floral tablecloths, and such local touches as wind chimes, Antiguan pottery, conch shells, and historic maps. Specials might include whelks in garlic butter, bacon-wrapped plantains in mustard sauce, snapper in lobster sauce, marinated conch, or shrimp creole. Local seafood is the obvious choice, although beef and poultry are also reliable. ⊠ *Commissioner Alley and Redcliffe St., St. John's,* ☎ *268/462–1883. AE, DC, MC, V.*

CONTEMPORARY

$$ ✕ **Bay House.** This romantic hilltop, alfresco eatery (request Table 10 for the best views) is located in the estimable Tradewinds Hotel above Dickenson Bay. Its menu received a welcome infusion of energy and creativity from the Italian-born, New York–savvy new chef, Giorgio Rocchi. His dishes run the culinary gamut from Thailand to Tuscany, with a healthy dollop of West Indian spice. Excellent starters range from deep-fried pork and prawn gow gees (wontons) in sweet-and-sour chile peanut sauce to seafood boudin set on a leek fondue edged with lobster sauce. Main dishes are just as eclectic: witness pan-fried snapper with passionfruit salsa or pork tenderloin marinated with honey, soy, ginger, and banana then wrapped in bacon and placed on handmade sugarcane skewers. After your meal, head to the hip, hopping, happening bar, a local favorite, for a cordial. ⊠ *Dickenson Bay,* ☎ *268/462–1223. AE, MC, V.*

$$ ✕ **Coconut Grove.** Coconut palms grow up through the roof of this
★ open-air thatched restaurant, part of the Siboney Beach Club. Candles flicker gently in lanterns that illuminate colorful local artwork, waves lap the white-coral sand a few feet away, and the waitstaff is warm and unpretentious. Although the signature dish has long been beer-battered shrimp with coconut cream and chili sauces, try such superbly presented, imaginative dishes as honey-glazed duck in pepper beurre blanc or (or sugar-cured in mango rum sauce), spiced red snapper layered with sweet potato gaufrette in ginger and Chablis sauce, and lobster flambéed with pineapple. Cap a memorable meal with an old rum or Cuban cigar. ⊠ *Dickenson Bay,* ☎ *268/462–1538. AE, MC, V.*

$$ ✕ Coco's. Overlooking the headlands of Five Islands Bay, Coco's could
★ be recommended simply for its ravishing sunsets followed by the spec-
tacular show of moonlight on water; the bay seems dappled by thou-
sands of silver coins. But it's also an uncommonly handsome place, whose
cheerful aquamarine trim, bleached-wood deck, gingerbread fretwork,
and blue tile tables replicate the feeling of an old chattel house. Although
it's part of an all-inclusive resort, the restaurant welcomes outside
diners. Globetrotting chef Nigel Martin presents a virtual United Na-
tions of influences: sweet-potato gnocchi and warm smoked salmon
with crème fraîche and tomato-lime-basil salsa or Guyanese shrimp with
lavender-perfumed barley risotto and sweet-chili hoisin sauce, for ex-
ample. ✉ *Mt. Prospect, Jolly Bay,* ☎ *268/462–9700. Reservations es-
sential. AE, MC, V.*

$$ ✕ HQ. This casually elegant eatery occupies part of the Officers' Quar-
★ ters building in Nelson's Dockyard: its polished hardwood floors,
brickwork, and beamed ceilings are offset by local Creole artworks by
Gillie Gobinet (for sale) and the contemporary open kitchen. The
water view from both the main dining room and the vast colonnaded
terrace is delightful. The canny, fairly priced wine list features over 150
selections (10 by the glass). The chef, Darryn Pitman, is a young, adventuresome, typically peripatetic Aussie. He utilizes indigenous
Caribbean ingredients whenever possible, but many dishes inventively
incorporate star anise, soy, Chinese red vinegar, brown sugar, tamarind,
and lemongrass. Enterprising signature dishes include rare, seared,
Cajun-rubbed wahoo with ginger-lime dressing, meltingly tender sugar-
cured beef salad with curry oil dressing, and cumin-crusted pork tenderloin with spicy apple-orange chutney. Sides include perfectly crunchy
home fries. Finish it off with a smashing white chocolate passion fruit
crème brulée, or the unusual stunner, chocolate and beetroot cake
with vanilla mascarpone. ✉ *Nelson's Dockyard, English Harbour,* ☎
268/562–2563. AE, MC, V.

ECLECTIC

$$ ✕ Admiral's Inn. This historic English Harbour tavern in the Admi-
★ ral's Inn hotel is a must for Anglophiles and mariners. At the bar in-
side, you can soak up the centuries under dark timbers (the bar top
even has the names of sailors from Nelson's fleet carved into it), but
most guests tend to sit on the terrace under shady Australian gums to
enjoy the views of the harbor complex and Clarence House opposite.
Specialties include curried conch, fresh snapper with equally fresh
limes, and lobster thermidor. The pumpkin soup is not to be missed.
✉ *Nelson's Dockyard,* ☎ *268/460–1027. Reservations essential. AE,
MC, V.*

$$ ✕ Redcliffe Tavern. Nigel Martin of Coco's also oversees this St.
John's charmer, which offers simpler but similar dishes. The dining room,
on the second floor of a colonial warehouse set amid the courtyards
of Redcliffe Quay, sports brick-and-stone walls decorated with antique
water-pumping equipment that still bears the original English maker's
crests. Salvaged from all over the island, the old machines, with their
flywheels and pistons, have been imaginatively integrated—one supports the buffet bar. Dinner appetizers include creole crab puffs with
cucumber, onion, and sesame relish; for a main dish try prosciutto-
wrapped roasted scallops and catfish, chicken with papaya and pistachios in mild curry cream, or entrecôte in rum and green peppercorn
sauce. The lunch menu also lists salads, sandwiches, and burgers. ✉
Redcliffe Quay, St. John's, ☎ *268/461–4557. AE, MC, V.*

$ ✕ Averill's. This place has all the essential elements of a casual ma-
rina eatery: sleek yachts moored at the deck, fresh sea breezes, exuberant boating barflies, and simple yet scrumptious food. Fresh daily

fish dishes include wahoo in caper, butter, and lemon sauce or dolphinfish in shrimp sauce. Excellent starters include cumin-crusted shrimp and sesame chicken. The ambience is particularly fun and raucous on Monday (roast pork barbecue night). ⊠ *Catamaran Marina, Falmouth Harbour,* ☎ *268/463–8866. AE, MC, V. Closed June–Sept.*

FRENCH

$$$ ✕ **Chez Pascal.** Pascal and Florence Milliat built this hilltop charmer
★ themselves. The flagstone terrace overlooks a tinkling fountain and lighted pool (there are also four guest rooms, with whirlpool baths and splendid sea views), and the elevated dining room is tastefully decorated with dark rattan furnishings, ceramics, local paintings, and copper pots. Pascal's classic Lyonnaise cuisine with tropical touches will put you in an even more romantic mood. He has a remarkably deft hand with subtle sauces. Witness the gossamer chicken-liver mousse in thyme sauce, the chicken breast in port and fresh cream with sweet-corn crepe, and a sublime steamed grouper in beurre blanc. Finish with a heavenly flourless chocolate cake with strawberry coulis (sauce) or a classic tarte Tatin. ⊠ *Galley Bay Hill,* ☎ *268/462–3232. Reservations essential. AE, D, MC, V. Closed Aug.*

$$$ ✕ **Le Bistro.** This Antiguan institution is remarkably consistent in every aspect. Its casually elegant decor has accents of peach and pistachio that subtly match the tile work, jade chairs, and painted lighting fixtures. Trellises cannily divide the large space into intimate sections, with tables staggered just the right distance apart. Chef Patrick Gaducheau delights in blending regional fare with indigenous ingredients. You might start with salmon and scallop carpaccio in raspberry vinaigrette, then drift into such sterling entrées as Cornish hen sautéed with fresh pineapples and rum or snapper in ginger cream. Classic bistro fare, from escargots *à la bourguignonne* to duck à l'orange, is also served. As for dessert, the exquisite Death by Chocolate teasingly tortures the taste buds. ⊠ *Hodges Bay,* ☎ *268/462–3881. Reservations essential. AE, MC, V. Closed Mon. No lunch.*

$ ✕ **Catherine's Café.** Occupying a wooden deck that overlooks English Harbour marina, this charming little café brims with Gallic brio thanks to its energetic, ebullient hostess, Catherine Ricard. The food is simple: ham-and-leek quiche, a proper *salade niçoise,* steak *à la moutarde* (with mustard) sandwich, and crêpes even airier than Catherine herself. Afternoon tapas—from charcuterie (smoked meats) to shrimp mousse—are also offered. In the evening you may find such specials as *moules mariniéres* (marinated mussels) or *gratin de cèpes* (wild mushrooms in a cheese sauce). The fairly priced, surprisingly extensive wine list offers Catherine's pert comments (For Solaia, she writes, "Just to show we're not narrow-minded Frogs, here is the top from Italy . . . "). This place is a delight, always percolating with life and good strong espresso. ⊠ *English Harbour,* ☎ *268/460–5050. MC, V. Closed Tues. and Sept.–Oct. No dinner Mon.*

ITALIAN

$$ ✕ **Abracadabra.** This busy, bright trattoria always has a party atmosphere. The courtyard is usually strung with lights; R&B and 1980s dance music play in the background; and the cheery rooms are daubed in sea-foam green and full of hand-painted tables and murals of jamming jazz musicians. The food, like the ambience, sings with flavor and color. Specialties include an amazing antipasto, eggplant parmigiana, bonito marinated in sweet onions and capers, and homemade crab ravioli in pesto. The wine list has some real finds from lesser-known areas of Italy (the owners confide—or rather joke—"We smuggle them in"). Beware the *limoncello:* it's really a grappa slammer infused with sugar and lime. ✉ *English Harbour,* ☎ *268/460–1732. AE, MC, V. Closed July–Sept.*

$$ ✕ **Alberto's.** Above Willoughby Bay on Antigua's southeast side, this
★ superior Italian restaurant is a bit out of the way but popular never-theless. The vivacious owner, Alberto, taught his culinary secrets to his English wife, Vanessa, and she now bests her mentor with her Italian and French inspirations (and beyond—sushi is her latest conquest). Try island lobster (grilled with basil and garlic); leek and Parmesan souf-flé; or veal medallions in mushroom crust; or more traditional dishes such as eggplant parmigiana or linguine with clams. For dessert, the homemade, lusciously textured sorbets are a must: tangy passion fruit, creamy coconut, lip-smacking lemon. Tables line a trellised balcony open to the breezes and hung with bougainvillea, and painted china graces the walls (check out the octopuses and squid on the plates by the bar). ✉ *Willoughby Bay,* ☎ *268/460–3007; via VHF 68. Reservations es-sential. AE, D, MC, V. Closed Mon. and May–Oct. No lunch.*

$ ✕ **Big Banana–Pizzas on the Quay.** This tiny, often crowded spot is tucked into one side of a restored warehouse with broad plank floors, wood beams, and stone archways. Cool Benetton-style photos of lo-cals and jamming musicians adorn the brick walls. It serves some of the island's best pizza (try the lobster or the seafood variety) as well as such tasty specials as conch salad. There's live entertainment some nights. ✉ *Redcliffe Quay, St. John's,* ☎ *268/480–6985. AE, MC, V. Closed Sun.*

Beaches

Antigua's beaches are public, and many are dotted with resorts that have water-sports outfitters and beach bars. Sunbathing topless or in the buff is strictly illegal except on one of the small beaches at Hawks-bill Beach Hotel. Beware that when cruise ships dock in St. John's, buses drop off loads of passengers on most of the west-coast beaches. Choose such a time to tour the island by car, visit one of the more remote east-end beaches, or take a day trip to Barbuda.

ANTIGUA

Darkwood Beach is a delightful taupe ribbon on the southwest coast.

Dickenson Bay has a lengthy stretch of powder-soft white sand and ex-ceptionally calm water. Here you'll find small and large hotels, water sports, concessions, and beachfront restaurants.

Five Islands Peninsula has four secluded beaches (including one nude) of fine tan sand and coral reefs for snorkeling at the Hawksbill Beach Hotel.

Half Moon Bay, a ¾-mi (1-km) crescent, is a prime snorkeling and wind-surfing area. On the Atlantic side of the island the water can be quite rough at times.

Johnson's Point is a deliciously deserted beach of bleached white sand on the southwest coast overlooking Montserrat.

Long Bay, on the far-eastern coast, has coral reefs in water so shallow that you can actually walk out to them. Along the beach are the Long Bay Hotel and the rambling Allegro Pineapple Beach Club.

Pigeon Point, near English Harbour, has two fine white-sand beaches; the leeward side is calmer, while the windward side is rockier, with sen-sational views and snorkeling around the point. Several restaurants and bars are nearby.

Runaway Beach is home to the Barrymore Beach Hotel, Lashings, and the Runaway Beach Hotel, so its stretch of white sand can get crowded.

Pink Beach on Barbuda, is an uncrowded 8-mi (13-km) stretch of white sand that reaches from Coco Point to Palmetto Point. Barbuda, encircled by reefs and shipwrecks, is great for scuba diving.

Outdoor Activities and Sports

Participant Sports

BICYCLING

Bicycling isn't terribly arduous on Antigua, except in the southernmost region, where the roads soar, dip, and corkscrew. Try **Bike Plus** (⌧ St. John's, ☎ 268/462–2453) for rentals, which run about $25–$30 a day. Everything from racing models to mountain bikes is available.

BOATING

Whether in a skiff or a schooner, Antigua's waters are delightful for cruising. Experienced boaters will particularly enjoy the east coast, which is far more rugged and has several offshore islets; be sure to get a good nautical map as there are numerous minireefs that can be treacherous. If you're just looking for a couple of hours of wave hopping, stick to the Dickenson Bay/Runaway area.

Nicholson Yacht Charters (☎ 800/662–6066) are real professionals. A long-established island family, they can charter you anything from a 20-ft ketch to a giant schooner. **Sea Sports** (⌧ Dickenson Bay, ☎ 268/462–3355) rents Jet Skis and Sunfish and offers parasailing and waterskiing trips. The atmosphere here can be hectic. **Sunsail Club Colonna** (☎ 268/462–6263 or 800/327–2276) has an extensive modern fleet of dinghies and 32-foot day sailers available for $25 per half day, $50 per full day.

Not a sailor yourself? Consider signing up for one of the following boat tours. Each provides a great opportunity to enjoy the seafaring life while someone else captains the ship. **Jolly Roger** cruises (☎ 268/462–2064), on a true-to-life replica of a pirate ship, come complete with "pirate" crew, limbo dancing, plank walking, and other pranks. Their Saturday night boozecruises with open bar and live bands are legendary for their frat party atmosphere. **Kokomo Cats** (☎ 268/462–7245) runs several cruises, including one to deserted beaches and islets, one to English Harbour, and one to sunset-gazing spots. **Miguel's Holiday Adventures** (☎ 268/461–0361; 268/724–0416 for cellular) leaves every Tuesday, Thursday, and Saturday morning at 10 AM from the Hodges Bay jetty for snorkeling, rum punches, and lunch at Prickley Pear Island. The glass-bottom **Shorty's** (☎ 268/462–6326) offers various snorkeling trips to Bird Island, as well as sunset cruises and lobster picnics. **Wadadli Cats** (☎ 268/462–4792) offers several cruises, including a circumnavigation of the island and snorkeling at Bird Island, on its four sleek catamarans, including the handsome *Spirit of Antigua*.

FISHING

Antigua's waters teem with such game fish as marlin, wahoo, and tuna. Most boats include equipment, lunch, and drinks. Figure at least $400 for a half day, $600 for a full day, for up to six people. The 45-ft Hatteras Sportfisherman **Obsession** (☎ 268/462–2824) has top-of-the-line equipment, including an international standard fighting chair, outriggers, and handcrafted rods. **Overdraft** (☎ 268/464–4954 or 268/463–3112) is a sleek, spacious 40-footer operated by a knowledgeable professional fisherman.

GOLF

Cedar Valley Golf Club (⊠ Friar's Hill, northeast of St. John's, ☎ 268/462–0161) has a 6,100-yard, 18-hole course. The bland, not terribly well-maintained terrain offers some challenge with tight hilly fairways and numerous doglegs. Greens fees are $35, including cart. **Jolly Harbour Golf Course** (⊠ Jolly Harbour, ☎ 268/480–6950) is a par-71, 6,001-yard, 18-hole course designed by Karl Litten. It's a lushly tropical course, with seven lakes adding to the challenge. At press time, greens fees were $60 (including cart), but new management may raise prices, so call to confirm.

HORSEBACK RIDING

Comparatively dry Antigua is best for beach rides, though you won't find anything wildly romantic and deserted à la *The Black Stallion*. **Spring Hill Riding Stables** (⊠ Falmouth, ☎ 268/463–8041) offers $35 trail rides on the beach or through the bush; half-hour private lessons are $20.

SCUBA DIVING

With all the wrecks and reefs, there are lots of undersea sights to explore. The most accessible wreck is the schooner ***Andes,*** not far out in Deep Bay, off Five Islands Peninsula. Among the favorite sites are **Green Island, Cades Reef,** and **Bird Island** (a national park).

Big John's Dive Antigua (⊠ Rex Halcyon Cove Beach Resort, Dickenson Bay, ☎ 268/462–3483) offers certification courses and day and night dives. **Dockyard Divers** (⊠ Nelson's Dockyard, English Harbour, ☎ 268/464–8591 or 268/460–1178), owned by British ex-merchant seaman Captain A. G. Fincham, is one of the island's most established outfits and offers diving and snorkeling trips, PADI courses, and dive packages with accommodations. Another top option is **Octopus Divers** (⊠ English Harbour, ☎ 268/460–6286), which provides PADI certification and snorkeling trips.

TENNIS AND SQUASH

The **Temo Sports Complex** (⊠ Falmouth Bay, ☎ 268/460–1781) has four floodlighted synthetic grass tennis courts, two glass-backed squash courts, showers, a sports shop, and snack bars. Court time is generally $25 per hour.

Many of the larger resorts have their own tennis courts. Guests have top priority. The only hotel that rents to nonguests on a regular basis is **Royal Antiguan Resort** (⊠ Deep Bay, ☎ 268/462–3733), which has eight lighted courts. You can also try **Rex Halcyon Cove Beach Resort** (⊠ Dickenson Bay, ☎ 268/462–0256), with four lighted courts.

WINDSURFING

Most major hotels offer windsurfing equipment. The best areas are Nonsuch Bay and the northern coast, which is slightly less protected and has a challenging juxtaposition of sudden calms and gusts. **Sea Sports** (☎ 268/462–3355), at Dickenson Bay, rents top-quality boards for $25 per hour. **Sunsail Club Colonna** (☎ 268/462–6263 or 800/327–2276) allows use of its top-of-the-line equipment for $50 a day and $25 a half day.

Shopping

Antigua's duty-free shops are at Heritage Quay; they're the reason so many cruise ships call here. Bargains can be found on perfumes, liqueurs and liquor (including, of course, Antiguan rum), jewelry, china, and crystal. As for other local items, look for straw hats, baskets, batik, pottery, and hand-printed cotton clothing.

Areas

Redcliffe Quay, on the waterfront at the south edge of St. John's, is by far the most appealing shopping area. Several restaurants and more than 30 boutiques, many with one-of-a-kind items, are set around land-scaped courtyards shaded by colorful trees. **Heritage Quay,** in St. John's, has 35 shops—including many that are duty-free—that cater to the cruise-ship crowd, which docks almost at its doorstep. Outlets here include Benetton, the Body Shop, Sunglass Hut, Dolce and Gabbana, and Oshkosh B'Gosh. There are also shops along **St. John's, St. Mary's, High,** and **Long Streets.** In addition, there are so many vendors cluttering the streets—disrupting traffic and pestering tourists—that the government has constructed a three-story Vendors' Mall at the intersection of Redcliffe and Thames streets—but ramshackle stalls still line the streets.

Specialty Items

ART

At **Harmony Hall** (⊠ Brown's Bay Mill, near Freetown, ☎ 268/460–4120) you'll find hand-painted Annabella boxes, books and cards, pottery and ceramic pieces (look for the ravishing cerulean blue, freestyle fish-motif work of Nancy Nicholson), carved wooden birds, and everchanging exhibits. There's also a marvelous Italian restaurant that's open for lunch and on weekends for dinner. **Island Arts Galleries** (⊠ Alton Pl., Sandy La., behind Hodges Bay Club, Hodges Bay, ☎ 268/461–3332; ⊠ Heritage Quay, St. John's, ☎ 268/462–2787), run by artist-filmmaker Nick Maley, showcases a variety of artists from throughout the Caribbean. Some of the art naïf pieces are stunning, and the genre paintings of local life often have a raw elemental power. Call first to ensure that Nick is around.

Lydia Llewellyn Art (⊠ Fort Rd., inside Chutney's Restaurant, St. John's, ☎ 268/560–0062) carries Lydia's striking marine art, where the iridescent fish actually extend onto the frames; avid celeb collectors include Robin Leach, Eric Clapton, and Viscount Portman.

BOOKS AND MAGAZINES

Map Shop (⊠ St. Mary's St., St. John's, ☎ 268/462–3993) has a "must" buy for those interested in Antiguan life: the paperback *To Shoot Hard Labour: The Life and Times of Samuel Smith, an Antiguan Workingman.* Also check out any of the books of Jamaica Kincaid, whose works on her native Antigua have won international acclaim. The shop also offers a fine assortment of books on Caribbean cuisine, flora, fauna, and history.

CIGARS, LIQUOR, AND LIQUEURS

La Casa Habana (⊠ Heritage Quay, St. John's, ☎ 268/462–2677) sells Cuban cigars (just remember that it's illegal to take them into the United States). **Manuel Dias Liquor Store** (⊠ Long and Market sts., St. John's, ☎ 268/462–0490) has a wide selection of Caribbean rums and liqueurs. **Quin Farara** (⊠ Long St., St. John's, ☎ 268/462–0463) has terrific deals on both hard liquor and wines.

CLOTHING

The hand-dyed clothing and scarves of the famed **Caribelle Batik** (⊠ St. Mary's St., St. John's, ☎ 268/462–2972) are done in the festive colors of a Caribbean Carnival. **Exotic Antigua** (⊠ Redcliffe Quay, St. John's, ☎ 268/462–2972) sells everything from antique Indonesian ikat throws to crepe de chine caftans to Tommy Bahama resort wear. **Jacaranda** (⊠ Redcliffe Quay, St. John's, ☎ 268/462–1888) sells batik, sarongs, and swimwear, as well as Caribbean gourmet items and local artwork. **New Gates** (⊠ Redcliffe Quay, St. John's, ☎ 268/562–1627) is a duty-free authorized dealer for such name brands as Ralph Lauren, Calvin Klein, and Tommy Hilfiger. **Noreen Phillips** (⊠ Redcliffe Quay, St. John's, ☎ 268/462–3127) creates glitzy appliquéd and beaded evening wear—inspired by the colors of the sea and sunset—in sensuous fabrics ranging from chiffon and silk to Italian lace and Indian brocade. **Sunseakers** (⊠ Heritage Quay, St. John's, ☎ 268/462–3618) racks up every conceivable bathing suit and cover-up—from bikini thongs to sarongs—by top designers and in a variety of colors, styles, and sizes. **A Thousand Flowers** (⊠ Redcliffe Quay, St. John's, ☎ 268/462–4264) carries resort wear made of comfortable silks, linens, and batiks from all over the world.

DUTY-FREE GOODS

Abbott's (⊠ Heritage Quay, St. John's, ☎ 268/462–3108 or 268/462–3073) sells pricey items from Baume and Mercier watches to Belleek china to Kosta Boda art glass in a luxurious, air-conditioned setting. **La Parfumerie** (⊠ Heritage Quay, St. John's, ☎ 268/462–2601) imports high-priced scents, from Armani to Zegna. The **Scent Shop** (⊠ High St., St. John's, ☎ 268/462–0303) offers scent-sational buys in perfumes and cosmetics.

HANDICRAFTS

Cedars Pottery (⊠ Buckleys, ☎ 268/460–5293) is the airy studio of Michael and Imogen Hunt. Michael produces a vivid line of domestic ware and Zen-simple teapots, vases, and water fountains featuring rich earth hues and sensuous lines. Imogen fashions ethereal paper clay fish sculptures and mask-shaped, intricately laced light fixtures and candelabras. **Ego** (⊠ Redcliffe Quay, St. John's, ☎ 268/562–1591) is a veritable United Nations of *objets,* including Thai Sa paper notebooks (pounded from mulberry bark), Ethiopian bread baskets, appliquéd Indian purses, even Japanese metalwork. The **Gazebo** (⊠ Redcliffe Quay, St. John's, ☎ 268/460–2776) is a vast, bilevel jumble of Mexican pottery and ceramics, Indonesian furnishings, gorgeous blue-glaze plates that rival delftware in both beauty and craftsmanship, handpainted rocking horses, basketry, hammocks, and more. **Isis** (⊠ Redcliffe Quay, St. John's, ☎ 268/462–4602) sells a range of island and international bric-a-brac, such as antique jewelry, hand-carved walking sticks, and glazed pottery. **Kate Designs** (⊠ Redcliffe Quay, St. John's, ☎ 268/460–5971) sells acclaimed artist Kate Spencer's distinctive work—lovely silk-screened scarves and sarongs, vividly colored place mats, paintings, prints, note cards—from neighboring St. Kitts as well as Dale Isaac's whimsical hats. **Mimosa** (⊠ Heritage Quay, St. John's, ☎ 268/462–2923) sells hand-painted wind chimes and porcelain clowns in island dress. The **New Pottery** (⊠ Cedar Grove, ☎ 268/461–3085) features the work of gifted potter Sarah Fuller, whose cobalt-blue glazes are striking. **Pigeon Point Pottery** (⊠ Pigeon Point, ☎ 268/460–1614) is the atelier of Nancy Nicholson, who's renowned for her exquisite glazed and matte finished ceramics, featuring Caribbean-pure shades, as well as her black-and-white yachting photos. The delightfully whimsical **Sofa** (⊠ English Harbour, ☎ 268/463–0610) carries some of the quirkier creations of island artisans, including handpainted furniture, mosaic vases, and recycled paper books—justifying the name (an acronym for Sculpture, Objects, Functional Art). **Things Local** (⊠ Nelson's Dockyard, English Harbour, ☎ No phone) is the bailiwick of local woodcarver, Carl Henry, who recycles dead trees into figurative yet intriguingly gnarled sculpture. He also makes splendid warri boards (an ancient African game played with large pods) and painted gourds.

Colombian Emeralds (✉ Heritage Quay, St. John's, ☎ 268/462–3462) is the largest retailer of Colombian emeralds in the world. The **Goldsmitty** (✉ Redcliffe Quay, St. John's, ☎ 268/462–4601) is Hans Smit, an expert goldsmith who turns gold, black coral, and precious and semi-precious stones into one-of-a-kind works of art.

Nightlife and the Arts

Most of Antigua's evening entertainment takes place at the resorts, which regularly present calypso singers, steel bands, limbo dancers, and folk-loric groups. Check with the tourist office for up-to-date information.

Nightlife

BARS

The Beach (✉ Dickenson Bay, ☎ 268/460–6940) is a sophisticated-funky combination of casual beach bar, lounge (with pianist or jazz trios playing nightly), and bistro (with Asian-Euro fusion cuisine and—a welcome rarity—a late-night bar menu). **Colombo's** (✉ Galleon Beach Club, English Harbour, ☎ 268/460–1452) is the place to be on Wednesday night for live reggae. It's also a yachty hangout, with pennants of various boats hanging from the rafters. Beware: the once-fine Italian fare is overrated. **Hype** (✉ Nelson's Dockyard, English Harbour, ☎ 268/562–2353), right outside the entrance to Nelson's Dockyard, is a semi-enclosed wooden pier that groans under the weight of yachties and their groupies during the 2-for-1 happy hours and Caribbean party nights with live bands. **Lashings** (✉ Runaway Bay, ☎ 268/462–4438) is a funky place that attracts world-renowned cricketers, as well as a jovial crowd for liberal happy hours, dirt-cheap Tex-Mex and local cuisine, and dirty dancing on the sand.

The **Mad Mongoose** (✉ Falmouth Harbour, ☎ 268/463–7900) is a wildly popular yachty (and singles) joint, splashed in vivid Rasta colors, with a game room and satellite TV. Right inside Nelson's Dockyard and part of the restored Copper and Lumber Store Hotel, the lively **Mainbrace Pub** (✉ English Harbour, ☎ 268/460–1058) offers proper fish-and-chips, darts, Bass on tap, and occasional live jazz. The crowd at **Millers by the Sea** (✉ Fort James Beach, ☎ 268/462–9414) spills over onto the beach during the ever-popular happy hour and live nightly entertainment. It's packed with cruise-ship passengers tanning and noshing on barbecue and burgers during the day. You can hike to the 18th-century ruins of Fort James at the other end of the beach for stunning views of St. John's. **Putter's** (✉ Dickenson Bay Rd., ☎ 268/463–4653 or 268/773–1234) is wildly popular with Brits, even though it's essentially just an open deck overlooking a lagoon that's really a swamp. There are also a playground, video arcade, and a lighted miniature golf course where you can access your inner child between brews. **Southern Cross** (✉ English Harbour Yacht Club Marina, ☎ 268/460–1797) is an overpriced Italian eatery, but its brick-and-mahogany bar, vaulted ceilings, stylish scrap-metal artworks, and phenomenal location make it a primo yachty hangout. Owner Flavio Scala has been a helmsman on several Italian entries in the America's Cup.

CASINOS

There are three true casinos on Antigua, as well as several holes-in-the-wall that mainly feature one-armed bandits. Hours depend on the season, so it's best to inquire upon your arrival. You'll find abundant slots and gaming tables at the somewhat dilapidated, unintentionally retro (icicle chandeliers, naugahyde seats, and 1970s soul crooners on the sound system), smoky **King's Casino** (✉ Heritage Quay, St. John's, ☎ 268/462–1727). **Riviera Casino** (✉ Runaway Bay, ☎ 268/562–

6262) has pretensions to elegance (Palladian doorways, a spiral stair-case leading to a cozier bar, gourmet cuisine) undercut by blue neon and early-bird dinner specials. Galoots in suits scan the room as if it were Vegas. Still, you can indulge in blackjack, roulette, Caribbean stud poker, slots, and the sport book, for placing bets on international jock events. The **St. James's Club** (✉ Mamora Bay, ☎ 268/463–1113) has an elegant, almost Bondian casino with a European ambience.

DANCE CLUBS

La Galleria (✉ Five Islands, ☎ 268/562–2981) is a welcome blend of romantic lounge and pulsating disco, with everything from live jazz to R&B and a fab sound system with DJ on weekends; the terrace offers spectacular views. At **Ribbit** (✉ Donovans, Green Bay, ☎ 268/462–7996) a lively crowd dances under a pulsating laser-light system that could provoke as much of a headache as the beers and blaring sound system. It's open Friday–Saturday at 10:30 PM. Admission is EC$10 Friday, EC$20 Saturday, when there's usually a live band. Semiformal attire (no jeans, shorts, or halter tops) is rather pretentiously requested on weekends. Guards and metal detectors ensure a safe party atmo-sphere. The **Web** (✉ Old Parham Rd., St. John's, ☎ 268/462–3186) attracts a somewhat rowdy local crowd and spins ethnic sounds such as reggae, soca, and salsa.

Exploring Antigua

Major hotels provide free maps but you should get your bearings be-fore heading out on the road. Street names aren't posted, so orient your-self in advance; look to see if a popular restaurant is near your destination, because easy-to-spot signs leading the way to restaurants are posted all over the island. Locals generally give directions in terms of landmarks (turn left at the yellow house, or right at the big tree). Wear a swimsuit under your clothes—one of the sights to strike your fancy might be a secluded beach.

Numbers in the margin correspond to points of interest on the Antigua and Barbuda map.

SIGHTS TO SEE

⑪ **Barbuda.** This flat 62-square-mi (161-square-km) coral atoll—with 17 mi (27 km) of pinkish white-sand beaches—is 26 mi (42 km) north of Antigua. Most of the island's 1,200 people live in Codrington. Coco Point Beach lures beachcombers, a bird sanctuary attracts ornitholo-gists, and offshore wrecks and reefs draw divers and snorkelers. Carib Aviation (☎ 268/462–3147) flies here daily from Antigua, and air and boat charters are available. Overnight guests can choose from two su-perluxury resorts, a more moderate hotel, and several guest houses. Contact the department of tourism (☎ 888/268–4227) for details.

The sole historic ruin here is **Martello Tower,** which is believed to have been a lighthouse built by the Spaniards before the English occupied the island.

The **Bird Sanctuary,** a wide mangrove-filled lagoon, is home to an es-timated 170 species of birds, including frigate birds with 8-ft (2½-m) wingspans. Tours commonly take you here and to a beach for snorkel-ing.

⑧ **Betty's Hope.** Just outside the village of Pares, a marked dirt road leads to Betty's Hope, Antigua's first sugar plantation, founded in 1650. You can tour the twin windmills, and the visitor center has exhibits on the island's sugar era. The village isn't much now, but the private trust overseeing its restoration has ambitious plans. ✉ *Pares,* ☎ *268/462–1469.* 📷 *Free.* ⏱ *Tues.–Sat. 9–4.*

❾ Devil's Bridge. This formation, sculpted by the crashing breakers of the Atlantic at Indian Creek, is a national park. Blowholes have been carved by the hissing, spitting surf. They may be hard to spot at first, but just wait until a wave bursts through!

❺ English Harbour. The most famous of Antigua's attractions lies on the coast, just south of Falmouth. In 1671 the governor of the Leeward Islands wrote to the Council for Foreign Plantations in London, pointing out the advantages of this landlocked harbor. By 1704 English Harbour was in regular use as a garrisoned station.

In 1784, 26-year-old Horatio Nelson sailed in on the HMS *Boreas* to serve as captain and second-in-command of the Leeward Island Station. Under him was the captain of the HMS *Pegasus,* Prince William Henry, duke of Clarence, who was to ascend the throne of England as William IV. The prince was Nelson's close friend and acted as best man when Nelson married Fannie Nisbet on Nevis in 1787.

When the Royal Navy abandoned the station at English Harbour in 1889, it fell into a state of decay. The Society of the Friends of English Harbour began restoring it in 1951, and on Dockyard Day, November 14, 1961, **Nelson's Dockyard** was re-opened with much fanfare. Today it's reminiscent, albeit on a much smaller scale, of Williamsburg, Virginia. Within the compound are crafts shops, restaurants, and two splendidly restored 18th-century hotels, the Admiral's Inn and The Copper and Lumber Store Hotel, worth peeking into. (The latter, occupying a supply store for Nelson's Caribbean fleet, is a particularly fine example of Georgian architecture, with warm brick, hardwood floors, timber ceilings, sailing prints, nautical maps, burgundy leather armchairs and sofas, and an interior courtyard evoking Old England in the public spaces.) The Dockyard is a hub for oceangoing yachts and serves as headquarters for the annual Sailing Week Regatta. Beach lovers tend to stay elsewhere, but visitors who enjoy history and the nautical scene often choose one of the nearby hotels. Water taxis will ferry you between points for EC$5.

The **Admiral's House Museum** displays ship models, a model of English Harbour, silver trophies, maps, prints, and Nelson's very own telescope and tea caddy, as well as recent regatta trophies. ✉ *Nelson's Dockyard,* ☎ *268/463–1053 or 268/463–1379.* 📷 *$2, suggested donation.* ⏱ *Daily 8–6.*

❹ Falmouth. This town sits on a lovely bay backed by former sugar plantations and sugar mills. **St. Paul's Church** was rebuilt on the site of a church once used by troops during the Nelson period.

Fig Tree Drive. This road takes you through the rain forest, which is rich in mangoes, pineapples, and banana trees (*fig* is the Antiguan word for "banana"). The rain-forest area is the hilliest part of the island— **Boggy Peak,** to the west, is the highest point, at 1,319 ft (439 m).

❸ Ft. George. East of Liberta—one of the first settlements founded by freed slaves—on Monk's Hill, this fort was built from 1689 to 1720. Among the ruins are the sites for 32 cannons, water cisterns, the base of the old flagstaff, and some of the original buildings.

❼ Harmony Hall. Northeast of Freetown (follow the signs) is this interesting art gallery built on the foundation of a 17th-century sugar-plantation great house. Artists Graham Davis and Peter and Annabella Proudlock, who founded the sister gallery in Jamaica, teamed up with local entrepreneur Geoffrey Pidduck to create this Antiguan establishment, which specializes in high-quality West Indian art. A large exhibit space is used for one-person shows; another space displays watercolors. A small bar in a sugar mill and a superlative Italian restaurant occupying the courtyard are open in season. Both are run by the enterprising Italians who operate the top-notch Abracadabra restaurant. There's also a pool, the beach is a five-minute walk down the hill, and you can arrange boat rides to nearby islets. You can also spend the night in one of the six comfortable, spacious cottages, which rent for $160 CP; the owners will graciously keep the kitchen open for dinner during the week. ⊠ *Brown's Mill Bay,* ☎ *268/463–2057 or 268/460–4120.* ⊘ *Daily 10–6.*

② Megaliths of Greencastle Hill. It's an arduous climb to these eerie rock slabs in the south-central part of the island. Some say the megaliths were set up by early inhabitants for their worship of the sun and moon; others believe they're nothing more than unusual geological formations.

⑩ Parham. This tiny village is a splendid, sleepy example of a traditional colonial settlement. **St. Peter's Church,** built in 1840 by Thomas Weekes, an English architect, is an octagonal Italianate building whose facade was once richly decorated with stucco and keystone work, though it suffered considerable damage during the earthquake of 1843.

① St. John's. Antigua's capital, home to some 40,000 people (approximately half the island's population), lies at sea level at the inland end of a sheltered northwestern bay. Although it has seen better days, a couple of notable historic sights and some good waterfront shopping areas and restaurants make it worth a visit.

Signs at the **Museum of Antigua and Barbuda** say PLEASE TOUCH, encouraging you to explore Antigua's past. Try your hand at the educational video games or squeeze a cassava through a *matapi* (a grass sieve). Exhibits interpret the nation's history, from its geological birth to its political independence in 1981. There are fossil and coral remains from some 34 million years ago; models of a sugar plantation and a wattle-and-daub house; an Arawak canoe; a wildly eclectic assortment of objects from cannonballs to 1920s telephone exchanges; and a small shop with handicrafts, books, prints, and paintings. The colonial building that houses the museum is the former courthouse, which dates from 1750. The museum gift shop carries such unusual items as calabash purses, seed earrings, and lignum vitae pipes. ⊠ *Church and Market sts.,* ☎ *268/462–1469.* ⊠ *$2 suggested donation.* ⊘ *Weekdays 8:30–4, Sat. 10–1.*

At the south gate of the **Anglican Cathedral of St. John the Divine** are figures of St. John the Baptist and St. John the Divine said to have been taken from one of Napoléon's ships and brought to Antigua. The original church was built in 1681, replaced by a stone building in 1745, and destroyed by an earthquake in 1843. The present building dates from 1845. With an eye to future earthquakes, the parishioners had the interior completely encased in pitch pine, hoping to forestall heavy damage. The church was elevated to the status of cathedral in 1848. ⊠ *Between Long and Newgate sts.,* ☎ *268/461–0082.*

Shopaholics head directly for **Heritage Quay,** a continually expanding multimillion-dollar complex. The two-story buildings contain stores that sell duty-free goods, sportswear, T-shirts, imports from down-island (paintings, T-shirts, straw baskets), and local crafts. There are also several restaurants and a casino. Cruise-ship passengers disembark here from the 500-ft-long (153-m-long) pier. ⊠ *High and Thames sts.*

Redcliffe Quay, set at the water's edge just south of Heritage Quay, is the most appealing part of St. John's. Attractively restored (and superbly re-created) buildings in a riot of cotton-candy colors house shops, restaurants, and boutiques and are linked by courtyards and landscaped walkways.

At the far south end of town, where Market Street forks into Valley Road and All Saints Road, a whole lot of haggling goes on every Friday and Saturday, when locals jam the public **marketplace** to buy and sell fruits, vegetables, fish, and spices. Be sure to ask before you aim a camera; expect your subject to ask for a tip. This is shopping the old-time Caribbean way, a jambalaya of sights, sounds, and smells.

❻ Shirley Heights. This bluff affords a spectacular view of English Harbour. The heights are named for Sir Thomas Shirley, the governor who fortified the harbor in 1787. You can stop in at **Shirley Heights Lookout,** a restaurant built into the remnants of the 18th-century fortifications. Most notable for its boisterous Sunday barbecues that often continue well into the night with live music and dancing; it serves dependable burgers, pumpkin soup, grilled items, and rum punches.

Not far from Shirley Heights is the **Dows Hill Interpretation Centre,** where observation platforms provide still more sensational vistas of the whole English Harbour area. There's a multimedia sound-and-light presentation on the island's history and culture, in which illuminated displays, incorporating lifelike figures and colorful tableaux, are presented with running commentary and music—resulting in a cheery, if bland, portrait of Antiguan life from the days of the Amerindians to the present. ☎ *268/460–2777 or 268/460–1773 (National Parks Authority).* 🖃 *EC$15.* ⊙ *Daily 9–5.*

ANTIGUA A TO Z

To research prices, get advice from other travelers, and book travel arrangements, visit www.fodors.com.

AIR TRAVEL
American Airlines has daily direct service from New York, nonstop service from Miami, and several flights from San Juan that connect with flights from more than 100 U.S. cities. Continental Airlines offers nonstop service from Newark and Miami. Air Canada has nonstop service from Toronto. Air France flies nonstop from Paris. British Airways has nonstop service from London. Virgin Atlantic also offers nonstop London flights. BWIA has nonstop service from New York, Miami, and Toronto. Carib Aviation flies daily to Barbuda, as well as neighboring islands. LIAT has daily flights to and from many other Caribbean islands.
➤ AIRLINES AND CONTACTS: **American Airlines** (☎ 268/462–0950); **Air Canada** (☎ 268/462–1147); **Air France** (☎ 268/462–1763); **British Airways** (☎ 268/462–0876); **BWIA** (☎ 268/480–2925 or 268/480–2942); **Carib Aviation** (☎ 268/462–3147); **Continental Airlines** (☎ 268/462–5355); **LIAT** (☎ 268/480–5600); **Virgin Atlantic** (☎ 268/560–2079).

AIRPORTS
Antigua's V. C. Bird International Airport, on the northeast coast, is a major hub for traffic between Caribbean islands and for international flights.

Taxis meet every flight, and drivers will offer to guide you around the island. The taxis are unmetered, but rates are posted at the airport, and drivers must carry a rate card with them. The fixed rate from the airport to St. John's is US$12 (although drivers have been known to *quote* in EC dollars); to English Harbour it's $21.

➤ AIRPORT INFORMATION: **V. C. Bird International Airport** (☎ 268/462–4672).

BIKE AND MOPED TRAVEL

You can rent Honda or Yamaha motorcycles for $35 per day ($150 per week) at Shipwreck Scooters.

➤ BIKE AND MOPED RENTALS: **Shipwreck** (✉ English Harbour, ☎ 268/464–7771).

BUSINESS HOURS

BANKS

Banks have varying hours but are generally open Monday–Thursday 8–2 and Friday 8–4.

POST OFFICES

Post offices are open Monday–Saturday 9–4.

SHOPS

Although some stores still follow the tradition of closing for lunch, most are open Monday–Saturday 9–5, especially in season; if a cruise ship is in port, shops in Heritage and Redcliffe Quays are likely to open Sunday.

CAR RENTALS

To rent a car, you need a valid driver's license and a temporary permit ($20), available through the rental agent. Costs average about $50 per day in season, with unlimited mileage, though you may get a better rate if you rent for several days. Most agencies offer automatic, stick-shift, and right- and left-hand-drive. Although four-wheel-drive vehicles ($55 per day) will get you more places and are refreshingly open, many roads are full of potholes.

Among the agencies are Avis, Budget, Dollar, Hertz, National, and Thrifty.

➤ MAJOR AGENCIES: **Avis** (✉ Airport, ☎ 268/462–2840; ✉ St. James's Club, Mamora Bay, ☎ 268/462–5000); **Budget** (✉ Airport, ☎ 268/462–3009); **Dollar** (✉ Factory Rd., St. John's, ☎ 268/462–0362); **Hertz** (✉ Airport, ☎ 268/462–6450; ✉ All Saints Rd., St. John's, ☎ 268/462–4114; ✉ Jolly Harbour, ☎ 268/462–6268); **National** (✉ Coolidge St., St. John's, ☎ 268/462–2113); **Thrifty** (✉ Airport, ☎ 268/462–8803).

CAR TRAVEL

GASOLINE

At press time, gasoline cost approximately $2.50 per gallon.

ROAD CONDITIONS

The main roads, by and large, are in good condition, although there are bronco-busting dirt stretches leading to some more remote locations and a few hilly areas that flood easily and become impassable for a day or two.

RULES OF THE ROAD

Driving is on the left, although many locals drive in the middle—or think nothing of stopping at roadside to chat. Don't be flustered by honking: it's the Caribbean version of hello.

ELECTRICITY

Antigua runs on 110 volts, allowing the use of most small North American appliances. Outlets are both two- and three-pronged, so bring an adapter.

EMBASSIES AND CONSULATES

➤ UNITED KINGDOM: The **British High Commission** (✉ Old Parham Rd., St. John's, ☎ 268/462–0008, WEB www.fco.gov.uk) looks after the requirements and safety of both U.K. and Commonwealth nationals (including those of Australia, Canada, and New Zealand). It's open Mon–Fri, 8:30 AM–12:30 PM.

➤ UNITED STATES: The **United States Consulate** (✉ U.S. Consulate, Hospital Hill, English Harbour, ☎ 268/463–6531, FAX 268/460–1569, WEB usembassy.state.gov) is open for appointments Mon–Fri, 9 AM–2 PM.

EMERGENCIES

➤ AMBULANCE AND FIRE: Dial ☎ 268/462–0251 for the ambulance. In the event of fire, dial ☎ 268/462–0044.

➤ HOSPITALS: **Holberton Hospital** (✉ Hospital Rd., St. John's, ☎ 268/462–0251) has a 24-hour emergency room.

➤ PHARMACIES: **City Pharmacy** (✉ St. Mary's St., St. John's, ☎ 268/480–3314); **Woods Pharmacy** (✉ Woods Centre, Friar's Hill Rd., St. John's, ☎ 268/462–9287).

➤ POLICE: Dial ☎ 268/462–0125.

ETIQUETTE AND BEHAVIOR

Antiguans are extremely proud and don't take kindly to strangers snapping photos without asking permission first.

FESTIVALS AND SEASONAL EVENTS

Antigua Sailing Week, which takes place at the end of April and in early May, draws more than 300 yachts for a series of races in several boat classes. The salt air crackles with excitement like a nautical Kentucky Derby. Late April sees the Antigua Classic Yacht Regatta, a five-day event including the Parade of Classics and Tall Ships race. Antigua Tennis Week, usually held the second week of May, features exhibitions by such masters as Billie Jean King, Kathy Rinaldi, Fred Stolle, and Bob Lutz, plus a pro-am tournament. Carnival runs from the end of July to early August and is one of the Caribbean's more elaborate, with eye-catching costumes, fiercely competitive bands, and the only Caribbean Queen show (a.k.a. the Miss Antigua Contest). Antigua International Hot Air Balloon Festival attracts dozens of fancifully shaped and colored hot air balloons in late November.

HEALTH

Exercise the usual precautions regarding sunburn in the tropics: use SPF15 or higher tanning lotion, and reapply at regular intervals or after swimming. There are no insect vectors, but on still days mosquitoes and no-see-ums can be a nuisance. Some beaches are shaded by manchineel trees, whose leaves and applelike fruit are poisonous to the touch; even raindrops falling from them can cause painful blisters. Most of the trees are posted with warning signs. If you come in contact with one, rinse the affected area and contact a doctor.

HOLIDAYS

Public holidays for 2002 are: New Year's Day, Good Friday (Mar. 29), Easter Sunday and Monday (Mar 31 and April 1), Labour Day (1st Mon. in May), Whit Monday (2nd Monday in June), Independence Day (Nov. 1), Christmas, and Boxing Day (Dec. 26).

LANGUAGE

Antigua's official language is English, and it's often spoken with a heavy West Indian lilt.

MAIL AND SHIPPING

Airmail letters to North America cost EC90¢; postcards, EC45¢. Letters to the United Kingdom cost EC90¢; postcards are EC45¢. Letters to Australia and New Zealand are EC1.20, postcards EC60¢. The main post office is at the foot of High Street in St. John's. Note that when addressing letters to the island, there are no postal codes; you need only indicate the address and "Antigua, West Indies."

➤ CONTACTS: **Main Post Office** (☎ 268/462–0992).

MONEY MATTERS

Note: prices quoted throughout this chapter are in U.S. dollars unless otherwise indicated.

ATMS

ATMs are available at the island's banks (listed below) and at the airport.

CREDIT CARDS

Most hotels, restaurants, and duty-free shops take major credit cards; all accept traveler's checks.

CURRENCY

Local currency is the Eastern Caribbean dollar (EC$), which is tied to the U.S. dollar and fluctuates only slightly. At hotels, the rate is EC$2.60 to US$1; at banks, it's about EC$2.70. American dollars are readily accepted, although you'll usually receive change in EC dollars.

➤ CONTACTS: **Bank of Antigua** (✉ High and Thames sts., ☎ 268/480–5300); **Barclays Bank** (✉ High St., ☎ 268/480–5000).

PASSPORTS AND VISAS

U.S. and Canadian citizens need proof of identity. A valid passport is most desirable, but a birth certificate is acceptable provided it has a raised seal and has been issued by a county or state (not a hospital) and provided that you also have some type of photo identification, such as a driver's license. A driver's license by itself isn't sufficient. Citizens of Australia, New Zealand, and the United Kingdom need passports. All visitors must present a return or ongoing ticket.

SAFETY

Throughout the Caribbean, incidents of petty theft are increasing. Leave your valuables in the hotel safe-deposit box; don't leave them unattended in your room, on a beach, or in a rental car. Also, the streets of St. John's are fairly deserted at night, so it's not a good idea to wander about alone.

SIGHTSEEING TOURS

GUIDED TOURS

Virtually all taxi drivers double as guides, and you can arrange an island tour with one for about $25 an hour. Every major hotel has a cabbie on call and may be able to negotiate a discount, particularly off-season.

ORIENTATION

Antours, by far the most professional outfit on Antigua, gives half- and full-day island tours that focus on such highlights as Shirley Heights and English Harbour. Antours is also the island's American Express representative.

➤ CONTACTS: **Antours** (✉ Long and Thames sts., St. John's, ☎ 268/462–4788).

SPECIAL-INTEREST

Estate Safari Adventure operates tours to the interior, where there are few marked trails and roads are rough. The cost (about $60 per person) includes lunch and snorkeling at a secluded beach. Tropikelly's four-wheel-drive off-road adventures enable you to fully appreciate the island's topography and rich history. Hiking is involved, though it's not strenuous. Four-wheel-drive tours with hikes are $65; bike tours cost $35; and hikes through the rain forest run $20.

The adventuresome and morbidly curious may enjoy visiting neighboring Montserrat. Jenny's Tours arranges day trips—including the ferry ride from Antigua's Heritage Quay, an island tour, breakfast, and lunch—for $150 per person (departure taxes not included; weekend rate $130 per person).

Montserrat's Soufriere Hills Volcano erupted in 1995, throwing the unfortunate island into the fire and wiping out much of its infrastructure. Though eruptions have subsided and residents returned, the volcano remains active, often spewing hot lava and plumes of ash visible from Antigua and other surrounding islands (plucky locals joke that new beachfront is being created; indeed a new mountain is sprouting). The tourism industry is making a tentative comeback, with simple guest houses, inns, rental villas, restaurants, and water-sports concessions opening. The tour takes in some of Montserrat's lush green forests, often compared to those of Ireland; the island's glistening, black-sand coast; lookout points showing the vast devastation, including the airport and Plymouth, the capital city buried under gray ash like a latter-day Pompeii; and the Montserrat Volcano Observatory to learn about volcanoes. Since the "safe zones" do change, it's strongly recommended that you go with a tour operator. However, hardy travelers do overnight and hike, kayak, and dive (check the Montserrat Tourist board Web site for information). The daily ferry (and occasionally, helicopter) from Antigua is met by island cabbies (the most reliable, friendly, and knowledgeable is Joe Phillips).
➤ CONTACTS: **Estate Safari Adventure** (☎ 268/462–4713); **Jenny's Tours** (✉ Box W471, St. John's, ☎ 268/461–9361); **Montserrat Tourist Board website** (WEB www.mrat.com); **Tropikelly** (☎ 268/461–0383).

TAXES
DEPARTURE TAX
The departure tax is $20.

SALES TAX
Hotels collect an 8½% government room tax; some restaurants will add a 7% tax.

TAXIS
Taxis are unmetered, and although fares mount up quickly, rates are fixed (your driver should have a rate card). Some cabbies may take you from St. John's to English Harbour and wait for a "reasonable" amount of time (about a half hour) while you look around, for about $40. You can always call a cab from the St. John's taxi stand.
➤ CONTACTS: **St. John's taxi stand** (☎ 268/462–0711; 268/462–5190 after 6 PM).

TELEPHONES
Few hotels have direct-dial phones, but it's easy enough to make connections through the switchboard. You can use the Caribbean Phone Card (available in $5, $10, and $20 amounts in most hotels and post offices) for local and long-distance calls and for access to AT&T USA Direct lines. Phone-card phones work much better than the regular pay phones. Some phone-card booths can now access Sprint and MCI. In addition, there are Boatphones at major tourist sights; simply pick up the receiver, and the operator will take your credit-card number (any

major card) and assign you a PIN (personal identification number). Calls using your PIN are then charged to that credit card.

To call Antigua from the United States, dial 1, then area code 268, then the local seven-digit number.

To call the United States and Canada, dial 1, the area code, and the seven-digit number, or use the phone card or one of the AT&T USA Direct phones, which are available at several locations, including the airport departure lounge, the cruise terminal at St. John's, and the English Harbour Marina.

To place a local call, simply dial the local seven-digit number.

TIPPING
Hotels and restaurants usually add a 10% service charge to your bill. In restaurants it's customary to leave another 5% if you're pleased with the service. Taxi drivers expect a 10% tip, porters and bellmen about $1 per bag. Maids are rarely tipped, but if you think the service exemplary, figure $2–$3 per night. Staff at all-inclusives aren't supposed to be tipped unless they've truly gone out of their way.

TRANSPORTATION AROUND ANTIGUA
You'll see two bus stations in St. John's, near the Botanical Gardens and near Central Market, but don't expect to see many buses. Schedules follow "island time," which is to say that privately owned vehicles roll when the spirit (infrequently) moves them. Taxis are generally your best bet.

VISITOR INFORMATION
There is a tourist-information desk at the airport, just beyond the immigration checkpoint. The tourist office gives limited information. You may have more success with the Antigua Hotels and Tourist Association.
➤ BEFORE YOU LEAVE: **Antigua and Barbuda Tourist Offices** in the United States (✉ 610 5th Ave., Suite 311, New York, NY 10020, ☎ 212/541–4117 or 888/268–4227, www.antigua-barbuda.org and WEB www.antiguanice.com; ✉ 25 S.E. 2nd Ave., Suite 300, Miami, FL 33131, ☎ 305/381–6762); in Canada (✉ 60 St. Clair Ave. E, Suite 304, Toronto, Ontario M4T 1N5, ☎ 416/961–3085); in the United Kingdom (✉ Antigua House, 15 Thayer St., London W1M 5LD, ☎ 0171/486–7073).
➤ IN ANTIGUA: **Antigua and Barbuda Department of Tourism** (✉ Nevis St., St. John's, ☎ 268/463–0125,6,7, FAX 268/462–2483); **Antigua Hotels and Tourist Association** (✉ Lower St. Mary's St., St. John's, ☎ 268/462–0374).

3 ARUBA

Updated by
Karen W.
Bressler and
Elise Rosen

A natural coral limestone bridge, burnished beige in the golden sun, straddles a perfect crescent of ecru sand and sapphire surf. Terns and snowy egrets dive-bomb for their lunch. To one side, towering cacti and rock formations and boulders, like jagged Henry Moore sculptures, stretch as far as the eye can see. To the other side . . . a parking lot with safari vans, a sea of wildly colored T-shirts (with even wilder slogans), and a ramshackle building advertised in big hand-painted letters as the THIRST AID STATION. Welcome to Aruba—an uneasy truce between natural beauty and tourism.

That delicate balance is the key to Aruba's undeniable success. Most of the island gleams with a fierce, extraterrestrial beauty, its battered coast defying development. But balmy sunshine, silky sand, aquamarine waters, and constant trade winds (so strong they've bent Aruba's trademark watapana tree—commonly known as the divi-divi tree—at a surreal 45-degree angle) have made the calmer southwest coast a tourist mecca. Most of its 28 major hotels sit side by side down a single strip of shore, with restaurants, exotic boutiques, fiery floor shows, and glitzy casinos on the premises. Nearly every night there are theme parties, treasure hunts, beachside barbecues, and fish fries with steel bands and limbo or Carnival dancers. Surround all this with warm blue-green waters whose visibility extends up to 100 ft (30 m), and you've got the perfect destination for anyone who wants sun salted with lots of activities.

The *A* in the ABC Islands (the other two being Bonaire and Curaçao), Aruba is small—only 19½ mi (31½ km) long and 6 mi (9½ km) across at its widest point. Once a member of the Netherlands Antilles, it became an independent entity within the Netherlands in 1986, with its own royally appointed governor and a 21-member elected parliament.

Aruba's stable economy was once based on oil, after a refinery was built in San Nicolas in 1924. The refinery supplied oil to the Allies in World War II, and by 1949 it employed 8,300 people. With its closing in 1985 the oil-boom days were laid to rest, though a new refinery opened in 1991. These days, education, housing, and health care are financed by tourism, and the island's population of 95,000 recognizes visitors as valued guests. The national anthem proclaims, "The greatness of our people is their great cordiality," and this is no exaggeration. Waiters serve you with smiles, English is spoken everywhere, and hotel hospitality directors appear delighted to fulfill your special needs.

The island's distinctive beauty lies in its countryside—full of rocky deserts, divi-divi trees, cactus jungles alive with the chattering of wild parakeets, secluded coves, and blue vistas with crashing waves. With its low humidity and average temperature of 82°F (28°C), Aruba has the climate of a paradise. Sun, cooling trade winds, friendly and courteous service, efficient amenities, golf and tennis clubs, modern casinos, glorious beaches, duty-free shopping, and remarkably varied cuisine help fill Aruba's more than 7,500 hotel rooms.

Lodging

Hotels are fairly expensive. To save money, take advantage of airline and hotel packages, which are plentiful. Or go during low season (summer), when rates are discounted by as much as 40%.

Most hotels are west of Oranjestad along L. G. Smith and J. E. Irausquin boulevards and are miniresort complexes, with their own drugstores, boutiques, fitness centers, beauty parlors, casinos, restaurants, gourmet delis, water-sports centers, and car-rental and travel desks. Meeting rooms, room service, laundry and dry cleaning services, in-room safe and minibar or refrigerator, and baby-sitting are standard amenities at all but the smallest properties, and many daily activities are usually part of the package. Children often get free accommodation in their parents' room; check for age qualifications. Most hotels, unless specified, don't include meals in their room rates.

CATEGORY	COST*
$$$$	over $325
$$$	$250–$325
$$	$175–$250
$	under $175

All prices are for a standard double room during high season, excluding 6% government tax and 11% service charge.

$$$$ ⬚ **Aruba Marriott Resort and Stellaris Casino.** You'll hear the sound of water everywhere at this high-rise resort, whether it's the beating of the surf or the trickling of waterfalls in the marble lobby and around the tropically landscaped free-form pool. Newly remodeled rooms are spacious and attractively appointed. Green, red, and yellow floral bedspreads cheerfully offset crisp white-tile floors, and light wood furniture and watercolor paintings add to the summery ambience. Most rooms have an ocean view and a large balcony; extras include hair dryers, scales, and irons. With its 18 treatment rooms, the Mandara Spa (opened in December 2000) provides the perfect respite from the midday sun, and an excellent opportunity for pampering and relaxing. Hungry? The Champions Sports Bar offers casual fare and lures fun-seekers with a mesmerizing display of memorabilia, 18 TV monitors, and a video arcade, pool table, and disco. For a more upscale dining experience, Tuscany restaurant serves superlative Italian cuisine. Guests at the Ocean Club, an adjacent time-share property, have access to the restaurants and shops in the main resort. ✉ *L. G. Smith Blvd. 101, Palm Beach,* ☎ *297/8–69000 or 800/223–6388,* ℻ *297/8–60649,* 🌐 *www.marriott.com. 372 rooms, 41 suites. 4 restaurants, 4 bars, café, air-conditioning, in-room data ports, in-room safes, minibars, no-smoking floor, refrigerators, pool, hair salon, 2 tennis courts, massage, sauna, spa, aerobics, health club, volleyball, beach, dive shop, windsurfing, boating, jet skiing, shops, casino, concierge, meeting rooms, car rental. AE, D, DC, MC, V. EP, FAP, MAP.*

$$$$ ☒ **Bushiri Beach Resort.** Indulge your vacation whims at this all-inclusive resort set on a secluded white-sand beach. A full activities center keeps guests of all ages on the go. The Chuchubi Kids' Club runs supervised daily programs for children ages 5–13, while grown-up water buffs can make a splash snorkeling, scuba diving (there are clinics for beginners), or taking out a paddleboat. For landlubbers, tennis is an option day or night. More energy to spare? Work out at the expanded fitness center. Or unwind with unlimited tropical drinks (or your beverages of choice) at the bars: one's at the pool, the other at the Jacuzzi. Nightly entertainment is always changing here. Beach games, Carnival Night, Limbo Night, and Talent Night are just some of the events you might enjoy. Or, if you prefer, you can always catch a complimentary ride to a nearby casino. Recent improvements at the hotel include a face-lift to the lobby (making it open-air) and a fresh painting of the exterior. At press time, all guest rooms—including 4 wheelchair-accessible accommodations—were undergoing renovations (10 at a time). ☒ *L. G. Smith Blvd. 35, Oranjestad,* ☎ *297/8–25216,* FAX *297/8–26789,* WEB *www.bushiri.com. 155 rooms. Restaurant, 2 bars, grill, air-conditioning, in-room safes, 2 pools, 3 outdoor hot tubs, 2 tennis courts, basketball, health club, volleyball, beach, boating, snorkeling, shop, baby-sitting, children's programs, laundry service, car rental. AE, D, DC, MC, V. All-inclusive.*

$$$$ ☒ **Hyatt Regency Aruba Beach Resort & Casino.** A top choice for hon-
★ eymooners, this truly romantic resort looks like a Spanish grandee's palace, with art deco–style flourishes and a multilevel pool with waterfalls, a two-story water slide, and a lagoon stocked with tropical fish and black swans. Rooms, done in gemstone color schemes and dark mahogany furnishings, have tiny balconies and lots of extras; those on the Regency Club floor have such amenities as free Continental breakfast and concierge service. You can relax on the beach, have a game of tennis, or head out for a horseback ride before an afternoon hydrotherapy treatment and a stop at the juice bar or yogurt shop. For a full meal choose from four excellent restaurants: Olé (Spanish), The Palm (contemporary Caribbean), Piccolo (Italian), and Ruinas del Mar (Continental). Families will appreciate Camp Hyatt, which imaginatively incorporates Aruban storytelling, cooking, and arts and crafts for kids ages 3–12. ☒ *J. E. Irausquin Blvd. 85, Palm Beach,* ☎ *297/ 8–61234 or 800/554–9288,* FAX *297/8–61682,* WEB *www.hyatt.com. 342 rooms, 18 suites. 4 restaurants, 5 bars, snack bar, air-conditioning, fans, in-room safes, minibars, no-smoking floor, room service, pool, hair salon, 2 outdoor hot tubs, massage, sauna, spa, steam room, 2 tennis courts, basketball, health club, horseback riding, volleyball, beach, dive shop, dock, snorkeling, water slide, windsurfing, boating, jet skiing, waterskiing, shops, casino, baby-sitting, children's programs, playground, concierge, business services, travel services, car rental. AE, D, DC, MC, V. EP, MAP.*

$$$$ ☒ **Radisson Aruba Resort & Casino.** Aruba's newest and largest hotel
★ stretches out over 14 acres on Palm Beach. It reopened at the start of this century (after a $55-million transformation). The colonial Caribbean–style guest rooms (each with an ocean or garden view) feature mahogany four-poster beds with regal-size throw pillows. The designers have thought of everything: blue accent lighting, wood furniture on the balconies, and plantation shutters. Other in-room perks include two phones, 27-inch TVs, minibars, coffeemakers, hair dryers, and fresh-baked cookies at turn-down. At night, take a peek at the heavens—with the help of a NexStar 8 telescope—in the resort's stargazing program. During NFL season, drop by the tailgate party at Gilligan's Beach Bar & Grill and enjoy barbecue and beer while you watch the Sunday afternoon games. ☒ *J. E. Irausquin Blvd. 81, Palm Beach,* ☎

Aruba

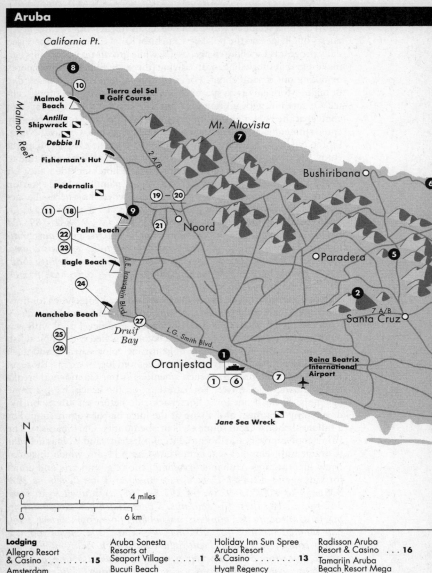

California Pt.

⑧
⑩
Malmok
Beach
*Antilla
Shipwreck* ◣
Debbie II
Fisherman's Hut ◣
Malmok Reef
2 A/B
Tierra del Sol
■ Golf Course
Mt. Altovista
⑦
Bushiribana ○
⑥
Pedernalis ◣
⑪ – ⑱
⑨
⑲ – ⑳
㉑
Noord
Palm Beach
㉒
㉓
Eagle Beach
㉔
J.E. Irausquin Blvd.
○ Paradera
⑤
Manchebo Beach
㉗
Druif
Bay
㉕
㉖
L.G. Smith Blvd.
Oranjestad
①
① – ⑥
⑦
②
7 A/B
Santa Cruz ○
Reina Beatrix
International
Airport
Jane Sea Wreck ◣

N

0 _____ 4 miles
0 _____ 6 km

Lodging

Allegro Resort & Casino	15
Amsterdam Manor Beach Resort	22
Aruba Grand Beach Resort & Casino	17
Aruba Marriott Resort and Stellaris Casino	12
Aruba Sonesta Resorts at Seaport Village	1
Bucuti Beach Resort	24
Bushiri Beach Resort	27
Divi Aruba Beach Resort Mega All Inclusive	25
Holiday Inn Sun Spree Aruba Resort & Casino	13
Hyatt Regency Aruba Beach Resort & Casino	14
La Cabana All Suite Beach Resort & Casino	23
Mill Resort & Suites	21
Radisson Aruba Resort & Casino	16
Tamarijn Aruba Beach Resort Mega All Inclusive	26
Vistalmar	7
Wyndham Aruba Beach Resort and Casino	18

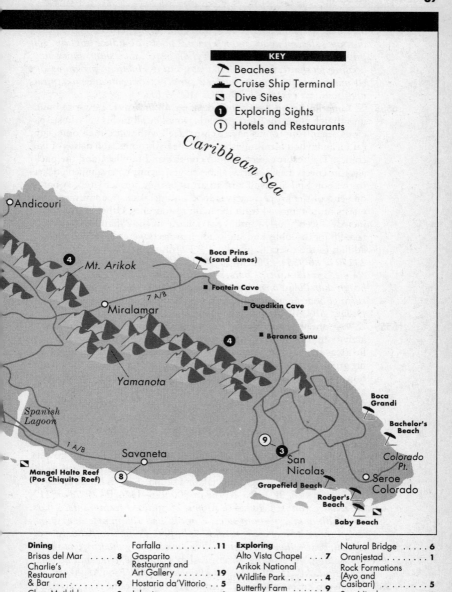

KEY

↗ Beaches
🚢 Cruise Ship Terminal
◥ Dive Sites
❶ Exploring Sights
① Hotels and Restaurants

Caribbean Sea

Andicouri

❹ Mt. Arikok

Boca Prins
(sand dunes)

7 A/B

■ Fontein Cave

Miralamar

■ Guadikin Cave

❹

■ Baranca Sunu

Yamanota

Boca
Grandi

Spanish
Lagoon

Bachelor's
Beach

1 A/B

⑨

Savaneta

❸

Colorado
Pt.

San
Nicolas

Mangel Halto Reef
(Pos Chiquito Reef)

⑧

Seroe
Colorado

Grapefield Beach

Rodger's
Beach

Baby Beach

Dining
Brisas del Mar **8**
Charlie's
Restaurant
& Bar **9**
Chez Mathilde **3**
Le Dôme **4**
L'Escale **1**
El Gaucho
Argentine Grill **2**

Farfalla **11**
Gasparito
Restaurant and
Art Gallery **19**
Hostaria da'Vittorio . . **5**
Jakarta **6**
Papiamento **20**
Ventanas
del Mar **10**

Exploring
Alto Vista Chapel . . . **7**
Arikok National
Wildlife Park **4**
Butterfly Farm **9**
California
Lighthouse **8**
Hooiberg **2**

Natural Bridge **6**
Oranjestad **1**
Rock Formations
(Ayo and
Casibari) **5**
San Nicolas **3**

297/8–66555, FAX *297/8–63260,* WEB *www.radisson.com. 358 rooms, 32 suites. 3 restaurants, 2 bars, air-conditioning, in-room data ports, in-room safes, minibars, room service, 2 pools, 2 outdoor hot tubs, golf privileges, 2 tennis courts, health club, beach, dive shop, snorkeling, boating, jet skiing, shops, casino, baby-sitting, children's programs, dry cleaning, laundry service, business services, convention center, meeting room, car rental. AE, D, DC, MC, V. BP.*

$$$$ 🏨 **Tamarijn Aruba Beach Resort Mega All Inclusive.** Low-rise buildings stretch along the property of this low-key all-inclusive, whose spacious oceanfront rooms have a casual feel, with white-tile floors, light rattan and wood furnishings, painted tile bathrooms, and patios or balconies. The resort caters to both couples and families, and the package here covers meals, snacks, all beverages, nightly entertainment, tickets to the Bon Bini Festival, and an array of outdoor activities. A bar at one end of the property serves food and drinks as a convenience for guests more removed from the main restaurants. Other conveniences include a free hourly (until 3 AM) shuttle to the Alhambra Casino. A face-lift for the lobby and landscaping projects were recently completed, adding to the overall appeal. ✉ *J. E. Irausquin Blvd. 41,* ☎ *297/8–24150 or 800/554–2008,* FAX *297/8–31940,* WEB *tamarijnaruba.com. 236 rooms. 3 restaurants, 2 bars, snack bar, fans, 2 pools, 2 tennis courts, health club, Ping-Pong, shuffleboard, volleyball, beach, snorkeling, windsurfing, boating, waterskiing, fishing, bicycles, shops, car rental. AE, D, DC, MC, V. All-inclusive.*

$$$$ 🏨 **Wyndham Aruba Beach Resort and Casino.** If bustle and nonstop activity make your day, you'll be right at home here. The grand public areas are cavernous enough to accommodate conventioneers and big groups from North and South America, which make up a good portion of the clientele. Rooms, which are average in size, have gold, khaki, and blue bedspreads; mustard-color stucco walls; and handsome dark-wood furniture. All have ocean-view balconies and are equipped with coffeemakers, irons, refrigerators, and hair dryers. A day at the pool means more than swimming and sunning; a "pool concierge" makes the rounds, lending out books, magazines, CDs, and CD players for the day; pool attendants spritz you with Evian, offer chilled towels, and serve frozen drinks. If you still don't feel pampered, head to the health club for a massage, a facial, or a sauna. ✉ *J. E. Irausquin Blvd. 77, Palm Beach,* ☎ *297/8–64466 or 800/996–3426,* FAX *297/8–68217,* WEB *www.wyndham.com. 478 rooms, 78 suites. 4 restaurants, 5 bars, air-conditioning, in-room safes, 2 pools, hair salon, massage, sauna, steam room, tennis court, health club, Ping-Pong, shuffleboard, volleyball, beach, dive shop, snorkeling, windsurfing, boating, jet skiing, parasailing, waterskiing, shops, casino, concierge, convention center, car rental. AE, D, DC, MC, V. All-inclusive, CP, EP, FAP, MAP.*

$$$ 🏨 **Allegro Resort & Casino.** Teeming activity surrounds the cloverleaf-shape pool (with its waterfall and whirlpool tubs) at the heart of this resort. It's a popular place with American and Canadian tour groups, and the buzzing atmosphere includes everything from beer-drinking contests to bikini shows. Burn off some calories at the recently expanded fitness center, or indulge your senses at the Intermezzo spa. In guest rooms (which are simple but clean) the white-tile bathrooms are a bit tight, and the balconies are tiny. But repeat visitors are lured by the attentive service, the attractive beachfront, and the festive mood. A new palazzo on the beach is a great spot for a cocktail party—honeymooners gather at 6 PM on Tuesdays. The Kids' Club, open from 9 to 5 daily, is for ages 4–12. ✉ *J. E. Irausquin Blvd. 83, Palm Beach,* ☎ *297/8–64500 or 800/447–7462,* FAX *297/8–63191,* WEB *www. allegroresorts.com. 405 rooms, 14 suites. 3 restaurants, 4 bars, air-conditioning, in-room safes, pool, 2 outdoor hot tubs, 2 tennis courts, bas-*

ketball, gym, Ping-Pong, volleyball, beach, snorkeling, boating, waterskiing, shops, casino, dance club, children's programs. AE, D, DC, MC, V. All-inclusive, EP.

$$$ 🏨 **Aruba Grand Beach Resort & Casino.** The atmosphere at this privately owned resort is low-key, and the repeat business is high. The yellow and white building complements a jade green roof. Spacious rooms and suites have such amenities as large walk-in closets and balconies that overlook either the ocean, the pool, or the garden. The Seawatch Restaurant offers international cuisine for breakfast, lunch, and dinner; the Whale's Rib entices guests seeking seafood fare in a more casual setting. Ask about special packages: discounts are available for children under 12. Plans to add a spa are in the works. In the meantime, guests may use the spa at the nearby Wyndham Resort for $5. ✉ *J. E. Irausquin Blvd. 79, Palm Beach,* ☎ *297/8–63900 or 800/345–2782,* FAX *297/8–61941,* WEB *www.apbresv.com. 130 rooms, 41 suites. 2 restaurants, 3 bars, deli, ice cream parlor, air-conditioning, refrigerators, room service, 2 pools, 2 tennis courts, volleyball, beach, dive shop, snorkeling, windsurfing, boating, waterskiing, shops, casino, baby-sitting, dry cleaning, laundry service, concierge, meeting room. AE, D, DC, MC, V. All-inclusive, EP, MAP.*

$$$ 🏨 **Aruba Sonesta Resorts at Seaport Village.** For those who enjoy being
★ in the thick of things (like Dutch Queen Beatrix, who has stayed here), this lively Oranjestad property is surrounded by shops, restaurants, and casinos. It's a top choice for singles, yet it also has plenty for families, and offers discounted rates to senior citizens. Suites in the newer Beach Tower have kitchenettes and ceiling fans. The original high-rise hotel (the Marina Tower) has compact but attractive accommodations; choose the quieter garden-view rooms here. In the lobby, which is connected to the Seaport Village Mall, you can board a motor skiff for a day trip along a landscaped canal to the resort's 40-acre private island. For the ultimate in self-pampering, visit the new Okeanos Spa. The resort's gourmet restaurant, L'Escale, is one of Aruba's best. ✉ *L. G. Smith Blvd. 9, Oranjestad,* ☎ *297/8–36000 or 800/766–3782,* FAX *297/8–25317,* WEB *www.arubasonesta.com. 285 rooms, 265 suites. 4 restaurants, 6 bars, air-conditioning, kitchenettes, minibars, no-smoking rooms, room service, 3 pools, massage, spa, golf privileges, tennis court, 2 health clubs, volleyball, beach, dive shop, snorkeling, jet skiing, marina, waterskiing, fishing, shops, 2 casinos, nightclub, baby-sitting, children's programs, playground, coin laundry, concierge, convention center. AE, D, DC, MC, V. All-inclusive, EP, FAP, MAP.*

$$$ 🏨 **Divi Aruba Beach Resort Mega All Inclusive.** At this Mediterranean-style resort, you can choose from standard guest rooms, beachfront lanai rooms, and *casitas* (garden bungalows) that look out onto individual courtyards and are only steps from the beach. The new sunny yellow, bright pink, and jade color schemes are cheerful, and the whole place has been spruced up with fresh landscaping, reconfigured walkways, a new pool deck, and refurbished oceanfront rooms. For a refreshing break, drop by the make-your-own piña colada and daiquiri station at the poolside bar (open round-the-clock). In addition to the many on-site facilities, you can also use those at the adjacent Tamarijn Aruba. Note that despite the "mega all-inclusive" label, getting your laundry done, having your hair cut, or hiring a baby-sitter cost extra. ✉ *L. G. Smith Blvd. 93, Manchebo Beach,* ☎ *297/8–23300 or 800/554–2008,* FAX *297/8–31940,* WEB *diviaruba.com. 203 rooms. 5 restaurants, 3 bars, air-conditioning, fans, refrigerators, 2 pools, hair salon, outdoor hot tub, tennis court, gym, shuffleboard, volleyball, beach, dive shop, snorkeling, windsurfing, boating, waterskiing, bicycles, shops, baby-sitting, laundry service. AE, D, DC, MC, V. All-inclusive.*

$$$ ☷ **La Cabana All Suite Beach Resort & Casino.** This completely self-contained, well-maintained resort village sits across the street from Eagle Beach. The original four-story building faces the beach and forms a horseshoe around a huge free-form pool with a water slide, a bar, a restaurant, and a water-sports center. One-third of the studio and one-bedroom suites have full sea views. All are comfortable and have fully equipped kitchenettes, balconies, and Jacuzzis. Pricier suites and villas are separated from the main building by a parking lot, making them more secluded. With the Home Food Shopping Program here, for a $5 fee, you can order groceries on-line up to two days prior to travel, and they'll be delivered to your door upon your arrival. ✉ *J. E. Irausquin Blvd. 250, Eagle Beach,* ☎ *297/8–79000; 212/251–1710 in NY; 800/ 835–7193;* FAX *297/8–70834,* WEB *www.lacabana.com. 803 suites. 4 restaurants, 3 bars, grocery, ice cream parlor, air-conditioning, in-room safes, kitchenettes, 3 pools, 3 outdoor hot tubs, massage, sauna, 5 tennis courts, aerobics, basketball, health club, racquetball, shuffle-board, squash, volleyball, dive shop, water slide. AE, DC, MC, V. All-inclusive, EP, FAP, MAP.*

$$ ☷ **Amsterdam Manor Beach Resort.** This mustard-color hotel—all gables and turrets—looks like part of a Dutch colonial village. It's a cozy enclave that surrounds a lovely pool with a waterfall, and glorious Eagle Beach is just across the street. Rooms are furnished in either Dutch modern or provincial style and range from small studios—some with a balcony and/or a whirlpool tub—to two-bedroom suites with peaked ceilings, whirlpool tubs and showers, and full kitchens. Up to two children under 12 stay free with their parents. Free diving lessons are available twice a week, and the hotel can arrange a variety of activities. ✉ *J. E. Irausquin Blvd. 252, Eagle Beach,* ☎ *297/8–71492,* FAX *297/8–71463,* WEB *www.amsterdammanor.com. 35 studios, 35 suites. Restaurant, bar, air-conditioning, fans, in-room safes, kitchenettes, 2 pools, snorkeling, playground, coin laundry, car rental. AE, DC, MC, V. CP, EP, MAP.*

$$ ☷ **Bucuti Beach Resort.** The owners' close attention to guest satisfac-
★ tion and care of the property is apparent throughout this intimate European-style resort. And it's all done with environmentally conscious élan. In fact, for its dedication to sustainable tourism, the hotel earned the prestigious "Green Globe 21" certificate in 2000, an honor bestowed upon only 18 tourism organizations worldwide (stringent global standards apply). Among the special efforts at the resort: rooms are equipped with bins for recyclables; water-saving devices are installed in the shower and toilet; options are displayed for guests to reuse towels and bed sheets; shampoo, lotion, and soap are supplied in dispensers (instead of individual bottles); energy-saving lightbulbs are used; solar panels heat water; and a treatment facility recycles water for garden use. Even Aruba's native terns feel welcome: a stretch of Bucuti's beach is roped off and guarded each spring to allow them to nest. Popular with honeymooners (their doorways are charmingly decorated), the hacienda-style buildings house enormous, sunny rooms that have bright tropical decor, handsome cherry-wood furnishings, sparkling tile floors, and a terrace or balcony with an ocean view. Room extras include coffee/tea makers, microwave ovens, hair dryers, irons, and devices for people with hearing impairments. The grounds are lushly landscaped, and the resort has an enviable location on the widest, most secluded section of Eagle Beach. The oceanfront Pirate's Nest restaurant looks like a beached galleon and is known for its dinners of lobster-size shrimp and expansive salad bar. If you feel like working off the calories from a meal or two, head for the open-air exercise pavilion. Need to stay connected to the real world? The hotel has a 24-hour business center with computers, Internet access, faxes, and phones. ✉ *L. G. Smith*

Blvd. 55-B, Eagle Beach (Box 1299), ☎ *297/8–31100 or 800/223–1108,* 🖷 *297/8–25272,* 🌐 *www.bucuti.com. 58 rooms, 5 suites. Restaurant, bar, grocery, air-conditioning, fans, in-room safes, minibars, refrigerators, pool, beach, bicycles, shops, coin laundry, business services, travel services. AE, D, DC, MC, V. CP, MAP.*

$$ 🎰 **Holiday Inn SunSpree Aruba Resort & Casino.** This is one of the larger properties on Palm Beach, with three buildings set apart from one another along a sugary, palm-dotted beach. Rooms are clean, spacious, and attractive in shades of deep green, royal blue, yellow, and orange. The pool's cascades and sundeck draw as large a crowd as the wide beach, where such activities as the Monday evening managers' cocktail party and the BBQ Beach Bash take place. This friendly resort is a reliable choice for families; as many as two children (under 17) can stay with their parents at no additional charge, and the resort has a complimentary Little Rascals Club for kids 5–12. Enjoy live entertainment as you try your luck at the casino. The Intermezzo spa (opened in 2000) features massages, wraps, and facials. ✉ *J. E. Irausquin Blvd. 230, Palm Beach,* ☎ *297/8–63600; 800/934–6750 (direct to hotel);* 🖷 *297/8–65165,* 🌐 *www.holiday-inn.com. 600 rooms, 7 suites. 4 restaurants, 4 bars, air-conditioning, no-smoking rooms, refrigerators, 2 pools, massage, spa, 4 tennis courts, basketball, health club, Ping-Pong, volleyball, beach, dive shop, dock, snorkeling, windsurfing, boating, waterskiing, shops, casino, children's programs, concierge, business services, meeting rooms, car rental. AE, DC, MC, V. All-inclusive, EP, FAP, MAP.*

$ 🏨 **Mill Resort & Suites.** This small, award-winning resort's whitewashed, red-roof buildings flank its open-air common areas. The architecture is striking: clean geometric lines, skylights, and wood-beam ceilings. The rooms are appealing, with blond-wood and rattan furnishings and a cool powder-blue color scheme. Junior suites have a king-size bed, a sitting area, and a kitchenette. Studios have a full kitchen, a convertible sofa bed or twin beds, a tiny bathroom, and no balcony. The beach is only a five-minute walk away; the Intermezzo spa (opened in 2000), a morning coffee hour, and a weekly scuba lesson are among the on-site amenities. At the Garden Cafe a special tourist menu offers three courses at affordable prices. ✉ *J. E. Irausquin Blvd. 330, Oranjestad,* ☎ *297/8–67700,* 🖷 *297/8–67271,* 🌐 *www.millresort. com. 64 studios, 128 suites. Restaurant, bar, grill, grocery, air-conditioning, in-room safes, kitchenettes, 3 pools, hair salon, massage, sauna, spa, 2 tennis courts, gym, shops, coin laundry, travel services, car rental. AE, D, DC, MC, V. EP.*

$ 🏨 **Vistalmar.** There's no beach here, but the sea and a swimming pier are just across the street. The simply furnished one-bedroom apartments have a full kitchen, a living-dining room, and a broad sunporch. The friendly owners, Alby and Katy Yarzagaray, provide snorkel gear and stock the refrigerator with breakfast fixings. A drawback is the distance from town, but a rental car can be provided at a reasonable cost, or you can ride the bus ($1.25) that departs from the hotel every two hours. ✉ *Bucutiweg 28, south of Oranjestad,* ☎ *297/8–28579,* 🖷 *297/ 8–22200. 8 rooms. Air-conditioning, kitchenettes, coin laundry, car rental. No credit cards. CP.*

Dining

Expect outstanding meals and cuisines and restaurateurs from around the world. Although most resorts offer better-than-average dining, don't be afraid to try one of the many excellent, reasonably priced independent restaurants. Ask locals about their favorite spots; some of the lesser-known eateries offer food that's definitely worth sampling.

Be sure to try such Aruban specialties as *pan bati* (a mildly sweet bread that resembles a pancake) and *keshi yena* (a baked concoction of Gouda cheese, spices, and meat or seafood in a rich brown sauce).

On Sunday you may have a hard time finding a restaurant outside a hotel that's open for lunch, and many restaurants are closed for dinner on Sunday or Monday. Reservations are essential for dinner in high season.

What to Wear
Even the finest restaurants require at most a jacket for men and a sundress for women. If you plan to eat in the open air, remember to bring along insect repellent—in case the mosquitoes get unruly.

CATEGORY	COST*
$$$$	over $30
$$$	$20–$30
$$	$10–$20
$	under $10

*per person for a main course at dinner

ARGENTINE
$$$ ✕ **El Gaucho Argentine Grill.** Faux-leather-bound books, tulip-top lamps, and wooden chairs adorn this Argentine steak house, which has been in business for more than 20 years. Main dishes include thick *churrasco* (Argentine steak) smothered in peppers and onions, and the catch of the day (perhaps grouper). Choose a bottle of rich red wine from the extensive cellar. For dessert, try the *helado Argentino* (vanilla ice cream with sweet-potato marmalade and caramel) or the *torta de queso*, otherwise known as cheesecake. ✉ *Wilhelminastraat 80,* ☎ *297/8–23677. AE, D, MC, V. Closed Sun.*

ASIAN
$$$ ✕ **Jakarta.** Brightly painted stone walls, fringed lamp shades, and clusters of candles bring this restaurant to life with a chic contemporary feel. The signature rijsttafel is a standout. It consists of 20 miniature meat, fish, vegetable, and fruit dishes that you share with others at your table. A full vegetable rijsttafel is available, too. Another popular choice is Indonesian-style chicken soup, made with hard-boiled eggs and chicken liver. The back patio is bedecked with a bamboo bar, wind chimes, and clay pots. ✉ *Wilhelminastraat 64,* ☎ *297/8–38737. AE, D, DC, MC, V. Closed Tues.*

CARIBBEAN
$$ ✕ **Brisas del Mar.** This friendly 32-table place overlooking the sea—accessible from the hotels by bus—makes you feel as if you're dining in an Aruban home. Old family recipes use such indigenous ingredients as the aromatic *yerbiholé* leaf (it has a somewhat minty basil flavor) and the sizzling Madame Jeanette pepper. Try the smashing steamy fish soup, *keri keri* (shredded fish kissed with annatto seed), or some of the island's best pan bati. The terrace is inviting on a breezy night; make reservations early to watch the sunset. ✉ *Savaneta 222A, Savaneta,* ☎ *297/8–47718. AE, MC, V.*

$$ ✕ **Gasparito Restaurant and Art Gallery.** This charming no-smoking
★ restaurant is also a gallery that showcases the works of local artists on softly lighted white walls. It's set in a *cunucu* (country house) in Noord, not far from the hotel strip, with lovely high-back hardwood chairs and steel lamps. The Aruban specialties—pan bati, keshi yena, fish croquettes, conch stew, stewed chicken, creole-style fish fillet—are a feast for both the eye and the palate, so it comes as no surprise that Gasparito's chefs walk away with top awards in Caribbean culinary competitions. One standout dish is the Gasparito chicken; the recipe, from

the owner's ancestors, features seven special ingredients including brandy, white wine, and pineapple juice (the rest are secret). Enjoy live local music on the patio, where a light menu is served. ✉ *Gasparito 3, Noord,* ☎ *297/8–67044. AE, D, MC, V. Closed Sun. No lunch.*

CONTEMPORARY

$$$$ ✕ **L'Escale.** You're missing out if you don't make a reservation for at least one meal in this upscale Aruba Sonesta Resort eatery (it was rated the island's best in 2000 by the Aruba Gastronomical Association). Sip wine and look out over bustling L. G. Smith Boulevard while waiting for your sautéed baby snails and Caribbean-style walnut-crusted snapper; for dessert try the rich chocolate soufflé. Sparkles and streamers will decorate your table for a special occasion, and the extensive cigar list can help turn any night into a celebration. If time is short (perhaps you're scurrying off to the Crystal Casino show), opt for the pre-theater menu. ✉ *L. G. Smith Blvd. 82, Oranjestad,* ☎ *297/8–36000. Reservations essential. AE, D, MC, V. No lunch.*

CONTINENTAL

$$$$ ✕ **Chez Mathilde.** This elegant restaurant occupies one of Aruba's last surviving 19th-century houses. Ask to sit in the swooningly romantic Pavilion Room, which has an eclectic mix of Italian and French decor, heavy damask drapes, brass gas lamps, and ivy-covered walls. The backroom greenhouse atrium is an appealing second choice. The outstanding French-style menu is constantly re-created. Feast on artfully presented baked escargots, roasted breast of duck on a lentil puree, or breaded ostrich fillet with sesame and soy dressing on Belgian endive. The crêpes suzette and chocolate layer cake with mocha and *ponche crema* sauce (Venezuelan eggnog made with brandy) will also please your taste buds. ✉ *Havenstraat 23, Oranjestad,* ☎ *297/8–34968. Reservations essential. AE, DC, MC, V. No lunch Sun.*

$$$ ✕ **Le Dôme.** Belgian Peter Ballière and his two partners imported
★ 11,000 bricks from Antwerp to authenticate the Continental interior of this fine dining spot. The service is polished, the maroon decor in the main room is sumptuous, and a local harpist and guitarist add considerable ambience. The Belgian endive soup is delicious; the *tournedos Rossini* (prime-cut beef in a port sauce with a goose-liver mousse), downright decadent. A seven-course set menu is also available. Try one of the eight imported Belgian beers or one of the wine list's 65 varieties. Savor champagne and a cup of coffee with the prix-fixe Sunday brunch. Note that this is a place where shorts are a no-no. The restaurant also caters a gourmet dinner cruise. ✉ *J. E. Irausquin Blvd. 224, Oranjestad,* ☎ *297/8–71517. Reservations essential. AE, D, DC, MC, V. Closed Mon. and Sept.*

ECLECTIC

$$$ ✕ **Papiamento.** Longtime restaurateurs Lenie and Eduardo Ellis con-
★ verted their 130-year-old home into a bistro that is elegant, intimate, and always romantic. You can feast sumptuously indoors surrounded by antiques or outdoors in a patio garden. The chefs mix Continental and Caribbean cuisines to produce favorites that include seafood and meat dishes. Try the clay-pot seafood medley for two. ✉ *Washington 61, Noord,* ☎ *297/8–64544. Reservations essential. AE, MC, V. Closed Mon. No lunch.*

$$$ ✕ **Ventanas del Mar.** The floor-to-ceiling windows of this elegant restaurant look out across a golf course and beyond to rolling sand dunes and the sea off the island's western tip. Dining on the intimate terrace amid flickering candlelight is very romantic. Sandwiches, salads, conch fritters, nachos, and quesadillas fill the midday menu; at night the emphasis is on seafood and meat. The sea bass in orange sauce is a must-try. ✉ *Tierra del Sol Golf Course, Malmokweg,* ☎ *297/8–67800. AE, MC, V.*

$$ ✕ **Charlie's Restaurant & Bar.** Charlie's has been a San Nicolas hangout for more than 50 years. Tourists flock here to gawk at the decor: the walls and ceiling are *covered* with license plates, hard hats, sombreros, life preservers, baseball pennants, intimate apparel, credit cards—you name it. Decent but somewhat overpriced specialties are Argentine tenderloin and "shrimps jumbo and dumbo" (dumb because they were caught). And don't leave before trying Charlie's special "honeymoon sauce" (so called because it's really hot). The real draw here is the nonstop party atmosphere—an oddly endearing hybrid between a frat house and a beach bar. ✉ *Zeppenfeldstraat 56, San Nicolas,* ☎ *297/8–45086. AE, D, MC, V. Closed Sun.*

$$ ✕ **Farfalla.** The culinary influences at this artful newcomer lean toward
★ French-Mediterranean, but also include Spain, Italy, Greece, and the Middle East. Creativity is apparent not only in the delectable preparation and presentation of dishes, but also in the decor—much of it handcrafted by the owner himself (like the woven Indonesian mats used as shades in the outdoor seating area). Even the menu is unique: rather than printed on paper, the food options are listed on replicas of an artist's palette. The restaurant hosts "action painting" sessions from time to time, where patrons are invited to contribute to a communal canvas posted in the dining room (the painting is then sold and the proceeds donated to charity). ✉ *Havenstraat 4,* ☎ *297/8–87900. AE, D, DC, MC, V. No lunch Sun.*

ITALIAN

$$$ ✕ **Hostaria da' Vittorio.** Everything here is enticing: terra-cotta floors, stone walls with arches, pale yellow beams, and light wood furniture create a warm ambience. The chef, Vittorio Muscariello, serves up culinary wonders including *ossobuco di vitello* (veal shank braised in dry white wine with fresh herbs and spices), *linguine dello scoglio* (with clams, mussels, squid, baby octopus, and shrimp), and a luscious tiramisu, all created on display in an open kitchen. A shop in the entryway sells gourmet Italian goods—wine, grappa, lemoncello, prosciutto, olive oil, risotto—at supermarket prices. Note that men aren't permitted to wear sleeveless shirts. ✉ *L. G. Smith Blvd. 380,* ☎ *297/8–63838. AE, MC, V.*

Beaches

Beaches in Aruba are legendary: white sand, turquoise waters, and virtually no litter—everyone takes the NO TIRA SUSHI (NO LITTERING) signs very seriously, especially with a $280 fine. The major beaches, which back up to the hotels along the southwestern strip, are public and crowded. You can make the hour-long hike from the Holiday Inn to the Tamarijn without ever leaving sand. Make sure you're well protected from the sun—it scorches fast despite the cooling trade winds. Luckily, there's at least one covered bar (and often an ice cream stand) at virtually every hotel. If you stroll at night, you can hotel-hop for dinner, dancing, gambling, and late-night entertainment. On the northeastern side, wind makes the waters too choppy for swimming, but the vistas are great, and the terrain is wonderful for exploring.

Palm Beach is the center of Aruban tourism, offering the best in swimming, sailing, and other water sports. It runs from the Wyndham Aruba Beach Resort to the Aruba Marriott Resort. On the southwestern coast, across the highway from what is known as Time-Share Lane, **Eagle Beach** (more than a mile long) has been designated one of the 10 best beaches in the world by *Travel & Leisure* magazine. Impressively wide **Manchebo Beach (Punta Brabo),** in front of the Manchebo Beach Resort, is where officials turn a blind eye to the occasional top-free sunbathers.

On the northwestern shore, small, nondescript **Malmok Beach** (where some of Aruba's wealthiest families have built tony residences) borders shallow waters that stretch 300 yards from shore. It's the perfect place to learn to windsurf. Right off the coast here is a favorite haunt for divers and snorkelers—the wreck of the German ship *Antilla,* scuttled in 1940. Next to the Holiday Inn, **Fisherman's Hut** is a windsurfer's haven. Swimming conditions are good, too. Take a picnic lunch (tables are available) and watch the elegant purple, aqua, and orange sails struggle in the wind.

On the island's eastern tip, semicircular **Baby Beach** borders a bay that's as placid and just about as deep as a wading pool—perfect for tots and terrible swimmers. Thatched shaded areas are good for cooling off. Just down the road is the island's rather unusual pet cemetery. You may see some shore divers here. Stop by the nearby snack truck for chicken legs, burgers, hot dogs, beer, and soda. Next to Baby Beach on the island's eastern tip, beautiful curving **Rodger's Beach** is only slightly marred by the view of the oil refinery at the far side of the bay. Swimming conditions are excellent, and there's live entertainment at the water's edge. To the northeast of San Nicolas, **Grapefield Beach,** a sweep of blinding white sand in the shadow of cliffs and boulders, is marked by a statue of an anchor dedicated to all seamen. Pick sea grapes in high season (January–June). Swim at your own risk; the waves here can be rough.

Strong swimming skills are a must at **Boca Grandi,** near Seagrape Grove and the Aruba Golf Club toward the island's eastern tip. You'll need a four-wheel-drive vehicle to make the trek to **Boca Prins.** Near the Fontein Cave and Blue Lagoon, this beach is about as large as a Brazilian bikini, but with two rocky cliffs and tumultuously crashing waves, it's as romantic as you get in Aruba. Boca Prins is famous for its backdrop of enormous vanilla sand dunes. This isn't a swimming beach, however. Bring a picnic, a beach blanket, and sturdy sneakers, and descend the rocks that form steps to the water's edge.

Outdoor Activities and Sports

On Aruba you can participate in every conceivable water sport as well as play tennis and golf or go on a fine hike through Arikok National Park. An up-and-coming sport popular with locals is bouldering. It's similar to mountain climbing and rappelling, only up and down the boulders of the Ayo rock formations or the eastern cliffs, which are more porous and can be dangerous. The Hyatt Regency Aruba Beach Resort & Casino can make arrangements for large groups to be guided, by sergeants of the Royal Dutch Marines, no less.

BOWLING

The **Eagle Bowling Palace** (⊠ Sasakiweg, Pos Abou, Oranjestad, ☎ 297/8–35038) has 16 lanes, a cocktail lounge, and a snack bar; it's open daily 10 AM to 2 AM. One lane for one hour will cost you $5.75–$11.50, depending on the time you play; shoes rent for $1.20.

FISHING

With catches including barracuda, kingfish, bonito, and black and yellow tuna, deep-sea fishing is great sport on Aruba. Many charter boats are available for half- or full-day sails. Half-day tours, including all equipment, soft drinks, and a box lunch, are around $250 for up to four people; full-day tours run about $500.

De Palm Tours (✉ L. G. Smith Blvd. 142, ☎ 297/8–24400 or 800/766–6016) runs deep-sea fishing tours seven days a week. It costs $275 to charter a boat for four hours. **Pelican Watersports** (✉ J. E. Irausquin Blvd. 230, ☎ 297/8–72302) offers daily boat charters from 8 AM to noon for deep-sea fishing, mostly on the south coast. **Red Sail Sports** (✉ J. E. Irausquin Blvd. 83, Oranjestad, ☎ 297/8–61603; 877/RED-SAIL in the U.S.) offers half-day fishing trips for $300 and full-day trips for $600 through **Northern Lights fishing company**. The price includes all fishing equipment; add $25 per person for more than four people.

GOLF

Aruba Golf Club (✉ Golfweg 82, near San Nicolas, ☎ 297/8–42006) has a 9-hole course with 20 sand traps and 5 water traps, roaming goats, and lots of cacti. There are 11 AstroTurf greens, making 18-hole tournaments a possibility. The clubhouse has a bar and locker rooms. The course's official U.S. Golf Association rating is 67; greens fees are $10 for 9 holes, $18 for 18 holes. Caddies and club rentals are available.

The driving range is the key feature of **Brown Golf & Leisure** (✉ J. E. Irausquin Blvd. 326, ☎ 297/8–64589), a massive new family fun center. The complex (open from 7 AM to 11 PM) also offers putting greens, a chipping area, and golf clinics for players seeking to perfect their game. Not golfing? Hit the batting cages, the game room, or the playground.

The **Tierra del Sol** (✉ Malmokweg, ☎ 297/8–60978) is on the northwest coast near the California Lighthouse. Designed by Robert Trent Jones, Jr., this 18-hole, par-71, 6,811-yard championship course combines Aruba's native beauty—flora, cacti, and rock formations—with the lush greens of the world's best courses. The $130 greens fee includes a golf cart; club rentals are $35.

Two elevated 18-hole miniature golf courses surrounded by a moat are available at **Joe Mendez Miniature Adventure Golf** (✉ Sasakiweg, ☎ 297/8–76625). There are also paddleboats and bumper boats, a bar, and a snack stand. A round of 18 holes costs $6.50, and you can play between 5 PM and 1 AM during the week; from noon on the weekends.

HIKING

Hiking in **Arikok National Wildlife Park** is generally not too strenuous, although you should exercise caution with the strong sun—bring plenty of water and wear sunscreen and a sun hat or visor. Sturdy, cleated shoes are a must to grip the granular, occasionally steep terrain. There are more than 20 mi (34 km) of trails, and it's important to stick to them. Look for different colors on signs to determine the degree of difficulty. The park is crowned by Aruba's second-highest mountain, the 577-ft (176-m) Mt. Arikok, so climbing is also a possibility.

De Palm Tours (☎ 297/8–24400 or 800/766–6016) offers a guided three-hour trip to sites of unusual natural beauty that are accessible only on foot. The fee is $25 per person, including refreshments and transportation; a minimum of four people is required.

HORSEBACK RIDING

Four ranches offer short jaunts along the beach or longer trail rides through countryside flanked by cacti, divi-divi trees, and aloe vera plants. Ask if you can stop off at Conchi, a natural pool that's reputed to have restorative powers. Rides are also possible in the Arikok National Wildlife Park. Rates run from $25 for an hour-long trip to $65 for a 3½-hour tour. Private rides cost slightly more. Some tour operators, like **De Palm Tours,** can arrange treks.

Rancho del Campo (✉ Sombre 22E,☎ 297/8–50290) offers rides to the natural bridge (Tuesday and Friday, $60), or the natural pool and Arikok Hill—including snorkeling and galloping around the sand dunes (seven days a week at 9 AM or 3 PM, $50). **Rancho Daimari** (✉ Plantage Daimari, ☎ 297/8–60239) escorts riders to the national park and the natural pool seven days a week, 8:30 AM and 2 PM for $50. **Rancho Notorious** (✉ Boroncana, Noord, ☎ 297/8–60508) offers trips that last 3¼ hours around the western side of the island, seven days a week. For $65 per person, the tour includes views of the countryside, beach, and lighthouse, with free hotel pickup (morning or afternoon). **Rancho el Paso** (✉ Washington 44, ☎ 297/8–73310) offers two-hour rides to the beach, with a break for swimming and drinks, every day except Sunday, for $45. Private rides are available for an extra $20.

KAYAKING

Kayaking is a popular sport on Aruba's calm waters. **De Palm Tours** (☎ 297/8–24400 or 800/766–6016) offers the Aruba Kayak Adventure—a four-hour guided kayaking tour with lunch and snorkeling Monday–Saturday; the cost is $65.

PARASAILING

Motorboats from Palm and Eagle beaches tow people up and over the water for about 12 minutes ($45 for a single-seater, $75 for a tandem). There's no official center where you can make arrangements, just independent operators stationed on the beaches. **Caribbean Parasail** (☎ 297/8–60505) is one operator you can call.

SCUBA DIVING AND SNORKELING

With visibility of up to 90 ft (27 m), Aruban waters are excellent for snorkeling and diving. Certified divers can go wall or reef diving or explore wrecks sunk during World War II. All sites have several varieties of coral, fish ranging in size from grunts to groupers, sensuously waving sea fans, giant sponge tubes, gliding manta rays, sea turtles, lobsters, octopuses, and green moray eels. Pick up the Aruba Tourism Authority's brochure "The Island for Water Sports," which describes many more sites for novice and professional divers.

The *Antilla*—a German freighter sunk off the northwest coast of Aruba near Malmok Beach—is popular with both divers and snorkelers. From Malmok Reef you can see the *Debbie II,* a 120-ft barge sunk in 1992. **Mangel Halto Reef** (also known as Pos Chiquito Reef or Bao Baranca) is excellent for night diving. The *Jane Sea Wreck* is a 200-ft freighter lying in an almost vertical position at a depth of 90 ft (27 m). **Pedernalis,** for novice divers, has large pieces of wreck spread out among coral formations. The best shore diving is at **Baby Beach.**

Expect snorkel gear to rent for about $15 per day and trips to cost around $40. Scuba rates are around $40 for a one-tank reef or wreck dive, $65 for a two-tank dive, and $45 for a night dive. Resort courses (introduction to scuba diving) average $70; complete open-water certification costs around $300.

De Palm Tours (☎ 297/8–24400 or 800/766–6016) offers daily snorkeling and scuba-diving trips ($35–$50). The Fun Factory snorkeling adventure ($45; Tuesday–Sunday) is a four-hour catamaran ride to shipwrecks and snorkeling sites and includes an open bar, lunch, equipment, and lessons. For a real treat, try the four-hour snorkel, sail, open-bar, and lunch cruise aboard the *Mi Dushi* (☎ 297/8–28919), a beautifully restored 1925 Swedish sailboat. Two stops are made for snorkeling; save your energy for the second one at the wreck of the *Antilla*. The cost is $45. **Pelican Watersports** (☎ 297/8–72302) offers snorkeling and scuba diving, as well as scuba instruction and certification. It also leads wreck and night dives at reasonable rates. **Red Sail Sports** (☎ 297/8–61603; 877/REDSAIL in the U.S.) offers scuba packages, resort courses, PADI-certification courses, night diving, and underwater camera rental. Four-hour snorkeling trips to Antilla, Catalina Bay, and Arashi include lunch and equipment for $49.50. The 1½-hour sunset sail ($29.50) has an open bar and snacks.

Through **Aruba Pro Dive** (✉ Ponton 88, ☎ 297/8–25520) divers can book one-tank dives ($35 with BC and regulators), or two-tank dives ($55 with BC and regulators) to the Antilla shipwreck, the Sonesta airplane, and other dive sites. **Scuba Aruba** (✉ Seaport Village Mall, L. G. Smith Blvd. 82, Oranjestad, ☎ 297/8–34142) sells diving equipment, snorkels, and masks, and books diving trips with other dive operators. **Unique Sports of Aruba (USA)** (✉ L. G. Smith Blvd. 79, Oranjestad, ☎ 297/8–63900) offers an assortment of dive packages for all levels, from novice to expert.

TENNIS

Aruba's winds make tennis a challenge even if you have the best of swings, but world-class tennis facilities are available at the **Aruba Racquet Club** (✉ Rooisanto 21, Palm Beach, ☎ 297/8–60215). The $1.4-million club was designed by Stan Smith Design International and is near the Aruba Marriott. Host to a variety of international tournaments, the club has eight courts (six lighted), as well as a swimming pool, an aerobics center, and a restaurant. Court fees are $10 per hour; a lesson with a pro costs $20 for ½ hour, $35 for 1 hour.

WINDSURFING

The southwestern coast's tranquil waters make it ideal for both beginners and intermediates, as the winds are steady but sudden gusts rare. Experts will find the Atlantic coast, especially around Grapefield and Boca Grandi beaches, more challenging; winds are fierce and often shift course without warning. Most operators also offer complete windsurfing vacation packages.

Fisherman's Huts Windsurf Center (✉ Aruba Marriott Resort, L. G. Smith Blvd. 101, ☎ 297/8–69000) rents Mistrals and Fanatic boards for $60 per day ($40 for two hours). Beginner lessons are $45, including rental; private lessons are $75. **Pelican Watersports** (☎ 297/8–72302) rents equipment and offers classes with a certified Mistral instructor. Beginner group lessons cost about $45; rentals start at $60 per day. At Malmok Beach, instruction and board rental are available through **Roger's Windsurf Place** (✉ L. G. Smith Blvd. 472, ☎ 297/8–61918). **Sailboard Vacations** (✉ L. G. Smith Blvd. 462, ☎ 297/8–61072) offers lessons and equipment rental.

Shopping

"Duty free" *is* a magic term here. Major credit cards are welcome virtually everywhere, U.S. dollars are accepted almost as readily as local currency, and traveler's checks can be cashed with proof of identity.

Aruba's souvenir and crafts stores are full of Dutch porcelains and figurines, as befits the island's heritage. Dutch cheese is a good buy (you're allowed to bring up to 10 pounds of hard cheese through U.S. customs), as are hand-embroidered linens and any products made from the native aloe vera plant—sunburn cream, face masks, skin refreshers. Local arts and crafts run toward wood carvings and earthenware emblazoned with ARUBA: ONE HAPPY ISLAND and the like. Since there's no sales tax, the price you see on the tag is what you pay. (Note that although large stores in town and at hotels are duty free, in tiny shops and studios, you may have to pay the ABB, or value-added tax of 6.5%.) Don't try to bargain. Arubans consider it rude to haggle, despite what you may hear to the contrary.

Areas and Malls

Oranjestad's **Caya G. F. Betico Croes** is Aruba's chief shopping street, lined with several duty-free boutiques and jewelry stores noted for the aggressiveness of their vendors on cruise-ship days.

For late-night shopping, head to the **Alhambra Casino Shopping Arcade** (⊠ L. G. Smith Blvd. 47, ☎ 297/8–35000), open 5 PM–11 PM. Souvenir shops, art boutiques, and fast-food outlets fill the arcade, which is attached to the busy casino. The **Aquarius Mall** (⊠ Elleboogstraat 1) is small but relatively upscale. The **Holland Aruba Mall** (⊠ Havenstraat 6) houses a collection of smart shops and eateries.

Port of Call Marketplace (⊠ L. G. Smith Blvd. 17, ☎ 297/8–36706) sells fine jewelry, perfumes, duty-free liquors, batiks, crystal, leather goods, and fashionable clothing. At **Royal Plaza Mall** (⊠ L. G. Smith Blvd. 94), across from the cruise-ship terminal, you'll find cafés, a post office branch (open Monday–Saturday 7 AM–6:45 PM), and such stores as Nautica, Benetton, Tommy Hilfiger, and Gandelman Jewelers. There's also the Internet Café, where you can send e-mail home and get your caffeine fix all in one stop.

Seaport Village Mall (⊠ L. G. Smith Blvd. 82, across from harbor, ☎ 297/8–36000) is five minutes from the cruise-ship terminal. It includes the Crystal Casino and more than 120 stores, with merchandise to meet every taste and budget. The **Strada I and Strada II** (⊠ Corner of Klipstraat and Rifstraat) are two complexes in tall Dutch buildings painted in pastels.

Specialty Items

CLOTHES

Confetti (⊠ Seaport Village Mall, L. G. Smith Blvd. 82, Oranjestad, ☎ 297/8–38614) has the hottest European and American swimsuits, cover-ups, beach hats, and other beach essentials. **J. L. Penha & Sons** (⊠ Caya G. F. Betico Croes 11/13, Oranjestad, ☎ 297/8–24160 or 297/8–24161), a venerated name in Aruban merchandising, sells clothes, perfumes, and cosmetics and offers such brands as Boucheron, Swiss Army, Dior, Cartier, and Givenchy. **Wulfsen & Wulfsen** (⊠ Caya G. F. Betico Croes 52, Oranjestad, ☎ 297/8–23823) has been one of the most highly regarded clothing stores in the Netherlands Antilles for three decades (and for a century in Holland).

DUTY-FREE GOODS

For leather goods (including Bally shoes), perfumes, cosmetics, and men's and women's clothing, stop in at **Aruba Trading Company** (ATC; ⊠ Caya G. F. Betico Croes 12, Oranjestad, ☎ 297/8–22602), which has been in business more than 70 years. **Little Switzerland** (⊠ Caya G. F. Betico Croes 14, Oranjestad, ☎ 297/8–21192; ⊠ Royal Plaza Mall, L. G. Smith Blvd. 94, Oranjestad, ☎ 297/8–34057), the St. Thomas-based giant, has china, crystal, and fine tableware. You'll find good buys on Omega and Rado watches, Swarovski and Baccarat crystal, and Lladro figurines.

HANDICRAFTS

Art and Tradition Handicrafts (⊠ Caya G. F. Betico Croes 30, Oranjestad, ☎ 297/8–36534; ⊠ Royal Plaza Mall, L. G. Smith Blvd. 94, Oranjestad, ☎ 297/8–27862) sells intriguing items that look handpainted but aren't. Buds from the *mopa mopa* tree are boiled to form a resin, to which artists add vegetable colors. This resin is then stretched by hand and mouth. Tiny pieces are cut and layered to form intricate designs on wooden boxes—truly unusual gifts. Also unique are Tano boxes and plates made from wheat, banana leaves, dried cactus, and mushroom.

The **Artistic Boutique** (⊠ Caya G. F. Betico Croes 25, Oranjestad, ☎ 297/8–23142; ⊠ Wyndham Aruba Beach Resort and Casino, J. E. Irausquin Blvd. 77, ☎ 297/8–64466, ext. 3508; ⊠ Seaport Village Mall, L. G. Smith Blvd. 82, Oranjestad, ☎ 297/8–32567; ⊠ Holiday Inn Sun-SpreeAruba Resort & Casino, J. E. Irausquin Blvd. 230, ☎ 297/8–33383) has been in business for 30 years and is known for selling Giuseppe Armani figurines from Italy, usually at a 20% discount; Aruban hand-embroidered linens; gold and silver jewelry; and porcelain and pottery from Spain.

Creative Hands (⊠ Socotorolaan 5, Oranjestad, ☎ 297/8–35665) sells porcelain and ceramic miniature cunucu houses and divi-divi trees, but the store's real draw is its exquisite Japanese dolls.

JEWELRY

In business for 25 years, **Boolchand's** (⊠ Seaport Village Mall, L. G. Smith Blvd. 82, Oranjestad, ☎ 297/8–30147) fills its 6,000-square-ft space with jewelry, leather goods, watches, sunglasses, games, cameras, and electronics. If green fire is your passion, **Colombian Emeralds** (⊠ Seaport Village Mall, L. G. Smith Blvd. 82, Oranjestad, ☎ 297/8–36238) has a dazzling array of emeralds, as well as watches by Breitling, Baume & Mercier, Jaeger, and more. **Gandelman Jewelers** (⊠ Royal Plaza Mall, L. G. Smith Blvd. 94, Oranjestad, ☎ 297/8–34433) sells Gucci and Rolex watches at reasonable prices, gold bracelets, and a full line of Lladro figurines. **Kenro Jewelers** (⊠ Seaport Village Mall, L. G. Smith Blvd. 82, Oranjestad, ☎ 297/8–34847 or 297/9–33171) has two stores in the same mall, attesting to the popularity of such merchandise as Mikimoto pearls, the Ramon leopard collection, and various brands of watches.

Nightlife and the Arts

Nightlife

Unlike on many islands, nightlife isn't confined to the touristic folk-loric shows at the hotels. Arubans like to party, and the more the merrier. They usually start celebrating late; the action (mostly on weekends) doesn't pick up till around midnight. For information on specific events—as well as shopping, sightseeing, sports, and dining recommendations (and a few coupons)—check out the free magazines *Aruba Nights, Aruba Events, Aruba Experience,* and *Aruba Holiday,* all available at the airport and at hotels.

BARS

At **Carlos & Charlie's** (⊠ Westraat 3A, Oranjestad, ☎ 297/8–20355), you'll find Mexican fare; American music from the 60s, 70s, and 80s; and a mike-toting emcee. **La Fiesta** (⊠ Aventura Mall, Plaza Daniel Leo, ☎ 297/8–35896), an upscale bar with a wraparound terrace, attracts a hip crowd. A DJ spins tunes of all types according to mood, and dancing is encouraged. **Iguana Joe's** (⊠ Royal Plaza Mall, L. G. Smith Blvd. 94, Oranjestad, ☎ 297/8–39373) has a creative reptilian-theme decor and a color scheme featuring such planter's punch colors as lime and grape. A uniquely Aruban institution is the **Kukoo Kunuku** (☎ 297/8–62010), a psychedelically painted 1957 Chevy bus. Weeknights, as many as 40 passengers board to carouse six local bars from sundown to midnight, with a refueling stop for dinner. Group and private charter rates are available; these include picking you up (and pouring you off) at your hotel. **Mambo Jambos** (⊠ 2nd floor, Royal Plaza Mall, L. G. Smith Blvd. 94, Oranjestad, ☎ 297/8–33632) is daubed in sunset colors, with parrots painted on the ceiling. It offers several house-specialty libations, and you can buy Mambo Jambos memorabilia at a shop next door. **Tzapagaga** (⊠ Wilhelminastraat 18A, Oranjestad, ☎ 297/8–31888) attracts locals and visitors with its eclectic drinks and tasty finger food.

CASINOS

Aruban casinos offer something for both high rollers and low-stakes types, as well as live, nightly entertainment in their lounges. Diehard gamblers might look for the largest or the most active casinos, but many simply visit the casino closest to their hotel.

In the casual **Alhambra Casino** (⊠ L. G. Smith Blvd. 47, Oranjestad, ☎ 297/8–35000), a "Moorish slave" named Roger gives every gambler a hearty handshake upon entering. Smart money is on the Wyndham's **Casablanca Casino** (⊠ J. E. Irausquin Blvd. 77, ☎ 297/8–64466). It's quietly elegant and has a Bogart theme. The **Centurion Casino** (⊠ J. E. Irausquin Blvd. 79, ☎ 297/8–63900) at the Aruba Grand Beach Resort is decorated with musical instruments. It opens at 10 AM for slots, 6 PM for all games. The Hyatt Regency's ultramodern **Copacabana Casino** (⊠ J. E. Irausquin Blvd. 85, ☎ 297/8–61234) is an enormous complex with a Carnival in Rio theme and live entertainment. The Sonesta's **Crystal Casino** (⊠ L. G. Smith Blvd. 82, ☎ 297/8–36000) is open 24 hours. The **Excelsior** (⊠ Holiday Inn SunSpreeAruba Resort & Casino, J. E. Irausquin Blvd. 230, ☎ 297/8–67777) has sports betting in addition to the usual slots and table games.

Overhead at the **Radisson Aruba Caribbean Resort** (⊠ J. E. Irausquin Blvd. 81, ☎ 297/8–64045), thousands of lights simulate shooting stars that seem destined to carry out your wishes for riches. The slots here open at 10 AM, and table action begins at 4 PM. The **Royal Cabana Casino** (⊠ J. E. Irausquin Blvd. 250, ☎ 297/8–77000) is the largest in the Caribbean. It has an expansive, sleek interior, 400 slot machines, nosmoking gaming tables and slot room, and the Tropicana nightclub. The **Royal Palm Casino** (⊠ Allegro Resort & Casino, J. E. Irausquin Blvd. 83, ☎ 297/8–69039) opens daily at noon for slots, 5 PM for all games. Low-key gambling can be found at the waterside **Seaport Casino** (⊠ L. G. Smith Blvd. 9, Oranjestad, ☎ 297/8–35027 Ext. 4212). The Marriott's **Stellaris Casino** (⊠ L. G. Smith Blvd. 101, ☎ 297/8–69000) is one of the island's most popular.

DANCE AND MUSIC CLUBS

At **Café Bahia** (⊠ Weststraat 7, Oranjestad, ☎ 297/8–89982), an elegant spiral staircase leads up to a bar and dance floor backed by a mural of colorful cacti against a blue, cloud-smattered Aruban sky. Locals and tourists drink cocktails and salsa to music played by island bands. At the **Cellar** (⊠ Klipstraat 2, Oranjestad, ☎ 297/8–28567) live bands perform Monday and Thursday–Saturday; the music du jour might be blues, jazz, funk, reggae, or rock. **Club E-Zone** (⊠ Bayside Mall, Westraat 5, Oranjestad, ☎ 297/9–36784) has a huge dance floor, walls decorated with hair-dryer tubes and Slinky toys, bartenders in hard hats, and a cozy VIP lounge. For jazz and local music try the **Garufa Cocktail Lounge** (⊠ Wilhelminastraat 63, Oranjestad, ☎ 297/8–27205). Take in the striking decor (leopard-print carpet, Nicole Miller–style bar stools) at this cozy cigar bar, which also serves as a lounge for customers awaiting a table at El Gaucho Argentine Grill, across the street. Stop by the cozy **Sirocco Lounge** (⊠ Wyndham Aruba, L. G. Smith Blvd. 77, Palm Beach, ☎ 297/8–64466) for jazz performances Thursday–Saturday evenings until midnight.

MOVIES

The **Seaport Cinema** (✉ Seaport Market Place, ☎ 297/8–30318) has six theaters showing the latest American movies in English.

THEME NIGHTS

At last count there were more than 30 theme nights offered during the course of a week, like Carnival Night and BBQ Buffets. Each "party" features a buffet dinner, entertainment (usually of the limbo, steel-band, stilt-walking variety), and dancing. The top groups tend to rotate among the resorts. For a complete list contact the Aruba Tourism Authority.

Check out **Carnival Night** (✉ Wyndham Aruba Beach Resort and Casino, J. E. Irausquin Blvd. 77, Palm Beach, ☎ 297/8–64466), which is a big hit on Wednesdays, with revelers dancing in costume. On Monday nights, you can stop by the **Caribbean Beach BBQ** (✉ Aruba Sonesta Resorts at Seaport Village, L. G. Smith Blvd. 9, Oranjestad, ☎ 297/8–36000), featuring traditional Caribbean barbecue and live music on the beach. Fridays at the same hotel, drop anchor for the seafood clambake buffet in the Brasserie Restaurant.

The Arts

ISLAND CULTURE

An Aruban must is the **Bon Bini Festival,** held every Tuesday from 6:30 PM to 8:30 PM in the outdoor courtyard of the Ft. Zoutman Museum. Stop by to check out local arts and crafts, food, drink, music, and dance. ✉ *Oranjestraat, look for clock tower,* ☎ *297/8–22185.* ☜ *$3.*

At the **Watapana Food and Art Festival** (☎ no phone), listen to live music, see local art, and sample authentic Aruban foods and beverages. The event is on the grounds between the Hyatt Regency Aruba Beach Resort & Casino and the Allegro Aruba Beach Resort & Casino, every Wednesday from 6 PM to 8 PM, from May through October. Admission is free.

THEATER

The term *theater* is used advisedly, referring primarily to glitzy Vegas-style revues and "everybody rumba"–type audience participation cabarets. The **Cabaret Royale** (✉ Wyndham Aruba Beach Resort and Casino, J. E. Irausquin Blvd. 77, Palm Beach, ☎ 297/8–64466) has an entertaining Cuban review (with a bit of flesh) Tuesday through Saturday at 9 PM. Dinner (seating at 7:30) and the show cost $34; $20 gets you two cocktails (starting at 8:30) and admission to the show. The **Tropicana Showroom** (✉ J. E. Irausquin Blvd. 250, ☎ 297/8–77000, ext. 731 or 727), the Royal Cabana Casino's cabaret theater and nightclub, features first-class Las Vegas–style revues, usually showcasing female impersonators, Monday, Tuesday, Thursday, and Saturday at 9 PM and Wednesday and Friday at 10 PM; the cost is $35 per person. Dinner/show combinations are available ($119 for two people).

Twinklebone's House of Roast Beef (✉ Noord 124, Noord, ☎ 297/8–26780) does serve succulent prime rib and the like. But it's best known for the fun, impromptu cabaret of Carnival music put on by the staff every night but Sunday. Some customers find it hokey; others eat it up.

Exploring Aruba

Oranjestad, the capital of Aruba, is good for shopping by day and dining by night, but the real Aruba—what's left of a wild, untamed beauty—can be found only in the countryside. Rent a car, take a sightseeing tour, or hire a cab for $30 an hour (for up to four people). The main highways are well paved, but on the windward side (the north-

and east-facing side) some roads are still a mixture of compacted dirt and stones. Although a car is fine, a four-wheel-drive vehicle will allow you to explore the unpaved interior.

Traffic is sparse, and you can't get lost. Signs leading to sights are often small and hand-lettered (though this is slowly changing as the government puts up official road signs), so watch closely. Remember that Highway 1A travels southbound along the western coast, and 1B is simply northbound along the same road. If you lose your way, just follow the divi-divi trees (because of the direction of the trade winds, the trees are bent toward the island's leeward, or western, side, where all the hotels are). Few beaches outside the hotel strip have refreshment stands, so take your own food and drink. Note that except in the infrequent restaurant there are no public toilets outside Oranjestad.

Numbers in the margin correspond to points of interest on the Aruba map.

SIGHTS TO SEE

❼ Alto Vista Chapel. Alone near the island's northwest corner sits the scenic little Alto Vista Chapel. The wind whistles through the simple mustard-color walls, eerie boulders, and looming cacti. Along the side of the road back to civilization are miniature crosses with depictions of the stations of the cross and hand-lettered signs exhorting PRAY FOR US, SINNERS and the like—a simple yet powerful evocation of faith. To get here, follow the rough, winding dirt road that loops around the island's northern tip, or, from the hotel strip, take Palm Beach Road through three intersections and watch for the asphalt road to the left just past the Alto Vista Rum Shop.

❹ Arikok National Wildlife Park. Nearly 20% of Aruba has been designated part of this national park (☎ 297/8–28001), which sprawls across the eastern interior and the northeast coast. The park is the keystone of the government's long-term ecotourism plan to preserve resources, and showcases the island's flora and fauna as well as ancient Arawak petroglyphs, the ruins of a gold mining operation at Miralmar, and the remnants of Dutch peasant settlements at Masiduri. At the park's main entrance, Arikok Center houses offices, rest rooms, and food facilities. All visitors must stop here upon entering so that officials can manage the traffic flow and hand out information on park rules and features. Within the confines of the park is Mt. Arikok, as well as the 620-ft (188-m) Mt. Yamanota, Aruba's highest peak.

Anyone looking for geological exotica should head for the caves on the northeastern coast. **Baranca Sunu**, the so-called Tunnel of Love, has a heart-shape entrance and, within, naturally sculpted rocks that look like the Madonna, Abe Lincoln, and even a jaguar. The **Guadirikiri** and **Fontein** caves are marked with ancient drawings (rangers are on hand to offer explanations), as both were used by native Indians centuries ago. Bats are known to make appearances (but don't worry—they won't bother you). Although you don't need a flashlight (paths here are well lighted), it's best to wear sneakers.

❾ Butterfly Farm. Hundreds of butterflies from around the world flutter about this spectacular garden. Guided 20- to 30-minute tours (included in the price of admission) provide an entertaining look into how these creatures complete their life cycle: from egg to caterpillar to chrysalis to butterfly. There's a special deal offered here: after your initial visit, you can return as often as you like for free. ⊠ *J. E. Irausquin Blvd., Palm Beach,* ☎ *297/8–63656.* 🎫 *$10.* ☉ *Daily 9–4:30 (last tour at 4).*

8 **California Lighthouse.** Built in 1910, the lighthouse stands at the island's far northern end. Although the interior is closed to the public, you can ascend the hill to its base for some magnificent views: huge boulders that look like extraterrestrial monsters and sand dunes embroidered with scrub that resemble tawny, undulating sea serpents. In this stark landscape you'll feel as though you've just landed on the moon. Next to the trattoria there's a placard explaining the history of the lighthouse and the wreck of a German ship (just offshore here).

2 **Hooiberg.** Named for its shape (*hooiberg* means "haystack" in Dutch), this 541-ft (165-m) peak lies inland just past the airport. If you have the energy, climb the 562 steps to the top for an impressive view of the city. To get here from Oranjestad, turn onto Caya G. F. Croes (shown on island maps as 7A) toward Santa Cruz; the peak will be on your left.

6 **Natural Bridge.** Centuries of raging wind and sea sculpted this coral rock bridge in the center of the windward coast. To reach it, follow the main road inland (Hospitalstraat) and then follow the signs that lead the way. Just before you reach the natural bridge, you'll pass the massive, intriguing stone ruins of the **Bushiribana Gold Smelter**, which resembles a crumbling fortress, and a section of surf-pounded coastline called Boca Mahos. Near the natural bridge are a café overlooking the water and a souvenir shop.

1 **Oranjestad.** Aruba's charming capital is best explored on foot. The palm-lined thoroughfare in the center of town runs between pastel-painted buildings, old and new, of typical Dutch design. There are many malls with boutiques and shops.

At the **Archaeological Museum of Aruba** you'll find two rooms chock-full of fascinating Indian artifacts, farm and domestic utensils, and skeletons. ☒ *J. E. Irausquinplein 2A,* ☎ *297/8–28979.* ☒ *Free.* ☉ *Weekdays 8–noon and 1–4.*

One of the island's oldest edifices, **Ft. Zoutman** was built in 1796 and played an important role in skirmishes between British and Curaçao troops in 1803. The Willem III Tower, named for the Dutch monarch of that time, was added in 1868 to serve as a lighthouse. The fort's historical museum displays Aruban relics and artifacts in an 18th-century house. ☒ *Zoutmanstraat,* ☎ *297/8–26099.* ☒ *Free.* ☉ *Weekdays 8–noon and 1–4.*

The tiny **Numismatic Museum**, next to the St. Francis Roman Catholic Church, displays coins and currencies—some of it salvaged from shipwrecks in the region—from more than 100 countries. The museum was spawned by one Aruban's private collection, and is now family-run. Some of the coins on display circulated during the Roman Empire, the Byzantine Empire, and the ancient Chinese dynasties; a few date as far back as the 5th century BC. ☒ *Zuidstraat 7,* ☎ *297/8–28831.* ☒ *Free.* ☉ *Weekdays 7:30–noon and 1–4:30.*

5 **Rock Formations.** The massive boulders at **Ayo** and **Casibari** are said to be a mystery since they don't match the island's geological makeup. You can climb to the top for fine views of the arid countryside, passing Aruba whip-tail lizards—the males are cobalt blue, the females blue with dots. The main path to Casibari has steps and handrails (except on one side), and you must move through tunnels and on narrow steps and ledges to reach the top. At Ayo you'll find ancient pictographs in a small cave (the entrance has iron bars to protect the artifacts from vandalism). You may also encounter a local boulder climber, one of many who are increasingly drawn to Ayo's smooth surfaces. Access to Casibari is via Tanki Highway 4A to Ayo via Highway 6A; watch carefully for the turnoff signs near the center of the island on the way to the windward side.

❸ San Nicolas. During the heyday of the oil refineries, Aruba's oldest village was a bustling port; now it's dedicated to tourism. The main promenade is full of interesting kiosks, and the whole district is undergoing a revitalization project that will introduce parks, a cultural center, a central market, a public swimming pool, and an arts promenade. *The* institution in town is **Charlie's Restaurant & Bar,** a San Nicolas hangout for more than 50 years. Stop in for a drink and advice on what to see and do.

ARUBA A TO Z

To research prices, get advice from other travelers, and book travel arrangements, visit www.fodors.com.

AIR TRAVEL

Aruba is 2½ hours from Miami and 4½ hours from New York. Flights leave daily to Aruba's Reina Beatrix International Airport from New York area airports and Miami International Airport, with easy connections from most American cities.

Air ALM flies daily from Miami via Curaçao; twice a week nonstop from Atlanta; and twice a week from San Juan, Puerto Rico, through Curaçao. The airline also has connecting flights to Caracas, Bonaire, Curaçao, St. Maarten, and other islands, and it offers the Visit Caribbean Pass for interisland travel.

American Airlines offers daily nonstop service from New York and Miami, Saturday nonstop flights from Boston, and twice-daily flights from San Juan. From Toronto and Montréal the flights are via San Juan. Continental Airlines has nonstop service four times a week from Newark and twice a week from Houston. Delta flies nonstop daily from Atlanta and New York. KLM offers regular service from Amsterdam. United flies from Chicago nonstop to Aruba on Saturday and Sunday. US Airways has daily nonstop flights from Philadelphia to Aruba.
➤ AIRLINES AND CONTACTS: **Air ALM** (☎ 297/8–23546); **American Airlines** (☎ 297/8–22700); **Continental Airlines** (☎ 800/525–0280); **Delta** (☎ 297/8–80044); **KLM** (☎ 297/8–23546); **United** (☎ 800/241–6522); **US Airways** (☎ 297/8–84167).

AIRPORTS

In 2000, the island celebrated the grand opening of its new state-of-the-art Reina Beatrix International Airport, after a multimillion-dollar renovation and expansion. The three-level concourse is triple the size of the previous airport, and is equipped with new security, flight display, and baggage handling systems. The U.S. Customs checkpoint is now able to handle 2.5 million passengers annually. Several airlines have responded by expanding their service to Aruba.

A taxi from the airport to most hotels takes about 20 minutes. It will cost about $16 to get to Eagle Beach, $18 to the high-rise hotels on Palm Beach, and $9 to the hotels downtown. You'll find a taxi stand right outside the baggage claim area.
➤ AIRPORT INFORMATION: **Reina Beatrix International Airport** (☎ 297/8–24800).

BIKE AND MOPED TRAVEL

Pedal pushing is a great way to get around the island; the climate is perfect and the trade winds help to keep you cool. If you prefer to exert less energy while reaping the rewards of the outdoors, a motorized scooter may do the trick. Or let your hair down completely and cruise around on a motorcycle. Big Twin Aruba rents Harley Davidsons to fulfill any biker's fantasy. Rates are $150 for a day, $95 for a half day. The dealership also sells Harley clothing and collectibles. Be sure to pose for a photo next to the classic 1939 Liberator on display in the showroom.

➤ BIKE AND MOPED RENTALS: **Big Twin Aruba** (⊠ L. G. Smith Blvd. 124-A, Oranjestad, ☎ 297/8–28660); **Donata Car and Cycle** (⊠ Catiri 59, Tanki Leendert, ☎ 297/8–34343); **George's Cycle Center** (⊠ L. G. Smith Blvd. 124, Oranjestad, ☎ 297/9–32202); **Pablito's Bike Rental** (⊠ L. G. Smith Blvd. 234, Oranjestad, ☎ 297/8–78655); **Ron's Motorcycle Rental** (⊠ Bakval 17A, Noord, ☎ 297/8–62090); **Semver Cycle Rental** (⊠ Noord 22, Noord, ☎ 297/8–66851).

BUSINESS HOURS
BANKS
Bank hours are weekdays 8:15–5:45; some close from noon to 1 (the Caribbean Mercantile Bank at the airport is open Saturday 9–4 and Sunday 9–1).

POST OFFICES
The central post office in Oranjestad is across from the San Francisco Church and is open weekdays 7:30 to noon and 1 to 4:30. The post office in the Royal Plaza mall is open Monday–Saturday, 7 to 6:45.

SHOPS
Shops are generally open Monday–Saturday 8:30–6. Some stores stay open through the lunch hour, noon–2, and many open when cruise ships are in port on Sunday and holidays.

CAR RENTALS
You'll need a valid driver's license to rent a car, and you must meet the minimum age requirements of each rental service (Budget, for example, requires drivers to be over 25; Avis, between the ages of 23 and 70; and Hertz, over 21). A deposit of $500 (or a signed credit-card slip) is required. Rates are between $35 and $65 a day (local agencies generally have lower rates). Insurance is available starting at $10 per day, and all companies offer unlimited mileage. Try to make reservations before arriving, and opt for a four-wheel-drive vehicle if you plan to explore the island's natural sights.

➤ MAJOR AGENCIES: **Avis** (⊠ Kolibristraat 14, Oranjestad, ☎ 297/8–28787; ⊠ Airport, ☎ 297/8–25496); **Budget Rent-a-Car** (⊠ Kolibristraat 1, Oranjestad, ☎ 297/8–28600 or 800/472–3325); **Dollar Rent-a-Car** (⊠ Grendeaweg 15, Oranjestad, ☎ 297/8–22783; ⊠ Airport, ☎ 297/8–25651; ⊠ Manchebo Beach Resort, J. E. Irausquin Blvd. 55, ☎ 297/8–26696); **Hedwina Car Rental** (⊠ Bubali 93A, Noord, ☎ 297/8–76442; ⊠ Airport, ☎ 297/8–30880); **Hertz** (⊠ Sabana Blanco 35, near the airport, ☎ 297/8–21845; ⊠ Airport, ☎ 297/8–29112); **National** (⊠ Tanki Leendert 170, Noord, ☎ 297/8–71967; ⊠ Airport, ☎ 297/8–25451); **Thrifty** (⊠ Balashi 65, Santa Cruz, ☎ 297/8–55300; ⊠ Airport, ☎ 297/8–35335).

CAR TRAVEL
GASOLINE
Gas prices average $1 a liter (roughly ⅓ gallon), which is reasonable by Caribbean standards.

ROAD CONDITIONS
Aside from the major highways, the island's winding roads are poorly marked (though this is slowly changing). International traffic signs and

Dutch-style traffic signals (with an extra light for a turning lane) can be misleading if you're not used to them; use extreme caution, especially at intersections, until you grasp the rules of the road.

RULES OF THE ROAD
Speed limits are rarely posted, but are usually 80 kph (50 mph).

ELECTRICITY
Aruba runs on a 110-volt cycle, the same as in the United States; outlets are usually the two-prong variety. Total blackouts are rare, and most large hotels have backup generators.

EMERGENCIES
➤ AMBULANCE AND FIRE: Dial ☎ 115.
➤ HOSPITALS: **Dr. Horacio Oduber Hospital** (✉ L. G. Smith Blvd., across from Costa Linda Beach Resort and the Alhambra Bazaar and Casino, ☎ 297/8–74300).
➤ PHARMACIES: **Botica Eagle** (✉ L. G. Smith Blvd., near hospital, ☎ 297/8–76103).
➤ POLICE: Dial ☎ 111000.

ETIQUETTE AND BEHAVIOR
It's best not to mention to residents how "American" everything is—many have settled here from South America and Europe.

FESTIVALS AND SEASONAL EVENTS
February or March witnesses a spectacular Carnival, a riot of color whirling to the tunes of steel bands and culminating in the Grand Parade, where some of the floats rival the extravagance of those in the Big Easy's Mardi Gras. Held May–October, One Cool Summer is a series of culinary, athletic, musical, cultural, and other events. Check with your hotel for specifics.

HOLIDAYS
Public holidays for 2002 are New Year's Day, Betico Croes's Birthday (a politician who aided Aruba's transition to semi-independence; Jan. 25), Carnival Monday (Feb. 11), National Anthem and Flag Day (Mar. 18), Good Friday (Mar. 29), Easter Monday (Mar. 31), Queen's Birthday (Apr. 30), Labor Day (May 1), Ascension Day (May 9), Christmas (Dec. 25–26).

LANGUAGE
Everyone on the island speaks English, but the official language is Dutch. Most locals, however, speak Papiamento—a fascinating, rapid-fire mix of Spanish, Dutch, English, French, and Portuguese—in normal conversation. Here are a few helpful phrases: *bon dia* (good day), *bon nochi* (good night), *masha danki* (thank you very much).

MAIL AND SHIPPING
You can send an airmail letter from Aruba to the United States or Canada for AFl2, and a postcard for AFl1.15; a letter to Europe is AFl1.75, a postcard AFl1. Prices to Australia and New Zealand may be slightly higher. When addressing letters to Aruba, don't worry about the lack of "formal" addresses (in some places) or postal codes; the island's postal service knows where to go.

MONEY MATTERS
Prices quoted throughout this chapter are in U.S. dollars unless otherwise noted.

ATMS

If you need fast cash, you'll find ATMs that accept international cards at banks in Oranjestad, at the major malls, and along the roads leading to the hotel strip.

➤ BANKS WITH ATMS: **ABN/Amro Bank** (✉ Caya G. F. Betico Croes 89, ☎ 297/8–21515); **Caribbean Mercantile Bank** (✉ Caya G. F. Betico Croes 5, ☎ 297/8–23118).

CURRENCY

The official currency is the Aruban florin (AFl), also called the guilder; at press time exchange rates were AFl1.77 per U.S. dollar for cash, AFl1.79 for traveler's checks, and AFl1.51 per Canadian dollar. The Dutch Antillean florin—used on Bonaire and Curaçao—isn't accepted here. Arubans happily accept U.S. dollars virtually everywhere, so there's no real need to exchange money, except for necessary pocket change (for soda machines or pay phones).

PASSPORTS AND VISAS

U.S. and Canadian citizens need a valid passport or a birth certificate with a raised seal and a government-issued photo ID. Visitors from the member countries of the European Union must carry their European Union Travel Card as well as a passport. All other nationalities must have a valid passport.

SAFETY

Arubans are very friendly, so you needn't be afraid to stop and ask anyone for directions. It's a relatively safe island, but commonsense rules still apply. Lock your rental car and leave valuables in your hotel safe. Don't leave bags unattended in the airport, on the beach, or on tour transports.

Mosquitoes and flies can be bothersome during the odd rain shower, so pack some repellent. The strong trade winds are a relief in the subtropical climate, but don't hang your bathing suit on a balcony—it will probably blow away. Help Arubans conserve water and energy: turn off air-conditioning when you leave your room, and don't let water run unnecessarily. Tap water is okay to drink.

SIGHTSEEING TOURS

BOATS

If you try a cruise around the island, know that—on choppy waters stirred up by trade winds—catamarans are much smoother than monohulls. Sucking on a peppermint or lemon candy may help a queasy stomach; avoid going with an empty or overly full stomach. Moonlight cruises cost about $25 per person (be prepared to sail with a lot of honeymooners). There are also a variety of snorkeling, dinner and dancing, and sunset party cruises to choose from, priced from $25 to $60 per person. Many smaller operators work out of their homes; they often offer to pick you up (and drop you off) at your hotel or meet you at a particular hotel pier.

➤ CONTACTS: **De Palm Tours** (✉ L. G. Smith Blvd. 142, ☎ 297/8–24400 or 800/766–6016); **Jolly Pirates** (☎ 297/8–37355); **Pelican Watersports** (✉ J. E. Irausquin Blvd. 230, ☎ 297/8–72302); **Red Sail Sports** (✉ J. E. Irausquin Blvd. 83, Oranjestad, ☎ 297/8–61603; 877/REDSAIL in the U.S.); **Tattoo Party Cruises** (☎ 297/8–62010).

ORIENTATION

You can see the main sights in one day, but set aside two days to really meander. Guided tours are your best option if you have only a short time. Aruba's Transfer Tour & Taxi C.A. takes you to the main sights on personalized tours that cost $30 per hour.

De Palm Tours has a near monopoly on Aruban sightseeing; you can make reservations through its general office or at hotel tour-desk branches. The basic 3½-hour hits such highlights as the Santa Anna Church, the Casibari Rock Formation, the Natural Bridge, and the Gold Smelter Ruins. Wear tennis or hiking shoes, and bring a lightweight jacket or wrap (the air-conditioned bus gets cold). The tour, which begins at 9:30 AM, picks you up in your hotel lobby and costs $22.50 per person. A full-day Jeep Adventure tour ($59.50 per person) takes you to sights that would be difficult for you to find on your own. Bring a bandanna to cover your mouth; the ride on rocky dirt roads can get dusty. De Palm also offers full-day tours of Curaçao ($219) every Friday. Prices include round-trip airfare, transfers, sightseeing, and lunch; there's free time for shopping.

➤ CONTACTS: **Aruba's Transfer Tour & Taxi C.A.** (✉ Pos Abao 41, Oranjestad, ☎ 297/8–22116); **De Palm Tours** (✉ L. G. Smith Blvd. 142, ☎ 297/8–24400 or 800/766–6016).

SPECIAL-INTEREST

Explore an underwater reef teeming with marine life without getting wet. Atlantis Submarines operates a 65-ft air-conditioned sub that takes 48 passengers 95–150 ft (29–46 m) below the surface along Barcadera Reef. The two-hour trip (including boat transfer to the submarine platform and 50-minute plunge) costs $72. Make reservations one day in advance. Another option is the *Seaworld Explorer,* a semisubmersible that allows you to sit and view Aruba's marine habitat from 5 ft (1½ m) below the surface. The cost is $35 for a 1½-hour tour.

Board the Chiva Arubanita Party Bus and paint the town red for six hours. The island nightlife tour kicks off with a sunset salute toast, followed by a traditional Aruban meal at Joey's Restaurant, and dance club–hopping 'til you drop. A live band plays on the bus and keeps the spirit alive during the drive. Le Dôme on the Ocean is a two-hour dinner cruise aboard the *Sea Star* catamaran offered by De Palm Tours. Feast on a three-course gourmet meal catered by Le Dôme Restaurant with glorious island views in the background. Enjoy appetizers such as smoked salmon with onions and capers, entrées including lamb in wine sauce or filet of grouper in lobster sauce, and your choice of wine. Cruises sail on Thursdays and cost $89 per person.

Romantic horse-drawn-carriage rides through the city streets of Oranjestad run $30 for a 30-minute tour; hours of operation are 7 PM–11 PM, and carriages depart from the clock tower at the Royal Plaza Mall.

➤ CONTACTS: **Atlantis Submarines** (✉ Seaport Village Marina, ☎ 297/8–36090); **Chiva Arubanita Party Bus** (☎ 297/8–24785); **Le Dôme on the Ocean** (☎ 297/8–24400); *Seaworld Explorer* (☎ 297/8–62416).

TAXES

DEPARTURE TAX

The airport departure tax is a whopping $34.50, but the fee is usually included in your ticket price.

SALES TAX

Hotels usually add an 11% service charge to the bill and collect a 6% government tax.

VALUE ADDED TAX (V.A.T.)

For purchases you'll pay a 6.5% ABB tax (value-added tax) in all but the duty-free shops.

TAXIS

There's a dispatch office at the airport (☎ 297/8–22116); you can also flag down taxis on the street (look for license plates with a "TX" tag).

Rates are fixed (i.e., there are no meters), though you and the driver should agree on the fare before your ride begins. Add $1 to the fare after midnight and $1–$3 on Sunday and holidays. An hour-long island tour costs about $30, with up to four people. Rides into town from Eagle Beach run about $5; from Palm Beach, about $8.

TELEPHONES
When making calls on Aruba, simply dial the five-digit number. AT&T customers can dial 800–8000 from special phones at the cruise dock and in the airport's arrival and departure halls. From other phones dial 121 to contact the SETAR International Operator to place a collect or AT&T Calling Card call.

COUNTRY AND AREA CODES
To call Aruba direct from the United States, dial 011–297–8, followed by the five-digit number in Aruba. (To call from elsewhere abroad, substitute 011 with the country of origin's international access code.)

LOCAL CALLS
Local calls from pay phones, which accept both local currency and phone cards, cost AFl.25.

TIPPING
Restaurants generally include a 10%–15% service charge on the bill; when in doubt, ask. If service isn't included, a 10% tip is standard; if it is included, it's still customary to add something extra, usually small change, at your discretion. Taxi drivers expect a 10%–15% tip, but it isn't mandatory. Porters and bellmen should receive about $2 per bag; chambermaids about $2 a day.

TRANSPORTATION AROUND ARUBA
Buses run hourly trips between the beach hotels and Oranjestad. The one-way fare is $1.15 ($2 round-trip), and exact change is preferred. Buses also run down the coast from Oranjestad to San Nicolas for the same fare. Contact the Aruba Tourism Authority for schedules.

VISITOR INFORMATION
➤ BEFORE YOU LEAVE: **Aruba Tourism Authority** (☎ 800/862–7822, WEB www.arubatourism.com; ⊠ 1 Financial Plaza, Suite 136, Fort Lauderdale, FL 33394, ☎ 954/767–6477; ⊠ 3455 Peach Tree Rd. NE, Suite 500, Atlanta, GA 30326, ☎ 404/892–7822; ⊠ 5901 N. Cicero, Suite 301, Chicago, IL 60646, ☎ 773/202–5054; ⊠ 1000 Harbor Blvd., Ground Level, Weehawken, NJ 07087, ☎ 201/330–0800; ⊠ 12707 North Freeway, Suite 138, Houston, TX 77060-1234, ☎ 281/872–7822; ⊠ Business Centre 5875, Suite 201, Hwy. 7, Vaughan, Ontario L4L 8Z7, Canada, ☎ 905/264–3434).
➤ IN ARUBA: **Aruba Tourism Authority** (⊠ L. G. Smith Blvd. 172, Eagle Beach, ☎ 297/8–23777).

Updated by
Jane E. Zarem

Head wrapped neatly in a kerchief and her skirt just sweeping the sand, the doll lady trudges along the beach to the shade of a mahogany tree and settles in for the day. Her bag is full of unfinished poppets and bits of cloth. Today she's creating eyes. Cutting deftly with oversize shears, one tip broken off, she makes white and black snippets that give expression to blank faces. "Doll, lady?" she beckons to passersby. Surrounded by a sea of luxury, the doll lady and her work are the cultural anchors.

Barbadians (Bajans) are a warm, friendly, and hospitable people who are genuinely proud of their country and culture. Tourism is the island's number one industry, but with a sophisticated business community and stable government, life here doesn't skip a beat after visitors pack up their sunscreen and return home. Financial services, agriculture (sugar), and light manufacturing (rum, chemicals, and electrical components) are predominant industries.

Most of the 266,000 Bajans (about 85%) live in the urban area around the capital city of Bridgetown, along the west coast north to Speightstown, and along the south coast down to Oistins. Others reside inland, in tiny hamlets scattered throughout the island's 11 parishes.

Barbados stands apart both physically and geographically from its Caribbean neighbors; it's a full 100 mi (161 km) east of the Lesser Antilles chain that arcs from the Virgin Islands to Trinidad. Although many neighboring islands are the peaks of a volcanic mountain range, Barbados is the top of a single mountain of coral and limestone, sources of building blocks for many a plantation manor. Barbados is 21 mi (34 km) long, 14 mi (22½ km) wide, and relatively flat; the highest point, Mt. Hillaby, is in the north and has an elevation of 1,115 ft (341 m). The interior hills and valleys are covered by impenetrable acres of sugarcane, punctuated only by the sugar factories and great houses that the crop has sustained for centuries.

Besides picturesque rolling hills, a perimeter of white-sand beaches, a central flatland, and even deposits of underground oil (providing 60% of the island's petroleum requirements), Barbados's unique geology has created its most popular attraction, Harrison's Cave. This natural phenomenon has bubbling underground streams, cascading waterfalls, and stalactites and stalagmites created through the millennia by the constant drip of calcite-laden water.

Actually, it was during a search for fresh water that Barbados was "discovered" by the Portuguese in 1536. They didn't stay but did give the island its name: Barbados, or "the bearded ones," after native fig trees with beardlike roots. A century later—and quite by accident—the British landed on the west coast at what is now Holetown. The first British settlement was established two years later, in 1627. Unlike the turbulent history of most of the Caribbean islands, British rule sustained uninterrupted until 1966, when Barbados became independent. The island has since had an elected prime minister and membership in the British Commonwealth of Nations.

Facilities here are top-notch. Beaches along the tranquil west coast, facing the Caribbean, are lined with posh resorts and residences that are virtually enveloped in lush foliage and a quiet atmosphere. This luxurious area, appropriately called the Platinum Coast, is a favorite destination of British vacationers. North Americans tend to prefer the hotels and resorts stretched along the beaches of the trendier south coast, which has shopping opportunities, countless restaurants, and an active nightlife. Bajans, however, spend their holidays along the rugged east coast, where the Atlantic surf pounds the dramatic shoreline with unrelenting force.

Barbados retains a noticeable British atmosphere. Most islanders are members of the Anglican church, afternoon tea is a ritual, polo ("the sport of kings") is played all winter, and cricket is the national passion—Barbados has produced some of the world's top cricketers. The tradition of dressing for dinner is firmly entrenched, yet the island's atmosphere is hardly stuffy. You can dine by candlelight facing the sea, in festive company at a sumptuous Bajan buffet, or casually with a burger at the beach. This is still the Caribbean, after all.

Lodging

Most visitors stay on either the fashionable west coast, north of Bridgetown, or the action-packed south coast. The west coast beachfront resorts in the parishes of St. Peter, St. James, and St. Michael are mostly self-contained enclaves. Highway 1, a two-lane road with considerable traffic, runs past these resorts, which makes strolling to a nearby bar or restaurant difficult. Along the south coast, in Christ Church Parish, many hotels are clustered near the busy strip known as the St. Lawrence Gap, with its dozens of small restaurants, bars, and nightclubs. On the much more remote east coast, a couple of small inns offer oceanfront views, cool breezes, and get-away-from-it-all tranquillity. Accommodations range from elegant resorts and private villas to modest but comfortable small hotels and inns. Another popular option is renting a time-share condominium, apartment, or private home. Hotels usually operate on the EP but also offer CP or MAP if you wish; some require MAP in winter, and others are all-inclusive. The hotels below all have TVs and radios in guest rooms unless otherwise noted.

CATEGORY	COST*
$$$$	over $500
$$$	$350–$500
$$	$200–$350
$	under $200

*All prices are for a standard double room, excluding 7½% government tax and 10% service charge. Note when comparing rates: the price categories for all-inclusive resorts reflect the inclusion of all meals, beverages, and activities.

Hotels

$ **Atlantis Hotel.** The Atlantis has a spectacular cliffside location over-looking the rocky Atlantic coast, where the sea views are mesmerizing. The hotel began as a modest family guest house more than a century ago. It's still small and congenial, with most of the activity happening around midday, when folks touring the east coast stop for a traditional Bajan buffet lunch at the Atlantis Hotel restaurant. Rooms are modest, and some have balconies overlooking that great view. You won't find a TV, and there's no air-conditioning—although the fresh Atlantic breeze that usually wafts through the open windows makes that no problem. There's a beachfront, but Bathsheba Beach—the island's premier surfing spot—is right next door. ⊠ *Tent Bay, Bathsheba, St. Joseph,* ☎ *246/433–9445. 8 rooms. Restaurant, bar, beach. AE. EP, MAP.*

$ **Edgewater Inn.** The perfect place for watching birds and butterflies, hiking, and surfing the Soup Bowl, this secluded hideaway is on a cliff overlooking the pounding surf and unusual rock formations at Bathsheba Beach. Despite its proximity to the sea, it resembles a rustic mountain lodge in both appearance and ambience. Bounded by Joe's River, a national park, and a 9-mi (14½-km) strip of sand, the property also backs up to an 85-acre rain forest. Yoga classes, nature walks, and guided hikes are available to guests. And you can swim in a unique Barbados-shape pool. All rooms and the dining room have ocean views and hand-hewn mahogany doors, moldings, and furniture; some rooms are air-conditioned. ⊠ *Bathsheba Beach, Bathsheba, St. Joseph,* ☎ *246/433–9900,* FAX *246/433–9902,* WEB *www.edgewaterinn.com. 20 rooms. Restaurant, bar, air-conditioning (some), pool, beach. AE, MC, V. CP, FAP, MAP.*

$$$$ **Turtle Beach Resort.** The truly elegant flagship of the Elegant Ho-★ tels Group is named for the sea turtles that lay their eggs on the broad strand of beach visible from the three-story open-air lobby. Everything you could wish for is here to enjoy—all the time, all included. Kayaks, Hobie Cats, and boogie boards are fun at the beach; scuba lessons are given in the pool; tennis equipment is provided; golfers get special rates and tee times at the nearby Barbados Golf Club. The Kids Club, which operates daily from 9 to 9, offers games, activities, and equipment (including computers with video games and Internet access) that appeal to all ages. Suites are large and attractively decorated with wicker furniture and subtle tropical color schemes; all have ocean views. With a choice of three restaurants (or dine around at four sister hotels) and with three bars for socializing and nightly entertainment, you won't want to go home. ⊠ *St. Lawrence Gap, Dover, Christ Church,* ☎ *246/428–7131 or 800/326–6898,* FAX *246/428–6089,* WEB *www.eleganthotels.com. 149 junior suites, 18 1-bedroom suites. 2 restaurants, 2 bars, snack bar, sports bar, air-conditioning, fans, in-room safes, refrigerators, room service, 3 pools, hair salon, massage, golf privileges, 2 tennis courts, gym, beach, snorkeling, windsurfing, boating, shops, cabaret, babysitting, children's programs, playground, dry cleaning, laundry service, business services. AE, DC, MC, V. All-inclusive.*

$$$ **Club Rockley Barbados.** On 65 acres near one of the island's most popular beach areas, this all-inclusive resort offers extensive amenities. The resort's 9-hole, par-36 golf course is challenging, attractive, and open to the public. The one- and two-bedroom accommodations are former time-share condominiums, and those time-shares that remain are set apart from the hotel. Each room has a balcony or patio. There's free shuttle service to the beach, just five minutes away. ⊠ *Golf*

114

Lodging

Accra Beach
Hotel & Resort 4
Almond Beach
Club 34
Almond Beach
Village 20
Atlantis Hotel 16
Bougainvillea
Beach Resort 13
Casuarina Beach
Club 11
Club Rockley
Barbados 3
Cobblers Cove
Hotel . : 21
Coconut Creek
Hotel 40
Colony Club
Hotel 29
Coral Reef Club . . . 25
Crane Beach
Hotel 14
Crystal Cove Hotel . 42
Divi Southwinds
Beach Resort 8
Edgewater Inn 17
Glitter Bay 26
Lone Star
Garage Motel 24
Mango Bay Hotel
& Beach Club 30
Port St. Charles . . . 19
Royal Pavilion 27
Royal Westmoreland
Villas 23
Sam Lord's
Castle 15
Sandridge Beach
Hotel 22
Sandy Beach
Island Resort 5
Sandy Lane 35
Tamarind Cove
Hotel 38
Treasure Beach 37
Turtle Beach
Resort 12

Dining

Angry Annie's 33
Atlantis Hotel 16
Baku Beach Bar 36
Bellini's Trattoria 7
Bonito Beach Bar &
Restaurant 18
Brown Sugar 2
Carambola 41
The Cliff 39
The Crane 14
David's Place 6
Josef's Resturant 9
Lone Star Garage
Restaurant 24
La Maison 28
Olives Bar
& Bistro 31
Pisces 10
Ragamuffins 32
Waterfront Cafe 1

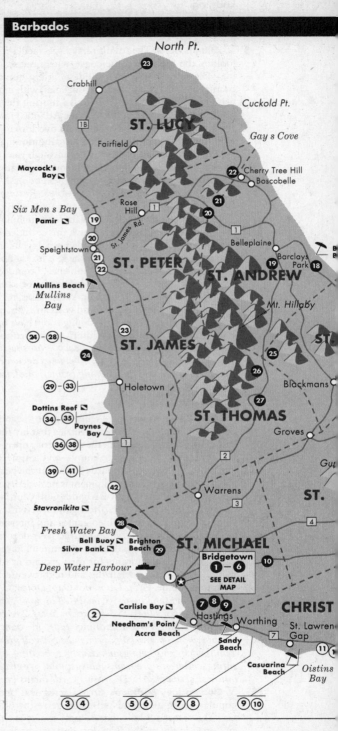

Barbados

KEY

- Beaches
- Cruise Ship Terminal
- Dive Sites
- ❶ Exploring Sights
- ① Hotels and Restaurants

ATLANTIC OCEAN

N

Barclays Park
Beach

⑱ *Tent Bay*

⑯⑰⑰

Bathsheba
Bathsheba
Soup Bowl

JOSEPH

*Consett
Bay*

Four
Crossroads

⑯

*Ragged
Pt.*

Marley
Vale

ST. JOHN

4

p Hill

⑪
⑫

4B

GEORGE

Edgecumbe

⑬

ST. PHILIP

Bottom
Bay

⑮
⑮

⑭

The Crane

⑭

Crane Beach

*Crane
Bay*

COBBLER'S REEF

CHURCH

⑬
⑫

ce

7

Oistins

✈ Grantley Adams
International
Airport

*Long
Bay*

Silver Sands
Beach

South Pt.

0   3 miles
0   3 km

Exploring

Andromeda Gardens 17
Animal Flower Cave 23
Barbados Museum 7
Barbados Wildlife Reserve 21
Barclays Park 18
Chalky Mount 19
Codrington Theological College 16
Emancipation Statue 10
Farley Hill 20
Flower Forest 25
Folkestone Marine Park & Visitor Centre 24
Francia Plantation House 11
Gun Hill Signal Station 12
Harrison's Cave . . . 27
Harry Bayley Observatory 8
Malibu Beach Club 28
Mount Gay Rum Visitors Centre 29
Rum Factory and Heritage Park 14
St. Nicholas Abbey 22
Sam Lord's Castle . . . 15
Sunbury Plantation House & Museum 13
Tyrol Cot Heritage Village 9
Welchman Hall Gully 26

Club Rd., Rockley, Christ Church, ☎ *246/435–7880 or 800/777–1250,* FAX *246/435–8015,* WEB *www.clubrockley.com. 164 rooms. 2 restaurants, 3 bars, air-conditioning, kitchenettes, 7 pools, hair salon, 9-hole golf course, 5 tennis courts, squash, shops, baby-sitting, children's programs, meeting room. AE, DC, MC, V. All-inclusive.*

$$$ 🏨 **Crane Beach Hotel.** High on a cliff overlooking the dramatic Atlantic (the panoramas are breathtaking), this remote coral-stone inn dates back more than a century. It was Barbados's first resort and has recently undergone a $6 million renovation. Suites, originally designed for turn-of-the-20th-century guests who stayed a month or two, are large and decorated with antiques. Some have four-poster beds and kitchenettes; all have ocean views (though there are no TVs). Corner suites have two walls of windows and broad patios. Only a couple of the rooms have air-conditioning, but there's a constant ocean breeze. The pool is so magnificently perched above the sea that it has served as the backdrop for numerous fashion photo shoots. To reach the beach, which is thumped by waves that are good for both bodysurfing and swimming, walk down some 200 steps onto a beautiful stretch of pink-tinged sand. ✉ *The Crane, Crane Bay, St. Philip,* ☎ *246/423–6220 or 800/223–6510,* FAX *246/423–5343,* WEB *www.thecrane.com. 4 rooms, 5 junior suites, and 9 1-bedroom suites. Restaurant, bar, fans, kitchenettes (some), minibars, 2 pools, 4 tennis courts, beach, meeting room. AE, DC, MC, V. EP, MAP.*

$$$ 🏨 **Sam Lord's Castle.** Set on the Atlantic coast about 14 mi (22½ km) east of Bridgetown, Sam Lord's Castle is not a castle with moat and towers but a great house surrounded by 72 acres of grounds, gardens, and beach. The seven rooms in the main house have canopied beds; downstairs, the public rooms have furniture by Sheraton, Hepplewhite, and Chippendale—for admiring, not for sitting. Guest rooms in surrounding cottages have conventional hotel furnishings, and some have kitchenettes. The beach is 1 mi (1½ km) long, the Wanderer Restaurant offers Continental cuisine, and there are even a few slot machines—as befits a pirate's lair. An all-inclusive package includes unlimited daytime tennis, all beverages, airport transfers, and a Thursday Shipwreck party in addition to accommodations and all meals. ✉ *Long Bay, St. Philip,* ☎ *246/423–7350,* FAX *246/423–6361,* WEB *www.samlordscastle.com. 236 rooms, 12 suites. 3 restaurants, air-conditioning, 3 pools, 7 tennis courts, beach, shops, meeting room. AE, D, DC, MC, V. All-inclusive.*

$$ 🏨 **Accra Beach Hotel & Resort.** The beautifully appointed rooms in the four-story Accra have balconies facing sandy, white Accra Beach. Six duplex penthouse suites have ocean-view sitting rooms downstairs, refrigerators, and a spacious bedroom and huge baths with whirlpools upstairs. All rooms are decorated in soft pastel colors and have handcrafted furniture. Between the hotel and its beach are a large cloverleaf-shape pool, a snack bar, and a poolside bar. In the evening, sumptuous dining in Wytukai (pronounced Y2K)—the island's first Polynesian restaurant—take a turn on a dance floor that's open to the stars. Children under 12 stay free in their parents' room. Rooms and facilities are accessible to people with disabilities. ✉ *Hwy. 7 (Box 73W), Rockley, Christ Church,* ☎ *246/435–8920 or 800/223-6510,* FAX *246/435–6794. 122 rooms, 6 suites. Restaurant, 2 bars, snack bar, air-conditioning, fans, pool, hair salon, gym, squash, beach, meeting rooms. AE, MC, V. CP, EP, MAP.*

$$ 🏨 **Casuarina Beach Club.** The Casuarina Beach Club, 20 minutes from Bridgetown, is popular among those who prefer self-catering vacations yet want to be close to the action. The setting is peaceful—unique among south coast resorts—but you're within walking distance of restaurants, nightlife, and shopping. The luxury four-story apartment hotel

consists of five clusters of Spanish-style buildings in 7½ acres of gardens surrounded by casuarina pines. The restaurant and one of two bars are on the beach—900 ft (275 m) of soft, fine sand. A reception area includes small lounges where you can get a dose of TV (there aren't any TVs in the rooms). All rooms and one- or two-bedroom suites have kitchenettes and large balconies. Scuba diving, golf, and other activities can be arranged. All facilities are accessible to people with disabilities. ✉ *St. Lawrence Gap, Dover, Christ Church,* ☎ *246/428–3600, 800/742–4276, or 800/223–9815;* FAX *246/428–1970,* WEB *www.casuarina. com. 124 rooms, 34 suites. Restaurant, 2 bars, air-conditioning, fans, kitchenettes, pool, 2 tennis courts, squash, beach, shops, children's programs, meeting room. AE, D, MC, V. CP, EP, MAP.*

$$ 🏨 **Divi Southwinds Beach Resort.** The toss-up here is whether to take one of the larger rooms—with a kitchenette and a balcony that overlooks the gardens and pool—or one of the smaller, older rooms just steps from the sandy, white beach. Though all the rooms are pleasant, the buildings themselves are plain. Guests come for the action, and that includes making full use of the water-sports facilities and 20 lush acres. ✉ *St. Lawrence Gap, Dover, Christ Church,* ☎ *246/428–7181 or 800/367–3484,* FAX *246/428–4674. 155 rooms. 2 restaurants, 2 bars, air-conditioning, kitchenettes, 2 pools, hair salon, putting green, 2 tennis courts, basketball, volleyball, beach, dive shop, shops, meeting room. AE, DC, MC, V. CP, EP, FAP, MAP.*

$$ 🏨 **Sandy Beach Island Resort.** On a wide, white beach, this comfortable hotel has modern rooms done in tropical colors, and one- and two-bedroom suites with full kitchens and dining areas. The Beachfront Restaurant serves a West Indian buffet Tuesday and Saturday nights, and you'll also find a boardwalk gazebo, a roof garden, and a free-form pool with a poolside bar on the grounds. Dive certification, deep-sea fishing, harbor cruises, and catamaran sailing can be arranged. It's a short walk to the shops, restaurants, and nightspots at St. Lawrence Gap. ✉ *Hwy. 7, Worthing, Christ Church,* ☎ *246/435–8000, 800/742–4276, 800/448–8355, 800/223–9815, or 800/462–2526;* FAX *246/435–8053. 41 rooms, 87 suites. Restaurant, 2 bars, air-conditioning, kitchenettes, pool, beach, snorkeling, windsurfing, boating, shops, meeting room. AE, DC, MC, V. CP, EP, MAP.*

WEST COAST

$$$$ 🏨 **Almond Beach Club.** This west coast resort is perfect for couples, honeymooners, and singles who want luxurious surroundings and no extra expenses. In addition to food, beverages, and sporting activities, the price of a room here gets you shopping excursions to Bridgetown, privileges at Almond Beach Village (which has a golf course), and transportation to the airport. All rooms have coffeemakers, hair dryers, and views of the ocean or the pool and gardens; junior suites have balconies. Meals are excellent, from the lavish breakfast buffets and four-course lunches to the afternoon teas and intimate dinners. There's also Enid's, a colorful West Indian restaurant that's on-site, and some area restaurants that are part of the dine-around program (for guests staying seven days or more). A small shopping center, with a branch of Cave Shepherd (the Bridgetown department store), is across the street; Holetown is within strolling distance. ✉ *Hwy. 1, Vauxhall, St. James,* ☎ *246/432–7840 or 800/425–6663,* FAX *246/432–2115,* WEB *www. almondresorts.com. 133 rooms, 28 junior suites. 2 restaurants, 4 bars, air-conditioning, in-room safes, 3 pools, sauna, tennis court, squash, beach, snorkeling, windsurfing, boating, waterskiing, airport shuttle. AE, MC, V. All-inclusive.*

$$$$ 🏨 **Almond Beach Village.** There's plenty to keep everyone in the family busy on these 30 landscaped acres near Speightstown: a 1-mi-long

(1½-km-long) beach; an executive par-3 golf course; nine pools; restaurants that serve Continental, Italian, and local cuisine; and such activities as shopping excursions, island tours, Caribbean cooking classes, and a dine-around program. The family section has junior and one-bedroom suites, a nursery, a play area, a wading pool, and a supervised Kid's Klub with extensive (and separate) programs for infants–age 12. A historic sugar mill on the property is a lovely spot for weddings. If all this isn't enough, you can hop the shuttle to the Almond Beach Club and use the facilities there. Seven low-rise buildings house the large, comfortable guest rooms; each has a coffeemaker and a hair dryer. All meals (including all beverages), activities, and departure transfers are included in the rates. ⊠ *Hwy. 1B, Heywoods, St. Peter,* ☎ *246/422–4900 or 800/425–6663,* FAX *246/422–0617,* WEB *www.almondresorts.com. 289 rooms, 41 suites. 4 restaurants, 5 bars, air-conditioning, in-room safes, 9 pools, wading pool, 9-hole golf course, 5 tennis courts, health club, racquetball, squash, beach, snorkeling, windsurfing, boating, waterskiing, fishing, shops, dance club, children's programs. AE, MC, V. All-inclusive.*

$$$$ 🏨 **Coconut Creek Hotel.** The atmosphere is quiet and secluded at this small, picturesque resort set on handsomely landscaped grounds overlooking the ocean. From a low bluff, steps lead down to two tiny coves and a sandy beach. Rooms have whitewashed wooden ceilings, rattan furnishings, and tropical accents. Some have spectacular ocean views; others overlook the garden or pool. TV is available in the lounge. Sunfish, kayaks, and other nonmotorized water-sports equipment are available. Meals are served at the open-air Pavilion restaurant; entertainment and dancing take place nightly at the Cricketers Bar. A free water taxi provides transportation to the sister Elegant hotels on the west coast. ⊠ *Hwy. 1, Derricks, St. James (Box 249, Bridgetown),* ☎ *246/432–0803 or 800/326–6898,* FAX *246/432–0272,* WEB *www. eleganthotels.com. 41 rooms, 12 suites. Bar, dining room, air-conditioning, in-room safes, refrigerators, pool, golf privileges, beach, snorkeling, windsurfing, boating, waterskiing, baby-sitting, dry cleaning, laundry service. AE, DC, MC, V. All-inclusive.*

$$$$ 🏨 **Crystal Cove Hotel.** A colony of attached duplex cottages, painted white and trimmed in the perky pastels typical of the Caribbean, spill down a hillside to the beach. Winding garden paths connect the units, which are quite private despite being close together. Each room has a balcony or patio, most have a water view, and some are literally inches from the beach. Rooms are bright, spacious, and pleasantly decorated with bleached wood and rattan furniture; bedcovers, drapes, and upholstery are in tropical pastels. During the day, there's plenty of activity at the water-sports center. Sail on a Hobie Cat, have a scuba lesson, or go waterskiing, windsurfing, or kayaking to your heart's content. For a change of scene, a free water taxi travels all day long among the four west-coast Elegant Hotels properties. And each weekday morning, there's a shopping excursion to Bridgetown. Luncheon is generally a beachside buffet; the table d'hôte dinner at Reflections Restaurant is superb, with service to match. Each night there's entertainment—a steel band or other live music. Crystal Cove guests can also participate in a dine-around program at its sister resorts. ⊠ *Hwy. 1, Appleby, St. James,* ☎ *246/432–2683 or 800/326–6898,* FAX *246/432–8290,* WEB *www.eleganthotels.com. 88 rooms. Restaurant, 2 bars, grill, air-conditioning, fans, in-room safes, refrigerators, room service, 3 pools, golf privileges, 2 tennis courts, gym, beach, snorkeling, windsurfing, boating, waterskiing, shop, baby-sitting, children's programs, laundry service. AE, D, DC, MC, V. All-inclusive.*

$$$$ 🏨 **Colony Club Hotel.** A stately parade of casuarina trees lines the en-
★	trance to what was once a gentlemen's private club. The stylish, sooth-

ing colonial decor suits the sophisticated, mature clientele, who enjoy relaxing on a quiet stretch of beach, soaking in one of four pools, admiring 7 acres of tropical gardens, and enjoying an exquisite meal in The Orchid Room or a more informal repast at the open-air Laguna Restaurant. Rooms are spacious, with whitewashed wood and rattan furniture and soft pink, beige, and green fabrics. Twenty luxurious and romantic ocean-view rooms have private access to one of two lagoon pools, which cascade down to lovely tropical gardens. TV is available only in the lounge, which doubles as a kids' club during the Christmas and Easter holiday seasons. In February, families with children under 12 would be happier at a hotel more suitable for children. That's not to say there's not plenty to do here. Nonmotorized water sports, an in-pool scuba-diving lesson, tennis, golf privileges at Royal Westmoreland Golf Course, water aerobics, and use of the fitness center are all included in the rates. A free water taxi provides transportation among four sister hotels on the west coast. ⊠ *Hwy. 1, Porters, St. James,* ☎ *246/422–2335 or 800/326–6898,* 𝔽𝔸𝕏 *246/422–0667,* 𝕎𝔼𝔹 *www. eleganthotels.com. 64 rooms, 34 junior suites. 2 restaurants, 3 bars, air-conditioning, fans, in-room safes, minibars, room service, 4 pools, hair salon, golf privileges, 2 tennis courts, gym, beach, snorkeling, windsurfing, boating, waterskiing, shops, laundry service, dry cleaning, baby-sitting, meeting room. AE, D, DC, MC, V. CP, EP, FAP, MAP.*

$$$$ 🏨 **Coral Reef Club.** As a guest at this small family-owned and -managed resort, you'll spend your days relaxing on the white-sand beach or around the pool, taking time out for the hotel's superb afternoon tea. The public areas ramble along the beach, and small coral-stone cottages are scattered over 12 flower-filled acres (the cottages farthest from the beach are a bit of a hike from the main house). The spacious accommodations are graced with fresh flowers, and each room has a small patio and amenities such as hair dryers. Junior suites have sitting areas and large private balconies or patios; cottage-style suites have an additional single bed and dressing room. TV is available by request only and carries an extra charge. Guests on MAP have dining and golf privileges at Royal Westmoreland Golf Club. The nearby Folkestone Underwater Marine Park is great for snorkeling, and there's a free weekday shuttle into Bridgetown. ⊠ *Hwy. 1, Holetown, St. James,* ☎ *246/ 422–2372 or 800/525–4800,* 𝔽𝔸𝕏 *246/422–1776. 34 rooms, 30 suites. Restaurant, bar, air-conditioning, fans, in-room safes, refrigerators, room service, 2 pools, hair salon, massage, golf privileges, 3 tennis courts, gym, beach, dive shop, snorkeling, windsurfing, boating, waterskiing, shops, billiards, baby-sitting. AE, MC, V. EP, FAP, MAP.*

$$$$ 🏨 **Glitter Bay.** Sir Edward Cunard of the English shipping family built this estate in the 1930s to resemble his palazzo in Venice; visiting aristocrats and celebrities gave Glitter Bay an early reputation for grandeur and style. Today, newer buildings, angled back from the beach, contain one- and two-bedroom suites and duplex penthouses, all with one king-size or two twin beds and private balconies or terraces; some have full kitchens. Manicured gardens separate the reception area and lounge from an alfresco dining room (where evening entertainment is presented), pools with a waterfall and footbridge, and ½ mi (1 km) of beach. Glitter Bay is more casual and family-oriented than its next-door sister property, the Royal Pavilion, but the resorts share facilities, including water sports and dining privileges. Guests also enjoy privileges at Royal Westmoreland Golf Club (with complimentary transportation). ⊠ *Hwy. 1, Porters, St. James,* ☎ *246/422–5555 or 800/223– 1818,* 𝔽𝔸𝕏 *246/422–1367,* 𝕎𝔼𝔹 *www.fairmont.com. 69 suites. Restaurant, air-conditioning, fans, in-room safes, minibars, room service, 2 pools, hair salon, massage, golf privileges, 2 tennis courts, gym, beach,* *snorkeling, windsurfing, boating, waterskiing, shops, baby-sitting, meeting room. AE, D, DC, MC, V. CP, EP, MAP.*

$$$$ 🗔 **Lone Star Garage Motel.** For something completely different, the house adjacent to the Lone Star Garage Restaurant—a renovated 1940s-era gas station—is now a four-suite motel. Two rooms are at beach level; two are upstairs. The Lincoln Bedroom is named for the car; other suites are appropriately dubbed Buick, Cord, and Studebaker. All are large and beautifully furnished in Bajan mahogany and Italian-designed upholstered furniture. Each suite has its own communications center, with a data port, a fax machine, a stereo/CD player, and a TV. On arrival you receive personalized stationery, business cards, and an assistant. The beach is at the door; golf, tennis, fishing, snorkeling, scuba diving, and horseback riding are available nearby. The restaurant is terrific. ⊠ *Hwy. 1, Mount Standfast, St. James,* ☎ *246/419–0599,* ℻ *246/419–0597,* ⊞ *www.thelonestar.com. 4 suites. Restaurant, bar, air-conditioning, fans, in-room data ports, in-room fax, refrigerators, room service, golf privileges, beach. AE, D, DC, MC, V. CP, EP, MAP.*

$$$$ 🗔 **Royal Pavilion.** The Royal Pavilion attracts sophisticated guests who want serenity (it's best to leave the kids at home). Of the 75 suites here, 72 are oceanfront; the remaining three are nestled in a two-story garden villa. Ground-floor rooms allow you to simply step through sliding doors, cross your private patio, and walk onto the sand. Second- and third-floor suites have king-size or two twin beds and amenities such as hair dryers. Breakfast and lunch are served alfresco at the edge of the beach; afternoon tea and dinner are in the Palm Terrace. Recreational facilities and dining privileges are shared with the adjoining and more informal sister hotel, Glitter Bay. ⊠ *Hwy. 1, Porters, St. James,* ☎ *246/422–4444 or 800/223–1818,* ℻ *246/422–3940,* ⊞ *www.fairmont.com. 75 suites. 2 restaurants, 2 bars, air-conditioning, room service, pool, hair salon, golf privileges, 2 tennis courts, beach, snorkeling, windsurfing, boating, waterskiing, shops, laundry service, concierge, meeting room. AE, D, DC, MC, V. CP, EP, MAP.*

$$$$ 🗔 **Sandy Lane Hotel.** Not only did the legendary Sandy Lane Hotel
★ close its doors in 1998, but its new owners leveled it. But like the phoenix, rising from the ashes of destruction, a spectacular new Sandy Lane Hotel has emerged on the site of its namesake. The $350 million result is undeniably magnificent. Former guests will find comfort in the similarities: a classical coral-stone mansion, set in a mahogany grove overlooking a sweeping stretch of beach. But the guest rooms are even larger now, with more modern amenities—such as remote-controlled lighting and air-conditioning; flat-screen TV, DVD player, and stereo; fax machines, e-mail, and high-speed Internet access; an individually stocked private bar; and generous bathrooms with multispray showers and separate bathtubs. There's an entirely new spa facility and fitness center, a brand new tennis center, and two new championship golf courses (bringing the total to 45 holes). One restaurant features haute cuisine in a formal setting; another, at beach level, is relaxed; others are located at the spa and at the golf clubhouse. ⊠ *Hwy. 1, Paynes Bay, St. James,* ☎ *246/432–2954,* ℻ *246/432–2954,* ⊞ *www.sandylane.com. 102 rooms, 10 suites. 4 restaurants, 3 bars, air-conditioning, fans, in-room data ports, in-room fax, in-room safes, minibars, room service, pool, hair salon, massage, spa, steam room, 2 18-hole golf courses, 1 9-hole golf course, 9 tennis courts, beach, snorkeling, windsurfing, boating, shops, children's programs, dry cleaning, laundry service, concierge, business services, meeting rooms AE, DC, MC, V. EP.*

$$$$ 🗔 **Tamarind Cove Hotel.** This Mediterranean-style hotel stretches along 750 ft (229 m) of prime beachfront. The center section was originally a private mansion owned by the honorable Janet Kidd, founder of the Holders Opera Season and daughter of British newspaper mogul Lord

Beaverbrook. Over the years, new construction and the incorporation of an adjacent resort have created a large, rambling property with lots of facilities and accommodations either close to the action or in cozy privacy. Rooms, which are on three floors (some are wheelchair accessible), are spacious and attractively decorated in subdued colors, with tropical accents and rattan furnishings. Ten luxury ocean-view suites have four-poster beds, marble floors, and coral-stone walls. Four suites have private outdoor Jacuzzis. Tangiers is the main restaurant, open for breakfast and lunch, and Bamboo is a casual beachfront bar serving lunch and dinner. Sasso, with contemporary decor and a blend of Italian, Mediterranean, and Caribbean cuisine at dinner, is the most elegant. Any dietary requirement can be accommodated. Besides golf privileges at the Royal Westmoreland Golf Club and a full complement of water sports, including sailing and kayaking, a free water taxi operates between the four Elegant hotels on the west coast. ⊠ *Hwy. 1, Paynes Bay, St. James,* ☎ *246/432–1332 or 800/326–6898,* FAX *246/432–6317,* WEB *www.eleganthotels.com. 58 rooms, 108 suites. 3 restaurants, 3 bars, air-conditioning, in-room safes, refrigerators, room service, 4 pools, hair salon, golf privileges, 2 tennis courts, gym, beach, snorkeling, windsurfing, boating, waterskiing, shops, cabaret, babysitting, children's programs, dry cleaning, laundry service, meeting room. AE, D, DC, MC, V. EP, MAP.*

$$$$ 🛏 **Treasure Beach.** The atmosphere here is quiet, upscale, friendly, and primarily adult. Guests, particularly British vacationers, often stay two or three weeks, giving the hotel a residential quality. One-bedroom suites create a staggered horseshoe around a small garden and pool. Most have sea views, but all are just steps from the beach. The superdeluxe Hemmingway Suite is a blend of antiques and modern luxury, with an enormous terrace and special amenities. All other suites have sitting rooms with comfortable sofa beds and chairs upholstered in pastel hues, glass-top tables, full kitchenettes, and a few books; one entire wall opens to the cooling ocean breezes but can be shuttered at night for privacy. Bedrooms are air-conditioned. Rooms have neither radio nor TV—except for the Hemmingway Suite—but you can read a complimentary local newspaper at breakfast. The restaurant's gourmet meals and fine service attract an outside clientele for dinner. Hotel guests on MAP enjoy an exchange plan with neighboring hotels. ⊠ *Hwy. 1, Paynes Bay, St. James,* ☎ *246/432–1346, 800/742–4276, or 800/223–6510;* FAX *246/432–1094. 29 1-bedroom suites. Restaurant, bar, air-conditioning, fans, in-room safes, kitchenettes, room service, pool, beach, snorkeling, dry cleaning, laundry service. AE, D, DC, MC, V. CP, EP, MAP.*

$$$ 🛏 **Cobblers Cove Hotel.** A pink-and-white, English-style country house
★ is the focal point of this intimate, elegant resort. Three acres of tropical gardens bordered by stone walls give the property privacy. Most suites are in 10 two-story cottages arranged in a V-shape around the great house. Each has a sitting room with a wet bar and louvered shutters that open onto a large patio or wooden balcony. Bedrooms are air-conditioned. The hotel has an excellent restaurant, a sociable bar, and a clubby lounge-library. For all-out luxury stay in the great house's stylish Colleton or Camelot suite. Each has a king-size four-poster bed, a whirlpool bath, and a large sitting room with spiral staircase leading to a secluded rooftop sundeck and private plunge pool. All guests enjoy special rates and guaranteed tee times at the nearby Royal Westmoreland Golf Club. From January to March the atmosphere is primarily adults only. ⊠ *Road View, Speightstown, St. Peter,* ☎ *246/422–2291 or 800/890–6060,* FAX *246/422–1460. 40 suites. Restaurant, bar, snack bar, air-conditioning, in-room safes, minibars, pool, golf privileges, tennis court, gym, beach, snorkeling, windsurfing, boating, wa-*

terskiing, library, baby-sitting, meeting room. AE, MC, V. CP, EP, FAP, MAP.

$$$ ⚓ **Mango Bay Hotel & Beach Club.** In central Holetown and within walking distance of shops and historic sights, Mango Bay's whitewashed buildings face the beach and are surrounded by gardens. Each room has a private terrace or balcony and a picturesque view of the garden, pool, or beach; all rooms are decorated in bright Caribbean colors and have wicker furniture. The all-inclusive price extends to beverages and a dine-around program at two local restaurants for guests staying a week or more. Activities include water sports, scuba instruction in the pool, aquacise classes, a catamaran cruise, glass-bottom boat rides, snorkeling trips, walking tours, and a shopping excursion to Bridgetown. There are always nightcaps along with after-dinner entertainment at the piano bar. Children three years and under stay free. ✉ *2nd St., Holetown, St. James,* ☎ *246/432–1384 or 877/626–4648,* FAX *246/432–5297,* WEB *www.mangobaybarbados.com. 64 rooms. Restaurant, bar, piano bar, air-conditioning, in-room safes, 2 pools, beach, snorkeling, windsurfing, boating, waterskiing. AE, MC, V. All-inclusive.*

$ ⚓ **Sandridge Beach Hotel.** The rooms and suites at this beachfront property near Speightstown are styled in bright colors and tropical furnishings. You can stay in a basic hotel room or a studio or one-bedroom suite with a kitchenette (ground-floor rooms have wide doors and ramps). Among the water activities is a glass-bottom boat ride, and one of the pools has a dramatic waterfall and deck of coral stone. ✉ *Road View, St. Peter,* ☎ *246/422–2361,* FAX *246/422–1965. 28 rooms, 30 suites. 2 restaurants, 2 bars, air-conditioning, kitchenettes, 2 pools, beach, snorkeling, windsurfing, boating, baby-sitting, meeting room. AE, DC, MC, V. CP, EP, FAP, MAP.*

Villas, Apartments, and Condominiums

Villas, private homes, and condos are available south of Bridgetown, in the Hastings-Worthing area, and along the west coast in St. James and in St. Peter. Most include maid service, and the owner or manager can arrange for a cook.

The **Barbados Tourism Authority** (☎ 246/427–2623) on Harbour Road in Bridgetown has a listing of apartments, along with the facilities offered and the rates. Some apartment complexes are small, with only three or four units; others range up to 30 units or more. They're in prime resort areas on both the south and west coasts.

A handful of time-share resorts have cropped up along the south and west coasts. Nonowner vacationers can rent the units by the week from the property managers. Two- and three-bedroom condos run $800–$1,400 per week in the summer—double that in winter. This is an economical option for family groups or couples vacationing together.

Among the condominium resorts are the following: **Royal Westmoreland Villas** (✉ Hwy. 2A, Westmoreland, St. James, ☎ 246/422–4653, WEB www.royal-westmoreland.com); **Port St. Charles.** (✉ Hwy. 1B, Heywoods, St. Peter, ☎ 246/419–1000, WEB www.portstcharles.com); **Bougainvillea Beach Resort** (✉ Maxwell Coast Rd., Maxwell, Christ Church, ☎ 246/418–0990 or 800/988–6904).

Dining

Bajan staples include rice, peas, and okra—often added to slowly cooked meat and fish dishes. Local specialty dishes include *buljol* (a cold salad of pickled codfish, tomatoes, onions, sweet peppers, and celery) and *conkies* (cornmeal, coconut, pumpkin, raisins, sweet potatoes, and spices, mixed together, wrapped in a banana leaf, and steamed).

Cou-cou, often served with steamed flying fish, is a mixture of cornmeal and okra topped with a spicy creole sauce made from tomatoes, onions, and sweet peppers. To make a Bajan-style pepper-pot stew, you must simmer (overnight) a hearty mix of oxtail, beef chunks, and "any other meat" in a rich, spicy gravy.

In addition to regional dishes, many first-class restaurants and hotel dining rooms serve quite sophisticated cuisine—prepared by chefs with international experience—to rival that served in the world's best restaurants. Most menus include seafood—dorado, kingfish, snapper, and flying fish are prepared every way imaginable. Flying fish is so popular a delicacy that it has become a national symbol. Shellfish abounds; on the other hand, so do steak, local black-belly lamb, and fresh fruits and vegetables.

For lunch, restaurants often offer a traditional Bajan buffet of fried fish, baked chicken, salads, and a selection of local roots and vegetables. Be cautious with the West Indian condiments; like the sun, they're hotter than you think. Typical Bajan drinks, besides Banks beer and Mount Gay rum, are *falernum* (a liqueur concocted of rum, sugar, lime juice, and almond essence) and *mauby* (a nonalcoholic drink made by boiling bitter bark and spices, straining the mixture, and sweetening it). You're sure to enjoy the fresh fruit punch, with or without the rum.

What to Wear

Barbados's dress code is conservative and, on occasion, formal—a jacket and tie for gentlemen and a cocktail dress for ladies in the fanciest restaurants, particularly in winter. Other places are more casual, although jeans and shorts are always frowned upon at dinner. Beach attire should be worn only at the beach.

CATEGORY	COST*
$$$$	over $35
$$$	$25–$35
$$	$15–$25
$	under $15

per person for a main course at dinner

Bridgetown

CARIBBEAN

$ ✕ **Waterfront Cafe.** Alongside the busy Careenage, this friendly bistro is the perfect place to enjoy a drink, snack, or meal—and to people-watch. Locals and tourists gather at outdoor café tables for all-day dining on sandwiches, salads, fish, pasta, pepper-pot stew, and tasty Bajan snacks such as buljol, fish cakes, or plantation pork (plantains stuffed with spicy minced pork). The panfried flying-fish sandwich is especially popular. In the evening you can gaze from the brick and mirrored interior through the arched windows while savoring nouvelle creole cuisine, enjoying cool trade winds, and listening to live jazz. There's a special Carib Buffet and steel-pan music on Tuesday night from 7 to 9. ⊠ *Bridge House, The Careenage, Bridgetown, St. Michael,* ☎ *246/427–0093. AE, DC, MC, V. Closed Sun.*

East Coast

CARIBBEAN

$ ✕ **Atlantis Hotel.** People have enjoyed lunch with a view at this hotel's restaurant for more than 40 years. Under the direction of owner-chef Enid Maxwell, the staff serves up an enormous Bajan buffet daily, with pumpkin fritters, spinach cake, pickled breadfruit, fried flying fish, roast chicken, pepper-pot stew, and fried okra and eggplant. Homemade coconut pie tops the dessert list. The Atlantis is a lunch stop for many organized day tours. ⊠ *Tent Bay, Bathsheba, St. Joseph,* ☎ *246/433–9445. AE.*

$ ✕ **Bonito Beach Bar & Restaurant.** When you tour the rugged east coast, plan to lunch on Mrs. Enid Worrell's wholesome West Indian home cooking. The view of the Atlantic from the second-floor dining room is striking, and the Bajan buffet lunch includes fried fish and baked chicken accompanied by salads and vegetables fresh from the family garden. If your timing is right, Mrs. Worrell might have homemade cheesecake for dessert. The fresh fruit punch—with or without rum—is great. ⊠ *Coast Rd., Bathsheba, St. Joseph,* ☎ *246/433–9034. No credit cards.*

South Coast

CARIBBEAN

$$$ ✕ **Brown Sugar.** Ferns, hanging plants, and cascading waterfalls decorate this breezy multilevel restaurant in a restored Barbadian home, five minutes south of Bridgetown. At midday, local businesspeople come for the extensive Planters Buffet Luncheon—from cou-cou to pepper-pot stew. Dinner entrées include local black-belly lamb, creole orange chicken, and homemade desserts such as angel food chocolate mousse cake, passion fruit or nutmeg ice cream, and lime cheesecake. ⊠ *Bay St., Aquatic Gap, St. Michael,* ☎ *246/426–7684. AE, DC, MC, V. No lunch Sat.*

$$ ✕ **David's Place.** Come here for sophisticated Bajan cuisine in a prime
★   waterfront location on St. Lawrence Bay. Waves slap against the pilings of the open-air deck—a rhythmic accompaniment to the soft classical background music. To start, the pumpkin soup is divine. Specialties such as flying fish, pepper-pot stew, curried shrimp, and vegetarian dishes come with homemade cheddar-cheese bread. Dessert might be bread pudding, carrot cake with rum sauce, or coconut cream pie. David's has an extensive wine list. ⊠ *St. Lawrence Main Rd., Worthing, Christ Church,* ☎ *246/435–9755. AE, MC, V. Closed Mon. No lunch.*

CONTEMPORARY

$$$ ✕ **Josef's Restaurant.** The signature restaurant of Austrian restaura-
★   teur Josef Schwaiger is, perhaps, the most upscale dining spot on the south coast, in a fabulous seaside location that is perfect day or night. Fruits of the sea—fresh tuna, say, or red snapper fillet—are prominent on the menu, along with interesting selections prepared with a Caribbean-Asian twist. Grilled calamari with Oriental spice dressing is a starter that combines all those elements. And free-range chicken teriyaki with stir-fry noodles will tingle your taste buds. Pasta dishes assuage the vegetarian palate. ⊠ *St. Lawrence Gap, Dover, Christ Church,* ☎ *246/435–8245. Reservations essential. AE, DC, MC, V. No lunch Sat.*

ITALIAN

$$ ✕ **Bellini's Trattoria.** Soft Italian music and waves gently lapping beneath the Mediterranean-style veranda set the stage for informal yet romantic dining. The cuisine is classic northern Italian with a contemporary flair. Toast the evening with a Bellini cocktail (sparkling wine with a splash of fruit nectar), and start your meal with antipasto, a small gourmet pizza, or a tasty homemade pasta dish. Move on to the signature shrimp, veal, steak, or seafood dishes, and top it all off with excellent tiramisù. ⊠ *Little Bay Hotel, St. Lawrence Gap, Dover, Christ Church,* ☎ *246/435–7246. AE, DC, MC, V.*

SEAFOOD

$$ ✕ **Pisces.** Seafood is prepared here in every way—from charbroiled to sautéed. Specialties include conch strips in tempura, rich fish chowder, panfried fillets of flying fish with a toasted almond crust and a light mango-citrus sauce, and seared prawns in a fragrant curry sauce. There are also some chicken, beef, and pasta dishes. Whatever your selection, the herbs that flavor it and the accompanying vegetables will have come from the chef's garden. For dessert, if you're too full to try the bread pudding or yogurt lime cheesecake, the homemade rum-raisin ice cream is delicious. The restaurant has contemporary decor and is filled with hanging tropical plants and twinkling white lights that reflect on the water. ⊠ *St. Lawrence Gap, Dover, Christ Church,* ☎ *246/435–6564. AE, DC, MC, V. No lunch.*

$$ ✕ **The Crane.** Perched on a cliff with arguably the most striking setting on Barbados, The Crane in the Crane Beach Hotel is an informal luncheon spot during the day. You might dine on Crane seafood chowder—prepared with lobster, shrimp, dolphinfish, local vegetables, and a dash of sherry—or enjoy a light salad or sandwich while taking in the breathtaking view. In the evening, there's candlelight, a soft guitar, and fabulous grilled Caribbean lobster, seasoned with herbs, lime juice, and garlic butter and served in its shell. Landlubbers can order a perfect filet mignon, too. Sundays are really special: from 10 to 11 AM, there's a Gospel Brunch; from 12:30 to 3 PM, there's a traditional Bajan buffet, accompanied by steel-pan music. ⊠ *Crane Bay, St. Philip,* ☎ *246/423–6220. Reservations essential. AE, D, DC, MC, V.*

West Coast
CONTEMPORARY

$$$$ ✕ **The Cliff.** The mastery of Chef Paul Owens is the foundation of one
★ of the finest dining establishments in Barbados. Every candlelit table has a sea view. In fact, steep steps hug the cliff to which the restaurant clings and reach down to the sea to accommodate guests arriving by yacht. Imaginative art accents the tiered dining terrace. The artistry extends to the innovative menu, which offers excellent cuts of prime meat and fresh fish, creatively presented with nouvelle accents and accompanied by fresh local vegetables. Don't skip dessert, which falls in the sinful category. Service is impeccable, of course. ⊠ *Hwy. 1, Derricks, St. James,* ☎ *246/432–1922. AE, DC, MC, V. No lunch.*

$$ ✕ **Carambola.** Dramatic lighting, alfresco dining, and a cliffside set-
★ ting overlooking the sea make this restaurant one of the island's most romantic. The menu is a mix of classic French and Caribbean cuisines—with Asian touches for good measure. Start with a spicy crab tart, served with hollandaise sauce on a bed of sweet red peppers. For an entrée, try fillet of mahimahi broiled with Dijon mustard sauce, or sliced duck breast with a wild mushroom fumet served with stuffed tomatoes and *gratin dauphinoise* (potatoes au gratin). When you think you can't eat another bite, the *citron gâteau* (lime mousse on a pool of lemon coulis) is a wonderfully light finish. ⊠ *Hwy. 1, Derricks, St. James,* ☎ *246/432–0832. Reservations essential. AE, MC, V. Closed Sun. No lunch.*

ECLECTIC

$$ ✕ **Olives Bar & Bistro.** Owner-chef Larry Rogers and his wife, Michelle, have turned a quaint Bajan house in the center of Holetown into an intimate restaurant. Mediterranean and Caribbean flavors enliven gourmet pizzas and tasty salads at lunch or dinner; special dishes on the menu might include fresh seafood, such as seared yellowfin tuna with ratatouille, and tasty Swiss-style *rösti* potatoes (shredded and fried like a pancake) with smoked salmon and sour cream. Dine inside or on the courtyard; the popular upstairs bar is a great spot to mingle over coffee, refreshing drinks, or snacks (pizza, pastas, salads). ⊠ *2nd St., Holetown, St. James,* ☎ *246/432–2112. AE, MC, V.*

$$ ✕ **Ragamuffins.** The only restaurant on Barbados within an authentic chattel house, Ragamuffins is funky, lively, and affordable. The menu offers seafood, perfectly broiled T-bone steaks, West Indian curries, and vegetarian dishes such as Bajan stir-fried vegetables with noodles. Dine

inside or out. The kitchen is within sight of the bar—which is a popular meeting spot most evenings. ⊠ *1st St., Holetown, St. James,* ☎ *246/432–1295. AE, MC, V. No lunch.*

$ ✕ Angry Annie's. You can't miss this place, as it's just steps from the main road. Outside and inside, everything's painted in bright Caribbean pinks, blues, greens, and yellows. The food is just as lively: great barbecued "jump-up" ribs and chicken, grilled fresh fish or juicy steaks, "Rasta pasta" for vegetarians, and a variety of spicy curries. Eat inside on gaily colored furniture or outside under the stars—or take it away with you. ⊠ *1st St., Holetown, St. James,* ☎ *246/432–2119. AE, DC, MC, V.*

$ ✕ Baku Beach Bar. Whether you're going to the beach, coming from the beach, or just wanting to be near the beach, this is a great place for lunch or an informal dinner. Tables spill onto the courtyard, through tropical gardens, and out to a boardwalk by the sea. Try Caesar salad (with or without grilled flying fish or chicken), burgers, spareribs, or grilled fish served with the salsa of your choice: BBQ, fruit, pesto, herb lemon, béarnaise, ginger soy, fresh and sun-dried tomatoes, and more. On the side, you might want garlic bread, sautéed onions, rice pilaf, or spicy potato wedges. Got room for crème brûlée, lemon tart, or a brownie with ice cream? Maybe just dawdling over a cappuccino is enough. ⊠ *Hwy. 1, Holetown, St. James,* ☎ *246/432–2258. AE, MC, V.*

FRENCH

$$$ ✕ La Maison. Save this elegant dining terrace for a special occasion. ★ It appears to be shored up by enormous casuarina tree trunks actually growing through the roof, and it overlooks tranquil Paynes Bay. The French chef creates terrific seafood dishes, including a succulent grilled red snapper marinated with lime and herbs and sautéed spiced shrimp in a mango-and-lime salsa; or try the perfect rack of black-belly lamb with a garlic-herb crust. Chocolate soufflé with white-chocolate ice cream is a special dessert, but you also can't go wrong with homemade coconut flan. ⊠ *Hwy. 1, Holetown, St. James,* ☎ *246/432–1156. Reservations essential. AE, DC, MC, V. Closed Mon. No lunch.*

SEAFOOD

$$$$ ✕ Lone Star Garage Restaurant. In the 1940s this was the only garage ★ on the west coast; today it's a snazzy restaurant, where top chefs turn the finest raw ingredients into gastronomic delights and where celebrities may be seated at the next table (or staying in the adjacent Lone Star Garage Motel). Dinner might start with seafood ravioli with dill and lemon oil, or Thai crab cakes with sweet-and-sour dressing. Or break the bank and opt for the Iranian beluga caviar, served with blinis, new potatoes, and sour cream. Chilled shellfish with special dips, grilled soft-shell crabs with rosemary, or seared tuna are offered at both lunch and dinner. Steak or herb-basted chicken, with creamed potatoes or fries, and vegetarian dishes are also tasty choices. The extensive à la carte menu will please any palate. ⊠ *Hwy. 1, Mount Standfast, St. James,* ☎ *246/419–0598. AE, MC, V.*

Beaches

Bajan beaches have fine, white sand, and all are open to the public. Most have access from the road, so nonguest bathers don't have to pass through hotel properties.

EAST COAST

With long stretches of open beach, crashing ocean surf, rocky cliffs, and verdant hills, the windward side of Barbados is full of dramatic views. This is also where many Barbadians have second homes and spend their holidays. But be cautioned: swimming at east coast beaches is treacherous, even for strong swimmers, and *not* recommended. The waves are high, the bottom tends to be rocky, the currents are unpredictable, and the undertow is strong.

The rolling surf at **Bathsheba Soup Bowl** attracts surfers (it's the site of the Independence Classic Surfing Championships each November) and daydreamers. Along the Ermy Bourne Highway on the East Coast, **Barclays Park** has a beachfront where you can dip, wade, and play in tide pools, but serious swimming is unwise; there's a lovely shaded picnic area across the road.

SOUTH COAST

A young, energetic crowd favors the south coast beaches, which are broad, blessed with white, powdery sand, and dotted with tall palms. The reef-protected waters are crystal clear and safe for swimming and snorkeling. The surf is medium to high, and the waves get bigger and the winds stronger (windsurfers take note) the farther southeast you go.

Near popular **Accra Beach,** in Rockley, you'll find plenty of places to indulge in a meal or have a drink. You can rent equipment for snorkeling and other water sports, and there's a convenient parking lot. **Casuarina Beach,** at the east end of the St. Lawrence Gap area, always has a nice breeze and a fair amount of surf. Public access is from Maxwell Coast Road. Refreshments are available at the Casuarina Beach Hotel. **Needham's Point** and its lighthouse are at the south end of Carlisle Bay. One of the best beaches, it's crowded with locals on weekends and holidays. The Carlisle Bay Centre has changing rooms and showers to accommodate cruise-ship passengers spending a day at the beach. In Worthing, next to the Sandy Beach Island Resort, **Sandy Beach** has shallow, calm waters and a picturesque lagoon, making it an ideal location for families. There's parking on the main road, and plenty of places nearby sell food and drink.

The cove at **Bottom Bay,** north of Sam Lord's Castle, is mesmerizing. Follow the steps down the cliff to a strip of white sand lined by coconut palms and washed by an aquamarine sea. There's even a cave to explore. It's out of the way and not near restaurants, so bring a picnic lunch. **Crane Beach** is an exquisite crescent of pink sand protected by steep cliffs. As attractive as this location is now, it was named not for any elegant long-legged wading birds but for the crane used for hauling and loading cargo when this area was a busy port. There's a lifeguard on duty, but the water can be rough. The rolling surf is great for bodysurfing if you're an experienced swimmer. Lunch and changing rooms are available at Crane Beach Hotel for $2.50 per person (which you can apply toward drinks or a meal) for beach access—through the hotel and down about 200 steps. **Silver Sands Beach,** close to the southernmost tip of the island, is a beautiful strand of white sand that always has a stiff breeze, which attracts intermediate and advanced windsurfers.

WEST COAST

Gentle Caribbean waves lap the west coast, and the stunning coves and sandy beaches are shaded by leafy mahogany trees. The water is calm and clear—perfect for swimming and other water sports. An almost unbroken chain of beaches runs between Speightstown, in the north, and Bridgetown. Elegant homes and luxury hotels take up most of the beachfront property in this area, Barbados's Platinum Coast.

Although west coast beaches are seldom crowded, they aren't isolated. Vendors stroll by, selling handmade baskets, hats, dolls, jewelry—

even original watercolors; owners of private boats offer waterskiing, parasailing, and snorkeling opportunities. There are no concession stands, but hotels welcome nonguests for terrace lunches (wear a cover-up), and you can buy picnic items at supermarkets in Holetown.

Brighton Beach, just north of Bridgetown, is large, open, and convenient to the port. Locals often take quick swims here on hot days. **Mullins Beach,** just south of Speightstown at Mullins Bay, is a good place to spend the day. The calm water is safe for swimming and snorkeling, there's easy parking on the main road, and Mullins Beach Bar (☎ 246/422–1878) serves snacks, meals, and drinks. **Paynes Bay,** south of Holetown, is lined with luxury hotels. It's a very pretty area, with plenty of beach to go around and good snorkeling. Parking areas and public access are available opposite the Coach House. Grab a bite to eat and liquid refreshments at Bomba's Beach Bar (☎ 246/432–0569).

Outdoor Activities and Sports

Participant Sports

FISHING

Fishing is great year-round—but ideal from January to April. Half- or full-day charter trips are available for serious deep-sea fishers looking for billfish or for those who prefer angling in calm coastal waters where wahoo, barracuda, and other small fish reside. Charters depart from the Careenage, in Bridgetown. Expect to pay $60–$120 per person, depending on the length of time, size of the boat, and whether it's a shared or private charter.

Billfisher II (✉ Bridge House, the Careenage, Bridgetown, ☎ 246/431–0741) is a 40-ft Pacemaker that can accommodate up to six people; trips include drinks and transportation to and from the boat. Full-day charters include a full lunch and guaranteed fish. **Blue Jay** (✉ St. James, ☎ 246/422–2098) is a fully equipped 45-ft Sport Fisherman, with a crew that knows where blue marlin, sailfish, barracuda, and king-fish play. Four people can be accommodated; each is guaranteed his or her own rod and chair and can invite, free of charge, a spouse or guest. Drinks and snacks are provided. **Blue Marlin Charters** (✉ Christ Church, ☎ 246/436–4322) operates *Blue Marlin*, a tournament-rigged, custom-built 36-ft Sport Fisherman, and *Idyll Time*, a 42-ft fishing boat. Both are fully equipped, and transportation, snacks, and beverages are included; lunch is served on full-day charters.

GOLF

Barbadians love golf, and golfers love Barbados. If you want to learn to play or improve your game, the **Barbados Academy of Golf & Public Driving Range** (✉ ABC Hwy., Balls Complex, Christ Church, ☎ 246/420–7405) has a chipping and putting green, with sand bunkers and 50 hitting bays. The adjacent 18-hole miniature golf course is fun for the whole family. Both are open daily 8 AM–11 PM, and snacks are available.

Almond Beach Village (✉ Hwy. 1B, Heywoods, St. Peter, ☎ 246/422–4900), on the island's northwest corner, has a 9-hole, par-3 executive course for guest use only; there's no fee, and clubs are provided. **Barbados Golf Club** (✉ Hwy. 7, Durants, Christ Church, ☎ 246/426–8463), the first public golf course on Barbados, opened in summer 2000. The par-72, 18-hole championship course was originally designed in 1974 and redesigned and reconstructed by noted golf architect Ron Kirby. Greens fees are $115 for 18 holes, $70 for 9 holes. Several hotels offer golf privileges, with preferential tee-time reservations and reduced rates. Club and shoe rentals are available. **Club Rockley Barbados** (✉

Golf Club Rd., Rockley, Christ Church, ☎ 246/435–7873), on the southeast coast near Sam Lord's Castle, has a challenging 9-hole course that can be played as 18 from varying tee positions. It's open to the public daily, and club rentals are available. Greens fees are $27.50 for 9 holes. The **Royal Westmoreland Golf Club** (✉ Hwy. 2A, Westmoreland, St. James, ☎ 246/422–4653) has a world-class Robert Trent Jones Jr., 18-hole championship course that meanders through the former 500-acre Westmoreland Sugar Estate. Greens fees include use of an electric cart; equipment rental is available. To play here, you must stay here or at a hotel with access privileges. Greens fees are $92 for 9 holes or $150 for 18 holes. The prestigious **Sandy Lane Golf Club** (✉ Hwy. 1, Paynes Bay, St. James, ☎ 246/432–2829) has undergone a dramatic redesign by renowned architect Tom Fazio. Golfers can play on its bottom 9 or its 18-hole Mollyneux course; another 18 holes should be complete by 2003. Greens fees are $60 for 9 holes or $100 for 18 holes.

HIKING

Hilly but not mountainous, the northern interior and the east coast are ideal for hiking. The **Arbib Heritage and Nature Trail** (✉ Speightstown, St. Peter, ☎ 246/426–2421), maintained by the Barbados National Trust, is actually two trails—one offers a rigorous hike through gullies and plantations to old ruins and little-known north-country areas; the other is a shorter, easier walk through Speightstown's side streets and past an ancient church and chattel houses. Guided hikes take place on Wednesday, Thursday, and Saturday 9–2:30 (book by 3 PM the day before) and cost $7.50. The **Barbados National Trust** (✉ Wildey House, Wildey, St. Michael, ☎ 246/426–2421) sponsors free 5-mi (8-km) walks year-round on Sunday from 6 AM to about 9 AM and from 3:30 PM to 6 PM, as well as monthly moonlight hikes. Experienced guides group you with others of similar levels of ability. Wear sensible shoes and a hat, and bring your camera. Hikes start and finish at the same location. Check newspapers or call the trust for the meeting place.

HORSEBACK RIDING

A ride through the hilly north country or along the beach is exhilarating, and equestrian tours can accommodate any level of experience. The **Caribbean International Riding Center** (✉ Auburn, St. Joseph, ☎ 246/422–7433 or 246/420–1246) offers one- and two-hour rides through the Scotland District and longer treks that continue on to Morgan Lewis Beach, on the Atlantic coast. Prices range from $40 for a one-hour trail ride to $82.50 for a 2½-hour trek; transportation to and from your hotel is included.

PARASAILING

Parasailing is available, wind conditions permitting, on the beaches of St. James and Christ Church. The chute is attached to a speedboat with a launching and landing platform; a hydraulic winch system hauls you in simply and safely. **Skyrider Parasail** (☎ 246/435–0570) operates from Bay Street in Bridgetown, but the boat picks people up all along either coast; just wave to the boatman. Rates are $45 per flight; MasterCard and Visa are accepted.

SCUBA DIVING AND SNORKELING

There are more than two dozen dive sites along the west coast between Maycocks Bay and Bridgetown and off the south coast as far as the St. Lawrence Gap. Certified divers can explore flat coral reefs and see sea fans and corals, huge barrel sponges, and more than 50 varieties of fish. Nine sunken wrecks are dived regularly, and at least 10 more are accessible to experts. Underwater visibility is generally 80–90 ft (24–28 m). The calm waters along the west coast are also ideal for snorkeling. The marine reserve, a stretch of protected reef between Sandy Lane and the Colony Club, contains beautiful coral formations accessible from the beach.

On the west coast, **Bell Buoy** is a large dome-shaped reef where huge brown coral tree forests and schools of fish delight all categories of divers at depths ranging from 20 to 60 ft (6 to 18 m). The 165-ft freighter *Pamir* lies in 60 ft of water off Six Men's Bay; still intact, you can peer through its portholes and view dozens of varieties of tropical fish. **Maycocks Bay,** on the northwest coast, is a particularly enticing site; large coral reefs are separated by corridors of white sand, and visibility is often 100 ft (30 m) or more. At **Dottins Reef,** off Holetown, you'll see schooling fish, barracudas, and turtles at depths of 40–60 ft (12–18 m). **Silver Bank** is a healthy coral reef with beautiful fish and sea fans; you may get a glimpse of the *Atlantis* submarine at 60–80 ft (18–24 m). Not to be missed is the **Stavronikita,** a scuttled Greek freighter at about 135 ft (41 m); hundreds of butterfly fish hang out around its mast, and the thin rays of sunlight filtering down through the water make fully exploring the huge ship a wonderfully eerie experience.

Farther south, **Carlisle Bay** is a natural harbor and marine park just below Bridgetown. Here you can retrieve empty bottles thrown overboard by generations of sailors and see cannons and cannonballs, anchors, and three unique shipwrecks (*Berwyn, Fox,* and *CTrek*) lying in 25–40 ft (8–12 m) of water, all close enough to visit on the same dive. The **Eilon,** a freighter confiscated for drug running, is the island's newest wreck. Sunk in 1996, it sits in 60 ft (18 m) of water in Carlisle Bay near three earlier wrecks.

Dive shops provide a two-hour beginner's "resort" course ($70–$75) or a weeklong certification course (about $350), followed by a shallow dive. Once you're certified, a one-tank dive runs about $50–$55; a two-tank dive is $70–$80. All equipment is supplied, and you can purchase multidive packages. Gear for snorkeling is available (free or for a small rental fee) from most hotels. Snorkelers can usually accompany dive trips for $20 for a one- or two-hour trip.

On the south coast, **Dive Boat Safari** (⊠ Grand Barbados Beach Resort, Needham's Point, Bridgetown, St. Michael, ☎ 246/427–4350) offers full dives and instruction. The **Dive Shop, Ltd.** (⊠ Aquatic Gap, St. Michael, ☎ 246/426–9947; 800/693–3483 in the U.S.; 888/575–3483 in Canada) is the island's oldest dive shop. On the west coast, **Hightide Watersports** (⊠ Coral Reef Club, Holetown, St. James, ☎ 246/432–0931 or 800/513–5763) offers one- and two-tank dives, night reef/wreck/drift dives, the full range of PADI instruction, and free transportation. **West Side Scuba Centre** (⊠ Sunset Crest Beach Club, Baku Beach, Holetown, St. James, ☎ 246/432–2558) offers all levels of PADI instruction, reef and wreck dives, night dives, underwater video and camera rental, and free transportation.

SEA EXCURSIONS

Minisubmarine voyages are enormously popular with families and those who enjoy watching fish but can't snorkel or dive. The 48-passenger **Atlantis III** turns the Caribbean into a giant aquarium. The 45-minute trip aboard the 50-ft submarine takes you to wrecks and reefs as deep as 150 ft (46 m). Special nighttime dives, using high-power searchlights, are spectacular. ⊠ *Shallow Draft Harbour, Bridgetown,* ☎ *246/436–8929.* ☞ *$80.*

The **Atlantis SEATREC** (Sea Tracking and Reef Exploration Craft; ⊠ Shallow Draft Harbour, Bridgetown, ☎ 246/436–8929) is a 46-passenger vessel with large windows below the surface through which you can view the underwater marine life on a near-shore reef. Trips last an hour and cost $35.

Party boats depart from Bridgetown's harbor, near the Careenage, for lunchtime snorkeling or sunset cruises. Prices are $65 per person and include transportation to and from the dock. The 44-ft catamaran **Limbo Lady** (☎ 246/420–5418) sails along the captivating west coast, stopping for a swim, snorkeling, and a Bajan buffet lunch. Sunset cruises are another option. A five-hour cruise on the 54-ft custom-built catamaran **Cool Runnings** (☎ 246/436–0911) includes stops along the coast for snorkeling on a coral reef, exploring a shallow shipwreck, and visiting sea turtles in a quiet bay; lunch is served on board. The 53-ft catamaran **Tiami** (☎ 246/430–0900) offers an early morning breakfast cruise, a luncheon cruise to a secluded bay, or a romantic sunset and moonlight cruise with special catering and live music; all cruises last four hours. **Secret Love** (☎ 246/432–1972), a 41-ft Morgan sailboat, offers daily lunchtime or evening snorkeling cruises for no more than 14 people.

The red-sail **Jolly Roger** (☎ 246/436–6424) "pirate" ship runs lunch-and-snorkeling sails along the west coast. Be prepared for a rather raucous time, with rope swinging, plank walking, and other games—and plenty of calypso music. The cruise costs about $65 per person, with complimentary drinks. Four- and five-hour daytime cruises along the west coast on the 100-ft MV **Harbour Master** (☎ 246/430–0900) stop in Holetown and land at beaches along the way; evening cruises are shorter but add a buffet dinner and entertainment. Day or night you can view the briny deep from the ship's onboard 34-seat semisubmersible. Either cruise runs about $65 per person.

SURFING

The best surfing is on the east coast, at Bathsheba Soup Bowl, where the Independence Classic Surfing Championship (an international competition) is held every November—when the surf is at its peak. For information, call the **Barbados Surfing Association** (☎ 246/228–5117).

TENNIS AND SQUASH

Most hotels have tennis courts that can be reserved day and night. Appropriate dress is expected on the courts. On the west coast public tennis courts are available for free on a first-come, first-served basis at **Folkestone Park** (✉ Holetown, ☎ 246/422–2314). On the south coast, the **National Tennis Centre** (✉ Sir Garfield Sobers Sports Complex, Wildey, St. Michael, ☎ 246/437–6010) charges $12 per hour and requires reservations.

At **Club Rockley Barbados** (✉ Golf Club Rd., Rockley, Christ Church, ☎ 246/435–7880) nonguests can reserve courts for $10 per hour. At the **Barbados Squash Club** (✉ Marine House, Hastings, Christ Church, ☎ 246/427–7913), court fees run $9 for 45 minutes; games can be set up with players of similar ability.

WINDSURFING

Barbados is part of the World Cup Windsurfing Circuit and one of the best locations in the world for windsurfing. Winds are strongest November through April at the island's southern tip, which is where the Barbados Windsurfing Championships are held in mid-January. Use of boards and equipment is often among the amenities included in the room rate at larger hotels, and these can usually be rented by nonguests.

Club Mistral (✉ Oistins, Christ Church, ☎ 246/428–7277) is a great place to learn to windsurf because the waves here are usually flat. More experienced windsurfers congregate at **Silver Rock Windsurfing Club**

(⊠ Silver Rock Hotel, Silver Sands Beach, Christ Church, ☎ 246/428–2866), where the surf ranges from 3 to 15 ft (1 to 5 m), providing an exhilarating windsurfing experience.

Spectator Sports

CRICKET

Barbados is mad for cricket. Young or old, male or female—Bajans love it. Although the season is from May to late December, international test matches are usually played from January to April. The Sandy Lane Gold Cup is held in March. Tickets to cricket matches at Kensington Oval, Bridgetown, range from $7.50 to $30. For information call the **Barbados Cricket Association** (☎ 246/436–1397).

HORSE RACING

Horse racing is administered by the **Barbados Turf Club** (☎ 246/426–3980) and takes place on alternate Saturdays most of the year at the **Garrison Savannah,** a six-furlong grass oval in Christ Church, about 3 mi (5 km) south of Bridgetown. The important races are the 5000 run in February, the Sandy Lane Gold Cup in May, the United Barbados Derby Day in August, and the Heineken Stakes on Boxing Day (day after Christmas). Post time is 12:30 PM, and general admission is $1 (grandstand seats are $5; those in the Club House are $12.50).

POLO

Polo matches are inexpensive (about $2.50) and are played at the **Barbados Polo Club** in Holders Hill, St. James (☎ 246/432–1802), on Wednesday and Saturday from October through April.

Shopping

Areas and Malls

Bridgetown's **Broad Street** is the primary shopping area. **DaCostas Mall,** in the historic Colonnade Building on Broad Street, has more than 25 shops that sell everything from Piaget to postcards. Broad Street's **Mall 34** has 22 shops where you can buy duty-free goods, souvenirs, and snacks. At the **Cruise Ship Terminal** shopping arcade, passengers can buy both duty-free goods and Barbadian-made merchandise at more than 30 boutiques and a dozen vendor carts and stalls.

Holetown and St. Lawrence Gap each have a **Chattel House Village,** a cluster of brightly colored shops selling local products, fashions, beachwear, and souvenirs. In Holetown's **DaCostas West Mall,** a miniversion of the Bridgetown mall, you'll find duty-free goods, island wear, and groceries. **Sunset Crest,** also in Holetown, has a branch of the Cave Shepherd department store, a supermarket, a pharmacy, and several small shops. The **Quayside Shopping Center,** in Rockley, Christ Church, has a small group of boutiques.

Department Stores

Cave Shepherd (⊠ Broad St., Bridgetown, ☎ 246/431–2121) offers a wide selection of luxury goods; branch stores are in Holetown, at the airport, and in the Cruise Ship Terminal. **Harrison's** (⊠ Broad St., Bridgetown, ☎ 246/431–5500) has 11 locations—including its two large stores on Broad Street and one each at the airport and the Cruise Ship Terminal—offering luxury name-brand goods from the fashion corners of the world.

Specialty Items

ANTIQUES

You'll find British antiques as well as wonderful local pieces—particularly mahogany furniture. Look for planters' chairs and the classic Barbadian rocking chair, as well as old prints and paintings. **Anti-**

quaria (✉ Spring Garden Hwy., St. Michael's Row, Bridgetown, ☎ 246/426–0635; ✉ Opposite Sandpiper Inn, Holetown, St. James, ☎ 246/432–2647) sells antique silver, brassware, mahogany furniture, and maps and engravings. Both branches are open every day but Sunday. **Greenwich House Antiques** (✉ Greenwich Village, Trents Hill, St. James, ☎ 246/432–1169) fills an entire plantation house with Barbadian mahogany furniture, crystal, silver, china, books, and pictures; it's open daily 10:30–5:30.

CLOTHES

Dresses and resort wear are often handmade of hand-printed fabrics. **Coconut Junction & Lazy Days** (✉ Quayside Shopping Center, Rockley, Christ Church, ☎ 246/435–8115), actually two shops in one, has top-quality beachwear, beach accessories, and beach equipment. Try **Colours of de Caribbean** (✉ Waterfront Marina, Bridgetown, ☎ 246/436–8522) for "wearable art"—original hand-painted and batik fashions—as well as handmade jewelry and accessories, decorative art that represents the Caribbean lifestyle and experience. Everything is designed and made in the Caribbean. Chances are you'll buy at least one T-shirt to commemorate your visit to Barbados. Check out the colorful ones from **Irie Blue**, which are designed and made in Barbados. You'll find them in many gift shops or at their own shops (✉ DaCostas Mall, Broad St., Bridgetown, St. Michael, ☎ 246/431–0017; or Worthing, Christ Church, ☎ 246/435–7699).

DUTY-FREE GOODS

Duty-free luxury goods—china, crystal, cameras, porcelain, leather items, electronics, jewelry, perfume, and clothing—are found in Bridgetown's Broad Street department stores and their branches, at the Cruise Ship Terminal (for passengers only), and in the departure lounge at Grantley Adams International Airport. Prices are often 30% to 40% less than at home. To buy items at duty-free prices, you must produce your outbound travel ticket and passport at the time of purchase—or you can have your purchases delivered free to the airport or harbor for pickup. Duty-free alcohol, tobacco products, and some electronic equipment *must* be delivered to you at the airport or harbor.

Little Switzerland (☎ 246/431–0030) is the anchor shop at DaCostas Mall on Broad Street in Bridgetown and has a branch at the Cruise Ship Terminal. You'll find perfume, jewelry, cameras, audio equipment, Swarovski and Waterford crystal, and Wedgwood china. The **Royal Shop** (✉ 32 Broad St., Bridgetown, ☎ 246/429–7072) carries fine watches and jewelry fashioned in Italian gold, Caribbean silver, diamonds, and other gems.

HANDICRAFTS

Typical crafts include pottery; items made of metal, wood, glass, shells, or paper; jewelry; hand-printed fabrics; handmade dolls; and watercolors and other paintings (originals and prints). You can buy such handicrafts in stores year-round, at the Barbados Museum Annual Craft Fair in December, and at major festivals (Crop Over, Oistins Fish Festival, Holetown Festival, etc.).

The **Best of Barbados** (✉ Worthing, Christ Church, ☎ 246/421–6900), which has a total of 13 locations, offers high-quality artwork and crafts, in both "native style" and modern designs; everything is made or designed on Barbados. Local artist Jill Walker's cheerful watercolors and prints are featured here. **Earthworks Pottery** (✉ Edgehill Heights, No. 2, St. Thomas, ☎ 246/425–0223) is a family-owned and -operated pottery where you can purchase anything from a dish or knickknack to a complete dinner service or one-of-a-kind art piece.

The products are sold in gift shops throughout the island, but the biggest selection is at the pottery, where you also can watch the potters work. **Fairfield Pottery & Gallery** (✉ Bridgetown, St. Michael, ☎ 246/424–3800) is in an old syrup boiling house. Each piece here is handcrafted of local clay and individually painted; call for a tour of the works. Items are for sale on-site and in island gift shops.

Pelican Craft Centre (✉ Harbour Rd., Bridgetown, ☎ 246/427–5350) is a cluster of workshops halfway between the Cruise Ship Terminal and downtown Bridgetown, where craftspeople create and sell "100% Barbadian-made" leather goods, batik, basketry, carvings, jewelry, glass art, paintings, pottery, and other items. It's open weekdays 9–6 and Saturday 9–2, with extended hours during holidays or to accommodate cruise-ship arrivals. In the chattel houses at **Tyrol Cot Heritage Village** (✉ Codrington Hill, St. Michael, ☎ 246/424–2074) you can watch local artisans make hand-painted figurines, straw baskets, clothing, paintings, pottery, etc.—and, of course, buy their wares.

Nightlife and the Arts

Nightlife

When the sun goes down, the musicians come out and folks in Barbados "lime" (which can be anything from a "chat-up" to a full-blown "jump-up"). Performances by reggae groups and calypso singers are major events, and tickets can be hard to come by—but give it a try. Most large resorts have nightly entertainment in season, and nightclubs often have live bands for listening and dancing. The busiest bars and dance clubs rage until 3 AM. On Saturday nights, some clubs—especially those with live music—charge a cover of about $10.

Party animals will want to make a late-night (after 11) excursion to **Baxter Road** for Bajan street snacks, local rum, great gossip, and good storytelling. The **Oistins Fish Fry** is the place to be on weekend evenings, when the south coast fishing village becomes an outdoor street fair. Barbecued chicken and flying fish are served right from the coal pot; servings are huge and inexpensive. Drinks, music, and dancing add to the fun.

BARS

Barbados supports the rum industry in more than 1,200 "rum shops," simple bars where men (mostly) congregate to discuss the world's ills, and in more sophisticated inns, where you'll find world-class rum drinks made with the island's renowned Mount Gay and Cockspur brands.

The **Boatyard** (✉ Bay St., Bridgetown, ☎ 246/436–2622) has a pub atmosphere, with both a DJ and live bands; from happy hour until the wee hours, the patrons are mostly local and visiting professionals. Head for the **Rusty Pelican** (✉ The Careenage, Bridgetown, St. Michael, ☎ 246/436–7778), overlooking the bustling waterfront, to see and be seen while listening to the light strains of a guitar. **Waterfront Cafe** (✉ The Careenage, Bridgetown, ☎ 246/427–0093) has live jazz in the evening, with a small dance floor for dancing. The wharf-side location adds to the atmosphere.

On the south coast, **Bubba's Sports Bar** (✉ Rockley Main Rd., Rockley, Christ Church, ☎ 246/435–6217) has three 10-ft (3-m) video screens and a dozen TVs tuned in to sporting events. You can take in the action while you sip a Banks and enjoy a Bubba burger, kebabs, or a juicy steak. **Café Sol** (✉ St. Lawrence Gap, Dover, Christ Church, ☎ 246/435–9531) has a wraparound terrace with a great view of the St. Lawrence Gap strip. Margaritas (rubbed with sugar not salt) will fortify you for the late-night complimentary Spanish dance lessons. **Champers** (⊠ Hwy. 1, Hastings, Christ Church, ☎ 246/435–6644) is a waterfront wine bar, where folks gather for good conversation, a great view, snacks, and a selection from the extensive wine list.

On the west coast, **Coach House** (⊠ Hwy. 1, Paynes Bay, St. James, ☎ 246/432–1163) has live entertainment nightly and live sports via satellite TV. **Upstairs at Olives** (⊠ 2nd St., Holetown, St. James, ☎ 246/432–2112) is a sophisticated watering hole. Enjoy cocktails and conversation seated amid potted palms and cooled by ceiling fans—either before or after dinner downstairs.

DANCE CLUBS

The most popular club is still **After Dark** (⊠ St. Lawrence Gap, Dover, Christ Church, ☎ 246/435–6547), with the longest bar on the island; a jazz-club annex; and an outdoor area featuring live appearances of reggae, calypso, and *soca* (an upbeat, sexy variation of calypso) headliners such as Krosfyah and Red Plastic Bag. **Harbour Lights** (⊠ Marine Villa, Bay St., Bridgetown, St. Michael, ☎ 246/436–7225) claims to be the "home of the party animal" and, most any night, features dancing under the stars to live reggae and soca music. The **Ship Inn** (⊠ St. Lawrence Gap, Dover, Christ Church, ☎ 246/435–6961) is a large, friendly pub with local band music for dancing.

THEME NIGHTS

On Wednesday and Friday evenings at the **Plantation Restaurant and Garden Theater,** the Tropical Spectacular calypso cabaret features dancing, fire eating, limbo, steel-band music, and the sounds of a top reggae and soca band. The fun begins at 6:30 PM. A Barbadian buffet dinner, unlimited drinks, transportation, and the show cost $75; for the show and drinks only, it's $37.50. ⊠ *St. Lawrence Rd., Dover, Christ Church,* ☎ *246/428–5048. AE, MC, V.*

The Arts

GALLERIES

The **Barbados Gallery of Art** (⊠ The Garrison, Bush Hill, St. Michael, ☎ 246/228–0149) is the only museum on Barbados dedicated to the visual arts. Its permanent collection includes artwork from the Caribbean, South America, and the United States. Admission is $2.50 weekdays and $1 on Saturday. The gallery is closed Sunday and Monday. The Cunard Gallery at the **Barbados Museum** (⊠ The Garrison, Bush Hill, St. Michael, ☎ 246/427–0201 or 246/436–1956) has a permanent collection of 20th-century Barbadian and Caribbean paintings and engravings; the Connell Gallery houses European decorative arts. The galleries are closed on Sunday and Monday, and there's a small entrance fee. **Queen's Park Art Gallery** (⊠ Queen's Park, Bridgetown, St. Michael, ☎ 246/427–2345), managed by the National Culture Foundation, is the island's largest gallery. It's open daily, and exhibits change monthly.

THEATER

The Thursday night (6:30–10) folkloric show *1627 and All That* traces island culture from colonization through slavery and emancipation to the present time. It's performed by energetic dancers dressed in period costumes and accompanied by lively steel-band music. Unlimited complimentary drinks are included; pay more for a Bajan buffet dinner and transportation. ⊠ *Barbados Museum, Hwy. 7, Garrison, St. Michael,* ☎ *246/428–1627.* ⊟ *$27.50 for show and drinks; $60 for show, drinks, dinner, and transportation. AE, MC, V.*

Exploring Barbados

The terrain of the island's 11 parishes changes dramatically from one to the next, and so does the pace and ambience. Bridgetown, the capital, is a rather sophisticated city. West coast resorts and private homes ooze luxury, whereas the small villages and vast sugar plantations found throughout central Barbados mark the island's history. The heavy Atlantic surf designed the cliffs of the dramatic east coast, and the northeast is called Scotland because of its hilly landscape. Along the lively south coast a palpable energy continues day and night.

The **Barbados National Trust** (✉ Wildey House, Wildey, St. Michael, ☎ 246/426–2421) has designed the Heritage Passport to some of Barbados's most popular attractions. When the holder pays full admission to visit some attractions, the passport will be stamped to validate free admission to other sights. Passports are free, and you can pick them up at displays in shops, hotels, and restaurants.

Bridgetown

This bustling city is a major duty-free port. The principal thoroughfare is Broad Street, which leads west from National Heroes Square (formerly Trafalgar Square). The busy capital is complete with rush hours and traffic congestion. The shopping area is compact.

Numbers in the margin correspond to points of interest on the Bridgetown map.

SIGHTS TO SEE

❶ **Barbados Synagogue.** Representing one of the oldest Jewish congregations in the Western Hemisphere, this synagogue began with Jews who left Brazil in the 1620s and introduced sugarcane to Barbados. The adjoining cemetery has tombstones dating from the 1630s. The original house of worship, built in 1654, was destroyed in an 1831 hurricane. The building was rebuilt in 1833 and restored by the Barbados National Trust in 1992. Services are held, and the building is open to the public. ✉ *Synagogue La., St. Michael,* ☎ *246/426–5792.* ☞ *Donation requested.* ⏰ *Weekdays 9–4.*

❷ **The Careenage.** Bridgetown's natural harbor and gathering place is where, in the early days, schooners were careened (turned on their sides) to be scraped of barnacles and repainted. Today the Careenage serves as a marina for pleasure yachts and excursion boats. The Chamberlain Bridge and the Charles O'Neal Bridge cross the Careenage.

❸ **National Heroes Square.** Renamed in 1999 (formerly Trafalgar Square), this square lies between the Parliament Buildings and the Careenage and marks the center of town. Its monument to Lord Horatio Nelson predates Nelson's Column in London's Trafalgar Square by 27 years. (Nelson was in Barbados briefly in 1777, when he was a 19-year-old navy lieutenant.) Also here are a war memorial and a fountain that commemorates the 1865 advent of running water on Barbados.

❹ **Parliament Buildings.** Adjacent to National Heroes Square, these Victorian buildings were built around 1870 to house the British Commonwealth's third-oldest parliament. A series of stained-glass windows depicts British monarchs from James I to Victoria. Like so many of Bridgetown's oldest buildings, they stand beside a growing number of modern offices.

❻ **Queen's Park.** Northeast of Bridgetown, Queen's Park contains one of the island's largest trees, an immense baobab more than 10 centuries old. Queen's Park House, the historic home of the British troop commander, has been converted into a theater with an exhibition room on

Barbados
Synagogue. . . **1**

The
Careenage . . **2**

National
Heroes
Square **3**

Parliament
Buildings **4**

Queen's
Park **6**

St. Michael's
Cathedral . . . **5**

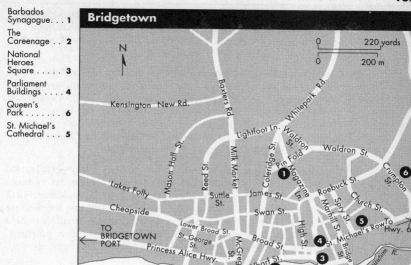

Bridgetown

the lower floor and a restaurant. ⊠ *Constitution Rd., St. Michael.* 📮 *Free.* ☉ *Daily 9–5.*

⑤ St. Michael's Cathedral. Although no one has proved it conclusively, George Washington, on his only visit outside the United States, is said to have worshiped at St. Michael's Cathedral. The original structure was nearly a century old when Washington presumably visited in 1751. Destroyed twice by hurricanes, it was rebuilt in 1784 and again in 1831. ⊠ *Spry St., east of National Heroes Sq., St. Michael.*

Southern Barbados

In Christ Church, on the heavily traveled south coast, you'll find the St. Lawrence Gap; condos; high-rise hotels; beach parks; and many places to eat, drink, and shop. This area is much busier and more developed than the west coast. In contrast, the broad, flat terrain in the southeast comprises acre upon acre of cane fields, interrupted only by an occasional oil rig and a few tiny villages hugging crossroads. Along the byways are colorful chattel houses, the property of tenant farmers. Historically, these typically Barbadian, ever-expandable houses were built to be dismantled and moved as required.

Numbers in the margin correspond to points of interest on the Barbados map.

SIGHTS TO SEE

✋ ⑦ Barbados Museum. This intriguing museum, in the former British Military Prison (1815) in the historic Garrison area, has artifacts from Arawak days (around 400 BC) and galleries that depict 19th-century military history and everyday life. You'll see cane-harvesting tools, wedding dresses, ancient (and frightening) dentistry instruments, and slave sale accounts kept in a spidery copperplate handwriting. You'll also find wildlife and natural history exhibits, an art gallery, a children's gallery, a gift shop, and a café. ✉ *Hwy. 7, Garrison Savannah, St. Michael,* ☎ *246/427–0201 or 246/436–1956.* ✉ *$5.* ☉ *Mon.–Sat. 9–5, Sun. 2–6.*

⑯ Codrington Theological College. An impressive stand of royal palms lines the road leading to the coral-stone buildings and serene grounds of Codrington College, an Anglican seminary founded in 1745 on a cliff overlooking Consett Bay. You're welcome to tour the buildings and walk the nature trails. Keep in mind, though, that this is a theological college; beachwear isn't appropriate. ✉ *Sargeant St., Conset Bay, St. John,* ☎ *246/433–1274.* ✉ *$2.50.* ☉ *Daily 10–4.*

⑩ Emancipation Statue. This larger-than-life statue of a slave—with raised hands, evoking both contempt and victory, and broken chains hanging from each wrist—is commonly referred to as the Bussa Statue. Bussa was the man who, in the early part of the 19th century, led the first slave rebellion in Barbados. The statue overlooks a broad cane field just outside Bridgetown, making the monument all the more poignant. ✉ *St. Barnabas Roundabout (intersection of ABC Hwy. and Hwy. 5), St. Michael.*

⑧ Harry Bayley Observatory. Built in 1963, this is the headquarters of the Barbados Astronomical Society. The observatory, equipped with a 14-inch reflector telescope, is the only one in the Eastern Caribbean. ✉ *Off Hwy. 6, Clapham, St. Michael,* ☎ *246/426–1317 or 246/422–2394.* ✉ *$4.* ☉ *Fri. 8:30 AM–11:30 PM.*

㉘ Malibu Beach Club. Located just north of Bridgetown, the fun-loving Malibu Rum people encourage visitors taking a distillery tour to make a day of it. The beach and water sports are adjacent to the Visitors Centre. Lunch and drinks are served at the beachside grill. ✉ *Black Rock, Brighton, St. Michael,* ☎ *246/425–9393.* ✉ *$7.50; $27.50 with lunch; $37.50 day pass.* ☉ *Weekdays 9–5.*

㉙ Mount Gay Rum Visitors Centre. On this popular 45-minute tour you learn the colorful story behind the world's oldest rum. Although the distillery is elsewhere, tour guides explain the rum-making procedure; historic and modern equipment are on display, and rows and rows of barrels are stored in this location. The tour concludes with a tasting and an opportunity to buy bottles of rum and gift items. ✉ *Spring Garden Hwy., Brandons, St. Michael,* ☎ *246/425–8757.* ✉ *$6; $27.50 with lunch.* ☉ *Weekdays 9–4.*

⑭ Rum Factory and Heritage Park. A long road through acres of cane fields brings you to the first rum distillery to be built in Barbados in the 20th century. Opened in late 1996 on a 350-year-old sugar plantation, the spotless, environmentally friendly, high-tech distillery produces ESA Field white rum and premium Alleyne Arthur varieties. Adjacent is the 7-acre Heritage Park, which showcases Bajan skills and talents in its Art Foundry and Cane Pit Amphitheatre; a row of shops and vendor carts are filled with local products, crafts, and foods. ✉ *Foursquare Plantation, St. Philip,* ☎ *246/420–1977.* ✉ *$5.* ☉ *Daily 9–5.*

⑮ Sam Lord's Castle. The Regency house built by the buccaneer Sam Lord is considered one of the island's finest mansions. Built in 1820 and now the centerpiece of a resort, the opulent estate features double verandas on all sides and magnificent plaster ceilings created by Charles Rutter, who also crafted some of the ceilings in England's Windsor Castle. Rooms are furnished with fine mahogany furniture and gilt mirrors that Sam Lord is reputed to have pillaged from passing ships. It's said he lured them onto treacherous reefs just offshore by hanging lanterns in palm trees to simulate harbor lights. ⊠ *Long Bay, St. Philip,* ☎ *246/ 423–7350.* ☞ *$5; hotel guests free.* ⊙ *Daily 10–4.*

⑬ Sunbury Plantation House & Museum. Lovingly rebuilt after a 1995 fire destroyed everything but the thick flint-and-stone walls of this 300-year-old plantation house, Sunbury offers an elegant glimpse of the 18th and 19th centuries on a Barbadian sugar estate. Period furniture, old prints, and a collection of horse-drawn carriages have been donated to lend an air of authenticity. Luncheon is served in the back garden. ⊠ *Off Hwy. 5, near Six Cross Roads, St. Philip,* ☎ *246/423–6270.* ☞ *$6.* ⊙ *Daily 10–5.*

⊙ ⑨ Tyrol Cot Heritage Village. This interesting coral-stone cottage just south of Bridgetown was constructed in 1854 and has been preserved as an example of period architecture. In 1929 it became home to Sir Grantley Adams, the first premier of Barbados and the only prime minister of the short-lived West Indies Federation. Part of the Barbados National Trust, the cottage is now filled with antiques and memorabilia that belonged to the late Sir Grantley and Lady Adams. It's the centerpiece of an outdoor "living" museum of colorful chattel houses, each with a traditional artisan or craftsman at work inside. The crafts are for sale, and refreshments are available at the "rum shop." ⊠ *Rte. 2, Codrington Hill, St. Michael,* ☎ *246/424–2074 or 246/436–9033.* ☞ *$6.* ⊙ *Weekdays 9–5.*

Northern Barbados

Speightstown, the north's commercial center and once a thriving port city, is characteristically West Indian. It's still busy, but with the traffic into and out of quaint local shops and informal restaurants. Many of Speightstown's 19th-century buildings, with typical overhanging balconies, have been or are being restored. The island's northernmost reaches, St. Peter and St. Lucy parishes, are varied and lovely. Between the tiny fishing towns along the northwestern coast and the sweeping views out over the Atlantic to the east are forest and farm, moor and mountain. Most guides include a loop through this area on a daylong island tour—it's a beautiful drive.

SIGHTS TO SEE

⊙ ㉓ Animal Flower Cave. Small sea anemones, or sea worms, resemble jewel-like flowers when they open their tiny tentacles. They live in small pools—some large enough to swim in—in this cave at the island's very northern tip. The view of breaking waves from inside the cave is magnificent. ⊠ *North Point, St. Lucy,* ☎ *246/439–8797.* ☞ *$1.50.* ⊙ *Daily 9–4.*

⊙ ㉑ Barbados Wildlife Reserve. The reserve is home to herons, innumerable land turtles, screeching peacocks, shy deer, sometimes elusive green monkeys, brilliantly colored parrots (in a large walk-in aviary), a snake, and a caiman. The animals run or fly freely, except for the snake and caiman, so step carefully and keep your hands to yourself. Late afternoon is your best chance to catch a glimpse of a green monkey. ⊠ *Farley Hill, St. Peter,* ☎ *246/422–8826.* ☞ *$11.50.* ⊙ *Daily 10–5.*

㉀ Farley Hill. At this national park in northern St. Peter, across the road from the Barbados Wildlife Reserve, the imposing ruins of a plantation great house are surrounded by gardens and lawns; an avenue of towering royal palms; and gigantic mahogany, whitewood, and casuarina trees. Partially rebuilt for the filming of *Island in the Sun,* the classic 1957 film starring Harry Belafonte and Dorothy Dandridge, the structure was later destroyed by fire. Behind the estate, there's a sweeping view of the region called Scotland for its rugged landscape. ⊠ *Farley*

Hill, St. Peter. ☎ 246/422–3555. ⌨ $1.50 per car; walkers free. ☉
Daily 8:30–6.

★ ㉒ **St. Nicholas Abbey.** With no religious connection at all, the name of
the island's oldest great house (circa 1650) is an amalgamation of the
owners' ancestral British home, St. Nicholas parish near Bristol, and
Bath Abbey nearby. Its stone-and-wood architecture makes it one of
only three original Jacobean-style houses still standing in the Western
Hemisphere. It has Dutch gables, finials of coral stone, and beautiful
grounds. The first floor, fully furnished with period furniture and portraits of family members, is open to the public. Fascinating home
movies, shot by the current owner's father, record Bajan town and plantation life in the 1930s. The Calabash Café, in the rear, serves snacks,
lunch, and afternoon tea. ⌧ *Near Cherry Tree Hill, St. Lucy,* ☎ 246/
422–8725. ⌨ $5. ☉ *Weekdays 10–3:30.*

Central Barbados

On the west coast, Holetown, in St. James Parish, is the center of the
Platinum Coast—so called for the vast number of luxurious resorts and
mansions that face the sea. Holetown is also where British captain John
Powell landed in 1625 to claim the island for King James. On the east
coast the crashing Atlantic surf has eroded the shoreline, forming steep
cliffs and rocks that look like giant mushrooms. Bathsheba and Cat-
tlewash are favorite local seacoast destinations on weekends and holidays. In the interior, narrow roads weave through tiny villages and
along and between the ridges. The landscape is covered with tropical
vegetation and riddled with fascinating caves and gullies.

SIGHTS TO SEE

★ ⑰ **Andromeda Gardens.** An intriguing collection of unusual and beautiful plant specimens from around the world is cultivated in 6 acres of
gardens nestled among streams, ponds, and rocky outcroppings overlooking the sea above the Bathsheba coastline. The gardens were created in 1954 with flowering plants collected by the late horticulturist
Iris Bannochie. They're now administered by the Barbados National
Trust. The Hibiscus Café serves snacks and drinks, and there's a Best
of Barbados gift shop on the property. ⌧ *Bathsheba, St. Joseph,* ☎
246/433–9261. ⌨ $6. ☉ *Daily 9–5.*

⑱ **Barclays Park.** Straddling the Ermy Bourne Highway, just north of
Bathsheba, this public park was donated by Barclays Bank. Pack a picnic or stop at the popular bar-restaurant and enjoy lunch with a gorgeous ocean view.

⑲ **Chalky Mount.** A handful of potters have workshops in this tiny east
coast village, high in the hills that produce the clay that has supplied
generations of potters for 300 years. The potteries are open daily to
visitors. You can watch as artisans create bowls, vases, candleholders,
and decorative objects that they, of course, offer for sale.

㉕ **Flower Forest.** It's a treat to meander among fragrant flowering bushes,
canna and ginger lilies, puffball trees, and more than 100 other species
of tropical flora in a cool, tranquil setting. A ½-mi-long (1-km-long)
path winds through the 50 acres of grounds, a former sugar plantation; it takes about 30–45 minutes to follow the path—or you can wander freely for as long as you wish. Seats, where you can pause and reflect,
are located throughout the forest. You'll also find a snack bar, gift shop,
and beautiful view of Mt. Hillaby. ⌧ *Richmond Plantation, Hwy. 2,
St. Joseph,* ☎ 246/433–8152. ⌨ $7. ☉ *Daily 9–5.*

㉔ **Folkestone Marine Park & Visitor Centre.** At this park north of Holetown there's a lot for the whole family to enjoy—both on land and
offshore. A museum illuminates some of the island's marine life; and

for some firsthand viewing there's an underwater snorkeling trail around Dottin's Reef (glass-bottom boats are available for nonswimmers). A barge sunk in shallow water is home to myriad fish, making it a popular dive site. ⊠ *Church Point, Holetown, St. James,* ☎ *246/ 422–2314.* ☞ *Free.* ⊘ *Weekdays 9–5.*

⑪ **Francia Plantation House.** Built of large coral-stone blocks in 1913, the architecture of this great house blends French, Brazilian, and Caribbean influences. You can tour the house (descendents of the original owner still live here) and gardens. The antique furniture was mostly made in Barbados of local mahogany; 17th- and 18th-century maps, watercolors, and prints grace the walls. ⊠ *Gun Hill, St. George,* ☎ *246/429–0474.* ☞ *$4.50.* ⊘ *Weekdays 10–4.*

☞ ⑫ **Gun Hill Signal Station.** The 360-degree view from Gun Hill, 700 ft (215 m) above sea level, was what made this location of strategic importance to the 18th-century British army. Using lanterns and semaphore, soldiers based here could communicate with their counterparts at the south coast garrison and at Grenade Hill in the north. Time moved slowly in 1868, and Captain Henry Wilkinson whiled away his off-duty time by carving a huge lion from a single rock—which is on the hillside just below the tower. Come for a short history lesson but mainly for the view; it's so gorgeous, military invalids were once sent here to convalesce. ⊠ *Gun Hill, St. George,* ☎ *246/429–1358.* ☞ *$6.* ⊘ *Weekdays 9–5.*

☞ ㉗ **Harrison's Cave.** This limestone cavern, complete with stalactites, stalagmites, subterranean streams, and a 40-ft (12-m) waterfall, is a rare find in the Caribbean—and one of Barbados's most popular attractions. The one-hour tours are on electric trams, which fill up fast; reserve ahead of time. Hard hats are required and provided, but all that may fall on you is a little dripping water. ⊠ *Hwy. 2, St. Thomas,* ☎ *246/438–6640.* ☞ *$12.50.* ⊘ *Daily 9–6; last tour at 4.*

㉖ **Welchman Hall Gully.** This 1-mi-long (2-km-long) natural gully is really a collapsed limestone cavern, once part of the same underground network as Harrison's Cave. The national trust protects the peace and quiet here, making it a beautiful place to hike among acres of labeled flowers and stands of trees. You'll see and hear some interesting birds and, with luck, a native green monkey. ⊠ *Welchman Hall, St. Thomas,* ☎ *246/438–6671.* ☞ *$6.* ⊘ *Daily 9–5.*

BARBADOS A TO Z

To research prices, get advice from other travelers, and book travel arrangements, visit www.fodors.com.

AIR TRAVEL

Several international carriers serve Barbados from North America and Europe. Air Canada flies nonstop from Toronto and Montréal. Air Jamaica has nonstop service from New York and also from other cities through its Montego Bay hub. American Airlines has nonstop service from New York and Miami and direct service from other U.S. cities, connecting with American Eagle in San Juan. British Airways offers daily service from London Heathrow. BWIA flies nonstop from New York and Miami daily, and from Washington Dulles, Atlanta, and Houston several times a week; the airline also has weekly flights from Toronto and thrice-weekly flights from the United Kingdom through Trinidad. Virgin Atlantic flies nonstop from London Gatwick.

Barbados is also well connected to other Caribbean destinations. BWIA Express flies from Grenada, Guyana, St. Lucia, St. Vincent, and Trinidad and Tobago. Caribbean Star flies three times daily between Barbados and Antigua via Dominica. HelenAir flies regional charters between Barbados and St. Lucia. LIAT connects Barbados with Anguilla, Antigua, Dominica, Grenada, Guadeloupe, Guyana, Martinique, Nevis, Puerto Rico, St. Croix, St. Kitts and Nevis, St. Lucia, St. Maarten, St. Thomas, Trinidad and Tobago, and St. Vincent and the Grenadines. Mustique Airways links Barbados with St. Vincent and the Grenadines (Bequia, Canouan, Carriacou, Mustique, and Union) on scheduled charter flights. SVG Air flies between Barbados and St. Vincent and the Grenadines. Trans Island Air flies regional charters between Barbados and the Grenadines.

➤ AIRLINES AND CONTACTS: **Air Canada** (☎ 246/428–5077); **Air Jamaica** (☎ 246/420–1956 or 800/523-5585); **American Airlines** (☎ 246/428–4170); **British Airways** (☎ 246/436–6413); **BWIA/BWIA Express** (☎ 246/426–2111); **Caribbean Star** (☎ 268/480–2561); **HelenAir** (☎ 758/452–7196); **LIAT** (☎ 246/434–5428); **Mustique Airways** (☎ 246/428–1638 or 246/435–7009); **SVG Air** (☎ 784/457–5124); **Trans Island Air** (☎ 246/418–1650); **Virgin Atlantic** (☎ 246/418–8505).

AIRPORTS

Grantley Adams International Airport, a major hub for airlines serving Eastern Caribbean destinations, is situated in Christ Church Parish, on the south coast. It's a large, modern facility; taxis and other ground transportation (such as vans from hotels that provide airport transfers) are available immediately upon exiting the customs area. The airport is about 15 minutes from hotels situated along the south coast, 45 minutes from the west coast, and about 30 minutes from Bridgetown.

Note that airport taxis aren't metered, but fares are regulated (about $28 to Speightstown, $20–$22 to west coast hotels, $10–$13 to south coast ones). Be sure, however, to establish the fare before getting into the cab and that you understand whether the price quoted is in U.S. or Barbadian dollars.

➤ AIRPORT INFORMATION: **Grantley Adams International Airport** (☎ 246/428–7101).

BOAT AND FERRY TRAVEL

Half the annual visitors to Barbados are cruise passengers. Bridgetown's Deep Water Harbour is on the northwest side of Carlisle Bay, and up to eight cruise ships can dock at the snazzy Cruise Ship Terminal. Downtown Bridgetown is a ½-mi (1-km) walk from the pier; a taxi costs about $3 each way.

BUSINESS HOURS

BANKS

Banks are open Monday–Thursday 8–3, Friday 8–5 (some branches in supermarkets are open Saturday morning 9–noon), and at the airport the Barbados National Bank is open from 8 AM until the last plane leaves or arrives, seven days a week (including holidays).

POST OFFICES

The general post office, in Cheapside, Bridgetown, is open weekdays 7:30–5; the Sherbourne Conference Center branch is open weekdays 8:15–4:30 during conferences; and branches in each parish are open weekdays 8–3:15.

SHOPS

Most stores in Bridgetown are open weekdays 8:30–5, Saturday 8:30–1. Out-of-town locations may stay open later. Some supermarkets are open daily 8–6 or later.

Bus service is efficient, inexpensive, and plentiful. Blue buses with a yellow stripe are public, yellow buses with a blue stripe are private, and private "zed-R" vans (so called for their ZRlicense plate designation) are white with a maroon stripe. All travel frequently along Highway 1 (St. James Road) and Highway 7 (South Coast Main Road), as well as inland routes. The fare is Bds$1.50 (75¢) for any one destination; exact change is required on public buses and appreciated on private ones. Buses pass along main roads about every 20 minutes and are usually packed. Stops are marked by small signs on roadside poles that say TO CITY or OUT OF CITY, meaning the direction relative to Bridgetown. Flag down the bus with your hand, even if you're standing at the stop. In Bridgetown terminals are at Fairchild Street for buses to the south and east and at Lower Green for buses to Speightstown via the west coast.

CAR RENTALS

To rent a car you must have an international driver's license or Barbados driving permit, obtainable at the airport, police stations, and major car-rental firms for $5 with a valid driver's license. Nearly 30 agencies rent cars, Jeeps, or minimokes (small, open-air vehicles) for $55–$105 a day (or $250–$400 a week), depending on the vehicle and whether it has air-conditioning. Most firms also offer discounted three-day rates as well. The rental generally includes insurance. Companies provide pickup and delivery service, offer unlimited mileage, and accept major credit cards. Baby seats are usually available upon request.

Barbados is served by several reputable local companies, and the cars they rent are in good condition.
➤ MAJOR AGENCIES: **Courtesy Rent-A-Car** (✉ Grantley Adams International Airport, ☎ 246/418–2500); **Coconut Car Rentals** (✉ Bay St., Bridgetown, ☎ 246/437–0297); **Corbins Car Rentals** (✉ Lipp Collymore Rock, Bridgetown, ☎ 246/427–9531); **Drive-a-Matic** (✉ Lower Carlton, St. James, ☎ 246/422–3000); **National Car Rentals** (✉ Lower Carlton, St. James, ☎ 246/426–0603); **Sunny Isle Motors** (✉ Worthing, Christ Church, ☎ 246/435–7979).

CAR TRAVEL

Visitors staying in a remote location, such as the east coast, will find it practical to rent a car for the duration of their stay. Even those folks staying in more populated areas, where taxis and public transportation are available at the door, will find it fun to rent a car or minimoke for a day or two of exploring on their own. Bathing suits and beach towels—and a map—are requisite gear for such an adventure; hotels can supply a picnic lunch.

Gas costs about 80¢ per liter (approximately $3 per gallon), and there are stations in Bridgetown, on the main highways along the west and south coasts, and in most inland parishes. Although times vary, you'll find most open daily with hours that extend into the evening; some are open 24 hours a day.

Barbados has nearly 2,400 mi (1,475 km) of paved roads that follow the coastline and meander throughout the countryside. A network of main highways facilitates traffic flow into and out of Bridgetown; the Adams-Barrow-Cummins (ABC) Highway bypasses Bridgetown, which saves time getting from coast to coast. Although small signs tacked to trees and poles at intersections point the way to most attractions, be sure to study a map. Remote roads are in fairly good repair, yet few are well lighted at night—and night falls quickly, at about 6 PM year-round. Even in full daylight, the tall sugarcane fields lining both sides of the road in interior sections can make visibility difficult.

RULES OF THE ROAD
Pedestrians and an occasional sheep or goat often walk in the roads. When someone flashes headlights at you at an intersection, it means "after you." Remember to drive on the left, and be especially careful negotiating roundabouts (traffic circles). The speed limit, in keeping with the pace of life and the narrow roads, is 30 mph in the country, 20 mph in town. Bridgetown actually has rush hours: 7:30–8:30 and 4:30–5:30. Park only in approved parking areas; downtown parking costs Bds75¢–Bds$1 per hour.

ELECTRICITY
Electric current on Barbados is 110 volts/50 cycles, U.S. standard. Hotels generally have adapters/transformers for guests from the United Kingdom or other countries that operate on 220-volt current.

EMBASSIES
➤ AUSTRALIA: **Australian High Commission** (✉ Bishop's Court Hill, St. Michael, ☎ 246/435–2834).
➤ CANADA: **Canadian High Commission** (✉ Bishop's Court Hill, St. Michael, ☎ 246/429–3550).
➤ UNITED KINGDOM: **British High Commission** (✉ Collymore Rock, St. Michael, ☎ 246/436–6694).
➤ UNITED STATES: **Embassy of the United States** (✉ Broad St., Bridgetown, St. Michael, ☎ 246/436–4950).

EMERGENCIES
➤ AMBULANCE: Dial ☎ 511.
➤ FIRE: Dial ☎ 311.
➤ HOSPITALS: **Bayview Hospital** (✉ St. Paul's Ave., Bayville, St. Michael, ☎ 246/436–5446) is south of the city, along the coast. **Queen Elizabeth Hospital** (✉ Martindales Rd., St. Michael, ☎ 246/436–6450) is just east of the Careenage.
➤ PHARMACIES: **Collins Ltd.** (✉ Broad St., ☎ 246/426–4515). **Grant's** (✉ Fairchild St., Bridgetown, ☎ 246/436–6120; ✉ Main Rd., Oistins, ☎ 246/428–9481). **Knight's** (✉ Lower Broad St., Bridgetown, ☎ 246/426–5196; ✉ Super Centre Shopping Center, Main Rd., Oistins, ☎ 246/428–6057; ✉ Suncrest Mall, Hwy. 1, Holetown, ☎ 246/432–1290; and ✉ Hwy. 1, Speightstown, ☎ 246/422–0048).
➤ POLICE: ☎ 211; 242/430–7100 for nonemergencies.
➤ SCUBA-DIVING ACCIDENTS: Barbados has excellent resources available for immediate assistance in case of diving emergencies. If you are aware of a diving emergency, call **Divers' Alert Network** (☎ 246/684–8111 or 246/684–2948). The Coast Guard Defence Force has a **24-hour hyperbaric chamber,** the only one in the region (✉ St. Ann's Fort, Garrison, St. Michael, ☎ 246/427–8819; 246/436–6185 for nonemergencies).

ETIQUETTE AND BEHAVIOR
The British influence remains strong, in part because Barbados is the favorite island retreat of most Brits and the retirement choice of many. Most hotels serve afternoon tea, cricket is the national pastime, and patrons at some bars are as likely to order a Pimm's Cup as a rum and Coke. British-style manners combine with a Caribbean friendliness and openness to give Bajans their special charm. Dress appropriately and discreetly, saving swimwear for the beach. Shorts and T-shirts are fine for sightseeing and shopping but frowned upon in restaurants in the evening.

FESTIVALS AND SEASONAL EVENTS

In mid-January, the **Barbados Jazz Festival** (☎ 246/437–4537, WEB www.barbadosjazzfestival.com) is a weekend jammed with performances by international artists, jazz legends, and local talent. In February the weeklong **Holetown Festival** (☎ 246/435–6264) is held at the fairgrounds to commemorate the date in 1627 when the first European settlers arrived in Barbados; food, carnival rides, the Royal Barbados Police Force Band, and mounted troops add to the enjoyment.

Three weeks of opera, concerts, and theatrical performances are presented each March during **Holders Opera Season** (☎ 246/432–6385, WEB www.holders.net). The open-air theater at Holders House, St. James, seats 600, and the program has won acclaim for its productions, which have included headliner Luciano Pavarotti. Around Easter weekend, **Oistins Fish Festival** (☎ 246/427–3272) celebrates the rich history of this south coast fishing village; events include fishing, boat racing, fish-boning competitions, food, arts and crafts presentations, dancing, and road racing. Dubbed the "world's greatest street party," the **Congaline Street Festival** is a festive celebration of music, dance, and local arts and crafts; held at the end of April, the highlight of this terrific street party is the Caribbean's longest conga line. For more information, call The National Cultural Foundation (☎ 246/424–0909).

Gospelfest (☎ 246/426–5940) occurs in May and features performances by gospel headliners from around the world. Dating from the 19th century, the **Crop Over Festival,** a monthlong event beginning in July and ending on Kadooment Day, a national holiday, marks the end of the sugarcane harvest with competitions, music and dancing, Bajan food, and arts and crafts. Get more details from he National Cultural Foundation (☎ 246/424–0909).

HEALTH

When swimming, avoid stepping on black sea urchins (locally called "cobblers"), which have needle-sharp spines. Insects aren't much of a problem, but if you plan to hike or spend time on secluded beaches in late afternoon, use insect repellent. Beware of the little green apples that fall from the manchineel tree—they may look tempting, but they're poisonous to eat and toxic to the touch. Even taking shelter under the tree when it rains can give you blisters. Most manchineels are identified with signs or a red-painted band around the trunk. If you do come in contact with one, immediately wash yourself off with water, go to the nearest hotel, and have someone there phone for a physician. The water on the island is plentiful and pure. It's naturally filtered through 1,000 ft (305 m) of pervious coral and safe to drink from the tap.

HOLIDAYS

New Year's Day, Errol Barrow Day (Jan. 21), Good Friday (Mar. 29, 2002), Easter Monday (Apr. 1, 2002), National Heroes Day (Apr. 28), Labour Day (May 1), Whit Monday (May 20, 2002), Emancipation Day (Aug. 1), Kadooment Day (first Mon. in Aug.), Independence Day (Nov. 30), Christmas, and Boxing Day (Dec. 26).

LANGUAGE

English is the official language and is spoken by everyone, everywhere. A 98% literacy rate is a sign of the island's sophistication. The Bajan dialect is based on Afro-Caribbean rhythms, but you'll notice a distinctly Irish or Scottish lilt, which differentiates the Bajan accent from its Caribbean neighbors. As for the African influence, you'll see it in names of typical Bajan foods, such as cou-cou and buljol.

MAIL AND SHIPPING

An airmail letter from Barbados to the United States or Canada costs Bds$1.15 per half ounce; an airmail postcard, Bds45¢. Letters to the United Kingdom cost Bds$1.40; postcards, Bds75¢. Letters to Australia and New Zealand cost Bds$2.75; postcards, Bds$1.75. When sending mail to Barbados, be sure to include the parish name in the address.

MONEY MATTERS

Prices quoted throughout this chapter are in U.S. dollars unless otherwise noted.

ATMS

Automated teller machines (ATMs) are available 24 hours a day at bank branches, transportation centers, shopping centers, gas stations, and other convenient spots throughout the island.

CREDIT CARDS

Major credit cards readily accepted throughout Barbados include American Express, BarclayCard, Carte Blanche, Diners Club, En-Route, Eurocard, MasterCard, and Visa. You can use major credit cards to obtain cash advances (in Barbadian dollars), if you have a PIN, from most ATM machines.

CURRENCY

The Barbados dollar is tied to the U.S. dollar at the rate of Bds$1.98 to $1. U.S. paper currency, major credit cards, and traveler's checks are all accepted islandwide. Be sure you know which currency you're dealing in when making a purchase.

➤ BANKS: **Barbados National Bank** (☎ 246/431–5700) has a branch at Grantley Adams International Airport that is open every day from 8 AM until the last plane lands or arrives. **Barclays Bank** (☎ 246/431–5151) is an international bank with several branches. The **Bank of Nova Scotia** (☎ 246/431–3000), also called Scotiabank, is a major Canadian bank that is represented throughout the Caribbean. **Caribbean Commercial Bank** (☎ 246/431–2500) has convenient Saturday morning hours at its branch at Sunset Crest Mall, in Holetown (☎ 246/419–8530). **CIBC** (☎ 246/431–3700) has a branch office at the Cruise Ship Terminal.

PASSPORTS AND VISAS

U.S. and Canadian citizens can enter Barbados for visits of up to three months with proof of citizenship and a return or ongoing ticket. Acceptable proof is a valid passport or a birth certificate with a raised seal and a government-issued photo ID; no other documents, including voter registration cards or baptismal certificates, are acceptable. British subjects and citizens of countries that are members of the British Commonwealth must present a valid passport and ongoing ticket.

SAFETY

Crime isn't a major problem, but take normal precautions. Don't leave valuables unattended on the beach or in plain sight in your room, and don't pick up hitchhikers.

SIGHTSEEING TOURS

A half- or full-day bus or taxi tour is a good way to get your bearings and can be arranged by your hotel. The price varies according to the number of attractions included; an average full-day tour (five to six hours) costs about $50–$60 per person and generally includes lunch and admissions.

Family-run **Bajan Tours** offers eight coach or minivan tours, including cultural, historic, ecological, and general sightseeing routings. Full-day tours include hotel transfers, all admissions, and a Bajan buffet lunch in Bathsheba. Prices are $40 for half-day and $56 for full-day tours.

Island Safari Tours will take you to all the popular spots and some that are out-of-the-way and inaccessible by buses or normal vehicles, but you'll be riding in a 4x4 Land Rover. Discovery tours last about three hours and cost $40 per person; Adventure tours, which last about four hours and include lunch, cost $57.50; an all-day (7 ½-hour) Land and Sea Safari includes the land portion, lunch, plus an afternoon cruise on a catamaran—with time for swimming and snorkeling, too—for $90 per person.

L. E. Williams Tour Co. offers island bus tours, which cost $30–$85 per person. Points of interest include Bridgetown, the St. James beach area, Animal Flower Cave, Farley Hill, Earthworks Pottery, Morgan Lewis Mill, St. John's Church, Sam Lord's Castle, Oistins fishing village, and the Mount Gay Rum Visitors Centre—with a West Indian buffet lunch at the Atlantis Hotel in Bathsheba.

Sally Shearn operates **VIP Tour Services.** Up to four people are picked up in an air-conditioned Mercedes-Benz and charged $40 per hour for a minimum of four hours. Your choice of tours (coastal, inland, cultural, naturalist, architectural, or customized) includes refreshment stops.

Bajan Helicopters offers an eagle's-eye view of the island. The prices per person are $75 for a 20-minute Discover Barbados tour and $125 for a 30-minute island tour that makes a full circuit of the coastline.

Every Wednesday afternoon from mid-January through mid-April, the **Barbados National Trust** offers a bus tour that stops at historic great houses and private homes, including Tyrol Cot Heritage Village (St. Michael); St. Nicholas Abbey (St. Peter); Francia Plantation, Drax Hall, and Brighton Great House (St. George); Villa Nova (St. John); and Sam Lord's Castle and Sunbury Plantation House (St. Philip). The cost is $18 per person, which includes transportation to and from your hotel. (If you wish to visit the homes on your own, they're open on those Wednesday afternoons from 2:30 to 5:30; entrance fees range from $1.25 to $5.)

➤ CONTACTS: **Bajan Helicopters** (✉ Bishop's Court Hill, St. Michael, ☎ 246/431–0069); **Bajan Tours** (✉ Gleayre, Locust Hall, St. George, ☎ 246/437–9389); **Barbados National Trust** (✉ Wildey House, Wildey, St. Michael, ☎ 246/426–2421); **Island Safari Tours** (✉ Bush Hall Main Rd., Bush Hall, St. Michael, ☎ 246/429–5337); **L. E. Williams Tour Co.** (☎ 246/427–1043); **VIP Tour Services** (✉ Hillcrest Villa, Upton, St. Michael, ☎ 246/429–4617).

TAXES

DEPARTURE TAX

At the airport, before leaving Barbados, each passenger must pay a departure tax of $12.50 (Bds$25), payable in either currency; children 12 and under are exempt.

SALES TAX

A 7½% government tax is added to all hotel bills. A 10% service charge is usually added to hotel bills and restaurant checks in lieu of tipping. At your discretion, tip beyond the service charge to recognize extraordinary service.

VALUE ADDED TAX (V.A.T.)

A 15% VAT is imposed on restaurant meals, admissions to attractions, and merchandise sales (other than duty-free). Prices are often tax inclusive; if not, the VAT will be added to your bill.

TAXIS

Taxis operate 24 hours a day. They aren't metered but operate according to fixed rates set by the government. They carry up to four passengers, and the fare may be shared. For short trips, the rate per mile (or part thereof) should not exceed $1.50. Drivers are courteous and knowledgeable; most will narrate a tour at an hourly rate of $20 for up to three people. Be sure to settle the price before you start off and agree on whether it's in U.S. or Barbados dollars.

TELEPHONES

COUNTRY AND AREA CODES

The area code for Barbados is 246.

INTERNATIONAL CALLS

Direct-dialing to the United States, Canada, and other countries is efficient, and the cost is reasonable, but always check with your hotel to see if a surcharge is added. To charge your overseas call on a major credit card without incurring a surcharge, dial 800/744–2000 from any phone.

LOCAL CALLS

Local calls are free from private phones and some hotels; for directory assistance dial 411. From pay phones the charge is Bds25¢ for five minutes. Prepaid phone cards, which can be used in pay phones throughout Barbados and other Caribbean islands, are sold at shops, attractions, transportation centers, and other convenient outlets.

TIPPING

If no service charge is added to your restaurant bill, tip waiters 10%–15% and maids $1 per room per day. Bellhops and airport porters should be tipped $1 per bag. Taxi drivers appreciate a 10% tip.

VISITOR INFORMATION

➤ BEFORE YOU LEAVE: **Barbados Tourism Authority** (✉ 800 2nd Ave., 2nd floor, New York, NY 10017, ☎ 212/986–6516 or 800/221–9831; ✉ 150 Alhambra Circle, Suite 1270, Coral Gables, FL 33134, ☎ 305/442–7471; ✉ 3440 Wilshire Blvd., Suite 1215, Los Angeles, CA 90010, ☎ 213/380–2198; in Canada: ✉ 105 Adelaide St., Suite 1010, Toronto, Ontario M5H 1P9, ☎ 416/214–9880 or 800/268–9122; in the U.K.: ✉ 263 Tottenham Court Rd., London W1P OLA, U.K., ☎ 020/7636–9448; WEB www.barbados.org).

➤ IN BARBADOS: The **Barbados Tourism Authority** (Harbour Road, Bridgetown, ☎ 246/427–2623) is open weekdays 8:15–4:30. Information bureaus, staffed by Tourism Authority representatives, are at **Grantley Adams International Airport** (☎ 246/428–5570) and at Bridgetown's **Cruise Ship Terminal** (☎ 246/426–1718).

5   BONAIRE

Updated by
Karen W.
Bressler and
Elise Rosen

The tranquil, otherworldly landscape here resembles a Dalí canvas, its colors so primary they seem artificial. Joshua trees pierce an azure sky like cathedral spires. On one side, a salt pond, the delicate hue of Cristal Rosé champagne, shimmers. On the other, psychedelic-green parrot fish glide through ocean shallows near the sand, where tangles of tortured driftwood—bleached stark white—rise like the Earth's bones. Just a hint of rose signals the arrival of dusk; a flock of pink flamingos darkens the sky like an eclipse, blends into the deepening blush of the setting sun, and then disappears.

For years Bonaire was regarded simply as a diving mecca, with most visitors practically oblivious to the equally rich beauty on land. But the government embarked on a program to expand its ecotourism base without succumbing to overdevelopment. Now there are facilities and tours geared toward snorkelers, hikers, bikers, and kayakers, as well as luxury resorts that offer pampering, fine dining, and solitude.

Bonaire, on land, is a stark desert island, perfect for those who are turned off by the overcommercialized high life of the other Antillean islands. There's an array of wildlife—from fowl to flowers—that will keep you awestruck for days. You'll want to rent a four-wheel-drive vehicle and go off in search of flamingos, iguanas, or the yellow-winged parrot named the Bonairean lora. Bolstering efforts to preserve the region's natural wonders, Bonaire in 1999 purchased the neighboring island of Klein Bonaire from its private owner, protecting it against development.

Divers still come to Bonaire as pilgrims to a holy land. Here diving is learned and perfected. Even Bonaire license plates tout the island as "Divers' Paradise." But the residents have worked hard to preserve this paradise (any diver with a reckless streak should go elsewhere). Back in 1979 the government made all the waters surrounding Bonaire part of a marine park. These areas were granted National Park status in 1999, meaning that anyone who disobeys the area's regulations could face legal action. The entire coastline—from the high-water tidemark to a depth of 200 ft (61 m)—is protected by strict regulations such as mandatory warm-up dives with a local instructor and bans on spearfishing and coral collecting. But certain hazards can't be avoided, as the people of Bonaire discovered in November 1999, when a major storm wrecked havoc on some of the island's coastal reefs. Conditions for divers, who typically descend below 30 ft, have not been significantly affected, but snorkelers who seek out the sea's wonders in the shallow waters will likely notice the damage: while the coral reefs are naturally regenerating (which could take several years), the views may be disappointing.

Most Bonaireans live on the west coast, an area that's also home to the capital city, Kralendijk, as well as many hotels, dive sites, and beaches. In the southeast you'll find mangrove swamps, windsurfing schools, and two small resorts in the Lac Bay area; south of here are a rocky, windswept coast, the magnificent salt ponds, and a flamingo sanctuary. The highest elevation is Brandaris Hill (784 ft/239 m) in the north. With just over 15,000 inhabitants, this little (112-square-mi/290-square-km) island has the feeling of a small community with a gentle pace. As the locals say, folks come here to dive, eat, dive, sleep, and dive. But they also come to kayak, mountain bike, hike, snorkel, and simply soak in the sunshine and natural beauty.

Lodging

Hotels on Bonaire—with several exceptions—cater primarily to avid divers who spend their days underwater and come up for air only for evening festivities. Hence, facilities tend to be modest, with clean but unadorned rooms (often without phones), pools, a restaurant, and perhaps a bar. Amenities are often limited to laundry, baby-sitting, car rental, and travel services; unless noted below, room service is usually unavailable. Groomed sandy beaches aren't a requisite for a hotel, but an efficient dive shop is. Many resorts have fully equipped kitchens and in-room safes. Although the larger hotels offer a variety of meal plans, most are on the EP; and as a rule, hotel restaurants are more expensive than restaurants in town. Many properties offer all-inclusive packages for an extra per-day charge.

Rental Apartments

If you prefer do-it-yourself homestyle comfort over the pampering and services offered by a hotel, rental apartments are also available.

➤ RENTAL AGENCIES: **Black Durgon Inn Properties** (☎ 599/717–5736 or 800/526–2370 in the U.S.) is a small, noncommercial community with its own pier on the water, though no beach. **Bonaire Intimate Stays** (☎ 800/388–5951) manages 13 small, non-resort-style budget properties (only one is on the water), all with 12 rooms or less. **Sun Rentals** (☎ 599/717–6130) has a range of accommodations. You can choose from private ocean view villas in luxurious areas like Sabadeco, furnished oceanfront apartments with a pool in town, or bungalows in Lagoenhill, set inland.

CATEGORY	Cost*
$$$$	over $225
$$$	$150–$225
$$	$100–$150
$	under $100

All prices are for a standard double room in high season, excluding a $6.50-per-person, per-night government room tax; 6% VAT; and 10%–15% service charge.

HOTELS

$$$$ 🏨 **Harbour Village Beach Resort.** This well-run, upscale resort on a

★   lovely palm tree–lined beach has it all—for divers and nondivers alike. Wide walkways bordered by foliage and flowers separate nine low-rise Mediterranean-style buildings with Moorish arches, mustard-color stucco walls, and red barrel-tile roofs. Pleasant rooms and suites are done in dusty rose and aqua with white tile floors, straw mats, and natural-wood furniture. French doors lead to a terrace or patio overlooking the sea or the marina. A European spa offers massage and Bonairean salt exfoliation. In the mood to merengue? Sign up for lessons. Or get in shape with tae bo or water aerobics. There's also a water-sports center with a dive shop, an underwater photo and video shop, and a Peter Burwash International tennis program. The Wine Club at Harbour Village hosts tastings, dinners, cooking classes, and culinary festivals. ⊠ *Kaya Gobernador N. Debrot 72 (Box 312, Kralendijk),* ☎ *599/717–7500 or 800/424–0004,* FAX *599/717–7507. 64 rooms, 8 suites, 70 condominiums. 4 restaurants, 3 bars, café, air-conditioning, fans, refrigerators, room service, pool, 4 tennis courts, outdoor hot tub, sauna, spa, steam room, aerobics, health club, beach, dive shop, dock, snorkeling, windsurfing, boating, waterskiing, bicycles, shops, babysitting, laundry service, business services, meeting rooms, travel services. AE, D, DC, MC, V. CP, FAP, MAP.*

$$$$ ☷ **Port Bonaire Resort.** Adjacent to the airport, Port Bonaire has 26 luxury apartments and penthouses with sea-view patios or balconies (though no beach). The Dutch Mediterranean design is evident in the tile roofs and pastel exteriors. Inside, florals and a powder-blue color scheme complement cream tile floors and blond-wood furnishings. Kitchens are well equipped with microwaves, dishwashers, and washing machines. Daily maid service is another welcome convenience. There are few on-site facilities, but you can use the facilities at the Plaza Resort Bonaire (you'll need a car to get there and into town). ⊠ *c/o Plaza Resort Bonaire, J. A. Abraham Blvd. 80,* ☎ *599/717–2500 or 800/766–6016,* FAX *599/717–7133. 10 2-bedroom apartments, 8 1-bedroom apartments, 4 beach houses, 4 penthouses. Pool, dock. AE, D, DC, MC, V. EP.*

$$$ ☷ **Bel-Mar Bonaire Oceanfront Hotel & Apartments.** Say goodbye to stress at this peaceful, intimate resort. Painted in bright, warm tropical colors and adorned with dried flowers, rooms here offer all the amenities of home and a large terrace or balcony where you can gaze at the sparkling Caribbean and marvel at the breathtaking sunsets. From some rooms you'll be tempted to (and can) swim, snorkel, or scuba right onto your "private" reef. Some penthouse units have Jacuzzis. ⊠ *E.E.G. Blvd. 88,* ☎ *599/717–7878,* FAX *599/717–7899,* WEB *www.belmar-bonaire. com. 22 rooms. Air-conditioning, in-room safes, kitchenettes, pool, dive shop, dock, snorkeling, bicycles, coin laundry. AE, MC, V. EP.*

$$$ ☷ **Captain Don's Habitat.** Captain Don Stewart's Habitat is no longer
★ merely a guest house for divers. Its upscale rooms are really junior suites, and its spacious Mediterranean-style villas (the Hamlet section) have ocean-view verandas, full kitchens, and stylish appointments. The Antillean-style cottages have fully stocked kitchens, wicker furnishings, and garden views; deluxe cottages have Indonesian and Italian wood and furnishings. The atmosphere here is laid-back (most rooms have no TVs or phones), and the emphasis is on round-the-clock diving— PADI 5-star training, SSI referral, Nitrox diving, and more than 20 specialty courses are at your fingertips. There are charges for using the in-room safes and for removing food from the breakfast buffet. The Rum Runners restaurant offers breakfast, lunch, and dinner, and a pizza oven serves up sizzling slices from 3 PM until 10. The beach is postage-stamp size but fine for shore dives or snorkeling, with mesmerizing reef formations just 90 ft from shore. ⊠ *Kaya Gobernador N. Debrot 85 (Box 88, Kralendijk),* ☎ *599/717–8290 or 800/327– 6709,* FAX *599/717–8240. 24 suites, 11 villas, 21 cottages. Restaurant, 2 bars, air-conditioning, fans, in-room safes, kitchenettes, pool, vol-*

Bonaire

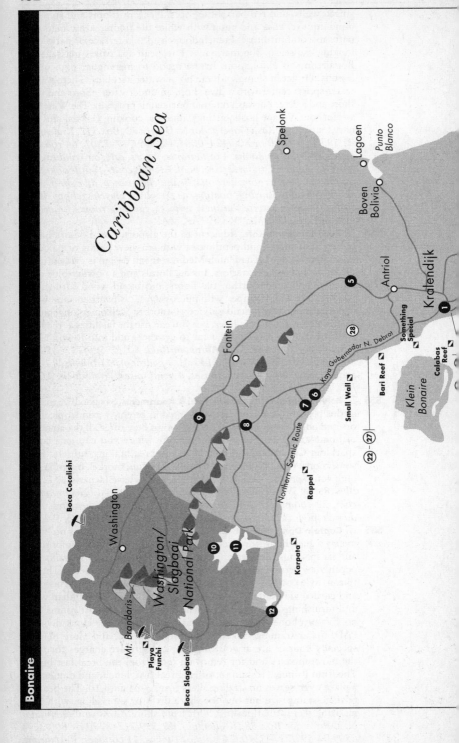

Caribbean Sea

Boca Cocalishi

Washington

Mt. Brandaris

Washington/
Slagbaai
National Park

Playa
Funchi

Boca Slagbaai

Karpata

Rappel

Northern Scenic Route

Spelonk

Fontein

Lagoen

Punto
Blanco

Boven
Bolivia

Antriol

Kralendijk

Kaya Gubernador N. Debrot

Small Wall

Bari Reef

Something
Special

Klein
Bonaire

Calabas
Reef

5

28

7 6

8

9

10

11

12

1

22 – 27

22 – 27

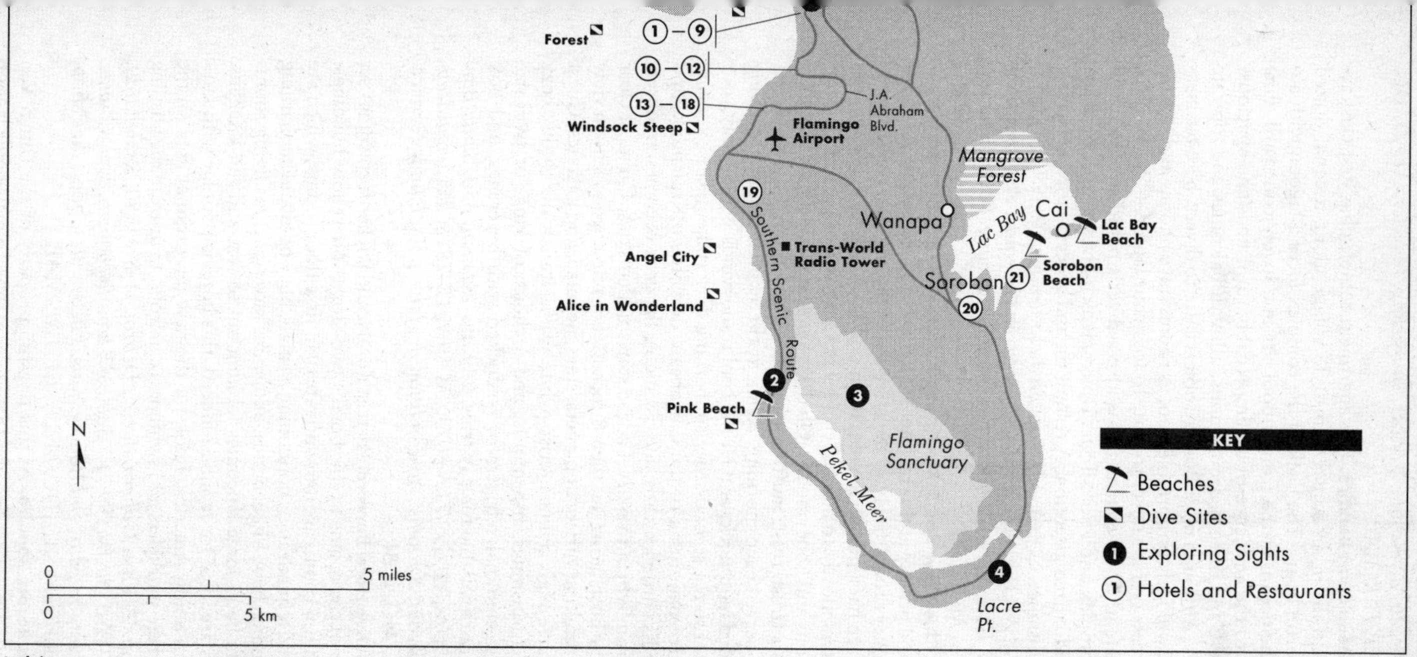

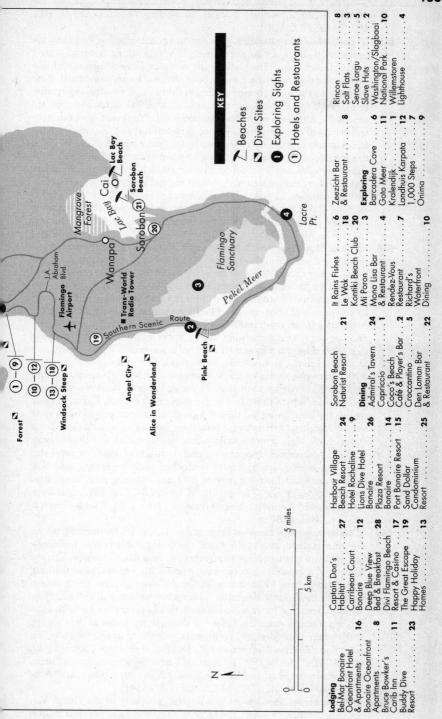

Forest
1 – 9
10 – 12
13 – 18
Windsock Steep
Flamingo Airport
J.A. Abraham Blvd.
Mangrove Forest
Wanapa
Lac Bay
Cai
Lac Bay Beach
Sorobon Beach
Sorobon
21
20
19
Southern Scenic Route
Trans-World Radio Tower
Angel City
Alice in Wonderland
Pink Beach
2
3
Flamingo Sanctuary
Pekel Meer
4
Lacre Pt.
N
0
5 miles
0
5 km
KEY
Beaches
Dive Sites
Exploring Sights
Hotels and Restaurants

Lodging
Bel-Mar Bonaire Oceanfront Hotel & Apartments 16
Bonaire Oceanfront Apartments 8
Bruce Bowker's Carib Inn 11
Buddy Dive Resort 23
Captain Don's Habitat 27
Carribean Court Bonaire 12
Deep Blue View Bed & Breakfast . . . 28
Divi Flamingo Beach Resort & Casino . . . 17
The Great Escape . . 19
Happy Holiday Homes 13
Harbour Village Beach Resort 24
Hotel Rochaline 9
Lions Dive Hotel Bonaire 26
Plaza Resort Bonaire 14
Port Bonaire Resort . 15
Sand Dollar Condominium Resort 25
Sorobon Beach Naturist Resort 21

Dining
Admiral's Tavern . . . 24
Capriccio 1
Coco's Beach Café & Player's Bar . . 2
Croccantino 5
Den Laman Bar & Restaurant 22
It Rains Fishes 6
Le Wok 18
Kontiki Beach Club . 20
Mi Poron 3
Mona Lisa Bar & Restaurant 4
Rendez-Vous Restaurant 7
Richard's Waterfront Dining 10
Zeezicht Bar & Restaurant 8

Exploring
Barcadera Cave 6
Goto Meer 11
Kralendijk 1
Landhuis Karpata . . 12
1,000 Steps 7
Onima 9
Rincon 8
Salt Flats 3
Seroe Largu 5
Slave Huts 2
Washington/Slagbaai National Park 10
Willemstoren Lighthouse 4

*leyball, beach, dive shop, 2 docks, snorkeling, bicycles. AE, D, DC,
MC, V. EP, FAP, MAP.*

$$$ ☰ **Caribbean Court Bonaire.** This apartment complex has first-class ac-
commodations in an Amsterdam-style village along a canal dotted
with colorful boats. The back of the complex faces a lagoon with ac-
cess to the ocean; at the front a pool sits in a lovely courtyard. Fine
art adds to the ambience of the impeccably furnished (and spacious)
one-, two-, and three-bedroom units, all with balconies and top-rate
amenities. Although most Bonaire hotels cater to divers, here business
travelers will feel comfortable, too, as rooms have phones and free In-
ternet access (yet it's never too late to toss your laptop—"Sorry, boss,
the fish ate it!"). Of course, this is also a diver's paradise: you'll find
a dive complex and Photo Tours Divers, which gives divers of all lev-
els individualized attention. A restaurant and grocery store are within
walking distance. ⊠ *J. A. Abraham Blvd., Kralendijk,* ☎ *599/717–5353,*
FAX *599/717–5363,* WEB *caribbeancourt.com. 21 units. Air-condition-
ing, fans, kitchenettes, 2 pools, dive shop, snorkeling, boating, moun-
tain bikes. MC, V. EP.*

$$$ ☰ **Deep Blue View Bed & Breakfast.** Experience the ultimate in tran-
★   quillity and privacy at this remote, Santa Barbara Heights resort (where
wild donkeys roam freely in the streets). With only four guest rooms
in the large hacienda-style villa, the mood is of laid-back luxury. The
B&B caters mostly to aquatic enthusiasts, but is also perfect for family reunions and honeymoons. On the tropical patio, delicious, healthy
breakfasts (fresh fruit, muffins, eggs, pancakes, granola, juice, coffee,
etc.) are served each morning. Relax at the swimming pool or swing
in a shaded hammock, and let the cool trade winds whisk away your
troubles. From a second-story sunbathing deck, take in the exquisite
300-degree panorama of the Caribbean, downtown Kralendijk, and
the island's entire leeward side. By night, the deck becomes an observatory from which to marvel at the star-studded skies. On most clear
nights, the hosts bring out their 8-inch Meade telescope to let you view
the breathtaking variety of planets, stars, nebulae, and galaxies. Guest
rooms have high ceilings, crisp white walls, Italian tile floors, cozy
wooden furnishings, fish motifs, and a choice of king- or twin-size
beds. A communal refrigerator is stocked with beverages, and box
lunches are available for day trips. ⊠ *Kaya Diamanta 50, Santa Barbara Heights,* ☎ *599/717–8073,* FAX *599/717–7826,* WEB *www.deep-
blueview.com. 4 rooms. Air-conditioning, fans, pool, laundry service.
AE, DC, MC, V. BP.*

$$$ ☰ **Lions Dive Hotel Bonaire.** Pastels, florals, and wicker furnishings set
✋   the tone of the rooms in this hotel's two-story, soft-yellow buildings.
Second-floor rooms are more private than first-floor rooms, which are
set around a quadrangle containing a small, busy pool and sunbathing
area. Studios have kitchenettes, and suites have spacious living rooms
with sofa beds, large balconies looking out to sea, and full kitchens.
All units are ideal for families; indeed, this hotel is popular with fam-
ilies from South America. Look for the new recreational area on the
beach where snorkelers and swimmers can frolic apart from the bustling
dive shop. ⊠ *Kaya Gobernador N. Debrot 91(Box 380, Kralendijk),*
☎ *599/717–5580,* FAX *599/717–5680,* WEB *lionsdivebonaire.com. 42 units.
Restaurant, bar, air-conditioning, fans, kitchenettes, pool, dive shop,
dock, snorkeling. AE, DC, MC, V. CP, FAP, MAP.*

$$$ ☰ **Plaza Resort Bonaire.** At this flagship property of the Dutch Van
der Valk chain, lush landscaped grounds surround a man-made lagoon
with bridges. You can also enjoy a gorgeous beach (open to nonguests
for $10 per day), loads of amenities, an activities program, and very
large guest rooms. Each has terra-cotta tile floors, green rattan furnishings, pastel floral bedspreads, coffeemakers, big TVs, and enor-

mous bathrooms with deep tubs, marble vanities, and bidets. One- and two-bedroom villas have full kitchens. Great expense and care have been lavished on the resort, which sprawls over 12 acres. It caters to Dutch and American tourists, and it's where the Dutch Queen Beatrix stays when she's in town. Monday is Bonairean folklore night, with live island music, dancing, and typical local foods. ✉ *J. A. Abraham Blvd. 80,* ☎ *599/717–2500 or 800/766–6016,* FAX *599/717–7133. 200 rooms, 48 villas. 3 restaurants, 4 bars, grocery, air-conditioning, fans, in-room safes, refrigerators, room service, 2 pools, beauty salon, massage, 4 tennis courts, aerobics, gym, beach, dive shop, dock, windsurfing, boating, bicycles, shops, casino, children's programs, business services, convention center, meeting rooms. AE, DC, MC, V. EP, FAP, MAP.*

$$$ ⊡ **Sand Dollar Condominium Resort.** These spacious time-share apartments combine a European design with a tropical rattan decor, though this varies according to the individual owner's taste. Studio, one-, two-, and three-bedroom units are available. Each has cable TV, a full kitchen, a large bathroom, a queen-size sofa bed, and a patio or terrace that looks out to the sea (some ground-floor units offer just a glimpse of the ocean through the foliage). Kitchen and bathroom upgrades have been completed or scheduled for many of the condos; phones and data ports for Internet connections will be installed in every unit by mid-2002. The minuscule beach disappears at high tide, but this doesn't faze the serious divers and their families, who often book stays here months in advance. When renovations are completed, the Sand Dollar Terrace Sports Bar & Restaurant will broadcast sporting events on a big screen satellite TV and serve 3 meals a day. There's also a grocery store if you'd rather cook for yourself. ✉ *Kaya Gobernador N. Debrot 79 (Box 262, Kralendijk),* ☎ *599/717–8738 or 800/288–4773,* FAX *599/717–8760,* WEB *www.sanddollarbonaire.com. 85 condos. Restaurant, bar, grocery, ice cream parlor, air-conditioning, kitchenettes, pool, 2 tennis courts, beach, dive shop, children's programs. AE, D, DC, MC, V. EP, FAP, MAP.*

$$$ ⊡ **Sorobon Beach Naturist Resort.** Guests at this secluded southeast-shore cluster of chalets must bare all at the beach (the island's only nudist beach) but can wear clothing throughout the rest of the premises. Each chalet has two one-bedroom units with light-wood Scandinavian-style furnishings, fully equipped kitchens, and shower-only baths. In keeping with the back-to-basics concept, rooms lack air-conditioning, TVs, phones, and radios. The shallow water in the crystal-clear bay is perfect for snorkeling. Yoga classes, kayaking, and nude cruises are available, and you can get a manicure and/or pedicure by appointment. A daily shuttle will take you to town. ✉ *Sorobon Beach (Box 14, Kralendijk),* ☎ *599/717–8080 or 800/828–9356,* FAX *599/717–6080. 30 1-bedroom units. Restaurant, bar, fans, in-room safes, kitchenettes, hair salon, massage, Ping-Pong, beach, snorkeling, boating, library, laundry service, airport shuttle. AE, MC, V. EP, MAP.*

$$ ⊡ **Bonaire Oceanfront Apartments.** These simply furnished but immaculate one- and two-bedroom apartments are just a three-minute walk from central Kralendijk. Though small, they're fully equipped with every conceivable amenity, including a balcony or a patio with smashing views of the bay and Klein Bonaire. Closed for rebuilding and renovations at press time, the apartments were scheduled to reopen by the end of 2001. ✉ *Kaya Grandi 65, Kralendijk,* ☎ *599/717–4000,* FAX *599/ 717–2211. 12 apartments. Air-conditioning, fans, in-room safes, kitchenettes, pool, baby-sitting. MC, V. EP.*

$$ ⊡ **Bruce Bowker's Carib Inn.** American diver Bruce Bowker started this ★ small diving lodge out of a private home about a mile from the airport. Rattan furnishings, cable TVs, kitchens (in all but standard rooms), and a family-style atmosphere have turned his homey hostelry

into one of the island's best bets—one that's booked more than a year in advance by repeat guests. Bruce knows everybody by name and loves to fill special requests. Novice divers will enjoy his very small scuba classes, and PADI certification is available. The beach is just a sliver but is fine for shore entries. ⊠ *J. A. Abraham Blvd. 46 (Box 68),* ☎ *599/717–8819,* ℻ *599/717–5295. 10 units. Air-conditioning, fans, kitchenettes, refrigerators, pool, beach, dive shop, snorkeling. MC, V. EP.*

$$ 🖾 **Buddy Dive Resort.** Reasonable rates and cozy, well-equipped accommodations keep guests coming back. The small, raised beach and its superb shore snorkeling is a major draw, as well. The dive shop has a drive-through air-fill station for Nitrox or compressed air tanks. Each apartment has a phone and a balcony or patio with an ocean or garden view. The original 10 apartments are small, but they're clean and offer the same amenities as newer units, including telephones. ⊠ *Kaya Gobernador N. Debrot 85 (Box 231, Kralendijk),* ☎ *599/717–5080 or 800/786–3483,* ℻ *599/717–8647,* 🕸 *www.buddydive.com. 6 rooms, 40 apartments. Restaurant, bar, air-conditioning, kitchenettes, 2 pools, beach, dive shop, coin laundry, car rental. AE, D, MC, V. CP, EP, FAP, MAP.*

$$ 🖾 **Divi Flamingo Beach Resort & Casino.** Aglow in radiant shades of yellow, fuchsia, and teal blue, this informal resort paints a happy picture against the backdrop of the crystalline Caribbean waters. After suffering major damage in a storm, the hotel underwent extensive renovations in 2000. All of the guest rooms (each with a balcony or terrace offering views of the ocean, pool, or garden) have been remodeled with new furniture, bathrooms, tile floors, and air-conditioning units. The pool and front service areas have also been renovated, and the grounds meticulously landscaped with tropical flora. The bi-level waterfront Chibi Chibi Restaurant has been restored as well, and has a fiber optics lighting system over the water for tableside fish viewing. Whether you're a novice or an expert diver, the first-rate dive facility here offers instruction, certification, and excursions to meet your needs. For kicks while you're not diving, drop by the weekly rum punch party. Or try your luck at the casino's slot machines, blackjack tables, and roulette wheels. ⊠ *J. A. Abraham Blvd. 40 (Box 143, Kralendijk),* ☎ *599/717–8285,* ℻ *599/717–8238,* 🕸 *www.divibonaire. com. 89 rooms, 40 time-share units. 2 restaurants, bar, grocery, air-conditioning, in-room safes, 2 pools, outdoor hot tub, spa, tennis court, volleyball, dive shop, dock, snorkeling, shops, casino, meeting rooms, car rental. AE, MC, V. BP, CP, EP, FAP, MAP.*

$$ 🖾 **The Great Escape.** Honeymooners from Venezuela and others in the know come here, a few minutes' walk from Pink Beach, for peace and privacy. The spotless rooms have pastel and beige color schemes and overlook flowers and foliage. Superior rooms have king-size beds and cost only $10 more than standard rooms. The courtyard contains a small waterfall, an open-air bar and grill restaurant, a freshwater pool, and a kids' pool with a small playground. ⊠ *E. E. G. Blvd. 97, Belnem,* ☎ *599/717–7488,* ℻ *599/717–7412. 8 rooms, 2 suites. Restaurant, bar, air-conditioning, fans, refrigerators, 2 pools, shops, playground. AE, MC, V. CP.*

$ 🖾 **Happy Holiday Homes.** Just south of the airport, this small complex of bungalows is across the street from the ocean in a quiet residential area. The comfortable accommodations are spic-and-span and have wooden ceilings, white tile floors, colorful pillows and throw rugs, fully equipped kitchens, living-dining areas, air-conditioned bedrooms, and cable TV. Each unit also has a barbecue and deck furniture on a sun terrace or garden patio. (Divers take note: the roomy patios are perfect for storing gear.) The friendly owners, Louise and Mel Villanueva, go all out for their guests, from buying groceries to arranging car rental or diving and windsurfing packages. ✉ *Punt Vierkant 9, Belnem (Box 216, Kralendijk),* ☎ *599/717–8405,* FAX *599/717–8605,* WEB *www.happyholidayhomes.com. 12 1- and 2-bedroom bungalows. Air-conditioning, in-room safes, kitchenettes, coin laundry, airport shuttle. MC, V. EP.*

$ 🏨 **Hotel Rochaline.** This small hotel in the heart of Kralendijk and above the popular City Café is a good bet for budget travelers who want to be downtown. The clean rooms have single beds, TVs, shower-only baths, and small balconies overlooking the harbor. ✉ *Kaya Grandi 7, Kralendijk,* ☎ *599/717–8286,* FAX *599/717–8258,* WEB *www.bonairenet. com. 25 rooms. 2 restaurants, bar, air-conditioning, meeting rooms. AE, MC, V. EP.*

Dining

Dining on Bonaire is far less expensive than on neighboring islands, and you'll find everything from Continental to Mexican to Asian fare. Most restaurants offer seafood fresh from the surrounding waters; in season try the snapper, wahoo, or dorado (a mild white fish). Meat lovers will appreciate the availability of Argentinian beef, and vegetarians will be pleased by the abundance of fresh Venezuelan produce. Many restaurants only serve dinner—only a few establishments not affiliated with hotels are open for breakfast, so check ahead.

What to Wear

Dress on the island is casual but conservative. Most places don't allow beachwear; even casual poolside restaurants prefer a cover-up.

CATEGORY	COST*
$$$$	over $30
$$$	$20–$30
$$	$10–$20
$	under $10

*per person for a main course at dinner

CARIBBEAN

$ ✕ **Mi Poron.** In the courtyard of a traditional Bonairean home, Mi Poron serves up island flavor in dishes such as stewed conch or goat and fried fish. Vegetarian options are also available. As you pass through the house to the courtyard, look at the decor and furnishings typical of the island in the not-so-distant past. ✉ *Kaya Caracas 1 (near town church), Kralendijk,* ☎ *599/717–5199. MC, V. Closed Mon.*

CONTINENTAL

$$ ✕ **Admiral's Tavern.** This marina tapas bar, part of the Harbour Village Beach Resort, has a soothing ambience. The rough-wood terrace overlooks the twinkling lights of the boats in the marina (so close you can spy on their occupants). The interior is draped with fishnets, buoys, and ships' steering wheels; a gorgeous carved Venezuelan mahogany bar dominates the decor. Three or four tapas—say, tuna empanadas, shrimp in garlic sauce, and tortillas—make a meal. Or you can choose larger dishes such as seared, sesame-crusted tuna with wasabi sauce. ✉ *Kaya Gobernador N. Debrot,* ☎ *599/717–7500. AE, D, DC, MC, V. Closed Tues.*

$$ ✕ **Rendez-Vous Restaurant.** People (Queen Beatrix among them) come
★ to Rendez-Vous for the hearty, consistently well-prepared food: warm French bread with garlic butter, conch chowder, creole-style fresh fish, and seafood, steak, and vegetarian entrées. Enjoy your meal indoors— the dining room showcases works by a local artist—or on the outdoor patio. Also marvel at the collection of hundreds of cigarette lighters

from around the world on display in the bar area. Live local music is performed on Friday. ⊠ *Kaya L. D. Gerharts 3, Kralendijk,* ☎ *599/ 717–8454. AE, MC, V. Closed Sun.*

ECLECTIC

$$ ✕ **Kontiki Beach Club.** The decor at the Kontiki, on the island's southern end and within the Lac Bay Resort apartment complex, is a harmonious blend of terra-cotta tile floors and rattan furnishings, set around the half-moon bar. There's also a brick terrace for alfresco dining. Dutch chef-owners Miriam and Martin serve dishes such as *smookie,* a delicious salmon carpaccio in a lemon-dill sauce, and "Catch Original," panfried local fish in red pepper sauce. If you're sick of wahoo— or just homesick—ask for the tuna toast or grilled cheese. The homemade cheesecakes are mouthwatering. (Note that the service charge is *not* included in the bill—unusual for Bonaire.) Seven studio apartments on premises rent for a very reasonable $50 per night. ⊠ *Kaminda Sorobon 64, Lac Bay,* ☎ *599/717–5369. AE, MC, V. Closed Mon.*

$$$ ✕ **Mona Lisa Bar & Restaurant.** Here you'll find Continental, Caribbean, and Indonesian fare. Popular bar dishes include Wiener schnitzel and fresh fish with curry sauce. Among the favorite seasonal choices in the main dining room are the grouper in papaya sauce and smoked chicken with mustard dressing and pineapple. The intimate stucco-and-brick dining room, presided over by a copy of the famous painting of the eponymous lady, is decorated with Dutch artwork, lace curtains, and whirring ceiling fans. The colorful bar adorned with baseball-style caps is a great place for late-night schmoozing and munching on light snacks or the catch of the day, served until 10 PM. ⊠ *Kaya Grandi 15, Kralendijk,* ☎ *599/717–8718. AE, MC, V. No lunch. Closed Sun.*

$$$ ✕ **Zeezicht Bar & Restaurant.** Zeezicht (pronounced zay-zeekt and meaning "sea view") serves three meals a day. At breakfast and lunch you'll get basic American fare with an Antillean touch, such as a fish omelet. Dinner is either on the terrace overlooking the harbor or in the homey, rough-hewn main room, which has fishnets, pirate murals, and mermaids carved into the wood-beam columns. Locals are dedicated to this hangout, especially for the seviche, conch sandwiches, and the Zeezicht special soup with conch, fish, shrimp, and oysters. There's also an Italian dining room upstairs. ⊠ *Kaya Corsow 10 (across from Karel's Beach Bar), Kralendijk,* ☎ *599/717–8434. AE, MC, V.*

$ ✕ **Coco's Beach Café and Players Bar.** This outdoor waterfront eatery with umbrella-shaded tables is a colorful, fun place to grab a bite any time of day. For breakfast, enjoy bagels, croissants, muffins, and pastries. The lunch and dinner menus include grilled options like fish, chorizo, chicken, and ribs. Banana and strawberry smoothies are popular heat-beaters. Open until 2 AM, the indoor bar features four pool tables (where any sharks you might encounter are not the underwater kind). ⊠ *Kaya Jan Craane Z/N,* ☎ *599/717–5087. AE, D, MC, V.*

INTERNATIONAL

$$ ✕ **Le Wok.** This popular newcomer serves satisfying French, Thai, and Indian fusion dishes and is open for dinner only. The restaurant is housed in an early 20th-century building featuring typical Bonairean architecture. ⊠ *Kaya C. E. B. Hellmund 19,* ☎ *599/717–7884. D, MC, V. Closed Tues.*

ITALIAN

$$$ ✕ **Croccantino.** At this casual restaurant decorated in splashes of purple and green, you can indulge in authentic Italian food on the expanded outdoor terrace or in the air-conditioned indoor smoking or nonsmoking rooms. For an appetizer, the *involtini di melanzane* (grilled eggplant with cream cheese and garlic) is excellent, and of the 12 pastas, the fettuccine *all'aragosta* (with lobster and a creamy seafood sauce) is the most succulent. Main dishes include *filetto ripieno* (filet mignon stuffed with prosciutto and cheese), and there are vegetarian choices, too. ⊠ *Kaya Grandi 48, Kralendijk,* ☎ *599/717–5025. MC, V. Closed Sun. No lunch Sat.*

$$ ✕ **Capriccio.** This splendid, family-run Italian eatery has plenty to
★ boast about. The pastas are handmade daily, fresh mozzarella is imported from Italy once a week, and there's a true climate-controlled wine cellar. Even the house red and white, bottled especially for the restaurant, are fine choices. You can opt for casual à la carte dining on the terrace or a romantic meal in the tonier air-conditioned dining room, which has lace curtains, candles, and floral sprays. The simple yet hefty portions are well-suited to the diving crowd's appetite, and the menu has changed little over time so as not to disappoint the many repeat visitors. If your appetite is hearty, go for the six-course prix-fixe "tour of the menu." Otherwise choose from the numerous pasta, meat, fish, or thin-crust pizza dishes. ⊠ *Kaya Isla Riba 1, Kralendijk,*☎ *599/717–7230. AE, MC, V. Closed Tues. No lunch Sun.*

SEAFOOD

$$ ✕ **Den Laman Bar & Restaurant.** A large aquarium and a nautical-theme decor are the backdrop at this casual restaurant. Eat indoors next to the glass-enclosed "ocean show" (request a table in advance) or outdoors on the noisier patio overlooking the sea. Pick a fresh Caribbean lobster from the tank or order red snapper creole, a hands-down winner. Homemade cheesecake is a draw, as is the live entertainment each Saturday night. ⊠ *Kaya Gobernador N. Debrot 77,* ☎ *599/717–8955. AE, MC, V. No lunch. Closed Tues.*

$$ ✕ **It Rains Fishes.** The mood is vivacious at this popular eatery situated on the terrace of a converted mansion overlooking the water. The friendly owners set the tone, and it's mirrored by the content diners. In the decor, the fish motif is evident: near the bar stands a mural of colorful underwater creatures, each uniquely conceived and hand-painted by a member of the staff or one of the owners. While the menu focuses on fish, other options include beef tenderloin, chicken sate, and pasta. Among the tasty tapas are sate beefsticks, seafood medley with garlic butter and lemon, and mushrooms panfried with garlic, parsley, and sherry. An outdoor bar and party space in the back is well-suited to private events. ⊠ *Kaya Jan N. E. Craane 24,* ☎ *599/717–8780. MC, V.*

$$ ✕ **Richard's Waterfront Dining.** Animated, congenial Richard Beady
★ owns this casually romantic waterfront eatery. It has become the island's most-recommended restaurant—a reputation that's well deserved. Richard, originally from Boston, sets the tone by personally checking on every table. The daily menu is listed on large blackboards, and the food is consistently excellent, catering to American palates with flavorful, though not spicy, preparations. Among the best dishes are conch *alajillo* (with garlic and butter), shrimp primavera, and grilled wahoo. Filet mignon béarnaise satisfies those seeking something other than creatures from the deep. ⊠ *J. A. Abraham Blvd. 60,* ☎ *599/717–5263. MC, V. Closed Mon. No lunch.*

Beaches

Don't expect long stretches of glorious powdery sand. Bonaire's beaches are small, and though the water is blue (several shades of it, in fact), the sand isn't always white. You have your pick of beaches according to color: pink, black, or white. The best hotel beaches are found at Harbour Village Beach Resort (open to nonguests for $25 per day, including towels and use of facilities) and Sorobon (the island's only nude beach, reserved for the exclusive use of hotel guests).

Boca Cocolishi. You'll find hermit crabs along the shore of this black-sand beach in Washington/Slagbaai National Park, on the northeast coast. The term *windswept* has true meaning here: cooling breezes whip the water into a frenzy as the color of the sea changes from midnight blue to aquamarine. The water is too rough for anything more than wading, but the spot is perfect for an intimate picnic *à deux*. To get here, take the Northern Scenic Route to the park; ask for directions at the gate.

Boca Slagbaai. Inside Washington/Slagbaai Park is this beach of coral fossils and rocks with interesting offshore coral gardens that are good for snorkeling. Bring scuba boots or canvas sandals to walk into the water because the beach is rough on bare feet. The gentle surf makes it an ideal place for swimming and picnicking.

Lac Bay Beach. Known for its festive music on Sunday nights, this open bay area with pink-tinted sand is equally dazzling by day. It's a bumpy drive (10–15 minutes on a dirt road) to get here, but you'll be glad when you arrive. It's a good spot for diving, snorkeling, and kayaking (bring your own), and there are public rest rooms and a restaurant for your convenience.

Pink Beach. As the name suggests, the sand here has a pinkish tint that takes on a magical shimmer in the late-afternoon sun. The water is suitable for swimming, snorkeling, and scuba diving. Take the Southern Scenic Route on the island's western side; the beach is past the Trans-World Radio station, close to the slave huts. It's a favorite Bonairean hangout on the weekend, but it's almost deserted during the week.

Playa Funchi. This Washington Park beach is notable for the lagoon on one side, where flamingos nest, and the superb snorkeling on the other, where iridescent green parrot fish swim right up to shore.

Sorobon Beach. Adjacent to the Sorobon Beach Resort's private stretch of sand, this is *the* windsurfing beach. You'll find a restaurant-bar next to the resort and a couple of windsurfing outfitters on the beach. The public beach area has rest rooms and huts for shade.

Windsock Beach. Near the airport, this pretty little spot, also known as Mangrove Beach, looks out toward the north side of the island and features about 200 m of white sand along a rocky shoreline. It's a popular dive site and swimming conditions are good.

Outdoor Activities and Sports

CYCLING

Twenty-one-speed mountain bikes are the perfect way to travel Bonaire's more than 180 mi (290 km) of unpaved routes (as well as the many paved roads). For mountain bikes try **Captain Don's Habitat** (⊠ Kaya Gobernador N. Debrot 103, ☎ 599/717–8290 or 599/717–8913). Rates average around $15–$20 per day, and a credit card or cash deposit is usually required. **Cycle Bonaire** (⊠ Kaya L. D. Gerharts 11D, next to Cultimara Supermarket, Kralendijk, ☎ 599/717–7558) rents mountain bikes and gear (trail maps, water bottles, helmets, locks, repair and first-aid kits) for $15–$20 a day or $75–$100 a week; half-day and full-day guided excursions start at $40, not including bike rental. **Hot Shot Rentals** (⊠ Kaya Bonaire 4, ☎ 599/717–7166) rents regular, hybrid, and Dutch touring bikes for $9 a day.

FISHING

Bonaire's waters teem with big game fish, from marlin to tuna to sail-fish. Captain Cornelis of **Big Game Sportfishing** (⊠ Kaya Warawara 3, ☎ FAX 599/717–6500) offers deep-sea charters for those in search of wahoo, marlin, tuna, swordfish, and sailfish. His rates—which cover bait, tackle, and refreshments—average $350 for a half day, $500 for a full day for as many as four people. **Multifish Charters** (☎ 599/717–7033) has day or night reef fishing on a 32-ft Permacraft twin diesel; the cost for six hours is $300 (four-person maximum). A nine-hour day of deep-sea fishing costs $450 (six-person maximum). **Piscatur Charters** (✉ Kaya H. J. Pop 4,☎ 599/717–8774) offers light-tackle angler reef fishing for jacks, barracuda, and snapper from a 15-ft skiff. Rates are $225 for a half day, $300 for a full day. You can charter the 42-ft Sport Fisherman *Piscatur,* which carries up to six people, for $350 for a half day, $500 for a full day. Bonefishing runs $200 for a half day.

HORSEBACK RIDING

Hour-long trail rides ($20) at the 166-acre **Kunuku Warahama Ranch** (✉ Kaminda Lac, north of Kralendijk along Kaya Nikiboko Zuid, ☎ 599/717–6786) take you through groves of cacti where iguanas, wild goats, donkeys, and flamingos reside. Reserve one of the gentle pintos or palominos a day in advance, and try to go early in the morning, when it's cool. The ranch, open Tuesday–Sunday 10–6, also has an alfresco restaurant, a golf driving range, and two playgrounds.

KAYAKING

Divers and snorkelers use the kayak to reach new and different dive sites and simply tow the craft along during their dive. Nondivers use kayaks to explore the flora and fauna of the island's rich mangrove forests (apply plenty of insect repellent before touring).

At **Jibe City** (✉ Sorobon Beach, ☎ 599/717–5233 or 800/748–8733 for a U.S. representative) kayaks go for $10 (single) and $15 (double) per hour; $25 and $35, respectively, per half day (note that the operation closes in October). Guided trips and kayak rentals are available from **Sand Dollar Dive and Photo. Discover Bonaire** (✉ Box 361, ☎ 599/717–5433 or 599/717–5252) offers kayaking trips (beginning at $35 for a half-day, single kayak trip), nature tours to explore Bonaire's unique flora and fauna (led by biologist Jerry Ligon, $45 per person), snorkeling adventures, special children's programs, and mountain biking trips. Guided tours are available.

SAILING

ABC Yachting (✉ Kaya Gobernador N. Debrot 18A, ☎ 599/560–7897), offers half- or full-day charters aboard a luxury 40-ft sailing yacht ($375 and $675, respectively) or the private charter of a 26-ft Bayliner day cruiser for $295 for four hours.

SCUBA DIVING

Bonaire has some of the best reef diving this side of Australia's Great Barrier Reef. It takes only 5–25 minutes to reach many sites, the current is usually mild, and although some reefs have sudden, steep drops, most begin just offshore and slope gently downward at a 45-degree angle. General visibility runs 60–100 ft (18–30 m), except during surges in October and November. You can see an enormous range of coral: knobby-brain, giant-brain, elkhorn, staghorn, mountainous star, gorgonian, and black. You'll also encounter schools of parrot fish, surgeonfish, angelfish, eels, snappers, and groupers. Beach diving is excellent just about everywhere on the leeward side, so night diving is popular. There are sites here suitable for every skill level; they're clearly marked by yellow stones on the roadside.

In the well-policed Bonaire Marine Park, which encompasses the entire coastline around Bonaire and Klein Bonaire, divers take the rules seriously. Don't even *think* about (1) spearfishing; (2) dropping anchor; or (3) touching, stepping on, or collecting coral. You must pay an admission of $10 (used to maintain the park), for which you receive a colored plastic tag (to attach to an item of scuba gear) entitling you to one calendar year of unlimited diving. Tags are available at all scuba facilities and from the **Marine Park Headquarters** (☎ 599/717–8444) at Karpata. Checkout dives—diving first with a master before going out on your own—are required, and you can arrange them through any dive shop. All dive operations offer classes in free buoyancy control, advanced buoyancy control, and photographic buoyancy control.

The *Guide to the Bonaire Marine Park* lists 86 dive sites (including 16 shore-dive-only and 35 boat-dive-only sites). Another fine reference book is the *Diving and Snorkeling Guide to Bonaire,* by Jerry Schnabel and Suzi Swygert. Guides associated with the various dive centers can give you more complete directions. It's difficult to recommend one site over another; to whet your appetite, here are a few of the popular sites.

Angel City. Take the trail down to the shore adjacent to the Trans-World Radio station; dive in and swim south to Angel City, one of the shallowest and most popular sites in a two-reef complex that includes Alice in Wonderland. The boulder-size green-and-tan coral heads are home to black margates, Spanish hogfish, gray snappers, and large purple tube sponges.

Bari Reef. Go to the free slide show on Tuesday at the Sand Dollar Condominium Resort to catch a glimpse of the elkhorn and fire coral, queen angelfish, and other wonders of Bari Reef, just off the resort's pier.

Calabas Reef. Off the coast from the former Divi Flamingo Beach Resort, this is the island's busiest dive site. It's replete with Christmas-tree worms, sponges, and fire coral adhering to a ship's hull. Fish life is frenzied, with the occasional octopus putting in an appearance.

Forest. You'll need to catch a boat to reach Forest, a dive site off the southwest coast of Klein Bonaire. Named for the abundant black-coral forests found in it, the site gets a lot of fish action, including a resident spotted eel that lives in a cave.

Rappel. This spectacular site is near the Karpata Ecological Center. The shore is a sheer cliff, and the lush coral growth is home to an unusual variety of marine life, including occasional orange sea horses, squid, spiny lobsters, and spotted trunkfish.

Small Wall. One of Bonaire's three complete vertical wall dives (and one of its most popular night-diving spots), Small Wall is offshore from the road north of Captain Don's Habitat, near Barcadera Beach. The 60-ft (18-m) wall is frequented by squid, turtles, tarpon, and barracudas, and has dense hard and soft coral formations; it also allows for excellent snorkeling.

Something Special. South of the marina entrance at Harbour Village Beach Resort, this spot is famous for its garden eels. They wave about from the relatively shallow sand terrace looking like long grass in a breeze.

Windsock Steep. This excellent shore-dive site (from 20 to 80 ft/6 to 24 m) is in front of the small beach opposite the airport runway. It's a popular place for snorkeling. The current is moderate, the elkhorn coral profuse; you may also see angelfish and rays.

DIVE CENTERS

Many of the dive shops listed below offer PADI and NAUI certification courses and SSI, as well as an array of underwater photography and videography courses. Some shops are also qualified to certify dive instructors. Full certification courses cost approximately $370; open water refresher courses run about $185; a one-tank boat dive with un-limited shore diving costs about $37; a two-tank boat dive with un-limited shore diving is about $55. As for equipment, renting a mask, fin, and snorkel costs about $8.50 all together; for a BC and regulator, expect to pay about $16.

Bonaire Scuba Center (⊠ Black Durgon Inn, Kaya Gobernador N. Debrot 145, ☎ 599/717–5736; in the U.S.: ⊠ Box 775, Morgan, NJ 08879, ☎ 908/566–8866 or 800/526–2370).

Bon Bini Divers (⊠ Lions Dive Hotel Bonaire, Kaya Gobernador N. Debrot 91, ☎ 599/717–5580 or 800/327–5425).

Bruce Bowker's Carib Inn Dive Center (⊠ J. A. Abraham Blvd. 46 [Airport Rd.], ☎ 599/717–8819).

Buddy Dive Resort (⊠ Kaya Gobernador N. Debrot 85, ☎ 599/717–5080).

Captain Don's Habitat Dive Shop (⊠ Kaya Gobernador N. Debrot 103, ☎ 599/717–5390).

Dee Scarr's Touch the Sea (⊠ Box 369, Kralendijk, ☎ 599/717–8529).

Dive Inn (⊠ Close to South Pier, Kaya C. E. B. Hellmund, ☎ 599/717–8761).

Great Adventures at Harbour Village (⊠ Harbour Village Bonaire, Kaya Gobernador N. Debrot 72, ☎ 599/717–7500 or 800/424–0004).

Habitat Dive Center (⊠ Captain Don's Habitat, Kaya Gobernador N. Debrot 85, ☎ 599/717–8290).

Photo Tours Divers (⊠ Caribbean Court Bonaire, J. A. Abraham Blvd., ☎ 599/717–5353 ext. 328).

Sand Dollar Dive and Photo (⊠ Sand Dollar Condominium Resort, Kaya Gobernador N. Debrot 79, ☎ 599/717–5252).

Toucan Diving (⊠ Plaza Resort Bonaire, J. A. Abraham Blvd. 80, ☎ 599/717–2500).

SNORKELING

Bonaire, in conjunction with *Skin Diver Magazine,* developed the world's first **Guided Snorkeling Program** in 1996. The highly educational and entertaining program begins with a slide show presenting a variety of topics, from a beginner's look at reef fish, coral, and sponges to advanced fish identification and night snorkeling. Guided snorkeling for all skill levels can be arranged through most resort dive shops; the cost is $25 (discounts available for more than one session) and includes slide presentations, transportation to the site, and a guided tour. Gear is an additional $9 per 24-hour period. The best snorkeling spots are on the island's leeward side, where you have shore access to the reefs, and along the west side of Klein Bonaire, where the reef is better developed.

In addition to the dive shops, **SeaCow WaterTaxi** (⊠ Club Nautico Pier, at the waterfront in Kralendijk, ☎ 599/780–7126) has snorkel trips (day and night), and daily excursions to Klein Bonaire.

TENNIS

Tennis isn't a common activity on tiny Bonaire, but you do have a few options to volley about. At **Plaza Resort Bonaire** and the **Sand Dollar Condominium Resort,** court prices generally run about $20 per hour for nonguests (free for guests), but pros aren't available. **Harbour Village Beach Resort** has a complex managed by Peter Burwash International and staffed by pro Mark Brinson. The hotel offers tennis packages as well. Plan to play in the early morning or evening hours to avoid the worst of the day's heat.

WATERSKIING
If you're looking to make a splash on water skis, **Great Adventures at Harbour Village** (☎ 599/717–7500 or 800/424–0004) can make arrangements for you. The cost is around $20 for 15 minutes of skiing.

WINDSURFING
Lac Bay, a protected cove on the east coast, is ideal for windsurfing. Novices will find it especially comforting since there's no way to be blown out to sea. The **Bonaire Windsurf Place** (⊠ Lac Bay, Box 63, ☎ 599/717–2288 or 800/225–0102), commonly referred to as "the place," rents the latest Mistral, ProTech, and Naish equipment for $35–$60 per hour. A two-hour group lesson costs $35. Private lessons are $45 per hour (rates include equipment for beginners only). The three-day lesson package is a real bargain at $120 per individual, $95 per group.

Jibe City (⊠ Sorobon Beach, ☎ 599/717–5233 or 800/748–8733 for a U.S. representative) offers lessons for $45 (includes board and sail for beginners only); board rentals start at $20 an hour, $40 for a half day. There are pickups at all the hotels at 9 AM and 1 PM; ask your hotel to make arrangements.

Shopping

You can get to know all the shops in Kralendijk in an hour or so. But sometimes there's no better way to enjoy some time out of the sun and sea than to go shopping (particularly if your companion is a dive fanatic and you're not). Almost all the shops are on the Kaya Grandi and adjacent streets and in tiny malls. Harborside Mall is a pleasant, airy, air-conditioned mall with several fine shops. The most distinctive local crafts are fanciful painted pieces of driftwood and hand-painted *cunucu,* or little wilderness houses. One word of caution: Buy as many flamingo T-shirts as you want, but don't take home items made of goatskin or tortoiseshell; they aren't allowed into the United States. Remember, too, that it's forbidden to take sea fans, coral, conch shells, and *all* forms of marine life off the island.

Specialty Items

CLOTHES
Benetton (⊠ Kaya Grandi 49, ☎ 599/717–5107) claims that its prices for men's, women's, and children's clothes are 30% lower than in New York. **Best Buddies** (⊠ Kaya Grandi 32, ☎ 599/717–7570) stocks a selection of Indonesian batik shirts, *pareos* (beach wraps), and T-shirts. Colorful cotton resort wear and T-shirts are available at **Bye-Bye Bonaire** (⊠ Harborside Mall, ☎ 599/717–7578). At **Island Fashions** (⊠ Kaya Grandi 5, ☎ 599/717–7565) you can buy swimsuits, sunglasses, T-shirts, and costume jewelry.

DUTY-FREE GOODS
Cigar smokers will find friends at **Little Holland** (⊠ Harborside Mall, ☎ 599/717–5670) as they breathe in the smoky splendor of Havanas. Montecristo, H. Upmann, Romeo & Juliet, and Cohiba are all here. Far from being banished to the porch, smokers are welcomed into the acclimatized Cedar Cigar Room. **Perfume Palace** (⊠ Harborside Mall, ☎ 599/717–5288) sells perfumes and makeup from Lancôme, Estée Lauder, Chanel, Ralph Lauren, and Clinique.

HANDICRAFTS
Bon Tiki (⊠ Kaya C. E. B. Hellmund 3, Kralendijk, ☎ 599/717–6877) offers a variety of unique works from Bonaire's finest artists. The **Har-**

mony Art Gallery (⊠ Kaya L. D. Gerharts 10, ☎ 599/717–8539) showcases the works of local, Dutch, and American artists and will ship artwork (shrink-wrapped but unframed) to the United States. **Roselord Souvenir & Gift Shop** (⊠ Kaya Kanari 42, North Nikiboko, ☎ 599/717–6765), outside Kralendijk, sells plates and woodwork painted by local artists. **Things Bonaire** (⊠ Kaya Grandi 38C, ☎ 599/717–8423) purveys T-shirts, earrings, batik dresses, souvenirs, and guidebooks.

JEWELRY

Littman's (⊠ Kaya Grandi 33, ☎ 599/717–8160) is an upscale jewelry and gift shop where many items are handpicked by owner Steven Littman on his regular trips to Europe. Look for Rolex, Omega, Cartier, and Tag Heuer watches, fine gold jewelry, antique coins, nautical sculptures, resort clothing, and accessories. There's a second outlet a few doors down in Harborside Mall.

Nightlife and the Arts

Nightlife

Most divers are exhausted after they finish their third, fourth, or fifth dive of the day, which may explain why there are so few discos. Indeed, many people's idea of nightlife is looking for the elusive "green flash" just before sunset, a harbinger of luck (some swear it exists, others say that it can only be seen after several daiquiris) or else they go diving, snorkeling, windsurfing by the light of the moon.

On Sunday afternoon at Lac Cai enjoy the festive Sunday Party, where locals celebrate the day with music, dancing, and food from 3 to 11. Take a taxi, especially if you plan to imbibe a few rum punches. Top island performers, including the Kunuku Band and Duo Flamingo, migrate from one resort to another throughout the week. You'll find information in the free magazines (published once a year) *Bonaire Holiday, Bonaire Affair,* and *Bonaire Nights.* The twice-monthly *Bonaire Update Events & Activities* pamphlet is available at most restaurants.

BARS

Amadeus (⊠ Kaya Bonaire 4, ☎ 599/717–2888), a lively outdoor bar across the street from the waterfront, draws throngs of young partyers. The Thursday night happy hour at **Captain Don's Habitat** (⊠ Kaya Gobernador N. Debrot 85, ☎ 599/717–8290) is very popular. In downtown Kralendijk, **City Cafe** (⊠ Kaya Isla Riba 3, ☎ 599/717–8286) is a wacky hangout splashed in magenta, banana, and electric blue. Here you'll find cocktails like the Alabama Slammer (Amaretto, gin, Southern Comfort, lemon) and snack food. **Karel's** (⊠ Kaya J. N. E. Craane 12, ☎ 599/717–8434) sits on stilts above the sea and is *the* place for mingling—especially Friday and Saturday nights, when there's live island and pop music.

CASINOS

In the casino at the **Plaza Resort Bonaire** (⊠ J. A. Abraham Blvd. 80, ☎ 599/717–2450), the slot machines are open at 6 PM, the gaming tables at 7 PM; things don't close till 4 AM. At the **Divi Flamingo**'s casino (⊠ J. A. Abraham Blvd., ☎ 599/717–8285), you can try your hand at blackjack, roulette, and slot machines 'til 4 AM.

DANCE CLUBS

The spacious **Fantasy Disco** (⊠ Kaya L. D. Gerharts 11, ☎ 599/717–6345) is the island's main dance spot. It has big-screen TVs and taped merengue, jazz, rock, and reggae music; occasionally there's a live band. Thursday's Ladies Night is popular.

MOVIES

The **Bonaire Twin Cinema** (✉ Kaya Prinses Marie, Kralendijk, ☎ 599/
717–2400) has four to six daily showings of recent-release movies (primarily American hits). Tickets are about $6.

The Arts

Nature's artistry earns top billing on Bonaire. Slide shows of under-
water and above-water scenes fascinate both divers and nondivers. Dee
Scarr, a dive guide, presents the fascinating Touch the Sea show Mon-
day night at 8:45, November–June, at **Captain Don's Habitat** (✉ Kaya
Gobernador N. Debrot 85, ☎ 599/717–8290). Flora and fauna of the
Caribbean are the focus of the slide show presented by naturalist Jerry
Ligon on Thursday night at 8:15 at the **Sand Dollar Condominium Re-
sort** (✉ Kaya Gobernador N. Debrot 79, ☎ 599/717–8738).

Exploring Bonaire

Two routes, north and south from Kralendijk, the island's small capital, are possible on the 24-mi-long (39-km-long) island; either route
will take from a few hours to a full day, depending on whether you
stop to snorkel, swim, dive, or lounge.

*Numbers in the margin correspond to points of interest on the Bonaire
map.*

Kralendijk

❶ Bonaire's small, tidy capital city (population 3,000) is five minutes from
the airport and a short walk from Bruce Bowker's Carib Inn. The main
drag, J. A. Abraham Boulevard, turns into **Kaya Grandi** in the center
of town. Along it are most of the island's major stores, boutiques, and
restaurants. Across Kaya Grandi, opposite the Littman jewelry store,
is Kaya L. D. Gerharts, with several small supermarkets, the Air ALM
office, a handful of snack shops, and some of the better restaurants.
Walk down the narrow waterfront avenue called Kaya C. E. B. Hellmund, which leads straight to the **North and South piers.** In the center of town, the Harborside Mall has chic boutiques. Along this route
is **Ft. Oranje,** with its cannons. From December through April, cruise
ships dock in the harbor once or twice a week. The elegant white structure that looks like a tiny Greek temple is the **fish market;** local fishermen no longer bring their catches here (they sell out of their homes
these days), but you'll find plenty of fresh produce. Pick up the brochure
Walking and Shopping in Kralendijk from the tourist office to get a
map and full listing of all the monuments and sights in the town.

South Bonaire

The trail south from Kralendijk is chock-full of icons—both natural
and man-made—that tell Bonaire's minisaga. Rent a four-wheel-drive
vehicle (a car will do, but during the rainy season of October–November the roads can become muddy) and head out along the Southern
Scenic Route. The roads wind through dramatic desert terrain, full of
organ-pipe cacti and spiny-trunk mangroves—huge stumps of saltwater
trees that rise from the marshes like witches. Watch for long-haired
goats, wild donkeys, and lizards of all sizes.

SIGHTS TO SEE

❸ **Salt Flats.** You can't miss the salt flats—voluptuous white drifts that
look something like mountains of snow. Harvested once a year, the
"ponds" are owned by Cargill, Inc., which has reactivated the 19th-
century salt industry with great success (one reason for that success is
that the ocean on this part of the island is higher than the land—which
makes irrigation a snap). Keep a lookout for the three 30-ft (9-m)
obelisks—white, blue, and red—that were used to guide the trade

boats coming to pick up the salt. Look also in the distance across the pans to the abandoned solar salt works that's now a designated **flamingo sanctuary.** With the naked eye you might be able to make out a pink-orange haze just on the horizon; with binoculars you will see a sea of bobbing pink bodies. The sanctuary is completely protected, and no entrance is allowed (flamingos are extremely sensitive to disturbances of any kind).

2 **Slave Huts.** The salt industry's gritty history is revealed in Rode Pan, the site of two groups of tiny slave huts. The white grouping is on the right side of the road, opposite the salt flats; the second grouping, called the red slave huts (though they appear yellow), stretches across the road toward the island's southern tip. During the 19th century slaves worked the salt pans by day, then crawled into these huts at night. Each Friday afternoon they walked seven hours to Rincon to weekend with their families, returning each Sunday. Only very small people will be able to enter, but walk around and poke your head in for a look.

4 **Willemstoren Lighthouse.** Bonaire's first lighthouse was built in 1837 and is now automated (but closed to visitors). Take some time to explore the beach and notice how the waves, driven by the trade winds, play a crashing symphony against the rocks. Locals stop here to collect pieces of driftwood in spectacular shapes and to build fanciful pyramids from objects that have washed ashore.

North Bonaire

The Northern Scenic Route takes you into the heart of Bonaire's natural wonders—desert gardens of towering cacti (*kadushi,* used to prepare soup, and the thornier *yatu,* used to build cactus fencing), tiny coastal coves, and plenty of fantastic panoramas. The road also weaves between eroded pink-and-black limestone walls and eerie rock formations with fanciful names like the Devil's Mouth and Iguana Head (you'll need a vivid imagination and sharp eye to recognize them). Brazil trees growing along the route were used by Indians to make dye (pressed from a red ring in the trunk). Inscriptions still visible in several island caves were made with this dye.

A snappy excursion with the requisite photo stops will take about 2½ hours, but if you pack your swimsuit and a hefty picnic basket (forget about finding a Burger King), you could spend the entire day exploring this northern sector. Head out from Kralendijk on the Kaya Gobernador N. Debrot until it turns into the Northern Scenic Route. Note that once you pass the Radio Nederland towers you cannot turn back to Kralendijk. The narrow road becomes one-way until you get to Landhuis Karpata, and you have to follow the cross-island road to Rincon and return via the main road through the center of the island.

SIGHTS TO SEE

6 **Barcadera Cave.** Once used to trap goats, this cave is one of the oldest in Bonaire; there's even a tunnel that looks intriguingly spooky. It's the first sight along the northern route; watch closely for a yellow marker on your left before you reach the towering Radio Nederland antennas. Pull off across from the entrance to the Bonaire Caribbean Club, and you'll discover some stone steps that lead down into a cave full of stalactites and vegetation.

11 **Goto Meer.** This saltwater lagoon near the island's northern end is a popular flamingo hangout. Bonaire is one of the few places in the world where pink flamingos nest. The shy, spindly legged creatures—affectionately called "pink clouds"—are magnificent birds to observe, and there are about 15,000 of them in Bonaire (the same as the number of permanent island residents). The best time to catch them at home is

January–June, when they tend to their gray-plumed young. For the best view take the newly paved access road alongside the lagoon through the jungle of cacti to the parking and observation area on the rise overlooking the lagoon and Washington/Slagbaai Park beyond.

⑫ **Landhuis Karpata.** This mustard-color building was the manor house of an aloe plantation more than 100 years ago. The site was named for the *karpata* (castor oil) plants that are abundant in the area—you'll see them along the sides of the road as you approach. Notice the rounded outdoor oven where aloe was boiled down before exporting the juice. Although the government has built a shaded rest stop at Karpata, there's still no drink stand.

❼ **1,000 Steps.** Once you've passed the Radio Nederland towers on the main road north, watch closely for a short yellow marker on the opposite side of the road to locate these limestone stairs carved right out of the cliff. If you trek down the stairs, you'll discover a lovely coral beach and protected cove where you can snorkel and scuba dive. Actually, you'll count only 67 steps, but it feels like 1,000 when you walk back up carrying scuba gear.

❾ **Onima.** Small signposts direct the way to the Indian inscriptions found on a 3-ft (1-m) limestone ledge that juts out like a partially formed cave entrance. Look up to see the red-stained designs and symbols inscribed on the limestone, said to have been the handiwork of the Arawak Indians when they inhabited the island centuries ago. The pictographs are at least 500 years old. To reach Onima, pass through Rincon on the road that heads back to Kralendijk, but take the left-hand turn before Fontein.

❽ **Rincon.** The island's original Spanish settlement, Rincon became home to the slaves brought from Africa to work the plantations and salt fields. Superstition and voodoo lore still have a powerful impact here, more so than in Kralendijk, where the townspeople work hard at suppressing old ways. Rincon is now a well-kept cluster of pastel cottages and century-old buildings that constitute Bonaire's oldest village. Watch your driving here—goats and dogs often sit right in the middle of the main drag. There are a couple of local eateries, but the real temptation is **Prisca's Ice Cream** (☎ 599/717–6334), to be found at Prisca's house, on Kaya Komkomber (watch for the hand-lettered sign).

❺ **Seroe Largu.** Just off the main road, this spot, at 394 ft (120 m), is one of the highest on the island. A paved but narrow and twisting road leads to a magnificent daytime view of Kralendijk's rooftops and the island of Klein Bonaire. To commemorate the new millennium, a large cross and figure of Christ were erected here, with inscriptions reading AD 2000, *ayera* (past), *awe* (present), and *semper* (future).

🖑 ❿ **Washington/Slagbaai National Park.** Once a plantation producing divi-divi trees (the pods were used for tanning animal skins), aloe (used for medicinal lotions), charcoal, and goats, the park is now a model of conservation. It's easy to tour the 13,500-acre tropical desert terrain on the dirt roads. As befits a wilderness sanctuary, the well-marked, rugged routes force you to drive slowly enough to appreciate the animal life and the terrain. A four-wheel-drive vehicle is a must. (Think twice about coming here if it rained the day before—the mud you may encounter will be more than inconvenient.) If you're planning to hike, bring a picnic lunch, camera, sunscreen, and plenty of water. There are two routes: the long one, 22 mi (35½ km), is marked by yellow arrows; the short one, 15 mi (24 km), by green arrows. Goats and donkeys may dart across the road, and if you keep your eyes peeled, you may catch sight of large iguanas camouflaged in the shrubbery.

Bird-watchers are really in their element here. Right inside the park's gate, flamingos roost on the salt pad known as **Salina Mathijs,** and exotic parakeets dot the foot of **Mt. Brandaris,** Bonaire's highest peak, at 784 ft (239 m). Some 130 species of birds fly in and out of the shrubbery in the park. Keep your eyes open and your binoculars at hand. Swimming, snorkeling, and scuba diving are permitted, but you're requested not to frighten the animals or remove anything from the grounds. Absolutely no hunting, fishing, or camping is allowed. A useful guide to the park is available at the entrance for about $6. ☎ 599/717–8444. ☜ $10.☉ Daily 8–5, but you must enter before 3.

BONAIRE A TO Z

To research prices, get advice from other travelers, and book travel arrangements, visit www.fodors.com.

AIR TRAVEL

Air ALM has daily flights via Curaçao from Miami. It also has flights to Aruba, Caracas, Venezuela, St. Maarten, Trinidad, and other Caribbean islands—using Curaçao as its hub. The airline's Visit Caribbean Pass allows easy interisland travel. Air Jamaica flies to Bonaire on Wednesday and Saturday from its hub in Montego Bay. Travelers can also connect to the nonstop flight from Montego Bay from eight of the airline's U.S. gateways: New York (JFK); Newark; Philadelphia; Baltimore; Atlanta; Chicago; Los Angeles; and Miami.
➤ AIRLINES AND CONTACTS: **Air ALM** (☎ 599/717–8500); **Air Jamaica** (☎ 800/523–5585).

AIRPORTS

Bonaire's Flamingo Airport is tiny but welcoming. Rental cars and taxis are available, but try to arrange for pickup through your hotel. A taxi will run between $9 and $12 (for up to four people) to most hotels; $16 to the Lac Bay Resort or Sorobon Beach Resort. Fares are 25% extra from 7 PM to midnight and 50% extra from midnight to 6 AM.
➤ AIRPORT INFORMATION: **Flamingo Airport** (☎ 599/717–3800).

BIKE AND MOPED TRAVEL

Scooters are a great way to zip around the island. Rates are about $18 per day for a 1-seater, and up to $38 for a deluxe 2-seater. A valid driver's license and cash deposit or credit card are required.
➤ BIKE AND MOPED RENTALS: **Hot Shot Rentals** (✉ Kaya Bonaire 4, ☎ 599/717–7166). **Macho!** (✉ Plaza Resort Bonaire, ☎ 599/717–2500).

BUSINESS HOURS

BANKS
Banks are generally open weekdays 8:30–noon and 1:15–3:30. The bank at the airport has extended hours: weekdays 6:30 AM–11:30 PM and weekends 6 AM–11:30 PM.

POST OFFICES
Post offices are open weekdays 7:30–noon and 1:30–4.

SHOPS
Stores in the Kralendijk area are generally open Monday–Saturday 8–noon and 2–6.

CAR RENTALS

You'll need a valid U.S., Canadian, or international driver's license to rent a car, and you must meet the minimum and maximum age requirements (usually 25 and 70) of each rental company. There's a government tax of $3.50 per day per car rental; no cash deposit is needed if you pay by credit card.

➤ MAJOR AGENCIES: **Avis** (✉ Flamingo Airport, ☎ 599/717–5795); **Budget** (✉ Flamingo Airport, ☎ 599/717–7424); **Flamingo Car Rental** (✉ Kaya Grandi 86, ☎ 599/717–8888 or 599/717–5588 at the airport); **Hertz** (☎ 599/717–7221); **Island Rentals** (✉ Kaya Industria 31, ☎ 599/717–2100); **National** (☎ 599/717–7940).

CAR TRAVEL

GASOLINE

Gas costs $2.50–$3 per gallon (NAf1.11 per liter), and you'll find stations in Kralendijk, Rincon, and Antriol.

ROAD CONDITIONS

Remember that there are miles of unpaved road; the roller-coaster hills at the national park require a strong stomach, and during the rainy season (October–November), mud—called Bonairean snow—can be difficult to navigate.

RULES OF THE ROAD

All traffic stays to the right, and there's not a single traffic light. Signs or green arrows are usually posted to leading attractions; if you stick to the paved roads and marked turnoffs, you won't get lost.

ELECTRICITY

Bonaire runs on 120 AC/50 cycles. A transformer and occasionally a two-prong adapter are required. Note that some appliances may work slowly (60 cycles are typical in North America).

EMERGENCIES

➤ AMBULANCE AND FIRE: Dial ☎ 599/717–8900 for the ambulance and ☎ 599/717–8000 for fire emergencies.

➤ HOSPITALS: **St. Franciscus Hospital** (✉ Kaya Soeur Bartola 2, Kralendijk, ☎ 599/717–8900).

➤ PHARMACIES: **Botika Bonaire** (✉ Kaya Grandi 27, by Harborside Mall, ☎ 599/717–8905).

➤ POLICE: Dial ☎ 599/717–8000.

➤ SCUBA-DIVING EMERGENCIES: There's a hyperbaric chamber (☎ 599/717–8187) next to the hospital in Kralendijk.

FESTIVALS AND SEASONAL EVENTS

Carnival, generally held in February, is the usual nonstop parade of steel bands, floats, and wild costumes, albeit on a much smaller scale than on some other islands. It culminates in the ceremonial burning in effigy of King Momo, representing the spirit of debauchery. April ushers in the festival of Simadan, a celebration of the corn harvest, with special songs paying tribute to the farmers. The week-long Bonaire Dive Festival is held in June, filled with educational and fun activities to raise people's awareness of the importance of the world's coral reefs. Early October sees the well-attended International Sailing Regatta. December marks the beginning of the Bari (Drum) Festival, for which local bands write and play songs about events of the past year.

HOLIDAYS

Public holidays for 2002 are: New Year's Day, Carnival Monday (Feb. 26), Good Friday (Apr. 13), Rincon Day and Queen's Birthday (Apr. 30), Labor Day (May 1), Bonaire Day (Sept. 6), Christmas and the day after (Dec. 25–26).

LANGUAGE

The official language is Dutch, but few speak it, and even then only on official occasions. The street language is Papiamento, a mix of

Spanish, Portuguese, Dutch, English, and French as well as African tongues. You'll light up your waiter's eyes if you can say *masha danki* (thank you very much) and *pasa un bon dia* (have a nice day). English is spoken by most people working at the hotels, restaurants, and tourist shops, but a Spanish phrase book may come in handy. Many members of the Dutch expat community have learned to read and write Papiamento, so the island doesn't feel like a *colony* of the Netherlands.

MAIL AND SHIPPING
Airmail postage to North America is NAf1.75 for letters and NAf1.10 for postcards; to the United Kingdom, letters cost Naf1.30, and postcards are Naf.65. The main post office is at the southeast corner of Kaya Grandi and Kaya Libertador S. Bolivar in Kralendijk.

MONEY MATTERS
Prices quoted in this chapter are in U.S. dollars unless otherwise noted.

ATMS
You'll find ATMs at the airport, Kralendijk, and Hato branches of MCB, as well as at the Sand Dollar Resort and the Plaza Resort; at the Kaya Grandi branch of the ABN-AMRO; at Banco di Caribe on Kaya Grandi; and at the Antilles Banking Corp on Kaya P. L. Brion. The **Cultimara Supermarket** (✉ Kaya L. D. Gerharts 13, at Kaya Soeur Bartola and behind Valerie's Gifts, Kralendijk) also has an ATM.

BANKS
ABN-AMRO Bank (✉ Kaya Grandi and Kaya Libertador S. Bolivar, Kralendijk, ☎ 599/717–8417; ✉ Kaya Grandi 22, Kralendijk, ☎ 599/717–7595; ✉ Kaya Grandi 49, Kralendijk, ☎ 599/717–7660). **Maduro & Curiel's Bank Bonaire N. V.** (MCB; ✉ Flamingo Airport, ☎ 599/717–5522; ✉ Kaya L. D. Gerharts, Kralendijk, ☎ 599/717–5520; ✉ Rincon, ☎ 599/717–6266; ✉ Hato, ☎ 599/717–5520).

CURRENCY
You don't need to convert your American dollars into the local currency, the NAf guilder. U.S. currency and traveler's checks are accepted everywhere, and the difference in exchange rates is negligible. Banks accept U.S. dollar banknotes at the official rate of NAf1.78 to the U.S. dollar, traveler's checks at NAf1.80. This rate is practically fixed. The rate of exchange at shops and hotels ranges from NAf1.75 to NAf1.80. The guilder is divided into 100 cents.

PASSPORTS AND VISAS
U.S. and Canadian citizens need only proof of identity (a valid passport or a birth certificate with a raised seal along with a photo ID). All other visitors must carry valid passports. In addition, all visitors must have a return or ongoing ticket and are advised to confirm reservations 48 hours before departure. The maximum stay is up to 90 days.

SAFETY
Because of strong trade winds pounding against the rocks, the windward (eastern) side of Bonaire is much too rough for diving. The *Guide to the Bonaire Marine Park* (available at dive shops around the island) specifies the level of diving skill required for 44 sites and knows what it's talking about. No matter how beautiful a beach may look, heed all warning signs regarding the rough undertow. Also get an orientation on what stings underwater and what doesn't.

During Bonaire's rainy season (October–November), mosquitoes can be fierce. Smart, happy people douse themselves with repellent and also spray their hotel room before going to bed. Open-air restaurants usually have a can of repellent handy.

Bonaire has a reputation for being friendly and safe, but lately people have taken to locking their car doors, especially in the heart of town. Don't leave your camera in an open car, and keep your money, credit cards, jewelry, and other valuables in your hotel's safety-deposit box.

SIGHTSEEING TOURS
BOAT TOURS AND CRUISES
On Bonaire, the myriad of choices for getting out and enjoying the deep blue sea seems as limitless as the ocean itself. Among them: snorkeling, picnicking, and sunset cruises (prices range from $25 to $50 per person), and private or group sails (expect to pay about $425 per day for a party of four). Glass-bottom boat trips are another highlight: The 1½-hour trip costs $23 per person and leaves twice daily, except Sunday, from the Harbour Village Marina.

➤ CONTACTS: *Samur* (☎ 599/717–5592), is a 56-ft Siamese junk. *Sea Witch* (☎ 599/9–560–7449) is a 56-ft ketch. *Woodwind* (☎ 599/9–560–7055) is a 37-ft trimaran. *Oscarina* (☎ 599/9–560–7674) is a 42-ft sloop.

➤ GLASS-BOTTOM BOAT TRIPS: *Bonaire Dream* (✉ Harbour Village Marina, Kaya Gobernador N. Debrot, ☎ 599/717–8239 or 599/717–4514).

ORIENTATION
➤ CONTACTS: **Achie Tours** (✉ Kaya Nikiboko Noord 33, ☎ 599/717–8630) has several half- and full-day island tours. **Baranka Tours** (✉ Kaya Gobernador N. Debrot 79A, ☎ 599/717–2200) offers several island tours at reasonable prices. **Bonaire Sightseeing Tours** (✉ Kaya General Manuel Piar, next to the main Air ALM office, Kralendijk, ☎ 599/717–8778) will chauffeur you around on two-hour tours of either the island's north or south or on a half-day city-and-country tour ($25), which visits sights in both regions.

TAXES
DEPARTURE TAX
The departure tax when going to Curaçao is $5.75. For all other destinations it's $20.

SALES TAX
Hotels charge a room tax of $6.50 per person, per night. Many hotels add a 10%–15% maid-service charge to your bill.

VALUE ADDED TAX (V.A.T.)
A V.A.T (value-added tax) of 6% is tacked on to dining and lodging costs.

TAXIS
Taxis are unmetered; they have fixed rates controlled by the government. A trip from the airport to your hotel will cost between $9 and $12 for up to four passengers. A taxi from most hotels into town costs between $5 and $8. Fares increase from 7 PM to midnight by 25% and from midnight to 6 AM by 50%. Drivers are usually knowledgeable enough about the island to conduct half-day tours; they charge about $30 for up to four passengers for half-day northern- or southern-route tours. Call **Taxi Central Dispatch** (☎ 599/717–8100 or dial 10) or inquire at your hotel.

TELEPHONES
It's difficult for visitors to Bonaire to get involved in dramatic, heart-wrenching phone conversations or *any* phone discussions requiring a degree of privacy. Many hotels don't have phones in the rooms, though in recent years the convenience has been added to a number of the major resorts. You can make calls from hotel front desks or from the Telbo

central phone company office (located next to the tourism office in Kralendijk), which is open 24 hours a day. Telephone connections have improved, but static is still common.

COUNTRY AND AREA CODES
The area code is 599; 717 is the exchange for every four-digit telephone number on Bonaire.

INTERNATIONAL CALLS
Forget about trying to use your phone cards; it's theoretically possible but utterly maddening trying to get connected to the right operator. You can try AT&T by dialing 001–800/872–2881 from public phones, but there are no guarantees. To call Bonaire from the United States, dial 011–599–717 + the local four-digit number.

LOCAL CALLS
When making interisland calls, dial 717 + the local four-digit number. Local phone calls cost NAf25¢.

TIPPING
Most restaurants add a 10%–12% service charge. Taxi drivers like a 10% tip, but it isn't mandatory (unless you can't stand to be glared at!). Bellhops should receive $1 per bag.

VISITOR INFORMATION
➤ BEFORE YOU LEAVE: Contact the **Bonaire Government Tourist Office** (✉ 10 Rockefeller Plaza, Suite 900, New York, New York10020, ☎ 212/956–5913 or 800/266–2473, WEB www.infobonaire.com; ✉ Interreps BV, Visserring-laan 24, 2288ER, Rijswijk, The Netherlands, ☎ 70/395–4444) for information on planning your trip.
➤ IN BONAIRE: Stop by the **Tourism Corporation Bonaire** office (✉ Kaya Grandi 2, ☎ 599/717–8322 or 599/717–8649), in Kralendijk for a list of weekly events.

6 BRITISH VIRGIN ISLANDS

Updated by Pamela Acheson

The eight-seater Cessna took off smoothly and on schedule for the 20-minute flight from St. Thomas. As it flew up the Sir Francis Drake Channel to the Beef Island/Tortola Airport, passengers gazed out at stunning views of island and channel. Suddenly everyone turned from the windows and looked at each other quizzically. They sat in stunned silence as the plane flew past the airport and headed to the little runway on nearby Virgin Gorda. After this unscheduled landing, the pilot turned around nervously and said, "Sorry. I'm late for my wedding. Nelson, my copilot, will fly you back to Tortola."

The British Virgin Islands (BVI) consist of about 50 islands, islets, and cays. Most are remarkably hilly, and all but Anegada are volcanic, having exploded from the depths of the sea some 25 million years ago. The BVI are serene, seductive, spectacularly beautiful, and still remarkably laid-back. At some points they lie only a mile or so from the U.S. Virgin Islands (USVI), but they remain unique and have maintained their quiet, friendly, casual character.

The pleasures here are understated: sailing around the multitude of tiny nearby islands; diving to the wreck of the RMS *Rhone*, sunk off Salt Island in 1867; snorkeling in one of hundreds of wonderful spots; walking empty beaches; taking in spectacular views from the island peaks; and settling in on a breeze-swept terrace to admire the sunset.

Several factors have enabled the BVI to retain the qualities of yesteryear's Caribbean: no building can rise higher than the surrounding palms, and there are no direct flights from the mainland United States, so the tourism tide is held back. Many visitors travel here by water, aboard their own ketches and yawls or on one of the ferries that cross the waters between St. Thomas and Tortola. Such a passage is a fine prelude to a stay in these unhurried havens.

Tortola, about 10 square mi (26 square km), is the largest and most populated of the islands; Virgin Gorda, with 8 square mi (21 square km), ranks second. The islands scattered around them include Jost Van

Dyke, Great Camanoe, Norman, Peter, Salt, Cooper, Ginger, Dead Chest, and Anegada. Tortola has the most hotels, restaurants, and shops. Virgin Gorda offers a few restaurants, shops, and resorts (many are self-contained). Jost Van Dyke is a major charter-boat anchorage; little bars line the beach at Great Harbour, but there are few places to stay. The other islands are either uninhabited or have a single hotel or resort—or even just a restaurant. Many of these, such as Peter Island, offer excellent anchorages, and their bays and harbors are popular with overnighting boaters.

Sailing has always been a popular activity in the BVI. The first arrivals here were a romantic seafaring tribe, the Ciboney Indians. They were followed (circa AD 900) by the Arawaks, who sailed from South America, established settlements, and farmed and fished. Still later came the mighty Caribs.

In 1493 Christopher Columbus was the first European visitor. Impressed by the number of islands dotting the horizon, he named them *Las Once Mil Virgines*—the 11,000 Virgins—in honor of the 11,000 virgin companions of St. Ursula, martyred in the 4th century. In the ensuing years, the Spaniards passed through, fruitlessly seeking gold. Then came pirates and buccaneers, who found the islands' hidden coves and treacherous reefs ideal bases from which to prey on passing galleons crammed with gold, silver, and spices. Among the most notorious of these fellows were Blackbeard Teach, Bluebeard, Captain Kidd, and Sir Francis Drake, who lent his name to the channel that sweeps through the BVI's two main clusters. In the 17th century the colorful cutthroats were replaced by the Dutch, who, in turn, were sent packing by the British. It was the British who established a plantation economy and for the next 150 years developed the sugar industry. When slavery was abolished in 1838, the plantation economy faltered, and the majority of the white population left for Europe.

The islands dozed, a forgotten corner of the British empire, until the early 1960s. In 1966 a new constitution granting the islands greater autonomy was approved. Still appointed by the queen of England, the governor has limited powers, concentrated on external affairs and local security. The legislative council, with representatives from nine districts, administers other matters. General elections are held every four years. The arrangement seems to suit the islanders just fine: the political mood is serene. It was also in the 1960s that Laurence Rockefeller and American expatriate Charlie Cary brought tourism to the BVI. In 1965 Rockefeller set about creating the Little Dix Bay resort on Virgin Gorda. Dedicated to preserving the island's natural beauty while providing guests with unpretentious yet elegant surroundings, Little Dix set the standard that still prevails in the BVI. A few years later Cary and his wife, Ginny, established the Moorings marina complex on Tortola, and sailing in the area burgeoned.

Although offshore banking is currently the BVI's number one industry, tourism is the second major source of income. The majority of the islands' jobs are tourism-related, and there may well be even more such jobs by 2003, when the Beef Island airport expansion is slated for completion. The runway enlargement will accommodate larger prop planes and small regional jets but will still be too small for full-size jets, so there's no doubt that BVIers—who so love their unspoiled tropical home—will maintain their islands' easygoing charms for both themselves and their guests.

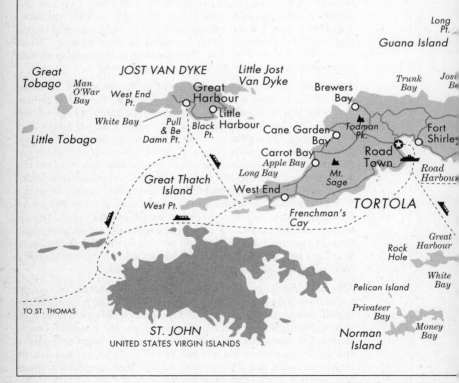

ATLANTIC

Long Pt.

Guana Island

Great Tobago

Man O'War Bay

JOST VAN DYKE

West End Pt.

Little Jost Van Dyke

Trunk Bay

Josi Be

Brewers Bay

Great Harbour

White Bay

Pull & Be Damn Pt.

Little Harbour

Black Pt.

Cane Garden Bay

Todman Pk.

Fort Shirley

Little Tobago

Carrot Bay

Apple Bay

Road Town

Road Harbour

Great Thatch Island

Long Bay

Mt. Sage

West Pt.

West End

TORTOLA

Frenchman's Cay

Great Harbour

Rock Hole

White Bay

Pelican Island

TO ST. THOMAS

Privateer Bay

Money Bay

ST. JOHN
UNITED STATES VIRGIN ISLANDS

Norman Island

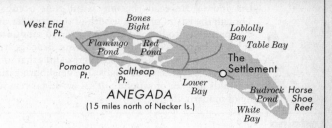

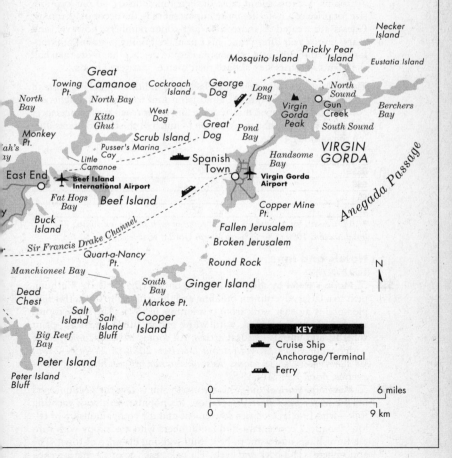

TORTOLA

Unwinding can easily become a full-time occupation on Tortola. Though the island offers a wealth of things to see and do, many visitors prefer just to loll about on its deserted sands or linger over lunch at one of its many delightful restaurants. Beaches are never more than a few minutes away, and the steep green hills that form Tortola's spine are fanned by gentle trade winds. The neighboring islands glimmer like emeralds in a sea of sapphire. It's a world far removed from the hustle of modern life.

Lodging

Luxury on Tortola is more a state of mind—serenity, seclusion, gentility—than state-of-the-art amenities and facilities. Hotels in Road Town don't have beaches, but they do have pools and are within walking distance of restaurants, nightspots, and shops. Accommodations outside Road Town are relatively isolated but are on beaches (some of them are exquisite; others are small or have been enlarged by bringing in sand). The BVI resorts are intimate: none are large—only four have more than 50 rooms. Visitors spend most of their time outside, so the location, size, or price of a hotel are more important than the decor of its rooms. Guests are treated as more than just room numbers, however, and many return year after year. This can make booking a room at popular resorts difficult, even off-season, despite the fact that more than half the island's visitors stay aboard their own or chartered boats.

Throughout the BVI a few hotels lack air-conditioning, relying instead on ceiling fans to capture the almost constant trade winds. Nights are cool and breezy, even in midsummer, and never reach the temperatures or humidity levels that are common in much of the United States during the summer.

CATEGORY	COST*
$$$$	over $225
$$$	$150–$225
$$	$75–$150
$	under $75

All prices are for a standard double room in high season, excluding 7% hotel tax and 10% (5%–15% on Virgin Gorda) service charge.

Hotels and Inns

ROAD TOWN

$$$ 🏨 **Maria's Hotel by the Sea.** Perched on the edge of Road Harbour, next to a large government building and the cruise ship dock, this simple hotel is an easy walk from restaurants in town. The small rooms are minimally decorated, with white rattan furniture, floral-print spreads, and murals by local artists. All rooms have balconies, some with harbor views. ⊠ *Waterfront Dr. (Box 206),* ☎ *284/494–2595,* FAX *284/494–2420. 38 rooms. Restaurant, bar, air-conditioning, kitchenettes, pool. AE, MC, V. EP.*

$$$ 🏨 **Moorings-Mariner Inn.** This two-story inn is also the headquarters for the Moorings Charter operation. It's popular with both yachting folk—who find its facilities convenient and the companionship of fellow "boaties" congenial—and landlubbers who are happy with simple furnishings and want to be within walking distance of town. The atmosphere is laid-back *and* lively. The pale peach color scheme is picked up in the floor tiles, and tropical-print fabrics add splashes of contrasting color. All units are on the large side and have small kitchenettes and balconies, and you'll face the marina in all but the eight rooms that overlook the pool or the tennis court. ⊠ *Waterfront Dr. (Box 139),*

☎ 284/494–2332 or 800/535–7289, FAX 284/494–2226. *38 rooms, 4 suites. Air-conditioning, kitchenettes, pool, tennis court, volleyball, dive shop, dock, marina, shops. AE, MC, V. EP.*

$$$ 🏨 **Pusser's Fort Burt Hotel.** Originally a fort built by the Dutch in the 17th century, this hillside landmark is at the edge of town and—like all good Caribbean forts and hotels—overlooks the harbor; some rooms have stunning views. The exterior is primarily handsome island stonework. Rooms are painted in pale pastels, cushions and bedspread fabrics are floral prints, and balconies are private. You could also go all out and book one of the two suites that have their own private pools. Now owned by Pusser's, of Pusser's Company Store fame, this hotel is a comfortable choice if you want to be close to town. Two-line dataport telephones and printer/fax machines in every room make it Tortola's only true business hotel. ✉ *Waterfront Dr. (Box 3380),* ☎ *284/494–2587,* FAX *284/494–2002,* WEB *www.pussers.com. 12 rooms, 5 suites. Restaurant, bar, air-conditioning, pool. AE, MC, V. EP.*

$$$ 🏨 **Village Cay Resort and Marina.** Right in town, this pleasant, compact hotel looks out on Road Harbour and several marinas. It's popular with yachters and those who love to shop and dine. Rooms have natural rattan furniture and pastel prints. Some units have cathedral ceilings and harbor views; others are quite small. After shopping in town, you can have a swim in the tiny pool and then head for the bar. ✉ *Wickham's Cay I (Box 145),* ☎ *284/494–2771,* FAX *284/494–2773,* WEB *www.villagecay.com. 19 rooms. Restaurant, bar, air-conditioning, pool, marina. AE, MC, V. EP.*

$$ 🏨 **Hotel Castle Maria.** You can spend all the money you save here at the nearby in-town attractions. And these very simple accommodations have everything most folks need: a refrigerator and cable TV; some rooms also have full kitchenettes, balconies, and air-conditioning. Refresh yourself either in the bar or the freshwater pool. ✉ *Waterfront Dr. (Box 206),* ☎ *284/494–2553,* FAX *284/494–2111. 30 rooms. Bar, pool. AE, MC, V. EP.*

OUTSIDE ROAD TOWN

$$$$ 🏨 **Frenchman's Cay Hotel.** This small, casual collection of one- and two-bedroom condos overlooks Drake's Channel. Each unit includes a full kitchen, a dining area, and a sitting room—ideal for families or couples who want the convenience of an apartmentlike setting. Rooms are done in neutral colors, with cream-color curtains and bedspreads and tile floors. Ceiling fans and breezes keep things cool. There are a small pool and a modest-size artificial beach that's sandy to the water's edge but rocky offshore (snorkelers will enjoy the reef here). The alfresco bar and dining room are breeze-swept and offer simple fare. ✉ *Frenchman's Cay (Box 1054), West End,* ☎ *284/495–4844 or 800/235–4077 (direct to hotel),* FAX *284/495–4056,* WEB *www.frenchmans.com. 9 units. Restaurant, bar, kitchenettes, fans, pool, tennis court, beach, snorkeling. AE, MC, V. EP.*

$$$$ 🏨 **Long Bay Beach Resort.** Spectacularly set on a 1-mi-long (1½-km-★ long) arc of white sand, this resort is one of Tortola's best. Beachfront accommodations include tropical hideaways set on stilts and within feet of the water's edge and spacious deluxe units with marble-top wet bars and showers and roomy dressing areas with Italian tiles. Hillside choices have balconies or decks and dramatic views of distant islands. Some look out over the pool and some have comfortable seating areas and in-room whirlpools. In addition, spacious one- and two-bedroom hillside villas with full kitchens are available. Floral prints and rattan furniture are used throughout. The casual Beach restaurant offers all-day dining inside and around the beachside pool and is the spot for twice-weekly West Indian barbecues. The Garden Restaurant serves ro-

Tortola

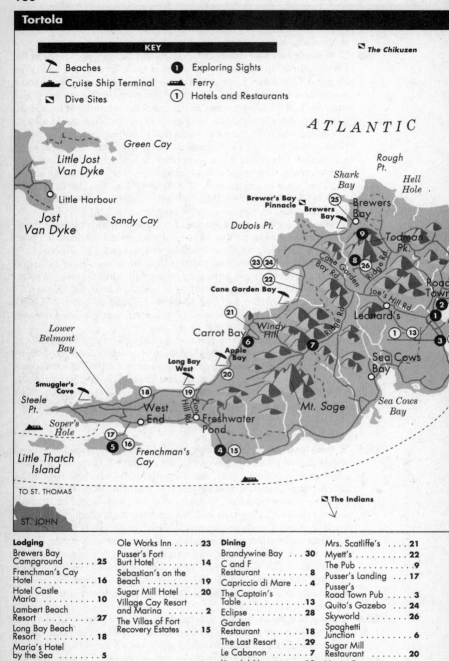

KEY

- ⟿ Beaches
- 🚢 Cruise Ship Terminal
- ◼ Dive Sites
- ❶ Exploring Sights
- ⛴ Ferry
- ① Hotels and Restaurants

◼ *The Chikuzen*

ATLANTIC

Green Cay

Little Jost Van Dyke

Rough Pt.

Shark Bay

Hell Hole

Little Harbour

Jost Van Dyke

Sandy Cay

Brewer's Bay Pinnacle ◼
Brewers Bay ㉕ *Brewers Bay*

Dubois Pt.

㉓ ㉔

⑨

㉒ ⑧ ㉖

Cane Garden Bay

Cane Garden Bay Rd

Todman Pk.

Ridge Rd.

Road Town

②

Joe's Hill Rd.

Leonard's

①

Lower Belmont Bay

㉑

Carrot Bay

⑥ *Windy Hill*

Apple Bay

⑦

Ridge Rd

① ⑬

③

Sea Cows Bay

Smuggler's Cove

Long Bay West

⑳

⑱ ⑲

Zion Hill Rd.

West End

Freshwater Pond

Mt. Sage

Sea Cows Bay

Steele Pt.

Soper's Hole

⑰

⑤ ⑯

Frenchman's Cay

④ ⑮

Little Thatch Island

TO ST. THOMAS

◼ *The Indians*

ST. JOHN

Lodging
Brewers Bay Campground **25**
Frenchman's Cay Hotel **16**
Hotel Castle Maria **10**
Lambert Beach Resort **27**
Long Bay Beach Resort **18**
Maria's Hotel by the Sea **5**
Moorings-Mariner Inn **11**

Ole Works Inn **23**
Pusser's Fort Burt Hotel **14**
Sebastian's on the Beach **19**
Sugar Mill Hotel . . . **20**
Village Cay Resort and Marina **2**
The Villas of Fort Recovery Estates . . . **15**

Dining
Brandywine Bay . . . **30**
C and F Restaurant **8**
Capriccio di Mare . . **4**
The Captain's Table **13**
Eclipse **28**
Garden Restaurant **18**
The Last Resort . . . **29**
Le Cabanon **7**
Lime 'n' Mango **12**

Mrs. Scatliffe's **21**
Myett's **22**
The Pub **9**
Pusser's Landing . . . **17**
Pusser's Road Town Pub **3**
Quito's Gazebo **24**
Skyworld **26**
Spaghetti Junction **6**
Sugar Mill Restaurant **20**
Virgin Queen **1**

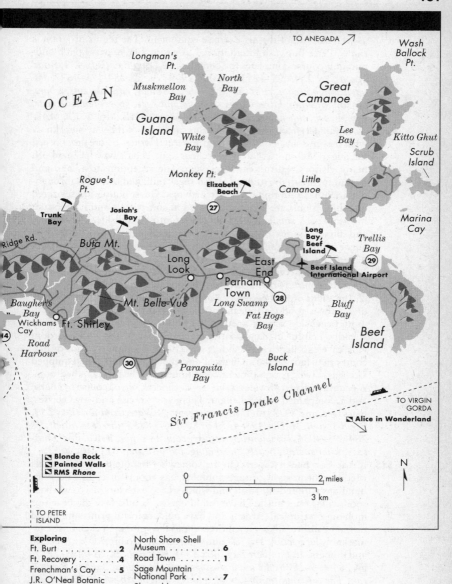

TO ANEGADA ↗

Wash
Ballock
Pt.

Longman's
Pt.

North
Bay

Great
Camanoe

O C E A N

Muskmellon
Bay

Lee
Bay

Kitto Ghut

Guana
Island

White
Bay

Scrub
Island

Monkey Pt.

Elizabeth
Beach ☂

Little
Camanoe

Marina
Cay

Rogue's
Pt.

㉗

Trunk ☂
Bay

Josiah's ☂
Bay

Long
Bay,
Beef
Island ⚓

Trellis
Bay

Ridge Rd.

Bufa Mt.

Long
Look

East
End

Beef Island
International Airport

㉙

Baugher's
Bay

Mt. Belle-Vue

Parham
Town
Long Swamp

㉘

Bluff
Bay

Wickhams
Cay

Ft. Shirley

Fat Hogs
Bay

Beef
Island

㉔

Road
Harbour

㉚

Paraquita
Bay

Buck
Island

🚢
TO VIRGIN
GORDA

Sir Francis Drake Channel

⚓ Alice in Wonderland

⚓ Blonde Rock
⚓ Painted Walls
⚓ RMS *Rhone*

0 _____ 2 miles
0 _____ 3 km

N
↑

TO PETER
ISLAND

Exploring
Ft. Burt **2**
Ft. Recovery **4**
Frenchman's Cay . . . **5**
J.R. O'Neal Botanic
Gardens **3**
Mt. Healthy
National Park **9**

North Shore Shell
Museum **6**
Road Town **1**
Sage Mountain
National Park **7**
Skyworld **8**

mantic gourmet dinners by candlelight five nights a week. The new spa and fitness center offers a full array of massage, facials, and body scrubs, as well as state-of-the-art exercise equipment. The tennis program is run by Peter Burwash International. A rustic 9-hole, par-3 pitch-and-putt golf course completes the complex. ✉ *Long Bay (Box 433, Road Town),* ☎ *284/495–4252 or 800/729–9599,* [FAX] *284/495–4677,* [WEB] *www.longbay.com. 78 rooms, 12 suites, 26 villas. 2 restaurants, 2 bars, air-conditioning, kitchenettes, 2 pools, massage, spa, 3 tennis courts, gym, beach, snorkeling, shops, meeting rooms. AE, MC, V. EP, MAP.*

$$$$ 🏨 **Sugar Mill Hotel.** The owners of this small, out-of-the-way hotel know
★ what they're doing—they were food and travel writers before they opened the Sugar Mill more than two decades ago. Their savvy has paid off: many visitors return year after year. The reception area, bar, and restaurant are in the ruins of an old sugar mill, and the walls throughout are hung with bright Haitian artwork. Guest houses are scattered up a hill; rooms are simply decorated in soft pastels and have rattan furnishings. A small circular pool is set into the hillside, and lunches and dinners (in season) are served on a terrace at the tiny beach. The Sugar Mill Restaurant is well known on the island. ✉ *Apple Bay (Box 425, Road Town),* ☎ *284/495–4355,* [FAX] *284/495–4696,* [WEB] *www.sugarmillhotel.com. 16 rooms, 4 suites, 2 villas. 2 restaurants, 2 bars, air-conditioning, pool, beach, snorkeling. AE, MC, V. EP, MAP.*

$$$$ 🏨 **The Villas of Fort Recovery Estates.** This complex has all the ingre-
★ dients for a good Caribbean vacation: grounds full of flowers; a remote beachside setting around the remnants of a Dutch fort; and friendly, helpful management. All the suites and the four-bedroom villa have excellent views (sliding glass doors open onto patios or balconies that face Drake's Channel and the beach) and fully equipped kitchens. Living rooms (not air-conditioned) can be used as a bedroom. A gourmet kitchen provides room-service dinners, served course by course and accompanied by candlelight. There are exercise and yoga classes, massages, and VCRs and videos for rent. ✉ *Waterfront Dr. (Box 239, Road Town),* ☎ *284/495–4354 or 800/367–8455 (direct to hotel),* [FAX] *284/495–4036,* [WEB] *www.fortrecovery.com. 14 suites, 1 villa. Pool, massage, kitchenettes, beach, snorkeling, baby-sitting. AE, MC, V. EP.*

$$$ 🏨 **Lambert Beach Resort.** On the somewhat remote north shore, this Mediterranean-style cottage complex has rooms in eight one-story buildings with red-tile roofs and white stucco exteriors. Two two-bedroom villas on a hillside have full kitchens. Rooms face the beach or look out on tropical gardens and have bold, colorful prints and blond rattan furniture. It's a very short walk to the stunning beach or the remarkably large pool. The restaurant offers alfresco breakfasts, lunches, and dinners. ✉ *Lambert Bay (Box 534), East End,* ☎ *284/495–2877,* [FAX] *284/495–2876,* [WEB] *www.pussers.com. 34 rooms, 2 villas. Restaurant, bar, air-conditioning, pool, tennis court, beach, snorkeling, windsurfing, shop. AE, MC, V. EP.*

$$$ 🏨 **Sebastian's on the Beach.** The best rooms here are the eight small rooms that open onto the beach. Although compact, they're airy and white, very simply decorated with floral-print curtains and bedspreads, and have terraces or balconies and great breezes and views (the ocean lulls you to sleep). Tiny bathrooms have only stall showers. The other 18 rooms are very basic, lack views, and can be noisy, but these are all air-conditioned. Some of these are across the street and are considerably cheaper than the beach rooms. The casual restaurant looks out over the water; at lunch you can order fresh salads, grilled vegetables, or soups and sandwiches; the dinner menu includes grilled fish, lobster, and steak. ✉ *Apple Bay (Box 441, Road Town),* ☎ *284/495–4212 or 800/336–4870,* [FAX] *284/495–4466,* [WEB] *www.sebastiansbvi.com. 26 rooms. Restaurant, bar, snack bar, fans, beach. AE, EP.*

$$ ▣ **Ole Works Inn.** Tucked against a hill and across the road from a beautiful beach is this rustic, appealing inn—owned by local recording star Quito Rhymer. A steeply pitched roof along with wood and stonework add contemporary flair to what was once an old sugar mill that dates from the 18th century. Rooms are simply decorated, but some have private balconies and kitchenettes, and you can't beat the Cane Garden Bay location. The Honeymoon Suite has an indoor swing for two. ✉ *Cane Garden Bay (Box 560, Road Town)*, ☎ *284/495–4837,* FAX *284/495–9618. 15 rooms, 3 suites. Air-conditioning, fans, refrigerators. MC, V. EP.*

Private Homes and Villas

Areana Villas (✉ Box 263, Road Town, ☎ 284/494–5864, FAX 284/494–7626, WEB www.areanavillas.com) represents top-of-the-line properties. Homes offer accommodations for 2 to 10 people in one- to five-bedroom villas decorated in soothing pastels. Many have pools, Jacuzzis, and glazed terra-cotta courtyards. On Long Bay, Areana represents Sunset House and Villas, an exquisite hideaway whose first guest was Britain's Princess Alexandra (but you needn't be royalty to receive the royal treatment here). The company also works with Equinox House, also on Long Bay, a handsome three-bedroom estate set amid lavish tumbling gardens. Rates range from expensive ($$$) to very expensive ($$$$) in season. **Lambert Beach Villas** (✉ Lambert Estate Box 534, East End, ☎ 284/495–2877, FAX 284/495–2876) rents two- and three-bedroom villas on the hills overlooking Elizabeth Beach.

Campground

$ ⛰ **Brewers Bay Campground.** Both prepared and bare sites are on Brewers Bay, one of Tortola's prime snorkeling spots. Check out the ruins of the distillery that gave the bay its name. You'll find a small commissary and public bathrooms but no showers. ✉ *Brewers Bay (Box 185, Road Town)*, ☎ *284/494–3463. 28 sites. Restaurant, bar, beach, windsurfing, baby-sitting. No credit cards.*

Dining

On Tortola local seafood is plentiful, and although other fresh ingredients are scarce, the island's chefs are a creative lot, who apply genius to whatever the weekly supply boat delivers. Contemporary American dishes prepared with a Caribbean influence are very popular. The fancier, more expensive restaurants have dress codes: long pants and collared shirts for men, and elegant, casual resort wear for women.

CATEGORY	COST*
$$$$	over $35
$$$	$25–$35
$$	$15–$25
$	under $15

per person for a main course at dinner

Road Town

AMERICAN/CASUAL

$$ ✕ **The Pub.** At this lively waterfront spot, tables are arranged along a terrace facing a small marina and the Road Town harbor. Hamburgers, salads, and sandwiches are typical lunch offerings. In the evening you can also choose grilled fish, steak, chicken, sautéed conch, or barbecued ribs. In fact, head here on Saturday night for all-you-can-eat ribs. There's entertainment on weekends, and locals gather here nightly for spirited dart games. ✉ *Waterfront Dr.,* ☎ *284/494–2608. Reservations not accepted. AE, DC, MC, V. No lunch Sun.*

$ ✕ **Pusser's Road Town Pub.** Almost everyone who visits Tortola stops here at least once to have a bite to eat and to sample the famous Pusser's Rum Painkiller (fruit juices and rum). The menu includes cheesy pizza, shepherd's pie, fish-and-chips, and deli sandwiches. Dine inside in air-conditioned comfort or outside on the veranda, which looks out on the harbor. Stop by on Fridays for nickel beer night. ✉ *Waterfront Dr.,* ☎ *284/494–3897. AE, MC, V.*

CARIBBEAN

$$ ✕ **C and F Restaurant.** Crowds head to this casual spot for the best
★ barbecue in town (chicken, fish, and ribs), fresh local fish prepared your way, and excellent curries. Sometimes there's a wait for a table, but it's worth it. The restaurant is just outside Road Town, on a side street past the Moorings and Riteway. ✉ *Purcell Estate,* ☎ *284/494–4941. Reservations not accepted. AE, MC, V. No lunch.*

ECLECTIC

$$ ✕ **Virgin Queen.** The sailing and rugby crowds head here to play
★ darts, drink beer, and eat Queen's Pizza—a crusty, cheesy pie topped with sausage, onions, green peppers, and mushrooms. Also on the menu is excellent West Indian and English fare: salt fish, barbecued ribs with beans and rice, bangers and mash, shepherd's pie, chili, and grilled sirloin steak. ✉ *Fleming St.,* ☎ *284/494–2310. Reservations not accepted. No credit cards. Closed Sept. and Sun.*

FRENCH

$$ ✕ **Le Cabanon.** Birds and bougainvillea brighten the patio setting of this breezy French restaurant and bar, a popular gathering place for locals and visitors alike. Fresh oysters or fried mozzarella with tomatoes is a good appetizer choice. Then move on to the rack of lamb, the grilled salmon, or the rib-eye steak. Or try the shepherd's pie made with a French twist—duck instead of ground beef. Save room for such tasty dessert offerings as chocolate mousse, coconut mousse, apple tart, and a platter of French cheeses. ✉ *Waterfront Dr.,* ☎ *284/494–8660. MC, V. Closed Sun.*

ITALIAN

$$ ✕ **Spaghetti Junction.** Popular with the boating crowd, this well-
★ known island favorite moved to new and roomier upstairs digs near the cruise ship dock. Join the crowd outside on the deck overlooking the marina or inside, where it's bustling. The expanded menu includes more fresh seafood and more nightly specials but still features house specialties such as penne with a spicy tomato sauce, spinach-mushroom lasagna, *cappellini* (very thin spaghetti) with shellfish, and jambalaya pasta. ✉ *Inner Harbour Marina,* ☎ *284/494–4880. MC, V. Closed Sun. No lunch.*

$ ✕ **Capriccio di Mare.** The owners of the well-known Brandywine Bay
★ restaurant also run this authentic little Italian outdoor café. People stop by in the morning for an espresso and fresh pastry and all day long for a cappuccino or a tiramisù, delicious toast Italiano (a grilled ham and Swiss cheese sandwich), a fresh salad, a bowl of perfectly cooked linguine or penne with a variety of sauces, or a crispy tomato and mozzarella pizza. Drink specialties include the Mango Bellini, an adaptation of the famous Bellini cocktail served by Harry's Bar in Venice. ✉ *Waterfront Dr.,* ☎ *284/494–5369. Reservations not accepted. No credit cards. Closed Sun.*

MEXICAN

$$ ✕ **Lime 'n' Mango.** A long veranda is the romantic setting for this popular restaurant in the Treasure Isle Hotel. The menu features local specialties and surprisingly authentic Mexican cuisine. Try the conch fritters, salt fish cakes, or Jamaican calamari for an appetizer. The fajitas—chicken, beef, or vegetarian—are the best Mexican entrée; they arrive at your table sizzling in a hot iron frying pan, with a side of warm tortillas. The coconut shrimp is also popular. Saturday night crowds form here to enjoy the popular West Indian barbecue. ⊠ *Waterfront Dr.,* ☎ *284/494–2501. AE, MC, V.*

SEAFOOD

$$$ ✕ **The Captain's Table.** Select the lobster you want from the pool here, and be careful not to fall in—it's in the floor right in the middle of the dining room. The menu also includes traditional escargots, fresh local fish, filet mignon with béarnaise sauce, duckling with berry sauce, and creative daily specials. Ceiling fans keep the dining room cool, but there are also tables on a breezy terrace overlooking the harbor. ⊠ *Columbus Centre, Wickham's Cay I,* ☎ *284/494–3885. AE, MC, V. No lunch Sat.*

Outside Road Town

AMERICAN/CASUAL

$$ ✕ **Pusser's Landing.** Yachters flock to this waterfront restaurant. Downstairs, from late morning to well into the evening, belly up to the outdoor mahogany bar or choose a waterside table for drinks, sandwiches, rotis, fish and chips, and pizzas. At dinnertime head upstairs for a harbor view and a quiet alfresco meal of grilled steak or local fish. ⊠ *Soper's Hole,* ☎ *284/495–4554. AE, MC, V.*

CARIBBEAN

$$ ✕ **Mrs. Scatliffe's.** The island's best West Indian cooking is here, according to many Tortolans (though some bemoan, "She's gone Continental"). Lunch and dinner are served on the upstairs terrace of Mrs. Scatliffe's home. The food is freshly prepared (vegetables come from the family garden); the baked chicken in coconut is meltingly tender. If you're lucky, after dinner you'll be treated to a lively *fungi* (bands that make music using household items—washboards, spoons, and the like—as instruments) performance by members of Mrs. Scatliffe's family. ⊠ *Carrot Bay,* ☎ *284/495–4556. Reservations essential. No credit cards.*

$$ ✕ **Quito's Gazebo.** This rustic beachside bar and restaurant is owned and operated by Quito Rhymer, a multitalented BVI recording star who plays the guitar and sings Calypso ballads and love songs Tuesday, Thursday, Friday, and Sunday; a reggae band performs Saturday. The menu is Caribbean with an emphasis on fresh fish. Try the conch stew or the curried chicken. A Caribbean buffet is featured on Sunday night, and Friday is fish-fry night. The atmosphere is so convivial that by the time you finish dinner you may find yourself swapping yarns with some colorful local personalities. ⊠ *Cane Garden Bay,* ☎ *284/495–4837. MC, V. Closed Mon.*

$ ✕ **Myett's.** Right on the beach, this bi-level restaurant-bar is hopping
★ day and night. Chowder made with fresh Anegada lobsters is the specialty, though the menu includes everything from hamburgers to fruit platters and vegetarian dishes to grilled shrimp, steak, and tuna. There's live entertainment on Saturday, Sunday, and Monday nights. ⊠ *Cane Garden Bay,* ☎ *284/495–9649. Reservations not accepted. AE, MC, V.*

CONTEMPORARY

$$$ ✕ **Eclipse.** Dine under a canopy of stars at this popular spot that isn't
★ much more than an outdoor terrace filled with tables. The menu is a mixture of fusion and Caribbean cuisine. Spend the evening sampling one dish after another—cracked conch, baked chevre, tuna carpaccio—as you order off the two-page grazing menu, or dig into the spicy cur-

ries, fusion chicken, fresh grilled Anegada swordfish, and vegetarian dishes on the regular menu. ⊠ *Fat Hog's Bay, East End,* ☎ *284/495–1646. AE, MC, V. No lunch Aug.*

$$$ ✕ **Skyworld.** Come to this mountaintop aerie at sunset and watch the
★ western horizon go ablaze with color, then settle back in the casually elegant dining room to feast. The superbly cooked filet mignon with port wine and mushroom sauce is truly exceptional. Other specialties include the smoked salmon in whiskey sauce appetizer, grilled local fish, roast duck, cinnamon roast pork loin with pears and rosemary, and key lime pie. The very simple lunch menu features hamburgers and sandwiches, though the restaurant can be crowded at this time when a cruise ship docks. ⊠ *Ridge Rd.,* ☎ *284/494–3567. AE, MC, V.*

$$$ ✕ **Sugar Mill Restaurant.** Candles gleam, and the background music is peaceful in this romantic restaurant. Inside a 360-year-old mill that's part of their Sugar Mill Hotel, owners Jeff and Jinx Morgan never disappoint. Well-prepared selections on the à la carte menu, which changes nightly, include pasta and vegetarian entrées. Crab bisque with crab rolls or Caribbean sweet-potato soup are good starters. House favorite entrées include the Jamaican jerk pork roast, the regimental beef curry with *poppadoms* (Indian popovers), marinated roast duck, and fresh fish with spicy creole sauce. ⊠ *Apple Bay,* ☎ *284/495–4355. AE, MC, V. No lunch.*

$$ ✕ **Garden Restaurant.** Relax over dinner in this dimly lit, open-air restau-
★ rant at Long Bay Beach Resort. Tables are well-spaced on several levels, and the atmosphere is intimate. The extensive menu changes daily. Appetizers might include escargots and Portobello mushrooms in pastry, curried cauliflower soup, or shrimp fritters; the list of entrées could feature grilled Anegada swordfish steak with avocado hollandaise, pan-roasted duck with Portobello mushrooms, or a filet mignon served with artichoke duxelle. There are always at least five desserts to choose from, such as Belgian chocolate mousse, cherry cheesecake, and carrot cake. ⊠ *Long Bay,* ☎ *284/495–4252. AE, MC, V. No lunch.*

ENGLISH

$$ ✕ **The Last Resort.** Actually on Bellamy Cay, just off Beef Island (free ferry service is provided to and from Trellis Bay/Beef Island), this spot features an English buffet, complete with pumpkin soup, prime rib, and Yorkshire pudding, as well as vegetarian selections. This is also the site of the longest-running show in the BVI. For nearly 30 years, guests have been laughing at the inimitable cabaret humor and ribald ditties of owner Tony Snell, the BVI's answer to Benny Hill. He performs nightly at 9:30. ⊠ *Bellamy Cay,* ☎ *284/495–2520. AE, MC, V.*

ITALIAN

$$$ ✕ **Brandywine Bay.** Here, candlelit outdoor tables have sweeping
★ views of neighboring islands, and owner-chef Davide Pugliese prepares foods the Tuscan way: grilled with lots of fresh herbs. The remarkable menu can include homemade mozzarella, foie gras, grilled local wahoo, and grilled veal chop with ricotta and sun-dried tomatoes; it always includes duck with an exotic fruit sauce. The wine list is excellent, and the lemon tart and the tiramisu are irresistible. ⊠ *Sir Francis Drake Hwy., east of Road Town,* ☎ *284/495–2301. Reservations essential. AE, MC, V. No lunch. Closed Sun.*

Beaches

Beaches in the BVI are less developed than those on St. Thomas or St. Croix. Try to get out on a dive-snorkeling boat or a day-trip sailing vessel at least once. This is often the best way to reach the most virgin Virgin beaches, which are on deserted islands. Tortola's north side has several perfect palm-fringed white-sand beaches that curl around turquoise bays and coves. Nearly all are accessible by car (preferably one with four-wheel-drive), albeit down bumpy roads that corkscrew precipitously. Facilities run the gamut, from absolutely none to a number of beachside bars and restaurants as well as places to rent watersports equipment.

If you want to surf, the area of **Apple Bay** (⊠ North Shore Rd.), which includes Little Apple Bay and Capoon's Bay, is the spot—although the beach itself is pretty narrow. Sebastian's, the very casual hotel here, caters to those in search of the perfect wave. Good surf is never a sure thing, but you're more apt to find it in January and February.

The water at **Brewers Bay** (⊠ Brewers Bay Rd. W or Brewers Bay Rd. E) is good for snorkeling, and there are a campground and beach bar here. The beach and its old sugar mill and rum-distillery ruins are just north of Cane Garden Bay, just past Luck Hill. There's another entrance just east of the Skyworld restaurant.

The enticing **Cane Garden Bay** (⊠ Cane Garden Bay Rd.) has exceptionally calm, crystalline waters and a silky stretch of sand. It's the closest beach to Road Town—one steep uphill and downhill drive—and is one of the BVI's best-known anchorages (unfortunately, it can be very crowded when cruise ships are in town). You can rent sailboards and such, stargaze from the bow of a boat, and nosh or sip at a variety of places, including Quito's Gazebo.

Lined with palm trees, wide, sandy **Elizabeth Beach** (⊠ Ridge Rd.) is accessible by walking down a private road. However, the undertow can be severe here in winter. The oft-deserted **Josiah's Bay** (⊠ Ridge Rd.) is a favored place to picnic or to hang ten, although in winter the undertow is often strong.

The scenery at **Long Bay, Beef Island** (⊠ Beef Island Rd.) draws superlatives: you can catch a glimpse of Little Camanoe and Great Camanoe islands, and if you walk around the bend to the right, you can see little Marina Cay and Scrub Island. Long Bay is also a good place to find seashells. Take the Queen Elizabeth II Bridge to Beef Island and watch for a small dirt turnoff on the left before the airport. Follow the road that curves along the east side of the dried-up marsh flat; don't drive directly across the flat as you can damage it.

Long Bay West (⊠ Long Bay Rd.) is a stunning 1-mi (1½-km) stretch of white sand. Have your camera ready for snapping the breathtaking approach. Although Long Bay Resort sprawls along part of it, the entire beach is open to the public. The water isn't as calm here as at Cane Garden or Brewers Bay, but it's still swimmable.

After bouncing your way to the beautiful **Smuggler's Cove** (⊠ Belmont Rd.), you'll feel as if you've found a hidden piece of the island, although you probably won't be alone on weekends. There's a fine view of Jost Van Dyke Island, and the snorkeling is good.

About the only thing you'll find moving at **Trunk Bay** (⊠ Ridge Rd.) is the surf. It's directly north of Road Town, midway between Cane Garden Bay and Beef Island, and to reach it you have to hike down a *ghut* (gully) from Ridge Road.

Outdoor Activities and Sports

Participant Sports

FISHING

The deep-sea fishing here is so good that tournaments draw competitors from around the world for the largest bluefish, wahoo, and shark. You can bring a catch back to your hotel's restaurant, and the staff will prepare it for you for dinner. A half-day of deep-sea fishing runs $300–$350, a full day $500–$600. For a few hours of reel fun, try **Persistence** (⌧ Towers, West End, ☏ 284/495–4122). If bone fishing is your cup of tea, call **Caribbean Fly Fishing** (⌧ Nanny Cay, ☏ 284/499–1590).

HORSEBACK RIDING

If you've ever wanted to ride a horse along a deserted beach, now's your chance. Or you can head up to Tortola's ridges for spectacular views. **Shadow Stables** (⌧ Ridge Rd., ☏ 284/494–2262) offers small group rides for $20 per person per hour.

SAILING

The BVI are among the world's most popular sailing destinations. They're close together and surrounded by calm waters, so it's fairly easy to sail from one anchorage to the next. If you know how to sail, you can charter a bare boat (perhaps for your entire vacation); if you're unschooled, you can hire a boat with a captain or learn to sail. Prices vary quite broadly depending on the type and size of the boat you wish to charter. In season, a weekly charter runs $1,500–$35,000.

BVI Yacht Charters (⌧ Inner Harbour Marina, Road Town, ☏ 284/494–4289) offers 38-ft to 51-ft sailboats for charter—with or without a captain, whichever you prefer. **Catamaran Charters** (⌧ Nanny Cay Marina, Nanny Cay, ☏ 284/495–6661) charters catamarans with or without captains. **Full Sail Sailing School** (⌧ Seabreeze Marina, East End, ☏ 284/494–0512) offers beginner and advanced sailing lessons. **The Moorings** (⌧ Wickham's Cay II, Road Town, ☏ 284/494–2501 or 800/535–7289), considered one of the best bareboat operations in the world, has a large fleet of well-maintained, mostly Beneteau yachts. Hire a captain or sail the boat yourself. If you prefer a powerboat, call **Regency Yacht Vacations** (⌧ Hodge's Creek, ☏ 284/495–1970) for both bareboat and captained charters.

SCUBA DIVING AND SNORKELING

Clear waters and numerous reefs afford some wonderful opportunities for underwater exploration. **Alice in Wonderland** is a deep dive south of Ginger Island with a wall that slopes gently from 15 ft (5 m) to 100 ft (30 m). It features huge mushroom-shape coral, hence its name.

Crabs, lobsters, and shimmering fan corals make their home in the tunnels, ledges, and overhangs of **Blonde Rock,** a pinnacle that goes from just 15 ft (5 m) below the surface to 60 ft (18 m) deep. It's between Dead Chest and Salt Island.

When the currents aren't too strong, **Brewer's Bay Pinnacle** (20–90 ft/6–27 m down) teems with sea life.

The *Chikuzen,* sunk northwest of Brewer's Bay in 1981, is a 246-ft vessel in 75 ft (23 m) of water; it's home to thousands of fish, colorful corals, and big rays.

At **The Indians,** near Pelican Island, colorful corals decorate canyons and grottoes created by four large, jagged pinnacles that rise 50 ft (15 m) from the ocean floor.

In 1867 the RMS *Rhone,* a 310-ft-long royal mail steamer, split in two when it sank in a devastating hurricane. It's so well preserved that it was used in the movie *The Deep.* You can see the crow's nest and bowsprit, the cargo hold in the bow, and the engine and enormous propeller shaft in the stern. Its four parts are at various depths from 30 to 80 ft (9 to 24 m; nearby Rhone Reef is only 20–50 ft/6–15 m down). Get yourself some snorkeling gear and hop a dive boat to this wreck, off Salt Island (across the channel from Road Town) and part of the BVI National Parks Trust. Every dive outfit in the BVI runs superlative scuba and snorkel tours here.

The **Painted Walls** is a shallow dive site where corals and sponges create a kaleidoscope of colors on the walls of four long gullies. It's northeast of Dead Chest.

Baskin' in the Sun (⊠ Prospect Reef, ☎ 284/494–2858) offers beginner and advanced diving courses and daily trips. Trainers teach openwater, rescue, advanced diving, and resort courses. The resort course costs $96; a one-tank dive is $76 and a two-tank dive is $96, including equipment.

Blue Waters Divers (⊠ Nanny Cay, ☎ 284/494–2847) teaches resort, open-water, rescue, and advanced diving courses and also makes daily trips. Resort courses cost $90, one-tank dives run $70, two-tank dives cost $90, including equipment.

Underwater Safaris (⊠ The Moorings, ☎ 284/494–3235) has resort and advanced diving courses, including rescue and open water, and scheduled day and night dives. The resort course fee is $101; one-tank dives are $68 with your own equipment, $78 including equipment. Two-tank dives cost $84 with your own equipment, $94 including equipment.

TENNIS
Tortola's tennis options range from simple, untended, concrete courts to professionally maintained facilities that host organized tournaments. The courts listed below are all open to the public; some have restrictions for nonguests.

Frenchman's Cay Hotel (⊠ West End, ☎ 284/495–4844) has an artificial-grass court with a pretty view of Sir Francis Drake Channel. Patrons of the hotel or restaurant can use the court free of charge; for others there's an hourly fee of $5. Although the court is night-lit, there's no pro available to be your guiding light, so to speak.

Long Bay Beach Resort (⊠ Long Bay, ☎ 284/495–4252) features two courts and a tennis program run by Peter Burwash International. Private lessons are $55 per hour. Nonguests may rent a court for $10 an hour. Tennis rackets can be rented for $7 an hour.

Moorings-Mariner Inn (⊠ Waterfront Dr., Road Town, ☎ 284/494–2332) has one all-weather hard court to which inn, marina, and Treasure Isle Hotel guests have free access; if it's empty, nonguests can use it at no charge. The lack of lights and a pro staffer may leave you in the dark, though.

Prospect Reef Resort (⊠ Waterfront Dr., Road Town, ☎ 284/494–3311) guests can play free by day (there's a fee for lights) on any of six hard-surface courts; nonguests pay $7 an hour. You can make an appointment for lessons ($40 an hour) with the island's most famous pro, Mike Adamson.

WINDSURFING

The winds are so steady here that some locals use sailboards to get from island to island. Three of the best spots for sailboarding are Nanny Cay, Slaney Point, and Trellis Bay on Beef Island.

Boardsailing BVI (☒ Nanny Cay, ☎ 284/495–0422; ☒ Trellis Bay, Beef Island, ☎ 284/495–2447) rents equipment for $30 a half-day and offers private and group lessons.

With **HIHO** (☒ Prospect Reef Resort, Waterfront Dr., Road Town, ☎ 284/494–0337) you can take private or group lessons or rent equipment for $30 a half-day.

Spectator Sports

BASKETBALL

The NBA games are a national passion and folks also play pretty good basketball here. Diehard fans can catch games at the New Recreation Grounds on Monday, Wednesday, Friday, or Saturday between May and August.

CRICKET

Fans of this sport are fiercely loyal and exuberant. Matches are held at the New Recreation Grounds, next to the J. R. O'Neal Botanic Gardens weekends February–April.

SOFTBALL

If you enjoy watching softball, you can catch local games on weekend evenings at the Old Recreation Grounds between Long Bush Road and Lower Estate Road. The season runs February–August.

Shopping

The BVI aren't really a shopper's delight, but there are many shops showcasing original items—from jams and spices to resort wear to excellent artwork. Don't be put off by an informal shop entrance; some of the best finds in the BVI lie behind shabby doors.

Areas

Many shops and boutiques are clustered along and just off Road Town's **Main Street.** You can shop in Road Town's **Wickham's Cay** area adjacent to the marina. There's an ever-growing number of art and clothing stores at **Soper's Hole,** in West End.

Specialty Items

ART

Caribbean Fine Arts Ltd. (☒ Main St., Road Town, ☎ 284/494–4240) carries a wide range of Caribbean art, including original watercolors, oils, and acrylics, as well as signed prints, limited-edition serigraphs, and turn-of-the-century sepia photographs. **Fluke's** (☒ Trellis Bay, East End, ☎ no phone) is the place to come for unique island maps, appealing prints, and colorful T-shirts. **Sunny Caribbee Art Gallery** (☒ Main St., Road Town, ☎ 284/494–2178) has many paintings, prints, and watercolors by artists from throughout the Caribbean.

CLOTHES AND TEXTILES

Arawak (☒ On the dock at Nanny Cay, ☎ 284/494–5240) carries gifts, batik sundresses, sportswear and resort wear for men and women, accessories, and children's clothing. **Caribbean Handprints** (☒ Main St., Road Town, ☎ 284/494–3717) creates Caribbean-theme silk-screened fabric and sells it by the yard or in all forms of clothing and beach bags. **Latitude 18°** (☒ Main St., Road Town, ☎ 284/494–7807; ☒ Soper's Hole Marina, ☎ 284/495–4347) sells Maui Jim, Smith, Oakley, and Revo sunglasses; Freestyle, Quiksilver, and Roxy watches; and a fine collection of sandals, beach towels, sundresses, and sarongs. **Pusser's**

Company Store (⊠ Main St. and Waterfront Rd., Road Town, ☎ 284/494–2467; ⊠ Soper's Hole Marina, ☎ 284/495–4603) features nautical memorabilia, ship models, marine paintings, an entire line of clothes and gift items bearing the Pusser's logo, handsome decorator bottles of Pusser's rum, Caribbean books, and luggage. **Sea Urchin** (⊠ Waterfront, Columbus Centre, Road Town, ☎ 284/494–2044; ⊠ Mill Mall, Road Town, ☎ 284/494–4108; ⊠ Soper's Hole Marina, ☎ 284/495–4850) is the source for local books, island jewelry, sunglasses, and resort wear—print shirts and shorts, colorful swimsuits, cover-ups, sandals, T-shirts—for the whole family. **Serendipity/Domino** (⊠ Main St., Road Town, ☎ 284/494–5879) showcases a colorful array of comfortable, light cotton clothing—including selections from Indonesia—as well as island jewelry and gift items. **Turtle Dove Boutique** (⊠ Flemming St., Road Town, ☎ 284/494–3611) is one of the best shops in the BVI for swimwear, silk and linen dresses, and gifts and accessories for the home. **Violet's** (⊠ Wickham's Cay I, ☎ 284/494–6398) features a collection of beautiful silk lingerie and a small line of designer dresses. **Zenaida's of West End** (⊠ Frenchman's Cay, ☎ 284/495–4867) displays the fabric finds of Argentine Vivian Jenik Helm, who travels through South America, Africa, and India in search of batiks, hand-painted and hand-blocked fabrics, and interesting weaves that can be made into pareos (women's wraps) or wall hangings. The shop also sells unusual bags, belts, sarongs, scarves, and ethnic jewelry.

FOODSTUFFS

Ample Hamper (⊠ Village Cay Marina, Wickham's Cay I, ☎ 284/494–2494; ⊠ Soper's Hole Marina, ☎ 284/495–4684) has cheeses, wines, fresh fruits, and canned goods from the United Kingdom and the United States. You can have the management here provision your yacht or rental villa. **Gourmet Galley** (⊠ Wickham's Cay II, Road Town, ☎ 284/494–6999) sells wines, cheeses, fresh produce, and provides full provisioning for yachtspeople and villa renters.

GIFTS

Buccaneer's Bounty (⊠ Main St., Road Town, ☎ 284/494–7510) purveys greeting cards, pirate memorabilia, nautical and tropical artwork, books on seashells and the islands, and Christmas ornaments. **Caribbean Corner Spice House** (⊠ Soper's Hole, ☎ 284/495–4498) sells exotic herbs and spices and homemade jams, jellies, hot sauces, and natural soaps. You'll find Cuban cigars here, too. **J. R. O'Neal, Ltd.** (⊠ Main St., Road Town, ☎ 284/494–2292) stocks the shelves of its somewhat hidden shop with fine crystal, Royal Worcester china, hand-painted Italian dishes, handblown Mexican glassware, Spanish ceramics, and Indian woven rugs and tablecloths. **Sunny Caribbee Herb and Spice Company** (⊠ Main St., Road Town, ☎ 284/494–2178), in a brightly painted West Indian house, packages its own herbs, teas, coffees, vinegars, hot sauces, soaps, skin and suntan lotions, and exotic concoctions—Arawak Love Potion and Island Hangover Cure, for example. You'll also find Caribbean books and art and hand-painted decorative accessories.

JEWELRY

Columbian Emeralds International (⊠ Wickham's Cay I, Road Town, ☎ 284/494–7477), a Caribbean chain catering to the cruise-ship crowd, is the source for duty-free emeralds plus other gems, gold jewelry, crystal, and china. **Samarkand** (⊠ Main St., Road Town, ☎ 284/494–6415) crafts charming gold and silver pendants, earrings, bracelets, and pins—many with an island theme: seashells, lizards, pelicans, palm trees. You'll also find genuine Spanish pieces of eight (coins—old Spanish pesos worth eight reals—from sunken galleons).

Flamboyance (⊠ Main St., Road Town, ☎ 284/494–4099; ⊠ Soper's Hole Marina, ☎ 284/495–5946) carries designer fragrances and up-scale cosmetics.

Nightlife and the Arts

Nightlife

Like any good sailing destination, Tortola has watering holes that are popular with salty and not-so-salty dogs. Many offer entertainment; check the weekly *Limin' Times* for schedules. The local beverage is the painkiller, an innocent-tasting mixture of fruit juices and rums. It goes down smoothly but packs quite a punch, so give yourself a moment before you order another.

Bing's Drop In Bar. This rollicking local hangout has a DJ nightly in season. ⊠ *Fat Hog's Bay, East End,* ☎ *284/495–2627.*

Bomba's Surfside Shack. By day this little shack—covered with everything from crepe-paper leis to license plates to colorful graffiti—looks like a pile of junk; by night it's one of Tortola's liveliest spots and one of the Caribbean's most famous beach bars. Sunday at 4 there's always some sort of live music, and Wednesday at 8 the locally famous Blue Haze Combo shows up to play everything from reggae to Top 40 tunes. Every full moon, bands play all night long and people flock here from all over. ⊠ *Apple Bay,* ☎ *284/495–4148.*

Ceta's Place. Every Thursday night there's a fish fry and a live band at this informal spot. ⊠ *Capoon's Bay,* ☎ *No phone.*

Jolly Roger. An ever-changing array of local, U.S., and down-island bands plays everything from rhythm and blues to reggae to country to good old rock and roll Friday and Saturday—and sometimes Sunday—starting at 8. ⊠ *West End,* ☎ *284/495–4559.*

Myett's. Local bands play here Saturday, Sunday, and Monday evenings, and there's usually a lively dance crowd. ⊠ *Cane Garden Bay,* ☎ *284/495–9543.*

The Pub. Here you'll find an all-day happy hour on Friday, and Ruben Chinnery on the guitar Friday and Saturday evenings from 6 to 9. ⊠ *Waterfront St., Road Town,* ☎ *284/494–2608.*

Pusser's Deli. Thursday is nickel-beer night, and crowds gather here for courage (John Courage, that is) by the pint. Other nights try Pusser's famous mixed drinks—painkillers—and snack on the excellent pizza. ⊠ *Waterfront St., Road Town,* ☎ *284/494–4199.*

Pusser's Landing. The schedule varies nightly, but you can usually count on some kind of live music (it could be reggae, rock, or a steel band) on Friday and Saturday evenings and Sunday afternoons. ⊠ *Soper's Hole, West End,* ☎ *284/495–4554.*

Quito's Gazebo. BVI recording star Quito Rhymer sings island ballads and love songs, accompanied by the guitar at this rustic beachside bar-restaurant. Solo shows are on Sunday, Tuesday, and Thursday nights at 8:30; Friday and Saturday, Quito and the band—The Edge—pump out a variety of tunes. ⊠ *Cane Garden Bay,* ☎ *284/495–4837.*

Sebastian's. There's often live music here on Saturday and Sunday, and you can dance under the stars. ⊠ *Apple Bay,* ☎ *284/495–4214.*

The Arts

Classics in the Atrium. Musicians from around the world perform here October–February each year. Past artists have included Britain's premier a cappella group, Black Voices; New Orleans jazz pianist Ellis Marsalis; and Keith Lockhart and the Serenac Quartet (from the Boston Pops Symphony). ⊠ *The Atrium at the H. Lavity Stoutt Community College, Paraquita Bay,* ☎ *284/494–4994.*

Exploring Tortola

Tortola doesn't have many historical sights, but it does have lots of beautiful natural scenery. Although you could explore the island's 10 square mi (26 square km) in a few hours, opting for such a whirlwind tour would be a mistake. Life in the fast lane has no place amid some of the Caribbean's most breathtaking panoramas and beaches. Also the roads are extraordinarily steep and twisting, making driving demanding. The best strategy is to explore a bit of the island at a time. For example, you might try Road Town (the island's main town) one morning and a drive to Cane Garden Bay and West End (a little town on, of course, the island's west end) the next afternoon. Or consider a visit to East End, a *very* tiny town located exactly where its name suggests. The north shore is where you'll find all the best beaches.

Numbers in the margin correspond to points of interest on the Tortola map.

Sights to See

❷ **Ft. Burt.** The most intact historic ruin on Tortola was built by the Dutch in the early 17th century to safeguard Road Harbour. It sits on a hill at the western edge of Road Town and is now the site of a small hotel and restaurant. The foundations and magazine remain, and the structure offers a commanding view of the harbor. ⊠ *Waterfront Dr.,* ☎ *No phone.* ⎘ *Free.* ☉ *Daily dawn–dusk.*

❹ **Ft. Recovery.** The unrestored ruins of a 17th-century Dutch fort, 30 ft in diameter, sit amid a profusion of tropical greenery on the Villas of Fort Recovery Estates grounds. There's not much to see here, and there are no guided tours, but you're welcome to stop by and poke around. ⊠ *Waterfront Dr.,* ☎ *284/485–4467.* ⎘ *Free.*

❺ **Frenchman's Cay.** On this little island connected by a causeway to Tortola's western end, there are a marina and a captivating complex of pastel West Indian–style buildings with shady balconies, shuttered windows, and gingerbread trim that house art galleries, boutiques, and restaurants. Pusser's Landing here is a lively place to stop for a cold drink (many are made with Pusser's famous rum) and a sandwich and watch the boats in harbor.

❸ **J. R. O'Neal Botanic Gardens.** Take a walk through this 4-acre showcase of lush plant life. There are sections devoted to prickly cacti and succulents, hothouses for ferns and orchids, gardens of medicinal herbs, and plants and trees indigenous to the seashore. From the tourist board office in Road Town, cross Waterfront Drive and walk one block over to Main Street and turn right. Keep walking until you see the high school. The gardens are on your left. ⊠ *Botanic Station,* ☎ *No phone.* ⎘ *Free.* ☉ *Mon.–Sat. 9–4:30.*

❾ **Mt. Healthy National Park.** The remains of an 18th-century sugar plantation are here. The windmill structure has been restored, and you can see the ruins of a mill, a factory with boiling houses, storage areas, stables, a hospital, and many dwellings. This is a nice place to picnic. ⊠ *Ridge Rd.,* ☎ *No phone.* ⎘ *Free.* ☉ *Daily dawn–dusk.*

❻ **North Shore Shell Museum.** On Tortola's north shore, this casual museum has a very informal exhibit of shells, unusually shaped driftwood, fish traps, and traditional wooden boats. ⊠ *North Shore Rd.,* ☎ *284/495–4714.* ▣ *Free.* ☉ *Daily dawn–dusk.*

❶ Road Town. The laid-back capital of the BVI looks out over Road Harbour. It takes only an hour or so to stroll down Main Street and along the waterfront, checking out the traditional West Indian buildings, painted in pastel colors and with high-pitched, corrugated-tin roofs; bright shutters; and delicate fretwork trim. For hotel and sightseeing brochures and the latest information on everything from taxi rates to ferry-boat schedules, stop in the BVI Tourist Board office. Or just choose a seat on one of the benches in Sir Olva Georges Square, on Waterfront Drive, and watch the people come and go from the ferry dock and customs office across the street.

❼ Sage Mountain National Park. At 1,716 ft (525 m) Sage Mountain is the highest peak in the BVI. From the parking area a trail leads you in a loop not only to the peak itself (and extraordinary views) but also to a small rain forest, sometimes shrouded in mist. Most of the forest was cut down over the centuries to clear land for sugarcane, cotton, and other crops; to create pastureland; or to simply utilize the stands of timber; in 1964 this park was established to preserve what rain forest remained. Up here you can see mahogany trees, white cedars, mountain guavas, elephant-ear vines, mamey trees, and giant bullet woods, to say nothing of such birds as mountain doves and thrushes. Take a taxi from Road Town or drive up Joe's Hill Road and make a left onto Ridge Road toward Chalwell and Doty villages. The road dead-ends at the park. ⊠ *Ridge Rd.,* ☎ *No phone.* ▣ *Free.*

★ ❽ Skyworld. Drive up here and climb the observation tower for a stunning, 360-degree view of numerous islands and cays. On a clear day you can even see St. Croix (40 mi/64½ km away) and Anegada (20 mi/32 km away). ⊠ *Ridge Rd.,* ☎ *No phone.* ▣ *Free.*

VIRGIN GORDA

Virgin Gorda, with its mountainous central portion connected by skinny necks of land to southern and northern appendages—on a map it looks like the slightest breeze would cause the whole island to splinter apart—is quite different from Tortola. The pace is even slower here, and Virgin Gorda receives less rain, so some areas are more arid and home to scrub brush and cactus. Goats and cattle own the right of way, and the unpretentious friendliness of the people is winning.

Lodging

Virgin Gorda's charming hostelries appeal to a select, appreciative clientele; repeat business is extremely high. Visitors who prefer Sheratons, Marriotts, and the like may feel they get more for their money on other islands, but the peace and pampering offered on Virgin Gorda are priceless to the discriminating traveler.

For approximate costs, *see* the lodging price chart *in* Tortola.

Hotels and Inns

$$$$ ★ 🏨 **Biras Creek Hotel.** A long-time guest purchased this 140-acre hideaway and has made it so classy that it's accepted by the exclusive Relais & Chateaux family of hotels. Units are in duplex cottages, and each has a bedroom and a living room with terra-cotta floor tiles and a decor of soft Caribbean colors. Off the bath is an enclosed garden shower that's open to the sky. Although entrances are hidden among the trees, many cottages are feet from the water's edge. Bike paths and trails lead to the beaches and the outstanding Biras Creek restaurant. On a hilltop affording stunning views of North Sound is the open-air stonework bar-restaurant area. A sailaway package includes two nights on a private yacht. ⊠ *North Sound (Box 54)*, ☎ *284/494–3555 or 800/223– 1108*, FAX *284/494–3557*, WEB *www.biras.com. 33 suites, 2 villas. 3 restaurants, bar, air-conditioning, pool, 2 tennis courts, hiking, beach, snorkeling, windsurfing, boating, bicycles, shops. AE, MC, V. FAP.*

$$$$ 🏨 **Bitter End Yacht Club and Marina.** This family-oriented, convivial resort-cum-marina is accessible only by boat. Accommodations range from comfortable hillside or beachfront rooms with spacious balconies to live-aboard yachts. Your day can include snorkeling and diving trips to nearby reefs, cruises, windsurfing lessons, excursions to local attractions, and lessons at the well-regarded Nick Trotter Sailing School. When the sun goes down, the festivities continue at The Clubhouse, an open-air restaurant-bar overlooking North Sound. ⊠ *North Sound (Box 46)*, ☎ *284/494–2746 or 800/872–2392*, FAX *284/494–4756*, WEB *www.beyc.com. 95 rooms. 2 restaurants, bar, air-conditioning (some), pool, beach, dive shop, snorkeling, windsurfing, boating, waterskiing, children's programs. AE, MC, V. EP, FAP.*

$$$$ 🏨 **Drake's Anchorage Resort Inn.** Set on the edge of its own, very hilly,
★ 125-acre island (on the northwest side of North Sound), this tiny, secluded, and delightful getaway provides the true privacy of an elegant resort, but without the pampering or the formality. Dinner attire here means changing from bathing suit to comfortable cottons. Three West Indian–style waterfront bungalows contain 4 rooms and 5 suites that are simply furnished in rattan, wicker, and pastel prints. Three villas with full kitchens are also available. The appealing Drake's Anchorage Resort Inn restaurant is an elegant stop for all meals. Hiking trails, water-sports facilities, four delightful beaches, and hammocks here and there make this a place you never want to leave. In 2000, rooms and suites and the restaurant were completely refurbished and it shows. ⊠ *North Sound (Box 2510)*, ☎ *284/494–2254 or 800/624–6651 (direct to hotel)*, FAX *284/495–2254*, WEB *www.drakesanchorage.com. 4 rooms, 5 suites, 3 villas. Restaurant, bar, hiking, beach, snorkeling, boating. AE, MC, V. MAP.*

$$$$ 🏨 **Little Dix Bay.** Relaxed elegance is the hallmark here. The resort sits
★ amid the mangroves, along a curving beach. Duplexes with hexagonal units and quadraplex cottages are tucked among the trees and on a little hill. Interiors have handsome fieldstone walls and are decorated in Caribbean prints. About half the rooms are air-conditioned. Lawns are beautifully manicured; the reef-protected beach is long and silken; and the candlelight dining in an open, peak-roof pavilion is memorable. This resort is popular with honeymooners and older couples who have been coming for years. The Little Dix Bay Pavilion is an unforgettable setting for any meal. ⊠ *Little Dix Bay (Box 70)*, ☎ *284/495–5555*, FAX *284/495–5661*, WEB *www.littledixbay.com. 94 rooms, 4 suites. 3 restaurants, 2 bars, air-conditioning, 7 tennis courts, beach, snorkeling, windsurfing, library, children's programs. AE, MC, V. EP, MAP.*

$$$ 🏨 **Olde Yard Inn.** Owners Charlie Williams and Carol Kaufman have
★ cultivated a friendly, refreshing atmosphere at this quiet retreat outside Spanish Town. Classical music plays in the bar, and books line the walls of the octagonal library cottage. Rooms are cozy and simply furnished (in warmer months request a room with air-conditioning). You can make arrangements for day sails and scuba excursions, and you can swim in the large pool, work out, or get a massage in the health club. There are two excellent restaurants: the Olde Yard Inn, for French-accented dinners, and the Sip and Dip Grill, for poolside lunches. The inn isn't on the beach, but free transportation is provided to nearby Savannah Bay. ⊠ *The Valley (Box 26)*, ☎ *284/495–5544; 800/653–9273 direct to hotel*, FAX *284/495–5986*, WEB *www.oldeyardinn.*

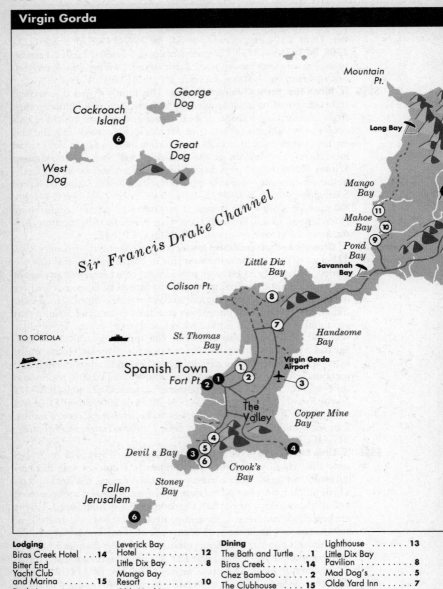

Mountain Pt.

George Dog

Cockroach Island

6

Long Bay

Great Dog

West Dog

Mango Bay

Sir Francis Drake Channel

Mahoe Bay

11

10

9

Pond Bay

Little Dix Bay

Colison Pt.

Savannah Bay

8

TO TORTOLA

St. Thomas Bay

7

Handsome Bay

Virgin Gorda Airport

Spanish Town

Fort Pt.

1

2

1

2

3

The Valley

Copper Mine Bay

4

Devil s Bay

4

5

6

4

3

Crook's Bay

Stoney Bay

Fallen Jerusalem

6

Lodging
Biras Creek Hotel . . .**14**
Bitter End
Yacht Club
and Marina **15**
Drake's
Anchorage **16**
Guavaberry
Spring Bay
Vacation Homes **4**

Leverick Bay
Hotel **12**
Little Dix Bay **8**
Mango Bay
Resort **10**
Olde Yard Inn **7**
Paradise Beach
Resort **11**
Virgin Gorda
Villa Rentals **13**

Dining
The Bath and Turtle . . .**1**
Biras Creek **14**
Chez Bamboo **2**
The Clubhouse **15**
Drake's Anchorage . . **16**
The Flying Iguana . . . **3**
Giorgio's Table **9**

Lighthouse **13**
Little Dix Bay
Pavilion **8**
Mad Dog's **5**
Olde Yard Inn **7**
Sip and Dip Grill **7**
Top of the Baths **6**

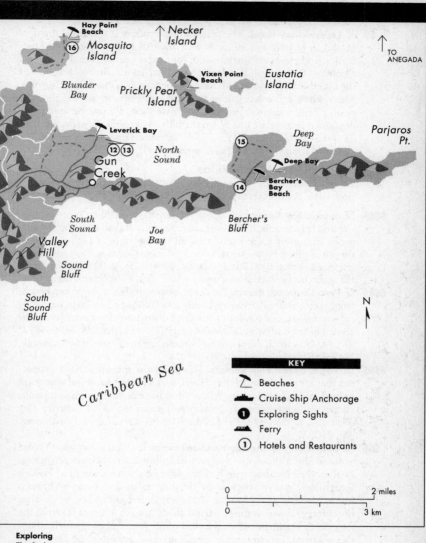

Necker Island

↑ TO ANEGADA

Hay Point Beach

(16)

Mosquito Island

Blunder Bay

Vixen Point Beach

Prickly Pear Island

Eustatia Island

Parjaros Pt.

Leverick Bay

(12)(13)

North Sound

Deep Bay

(15)

Gun Creek

Deep Bay

(14)

Bercher's Bay Beach

South Sound

Joe Bay

Bercher's Bluff

Valley Hill

Sound Bluff

South Sound Bluff

Caribbean Sea

N

KEY

Beaches

Cruise Ship Anchorage

1 Exploring Sights

Ferry

(1) Hotels and Restaurants

0   2 miles
0   3 km

Exploring
The Baths **3**
Coastal Islands **6**
Copper Mine
Point **4**
Little Fort
National Park **2**
Spanish Town **1**
Virgin Gorda Peak
National Park **5**

com. 14 rooms, 1 suite. 2 restaurants, bar, air-conditioning, pool, health club, croquet, shops, library. AE, MC, V. EP.

$$ ⬜ **Leverick Bay Hotel.** The small hillside rooms at this hotel are decorated in pastels and original artwork. All have refrigerators, balconies, and views of North Sound; four two-bedroom condos are also available. Down the hill, a Spanish colonial-style main building houses the Lighthouse restaurant and a store (operated by Pusser's of Tortola). The resort's office has games that you can borrow. Several shops, a pool, a beauty salon, a tiny beach, a dive shop, a coin-operated laundry, and a market are just down the hill. ✉ *Leverick Bay (Box 63),* ☎ *284/495–7421,* ℻ *284/495–7367,* 🌐 *www.virgingordabvi.com. 16 rooms, 4 condos. Ceiling fans, refrigerators. AE, D, MC, V. EP.*

Private Homes and Villas

Those craving seclusion would do well at a villa or even a private home. Both offer comfortable lodgings with full kitchens and maid service.

$$$$ ⬜ **Mango Bay Resort.** Sparkling white villas framed by morning glories and frangipanis, handsome contemporary Italian decor, and a gorgeous ribbon of golden sand that all but vanishes at high tide make this an idyllic family retreat. Even for Virgin Gorda it's a study in isolation. ✉ *Mahoe Bay (Box 1062),* ☎ *284/495–5672,* ℻ *284/495–5674,* 🌐 *www.mangobayresort.com. 5 villas. Beach. No credit cards.*

$$$$ ⬜ **Paradise Beach Resort.** These one-, two-, and three-bedroom beachfront suites and villas have a handsome Caribbean-style decor, pastel color schemes, and outdoor showers. Four-wheel-drive vehicles are included in the daily rate. ✉ *Mahoe Bay (Box 534),* ☎ *284/495–5871,* ℻ *284/495–5872,* 🌐 *www.paradisebeachresort.com. 9 units. Beach. No credit cards.*

$$$$ ⬜ **Virgin Gorda Villa Rentals.** This company manages many properties that are near Leverick Bay Hotel, so it's perfect for those who want to be close to some activity. Many villas have private swimming pools; all are well maintained and have spectacular views. ✉ *Leverick Bay (Box 63),* ☎ *284/495–7421. 26 villas, from studios to 3 bedrooms. AE, MC, V.*

$$$ ⬜ **Guavaberry Spring Bay Vacation Homes.** It's hard to say what's more unusual about these one- and two-bedroom units: their shape (hexagonal) or their location (perched on stilts and scattered about a hillside). Regardless, you're so close to chirping birds and breezes through leaves, you feel as if you're in a tree house. It's just a short walk from the cottages down to the tamarind-shaded beach and not far from the mammoth boulders and cool basins of the famed Baths, which adjoin this property. Eleven private houses are also available. ✉ *The Valley (Box 20),* ☎ *284/495–5227,* 🌐 *www.guavaberryspringbay.com. 12 1-bedroom units, 9 2-bedroom units. Beach. No credit cards.*

Dining

Restaurants range from simple to elegant. Hotels that are accessible only by boat will arrange transport in advance upon request for nonguests who wish to dine at their restaurants. It's wise to make dinner reservations almost everywhere except really casual spots.

For approximate costs, *see* the dining price chart *in* Tortola.

AMERICAN/CASUAL

$$ ✕ **The Flying Iguana.** In this charming restaurant's comfortable lounge, lifelike stuffed or colorfully painted wooden iguanas are perched in the plants, and local artwork is displayed. The open-air dining room looks out over Virgin Gorda's tiny airport to the sea. Sandwiches and thick, juicy hamburgers are served for lunch. The dinner menu includes a pasta special, grilled chicken, and steaks. ✉ *The Valley, at the airport,* ☎ *284/495–5277. AE, MC, V.*

$$ ✕ **Lighthouse.** This bi-level restaurant at the Leverick Bay Hotel looks out over North Sound. The upstairs is slightly less casual but definitely more expensive, with a menu that includes grilled steak, chops, and chicken dishes. Below, the Beach Bar offers light fare all day—starting with breakfast and moving on to hamburgers, salads, and pizzas until well into the evening. ✉ *Leverick Bay,* ☎ *284/495–7369. AE, MC, V.*

$$ ✕ **Top of The Baths.** At the entrance to The Baths, this popular restaurant starts serving at 8 AM. Tables are outside on a terrace or in an open-air pavilion; all have stunning views of the Sir Francis Drake Channel. Hamburgers, salads, and sandwiches are offered at lunch. Conch seviche and lentil soup are among the dinner appetizers. Entrées include Cornish hen with wild rice, grilled swordfish with fresh rosemary sauce, and local lobster. For dessert you can choose from such delectables as chocolate cheesecake or pecan pie. ✉ *The Valley,* ☎ *284/495–5497. AE, MC, V.*

$ ✕ **The Bath and Turtle.** You can really sit back and relax at this infor-
★ mal patio tavern with a friendly staff—although the TV noise can be a bit much. Burgers, well-stuffed sandwiches, pizzas, pasta dishes, and daily specials round out the casual menu. Live entertainers perform Wednesday and Sunday nights. ✉ *Virgin Gorda Yacht Harbour,* ☎ *284/495–5239. MC, V.*

$ ✕ **Mad Dog's.** Piña coladas are *the* thing at this breezy bar just outside The Baths. The menu includes great BLTs, hot dogs, and burgers. ✉ *The Valley, at the entrance to The Baths,* ☎ *284/495–5830. Reservations not accepted. MC, V. No dinner.*

$ ✕ **Sip and Dip Grill.** The pool at the Olde Yard Inn is the setting for
★ this pleasant, informal lunch spot. Come for the grilled fish, pasta salads, chilled soups, and ice cream. Sunday evening there's a barbecue with live entertainment. ✉ *The Valley,* ☎ *284/495–5544. Reservations not accepted. AE, MC, V. No dinner Mon.–Sat.*

CAJUN/CREOLE

$$ **Chez Bamboo.** This pleasant little hideaway isn't really that hard to find: look for the building with the purple and green latticework. Candles on the dining room tables and the patio create a mellow atmosphere in which to enjoy such dishes as conch gumbo, Chez B's bouillabaisse, and steak New Orleans. For dessert try the chocolate bourbon mint cake. Stop by Friday night for live jazz. ✉ *Across from and a little north of Virgin Gorda Yacht Harbour,* ☎ *284/495–5752. Reservations not accepted. AE, MC, V. Closed Mon. No lunch.*

CONTEMPORARY

$$$$ ✕ **Biras Creek.** This hilltop restaurant at the Biras Creek Hotel is stun-
★ ning: broad steps lead up to an open-air lounge and restaurant with beautiful views of North Sound. The three-course prix-fixe menu changes daily and includes several choices per course: appetizers might be chilled yellow-pepper soup, conch fritters with papaya sauce, or avocado and lobster salad. Roast duck breast with plum sauce, grilled swordfish with bacon and caper sauce, pan-seared snapper with a ginger beurre blanc, and a roast breast of pheasant are some of the enticing entrées. Delightful desserts include key lime pie with raspberry sauce and a rich chocolate brownie with chocolate sauce. Dinner ends with Biras Creek's signature offering of Stilton and port. ✉ *North Sound,* ☎ *284/494–3555. Reservations essential. AE, MC, V.*

$$$$ ✕ **Drake's Anchorage.** Waves lap almost within reach at tables strung
★ along the front of this waterside, open-air restaurant at Drake's Anchorage Resort Inn. At sunset you can see stunning North Sound and the surrounding hills, and at night the lights of neighboring resorts twinkle and

shimmer. Dinner is an elegant four-course affair. The evening begins with an exceptional soup of the evening. Next comes a salad, then the entrée you chose, such as boneless breast of duck with orange-pineapple sauce, roasted rack of lamb with Caribbean-spiced mustard sauce, filet of local red snapper, or a filet mignon with brandy cream sauce. Dessert choices change but are always tempting. ⊠ *North Sound,* ☎ *284/494–3555. Reservations essential. AE, MC, V. No lunch.*

$$$$ ✕ **Little Dix Bay Pavilion.** For an elegant evening at the Little Dix Bay
★ resort, you can't do better than this—the candlelight in the main open-air pavilion is enchanting, the menu sophisticated, the service attentive. The dinner menu changes daily, but there's always a fine selection of superbly prepared seafood, meat, and vegetarian entrées—gingered duck breast with Pacific Rim vegetables, black Angus rib eye with horseradish and mustard sauce, pan-seared snapper with christophene ratatouille. The breakfast and lunch buffets shine. ⊠ *Spanish Town,* ☎ *284/495–5555 ext. 174. AE, MC, V.*

$$$ ✕ **Olde Yard Inn.** The intimate dining room is suffused with gentle,
★ classical melodies and the scent of herbs; a cedar roof covers the breezy space, which is decorated with old-style Caribbean charm. The French-accented cuisine includes lamb chops with mango chutney, chicken breast in a rum cream sauce, grilled fish, steaks, and lobster. Chocolate mousse, cheesecake, and Key lime pie are sweet endings. ⊠ *The Valley, north of the marina,* ☎ *284/495–5544. AE, MC, V.*

ITALIAN

$$ ✕ **Giorgio's Table.** Gaze out at the stars and the lights of Tortola and listen to the water lap against the shore while dining on veal scallopini, filet mignon with mushrooms, fresh local fish, or penne with garlic and tomatoes. Lunch fare at this casual establishment includes pizzas and sandwiches. ⊠ *Mahoe Bay,* ☎ *284/495–5684. MC, V.*

SEAFOOD

$$ ✕ **The Clubhouse.** The Bitter End Yacht Club's open-air waterfront restaurant is a favorite rendezvous for the sailing set—busy day and night. At the lavish buffets you get your choice of an entrée for breakfast, lunch, and dinner. Dinner selections include grilled swordfish or tuna, chopped sirloin, scallops, and shrimp. ⊠ *Bitter End Yacht Club, North Sound,* ☎ *284/494–2746. AE, MC, V.*

Beaches

The best beaches are easily reached by water, although they're also accessible on foot, usually after a moderately strenuous 10- to 15-minute hike. Either way, your persistence is rewarded. Anybody going to Virgin Gorda must experience swimming or snorkeling among its unique boulder formations, which can be visited at several beaches along Lee Road. **The Baths** feature the most outstanding grouping of boulders but is usually quite crowded. From The Baths you can walk on Lee Road or swim north to less-populated **Spring Bay Beach,** which is a gem. Swim or walk north from **Spring Bay Beach** to reach **The Crawl,** a small and appealing beach.

From Biras Creek or Bitter End on the north shore, you can walk to **Bercher's Bay Beach** and along the windswept surf. Footpaths from Bitter End and foot and bike paths from Biras Creek also lead to **Deep Bay,** a calm, well-protected swimming beach. Mosquito Island's **Hay Point Beach** is a broad band of white sand accessible only by boat or by a path from a little dock on the island's east side.

Leverick Bay (⊠ Leverick Bay Rd.) is a tiny, busy beach-cum-marina that fronts a resort restaurant and pool. Come here if you want a break from the island's serenity. The view of Prickly Pear Island is a plus, and the dive facility here can arrange to motor you out to beautiful Eustatia Reef, just across North Sound.

It's worth heading out to **Long Bay** (✉ Plum Tree Bay Rd., near Virgin Gorda's northern tip, past the Diamond Beach Club), for the snorkeling (Little Dix Bay resort has outings here). The drive takes about half an hour after the turnoff from North Sound Road, and a dirt road makes up part of the route.

For a wonderfully private beach close to Spanish Town, try **Savannah Bay** (✉ North Sound Rd.). It may not always be completely deserted, but it's a lovely long stretch of white sand. Prickly Pear Island has a calm swimming beach at **Vixen Point Beach.**

Outdoor Activities and Sports

Participant Sports

FISHING

The sportfishing here is so good that anglers from around the world fly in for the annual tournaments. **Walford Ferrington** (✉ Leverick Bay, North Sound, ☎ 284/495–7612) will pick you up almost anywhere on Virgin Gorda and take you out on his 24-ft speedboat for half- or full-day fishing jaunts. Plan to spend $250–$600.

SAILING

The BVI waters are calm and, hence, are terrific places to learn to sail. The **Nick Trotter Sailing School** (✉ Bitter End Yacht Club, North Sound, ☎ 284/494–2745) offers beginner and advanced courses. Private lessons are $40 per hour.

SCUBA DIVING AND SNORKELING

Many of the breathtaking sites off Tortola can also be reached easily from Virgin Gorda. Also, note that the North Sound has some terrific snorkeling spots. The **Bitter End Yacht Club** (✉ North Sound, ☎ 284/494–2746) offers a number of snorkeling trips day and night. Costs range from $5 per person to $55 per person depending on the length and type of trip. Contact **Dive BVI** (✉ Virgin Gorda Yacht Harbour, ☎ 284/495–5513) for expert instruction, certification, and day trips. It costs $101 for a resort course, $85 for a two-tank dive, and $65 for a one-tank dive; equipment rental is an additional $15. **Kilbride's** (✉ Bitter End, North Sound, ☎ 284/495–9638) offers resort, advanced, and rescue courses. The fee for a resort course is $95. One-tank dives run $60; two-tank dives, $85. Equipment rental is an additional $15.

WINDSURFING

The North Sound is a good place to learn to windsurf: it's protected, so you can't be easily blown out to sea. The **Bitter End Yacht Club** (✉ North Sound, ☎ 284/494–2746) gives lessons and rents equipment for $20 per hour.

Spectator Sports

CRICKET

You can catch a match at the **Recreation Grounds** in Spanish Town February–April. The Virgin Gorda BVI Tourist Board office can give you information on game dates and times.

Shopping

Most boutiques are within hotel complexes. Two of the best are at Biras Creek and Little Dix Bay. Other properties—the Bitter End, Leverick Bay, and the Olde Yard Inn—have small but equally select boutiques, and there's a respectable and diverse scattering of shops in the bustling yacht harbor complex in Spanish Town.

CLOTHING

Dive BVI (✉ Virgin Gorda Yacht Harbour, ☎ 284/495–5513) sells books about the islands as well as sportswear, sunglasses, and beach bags. **Island Silhouette in Flax Plaza** (✉ Near Fischer's Cove Beach Hotel, ☎ no phone) is the place to go for resort wear hand-painted by Virgin Gorda artists and for locally made tie-dyed T-shirts. **Next Wave** (✉ Virgin Gorda Yacht Harbour, ☎ 284/495–5623) sells bathing suits, T-shirts, canvas tote bags, and locally made jewelry. **Pavilion Gift Shop** (✉ Little Dix Bay Hotel, ☎ 284/495–5555) has the latest in resort wear for men and women, as well as jewelry, books, housewares, and expensive T-shirts. **Pelican's Pouch Boutique** (✉ Virgin Gorda Yacht Harbour, ☎ 284/495–5477) is where you'll find a large selection of swimsuits plus cover-ups, T-shirts, and accessories. **Pusser's Company Store** (✉ Leverick Bay, ☎ 284/495–7369) has a trademark line of sportswear, rum products, and gift items.

FOODSTUFFS

Bitter End's Emporium (✉ North Sound, ☎ 284/494–2745) is the place for such edible treats as local fruits, cheeses, and baked goods. **Commissary and Ship Store** (✉ The Valley, ☎ 284/495–5555) offers daily specials prepared by Little Dix Resort chefs, as well as assorted cheeses, canned goods, wines, and gourmet items. **Wine Cellar and Bakery** (✉ Virgin Gorda Yacht Harbour, ☎ 284/495–5250) bakes bread, rolls, muffins, and cookies and has sandwiches and sodas to go.

GIFTS

Palm Tree Gallery (✉ Leverick Bay, ☎ 284/495–7479) sells attractive handcrafted jewelry, paintings, and one-of-a-kind gift items, as well as games and books about the Caribbean. **Thee Artistic Gallery** (✉ Virgin Gorda Yacht Harbour, ☎ 284/495–5104) features Caribbean jewelry, 14-karat-gold nautical jewelry, maps, collectible coins, and crystal. **The Reeftique** (✉ Bitter End, North Sound, ☎ 284/494–2745) carries island crafts and jewelry, clothing, and nautical odds and ends with the Bitter End logo.

HANDICRAFTS

Virgin Gorda Craft Shop (✉ Virgin Gorda Yacht Harbour, ☎ 284/495–5137) features the work of island artisans, and carries West Indian jewelry and crafts styled from straw, shells, and other local materials. It also stocks clothing and paintings by Caribbean artists.

Nightlife

The Bath and Turtle (✉ Virgin Gorda Yacht Harbour, ☎ 284/495–5239), one of the liveliest spots on Virgin Gorda, hosts island bands on Wednesday from 8 PM until midnight. **Bitter End Yacht Club** (✉ North Sound, ☎ 284/494–2746) features local bands most nights in season. Call for schedules. **Chez Bamboo** (✉ Across from Virgin Gorda Yacht Harbour, ☎ 284/495–5752) is the place for jazz on Friday nights and a live band Sunday nights. The **Lighthouse** (✉ Leverick Bay, ☎ 284/495–7370) has live bands on Saturday night and Sunday afternoon in season. **Little Dix Bay** (✉ Little Dix Bay, ☎ 284/495–5555) presents elegant live entertainment several nights a week in season. **Rock Café** (✉ The Valley, ☎ 284/495–5672) has live bands Friday, Saturday, and Sunday nights. **Sip and Dip Grill** (✉ Olde Yard Inn, ☎ 284/495–5544) has a live local band at their Sunday night barbecue.

Exploring Virgin Gorda

One of the most efficient ways to see Virgin Gorda is by sailboat. There are few roads, and most byways don't follow the scalloped shoreline.

The main route sticks resolutely to the center of the island, linking The Baths at the tip of the southern extremity with Gun Creek and Leverick Bay at North Sound and providing exhilarating views. The craggy coast, scissored with grottoes and fringed by palms and boulders, has a primitive beauty. If you drive, you can hit all the sights in one day. The best plan is to explore the area near your hotel (either The Valley or North Sound) first, then take a day to drive to the other end. Stop to climb Gorda Peak, in the island's center.

Numbers in the margin correspond to points of interest on the Virgin Gorda map.

Sights to See

❸ The Baths. At Virgin Gorda's most celebrated sight, giant boulders are scattered about the beach and in the water. Some are almost as large as houses and form remarkable grottoes. Climb between these rocks to swim in the many pools. Early morning and late afternoon are the best times to visit if you want to avoid crowds. (If it's privacy you crave, follow the shore northward to quieter bays—Spring, the Crawl, Little Trunk, and Valley Trunk—or head south to Devil's Bay.) ⊠ *Lee Rd.,* ☎ *No phone.* ☜ *Free.*

❻ Coastal Islands. You can easily reach the quaintly named Fallen Jerusalem Island and the Dog Islands by boat. They're all part of the BVI National Parks Trust, and their seductive beaches and unparalleled snorkeling opportunities display the BVI at their beachcombing, hedonistic best. ☎ *No phone.* ☜ *Free.*

❹ Copper Mine Point. Here you'll see a tall, stone shaft silhouetted against the sky and a small stone structure that overlooks the sea. These are the ruins of a copper mine established 400 years ago and worked first by the Spanish, then by the English, until the early 20th century. ⊠ *Copper Mine Rd.,* ☎ *No phone.* ☜ *Free.*

❷ Little Fort National Park. This 36-acre wildlife sanctuary has the ruins of an old fort. Giant boulders like those at The Baths are scattered throughout the park. ⊠ *Spanish Town Rd.,* ☎ *No phone.* ☜ *Free.*

❶ Spanish Town. Virgin Gorda's peaceful main settlement, on the island's southern wing, is so tiny that it barely qualifies as a town at all. Also known as The Valley, Spanish Town is home to a marina, some shops, and a couple of car-rental agencies. Just north of town is the ferry slip. At the **Virgin Gorda Yacht Harbour** you can stroll along the dock and do a little shopping.

❺ Virgin Gorda Peak National Park. There are two trails at this 265-acre park, which contains the island's highest point, at 1,359 ft (414 m). Small signs on North Sound Road mark both entrances; sometimes, however, the signs are missing, so keep your eyes open for a set of stairs that disappears into the trees. It's about a 15-minute hike from either entrance up to a small clearing, where you can climb a ladder to the platform of a wooden observation tower and a spectacular 360-degree view. ⊠ *North Sound Rd.,* ☎ *No phone.* ☜ *Free.*

JOST VAN DYKE

Named after an early Dutch settler, Jost Van Dyke is a small island northwest of Tortola and is *truly* a place to get away from it all. Mountainous and lush, the 4-mi-long (6½-km-long) island—home to only about 140 people—has one tiny resort, some rental houses, a campground, a handful of cars, and a single road. This is one of the Caribbean's most popular anchorages, and there's a disproportionately large number of informal bars and restaurants, which have helped earn Jost its reputation as the "party island" of the BVI.

Lodging

For approximate costs, *see* the lodging price chart *in* Tortola.

$$$ ⊡ **Sandcastle.** This six-cottage hideaway is on a ½-mi (¾-km) stretch of white-sand beach at remote White Bay. There's "nothing" to do here, except relax in a hammock, read, walk, swim, and enjoy sophisticated cuisine by candlelight in the Sandcastle restaurant. You can also make arrangements for diving, sailing, and sportfishing trips. ⊠ *White Bay,* ☎ *284/495–9888,* FAX *284/495–9999,* WEB *www.sandcastle-bvi.com. 6 cottages. Restaurant, bar, beach, shops. MC, V. EP.*

$$$ ⊡ **Sandy Ground Estates.** The eight privately owned one- and two-bedroom houses here are tucked into the foliage along the edge of a beach at the island's east end. Each house is architecturally different, and interiors range from spartan to stylish. The fully equipped kitchens can be pre-stocked if you supply a list of groceries (a good idea, as supplies are limited on the island), and there are four very casual restaurants on the other side of the hill—a long walk away. ⊠ *Sandy Ground,* ☎ *284/494–3391,* WEB *www.sandyground.com. 8 houses. Beach. AE, MC, V. EP.*

$ ⚿ **White Bay Campground.** On the east end of White Bay Beach, this simple campground has bare sites, equipped tent sites (with electricity and a lamp), and screened cabins. The owners will take you on nature walks and can arrange island tours and sailing and diving trips. ⊠ *White Bay,* ☎ *284/495–9312. 12 sites, 4 cabins. Restaurant, bar, beach. No credit cards.*

Dining

Restaurants on Jost Van Dyke are informal (some serve meals family style at long tables) but charming. The island is a favorite charter stop, and you're bound to hear people exchanging stories about the previous night's anchoring adventures. Most restaurants don't take reservations, and in all cases dress is casual.

For approximate costs, *see* the dining price chart *in* Tortola.

ECLECTIC

$$$ ✕ **Sandcastle.** Candlelit dinners in the tiny beachfront dining room of the sandcastle cottage complex are four-course prix-fixe affairs with seating at 7 PM. The menu changes but can include a West Indian pumpkin or curried-apple soup; curried shrimp or three-mustard chicken; and for dessert, rum bananas or Key lime pie. Reservations are requested by 4 PM. Sandwiches are served at lunch at the Soggy Dollar Bar, famous as the purported birthplace of the lethal painkiller drink. ⊠ *White Bay,* ☎ *284/495–9888. Reservations essential. MC, V.*

$$ ✕ **Abe's Little Harbour.** Specialties at this informal, popular spot include fresh lobster, conch, and spareribs. During most of the winter season there's a pig roast every Wednesday night. ⊠ *Little Harbour,* ☎ *No phone (boaters can use VHF Channel 16). No credit cards.*

$$ ✕ **Club Paradise.** The dinner menu at this casual beachfront establishment includes grilled local fish such as mahimahi, red snapper, and grouper, grilled steak, and barbecued chicken and ribs. Hamburgers, West Indian conch stew, and curried chicken are the luncheon fare. ⊠ *Great Harbour,* ☎ *284/495–9267. No credit cards.*

$$ ✕ **Foxy's Tamarind.** One of the true hot spots in the BVI—and a must-
★ stop for yachters from the world over—Foxy's hosts the madcap Wooden Boat Race every May and throws big parties on New Year's

Eve, April Fools' Day, and Halloween. This lively place serves local dishes and terrific barbecue, and it makes a rum punch that's all its own. Foxy plays the guitar and creates calypso ditties about his guests. Next door is Foxy's Store, which sells clothing, sundries, souvenirs, and cassettes of Foxy performing. ⊠ *Great Harbour,* ☎ *284/495–9258. AE, MC, V. No lunch weekends.*

$$ ✕ **Harris' Place.** Owner Harris Jones is famous for his pig-roast buffets and Monday night Lobstermania. Harris' Place is a great spot to rub elbows with locals and the charter-boat crowd. ⊠ *Little Harbour,* ☎ *284/495–9302. AE, MC, V.*

$$ ✕ **Sydney's Peace and Love.** Here you'll find great lobster, barbecue, and a sensational (for the BVI) jukebox. The cognoscenti sail here for dinner since there's no beach—meaning no irksome sand fleas. ⊠ *Little Harbour,* ☎ *284/495–9271. No credit cards.*

$ ✕ **Happy Laurry.** Hamburgers, cheeseburgers, and honey-dipped fried chicken are the specialties at this beachfront spot. ⊠ *Great Harbour,* ☎ *284/495–9259. No credit cards.*

Beaches

White Bay, on the south shore, west of Great Harbour, has a long stretch of white sand. Just offshore, the little islet known as **Sandy Cay** is a gleaming scimitar of white sand, with marvelous snorkeling.

PETER ISLAND

Dramatic, hilly, and with wonderful anchorages and beautiful beaches, privately owned Peter Island is about 5 mi (8 km) directly south across the Sir Francis Drake Channel from Road Town, Tortola. Set amid the string of islets that stream from the southern tip of Virgin Gorda, the island is an idyllic hideaway replete with white sand beaches, stunning views, and the Peter Island Resort. You can sail here on your own craft or take a launch from the Peter Island dock east of Road Town, Tortola ($15 each way or free if you're coming for dinner; just mention that you have a reservation). Note that the resort discourages nonguests from using hotel facilities other than the restaurants.

Lodging

For approximate costs, *see* the lodging price chart *in* Tortola.

$$$$ ▦ **Peter Island Resort and Yacht Harbour.** This casually elegant retreat ★ has recently undergone a major renovation, and it sparkles. Fifty-two guest rooms, in four-unit cottages tucked amid beds of radiant flowers, are either at the far end of the main beach or clustered near the main building. Beachfront Junior Suites are beautiful stone-and-wood structures with French doors that open onto balconies or patios, a few steps from a lovely stretch of sand. The less expensive, second-floor Ocean View units, and more spacious first-floor Garden Terrace rooms, look across the pool and gardens toward the hills of Tortola. A spectacular hilltop villa, the Crow's Nest, has four bedrooms, a living room, a state-of-the-art kitchen, a dining room, a huge terrace with panoramic views, an inner courtyard, an entertainment system, domestic help, vehicles, and a private pool. There's lots to do here: facilities include a tennis program run by Peter Burwash, a water sports center, a beachfront spa, mountain bicycles, a 20-station fitness trail, and a 5-star PADI dive facility. After dinner in the Tradewinds Restaurant, you can often dance under the stars. If you seek seclusion, take note: some of the resort's beaches are on bays that are popular charter-boat anchorages, and although no longer owned and run by Amway Hotel Cor-

poration, this property is still used for Amway incentive trips. ⊠ *Sprat Bay (Box 211, Road Town, Tortola)*, ☎ *284/495–2000 or 800/346–4451*, FAX *284/495–2500*, WEB *www.peterisland.com. 52 rooms, 3 villas. 2 restaurants, 2 bars, pool, spa, 4 tennis courts, basketball, gym, beach, dive shop, windsurfing, mountain bikes, laundry service, helipad. AE, MC, V. FAP.*

Dining

For approximate costs, *see* the dining price chart *in* Tortola.

ECLECTIC

$$$$ ✕ **Tradewinds Restaurant.** The Peter Island Resort's air-conditioned dining room overlooks the Sir Francis Drake Channel and is an enchanting dinner setting. The à la carte menu offers mostly Continental selections with subtle Caribbean touches; Saturday night is buffet night. After dinner, dance under the stars to soft, rhythmic tunes performed by local musicians three or four nights a week in season. ⊠ *Sprat Bay*, ☎ *284/495–2000. Reservations essential. AE, MC, V. No lunch.*

$$$ ✕ **Deadman's Bay Bar and Grill.** This casual beach grill serves lunches of thick and juicy burgers, grilled fish, light salads, and individual pizzas freshly made in the new pizza oven. Sunday lunch features a lavish West Indian buffet and a steel band. A dinner with a choice of grilled local fish, steak, or chicken is served most evenings. Try one of the many delicious frozen tropical drinks. ⊠ *Sprat Bay*, ☎ *284/495–2000. Reservations essential. AE, MC, V.*

Beaches

Palm-fringed **Dead Man's Bay,** considered by many to be one of the world's 10 most romantic beaches, is a short hike from the dock. Snorkeling is good at both ends of the beach, and you'll find a bar and restaurant for lunch. If you feel like taking a hike instead of heading down to Dead Man's Bay, follow the road up, and when it levels off, bear right and head down to the other side of the island and secluded **White Bay.**

ANEGADA

Anegada lies low on the horizon about 14 mi (22½ km) north of Virgin Gorda. Unlike the hilly volcanic islands in the chain, this is a flat coral and limestone atoll. Nine miles (14 km) long and 2 mi (3 km) wide, the island rises no more than 28 ft (9 m) above sea level. In fact, by the time you're able to see it, you may have run your boat onto a reef. (More than 300 captains unfamiliar with the waters have done so since exploration days; note that bareboat charters don't allow their vessels to head here without a trained skipper.) Although the reefs are a sailor's nightmare, they (and the shipwrecks they've caused) are a scuba diver's dream. Snorkeling, especially in the waters around Loblolly Bay on the north shore, is also a transcendent experience. You can float in shallow, calm, reef-protected water just a few feet from shore and see one coral formation after another, each shimmering with a rainbow of colorful fish. Such watery pleasures are complemented by ever-so-fine, ever-so-white sand (the northern and western shores have long stretches of the stuff) and the occasional beach bar (stop in for burgers, Anegada lobster, or a frosty beer). The island's population of about 150 lives primarily in a small south-side village called The Settlement. Many local fisherfolk are happy to take visitors out bonefishing.

Lodging

For approximate costs, *see* the lodging price chart *in* Tortola.

$$$$ 🏨 **Anegada Reef Hotel.** If you favor laid-back living (meaning, among other things, absolutely no schedules), this is the spot for you. Pack a bathing suit and a few warmer garments for the evening, and you're good to go. The hotel's simply furnished rooms are laid out in motel fashion. It has its own narrow strip of beach, but beach lovers will want to spend their days on the deserted strands at the other side of the island; you can ask to be dropped off with a picnic lunch or be picked up and returned to the hotel for lunch. Snorkeling and diving are popular activities, as are deep-sea fishing or bonefishing in the flats. Cool down with a drink in the outdoor bar, and be sure to try the island's famous lobster—freshly grilled in the Anegada Reef restaurant. ✉ *Setting Point,* ☎ *284/495–8002,* FAX *284/495–9362,* WEB *www.anegadareef.com. 16 rooms. Restaurant, bar, beach. MC, V. FAP.*

$$ 🏨 **Neptune's Treasure.** This little guest house offers simple double and single rooms that are very basically furnished. However, all have private baths. You'll find a restaurant, Neptune's Treasure, and a little gift shop on the premises. ✉ *Between Pomato and Saltheap points,* ☎ *284/495–9439. 4 rooms. Restaurant, beach. AE, MC, V. EP.*

$ ⛺ **Anegada Beach Campground.** The tents (8×10 ft or 10×12 ft/2×3 m or 3×4 m) here are pitched in a marvelously serene setting. Bare sites cost $7 per person, per night; equipped sites are $20 per person. ✉ *The Settlement,* ☎ *284/495–9466. 18 sites. Restaurant, bar, beach. No credit cards.*

Dining

There are between 6 and 10 restaurants open at any one time, depending on the season and also on whim. Check when you're on the island.

For approximate costs, *see* the dining price chart *in* Tortola.

SEAFOOD

$$$ ✗ **Anegada Reef Hotel.** Seasoned yachters gather nightly at the Anegada Reef Hotel's bar-restaurant to converse and dine with hotel guests. Dinner is by candlelight and always includes famous Anegada lobster, steaks, and chicken—all prepared on the large grill by the little open-air bar. ✉ *Setting Point,* ☎ *284/495–8002. Reservations essential. No credit cards.*

$$ ✗ **Big Bamboo.** Ice-cold beer, island drinks, burgers, and grilled lobster entice a steady stream of barefoot diners to this beach bar for lunch. Dinner is by request. ✉ *Loblolly Bay,* ☎ *284/495–2019. AE.*

$$ ✗ **Neptune's Treasure.** The owners catch, cook, and serve the seafood (lobster is a specialty) at this casual bar and restaurant in the Neptune's Treasure guest house. ✉ *Between Pomato and Saltheap points,* ☎ *284/495–9439. AE.*

$$ ✗ **Pomato Point.** This relaxed restaurant-bar is on a narrow beach, a short walk from the Anegada Reef Hotel. Entrées include steak, chicken, lobster, and fresh-caught seafood. Owner Wilfred Creque displays various island artifacts, including shards of Arawak pottery and 17th-century coins, cannonballs, and bottles. ✉ *Pomato Point,* ☎ *284/495–8038. Reservations essential. No credit cards.*

Shopping

Anegada Reef Hotel Boutique (✉ Setting Point, ☎ 284/495–8002) has a bit of everything: resort wear, hand-painted T-shirts, locally made jewelry, books, and one-of-a-kind gifts. **Pat's Pottery** (✉ Nutmeg Point,

☎ 284/495–8031) sells bowls, plates, cups, candlestick holders, original watercolors, and more.

OTHER BRITISH VIRGIN ISLANDS

Cooper Island

This small hilly island on the south side of the Sir Francis Drake Channel, about 8 mi (13 km) from Road Town, Tortola, is popular with the charter-boat crowd. There are no roads (which doesn't really matter because there aren't any cars), but you will find a beach restaurant, a casual little hotel, a few houses (some are available for rent), and great snorkeling at the south end of Manchioneel Bay.

Dining and Lodging

For approximate costs, *see* the dining and lodging price charts *in* Tortola.

$$$ ✕☎ **Cooper Island Beach Club.** Six West Indian-style cottages—set back from the beach among the palm trees—house 12 no-frills units, each with a living area, a small but complete kitchen, and a balcony. A stay here takes you back to the basics: you use rainwater that has been collected in a cistern, and you can't use any appliances because electricity is so limited (who needs pressed clothes and blow-dried hair anyway?). There's plenty of "civilization," however, at the on-site bar, which fills nightly with boaters. The restaurant is also popular with the boating crowd (if you don't have your own vessel, note that ferry service from Road Town is available only to hotel guests). The restaurant serves great ratatouille (it's a main course at lunch, an appetizer at dinner); grilled fish, chicken and vegetable rotis, penne pasta, steak, and conch creole. For lunch there are hamburgers, conch fritters, sandwiches, and pasta salad. Reservations are essential. ✉ *Manchioneel Bay (Box 859, Road Town, Tortola),* ☎ *413/659–2602 or 800/542–4624,* WEB *www.cooper-island.com; No phone to restaurant (boaters can use VHF Channel 16). 12 rooms. Restaurant, fans, beach, dive shop. AE, MC, V. EP.*

Guana Island

Guana Island is very quiet and because the whole island is owned by the resort, *very* private. There are *no* public amenities, and access is limited (the hotel sends a private launch to pick up its guests on Beef Island). If you arrive on your own boat, the only place you're allowed is on the beach.

Dining and Lodging

For approximate costs, *see* the dining and lodging price charts *in* Tortola.

$$$$ ✕☎ **Guana Island.** The hotel complex is atop a hill, a 10-minute walk from the beach, and views of neighboring islands are stunning. The 15 comfortable rooms are in seven houses scattered throughout the grounds. The houses are decorated in Caribbean style, with rattan furniture, and each has its own porch. You can observe more than 50 species of birds on this island, and the terrain is a verdant collection of plants ringed by six deserted beaches. Guests mingle during cocktail hour and often dine together at several large tables in the main house, but there are small tables if you prefer a more intimate meal. Daily rates include three meals, afternoon tea, and house wine with lunch and dinner. ✉ *Hilltop (Box 32, Road Town, Tortola),* ☎ *284/494–2354 or 914/ 967–6050,* FAX *284/495–2900,* WEB *www.guana.com. 15 rooms. Restaurant, fans, tennis court, croquet, hiking. No credit cards. FAP.*

Little Thatch Island

Just west of Tortola is Little Thatch Island, a petite private island with an elegant hideaway.

Lodging

For approximate costs, *see* the lodging price chart *in* Tortola.

$$$$ ⊡ **Little Thatch Island.** When you want to be pampered and don't care about the price (the cost per day is $10,450 for 1–4 guests and $11,755 for 5–10 guests), this stunning hilltop hideaway can be all yours. The four octagonal one-bedroom cottages have Douglas fir roofs and broad terraces. Three of the four have handsome outdoor (but exceedingly private) stonework showers. Rattan furnishings are of the highest quality and are extremely comfortable. Views from the open-air living room, the dining room, and the pool are breathtaking. A gourmet chef prepares all your meals, and unobtrusive staff members provide impeccable service, seeing to your every need. ⊠ *Box 861, Road Town, Tortola,* ☎ *284/495–9227,* F̅A̅X̅ *284/495–9212,* W̅E̅B̅ *www.littlethatchisland. com. Pool, beach, windsurfing, boating. AE, MC, V. FAP. Closed Aug.–Oct.*

Necker Island

Necker Island, just north of Virgin Gorda, is yet another private isle. Accommodations here are luxurious, but you can only stay if you rent the whole island.

Lodging

For approximate costs, *see* the lodging price chart *in* Tortola.

$$$$ ⊡ **Necker Island.** You and as many as 25 friends can lease the whole island, including its five beaches, many walks, tennis courts, luxurious villa with 10 spacious guest rooms, and two Balinese cottages. The common living area is anything but common: the huge room is lined with doors that open to the breezes. Here and there are oversize couches and chairs, surrounded by potted plants, artwork, and sculptures. Bedrooms have slate floors, stonework walls, and stunning views. A chef prepares gourmet meals for you in the state-of-the-art kitchen; a full staff takes care of everything else. ⊠ *Box 1091, The Valley, Virgin Gorda,* ☎ *284/494–2757,* F̅A̅X̅ *284/494–4396,* W̅E̅B̅ *www. virgin.com/limitededition. 2 pools, 2 tennis courts, gym, beach, windsurfing, boating. AE, MC, V.*

Marina Cay

Beautiful little Marina Cay is in Trellis Bay, not far from Beef Island. Sometimes you can see it and its large J-shape coral reefs—a most dramatic sight—from the air soon after takeoff from the airport on Beef Island. With only 6 acres, this islet is considered small even by BVI standards. You'll find a restaurant, Pusser's Store, and a six-unit hotel here. Ferry service is free from the dock on Beef Island.

Lodging

For approximate costs, *see* the lodging price chart *in* Tortola.

$$$ ⊡ **Pusser's Marina Cay Hotel and Restaurant.** The tiny island's only hotel has four rooms and two villas, all with lovely views of the water and neighboring islands. Each has its own porch. The restaurant's menu ranges from fish and lobster to steak, chicken, and barbecued ribs. Pusser's Painkiller Punch is the house specialty. There's free ferry service from the Beef Island dock for anyone visiting the island (call for ferry times, which vary with the season). ✉ *West side of Marina Cay (Box 76, Road Town, Tortola),* ☎ *284/494–2174,* FAX *284/494–4775,* WEB *www.pussers.com. 4 rooms, 2 villas. Restaurant, bar, beach. AE, DC, MC, V. EP.*

BRITISH VIRGIN ISLANDS A TO Z

To research prices, get advice from other travelers, and book travel arrangements, visit www.fodors.com.

AIR TRAVEL

Both the Beef Island/Tortola and Virgin Gorda airports are classic Caribbean—almost always sleepy. However, the Beef Island terminal can get crowded when several departures are scheduled close together, and lines at service desks move slowly when this happens; give yourself at least an hour. There's no nonstop service from the continental United States to the BVI; connections are usually made through San Juan, Puerto Rico, or St. Thomas, USVI. Several airlines serve either San Juan and St. Thomas or both. Air St. Thomas flies between St. Thomas and San Juan and Virgin Gorda. Air Sunshine flies back and forth from St. Thomas and San Juan to Beef Island/Tortola and Virgin Gorda. American Eagle flies between St. Thomas and Beef Island/Tortola, and between San Juan and Beef Island/Tortola. Cape Air flies to both San Juan and St. Thomas from Beef Island/Tortola. Clair Aero Services flies back and forth to St. Thomas from Beef Island/Tortola. Continental flies between San Juan and Beef Island/Tortola.

Regularly scheduled flights between the BVI and most other Caribbean islands are provided by LIAT. Many Caribbean islands can also be reached through Fly BVI, a charter service on Virgin Gorda.
➤ AIRLINES AND CONTACTS: **Air St. Thomas** (☎ 284/495–5935); **Air Sunshine** (☎ 284/495–8900); **American Eagle** (☎ 284/495–1122); **Cape Air** (☎ 284/495–2100); **Clair Aero Services** (☎ 284/495–2271); **Continental** (☎ 340/777–8190); **Fly BVI** (☎ 284/495–1747); **LIAT** (☎ 284/495–2577).

AIRPORTS

At the Beef Island/Tortola Airport, taxis hover at the exit from customs. Fares are officially set; they're not negotiable and are lower per person when there are several passengers. Figure about $15 for up to three people and $5 for each additional passenger for the 20-minute ride to Road Town and about $20–$30 for the 45-minute ride to West End. Expect to share your taxi, and be patient if your driver searches for people to fill his cab—only a few flights land each day, and this could be your driver's only run. You can also call the BVI Taxi Association.

On Virgin Gorda call Mahogany Rentals and Taxi Service. If you are staying on North Sound, a taxi will take you from the airport to the dock where your hotel launch will meet you, but be sure to make launch arrangements with your hotel before your arrival. If your destination is Leverick Bay, your land taxi will take you there directly. Note that if your destination is Virgin Gorda you can also fly to Beef Island/Tortola and catch the nearby North Sound Express, which will take you to Spanish Town or North Sound.
➤ AIRPORT INFORMATION: **BVI Taxi Association** (☎ 284/495–1982); **Mahogany Rentals and Taxi Service** (✉ The Valley ☎ 284/495–5469).

BOAT AND FERRY TRAVEL
FARES AND SCHEDULES
Ferries connect St. Thomas, USVI, with Tortola and Virgin Gorda. Inter-Island Boat Services' *Sundance II* connects St. John and West End, Tortola, daily. Native Son, Inc. operates three ferries (*Native Son, Oriole,* and *Voyager Eagle*) and has daily service between St. Thomas and Tortola (West End and Road Town). The *Nubian Princess* operates between Red Hook, St. Thomas; Cruz Bay, St. John; and West End, Tortola, daily. Smiths Ferry Services operates between downtown St. Thomas and Road Town and West End daily. Speedy's Ferries runs between Virgin Gorda, Tortola, and St. Thomas on Tuesday, Thursday, and Saturday, and its *Speedy's Fantasy* runs between Road Town, Tortola, and Spanish Town, Virgin Gorda, daily.

North Sound Express boats run daily between Virgin Gorda's North Sound and Spanish Town and Beef Island/Tortola. The Peter Island Ferry runs daily between Peter Island's private dock on Tortola (just east of Road Town) and Peter Island. Jost Van Dyke Ferry Service makes the Jost Van Dyke–Tortola run several times daily. New Horizon Ferry Service makes the Jost Van Dyke–Tortola trip a number of times each day.
➤ BOAT AND FERRY INFORMATION: **Inter-Island Boat Services** (☎ 284/495–4166); **Jost Van Dyke Ferry Service** (☎ 284/494–2997); **Native Son, Inc.** (☎ 284/495–4617); **New Horizon Ferry Service** (☎ 284/495–9477); **North Sound Express** (☎ 284/495–2271); *Nubian Princess* (☎ 284/495–4999); **Peter Island Ferry** (☎ 284/495–2000); **Smiths Ferry Services** (☎ 284/495–4495); **Speedy's Ferries** (☎ 284/495–5240).

BUSINESS HOURS
BANKS
Banks usually have hours Monday–Thursday 9–2:30 and Friday 9–2:30 and 4:30–6.

POST OFFICES
Post offices are open weekdays 9–5 and Saturday 9–1.

SHOPS
Stores are generally open Monday–Saturday 9–5. You may find some open on Sunday.

CAR RENTALS
You'll need a temporary BVI license, available at the rental car company for $10 with a valid license from another country. Most agencies offer both four-wheel-drive vehicles and cars (often compacts).

On Tortola try Avis, Hertz, or Itgo Car Rental. On Virgin Gorda contact Mahogany Rentals and Taxi Service or L&S Jeep Rental.
➤ MAJOR AGENCIES: **Avis** (✉ Botanic Gardens, Road Town,Tortola, ☎ 284/494–3322); **Hertz** (✉ West End, Tortola, ☎ 284/495–4405); **Itgo Car Rental** (✉ Wickham's Cay I, Road Town, Tortola, ☎ 284/494–2639); **L&S Jeep Rental** (✉ Spanish Town, Virgin Gorda, ☎ 284/495–5297); **Mahogany Rentals and Taxi Service** (✉ Spanish Town, Virgin Gorda, ☎ 284/495–5469).

CAR TRAVEL
Both Tortola and Virgin Gorda have a number of car rental agencies. Although taxi service is good on these two islands, many people who want to explore the islands and try a different beach every day opt for renting a vehicle. On Anegada it is possible to rent a car, but most visitors rely on taxis for transportation. Jost Van Dyke has a single road, and visitors travel by foot or local taxi. On the other islands there are no roads.

GASOLINE

Gas costs about $2.50 a gallon.

ROAD CONDITIONS

Tortola's main roads are, for the most part, well paved, but there are exceptionally steep hills and sharp curves; driving demands your complete attention. A main road encircles the island and several roads cross it, almost always through mountainous terrain. Virgin Gorda has a smaller road system, and a single, very steep road links the north and south ends of the island.

RULES OF THE ROAD

Driving in the BVI is on the left side of the road. Speed limits (rarely enforced) are 20 mph in town and 40 mph outside town.

ELECTRICITY

Electricity is 110 volts, the same as in North America, so European appliances will require adaptors. The electricity is quite reliable.

EMERGENCIES

➤ AMBULANCE AND FIRE: For general emergencies, dial ☎ 999.
➤ HOSPITALS: **Medicure Health Center** (✉ Spanish Town, Virgin Gorda, ☎ 284/495–5479); **Peebles Hospital** (✉ Road Town, Tortola, ☎ 284/494–3497).
➤ PHARMACIES: In Road Town, Tortola: **Cay Pharmacy** (✉ Road Town, Tortola, ☎ 284/494–8128); **J. R. O'Neal Drug Store** (✉ Road Town, Tortola, ☎ 284/494–2292); **Island Drug Centre** (✉ Spanish Town, Virgin Gorda, ☎ 284/495–5449); **Medicure** (✉ Spanish Town, Virgin Gorda, ☎ 284/495–5479).
➤ POLICE: For general emergencies, dial ☎ 999.

ETIQUETTE AND BEHAVIOR

Islanders are religious, and churches fill up on Sunday. You're welcome to attend services, but be sure to dress up. If you encounter any rudeness, you probably didn't begin the conversation properly: only after courteous exchanges ("Hello, how are you today?" and "Not too bad, and how are you?") should you get down to the business of buying groceries, ordering lunch, or hiring a taxi.

FESTIVALS AND SEASONAL EVENTS

In March catch the breathtaking displays of local foliage at the Horticultural Society Show at the botanical gardens; also in March, gather together with locals and yachties at Foxy's Annual St. Patrick's Celebration on Jost Van Dyke. In April, join the fun at the Virgin Gorda Festival, which culminates with a parade on Easter Sunday; also in April, glimpse the colorful spinnakers as sailing enthusiasts gather for the internationally known BVI Spring Regatta. May is the time for partying at Foxy's Wooden Boat Regatta, on Jost Van Dyke. In August try your hand at sportfishing as anglers compete to land the largest catch at the BVI Sportfishing Tournament; August sees two weeks of joyful revelry during Tortola's BVI Emancipation Festival Celebrations. If you've always wanted to escape to the islands and live on a boat, then the November BVI Boat Show is for you. To compete in sailing races and games, drop in on Virgin Gorda's North Sound during the last six weeks of the year for the Bitter End Yacht Club's Competition Series, including the Invitational Regatta. For the best in local *fungi* bands (bands that make music using household items as instruments), stop by the Scratch/Fungi Band Fiesta in December.

HEALTH

The manchineel tree's fruit, which resembles small green apples, is poisonous, and the tree's sap can blister skin badly. These trees are found all over the Caribbean, and trees on resort property or trails are usually marked. No-see-ums (fleas) can be a bother at twilight, especially along the beaches. Use insect repellent if there's no wind to blow them away. Underwater, watch out for those black spiny-looking things you see around rocks. They're called sea urchins and have a powerful sting.

HOLIDAYS

Public holidays for 2002 are: New Year's Day, Commonwealth Day (Mar. 14), Good Friday (Mar. 29), Easter Monday (Apr. 1), Whit Monday (May 22), Sovereign's Birthday (June 16), Territory Day (July 1), BVI August Festival Days (July 26–Aug. 7), St. Ursula's Day (Oct. 21), Christmas, and Boxing Day (Dec. 26).

LANGUAGE

English is the official language, and it's often spoken with a West Indian accent and with a few idiomatic expressions. If someone says he's just limin', it means he's hanging out. If you ask for an item in a store, and the shopkeeper replies, "It's finished," then the shop has temporarily run out.

MAIL AND SHIPPING

There are post offices in Road Town on Tortola and in Spanish Town on Virgin Gorda (note that postal service in the BVI isn't very efficient). Postage for a first-class letter to the United States, Canada, Australia, New Zealand, or the United Kingdom is 55¢; for a postcard, 35¢. For a small fee Rush It, in Road Town and in Spanish Town, offers most U.S. mail and UPS services (via St. Thomas the next day). If you wish to write to an establishment in the BVI, be sure to include the specific island in the address; there are no postal codes.

➤ CONTACTS: **Rush It** (✉ Road Town, Tortola, ☎ 284/494–4421; ✉ Spanish Town, Virgin Gorda, ☎ 284/495–5822).

MONEY MATTERS

BANKS AND ATMS

On Tortola you'll find a Barclays Bank near the waterfront in Road Town. The Chase Manhattan Bank is also near Road Town's waterfront and has an ATM machine. On Virgin Gorda, Barclays Bank isn't far from the ferry dock in Spanish Town.

➤ CONTACTS: **Barclays Bank** (✉ Wickham's Cay I, Road Town, Tortola, ☎ 284/494–2171; ✉ Virgin Gorda Yacht Harbour, Spanish Town, Virgin Gorda, ☎ 284/495–5271). **Chase Manhattan Bank** (✉ Wickham's Cay I, Road Town, Tortola, ☎ 284/494–2662).

CREDIT CARDS

Most hotels and restaurants in the BVI accept MasterCard and Visa, and some also accept American Express, Diner's Club, and Discover. Beware that a few accept only cash or traveler's checks.

CURRENCY

The currency is the U.S. dollar. Any other currency must be exchanged at a bank.

PASSPORTS AND VISAS

U.S. and Canadian citizens need a valid passport, or a birth certificate with a raised seal along with a government-issued photo ID. Visitors from all other countries need a valid passport.

SAFETY

Although crime is almost nonexistent, use common sense: don't leave your camera on the beach while you take a dip or your wallet on a hotel dresser when you go for a walk.

SIGHTSEEING TOURS

Travel Plan Tours can arrange island tours, boat tours, and yacht charters from its Tortola base. Or you can just rent a taxi (minimum of three people) on either Tortola or Virgin Gorda.

➤ CONTACTS: **Travel Plan Tours** (☎ 284/494–2872).

TAXES

DEPARTURE TAX

The departure tax is $5 by boat and $10 by plane. There is a separate booth at the airport to collect this tax.

SALES TAX

There's no sales tax in the BVI. However, there's a 7% government tax on hotel rooms; hotel service charges range from 5% to 15%.

TAXIS

Your hotel staff will be happy to summon a taxi for you. Rates aren't published, so you should negotiate the fare with your driver before you start your trip. It's cheaper to travel in groups because there's a minimum fare to each destination, which is the same whether you are one, two, or three people. The taxi number is also the license plate number. On Tortola, there are BVI Taxi Association stands in Road Town near the ferry dock, at Wickham's Cay I, and at the Beef Island/Tortola airport. You can also usually find a taxi at the ferry dock at Soper's Hole, West End, where ferries arrive from St. Thomas.

Andy's Taxi and Jeep Rental offers service from one end of Virgin Gorda to the other. Mahogany Rentals and Taxi Service provides taxi service all over Virgin Gorda.

➤ CONTACTS: **Andy's Taxi and Jeep Rental** (✉ The Valley, Tortola, ☎ 284/495–5511); **BVI Taxi Association** (✉ Near the ferry dock, Road Town, Tortola, ☎ 284/494–7519; ✉ Wickham's Cay I, Road Town, Tortola, ☎ 284/494–2322; ✉ Beef Island Airport, Tortola, ☎ 284/495–1982); **Mahogany Rentals and Taxi Service** (✉ The Valley, Virgin Gorda, ☎ 284/495–5469).

TELEPHONES

COUNTRY AND AREA CODES

The area code for the BVI is 284; when you make calls from North America, you need only dial the area code and the number. From the United Kingdom you must dial 001 and then the area code and the number. From Australia and New Zealand you must dial 0011 followed by 1, the area code, and the number.

INTERNATIONAL CALLS

For credit card or collect long-distance calls to the United States, use a phone-card telephone or look for special USADirect phones, which are linked directly to an AT&T operator. For access dial 800/872–2881, or dial 111 from a pay phone and charge the call to your MasterCard or Visa. USADirect and pay phones can be found at most hotels and in towns.

LOCAL CALLS

To call anywhere in the BVI once you've arrived, dial all seven digits. A local call from a pay phone costs 25¢, but such phones are sometimes on the blink. An alternative is a Caribbean phone card, available in $5, $10, and $20 denominations. It's sold at most major hotels and many stores and can be used to call within the BVI as well as all over the Caribbean and to access USADirect from special phone-card phones.

TIPPING

Tip porters and bellhops $1 per bag. Sometimes a service charge (10%) is included on restaurant bills; it's customary to leave another 5% if you liked the service. If no charge is added, 15% is the norm. Cabbies normally aren't tipped because most own their cabs; add 10%–15% if they exceed their duties.

TRANSPORTATION AROUND
THE BRITISH VIRGIN ISLANDS

There's limited bus service on Tortola. For information about schedules, call Wheatley's Bus Service. The bus runs in a loop from East End on Beef Island to Road Town along Blackburn Highway and then back to East End via Ridge Road. The fare is $1.

Speedy's Ferries runs between Road Town, Tortola, and Spanish Town, Virgin Gorda, daily. North Sound Express boats run daily between Virgin Gorda's North Sound and Spanish Town and Beef Island/Tortola. The Peter Island Ferry runs daily between Peter Island's private dock on Tortola (just east of Road Town) and Peter Island. Jost Van Dyke Ferry Service makes the Jost Van Dyke–Tortola run several times daily. New Horizon Ferry Service makes the Jost Van Dyke–Tortola trip a number of times each day.

Clair Aero Services flies between Tortola and Anegada on Monday, Wednesday, Friday, and Sunday.
➤ CONTACTS: **Clair Aero Services** (☎ 284/495–2271); **Jost Van Dyke Ferry Service** (☎ 284/494–2997); **New Horizon Ferry Service** (☎ 284/495–9477); **North Sound Express** (☎ 284/495–2271); **Peter Island Ferry** (☎ 284/495–2000); **Speedy's Ferries** (☎ 284/495–5240); **Wheatley's Bus Service** (☎ 284/495–2421).

VISITOR INFORMATION

➤ BEFORE YOU LEAVE: **BVI Tourist Board (U.S.)** (✉ 370 Lexington Ave., Suite 1605, New York, NY 10017, ☎ 212/696–0400 or 800/835–8530; ✉ 3450 Wilshire Blvd., Suite 1202 Los Angeles, CA 90010, ☎ 213/736–8931; ✉ 3390 Peachtree Rd. NE, Suite 1000, Atlanta, GA 30326, ☎ 404/240–8018); **BVI Tourist Board (U.K.)** (✉ 55 Newman St., London W1P 3PG, U.K., ☎ 011–44–207–947–8200).
➤ IN THE BRITISH VIRGIN ISLANDS: **BVI Tourist Board** (✉ Box 134, Road Town, Tortola, ☎ 284/494–3134); **Virgin Gorda BVI Tourist Board** (✉ Virgin Gorda Yacht Harbor, Spanish Town, Virgin Gorda, ☎ 284/495–5181).

7 CAYMAN ISLANDS

Updated by
JoAnn
Milivojevic

The signpost just past the airport/post office/fire station reads, "Iguanas have the right of way." Many of these prehistoric-looking lizards lurk about Little Cayman, the smallest of the Cayman Islands' trio. According to Gladys of Pirates Point, iguanas love grapes. She keeps extras on hand just so her guests can feed them to the iguanas. That kind of hospitality is the norm on an island where the repeat guest list is high and the island's recently appointed police officer has yet to use his siren. Each of the three Cayman Islands has its own rhythm from Grand Cayman to the Brac to the Little Cayman, it's slow, slower, slowest.

This British colony, which consists of Grand Cayman, smaller Cayman Brac, and Little Cayman, is one of the Caribbean's most popular destinations. Columbus is said to have sighted the islands in 1503, but he didn't stop off to explore. He did note that the surrounding sea was alive with turtles, so the islands were named Las Tortugas. The name was later changed to Cayman, referring to the caiman crocodiles that once roamed the islands. The Cayman Islands remained largely uninhabited until the late 1600s, when England took them and Jamaica from Spain under the Treaty of Madrid. Emigrants from England, Holland, Spain, and France then arrived, as did refugees from the Spanish Inquisition and deserters from Oliver Cromwell's army in Jamaica. The Caymans' caves and coves were also perfect hideouts for the likes of Blackbeard, Sir Henry Morgan, and other pirates out to plunder Spanish galleons. Many ships fell afoul of the reefs surrounding the islands, often with the help of Caymanians who lured vessels to shore with beacon fires.

The legend of one wreck in particular—the Wreck of the Ten Sails—has remained popular with Caymanians through the years. In 1794 a convoy of 10 Jamaican ships bound for England foundered on the reefs. The islanders saved everyone, including, it was said, a few members of royalty. The tale has it that a grateful King George III decreed that Caymanians would forever be exempt from conscription and would never have to pay taxes. However, though Caymanians don't pay taxes, this tale has been proven pure fiction.

As for current politics, this British colony has a governor, who appoints three official members to the Legislative Assembly. He must also accept the advice of the Executive Council in all matters except foreign affairs, defense, internal security, and civil-service appointments. Though the governor is appointed from England, locally elected Caymanians greatly influence how their islands are run.

Today's Caymans may be seasoned with suburban prosperity, particularly Grand Cayman (residents joke that the national flower is the satellite dish), and stuffed with crowds (the hotels that line the famed Seven Mile Beach are often full, even in the slow summer season), but the 31,000 Cayman Islanders—most of whom live on Grand Cayman—add considerable flavor with their renowned courtesy and civility. The cost of living may be about 20% higher here than in the United States (one U.S. dollar is worth only about 80 Cayman cents), but you won't be hassled by panhandlers or feel afraid to walk around on a dark evening (the crime rate is very low). Add political and economic stability to the mix, and you have a fine island recipe indeed.

GRAND CAYMAN

Grand Cayman is world-renowned for two offshore activities: banking and scuba diving. The former pays dividends in the manicured capital of George Town, which bulges with some 554 banks. The latter offers its rewards in translucent waters that are full of colorful and varied life—much of it protected by a marine parks system. Although about a third of Grand Cayman's visitors come for the diving, a growing number are young honeymooners. The island offers many additional pleasures, from shopping for jewelry to fine dining to simply strolling hand-in-hand on a powder-soft beach.

Lodging

In the off-season (summer) it's easy to find lodgings, even on short notice, but for peak-season and holiday visits book well in advance. Note that most hotels require a 7- or 14-day minimum stay at Christmas time, though condominiums will let you book on a day-to-day basis for stays of any length.

Brace yourself for resort prices—there are few accommodations in the economy range. Most of the larger hotels along Seven Mile Beach don't offer meal plans. Smaller properties that are farther from restaurants usually offer MAP or FAP (to estimate rates for hotels offering MAP or FAP, add about $40 per person, per day to the average price ranges below).

CATEGORY	COST*
$$$$	over $275
$$$	$225–$275
$$	$150–$225
$	under $150

All prices are for a standard double room in winter, excluding 10% government room tax and 10% service charge.

Hotels

$$$$ ★ **Hyatt Regency Grand Cayman.** Elegant ocean-view suites, an archway over the road, and a concourse of shops have been recently added to this posh property. The one-bedroom ocean-view suites can sleep up to four and are painted in soft lime green with teak furnishings, mar-

Grand Cayman

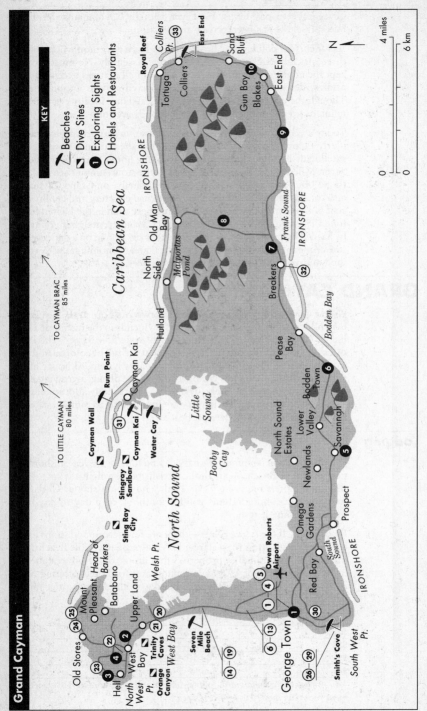

KEY

⌇ Beaches

◣ Dive Sites

① Exploring Sights

① Hotels and Restaurants

Caribbean Sea

TO CAYMAN BRAC
85 miles

TO LITTLE CAYMAN
80 miles

N

4 miles

6 km

Royal Reef

Colliers

East End **㉝**

Sand Bluff

Tortuga

Colliers

Gun Bay **⑩**

Blakes

East End

IRONSHORE

⑨

Frank Sound

IRONSHORE

Old Man Bay

North Side

⑧

Malportas Pond

⑦

Breakers

Hutland

㉜

Bodden Bay

Rum Point

Cayman Wall

Cayman Kai **㉛**

Cayman Kai

Water Cay

Stingray Sandbar

Sting Ray City

North Sound

Little Sound

Booby Cay

Pease Bay

⑥

Bodden Town

Savannah

Lower Valley

North Sound Estates

Newlands

⑤

Head of Barkers

Mount Pleasant

Batabano

Upper Land

Welsh Pt.

Omega Gardens

Prospect

South Sound

IRONSHORE

Old Stores **㉕**

㉔

㉒ **②**

North West
West Bay
Pt.

Hell **③**
④
㉓

Trinity Caves

Orange Canyon

West Bay

⑳

㉑

Seven Mile Beach

⑭ **⑲**

⑥ **⑬**

① **④**

⑤

Owen Roberts Airport

✈

Red Bay

①

㉚

㉖ ㉙

Smith's Cove

South West Pt.

George Town

Cayman Brac and Little Cayman

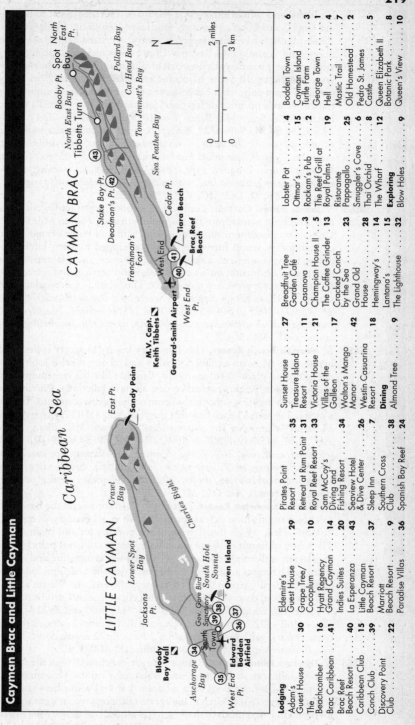

Lodging
Adam's Guest House ... 30
The Beachcomber ... 16
Brac Caribbean Beach Resort ... 41
Brac Reef Beach Resort ... 40
Caribbean Club ... 15
Conch Club ... 39
Discovery Point Club ... 22
Eldemire's Guest House ... 29
Grape Tree/Cocoplum ... 10
Hyatt Regency Grand Cayman ... 14
Indies Suites ... 20
La Esperanza ... 43
Little Cayman Beach Resort ... 37
Marriott Beach Resort ... 9
Paradise Villas ... 36
Pirates Point Resort ... 35
Retreat at Rum Point ... 31
Royal Reef Resort ... 33
Sam McCoy's Diving and Fishing Resort ... 34
Seaview Hotel & Dive Center ... 26
Sleep Inn ... 7
Southern Cross Club ... 38
Spanish Bay Reef ... 36
Sunset House ... 27
Treasure Island Resort ... 11
Victoria House ... 21
Villas of the Galleon ... 17
Walton's Mango Manor ... 42
Westin Casuarina Resort ... 18

Dining
Almond Tree ... 9
Breadfruit Tree Garden Café ... 27
Casanova ... 11
Champion House II ... 21
The Coffee Grinder ... 17
Cracked Conch by the Sea ... 42
Grand Old House ... 7
Hemingway's ... 26
Lantana's ... 37
Lobster Pot ... 4
Ottmar's ... 15
Rackam's Pub ... 2
The Reef Grill at Royal Palms ... 19
Ristorante Pappagallo ... 25
Smuggler's Cove ... 6
Thai Orchid ... 8
The Wharf ... 12

Exploring
Blow Holes ... 9
Bodden Town ... 6
Cayman Island Turtle Farm ... 3
George Town ... 1
Hell ... 4
Mastic Trail ... 7
Old Homestead ... 2
Pedro St. James Castle ... 5
Queen Elizabeth II Botanic Park ... 8
Queen's View ... 10

ble baths, and formal entryways. The main resort, adjacent to Britannia Golf Course, has gorgeously landscaped grounds. Moderate-size standard rooms have marble entranceways, oversized bathtubs, French doors, and verandas; 44 Regency Club rooms include concierge services and complimentary Continental breakfast, early evening hors d'oeuvres, and cocktails. Some balconies are small "step outs," meaning standing room only, while others have a table and chairs—inquire carefully as there's no price difference. Hemingway's is the hotel's stellar restaurant. ⊠ *Seven Mile Beach (Box 1698)*, ☎ *345/949–1234 or 800/233–1234*, ℻ *345/949–8528*, WEB *grandcayman.hyatt.com/cayman. 112 rooms, 63 suites, 70 villas. 3 restaurants, 4 bars, air-conditioning, minibars, 7 pools, hair salon, hot tub, massage, spa, 9-hole golf course, 4 tennis courts, croquet, gym, beach, dive shop, snorkeling, windsurfing, boating, parasailing, waterskiing, shops, children's programs, car rental. AE, D, DC, MC, V. CP, EP, MAP.*

$$$$ ★ 🏨 **Indies Suites.** Cayman's only all-suite hotel is attractive, comfortable, and right across from the quieter north end of Seven Mile Beach. One- or two-bedroom suites, done in cream and burnt orange, have contemporary wood furniture, a fully equipped modern kitchen, a dining-living room (with a sleeper sofa), a terrace, and a storeroom for dive gear. Continental buffet breakfast, maid service, and a free sunset cruise once a week are nice extras. The lobby is spectacular, with vintage 1930s Fords on display. ⊠ *Seven Mile Beach (Box 2070 GT)*, ☎ *345/945–5025 or 800/654–3130*, ℻ *345/945–5024. 38 suites. Bar, snack bar, air-conditioning, pool, hot tub, dive shop, snorkeling, coin laundry. AE, MC, V. CP.*

$$$$ 🏨 **Marriott Beach Resort.** This five-story luxury property is designed in colonial style with arched doorways and an airy marble lobby that opens onto a plant-filled courtyard. Families like the large adjoining rooms done in bright tropical colors; all have balconies. Price varies according to the view, which is the ocean or the garden courtyard. There's a snorkeling reef, a beach bar near the pool, and a full-service spa. The Marriott is popular for conventions. ⊠ *Seven Mile Beach (Box 30371)*, ☎ *345/949–0088 or 800/228–9290*, ℻ *345/949–0288*, WEB *www.marriott.com. 309 rooms, 4 suites. Restaurant, bar, snack bar, air-conditioning, pool, hair salon, hot tub, spa, beach, dive shop, snorkeling, windsurfing, shops, dry cleaning, laundry service, meeting rooms, car rental. AE, DC, MC, V. EP.*

$$$$ 🏨 **Westin Casuarina Resort.** Part of the Casuarina is on the beach, so its choice rooms have at least partial ocean views (standards have an "island" view, which translates into the parking lot and main drag). The lobby spills out onto the waterfront, where tall royal palms shade the elegant walkway. Rooms have bleached-wood furniture and stucco ceilings. The suites aren't much different from one-bedroom lodgings, so they're hardly worth the extra money. Havana, the Westin's high-end restaurant, deserves praise for its excellent Cuban/Caribbean fare. ⊠ *Seven Mile Beach (Box 30620)*, ☎ *345/945–3800 or 800/228–3000*, ℻ *345/949–5825*, WEB *www.westin.com. 339 rooms, 2 suites. 2 restaurants, 3 bars, grill, pool, hair salon, 2 hot tubs, 2 tennis courts, gym, beach, dive shop, shops, meeting rooms. AE, MC, V. EP.*

$$$ 🏨 **Treasure Island Resort.** Rooms here are functional, with tile floors, stucco walls, rattan furniture, and watercolor prints. This sprawling complex has a huge pool with adjacent bar and also offers guests a section of Seven Mile Beach to lounge on (although recent weather hasn't been kind, and much of the beach has eroded). ⊠ *Seven Mile Beach (Box 1817)*, ☎ *345/949–7777 or 800/203–0775*, ℻ *345/949–8672. 278 rooms. Restaurant, bar, air-conditioning, 2 tennis courts, 2 pools, beach, snorkeling, windsurfing. AE, DC, MC, V. EP.*

$$ ☷ **Spanish Bay Reef.** Flowering trees and bushes surround pale pink two-story stucco units at this resort on a small, sandy beach at the northwest tip of the island near 27 spectacular north wall scuba diving sites. Boardwalks connect simple, comfortable guest rooms, which have bright Caribbean-print spreads and curtains. The outdoor bar-dining area surrounds the pool and has views of the ocean; the indoor bar-dining area is spacious and made of coral stone. Spanish Bay Reef is a deep drop-off, which means superior diving and snorkeling. Rates include round-trip transfers, taxes and gratuities, shore diving, boat dives, and use of bicycles (not in mint condition). ✉ *167 Conch Point Rd. (Box 903),* ☏ *345/949–3765,* ℻ *345/949–1842. 67 rooms. Restaurant, bar, pool, hot tub, beach, dive shop, snorkeling. AE, MC, V. All-inclusive.*

$$ ☷ **Sunset House.** Low-key and laid-back describe this resort with
★ motel-style rooms on the ironshore. A congenial staff, a happening bar, and a seafood restaurant are pluses, but the diving (and the dive packages) attract most guests. Full dive services include free waterside lockers, two- and three-tank dives at the better reefs around the island, Cathy Church's U/W Photo Centre, and a made-to-order full hot breakfast. The latest dive attraction is a newly sunk 9-ft bronze mermaid sculpture dubbed Aphrodite. It's a five-minute walk to a sandy beach. ✉ *S. Church St. (Box 479),* ☏ *345/949–7111 or 800/854–4767,* ℻ *345/949–7101. 58 rooms, 2 suites. Restaurant, bar, air-conditioning, pool, hot tub, dive shop. AE, MC, V. CP, EP, MAP.*

$ ☷ **Seaview Hotel & Dive Center.** South of George Town, this perfectly pleasant and affordable hotel is for people on a tight budget. The staff is friendly, and the amenities are quite adequate. It's a perfect place to go if you're interested in a hotel from which to base yourself for a diving vacation. It's on the water, so the best rooms have ocean views; most are decorated with tropical-patterned bedspreads and pale blue walls. ✉ *S. Church St. (Box. 260),* ☏ *345/945–0558 or 945–0577,* ℻ *345/945–0559. 18 rooms. Restaurant, bar, air-conditioning, pool, snorkeling. AE, MC, V.*

$ ☷ **Sleep Inn.** This two-story hotel is a quick stroll from Seven Mile Beach, close to the airport, and a mile from George Town's shops. Rooms are motel-modern, with maroon, mauve, and beige color schemes and contemporary wood furnishings. All rooms have mini refrigerators and microwaves, a nice extra. The Dive Inn dive shop is here, as are tour agencies, and car and motorcycle rental offices. ✉ *Seven Mile Beach (Box 30111),* ☏ *345/949–9111 or 800/753–3746,* ℻ *345/949–6699. 115 rooms. Bar, grill, air-conditioning, pool, hot tub, dive shop, shops, laundry service, meeting rooms, travel services, car rental. AE, D, DC, MC, V. EP.*

Guest Houses

They may be some distance from the beach and short on style and facilities, but these lodgings offer rock-bottom prices (all fall well below the $ category), a friendly atmosphere, and your best shot at getting to know the locals. Rooms are clean and simple, often with cooking facilities, and most have private bathrooms. These establishments do not accept personal checks or credit cards but do take reservations.

$ **Adam's Guest House** (✉ Melnac Ave. near Seaview Hotel [Box 312], ☏ 345/949–2512, ☏ ℻ 345/949–0919), 1 mi (1½ km) south of George Town and 4 mi (6½ km) from the beach, has five rooms, all with kitchenettes.

$ **Eldemire's Guest House** (✉ S. Church St. [Box 482], ☏ 345/949–5387, ℻ 345/949–6987), Grand Cayman's first guest house, has 12 units starting at $85. It's a 15-minute drive to Seven Mile Beach, but less than a mile (1½ km) south of pretty Smith Cove Bay.

Villas and Condominiums

The **Cayman Islands Department of Tourism** (www.caymanislands.ky) provides a list of condominiums and small rental apartments. Rates are higher in winter, and there may be a three- or seven-night minimum. These complexes are all similar, with fully equipped kitchens, telephones, satellite TV, air-conditioning, living and dining areas, and patios. Differences arise in property amenities and proximity to town.

$$$$ 🏨 **The Beachcomber.** Each of the simply furnished two-bedroom apartments in this older condo community has a view of the ocean from a private screened patio. When the sun gets too warm, you can retreat to the shade of the palabas on Seven Mile Beach or go snorkeling in the reef offshore. A grocery store is across the street, and there are countless shopping and dining opportunities within walking distance, so you don't really need a car. ⊠ *Seven Mile Beach (Box 1799),* ☎ *345/945–4470,* ℻ *345/945–5019. 23 units. Grill, air-conditioning, pool, beach, coin laundry. AE, MC, V. EP.*

$$$$ 🏨 **Caribbean Club.** Eighteen one- and two-bedroom villas (six on the beach) make up this quiet condominium getaway. Although these units are not necessarily deluxe, they are secluded and have tidy tiled baths and simple wicker furniture. There's also maid service—always a plus. In the same complex, Lantana's restaurant serves Caribbean and American fare. ⊠ *Seven Mile Beach (Box 30499),* ☎ *345/945–4099,* ℻ *345/ 945–4443,* 🌐 *www.caribclub.com. 18 villas. Restaurant, bar, air-conditioning, tennis court, beach, coin laundry, dry cleaning, laundry service. AE, MC, V. EP, MAP.*

$$$$ 🏨 **Discovery Point Club.** This secluded complex—all ocean-front suites—is at the far north end of Seven Mile Beach in West Bay, 6 mi (9½ km) from George Town. It has a lovely beach and great snorkeling in the protected waters of nearby Cemetery Reef. Tennis courts, a hot tub, a pool, and screened-in private porches add to the appeal here. Kids 6 and under stay free April–December. ⊠ *West Bay (Box 439),* ☎ *345/945–4724,* ℻ *345/945–5051. 45 units. Grill, pool, hot tub, 2 tennis courts, beach, coin laundry. AE, MC, V. EP.*

$$$$ 🏨 **Villas of the Galleon.** The exteriors of these deluxe stucco cottages look shabby, but the interiors are attractive and beautifully maintained, and their location—on the widest section of Seven Mile Beach, just across from the Jack Nicklaus–designed Links Golf Club—couldn't be better. Each one- or two-bedroom unit has a full kitchen, a terrace, and enormous closets (a big plus for families); decor varies, though such tasteful touches as eggshell-tile floors, pastel finishes, and rattan furnishings are common. ⊠ *Seven Mile Beach (Box 1797),* ☎ *345/945–4433,* ℻ *345/945–4705,* 🌐 *www.villasofthegalleon.com. 74 units. Grill, air-conditioning, beach, coin laundry. AE, D, MC, V. EP.*

$$$ 🏨 **Grape Tree/Cocoplum.** A half mile (¾ km) from George Town on Seven Mile Beach, these sister condos are adjacent to one another. Grapetree's units are carpeted and have traditional wicker furnishings and a beige-and-brown decor. Cocoplum's units are similar, though they're decorated with Caribbean pastel prints, and their grounds have more plants and trees. ⊠ *Seven Mile Beach (Box 1802),* ☎ *345/949–5640,* ℻ *345/949–0150,* 🌐 *www.grapetree.ky. 51 units. Air-conditioning, 2 pools, tennis court, beach. AE, MC, V. EP.*

$$$ 🏨 **Retreat at Rum Point.** The Retreat has its own narrow beach with casuarina trees, far from the crowd. Up to six people can rent a two-bedroom villa here, and two or three people will be comfortable in a one-bedroom unit. The decor in these privately owned condos varies—for the most part you'll find tropical motifs and wicker furniture. All units are spacious and have a washer and dryer. Take advantage of superb offshore diving (there are dive facilities nearby), including the famed

North Wall. You'll be stranded without a car; it's a 35-minute drive to town or the airport. ⊠ *North Side (Box 46),* ☎ *345/947–9135,* FAX *345/947–9058,* WEB *www.retreatcondos.com. 23 units. Restaurant, bar, air-conditioning, pool, sauna, tennis court, gym, racquetball, beach. AE, MC, V. EP.*

$$$ 🏠 **Victoria House.** The one-, two-, and three-bedroom units in this simple building have white walls and tile floors and are decorated with muted Caribbean prints and rattan furniture. You may choose from a range of activities including tennis and water sports. The Victoria is 3 mi (5 km) north of town on a quiet stretch of Seven Mile Beach; if you're an early riser, you may catch a glimpse of giant sea turtles on the sand. ⊠ *Seven Mile Beach, near West Bay (Box 30571),* ☎ *345/945–4233,* FAX *345/945–5328,* WEB *www.victoriahouse.com. 25 units. Air-conditioning, tennis, beach, snorkeling, coin laundry. AE, MC, V. EP.*

$$ 🏠 **The Royal Reef.** This small, well-run timeshare property on the less hectic east end of Grand Cayman presents superior value for the price. It's a 45-minute drive back to George Town from here, so a car is a must. But if you want a get-away-from-it-all trip, then that's not so much of a problem. Each of the tile-floored villas has a roomy terrace facing the sea and can be divided into a large one-bedroom and studio for weekly rental throughout the year; the entire unit can sleep up to six. All units have satellite TV; the larger ones have separate dining areas and stereos. Having a full kitchen in the larger unit or a kitchenette in the smaller will help offset the cost of expensive meals. ⊠ *Queen's Hwy., East End (Box 20865 SMB),* ☎ *345/345–3100 (direct to hotel), 800/221–8090 or 954/485–5412 (reservations),* FAX *345/947–3191,* WEB *www.royalresorts.com. 32 villas. Restaurant, bar, grocery, air-conditioning, fans, kitchenettes, refrigerators, pool, hair salon, outdoor hot tub, massage, spa, tennis court, gym, beach, dive shop, dock, snorkeling, boating, bicycles, coin laundry, concierge. AE, MC, V. EP.*

Dining

Grand Cayman's restaurants satisfy every palate and pocketbook. Big spenders will find gourmet cuisine, and those on a budget will appreciate the abundance of moderately priced ethnic eateries. Local hangouts that serve West Indian fare offer the most in both flavor and value.

Fish—including grouper, snapper, tuna, wahoo, and marlin—is served either simply baked, broiled, steamed, or Cayman style (with peppers, onions, and tomatoes). Conch, the meat of a large pink mollusk, is ubiquitous in stews and chowders and as fritters or panfried (cracked). Caribbean lobster is available but is often quite expensive, and other shellfish are in short supply in local waters. The only traditional culinary treat of the islands is turtle—served in soup or stew or as a steak—though fewer restaurants offer it these days.

Dining out here can be expensive, so replenish your cash reserves because some places do not accept plastic. Many restaurants add a 10%–15% service charge to the bill, so check before leaving a tip.

What to Wear

Smart casual wear (slacks and sundresses) is acceptable for dinner in all but a few places. The nicer resorts and more expensive restaurants may require a jacket, especially in high season; ask when making reservations. Shorts are usually acceptable during the day, but unless you're going to an ultracasual beach bar, beachwear (bathing suits, cover-ups, tank tops, etc.) is a no-no. Most restaurants have an alfresco dining section, and if you plan to dine under the stars, you may need a spritz of bug spray (mosquitoes can be pesky, especially at sunset), which most places provide.

CATEGORY	COST*
$$$$	over $30
$$$	$20–$30
$$	$10–$20
$	under $10

per person for a main course at dinner

ASIAN

$$ ✕ **Thai Orchid.** It looks like a typical Thai restaurant, but the food more than makes up for the ordinary decor. Try the delicious *pad thai,* the *ped phad khing* (crispy duck stir-fried with ginger and vegetables), or the Thai spring rolls with marinated pork. Many vegetarian dishes are offered as well. The main difference between the lunch and dinner menus is the price. ⊠ *Queens Court Shopping Plaza,* ☎ *345/949–7955. AE, MC, V. No lunch Sun.*

CAFÉS

$ ✕ **The Coffee Grinder.** For breakfast or lunch that's tasty and light on your wallet, this bakery and deli won't disappoint. Everything is baked fresh daily from scratch. On the menu are wraps with ingredients like black beans, seasoned rice, and cheese; sandwich choices include Italian subs, Reubens, and roast turkey Waldorf on a sourdough walnut roll. For breakfast it's bagels with toppings like eggs, meats, and cheeses. There are plenty of rolls, sweet pastries, and excellent coffees. You can dine at small tables indoors or out on the sidewalk. ⊠ *Seven Mile Shops,* ☎ *345/949–6294. AE, MC, V. No dinner.*

CARIBBEAN

$$$ ✕ **Almond Tree.** The large patio dining area combines architecture from the South Seas isle of Yap with bones, skulls, and bric-a-brac from Africa, South America, and the Pacific. Good-value seafood entrées include turtle steak and fresh snapper breaded with crushed almonds. For an after-dinner drink or a late dinner menu (served until 1 AM most nights) try their neighboring beach-side bar and grill, the Tree House Beach Bar. ⊠ *N. Church St.,* ☎ *345/949–2893 Almond Tree; 345/945–0155 Tree House. AE, D, MC, V.*

$$$ ✕ **Hemingway's.** Sea views and breezes attract diners to this elegant
★ open-air restaurant in the Hyatt Regency Grand Cayman complex on Seven Mile Beach. Nouvelle Caribbean and seafood dishes include lemongrass-crusted grouper with *udon,* noodles and baby Portobello mushrooms in a coconut sauce, Boniato-wrapped prawns with grilled chayote slaw and red grapefruit reduction, and sugarcane-skewered tempura lobster with basil mashed potatoes and *ponzu* butter. Portions are large, and service is superb. For a tropical drink try the Banana Mud Slide (with dark rum, Bailey's, Kahlua, vodka, banana oasis, and chocolate sauce). ⊠ *West Bay Rd.,* ☎ *345/945–5700. AE, D, DC, MC, V.*

$$ ✕ **Breadfruit Tree Garden Cafe.** This spot is favored by locals—as much for the delicious food as for the reasonable prices. The jerk chicken rivals any on the island. Also on the menu are curry chicken and stewed pork, oxtail, rice and beans, and homemade soups. Drinks include breadfruit, mango, passion fruit, and carrot juices. The interior is kitschy, with silk roses, white porch swings, straw hats, empty birdcages, and fake ivy crawling along the ceiling. It's open until the wee hours, which makes it a good midnight munchie stop. ⊠ *58 Eastern Ave.,* ☎ *345/945–2124. No credit cards.*

$ ✕ **Champion House II.** Tucked back behind the original Champion House restaurant is this more comfortable, spacious restaurant surrounded by lush outdoor plants. Tasty traditional island dishes include marinated conch, curried goat, turtle stew, ackee, and cod fish—all served with rice and beans, plantains, and veggies. Try one of the fruit juices like tamarind, Irish moss, or soursop, or a spicy, homemade ginger beer. The entrées are large, and half portions are available. The breakfast and lunch buffets are quite popular and reasonably priced. ⊠ *43 Eastern Ave.,* ☎ *345/949–7882. AE, MC, V.*

CONTEMPORARY

$$$$ ✕ **Lantana's.** This restaurant—on the edge of the Caribbean Club villa complex in the heart of Seven Mile Beach—creates excellent American-Caribbean dinners. Enjoy lobster quesadillas, homemade lamb sausage, or Cayman mahimahi with cardamom-scented tabbouleh and cassava fritters. If you come for nothing else, *don't* miss the incredible roasted garlic soup and the apple pie. The decor of the bi-level restaurant—potted plants, teak furniture, painted wooden fish—places you in the perfectly serene island state of mind. ⊠ *West Bay Rd.,* ☎ *345/ 945–5595. AE, D, MC, V.*

CONTINENTAL

$$$$ ✕ **Grand Old House.** The menu here consists of Continental entrées and a few local specialties. Among the spicier appetizers is fried coconut shrimp with mustard apricot sauce. On the milder side are lobster served "the chef's way" (dipped in egg batter and sautéed with shallots, mushrooms, and white wine) and duck with fresh pear chutney. The ocean-side gazebos, surrounded by palms and cooled by ceiling fans, are refreshing and lively; stellar service makes a meal here all the more enjoyable. ⊠ *S. Church St.,* ☎ *345/949–9333. Reservations essential. DC, MC, V. Closed Sun. May–Nov. No lunch weekends.*

$$$$ ✕ **Ottmar's.** This quietly elegant restaurant in the Grand Pavillion ★ Commercial Centre is styled after a West Indian great house. Jade carpeting, peach walls, mahogany furniture, glass chandeliers, and a trickling fountain create an attractive setting for the excellent service. Favorites on the international menu include bouillabaisse, the Indonesian rijsttafel, and French pepper steak (flamed in cognac and doused with green peppercorn sauce and crème fraîche). ⊠ *West Bay Rd.,* ☎ *345/945–5879 or 345/945–5882. Reservations essential. AE, MC, V.*

ECLECTIC

$$ ✕ **Rackam's Pub.** North of George Town, jutting out onto a jetty, this low-key bar and grill has terrific views on its outdoor deck. The surf-and-turf fare is delicious—and surprisingly affordable. The young, friendly staff serves good jerk burgers (basted with Jamaican jerk sauce), grouper fish-and-chips, and tasty chiles *rellenos.* ⊠ *N. Church St.,* ☎ *345/945–3860. AE, MC, V.*

ITALIAN

$$$ ✕ **Lighthouse at Breakers.** About a 25-minute drive from Seven Mile Beach, this south shore restaurant offers seaside dining with good food, a well-chosen wine list (with an especially good selection of wines by the glass), and stellar desserts. The rustic, shipboard setting draws a steady stream of locals and visitors. Start with the salad of green asparagus points and baby field greens or flash-fried calamari; pastas are all a good bet as are yellowfin tuna with a brandy peppercorn sauce or the char-grilled veal chop. Save room for dessert, especially the hot chocolate soufflé or some of the homemade ice creams. ⊠ *Breakers,* ☎ *345/947–2047,* ⓦⓔⓑ *www.lighthouse.ky. Reservations essential for dinner. AE, MC, V.*

$$$ ✕ **Ristorante Papagallo.** If you're not taking a cab, be sure to pack a map for the journey down twisted, unmarked roads to this oversize Polynesian hut at the northernmost tip of the island. Try the arugula salad with mango vinaigrette, followed by the blackened yellowtail or the snapper fillet with pineapple salsa. Caymanians and tourists alike say it's worth the trip for the island's best Italian-Caribbean fusion cuisine. ⊠ *Conch Point Rd. (Box 184),* ☎ *345/949–1119,* ☏ *345/949–1114. Reservations essential. AE, MC, V. No lunch.*

SEAFOOD

$$$$ ✕ **The Reef Grill at Royal Palms.** The impeccable service by the knowledge wait staff is only surpassed by the divine food served in an elegant dining room or on the more casual garden patio accented with baby royal palm trees. Try the signature honey-soy glazed sea bass in a mild Thai curry sauce; it's tender, succulent, and served with coconut rice and a spicy sauteed red cabbage. Other creative dishes include pepper-crusted yellowfin tuna and plank-roasted BBQ salmon. Among the desserts are fresh sorbets, crème brûlée and chocolate almond mousse. The adjoining beach bar is a popular night spot with live bands most evenings. ⊠ *Seven Mile Beach,* ☎ *345/945–6358. Reservations essential. AE, D, MC, V. No lunch.*

$$$$ ✕ **The Wharf.** Owned and operated by a group of Austrians, this large, tidy blue-and-white restaurant spills out onto a multitiered veranda that overlooks the sea. On the surf-and-turf menu are conch fritters, home-smoked salmon, turtle steak, broiled lobster, and steak fillet béarnaise; anything on the fresh daily menu is also recommended. A harpist entertains after a lively happy hour band. The Ports of Call bar is a perfect spot from which to watch the sun set, and tarpon feeding off the deck is a nightly (9 PM) spectacle here. ⊠ *West Bay Rd.,* ☎ *345/949–2231. AE, MC, V.*

$$$ ✕ **Cracked Conch by the Sea.** This island favorite provides patio din-
   ★   ers with panoramic sea views. Specialties include cracked (tenderized and panfried) conch, conch fritters, conch chowder, spicy Cayman-style snapper, and turtle steak. The Sunday buffet is a divine array of island-style curries and jerk meats; don't miss the cassava cake, a thick, sweet, spongy dessert. ⊠ *West Bay Rd. (next to the Turtle Bay Farm),* ☎ *345/945–5217. MC, V.*

$$$ ✕ **Smuggler's Cove.** One of the best on the island and certainly the most
   ★   romantic, this small restaurant is right on the water near downtown George Town. The comfortable, candlelit dining room and lovely deck overlooking the ocean are perfect spots to bring someone for a special dinner. Excellent appetizers include tuna carpaccio marinated in basil and dill, and jerk duck seasoned with pimiento and scotch bonnet peppers. The best entrées are those with Caribbean lobster—particularly the Smuggler's Fillet, a lobster-stuffed beef tenderloin seared in rosemary butter and glazed with port. ⊠ *George Town,* ☎ *345/949–6003. Reservations essential. AE, D, MC, V. No lunch weekends.*

$$ ✕ **Lobster Pot.** The second-floor terrace of this cozy restaurant overlooks the bay downtown, so the sunsets are an extra attraction. The menu includes Continental dishes and such Caribbean specialties as conch chowder, seafood curry, shrimp Diane, and, of course, lobster. This place is popular, and the constant turnover creates a frenzied atmosphere. If you can't make it for dinner, drop by the pub and have a frozen banana daiquiri. ⊠ *N. Church St.,* ☎ *345/949–2736. AE, D, MC, V.*

Beaches

You may read or hear about the "dozens of beaches" on these islands, but that's more exaggeration than reality. Grand Cayman's west coast, the most developed area of the entire colony, is where you'll find the famous **Seven Mile Beach**—5½ mi (9 km) long—and its expanses of powdery white sand. The beach is litter-free and sans peddlers, so you can relax in an unspoiled, hassle-free (if somewhat crowded) atmosphere. This is also Grand Cayman's busiest vacation center, and most of the island's accommodations, restaurants, and shopping centers are on this strip. You'll also find headquarters for the island's aquatic activities here.

Grand Cayman also has several smaller beaches—coves, really. **Smith's Cove,** off South Church Street and south of the Grand Old House, is a popular local bathing spot on weekends. The best windsurfing is just off the beaches of **East End,** at Colliers, by Morritt's Tortuga Club.

Cayman Kai, is a favored hideaway on the north side of the island. **Rum Point** is convenient for snorkeling and has a bar and grill especially popular on Sundays. If you seek a little more privacy, head to **Water Cay,** a more isolated, unspoiled beach.

Outdoor Activities and Sports

Participant Sports

FISHING

If you enjoy action fishing, Cayman waters have plenty to offer. Some 25 boats are available for charter, offering fishing options that include deep-sea, reef, bone, tarpon, light-tackle, and fly-fishing. These are among the Grand Cayman charter operators to contact. **Bayside Watersports** (☎ 345/949–3200) offers half-day snorkeling trips, North Sound Beach lunch excursions, and full-day deep-sea fishing and dinner cruises. **Burton's Tourist Information & Activity Services** (☎ 345/949–6598) can hook you up with a number of different charters and tours. **Captain Alphonso Ebanks** (☎ 345/949–1012) specializes in fishing and snorkeling tours to Stingray City and has half- and full-day tours. Finally, **Island Girl** (☎ 345/947–3029) offers customized private fishing and snorkeling charters; deep-sea fishing excursions include trolling, live bait, and drift fishing for yellowfin tuna and marlin; night fishing trips are also available.

GOLF

The **Grand Cayman–Britannia** golf course (☎ 345/949–8020), next to the Hyatt Regency, was designed by Jack Nicklaus. The course is really three in one—a nine-hole, par-70 regulation course, an 18-hole, par-57 executive course, and a Cayman course (played with a Cayman ball that goes about half the distance of a regulation ball). Greens fees run $40–$90, and golf carts ($15–$25) are mandatory.

Windier, and therefore more challenging, than most courses is the **Links at Safe Haven** (☎ 345/949–5988), Cayman's first 18-hole championship golf course, which is a botanical garden of indigenous trees, plants, and flowering shrubs. The Roy Case–designed, par-71, 6,605-yard course also has an aqua driving range (the distance markers and balls float), a clubhouse, pro shop, and restaurant. Greens fees run to $60. Golf carts ($15–$20 per person) are mandatory.

HORSEBACK RIDING

Nicki's Beach Rides (✉ Box 482, ☎ 345/945–5839) offers 1½-hour leisurely family horseback rides along one of the many white-sand beaches; the guides provide bits of island history and lore as you ride. **Pampered Ponies** (✉ Box 455, ☎ 345/945–2262 or 345/916–2540) features horses trained to walk, trot, and canter along the beaches and beach trails. Private rides, early mornings, sunsets, and evenings under the moonlight available.

HIKING

Nature trails abound on all three islands, and it's best to ask locals for directions. Guided nature walks are available at the National Trust's **Mastic Trail** on Grand Cayman (✉ Off Frank Sound Rd., ☎ 345/945–6588), a rugged 2-mi (3-km) slash through pristine woodlands, mangrove swamps, and ancient rock formations. There is no entry fee; guided hikes are $45 and run daily 9–5 by appointment only.

SCUBA DIVING AND SNORKELING

Pristine water (visibility often exceeding 100 ft), breathtaking coral formations, and plentiful and exotic marine life mark the **Great Wall**—a world-renowned dive site just off the north side of Grand Cayman. Many top-notch dive operations offer a variety of services, instruction, and equipment. A must-see for adventurous souls is **Stingray City** in the North Sound, noted as the best 12-ft dive in the world; it features dozens of stingrays tame enough to suction squid from your outstretched palm. **Trinity Caves** in West Bay is a deep dive with numerous canyons starting at about 60 ft. **Orange Canyon** starts at the edge of a wall at about 40 ft and is an easy shallow dive. The best shore-entry snorkeling spots are off the ironshore south of George Town, at **Eden Rock** and **Parrot's Landing**; north of town, at the reef off the West Bay Cemetery on Grand Cayman's **west coast**; and in the reef-protected shallows of the island's **north and south coasts,** where coral and fish life are much more varied and abundant.

Divers are required to be certified and possess a "C" card. Otherwise, you can take a full certification course, which costs $350–$400, lasts four to six days, and includes classroom, pool, boat sessions, and checkout dives. A short resort course lasts a day, costs about $80–$100, and introduces novices to the sport and teaches the rudimentary skills needed to make a shallow, instructor-monitored dive. A single-tank dive averages $50; a two-tank dive, about $75. Snorkel-equipment rental runs $5–$15 a day. Most operations rent gear and underwater photography equipment.

There are many dive operators in Grand Cayman. Call the **Cayman Islands Watersports Operators Association** (☎ 345/949–8522) for details on local providers. Or you can get complete information on all of them from the Department of Tourism.

Here are some reliable operations. **Aquanauts** (☎ 345/945–1990 or 888/786–6887) is at Morgans Harbour just minutes from spectacular North and West Walls; complimentary shuttle service is available. **Bob Soto's** (☎ 345/949–2871 or 800/BOB–SOTO) was the first dive operation in Cayman and now has several island locations; it has film-processing facilities and underwater photo courses. **Don Foster's** (☎ 345/949–5679 or 800/833–4837) is headquartered in George Town and offers both film processing and underwater photo courses. **Eden Rock** (☎ 345/949–7243) provides easy access to excellent George Town shore diving at Eden Rocks and Devil's Grotto; both reefs are a short swim from shore. **Parrot's Landing** (☎ 345/949–7884 or 800/448–0428) is near four offshore dive sites accessible from shore. **Red Sail Sports** (☎ 345/949–8745 or 800/255–6425) offers daily trips to Stingray City and has locations at many Grand Cayman hotels along Seven Mile Beach. **Sunset Divers** (☎ 345/949–7111 or 800/854–4767) has six dive boats, great shore diving, nitrox tanks, and rebreathers. **Turtle Reef Divers** (☎ 345/949–1700) offers Nitrox dives and certification; it is next to the Turtle Farm, where there are some excellent shore dives. One-week live-aboard dive cruises are available on the 110-ft **Cayman Aggressor III** (☎ 800/348–2628), which cruises around all three of the Cayman Islands. The luxury yacht **Little Cayman Diver II**

(☎ 800/458–2722) offers one-week dive cruises focusing on the pristine dive sites around Little Cayman.

TENNIS AND SQUASH
Most hotels and condo complexes have tennis courts (some lighted) for guests. Contact yours, or one that does, to reserve time or lessons.

The **South Sound Squash Club** (✉ S. Sound Rd., ☎ 345/949–9469) has courts available to the general public. Call the resident pro, John McCrury, for a court or game.

WINDSURFING
Cayman Windsurf (☎ 345/947–7492) offers lessons and rentals on the east end of the island at Morritt's Tortuga Beach Club and on North Sound by Safe Haven. **Sailboards Caribbean** (✉ West Bay Rd., ☎ 345/ 949–1068) offers windsurfing rentals and lessons for everyone in West Bay.

Shopping

On Grand Cayman the good news is that there's no sales tax *and* there's plenty of duty-free merchandise. The bad news is that prices on imported merchandise—English china, Swiss watches, French perfumes, and Japanese cameras and electronic goods—are not always lower than elsewhere. Locally made items to watch for include woven mats, baskets, jewelry made of a marblelike stone called caymanite (from the cliffs of Cayman Brac), and authentic sunken treasure. Cigar lovers take note: some shops carry Cohiba and Partagas brands (but enjoy them on the island, as bringing them back to the United States is a no-no).

Although you'll find black coral products in Grand Cayman, they're controversial. Most of the coral used to make items sold here comes from Belize and Honduras because Cayman Islands marine law prohibits the removal of live coral from its own sea. Black coral grows at a very slow rate (3 inches every 10 years), it is often designated as an endangered species, and reefs are not always harvested carefully. Environmental groups generally discourage people from purchasing coral products.

Areas and Malls

The main shopping areas are **Elizabethan Square, Cardinal Avenue,** and the chic **Kirk Freeport Plaza,** known for its fine jewelry, plus duty-free china, crystal, Gucci items, perfumes, and fine cosmetics. The **Queen's Court Shopping Centre,** on Seven Mile Beach close to town, has shops that sell an array of souvenirs, crafts, and gifts. At the **West Shore Shopping Centre** or the **Galleria Shopping Plaza,** both on Seven Mile Beach, you'll find good-quality island art, beachwear, and more.

Specialty Items

ART
The waterfront **Artifacts** gallery (☎ 345/949–2442) sells Spanish pieces of eight, doubloons, and Halcyon Days' enamels, which are handpainted collectible pillboxes made in England. **Cathy Church's Underwater Photo Centre and Gallery** (✉ S. Church St., ☎ 345/949–7415) has a collection of spectacular underwater photos by the famed photographer Cathy Church. At **Cayman Glassblowing Studio** (✉ N. Church St., ☎ 345/949–7020) you can watch artisans create vibrantly colored glass sculptures, vases, and more. You'll find original prints, paintings, and sculpture with a tropical theme at **Island Art Gallery** (✉ Anchorage Shopping Centre, ☎ 345/949–9861). The **Kennedy Gallery** (✉ West Shore Centre, West Bay Rd., ☎ 345/949–8077) features lithographs and prints depicting the Cayman Islands by local artists. Debbie van

der Bol runs the arts-and-crafts shop **Pure Art** (⊠ S. Church St., ☎ 345/949–9133; ⊠ Hyatt Regency, ☎ 345/945–5633), which sells watercolors, wood carvings, and lacework by local artists, as well as her own sketches and cards.

CLOTHES

Calico Jack's (⊠ West Bay Rd., ☎ 345/949–4373) is a good source for T-shirts, casual resort wear, and dive gear. **St. Michael** (⊠ Galleria Plaza, off West Bay Rd., ☎ 345/945–5165) sells clothes and other items.

FOODSTUFFS

For groceries and pharmaceutical needs, try **Foster's Food Fair** (⊠ Strand Shopping Center, ☎ 345/945–4748 store; 345/945–7759 pharmacy), a huge modern supermarket just off Seven Mile Beach. The **Tortuga Rum Company** (⊠ N. Sound Rd., ☎ 345/949–7701or 345/949–7867) has scrumptious rum cake (sealed fresh) that's sweet and moist and makes a great souvenir.

HANDICRAFTS

The coral creations of **Bernard Passman** (⊠ Fort St., ☎ 345/949–0123) have won the approval of the British royal family, and the pope even owns a piece of Passman's work. **Carey Cayman Coral** (⊠ S. Sound Rd., ☎ No phone) is a workshop run by Carey Hurlstone, who carves glass and makes black coral jewelry and figurines. The **Heritage Crafts Shop** (☎ 345/945–6041), near the harbor in George Town, sells local crafts and gifts. You'll find beautiful coral pieces at **Richard's Fine Jewelry** (⊠ Harbour Dr., ☎ 345/949–7156), where designers Richard and Rafaela Barile attract a share of celebrities.

Nightlife

Look at the free *What's Hot* or check the Friday edition of the *Caymanian Compass* for listings of music, movies, theater, and other entertainment.

On Tuesdays and Wednesdays locals go to **Legendz** (⊠ West Bay Rd., ☎ 345/945–1950) for the live bands and comedy night, respectively. The **Cracked Conch** (⊠ West Bay Rd., near Turtle Farm, ☎ 345/945–5217) is where islanders congregate on Thursday night for karaoke, classic dive films, and happy hour. On Friday nights the locals head to **Bed** (⊠ Harquail Bypass, ☎ 345/949–7199), a popular bar and restaurant with a comfortable lounge atmosphere and servers in pajamas. **Royal Palms** (⊠ West Bay Rd., ☎ 345/945–6358) is where local bands play Wednesday through Saturday nights; it's an outdoor beach bar with plenty of room for dancing under the stars. If you are dying to see a film, **Cinema 1 & 2** (⊠ Harquail Bypass, ☎ 345/949–4011 for show times) is across from Bed.

Exploring Grand Cayman

The historic capital of George Town, which is at one end of Seven Mile Beach, is easy to explore on foot. If you're a shopper, you can spend days here; otherwise, you can tour downtown in an hour. To see the rest of the island, rent a car or scooter or take a guided tour. The portion of the island called West Bay is noted for its jumble of affluent colonial neighborhoods and rather tawdry tourist attractions. A drive along West Bay Road will take you past the dense Seven Mile Beach area and into a less congested scene. It's about a half hour to West Bay from George Town. The less developed East End has natural attractions, from blowholes to botanical gardens, as well as the remains of the original settlements. Plan on at least 45 minutes for the drive out from George Town. You need a day to circle and explore the entire island—including a stop at a beach for a picnic or swim.

Numbers in the margin correspond to points of interest on the Grand Cayman, Cayman Brac, and Little Cayman maps.

Sights to See

⑨ Blow Holes. These make the ultimate photo opportunity as crashing waves force water into caverns and send geysers shooting up through the ironshore.

⑥ Bodden Town. In the island's original capital you'll find an old cemetery on the shore side of the road. Graves with A-frame structures are said to contain the remains of pirates. There are also the ruins of a fort and a wall erected by slaves in the 19th century. A curio shop serves as the entrance to what's called the Pirate's Caves, partially underground natural formations that are more hokey (decked out with fake treasure chests and mannequins in pirate garb) than spooky.

③ Cayman Island Turtle Farm. Started in 1968 as both a conservation and a commercial enterprise, the farm has become the island's most popular attraction (almost 350,000 visitors a year). You'll find turtles of all ages and sizes, from Ping Pong ball–size eggs to elderly 600-pounders (some turtles live as long as 100 years). The farm releases about 5% of its stock out to sea every year and harvests turtles for local restaurants. (Note: U.S. citizens cannot take home any turtle products because of a U.S. ban.) In the adjoining café you can sample turtle soup or turtle sandwiches while viewing an exhibit about turtles. ✉ *West Bay Rd.,* ☎ *345/949–3893.* 🎟 *$6.* ☉ *Mon.–Sat. 8:30–5.*

① George Town. Begin exploring the capital by strolling along the waterfront, Harbour Drive. The circular gazebo is where visitors from the cruise ships disembark. Diagonally across the street from the cruise ship dock is the **Elmslie Memorial United Church,** named after Scotsman James Elmslie, the first Presbyterian missionary to serve in the Caymans. The church was the first concrete-block building built in the Cayman Islands. Its vaulted ceiling, wooden arches, and sedate nave reflect the quietly religious nature of island residents. Along your rambles in George Town you'll easily come across **Fort Street,** a main shopping street where you'll also notice the small clock tower dedicated to Britain's King George V and the huge fig tree manicured into an umbrella shape. Here, too, is a statue (unveiled in 1994) of national hero James Bodden, the father of Cayman tourism. Across the street is the Cayman Islands Legislative Assembly Building, next door to the 1919 Peace Memorial Building. That the Caymanians built a memorial to peace rather than war speaks to their character.

On **Edward Street** you'll find the charming library, built in 1939; it has English novels, current newspapers from the United States, and a small reference section. It's worth a visit just for the Old World atmosphere and a look at the shields with insignias of Britain's prominent institutions of learning; they decorate the ceiling beams. Across the street is the courthouse. Down the next block is the financial district, where banks from all over the world have offices.

Down from the financial district is the **General Post Office,** also built in 1939, with its strands of decorative colored lights and some 2,000 private mailboxes on the outside (mail is not delivered on the island). Behind the post office is **Elizabethan Square,** a shopping and office complex on Shedden Road with food, clothing, and souvenir establishments. The courtyard has benches placed around a garden and a fountain; it's a pleasant place to rest your feet.

Built in 1833, the **Cayman Islands National Museum** was used as a courthouse, a jail (now the gift shop), a post office, and a dance hall before reopening in 1990 as a museum. It's small but fascinating, with excellent displays and videos that illustrate local geology, flora, fauna, and island history. Pick up a walking-tour map of George Town at the museum gift shop before leaving. ✉ *Harbour Dr.,* ☎ *345/949–8368.* ✉ *$5.* ⊙ *Weekdays 9–5, Sat. 10–2.*

❹ **Hell.** This tiny village is little more than a patch of incredibly jagged rock formations called ironshore. The big attraction here is the small post office where you can get cards and letters postmarked from Hell (a postcard of bikini-clad beauties emblazoned with WHEN HELL FREEZES OVER gives you a picture of what this place is like).

❼ **Mastic Trail.** In the 1800s this woodland trail was often used as a shortcut to and from the North Side. The low-lying area was full of hardwood trees, including mahogany, West Indian cedar, and the mastic that early settlers used in building their homes. Along the trail you'll see an abundance of trees, birds, and plants unique to this old-growth forest. It's on National Trust territory, and you must call to book a guide. ✉ *Frank Sound Rd.,* ☎ *345/949–0121.*

❷ **Old Homestead.** Formerly known as the West Bay Pink House, this is probably the most photographed home in Grand Cayman. The pink-and-white Caymanian cottage was built in 1912 of wattle and daub around an ironwood frame. Cheery Mac Bothwell, who grew up in the house, takes you on tours that present a nostalgic and touching look at life in Grand Cayman before the tourism and banking booms. ✉ *West Bay Rd.,* ☎ *345/949–7639.* ✉ *$5.* ⊙ *Mon.–Sat. 8–5.*

❺ **Pedro St. James Castle.** Built in 1780, the great house is not only Cayman's oldest stone structure, it's the only remaining late-18th-century residence on the island. The buildings are surrounded by 8 acres of natural parks and woodlands. You can stroll through landscaping of native Caymanian flora and experience one of the most spectacular views on the island from atop the dramatic Great Pedro Bluff. Not to be missed is the impressive multimedia theater show complete with smoking pots, misting rains, and two film screens where the story of Pedro's Castle is presented. The show plays on the hour; plan to see it before you tour the site. ✉ *S. Sound Rd., Savannah,* ☎ *345/947–3329.* ✉ *$8.*

❽ **Queen Elizabeth II Botanic Park.** This 65-acre wilderness preserve showcases the variety of indigenous habitats and vegetation as well as other nonindigenous tropical plants. Interpretive signs identify the flora along the walking trail. Rare blue iguanas are bred and released in the gardens; there's usually one named Charlie hanging around the entrance gate. You can also see native orchids and, if you're lucky, the brilliant green Cayman parrot. ✉ *Frank Sound Rd.,* ☎ *345/947–9462 or 345/947–3558 (info line),* FAX *345/947–7873.* ✉ *$3.* ⊙ *Daily 9–6:30 (last admission at 5:30).*

❿ **Queen's View.** This functions as both an eastern lookout point and a monument dedicated by Queen Elizabeth in 1994 to commemorate the legendary Wreck of the Ten Sails, which took place just offshore.

CAYMAN BRAC

Brac, the Gaelic word for "bluff," aptly identifies this island's most distinctive feature, a rugged limestone cliff that runs down the center of the 12-mi (19-km) island and soars to 140 ft at its eastern end. Lying 89 mi (143 km) northeast of Grand Cayman, Brac is accessible via Cayman Airways and Island Air. Only 1,200 people live on the island, in communities such as Watering Place and Spot Bay. Residents are very friendly, so it's easy to strike up conversation; in fact, you'll often have to be the one to end the chat if you expect to do anything else that day.

Lodging

Hotels here are usually a better value than their prices indicate at first glance. Rates often include meals, if not drinks and diving. In addition, lodgings are much cozier and more intimate than their Grand Cayman counterparts, and hoteliers often treat guests like family. Most hotels give you the option of including all meals in your stay, but there are a few restaurants on the island. To reach them, however, you'll need a taxi or a bike (most hotels have these for guest use). Most restaurants serve island fare (stewed fish, conch fritters, curries), and portions are generally large.

For approximate costs, *see* the lodging price chart *in* Grand Cayman.

Hotels

$$ ⚐ **Brac Caribbean.** This condo complex offers all the comforts of
★ home in one- to four-bedroom units. Each unit has white tile floors, light peach stucco walls, and a private balcony overlooking the sea. ⊠ *Stake Bay (Box 4),* ☎ *345/948–2265 or 800/791–7911,* FAX *345/ 948–2206. 14 units. Restaurant, bar, air-conditioning, pool, hot tub, dive shop, fishing, bicycles. AE, MC, V. CP.*

$$ ⚐ **Brac Reef Beach Resort.** Because of its all-inclusive dive package, this resort is popular. That said, it seems ironic that the main building is set back from the shore and that none of the rooms has a water view (though rooms on the ground floor have patios, and some on the second floor have balconies). The resort does have a pretty beach, however, and many amenities, including a pool, guest bicycles, a dive shop, and a two-story dock (its gazebo is glorious on a star-filled night, when you can see brilliantly hued fish darting about). The modest all-inclusive package rates include three buffet meals daily, all drinks, airport transfers, and taxes and service charges for two persons; dive packages cost a little more. There are also theme events such as English high tea as well as weekly cocktail parties. ⊠ *Brac Reef Beach (Box 56),* ☎ *345/948–1323, 800/327–3835, or 727/323–8727 in FL;* FAX *727/323–8827,* WEB *www.bracreef.com. 40 rooms. Restaurant, bar, air-conditioning, pool, hot tub, tennis court, beach, dive shop, dock, snorkeling, bicycles, gym, meeting rooms. AE, D, MC, V. All-inclusive, EP, FAP, MAP.*

$ ⚐ **La Esperanza.** *Esperanza* is the Spanish word for "hope," and after you've stayed at this rustic establishment in Stake Bay, you hope that Ethan Dilbert (better known as Mr. Bussy) makes a go of his modest little resort. The property is on the north side of the island, and you're treated more as family than guest when you stay here. The compound offers four two-bedroom apartments with fully equipped kitchens and a three-bedroom house with two baths. Guest quarters have white tile floors and simple furnishings. His seaside restaurant terrace offers breathtaking Cayman Brac sunsets—and, of course, there's always the owner's famous jerk chicken, which he prepares by the side of the road every Friday and Saturday night. ⊠ *Stake Bay (Box 28),* ☎ *345/ 948–0531 or 345/948–0591,* FAX *345/948–0525,* WEB *www.candw.ky/ users/cay06865. 11 rooms. Restaurant, bar, shop. AE, MC, V. MAP.*

$ ⚐ **Walton's Mango Manor.** This two-story traditional West Indian
★ home has five rooms (with bath) and a tranquil setting. Beautiful antique furnishings and architectural details abound, including the stairway handrail, which is a relic from an old ship. The nearby ironshore

beach is the perfect place for a sunrise walk. The proprietors love to relate Brac history and help you make arrangements for game-fishing trips, scuba-diving excursions, and other activities. As only breakfast is included, you'll need a car so you can get out for other meals and exploring the island. ⊠ *Stake Bay (Box 56),* ☎ FAX *345/948–0518. 5 rooms. Air-conditioning, fans. AE, MC, V. CP.*

Beaches

The accommodations on the **southwest coast** have fine small beaches, better for sunning than for snorkeling because of the abundance of turtle grass in the water. Everyone is welcome on hotel beaches.

Outdoor Activities and Sports

SCUBA DIVING AND SNORKELING

The waters off Cayman Brac are more pristine than those off Grand Cayman, so you'll see more (and larger) critters. The snorkeling is excellent off the **north coast.** Many fish have taken to the Russian warship that was scuttled offshore from the now-defunct Buccaneer's Inn. (Look for the beautiful queen angelfish that makes its home between two of the guns.) All the ship's doors have been removed, so you can swim through it—not for the faint of heart as it's pitch black in some spaces.

Two-tank dives cost $60–$70 at **Brac Aquatics** (☎ 345/948–1429 or 800/544–2722), a full-service dive operation that offers courses in addition to daily and packaged dive rates. **Brac Reef Divers** (☎ 345/948–1323) offer scuba and snorkeling gear and courses, with two-tank dives priced around $60–$70.

SPELUNKING

If you plan to explore any of Cayman Brac's caves, wear sneakers as some of the paths are steep and rocky. **Peter's Cave** is a great place to view the south side bluffs. **Great Cave** is near the old lighthouse and has numerous stalagmites and stalactites. **Bat Cave** is well-lighted and where you'll most likely see bats hanging from the ceiling. **Rebeka's Cave** has a grave site where a Cayman Brac family buried baby Rebeka who lost her life during a hurricane in the 1930s.

Exploring Cayman Brac

Cayman Brac Museum. In addition to displaying implements used in the daily lives of Bracers in the 1920s and '30s, this two-room museum exhibits a few oddities, such as a 4,000-year-old ax. The variety of Brac flora on the property includes unusual orchids, mangoes, papaya, agave, and cacti. ⊠ *Old Government Administration Bldg., Stake Bay,* ☎ *345/948–2622.* ☜ *Free.* ☉ *Weekdays 9–noon and 1–4, Sat. 9–noon, Sun. 1–4.*

Parrot Preserve. The easiest place to spot the endangered Cayman Brac parrot is in this preserve on Major Donald Drive (also known as Lighthouse Road). This 6-mi (9½-km) dirt road also leads to ironshore cliffs that offer the best panoramic view of North East Point and the open ocean. Swimming is possible, but the bottom is rocky and clogged with turtle grass.

LITTLE CAYMAN

Only 7 mi (11 km) from Cayman Brac, Little Cayman Island has a population of about 100 on its 12 square mi (31 square km). This is a true hideaway: few phones, fewer shops, no man-made sights or nightlife to speak of—just spectacular diving, great fishing, fantastic bird-watching, placid beaches, and laid-back camaraderie. The newest attraction is a luxurious nature spa, which offers pampering services like full massages, body wraps, and facials; it's fast becoming a popular indulgence for locals and visitors.

Lodging

Accommodations are mostly in small lodges, many of which offer meal and dive packages. The meal packages are a good idea; the chefs in most places are impeccably trained.

For approximate costs, *see* the lodging price chart *in* Grand Cayman.

Hotels

$$$ ☐ **Southern Cross Club.** The stunning beach is dotted with brightly col-
★ ored cottages, all with fabulous sea views. Pastel colors and wicker furniture keep you comfortable, while tile floors and swirling fans keep you cool. Service and meals are impeccable, though diving and fishing are the true draws here. Wading through seagrass is the norm on all resort beaches. But this resort is near secluded Owen Island, which has a lovely sandy beach; it's a short kayak away, making this property especially attractive. ⊠ *South Hole Sound (Box 44),* ☎ *345/948–1099 or 800/899–2582,* FAX *317/636–9503. 10 rooms. Restaurant, bar, dive shop, snorkeling, fishing, bicycles, airport shuttle. AE, MC, V. FAP.*

$$ ☐ **Little Cayman Beach Resort.** This two-story property is considerably less rustic than other Little Cayman resorts. Rooms have contemporary furnishings and tropical, jewel-tone color schemes. Numbers 115, 116, 215, 216, and 301–308 have water views and will be quieter than rooms facing the bar. If you're the active type, the resort offers fishing and diving packages and also caters to bird-watchers and soft-adventure ecotourists. If you want some pampering, be sure to check out the affiliated Nature Spa, which has treatments like marine algae body masks, sea salt body polishes, and relaxing massages. All-inclusive packages (for spa-goers, divers, and nondivers) include three meals daily, all alcoholic and soft drinks, airport transfers, taxes, and gratuities. ⊠ *Blossom Village (Box 51),* ☎ *345/948–1033 or 800/327–3835,* FAX *345/948–1040,* WEB *www.littlecayman.com. 40 rooms. Restaurant, bar, pool, hot tub, spa, tennis court, gym, dive shop, fishing, bicycles, shops, meeting rooms. AE, MC, V. All-inclusive, EP, FAP, MAP.*

$$ ☐ **Pirates Point Resort.** The guest-house feel of this informal resort generates almost instant camaraderie among those who stay here—and many return. Owner Gladys Howard is no doubt another reason for the repeat business. Her down-home welcome (she's originally from Texas) belies her upscale meals (she trained at Cordon Bleu with Julia Child, James Beard, and Jacques Pepin). Rooms have tile floors, ceiling fans, and white rattan and wicker furnishings. "Relaxing" rates (for nondivers) include the mouthwatering meals and wine; all-inclusive rates include meals, alcoholic beverages, and two daily boat dives. Not all rooms have air-conditioning. ⊠ *Preston Bay (Box 43),* ☎ *345/948–1010,* FAX *345/948–1011. 10 rooms. Restaurant, bar, air-conditioning (some), gym, dive shop, bicycles, airport shuttle. MC, V. All-inclusive, FAP.*

$$ ☐ **Sam McCoy's Diving and Fishing Resort.** Stays here are ultracasual. Bedrooms (all with bath) are simple but cheerful and are done in royal and powder blues. You eat at beachside barbecues or with Sam, the good-natured owner, and his family. "Relaxing" rates (for nondivers)

include three meals a day and airport transfers; all-inclusive rates also include beach and boat diving. Sam is a *very* experienced fishing guide; his bonefishing trips cost around $45 an hour for two (slightly less for one). ✉ *North Side (Box 12),* ☎ *345/948–0026 or 800/626–0496,* FAX *345/948–0057,* WEB *mccoyslodge.com.ky. 8 rooms. Air-conditioning, fans, pool. AE, MC, V. All-inclusive, FAP.*

Villas

$$$$ ⊞ **Conch Club.** These two- to three-bedroom town homes can sleep four
★   to six people and have well-appointed furnishings, pretty aqua floor tiles, vaulted ceilings, fully equipped kitchens, decks, and patios overlooking the sea. As a guest here, you can use all the facilities of the Little Cayman Beach Resort less than ¼ mi away. These spacious units are a good option for families and couples traveling together. There's also a dock and huts for dive gear. ✉ *Blossom Village (Box 51),* ☎ *345/948–1033 or 800/327–3835. 15 units. Kitchenettes, pool, hot tub, spa, dive shop, bicycles, gift shop. AE, MC, V. All-inclusive, MAP, FAP.*

$$ ⊞ **Paradise Villas.** The cozy one-bedroom units have full kitchens, air-
★   conditioning, and terraces that open onto the beach. Your quarters are simply but immaculately appointed with rattan furnishings and muted abstract fabrics. Each cottage has a few hammocks for those lazy days when you don't want to go on a dive. If you get tired of cooking for yourself in the well-equipped kitchenettes, delicious island-style food (not to mention the island's only bar) is just steps away at the Hungry Iguana restaurant. ✉ *Southern Hole Sound (Box 48),* ☎ *345/948–0001,* FAX *345/948–0002. 12 units. Kitchenettes, pool, dive shop, bicycles, gift shop. AE, MC, V.*

Beaches

The beach at **Sandy Point,** on the eastern tip of Little Cayman, is an isolated patch of powder and worth every effort to reach by boat, car, or bike. **Owen Island,** which is rowboating distance (200 yards) from the south coast, has a sandy beach. You can pack a picnic lunch and spend the day.

Outdoor Activities and Sports

BIRD-WATCHING

Governor Gore Bird Sanctuary, established in 1994, is home to 5,000 pairs of red-footed boobies (the largest colony in the western hemisphere) and 1,000 magnificent frigate birds. You may catch black frigates and snowy egrets competing for lunch in dramatic dive-bombing battles. The sanctuary is near the airport.

FISHING

Bloody Bay, off the north coast, has spectacular fishing, including angling for tarpon and bonefish. Sam McCoy, of **Sam McCoy's Fishing & Diving** (☎ 345/948–0026 or 800/626–0496), is among the premier fishermen on the island. The **Southern Cross Club** (☎ 800/899–2582), a resort near South Hole Sound, also offers deep-sea fishing trips for nonguests.

SCUBA DIVING AND SNORKELING

Jacques Cousteau considered **Bloody Bay Wall,** just 15 minutes from Little Cayman by boat, one of the world's top dives. The drop begins at a mere 18 ft (6 m) and plunges to more than 1,000 ft (306 m), with visibility often reaching 150 ft (46 m)—diving doesn't get much better than this. Expect to pay $60–$75 for a two-tank boat dive. Most hotels have diving instructors and equipment. **Paradise Divers** (☎ 345/948–0001), runs a 46-ft pontoon boat from the North Coast of

Little Cayman to Bloody Bay and Jackson Bay. **Reef Divers** (☎ 345/948–1033) has its own dock and a full-service photo and video center. **Sam McCoy's Fishing & Diving** (☎ 345/948–0026 or 800/626–0496) is run by a Little Cayman family that will transport you to dive boats and shore locations. The **Southern Cross Club** (☎ 800/899–2582) limits each of its boats to 12 divers and has its own dock.

Guided snorkeling trips usually include stops at Stingray City Sandbar, Coral Garden, and Conch Bed, the top snorkel sites. Full-day trips include lunch prepared on the boat or onshore and cost under $40 per person; half-day trips average $25. Trips are available through several outfits, including **Red Sail Sports** (☎ 345/945–5965 or 800/733–7245; WEB www.redsail.com), **Captain Bryan's Sail and Snorkel Tours** (☎ 345/949–0038; WEB www.cayman.org/captainbryan), and **Kirk Sea Tours** (☎ 345/949–6986).

CAYMAN ISLANDS A TO Z

To research prices, get advice from other travelers, and book travel arrangements, visit www.fodors.com.

AIR TRAVEL
American Airlines has daily nonstop flights from both Miami and Raleigh/Durham, NC. British Airways offers twice-weekly service from London (Gatwick) to Grand Cayman with an intermediate stop in Nassau, Bahamas. Cayman Airways flies nonstop to Grand Cayman from Miami two or three times daily, from Tampa four times a week, from Orlando three times a week, and from Houston and Atlanta three times a week. Continental flies nonstop to Grand Cayman from Newark, NJ, three times a week. Delta has daily nonstops from Atlanta and New York (JFK) to Grand Cayman. Northwest has nonstops from Minneapolis and Detroit to Grand Cayman. USAirways flies nonstop daily to Grand Cayman from Charlotte, NC, and Philadelphia. Air service from Grand Cayman to Cayman Brac and Little Cayman is offered by two airlines: Cayman Airways has daily morning and evening service to both Cayman Brac and Little Cayman, and Island Air offers morning and afternoon service from Grand Cayman to both Cayman Brac and Little Cayman.
➤ AIRLINES AND CONTACTS: **American Airlines** (☎ 345/949–8799 or 800/433–7300); **Cayman Airways** (☎ 345/949–2311 or 800/422–9626); **Continental** (☎ 345/916–5545 or 800/231–0856); **Delta** (☎ 800/221–1212); **Island Air** (☎ 345/949–5252); **Northwest** (☎ 345/949–2956 or 800/447–4747); **US Airways** (☎ 800/428–4322).

AIRPORTS
Flights land at Owen Roberts Airport (Grand Cayman), Gerrard-Smith Airport (Cayman Brac), or Edward Bodden Airstrip (Little Cayman). Upon arrival some hotels offer free pickup at the airport, particularly on Cayman Brac and Little Cayman. Taxi service and car rentals are also available.
➤ AIRPORT INFORMATION: On Grand Cayman contact **Owen Roberts Airport** (☎ 345/949–5252 or 345/949-7811); on Cayman Brac **Gerrard Smith International Airport** (☎ 345/948–1222); and on Little Cayman **Edward Bodden Airstrip** (☎ 345/948–0021).

BIKE AND MOPED TRAVEL
When renting a motor scooter or bicycle, remember to drive on the left—and wear sunblock. Bicycles ($10–$15 a day) and scooters ($30–$35 a day) can be rented from several outlets on Grand Cayman. Since the island is fairly flat, riding is generally not a problem. On Cayman

Brac or Little Cayman, your hotel can make arrangements for you. Many resorts also offer bicycles for local sightseeing.

➤ BIKE AND MOPED RENTALS: **Bicycles Cayman** (☏ 345/949–0608); **Cayman Cycle** (☏ 345/945–4021); **Eagles Nest** (☏ 345/949–4866) specializes in renting Harley Davidson motorcycles; **Soto Scooters** (☏ 345/945–4652).

BUSINESS HOURS

BANKS

Banks are open Monday–Thursday 9–2:30 and Friday 9–1 and 2:30–4:30.

POST OFFICES

Post offices are generally open weekdays from 8:30 to 3:30 and Saturday from 8:30 to 11:30.

SHOPS

Shops are open weekdays 9–5, and Saturday in George Town from 10 to 2; in outer shopping plazas they are open from 10 to 5. Shops are usually closed Sunday except in hotels.

CAR RENTALS

To rent a car, bring your current driver's license, and the car-rental firm will issue you a temporary permit ($7.50). Most firms have a range of models, from compacts to Jeeps to minibuses. Rates range from $35 to $65 a day. The major agencies have offices in a plaza across from the airport terminal in Grand Cayman, where you can pick up and drop off vehicles. You can rent a car from Ace Hertz, Budget, Coconut, Economy, Soto's, and Thrifty on Grand Cayman. Ace Hertz also has an office on Cayman Brac. McLaughlin operates on Little Cayman, though you probably won't need to rent a car there.

➤ MAJOR AGENCIES: **Ace Hertz** (☏ 345/949–2280 or 800/654–3131); **Budget** (☏ 345/949–5605 or 800/472–3325); **Coconut Car Rentals** (☏ 345/949–4377 or 800/941–4562); **Economy** (☏ 345/949–9550); **McLaughlin Rentals** (☏ 345/948–1000); **Soto's 4X4** (☏ 345/945–2424 or 800/625–6174); **Thrifty** (☏ 345/949–6640 or 800/367–2277).

CAR TRAVEL

Traffic on West Bay Road in Grand Cayman can be congested, especially during high season as it's the only thoroughfare on the Seven Mile Beach strip. Head out of the strip and get beyond George Town, and traffic will be sparse. Exploring Cayman Brac on a scooter is easy and fun. You won't really need a car on Little Cayman, though there are a limited number of Jeeps for rent.

GASOLINE

Gas prices at press time were about $2.40 for an imperial gallon, slightly more than a U.S. gallon.

ROAD CONDITIONS

If you're touring Grand Cayman by car, there's a well-maintained road that circles the island; it's hard to get lost. Grand Cayman is relatively flat and fairly easy to negotiate if you're careful in traffic. Roads are well-marked and in decent condition on all three islands.

RULES OF THE ROAD

Remember—driving in the Cayman Islands is on the left, so when pulling out into traffic, look to your right.

ELECTRICITY

Electricity is the same in the Caymans as it is in the United States (110 volts, 60 cycles); it's reliable throughout the islands.

EMBASSIES AND CONSULATES
➤ CONTACTS: **U.S. Consular Representative** is Mrs. Gail Duquesney at Adventure Travel (☎ 345/945–1511).

EMERGENCIES
➤ AMBULANCE AND FIRE: ☎ 911.
➤ DENTISTS: **David Godfrey** (☎ 345/949–7623); **David Wolfe** (☎ 345/945–4388).
➤ HOSPITALS: **George Town Hospital** has a 24-hour two-person, double-lock hyperbaric chamber (⊠ Hospital Rd., ☎ 345/949–4234).
➤ PHARMACIES: **Island Pharmacy** (⊠ West Shore Centre, ☎ 345/949–8987).
➤ POLICE: ☎ 911.

ETIQUETTE
You'll hear first names preceded by "Mr." or "Miss" (e.g., Mr. Sam)—these are terms of respect generally used for Caymanian senior citizens.

FESTIVALS AND SEASONAL EVENTS
During April's colorful Batabano Carnival, revelers dress up as dancing flowers and swimming stingrays. If you want to see an utterly British parade spiced with island-style panache, check out the Queen's Birthday bash in June. During Million Dollar Month in June, you'll find fishing tournaments on all three islands (five tournaments in all), each with its own rules, records, and entrance fees; huge cash prizes are awarded, including one for a quarter of a million dollars that's given to the angler who breaks the existing Blue Marlin record. The record as of the end of 1999 was 584 pounds. The end of October sees the carnival-like atmosphere of Pirates Week (which really lasts 10 days and includes a mock invasion of Hog Sty Bay by a mock Blackbeard and company). Visitors and locals dress up like pirates and wenches; music, fireworks, and a variety of competitions take place island-wide.

HEALTH
Poisonous plants on the island include the maiden plum, the lady hair, and the manchineel tree. If in doubt, don't touch. The leaves and applelike fruit of the manchineel are poisonous to touch and should be avoided; even raindrops falling from them can cause painful blisters.

HOLIDAYS
Public holidays include New Year's Day, Ash Wednesday (Mar. 8), Good Friday (Apr. 21), Easter Sunday (Apr. 23), Discovery Day (May 19), Queen's Birthday (June 16), Constitution Day (July 7), Christmas, and Boxing Day (Dec. 26).

LANGUAGE
English is the official language in the Cayman Islands, and it is spoken with a distinctive brogue that reflects Caymanians' Welsh, Scottish, and English heritage. For example, *three* is pronounced "tree"; *pepper* is "pep-ah"; and *Cayman* is "K-*man*." The number of Jamaican residents in the workforce means the Jamaican patois and heavier accent are also common (other Jamaican influences are tales about the *duppy*—pronounced like "puppy"—a scary night creature that haunts the Caymans).

MAIL AND SHIPPING
Beautiful stamps are available at the General Post Office in downtown George Town and at the philatelic office in West Shore Plaza. Sending a postcard to the United States, Canada, the Caribbean, or Central America costs CI20¢. An airmail letter is CI30¢ per half ounce. To Europe

and South America, rates are CI25¢ for a postcard and CI40¢ per half ounce for airmail letters. When addressing letters to the Cayman Islands, be sure to include "BWI" (British West Indies) at the bottom of the envelope. Note that the islands don't use postal codes, but don't let this worry you; your letter should arrive fine without one.

MONEY MATTERS

All prices quoted in this book are in U.S. dollars unless otherwise noted.

ATMS

ATMs are readily available, particularly on Grand Cayman; they usually give the option of U.S. or Cayman dollars.

CREDIT CARDS

Major credit cards are widely accepted except for Discover.

CURRENCY

The Cayman dollar is divided into a hundred cents with coins of 1¢, 5¢, 10¢, and 25¢ and notes of $1, $5, $10, $25, $50, and $100. There is no $20 bill. Although the American dollar is accepted everywhere, you'll often get your change in Cayman dollars.

PASSPORTS AND VISAS

It is always best when traveling abroad to carry a valid passport. However, U.S., U.K., and Canadian citizens, as well as citizens of Commonwealth countries, may carry an original birth certificate and a valid picture ID. A voter registration card is no longer acceptable identification. Citizens of all other countries need a valid passport, and all visitors must have a valid return ticket.

SAFETY

Penalties for importing drugs and firearms and possession of controlled substances include large fines and prison terms. Theft is not widespread, but be smart: lock your room and car and secure valuables as you would at home. Outdoors, marauding blackbirds called ching chings have been known to carry off jewelry if it is left out in the open.

Locals conserve fresh water, so don't waste this precious commodity. Caymanians also strictly observe and enforce laws that prohibit collecting or disturbing endangered animal, marine, and plant life and historical artifacts found throughout the islands and surrounding marine parks; simply put, take only pictures, and don't stand on reefs because that kills them.

SIGHTSEEING TOURS

Half-day tours average $30–$50 a person and generally include a visit to the Turtle Farm and Hell in West Bay, drives along Seven Mile Beach and through George Town, and time for shopping downtown. In addition to those stops, full-day tours, which average $55–$75 per person and include lunch, also visit Bodden Town to see pirate caves and graves and the East End, where you visit blowholes on the ironshore and the site of the famous Wreck of the Ten Sails.
➤ CONTACTS: **A. A. Transportation Services** (☎ 345/949–7222 (ask for Burton Ebanks); **Majestic Tours** (☎ 345/949–7773); **Reid's Premier Tours** (☎ 345/949–3345); **Rudy's Travellers Transport** (☎ 345/949–3208); and **Tropicana Tours** (☎ 345/949–0944).

BOAT TOURS

The most impressive sights in the Cayman Islands are underwater, and several submarine trips will allow you to see these wonders. On Grand

Cayman don't miss a trip on the *Atlantis* submarine, which takes 48 passengers, a driver, and two guides down along the Cayman Wall to depths of up to 100 ft (31 m). Through its large windows you can see huge barrel sponges, corals in extraterrestrial-like configurations, strange eels, and schools of beautiful and beastly fish. Night dives are especially dramatic; the artificial lights of the sub make the colors more vivid than they look during daytime excursions. Costs range around $72–$85 per person for trips lasting 1–1½ hours. The company also operates private trips on a research submersible that reaches depths of 800–1,000 ft (245–806 m). The *Nautilus* is a semisubmersible (part of the craft remains above water). You can catch some sun on the deck or venture to the cabin below, where windows allow you to see the reefs and marine life. Theme cruises (mystery theater, dinner at sunset, etc.) are also offered. A one-hour undersea tour is $35. In the semisubmersible *Seaworld Explorer,* you sit before windows in the hull of the boat just 5 ft (1½ m) below the surface, observing divers who swim around with food, attracting fish to the craft. The cost of this hourlong trip is $38.

Glass-bottom-boat trips cost around $25 and are available through several companies, including Acqua Delights, the *Cayman Mermaid,* and Kirk Sea Tours.

Sunset sails, dinner cruises, and other theme (dance, booze, pirate, etc.) cruises are available aboard several vessels. Party cruises typically run $20–$50 per person. The *Jolly Roger* is a replica of a 17th-century Spanish galleon offering afternoon, sunset, and dinner cruises. *Blackbeard's Nancy* is a 1912 topsail schooner, offering dinner cruises among others. The *Spirit of Ppalu* is a 65-ft glass-bottom catamaran offering dinner cruises.
➤ CONTACTS: **Aqua Delights** (☎ 345/945–4786); **Atlantis** submarine (☎ 345/949–7700 or 800/877–8571, WEB www.goatlantis.com/cayman); **Blackbeard's Nancy** (☎ 345/949–8988); **Cayman Mermaid** (☎ 345/949–8100); **Jolly Roger** (☎ 345/949–8534); **Kirk Sea Tours** (☎ 345/949–6986); **Nautilus** (☎ 345/945–1355, WEB www.nautilus.ky); **Seaworld Explorer** (☎ 345/949–8534); **Spirit of Ppalu** (☎ 345/949–1234).

TAXES
DEPARTURE TAX
There is a departure tax of $12.50, included in your airline ticket.

SALES TAX
A 10% government tax is added at all accommodations. Otherwise, there is no tax on goods or services.

TAXIS
Taxis offer 24-hour island-wide service. Fares are determined by an elaborate rate structure set by the government, and although it may seem pricey for a short ride (the fare from Seven Mile Beach for four people to the airport is $15 to $25), cabbies rarely try to rip off tourists. Ask to see the chart if you want to double-check the quoted fare.
➤ CONTACTS: **A. A. Transportation** (☎ 345/949–7222); **Cayman Cab Team** (☎ 345/945–1173).

TELEPHONES
COUNTRY AND AREA CODES
For international dialing to Cayman, the area code is 345.

INTERNATIONAL CALLS
To call outside the Caymans, dial 0 + 1 + area code and number. You can call anywhere, anytime through the cable and wireless system and

local operators. To place credit-card calls, dial 110; credit card and calling card calls can be made from any public phone and most hotels. Beware though, most hotels add huge surcharges to all calls local and international, even to toll-free access numbers for prepaid phone cards.

➤ ACCESS NUMBERS: **AT&T USADirect** (☎ 800/872–2881); **MCI Direct** (☎ 800/888–8000); **Sprint Direct** (☎ 800/366–4663).

LOCAL CALLS

To make local calls (on or between any of the three islands), dial the seven-digit number.

TIPPING

At large hotels a service charge is generally included and can be anywhere from 6% to 10%; smaller establishments and some villas and condos leave tipping up to you. Although tipping is customary at restaurants, note that some automatically include 15% on the bill—so check the tab carefully. Taxi drivers expect a 10%–15% tip.

TRANSPORTATION AROUND THE CAYMAN ISLANDS

If your accommodations are along Grand Cayman's Seven Mile Beach, you can walk or bike to the shopping centers, restaurants, and entertainment spots along West Bay Road. George Town is small enough to see on foot. If you want to see Grand Cayman, renting a car for a day is an option. You can also take a taxi, though the cost might be substantial. On Cayman Brac and Little Cayman, renting a car, bike, or moped is a must if you want to see more of the islands. There is no ferry service between Grand Cayman and Little Cayman or Cayman Brac; you must fly. Nor is there ferry service between the two smaller islands.

VISITOR INFORMATION

➤ BEFORE YOU LEAVE: **Cayman Islands Department of Tourism** (✉ 6100 Blue Lagoon Dr., Suite 150, Miami, FL 33126-2085, ☎ 305/266–2300; ✉ 2 Memorial City Plaza, 820 Gessner, Suite 170, Houston, TX 77024, ☎ 713/461–1317; ✉ 420 Lexington Ave., Suite 2733, New York, NY 10170, ☎ 212/682–5582; ✉ 9525 W. Bryn Mawr Ave., Suite 160, Rosemont, IL 60018, ☎ 847/678–6446; ✉ 3440 Wilshire Blvd., Suite 1202, Los Angeles, CA 90010, ☎ 213/738–1968; ✉ 234 Eglinton Ave. E, Suite 306, Toronto, Ontario M4P 1K5, ☎ 416/485–1550; and ✉ Trevor House, 100 Brompton Rd., Knightsbridge, London SW3 1EX, ☎ 0171/491–7771; WEB www.caymanislands.ky).

➤ IN THE CAYMAN ISLANDS: **Department of Tourism** (✉ Cricket Sq. and Elgin Ave., George Town, ☎ 345/949–0623; ✉ Grand Cayman Airport, ☎ 345/949–2635; ✉ George Town Craft Market, Cardinal Ave., George Town, ☎ 345/949–8342 [open when cruise ships are in port]; ✉ kiosk at the cruise-ship dock, George Town, ☎ no phone). **Islands-wide tourist hot line** (☎ 345/949–8989). **Tourist Information and Activities Service** (☎ 345/949–6598, FAX 345/945–6222).

Updated by
Karen W.
Bressler and
Elise Rosen

Creaking, rickety boats line the waterfront; all have made the improbable journey here from Venezuela at the crack of dawn. Vendors cackle, assailing passersby with pleas to buy everything from fish to straw hats. Stout, unconcerned matrons in hair curlers haggle in three languages. Tourists fumble for their cameras, trying frantically to capture the moments on film. This is Willemstad's famed Floating Market, as astonishing a parade of humanity as any in New York or Cairo.

Despite such bustling, colorful, multiethnic sights as the Floating Market, Curaçao—the largest island of the Netherlands Antilles (38 mi/ 61 km long and 2–7½ mi/3–12 km wide)—is also the most staunchly Dutch in its culture and its architecture. Although Dutch is the official language, Papiamento is the tongue common to all the Netherland Antilles and spoken most often by locals. Curaçao's charming capital of Willemstad, its underwater park, and its dozens of little cove beaches make it ideal for exploring. Willemstad's historic city center and the island's natural harbor (Schottegat) were inscribed on UNESCO's World Heritage List in 1997, a coveted distinction reserved for the likes of the Palace of Versailles and the Taj Mahal.

Thirty-five miles (56 kilometers) north of Venezuela and 42 mi (68 km) east of Aruba, Curaçao sits below the so-called hurricane belt. The sun smiles down on the island, but it's never stiflingly hot thanks to the gentle trade winds. Water sports—including outstanding reef diving— attract enthusiasts from all over the world. Curaçao claims 38 beaches, though only a handful are long strips of silky sand; most are stretches of washed-up coral that have broken down into white or pink sand, to varying degrees of smoothness. The island is dominated by arid countryside, rocky coves, and a sprawling capital built around a natural harbor. Until recently, the economy was based on oil refining, and it catered to offshore corporations seeking tax hedges. Although tourism has become a major economic force, with millions of dollars invested in restoring old colonial landmarks and modernizing hotels, Curaçao's atmosphere remains low-key.

In Willemstad, Curaçao's "face" is a surprise—spiffy rows of brightly colored town houses that look transplanted from Holland. Although the gabled roofs and red tiles show a Dutch influence, the gay colors of the facades are peculiar to Curaçao. It's said that a popular governor suffered from migraines, a condition irritated by the color white, so all the houses were painted in colors. In the countryside, the doll-house look of the plantation houses, or *landhuizen* (literally, "land houses"), makes a cheerful contrast to the stark cacti and the austere shrubbery.

The history books still can't agree on who discovered Curaçao—one school believes it was Alonzo de Ojeda, while another says it was Amerigo Vespucci—but they agree that it was around 1499. The first Spanish settlers arrived in 1527. In 1634 the Dutch came via the Netherlands West India Company. They promptly shipped off the Spaniards and the few remaining Indians—survivors of the battles for ownership of the island, famine, and disease—to Venezuela. Eight years later Peter Stuyvesant began his rule as governor, which lasted until he left for New York around 1645. Twelve Jewish families arrived from Amsterdam in 1651, and by 1732 there was a synagogue; the present structure is the oldest synagogue still in use in the western hemisphere. Over the years the city built fortresses to defend against French and British invasions—many of those ramparts now house restaurants and hotels. The Dutch claim to Curaçao was recognized in 1815 by the Treaty of Paris. In 1954 Curaçao became an autonomous part of the Kingdom of the Netherlands, with a governor appointed by the queen, an elected parliament, and an island council.

Today Curaçao's population is derived from more than 50 nationalities in an exuberant mix of Latin, European, and African roots and with a Babel of tongues, resulting in superb restaurants and an active cultural scene. The island, like its Dutch settlers, is known for its religious tolerance, and tourists are warmly welcomed.

Lodging

Beach hotels on the island's southwestern end tend to be small, secluded, and peaceful, but are a 30- to 45-minute drive from town. Those east and west of Willemstad proper tend to be large-scale luxury resorts. In town you'll find places that cater to budget and business travelers. Most hotels provide beach or shopping shuttles. The larger ones provide kids' programs and allow children to stay in their parents' room for free or at a discounted rate. These hotels also include a Continental breakfast or a large buffet breakfast. Full American Plans aren't popular because of the abundance of good restaurants. At press time, construction had begun on two major developments: the 70-room Curaçao Howard Johnson Plaza Hotel at the Brionplein in historic downtown Otrabanda, expected to open in August 2001, and the Royal Seaquarium Curaçao, a new luxury timeshare property with 174 villas, expected to open in December 2001. The Hotel Kurá Hulanda was closed for renovations after changing hands (Jacob Dekker, creator of the Kurá Hulanda museum, is the new owner).

Rentals are popular with European visitors. Contact the **Curaçao Tourism Development Bureau** (⊠ Pietermaai 19, Willemstad, ☎ 5999/461–6000 ext. 117) at least two months in advance for a list of available properties. The Curaçao Apartments and Small Hotels Association, in conjunction with the CTDB, publishes a brochure on quality accommodations.

CATEGORY	COST*
$$$$	over $325
$$$	$225–$325
$$	$125–$225
$	under $125

All prices are for a standard double room, including 7% government tax and 12% service charge.

$$$ ⊞ **Curaçao Marriott Beach Resort & Emerald Casino.** One of the island's
★ most elegant resorts, the Marriott lies on landscaped grounds brimming with oleander, hibiscus, and palms. Its beach is beautiful; facilities include a lively pool with a swim-up bar, tennis courts, a fitness center, an alluring albeit small casino, and a 3,000-square-ft (279-square-m) ballroom. Rooms are as well-equipped as the grounds, with hair dryers, irons and ironing boards, and balconies or patios. Besides an array of water sports, including spectacular diving, there's a golf course nearby and a children's program on site. The Curaçao World Trade Center is a stone's throw away, and the hotel's conference service staff will help you coordinate business engagements. The sophisticated Emerald Grille steak house has candlelit tables, rich wood paneling, and a pianist during dinner. There are vegetarian offerings and some seafood dishes on the menu, and the bar offers a fine selection of single-malt Scotches and brandies. For upscale Northern Italian cuisine, try the pleasing Portofino restaurant. ⊠ *Piscadera Bay (Box 6003),* ☎ *5999/736–8800,* ℻ *5999/462–7502,* 🕸 *www.marriott.com. 237 rooms, 10 suites. 3 restaurants, 2 bars, air-conditioning, minibars, no-smoking rooms, room service, pool, barbershop, hair salon, 2 outdoor hot tubs, sauna, steam room, health club, 2 tennis courts, golf privileges, beach, dive shop, dock, snorkeling, windsurfing, business services, convention center, meeting rooms, car rental. AE, D, DC, MC, V. EP, FAP, MAP.*

$$$ ⊞ **Hotel Floris.** A blend of European colonial and Caribbean architecture is the framework for this luxurious, business-minded resort. It's within walking distance of the World Trade Center and also has its own well-equipped conference facilities. The meticulously designed—by famed Dutch architect Jan des Bouvrie—one-bedroom suites have kitchens, living rooms, and large porches. Solid mahogany woodwork and natural stone tiles contribute to the elegant, exclusive ambience. A tropical garden surrounds the pool and restaurant, and the beach is just across the street. ⊠ *J. F. Kennedy Blvd. (Box 6246), Piscadera Bay,* ☎ *5999/462–6111,* ℻ *5999/462–6211. 72 suites. Restaurant, air-conditioning, in-room data ports, pool, tennis court, golf privileges, beach, dive shop, business services, meeting room. AE, MC, V. EP.*

$$$ ⊞ **Sunset Waters Beach Resort.** Curaçao's first all-inclusive, this new hotel is removed from the bustle of downtown, set in a remote area on a luscious 400-yard stretch of beach. The sandy cove is the result of painstaking labor, months of digging out the rocky crags that once lined the waterfront here. Comforts on the beach now include thatched huts and lounge chairs, a beach bar and showers. The interior decor is bright and airy, with white tile floors, wooden slat ceilings, and sleeping sofas in shades of blue and mauve. Rooms have either an ocean or garden view, a terrace or patio, and direct dial phones. One small section of the shoreline is designated for nude sunbathing, and some of the guest rooms afford a full view, so do request a room elsewhere if you'd prefer less exposure. The casino debuted with slots only, but plans are to add card tables. Complimentary shuttles to town run twice a day, six days a week. Kids under 12 stay free. ⊠ *Santa Marta Bay,* ☎ *5999/864–1233,* ℻ *5999/864–1237,* 🕸 *www.sunsetwaters.com. 120 rooms. 2 restaurants, 3 bars, air-conditioning, refrigerators, pool, outdoor hot tub, miniature golf, tennis court, health club, jogging, beach, dive shop, snorkeling, boating, shop, casino, children's programs, meeting rooms, travel services, car rental. AE, D, MC, V. All-inclusive.*

$$ ⊞ **Avila Beach Hotel.** For privacy, peace, and personal service, Holland's royal family and its government ministers stay at this 200-year-old mansion overlooking the ocean. The Old World air begins in the lobby, with gilt mirrors, Asian rugs, porcelain figurines, and gas lamps. There's a room here for everyone, from budget-priced, basic rooms in

Curaçao

North Pt.

(23)

Westpunt

(21)

Westpunt

Savonet

Mt. Christoffel

(22)

(20)

San Hyronimo

Knip Bay

Jeremi Bay

Barber

Playa Lagun

Ascencion

Santa Cruz

(19)

(24)

Soto

Santa Marta Bay

San Juan Bay

Playa Porto Marie

St. Willibrordus

Boca St. Marie

Port Marie Bay

Banda Abou (Dive Area)

Daai Booi Bay

(25)

Bullen Bay

(22)

Juliana

St. Michiel

St. Michiel Bay

Central Curaçao (Di

N

0	10 miles
0	15 km

Lodging					
Avila Beach Hotel	. . . 7	Hotel Floris 2	Plaza Hotel and Casino 6	**Dining**	
Chogogo Resort	 5	Kurá Hulanda Hotel 18	Princess Beach Resort and Casino 15	Bistro Le Clochard 8	
Curaçao Marriott Beach Resort & Emerald Casino 3		Landhuis Daniel 22	Sheraton Curaçao Resort 1	Cactus Club 10	
Habitat Curaçao . . . 25		Lions Dive Hotel Curaçao 19	Sunset Waters Beach Resort 24	Fort Nassau Restaurant 20	
Holiday Beach Hotel and Casino . . . 4		Otrabanda Hotel & Casino 9		Froets Garden of Eaten 16	

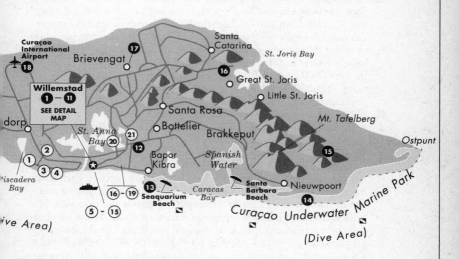

KEY

- ⚲ Beaches
- 🚢 Cruise Ship Terminal
- ◪ Dive Sites
- ❶ Exploring Sights
- ① Hotels and Restaurants

Caribbean Sea

Curaçao International Airport

Brievengat

Santa Catarina

St. Joris Bay

Great St. Joris

Little St. Joris

Willemstad
❶ — ❶❶
SEE DETAIL MAP

dorp

St. Anna Bay

Santa Rosa

Bottelier

Brakkeput

Mt. Tafelberg

Ostpunt

Bapor Kibra

Spanish Water

iscadera Bay

Seaquarium Beach

Caracas Bay

Santa Barbara Beach

Nieuwpoort

Curaçao Underwater Marine Park

ve Area)

(Dive Area)

Jaanchi's Restaurant **23**
Mambo Beach **17**
Otrabanda Bay Sight Terrace **9**
La Pergola **14**
Rijstaffel Indonesia Restaurant **21**

Scampi's **12**
Small World International Cuisine **13**
Time Out Café **11**

Exploring
Boka Tabla **21**
Christoffel Park **20**
Country House Museum **19**
Curaçao Seaquarium **13**
Curaçao Underwater Marine Park **14**

Hato Caves **18**
Landhuis Brievengat **17**
Landhuis Knip **22**
Ostrich Farm **16**
Den Paradera **15**
Senior Curaçao Liqueur Distillery . . . **12**

the original house to larger, more modern rooms in the moderately priced La Belle Alliance section to the luxurious rooms (with whirlpool tubs) in the Blues Wing. The outdoor area is adorned with statues by local artists and is often the setting for concerts by world-renowned classical musicians. The Belle Terrace restaurant, shaded by an enormous tree, serves imaginative international dishes. Saturday is Caribbean grill night, with music by mariachi or steel bands. At the Blues Seafood Restaurant and Cocktail Bar, live jazz takes center stage Thursday and Saturday evenings, and there's a terrific tapas buffet on Friday night. From your intimate booth in the covered, open-air pavilion you can watch stunning sunsets over the sea. ⊠ *Penstraat 130 (Box 791), Willemstad,* ☎ *5999/461–4377,* FAX *5999/461–1493,* WEB *www.avilahotel.com. 100 rooms, 8 suites. 3 restaurants, 2 bars, air-conditioning, in-room data ports, in-room safes, kitchenettes, refrigerators, tennis court, beach, business services, convention center, meeting rooms. AE, DC, MC, V. EP. MAP.*

$$ 🖫 **Chogogo Resort.** Vacationers who prefer bungalows over hotel rooms will appreciate Chogogo, on the island's eastern end and a two-minute walk from Jan Thiel Beach. All the accommodations are spotless and have fully equipped kitchens, TVs, CD players, and balconies or patios. It's a quiet, relaxing place with a European flair (you'll find mostly Dutch families here). ⊠ *Jan Thiel Beach,* ☎ *5999/747–2844,* FAX *5999/747–2424,* WEB *www.chogogo.com. 26 bungalows, 16 apartments, 12 studios. Restaurant, air-conditioning, fans, kitchenettes, refrigerators, pool, beach, laundry service. AE, D, MC, V. EP.*

$$ 🖫 **Habitat Curaçao.** The sprawling, beachfront Habitat is a diver's dream, with top-notch facilities and 24-hour diving. Clusters of canary yellow and red buildings are surrounded by tropical foliage and connected by stairways and winding paths. The raised pool next to the ocean affords grand vistas. Rooms are brightly outfitted with marine-life fabrics specially commissioned from local artist Nena Sanchez. Each room has a furnished terrace or balcony, a fully equipped kitchenette and a roomy bathroom with shower, but no TV. Request an ocean view (the price is the same and only 40 rooms feature one), and be aware of incidental room charges, such as the safe rental. ⊠ *Coral Estates, Rif St. Marie,* ☎ *5999/864–8800 or 800/327–6709,* FAX *5999/864–8464,* WEB *www.habitatdiveresorts.com. 56 suites, 20 2-bedroom cottages. Restaurant, bar, air-conditioning, in-room safes, pool, beach, dive shop, dock, shops, meeting rooms. AE, DC, MC, V. CP, EP.*

$$ 🖫 **Holiday Beach Hotel and Casino.** Although this is an older property, it's a reasonable choice if you're on a tight budget. Its four-story U-shape aquamarine building surrounds the pool. The lobby is spacious to permit the assembly of tour groups, and one of the island's largest casinos, Casino Royale, is right next door. The crescent beach is quite large for Curaçao and dotted with palm trees. There's a 24-hour Denny's on site, and the shops of Willemstad are within walking distance. There's also a free shuttle to and from town. ⊠ *Pater Euwensweg 31 (Box 2178), Otrabanda, Willemstad,* ☎ *5999/462–5400 or 800/444–5244,* FAX *5999/462–4397,* WEB *www.hol-beach.com. 200 rooms, 1 suite. 2 restaurants, 2 bars, pool, 2 tennis courts, health club, Ping-Pong, volleyball, beach, dive shop, casino, video games, playground, meeting rooms. AE, D, DC, MC, V. EP.*

$$ 🖫 **Kurá Hulanda Hotel.** This charming Otrabanda property is a remarkably peaceful, private place amid the city's bustle. At press time, the hotel was closed for renovations after changing hands (Jacob Dekker, creator of the Kurá Hulanda museum, is the new owner). The architectural style is Dutch Colonial; the grounds are adorned with sculptures and tropical gardens. Three museums are situated within the complex. Forty guest rooms were to open by end of summer 2001, 75 by

year's end, and 160 by end of 2002. ⊠ *Klipstraat 9, Willemstad,* ☎ *5999/462–7507 or 5999/462–7878,* FAX *5999/462–7969,* WEB *www. kurahulanda.com. 75 rooms. 3 restaurants, 2 bars, coffee shop, air-conditioning, 2 pools, health club, shops, business services, conference center. AE, MC, V. EP.*

$$ 🏨 **Lions Dive Hotel Curaçao.** This yellow-and-blue caravansary is a hop, skip, and plunge away from the Seaquarium (complimentary admission is given to guests), on ¼ mi (½ km) of private beach. Most guests are dive enthusiasts satisfied by the top-notch scuba center and the young, helpful staff. Rooms are airy, modern, and light-filled, with tile floors, wicker furnishings, and large bathrooms (showers only). French doors open onto a spacious balcony or terrace, and every room has a sea view. The Sunday-night happy hour is especially festive, with a merengue band playing poolside. By midnight, however, the only sound to be heard is the whir of your room's air-conditioner. Dive packages are offered with Ocean Encounters. ⊠ *Bapor Kibra,* ☎ *5999/461–8100,* FAX *5999/ 461–8200,* WEB *www.lionsdive.com. 72 rooms. Restaurant, bar, air-conditioning, fans, in-room safes, pool, health club, beach, dive shop, dock, windsurfing, boating. AE, DC, MC, V. EP.*

$$ 🏨 **Plaza Hotel and Casino.** PLEASE DON'T TOUCH THE PASSING SHIPS is the slogan at the island's first high-rise hotel and the only hotel in the world with marine collision insurance. The ships do come close: the structure is built right into the massive walls of a 17th-century fort at the entrance to Willemstad's harbor. You give up beachfront (you have beach privileges at Seaquarium, and there's a shuttle) for walking access to the city's center. Consequently, it's a business traveler's oasis (Internet access, fax machines, copiers, mobile phone rentals, and Microsoft Office applications are available in the business center), though there are loads of activities to satisfy vacationers, too. The lobby is laden with antiques, and a winding lagoon and waterfall give the hotel the air of an elegant colonial outpost. The hotel is just steps away from the strip of waterfront restaurants tucked into the Waterfort Arches. At press time, plans were in the works for construction of a new Plaza Hotel behind the Seaquarium. ⊠ *Plaza Piar (Box 813), Willemstad,* ☎ *5999/461–2500,* FAX *5999/461–6543,* WEB *www.plazahotelcura-cao.com. 205 rooms, 19 suites. 2 restaurants, 3 bars, air-conditioning, in-room safes, no-smoking rooms, room service, pool, dive shop, shops, casino, business services, meeting rooms, car rental. AE, MC, V. CP.*

$$ 🏨 **Princess Beach Resort and Casino.** You can't beat the location on one of Curaçao's most beautiful beaches, right near the Seaquarium. The hotel has been purchased by Lionstone Hotels & Resorts, owners of the Sheraton, and was recently renovated. Roughly half the rooms have fine ocean views, and some are accessible to people with disabilities. Amenities include cable TV, radios, direct-dial phones, coffeemakers, and balconies or patios. The path to the rooms is through lush tropical grounds; be forewarned, however, you may have quite a hike. This is a high-energy place, with lively happy hours, popular theme buffet dinners, and a slew of sports activities and nightly entertainment. The newest restaurant, Don Luigi, serves traditional Italian food in an air-conditioned dining room or on a terrace overlooking the crystal Caribbean. ⊠ *Martin Luther King Blvd. 8, Willemstad,* ☎ *5999/736–7888,* FAX *5999/461–4131,* WEB *www.princessbeach.com. 310 rooms, 9 suites, 22 timeshare units. 3 restaurants, 4 bars, air-conditioning, in-room data ports, in-room safes, no-smoking rooms, room service, 2 pools, hair salon, 2 tennis courts, gym, volleyball, beach, dive shop, dock, snorkeling, shops, casino, baby-sitting, children's programs, dry cleaning, laundry service, business services, meeting rooms, conference center, travel services, car rental.. AE, DC, MC, V. CP, EP, FAP, MAP.*

\$\$ ⊞ **Sheraton Curaçao Resort.** Bask in the glorious Caribbean sun on
★ one of the Sheraton's two private beaches, or create a splash at the free-
form pool, which creates the illusion of spilling over onto the shoreline. Retreat to your spacious room, with comforts to suit vacationers
and business travelers alike: a balcony with ocean or island view, satellite TV, direct-dial phone, coffeemaker, iron and ironing board. Some
rooms also have facilities for people with disabilities. On the executive floor, rooms feature fax machines and data ports. Action seekers
will find everything at their fingertips: water sports, a top-notch dive
center, tennis and beach volleyball. Night owls may find their niche at
the Las Vegas–style casino. Want to venture into town and get a feel
for the local life? The hotel is just five minutes from the shops, sights,
and eateries of Willemstad. Catch the free shuttle, twice daily (except
Sundays). When you get back, savor a meal at the tasty Calypso Terrace (international cuisine) or La Piazzetta (Italian). ✉ *J. F. Kennedy
Blvd. (Box 2133), Piscadera Bay,* ☎ *5999/462–5000,* FAX *5999/462–
5846,* WEB *www.ccresort.com. 184 rooms, 13 suites. 3 restaurants, 3
bars, air-conditioning, in-room safes, no-smoking rooms, room service,
2 pools, barbershop, hair salon, outdoor hot tub, spa, miniature golf,
golf privileges, 2 tennis courts, health club, volleyball, beach, dive
shop, dock, snorkeling, windsurfing, boating, jet skiing, waterskiing,
fishing, bookstore, shops, casino, baby-sitting, laundry service, business services, meeting rooms, travel services, car rental, free parking.
AE, DC, MC, V. EP, FAP, MAP.*

\$ ⊞ **Landhuis Daniel.** Dating from 1711, this mustard plantation house
with white colonnades and red-tile roof was never a part of a farm but,
rather, served as an inn. The property, near the narrow center of the
island, has a pool, dive shop, and a French-Caribbean restaurant, serving dishes made with organic fruits, vegetables, and herbs, grown right
on the plantation. The intriguing menu varies according to the seasonal
crop yield. Rooms are tiny but clean, with basic furnishings, and three
of them now have air-conditioning. You'll feel far more comfortable
in the original house; the row of claustrophobic rooms in the former
slave quarters has even less charm than a stateside motel. Join in the
fun at the poolside barbecue on Fridays, Saturdays, and Sundays. ✉
Weg Naar Westpunt, ☎ FAX *5999/864–8400,* WEB *www.best-caribbean.
com/landhuisdaniel. 8 rooms. Restaurant, bar, fans, pool, dive shop.
AE, MC, V. EP, MAP.*

\$ ⊞ **Otrabanda Hotel & Casino.** In the historic Otrabanda, this little hotel
offers superior value for the money. Standard rooms are cramped but
appealing, with terrific harbor views, rattan furnishings, and paintings
of country scenes. The most attractive and roomiest are those tucked
under the peaked roof. For a good meal and a good view, stop by the
Otrabanda Bay Sight Terrace. ✉ *Breedestraat, Otrabanda, Willemstad,*
☎ *5999/462–7400,* FAX *5999/462–7299. 42 rooms, 3 suites. Restaurant, bar, air-conditioning, pool, shops, casino, baby-sitting. AE, DC,
MC, V. CP.*

Dining

Dine beneath the boughs of magnificent old trees, in the romantic gloom
of wine cellars in renovated plantation houses, or on the ramparts of
18th-century forts. Curaçaoans partake of some of the best Indonesian food in the Caribbean, and you'll also find fine French, Swiss, Dutch,
and Swedish fare.

What to Wear

Dress in restaurants is almost always casual (though beachwear isn't
acceptable). Some of the resort dining rooms and nicer restaurants re-

quire that men wear jackets, especially in high season; ask when you make reservations.

CATEGORY	COST*
$$$$	over $30
$$$	$20–$30
$$	$10–$20
$	under $10

*per person for a main course at dinner

AMERICAN

$$ ✕ **Cactus Club.** A grove of aloes and cacti greets you in the courtyard of this Caribbean version of Bennigan's. The inside is subdued: faux Tiffany lamps, hanging plants, ceiling fans. Food is cheap and filling, including fettuccine Alfredo, fajitas, buffalo wings, Cajun snapper, and burgers. It's predictably popular with both locals and homesick Americans. There's also a branch at the Seaquarium (☏ 5999/465–1265). ✉ *Van Staverenweg 6, Willemstad,* ☏ *5999/737–1600. DC, MC, V.*

ASIAN

$$$ ✕ **Rijsttafel Indonesia Restaurant.** An antique rickshaw at the entrance
★   sets the mood. Exotic delicacies make up the traditional Indonesian banquet called rijsttafel, where some 16 to 25 dishes are set buffet style around you. Smaller appetites should opt for the *nasi rames,* with only eight dishes. A vegetarian rijsttafel is also available. An à la carte menu includes fried noodles and combination meat-and-fish platters. The walls are hung with batiks, *ikat* (a form of Indonesian fabric) tapestries, basketwork, copper pots, and *wajang* dolls and shadow puppets. ✉ *Mercurriusstraat 13–15, Saliña,* ☏ *5999/461–2606. AE, DC, MC, V. No lunch Sun.*

CARIBBEAN

$$ ✕ **Jaanchi's Restaurant.** This sheltered, open-air restaurant has lunches of mouthwatering Curaçaoan dishes. The specialty is a hefty platter of fresh seafood with sides of potatoes or funchi and vegetables. Curaçaoans joke that Jaanchi's iguana soup is "so strong it could resurrect the dead"—truth is, it tastes like chicken soup, only better. The place usually closes at 6:30 PM but will stay open later if you call ahead. If you can, call in advance to find out whether they expect huge tour groups that day; the food and service may deteriorate. An ATM is right outside the front door; a rarity on this side of the island. ✉ *Westpunt 15, Westpunt,* ☏ *5999/864–0126. AE, DC, MC, V.*

CONTINENTAL

$$$ ✕ **Bistro Le Clochard.** This romantic gem is built into the 19th-century
★   Riffort—an oasis of arched entryways, exposed brickwork, wood beams, and lace curtains. Cocktails and hors d'oeuvres (and dinner, if you choose) are served on the Waterside Terrace, with its view of the floating bridge and harbor. The French and Swiss dishes are consistently well prepared. Begin with the scrumptious, mildly spicy banana soup with chicken. Then try the specialty *La Potence,* a variation of boeuf Bourguignonne in which you dip skewered cubes of juicy tenderloin into tasty sauces surrounding a platter of rice, or the chicken in cream of curry sauce. Leave room for the heavenly homemade Swiss Toblerone chocolate mousse. ✉ *Harbourside Terrace, Riffort, Otrabanda, Willemstad,* ☏ *5999/462–5666,* ᴡᴇʙ *bistroleclochard.com. Reservations essential. AE, DC, MC, V. No lunch Sat. Closed Sun.*

$$$ ✕ **Fort Nassau Restaurant.** On a hill above Willemstad, the restau-
★   rant is built into an 18th-century fort with a 360-degree view. Go for a drink in the breezy Battery Terrace bar or dine in air-conditioned com-

fort beside huge bay windows. The variegated tile work throughout is stunning. Delicious highlights of the diverse menu include fillet of salmon glazed with cane sugar and served with stewed leek, saffron rice, and salsa and grilled sirloin steak with garlic mashed potatoes. Desserts here are delectable. ✉ *Schottengatweg 82, near Juliana Bridge, Willemstad,* ☎ *5999/461–3450 or 5999/461–3086. Reservations essential. AE, D, DC, MC, V. No lunch weekends.*

ECLECTIC

$$$ ✕ **Froets Garden of Eaten.** This fun, outdoor garden eatery across from the Princess Beach Resort is popular because of its tasty food and prix-fixe menu. Appetizers are all one price, as are all entrées and desserts. Try a salad of shrub celery with deep-fried Camembert covered with a sauce of walnuts and honey, followed by a ragoût of seafood with spinach tagliatelle. The *bolo de preimu,* a local plum cake with cinnamon sauce and lime sorbet, is wonderful. ✉ *Koraal Spechtweg 11,* ☎ *5999/465–7565. AE, MC, V. No lunch.*

$$$ ✕ **Small World International Cuisine.** For a tasty, pleasant dining experience, try this eclectic eatery, whose outdoor deck juts out over the ★ Caribbean. The menu is broken down into French, Spanish, Creole, and Chinese sections. *Gambas al ajillo* (shrimp in garlic sauce served with flavorful veggies and rice) is a savory choice, as is the salmon fillet papillote (the salmon is cooked in its own juices and wrapped in a foil pouch with carrots and onions). If you prefer indoor seating, request the nifty glass-top table with the built-in terrarium. ✉ *Waterfort Boogjes 18–19, Willemstad,* ☎ *5999/465–5575. AE, DC, MC, V.*

$$ ✕ **Mambo Beach.** On the west end of Seaquarium Beach, this hip, open-air bar and grill, spread over the sand, serves good food for breakfast, lunch, and dinner. Baguettes dominate the lunch menu; steaks, fresh seafood, and pasta fill the dinner menu. Creative offerings include smoked marlin with sun-dried tomatoes and salmon fried in couscous. This is a fantastic place to watch the sun set, but don't forget your insect repellent. ✉ *Seaquarium Beach,* ☎ *5999/461–8999. AE, MC, V.*

$$ ✕ **Otrabanda Bay Sight Terrace.** The best feature of this low-key eatery in the Otrabanda Hotel & Casino is its remarkable setting overlooking Santa Anna Bay with a full view of the colorful town-house facades. As you dine, you're so close to the passing ships, it seems you can almost touch them. The food here is fairly good—and fairly priced. One favorite is the keshi yena. ✉ *Breedestraat, Otrabanda, Willemstad,* ☎ *5999/462–7400. AE, MC, V.*

$ ✕ **Time Out Café.** Tucked into an alley in the shopping heartland of Punda, this low-key, outdoor eatery serves up light bites like tuna sandwiches and *tostis* (toasted cheese), as well as the omnipresent "catch of the day" option. There's no late night scene here, but drop by for a beer and a pool game before venturing out. Closing time is at 9:30 PM in low season, midnight in high season. ✉ *Keukenplein 8,* ☎ *5999/465–6633. No credit cards.*

ITALIAN

$$$ ✕ **La Pergola.** Built into the stuccoed walls of the Waterfort Arches, with huge picture windows fronting the rambunctious sea, copper pots hanging everywhere, and a pretty pink-and-white arbor wound with bunches of grapes, La Pergola offers creative variations on Italian standards and no fewer than 14 pastas and 11 pizza options. ✉ *Waterfort Archesboog 12, Willemstad,* ☎ *5999/461–3482. AE, DC, MC, V. No lunch Sun.*

SEAFOOD

$$ ✕ **Scampi's.** Feast on fish, fish, and more fish as you contemplate the vast Caribbean sea from your outdoor, front-row seat on water's edge.

Or enjoy a happy hour cocktail (like the signature Red Sunset—lemon rum with 7-Up) at the bar under a thatched hut. ⊠ *Waterfort Archesboog 7, Willemstad,* ☎ *5999/465–0769. AE, DC, MC, V.*

Beaches

Curaçao has some 38 beaches, many of them quite striking. Those along the southeast coast are often rocky (wear your flip-flops or reef shoes into the water), but in the west you'll find stretches of smooth sand at the shoreline. Rent a Jeep, motor scooter, or heavy-treaded car, ask your hotel to pack a picnic basket, and go exploring. You'll discover the joy of inlets: tiny bays marked by craggy cliffs, exotic trees, and small pebbly or sandy beaches. The government recently added rest rooms and snack bars to several public beaches, making them more inviting.

Among the hotels with the best beaches are the Sheraton Curaçao, the Curaçao Marriott Beach Resort, the Princess Beach Resort, Sunset Waters Beach Resort, and the Lions Dive Beach Resort. No matter where you're staying, beach hopping to other hotels can be fun. Nonguests are supposed to pay the hotels a beach fee, but often there's no one to collect.

Daai Booi Bay. Good for swimming and snorkeling, this sandy, public west shore crescent has a snack bar and washrooms. The narrow paved road to it (follow signs from the church of St. Willibrordus) is flanked by thick lush trees and huge organ-pipe cacti. Admission is $3 per car.

Knip Bay. At this protected cove, flanked by sheer cliffs, you'll find two beaches. Big (Groot) Knip has huts and hammocks for shade, and crystal-clear turquoise waters that are perfect for swimming. Little (Kleine) Knip is shaded with trees, but these are manchineels (raindrops or dewdrops dripping off their leaves can cause blisters), so steer clear of them. Both beaches have alluring white sand, changing facilities, and snack bars. On Sunday, families come here to barbecue, and sometimes there's live music. To get here, take the road to the Knip Land House, then turn right. Signs will direct you.

Playa Lagun. This northwestern cove is caught between gunmetal gray cliffs, which beautifully frame the Caribbean blue. Couples can steal quiet moments here on weekday mornings, but locals flock here on weekends. Canoe trips, dive sessions, and swimming lessons are available through the dive shop on the beach. Cognoscenti know this is one of the best places to snorkel.

Playa Porto Marie. A sandy stretch on a beautiful bay on the island's west coast, this public beach's calm, clear waters make it a great diving site, and food and drinks are served in a shaded beach pavilion. Admission is about $2 weekdays, $2.25 weekends and holidays.

Santa Barbara. To reach this popular family beach on the eastern tip, you can drive through one of Curaçao's toniest neighborhoods, Spanish Water, where gleaming white yachts replace humble fishing fleets. The beach has changing facilities and a snack bar but charges an admission fee, usually around $2.25 per person, but up to $7 per person on weekends. Around the bend, Caracas Bay is a popular dive site, with a sunken ship so close to the surface that snorkelers can view it clearly.

Seaquarium Beach. You'll pay a fee ($2.25 per person) to enter here, but the array of amenities (rest rooms, showers, boutiques, watersports center, snack bar, restaurants with beach bars, thatched shelters and palm trees for shade, security patrols) on this 1,600-ft (490-m) manmade sandy beach and the calm waters protected by a carefully placed breakwater are well worth it.

Westpunt. On the northwest tip of the island, Westpunt is shady in the morning. It doesn't have much sand, but you can sit on a shaded rock ledge. The Playa Forti Bar & Restaurant offers refreshing soft drinks and beer. Take in the view of the boats in the marina and watch the divers jump from the high cliff. Water-sports enthusiasts, take note: The All West Dive Shop is on the beach here.

Outdoor Activities and Sports

Participant Sports

For the full gamut of activities in one spot, nature buffs (especially bird-watchers), families, and adventure-seekers may want to visit the newest park, **Caracas Bay Island** (☎ 5999/747–0777). Things to do here include hiking, mountain biking, horseback riding, canoeing, kayaking, windsurfing, jetskiing, and snorkeling. There's a fully equipped dive shop, a restaurant, and a bar on premises. Admission to the scenic area is $3; activities cost extra.

BOATING, SAILING, AND WINDSURFING

Top Watersports Curaçao (✉ Seaquarium Beach, ☎ 5999/461–7343) rents smaller craft like Sunfish, as well as canoes, snorkel gear, and floating mats. It's also the island's top windsurfing center, offering both rentals and instruction. This section of coast tends to be calmer than most, making it ideal for beginners, although the breezes are sufficiently steady to keep experienced windsurfers on their toes.

FISHING

There are surprisingly few charter boats available for deep-sea fishing, but the small 18-ft *Hemingway* (☎ 5999/888–8086) offers Penn International, senator, and spinning reels as well as an experienced guide. It can accommodate no more than two people (one person $45, two $70) but can negotiate fairly deep water where shark, wahoo, tuna, barracuda, sailfish, and marlin are abundant. They'll pick up at your hotel.

GOLF

In the mood to hit the green? Try the **Blue Bay Curaçao Golf and Beach Resort** (✉ Landhuis Blauw, ☎ 5999/868–1755). The 18-hole, par-72 course, which opened in December 1999, beckons experts and novices alike. Facilities include a golf shop, locker rooms, and a snack bar. Greens fees range $65–$105 per person, and you can rent carts, clubs, and shoes. If you'd like to drive your game to a new level, take a lesson from the house pro ($30 for a half hour) or head for the driving range and putting green ($10 per person for unlimited range balls). At press time, plans were in the works to build a luxury resort at the site; currently studios and bungalows are available for rental, starting at $75 per night. **Curaçao Golf and Squash Club** (✉ Wilhelmenalaan, ☎ 5999/737–3590) welcomes visitors daily 8–8 in high season. The 9-hole course is a challenge because of the stiff trade winds and the sand greens. Greens fees are $20 for 18 holes.

HORSEBACK RIDING

Ashari's Ranch (☎ 5999/869–7755) offers rides for all levels. Trail rides on gentle, smooth-gaited "paseo" horses are available at **Christoffel Park** (☎ 5999/864–0363). Prices range from $25 to $70; make reservations well in advance.

SCUBA DIVING AND SNORKELING

The **Curaçao Underwater Marine Park** includes almost a third of the island's southern diving waters. Scuba divers and snorkelers can enjoy more than 12½ mi (20 km) of protected reefs and shores, with normal visibility from 60 to 150 ft (18 to 45 m). With water temperatures ranging from 75°F to 82°F (24°C to 28°C), wet suits are generally unnecessary. No coral collecting, spearfishing, or littering is allowed. An exciting wreck to explore is the SS *Oranje Nassau,* which ran aground more than 90 years ago. The other two main diving areas are **Banda Abou,** along the southwest coast between West Point and St. Marie, and along **central Curaçao,** which stretches between Bullen Bay to the Princess Beach Resort. The north coast is not recommended for diving because of the dangerously rough conditions found there.

Introductory scuba resort courses run about $60–$75. Full certification courses average $200 for three days and $325 for the advanced five-day version. Virtually every operator below charges $33–$35 for a single-tank dive and $55–$60 for a two-tank dive. Snorkel gear commonly rents for $12–$15 per day. For detailed information on dive sites and operators, call 800/328–7222 and ask for the brochure "Take the Plunge in Curaçao" or pick up the *DIP–Curaçao's Official Dive Guide* for a nominal cost from the CTDB.

The following operators can help get you started: **Caribbean Sea Sports** at the Marriott Beach Resort (✉ JFK Blvd., Box 6269, ☎ 5999/462–2620) takes divers to popular nearby sites including the *Superior Producer* wreck. **Curaçao Seascape** (✉ JFK Blvd., ☎ 5999/462–5000) offers shore dives and open water certification programs. The closest operation to the famous Mushroom Forest dive site, **Easy Divers Curaçao** (✉ Sunset Waters Beach Resort, Santa Marta Bay, ☎ 5999/864–2822), will customize dive trips for you, or you can take part in one of the daily two-tank dives from their 38-ft boat. PADI instruction is available. The dive center of **Habitat Curaçao** (✉ Coral Estates, Rif St. Marie, ☎ 5999/864–8800) offers everything from a two-day, three-dive introductory course to underwater video and photography courses ($275–$400). **Peter Hughes Ocean Encounters** (✉ Princess Beach Resort, Dr. Martin Luther King Blvd. 8, ☎ 5999/468–8991; Lions Dive Hotel, Bapor Kibra, ☎ 5999/461–8131) offers a variety of shore and boat dives and packages, as well as certified PADI instruction.

TENNIS

If you're not staying at a hotel with a tennis court, try the **Santa Catherina Sports Complex** (✉ Club Seru Coral, Koraal Partier 10, ☎ 5999/767–7028). Court time costs $20 an hour.

Spectator Sports

Centro Deportivo Curaçao (✉ Bonamweg 49, ☎ 5999/737–6620), a modern and comfortable stadium about 10 minutes from town, hosts soccer matches and baseball games March–October. It's open daily 9:30–12:30 and 1–6.

Shopping

Curaçao offers a number of exciting buys, from Dutch classics like embroidered linens, blue delft china, and clogs to local crafts (you can find some marvelous ceramic work). There are also fine local painters, most of whom work in the landscape mode. If you're looking for bargains on Swiss watches, cosmetics, cameras, crystal, perfumes, Nike or Reebok sneakers, or electronic equipment, do some comparison shopping back home and come armed with a list of prices. Willemstad is no longer a free port: there's now a tax, so prices are higher.

Areas

Most shops are concentrated in **Willemstad**'s Punda within about a six-block area. The main shopping streets are Heerenstraat, Breedestraat, and Madurostraat. Heerenstraat and Gomezplein are pedestrian malls, closed to traffic, and their roadbeds have been raised to sidewalk level and covered with pink inlaid tiles. **Riffort Village** is the talk of the town: a large shopping-entertainment complex under development in Otrabanda along prime waterfront space between the floating bridge and the Mega Pier.

Specialty Items

ART

Gallery Eighty Six (✉ Trompstraat, Punda, ☎ 5999/461–3417) features works by local artists and occasionally those of South Americans and Africans. **Kas di Alma Blou** (✉ De Rouvilleweg 67, ☎ 5999/462–8896) is in a gorgeous 19th-century indigo town house and presents the top local artists; you'll find shimmering landscapes, dazzling photographs, ceramics, even African-inspired Carnival masks.

CIGARS

The sweet smell of success permeates **Cigar Emporium** (✉ Gomezplein, ☎ 5999/465–3955), where you'll find the largest selection of cigars on the island, including H. Upmann, Romeo & Julietta, and Montecristo. Visit the climate-controlled cedar cigar room.

CLOTHES

Left your gym shoes at home? Step into **Athlete's Foot** (✉ Heerenstraat 10, ☎ 5999/461–3239) and you'll be up and running in no time. At the Willemstad branch of **Batik Exclusive** (✉ Handelskaade 6, ☎ 5999/461–0262), you can outfit yourself in vibrant Caribbean colors. The shop sells batik sarongs for adults and kids ($21), knapsacks, bathing suits, dresses, halter tops, and gift items, including mobiles with aquatic designs and hand puppets. **Benetton** (✉ Madurostraat 4, ☎ 5999/461–4619; Curaçao International Airport, ☎ 5999/869–6054, and other locations) has winter stock in July and summer stock in December, all of it 20% off the retail price. At **Big Low Center** (✉ Heerenstraat 6, ☎ 5999/461–1680) you'll find T-shirts galore. Special deals include three regular tees or two embroidered tees for $15. **Clog Dance** (✉ De Rouvilleweg 9B, ☎ 5999/462–3280) has Dutch clogs and fashions, cheeses, tulips, delftware, and chocolate. **Fendi** (✉ Breedestraat 9, ☎ 5999/461–2618) sells its merchandise for 25% less than in the United States.

FOODSTUFFS

Toko Zuikertuintje (✉ Zuikertuintjeweg, ☎ 5999/737–0188), a supermarket built on the site of the original 17th-century Zuikertuintje Landhuis, is where most of the local elite shop for all sorts of European and Dutch delicacies. Perfect on a sunny day or on an evening harbor-front stroll, **Vienna Ice Café** (✉ Handelskaade 14, Punda, ☎ 5999/736–1086) serves up scrumptious homemade ice cream. Indulge your sweet tooth with such flavors as green apple, mango, and rum plum. At press time, plans were to add an outdoor café offering salads, local food, grilled steaks, salmon, and more.

GIFTS

Boolchand's (✉ Heerenstraat 4B, ☎ 5999/461–2798) handles an interesting variety of merchandise behind a facade of red-and-white-checkered tiles. Stock up here on electronics, jewelry, Swarovski crystal, Swiss watches, and cameras. For a truly rewarding gift search, stop by **Galeria Den Tapara** (✉ De Ruyterkade Z/N, ☎ 5999/461–0766), where several merchants sell their wares under the same roof. Unique crafts include musician statuettes made from coconut shells, wooden rain sticks (pray for a shower by slowly turning the stick upside down, producing the soft sound of raindrops), incense, African cloths, textiles, and instruments. **Julius L. Penha & Sons** (⊠ Heerenstraat 1, ☎ 5999/461–2266), in front of the Pontoon Bridge, sells French perfumes and an array of cosmetics. At **Little Switzerland** (⊠ Breedestraat 44, ☎ 5999/461–2111) you'll find jewelry, watches, crystal, china, and leather goods at significant savings. The very first gift shop to open on Curaçao more than 60 years ago, **Warenhaus Van Der Ree** (⊠ Breedestraat 5, ☎ 5999/461–1645) still offers quite a selection of novelties. Look for stainless-steel wind chimes, dolls, frames, hammocks, Dutch cheese, and hand-painted whistles.

HANDICRAFTS

Arawak Craft Factory (⊠ Cruise Terminal, Otrabanda, ☎ 5999/462–7249) has a factory showroom of locally made crafts. You can purchase a variety of tiles, plates, pots, and tiny replicas of land houses. A special walkway allows you to watch the artisans at work and ask questions. **Bamali** (⊠ Breedestraat, Punda 2, ☎ 5999/461–2258) sells Indonesian batik clothing, leather bags, and charming handicrafts. **Caribbean Handcraft Inc.** (⊠ Kaya Kakina 8, Jan Thiel, ☎ 5999/767–1171) offers an elaborate assortment of locally handcrafted souvenirs. **Landhuis Groot Santa Martha** (⊠ Santa Martha, ☎ 5999/864–1559) is where artisans with disabilities fashion handicrafts. An open house is held every last Sunday of the month, when visitors can browse and buy. **Open Atelier** (⊠ F. D. Rooseveltweg 443, ☎ 5999/868–6027), just past Santa Maria on the road to the airport, promotes Curaçaoan artists' work, with an emphasis on watercolors.

JEWELRY

Freeport (⊠ Heerenstraat 13, ☎ 5999/461–9500) has a fine selection of duty-free watches and jewelry (lines include David Yurman, Christofle, Movado, and Maurice Lacroix) attracting shoppers who pour in from the cruise ships that dock nearby. **Gandelman** (⊠ Breedestraat 35, ☎ 5999/461–1854; ⊠ Marriott Beach Resort, Piscadera Bay, ☎ 5999/462–8386) has watches by Cartier and Rolex, leather goods by Prima Classe, and Baccarat and Daum crystal. **La Zahav N. V.** (⊠ Curaçao International Airport, ☎ 5999/868–9594) sells gold jewelry—with or without diamonds, rubies, and emeralds—at true discount prices. The shop is in the airport transit hall, just at the top of the staircase.

LINENS

New Amsterdam (⊠ Gomezplein 14, ☎ 5999/461–2437; ⊠ Breedestraat 29, ☎ 5999/461–3239) is the place to price hand-embroidered tablecloths, napkins, and pillowcases, as well as Italian gold and Hummel figurines.

PERFUMES AND COSMETICS

Perfume Palace (⊠ Braastraat 23, ☎ 5999/461–7462) carries all the major brands of cosmetics and perfume.

Nightlife

Friday is a big night out, with rollicking happy hours—most with live music—at several hotels, most notably the Holiday Beach Hotel and the Avila Beach Hotel. And while it might surprise you, Sunday night revelry into the wee hours is an island tradition. A museum by day, Landhuis Brievengat turns into a party paradise after dark—the night owls flock here Wednesday through Sunday for live music in the outdoor courtyard from 8 PM until dawn. Check with the tourist board for the schedule of events or pick up a copy of the weekly free entertainment listings, *K-Pasa,* available at most restaurants and hotels.

BARS

Live jazz electrifies the pier at the **Blues Bar & Restaurant** (⊠ Avila Beach Hotel, Penstraat 130, ☎ 5999/461–4377) Thursdays (*the* night to go) and Saturdays. **De Heeren** (⊠ Suikertuimtjeweg [Shopping Center], ☎ 5999/736–0491) is a great spot to grab a locally brewed Amstel Brite and meet a happy blend of tourists and transplanted Dutch locals. Meaning "Fort Alertness," **Fort Waakzaamheid Tavern & Restaurant** (⊠ Seru Domi, ☎ 5999/462–3633) is a pleasant place for a cocktail day or night, complete with a panoramic view of the island. By day **Hook's Hut** (⊠ Next to Marriott Beach Resort, Piscadera Bay, ☎ 5999/462–6575) is a local beach hangout. The daily happy hour from 5 to 6 kicks off a lively nighttime scene. The outdoor pool table is not in great shape, but it's one of the few bar tables around. There's a $3 flat fee per half hour; pay the bartender.

Anchor yourself at a dockside table at the **International Café** (⊠ Handelskaade 13, ☎ 5999/465–1056), and sip frozen cappuccinos as the ships pass by in Santa Anna Bay. Or, loosen up with a cocktail—specialties include the Blue Curaçao Margarita and the Pink Panther (Baileys, Amaretto, coconut liqueur, grenadine, Ponche Crema, coconut cream, and pineapple juice). **Keizershof,** a complex of renovated heritage buildings at the corner of Otrabanda's Hoogstraat and Rouvilleweg, has two restaurants and a café in addition to dancing under the stars at **Keizershof Terrace** (☎ 5999/462–3493) and sing-alongs at **Pianobar Kalimba** (☎ 5999/462–3583). Sunday Happy Hours are hot at **Rumors** (⊠ Lions Dive Hotel, Bapor Kibra, ☎ 5999/461–7555), featuring some of the best rock and reggae bands.

CASINOS

Gambling seems almost an afterthought on Curaçao. Although casinos are a staple at most hotels, even the biggest have only a few card tables, and some are limited to slot machines. The following hotels have casinos that are open daily 1 PM–4 AM: the Marriott Beach Resort & Emerald Casino, the Sheraton Curaçao, the Plaza Hotel, Holiday Beach Hotel, the Kurá Hulanda Hotel, and the Princess Beach. Of these, only the Marriott and Sheraton casinos even approach a small Vegas hotel in terms of variety of games and Bond-like elegance.

DANCE AND MUSIC CLUBS

Baya Beach (⊠ Caracas Bay Island Park, ☎ 5999/747–0777) is a festive newcomer luring guests with its pulsating blend of salsa, merengue, and hip-hop. Saturday nights are the liveliest. **De Tropen** (⊠ SBN Doormanweg 37, ☎ 5999/736–6880) is a trendy nightspot with the latest music, occasionally live. **Mambo Beach Club** (☎ 5999/461–8999), an open-air bar on Seaquarium Beach, draws a hip, young crowd that flocks here to dance the night away under the stars. Popular with tourists and locals throughout the week, insiders know this as *the* place to be on Sunday night; come in time for happy hour and warm up for the nightlong party with some beach volleyball.

Exploring Curaçao

Willemstad

What does the capital of Curaçao have in common with New York City? Broadway, for one thing. Here it's called Breedestraat, but the origin is the same. Dutch settlers came here in the 1630s, the same period when they sailed through the Narrows to Manhattan, bringing with them original red-tile roofs, first used on the trade ships as ballast and later incorporated into the architecture of Willemstad.

Curaçao
Museum . . . **11**

Floating
Market **6**

Ft.
Amsterdam . . **2**

Kurá
Hulanda
Museum . . . **10**

Maritime
Museum **8**

Mikveh Israel-
Emanuel
Synagogue . . **3**

Old Market
(Marche) **4**

Plaza Piar . . . **1**

Queen
Emma
Bridge **5**

Queen
Juliana
Bridge **9**

Scharloo **7**

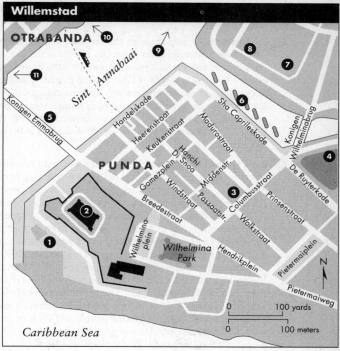

The city is cut in two by Santa Anna Bay. On one side is the Punda—crammed with shops, restaurants, monuments, and markets—and on the other is the less touristy Otrabanda (literally, the "other side"), with lots of narrow, winding streets full of private homes notable for their picturesque gables and Dutch-influenced designs. There are three ways to cross the bay: drive or take a taxi over the Juliana Bridge; traverse the Queen Emma Pontoon Bridge on foot; or ride the free ferry, which runs when the Pontoon Bridge is open for passing ships. All the major hotels outside town offer free shuttle service to town once or twice daily. Shuttles coming from the Otrabanda side leave you at Riffort. From here it's a short walk north to the foot of the pontoon bridge. Shuttles coming from the Punda side leave you near the main entrance to Ft. Amsterdam.

Numbers in the margin correspond to points of interest on the Willemstad map.

SIGHTS TO SEE

11 Curaçao Museum. Housed in a century-old plantation house, this small museum is filled with artifacts, paintings, and antiques that trace the island's history. This is also the venue for art exhibitions that visit the island. ✉ *V. Leeuwenhoekstraat, Otrabanda,* ☎ *5999/462–3873.* ✉ *$3.* ⊙ *Weekdays 9–noon and 2–5, Sun. 10–4.*

6 Floating Market. Each morning dozens of Venezuelan schooners laden with tropical fruits and vegetables arrive at this bustling market on the Punda side of the city. Mangoes, papayas, and exotic vegetables vie for space with freshly caught fish and herbs and spices. The buying is best at 6:30 AM—too early for many people on vacation—but there's plenty of action throughout the afternoon. Any produce bought here, however, should be thoroughly washed or peeled before eating. ⊠ *Sha Caprileskade.*

② Ft. Amsterdam. Step through the archway and enter another century. The entire structure dates from the 1700s, when it was the center of the city and the island's most important fort. Now it houses the governor's residence, the Fort Church, the ministry, and government offices. Outside the entrance a series of majestic gnarled *wayaka* trees are fancifully carved with androgynous human forms—the work of local artist Mac Alberto. ⊠ *Foot of Queen Emma Bridge,* ☎ *5999/461–1139.* ≊ *$1.75 (to church museum only).* ☉ *Weekdays 9–noon and 2–5, Sunday service, 10.*

★ ⑩ Kurá Hulanda Museum. Here you can step into a full-size reconstruction of a slave ship's hold and read gut-wrenching firsthand accounts of the era. Or you can see fascinating fossils and bone artifacts from Africa in the *Origin of Man,* another of the main exhibits. Opened in April 1999, this museum is housed in restored 19th-century buildings and is the largest of its kind in the Caribbean. It was founded by Dr. Jacob Gelt Dekker, a Netherlands native who lives in a house next door and whose extensive world travels, fascination with African history and culture, and business savvy made it all possible. Also on site, the Kurá Hulanda Conference Center features state-of-the-art facilities for lectures, seminars, and tutorials. The Jacob Gelt Dekker Institute for Advanced Cultural Studies is an international think tank and learning exchange center dedicated to the people and ideas of the Atlantic Rim, with an emphasis on African studies and the African diaspora. ⊠ *Klipstraat 9, Otrabanda,* ☎ *5999/462–1400,* 𝖶𝖤𝖡 *www.kurahulanda. com.* ≊ *$5.* ☉ *Mon.–Sat. 10–5.*

★ ⑧ Maritime Museum. The 40-odd chronological exhibits at this museum truly give you a sense of Curaçao's maritime history, using ship models, maps, nautical charts, navigational equipment, and audiovisual displays. Topics explored along the way include the development of Willemstad as a trading city, Curaçao's role as a contraband hub, the explosion of the *De Alphen* in 1776, the slave trade, the development of steam navigation, the rise of cruise tourism, and the role of the Dutch navy on the island. The third floor hosts temporary exhibits, and the museum also offers a two-hour guided tour on its "water bus" through Curaçao's harbor—a route familiar to traders, smugglers, and pirates. When you're ready for a break, drop anchor at the Harbor Café or browse through the souvenir shop. ⊠ *Van der Brandhofstraat 7, Scharloo,* ☎ *5999/465–2327.* ≊ *$6 museum only; $11 museum and harbor tour.* ☉ *Daily 10–5.*

③ Mikveh Israel-Emanuel Synagogue. The temple, the oldest still in use in the western hemisphere, is one of Curaçao's most important sights and draws 20,000 visitors a year. A unique feature is the brilliant white sand covering the synagogue floor, a remembrance of Moses leading his people through the desert and of the diaspora. The Hebrew letters on the four pillars signify the names of the Four Mothers of Israel: Sarah, Rebecca, Rachel, and Leah. The synagogue was dedicated in 1732 by the Jewish community that originally came from Amsterdam in 1651 to establish a new congregation and to seize opportunities that weren't generally afforded them in Europe at that time. They were later joined by Jews from Portugal and Spain fleeing persecution from the Inquisition (via Amsterdam). A number of Jews also came from Brazil, after the Portuguese reconquest of Recife—a Dutch trading post—raised fears that the Inquisition would be introduced there, too. By the early 1700s, more than 2,000 Jews resided on Curaçao. The fascinating **Jewish Cultural Museum** (☎ *5999/461–1633*), in the back, displays Jewish antiques (including a set of circumcision instruments) and artifacts collected from all over the world. English and Hebrew services are held Friday at 6:30 PM and Saturday at 10 AM. Men who attend should wear a jacket and tie. ⊠ *Hanchi Di Snoa 29, Punda,* ☎ *5999/461–1633.* 🖃 *Small donation expected in synagogue; Jewish Cultural Museum: $2.* ⊙ *Weekdays 9–11:45 and 2:30–4:45.*

❹ **Old Market (Marche).** Local women prepare hearty Antillean lunches at the Old Market behind the post office. Enjoy such Curaçaoan specialties as funchi, keshi yena, goat stew, fried fish, peas and rice, and fried plantains. Small portions cost $2.50; large plates for $7 are a feast for two. ⊠ *De Ruyterkade.*

❶ **Plaza Piar.** This plaza is dedicated to Manuel Piar, a native Curaçaoan who fought for the independence of Venezuela under the liberator Simón Bolívar. On one side of the plaza is the **Waterfort,** a bastion dating from 1634. The original cannons are still positioned in the battlements. The foundation, however, now forms the walls of the Plaza Hotel.

❺ **Queen Emma Bridge.** This bridge is affectionately called the Swinging Old Lady by the natives. If you're standing on the Otrabanda side, take a few moments to scan Curaçao's multicolor face, on the other side of Santa Anna Bay. If you wait long enough, the bridge will swing open (at least 30 times a day) to let seagoing ships pass through. The original bridge, built in 1888, was the brainchild of the American consul Leonard Burlington Smith, who made a mint off the tolls he charged for using it: 2¢ per person for those wearing shoes, free to those crossing barefoot. Today it's free to everyone.

❾ **Queen Juliana Bridge.** This 1,625-ft-long (497-m-long) bridge was completed in 1974 and stands 200 ft (61 m) above water—a great vantage point for photos of the city. It's the bridge you drive over to cross to the other side of the city, and although the route is time-consuming (and more expensive if you're going by taxi), the view is worth it. At every hour of the day, the sun casts a different tint, creating an ever-changing panorama; the nighttime view is breathtaking.

❼ **Scharloo.** The Wilhelmina Drawbridge connects Punda with the once-flourishing district of Scharloo, where the early Jewish merchants first built stately homes. The end of the district closest to Kleine Werf is now a red-light district and is pretty run-down, but the rest of the area is well worth a visit. The architecture along Scharlooweg (much of it from the 17th century) is intriguing, and, happily, many of the structures that had become dilapidated have been meticulously renovated.

The Rest of the Island

The Weg Maar Santa Cruz road through the village of Soto winds to the island's northwest tip through landscape that Georgia O'Keeffe might have painted—towering cacti, flamboyant dried shrubbery, and aluminum-roof houses. Throughout this *cunucu,* or countryside, you'll see fishermen hauling nets, women pounding cornmeal, and an occasional donkey blocking traffic. Land houses, large plantation houses from centuries past, dot the countryside, though most are closed to the public. To explore the island's eastern side, take the coastal road—Martin Luther King Boulevard—from Willemstad about 2 mi (3 km) to Bapor Kibra. Here you'll find the Seaquarium and the Underwater Park.

Numbers in the margin correspond to points of interest on the Curaçao map.

SIGHTS TO SEE

㉑ **Boka Tabla.** At Boka Tabla, the sea has carved a magnificent grotto. Safely tucked in the back, you can watch and listen to the waves crashing against the rocks. Several of the surrounding minicaverns serve as nesting places; watch flocks of parakeets emerge in formation, magnificent hawks soar and dip, and gulls dive-bomb for lunch. ✉ *Westpunt Hwy., just past village of Soto.*

★ ⓴ **Christoffel Park.** This fantastic 4,450-acre garden and wildlife preserve centers on the towering Mt. Christoffel. There are eight hiking trails in the park, which take anywhere from 20 minutes to 2 ½ hours to complete. You can drive your own car (if it has heavy-treaded tires) or rent a four-wheel-drive vehicle with an accompanying guide (NAf150 for up to five passengers). Start out early (by 10 AM the park starts to feel like a sauna), and if you're going solo, first study the *Excursion Guide to Christoffel Park,* sold at the front desk of the Savonet Museum. It outlines the various routes and identifies the flora and fauna found here. There's a 20-mi (32-km) network of roads, and no matter what route you take, you'll be treated to views of hilly fields full of prickly pear cacti, divi-divi trees, bushy-haired palms, and exotic flowers that bloom unpredictably after November showers. There are also caves—the strong at heart will revel in the rustling of bat wings and the sight of scuttling scorpion spiders (not poisonous)—and ancient Indian drawings. Spectacular birdwatching is abundant, and experts lead the way twice daily.

Watch for goats and small wildlife that might cross your path or dart in front of your car, and consider yourself lucky if you see any of the elusive, protected white-tail deer. The whip snakes and minute silver snakes you may encounter aren't poisonous. White-tail hawks may be seen on the green route, white orchids and crownlike passionflowers on the yellow route. Climbing the 1,239-ft (379-m) **Mt. Christoffel** on foot is an exhilarating challenge to anyone who hasn't grown up scaling the Alps. The park's guidebook claims the round-trip will take an hour, and Curaçaoan adolescent boys do make a sport of racing up and down, but it's really more like two (sweaty) hours from the mountain's base for a reasonably fit person who's not an expert hiker. The view from the peak, however, *is* thrilling—a panorama that includes Santa Marta Bay and the tabletop mountain of St. Hironimus. On a clear day you can even see the mountain ranges of Venezuela, Bonaire, and Aruba.

You might also enjoy one of the park's fascinating tours. Every Friday morning at 10, park rangers lead a 2½-mi (4-km) nature hike, discoursing on the indigenous flora and fauna. The fee ($9) includes an iguana presentation and a soft drink. Jeep tours ($100 for 1–5 people) go off the beaten track, raising plenty of dust. The 15-minute deer-watching expeditions (with no more than eight people to prevent startling the skittish creatures) track the herd of 150–200 small white-tail deer in the park for $6 per person (Saturdays and Sundays, beginning at 4:30 PM). ✉ *Savonet,* ☎ *5999/864-0363.* 🎟 *Park and museum $13.50, museum only $3.* ☉ *Mon.–Sat. 8–4, Sun. 6–3; last admission 1 hr before closing.*

⓳ **Country House Museum.** This thatched-roof cottage is a living museum demonstrating country life as it was in the 19th century. It's filled with antique furniture, farm implements, and clothing typical of colonial life. Out back is a minifarm with a vegetable garden, penned donkeys, and caged parrots, eagles, and iguanas. Look closely at the fence—it's made of living cacti. There's also a snack bar. A festival featuring live music and local crafts takes place here on the first Sunday of each month. ✉ *Dokterstuin 27,* ☎ *5999/864-2742.* 🎟 *$1.50.* ☉ *Tues.–Fri. 9–4, weekends 9–5.*

★ ⓒ ⑬ **Curaçao Seaquarium.** The Seaquarium is *the* place to see the island's underwater treasures without getting your feet wet. It's the world's only public aquarium where sea creatures are raised and cultivated naturally. Where else can you hand-feed a shark (or watch a diver do it)? The **Animal Encounters** section consists of a broad, 12-ft-deep (4-m-deep) open-water enclosure that brings you face to face with a variety of jaws. Snorkelers and divers are welcome to swim freely with stingrays, tarpon, groupers, and such. Diving instruction and equipment are part of the package; it's a thrilling introduction to the sport in a controlled environment, and, in fact, up to 75% of participants have never tried diving before. If shark feeding isn't your cup of tea, there's an underwater observatory. The cost is $55 for divers, $35 for snorkelers, which includes admission to the Seaquarium, training, use of equipment, and food for the fish, turtles, and sharks. Reservations for Animal Encounters must be made 24 hours in advance.

You can spend several hours mesmerized by the 46 freshwater tanks full of more than 400 varieties of fish and vegetation found in the waters around Curaçao. The Maritime Awareness Center offers hands-on discovery of the underworld wonders of coral reefs. In the minitheater, a high-tech, three-dimensional slide show makes you feel as if you're actually in the ocean. There are also glass-bottom-boat tours, feeding shows, and a viewing platform overlooking the wreck of the steamship SS *Oranje Nassau,* which sank in 1906. You can stop by the on-site snack bar and restaurant or browse in the souvenir shop. A nearby beach is well suited to novice swimmers and children. ⊠ *Bapor Kibra,* ☎ *5999/461–6666.* ⌷ *$13.25.* ⊙ *Daily 8:30–6.*

⑭ **Curaçao Underwater Marine Park.** About 12½ mi (20 km) of untouched coral reefs off the southeast shore have been granted the status of a national park. Mooring buoys placed at the most interesting dive sites provide safe anchoring and prevent damage to the reef. Several sunken ships lie awaiting visitors in the deep. The park stretches along the south shore from the Princess Beach Resort in Willemstad to the island's eastern tip.

⑱ **Hato Caves.** Hour-long guided tours wind down into various chambers to the water pools, a "voodoo" chamber, a wishing well, fruit bats' sleeping quarters, and Curaçao Falls, guarded by a limestone "dragon." Hidden lights illuminate the limestone formations (use your imagination, and you'll see such fantastic shapes as the Sleeping Giant, the Madonna, and the Woolly Mammoth) and gravel walkways. This is one of the better Caribbean caves open to the public, but keep in mind that there are 49 steep steps to reach the entrance, and the cave itself is dank and hot (though they've put electric fans in some areas to provide relief). ⊠ *Head northwest toward airport, take right onto Gosieweg, follow loop right onto Schottegatweg, take another right onto Jan Norduynweg, a final right onto Rooseveltweg, and follow signs,* ☎ *5999/ 868–0379.* ⌷ *$6.25.* ⊙ *Daily 10–5.*

⑰ **Landhuis Brievengat.** This mustard-color plantation house is a fine example of a home from the island's past. You can see the original kitchen still intact, the 18-inch-thick walls, fine antiques, and the watchtowers once used for lovers' trysts. The restaurant, open only on Wednesday and Friday, serves a tasty Indonesian rijsttafel. Friday night a party is held on the wide wraparound terrace, with bands and plenty to drink ($6 cover charge). On the last Sunday of the month (6 PM–7:30 PM), this estate holds an open house with crafts demonstrations and folkloric shows. ⊠ *15-min drive northeast of Willemstad, near Centro Deportivo stadium,* ☎ *5999/737–8344.* ⌷ *$1.* ⊙ *Mon.–Sat. 9:15–12:15 and 3–6.*

㉒ **Landhuis Knip.** In terms of slave population, this was once the island's largest plantation. It therefore comes as no surprise that the slave revolt took place here in 1795. The renovated plantation house near the island's western tip is filled with period furnishings, clothing, and household items. ⊠ *Weg Naar Santa Cruz,* ☎ *5999/864–0244.* 🎫 *$2.* ⊙ *Weekdays 9–4, weekends 10–5.*

🦢 ⑯ **Ostrich Farm.** If you (and the kids) are ready to stick your neck out for an adventure, visit one of the largest ostrich breeding farms outside Africa and the only one in the Caribbean. Every hour guided tours (reservations are essential) show the creatures' complete development from egg to mature bird. At the Restaurant Zambezi you can sample local ostrich specialties and other African dishes (reservations are suggested). Be sure to visit the Art of Africa shop, featuring crafts from Zimbabwe and South Africa including handmade wall hangings, exotic leather products, and wood carvings. ⊠ *Groot St. Joris,* ☎ *5999/747–2777; 5999/ 747–2777 to restaurant,* WEB *www.ostrichfarm.net.* 🎫 *$7.* ⊙ *Tues.– Sun. 8–5.*

⑮ **Den Paradera.** Dazzle your senses at this organic herb garden, where local plants are cataloged according to their traditional use in folk medicine. As part of owner Dinah Veeris's research, she interviewed dozens of older islanders about the plants and their use in treating everything from diabetes to stomach ulcers. A reconstructed settlement at the rear of the property consists of small huts with life-size rag dolls depicting traditional folkloric scenes. Top off your visit with a special refreshing beverage (made of aloe, ginger, and lemon). A shop sells natural perfumes and potpourri. ⊠ *Seru Grandi Kavel 105A, Banda'ariba,* ☎ *5999/767–5608.* 🎫 *$5.65 (with guided tour), $4.25 (without guided tour). Call ahead for tour appointment.* ⊙ *Daily 9–6.*

⑫ **Senior Curaçao Liqueur Distillery.** The charming 17th-century Landhuis Chobolobo (just outside Willemstad) is where the famed Curaçao liqueur, made from the peels of the bitter Iranha orange, is produced. Don't expect a massive factory—it's just a small showroom in an open-air foyer. There are no guides, but delightful old hand-painted posters explain the distillation, and you'll be graciously offered samples in assorted flavors. If you're interested in buying—the orange-flavored chocolate liqueur is delicious over ice cream—you can choose from a complete selection, bottled in a variety of fascinating shapes, including Dutch ceramic houses. ⊠ *Landhuis Chobolobo, Saliña Arriba,* ☎ *5999/461–3526.* 🎫 *Free.* ⊙ *Weekdays 8–noon and 1–5.*

CURAÇAO A TO Z

To research prices, get advice from other travelers, and book travel arrangements, visit www.fodors.com.

AIR TRAVEL

Air ALM, Curaçao's national airline, offers frequent service from Miami and Atlanta. For Atlanta departures Air ALM has connecting service to most U.S. gateways with Delta. Its Visit Caribbean Pass allows easy interisland travel. American Airlines flies direct daily from Miami. E Liner Airways has interisland service, including sightseeing and beach tours of Aruba and Bonaire. Guyana Air has nonstop service from New York. KLM flies direct from Amsterdam (to fly from Australia, New Zealand, or the United Kingdom, consider flying to Amsterdam for this flight to Curaçao).

➤ AIRLINES AND CONTACTS: **Air ALM** (☎ 5999/869–5533); **American Airlines** (☎ 5999/869–5707); **Guyana Air** (☎ 5999/461–3033 or 5999/869–5533); **KLM** (☎ 5999/465–2747).

AIRPORTS

The airport has car rental facilities, duty free shops, and a restaurant. It takes about 20 minutes to get to the hotels in Willemstad by taxi.

➤ AIRPORT INFORMATION: **Curaçao International Airport** (☎ no phone) has car rental facilities, duty free shops, and a restaurant.

BUSINESS HOURS

BANKS

Banks are open weekdays 8–3:30 or 8–11:30 and 1:30–4; the airport branch has extended hours: 8–8 Monday–Saturday and 9–4 on Sunday.

POST OFFICES

Post office hours are 7:30–noon and 1:30–5 weekdays. The Groot Kwartier branch is open 7–7 on weekdays and 7–3 on Saturday.

SHOPS

Some shops still remain shuttered on Monday. Many are open Monday–Saturday 8–noon and 2–6. Some stay open during the lunch hour and on Sunday and holidays when cruise ships are in port.

CAR RENTALS

You can rent a car from any of the major car agencies at the airport or have one delivered free to your hotel. Rates range from about $60 a day for a Toyota Tercel to about $75 for a four-door sedan or four-wheel-drive vehicle; add 6% tax and required $10 daily insurance.

➤ MAJOR AGENCIES: **Avis** (☎ 5999/461–1255 or 800/331–1212); **Budget** (☎ 5999/868–3466 or 800/472–3325); **Dollar** (☎ 5999/461–3144); **National Car Rental** (☎ 5999/868–3489 or 800/328–4567).

CAR TRAVEL

If you're planning to do country driving or rough it through Christoffel Park, a four-wheel-drive vehicle is best. All you need is a valid U.S., Canadian, or British driver's license.

GASOLINE

Gas prices in Curaçao are about NaFl 1.46 per liter for unleaded; NaFl 1.42 for regular; and NaFl1.50 for diesel. There are many gas stations in the Willemstad area as well as in the suburban areas, including two on the main road as you head to the western tip of the island.

RULES OF THE ROAD

Driving in the Netherlands Antilles is the same as in the U.S., on the right-hand side of the road. Right turns on red are prohibited. Local laws require drivers and passengers to wear seat belts and motorcyclists to wear helmets. Children under 4 years of age should be in child safety seats; if older they should ride in the back seat.

ELECTRICITY

The current is 110–130 volts/50 cycles, which is compatible with such small North American appliances as electric razors and blow dryers.

EMBASSIES

➤ CANADA: **Consulate of Canada** (✉ Plaza Jojo Correa 2–4, ☎ 5999/466–1295).

➤ UNITED KINGDOM: **British Consulate** (✉ Jan Sofat 38, ☎ 5999/747–3322).

➤ UNITED STATES: **United States Consulate** (✉ J B Gorsiraweg 1, ☎ 5999/461–3066).

EMERGENCIES
➤ AMBULANCE AND FIRE: Dial ☎ 112. Dial ☎ 8888 for on-call dentists and ☎ 1111 for on-call doctors.
➤ HOSPITALS: **St. Elisabeth's Hospital** (✉ Breedestraat 193, ☎ 5999/462–4900 or 5999/462–5100).
➤ PHARMACIES: The centrally located **Botica Popular** (✉ Madurostraat 15, ☎ 5999/461–1269).
➤ POLICE: Dial ☎ 114.
➤ SCUBA-DIVING EMERGENCIES: **St. Elisabeth's Hospital** (✉ Breedestraat 193, ☎ 5999/462–4900 or 5999/462–5100) is equipped with a hyperbaric chamber.
➤ SEA EMERGENCIES: Dial (☎ 5999/463–7911).

ETIQUETTE AND BEHAVIOR
To guarantee a smile, wish someone *bon dia* (good day) or offer a warm *masha danki* (thank you very much) after someone has performed a service. Dutch culture is stronger on Curaçao than on many Antillean islands, so the island has a European flavor (note that topless sunbathing is tolerated at some hotels).

FESTIVALS AND SEASONAL EVENTS
Carnival lasts longer on Curaçao than on many islands: the revelries begin at New Year's and continue until midnight the day before Ash Wednesday. The highlight is the Tumba Festival (dates vary), a four-day musical event featuring fierce competition between local musicians for the honor of having their piece selected as the official road march during parades. Easter Monday's Seú Folklore Parade features groups celebrating the harvest in traditional costumes. The Curaçao Salsa Festival is held in June, July, or August and attracts international performers and audiences. October sees the Curaçao International Jazz Festival.

HEALTH
Mosquitoes are a presence on Curaçao, at least during the rainy season. The bad news is that the rainy season falls between October and February, coinciding with the tourist high season. To be safe, keep perfume to a minimum, use insect repellent before dining alfresco, and spray your hotel room at night—especially if you've opened a window. If you plan to go into the water, beware of long-spine sea urchins, which can be painful if you come in contact with them.

Don't eat any of the little green applelike fruits (they even smell like apples) of the manchineel tree: they're poisonous. In fact, steer clear of the trees altogether; raindrops or dewdrops dripping off the leaves can blister your skin. If contact does occur, rinse the affected area with water and, in extreme cases, get medical attention. Usually the burning sensation won't last longer than two hours.

HOLIDAYS
Public holidays for 2002 are: New Year's Day, Good Friday (Apr. 13), Easter Monday (Apr. 16), the Queen's Birthday (not Beatrix, but rather her mother, Juliana; Apr. 30), Labor Day (May 1), Curaçao Flag Day (July 2), and Christmas.

LANGUAGE
Dutch is the official language, but the vernacular is Papiamento—a mixture of Dutch, African, French, Portuguese, Spanish, and English. One theory holds that the language developed during the 18th century as a mode of communication between land owners and their slaves. These days English is studied by schoolchildren as well as Spanish and, of

course, Dutch, and anyone involved with tourism generally speaks English.

MAIL AND SHIPPING

There are post offices in Punda, Otrabanda, and Groot Kwartier on Schottegatweg (Ring Road), as well as small branches at the International Trade Center and the airport. Some hotels sell stamps and have letter drops; you can also buy stamps at some bookstores. An airmail letter to the United States, Canada, or the United Kingdom costs NAf2.25, a postcard NAf.90.

MONEY MATTERS

Prices quoted throughout this chapter are in U.S. dollars unless otherwise indicated.

ATMS

The airport has an ATM (it dispenses U.S. dollars) as do many bank branches.

CURRENCY

U.S. dollars—in cash or traveler's checks—are accepted nearly everywhere, so there's no need to worry about exchanging money. However, you may need small change for pay phones, cigarettes, or soda machines. The currency in the Netherlands Antilles is the florin (also called the guilder) and is indicated by fl or NAf on price tags. The florin is very stable against the U.S. dollar; the official rate of exchange at press time was NAf1.77 to US$1.

➤ BANKS: **ABN-AMRO Bank** (☎ 5999/763–8000); **Antilles Banking Corporation** (☎ 5999/461–2822); **Maduro & Curiel's Bank** (☎ 5999/466–1100).

PASSPORTS AND VISAS

U.S. and Canadian citizens need either a valid passport or a birth certificate with a raised seal along with a government-authorized photo ID. Citizens of Australia, New Zealand, and the United Kingdom must produce a passport. All visitors must show an ongoing or return ticket.

SAFETY

Crime is on the increase (but not rampant) in Curaçao, so common-sense rules apply. Lock rental cars, and don't leave valuables in the car. Use the in-room safe or leave valuables at the front desk of your hotel, and never leave bags unattended at the airport, on tours, or on the beach.

SIGHTSEEING TOURS

BOAT TOURS

Many sailboats and motorboats offer sunset cruises and daylong snorkel and picnic trips to Klein Curaçao, the "clothes-optional" island between Curaçao and Bonaire. Prices run $50–$65. Or for a unique vantage point, soak up the local marine life from one of Seaworld Explorer/Atlantis Adventures' semi-submersibles. An hour-long tour of the beautiful coral reefs is $33.

➤ CONTACTS: *Bounty* (☎ 5999/560–1887) is a 90-ft schooner. *Insulinde* (☎ 5999/560–1340) is a 120-ft Dutch sailing ketch. *Mermaid* (☎ 5999/560–1530) is a 66-ft motor yacht. *Seaworld Explorer/Atlantis Adventures* (☎ 5999/462–8833).

ORIENTATION

Casper Tours has very amiable service. For around $30 per person you'll be escorted around the island in an air-conditioned van, with stops at the Juliana Bridge, the salt pans, Knip Bay for a swim, the grotto at Boca Tabla, and Jaanchi's Restaurant for lunch (not included in price). Does Travel & Cadushi Tours takes you around in an air-conditioned coach with a knowledgeable guide. They can also arrange short hops to Aruba and Bonaire. Peter Trips offers full-day island tours ($37, meal not included) departing from the hotels Friday, Saturday, and Sunday at 9 AM, with visits to many points of interest, including Scharloo, Slavebridge, Jan Thiel, Fort Nassau, and Knip Bay. Or you can opt for 3½-hour tours of the island's east (Monday at 3 PM, $19) or west side (Tuesday and Thursday at 3 PM, $21). Rumba Tours offers shopping tours and "your imagination" tours (you design the itinerary), in addition to the traditional guided tours. Taber Tours offers a three-hour East Tour ($13) that includes the Curaçao Liqueur Factory at Landhuis Chobolobo, the Curaçao Museum, and the Bloempot shopping center. Day trips to Aruba ($175) and Bonaire ($165) are also available.

➤ CONTACTS: **Casper Tours** (✉ Matiustraat 3, ☎ 5999/465–3010); **Does Travel & Cadushi Tours** (✉ Caracasbaaiweg 164, ☎ 5999/461–1626); **Peter Trips** (☎ 5999/465–2703); **Rumba Tours** (✉ Hofi Abao 50, ☎ 5999/562–8619); **Taber Tours** (✉ Dokweg, ☎ 5999/737–6637).

SPECIAL INTEREST

For personalized history and nature tours contact Dornasol Tours; half-day tours run $25, and full-day tours are $40 per person. Dutch Dream Adventures targets the action-seeker with canoe safaris, mountain biking, and Jeep tours. The Ostrich Express visits one of the largest ostrich farms outside Africa and gives you a 60-minute guided tour. Kids enjoy the chance to hold an egg, stroke a fluffy day-old chick, and sit atop a fully grown ostrich for an unusual photo op. The price is $8.50 for adults, $5.60 for children 2–14, with pick-up at your hotel. Wild Curaçao offers expertly guided ecotourism adventures highlighting the island's flora and fauna, with stops at nature preserves, caves, salt lakes, and more. Or keep track of your surroundings as you visit key historic sites aboard the Willemstad Trolley Train.

➤ CONTACTS: **Christoffel National Park** (☎ 5999/864–0363); **Dornasol Tours** (☎ 5999/468–2735); **Dutch Dream Adventures** (☎ 5999/465–3575]); **Ostrich Express** (☎ 5999/560–1276); **Wild Curaçao** (☎ 5999/561–0027); **Willemstad Trolley Train** (☎ 5999/462–8833).

WALKING TOURS

Walking tours of historic Otrabanda, focusing on the unique architecture of this old section of town, are led by architect Anko van der Woude or art history expert Jenny Smit every Thursday (reservations are suggested), leaving from the central clock at Brionplein at 5:15 PM. Jopie Hart offers a walking tour that emphasizes the sociocultural aspects of Otrabanda; it begins at 5:15 PM on Wednesday and departs from the clock at Brionplein. Mention ahead to your tour leader that you speak English.

➤ CONTACTS: **Anko van der Woude/Jenny Smit** (☎ 5999/461–3554); **Jopie Hart** (☎ 5999/767–3798).

TAXES

DEPARTURE TAX

The airport international departure tax is NAf35 (or $20), and the interisland departure tax is NAf10 (about $5.65).

SALES TAX

Hotels add a 12% service charge to the bill and collect a 7% government room tax; restaurants add 10%–15%.

VALUE ADDED TAX (V.A.T.)

Most shops and restaurants also tack on 6% ABB tax (a value-added tax aimed specifically at tourists).

TAXIS

Drivers have an official tariff chart, with fares from the airport to Willemstad and the nearby beach hotels running about $10–$15 and those to hotels at the island's western end about $25–$40. Since there are no meters, you should confirm the fare with the driver before departure. There's an additional 25% surcharge after 11 PM. Taxis are readily available at hotels; in other cases, call Central Dispatch.

➤ CONTACTS: **Central Dispatch** (☎ 5999/869–0752).

TELEPHONES

Phone service through the hotel operators in Curaçao is slow, but direct-dial service, both on-island and to elsewhere in the world, is fast and clear. Hotel operators will put the call through for you, but if you make a collect call, do check immediately that the hotel does not charge you as well.

COUNTRY AND AREA CODES

To call Curaçao direct from the United States, dial 011–5999 plus the number in Curaçao.

INTERNATIONAL CALLS

AT&T Direct service is available by calling 001/800/872–2881, which connects you with an AT&T International operator, but it's nearly impossible from pay phones, and your hotel will likely add a surcharge.

LOCAL CALLS

To place a local call on the island, dial the seven-digit local number. Pay phones charge NAf.50 for a local call—far cheaper than what a hotel will charge you.

TIPPING

As service is usually included, tipping at restaurants isn't expected, though if you found the staff exemplary, you can add another 5%–10% to the bill. Taxi drivers normally receive a 10% gratuity, but this is at your discretion. Tip porters and bellmen about $1 a bag, the hotel housekeeping staff $2–$3 per day.

VISITOR INFORMATION

➤ BEFORE YOU LEAVE: **Curaçao Tourist Board** (✉ 475 Park Ave. S, Suite 2000, New York, NY 10016, ☎ 212/683–7660 or 800/270–3350; ✉ 330 Biscayne Blvd., Suite 808, Miami, FL 33132, ☎ 305/374–5811).
➤ IN CURAÇAO: **Curaçao Tourism Development Bureau** (✉ Pietermaai 19, Willemstad, ☎ 5999/461–6000 ext. 117, WEB www.curacao.com; at the ✉ Curaçao International Airport, ☎ 5999/868–6789).

9 DOMINICA

Updated by
Carla Armour

In the early hours of the morning—after the day's first rainfall has seemingly washed the whole world clean—the sun slides up into the sky over the mountains and under the arch of a faint rainbow. Aroused by the light, birds begin their wildly orchestrated chorus—nature's alarm clock. In breezes heavy with the scents of damp earth and lemongrass and not yet fully warmed by the sun, leaves quiver and sparkle with raindrops and dew and the promise of another beautiful day.

"Isle of beauty, isle of splendor," rings the first line of the national anthem of the Commonwealth of Dominica. Indeed, the intensity of the unspoiled beauty and splendor of this isle, dubbed "the nature island of the Caribbean," is truly inspiring as it turns and twists, towers to mountain crests, then tumbles to falls and valleys. The weather is equally dramatic: torrential rains, dazzling sunshine, and, above all, rainbows are likely to greet you in the course of a day.

In the center of the Caribbean archipelago, wedged between the two French islands of Gaudeloupe to the north and Martinique to the south, Dominica (pronounced dom-in-*ee*-ka) is a wild place. Wild Orchids, Anthurium lilies, Ferns, Heliconias, and myriad fruit trees sprout profusely. Water chutes cascade down cliff faces at roadside. Much of the interior is still covered by luxuriant rain forest and remains inaccessible by road. Here everything grows more intensely: greener, brighter, and bigger. The ideal environment that gave the early Caribs (the region's original inhabitants) a natural fortress against the European settlers also kept Dominica from being colonized like other Caribbean islands. Today the rugged northeast is reserved as home to the last survivors of the Caribs, as well as to some of their traditions and tales.

Dominica—just 29 mi (47 km) long and 16 mi (26 km) wide—is a former British colony; having attained its independence in November 1978, it now has a seat in the United Nations and the central Caribbean's only Natural World Heritage Site. Its capital is Roseau (pronounced rose-*oh*); the official language is English, although most locals communicate with each other in Creole; roads are driven on the left; family and place names are a melange of English, Carib, and French; and the religion is predominantly Catholic. The economy is still heavily dependent on agriculture—further testimony to the fertility of the soil and the bounty of Dominica's nature.

A newcomer on the tourism scene in the Caribbean, Dominica has no major hotel chains. With a population of just 70,000, and her National Forestry Division spending the last 50 years preserving and designating more national forests, and marine reserves, and parks, per capita, than almost anywhere on earth, Dominica is "the Alternative Caribbean." Dominicans realize the island's vast tourism potential, and development is on the rise. Ecotourism is at the forefront, mountain lodges and cottage retreats have been developed, and classic architecture is being restored.

It's an ideal place to go if you want to really get away and challenge yourself—hike, bike, trek, spot birds and butterflies in the rain forest; explore waterfalls and discover the world's largest boiling lake; experience a vibrant culture in Dominica's traditions; kayak, dive, snorkel, or sail in marine reserves; or go out in search of the many resident whale and dolphin species. From the Elfin Woodlands and dense luxuriant rainforest to the therapeutic geothermal springs and world-class dive sites that mirror her terrestrial terrain, to experience Dominica is really to know the earth as it was created.

Lodging

Dominica is an alternative Caribbean destination: Places to stay, amenities offered, and prices asked are as varied as the island's landscapes. Here you'll find intimate city hotels, mountain retreats, secluded bungalows, plantation houses, and seaside cottages. Most properties offer packages with dives, hikes, tours, and/or meal plans included. All the usual amenities abound: on-site restaurants and bars, in-room phones, cable-equipped TVs, air-conditioning, and private bathrooms. You will find many properties advertise winter rates with either a discount for summer or longer stays.

CATEGORY	COST*
$$$$	over $150
$$$	$125–$150
$$	$100–$125
$	under $100

All prices are for a standard double room, excluding 5% tax, 5% sales tax, and 10%–15% service charge.

$$$$ ★ 🏨 **Castle Comfort Lodge.** The wrought-iron gate and homey appearance of this property camouflage the hub of activity facing the sea. Once inside, there's no mistaking its purpose: the location on the water's edge, the Dive Dominica boats anchored out in the Caribbean, the telltale dive log, and the divers in the hot tub with mask imprints on their foreheads give it all away. This Lodge offers dive packages with everything included: dives, transfers, meals, accommodation, taxes, and all (extra nights are sold on a MAP basis only). Rooms are in two buildings: one directly on the sea, the other at the back of the property. Each has white rattan furnishings, fish-pattern fabrics, a telephone, a TV, and a veranda. Bountiful home-cooked meals are served on a large, airy terrace. Nondivers can spend the morning by the pool or kayaking in the bay. Inland adventures and nature walks can also be arranged. ✉ *1 mi (1½ km) south of Roseau (Box 2253, Roseau),* ☎ *767/448–2188 or 888/414–7626,* ℻ *767/448–6088,* 🌐 *www.divedominica.com. 15 rooms. Restaurant, pool, air-conditioning, fans, pool, hot tub, dive shop, boating. Closed September. AE, MC, V. MAP.*

$$$$ ★ 🏨 **Picard Beach Cottage Resort.** Eighteen hardwood cottages are nestled along Dominica's longest golden sand beach, fringing the remnants of an old coconut plantation. The warm and charming staff here live up to the words on the unpretentious promotional leaflet, which says

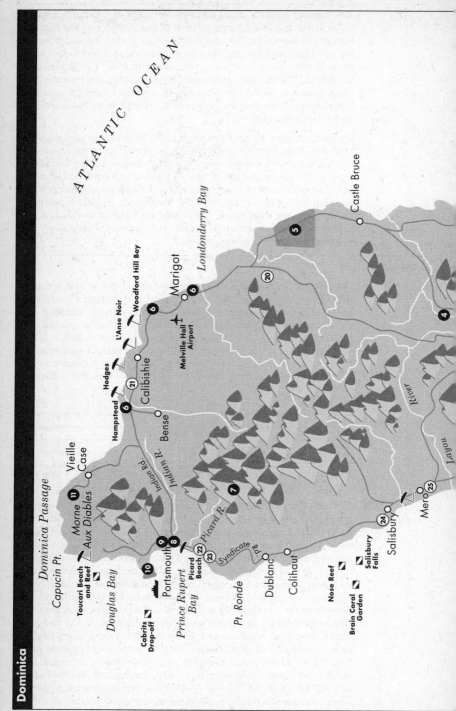

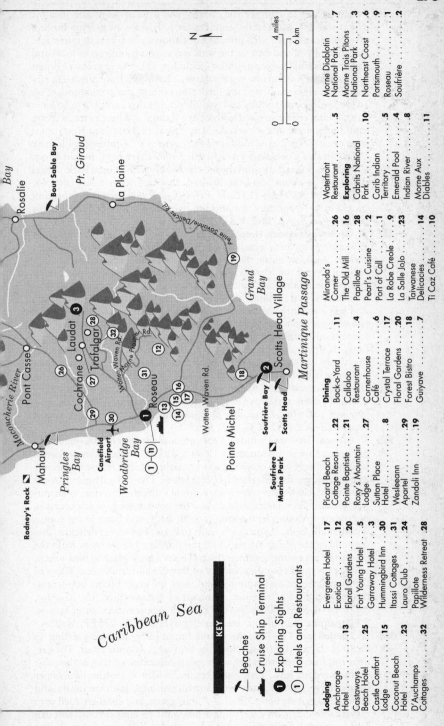

"come . . . let us pamper you." They will even arrange activities for you if you ask. Most of the cottages are only steps away from the sea, a white picket fence with private gates allows you access to the beach. All around you and among the walkways are a profusion of local and exotic trees and flowering shrubs—including Hibiscus in at least a dozen colors; at the entrance to your cottage, a basin is left for rinsing sandy feet. Each air-conditioned one-bedroom cottage can accommodate up to four people (two adults and two children or three adults); most have tubs, a kitchenette stocked with coffee fixings and herbal tea, a living and dining area, and a veranda. The casual Le Flambeau Restaurant next door serves creole food, and the resort is a 15-minute walk from Portsmouth's stores and a 10- to 20-minute drive from Indian River, Cabrits National Park, and the Morne Diablotin National Park. A taxi will cost you about $50 from Roseau. ⊠ *Prince Rupert Bay (Box 34, Roseau),* ☎ *767/445–5131,* 𝖥𝖠𝖷 *767/445–5599,* 𝖶𝖤𝖡 *www.delphis.dm/ picard.htm. 18 cottages. Restaurant, bar, air-conditioning, fans, kitchenettes, beach. AE, MC, V. CP, EP, MAP.*

$$$ 🏨 **Castaways Beach Hotel.** This beachfront hotel, 20 minutes from Roseau, draws an eclectic crowd: hikers, divers, athletes, and leisure seekers. Midway along the west coast, it's ideally situated so you can enjoy many of the island's popular attractions, either by tour bus or solo on mountain bikes rented at the hotel. Half of the spacious rooms were remodeled in 2000, adding minibars, hair dryers, drop ceilings, and tropical fabrics adorning the wooden and rattan furnishings. All rooms have balconies with views of the Caribbean through tropical gardens; although they are not all air-conditioned, rooms have ceiling fans, are open, comfortable, and cool. In the evening, guests gather either at the bar or in the terrace restaurant. On Sunday there's a beach barbecue with drinks and live music. ⊠ *11 mi (18 km) north of Roseau (Box 5, Roseau),* ☎ *767/449–6244 or 888/227–9292,* 𝖥𝖠𝖷 *767/449– 6246,* 𝖶𝖤𝖡 *www.castaways.dm. 26 rooms. Restaurant, 2 bars, fans, tennis court, volleyball, beach, dive shop, snorkeling, boating, fishing. Closed Sept.–mid-Oct. MC, V. CP, EP, MAP.*

$$$ 🏨 **Exotica.** The road winds up the mountain through lush vegetation
★ until you arrive at this sanctuary 1,600 ft (485 m) above sea level. Owned by a prominent local couple, Fae and Arthie Martin, these handsome bungalows are named after tropical fruits. The red galvanized roofs have solar panels; the rooms have bright, cheerful interiors with rattan furnishings and floral fabrics; and the bungalows have kitchenettes, bedrooms with two (extra-long) double beds, and large living rooms with trundle beds. If you don't want to cook, Fae serves delicious creole food at the Sugar Apple Café; the produce often comes from the property's sprawling organic garden. This is a great place to bird-watch, and the grounds contain a variety of flowers and fruit trees. Views of the distant ocean are stunning, and there are great hiking opportunities in the area. ⊠ *Gommier, southeast of Roseau (Box 109, Roseau),* ☎ *767/448–8839,* 𝖥𝖠𝖷 *767/448–8829,* 𝖶𝖤𝖡 *www.exotica-cottages.com. 8 bungalows. Restaurant, kitchenettes. AE, MC, V. CP, EP, MAP.*

$$$ 🏨 **Zandoli Inn.** This little three-story inn has a breathtaking setting on
★ an 80-ft (24-m) cliff overlooking the southeast Atlantic coast. The gardens roll from crest to valley, with spectacular views either of the coast or the verdant hills. Five guest rooms, which share the two upper floors, have locally made wooden furnishings, jalousie doors and blinds, and private baths. Shades of blue, green, and coral are used with remarkable effect on everything from walls to lampshades. You can take a soothing dip in the plunge pool—under a canopy of orchids that hang from the trees along the pathways—or go for a more adventurous swim among huge boulders in the aqua-blue Atlantic. Breakfasts and dinners feature fresh herbs and pungent seasonings, and the cozy

bar area serves as the perfect spot for a pre-dinner coconut punch or after dinner conversation. Car rentals can be arranged. ✉ *Roche Cassée (Box 2099, Roseau),* ☎ 767/446–3161, FAX 767/446–3344, WEB *www.zandoli.com. 5 rooms. Bar, dining room, fans, pool, hiking. AE, D, MC, V. CP.*

$$ 🏨 **Evergreen Hotel.** This small establishment, 1 mi (1½ km) from downtown Roseau, is a family-run home away from home. Jenny, the manager, and her family ensure your stay within these beautiful gardens is one you will want to repeat. Spacious rooms in the waterfront annex are decorated with bright floral prints and rattan furniture; all have cable TV, large showers, and balconies with sea views. The original stone-and-wood building holds a dining and meeting room, as well as the property's first guest rooms. Wooden furnishings and needlepoint hangings give these a quaint, cottage-y feel, and the modern facilities make up for the lack of sea views. The Honeymoon Hut is in a garden abloom with flowers and fruit trees. The Crystal Terrace Restaurant and Bar right over the ocean caters to hotel guests and visitors with a creative creole menu. Spicey crabbacks and melt-in-your-mouth breadfruit soufflé are just a couple items to sample. ✉ *Castle Comfort (Box 309, Roseau),* ☎ 767/448–3288, FAX 767/448–6800, WEB *www.delphis.dm/evergreen.htm. 16 rooms, 1 Honeymoon Hut. Restaurant, bar, air-conditioning, pool, meeting rooms. AE, MC, V. CP, MAP.*

$$ 🏨 **Fort Young Hotel.** Originally built in the late 1700s, Fort Young was ★ once the island's main military installation. With massive, 200-year-old walls encircling the original part of the hotel, cannons guarding entrances, and flagstone floors, a real sense of history is conveyed throughout the property. Guest rooms have modern furnishings, private baths, balconies, and spectacular sea views. As part of its 1999 expansion, along a dramatic cliff at the edge of the tranquil Caribbean, the hotel added 21 modern guest rooms and suites, along with a waterfall, a duty-free shopping complex, and a spa. The Waterfront Restaurant and Boardwalk Café and Bar offers excellent cuisine and a repose within the hustle of Roseau. ✉ *Victoria St. (Box 519), Roseau,* ☎ 767/448–5000, FAX 767/448–5006, WEB *www.fortyounghotel.com. 53 rooms. 2 restaurants, 2 bars, air-conditioning, fans, pool, spa, shops. AE, MC, V. CP, EP, MAP.*

$$ 🏨 **Garraway Hotel.** This hotel in downtown Roseau, with towering plants, fresh flowers, and original paintings by local and regional artists, is elegant and very tropical. So, too, are the guest rooms and suites, which are decorated in bright fabrics and cool colors. All have direct-dial phones and cable TV; some have in-room faxes. Perched on the western edge of the capital city, the higher floors and the roof terrace survey a colorful jumble of rooftops, which are a nostalgic foreground for the imposing mountains rising from the Roseau Valley. The second-floor Balizier Restaurant specializes in creative creole cuisine, featuring lunch buffets twice weekly. Downstairs are the Ole Jetty Bar and its sidewalk café, where you can sip the cocktail of the hour while the sun sets on the city's shoreline. ✉ *Bayfront (Box 789), Roseau,* ☎ 767/449–8800, FAX 767/449–8807, WEB *www.delphis.dm/garraway.htm. 20 rooms, 11 suites. Restaurant, bar, air-conditioning, fans, meeting rooms. AE, DC, MC, V. CP, EP, FAP, MAP.*

$$ 🏨 **Wesleeann Apartel.** With the red Spanish-tile roof of this five-story building juxtaposed within suburban development, it's hard to miss the Wesleeann. Once inside, everything slows down as the white walls and floors, rattan furnishings, and floral patterns immediately set the tone. Guest quarters include rooms, suites, and two- and three-bedroom apartments. Each unit has a small balcony, cable TV, a phone, a dining area, and a small kitchen. The top-floor restaurant and bar serves cocktails, as well as contemporary and creole cuisine; the hotel

also has a small breakfast room. ✉ *8th and 9th sts., Canefield (Box 1764, Roseau),* ☎ *767/449–0419,* FAX *767/449–2473,* WEB *www. wesleeann.com. 3 rooms, 4 suites, 5 apartments. Restaurant, bar, air-conditioning, kitchenettes, refrigerators, meeting rooms. AE, MC, V. CP, EP, MAP.*

$ 🏨 **Anchorage Hotel.** The Anchorage is a favorite nesting ground of adventure seekers of every age who come to use the on-site dive and whale-watching center and in-house tour company. A comfortable, inexpensive option for those wishing to stay close to Roseau who also enjoy being on the ocean. All of this family-run hotel's brightly decorated and locally furnished rooms have phones, cable TV, private baths, and balconies. Twenty superior rooms have Caribbean views and two double beds; 12 smaller, standard rooms face the pool and the ocean and have two twin beds or one double. The Ocean Terrace Restaurant and Carib Bar and Lounge, perched above the Caribbean, have a tropical, open-air setting where you can experience the dramatic sunsets with the visiting yachts in the foreground. Yachtsmen, locals, and visitors join in on the weekly buffet dinners with live music. The front desk will help arrange just about any activity for you: hiking, whale-watching, fishing, and bird-watching—on land or sea. ✉ *Castle Comfort (Box 34, Roseau),* ☎ *767/448–2638,* FAX *767/448–5680,* WEB *www. anchoragehotel.dm. 32 rooms. Restaurant, bar, air-conditioning, pool, squash, dive shop. AE, D, MC, V. CP, EP, FAP, MAP.*

$ 🏨 **Coconut Beach Hotel.** No matter where in the Portsmouth Bay you stand, you're likely to spot the bright green and orange of this activity hub. Nestled between hibiscus hedges and mango trees—and only yards from Dominica's longest beach—the 18 apartment-style suites and bungalows all have phones, satellite TVs, and verandas. La Salle JoJo Restaurant offers a mix of contemporary creole and interesting fast-food items, or try La Terrace Cocktail. Every Friday and Saturday night, the Palladium Nightclub comes alive with a selection of music that keeps you on your feet into the wee hours of the morning. The hotel also accommodates groups for functions and meetings. An on-site water-sports company arranges sailing, kayaking, waterskiing, and paddleboating, while the staff schedules land-based adventures. ✉ *Picard Beach (Box 37, Roseau),* ☎ *767/445–5393 or 767/445–5415,* FAX *767/445–5693,* WEB *www.coconutbeachhotel.com. 18 units. Restaurant, bar, air-conditioning, kitchenettes, beach, boating, waterskiing. AE, D, MC, V. CP, EP, MAP.*

$ 🏨 **D'Auchamps Cottages.** Just outside Roseau en route to Trafalgar is the home of Patricia Honychurch. In her lush gardens are three bungalows that provide a studio garden cabin with rustic fixtures like an outdoor bathroom. The two-bedroom, and one-bedroom bungalows are closer to the main house and consist of simple cozy furnishings, modern fixtures, kitchens, and covered patios. All are private and very comfortable. The gardens have marked walkways through exotic anthuriums and ferns. Mrs. Honychurch encourages guests to walk through and can offer her knowledge of the different shrubs, plants, and trees within the gardens. No meals are provided here, but it's not far from Roseau and shops where you can purchase basic supplies. ✉ *Trafalgar (Box 1889, Roseau),* ☎ *767/448–3346,* FAX *767/449–9637,* WEB *www.delphis. dm/dauchamps. 3 cottages. Kitchenettes. No credit cards. EP.*

$ 🏨 **Floral Gardens.** As you wind your way into the dense rain forest from Melville Hall Airport, you catch glimpses of the beautiful Pagua River. Bumping over a little yellow bridge that crosses a tributary to this river, you come to two chalet-style villas. Verdant gardens overflow with exotic plants and spouting fountains; rabbits, ducks, turkeys, and peacocks roam the gardens. Guest accommodations in the two main buildings are decorated with local furnishings, as are the larger self-contained apartments (four have kitchenettes). A boutique purveys souvenirs from Dominica and the region. The Floral Gardens restaurant and bar serves home-style creole fare and potent rum punches. ⊠ *Concord,* ☎ *767/445–7636,* FAX *767/445–7333,* WEB *www.floralgardens. dm. 5 rooms, 4 apartments. Restaurant, kitchenettes, shops, meeting rooms. MC, V. CP, EP, MAP.*

$ ⛱ **Hummingbird Inn.** The ambience of this small hilltop retreat, just north of Roseau, is created by owner Jean James Finucane, a patriotic Dominican with an endearing smile and a passion for hummingbirds. Two bungalows with outstanding Caribbean views stand amid a profusion of foliage in the yard. Ten rooms have tropical interiors; white walls, terra-cotta-tile floors, private baths, verandas, and peaked wooden ceilings. Wooden hurricane shutters can be left open all night to allow in fresh breezes and the sound of the ocean a few hundred yards below. No air-conditioning, TVs, or phones are found here. Instead, there are such tropical fixtures as ceiling fans, handmade quilts, hammocks, and tables fashioned out of local woods. The Honeymoon Suite has a stately mahogany four-poster bed, a bathroom, a private kitchen, and a patio. The reception area, lounge, and dining terrace are in the main house, as is the kitchen. Jean is an expert on creole cooking and ensures everything coming from her kitchen meets her approval. ⊠ *Morne Daniel, 2 mi (3 km) north of Roseau (Box 1901, Roseau),* ☎ FAX *767/449–1042,* WEB *www.delphis.dm/eiroxys.htm. 9 rooms, 1 suite. Restaurant, bar, fans. AE, MC, V. CP, EP, MAP.*

$ ⛱ **Itassi Cottages.** Run by the same family that owns the Sutton Place Hotel, these three self-contained cottages live up to the promise in the brochure: that they are "for discerning travelers who are not necessarily loaded." Set on beautifully landscaped grounds, the two-bedroom, two-bath cottage can house as many as six people; the one-bedroom, one-bath cottage accommodates up to four people; and the studio cottage comfortably sleeps two. Each cottage has a full kitchen and cable TV, and there's a shared laundry facility. The decor is homey, with a mix of antiques, straw mats, handmade floral bedspreads, and calabash lamps. Spacious porches have hammocks and sweeping views of Roseau, Scotts Head, and the Caribbean. ⊠ *Morne Bruce, about 1 mi (1½ km) southeast of Roseau (Box 2333, Roseau),* ☎ *767/448–7247,* FAX *767/448–3045,* WEB *www.delphis.dm/itassi.htm. 3 cottages. Fans, kitchenettes, laundry service. AE, MC, V. EP.*

$ ⛱ **Lauro Club.** The murmur of the sea and the sounds of nocturnal wildlife are all you're likely to hear at this charming cliff-top complex. The eight brightly painted, solar-powered bungalows are staggered up along the cliff and placed within the landscaped grounds, allowing lots of space between you and your neighbors as well as views of the tranquil Caribbean. Each unit is named after a Caribbean dance (for example, the Quadrille, the Limbo) and has a large sitting area with a trundle bed, a bedroom with a double bed, ceiling fans, and a well-equipped kitchenette on a spacious hardwood veranda (though none has a phone or a TV). Walkways wind through the property to the restaurant, bar, and swimming pool and hot tub, and a wooden stairway corkscrews down the cliff to a spot where you can swim among giant volcanic boulders. This property is a little isolated—about 12 mi (19 km) from Roseau and Portsmouth—so if you stay here, consider renting a car. ⊠ *Grand Savanne (Box 483), Salisbury,* ☎ *767/449–6602,* FAX *767/449–6603,* WEB *www.lauroclub.com. 8 bungalows, 10 apartments. Fans, kitchenettes, pool, hot tub, beach. MC, V. EP, CP, FAP, MAP.*

$ ⛱ **Papillote Wilderness Retreat.** Imbued with the commitment of its
★ owners and staffed by some of the island's friendliest people, Papillote retains its warmth even in the heights of the cool Trafalgar Mountains. Lush greenery abounds, the nearby river beckons you to take a dip,

and the 200-ft (61-m) Trafalgar Falls are a short hike from your room. Owner Anne Jean-Baptiste's botanical garden is a mind-boggling collection of rare and indigenous plants and flowers—all planted around secluded mineral pools and stone sculptures. Anne's walking tours of the garden end at the bird-watching station at the top of the property. The charming rooms are decorated with such local handicrafts as quilts, grass rugs, prints, and pottery. The terrace-style Papillote restaurant, which has spectacular mountain and valley views, serves excellent local cuisine. ✉ *Trafalgar Falls Rd. (Box 2287, Roseau),* ☎ *767/ 448–2287,* FAX *767/448–2285,* WEB *www.papillote.dm. 3 rooms, 2 suites, 1 2-bedroom cottage. Restaurant, bar, shops. Closed Sept.– mid-Oct. AE, D, MC, V. EP, MAP.*

$ ⊞ **Pointe Baptiste.** Alec Waugh, Noël Coward, and Princess Margaret were guests here when this hideaway was in its heyday. Although the garden has now grown woody with time and the weathered plantation house's antiques-filled interior is redolent with memories and dilapidated Old World charm, the setting above the windblown Atlantic coast with two secluded white sand beaches is divine. The main house has four bedrooms, a dining room, a kitchen with a pantry, and a large veranda with an inspiring view. In the garden is a whitewashed cottage—straight out of a Ralph Lauren catalog—containing an additional room, bathroom, and small kitchen. You can rent either one. A cleaner and cook will come daily to the main house, but otherwise you're on your own. This place is secluded and miles from any of the popular nature attractions, so you'll need a car—this can be arranged for you, and if you like, Annick will purchase your first day's supplies for you. ✉ *2 mi (3 km) northwest of village of Calibishie c/o Annick Giraud, Calibishie,* ☎ *767/445–8495 or 767/245–2460,* WEB *www.delphis. dm/pointeb.htm. 4 rooms, 1 cottage. D, MC, V.*

$ ⊞ **Roxy's Mountain Lodge.** What was once a family home has been transformed into a homey mountain retreat in the village of Laudat. The main lodge's hotel-style rooms have wood details and furnishings, well-crafted fittings, and grass mats. At the back of the property, a second, self-contained building offers suite-style guest quarters. The restaurant, which serves traditional Dominican cooking, opens onto a huge terrace that overlooks the gardens. The small bar has bottles of herbs steeped in rum and is a watering hole that's popular with hikers fresh from the nearby trails. This popular spot is used by nature enthusiasts as a gateway to the Morne Trois Pitons World Heritage Site. Laudat can get chilly during winter months so be sure to pack something warm. ✉ *Laudat, 4 mi (6½ km) north of Roseau (Box 265, Roseau),* ☎ FAX *767/448–4845,* WEB *www.delphis.dm/eiroxys.htm. 10 rooms, 1 suite. Restaurant, bar, hiking. AE, MC, V. CP, EP, MAP.*

$ ⊞ **Sutton Place Hotel.** The Harris family have transformed their grand-
★ parents' historic 1890s residence in the heart of Roseau into a small, painstakingly finished hotel. The wrought-iron gates at the entrance lead up stairs from the street into a cool foyer, reception area, and restaurant, which serves scrumptious contemporary creole cuisine. Up a couple of flights of hardwood stairs are the five standard rooms, superbly decorated with fabrics and fittings imported from New York. Guests share a lounge and a kitchenette, where a complimentary Continental breakfast is served in a setting overlooking the courtyard. Three spacious top-floor suites with kitchens have restored antiques and replicas, teak-louvered windows, and polished wood floors. The structure's original stonework can be seen in the cozy, air-conditioned Cellars Bar, a popular local hangout. ✉ *25 Old St. (Box 2333) Roseau,* ☎ *767/ 448–8700,* FAX *767/448–3045,* WEB *www.delphis.dm/sutton.htm. 5 rooms, 3 suites. Restaurant, bar, air-conditioning, fans. AE, D, MC, V. CP.*

Dining

With Dominica's strong agricultural tradition, you can expect a cornucopia of vegetables, fruits, and root crops to appear on menus around the island. Sweet ripe plantains, *kushkush* yams, breadfruit, and dasheen (a tuber similar to the potato, called "taro" elsewhere) are among the staples. You'll find fresh fish on almost every menu (often cooked in a creole *sancouche*, which uses coconut milk). The local drink is spiced rum—a cask rum steeped with herbs such as anisette (called "nanny") and *pweve* (lemongrass). And be sure that when you ask for a glass of juice it's going to come directly from the fruit and not a box.

Dominican cuisine is also famous for its use of local game, such as the "mountain chicken"—a euphemism for a large frog called *crapaud*—and for more intrepid diners, the *manicou* (a small opossum) and the *agouti* (a large indigenous rodent).

In and around Roseau and all over the island, throughout villages and hamlets you can find a myriad of tiny food shops, where the food is local, plentiful, and highly seasoned. So if what you are looking for is a quick bite to sample Dominica's local cuisine, make your way in and ask for the day's special. Otherwise, you could try roadside vendors making breakfasts of bakes and accras for the passerby.

What to Wear

Most Dominicans dress elegantly and practically when eating out—for dinner it's shirt and trousers for men and modest dresses for women. During the day, nice shorts are acceptable at most places; beach attire is frowned upon, unless of course you're eating on the beach.

CATEGORY	COST*
$$$$	over $35
$$$	$25–$35
$$	$15–$25
$	under $15

per person for a main course at dinner

CARIBBEAN

$$ ✕ **Crystal Terrace Restaurant and Bar.** At the Evergreen Hotel you can dine on a large, airy terrace perched right over the sea, or relax at the bar while sipping a tropical cocktail. Mrs. Winton sees to it that what is served is classic local food with a very elegant twist. Dinners are usually a prix-fixe menu, with an appetizer; a choice of soup, salad, or a local delicacy such as crab back; entrées of chicken, fish, or other meats are served with local produce and prepared in interesting combinations. For dessert there's fresh fruit or homemade cake and ice cream. Breakfast and lunch are also served here and reservations are advised. ✉ *Castle Comfort, Roseau,* ☎ *767/448–3288. AE, MC, V.*

$ ✕ **Guiyave.** This popular lunchtime restaurant in a quaint Caribbean town house also has a pastry shop downstairs serving chicken patties, spicy rotis, and a scrumptious selection of tarts and cakes. These can also be ordered at the upstairs restaurant, along with more elaborate fare such as fish court boullion or chicken in a sweet-and-sour sauce. You can dine indoors in the airy dining room or on the sunny balcony perched above Roseau's colorful streets—the perfect spot to indulge in one of the fresh-squeezed tropical juices. ✉ *15 Cork St., Roseau,* ☎ *767/448–2930. AE, MC, V. No dinner. Closed Sun.*

$$ ✕ **La Robe Creole.** An old cut-stone building near the Fort Young Hotel—
★ and only steps away from the Old Market Plaza—houses one of Dominica's best restaurants. Retreat into a cozy dining room with wood rafters, ladder-back chairs, and colorful madras tablecloths, which alternately jazz

up the daily lunch settings and make the evening dining more formal. You can dine on a meal selected from an eclectic à la carte menu. Callaloo soup is a specialty, as are lobster crêpes and salads. The downstairs take-out annex, Mouse Hole, is an inexpensive and tasty place to snack when you're on the run. The restaurant makes its own delicious mango chutney and plantain chips, which you can buy in local shops. ⊠ *3 Victoria St., Roseau,* ☎ *767/448–2896. D, MC, V. Closed Sun.*

$$ ✕ **La Salle JoJo.** This unexpectedly posh, air-conditioned beachfront bar and restaurant at the Coconut Beach Hotel is popular with visiting yachtsmen, students from the nearby medical school, and anyone interested in an afternoon or evening on a stretch of golden-sand beach. Fresh tropical drinks and local seafood dishes are the specialties; sandwiches, burgers, and rotis, and even a children's menu are offered here. On weekends this place really comes alive when the DJs crank up the latest hits at The Palladium Nightclub. ⊠ *Picard Beach,* ☎ *767/445–5393. AE, D, MC, V.*

$$ ✕ **Papillote.** Savor a lethal rum punch while lounging in a hot mineral
★   bath in the Papillote Wilderness Retreat gardens. Then try the bracing callaloo soup, dasheen puffs, fish "rain forest" (marinated with papaya and wrapped in banana leaves), or the succulent freshwater shrimp. This handsome caribbean restaurant has quite possibly one of the best views in the region. Dine at an altitude cool enough to need a throw and watch the glimmer of the moonlight on the Caribbean Sea in the distance. ⊠ *Trafalgar Falls Rd., Roseau,* ☎ *767/448–2287. Reservations essential. AE, D, MC, V.*

$ ✕ **Back–A–Yard.** Talk about down-home cooking. At the back ("in de yard") of a beautifully restored creole town house is this mouthwatering vegetarian restaurant. Seated on metal garden chairs, you are served a variety of vegetable, pasta, and grain dishes. This is a cool, cheap hangout with great people, food, and drinks. ⊠ *19 Castle St., Roseau,* ☎ *767/449–9736. No dinner. Closed Sun. No credit cards.*

$ ✕ **Callaloo Restaurant.** On one of the busiest streets in Roseau you can escape the bustle and step into a quaint informal eatery where the effervescent Marge Peters is Queen. Marge is proud to tell you that although she is a busy businesswoman, her place is in the kitchen, and that's where she spends most of her time. Taking pride in age-old cooking traditions, she uses only the freshest local produce. Changing lunch and dinner specials might include curried conch, mountain chicken, or callaloo (fragrant with cumin, coconut cream, lime, clove, and garlic). Don't miss the fresh fruit juices, ice creams, and desserts. ⊠ *66 King George V St., Roseau,* ☎ *767/448–3386. AE, D, MC, V.*

$ ✕ **Floral Gardens.** The sound of water falling in the background, rough-hewn timber beams, and vertivert mats create a rustic atmosphere. Dinner is served in the main building, but there are more tables in a building across the road overlooking the river. The home-style creole fare includes fresh fish and beef stews, fruits and vegetables, and tropical-flavored pies and tarts. ⊠ *Concord,* ☎ *767/445–7636. AE, D, MC, V.*

$ ✕ **Forest Bistro.** If you've been discovering Soufrière, be sure to stop by this naturalist's haven. Set on what remains of the island's finest lime orchard, with views of the lush mountains, this small bistro is quaint, charming, simple, and home to the Charleses. Here you feast on Dominican-style breakfasts: saltfish and bakes, fried plantains, accras, coffee, and fresh juice. Hearty lunches and dinners of fish or chicken are done with typical Dominican flair and served with local vegetables. If you like, Andre will set you up to dine on a table in a spot in his organic garden. ⊠ *Soufrière,* ☎ *767/448–7105. Reservations essential. No credit cards.*

$ ✕ **Miranda's Corner.** Just past Springfield on the way to Pont Casse, you'll begin to see hills full of flowers. At a big bend, a sign on a tree reads MIRANDA'S CORNER, referring to a bar, rum shop, and diner all in one. Here Miranda Alfred is at home, serving everyone from Italian tourists to banana farmers. The specialties are numerous—even the shrimp from her pond are prepared with a potion of passion and a fistful of flavor. This joint is open for breakfast, lunch, and dinner, and if you want something specially prepared, just call ahead and Miranda will help you out. ⊠ *Mount Joy, Springfield,* ☎ *767/449–2509. Reservations essential. No credit cards.*

$ ✕ **Pearl's Cuisine.** Inside a restored green-and-white creole town house, chef Pearl, with her robust and infectious character, prepares some of the island's best local cuisine. She offers everything—*sousse* (pickled pigs' feet), blood pudding, and rotis—in typical Dominican style. When sitting down to lunch or dinner, ask for a table on the open-air gallery that overlooks the streets of Roseau, prepare for an abundant portion served on a platter, but make sure you leave space for dessert. Enjoy a quick meal from the daily varied menu of soup, pelau, burgers and spicy rotis among other snack items in the ground-floor snackette. The fresh fruit juice choices are also varied. ⊠ *50 King George V St., Roseau,* ☎ *767/448–8707. AE, D, MC, V.*

$ ✕ **Port of Call Restaurant and Bar.** Just around the corner from the bayfront in downtown Roseau is a traditional stone building. The interior of this breezy restaurant has a soothing gray-and-white color scheme. The layout is such that you can have private seating or a laidback setting. Management here is always ready to meet your needs for homestyle local cuisine or a selection of à la carte items such as a hamburger with french fries or maybe just an exotic cocktail from the bar. ⊠ *3 Kennedy Ave., Roseau,* ☎ *767/448–2910. AE, D, MC, V.*

ECLECTIC/CONTEMPORARY

$$ ✕ **Waterfront Restaurant.** At the southern end of Roseau's bayfront
★ is the Fort Young Hotel. Upstairs, surveying the tranquil Caribbean coastline is this very elegant restaurant. The large upstairs veranda wraps around the air-conditioned formal dining room. The à la carte menu choices range from appetizers of smoked salmon and roasted vegetable quesadillas to mains of orange duck and rack of lamb. Tropical desserts include cheesecake and guava tart. ⊠ *Victoria St., Roseau,* ☎ *767/448–5000. AE, MC, V.*

$ ✕ **Cornerhouse Café.** Across the street from the Old Market Plaza is a beautifully restored Caribbean town house. The sign on the lattice veranda reads DOMINICA'S INFORMATION CAFÉ. Here a couple of young entrepreneurs offer an eclectic menu of snacks, meals, and other treats: bagels with an assortment of toppings, as well as delicious soups, sandwiches, salads, cakes, and coffee. Computers in the cybercafé are rented in 30-minute intervals; relax on soft chairs and flip through books and magazines while you wait. Wednesday is quiz night, and every night is game night—but arrive early, as there's always a full house. ⊠ *Corner of Old and King George V sts., Roseau,* ☎ *767/449–9000. No credit cards. Closed Sun.*

$ ✕ **The Old Mill Restaurant Bar & Beer Garden.** Just entering the village of Loubiere on the Southwest coast of the island is a beautifully restored old mill, the only one in Dominica where, until very recently, the aqueduct still functioned. A creative German couple have created a fine dining experience, an intimate bar in the cellar and the ultimate hangout spot tucked in the gardens outside. The menu is creatively eclectic with everything from German sausages to linguini with pesto to passion fruit sorbet. Part of the complex includes Dominica's latest nightspot, the Magic Disco & Club. The Mill is open for dinners only and closed on Sundays. ⊠ *Wallhouse, Loubiere,* ☎ *767/448–7778 or 767/448–7840. MC, V. Closed Sun. No lunch.*

$ ✕ **Taiwanese Delicacies.** Over the past 12 years a new ethnic group has been added to Dominica's melting pot culture. Taiwanese Dominicans are opening businesses and, of course, Chinese restaurants. This spot in Castle Comfort has drawn the biggest crowds for hot and spicy dishes, crispy vegetable and tofu selections, tender meats, elegant understated dining, and takeaway service. If you enjoy Chinese, you have to try it Dominican (Taiwanese) style. ⊠ *Castle Comfort,* ☎ *767/448–3497. No credit cards.*

FRENCH

$ ✕ **Ti Caz Café.** The brainchild of a young couple from Lille, this Parisian café–style restaurant sits on a prominent Bayfront corner in Roseau. It's hard to miss the umbrella-covered chairs and tables. The friendly team here starts at 8:30 each morning serving breakfast crêpes, croissants, baguette sandwiches, and piping hot café au lait. Throughout the day you can relax indoors or outdoors and enjoy any of the extensive menu's selections with the perfect glass of wine. In the Cellar downstairs, the Cocorico wine store houses a selection from more than eight countries; it also purveys a wide assortment of pâtés and cheeses, sausages, cigars, and French breads. ⊠ *Corner of Bayfront and Kennedy aves., Roseau,* ☎ *767/449–8686 or 767/449–9774. MC, V. No dinner. Closed Sun.*

Beaches

As a volcanic island, Dominica offers many powder-fine black-sand beaches. Found mostly in the north and east, they are windswept, dramatic, and uncrowded, lending themselves more to relaxation than swimming because many have undercurrents. There are also secluded white- or brown-sand beaches here. If you are adventuring on your own, the northeast coast offers beautiful, sandy beaches and bays, the most popular of which is **Woodford Hill Beach,** just past the village. On holidays Woodford Hill can be crowded, so if you're looking for a secluded spot, **Hodges Beach** is just a bit farther on, though it's not as white and clear because there's a river here; it is accessed through an estate road and private lands. **Hampstead Beach,** which actually encompasses three bays (one of which is sheltered and calm), is a bit off the beaten path. **L'Anse Noir** is also a favorite for the more adventurous; it sits on a cove just past Woodford Hill, and some days the odd surfer finds just the right wave. Although northeast coast beaches offer excellent shallow swimming, their wind-tossed beauty can be dangerous; there are sometimes strong currents with the whipped-cream waves. From these beaches you can see the islands of Marie Galante, Les Saintes, and parts of Guadeloupe. Along the northwest side of the island from Toucari, through Purple Turtle, and down to Picard are the best all-round beaches, which have great opportunities for windsurfing and snorkeling. **Picard Beach,** a 2-mi (3-km) stretch of brown sand, is fringed with coconut trees.

Heading south along the west coast are more opportunities for sea bathing, where the beaches are fewer and mostly made of black sand and rounded volcanic rocks. Swimming off these rocky shores has its pleasures, too: the water is usually as flat as a lake, deep and blue, and is especially good for snorkeling. **Mero Beach** and **Castaways.** At **Champagne,** volcanic vents puff steam into the sea (the experience has been described as "swimming in champagne"). At **Scotts Head** and **Soufrière Bay** you will find fine snorkeling and scuba diving.

Outdoor Activities and Sports

BOATING AND SAILING

West-coast waters are deep, and the coves here are numerous. Motorboat and sailing excursions include those to neighboring islands as well as to secluded spots on Dominica itself. A couple of companies organize trips either on an hourly or a daily basis, with costs ranging from $80 per hour to $750 for a full day. You can arrange trips through **Dominica Tours** (✉ Anchorage Hotel, Castle Comfort, ☎ 767/448–2638 or 767/448–0990). The **Castaways Beach Hotel** (✉ Mero, ☎ 767/449–6245), situated on the west coast, arranges boating, sportfishing, and sailing charters.

CYCLING

Cyclists find Dominica's rugged terrain to be an exhilarating challenge, but there are routes suitable for all levels of bikers. **Nature Island Dive** has a fleet of bikes in good condition. Knowledgeable guides lead tours for $30–$65.

FISHING

Anglers will delight in the numerous banks and drop-offs, as well as in the year-round fair weather. **Game Fishing Dominica** (✉ Box 2077, St. Joseph Roseau, ☎ FAX 767/449–6638, ☎ 767/235–6638) works off the Castaways dock in Mero. Eight years ago they started the Annual International Sportfishing Tournament in Dominica. Francis Cambran will take you out for between $450 and $700 for five to eight hours, providing all equipment, bait, and refreshments.

HIKING

Dominica's majestic mountains, clear rivers, and lush vegetation combine to offer opportunities for real adventure. The island is crisscrossed by ancient footpaths of the Arawak and Carib Indians and the Nègres Maroons, escaped slaves who established camps in the mountains. Existing trails range from easygoing to arduous. To make the most of your excursion, you'll need sturdy hiking boots, insect repellent, a change of clothes (kept dry), and a guide. Hikes and tours run $25 to $50 per person, depending on destinations and duration. Guides can be contacted through the **Dominican Tourist Office** (✉ Valley Rd., Roseau, ☎ 767/448–2045). The **Forestry Division** (☎ 767/448–2401) is responsible for the management of forests and wildlife and have a wealth of information and documents on Dominica as well as on reputable guides. Their offices are in the Botanical Gardens in Roseau.

For the hike to Boiling Lake or the climb up Morne Diablotin, you will need hiking boots, a guide, and water. Local bird and forestry expert **Betrand Jno Baptiste** (☎ 767/446–6358) leads hikes up Morne Diablotin and along the Syndicate Nature Trail; if he's not available, ask him to recommend another guide.

SCUBA DIVING AND SNORKELING

Voted one of the top 10 dive destinations in the world by *Skin Diver* and *Rodale's Scuba Diving* magazines, Dominica's dive sites are truly awesome. There are numerous highlights all along the west coast of the island, but the best are those in the southwest—within and around **Soufrière Scottshead Marine Park.** This bay is the site of a submerged volcanic crater; the Dominica Watersports Association has worked along with the Fisheries Division for years establishing this reserve and have set stringent regulations to prevent the degradation of the ecosystem. Within a half mile (¾ km) of the shore, there are vertical drops from 800 ft (240 m) to more than 1,500 ft (450 m), with visibility frequently extending to 100 ft (30 m). Shoals of boga fish, Creole wrasse, and blue cromis are common, and you might even see a spotted moray eel or a honeycomb cowfish. Crinoids (rare elsewhere) are also abundant here, as are giant barrel sponges. Other noteworthy dive sites outside this reserve are **Salisbury Falls, Nose Reef, Brain Coral Garden,** and— even farther north—at **Cabrits Drop-Off** and **Toucari Reef.** The opportunities for underwater photography, particularly macrophotography, are unparalleled.

The going rate is $65 for a two-tank dive or $100 for a resort course with an open-water dive. All scuba-diving operators also offer snorkeling; equipment rents for $10–$20 a day. The **Anchorage Dive & Whale Watch Center** (✉ Anchorage Hotel, Castle Comfort, ☎ 767/448–2638) has two dive boats that can take you out day or night. They also offer PADI instruction (all skill levels), snorkeling and whale-watching trips, and shore diving. **Dive Castaways** (✉ Castaway Beach Hotel, ☎ 767/449–6244), a PADI dive shop 11 mi (18 km) north of Roseau, offers diving, courses, snorkeling, and other water and beach activities. **Dive Dominica** (✉ Castle Comfort Lodge, ☎ 767/448–2188) conducts NAUI, PADI, and SSI courses, as well as dive, snorkeling, and whale-watching trips. **Nature Island Dive** (✉ Soufrière, ☎ 767/449–8181) is run by an enthusiastic crew. Some of the island's best dive sites are right outside their door, and they offer diving, snorkeling, kayaking, and mountain biking as well as resort and full PADI courses.

SWIMMING

Locals boast of having a river for every day of the year. Some are better for swimming than others, but all guarantee a pick-me-up during a hot day. As an extra treat, you can often find hot springs among the boulders; look for the telltale orange sulfur stains. **Escape** (✉ ☎ 767/448–5240) operates river-rafting, canyoning, rappelling, and tubing trips, with rates between $70 and $110 per person for five to eight hours.

WHALE AND DOLPHIN WATCHING

Dominica records the highest species counts of resident cetacea in the region, so it's not surprising that tours claim 90% sighting success for their excursions. Humpback whales, false killer whales, minke, and orcas are all occasionally seen, as are several species of dolphin. But the resident sperm whales (they calve in Dominica's 3,000-ft-deep/900-m-deep waters) are truly the stars of the show. During your 3½-hour expedition you may be asked to assist in recording sightings, which aid operators in collecting data that can be shared with local and international organizations. Although there are resident whales and dolphins and therefore year-round sightings, there are more species to be observed in November through February. The **Anchorage Dive & Whale Watch Center** (✉ Anchorage Hotel, Castle Comfort, ☎ 767/448–2638) is a major operator. **Dive Dominica** (✉ Castle Comfort Lodge, ☎ 767/448–2188) is a major whale-watching operator as well as a dive outfitter.

WINDSURFING

Although windsurfing isn't a very widely practiced sport in Dominica, there are a few individuals who will swear that the conditions are right for an exhilarating experience. You will need to bring your own gear with you and wait out the weather at beaches like Turtle Beach in the North East or down at Scottshead, where chances for waves on the Atlantic side can be mixed with the winds within the Soufrierè Bay. For windsurfing information contact **Andrew Armour** at the **Anchorage Dive & Whale Watch Center** (✉ Anchorage Hotel, Castle Comfort, ☎ 767/448–2638).

Shopping

Dominicans produce a variety of distinctive handicrafts, with various communities specializing in their specific products. The crafts of the

Carib Indians include traditional baskets made of dyed *larouma* reeds and waterproofed with tightly woven *balizier* leaves. These are sold in the Carib Indian Territory as well as in Roseau's shops. Vertivert straw rugs, screwpine tableware, fwije (the trunk of the forest tree fern), and wood carvings are just some examples. Also notable are local herbs, spices, condiments, and herb teas. Café Dominique, the local equivalent of Jamaican Blue Mountain coffee, is an excellent buy, as are the Dominican rums Macoucherie and Soca. Proof that the old ways live on in Dominica can be found in the number of herbal remedies available. One stimulating memento of your visit is rum steeped with bois bandé (scientific name *Richeria grandis*), a tree whose bark is reputed to have aphrodisiac properties. These are sold at shops, vendor's stalls, and supermarkets all over the island. Duty-free shopping is also available in specific stores around Roseau.

Stores are generally open from 8 until 4 or 5 on weekdays and from 8 to 1 on Saturdays. Most are closed on Sundays. Vendors are usually out on roadsides when there are French groups in for the day or on weekend excursions or when there are cruise ships in port.

Major Shopping Areas

One of the easiest places to pick up a souvenir is the Old Market Plaza, just behind the Dominica Museum, in Roseau. Slaves were once sold here, but today handcrafted jewelry, T-shirts, spices, souvenirs, and batiks are available from a group of vendors in open-air booths set up on the cobblestones. These are usually busiest when there is a cruise ship berthed across the street. On these days you can also find a vast number of vendors along the bay front.

Specialty Items

ART

Most artists work from their home studios and it often takes the right contact to find them. Contact the Old Mill Cultural Center or Earl Etienne, a Cultural Officer, and they will lead you on the right path. A couple of places where you are sure to see some interesting pieces are listed below, but work also adorns the walls of banks, restaurants, and some hotels.

Balisier's (✉ 35 Great George St., Roseau, ☎ no phone) is a real treasure. This is a showroom for the work of owner, Hilroy Fingol, a young artist who specializes in airbrush painting. **Gallery #4** (✉ 4 Hanover St., Roseau, ☎ 767/449–2484 or 767/449–1804) is the contact point for Dominica's most prominent artist, Earl Etienne, where he also shows pieces by local painters.

CLOTHING

With a plethora of clothing stores cropping up all over Roseau, it's easy to pick up something reasonably inexpensive. For classic Caribbean and designer clothing it's advisable to try **Ego Boutique** (✉ 9 Hillsborough St., Roseau, ☎ 767/448–2336), which is run by Florence Green, who proudly announces that the staff can communicate in Spanish, English, and French. The merchandise adds to the international atmosphere: along with the clothing are crafts and home accessories from the Caribbean and the rest of the world.

GIFTS AND SOUVENIRS

With tourism development comes the added benefits of increasing commerce; duty-free shops are cropping up in Roseau. Some name-brand stores carry jewelry, perfumes, crystals, and leather goods; several of these are within Roseau's bay front. **Ashbury's and Colombian Emeralds** (✉ Fort Young Hotel, Roseau) carries perfumes, crystals, emerald, diamond, gemstone, gold and silver jewelry, liquor, and a variety of special gifts. **Baroon International** (✉ Kennedy Ave., Roseau) sells a wide variety of unique jewelry from Asia, the U.S., and other Caribbean islands; there are also pieces that are assembled in the store, as well as personal accessories, souvenirs, and special gifts. For quality leather goods and other personal accessories, try **Land** (✉ Castle St., Roseau). **Rare Earth Treasures** (✉ Fort Lane, Roseau) is where you will find exactly what the name says, uniquely fashioned fine jewelry. Their collection of gemstones and crystals is a treat not to be missed, even when you can't afford to buy.

The Crazy Banana (✉ 17 Castle St., ☎ 767/449–8091) purveys everything from earthenware to doorstops, as well as other Caribbean-made crafts, rums, cigars, jewelry, and local art. **Frapi Souvenir & Gift Shop** (✉ 9 King George 5th St., ☎ 767/449–9294) has a line of whimsical T-shirts and postcards but also carries uniquely crafted gifts and souvenirs. **Island Stuff** (✉ 25 Hanover St., ☎ 767/449–9969), just a couple of blocks east of the ferry terminal, is a tiny Pandora's box, where you can find fine art, souvenirs, or the perfect hand-carved piece of furniture among the numerous items on sale.

HANDICRAFTS

Dominica Pottery (✉ Bayfront St. and Kennedy Ave., Roseau, ☎ no phone) is run by a local priest, whose products are fashioned with various local clays and glazes. **Papillote Wilderness Retreat** (✉ Trafalgar, ☎ 767/448–2287) has an intimate gift shop with an excellent selection of local handcrafted goods and particularly outstanding wood carvings by Louis Desire. **Tropicrafts** (✉ Corner of Queen Mary St. and Turkey La., Roseau, ☎ 767/448–2747) has a back room where you can watch local ladies weave grass mats. You'll also find a variety of arts and crafts from around the Caribbean, local wood carvings, rum, hot sauces, perfumes, and traditional Carib baskets, hats, and woven mats.

Nightlife and the Arts

The friendly, intimate atmosphere at the numerous bars and hangouts will keep you entertained for hours. If you're looking for jazz, calypso, reggae, steel-band, *soca* (a variation of calypso), cadence/zouk, or jing ping—a type of folk music featuring the accordion, the *quage* (a kind of washboard instrument), drums, and a "boom boom" (a percussive instrument)—you're guaranteed to find it. Wednesday through Friday nights are really lively, and during Carnival, Independence, and the summer celebrations, things can be intense. Indeed, Carnival, the pre-Lenten festival, is the most spontaneous in the Caribbean. The annual World Creole Music Festival in late October also packs in the action, with three days and nights of pulsating rhythm and music. Creole Music enthusiasts come from all over the world. Throughout the year, however, most larger hotels have live evening entertainment.

Nightlife

At **Cellars** (✉ Sutton Place hotel, Old St., Roseau, ☎ 767/449–8700), Wednesday night is Amateur Bartenders Soca Rum Night. Volunteer to be the bartender; taste tests of the feature cocktails are free, but there's a $4 minimum drink charge to enter. Friday is Kubuli Karaoke Night, entrance is free, but you might be made to sing for your drink. **Magic Discotheque & Club** (✉ Wallhouse, Loubiere, 767/448–7778), is Dominica's latest nightspot, drawing a crowd from every corner of the island to its air-conditioned comfort. Bouncers in black at the door, a long cocktail bar with masses of seating, and the old mill wheel dramatically juxtaposed against the futuristic lighting of the dance floor set the mood. Here the restored mill section of the Old Mill in Wallhouse has been opened by a German couple. It's open every weekend, on holiday nights, and for special celebrations. Entrance is $5. **Symes Zee's** (⊠ 34 King George V St., Roseau, ☎ 767/448–2494) draws a crowd on Thursday night from 10 until the wee hours of the morning, when there is a jazz/blues/reggae band. There's no cover, and the food, drinks, and cigars are reasonably priced. **Warehouse** (⊠ Outside Roseau, just past Canefield Airport, ☎ 767/449–1303) is *the* place to dance to disco on Saturday night. DJs are brought in from other islands to ensure there's variety to all the vibrations. The entrance fee is $5.

The Arts

Arawak House of Culture (⊠ Kennedy Ave. near Government Headquarters, Roseau, ☎ 767/449–1804), managed by Aileen Burton at the Cultural Division, is Dominica's performing-arts theater. A number of productions are staged here throughout the year, including plays, recitals, and dance performances. **Old Mill Cultural Center** (⊠ Canefield, ☎ 767/449–1804) is one of Dominica's historic landmarks. The Old Mill was once the home of the island's first sugarcane-processing mill and rum distillery. The main building was restored in 1997, and plans are afoot to develop the rest of the property. It's now the place to learn about Dominica's traditions. A variety of performances and events take place here throughout the year.

Exploring Dominica

Despite the small size of this almond-shape island, it can take a couple of hours to travel between the popular destinations. Many sights are isolated and difficult to find; you may be better off taking an organized excursion. If you do go it alone, drive carefully: the roads can be narrow and winding. Plan on eight hours to see the highlights; to fully experience the island, set aside a couple of days and work in some hikes.

Numbers in the margin correspond to points of interest on the Dominica map.

SIGHTS TO SEE

⓾ **Cabrits National Park.** Just north of the town of Portsmouth, this 250-acre park is—along with Brimstone Hill in St. Kitts, Shirley Heights in Antigua, and Ft. Charlotte in St. Vincent—among the most significant historic sites in the Caribbean. It also includes a marine park and herbaceous swamps, which are an important environment for several species of rare birds and plants. At the heart of the park is the Ft. Shirley military complex. Built by the British between 1770 and 1815, it once comprised 50 major structures, including storehouses that were also quarters for 500 men. With the help of the Royal Navy (which sends sailors ashore to work on the site each time a ship is in port) and local volunteers, historian Dr. Lennox Honychurch restored the fort and its surroundings, incorporating a small museum that highlights the natural and historic aspects of the park, and an open canteen-style restaurant.

❺ **Carib Indian Territory.** Today, more than 500 years after the Kalinago caught Columbus's men trespassing, the descendants we know as Carib Indians call this part of Dominica their final refuge. In 1903, after centuries of conflict, the Caribs were granted a portion of land (approximately 3,700 acres) on the island's northeast coast to establish a reservation with their own chief. Today it's known as Carib Territory, clinging to the northeasterly corner of Dominica, where a group of just over 3,000 Caribs, who resemble native South Americans, live like most other people in rural Caribbean communities. Many are farmers and fishermen; others are entrepreneurs who have opened restaurants, guest houses, and little shops where you can buy exquisite Carib baskets and other handcrafted items. The craftspeople retain knowledge of basket weaving, wood carving, and canoe building, which has been passed down from one generation to the next.

The Caribs' long, elegant canoes are created from the trunk of a single *gommier* tree. If you're lucky, you may catch canoe builders at work. Stop by the reservation's Catholic church in Salibia to see its unique altar. It was designed by Dr. Lennox Honychurch, a local historian, author, and artist, and was once a canoe.

Within the territory you'll also find **L'Escalier Tête Chien** (Snake's Staircase, Tête Chien is the name of a snake whose head resembles that of a dog), a hardened lava formation that runs down into the Atlantic. The ocean here is particularly fierce, and the shore is full of countless coves and inlets. According to Carib legend, at night the nearby Londonderry Islets metamorphose into grand canoes to take the spirits of the dead out to sea.

Though there's not currently much in the territory that demonstrates the Caribs' ancient culture and customs, plans for a museum showing early Carib life are in the works. In addition, the territory's Karifuna Cultural Group travels nationally and internationally, performing traditional dance and wearing traditional costumes—their bodies painted and adorned with feathers and beads.

❹ Emerald Pool. To reach this spot in the Morne Trois Pitons National Park, you follow a trail that starts at the side of the road near the reception center (it's an easy 20-minute walk). Along the way you'll pass lookout points with views of the windward (Atlantic) coast and the forested interior before ending at a swirling basin into which a 50-ft (15-m) waterfall splashes. If you don't want a crowd, check whether there are cruise ships in port before going out, as this spot is popular with cruise-ship tour groups.

❽ Indian River. Indian River, in Portsmouth, was once a Carib Indian settlement. A gentle rowboat ride for wildlife spotting along this river, lined with *terra carpus officinalis* trees, whose buttress roots spread up to 20 feet, is not only a relaxing treat but educational and most times entertaining. To arrange such a trip, stop by the Visitor Center at the mouth of the river and ask for one of the "Indian River Boys." These young, knowledgeable men are members of the Portsmouth Indian River Tour Guides Association (PIRTGA) and have for years protected and promoted one of Dominica's special areas. Most boat trips take you up as far as Rahjah's Jungle Bar. You can usually do an optional guided walking tour of the swamplands and the remnants of one of Dominica's oldest plantations. Tours last one to three hours and cost $15 to $30 per person.

⓫ Morne Aux Diables. In the far north of Dominica, this peak soars 2,826 ft (848 m) above sea level and slopes down to Toucari and Douglas bays and long stretches of dark-sand beach. To reach the mountain, take the road along the Caribbean coast. It twists by coconut, cocoa, and banana groves, past fern-festooned embankments, over rivers, and into villages where brightly painted shanties are almost as colorful as all the flora and fauna.

❼ Morne Diablotin National Park. After years of advocacy, research, preservation, land price negotiations, and fund-raising, 8,242 acres of land within the Northern Forest Reserve was dedicated as the Morne Diablotin National Park in January 2000. Dominica's highest summit at 4,747 ft (1,424 m) takes its name from a bird, known in English as the black-capped petrel, which was prized by hunters in the 18th century. Though there aren't any of these birds left today, Dominica is still a birder's paradise, whose aviary crown jewels are the green-and-purple Sisserou parrot (*Amazona imperialis*) and the Jaco, or red-neck, parrot (*Amazona arausiaca*), found here in greater numbers than in other parts of the island, but still Dominica's endemic endangered species. Before the establishment of the national park, the 200-acre site of Project Sisserou was the protected area, including the Syndicate Nature Trail, set aside with the help of some 6,000 schoolchildren, each of whom donated 25¢ to protect the habitat of the flying pride of Dominica, as well as countless other species of birds and other wildlife. The west-coast road (at the bend near Dublanc) runs through three types of forests and leads into the park. The trail offers a casual walk; just bring a sweater and binoculars. The five- to eight-hour hike up Morne Diablotin isn't for everyone. You need a guide, sturdy hiking shoes, warm clothing, and a backpack with refreshments and a change of clothes (including socks) that are wrapped in plastic to keep them dry. A good guide is local ornithology expert **Betrand Jno Baptiste** (☎ 767/446–6358).

③ **Morne Trois Pitons National Park.** Dedicated a national park in 1975 and named a UNESCO World Heritage Site in 1998, this 17,000-acre (covering 9% of Dominica) swath of lush, mountainous land in the south-central interior is the Nature Island's crown jewel. Named after one of the highest 4,600 ft (1,380 m) mountains on the island, it contains the world's largest boiling lake, majestic waterfalls, and cool mountain lakes. There are four types of vegetation zones here. Ferns grow 30-ft (9-m) tall and wild orchids sprout from trees, sunlight leaks through green canopies, and a gentle mist rises over the jungle floor. A system of trails has been developed in the park, and the Division of Forestry and Wildlife works hard to maintain it—with no help from the excessive rainfall and the profusion of vegetation that seems to grow right before your eyes. Access to the park is possible from most points of the compass, though the easiest approaches are via the small mountaintop villages of Laudat (pronounced low-*dah*) and Cochrane.

About 5 mi (8 km) out of Roseau, the Wotton Waven Road branches off toward Sulphur Springs, where you'll see the belching, sputtering, and gurgling releases of volcanic hot springs. At the base of Morne Micotrin, you'll find two crater lakes: the first, at 2,500 ft (750 m) above sea level, is **Freshwater Lake.** According to a local legend, it's haunted by a vindictive mermaid and a monstrous serpent. Farther on is **Boeri Lake,** fringed with greenery and with purple hyacinths floating on its surface. The undisputed highlight of the park is **Boiling Lake.** The world's largest such lake, it is a cauldron of gurgling gray-blue water, 70 yards wide and of unknown depth, with water temperatures from 180°F to 197°F. Although generally believed to be a volcanic crater, the lake is actually a flooded fumarole—a crack through which gases escape from the molten lava below. The two- to four-hour (one-way) hike up to the lake is challenging (on a very rainy day, be prepared to slip and slide the whole way up and back). You'll need attire appropriate for a strenuous hike, and a guide is a must. Most guided trips start early (no later than 8:30 AM) for this all-day, 7-mi (11-km) round-trip trek. On your way to Boiling Lake, you'll pass through the **Valley of Desolation,** a sight that definitely lives up to its name. Harsh sulfuric fumes have destroyed virtually all the vegetation in what must have once been a lush forested area. Small hot and cold streams with water of various colors—black, purple, red, orange—web the valley. Stay on the trail to avoid breaking through the crust that covers the hot lava. During this hike you'll pass rivers where you can refresh yourself with a dip (a particular treat is a soak in a hot-water stream on the way back). At the beginning of the Valley of Desolation trail is the **TiTrou Gorge,** where you can swim in the pool or relax in the hot-water springs along one side. If you're a strong swimmer, you can head up the gorge to a cave (it's about a five-minute swim) that has a magnificent waterfall; a crack in the cave about 50 ft (15 m) above permits a stream of sunlight to penetrate the cavern.

Also in the national park are some of the island's most spectacular waterfalls. The 45-minute hike to **Sari Sari Falls,** accessible through the east-coast village of La Plaine, can be hair-raising. But the sight of water cascading some 150 ft (45 m) into a large pool is awesome. So large are these falls that you feel the spray from hundreds of yards away. Just beyond the village of Trafalgar and up a short hill, there's the new reception facility where you can purchase passes to the national park and find guides to take you on a rain-forest trek to the twin **Trafalgar Falls.** If you like a little challenge, let your guide take you up the riverbed to the cool pools at the base of the falls (check whether there's a cruise ship in port before setting out; this sight is popular with the tour operators). You need a guide for the arduous 75-minute hike to **Middleham Falls.** The turnoff for the trailhead is just before the village of Laudat. The trail takes you to another spectacular waterfall, where water cascades 100 ft (30 m) over boulders and vegetation and then into an ice-cold pool (a swim here is absolutely exhilarating). Guides for these hikes are available at the trailheads; still, it's best to arrange a tour before even setting out.

❻ Northeast Coast. Steep cliffs, dramatic reefs, and rivers that swirl down through forests of mangroves and fields of coconut define this section of land. The road along the Atlantic, with its red cliffs and windswept trees, crosses the Hatton Garden River before entering the village of Marigot. In the northeastern region there are numerous estates—old family holdings planted with fruit trees. Beyond Marigot and the Melville Hall Airport is the beautiful Londonderry Estate. The beach here is inspiring, with driftwood strewn about its velvety black sands, which part halfway—where the Londonderry River spills into the Atlantic (swimming isn't advised because of strong currents, but a river bath here is a memorable treat). Farther along the coast, beyond the village of Wesley (which has a gas station and a shop that sells wonderful bread) and past Eden Estate, there are still more beautiful beaches and coves. The swimming is excellent at Woodford Hill Bay, Hodges Beach, Hampstead Estate, and L'Anse Noir. A stay in the charming community of Calibishie is a must; here you'll find bars and restaurants right on the beach, as well as new villas and guest houses. At Bense, a village in the interior just past Calibishie, you can take a connector road to Chaud Dwe (pronounced show-*dweh*), a beautiful bathing spot in a valley; the only crowd you're likely to encounter is a group of young villagers frolicking in the 15-ft-deep (4½-m-deep) pool and diving off the 25-ft-high (7½-m-high) rocks.

❾ Portsmouth. Portsmouth was once intended to be the capital of Dominica, thanks to its superb harbor on Prince Rupert Bay. In its heyday as many as 400 ships docked here at one time. In 1782 it was also the site of the Battle of Les Saintes, a naval engagement between the French and the English. The English won the battle but lost the much tougher fight against malaria-carrying mosquitoes that bred in the nearby swamps. As a result, Roseau, not Portsmouth, is the capital. Maritime traditions are continued here by the yachting set, and a 2-mi (3-km) stretch of sandy beaches fringed with coconut trees runs to the Picard Estate area.

❶ Roseau. Although it is one of the smallest towns in the Caribbean, Roseau has the highest concentration of inhabitants of any town in the eastern Caribbean islands. Classic architecture and a bustling marketplace transport visitors back in time. Although you can walk the entire town in about an hour, you'll get a much better feel for the place on a leisurely stroll.

For some years now, the Society for Historical Architectural Preservation & Enhancement (SHAPE) has organized programs and projects to preserve the city's architectural heritage. Several interesting buildings have already been restored. **Lilac House** (✉ Kennedy Ave.) has three types of gingerbread fretwork, latticed veranda railings, and heavy hurricane shutters. The **J. W. Edwards Building** (✉ Cnr. Old and King George V Sts.) has a stone base and a wooden second-floor gallery and is home to the cozy Cornerhouse Cafe. This area was laid out by the French on a radial plan rather than a grid, so streets such as Hanover, King George V, and Old radiate from one main section, called the marketplace. South of the marketplace is the Fort Young Hotel, built as a British fort in the 18th century; the nearby state house, public library, and Anglican cathedral are also worth a visit.

The 40-acre **Botanical Gardens,** founded in 1891 as an annex of London's Kew Gardens, is a great place to relax, stroll, or watch a cricket match. In addition to the extensive collection of tropical plants and trees, there's also a parrot aviary. At the Forestry Division office, which is also on the garden grounds, you'll find brochures and booklets on the island's flora, fauna, and national parks. One of the forestry officers, Arlington James, is particularly knowledgeable on these subjects. He or one of the other staff members can also recommend good hiking guides. ✉ *Forestry Division,* ☎ *767/448–2401 ext. 3417.* ☉ *Mon. 8–1 and 2–5, Tues.–Fri. 8–1 and 2–4.*

New developments at Bayfront on the Dame M. E. Charles Boulevard have brightened up the waterfront. The old post office now houses the **Dominica Museum.** This labor of love by local writer and historian Dr. Lennox Honychurch contains furnishings, documents, prints, and maps that date back hundreds of years; you'll also find an entire Carib hut as well as Carib canoes, baskets, and other artifacts. The museum is open weekdays 9–4 and Saturday 9–noon; admission is $2.

2 **Soufrière.** This lazy, sunbaked village lies within the bay that's part of the National Marine Park. First settled by French lumbermen in the 17th century, today Soufrière is primarily a fishing village whose residents are very laid-back. The Catholic church, built of volcanic stone, is one of the island's prettiest churches.

The owners of Nature Island Dive have bought the ruins of the L. Rose Lime Oil factory and are developing the site, which promises to be a gem when it is completed. With sulfur springs to the east, the best diving and snorkeling on the island within the marine park to the west, Bois Cotlette (a historic plantation house) and the current expansion of Petite Coulibrie farther southeast, and the Scotts Head Peninsula at the south tip of the island separating the Caribbean from the Atlantic, there's treasure here to suit every visitor.

DOMINICA A TO Z

To research prices, get advice from other travelers, and book travel arrangements, visit www.fodors.com.

AIR TRAVEL
American Eagle flies into Melville Hall Airport every afternoon from San Juan. The Carib Air Alliance, formed in 2001, brings a number of regional airlines together into Dominica from various hubs: Martinique, St. Lucia, and Antigua into Canefield Airport on scheduled flights

throughout the day. Whitchurch Travel is the agent for the Caribbean Star Airlines, a newer service into Dominica with direct flights from Barbados, Tortola, and St. Vincent with connections to Grenada, Trinidad, Antigua, and St. Kitts. Flights arrive and depart 2 to 4 times daily into Melville Hall Airport depending on the destination. Rates are competitive, and the service is really warm Caribbean. Air Guadeloupe and LIAT also connect with international flights arriving at Melville Hall Airport throughout the day.

➤ AIRLINES AND CONTACTS: **American/American Eagle** (☎ 767/448–6680); **Carib Air Aliance** (☎ 767/448–2181); **LIAT** (☎ 767/448–2421); **Whitchurch Travel (for Caribbean Star Airlines)** (☎ 767/448–2181 or 767/445–8841).

AIRPORTS
Canefield Airport, about 3 mi (5 km) north of Roseau, handles only small aircraft and daytime flights; landing here can be a hair-raising experience for those uneasy about flying. Melville Hall Airport is on the northeast coast, 75 minutes from Roseau, and handles larger planes.

Cab fare from Canefield Airport to Roseau is about $15. The 75-minute drive from Melville Hall Airport to Roseau takes you through the island's Central Forest Reserve and is a tour in itself. The trip costs about $55 by private taxi or $20 per person by co-op cab.

➤ AIRPORT INFORMATION: **Canefield Airport** (☎ 767/449–1199); **Melville Hall Airport** (☎ 767/445–7101).

BOAT AND FERRY TRAVEL
FARES AND SCHEDULES
Express des Isles has scheduled service Monday, Wednesday, and Friday–Sunday from Guadeloupe, in the north to Martinique, and on to St. Lucia in the south on specific days. The Jet Catamaran Ferry arrives and departs at the Roseau Ferry Terminal. The crossing costs $90–$110, takes approximately 90 minutes, and offers superb views of the other islands.

➤ BOAT AND FERRY INFORMATION: **Express des Isles** (✉ Roseau Ferry Terminal, c/o Whitchurch Shipping & Tours, ☎ 767/448–2181).

BUSINESS HOURS
BANKS
Banks are open Monday–Thursday 8–3, Friday 8–5.

POST OFFICES
Post offices are open Monday 8–5, Tuesday–Friday 8–4, Saturday 8–1.

SHOPS
Generally businesses are open Monday 8–5, Tuesday–Friday 8–4, Saturday 8–1. Some stores have longer hours, but you should call ahead to confirm them.

CAR RENTALS
Daily car-rental rates begin at $50 (weekly and long-term rates can be negotiated). Expect to add approximately another $7–$17 a day for optional collision damage insurance; otherwise, you will be asked to leave a credit card number or cash deposit. You'll need to buy a visitor's driving permit (EC$20) at one of the airports or at the Traffic Division office on High Street in Roseau.

The following companies are some of the most reliable with a variety of vehicles and offer airport and hotel pick-up and drop-off.

➤ MAJOR AGENCIES: **Best Deal Car Rental** (✉ 15 Hanover St., Roseau, ☎ 767/449–9204 or 767/235–3325); **Island Car Rentals** (✉ Goodwill

Rd., Goodwill, ☎ 767/448–2886 or 767/445–8789); **Wide Range Car Rentals** (✉ 79 Bath Rd., Roseau, ☎ 767/448–2198).

CAR TRAVEL
GASOLINE
Gasoline stations can be found all over the island; gas costs approximately $2.50 per gallon.

ROAD CONDITIONS
The roads can be narrow in places, and they meander around the coast and through mountainous terrain.

RULES OF THE ROAD
Driving in Dominica is on the left side, though you can rent vehicles with a steering wheel on either the left or right.

ELECTRICITY
Electric voltage is 220/240 AC, 50 cycles. North American appliances require an adapter and transformer; however, many establishments provide these and often have dual voltage fitting (110/120 and 220/240 volts).

EMBASSIES
➤ UNITED KINGDOM: Honorary Consul (☎ 767/448–7655).

EMERGENCIES
➤ AMBULANCE AND FIRE: Dial ☎ 1/800–4357.
➤ HOSPITALS: **Princess Margaret Hospital** (✉ Federation Dr., Goodwill, ☎ 767/448–2231 or 767/448–2233).
➤ PHARMACIES: **Jolly's Pharmacy** (✉ 12 King George V St., Roseau, ☎ 767/448–3388).
➤ POLICE: Dial ☎ 1/800–4357.

ETIQUETTE AND BEHAVIOR
Unlike neighboring Martinique and Guadeloupe, topless bathing is frowned upon in Dominica. In addition, swimsuits may not be worn on the street.

Dominicans, on the whole, are laid-back and polite. You will no doubt be greeted with a warm "good morning" or "good night" by anyone you pass on the street. Yet the people here are very private; it's better to ask permission before photographing someone. Note also that bargaining is not generally appreciated in Dominican shops.

FESTIVALS AND SEASONAL EVENTS
Dominica boasts the most spontaneous carnival in the region, Mas Domnik. It's great to join a band and get all costumed and painted. Revelling in the streets during Carnival Monday and Tuesday, it's one big family. Celebrations usually heat up the last 10 days or so before Ash Wednesday. The National Cultural Council hosts the Emancipation Celebrations in August. September and October see Independence celebrations, culminating on Independence Day on November 3. Another major event is the Annual World Creole Music Festival, held the last weekend in October. This three-day music and cultural festival draws performers and Creole music enthusiasts from around the globe. Community Day of Service is November 4.

HEALTH
If you're susceptible to motion sickness, be sure to pack some medication—the roads twist and turn dramatically. If you plan to hike, pack good sneakers and/or rugged hiking boots (trail conditions vary), a backpack, an extra set of hiking clothes, and insect repellent.

HOLIDAYS

Public holidays for 2002 are: New Year's (Jan. 1), Merchant's Holiday (Jan. 2), Carnival Jump-Up Days (two days before Ash Wednesday each year), Ash Wednesday, Labour Day (May 1), Whit Monday (May 24), Emancipation Day (Aug. 5), Independence Day (Nov. 3) and Community Service Day (Nov. 4), Christmas Day (Dec. 25), and Boxing Day (Dec. 26).

LANGUAGE

The official language is English. Most Dominicans also speak Creole (with roots in French, English, and African).

MAIL AND SHIPPING

First-class letters to North America cost EC95¢ and those to the U.K. cost EC90¢; postcards are EC55¢ to just about anywhere in the world. The general post office is opposite the ferry terminal in Roseau. Dominica is often confused with the Dominican Republic, so when addressing letters to the island, be sure to write: The Commonwealth of Dominica, Eastern Caribbean. Islands in this part of the Caribbean do not use postal codes.

MONEY MATTERS

Prices throughout this chapter are quoted in U.S. dollars unless indicated otherwise.

ATMS

You'll find ATMs in all the banks in Roseau—including Barclays Bank on Old Street, the Royal Bank of Canada near the cruise-ship berth, Banque Française Commerciale on Queen Mary Street, and the Bank of Nova Scotia on Hillsborough Street—as well as some in larger villages such as Portsmouth. They dispense EC dollars only and accept international bank cards.

CREDIT CARDS

Major credit cards are widely accepted, as are traveler's checks.

CURRENCY

The official currency is the Eastern Caribbean dollar (EC$) but U.S. dollars is readily accepted. The exchange rate will be EC$2.67 to the U.S. $1, but you'll usually get change in EC dollars.

PASSPORTS AND VISAS

U.S. citizens need a valid passport or an original birth certificate along with a government-issued photo ID. Visitors from other countries must have a valid passport, and all visitors need a return or ongoing ticket.

SAFETY

As with all destinations in the world, crime has been known to rear its ugly head on Dominica. It's always wise to secure valuables in hotel safes and not carry too much money or many valuables around. Remember that if you rent a car to tour the island, you may have to park it in a remote area, so don't leave valuables in your vehicle while you're off on a hike or a tour.

SIGHTSEEING TOURS

A plethora of certified guides are willing and able, and there are numerous tour and taxi companies; ask the staff at your hotel for a recommendation. A couple of the most reputed operators are Ken's Hinterland Adventure Tours & Taxi Service, which offers excursions in four-wheel-drive vans (with air-conditioning and two-way radios) with knowledgeable guides. Their botanical and ornithological trips

are good. Tours cost from $25 to $50 per person. Dominica Tours co-
ordinates a variety of terrestrial and aquatic excursions (including
tours tailored to your specific interests) in sturdy four-wheel-drive, air-
conditioned vehicles, boats, bikes, or on foot. Prices range from $25
to $65 per person.

➤ CONTACTS: **Ken's Hinterland Adventure Tours & Taxi Service** (✉
c/o Fort Young Hotel, Roseau, ☎ 767/448–4850 or 767/235–3517);
Dominica Tours (✉ Anchorage Hotel, Castle Comfort, ☎ 767/448–
2638 or 767/448–0990).

TAXES

DEPARTURE TAX
The departure tax is U.S.$20 or EC$50.

SALES TAX
Hotels collect a 5% government hotel occupancy tax, restaurants a 5%
government sales tax.

TAXIS
You can catch taxis at the airports and in Roseau. Rates are fixed by
the government, but prices can usually be negotiated. You could also
opt for a co-op, sharing a taxi (and the fare) with other passengers going
in the same direction. Drivers are also happy to offer their services as
guides at the cost of $20 an hour, per car of four, with tip extra. It's
good to get a recommendation from your hotel, the Dominica Hotel
and Tourism Association, or the Division of Tourism. For more information on reputable taxi companies contact the Dominica Taxi Association or Nature Island Taxi Association. Mally's Taxi & Tours Service
has been operating for over three decades and runs regular service to
airports as well as offers tour and taxi services at most hotels and guesthouses. Alwin's Taxi Service has some great guys who get to you
quickly and give courteous service. If you're in and around Roseau,
try them.

➤ CONTACTS: **Alwin's Taxi Service** (☎ 767/448–4260); **Dominica Taxi
Association** (☎ 767/449–8533); **Mally's Taxi & Tours Service** (☎ 767/
448–3114 or 767/448–3360—24 hrs); **Nature Island Taxi Association**
(☎ 767/448–1679).

TELEPHONES

COUNTRY AND AREA CODES
To call Dominica from the U.S., dial the area code, 767, and the local
access code, 44, followed by the five-digit local number.

INTERNATIONAL CALLS
The island has a very advanced telecommunication system and accordingly efficient direct-dial international service. All pay phones are
equipped for local, overseas dialing, and credit card calling, accepting
either EC coins or phone cards, which you can buy at many island stores
and at the airports.

LOCAL CALLS
On the island, dial the seven-digit number that follows the area code.

TIPPING
Most hotels and restaurants add a 10% service charge to your bill. A
5% tip for exceptionally good service on top of the service charge is
always welcomed; otherwise just tip accordingly.

VISITOR INFORMATION
➤ BEFORE YOU LEAVE: **Dominican Tourist Office** (✉ 800 2nd Ave., Suite
1802, New York, NY 10017, ☎ 212/949–1711, FAX 212/949–1714,

WEB www.dominica.dm); **The Dominica Tourist Office at MKI Ltd.,** (⊠ Mitre House, 66 Abbey Rd., Bush Hill Park, Enfield, Middlesex, EN1 2QE, U.K. ☎ 181/350–1000, FAX 181/350–1011); **Office of the Dominica High Commission, London** (⊠ 1 Collingham Gardens, London SW5 0HW, U.K., ☎ 0171/370–5194).

➤ IN DOMINICA: **Division of Tourism** (⊠ Valley Rd., Roseau, ☎ 767/ 448–2045; Old Post Office branch ⊠ Dame M. E. Charles Blvd., Roseau, ☎ 767/448–2045 ext. 118; Canefield Airport branch ☎ 767/ 449–1242; Melville Hall Airport ☎ 767/445–7051).

10 DOMINICAN REPUBLIC

Updated by
Eileen
Robinson Smith

Wearing nothing but a layer of Israeli mud, I was set out to dry on a chaise longue at Natura Cabanas. After dozing in the tropical sun, I opened my eyes to the music of a songbird making the rounds between the passion fruit and citrus trees. My primitive spa experience had begun with a steam bath in the "magic mushroom." After a break for juice therapy, there was the kind of deep, all-over body massage that puts you in another zone. Next, a skinny-dip off the deserted beach and it's back to the bungalow, the architect-owner's take on a native hut with a palm-thatched roof. Ten minutes from Cabarete, the spa looks like a century long past in a faraway paradise.

It's hard to say which is more likely to leave you breathless in the Dominican Republic (D.R.): the unspoiled scenery or the merengue—wonderful, sexy music that Dominicans seem to dance to 365 days a year. Sprawling over two-thirds of the island of Hispaniola, which it shares with Haiti, the D.R. is a delightful, almost magical place. Its people are friendly and hospitable by nature; if you return their courtesy, they'll do their best to ensure that your vacation is memorable. The D.R. also happens to be one of the least expensive Caribbean destinations.

Hispaniola has had a stormy history replete with revolutions, military coups, invasions, epidemics, and bankruptcy. Columbus happened upon this island on December 5, 1492, and on Christmas Eve his ship, the *Santa María*, was wrecked on its Atlantic shore. He named it La Isla Española (the Spanish Island), established a small colony, and sailed back to Spain on the *Pinta*. Santo Domingo was founded in 1496 by Columbus's brother, Bartholomeo Columbus, and Nicolás de Ovando, and during the 16th century it became the bustling New World hub of Spanish commerce and culture. In the 17th century the western third of the island was ceded to France. A slave revolt there in 1804 resulted in the establishment of Haiti—the first black republic. Dominicans and Haitians battled for control of the island throughout the 19th century. The Dominicans declared themselves independent from Haiti in 1844 and from Spain in 1865. The country was, however, bankrupt by the turn of the century.

The United States helped to administer the island's finances, and U.S. Marines occupied it from 1916 until 1924, when a new Dominican constitution was signed. Rafael Trujillo ruled the D.R. with an iron fist from 1930 until his assassination in 1961. A short-lived democracy was overthrown soon after, and U.S. Marines were sent down yet again in 1965. The country has been relatively stable since the early 1970s, and its government has been a staunch supporter of the United States. Indeed, American influence looms large in Dominican life. Major thoroughfares in the capital, Santo Domingo, are named after American presidents; many Dominicans speak at least rudimentary English and have relatives living in the States; and baseball is a national passion. Still, this is a vibrantly Latin country—at times cool, collected, and laid-back; at times fiery hot, frenetic, and chaotic.

Dominican towns and cities are generally not quaint, neat, or particularly pretty, and poverty is everywhere. However, the ever-increasing role of tourism in the economy is bringing about changes that benefit residents and visitors alike: major highways have been repaved; sidewalks, lighting, and signage in urban areas are being improved; and the banks are issuing low-interest loans to people who want to buy and restore colonial buildings. More projects are in the works, notably the restoration of Santo Domingo's Colonial Zone. Clearly the D.R. is realizing more of its vast potential.

The country has several areas with all the attractions and amenities necessary for the perfect island vacation. Santo Domingo is the oldest continuously inhabited city in this half of the globe, and many visitors find it difficult to tear themselves away from its 16th-century Colonial Zone. Sun worshipers head to one of the many beach resort areas, perhaps Boca Chica, Juan Dolio, or La Romana, on the southeast coast; Punta Cana, on the island's eastern tip; La Samaná, in the northeast; the Amber Coast and Puerto Plata, to the northwest; and Barahona, in the southwest. The highest peak in the West Indies, Pico Duarte (10,370 ft/3,171 m), lures hikers to the central mountain range. Ancient sunken galleons and coral reefs divert divers and snorkelers. And everywhere there's the breathtaking scenery, the land ever turning and twisting and towering into mountains before tumbling into the sea.

Lodging

The D.R. has the largest hotel inventory (49,000 rooms and growing; at press time 5,000 more were under construction) in the Caribbean. The options range from rustic country inns to posh beach resorts to chic Santo Domingo hotels. The growth is a reflection of confidence in the government.

Santo Domingo hotels generally base their tariffs on the EP and maintain the same room rates year-round. Beach resorts have high winter and low summer rates—with prices reduced by as much as 50%. Along the north coast you'll find many all-inclusive properties. Although it wasn't long ago that visitors wanted all-inclusive packages, the trend now is toward flexibility. Many Punta Cana resorts are once again offering the EP and MAP (occasionally, you'll also find the FAP). Sosua and Cabarete are strongholds of the small inn, which isn't all-inclusive, but that does not mean that larger, strictly all-inclusive resorts don't exist there. They do.

Most visitors take advantage of the many charter air-hotel packages available through travel agents and tour operators, particularly in winter. You can now get a direct flight to Punta Cana from, say, Connecticut or Missouri, and pay $700 for a week's vacation including air-fare and a stay at a brand-new, all-inclusive property.

CATEGORY	COST*
$$$$	over $175
$$$	$125–$175
$$	$75–$125
$	under $75

All prices are for a standard double room, in high season, excluding 10% service charge and 13% tax. If a hotel is all-inclusive, the rates include three meals, most sports and activities, and often alcoholic beverages.

Santo Domingo

$$$ 🏨 **Barcelo Gran Hotel Lina & Casino.** A steadfast city landmark for decades, now painted in bold Caribbean colors (from mango to hot pink), this hotel is near the Malecón and the Presidential Palace. Business and conventions are a large part of their repeat clientele because of the professional and helpful staff. Guests and the capital's movers and shakers still frequent the Restaurante Lina, with its classic continental dishes and piano bar. ⊠ *Av. Maximo Gomez and Av. 27 de Febrero (Box 1915)*, ☎ *809/563–5000*, FAX *809/686–5521*, WEB *www.barcelo-hotels.com. 202 rooms, 15 suites. 2 restaurants, piano bar, coffee shop, air-conditioning, minibars, hot tub, 2 pools, health club, casino, concierge, business services. AE, DC, MC, V. EP, FAP, MAP.*

$$$ 🏨 **Hotel Santo Domingo.** Surrounded by walled gardens and over-
★ looking the sea, this in-town getaway is favored by diplomats (many VIPs check into one of the Excel Club's eight business rooms with king-size beds and offices with speaker phones and modem lines). The Cafetel restaurant serves lunch and features an antipasto buffet and courtyard seating. Merengue combos draw locals to Las Palmas for dancing, and a sophisticated after-work crowd gathers at the Marrakesh Café & Bar, with its American music and Casablanca-style decor that complements the lobby's mahogany arches and potted palms. A trellised arcade leads to a large, peaceful pool that's surrounded by greenery. ⊠ *Avs. Independencia and Abraham Lincoln (Box 2112)*, ☎ *809/221–1511 or 800/877–3643*, FAX *809/533–8898*, WEB *www.hotel.stodgo.com.do. 220 rooms. 3 restaurants, 2 bars, air-conditioning, pool, hair salon, sauna, 3 tennis courts, health club, business services, meeting rooms, car rental, helipad. AE, MC, V. BP.*

$$$ 🏨 **Hotel Sofitel Frances.** A two-story, 16th-century structure, the facade has handsome native stonework, and the interior is done in pink stucco. Columned arches open to a European-style fountain and a courtyard furnished with teak and shaded by white umbrellas. Thanks to rattan furniture and potted plants, second-floor patios have a tropical, colonial feel. Guest rooms and baths are minimalistic, with rugs on tiled floors and stylish French bedspreads, plus satellite TV. The lobby restaurant specializes in French and international cuisine. ⊠ *Calle Las Mercedes and Arzobispo Merino*, ☎ *809/685–9331 or 800/221–45423*, FAX *809/685–1289*, WEB *www.sofitel.com. 19 rooms. Restaurant, bar, minibars. AE, MC, V. EP.*

$$$ 🏨 **Melia Santo Domingo Hotel and Casino.** Right on the Malecón, the
★ lobby, restaurants, and guest rooms—all of which were completely and lavishly renovated in late 2000—a look that is contemporary yet classic. There are wonderful ocean views from throughout the hotel. Royal Service Level guests lap in the luxury, with such special amenities as a full breakfast, complementary premium liquors, and fine hors d'oeuvres in the concierge lounge. The rooms are "beyond" comfortable, and your butler will even have your clothes pressed for free. The Restaurant Casabe serves noteworthy buffets as well as à la carte items and is open 24 hours; the impressive Da Vinci restaurant faces the ocean

Dominican Republic

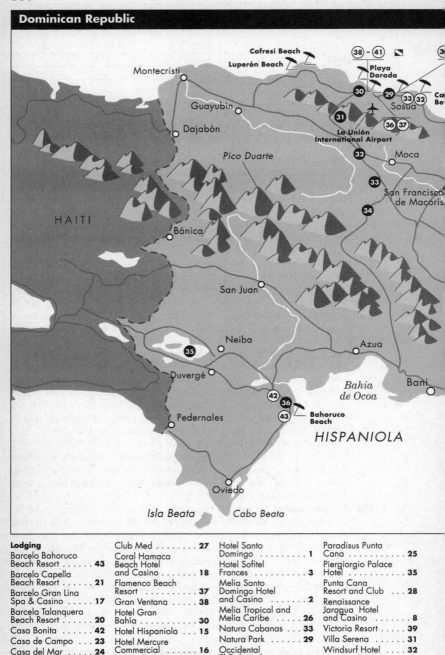

Lodging

Barcelo Bahoruco
Beach Resort 43

Barcelo Capella
Beach Resort 21

Barcelo Gran Lina
Spa & Casino 17

Barcela Talanquera
Beach Resort 20

Casa Bonita 42

Casa de Campo . . . 23

Casa del Mar 24

Club Med 27

Coral Hamaca
Beach Hotel
and Casino 18

Flamenco Beach
Resort 37

Gran Ventana 38

Hotel Gran
Bahía 30

Hotel Hispaniola . . 15

Hotel Mercure
Commercial 16

Hotel Occidental
Playa Dorada 40

Hotel Santo
Domingo 1

Hotel Sofitel
Frances 3

Melia Santo
Domingo Hotel
and Casino 2

Melia Tropical and
Melia Caribe 26

Natura Cabanas . . . 33

Natura Park 29

Occidental
El Embajador
and Casino 9

Paradisus Punta
Cana 25

Piergiorgio Palace
Hotel 35

Punta Cana
Resort and Club . . . 28

Renaissance
Jaragua Hotel
and Casino 8

Victoria Resort 39

Villa Serena 31

Windsurf Hotel 32

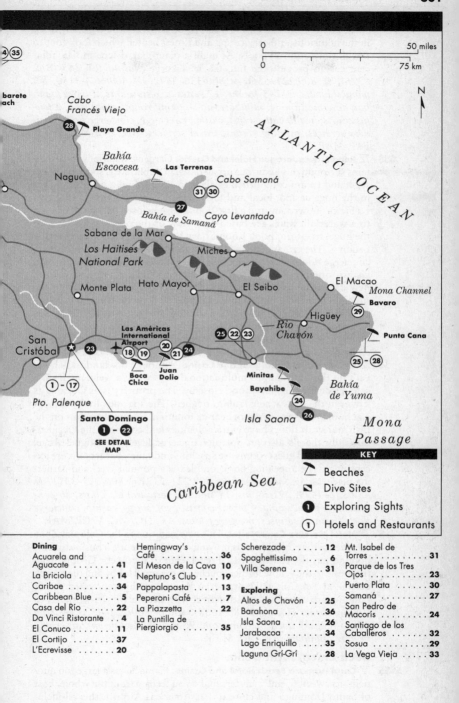

ATLANTIC OCEAN

N

0 ____ 50 miles
0 ____ 75 km

4 35

barete
ach

Cabo Francés Viejo

28 **Playa Grande**

Bahía Escocesa

Nagua

Las Terrenas

Cabo Samaná

31 30

27

Bahía de Samaná *Cayo Levantado*

Sabana de la Mar

Los Haitises National Park

Miches

Monte Plata Hato Mayor El Seibo

El Macao

Mona Channel

Bavaro

29

Higüey

Río Chavón

25 22 23

San Cristóbal

23

Las Américas International Airport

18 19

20

21 24

Punta Cana

25 - 28

Boca Chica

Juan Dolio

1 - 17

Pto. Palenque

Minitas

Bayahibe

24

26

Bahía de Yuma

Isla Saona

Mona Passage

Santo Domingo

1 - 22

SEE DETAIL MAP

Caribbean Sea

KEY

Beaches

Dive Sites

1 Exploring Sights

1 Hotels and Restaurants

Dining
Acuarela and
Aguacate **41**
La Briciola **14**
Caribae **34**
Caribbean Blue **5**
Casa del Río **22**
Da Vinci Ristorante . **4**
El Conuco **11**
El Cortijo **37**
L'Ecrevisse **20**

Hemingway's
Café **36**
El Meson de la Cava **10**
Neptuno's Club **19**
Pappalapasta **13**
Peperoni Café **7**
La Piazzetta **22**
La Puntilla de
Piergiorgio **35**

Scherezade **12**
Spaghettissimo **6**
Villa Serena **31**

Exploring
Altos de Chavón . . . **25**
Barahona **36**
Isla Saona **26**
Jarabacoa **34**
Lago Enriquillo **35**
Laguna Grí-Grí **28**

Mt. Isabel de
Torres **31**
Parque de los Tres
Ojos **23**
Puerto Plata **30**
Samaná **27**
San Pedro de
Macorís **24**
Santiago de los
Caballeros **32**
Sosua **29**
La Vega Vieja **33**

and specializes in contemporary Mediterranean cuisine. You can rent a cell phone from the business center, or flee from the world of work in the luxurious, full-service spa and fitness center, which looks out to the glorious rooftop pools. At night a piano bar, disco, and an adjacent casino provide the fun. ⊠ *Av. George Washington 365 (Box 8326),* ☎ *809/221–6666 or 800/336–3542,* FAX *809/687–8150,* WEB *www.solmelia.es. 245 rooms, 17 suites. 2 restaurants, 2 bars, piano bar, air-conditioning, minibars, no-smoking rooms, pool, spa, 2 tennis courts, health club, shops, casino, concierge, concierge floor, business services, meeting rooms, travel services. AE, DC, MC, V. EP, FAP, MAP.*

$$$ ★ 🏨 **Renaissance Jaragua Hotel and Casino.** Gardens, waterfalls, and fountains surround this luxurious urban oasis. In public areas soothing beige, sage, and cream color schemes abound. You'll find a grill restaurant in the huge casino; local and big-name performers in the 1,000-seat La Fiesta Showroom; and a first-floor glass-enclosed bar that looks out to a waterfall. Rates are based on a view of the ocean, garden, or of the huge, free-form pool. Rooms have been painted and boast all new bedding. The expanded Renaissance Club—53 rooms on executive, concierge floors with a separate lounge and terrace that affords ocean vistas—often sells out on weeknights. Suites have Club privileges and new data ports and larger desks. The business center is efficient; the fitness center is the largest in the city. ⊠ *Av. George Washington 367,* ☎ *809/221–2222 or 800/331–3542,* FAX *809/686–0528,* WEB *renaissancehotels.com. 292 rooms, 8 suites. 4 restaurants, 5 bars, air-conditioning, minibars, pool, hot tub, sauna, spa, golf, 4 tennis courts, casino, dance club, concierge floor, business services. AE, MC, V. EP, FAP, MAP.*

$$ 🏨 **Occidental El Embajador and Casino.** Although this landmark hotel isn't on the Malecón, its multinational flags wave a welcome from a safe residential neighborhood close by. The property is as glorious as it was in the days when Trujillo reigned. The spacious lobby is a social hub; orchestras perform near its fountain. Executive rooms on the fifth and sixth floors have extra amenities and comprise the Occidental Club; there's also an upscale concierge level, the Miguel Angel Club. Standard guest rooms are spacious and quiet; bathrooms are exceptional. The appealing pool complex is a popular weekend gathering place. ⊠ *Av. Sarasota 65,* ☎ *809/221–2131 or 800/843–3311,* FAX *809/532–4494. 291 rooms, 14 suites. 2 restaurants, 3 bars, air-conditioning, pool, sauna, 4 tennis courts, gym, shops, casino, concierge floor, business services, meeting rooms. AE, DC, MC, V. CP, MAP.*

$ 🏨 **Hotel Mercure Commercial.** This new addition to the Colonial Zone is evidence that the old city is moving on up! In theory, a businessmen's hotel, it has the characteristic French élan of the Accor Group, from the music to the yellow leather couches in the small lobby and the French cuisine at "el Colonial" brasserie. Rooms in this renovated 1940s building are cramped but attractive, with decorative tile work. ⊠ *El Conde, corner Hostos,* ☎ *809/688–5500 or 800/221–4523,* FAX *809/ 688–5522,* WEB *www.mercure.com. 96 rooms. Restaurant, air-conditioning, minibars. AE, MC, V. EP.*

Boca Chica/Juan Dolio

$$$$ 🏨 **Coral Hamaca Beach Hotel and Casino.** Hamaca has a large fun quotient, its sweet, friendly staffers make you feel a part of the whole. East of Santo Domingo and close to Las Américas Airport, this all-inclusive offers around-the-clock services. Its reception area has terra-cotta floors, wicker furnishings, works by Dominican artists, and huge floral arrangements. Opt for one of the 247 newer rooms. A lovely champagne-color beach has two bars, a juice bar, Mexican, Chinese, and

Italian restaurants, among others, and a *palapa* (thatched-roof, open-air structure) where live music is played nightly. For more fun head to the casino, amphitheater, or disco. ✉ *Boca Chica Beach*, ☎ *809/523–4611 or 888/942–6725*, ℻ *809/523–6767*, 🖩 *www.coralhotels.com. 630 rooms. 6 restaurants, 6 bars, grill, air-conditioning, 2 pools, 3 tennis courts, beach, dive shop, snorkeling, windsurfing, boating, bicycles, casino, dance club, theater, children's programs, playground, laundry service, meeting rooms. AE, DC, MC, V. All-inclusive.*

$$$ ★ 🖩 **Barcelo Capella Beach Resort.** Set on 17 acres punctuated with benches and manicured shrubbery, this grand resort is an eclectic mix of architectural styles—from Victorian to Moorish. Its yellow-stucco exterior is accented by white latticework and columns, coral stonework, and a peaked red-tile roof. The large, quiet rooms have a civilized, almost British colonial air; some have terraces or balconies and sea views. There's evening entertainment at the theater or one of the bars or a *folklórica* dance ensemble, performing. Capella has taken over Talenguera's tri-level, palapa disco on the beach and its water sports club. Also they added 200 new beach rooms, a theater, and a second buffet restaurant. ✉ *Villas Del Mar (Box 4750, Santo Domingo)*, ☎ *809/ 526–1080*, ℻ *809/526–1088*, 🖩 *www.barcelo-hotels.com. 271 rooms, 22 suites. 3 restaurants, 3 bars, air-conditioning, minibars, 2 pools, massage, sauna, 2 tennis courts, health club, beach, snorkeling, windsurfing, boating, shops, dance club, recreation room, theater, children's programs, concierge floor, meeting rooms. AE, MC, V. All-inclusive, EP, MAP.*

$$ 🖩 **Barcelo Talanquera Beach Resort.** At this relaxed resort guest quarters are in pink-stucco, low-rise buildings on 1,260 lushly landscaped acres. You can explore the grounds—perhaps resting beside a stream, a fish pond, or a swimming pool (one even has a waterfall). Opt for one of the 100 new rooms that are on the beach. Check out the new restaurant and disco. For a taste of fine contemporary Caribbean cuisine, a meal at L'Ecrevisse restaurant is a must. ✉ *Juan Dolio Beach*, ☎ *809/526–1510*, ℻ *809/526–2408*, 🖩 *www.barcelo-hotels.com. 435 rooms. 3 restaurants, 4 bars, air-conditioning, 3 pools, Ping-Pong, volleyball, beach, dive shop, snorkeling, windsurfing, bicycles, children's programs. AE, MC, V. All-inclusive.*

La Romana

$$$$ ★ 🖩 **Casa de Campo.** "House in the Country" is an understated appellation for this enormous complex. It sprawls over 7,000 acres and can accommodate 3,000 guests (indeed many wealthy Dominicans have luxurious second homes here). It includes 350 hotel rooms and 150 two-, three-, and four-bedroom villas with kitchens. A truly world-class property, always evolving, it has a tennis center considered The Wimbledon of the Caribbean and the best equestrian center in the islands, with hundreds of mounts for use on the riding trails, the polo grounds, and the school ring. But golf is the big draw here. On-site are two 18-hole courses (one of them—Teeth of the Dog—has seven holes that skirt the sea and is rated numero uno in the Caribbean). A third 18-hole course, also designed by famed architect Pete Dye, is being constructed around the artisan village of Altos de Chavon, with breathtaking views of the Chavon River and the Caribbean; the first nine holes are slated to open at the end of 2001. Also underway is a luxurious yacht marina and villa complex scheduled to open in the fall of 2001. Other resort amenities include a trap shooting center (with a great restaurant, the Afro/British Safari Club) and a 5,000-seat amphitheater, at which such big-name entertainers like Julio Iglesias perform. Two of the best optional activities are the sunset sea cruise and the very special cruise down the Rio Chavon. Excellent children's programs make this com-

plex perfect for families. Minibuses provide free transportation around the resort and Altos de Chavon, although you should definitely consider renting golf carts, scooters, and bicycles. The new La Romana/Casa de Campo International Airport has opened, with improved air service. Its creative design replicates a sugar mill factory, since the resort was originally a sugar cane plantation. ⊠ *5-min cab ride from La Romana (Box 140, La Romana),* ☎ *809/523–3333 or 800/877–3643,* ℻ *809/523–8548,* ⊞ *www.casadecampo.cc. 500 units. 10 restaurants, bar, air-conditioning, kitchenettes, 19 pools, sauna, 3 18-hole golf courses, 13 tennis courts, health club, horseback riding, dive shop, snorkeling, windsurfing, fishing, bicycles, shops, theater, children's programs. AE, MC, V. All-inclusive, EP, FAP, MAP.*

$$$$ ⊡ **Casa del Mar.** This deluxe resort, its whimsical gingerbread fretwork awash in Caribbean colors, is on an exceptional palm-fringed ribbon of white sand close to La Romana Airport and Casa de Campo. Most of the attractive guest rooms have views of the sea, the spectacular pools, or both. In the Bayahibe Restaurant, buffets of fresh, tasty dishes are served beneath stunning handcrafted chandeliers (be sure to check out the sundae bar, which has ice cream in such exotic flavors as coconut or corn). There's more fine dining to be found in the on-site Asian and Italian restaurants. The free half-day excursion to Saona Island is a treat. ⊠ *Bayahibe Bay,* ☎ *809/221–8880 or 877/227–2536,* ℻ *809/221–8881. 568 rooms. 4 restaurants, 4 bars, air-conditioning, 2 pools, hot tub, 4 tennis courts, archery, gym, horseback riding, volleyball, beach, dive shop, snorkeling, boating, windsurfing, bicycles, dance club. AE, MC, V. All-inclusive.*

Punta Cana

$$$$ ⊡ **Melia Tropical All-Inclusive Beach Resort and Melia Caribe All-In-**
★   **clusive Beach, Spa & Golf Resort.** Melia has done an exceptional job with these American-friendly resorts, designed with both couples and families in mind. Each of the two-story bungalows contains 12 junior suites per floor; all are decorated in soft Caribbean pastels and have balconies. The lobby has fountains, lagoons, boardwalks, pillars, and sculptures. The sprawling complex is beautified by waterscapes, mangroves, and palms. The hot-pink flamingos here aren't plastic, and the pond's white rotunda is positively presidential. (It is the site of many a wedding ceremony, as well as orchestral performances.) Surrounded by tall coconut trees, the pool (with a Jacuzzi at its center and a smaller pool for kids) looks like a lake. At the self-indulgent his-and-her spa, with its Grecian-style white columns, you can have an aromatherapy massage or relax in a whirlpool surrounded by classical sculptures. A cute little train regularly takes guests on the five-minute journey to beautiful Bavaro Beach (topless sunbathing allowed). Although golf is key at the adjacent Melia Caribe Resort (at press time there were 18 holes with an additional nine in the works), other facilities include guest villas, a shopping center, a movie theater, Gourmet Boulevard lined with numerous specialty restaurants, and a dine-around program to help you beat the all-inclusive-buffet blues. Top choices are Ma Maison (with an adjacent cappuccino/liqueur bar) and the Japanese restaurant. After dinner, men sink into the leather chairs at the Cigar Club, teenagers go to play the electronic games and to dance, while couples listen to the live jazz or watch one of the two professional animation shows. ⊠ *Punta Cana, near Higüey,* ☎ *809/221–1290 or 800/336–3542 (reservation service),* ℻ *809/221–4595,* ⊞ *www.solmelia.es. 1,044 units. 15 restaurants, 6 bars, 2 pools, 2 spas, golf, 6 tennis courts, health club, beach, snorkeling, windsurfing, boating, casino, dance club, children's programs, meeting rooms. AE, DC, MC, V. All-inclusive.*

$$$$ 🏨 **Natura Park.** Here's a new concept: an eco-sensitive all-inclusive. At this squeaky clean, environmentally correct establishment, meals are made from wholesome, all-natural ingredients, and furniture is handcrafted from the coco palms that were cut down to make room for the property's gardens, walkways, and man-made lakes. The grounds also have what remains of a coconut plantation as well as a mangrove forest and a natural lake. Guest rooms are in 13 buildings that put stone, wood, and cane to good use. The outdoor à la carte restaurant looks onto a spectacular lagoon-style pool (with a swim-up bar) and beyond to Bavaro Beach. Be renewed at the luxurious spa. ✉ *Bavaro Beach*, ☎ *809/538–3111 or 888/628–8727,* 𝔽𝔸𝕏 *809/221–6060. 518 rooms, 6 suites. 3 restaurants, 4 bars, 2 pools, spa, 3 tennis courts, beach, windsurfing, boating, dance club, children's programs. MC, V. All-inclusive.*

$$$$ 🏨 **Paradisus Punta Cana.** The Paradisus has an open-air lobby of lagoons and rock gardens. The path to the elegant casino (players dress accordingly) is punctuated by sculptures. Bi-level suites have tropical motifs and brightly painted wooden furnishings. If you don't feel pampered enough by your luxurious surroundings and the new spa, you will by the staff and trilingual concierges. From the simple grilled seafood and meats at the beach palapas to the sophisticated international fare (and complimentary cognacs and liqueurs) at the à la carte Romantico restaurant, the cuisine here is exceptional. You'll find everything from aquaerobics (often followed by rum cocktails at the swim-up bar) to painting lessons to PADI dive instruction. Honeymoon packages are exceptional, and weddings are blissful. (Love that white, horse-drawn marriage carriage.) ✉ *Bavaro Beach*, ☎ *809/687–9923 or 800/33–MELIA,* 𝔽𝔸𝕏 *809/687–0752. 497 suites. 7 restaurants, 4 bars, air-conditioning, spa, 4 tennis courts, archery, health club, beach, dive shop, snorkeling, windsurfing, boating, bicycles, casino, children's programs. AE, DC, MC, V. All-inclusive.*

$$$ 🏨 **Club Med.** Newly renovated in 2000, this "village" is looking fine, with the sleeping rooms particularly attractive. Put in for one of the 500 new rooms. Set on one of the island's best beaches, it is a great choice for families, what with a Petit Club Med (ages 2–4) and a Mini Club Med (ages 4–13). Though the resort is American-friendly, there is a lot that happens here in Spanish—and of course, many GO's (staffers) speak French and English. Ask about frequent specials. Most packages come with airfare. And have fun. P.S. Nonguests can pay for a day-pass, which includes lunch with complementary beer and wine service. ✉ *Punta Cana*, ☎ *809/686–5500 or 800/258–2633,* 𝔽𝔸𝕏 *809/685–5287. 2,000 rooms. 3 restaurants, 2 bars, air-conditioning, pool, aerobics, archery, volleyball, beach, windsurfing, kayaking, boating, waterskiing, nightclub, children's programs. AE, MC, V. All-inclusive.*

$$$ 🏨 **Punta Cana Beach Resort.** Those of us who knew the original resort from years past remember when the road was like a lunarscape, the lobby nautical-tacky, and the rooms quite ugly. Yet it was always endearing, with a charisma appreciated by die-hard Caribophiles. And there has always been that incredible beach, with breezy hammocks hanging from the seaswept coco palms and topless Euro-beauties. Well, it's come a long way, baby. This is one of the most ambitious and long-awaited resort developments in the country. Yes, there is still a hotel, the original totally renovated, the new beach wing upscale with hardwoods, marble, and chic tropical furnishings. Roofs of the main buildings are still made of woven palm fronds, and, yes, the beach with its beauties is as gorgeous as ever. Rooms are distributed in luxury golf villas, decorated by investor Oscar de La Renta and overlooking a spectacular Pete Dye 18-hole golf course, and in three-story buildings with views of tennis courts, lush gardens, or the beach. The first stage of La Marina Punta Cana is completed with 48 berths, the Yola Restaurant, and 46 ocean-view apartments. A nearby exclusive residential development is underway, where privacy and natural environment will dominate. The mansion of Julio Iglesias, another investor, is finished and awaiting more new and interesting neighbors on the next 55 sites. Much more is in the works. ⊠ *Playa Punta Cana,* ☎ *809/221–2262 or 888/442–2262,* FAX *809/687–8745,* WEB *www.puntacana.com. 418 rooms. 5 restaurants, 5 bars, pool, hair salon, 18-hole golf course, 4 tennis courts, aerobics, health club, horseback riding, beach, dive shop, snorkeling, windsurfing, boating, marina, fishing, children's programs, laundry services, business services, meeting rooms. AE, MC, V. MAP.*

Samaná

$$$$ 🏨 **Hotel Gran Bahía.** This seaside, Victorian-style building is all turrets, gables, and fretwork; it also has graceful verandas that overlook the pool. Rooms are very large and have cheerful floral prints, tile floors, and watercolor paintings. The grand yet welcoming reception area and three-story white, colonnaded atrium surround a spectacular fountain flanked by cozy nooks. The superb views make breakfast on your private balcony a treat. Dining in the alfresco restaurant is pleasant, or you can try a meal in the pastel-pretty indoor buffet dining room. (Note, however, that the food is not of the same caliber as the accommodations.) ⊠ *10 mins from Samaná (Box 2024, Santo Domingo),* ☎ *809/ 538–3111,* FAX *809/538–2764. 110 rooms. 2 restaurants, bar, air-conditioning, pool, hair salon, golf, 2 tennis courts, archery, gym, horseback riding. AE, MC, V. All-inclusive.*

$$ 🏨 **Villa Serena.** This little-known gem is down the beach from the fishing village of Las Galeras and at the end of the long, scenic road from Puerto Plata. Each room is individually decorated and has a lanai overlooking the Bahía de Rincón. Prices include breakfast, and the Villa Serena restaurant serves some of the best food on the peninsula. ⊠ *Las Galeras (Box 51–1),* ☎ *809/696–0065,* FAX *809/538–2545. 11 rooms. Restaurant, bar, air-conditioning, fans, pool, horseback riding, beach, dive shop, snorkeling, bicycles. AE, MC, V. CP.*

The Amber Coast

$$$$ 🏨 **Flamenco Beach Resort.** This high-energy (some would say busy and crowded) hotel has a variety of social and sports activities. Even though the hotel property fronts a white-sand beach, the only thing you'll find missing from the rooms is an ocean view because of the way the buildings are angled. Public spaces have cobblestone and Andalusian brick floors. The main free-form pool (with a swim-up bar) is designed to resemble a lake, complete with a waterfall and lapping waves. The Club Miguel Angel offers concierge service and premium wines and liquors. A meal in the highly regarded Spanish restaurant, El Cortijo, is a must. ⊠ *Playa Dorada (Box 532, Puerto Plata),* ☎ *809/320–5084,* FAX *809/ 320–6319. 582 units. 8 restaurants, 6 bars, air-conditioning, minibars, 2 pools, 2 tennis courts, horseback riding, beach, dive shop, snorkeling, windsurfing, boating, waterskiing, shops, concierge floor. AE, MC, V. All-inclusive.*

$$$$ 🏨 **Gran Ventana.** Set on 250 acres of creatively landscaped grounds, ★ this hotel is characterized by style and pizzazz. The lobby is a showpiece, with a central fountain surrounded by wicker chairs, handhewn wooden tables, and commodious white sofas. The main buffet dining area is divided into three spaces that are set in Victorian-style gazebos. Among the other à la carte dining options, the Italian restaurant serves authentic dishes. Rooms are in two handsome buildings with canopied entrances, ocher stucco facades, and red-tile roofs. Most rooms have sea views obstructed only by a few palms and a picket fence that keeps the beach private and tranquil. The 141 extra-large rooms in the new building don't have the sea views of those in the original

wing, but they do have oversized baths. You'll also find a lap pool, and peace and quiet. The hotel's packages are popular with those renewing vows or getting married; many opt to stay in the new penthouse. ✉ *Playa Dorada (Box 22, Puerto Plata),* ☎ *809/320–2111,* ℻ *809/ 320–2112,* 🌐 *www.victoriahoteles.com.do. 504 rooms, 2 suites. 5 restaurants, 6 bars, air-conditioning, 3 pools, hair salon, 2 hot tubs, sauna, 1 tennis court, gym, beach, snorkeling, windsurfing, boating, bicycles, shops, dance club, recreation room, convention center, car rental. AE, DC, MC, V. All-inclusive.*

$$$$ 🏨 **Hotel Occidental Playa Dorada.** To say that this property has had a face-lift doesn't begin to describe its highly successful renovation completed in late 2000. Everything is new. The handsome European tiles in the lobby bar and the gas lamps give public spaces a colonial ambience. Dark ceiling beams and exposed brick and stucco walls continue the Old World theme in the three specialty restaurants. The huge buffet area is enclosed with glass and air-conditioned. Two pools (one for kids) look out to a quiet stretch of Las Papas Beach. The new 150-room addition overlooks another huge pool. Guests can try to strike pay dirt at the strikingly renovated El Dorado Casino. ✉ *Playa Dorada, Puerto Plata,* ☎ *809/320–3988 or 800/545–8089,* ℻ *809/320– 1190. 501 rooms. 5 restaurants, 4 bars, 3 pools, beach, golf, 2 tennis courts, horseback riding, dive shop, windsurfing, boating, shops, casino. AE, DC, MC, V. All-inclusive.*

$$$$ 🏨 **Victoria Resort.** This study in pastels and gingerbread fretwork is
★ smack in the middle of the Playa Dorada golf course with a view of Isabel de Torres Mountain. The open, airy public areas have such touches as wicker furniture, marble floors, and carnival masks hung on mint green walls. Deluxe accommodations—in two-story buildings set apart from other structures to provide peace and quiet—are spacious and have plantation-style wicker furniture, tile floors, and balconies or terraces. The Grande Club House looks onto a lake, a pool, and a hot tub. The alfresco café has better-than-average buffets with international and Dominican dishes. At the Jardin Victoria you can enjoy traditional Continental cuisine, professional service, and strolling musicians. Another great dinner option is the pizzeria with brick ovens. The Victoria Beach Club is just a five-minute walk, or you can hop the shuttle to the restaurants at its sister hotel Gran Ventura. ✉ *Playa Dorada (Box 22, Puerto Plata),* ☎ *809/320–1200,* ℻ *809/320–4862,* 🌐 *www.victoriahoteles.com.do. 190 rooms. 4 restaurants, café, pizzeria, air-conditioning, minibars, 2 pools, outdoor hot tub, golf, tennis court, gym, horseback riding, dive shop, snorkeling, windsurfing, boating, jet skiing, parasailing, nightclub. AE, DC, MC, V. All-inclusive.*

$$$ 🏨 **Windsurf Hotel.** Loyal repeat guests to this young and fun, modest
★ hotel may soon be saying, "I knew it when." The Canadian owners have some big plans, including 48 new upscale rooms and 98 apartments (nine will be directly on the beach), which are currently under construction and due to open by spring of 2002. A great value for the peso, with hotel rooms on a par with the full-service resorts and a kicked-back atmosphere, it's the kind of place where American surfers dance with Scandinavian beauties at the welcome mixer. Guests will still be able to use the amenities at the CaribBic Beach Center, Cabarete's famous watersports school, on the beach across the street. ✉ *Carretera Principal (Cabarete),* ☎ *809/571–0718,* ℻ *809/571–0710,* 🌐 *www. sunsetresorts.com. 60 rooms. Restaurant, 2 bars, air-conditioning, fans, kitchenettes, refrigerators, room service, 2 bars, pool, boccie, volleyball, surfing, windsurfing, boating, playground, shop. MC, V. EP, MAP.*

$$ ⚏ **Natura Cabanas.** This spa getaway offers true paradise. There are no phones or TVs in the simple, criollo-style thatched-roof bungalows, though each has a fully equipped kitchen, can accommodate as many as six people, and is surrounded by centenary palms. The secluded swimming pool is separated from the private beach by exuberant vegetation. The owners' mantra is "peace, quiet, and health." There are yoga lessons, aromatherapy vapor baths, deep massages, mud baths, salt scrubs, facial and body peels, and a sauna. The economical room rates include airport transfers, a healthful breakfast, and maid service. You can rent mountain bikes, go on horseback-riding or four-wheel-drive treks. Afterward refresh yourself at the juice bar and head to the alfresco dining room for a candlelight dinner (vegetarian meals are available). Day guests to the spa are welcome. ⊠ *Playa Perla Marina, Cabarete,* ☎ *809/571–1507, 809/571–3346, or 809/470–1828;* FAX *809/571–3346,* WEB *www.caribecom.com/naturacab. 5 bungalows. Restaurant, bar, kitchenettes, pool, sauna, spa, beach, horseback riding, boating. No credit cards. CP.*

$$ ⚏ **Piergiorgio Palace Hotel.** The dream of an Italian fashion designer, Piergiorgio is a white-clapboard inn with a sweeping veranda and intricate fretwork. It replicates the Victorian splendor for which early Sosua was known. A gazebo is integrated into the front entrance, and a sweeping staircase rises from the marble-tiled lobby. Romantics take to the pink-and-white floral guest rooms; half have ocean views (the rest overlook the kidney-shaped pool and gardens). Piergiorgio's stretch limo whisks you from the Puerto Plata Airport to the inn, and the moderate rates include breakfast (and for $20 or so more, dinner) at the cliff-side La Puntilla de Piergiorgio restaurant. ⊠ *Calle La Puntilla 1, El Batey, Sosua,* ☎ *809/571–2626,* FAX *809/571–2786,* WEB *www. piergiorgio.com. 51 rooms. Restaurant, 2 bars, in-room safes, air-conditioning, 2 pools, hot tub. AE, MC, V. CP.*

Barahona

$$ ⚏ **Casa Bonita.** In the scenic southwest, this gentrified country inn is a charming alternative to high-rise hotels and busy all-inclusives. Julio and Virginia Schiffino expanded their vacation home and added 12 criollo-style cottages with roofs of thatched *cana* (a type of palm), rough-hewn walls, and simple furnishings. Six have air-conditioning, and all face the sea or the verdant forest of the Sierra de Bahoruco and two mountain rivers. The open-air gallery, adjacent sitting areas, and restaurant overlook the pool area and are tastefully appointed with comfortable sofas and scads of colorful throw pillows. The Schiffinos' dream vision, the spectacular Barcelo Barhoruco Hotel, is also now open. ⊠ *In foothills, 8 mi (13 km) from Barahona,* ☎ *809/696–0215,* FAX *809/223–0548. 12 cottages. Restaurant, bar, pool. AE, MC, V. EP, MAP.*

$ ⚏ **Barcelo Bahoruco Beach Resort.** "Maravilloso!" is just one guest's
★ reaction to this new resort on a gorgeous stretch of virgin beach staggered with rugged cliffs, that goes for miles. The dream-vision of Julio Schiffino, owner of the nearby inn, Casa Bonita, it is the most exciting thing to happen in tourism in the Southwestern region so far in the millennium. Seven years in the making, this four-star hotel came to fruition with the help of the Spanish Barcelo group, which is managing it. The interior design has been artistically done by co-owner, Virgina Schiffino. The tri-level lobby is an artistic mix of West Indian and African colonial and contemporary style. Classical music plays in the reception area, but it's lively Dominican dance music at the pool complex with its Jacuzzi and swim-up bar, all traversed by wooden bridges. The alfresco buffet restaurant, which, like the lobby, is topped by a huge palapa, serves an exceptional array of food. Guest rooms are in a series of stucco buildings, each with its own tasteful interior design

and balconies facing the sea. Eco-tours take guests to national parks and flamingo refuges, as well as on horseback riding safaris. Nonguests can buy day passes. ✉ *Carretera de la Costa KM. 17 Bahoruco, Barahona.* ☎ *809/524–1111,* ℻ *809/524–6060,* 🌐 *www.barcelo-hotels. com. 105 rooms. 2 restaurants, 2 pools, 3 bars, tennis court, meeting room. AE, MC, V. All-inclusive.*

Dining

The island's culinary repertoire includes Spanish, Latin American, Italian, Middle Eastern, Japanese, and Chinese cuisines. Every year there are more establishments that serve contemporary Caribbean dishes as well as places that offer *nueva cocina Dominicana* (contemporary Dominican cuisine). If seafood is on the menu, it's bound to be fresh.

Among the best Dominican specialties are *sancocho* (a thick stew usually made with five meats and served with rice and avocado slices), *arroz con pollo* (rice with chicken), and *plátanos* (plantains) in all their tasty varieties. Many meals are finished with *majarete*, a cornmeal custard. Shacks and stands that serve cheap eats are an integral part of the culture and landscape. They might offer johnnycakes (fried dough stuffed with everything from chicken to seafood) or pork sandwiches laden with onions, tomatoes, pickles, and seasonings. Presidente is the best local beer; Barceló *anejo* (aged) rum is as smooth as cognac.

What to Wear

In resort areas shorts and bathing suits under beach wraps are usually (but not always) acceptable at breakfast and lunch. For dinner, long pants, skirts, and collared shirts are the norm. Restaurants tend to be more formal in Santo Domingo, both at lunch and at dinner, with trousers required for men and dresses suggested for women. Ties aren't required anywhere but jackets are (even at the midday meal) in some of the finer establishments.

CATEGORY	COST*
$$$$	$30 or more
$$$	$20–$30
$$	$10–$20
$	under $10

per person for a main course at dinner

Santo Domingo

CARIBBEAN

$$ ✕ **El Conuco.** The name means "the countryside," and it *is* hard to be-
★ lieve that this thatched-roof patio—alive with hanging plants, hibiscus, and frangipani—is right in Santo Domingo. The Dominican dishes on the single prix-fixe menu here are superb, from *la bandera* (white rice, kidney beans, and stewed beef duplicating the colors of the flag) to a magnificent, delicately flaky *bacalao de la comai* (cod in white cream sauce with garlic and onions). The ambience is always celebratory; costumed waiters dance with you or take to makeshift drums, all in time with the merengue music. ✉ *Calle Casimiro de Moya 152,* ☎ *809/ 686–0129 or 809/689–4290. MC, V.*

CONTEMPORARY

$$$$ ✕ **Caribbean Blue.** Even if the food was not as good as it is, just being in this new, ultra-chic, 16th-century restoration worthy of *Architectural Digest,* is a thrill. Exquisite taste permeates the multistory renovation: steel shelves, amber tiles, mirrors, a circular staircase of cordova hardwood, bamboo plants, and oversized vases set in recessed arches; colonial artifacts are juxtaposed with contemporary artwork. It is another indicator that the Colonial Zone has it going on. New World Cui-

sine is the ticket here, anything from veal raviolis with a tomato ragoût, cream of vanilla, and orange reduction to mango barbecued Chilean sea bass, and prime steaks with caramelized hearts of palm and fried yucca. ✉ *C/Hostos 205,* ☎ *809/682–1238. AE, MC, V. Closed Mon.*

$$$$ ✕ **Peperoni Café.** This is one that has capitaleanos talking—a salute to cuisine from around the world. Fusion food—Thai beef salad, crab-encrusted Chilean sea bass, calamari salad, Szechuan steak, and things as "American pie" as hamburgers, but with unusual add-ons, like pancetta and barbecue sauce, in the Wyoming burger. It has an admirable *carta de vinos*—with French, Spanish, Californian, Argentine, and Italian selections—up to Dom Perignon for 2,600 pesos ($160). Finish with pecan pie or tiramisu and a piping Irish coffee, café latte, or chocolate Peperoni. In a commercial neighborhood, it is well worth finding. Most taxi drivers know of it. ✉ *Sarasota #25, Plaza Universitaria Santo Domingo,* ☎ *809/508–1330. AE, MC, V.*

CONTINENTAL

$$$$ ✕ **El Meson de la Cava.** A capital landmark since 1969, this cave, which has served as a hideaway for aborigines, pirates, and freedom fighters, continues to draw a crowd of loyal locals and tourists. Despite the chill and drips from the stalagmites, this is one warm cavern thanks to the hospitality of the owners, the veteran captains and waiters. Leave the high heels off, for the descending, circular staircase is tougher than a field sobriety test. The original owner's daughter, Laura Ricart, a graduate of New York's French Culinary Institute, is contemporizing the classic continental menu with such specials as a miso and sake–glazed Chilean sea bass, with mashed yucca and potatoes, and Taína salad with imported lettuces, watercress, avocado, mango, hearts of palm, and a rum balsamic vinaigrette. Finish with a cappuccino merengue. Chef Laura and her husband, Plinio Jacobs, are opening a new terrace topside to take advantage of the river views. ✉ *Av. Mirador del Sur #1,* ☎ *809/532–2615 or 809/533–2818. Reservations essential. AE, MC, V.*

ITALIAN

$$$ ✕ **Da Vinci Restorante.** The newest restaurant at the glamorous Melia
★ Hotel, this is one of those exceptional gourmet rooms that helps dispel the myth that hotel restaurants are not as good as free-standing ones. With its own entrance, the beautifully appointed space, accented with burnished hardwood, is a tribute to the Italian painter, with reproductions in the foyer and murals depicting his inventions. Table settings are elegantly simplistic. The menu is the same for lunch and dinner, with appetizers that could be "mains," such as the mussels (18) steamed with fresh tomato and basil, and Chilean sea bass with a creamy cilantro sauce. Quail stuffed with foie gras and pistachios is one fine entrée. Presentation is contemporary, and the plates are artfully painted, particularly for the outstanding desserts like fanned pears poached in red wine with a Galliano/Frangelica cream, and chocolate cappuccino cheesecake with crème de menthe glaze and rose petal ice cream. Friday and Saturday nights a pianist and violinist from the symphony perform. The wine list is admirable, the personalized service totally professional and very amiable. ✉ *Av. George Washington #365,* ☎ *809/221–6666, ext. 2510. AE, MC.*

$$$ ✕ **La Briciola.** The owners have done an exemplary job modernizing the interiors of these adjoining 16th-century colonial buildings. The vaulted-ceiling, stone-and-brick main dining room and the more casual piano bar overlook a courtyard whose trees are lighted romantically at night. A vocalist serenades, or there might be a flutist or pianist. Mahogany furnishings, wooden chandeliers, and Italian tile work create an elegant atmosphere. Celebrities from Julio Iglesias to Sammy

Sosa have been sighted. Excellent homemade pastas include velvety gnocchi *fume* (with Scamorze cheese, ham, and cream). The meat falls away from the bone on the osso buco; the mussels are flown in from Spain, the bluepoint oysters from Boston. Have the owner, Franco Riccobono, help you select from the all-Italian wine list. His son, Alessandro, can help you choose a grappa to complement the delicious tiramisu. ⊠ *Calle Arzobispo Merino 152-A, at Padre Bellini,* ☎ *809/688–5055. Jacket required. Reservations essential. AE, DC, MC, V. Closed Sun.*

$$$ ✕ **Pappalapasta.** Exceptional food, a highly professional waitstaff, and
★ a location around the corner from the Presidential Palace make this restaurant popular with politicians, diplomats, and those who seek their favor. A series of intimate dining rooms is handsomely decorated with polished hardwood furnishings, abstract artwork, and Tiffany-style lamps. Try the innovative shrimp and white bean salad with pesto and Parmesan. Pumpkin ravioli in almond butter, and snapper *chiaro di mare* (with olives, capers, garlic, tomatoes, and peppers) are standouts. Finish with some heady grappa *piccolo* while being mesmerized by the piano player. ⊠ *Calle Dr. Baez 23,* ☎ *809/682–4397. Jacket required. Reservations essential. AE, MC, V. Closed Mon.*

$$$ ✕ **Spaghettissimo.** This contemporary Italian spot deserves the word-
★ of-mouth fame it enjoys. Owner Frederic Gollong will charm you with his dry wit and welcoming ways. From the antipasto buffet to such delicacies as the meringue confection aptly named the cloud, the quality and freshness of the food are apparent. Savor Frederic's own Dover sole with almonds or rabbit Provençal. For a pasta course try the homemade ravioli with a porcini mushroom cream sauce. And don't overlook the specials. On Wednesday night live Italian and Brazilian music in the candlelit garden captures a devoted crowd. Brunch is *the* thing on Sunday. ⊠ *Paseo de los Locubres 13,* ☎ *809/565–3708 or 809/547–2650. AE, DC, MC, V.*

MIDDLE EASTERN

$$$ ✕ **Scherezade.** The exotic decor—Moorish arches, tile work, a terrace with orchids—is just one of the reasons why this restaurant is so popular. The excellent service is provided by waiters who wear embroidered vests and fez hats. Hummus, not butter, comes with the pita bread. Try the velvety cream of asparagus and watercress or the tabbouleh. Superb entrées include the Madagascar shrimp in green pepper and spinach sauce or the Arabian lobster, grilled simply with oil, garlic, and lemon. Desserts include baklava, orange soufflé, and ginger flan. Some nights flamenco dancers perform. ⊠ *Av. Roberto Pastoriza 226,* ☎ *809/ 227–2323. AE, DC, MC. Closed Mon.*

Boca Chica/Juan Dolio

CONTEMPORARY

$$$ ✕ **L'Ecrevisse.** The intimate dining room of the Barcelo Talanquera Beach
★ Resort is a stronghold of innovative contemporary Caribbean cuisine. It's also one of the few restaurants in the world to have earned two Awards of Excellence from *Wine Spectator* magazine for its wine list. The decor is formal and romantic, and the service is white glove, but the atmosphere is relaxed. ⊠ *Juan Dolio Beach,* ☎ *809/526–1510. AE, DC, MC, V. Closed Sun.*

SEAFOOD

$$ ✕ **Neptuno's Club.** This breezy seaside eatery is little more than a shack perched above the gin-clear waters. Stay with the simple, fresh fish dishes: paella, grilled sea bass and grouper, lobster, and the sautéed squid served sizzling in the pan. ⊠ *Boca Chica Beach,* ☎ *809/523– 4703. MC, V. Closed Mon.*

La Romana

CONTEMPORARY

$$$$ ✕ **Casa del Río.** You can look out over the Río Chavón while you dine
★ in the candlelit stone cellar of this re-creation of a medieval castle in
the vast Casa de Campo resort. The creative cuisine is a blend of classical French methodology and Asian influences, utilizing fresh, indigenous products. Desserts are extravaganzas in their complexity of
tastes and dramatic presentation. ✉ *Altos de Chavón,* ☎ *809/523–*
3333 ext. 2345. Reservations essential. AE, MC, V. No lunch.

ITALIAN

$$$ ✕ **La Piazzetta.** In the same re-created medieval castle as Casa del Río,
★ this restaurant is a salute to the best in contemporary cuisine found in
Italy today. An Italian accordionist sets the mood. The antipasto buf-
fet, with an amazing selection, from cold octopus to white bean salad
and rolled prosciutto, is the best way to begin the experience. A sim-
ple, fresh salad of arugula and radicchio (grown in the resort's gar-
den) with shaved Parmesan readies the palate for the principal course.
The menu is constantly evolving, and the chef, Mauro Ajmone, imported
from Italy, is known for his fresh pastas (the raviolis are the best) and
his seafood stew. The quality of meat served in this and all of Casa de
Campo's restaurants, is difficult to find elsewhere in the country. Save
room for the luscious creations of the pastry chef. ✉ *Altos de Chavón,*
☎ *809/523–3333 ext. 3559. Reservations essential. AE, MC, V. No*
lunch.

Samaná

SEAFOOD

$$ ✕ **Villa Serena.** At the very end of the long road from Puerto Plata is
this spot in the small Villa Serena hotel. On the beach, the restaurant's
specialties include fresh fish and delicious homemade desserts. ✉ *Las*
Galeras, ☎ *809/696–0065. MC, V.*

The Amber Coast

CONTEMPORARY

$$$ ✕ **Acuarela and Aquacate.** Named for the watercolors that adorn its
★ walls, the Acuarela café is in a 120-year-old home surrounded by a gar-
den. It's a hip, contemporary place with some very creative cuisine. The
clientele—well-heeled expats and Dominicans—is partial to such ap-
petizers as Thai carpaccio (beef) with peanut sauce. For an entrée, the
talented chef-owner, Rafael Vasquez, recommends the lobster medal-
lions with a Pernod cream served over fried polenta. Beef served at
Acuarela is certified Angus. The grand finale might be coconut crêpes
with Grand Marnier, coconut ice cream, and caramel sauce. Down the
garden path is the more affordable Aguacate, where Tex-Mex dinners
are served beneath rafters bedecked with saddles and ablaze with twin-
kling lights. Try the Plato Fiesta—a combination of seven appetizers,
then the house-smoked chicken or spareribs with barbecue sauce. Fin-
ish with a tamarind daiquiri. Saturday night after 11 the music
(merengue, salsa, vintage rock) begins, and people keep on coming. ✉
Calle Prof. Certad 3, at Calle Presidente Vasquez, Puerto Plata, ☎ *809/*
586–5314. MC, V. Closed Mon.

$$ ✕ **El Cortijo.** The restaurant in the Flamenco Beach Resort is a refreshing
change from Playa Doradas's all-inclusive buffets. Cane-back chairs,
tile floors, and subdued lighting create a serene atmosphere. Impeccable service prevails—the waitstaff even goes so far as to cut the
stems of vintage wine bottles with a hot "branding" iron. Classic
Spanish and Continental dishes are given a contemporary twist; you'll
find gazpacho with melon pearls and mint, wild boar with Roquefort
and Serrano ham, and *tejas* (cookies shaped like roof tiles) of coconut

stuffed with mangoes. The prix-fixe menu is a worthy option. ⊠ *Playa Dorada*, ☎ *809/320–5084. AE, DC, MC, V. No lunch.*

ECLECTIC

$$ ✕ **Hemingway's Café.** As much a meeting place as a memorial to the late great writer, this café is full of old photos that chronicle his life and dishes with names that bring to mind his work. Everyone, from long-haired expats to government VIPs, comes to savor For Whom the Bell Tolls fajitas (in chicken, shrimp, or beef versions) and drink sangria. More upscale items have been added, from shrimp dishes to Angus beef steaks. The atmosphere is fun, the crowd young. ⊠ *Playa Dorada Plaza*, ☎ *809/320–2230. AE, MC, V.*

ITALIAN

$$$ ✕ **La Puntilla de Piergiorgio.** Atop a seaside cliff at the Piergiorgio Palace
★ Hotel, this restaurant has waiters who will pamper you as you sit overlooking the precipice. Cascades of pink bougainvillea rustle about you in the cooling breeze. Gnocchi with a tomato-basil cream sauce, shrimp-laced fettuccine, or a simple grilled lobster are among the best choices. Live bands often play in the bandstand, and if you don't have a car, the restaurant will pick you up and drop you off in a festive horse-drawn wagon. ⊠ *Calle La Puntilla 1, El Batey, Sosua*, ☎ *809/571–2215. AE, MC, V.*

SEAFOOD

$$ ✕ **Caribae.** At this warm, hip, unassuming spot you'll find mostly locals in the know: artists, and fun expats. Quiet and away from the maddening crowds, the choice of music is always right on. The fish is fresh; the cuisine contemporary, yet criollo and Taíno specialties are also showcased. Sandwiches, fritters, and fresh salads are available. The charming, multilingual owner (a biologist) grows his own herbs and vegetables on the property. Bring your swimsuit and after dinner have a dip in the night-lit pool. ⊠ *Camino Libre 70, Sosua*, ☎ *809/470–1828. Reservations essential. AE, MC, V. Lunch only. Closed Tues.*

Beaches

The Dominican Republic has more than 1,000 mi (1,600 km) of beaches, including the Caribbean's longest stretch of white sand: Punta Cana/Bavaro. Many beaches are accessible to the public and may tempt you to stop for a swim. That's part of the uninhibited joy of this country. Do be careful, though: some have dangerously strong currents.

Boca Chica. The beach closest to Santo Domingo (2 mi/3 km east of Las Américas Airport, 21 mi/34 km from the capital) is crowded with city folks on weekends. In the early part of the last century it was developed by wealthy industrialist Juan Vicini. Entire families once moved their households here for the summer. The beach was an immaculate stretch of fine sand, and you could (and still can) walk far out into the gin-clear waters protected by coral reefs. Since then progress has made its mark; certain areas are cluttered with plastic furniture, pizza stands, and beach cottages. The strip with the mid-rise resorts is well kept but busy. The old Hamaca Hotel was the place to see and be seen; dictator Trujillo kept quarters here, and President Lionel Fernández now books the Presidential Suite.

Cabarete Beach. On the north coast, this beach has ideal wind and surf conditions. It's an integral part of the international windsurfing circuit.

Juan Dolio. A narrow beach of fine white sand, Juan Dolio is a 20-minute drive east of Boca Chica and is home to many different resorts.

Luperón Beach. About an hour's drive west of Puerto Plata, this wide white-sand beach is fit for snorkeling, windsurfing, and scuba diving. The Luperón Beach Resort is handy for rentals and refreshments.

Playa Grande. On the north coast, this long stretch of powdery sand is slated for development (the Playa Grande Hotel has already disturbed the solitude). For now, however, the entire northeast coast still seems like one unbroken golden stretch, littered only with kelp, driftwood, and the occasional beer bottle. If you don't mind the lack of facilities, you have your pick of deserted patches.

Puerto Plata. On the north's Amber Coast (so called because of its un-usual—and large—deposits of amber) this is one of the D.R.'s most established resort areas, especially along Playa Dorada. The beaches are of soft beige or white sand, with lots of reefs for snorkeling. The Atlantic waters are great for windsurfing, waterskiing, and fishing. The substantial city of Puerto Plata, with its Victorian vestiges, is a 10-minute cab ride.

Punta Cana. The gem of the Caribbean is a 20-mi (32-km) strand of pearl white sand shaded by swaying coconut palms. It's on the east-ernmost coast, which includes Bavaro Beach, and it's the home of nu-merous all-inclusive resorts. There's no major town close to this resort area, though.

La Romana. This is the site of the 7,000-acre Casa de Campo resort, so you're not likely to find any private place in the sun. The miniature Minitas Beach and lagoon are also here.

Sosua. Here calm waters gently lap a shore of soft white sand. Un-fortunately, the backdrop is a string of tents where hawkers push sou-venirs, snacks, and rental of water-sports equipment from the vendors.

Las Terrenas. On the north coast of the Samaná Peninsula, tall palms list toward the sea, the beach is narrow but sandy, and there's plenty of color—vivid blues, greens, and yellows. Two hotels are on the beach at Punta Bonita.

Outdoor Activities and Sports

Although there's hardly a shortage of activities here, the resorts have virtually cornered the market on sports, including every conceivable water sport. In some cases facilities may be available only to guests. You can check with the hotels or the tourist office for more details.

Participant Sports

BOATING

Sailing conditions are ideal, with a constant trade wind. Favorite ex-cursions include day trips to Catalina Island and sunset cruises on the Caribbean. Prices for crewed sailboats of 26 ft and longer with a ca-pacity from 4 to 12 people range from $120 to $700 a day. The pri-vate marina at **Casa de Campo** (✉ La Romana, ☎ 809/523–3333) has charter sailing vessels. Check with **Club Med** (✉ Punta Cana, ☎ 809/686–5500) about its boating options. Hobie Cats and pedal boats are available at **Heavens** (✉ Playa Dorada, ☎ 809/586–5250). The **Carib BIC Center** (✉ Cabarate, ☎ 809/571–0640) is a renowned windsurf-ing center that also rents Lasers, 17-ft catamarans, boogie boards, and sea kayaks.

CYCLING

Pedaling is easy on pancake-flat beaches, but there are also some steep hills in the D.R. Several resorts rent bikes to their guests: **Dorado Naco** (✉ Dorado Beach, ☎ 809/320–2019); **Hotel Cofresi** (✉ Puerto Plata,

☎ 809/586–2898); **Jack Tar Village** (✉ Puerto Plata, ☎ 809/586–3800);
Villas Doradas (✉ Playa Dorada, Puerto Plata, ☎ 809/320–3000).

FISHING

Marlin and wahoo are among the fish that folks angle for here (note
that fishing is best between January and June). Costs to charter a
boat—with a crew, refreshments, bait, and tackle—range from $300
to $500 for a half day and from $400 to $700 for a full day. You can
arrange fishing trips through **Actividas Acuaticás** (✉ Playa Dorada, ☎
809/586–3988). The marina at **Casa de Campo** (✉ La Romana, ☎ 809/
523–3333) arranges fishing charters.

GOLF

The **Barcelo Bavaro Beach Golf and Casino Resort** (✉ Bavaro Beach,
near Higüey, ☎ 809/686–5797) has an 18-hole course, open to its own
guests and those of other hotels. The greens fee for those not staying
at Bavaro is $32; golf carts rent for $50. *Golf* magazine has called **Casa
de Campo** (✉ La Romana, ☎ 809/523–3333) "the finest golf resort
in the Caribbean." Greens fees range from $85 to $125; if you're an
avid golfer, though, inquire about the resort's multi-day passes and golf
packages. Pete Dye has designed a third 18-hole course here, close to
Altos de Chávon. It will hug a cliff that overlooks the ocean as well as
Río Chávon and its palm groves. The first nine holes are scheduled to
open by the end of 2001. The **Metro Country Club** (☎ 809/526–3315),
east of Santo Domingo in Juan Dolio and on the road to La Romana,
has an 18-hole public course designed by Charles Ankrom. Greens fees
run $35 to $50, and a cart costs $16 to $20. **Playa Dorada**'s 18-hole
Robert Trent Jones–designed course (✉ Adjacent to Victoria Resort,
☎ 809/320–3344) is open to guests staying at all the hotels in the complex. Greens fees range from $15 (9 holes) to $27. Guests in Santo
Domingo hotels are usually allowed to use the 18-hole course at the
Santo Domingo Country Club (✉ Av. Isabella Guiar, in front of El Club
del Banco Reservo, 40 mins south of Santo Domingo, ☎ 809/530–6606)
on weekdays—*after* members have teed off—for $35 (9 or 18 holes).

HIKING

At 10,370 ft (3,171 m), Pico Duarte is the highest peak in the West Indies and a favorite for serious hikers and mountain climbers. Hire a
guide in La Ciénaga, one hour and 8½ mi (14 km) west of Jarabacoa,
if you're prepared and equipped for an arduous 12-mi (19-km) two-
day climb; you can also rent a mule here. The **park service** (☎ 809/
472–4204) can assist you in obtaining a guide to lead you up Pico Duarte.

HORSEBACK RIDING

The 250-acre Equestrian Center at **Casa de Campo** (✉ La Romana, ☎
809/523–3333) has something for both Western and English riders—
a dude ranch, a rodeo arena, guided trail rides, and jumping and riding lessons. Guided rides run about $20 an hour; lessons cost $40 an
hour. **Gran Chaparral** (✉ Puerto Plata, ☎ 809/320–4450) is a ranch
that offers beach rides of varying lengths and costs on its well-trained,
gaited horses. **Rancho Isabella** (✉ East of Playa Dorada, ☎ 809/707–
3627) conducts delightful six-hour trail rides in the country and on the
beach; a Dominican buffet lunch is included in the cost of $45.

SCUBA DIVING

Ancient sunken galleons, undersea gardens, and offshore reefs are
among the lures here. In the waters off **Sosua** alone you'll find a dozen
dive sites (for all levels of ability) with such catchy names as 3 Rocks
(a deep, 163-ft/50-m dive), Airport Wall (98 ft/30 m), and Pyramids.
Some 10 dive schools are represented on Sosua Beach. Most resorts
have dive shops on the premises or can arrange trips for you. **North-**

ern Coast Aquasports in Sosua (☎ 809/571–3883) is a five-star PADI instruction center and resort.

TENNIS

There must be a million nets around the island, and most of them can be found at the large resorts. **La Terraza Tennis Club** (☎ 809/523–8548, ask for tennis office) at the Casa de Campo resort has been called the "Wimbledon of the Caribbean." This 12-acre facility, perched on a hill with sea views, has 13 Har-Tru courts. Nonguests are welcome (just call in advance); court time costs $20 an hour; lessons are $40 an hour. The **Playa Naco Golf & Tennis Resort** (☎ 809/320–6226 ext. 2568), in Playa Dorada, allows nonguests to play on its four clay courts for $4 an hour—day or night. Lessons from a pro cost $14 an hour.

WINDSURFING

Between June and October, Cabarete Beach has what many consider to be optimal windsurfing conditions: wind speeds at 20–25 knots and 3- to 15-ft (1- to 5-m) waves. The Professional Boardsurfers Association has included Cabarete in its international windsurfing slalom competition. The novice is also welcome to learn and train on modified boards stabilized by flotation devices. **Carib BIC Center** (✉ Cabarete Beach, ☎ 809/571–0640, FAX 809/571–0649) offers equipment and instruction. Lessons are generally $30–$35 an hour; boards rent for $20 an hour. A gem of a windsurfing club, this family-owned business has many repeat clients, who have made a new expansion possible. Their adjacent retail surf shop sells beachwear, backpacks, sunscreen, hammocks, "shades," and snorkeling equipment.

Spectator Sports

BASEBALL

Baseball is a national passion, and these days Sammy Sosa is the island's superman. But he is just the latest in a string of baseball heroes. Triple-A Dominican and Puerto Rican players and some American major leaguers hone their skills in the D.R.'s Professional Winter League, which plays from October through January. As many as 20,000 fans often crowd the **Liga de Béisbol** stadium (☎ 809/567–6371) in Santo Domingo. If your Spanish is good, you can call the stadium or consult local newspaper listings for details on the five teams and game schedules; otherwise, you may want to ask staff at your hotel to arrange tickets for you. Games are also played in the Tetelo Vargas Stadium, in the town of San Pedro de Macorís.

HORSE RACING

There are races (flats) year-round at the **Hipódromo V Centenario** (✉ Av. Las Américas, Santo Domingo, ☎ 809/687–6060. 🎟 Free. ⊙ Daily 8–2:45).

POLO

Casa de Campo is a key place to play or watch the fabled sport of kings. The resort has always prided itself on the polo traditions it has kept alive since its opening some 20 years ago. (For many years a nephew of the Maharajah of Jodhpur, Jaber Singh, was an instructor. His pupils included Ramfis Trujillo, son of the former dictator.) Matches are scheduled from October to June, with high-goal players flying in from France and Argentina. Private polo lessons and clinics are available for those who always wanted to give it a shot. There is also a polo field in Santo Domingo.

Shopping

The hottest items right now are cigars. Many exquisite hand-wrapped smokes come from the island's rich Ciabo Valley, and Fuente cigars, handmade in Santiago, are highly prized. Dominican rum and coffee are also good buys. *Mama juana,* an herbal potion, is the Dominican answer to Viagra. The D.R. is the homeland of designer Oscar de la Renta, and you may want to stop at the chic shops that carry his creations. Hand-carved wooden rocking chairs are big sellers, and you can buy them boxed and unassembled for easy transport. La Vega is famous for its *diablos cajuelos* (devil masks), which are worn during Carnival. Look also for the delicate, faceless ceramic figurines that symbolize the Dominican culture.

Though locally crafted products are often of a high caliber (and often very affordable), expect to pay hundreds of dollars for designer jewelry made of amber and larimar. Larimar—a semiprecious stone that's the color of the Caribbean sea—is found on the D.R.'s south coast. Prices vary according to the stone's hue; the rarest and most expensive gems have a milky haze, and the less expensive are solid blue. Amber has been mined extensively between Puerto Plata and Santiago. A fossilization of resin from a prehistoric pine tree, it often encases ancient animal and plant life from leaves to spiders to tiny lizards. Beware of fakes, which are especially prevalent in street stalls. Visit a reputable dealer or store and ask how to tell the difference between real larimar and amber and imitations.

Bargaining is both a game and a social activity in the D.R., especially with street vendors and at the stalls in El Mercado Modelo. Vendors are disappointed and perplexed if you don't haggle. They're also tenacious, so unless you really plan to buy, don't even stop to look.

Areas and Malls

SANTO DOMINGO

The restored buildings of **La Atarazana** (⊠ Across from Alcazar in the Colonial Zone) are filled with shops, art galleries, restaurants, and bars. One of the main shopping streets in the Colonial Zone is **Calle El Conde,** a pedestrian thoroughfare. Some of the best shops on **Calle Duarte** are north of the Colonial Zone, between Calle Mella and Avenida de Las Américas. **El Mercado Modelo,** a covered market, borders Calle Mella in the Colonial Zone. Vendors here sell a dizzying selection of Dominican crafts. **Plaza Criolla** (⊠ Av. Maximo Gomez) is filled with shops that sell everything from scents to nonsense. **Plaza Central** (⊠ Avs. Winston Churchill and 27 de Febrero) has many top international boutiques. **Unicentro** (⊠ 406 Av. Abraham Lincoln) is a major Santo Domingo mall.

PUERTO PLATA

A popular shopping street for costume jewelry and souvenirs is **Calle Beller. Playa Dorada Plaza** (⊠ Calle Duarte at Av. 30 de Marzo) is a shopping center in the American tradition. Stores here sell everything from cigars, rum, coffee, and herbal remedies to ceramics, hand-carved wooden items, and T-shirts, and there are Nautica, Guess, and Bennetton stores. The seven showrooms of the **Tourist Bazaar** (⊠ Calle Duarte 61) are in an old mansion with a patio bar.

ALTOS DE CHAVÓN

In this re-creation of a Mediterranean village on the grounds of the Casa de Campo resort, you'll find art galleries, boutiques, and souvenir shops grouped around a cobbled square. Extra special are: El Club de Cigaro and the rotating art exhibits at the Museo Arqueológico Regional.

Specialty Items

ART

Arawak Gallery (✉ Av. Pasteur 104, Santo Domingo, ☎ 809/685–1661) specializes in pre-Columbian artifacts and contemporary pottery and paintings. **Casa Jardín** (✉ Balacer Gustavo Medjia Ricart 15, Santo Domingo, ☎ 809/565–7978) is the garden studio of abstract painter Ada Balacer. Works by other women artists are also shown; look for pieces by Yolarda Naranjo, known for her modern work that integrates everything from fiberglass, hair, rocks, and wood to baby dresses. **Galería de Arte Mariano Eckert** (✉ Av. Winston Churchill and Calle Luis F. Tomen, 3rd floor, Santo Domingo, ☎ 809/541–7109) focuses on the work of Eckert, an older Dominican artist who's known for his still lifes. **Galería de Arte Nader** (✉ Rafael Augusto Sanchez 22, Ensanche Pianttini and Plaza Andalucia II, Santo Domingo, ☎ 809/687–6674 or 809/544–0878) showcases top Dominican artists in a variety of media. The gallery staff is well known in Miami and New York and works with Sotheby's. **Lyle O. Reitzel Art Contemporaneo** (✉ Plaza Andalucia II, Santo Domingo, ☎ 809/227–8361) specializes in very contemporary art, such as the very dark paintings of José Garcia Cordero, a Dominican living in Paris. **Mi Pais** (✉ Calle Villanueva at Antera Mota, Puerto Plata, ☎ no phone) is an innovative gallery that showcases paintings and sculptures by such Dominican artists as Orlando Menicucci, Servio Certad, Pedro Terrero, and Celia Vargas Nadel.

CLOTHING

Plaza Central (✉ Avs. Winston Churchill and 27 de Febrero, Santo Domingo, ☎ 809/541–5929) is a major shopping center with a Jenny Polanco shop (an upscale Dominican designer) and other high-end stores.

DUTY-FREE ITEMS

Centro de los Héroes (✉ Av. George Washington, Santo Domingo) sells liquor, cameras, and the like.

HANDICRAFTS

Artesanía Lime (✉ Autopista Duarte, 2½ km, Santiago, ☎ 809/582–3754) is worth a visit for its mahogany carvings and Carnival masks. **Collector's Corner Gallery and Gift Shop** (✉ Plaza Shopping Center, Calle Duarte at Av. 30 de Marzo, Puerto Plata, ☎ no phone) offers a wide range of souvenirs, including many made of amber. **Taimascaros** (✉ Camino Libre 70, Sosua, ☎ 809/571–3138) is a group of artists and carnival goers organized by artist Jacinto Manuel Beard Gomez, to preserve both the event and Dominican culture. They make their own masks and costumes, and Jacinto's striking artwork incorporates carnival elements.

JEWELRY

Ambar Tres (✉ La Atarazana 3, Santo Domingo, ☎ 809/688–0474) carries a wide selection of items made with amber, including high-end jewelry. If you tour the in-house museum, you'll have an even deeper appreciation of the gem.

TOBACCO

Cigar King (✉ Calle Conde 208, Baguero Bldg., Colonial Zone, Santo Domingo, ☎ 809/686–4987) keeps Dominican and Cuban cigars in a temperature-controlled cedar room (note that Cuban stogies can't be brought through U.S. customs legally). **Santo Domingo Cigar Club** (✉ Av. George Washington 367, ☎ 809/221–1483), in the lobby of the Renaissance Jaragua Hotel and Casino, is a great place to find yourself a good smoke.

Nightlife

Get a copy of the *Vacation Guide* and the newspaper, *Touring*—both available free at the tourist office and at hotels—to find out what's happening around. Look in the *Santo Domingo News* and the *Puerto Plata News* for listings of events and the monthly *Dominican and Fiesta.*

CAFÉS

Cigarro Café (⊠ Av. Maximo Gomez and Av. 27 de Febrero, Santo Domingo, ☎ 809/688–7038) in the Grand Hotel Lina is the place to go for high-quality cigars and coffee, with an appealing assortment of gadgets for the smoker. Cigar brands include the country's best—Aurturo Fuente and Fuente Fuente Opus X.

Doubles (⊠ Calle Arzobispo Merino 54, Santo Domingo, ☎ 809/688–3833) looks like a friend's living room—that is, if you have a friend who has a hip sense of interior design and would mix rattan furniture, antiques, subdued lighting, and candles in a space that's centuries old. Spanish tiles add still more charm to this atmospheric piano bar.

Don't think of the sandwich when you visit **Monté Cristo** (⊠ Av. Jose Armado Soler, corner of Abraham Lincoln, Santo Domingo, ☎ 809/542–5000), although the crowds can sandwich you in at this pub. The clientele spans the decades, music crosses the Americas, and there is a small dance floor. Mondays there are movies and merengue videos, Tuesdays begin with free wine tastings, and midweek there is a Boston night. Both hot and cold tapas and sandwiches are served if you want a bite with your drink. Open "after work" 'til whenever, usually 4 or 5 AM, and there's no cover.

At **Punto Y Corcho** (⊠ Av. Abraham Lincoln at Gustavo Mejía Ricart, Santo Domingo, ☎ 809/683–0533), on Plaza Andalucia, wine (by the glass and bottle) and local and international liquors are the order of the night here. This is a great date and late-night spot.

CASINOS

Gambling here is more a sideline than a raison d'être. Most casinos are in the larger hotels of Santo Domingo. All offer blackjack, craps, and roulette and are generally open daily 3 PM–4 AM. Free buffets are sometimes set up at midnight, when some of the name entertainers come on. You must be 18 to enter, and jackets are required.

In Santo Domingo the most popular casinos are in large hotels: **Barcelo Gran Hotel Lina** (⊠ Av. Máximo Gomez and Av. 27 de Febrero, ☎ 809/563–5000); **Hispaniola** (⊠ Av. Independencia and Av. Abraham Lincoln, ☎ 809/221–7111); **Occidental El Embajador** (⊠ Av. Sarasota 65, ☎ 809/533–2131); and **Renaissance Jaragua Hotel** (⊠ Av. George Washington 367, ☎ 809/686–2222).

There are also a couple of options outside of Santo Domingo in the Playa Dorada area. The **American Casino** (⊠ Jack Tar Village, Playa Dorada, ☎ 809/320–6014) wants your pesos and will pay for your taxi, give you complimentary lessons to learn or perfect your game, and then give you free drinks and snacks. The casino at the **Hotel Occidental Playa Dorada** (⊠ Playa Dorada, Puerto Plata, ☎ 809/320–3988) is *the* most appealing gambling option, with a pleasing mix of CDs and live music that won't damage your eardrums.

DANCE CLUBS

Santo Domingo has more than its share of hot spots. As in other Latin countries, after dinner it's not a question of *whether* people will go dancing but *where* they'll go. Just about every resort in Puerto Plata has live entertainment, dancing, or both. You'll soon discover that closing time is "flexible."

Andromeda (✉ Playa Dorada, Puerto Plata, ☎ 809/586–5250) is a happening dance club–video bar with frenetic energy and a high-decibel Latin/Afro beat. Dominicans come here from town to "work out" and show visitors how dancing is done.

Bachata Rosa (✉ La Atarazana 9, Colonial Zone, Santo Domingo, ☎ 809/688–0969 or 809/682–7726) is named after a popular song by the Dominican merengue megastar Juan Luís Guerra (he's a part owner). It has three floors and includes a stage, a dance floor, a Caribbean restaurant, and often live music. Guerra has his videos going on three wide screens. Free transportation is available to and from hotels.

Bella Bleus (✉ George Washington Ave. Santo Domingo, ☎ 809/622–5452) is located on the Malecón, next to Vesuvio. This disco, owned by baseball star Jose Rio, attracts players, business types, and tourists. A study in blue, it has blue drapes, carpet, and walls, which are adorned with paintings of ballerinas (the bellas). It has an aquarium and a water view, particularly from its open-air terrace. Tuesday nights, local songsters croon. Wednesdays and weekends, it is happening from 10 PM on. Closed Mondays.

Crazy Moon (✉ Paradise Beach Club and Casino, Playa Dorada, Puerto Plata, ☎ 809/320–3663) is a megaspace that's often back to back, wall to wall. It features Latin music and hip-hop mixed with Euro sounds. Rest up from time to time at the horseshoe bar so that you can keep pace until the wee, wee hours.

The second floor of **Hemingway's Café** (✉ Playa Dorada Plaza, Puerto Plata, ☎ 809/320–2230) has been transformed into a new dance venue with both DJs and live bands, featuring everything from rock and reggae to merengue. It is enjoying the popularity that the café has always had.

The Monaco Disco Club (✉ John F. Kennedy Av. at the corner of Horacio Blanco Fonbona, Santo Domingo, ☎ 809/562–6613) is off the tourist path and populated primarily with young, upscale Dominicans. Large, yet still crowded on weekends, it has a sense of humor. For example, on Halloween, you could find mummies rising out of their coffins and crypts near the parking lot. Contemporary Latin music dominates. Older couples head to the VIP area. The room is closed on Tuesdays. No cover charge.

Trio Café (✉ Plaza Castilla, at Av. Lope de Vega and Av. Abraham Lincoln, Santo Domingo, ☎ 809/541–2781) is basically a classy bar. There's no dance floor per se, but around 1 AM the crowd really starts "feeling its dances," and everyone just goes with it. Fun theme nights have been inaugurated, like Crazy Hair Night. A terrace has been added, and this enables one to get away from the maddening crowds yet still hear the music loud and clear.

Zanzibars (✉ The waterfront at Av. del Puerto, Santo Domingo, ☎ 809/930–7343), a tri-level entertainment "yacht," is a creative concept, with a different theme working on each level. You'll find everything from African to Cuban to techno. The music is tasteful, danceable, and Dominican-loud, but the river water absorbs noise. Within the Colonial Zone, the boat faces the night-lit Casa Colon, which looks like a colonial stage set.

Exploring the Dominican Republic

Santo Domingo

Spanish civilization in the New World began in Santo Domingo's 12-block Colonial Zone. This historical district is now bustling and noisy, with narrow cobbled streets, shops, and restaurants. It's easy to imagine this old city as it was when the likes of Columbus, Cortés, Ponce de León, and pirates sailed in and out and colonists were settling themselves. Tourist brochures tout that "history comes alive here"—a surprisingly truthful statement.

A quick taxi tour of the old section takes about an hour; if you're interested in history, you'll want to spend a day or two exploring the many old "firsts," and you'll want to do it in the most comfortable shoes you own. Or you can jump on one of the green, open-air trolleys that pass the Parque Colón every hour; a 45-minute tour costs about $7, a full-blown two-hour excursion $20. Multilingual guides hit the highlights, and you can hop out to take photos. Now that the Zone is well lit at night, with new "gas" lanterns, more hotels and restaurants have opened, giving it much more to offer the visitor, particularly in the evenings.

Parque Independencia separates the old city from the new. Avenidas 30 de Marzo, Bolívar, and Independencia traverse the park and mingle with avenues named for George Washington, John F. Kennedy, and Abraham Lincoln. Modern Santo Domingo is a sprawling, noisy city with a population of close to 2 million. (Note: hours and admission charges to sights are erratic.)

Numbers in the margin correspond to points of interest on the Santo Domingo map.

SIGHTS TO SEE

㉑ Acuario Nacional. The largest aquarium in the Caribbean has an impressive collection of tropical fish, though its construction was a controversial public expenditure. ⊠ *In Sans Souci district, Av. España, San Souci,* ☎ *809/592–1509.* ☞ *Free.* ☉ *Weekdays 8–5, Sat. 8–4, Sun. 9–12:30.*

❺ Alcazar de Colón. The castle of Don Diego Colón, built in 1517, was painstakingly reconstructed and restored in 1955. Forty-inch-thick coral-limestone walls were patched and shored with blocks from the original quarry. The Renaissance-style structure, with its balustrade and double row of arches, has strong Moorish, Gothic, and Isabelline influences. There are 22 rooms, furnished in a style to which the viceroy of the island would have been accustomed—right down to the dishes and the viceregal shaving mug. Many of the period paintings, statues, tapestries, and furnishings were donated by the University of Madrid. ⊠ *Plaza de España (just off Calle Emiliano Tejera at foot of Calle Las Damas),* ☎ *809/687–5361.* ☞ *RD$10.* ☉ *Mon. and Wed.–Fri. 9–5, Sat. 9–4, Sun. 9–1.*

❷ La Atarazana. The Royal Mooring Docks made up the colonial commercial district, where naval supplies were stored. There are eight restored buildings, the oldest of which dates from 1507. They now house crafts shops, restaurants, and art galleries. ⊠ *Calle La Atarazana.*

❿ Calle Las Damas. The Street of the Ladies was named after the elegant ladies of the court who, in the Spanish tradition, promenaded in the evening. Here you'll see a sundial dating from 1753 and the Casa de los Jesuitas, which houses a fine research library for colonial history as well as the Institute for Hispanic Culture; admission is free, and it's open weekdays 8–4:30.

❼ Capilla de los Remedios. The Chapel of Our Lady of Remedies was built in the 17th century as a private chapel for the family of Francisco de Dávila. Early colonists also worshiped here before the completion of the cathedral. Its architectural details, particularly the lateral arches, are evocative of the Castilian Romanesque style. ⊠ *Calle Las Damas,*

Santo Domingo

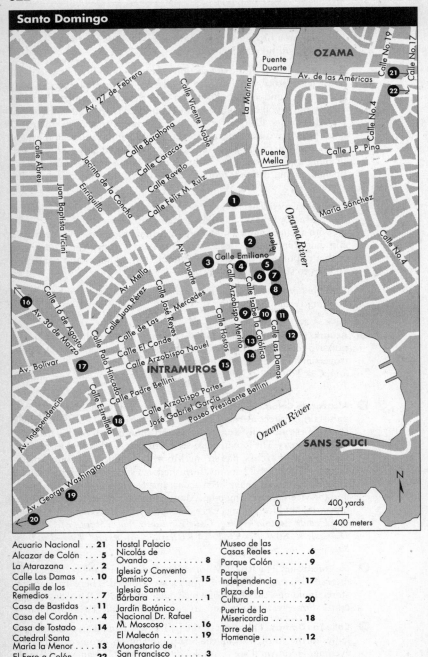

Acuario Nacional . . **21**
Alcazar de Colón . . . **5**
La Atarazana **2**
Calle Las Damas . . . **10**
Capilla de los
Remedios **7**
Casa de Bastidas . . **11**
Casa del Cordón **4**
Casa de Tostado . . . **14**
Catedral Santa
María la Menor **13**
El Faro a Colón **22**

Hostal Palacio
Nicolás de
Ovando **8**
Iglesia y Convento
Domínico **15**
Iglesia Santa
Bárbara **1**
Jardín Botánico
Nacional Dr. Rafael
M. Moscoso **16**
El Malecón **19**
Monastario de
San Francisco **3**

Museo de las
Casas Reales **6**
Parque Colón **9**
Parque
Independencia **17**
Plaza de la
Cultura **20**
Puerta de la
Misericordia **18**
Torre del
Homenaje **12**

at foot of Calle de Las Mercedes, ☎ *No phone.* 🎫 *Free.* ⏱ *Mon.–Sat. 9–6; Sun. masses begin at 6 AM.*

⑪ **Casa de Bastidas.** There's a lovely inner courtyard here with tropical plants and temporary-exhibit galleries. ✉ *Calle Las Damas, just off Calle El Conde,* ☎ *No phone.* 🎫 *Free.* ⏱ *Tues.–Sun. 9–5.*

❹ **Casa del Cordón.** This structure, built in 1503, is the western hemisphere's oldest surviving stone house. It's recognizable by the sash of the Franciscan order carved in stone over the arched entrance. Columbus's son, Diego Colón, viceroy of the colony, and his wife lived here until the Alcazar was finished. It was in this house, too, that Sir Francis Drake was paid a ransom to prevent him from totally destroying the city. ✉ *Corner of Calle Emiliano Tejera and Calle Isabel la Católica,* ☎ *No phone.* 🎫 *Free.* ⏱ *Weekdays 8:30–4:30.*

⑭ **Casa de Tostado.** The house was built in the early 16th century and was the residence of writer Don Francisco Tostado. Note its unique twin Gothic windows. It now houses the Museo de la Familia Dominicana (Museum of the Dominican Family), which features exhibits on the well-heeled 19th-century Dominican family. ✉ *Calle Padre Bellini, near Calle Arzobispo Meriño,* ☎ *809/689–5057.* 🎫 *RD$10.* ⏱ *Thurs.–Tues. 9–2.*

⑬ **Catedral Santa María la Menor.** The coral-limestone facade of the first cathedral in the New World towers over the south side of the Parque Colón. Spanish workmen began building the cathedral in 1514 but left off to search for gold in Mexico. The church was finally finished in 1540. Its facade is composed of architectural elements from the late Gothic to the lavish plateresque styles. Inside, the high altar is made of hammered silver, and the treasury contains a magnificent collection of gold and silver. Of interest is the Chapel of Our Lady of Antigua, which for more than four centuries guarded the magnificent bronze and marble sarcophagus containing (say Dominican historians) the remains of Christopher Columbus. The sarcophagus was most recently moved to El Faro a Colón (Columbus Memorial Lighthouse)—only the latest in the great navigator's posthumous journeys. ✉ *Calle Arzobispo Meriño,* ☎ *809/689–1920.* 🎫 *Free.* ⏱ *Mon.–Sat. 9–4; Sun. masses begin at 6 AM.*

👐 ㉒ **El Faro a Colón.** This striking lighthouse, monument, and museum dedicated to the great navigator is shaped like a pyramid cross (although from ground level it looks like a giant concrete casket). The lighthouse complex was completed in 1992, its inauguration coinciding with the 500th anniversary of Christopher Columbus's landing on the island. Along with its showpiece laser-powered lighthouse, the complex now holds the tomb of Columbus and six museums with exhibits on Columbus and the early exploration of the New World. One museum focuses on the long, rocky, and often controversial history of the lighthouse memorial itself and another on the great navigator's posthumous peregrinations (Cuba, Spain, and the D.R. have all laid claim to—and hosted—his remains, which even today are a subject of controversy). ✉ *Av. España,* ☎ *809/591–1492.* 🎫 *RD$10.* ⏱ *Tues.–Sun. 10–5.*

❽ **Hostal Palacio Nicolás de Ovando.** This was once the residence of Nicolás de Ovando, one of the principal organizers of the colonial city. It was later transformed into a hotel. This historic landmark is undergoing a multimillion-dollar restoration, and it will eventually be part of the Sofitel chain. ✉ *Calle Las Mercedes 44,* ☎ *800/221–4542 (Sofitel).*

⑮ **Iglesia y Convento Dominico.** This graceful building with the rose window is the Dominican Church and Convent, founded in 1510. In 1538

Pope Paul III visited here and was so impressed with the lectures on theology that he granted the church and convent the title of university, making it the oldest institution of higher learning in the New World. ✉ *Calle Padre Bellini and Av. Duarte,* ☎ *809/682–3780.* 🎫 *Free.* ☉ *Tues.–Sun. 9–6.*

❶ Iglesia Santa Bárbara. This combination church and fortress, the only one of its kind in Santo Domingo, was completed in 1562. ✉ *Av. Mella, between Calle Isabel la Católica and Calle Arzobispo Meriño,* ☎ *No phone.* 🎫 *Free.* ☉ *Weekdays 8–noon; Sun. masses begin at 6 AM.*

⓰ Jardín Botánico Nacional Dr. Rafael M. Moscoso. The Dr. Rafael M. Moscoso National Botanical Garden, the largest garden in the Caribbean, is north of town in the Arroyo Hondo district. Its 445 acres include a Japanese garden, a great ravine, a glen, a gorgeous display of orchids, and an enormous floral clock. You can tour the gardens by train, boat, or horse-drawn carriage. ✉ *Av. República de Colombia at Av. de los Proceres,* ☎ *809/687–6211.* 🎫 *RD$10.* ☉ *Tues.–Sun. 9–5.*

In the 320-acre **Parque Zoológico Nacional** (National Zoological Park), not far from the botanical gardens, animals roam free in natural habitats. There are an African plain, a children's zoo, and what the zoo claims is the world's largest birdcage. ✉ *Av. Máximo Gómez at Av. de los Proceres,* ☎ *809/562–2080.* 🎫 *RD$5.* ☉ *Tues.–Sun. 9–6.*

⓲ El Malecón. Avenida George Washington, better known as the Malecón, runs along the Caribbean and has tall palms, cafés, hotels, and sea breezes. The Parque Litoral de Sur borders the avenue from the colonial city to the Hotel Santo Domingo, a distance of about 3 mi (5 km)—watch out for pickpockets.

❸ Monasterio de San Francisco. Constructed between 1512 and 1544, the San Francisco Monastery contained the church, chapel, and convent of the Franciscan order. Sir Francis Drake's demolition squad significantly damaged the building in 1586, and in 1673 an earthquake nearly finished the job, but when it's floodlighted at night, the eerie ruins are dramatic, indeed. ✉ *Calle Hostos at Calle Emiliano.*

❻ Museo de las Casas Reales. The Museum of the Royal Houses has collections displayed in two early 16th-century palaces that have been altered many times. Exhibits cover everything from antique coins to replicas of the *Niña,* the *Pinta,* and the *Santa María.* There are sculpture and cartography galleries, coats of armor and coats of arms, coaches and a royal court room, gilded furnishings, and Indian artifacts. The first room of the former governor's residence has a wall-size map marking the routes sailed by Columbus's ships on expeditions beginning in 1492. ✉ *Calle Las Damas at Calle de Las Mercedes,* ☎ *809/682–4202.* 🎫 *RD$10.* ☉ *Tues.–Sat. 9–4:45, Sun. 10–1.*

❾ Parque Colón. The huge statue of Christopher Columbus in the park named after him dates from 1897 and is the work of French sculptor Gilbert. On the west side of the square is the old town hall and, on the east, the Palacio de Borgella, residence of the governor during the Haitian occupation of 1822–44. Gallery spaces house architectural and archaeological exhibits pertaining to the fifth centennial.

⓱ Parque Independencia. Independence Park, on the far western border of the Colonial Zone, is a big city park dominated by the marble and concrete Altar de la Patria. The impressive mausoleum was built in 1976 to honor the founding fathers of the country (Duarte, Sánchez, and Mella).

⓴ Plaza de la Cultura. Landscaped lawns, modern sculptures, and sleek buildings make up the Plaza de la Cultura. Among the buildings are the **Teatro Nacional** (National Theater; ☎ 809/687–3191), which stages performances in Spanish; the **Biblioteca Nacional** (National Library; ☎ 809/688–4086), in which the written word is Spanish; and museums and art galleries, whose notations are also in Spanish. The **Museo del Hombre Dominicano** (Museum of Dominican Man; ☎ 809/ 687–3623) traces the migrations of Indians from South America through the Caribbean islands. The **Museo de Historia Natural** (Museum of Natural History; ☎ 809/689–0106) examines the flora and fauna of the island. In the **Museo de Arte Moderno** (Museum of Modern Art; ☎ 809/682–8260), the works of 20th-century Dominican and foreign artists are displayed. Native sons include Elvis Aviles, an abstract painter whose works have a lot of texture. His art has obvious Spanish influences with Dominican symbols, such as those from the Taíno Indians. Tony Capellan is one of the best-known artists, representing the D.R. in major international exhibitions. 🖾 *Museums RD$10 each.* ☉ *Tues.–Sat. 10–5.*

⑱ **Puerta de la Misericordia.** The Gate of Mercy is part of the old city wall. It was here on the plaza, on February 27, 1844, that Ramón Mata Mella, one of the country's founding fathers, fired the shot that began the struggle for independence from Haiti. ⊠ *Calle Palo Hincado at Calle Arzobispo Portes.*

⑫ **Torre del Homenaje.** You won't have any trouble spotting the Tower of Homage in Ft. Ozama. The fort sprawls two blocks south of the Casa de Bastidas, with a brooding crenellated tower that still guards the Ozama River. Built in 1503 to protect the eastern border of the city, the sinister tower was the last home of many a condemned prisoner. ⊠ *Paseo Presidente Bellini,* ☎ *No phone.* 🖾 *RD$10.* ☉ *Tues.– Sun. 8–7.*

The East Coast

Las Américas Highway (built by the dictator Trujillo as a place for his son to race his sports cars) runs east along the coast from Santo Domingo to La Romana—about a two-hour drive. Midway are the well-established resort area of Juan Dolio and Sammy Sosa's hometown, San Pedro de Macorís. East of La Romana are Punta Cana and Bavaro, glorious beaches on the sunrise side of the island. Along the way is Higüey, an undistinguished collection of ramshackle buildings notable only for its controversial church and shrine (someone had a vision of the Virgin Mary here), consecrated by Pope John Paul II in 1984, which resembles a pinched, concrete McDonald's arch.

Numbers in the margin correspond to points of interest on the Dominican Republic map.

SIGHTS TO SEE

㉕ **Altos de Chavón.** Cattle and sugarcane used to be the two big mainstays around La Romana. That was before Gulf & Western created (and then sold) the Casa de Campo resort, which is a very big business, indeed. Altos de Chavón, a re-creation of a 16th-century Mediterranean village and an artists' colony, is on the resort grounds. It sits on a bluff overlooking the Río Chavón, about 3 mi (5 km) east of the main facility of Casa de Campo. There are cobblestone streets lined with lanterns, wrought-iron balconies and wooden shutters, and courtyards swathed with bougainvillea. More than a museum piece, this village is a place where artists live, work, and play. Dominican and international painters, sculptors, and artisans come here to teach sculpture, pottery, silk-screen printing, weaving, dance, and music at the art school, which is affiliated with New York's Parsons School of Design. They work in their studios and crafts shops and sell their finished wares.

The village also has an archaeological museum, five restaurants, and a 5,000-seat amphitheater where Julio Iglesias has entertained. The focal point of the village is **Iglesia St. Stanislaus,** which is named after the patron saint of Poland in tribute to Polish pope John Paul II, who visited the D.R. in 1979 and left some of the ashes of St. Stanislaus behind. The charmed chapel is the romantic setting of many a wedding, with honeymoons at the resort.

㉖ Isla Saona. Off the east coast of Hispaniola lies this island, now a national park inhabited by sea turtles, pigeons, and other wildlife. Caves here were once used by Indians. The beaches are beautiful, and legend has it that Columbus once strayed ashore here.

㉓ Parque de los Tres Ojos. About 1½ mi (2½ km) outside the capital is the Park of the Three Eyes. The "eyes" are cool blue pools peering out of deep limestone caves.

㉔ San Pedro de Macorís. The national sport and the national drink are both well represented in this city, an hour or so east of Santo Domingo. Some of the country's best baseball games are played in Tetelo Vargas Stadium. Many major-league players in the States have roots here. The grander homes in the area most likely belong to Dominican baseball stars such as George Bell, Tony Fernandez, and Sammy Sosa. The Macorís Rum distillery is on the eastern edge of the city. Outside town is Juan Dolio, a beach and resort area popular with Capitaleños and foreign visitors.

The Amber Coast

The Autopista Duarte ultimately leads (in three to four hours from Santo Domingo) to the Amber Coast, so called because of its large, rich amber deposits. The coastal area around Puerto Plata is a region of splashy resorts and megadevelopments; the north coast has more than 70 mi (110 km) of beaches, with condominiums and villas going up fast. The farther east from Puerto Plata and its little sister, Sosua, you get, the prettier and less spoiled the scenery becomes. The autopista runs past Cabarete, a neat village that's a popular windsurfing haunt, and Playa Grande. The white-sand beach is miraculously unspoiled.

SIGHTS TO SEE

㉘ Laguna Grí-Grí. This swampland looks as if it's smack out of Louisiana bayou country. It also has a cool blue grotto that almost outdoes the Blue Grotto of Capri. Laguna Grí-Grí is only about 90 minutes west of Puerto Plata, in Río San Juan (ask your hotel concierge for directions off the autopista).

㉛ Mt. Isabel de Torres. Southwest of Puerto Plata, this mountain soars 2,600 ft (795 m) above sea level. On it there are a botanical garden, a huge statue of Christ, and a spectacular view. Cable cars take you to the top. ⊠ *Follow signs from autopista,* ☎ *No phone.* 🎫 *$6.50 cable car.* ☉ *Cable car: Mon.–Tues. and Thurs.–Sun. 9–5.*

㉚ Puerto Plata. Although now quiet and almost sleepy, this was a dynamic city in its heyday. You can get a feeling for this past in the magnificent Victorian gazebo in the central Parque Independencia. On Puerto Plata's own Malecón, the Fortaleza de San Felipe protected the city from many a pirate attack and was later used as a political prison.

Puerto Plata is also the home of the **Museo de Ambar Dominicano** (Dominican Amber Museum), which is in a lovely galleried mansion. The museum displays and sells the D.R.'s national stone. Semiprecious, translucent amber is actually fossilized pine resin that dates from about 50 million years ago, give or take a few millennia. Shops on the museum's first floor sell amber, souvenirs, and ceramics. ⊠ *Calle Duarte 61,* ☎ *809/586–2848.* ⊡ *RD$15.* ⊙ *Mon.–Sat. 9–5.*

㉗ **Samaná.** Back in 1824, a sailing vessel called the *Turtle Dove,* carrying several hundred escaped American slaves from the Freeman sisters' underground railway, was blown ashore in Samaná. The escapees settled and prospered, and today their descendants number several thousand. The churches here are Protestant; the worshippers live in villages called Bethesda, Northeast, and Philadelphia; and the language spoken is an odd 19th-century form of English mixed with Spanish.

Sportfishing at Samaná is considered to be among the best in the world. In addition, about 3,000 humpback whales winter off the coast of Samaná from December to March. Major whale-watching expeditions are being organized and should boost the region's economy without scaring away the world's largest mammals.

Samaná makes a fine base for exploring the area's natural splendors. Most hotels on the peninsula arrange tours to Los Haitises National Park, a remote, unspoiled rain forest with limestone knolls, crystal lakes, mangrove swamps teeming with aquatic birds, and caves stippled with Taíno petroglyphs. Las Terrenas, a remote stretch of beautiful, nearly deserted beaches on the north coast of the Samaná peninsula attracts surfers and windsurfers. There are several modest seafood restaurants, a dusty main street in the town of Las Terrenas, a small airfield, an all-inclusive resort, and several congenial hotels right on the beach at Punta Bonita. If you're happy just hanging out, drinking beer, and soaking up the sun, this is the place for you.

㉙ **Sosua.** This small community was settled during World War II by 600 Austrian and German Jews. After the war many of them returned to Europe or went to the United States, and most who remained married Dominicans. Only a few Jewish families reside in the community today, and there's only a small one-room synagogue.

Sosua, called Puerto Plata's little sister, has become one of the country's most popular destinations. Hotels and condos are going up at breakneck speed. It actually consists of two communities—El Batey, the modern hotel development, and Los Charamicos, the old quarter—separated by a cove and one of the island's prettiest beaches. The sand is soft and white; the water, crystal clear and calm. The walkway above the beach is packed with tents filled with souvenirs, pizzas, and even clothing for sale—a jarring note in this otherwise idyllic setting.

The Cibao Valley

The heavily trafficked road north from Santo Domingo, known as the Autopista Duarte (now a four-lane, divided highway), cuts through the lush banana plantations, rice and tobacco fields, and royal poinciana trees of the Cibao Valley. Along the road are stands where, for a few centavos, you can buy ripe pineapples, mangoes, avocados, *chicharrones* (either fried pork rinds or chicken pieces), and fresh fruit drinks.

㉞ **Jarabacoa.** Nature lovers should consider a trip to Jarabacoa, in the mountainous region known rather wistfully as the Dominican Alps. There's little to do in the town itself but eat and rest up for excursions on foot, horseback, or by motorbike taxi to the surrounding waterfalls and forests—quite incongruous in such a tropical country. Other activities include adventure tours, particularly white-water raft or canoe trips, Jeep safaris, and paragliding. Accommodations in the area are rustic but comfortable.

㉝ **La Vega Vieja.** Founded in 1495 by Columbus, La Vega is the site of one of the oldest settlements in the New World. You may find the tour of the ruins of the original settlement, the Old La Vega, rewarding. About 3 mi (5 km) north of La Vega is Santo Cerro (Holy Mount), site of a miraculous apparition of the Virgin and therefore many local pilgrimages. The Convent of La Merced is here, and the views of the Cibao Valley are breathtaking. The new town's remarkable Concepción de la Vega Church was constructed in 1992 to commemorate the 500th anniversary of the discovery of America. The unusual modern Gothic style—all curvaceous concrete columns, arches, and buttresses—is striking.

La Vega is also celebrated for its Carnival, featuring haunting devil masks. These papier-mâché creations are intricate, fanciful gargoyles painted in surreal colors; spiked horns and real cow's teeth lend an eerie authenticity. Several artisans work in dark, cramped studios throughout the area; their skills have been passed down for generations. Closest to downtown is the **art studio of José Luís Gomez**. Ask any local (tip 10–20 pesos) to guide you to his atelier (no phone). José speaks no English but will show you the stages of a mask's development. He sells the masks for $50–$60, a great buy, considering the craftsmanship.

32 **Santiago de los Caballeros.** The second city of the D.R., where many past presidents were born, sits about 90 mi (145 km) northwest of Santo Domingo. This industrial center has a surprisingly charming, provincial ambience. A massive monument honoring the restoration of the republic guards the entrance to the city. Traditional yet progressive, Santiago is relatively new to the tourist scene, but try to set aside a day or two to explore this city, which dates from the 1500s. There are colonial-style buildings with wrought-iron details and tiled porticos as well as many homes reflecting a Victorian influence, with the requisite gingerbread latticework and fanciful colors. Santiago is a center for processing tobacco leaf. You can gain an appreciation of the art and skill of Dominican (similar to Cuban) cigar making with a tour of E. Leon Jiménez Tabacalera (☎ 809/563–1111 or 809/535–5555).

The Southwest

36 **Barahona.** Here mountains carpeted with rain forests and laced with streams slope down into white stretches of sand. You can bathe in the cascades of icy mountain rivers or in hot thermal springs surrounded by dense foliage, *llanai* vines, and fruit trees. Barahona is a tropical Garden of Eden. Be tempted to come while you and yours can still have it all to yourself.

35 **Lago Enriquillo.** The largest lake in the Antilles is near the Haitian border. The salt lake is also the lowest point in the Antilles: 114 ft (35 m) below sea level. It encircles wild, arid, and thorny islands that serve as sanctuary to such exotic birds and reptiles as flamingoes, iguanas, and caimans—the indigenous crocodile. The area is targeted by the government for improvements and infrastructure designed for ecotourists.

DOMINICAN REPUBLIC A TO Z

To research prices, get advice from other travelers, and book travel arrangements, visit www.fodors.com.

AIR TRAVEL

Air Atlantic has service from Miami and San Juan into Las Américas on Monday, Wednesday, and Friday. Air Caraïbes is a new airline that services Santo Domingo, connecting it with San Juan, the French West Indies, and other Caribbean "down" islands. Air Transat serves Santo Domingo from Montréal, Toronto, Vancouver, Victoria, and the maritime provinces; it now has three weekly flights into La Romana. Air ALM connects Santo Domingo to St. Martin and Curaçao. American Airlines has the most extensive service to the D.R. It flies nonstop from New York and Miami to Santo Domingo, Puerto Plata, and La Romana and offers connections to both Santo Domingo and Puerto Plata from San Juan, Puerto Rico. From San Juan, American Eagle has six daily flights to Santo Domingo, two daily flights to La Romana, two flights daily to Santiago, and several flights weekly to Punta Cana. Aeromar flies nonstop from Miami to Santo Domingo daily. Continental flies nonstop from Newark to Puerto Plata and Santo Domingo. Queen Air flies from New York to Santo Domingo four times a week. US Airways offers service into Santo Domingo directly from Philadelphia, once a day, seven days a week; flights from other U.S. cities must connect in Philadelphia.

➤ AIRLINES AND CONTACTS: **Air Atlantic** (☎ 809/572–1441); **Air Caraïbes** (☎ 809/549–0741); **Air Transat** (☎ 416/259–1118); **Air ALM** (☎ 809/687–4569); **American Airlines/American Eagle** (☎ 809/542–5151); **Aeromar** (☎ 877/237–6672); **Continental** (☎ 809/562–6688); **Queen Air** (☎ 809/565–4041); **US Airways** (☎ 809/540–0505).

AIRPORTS

The Barahona International Airport on the southwest coast is finished and awaits scheduled flights; for now, only private planes fly in. International flights generally arrive at Las Américas International Airport, about 20 mi (32 km) outside Santo Domingo, and La Unión International Airport, about 15 mi (24 km) east of Puerto Plata on the north coast. The Punta Cana International Airport is a unique experience. The terminal building is a thatched-roof structure with cane partitions; it covers several acres and is surrounded by gardens. The new La Romana/Casa de Campo International Airport has opened. Its creative design replicates a sugar mill factory; the area was originally a sugar cane plantation.

Anticipate long lines and allow 1½–2 hours for checking in for an international flight, especially at Las Américas. Do confirm your flight two days in advance. Keep a sharp eye on your luggage. If you fly out of a U.S. airport such as Miami, where a shrink-wrap service is offered—avail yourself of it (plastic-wrap your bag like meat in a supermarket, and no one is likely to tamper with it).

Taxis are available at the airports, and the 25-minute ride into Santo Domingo averages about $30. Some order has been imposed outside the airport—taxis line up and, for the most part, charge official, established rates. If you've arranged for a hotel transfer (a good idea), a representative should be waiting for you in the immigration hall. Fares from the Puerto Plata airport average $16 to Playa Dorada; expect to pay about $30 from Punta Cana airport to the hotels.

➤ AIRPORT INFORMATION: **Barahona International Airport** (☎ 809/524–4109); **Las Américas International Airport** (☎ 809/549–0450); **La Unión International Airport** (☎ 809/586–0107 or 809/586–0219); **Punta Cana International Airport** (☎ 809/668–4749); **La Romana/Casa de Campo International Airport** (☎ 809/556–5565).

BUSINESS HOURS

BANKS

Banks are open weekdays 8:30–4:30.

POST OFFICES

Post offices are open weekdays 7:30–2:30.

Offices and shops are open weekdays 8–noon and 2–6, Saturday 8–noon. About 50% of the stores stay open all day, no longer closing for a midday siesta.

CAR RENTALS
You'll need a valid driver's license from your own country and a major credit card (or cash deposit). Rates average US$70 and up per day. Ask around, as some local agencies give better rates. Both international and local companies rent cars in the D.R.
➤ Major Agencies: **Avis** (☎ 809/535–7191); **Budget** (☎ 809/562–6812); **Hertz** (☎ 809/221–5333); **McBeal** (☎ 809/688–6518); **National** (☎ 809/562–1444); **Nelly Rent-a-Car** (☎ 809/544–1800 or 800/526–6684 in the U.S.).

CAR TRAVEL
Fill up—and keep an eye on—the tank; gas stations are few and far between in rural areas. Gas prices are high by U.S. standards, approximately $2.33–$2.59 a gallon.

Many Dominicans drive recklessly, and their cars are often in bad shape (missing headlights, taillights, etc.). It's strongly suggested that you don't drive outside the major cities at night. If you must, use extreme caution, especially on the narrow, unlighted mountain roads. Watch out for pedestrians, bicycles, motorbikes, and the occasional stray cow or goat.

Traffic and directional signs are less than adequate; before setting out, consult with your hotel concierge about routes and buy a good road map. Although some roads are still full of potholes, the route between Santo Domingo and Santiago is now a four-lane divided highway, and the road between Santiago and Puerto Plata has a smooth new blacktop. Surprisingly, many of the scenic secondary roads, such as the "high road" between Playa Dorada and Santiago, are in good shape.

Driving is on the right. The 80-kph (50-mph) speed limit is strictly enforced. Note that outside Santiago you might be pulled over for speeding, even if you weren't. You'll be expected to pay a bribe of about $3. Pay it, smile, and moan about it later. The hassles just aren't worth it if you don't. The police count on these payoffs to augment their meager incomes. Upon taking office, the current president allegedly doubled the policemen's salaries and is hoping to increase them even more—perhaps eliminating the need for such "moonlighting."

ELECTRICITY
The current is 110 volts, 60 cycles—just like in North America. You'll hear much talk about electrical blackouts, but they occur less frequently and tend to last only one to two minutes (when they're over, everyone claps). Hotels and most restaurants have generators.

EMBASSIES
➤ Canada: **Canadian Embassy** (✉ Capitan Eugenia de Marchena, No. 39 (Box 2054), La Esperilla, Santo Domingo, ☎ 809/685–1136); **Canadian Consulate** (✉ Edificio Isabel de Torres, Suite 311C, Puerto Plata, ☎ 809/586–5761).
➤ United Kingdom: **British Embassy** (✉ Ave 27 de Fabrero No 233, Edificio Corominas Pepin, Santo Domingo, ☎ 809/472–7671 or 809/472–7373).

➤ UNITED STATES: **United States Embassy** (✉ Leopoldo Navarro esq. Cesar Nicolas Penson, Santo Domingo, ☎ 809/221–5511).

EMERGENCIES
➤ AMBULANCE AND FIRE: Dial ☎ 911.
➤ HOSPITALS: **Centro Médico Sosua** (✉ Av. Martinez, Sosua, ☎ 809/571–3949); **Centro Médico Universidad Central del Este** (✉ Av. Máximo Gómez 68, Santo Domingo, ☎ 809/221–0171); **Clínica Abreu** (✉ Calle Beller 42, Santo Domingo, ☎ 809/688–4411); **Clínica Dr. Brugal** (✉ Calle José del Carmen Ariza 15, Puerto Plata, ☎ 809/586–2519); **Clínica Gómez Patino** (✉ Av. Independencia 701, Santo Domingo, ☎ 809/685–9131); **Servimed** (✉ Plaza La Criolla, Sousa, ☎ 809/571–0964) is open 24 hours a day and has a medical staff that speaks five languages.
➤ PHARMACIES: **Farmacia Deleyte** (✉ Av. John F. Kennedy 89, Puerto Plata, ☎ 809/586–2583); **San Judas Tadeo** (✉ Av. Independencia 57, Santo Domingo, ☎ 809/689–6664).
➤ POLICE: Dial ☎ 809/586–2804 in Puerto Plata; 711 in Santo Domingo; 809/571–2233 in Sosua.

ETIQUETTE AND BEHAVIOR
Wearing shorts, miniskirts, and halter tops in churches is considered inappropriate. Men in Santo Domingo never wear shorts.

FESTIVALS AND SEASONAL EVENTS
Santo Domingo hosts a Carnival in late February. The renowned Festival del Merengue is held in late July and early August in Santo Domingo and showcases name entertainers, bands, and orchestras. During the last week in August the island's top restaurants compete in the capital city's Gastronomic Festival. In October the Puerto Plata Festival transforms the Amber Coast into one giant fiesta.

HEALTH
Though it's reasonably safe to drink water from the tap (especially in the better resorts), you're better off playing it safe with bottled water. Many resorts have adopted the Crystal Program, which sets strict guidelines for food service, particularly for hot and cold buffets. Still, try to arrive at the very start of a buffet meal, before the food has sat out for a while in the tropical heat.

HOLIDAYS
Public holidays for 2002 are: New Year's Day, Our Lady of La Altagracia Day (Jan. 21), Duarte's Birthday (Jan. 26), Independence Day (Feb. 27), Good Friday (Apr. 13), Labor Day (May 1), Corpus Christi (June 14), Restoration Day (Aug. 16), Our Lady of Las Mercedes Day (Sept. 24), Columbus Day (Oct. 26), Discovery of Hispaniola Day (Dec. 5), and Christmas.

LANGUAGE
Before you travel to the D. R., rent Spanish audiotapes from the library or study a quick guide to travel Spanish and take it with you. Staff at major tourist attractions and front-desk personnel in most major hotels speak a fascinating form of English, and you may have difficulty making yourself understood. Outside the popular tourist establishments, restaurant menus are in Spanish, as are traffic signs everywhere. Using smiles and gestures will help, and though you can manage with just English, people are even more courteous if you try to speak their language.

MAIL AND SHIPPING
Airmail postage to North America for a letter or postcard is RD$2, to Europe RD$4; letters may take up to three weeks to reach their desti-

nation. Or you can pay almost US$1.45 to buy a pale green stamp for "fast mail" in a gift shop (outside Santo Domingo, post offices aren't easy to find). The main branch of the post office in Santo Domingo is on Calle Heroes del Luperon at Rafael Damiron La Ferla.

MONEY MATTERS
Prices quoted in this chapter are in U.S. dollars unless noted otherwise.

ATMS
Banco Popular has many locations throughout the country; many have ATMs that accept international cards.

CREDIT CARDS
Major credit cards are accepted at most hotels, large stores, and restaurants.

CURRENCY
The coin of the realm is the Dominican peso (written RD$). At press time, RD$16.40 was equivalent to US$1. Always make certain you know in which currency any transaction is taking place. Carry a pocket calculator to make conversions easier. You'll find *cambios* (currency exchange offices) at the airports as well as in major shopping areas throughout the island. In addition, some hotels provide their guests with exchange services.

PASSPORTS AND VISAS
U.S. and Canadian citizens must have either a valid passport or proof of citizenship, such as an original birth certificate with a raised seal. Legal residents of the U.S. must have an alien registration card (green card) and a valid passport from their home country. Citizens of Australia, New Zealand, and the U.K. need a valid passport.

SAFETY
In general, the island is very safe, and you don't hear about violent crime against tourists. In Santo Domingo, however, be conscious of your wallet or pocketbook, especially around the Malecón, where pickpockets are a problem. Note that at night you may see men in civvies with shoulder rifles standing outside businesses or homes. Don't be unnerved by this. These men are the Dominican equivalents of private security guards. If you rent a car, don't drink and drive. Always lock your car and never leave valuables in it even if it is locked.

SIGHTSEEING TOURS
Apolo Tours offers a full-day tour of Playa Grande and tours to Santiago (including a casino excursion) and Sosua; all cost $35. The company will also arrange transfers between your hotel and the airport, day trips, and custom and small-group tours along the north coast, which include stops for swimming and a trip to Samaná ($49). Cabemba Tours runs various tours of the Cibao Valley and the Amber Coast, including Puerto Plata, Sosua, and Río San Juan. Caribbean Jeep Safaris is an English-speaking outfit that runs Jeep tours in the mountains behind Puerto Plata and Sosua, ending up at the Cabarete Adventure Park, where you can swim in an underground pool and explore caves with Taíno rock paintings. Buffet lunch and unlimited drinks are included in the $40 price.

At Ecotourismo, a Sosua-based operation, they say, "We love our country and invite you to share and discover the secrets of a land with a richer biodiversity than any in the Caribbean." They offer horse safaris, kayaking, bird-watching, mountain excursions to the Blue Moon Inn for Indian dinners, and more. Go Dominican Tours has tours to Jarabacoa for $85, which include lunch, drinks, and 3½ hours of river rafting; jumping off cliffs is optional. Jeep safaris trek to flower, fruit, and coffee plantations. Horseback riding in the Puerto Plata area is another option. Iguana Mama, Mountain Bike, Hiking & Cultural Vacations offers adventure tours with an ecological conscience: 20% of their profits are donated to local environmental projects and education.

Winchester Tours, a Massachusetts-based company, specializes in wildlife and bird-watching tours of Barahona for groups of 6–10 nature lovers. The company's president, Fred Sladen, also acts as tour leader. Having lived in the Caribbean for 15 years, he's a recognized authority on tropical birds and ecosystems and is a very personable host as well. He, too, donates to conservation organizations.

Prieto Tours, which operates Gray Line of the D.R., has half-day bus tours of Santo Domingo, nightclub tours, beach tours, trips to Cibao Valley and the Amber Coast, and a variety of other excursions; prices start at $30. Turinter offers a six-hour trip to Altos de Chavón ($45); a full-day of swimming and boating on Saona Island ($78); and specialty trips (museum, shopping, fishing).
➤ CONTACTS: **Apolo Tours** (☎ 809/586–5329); **Cabemba Tours** (☎ 809/586–2177); **Caribbean Jeep Safaris** (☎ 809/571–1924); **Ecotourismo** (☎ 809/571–3138); **Go Dominican Tours** (☎ 809/586–5969); **Iguana Mama, Mountain Bike, Hiking & Cultural Vacations** (☎ 800/571–0908); **Prieto Tours** (☎ 809/685–0102); **Turinter** (☎ 809/685–4020); **Winchester Tours** (☎ 800/391–2473).

TAXES
DEPARTURE TAX
The D.R. has a $10 departure tax (included in ticket prices if purchased in the U.S.); additionally, a tourist card *must* be bought upon arrival, which also costs $10 (paid in cash in U.S. dollars).

SALES TAX
A 10% service charge is added to restaurant checks and hotel bills, as is a 13% government tax.

TAXIS
Taxis, which are government regulated, line up outside hotels and restaurants. They're unmetered, and the minimum fare within Santo Domingo is about $4, but you can bargain for less if you order a taxi away from the major hotels. Some taxis aren't allowed to pick up from hotels, so they hang out on the street in front of them. On the average, they're $1 cheaper per ride. (Note: avoid unmarked street taxis, particularly in Santo Domingo—they're a little risky, and there have been incidents of robberies.)

Hiring a taxi by the hour—with unlimited stops—is $10 per hour with a minimum of two hours. Be sure to establish the time that you start; drivers like to advance the time a little. Always carry small denominations, like 5-, 10-, and 20-peso notes, because drivers rarely seem to have change. Taxis can also drive you to destinations outside the city. Rates are posted in hotels and at the airport. Sample fares from Santo Domingo are $80 to La Romana and $150 to Puerto Plata. If you're negotiating, the going rate is RD$5 per kilometer. Round-trips are considerably less than twice the one-way fare. Two good cab companies are El Conde Taxi and Tecni-Taxi.

Radio taxis are not only convenient but also a wise choice if you don't speak Spanish. The fare is negotiated over the phone when you make the appointment. The most reliable company is Apolo Taxi. The standard charge is about $7 per hour during the day and $8 at night, no minimum, and with as many stops as you like. Another option is to go in high-Dominican style and hire a limo, even if it's just for a night. Call P. Green Taxi for a courteous, English-speaking driver. Call the Limousine Connection, whose rates run around $50 per hour.

➤ CONTACTS: **Apolo Taxi** (☎ 809/541–9595); **El Conde Taxi** (☎ 809/563–6131); **P. Green Taxi** (☎ 809/251–0571); **Limousine Connection** (☎ 809/540–5304 or 809/567–3435); **Tecni-Taxi** (☎ 809/567–2010 in Santo Domingo; 809/320–7621 in Puerto Plata).

TELEPHONES
COUNTRY AND AREA CODES
To call the D.R. from the United States, dial 1 and then the area code 809 and the local number. From the D.R. there's also direct-dial service.

INTERNATIONAL CALLS
To reach the U.S. and Canada, dial 1, followed by the area code and number; to the U.K., dial 011, the country and city codes, and the number.

LOCAL CALLS
To make a local call, dial the 7-digit number.

TIPPING
If you found the service to your liking, tip an extra 5%–10%. It's customary to leave a dollar per day for the hotel maid. Taxi drivers expect a 10% tip, especially if they've had to lift luggage or to wait for you. Skycaps and hotel porters expect at least RD$10 per bag.

TRANSPORTATION AROUND THE DOMINICAN REPUBLIC
AIRPLANES
Air Century, flying out of Herrara Airport and La Romana Airport, offers charters, transfers, excursions, and sightseeing. Air Santo Domingo offers service between the capital and Puerto Plata, Punta Cana, La Romana, El Portillo, and Santiago. Each hop is about $60. Jimmy and Irene Butler of Air Taxi charter planes for trips around the island or to neighboring islands. Caribar has both planes and helicopters and offers general air service, ambulance service, and aerial photography trips.

➤ CONTACTS: **Air Century** (✉ Herrara Airport, Santo Domingo, ☎ 809/566–0888 or 809/567–6778; ✉ La Romana Airport, ☎ 809/550–6636 or 809/550–8201; ✉ Casa de Campo, ☎ 809/523–3333 ext. 8351); **Air Santo Domingo** (☎ 809/683–8020); **Air Taxi** (✉ Núñez de Cáceres 2, Santo Domingo, ☎ 809/227–8333 or 809/567–1555); **Caribar** (✉ Av. Luperon, Herrara Airport, Santo Domingo, ☎ 809/542–6688; ✉ La Romana Airport, ☎ 809/550–2585 in La Romana).

BUSES
Privately owned air-conditioned buses make regular runs to Santiago, Puerto Plata, and other destinations. You should make reservations by calling Metro Buses or Caribe Tours. One-way bus fare from Santo Domingo to Puerto Plata is about $6, and it takes four hours. Metro's buses have more of an upscale clientele. Although the coffee and cookies are complimentary, there are no movies. Caribe, which shows bilingual movies, is favored by locals; buses are often filled to capacity, especially on weekends.

Frequent service from Santo Domingo to the town of La Romana is provided by Express Bus. Buses depart from Revelos Street in front of Enriquillo Park every hour on the hour from 5 AM to 9 PM; the schedule is exactly the same from Romana. The office of this bus line is now closed, so there's no phone. But a ticket taker will take your $3 just before departure. Travel time is about 1¾ hours, and if luck is with you, you'll get the larger bus, which will show a first-rate American movie. Once in town you can take a taxi from the bus stop to Casa de Campo ($7) or Casa del Mar ($10).

➤ CONTACTS: **Metro Buses** (☎ 809/566–7126 in Santo Domingo; 809/586–6062 in Puerto Plata; 809/587–4711 in Santiago); **Caribe Tours** (☎ 809/221–4422).

OTHER OPTIONS

Traditionally, *públicos* or *conchos* are small blue-and-white or blue-and-red cars that run regular routes, stopping to let passengers on and off. But now everyone is getting into the act. Anyone who owns a car can operate it as a *público* and after 5 PM many do. The fare is RD$2. Competing with the públicos are the *colectivos* (privately owned vans), whose drivers coast around the major thoroughfares, leaning out of the window or jumping out to try to persuade you to climb aboard. It's a colorful if cramped way to get around. The fare is about RD$1.

Voladoras (fliers) are vans that run from Puerto Plata's Central Park to Sosua and Cabarete a couple of times each hour for RD$10. They have a reliable schedule but aren't always labeled with their destination.

Motoconchos are a popular, inexpensive way to get around such areas as Puerto Plata, Sosua, and Jarabacoa. You can flag one of these bikes down along rural roads and in town; rates vary from RD$3 to RD$20 per person, depending upon distance. Be careful: no helmets are provided, and the Dominicans drive like maniacs.

VISITOR INFORMATION

➤ BEFORE YOU LEAVE: **Dominican Republic Tourist Office** (✉ 136 E. 57th St., Suite 803, New York, NY 10022, ☎ 212/575–4966 or 888/374–6361, WEB www.dr1.com/travel.shtml; ✉ 2355 Salzedo Ave., Suite 307, Coral Gables, FL 33134, ☎ 305/444–4592 or 888/358–9594; ✉ 1464 Crescent St., Montréal, Québec H3A 2B6, Canada, ☎ 514/933–6126; ✉ 20 Hand Court, High Holborn, London WC1, U.K., ☎ 0171/723–1552).

➤ IN THE DOMINICAN REPUBLIC: **Secretary of Tourism** (✉ Secretaria de Estado de Turismo, Av. México, corner of Av. 30 de Marzo, Edificios Guberbamentales, Santo Domingo, ☎ 809/221–4660); **Ministry of Tourism** (✉ Av. Mexico, Santo Domingo, ☎ 809/221–4660); **Puerto Plata tourist office** (✉ Playa Long Beach, Puerto Plata, ☎ 809/586–3676).

11 GRENADA

By Jane E.
Zarem

It's cool, dark, and pungent inside the nutmeg co-op. In loose floral skirts and cotton shirts, bandanas around their heads, the ladies of Gouyave work hard for their money. Perched on stools, facing huge wooden chutes, they sort nutmegs all day. Fingers move like lightning, sorting thousands per hour. When sunlight briefly brightens the room, the chute wall reveals someone's handwritten message: GOD LOOKED AT MY WORK AND WAS PLEASED. THEN HE LOOKED AT MY SALARY, BOWED HIS HEAD, AND SADLY WALKED AWAY.

Grenada, a jewel of an island 21 mi (34 km) long and 12 mi (19 km) wide, boasts 45 beaches and countless secluded coves. It's crisscrossed by nature trails, laced with spice plantations, and its mountainous interior is lush rain forest. Select hotels cling to hillsides or skirt the sea; a mellow island spirit juxtaposes nicely with top facilities and sensible development. St. George's is one of the most picturesque capital cities in the Caribbean, and Grand Anse is one of the finest beaches. Nicknamed Isle of Spice, Grenada is a major producer of nutmeg, cinnamon, mace, cocoa, and other spices and flavorings. The aroma of spices fills the air in markets, in restaurants, and throughout the countryside.

Grenada lies in the eastern Caribbean, 12 degrees north of the equator, and is the southernmost of the Windward Islands. The nation of Grenada consists of three islands: Grenada, the largest, with 120 square mi (311 square km) and a population of just over 90,000; Carriacou (car-ree-a-coo), 23 mi (37 km) north of Grenada, with 13 square mi (34 square km) and a population of about 5,000; and Petite Martinique, 2 mi (3 km) northeast of Carriacou, with just 486 acres and a population of only 700. Carriacou and Petite Martinique are popular for day trips, fishing, or snorkeling excursions, but most of the tourist activity is on Grenada.

Although he never set foot on the island, Christopher Columbus sighted Grenada in 1498 and named it Concepción. Spanish sailors following in his wake renamed it Granada, after the city in the hills of their homeland. Adapted to Grenade by French colonists, the transformation to Grenada was completed by the British in the 18th century.

Throughout the 17th century, Grenada was the scene of many bloody battles between indigenous Carib Indians and the French. Rather than surrender upon losing their last battle in 1651, the Caribs committed mass suicide by leaping off a cliff in Sauteurs, at the island's northern tip. The French were later overwhelmed by the British in 1762, thus beginning a seesaw of power between the two nations. By the Treaty of Versailles in 1783, Grenada was granted to the British and, almost immediately, African slaves were brought in to work the sugar plantations. Slavery continued for 50 years until it was abolished in 1834.

On February 7, 1974, Grenada was granted total independence within the British Commonwealth. The socialist New Jewel Movement (NJM) party seized power in 1979, formed the People's Revolutionary Government, and named Maurice Bishop prime minister. A division within the party led to the murder of Bishop and many of his supporters, after which NJM deputy prime minister Bernard Coard and Army Commander Hudson Austin took over the government. Days later, on October 25, 1983, at the request of Grenada's governor general and the heads of state of neighboring islands, U.S. troops intervened. American students attending St. George's University Medical School were evacuated, and the revolution was quickly quelled. Coard and Austin (and others) were arrested, found guilty of murder, and are currently serving life sentences in prison, high on a hill overlooking St. George's Harbour and the scene of the crime.

The late Herbert A. Blaize was elected prime minister in December 1984. With millions of dollars in U.S. and Canadian aid, his government reorganized Grenada's economy to emphasize agriculture, light manufacturing, and tourism. The country rebuilt roads and installed a direct-dial phone system. Grenada's modern Point Salines International Airport, which was begun with Cuban assistance and completed by the new government in 1984, enables jets to land day or night.

The peaceful progress of this island nation continues. Grenada's popularity as a vacation destination increases each year as travelers seek new and exotic islands to visit. Hotels have expanded, and new ones are on the drawing board, but any expansion of the tourism industry is carefully controlled: no building can stand taller than a coconut palm. Many hotels, resorts, and restaurants are family-owned, run by people who get to know their guests. They're typical Grenadians—friendly, hospitable, and hardworking.

Lodging

Grenada's tourist accommodations are almost all in the southwest part of the island, primarily on or near Grand Anse Beach. Lodging options range from simply furnished, inexpensive kitchenette apartments to elegant suites just steps from the sea. Hotels tend to be small and intimate, with friendly management and attentive staff. All guest rooms are equipped with a TV unless indicated otherwise. Families should note that a few resorts may not welcome children during the winter season (December 15–April 15); during the off-season, on the other hand, many resorts allow children under 12 to share their parents' room for free. Prices may also be discounted up to 40% in the off-season.

CATEGORY	COST*
$$$$	over $325
$$$	$225–$325
$$	$150–$225
$	under $150

*All prices are for a standard double room in high season, excluding 8% government tax and 10% service charge.

Lodging

Allamanda
Beach Resort **8**

Blue Horizons
Cottage Hotel **12**

Calabash Hotel **24**

Caribbee Country
House **31**

Coyaba Beach
Resort **9**

Flamboyant Hotel
& Cottages **13**

Grenada Grand
Beach Resort **7**

Laluna **19**

LaSOURCE **18**

Mariposa Beach
Resort **15**

Rex Grenadian **16**

La Sagesse **28**

Secret Harbour
Resort **23**

Silver Beach
Resort **30**

Spice Island
Beach Resort **10**

True Blue Bay
Resort **22**

Twelve Degrees
North **26**

Dining

Aquarium Beach
Club and
Restaurant **17**

The Beach
House **20**

La Belle Creole **12**

The Boatyard **25**

La Boulangerie **11**

Brown Sugar **21**

Callaloo By
The Sea **29**

Cicely's **24**

Coconut Beach **6**

La Dolce Vita **14**

Mamma's **4**

The Nutmeg **1**

The Red Crab **27**

Rudolf's **2**

La Sagesse **28**

Scraper's **32**

Tout Bagay **3**

Tropicana **5**

Grenada and Carriacou

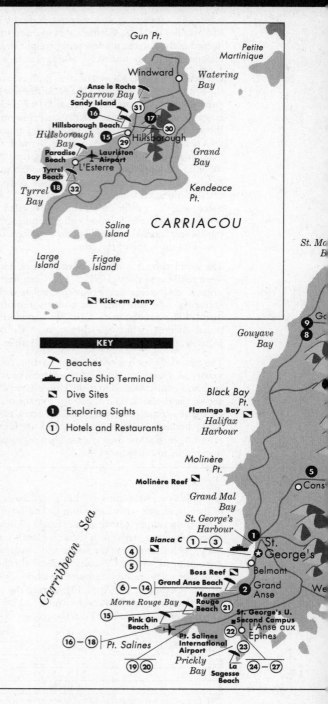

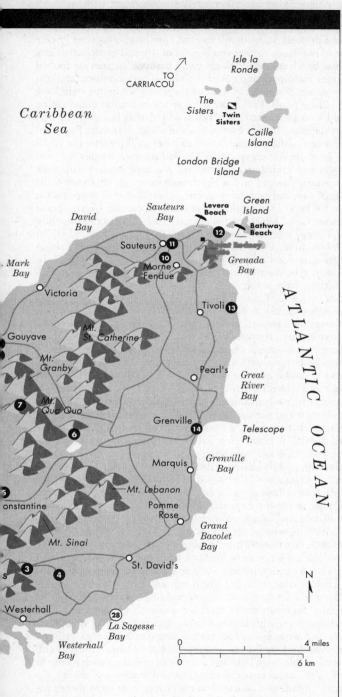

Caribbean Sea

Isle la Ronde

TO CARRIACOU

The Sisters

Twin Sisters

Caille Island

London Bridge Island

David Bay

Sauteurs Bay

Levera Beach

Green Island

Bathway Beach

Sauteurs ⑪

Morne Fendue ⑩

⑫

Grenada Bay

Mark Bay

Victoria

Tivoli ⑬

Mt. St. Catherine

Mt. Granby

Gouyave

⑦ Mt. Qua Qua

⑥

Pearl's

Great River Bay

Grenville

⑭

Telescope Pt.

Marquis

Grenville Bay

Mt. Lebanon

Pomme Rose

onstantine

Mt. Sinai

Grand Bacolet Bay

St. David's

③ ④

N

Westerhall

⑳

La Sagesse Bay

Westerhall Bay

A T L A N T I C   O C E A N

0   4 miles

0   6 km

Exploring

Annandale Falls **5**
Bay Gardens **3**
Belair **17**
Carib's Leap **11**
Concord Falls **7**
Dougaldston Spice Estate **8**
Gouyave **9**
Grand Anse **2**
Grand Étang National Park . . . **6**
Grenville **14**
Historical Museum **15**
Laura Herb and Spice Garden **4**
Levera National Park **12**
Mt. Rodney Estate **10**
River Antoine Rum Distillery **13**
St. George's **1**
Sandy Island **16**
Tyrrel Bay **18**

Hotels

$$$$ ⊞ **Calabash Hotel.** Suites in this elegant, comfortable hotel on Prickly
★   Bay are in two-story cottages on 8 acres of tropical gardens that hug
the curved beach and overlook the yacht harbor. Cottages are framed
by fragrant frangipani and colorful hibiscus, bougainvillea, and oleander blossoms. Twenty-two suites have whirlpool baths; eight have
private plunge pools. Each suite has a spacious bedroom and sitting
area, and a veranda where breakfast is served after being freshly prepared by the maid. Rooms have rattan and wicker furniture. Fans dan-
gle from whitewashed ceilings; each room has a CD player—but you'll
have to go to the library to watch TV. Bathrooms are equipped with
hair dryers and lighted makeup mirrors. A complimentary fruit plate
or fruit punch is served on the beach each morning; afternoon tea is
served each day; and each evening, canapés are delivered to your suite.
Cicely's, the hotel's restaurant, serves excellent cuisine. Greens fees at
the Grenada Golf Club are complimentary. ⊠ *L'Anse aux Épines (Box
382), St. George's,* ☎ *473/444–4334, 800/223–1108, or 800/742–4276;*
FAX *473/444–5050,* WEB *www.calabashhotel.com. 30 suites. Restaurant, 2 bars, air-conditioning, room service, pool, spa, golf privileges,
tennis court, gym, shuffleboard, beach, snorkeling, boating, shops, billiards, library, baby-sitting, dry cleaning, laundry service, concierge,
car rental. AE, MC, V. CP, MAP.*

$$$$ ⊞ **Laluna.** Brand-new in 2001, Laluna is an upscale cottage enclave
hidden away on a remote, pristine beach near Grenada's Quarantine
Point. Sixteen large cottages with thatched roofs—and each with its
own plunge pool—line the beachfront, with the wooded hillside as a
backdrop. Bedrooms, with king-size beds, open onto large verandas
that serve as indoor-outdoor sitting areas. In addition to a direct-dial
telephone and television set, each room has a VCR, stereo, and CD
player, computer modem outlets, and coffeemaker. Bathrooms have custom-made tubs and showers that partially open to the natural environment; thick bathrobes, a makeup mirror, and a hair dryer are
supplied as well. A main "club house" is the location of the restaurant, bar, a small CD and video library, and other services. There's weekly
entertainment, nightly sunset meditation, and yoga classes. ⊠ *Morne
Rouge (Box 1500),* ☎ *473/439–0001 or 800/628–8929,* FAX *473/439–
0600,* WEB *www.laluna.com. 16 cottages. Restaurant, bar, air-conditioning, fans, in-room data ports, in-room safes, in-room VCRs, minibars, pool, massage, beach, snorkeling, windsurfing, boating, bicycles,
shops, library, concierge, car rental. AE, DC, MC, V. BP, MAP.*

$$$$ ⊞ **LaSOURCE.** Five minutes from the airport, Grenada's first all-inclusive
★   resort unfolds on 40 acres facing Pink Gin Beach. The reception hall
leads to a breezy courtyard, the Oasis bar, the Great House restaurant
with its colonnaded terrace, a piano bar, and a two-level swimming
pool. Guest quarters are in four-story buildings, all facing the beach.
(Be prepared for lots of stairs; there are no elevators.) Bedrooms have
Oriental-design rugs on Italian marble floors, Jamaican mahogany
furniture and woodwork, four-poster king-size beds, high ceilings,
balconies overlooking the sea, and marble bathrooms. The chef's cuisine is memorable, with light and vegetarian dishes on each menu. In
addition to the usual resort sports, yoga and fencing are offered. An
"executive" 9-hole golf course is on the property. At night there's entertainment and live music. Rates include *everything*—even daily spa
treatments—and tipping isn't allowed. This is an adults only resort,
with a minimum age of 16 years. ⊠ *Pink Gin Beach (Box 852), St.
George's,* ☎ *473/444–2556 or 800/544–2883,* FAX *473/444–2561,* WEB
*www.lasourcegrenada.com. 91 rooms, 9 suites. 2 restaurants, bar,
piano bar, air-conditioning, fans, in-room safes, refrigerators, pool, hair*

salon, hot tub, sauna, spa, 9-hole golf course, 2 tennis courts, aerobics, archery, badminton, health club, jogging, Ping-Pong, volleyball, beach, dive shop, snorkeling, windsurfing, boating, waterskiing, shops, laundry service, concierge, travel services. AE, D, MC, V. All-inclusive.

$$$$ ⊞ **Spice Island Beach Resort.** In December 2000, the "jewel of Grand
★ Anse Beach" completed a $5.5-million renovation, which added 10 beachfront suites, a completely rebuilt grand entrance and reception area, free-form pool, spa, business center, and two shops. Returning guests can rest assured that even with all the changes and improvements— and its new peach-color paint—much remains the same. The resort still enjoys Grenada's premier location on Grand Anse Beach, the dining room and bar are still steps from the sand and open to sea breezes, and the impeccable service remains warm and friendly. Every guest room has been redecorated with new furniture and stylish fabrics in soft colors. And all have extra-large marble bathrooms with whirlpool tubs, hair dryers, irons and ironing boards, and plenty of plush towels. Each duplex beach house and garden suite has an ocean view from the terrace or balcony. Thirteen suites have private plunge pools. Four huge Royal Suites offer the ultimate luxury: a private 16×20-ft pool, garden, lounge, sundeck, and in-room fitness area with exercise bike and sauna. "Spice" is now an all-inclusive property, so guests enjoy all meals at the resort's Oliver's Restaurant, as well as drinks and unlimited use of water-sports gear—at no supplemental charge. Spice Island Diving is on-site, but dive instruction and dive trips are priced separately. Spa treatments are also extra. ⊠ *Grand Anse (Box 6), St. George's,* ☎ *473/ 444–4258, 800/223–6510, 800/223–9815, or 800/742–4276;* ℻ *473/ 444–4807,* 🌐 *www.spicebeachresort.com. 66 suites. Restaurant, bar, air-conditioning, fans, in-room safes, minibars, room service, pool, hair salon, spa, golf privileges, tennis court, gym, beach, dive shop, snorkeling, boating, bicycles, shops, library, laundry service, concierge, business services, meeting rooms. AE, D, DC, MC, V. All-inclusive.*

$$$ ⊞ **Grenada Grand Beach Resort.** The location (across from the Grand Anse Shopping Centre) is convenient, the 20 acres of grounds are lush, the rooms are comfortable, and the amenities are extensive. Best of all, this appealing resort complex also fronts on a broad section of Grand Anse Beach. Fresh-water lovers can swim in two attractive pools. Groups are attracted to the 800-seat convention center. Guest rooms have attractive mahogany furniture, king-size or twin beds, a balcony or patio, voice mail and data port, large-screen TV, and a hair dryer. The restaurant offers table d'hôte and à la carte menus—you can even get a New York–style steak. The weekly buffet is accompanied by a steel band. ⊠ *Grand Anse (Box 441), St. George's,* ☎ *473/444–4371 or 800/223–9815,* ℻ *473/444–4800,* 🌐 *www.grandbeach.net. 234 rooms, 2 suites. Restaurant, 2 bars, snack bar, room service, air-conditioning, 2 pools, barbershop, hair salon, 9-hole golf course, 2 tennis courts, gym, beach, dive shop, snorkeling, boating, shops, laundry service, business services, convention center, meeting rooms, travel services, car rental. AE, DC, MC, V. CP, EP, MAP.*

$$$ ⊞ **Rex Grenadian.** This massive resort on Tamarind Bay is just three minutes from the airport. Guests, many of whom are European, are welcomed into a glistening white reception area that has lofty ceilings, vast arched doorways, trellised walkways, and tiled terraces. Some rooms are in the main building, but most are in eight two-story buildings on a bluff overlooking the sea. Rooms have simple rattan furniture. Balconies have a view of the sea or of a lake and gardens. Superior rooms have air-conditioning, a tub, and a hair dryer; standard rooms have ceiling fans and showers. The pool, casual restaurant, and bar are near the beach but separated from the guest rooms by a large lawn and lake. Activities abound—water sports, nature walks, dance classes, dive

lessons, evening shows in the lounge, and happy hours. Buffet breakfast and dinner are served at the International restaurant. ⊠ *Point Salines
(Box 893), St. George's,* ☎ *473/444–3333 or 800/255–5859,* 𝐅𝐀𝐗 *473/
444–1111,* 𝐖𝐄𝐁 *www.rexcaribbean.com. 191 rooms, 21 suites. 3 restaurants, 3 bars, café, piano bar, air-conditioning, fans, pool, sauna, 2 tennis courts, health club, 2 beaches, dive shop, snorkeling, windsurfing,
boating, waterskiing, shops, cabaret, baby-sitting, business services, meeting rooms. AE, D, DC, MC, V. All-inclusive, CP, EP, MAP.*

$$$ ⊡ **Secret Harbour Resort.** Perched on a cliff above Mount Hartman Bay
(and away from the throng on the south coast), this resort attracts a
yachting crowd. The on-site Moorings' Club Mariner Watersports Cen-
tre has a fleet of small sailboats and yachts available for day or long-
term charters. But the setting is also quite romantic. The 20 suites are
each beautifully decorated, with two antique, full-size four-poster beds
and an Italian-tile bath. Guests have free use of water-sports equipment,
including Windsurfers, Sunfish, and sailboats; Aquanauts Grenada dive
shop is on-site. Just offshore, Calvigny Island is a 10-minute ride by speed-
boat; bring a picnic and spend the afternoon on your own deserted isle.
Be aware that the resort is not suitable for children under 12, as the
steps down to the beach are rather steep and the dock area can be quite
busy. ⊠ *L'Anse aux Épines (Box 11), St. George's,* ☎ *473/444–4439
or 800/437–7880,* 𝐅𝐀𝐗 *473/444–4819,* 𝐖𝐄𝐁 *www.secretharbour.com. 20
suites. 2 restaurants, bar, air-conditioning, room service, pool, tennis
court, beach, dive shop, dock, snorkeling, windsurfing, boating, wa-
terskiing. AE, D, DC, MC, V. EP, MAP.*

$$ ⊡ **Allamanda Beach Resort.** Right on Grand Anse beach, this small hotel
has some rooms with whirlpool baths; many also have connecting
doors, making it a good choice for families. All rooms have tropical decor,
tile floors, cable TV, and a balcony or patio; one is wheelchair accessible. The restaurant serves international cuisine, and a poolside snack
bar has great fresh-fruit smoothies. At the water-sports center, you'll
find Sunfish, snorkeling equipment, and Dive Grenada, a private scuba
operation. Shopping, restaurants, nightlife, and the minibus to town are
right at the doorstep. An all-inclusive option is available, which includes
all meals, nonalcoholic beverages, massage, airport transfers, and gratuities. ⊠ *Grand Anse (Box 1025), St. George's,* ☎ *473/444–0095 or
800/742–4276,* 𝐅𝐀𝐗 *473/444–0126,* 𝐖𝐄𝐁 *www.allamandaresort.com. 50
suites. 2 restaurants, snack bar, air-conditioning, fans, in-room safes,
refrigerators, pool, massage, tennis court, gym, volleyball, beach, dive
shop, snorkeling, boating, meeting rooms. AE, MC, V. EP.*

$$ ⊡ **Blue Horizons Cottage Hotel.** This sister hotel of Spice Island Beach
★   Resort, just 200 yards away, is an especially good value. Each suite or
studio has a fully equipped kitchenette, a private terrace, and a TV.
Deluxe suites have separate sitting-dining rooms and one king- or two
queen-size beds; studios have dining alcoves and king-size beds. Hand-
some mahogany furniture is set off by white walls, bright floral prints,
and white-tile floors with woven-grass mats. Palm trees and tropical
plants stud the 6 acres of grounds that are also home to 21 species of
birds. Lunch is served poolside, where the open-air bar is a friendly
gathering place. The hotel's restaurant, La Belle Creole, is renowned
for its contemporary West Indian cuisine. The resort is not directly on
the beach, but it's a very short walk to Grand Anse, where you can
use Spice Island's beach chairs and water-sports equipment at no cost,
and its tennis court, fitness room, dive shop and other facilities for a
nominal fee. Greens fees at the nearby Grenada Golf & Country Club
are complimentary. Children under 12 stay free in winter; those under
18 stay free in the off-season. ⊠ *Grand Anse (Box 41), St. George's,*
☎ *473/444–4316, 473/444–4592, 800/223–9815, or 800/742–4276;*
𝐅𝐀𝐗 *473/444–2815,* 𝐖𝐄𝐁 *www.bluegrenada.com. 26 suites, 6 studios.*

Restaurant, 2 bars, air-conditioning, fans, kitchenettes, pool, golf privileges, recreation room, library, baby-sitting, laundry service, meeting rooms, car rental. AE, MC, V. CP, EP, MAP.

$$ ★ **Coyaba Beach Resort.** Named with the Arawak word for "heaven," this attractive family-run resort is strategically located on Grand Anse Beach. It's also a remarkable value, particularly in the off-season when, considering the setting, rates are extremely reasonable. Rooms, decorated with natural wood and Arawak-inspired folk art, are in eight two-story buildings that surround 5½ acres of meticulously landscaped lawns and gardens. Guests have complimentary use of all nonmotorized water-sports equipment. There's tennis, volleyball, and a pool with a swim-up bar. Excellent West Indian cuisine is served at the bamboo-walled restaurant or on the poolside terrace; there's musical entertainment several nights a week. Each room has a king-size or two double beds, a balcony or patio, a TV, and a bathroom with a hair dryer; most have a water view, and three are wheelchair accessible. Complimentary golf is available at the 9-hole course at the nearby Grenada Grand Beach Resort. ⊠ *Grand Anse (Box 336), St. George's,* ☎ *473/444–4129, 473/444–2011, 800/223–9815, or 800/742–4276;* FAX *473/444–4808,* WEB *www.coyaba.com. 70 rooms. 2 restaurants, 2 bars, air-conditioning, room service, pool, golf privileges, tennis court, shuffleboard, volleyball, beach, dive shop, snorkeling, shops, baby-sitting, laundry service, meeting rooms. AE, D, DC, MC, V. CP, EP, FAP, MAP.*

$$ **Flamboyant Hotel & Cottages.** The rooms and suites of this Grenadian-owned hotel are built into a steep hillside. Each has a private veranda and a fabulous panoramic view of Grand Anse Bay. Self-catering one-bedroom suites and two-bedroom, two-bath cottages each have a fully equipped kitchen, sitting room with TV and sofa bed, and daily maid service, making this an excellent value for families. Be prepared for lots of stairs—you'll descend about 100 of them to get to Grand Anse Beach. But don't worry: halfway down—or on the way back up—you can stop for a dip in the pool or grab a bite at the Beachside Terrace restaurant. Golf privileges are available at the Grenada Golf & Country Club. Children under 12 stay free in winter; children under 18 stay free in the off-season. ⊠ *Grand Anse (Box 214), St. George's,* ☎ *473/444–4247, 800/223–9815, or 800/742–4276;* FAX *473/444–1234,* WEB *www.flamboyant.com. 38 rooms, 20 suites, 2 cottages. Restaurant, bar, grocery, air-conditioning, in-room safes, kitchenettes, minibars, room service, pool, golf privileges, beach, snorkeling, shops, billiards, cabaret, recreation room, baby-sitting, laundry service, meeting rooms, car rental. AE, D, DC, MC, V. CP, EP, MAP.*

$$ **True Blue Bay Resort.** Although its name refers to the fact that this area was once an indigo plantation, it could just as well describe the color of the bay. The small family-run cottage colony is on 2 acres of lawns and gardens that slope down to the bay. Some spacious one-bedroom apartments are perched cliff-side, and others are on the waterfront; each has a veranda that overlooks the sea. Private two-bedroom cottages are in gardens by the pool. Each has a dining area, a living room with a sofa bed, a fully equipped kitchen, air-conditioned bedrooms, ceiling fans, cable TV, and daily maid-laundry service. The bayside restaurant serves Mexican and Caribbean cuisine. The inn is a five-minute drive from Grand Anse Beach, but you can swim in True Blue Bay, arrange yacht charters at the marina, or dive excursions at the on-site EcoDive dive center. ⊠ *Old Mill Ave., True Blue Bay (Box 1414), Grand Anse,* ☎ *473/443–8783,* FAX *473/444–5929,* WEB *www.truebluebay.com. 11 1-bedroom units, 3 2-bedroom units. Restaurant, bar, air-conditioning, fans, kitchenettes, pool, dive shop, snorkeling, boating, marina, fishing, shop, baby-sitting, laundry service, car rental. AE, MC, V. EP.*

$$ ⊡ **Twelve Degrees North.** Named for Grenada's location 12 degrees north
★ of the equator, eight top-of-the-line one- and two-bedroom apartments,
all facing the sea, come with exceptional personal service—including
your own housekeeper, who will cook your breakfast and lunch, clean,
and tend to your laundry. Grocery items are stocked for your arrival,
and you're greeted with lovely flowers, a bottle of rum punch, and a
spice basket. Apartments are bright and airy, with modern furniture,
tropical art on the walls, and woven-grass rugs on the clay-tile floors.
There's no air-conditioning, but the trade winds will keep you cool. The
balcony or patio is perfect for breakfast (in the terry cloth robes pro-
vided), a quiet lunch, sunset drinks, or a romantic dinner for two. Ac-
tivities center on the private beach, pool, and tennis court. You have
free use of Sunfish and ocean kayaks; fishing, scuba diving, and day sails—
or an on-site massage—can be arranged. This is a small, secluded inn
(not appropriate for children under 15), with a minimum stay of one
week during peak season. ⊠ *L'Anse aux Épines (Box 241), St. George's,*
☎ *473/444–4580 or 800/322–1753,* FAX *473/444–4580,* WEB
*www.twelvedegreesnorth.com. 8 apartments. Pool, massage, tennis
court, beach, snorkeling, boating, laundry service. AE, V. EP.*

$ ⊡ **La Sagesse.** In a nature reserve on a bay 10 mi (16 km) east of the
airport—about a 30-minute drive, the grounds of this secluded coun-
try inn include a salt-pond bird sanctuary, thick mangroves, several na-
ture trails, and ½ mi (¾ km) of tree-shaded beach. Guest rooms are in
the manor house and a beach cottage; two small budget-price rooms
are located behind La Sagesse restaurant. Rooms are rustic but just 30
ft from the beach, with screened-in patios and ceiling fans. Be content
to relax and enjoy the natural surroundings or rent a car if you stay
this far out; although Mike Meranski, the cheerful American owner,
will run you into town for groceries. ⊠ *La Sagesse Nature Center (Box
44), St. David's,* ☎ *473/444–6458 or 800/322–1753,* FAX *473/444–6458,*
WEB *www.lasagesse.com. 8 rooms. Restaurant, bar, fans, kitchenettes,
hiking, beach, snorkeling, laundry service. MC, V. EP.*

$ ⊡ **Mariposa Beach Resort.** Over the hill from Grand Anse Beach, this
colony of Mediterranean-style coral-color villas covers the side of a hill
overlooking Morne Rouge Bay. The ambience is decidedly European,
and each stylishly decorated room and self-catering apartment has a
water view, a covered veranda or garden, and an Italian-tile bath-
room. It's a short walk downhill to Morne Rouge Beach or a water-
taxi ride to the beach club. The restaurant specializes in seafood and
international dishes. Children under 12 stay free. ⊠ *Morne Rouge Bay
(Box 857), St. George's,* ☎ *473/444–3171,* FAX *473/444–3172,* WEB
*www.mariposaresort.com. 30 rooms, 15 apartments. Restaurant, bar,
air-conditioning, fans, in-room safes, kitchenettes, room service, pool,
beach, laundry service. AE, MC, V. MAP.*

CARRIACOU

$$ ⊡ **Caribbee Country House.** This rambling country house is high on a
promontory overlooking the sea on the northwest side of the island; the
panoramas are magnificent, particularly at sunset. Hillside suites are decorated by theme (Colonial, South American, West Indian) and have
four-poster beds draped with netting, soft-pastel color schemes, and
Italian-tile floors. One suite has a step-up shower with an open-air view
of the bay; another has its own beach. Breakfast and dinner (French creole cuisine) are served in the dining room—and don't be surprised if one
of the owner's macaws joins you, looking for a treat. The inn is isolated
and not suitable for children, but it offers great opportunities for nature
walks, meditation, romance, and total relaxation. ⊠ *Prospect,* ☎ *473/
443–7380,* FAX *473/443–8142,* WEB *www.caribbee.cacounet.com. 6 rooms,*

3 suites. Bar, dining room, hiking, beach, snorkeling, library, laundry service, airport shuttle. No credit cards. CP, EP, MAP.

$ ⊠ **Silver Beach Resort.** Choose between a self-catering cottage, with sitting room and kitchenette, or an oceanfront double room at this laid-back beachfront resort, a short walk from the jetty in Hillsborough. All quarters have a patio or balcony; most have an ocean view. You can arrange fishing or spearfishing excursions on the resort's 30-ft Chris-Craft. From the dock you can see Sandy Island, a deserted islet a stone's throw from shore where you can picnic and snorkel. The open-air Ship-wreck Restaurant serves hearty breakfasts and Caribbean and seafood dinners. MAP guests may dine around at other local restaurants. Children under 12 stay free in the room with their parents. ⊠ *Silver Beach, Beausejour Bay, Hillsborough,* ☎ *473/443–7337, 800/742–4276, or 800/223–9815;* FAX *473/443–7165,* WEB *www.silverbeachhotel.com. 10 rooms, 6 cottages. Restaurant, bar, fans, kitchenettes, tennis court, dive shop, dock, snorkeling, windsurfing, boating, fishing, shops, laundry service, travel services, airport shuttle, car rental. AE, MC, V. CP, EP, MAP.*

Villa and Private-Home Rentals

For Grenada rental information contact: **Villas of Grenada** (⊠ Box 218, St. George's, ☎ 473/444–1896, FAX 473/444–4529). In-season rates range from about $600 a week for a two-bedroom home with a pool to about $3,500 for a six-bedroom home on the beach.

For Carriacou rental information contact: **Down Island Villa Rentals, Ltd.** (⊠ Craigston, ☎ 473/443–8182, FAX 473/443–8290, WEB www.islandvillas.com). In-season rates range from about $50 per day for a small cottage or in-town apartment suitable for two people to $215 per day for a villa with panoramic views and a swimming pool that accommodates up to six people.

Dining

Grenada grows everything from lettuce and tomatoes to plantains, mangoes, papaya (called *pawpaw*), callaloo (similar to spinach), citrus, yams, christophenes (like squash), breadfruit—the list is endless. And all dishes are prepared with local produce and seasoned with the many spices grown here. Be sure to try mango, soursop, guava, coconut (the best!), or nutmeg ice cream.

Soups—especially pumpkin and callaloo—are divine and often start a meal. Pepper pot is a savory stew of pork, oxtail, vegetables, and spices simmered for hours. Oildown, the national dish, is salted meat, breadfruit, onion, carrot, celery, dasheen (a root vegetable), and dumplings all boiled in coconut milk until the liquid is absorbed and the savory mixture becomes "oily."

Fresh seafood of all kinds, including lobster, is plentiful. Conch, known here as *lambi*, is popular and often appears curried or in a stew. Crab back, though, is not seafood—it's land crab. Almost all Grenadian restaurants serve seafood and at least some native dishes.

Rum punches are ubiquitous and always topped with grated nutmeg. Carib, the locally brewed beer, is refreshing, light, and quite good.

What to Wear

Dining in Grenada is casual. Collared shirts and long pants for men (even the fanciest restaurants don't require jacket and tie) and sundresses or slacks for women are appropriate. Beachwear, of course, should be reserved for the beach.

CATEGORY	COST*
$$$	over $18
$$	$10–$18
$	under $10

per person for a main course at dinner

Grenada

CAFÉ

$ ✕ **La Boulangerie.** This French bakery and coffee shop, convenient to the Grand Anse hotels, is a great place for breakfast or a light meal—to eat in, take out, or have delivered. You'll find croissants and other special breads and pastries, espresso, juices, baguette sandwiches, focaccia, roasted chicken, and homemade gelati. ⊠ *Le Marquis Complex, Grand Anse,* ☎ *473/444–1131. AE, MC, V.*

CARIBBEAN

$$ ✕ **Brown Sugar.** Up a steep hill and tucked on a terrace overlooking Grand Anse, this small restaurant has contemporized Grenadian recipes handed down over the generations. Thick, rich callaloo soup is a perfect starter, followed by a special entrée: perhaps fish fillet wrapped in callaloo leaves and steamed in coconut milk and local seasonings; oildown, the Grenadian national dish; Caribbean shrimp dredged in shredded coconut, deep-fried, and served with mango chutney; creole chicken; or a simple steak—all accompanied by local vegetables and warm fresh-baked bread. Vegetarian choices and a children's menu are always available. Dining is accompanied by steel-pan music on Tuesday, Friday, and Sunday evenings. Complimentary transportation is provided. ⊠ *Main Rd., Grand Anse,* ☎ *473/444–2374. Reservations essential. AE, D, DC, MC, V.*

$$ ✕ **Coconut Beach, the French Creole Restaurant.** Take local seafood,
★ add butter, wine, and Grenadian spices, and you have excellent French creole cuisine. Throw in a beautiful setting at the northern end of Grand Anse Beach, and this West Indian cottage becomes an even more delightful spot. Lobster is a specialty and may be wrapped in a crêpe, dipped in garlic butter, or added to pasta. There's also the seafood platter, lambi Calypso, and T-bone steak. Homemade coconut pie is a winner for dessert. Coconut Beach is casual enough that you can wander down the beach and stop by for an alfresco lunch. In season, there's a beach barbecue with live music Wednesday and Sunday nights. Free transportation can be arranged. ⊠ *Grand Anse Beach,* ☎ *473/444–4644. AE, D, MC, V. Closed Tues.*

$$ ✕ **Mamma's.** Mamma's has been a fixture in Grenada for years. Following the tradition of her late mother, one of Mamma's daughters will set generous helpings of truly local specialties before you—roast turtle, lobster salad, christophene salad, or fried plantain, as well as such exotica as *tatou* (armadillo), *manicou* (opossum), and sea urchin. There's no menu. Up to 25 native dishes are served family style at a fixed $18 (EC$45) per person. A sense of adventure is helpful, but you won't leave hungry. ⊠ *Lagoon Rd., Belmont, St. George's,* ☎ *473/440–1459. Reservations essential. No credit cards.*

$$ ✕ **The Nutmeg.** Fresh seafood, homemade West Indian dishes, great hamburgers, and the waterfront view make this a favorite with locals and visitors alike. It's upstairs on the Carenage (above Sea Change bookstore), with large open windows from which you can watch the harbor activity as you eat. Try the callaloo soup, curried lambi, lobster, shrimp—or just stop by for a rum punch and a roti, a fish sandwich and a Carib, or a hamburger and a Coke. ⊠ *The Carenage, St. George's,* ☎ *473/440–2539. AE, D, MC, V.*

CHINESE

$$ ✕ **Tropicana.** The chef-owner here hails from Trinidad and specializes in both Chinese and West Indian cuisine. Local businesspeople seem to be the best customers for the extensive menu of Chinese food, the tantalizing aroma of barbecued chicken notwithstanding. Eat in or take out—it's open from 7:30 AM until midnight. Tropicana is right at the Lagoon Road traffic circle, overlooking the marina. ⊠ *Lagoon Rd., St. George's,* ☎ *473/440–1586. AE, DC, MC, V.*

CONTEMPORARY

$$$ ✕ **Cicely's.** The small, open-air restaurant at the Calabash Hotel,
★ named for chef Cicely Roberts, is surrounded by palms, flowers, and twinkling lights. Cicely's culinary skills are complemented by those of Graham Newbould, former chef to the British royal family; the result is international cuisine with a Caribbean flair. The five-course table d'hôte dinner is a good bet; past menus have included chilled lobster mousse, cream of tannia (similar to potato) soup or christophene vichyssoise, followed by baked stuffed rainbow runner or charcoal-grilled pork fillet with piquant guava, garlic, and ginger sauce. Fresh-fruit sorbet or cheese and English-style biscuits top off your meal. ⊠ *L'Anse aux Épines,* ☎ *473/444–4334. Reservations essential. AE, MC, V. No lunch.*

$$$ ✕ **La Belle Creole.** The marriage of Continental and West Indian
★ cuisines and a splendid view of distant St. George's are the hallmarks of this romantic hillside restaurant at the Blue Horizons Cottage Hotel. The always-changing five-course table d'hôte menu is based on original recipes of the owner's mother, a pioneer in incorporating local products into "foreign" cuisines. Try Grenadian caviar (roe of the white sea urchin), cream of bread-nut soup, lobster-egg flan, or callaloo quiche, followed by lobster à la creole or ginger pork chops. The inspired cuisine, intimate atmosphere, and gracious service is impressive. ⊠ *Grand Anse,* ☎ *473/444–4316 or 473/444–4592. Reservations essential. AE, D, MC, V.*

$$ ✕ **The Beach House.** At this restaurant, next door to the new Laluna resort, a gleaming white-sand and sea view is the perfect backdrop for a salad or pasta luncheon on the deck. At dinner excellent steak and seafood, sashimi tuna and rack of lamb, blackened fish or prime rib of beef—accompanied by a superb wine—give "beach party" new meaning. A kids' menu is available, too. ⊠ *Airport Rd., Point Salines,* ☎ *473/444–4455. Reservations essential. AE, MC, V. Closed Sun.*

ECLECTIC

$$ ✕ **The Boatyard.** As its name implies, boaters frequent this lively restaurant and its Tiki Bar, at the Spice Island Marina. Burgers, fish-and-chips, and deep-fried shrimp are served at lunchtime. At dinner you can order charcoal-grilled club steaks, lobster, and meat or seafood brochettes. The menu always includes pasta, a vegetarian plate, West Indian dishes—and even some Mexican snacks. In season there's music and dancing on weekend nights. For quieter nights, there's a book-exchange library. ⊠ *L'Anse aux Épines,* ☎ *473/444–4662. MC, V.*

$$ ✕ **Rudolf's.** This busy, English-style waterfront pub offers West Indian fare, as well as fish-and-chips, sandwiches, and burgers. Skip the attempts at haute cuisine and enjoy the crab back, lambi, steak, and delectable nutmeg ice cream. The rum punches are lethal—even for Grenada. Rudolf's is a popular luncheon spot for local businesspeople, as well as visitors. It recently added an outside canopied terrace, where patrons can enjoy drinks or meals with a full view of the harbor. ⊠ *The Carenage, St. George's,* ☎ *473/440–2241. MC, V. Closed Sun.*

$$ ✕ **Tout Bagay Restaurant & Bar.** Its name means "everything is possible," and the eclectic menu proves the point. At lunch, for example, you might select a salad (lobster, shrimp, Caesar), or you might try a local specialty, such as a roti, flying fish sandwich, or creole-style fish. At dinner, the menu is equally broad—on the one hand, you might try lobster Thermidor, cappellini with red pepper pesto and shrimp, curry goat, or sweet and sour lambi. Tout Bagay is literally on the water at the northern end of The Carenage, and the view (day or night) is spectacular. It's a popular lunch choice for businesspeople, as well as visitors who want a break after touring the capital or shopping on the adjacent streets. ⊠ *The Carenage, St. George's,* ☎ *473/440–3000. AE, DC, MC, V.*

ITALIAN

$$$ ✕ **La Dolce Vita.** Now located at the southern end of Grand Anse Beach,
★   overlooking the sea and the twinkling lights of St. George's in the distance, this is *the* place to come for fine dining and delicious Italian cuisine. The chef is noted for his homemade pasta, prepared fresh daily. Start with a selection of cold and hot antipasti, then try lobster spaghetti, gnocchi, or fresh seafood. The restaurant is at the bottom of the 100-step beach access at the Flamboyant Hotel. ⊠ *Grand Anse Beach,* ☎ *473/444–3456. Reservations essential. D, MC, V. No lunch. Closed Mon.*

SEAFOOD

$$$ ✕ **The Red Crab.** Locals and expats love to gather at this pub, especially on Saturday night. The curried lambi and garlic shrimp keep the regulars coming back. Seafood, particularly lobster, and steak (imported from the U.S.) are staples of the menu; hot garlic bread comes with all orders. You can eat inside or under the stars. There's live music Monday and Friday in season. ⊠ *L'Anse aux Épines (near the Calabash),* ☎ *473/444–4424. Reservations essential. AE, MC, V. Closed Sun.*

$$ ✕ **Aquarium Beach Club and Restaurant.** The beach club rents ocean kayaks and snorkeling equipment. When you come up for air, enjoy fresh seafood or luncheon salads and a cool drink at the restaurant. On Friday, happy hour at the Bamboo Bar is from 4:30 to 6:30; then dinner is served. Besides fresh fish and lobster, the menu might include callaloo cannelloni or pepper steak. Saturday is volleyball day, and on Sunday there's a lobster barbecue. The atmosphere is congenial. ⊠ *La-Source Rd., Point Salines,* ☎ *473/444–1410. Reservations essential. AE, D, DC, MC, V. Closed Mon.*

$$ ✕ **La Sagesse.** The perfect spot to soothe a frazzled soul, La Sagesse resort's open-air, mostly seafood restaurant and beach bar are on a secluded cove in a nature preserve about 30 minutes from Grand Anse. You can combine your lunch or dinner with a hike or a day at the beach. Select from sandwiches, salads, or lobster for lunch. Lambi, smoked marlin, dolphinfish, and tuna steak are joined on the dinner menu by chicken française and a daily vegetarian special. Wash down your meal with a cold beer or a fresh-fruit smoothie. Transportation is available, complimentary if your meal is combined with a hike. ⊠ *La Sagesse Nature Center, St. David's,* ☎ *473/444–6458. Reservations essential. AE, MC, V.*

Carriacou

CARIBBEAN

       ✕ **Callaloo by the Sea Restaurant & Bar.** On the main road, south of town, diners enjoy extraordinary views of Sandy Island and Hillsborough Bay. The emphasis is on West Indian dishes and excellent seafood, including lobster thermidor. The callaloo soup, of course, is outstanding. Don't miss it! ⊠ *Hillsborough,* ☎ *473/443–8004. AE, MC, V. Closed Sept.*

SEAFOOD

$ ✕ **Scraper's.** Scraper's serves up lobster, conch, and the fresh catch of the day, along with a simple spirit and decor seasoned with occasional calypsonian serenades (by owner Steven Gay "Scraper," who's a pro). Order a rum punch and do nothing but enjoy yourself. ⊠ *Tyrrel Bay,* ☎ *473/443–7403. AE, D, MC, V.*

Beaches

Grenada

Grenada has some 80 mi (130 km) of coastline, 65 bays, and 45 white-sand (and a few black-sand) beaches—many in little coves. The best beaches are on the Caribbean, south of St. George's, where the resorts are also clustered.

At the island's north end, Levera National Park has two beaches: **Levera Beach** is pretty and remote but too rough for more than wading (note that it's closed from April to June, when turtle eggs are hatching). **Bathway Beach** is a beautiful strip of sand with a natural reef that protects swimmers from the rough Atlantic surf. Changing rooms are available at the park headquarters.

In the southwest, about 3 mi (5 km) south of St. George's, **Grand Anse Beach,** is Grenada's loveliest and most popular beach. It's a gleaming 2-mi (3-km) semicircle of white sand, lapped by clear, gentle surf. Seagrape trees and coconut palms provide shady escapes from the sun. Brilliant rainbows frequently spill into the sea from the high green mountains that frame St. George's Harbour to the north. The Grand Anse Craft & Spice Market is at the midpoint of the beach. **Morne Rouge Beach,** 1 mi (1½ km) south of Grand Anse Bay, forms a ½-mi-long (¾-km-long) crescent and has a gentle surf that is excellent for swimming. Light meals are available nearby. **Pink Gin Beach** is at Point Salines, near the airport.

Along the southeast coast, **La Sagesse Beach,** at La Sagesse Nature Center, is a lovely, quiet refuge with a strip of powdery white sand. Plan a full day of nature walks, with lunch at the small inn adjacent to the beach.

Carriacou

Anse La Roche is about a 15-minute hike from the village of Prospect, in the north. Like all the beaches on Carriacou, this one has pure white sand, sparkling clear water, and abundant marine life for snorkelers. It's never crowded here. In **Hillsborough,** day-trippers can take a dip at the beach adjacent to the jetty. The beach stretches for quite a distance in each direction, so there is plenty of room to swim without interference from the boat traffic. **Paradise Beach** is a long, narrow stretch of sand between Hillsborough and Tyrrel Bay. The calm, clear water is inviting, but there are no changing facilities. **Sandy Island** is a truly deserted island off Hillsborough—just a strip of white sand, with a few palm trees, surrounded by a reef and crystal-clear waters. Anyone hanging around the jetty with a motorboat will provide transportation for a few dollars. At **Tyrrel Bay,** a swath of sand follows the coastline. But beware the manchineel trees here; they drop poisonous green "apples," and their foliage can burn your skin.

Outdoor Activities and Sports

BOATING AND SAILING

As the "Gateway to the Grenadines," Grenada attracts significant numbers of seasoned sailors to its waters. Large marinas are in the lagoon area of St. George's, at Prickly Bay on Grenada's south coast, and at Tyrrel Bay in Carriacou. You can charter a yacht, with or without crew, for weeklong sailing vacations through the Grenadines or along the coast of Venezuela. Scenic half- or full-day sails along Grenada's coast cost $30–$60 per person (with a minimum of four passengers), including lunch or snacks and open bar; a full-day cruise from Grenada to Carriacou may cost $350–$700, depending on the boat, for one to six people.

On Grenada: **Carib Cats** (☎ 473/444–3222) departs from the Tropicana jetty in the lagoon area of St. George's for either a full-day sail along the southwest coast, a half-day snorkel cruise to Molinière Bay, or a 2-hr sunset cruise along the west coast. **Footloose Yacht Charters** (☎ 473/440–7949) has both sailing or motoring yachts available for day trips around Grenada or longer charters to the Grenadines. **Island Dreams** (☎ 473/443–3603) has a 45-ft sailing yacht available for private half- or full-day charters for up to 10 passengers or overnight sails around Grenada or to the Grenadines for two people. **Moorings "Club Mariner" Watersports Center** (☎ 473/444–4439 or 473/444–4549), at the Secret Harbour Resort, in L'Anse aux Epines, has half- and full-day skippered charters, rental sailboats, and a range of sailing programs for beginning and experienced sailors. **Starwind Enterprise** (☎ 473/440–3678) offers day, half-day, and sunset sailing trips along Grenada's southwest coast aboard *Starwind II*, a 43-ft sailing yacht, or the 42-ft catamaran *Starwind III*. **Tradewind Yacht Charters** (☎ 473/444–4924), at the Spice Island Marina on Prickly Bay, rents sailing or power yachts, with or without crew, by the day or week.

On Carriacou: **Carriacou Yacht Charters** (☎ 473/443–8599) has a 76-ft ketch, *Suvetar*, which cruises the Grenadines on either long- or short-term charters or for day trips.

CYCLING

Level ground is rare in Grenada, but that doesn't stop the aerobically primed. Roads are narrow and winding, however, and sharing lanes with fast-moving vehicles can be hazardous. You can rent bikes at **Ride Grenada** (✉ L'Anse aux Épines, ☎ 473/444–1157).

FISHING

Deep-sea fishing around Grenada is excellent, with marlin, sailfish, yellowfin tuna, and dolphin topping the list of good catches. You can arrange half- or full-day sportfishing trips—for $250–$500, depending on the type of boat, number of people, and length of trip. **Bezo Charters** (☎ 473/443–5477 or 473/443–5021), has a tournament-equipped Bertram 31 Flybridge Sport Fisherman, called *Bezo*, with air-conditioned cabin, fighting chair, and an experienced crew just waiting to take you blue-water fishing. Charters can be customized; equipment and beverages are included. **Evans Fishing Charters** (☎ 473/444–4422 or 473/444–4217) has a Bertram 35 Sport Fisherman, *Xiphias Seeker*, with an air-conditioned cabin; equipment includes Penn International and Shimano reels. **True Blue Sportfishing** (☎ 473/444–2048) offers big-game charters on its "purpose-built" 31-ft Sport Fisherman, *Yes Aye*. It has an enclosed cabin, fighting chair, and professional tackle. Refreshments and courtesy transport are included.

GOLF

Determined golfers might want to try the 9-hole course at the **Grenada Golf and Country Club** (☎ 473/444–4128), about halfway between St. George's and Grand Anse. Greens fees are EC$7, and club rental is available; your hotel can make arrangements for you. Guests at the **Grenada Grand Beach Resort** (☎ 473/444–4371) in Grand Anse can use its 9-hole course. **LaSOURCE** (☎ 473/444–2556), in Point Salines, has a 9-hole, par-3 course for the use of guests.

HIKING

Mountain trails wind through **Grand Étang National Park and Forest Preserve** (☎ 473/440–6160); if you're lucky, you may spot a Mona monkey or some exotic birds on your hike. There are trails for all levels—from a self-guided nature trail around Grand Étang Lake to a demanding one through the bush to the peak of Mount Qua Qua (2,373 ft/724 m) or a real trek up Mount St. Catherine (2,757 ft/841 m). Long pants and hiking shoes are recommended. The cost is $25 per person for a four-hour guided hike up Mount Qua Qua, $20 each for two or more, or $15 each for three or more; the Mount St. Catherine hike starts at $35 per person. **EcoTrek** (☎ 473/444–7777) takes small groups on day trips to the heart of the rain forest, where you'll find hidden waterfalls and hot spring pools. **Henry's Safari Tours** (☎ 473/444–5313) offers hiking excursions through rich agricultural land and rain forest to Upper Concord Falls and other fascinating locations. **Telfor Bedeau, Hiking Guide** (☎ 473/442–6200) is a Grenadian treasure. Over the years, he has walked up, down, or across nearly every mountain, trail, and pathway on the island. His experience and knowledge make him an excellent guide, whether it's an easy walk with novices or the most strenuous hike with experts.

RUNNING

At 4 PM on alternate Saturdays throughout the year, **Hash House Harriers** (☎ 473/440–3343) welcomes not-so-serious runners and walkers to join them for exercise and fun in the countryside.

SCUBA DIVING AND SNORKELING

You can see hundreds of varieties of fish and more than 40 species of coral at more than a dozen sites off Grenada's southwest coast, only 15–20 minutes by boat, and another 20 sites or so around Carriacou's reefs and neighboring islets.

Off Grenada: a spectacular dive is *Bianca C,* a 600-ft cruise ship that caught fire in 1961, sank to 100 ft (30½ m), and is now encrusted with coral and home to giant turtles, spotted eagle rays, barracuda, and jacks. **Boss Reef** extends 5 mi (8 km) from St. George's Harbour to Point Salines, with a depth ranging from 20 to 90 ft (6 to 27½ m). **Flamingo Bay** has a wall that drops to 90 ft (27½ m) and is teeming with fish, sponges, seahorses, sea fans, and coral. **Molinère Reef** slopes from about 20 ft (6 m) below the surface to a wall that drops to 65 ft (20 m). It's a good dive for beginners, and advanced divers can continue farther out to view the wreck of the *Buccaneer,* a 42-ft sloop.

Off Carriacou: **Kick-em Jenny** is an active underwater volcano, with plentiful coral and marine life and visibility up to 100 ft (31 m). **Sandy Island,** in Hillsborough Bay, is especially good for night diving and has fish that feed off its extensive reefs 70 ft (21 m) deep. For experienced divers, **Twin Sisters of Isle de Rhonde** is one of the most spectacular dives in the Grenadines, with walls and drop-offs of up to 185 ft (56½ m) and an underwater cave.

Most dive operators take snorkelers along on dive trips or have special snorkeling adventures. The best snorkeling in Grenada is at Molinère Point, north of St. George's; in Carriacou, Sandy Island is magnificent and just a few hundred yards offshore.

The PADI-certified dive operators listed below offer scuba and snorkeling trips to reefs and wrecks, including night dives and special excursions to the *Bianca C.* They also offer resort courses for beginning divers and certification instruction for more experienced divers. It costs about $40–$45 for a one-tank dive, $70–$75 for a two-tank dive, $50 for *Bianca C,* $75–$80 to dive Isle De Rhonde, and $50–$55 for night dives. Discounted 5- and 10-dive packages are also offered. Resort courses cost about $70, lifetime open-water certification about $350, and snorkeling trips about $15.

On Grenada: **Aquanauts Grenada** (⊠ Secret Harbour Resort, L'Anse aux Épines, ☎ 473/444–1126) has a multilingual staff, so instruction is available in English, German, Dutch, French, and Spanish. Two-tank dive trips, accommodating no more than eight divers, are offered each morning to both the Caribbean and Atlantic sides of Grenada.

Dive Grenada (⊠ Allamanda Beach Resort, Grand Anse Beach, ☎ 473/444–1092) offers dive trips twice daily (at 10 AM and 2 PM), specializing in diving the *Bianca C.*

EcoDive (⊠ Coyaba Beach Resort, Grand Anse Beach, ☎ 473/444–7777) offers two dive trips daily, both drift and wreck dives, as well as weekly day trips to dive Isle de Rhonde. The EcoDive Centre is also home to EcoTrek, Grenada's marine conservation and education center that conducts coral-reef monitoring and turtle projects.

EcoDive True Blue (⊠ True Blue Bay Resort, True Blue, ☎ 473/444–2133) offers trips to Atlantic sites.

Sanvics Scuba (⊠ Grenada Grand Beach Resort, Grand Anse Beach, ☎ 473/444–4753) offers daily one- and two-tank dive trips to coral reefs, walls, and wreck sites.

Scuba World (⊠ Rex Grenadian Resort, Point Salines, ☎ 473/444–3684) offers daily trips to the *Bianca C.*

Spice Island Diving (⊠ Spice Island Beach Resort, Grand Anse, ☎ 473/444–3483) offers a wide range of dives, including single- and two-tank dives to reefs and wrecks, the *Bianca C.*, night dives, and two-tank dives to Isle de Rhonde.

On Carriacou: **Arawak Divers** (⊠ Tyrrel Bay, ☎ 473/443–6906) has its own jetty at Tyrrel Bay; it takes small groups on daily dive trips and night dives, offers courses in German and English, and provides pickup service from yachts.

Carriacou Silver Diving (⊠ Main St., Hillsborough, ☎ 473/443–7882) accommodates up to 12 divers on one of its dive boats and up to six on another. The center operates two guided single-tank dives daily, as well as individually scheduled excursions.

Tanki's Watersport Paradise Ltd. (⊠ Paradise Beach, ☎ 473/443–8406) offers dive trips to nearby reefs and snorkeling trips to Sandy Island.

TENNIS

The larger resort hotels all have tennis courts for guests. Visitors staying at a hotel without tennis on-site may play on the unattended, first come–first "serve" public courts in Grand Anse and in Tanteen, St. George's.

Shopping

The best souvenirs of Grenada are little spice baskets filled with cinnamon, nutmeg, mace, bay leaves, cloves, turmeric, and ginger. You can buy them for as little as $2 in practically every shop, at the open-air produce market at Market Square in St. George's, at the vendor stalls near the pier, and at the Craft & Spice Market on Grand Anse Beach. Vendors also sell inexpensive handmade fabric dolls, coral jewelry, seashells, and hats and baskets handwoven from green palm fronds. Bargaining is not appropriate in the shops, and it isn't customary with vendors—although most will offer you "a good price."

Areas and Malls

In St. George's, vendor stalls and gift shops along the **Carenage** are particularly convenient for cruise-ship passengers. On the north side of the harbor, **Young Street** is a main shopping thoroughfare; it rises steeply from the Carenage, then descends just as steeply to the market area.

In Grand Anse, a short walk from the resorts, the **Grand Anse Shopping Centre** offers a supermarket-liquor store, a clothing store, a bank, a fast-food restaurant, a pharmacy, an art gallery, and several small gift shops. **Le Marquis Complex,** diagonally across the street, has restaurants, shops, an art gallery, and tourist services. The newest and most extensive Grand Anse shopping center is **Spice Island Mall.** It has a modern supermarket (with a liquor section), clothing and shoe boutiques for men and women, housewares, a wine shop, gift shops, a food court, bank, and a video-game arcade.

Specialty Items

DUTY-FREE GOODS

Duty-free shops at the airport sell liquor at impressive discounts of up to 50%, as well as perfumes, gifts, and crafts. You can shop duty free at some shops in town, but you must show your passport and outbound ticket to benefit from the duty-free prices. **Colombian Emeralds** has a large selection of fine jewelry, watches, and gift items at its shop on the Carenage (☎ 473/440–1746) and another at the airport departure lounge (☎ 473/444–1047). **The Gift Shop** sells crystal, china, watches, and leather goods at its shop at the Grand Anse Shopping Centre (☎ 473/444–4408). **Gitten's** carries perfume and cosmetics at its shop on the Carenage (☎ 473/440–3174), at Spiceland Mall (☎ 473/439–0860), and at the airport departure lounge (☎ 473/444–2549).

FOODSTUFFS

Marketing & National Importing Board (✉ Young St., St. George's, ☎ 473/440–1791) stocks fresh fruits and vegetables, spices, hot sauces, and local syrups and jams at lower prices than you'll find in gift shops. **Market Square** (✉ Foot of Young St., St. George's, ☎ no phone) is a bustling, open-air produce market that's open mornings; Saturday is the best—and busiest—time to stock up on fresh fruit to enjoy during your stay and spices to take home. Crafts, leather goods, and decorative items are also for sale. **The Wine Shoppe** (✉ Spiceland Mall, Grand Anse, ☎ 473/439–9463) stocks some 250 different premium wines (as well as a selection of *vin ordinaire*) from around the world.

GIFTS

Arawak Islands (✉ Upper Belmont Rd., St. George's, ☎ 473/444–3577) blends island perfumes, colognes, body oils, and herbal teas—all packaged for gift-giving. The workshop is on-site. **Figleaf** (✉ The Carenage, St. George's, ☎ 473/440–9771) is a small gift shop where you'll find an interesting selection of Caribbean arts and crafts, aromatherapy and herbal bath products, and resort wear. **Gifts Remembered** (✉ Cross St., St. George's, ☎ 473/440–2482; ✉ Coyaba Beach Resort, Grand Anse, ☎ 473/444–4129) is crammed with wonderful, inexpensive things, including hammocks, scrimshaw, wood carvings, beachwear, sundries, and hand-painted masks made from calabashes. **Pssst Boutique** (✉ Spiceland Mall, Grand Anse, ☎ 473/443–8783) will catch your eye; it's chock full of unusual costume jewelry, colorful island clothing, and fascinating gift items for the home.

HANDICRAFTS

Art Fabrik (✉ 9 Young St., St. George's, ☎ 473/440–0568) is a studio where you can watch artisans create batik before turning it into clothing or accessories. In the shop you'll find fabric by the yard or fashioned into dresses, shirts, shorts, hats, and scarves. The **Grand Anse Craft & Spice Market** (✉ Grand Anse Beach, Grand Anse, ☎ 473/440–3377 or 473/440–3780), managed by the Grenada Board of Tourism, is between the main road and the beach. The facility, opened in 1999, has 82 booths for vendors who sell arts, crafts, spices, music tapes, clothing, produce, and refreshments. It's open daily 7–7. **La Sagesse Arts & Crafts Market** (⊠ La Sagesse Natural Works, St. David's, ☎ 473/443–1695), in an 18th-century sugar factory, is a showcase for 28 Grenadian arts and craftspeople to display and sell their work. **Imagine** (⊠ Grand Anse Shopping Centre, ☎ 473/444–4028) specializes in island handicrafts, including straw work, ceramics, island fashions, and batik fabrics. **Tikal** (⊠ Young St.,St. George's, ☎ 473/440–2310) is well known for its exquisite baskets, artwork, jewelry, batik items, and fashions, both locally made and imported from Africa and Latin America. **White Cane Industries** (⊠ Scott St., St. George's, ☎ No phone) stocks bargain baskets, hats, and spectacularly colored rag rugs, all handwoven locally by sight-impaired craftspeople. They also have a booth at the Grand Anse Craft & Spice Market. Credit cards aren't accepted at either location.

RECORDS
Turbo Charge Records & Tapes (⊠ St. John's St., St. George's, ☎ 473/440–0586) is the place to buy the latest reggae, calypso, soca, and steelband music.

Nightlife and the Arts

Nightlife
Grenada's nightlife is centered on the resort hotels and a handful of nightspots in the Grand Anse area. During the winter season many hotels have a steel band or other local entertainment several nights a week.

BARS
Boatyard (⊠ L'Anse aux Épines, ☎ 473/444–4662), at the Spice Island Marina, is the place to be on Friday from 11 PM 'til sunup, when there's a steel band and international discs are spun by a smooth-talkin' local DJ; on Saturday, there's dancing to live band music. **Casablanca** (⊠ Grand Anse, ☎ 473/444–1631) is a sports bar, upstairs above the banks, where you can play chess, cards, dominoes, darts, pool, or snooker, and watch games on a big-screen TV while having a drink and a snack; Monday to Saturday, from 5 PM to 3 AM, you can listen and dance to a DJ or live music.

DANCE CLUBS
Dynamite Disco (⊠ The Limes, Grand Anse, ☎ 473/444–4056) has a party atmosphere every weekend, with disco, reggae, and calypso. **Fantazia 2001** (⊠ Morne Rouge Beach, ☎ 473/444–2288) is a popular nightspot; disco, soca, reggae, and international pop music are played from 9:30 PM until the wee hours on Thursday, Friday, and Saturday nights. Wednesday is always oldies night, and Friday night features a Cultural Cabaret designed to give visitors a taste of local folklore and traditional dances. There's a small cover charge of EC$10–$20 on weekends. **Le Sucrier** (⊠ Sugar Mill, Grand Anse Roundabout, ☎ 473/444–1068) is lively Wednesday–Saturday 9:30 PM–3 AM. Wednesday is oldies night, there's live jazz on Thursday, and a mostly young crowd gathers for dancing on Friday and Saturday.

THEME NIGHTS
Rhum Runner (⊠ The Carenage, St. George's, ☎ 473/440–4386), a 60-ft twin-deck catamaran, leaves from the Carenage at 7:30 PM each Friday and Saturday for a moonlight cruise in the waters around St. George's and Grand Anse, returning about midnight. Tickets are $8 (EC$20), and reservations are recommended. On Wednesday from 6 to 9 there's a sunset dinner cruise for $40 per person; reservations must

be made by 4:30 the day before. *Rhum Runner II,* a 72-ft sister ship, operates monthly moonlight cruises the Friday and Saturday nights nearest the full moon for $11 (EC$30) per person—add $3 (EC$6) for a barbecue dinner.

The Arts

GALLERIES

Art Grenada (⊠ Suite 7, Grand Anse Shopping Centre, ☎ 473/444–2317) displays and sells works exclusively by Grenadian artists. Exhibitions change monthly, and you can have your purchases shipped. At **United Artists Art Gallery** (⊠ No. 15, Le Marquis Complex, Grand Anse, ☎ 473/444–5022), you'll find wood and stone carvings, painted masks, paintings, furniture, and other objects d'art created by artists from Grenada, Carriacou, and Petite Martinique. **Yellow Poui Art Gallery** (⊠ Cross St., St. George's, ☎ 473/440–3001) displays and sells original paintings, sculpture, photography, lithographs, and antique engravings by artists from Grenada and elsewhere in the Caribbean.

On Carriacou, in the village of L'Esterre, hand-painted signs announce THIS WAY TO THE GREAT ARTIST, **Canute Caliste**. If you get lost, one of his 200 grandchildren will lead the way. Caliste's colorful watercolors of island scenes are also available at the Carriacou Museum and at galleries in Grenada.

ISLAND CULTURE

Marryshow Folk Theatre (⊠ Herbert Blaize St., St. George's, ☎ 473/440–2451) presents concerts, plays, and special cultural events. Call for a schedule.

Exploring Grenada

Numbers in the margin correspond to points of interest on the Grenada (and Carriacou) map.

Grenada

It may be hard to pull yourself away from the beach, but a day or more of exploring is time well spent: the scenery is stunning, and the scent of nutmeg fills the air. St. George's has a busy harbor, interesting shops, and several historic sites. Visit a spice plantation and a nutmeg processing plant, or if you're adventurous, take guided hikes into the rain forest, up a mountainside, or to hidden waterfalls.

SIGHTS TO SEE

5 **Annandale Falls.** A mountain stream cascades 50 ft into a pool surrounded by exotic vines, such as liana and elephant ears. This is a lovely, cool spot for swimming and picnicking. ⊠ *Main interior road, 15 min northeast of St. George's,* ☎ *473/440–2452.* ⚏ *$1.* ⊙ *Daily 9–5.*

3 **Bay Gardens.** Just 15 minutes from St. George's, on what was once a sugar plantation, some 450 species of flowers and plants have been cultivated in patterns mimicking their growth in the wild. Eight acres of paths are open to visitors. ⊠ *Morne Delice, St. Paul's,* ☎ *473/440–5291.* ⚏ *$1.* ⊙ *Daily 7–6.*

11 **Carib's Leap.** At Sauteurs (the French word for "leapers"), on the island's northernmost tip, Carib's Leap (or Leapers Hill) is the 100-ft vertical cliff from which the last of the indigenous Carib Indians flung themselves into the sea in 1651. After losing several bloody battles with European colonists, they chose to exterminate their race rather than surrender to the French. A commemorative display recounts the historical event.

7 **Concord Falls.** About 8 mi (13 km) north of St. George's, a turnoff from the west coast road leads to Concord Falls—actually three separate waterfalls. The first is at the end of the road; during the dry months (January–May) when the currents aren't too strong, you can take a dip under the cascade. Reaching the two other cascades requires an hour's hike into the forest reserve. The third and most spectacular waterfall, at Fountainbleu, thunders 65 ft over huge boulders and creates a small pool where you can cool off before hiking back down the trail. It's smart to hire a guide. The path is clear, but slippery boulders toward the end can be treacherous without assistance. ⊠ *West Coast Rd.* ☜ *$1 for changing room.*

❽ Dougaldston Spice Estate. Just south of Gouyave, this historic plantation, now primarily a living museum, still grows and processes spices the old-fashioned way. You can see cocoa, nutmeg, mace, cloves, and other spices laid out on giant racks to dry in the sun. A worker will be glad to explain the process (and will appreciate a small donation). You can buy spices for about $2 a bag. ⊠ *Gouyave,* ☏ *No phone.* ☜ *$1.* ☉ *Weekdays 9–4.*

✋ ❾ Gouyave. Gouyave (pronounced *gwahve*) is the center of Grenada's fishing industry. It's also been dubbed the "town that never sleeps": most nights there's a party going on, with plenty of local music. A tour of the **Gouyave Nutmeg Processing Cooperative,** in the center of town, is a fragrant, fascinating way to spend a half hour. Workers in the three-story plant, which turns out 3 million pounds per year of Grenada's most famous export, sort nutmegs by hand and pack them in burlap bags for shipping worldwide. ⊠ *Gouyave,* ☏ *473/444–8337.* ☜ *$1.* ☉ *Weekdays 10–1 and 2–4.*

❷ Grand Anse. A residential and commercial area about 5 mi (8 km) south of downtown St. George's, Grand Anse is named for the world-renowned beach it surrounds. Most of Grenada's tourist facilities—resorts, restaurants, some shopping, and most nightlife—are in this general area. **Grand Anse Beach** is a 2-mi (3-km) crescent of sand, shaded by coconut palms and seagrape trees, with gentle turquoise surf. A handful of resort hotels line the beachfront, and there's a public entrance at Camerhogne Park, just a few steps from the main road. **St. George's University,** which for years held classes at its enviable beachfront location in Grand Anse, has consolidated most of its facility in True Blue, a nearby residential area. The school's Grand Anse property is currently used only for administrative purposes.

✋ ❻ Grand Étang National Park and Forest Reserve. Deep in the interior of lush, mountainous Grenada is a bird sanctuary and forest reserve, with miles of hiking trails, lookouts, and fishing streams. **Grand Étang Lake** is a 36-acre expanse of cobalt-blue water that fills the crater of an extinct volcano 1,740 ft (530 m) above sea level. Although legend has it the lake is bottomless, maximum soundings are recorded at 18 ft (5½ m). The informative **Grand Étang Forest Center** has displays on the local wildlife and vegetation. A forest manager is on hand to answer questions. There's a small snack bar and souvenir stands nearby. ⊠ *Main interior road, between Grenville and St. George's,* ☏ *473/440–6160.* ☜ *$1.* ☉ *Daily 8:30–4.*

⓮ Grenville. The island's second-largest city retains its historical identity as a French colonial market town. Saturday is market day, and the town buzzes with people doing their weekly shopping. The **Grenville Cooperative Nutmeg Association** (☏ *473/442–7241*) is open to the public for guided tours. You can see and learn about the entire process of receiving, drying, sorting, and packing nutmegs. Just north of Grenville is **Pearl's Airport,** which was replaced in October 1984 by Point Salines International Airport. Deteriorating Cuban and Soviet planes sit at the end of the old runway, abandoned after the 1983 intervention, when Cuban "advisors" helping to construct the new airport were summarily removed from the island. There's a good view north to the Grenadines and a small beach nearby.

④ Laura Herb and Spice Garden. The 6½-acre gardens are part of an old plantation in the village of Laura, in St. David's, just 6 mi (10 km) east of Grand Anse. On the 45-minute tour, you'll learn all about Grenada's indigenous spices and herbs, including cocoa, clove, nutmeg, pimiento, cinnamon, turmeric, and tonka beans (vanilla). ⊠ *St. David's,* ☎ *473/ 443–2604.* ⊇ *$2.* ☉ *Weekdays 8–4.*

⑫ Levera National Park and Bird Sanctuary. This portion of Grenada's protected parkland encompasses 450 acres at the northeastern tip of the island, where the Caribbean Sea meets the Atlantic Ocean. Facilities include a visitors center, changing rooms, a small amphitheater, and a gift shop. A natural reef protects swimmers from the rough Atlantic surf at Bathway Beach. Thick mangroves provide food and protection for nesting seabirds and seldom-seen parrots. Some fine Arawak ruins and petroglyphs are on display, and the first islets of the Grenadines are visible from the beach. Admittance and use of the beaches and grounds are free; there's a small charge to view the displays in the visitors center. ⊠ *Levera,* ☎ *473/442–1018.* ⊇ *$1.* ☉ *Daily 8:30–4.*

⑩ Mt. Rodney Estate. When touring northern Grenada, plan to have lunch in Sauteurs. A road winds up a mountainside to an 1880s plantation house, lovingly restored by Lin and Norris Nelson. Sugar, coffee, and cocoa grew on the plantation in its heyday, and the fabulous views north to the Grenadines remain. Buffet luncheon is served from noon to 2 on the dining terrace. (This lunch stop is often included on a guided island tour; or call 473/442–9420 for reservations.)

⑬ River Antoine Rum Distillery. At this rustic operation, kept open primarily as a museum, Rivers rum is produced by the same methods used since the distillery opened in 1785. The process begins with the crushing of sugarcane from adjacent fields in the River Antoine (pronounced an-*twine*) Estate. The result is a potent overproof rum that will knock your socks off. ⊠ *River Antoine Estate, St. Patrick's,* ☎ *473/442–7109.* ⊇ *$1.* ☉ *Guided tours daily 9–4.*

① St. George's. Grenada's capital is a busy West Indian city, most of which remains unchanged from colonial days. Narrow streets lined with shops wind up, down, and across steep hills. Pastel-painted warehouses with roofs covered in orange tiles (brought over from Europe as ballast in 18th-century ships) cling to the waterfront. Small rainbow-hue houses rise from the waterfront and disappear into steep green hills.

St. George's Harbour is the center of town. Schooners, ferries, and tour boats tie up along the seawall or at the small dinghy dock. Cruise ships dock at the large pier at the harbor entrance or anchor just outside and transport passengers ashore by tender. On weekends, a tall ship is likely to be anchored in the middle of the harbor, giving the scene a 19th-century appearance.

The Carenage (pronounced car-a-*nahzh*), which surrounds horseshoe-shape St. George's Harbour, is the capital's main thoroughfare. Warehouses, shops, and restaurants line the waterfront. At the center of The Carenage, on the pedestrian plaza, sits the *Christ of the Deep* statue. It was presented to Grenada by Costa Cruise Line in remembrance of its ship *Bianca C,* which burned and sank in the harbor in 1961 and is now a favorite dive site. Near the cruise-ship welcome center, at the south end of The Carenage, the Grenada Board of Tourism has its offices, and you can buy inexpensive spices and crafts at vendor stalls nearby.

The **Grenada National Museum,** a block from The Carenage, is set in the foundation of a French army barracks and prison that was built in 1704. The small museum has exhibitions of news items, photos, and proclamations regarding the 1983 intervention, along with Empress Josephine's childhood bathtub and other memorabilia from earlier historical periods. ⊠ *Young and Monckton sts.,* ☎ *473/440–3725.* ▣ *$1.* ☉ *Weekdays 9–4:30, Sat. 10–1.*

An engineering feat for its time, the 340-ft-long (103-m-long) **Sendall Tunnel** was built in 1895 and named for an early governor. It separates the harborside of St. George's from the Esplanade on the bay side of town, where you'll find the open-air meat, fish, and produce markets. The Esplanade is also the terminus of the minibus route.

Don't miss picturesque **Market Square,** a block from The Esplanade at Granby Street. It's open every weekday morning but really comes alive on Saturday from 8 to noon. Vendors sell baskets, spices, brooms, clothing, knickknacks, coconut water, and heaps of fresh produce. Market Square is historically where parades and political rallies take place—and the beginning of the minibus routes to all areas of the island.

St. Andrew's Presbyterian Church, built in 1830, is at the intersection of Halifax and Church streets. Also known as Scots' Kirk, it was constructed with the help of the Freemasons. Built in 1825, the beautiful stone and pink stucco **St. George's Anglican Church,** on Church Street, is filled with statues and plaques depicting Grenada in the 18th and 19th centuries. **St. George's Methodist Church,** on Green Street near Herbert Blaize Street, was built in 1820 and is the oldest original church in the city. The Gothic tower of **St. George's Roman Catholic Church** dates from 1818, but the current structure was built in 1884; the tower is the city's most visible landmark.

On Church Street, **York House** (1801) is home to Grenada's Houses of Parliament and Supreme Court. It, the neighboring Registry Building (1780), and Government House (1802) are fine examples of early Georgian architecture.

Ft. George is high on the hill at the southern tip of Church Street. The fort, which rises above the entrance to St. George's Harbour, is Grenada's oldest—built by the French in 1705 to protect the harbor. No shots were fired here until October 1983, when Prime Minister Bishop and some of his followers were assassinated in the courtyard. The fort now houses police headquarters but is open to the public daily; admission is free. The 360-degree view of the capital city, St. George's Harbour, and the open sea is spectacular.

On Richmond Hill, high above the city of St. George's and the inland side of the harbor, historic **Ft. Frederick** provides a panoramic view of two-thirds of Grenada. The fort was completed in 1791; it was also the headquarters of the People's Revolutionary Government during the 1983 coup. Today, you can get a bird's-eye view of the prison, on top of an adjacent hill, where the rebels remain incarcerated—and have, by all accounts, one of the most picturesque views in all of Grenada.

In St. Paul's, five minutes outside St. George's, **de la Grenade Industries** produces syrups, jams, jellies, and liqueurs made from nutmeg and other homegrown fruits and spices. It began in 1960 as a cottage industry. You're welcome to watch the process and purchase gift items from the retail operation on-site. ☎ *473/440–3241.* ▣ *Free.* ☉ *Weekdays 8–5, Sat. 9–12:30.*

Carriacou

Carriacou, the land of many reefs, is a hilly island and (unlike its lush sister island of Grenada) has neither lakes nor rivers—only rainwater, caught in cisterns and purified with bleach. It gets arid during the dry season (January–May). Nevertheless, plenty of fruit is grown here, and the climate seems to suit the mahogany trees used for furniture-making and the white cedar critical to the boatbuilding that has made Carriacou famous.

This little island (13 square mi/34 square km) packs a lot of punch—rum punch, that is. With more than 100 rum shops, Carriacou brings the fastest metabolism down to a quiet purr and exudes the hallmark friendliness and peace of a Caribbean retreat. Simplicity, not luxury, is the pleasure here.

Hillsborough is the main town. Rolling hills cut a wide swath through the island's center, from Gun Point in the north to Tyrrel Bay in the south. The small town of Windward, on the northeast coast, is a boat-building community. You'll likely encounter half-finished hulls on the roadside. Originally constructed for interisland commerce, the boats are now built for fishing and pleasure sailing.

Interestingly, tiny Carriacou has several distinct cultures. Hillsborough is decidedly English; the southern region, around L'Esterre, reflects French roots; and the northern town of Windward has Scottish ties. African culture, of course, is the overarching influence.

SIGHTS TO SEE

❶❼ Belair. For a wonderful bird's-eye view of Carriacou's west coast, drive to Belair, 700 ft (213½ m) above sea level, in the north-central part of the island. On the way you'll pass the photogenic ruins of an old sugar mill. The Belair lookout is adjacent to **Princess Royal Hospital**, where patients surely find the view of Hillsborough, the harbor, and endless sea to be restorative.

❶❺ Historical Museum. Housed in a building that once held a cotton gin, one block from the waterfront, the museum has exhibitions of Amerindian, European, and African artifacts, a collection of watercolors by native artist Canute Caliste, and a gift shop loaded with local items. ✉ *Paterson St., Hillsborough,* ☎ *No phone.* 💵 *$2.* ☉ *Weekdays 9:30–4, Sat. 10–4.*

❶❻ Sandy Island. Just off Hillsborough Harbour, tiny Sandy Island is a gorgeous islet, lapped by crystal-clear water, with nothing more on it than powdery white sand and some palm trees. For a few dollars, any local fellow with a motorboat will transport you back and forth. Bring your snorkeling gear and, if you want, a picnic—and leave all your cares behind.

❶❽ Tyrrel Bay. Picturesque Tyrrel Bay is a large protected harbor in southwest Carriacou. The bay is almost always full of sailboats, powerboats, and working boats—coming, going, or bobbing at their moorings. Edging the bay is a beach with pure white sand; bars, restaurants, a guest house, and a few shops face the waterfront.

Petite Martinique

Petite Martinique, 10 minutes north of Carriacou by boat, is tiny and residential, with a guest house or two but no tourist facilities or attractions—just peace and quiet. Meander along the beachfront and watch the boatbuilders at work. And if by chance there's a boat launch, sailboat race, wedding, or cultural festival while you're there, you're in for a treat. The music is infectious, the food bountiful, the spirit lively.

GRENADA A TO Z

To research prices, get advice from other travelers, and book travel arrangements, visit www.fodors.com.

AIR TRAVEL

Air Jamaica has twice-weekly nonstop flights into Grenada's Point Salines International Airport from New York and connecting flights from its other gateway cities via Montego Bay, Jamaica, with a stop in St. Lucia. American Airlines/American Eagle has daily flights from major U.S. and Canadian cities via San Juan. BWIA flies to Grenada from New York, Miami, Washington, D.C., and Toronto via Trinidad. British Airways flies from London twice a week. J.M.C. has two weekly charter flights from London. From other parts of the world, connections must be made through U.S. cities, San Juan, Toronto, or London.

Caribbean Star flies daily to Grenada from its Antigua hub, via St. Vincent, Dominica, and Trinidad. LIAT has scheduled service between Grenada and several neighboring islands in the northeast Caribbean. SVG Air flies from Grenada and Carriacou to St. Vincent and the Grenadines (St. Vincent, Union, Canouan, and Bequia).

➤ AIRLINES AND CONTACTS: **Air Jamaica** (☎ 473/444–5975); **American Airlines/American Eagle** (☎ 473/444–2222) ; **BWIA** (☎ 473/444–1221); **British Airways** (☎ 473/444–1664); **Caribbean Star** (☎ 268/480–2561); **J.M.C.** (☎ 473/444–2796); **LIAT** (☎ 473/440–2796 or 473/440–4121); **SVG Air** (☎ 473/444–0328).

AIRPORTS

Point Salines International Airport, at the southwestern tip of Grenada, is a modern facility with an extra-long runway suitable for the largest jets. The departure lounge and gate areas were recently renovated and enlarged to accommodate increased traffic. Passenger amenities include a restaurant, snack bar, and several shops (including duty-free shopping in the departure lounge).

On Carriacou, five minutes south of Hillsborough, Lauriston Airport is a lighted landing strip suitable only for light planes, with a small building for ticket sales and shelter. What's particularly fascinating about this airport is that the main road between Hillsborough and Tyrrel Bay crosses the live runway at its midpoint. Look both ways before crossing!

There is no bus service between the Point Salines Airport and hotels, but taxis are always available. Fares to St. George's are $15; to the hotels of Grand Anse and L'Anse aux Epines, $10. Rides taken between 6 PM and 6 AM incur a $4 surcharge. From Carriacou's Lauriston Airport to Hillsborough, the taxi fare is $4.

➤ AIRPORT INFORMATION: On Grenada: **Point Salines Airport** (☎ 473/444–4101). On Carriacou: **Lauriston Airport** (☎ 473/443–6306).

BOAT AND FERRY TRAVEL

Approximately two-thirds of the annual visitors to Grenada arrive by sea. Small ships, including tall ships, tie up at the pier or anchor in St. George's Harbour. Cruise ships generally anchor offshore and bring passengers by launch to the welcome center on The Carenage. From there, they can easily explore the capital city on foot, take a taxi (land or water) or bus to Grand Anse Beach, or join a sightseeing tour of the island.

Passenger ferries and cargo schooners (that also take passengers) to Grenada's other islands, Carriacou and Petite Martinique, depart from The Carenage.

FARES AND SCHEDULES

Two high-speed power catamarans—*Lexianna Jet* and *Osprey Express*—each make two round-trip voyages daily (except Wednesday) from Grenada to Carriacou and on to Petite Martinique. The fare for the 90-minute one-way trip is $18 per person; round-trip, $35. For the 15-minute trip between Carriacou and Petite Martinique, the fare is $4 each way. The boat leaves from The Carenage in St. George's.

The schooners *Alexia II, Alexia III,* and *Adelaide B* leave from The Carenage in St. George's in the morning (except Monday and Thursday), ferrying cargo and passengers on the four-hour voyage to Carriacou; they return to Grenada daily (except Tuesday and Friday). The *Adelaide B* continues on from Carriacou to Petite Martinique (about a 1½-hour trip) on Wednesday and Saturday afternoons, returning early on Monday and Thursday mornings. The fare between Grenada and Carriacou is $7.50 one-way, $12 round-trip; between Carriacou and Petite Martinique, it's about $5 each way. Reservations aren't necessary.

The mail boat between Carriacou and Petite Martinique makes one round-trip on Monday, Wednesday, and Friday, leaving Petite Martinique at 8 AM and returning from Windward, Carriacou, at noon. The fare is about $5 each way.

BUSINESS HOURS

BANKS

Banks are open Monday–Thursday 8–3, Friday 8–5.

POST OFFICES

The main post office, at Burns Point by the port in St. George's, is open weekdays 8–3:30. Each town or village has a post office branch.

SHOPS

Stores are generally open weekdays 8–4 or 4:30 and Saturday 8–1; some close from noon to 1 during the week. Most are closed Sunday, although tourist shops usually open if a cruise ship is in port.

CAR RENTALS

To rent a car, you need a valid driver's license and a local permit (available at the Central Police Station on The Carenage and at some car-rental firms), which costs $12 (EC$30). Rental cars (including four-wheel-drive vehicles) cost $60–$75 a day or $300–$370 a week with unlimited mileage. In high season there may be a three-day minimum rental.

On Grenada, Avis is at Spice Island Rentals, on Paddock and Lagoon roads in St. George's. David's has offices at Point Salines International Airport, Renaissance Grenada Resort, Rex Grenadian Hotel, and the Limes in Grand Anse. Dollar Rent-a-Car is at Point Salines Airport. In the True Blue area, call McIntyre Bros. Ltd. On Carriacou, Barba's Auto Rentals, at Tyrrel Bay, will meet you at the airport.
➤ MAJOR AGENCIES: **Avis** (☎ 473/440–3936, 473/440–2624, or 473/444–5480 after hrs); **Barba's Auto Rentals** (☎ 473/443–7454); **David's** (☎ 473/444–3399 or 473/444–3038); **Dollar Rent-a-Car** (☎ 473/444–4786, or 473/443–2330 after hrs); **McIntyre Bros. Ltd.** (☎ 473/444–3944, or 473/443–5319 after hrs).

CAR TRAVEL

Having a car or Jeep is a convenience—particularly for visitors staying at resorts in locations other than Grand Anse, which has frequent minibus service. Otherwise, round-trip taxi rides can get expensive if you plan to leave the resort frequently for shopping, meals, or visiting other beaches. Driving is also a reasonable option if you want to explore the island on your own.

GASOLINE
Gasoline costs about $2.60 per gallon, and gas stations are located in St. George's, Grand Anse, Grenville, Gouyave, and Sauteurs.

ROAD CONDITIONS
Driving is a constant challenge in the tropics, but most of Grenada's 650 mi (1,050 km) of paved roads are kept in fairly good condition—albeit steep and narrow beyond the Grand Anse area. The main road between St. George's was recently reconstructed to make the road wider and travel safer. Directions are clearly posted, but having a map on hand is certainly a good idea when traveling in the countryside.

RULES OF THE ROAD
Driving is on the left, British-style.

ELECTRICITY
Electric current on Grenada is 220 volts/50 cycles. Appliances rated at 110 volts (U.S. standard) will work only with a transformer and adapter plug. For dual-voltage computers or appliances, you'll still need an adapter plug; some hotels will loan adapters to guests. Most hotels have 110 outlets for shavers; very few have 110 lines in guest rooms.

EMBASSIES
➤ UNITED KINGDOM: **British High Commission** (✉ 14 Church St., St. George's, ☎ 473/440–3536 or 473/440–3222).
➤ UNITED STATES: **Embassy of the United States** (✉ L'Anse Aux Epines Stretch, St. George's, ☎ 473/444–1173 or 473/444–1177).

EMERGENCIES
➤ AMBULANCE AND FIRE: For an ambulance in St. George's, Grand Anse, and L'Anse aux Epines, dial ☎ 434. In St. Andrew's, dial ☎ 724. On Carriacou, dial ☎ 774. For fire, dial ☎ 911.
➤ COAST GUARD: Dial ☎ 399; 473/444–1931 for nonemergencies.
➤ HOSPITALS: **Princess Alice Hospital** (☎ 473/442–7251) in Grenville; **St. George's General Hospital** (☎ 473/440–2051) is Grenada's main hospital, located on Fort George's Point, at northern end of The Carenage in St. George's.; **St. Augustine's Medical Services, Inc.** (☎ 473/440–6173) a modern, 18-bed private hospital located in Grand Anse. On Carriacou, **Princess Royal Hospital** (☎ 473/443–7400), in the Belair section, overlooking Hillsborough.
➤ PHARMACIES: **Gitten's** (✉ Halifax St., St. George's, ☎ 473/440–2165 or 473/440–2340 after hrs). **Gitten's Drugmart** (✉ Main Rd., Grand Anse, ☎ 473/444–4954 or 473/440–2340 after hrs). **Mitchell's Pharmacy** (✉ Grand Anse Shopping Centre, ☎ 473/444–3845). **Parris' Pharmacy Ltd.** (✉ Victoria St., Grenville, ☎ 473/442–7330). On Carriacou, try **Charles Pharmacy** (✉ Sea View, ☎ 473/443–7933).
➤ POLICE: Dial ☎ 911.

ETIQUETTE AND BEHAVIOR
A Grenadian will always greet you with a friendly "good morning," "good afternoon," or "good evening," and will be disappointed if the courtesy isn't returned. That's true whether it's a perfect stranger or someone you've met before. Though such greetings are common throughout the Caribbean, in Grenada they will often be followed by, "Are you enjoyin' it?" It seems everyone wants to make sure you're having a good time in Grenada.

Taking photos of local people, their boats, homes, or children isn't appreciated without first asking permission and offering a tip for the favor.

Dress appropriately and discreetly, saving swimwear for the beach. Shorts and T-shirts are fine for sightseeing and shopping, but frowned upon in restaurants in the evening.

FESTIVALS AND SEASONAL EVENTS
GRENADA

In late January the Spice Island Billfish Tournament is held. Sportfishermen vie for cash prizes for the biggest game fish (marlin, sailfish, yellowfin tuna). The Grenada Sailing Festival, held at the end of January and early February, includes six days of races and regattas and a daylong crafts market and street festival—all organized by the Grenada Yacht Club.

February 7 is Independence Day. Watch the float parade and fireworks at Queen's Park, on the north side of St. George's. Beginning around March 17 and lasting a week, the St. Patrick's Day Fiesta is celebrated in Sauteurs (St. Patrick's Parish), in the north of Grenada, with arts and crafts, agricultural exhibits, food and drink, and a cultural extravaganza with music and dancing.

Late April sees international triathletes compete in the annual Grenada International Triathlon. The competition starts and finishes at Grand Anse Beach. Participants swim 1½ km, cycle 25 km, and run 5 km on the first day. A three-person relay takes place on the second day. Teams must include at least one female and have a combined age of at least 100 years. Music lovers congregate at Grenada's Grenada Spice Jazz Festival, a four-day event in late May that showcases regional and international jazz greats.

Each June 29 the Fisherman's Birthday Celebration is a sort of mini-Carnival in villages on Grenada's west coast, particularly in Gouyave. There's a blessing of the boats, boat racing, fishing contests, and music and dancing in the street. In early August the Rainbow City Festival is held in Grenville; it's primarily an agricultural fair, with local arts and crafts and livestock.

The Grenada to Carriacou Yacht Race is a highlight of the Carriacou Regatta in August. A month of calypso road shows culminates in the Grenada Carnival the second week of August. It's the biggest celebration of the year, with a beauty pageant, a soca monarch competition, continuous steel-pan and calypso music, and a huge Parade of the Bands on the last Tuesday.

CARRIACOU

The biggest event of the year is the four-day Carriacou Carnival, held in mid-February. Revelers participate in parades, calypso contests, music and dancing, and general frivolity.

During the first weekend in August, the Carriacou Regatta attracts yachts and sailboats from throughout the Caribbean for three days of boat races. Festivities also include road relays, fashion shows, donkey rides, and greasy pole contests—and music and partying galore.

In December the week before Christmas, the Carriacou Parang Festival is a musical and cultural celebration. "Parang" is Spanish for ad-libbing. Costumed singers travel from village to village, creating spontaneous songs based on local gossip and accompanied by guitar, violin, and drums.

A highlight of most festivals on Carriacou is the Big Drum Dance, unique to this island (and neighboring Union Island). The term refers to the size of the gathering, not the drum. When the British took control of Carriacou in 1783, they banned the beating of drums for fear the former French slaves would use them to communicate and start a revolt. Despite the repression, the African tradition of drumming survived. Today on Carriacou, costumed dancers move to the rhythmic beat of pounding drums at social events, harvests, boat launches, weddings, and other happy occasions.

HEALTH
Insects can be a nuisance after heavy rains, when mosquitoes emerge, and on the beach after 4 PM, when tiny sand flies begin to bite. Use repellent, especially when hiking in the rain forest. Tap water in hotels and restaurants is perfectly safe to drink.

HOLIDAYS
New Year's Day, Independence Day (Feb. 7), Good Friday (Mar. 29, 2002), Easter Monday (Apr. 1, 2002), Labour Day (May 1), Whit Monday (May 20, 2002), Corpus Christi (May 30, 2002), Emancipation Holidays (1st Mon. and Tues. in Aug.), Carnival (2nd Mon. in Aug.), Thanksgiving Day (Oct. 25), Christmas, and Boxing Day (Dec. 26).

LANGUAGE
English—spoken with a fetching lilt with British intonations—is the official language here. Creole patois isn't commonly heard except, perhaps, among older folks in the countryside.

Here's some local terminology you should know: If you want a refreshing drink of coconut water at the market, for EC$1 or so the "jelly man" will hack off the top of a fresh green "jelly" (coconut) for you with one swipe of his machete. And if someone asks if you'd like a "sweetie," they're offering you a candy. When you're buying spices, you may be offered "saffron" and "vanilla." The saffron is really turmeric, a ground yellow root rather than the fragile pistils of crocus flowers; the vanilla is an essence made from locally grown tonka beans, a close substitute but not the real thing. No one is trying to pull the wool over your eyes; these are common local terms.

MAIL AND SHIPPING
Airmail rates for letters to the United States, Canada, and the United Kingdom are EC75¢ for a half-ounce letter and EC35¢ for a postcard; airmail rates to Australia are EC$1.10 for a half-ounce letter and EC45¢ for a postcard; to New Zealand, EC90¢ for a letter and EC45¢ for a postcard. When addressing a letter to Grenada, simply write "Grenada, West Indies" after the local address.

MONEY MATTERS
Prices quoted in this chapter are in U.S. dollars unless otherwise indicated.

Barclays Bank is a major international bank; its head office in Grenada is in downtown St. George's; branches are located in Grand Anse, Grenville, and Carriacou. National Commercial Bank is a regional bank, with branches in St. George's, Grand Anse, Grenville, and Carriacou. Scotiabank (The Bank of Nova Scotia), an international bank, has its head office in Grenada in St. George's, with branches in Grand Anse and Grenville.
➤ CONTACTS: **Barclays Bank** (⊠ Church and Halifax Sts., ☎ 473/440-3232); branches in Grand Anse (☎ 473/444-3322), Grenville (☎ 473/442-7733), Carriacou (☎ 473/443-7232). **National Commercial Bank** (⊠ True Blue, ☎ 473/444-2265); branches in St. George's (⊠ Halifax St., ☎ 473/440-3566), Grand Anse (☎ 473/444-2627), Grenville (☎ 473/442-7532), Carriacou (☎ 473/443-7289). **Scotiabank** (⊠ Halifax St., ☎ 473/440-3274); branches in Grand Anse (☎ 473/444-1917), Grenville (☎ 473/442-5507).

ATMS

ATMs are available 24 hours a day at bank branches, on the Carenage, and at the airport.

CREDIT CARDS

Major credit cards—including Access, American Express, Diner's Club, Discover, Eurocard, MasterCard, and Visa—are widely accepted.

CURRENCY

Grenada uses the Eastern Caribbean (EC) dollar. The official exchange rate is fixed at EC$2.67 to US$1; cabs, shops, and hotels sometimes have slightly lower rates (EC$2.50–EC$2.60). You can exchange money at banks and hotels, but U.S. and Canadian paper currency, traveler's checks, and major credit cards are widely accepted. You will often receive EC$ in change.

PASSPORTS AND VISAS

A valid passport and a return or ongoing ticket are required. An original birth certificate with raised seal and a valid, government-issued photo ID are also acceptable instead of a passport for U.S., Canadian, and British citizens only.

SAFETY

Crime isn't a big problem, but it's a good idea to secure your valuables in the hotel safe and not leave items unattended on the beach. Removing bark from trees, taking wildlife from the forest, and removing coral from the sea are all forbidden. Also, be careful when walking late at night in Grand Anse; it's dark enough to bump into one of the cows that graze silently by the roadside or to trip in a hole dug by a land crab!

SIGHTSEEING TOURS

Guided tours offer the sights of St. George's, Grand Étang National Park, spice plantations and nutmeg processing centers, rain forest hikes, snorkeling trips to offshore islands, and day trips to Carriacou.

On Adventure Jeep Tours, you drive safari fashion along scenic coastal roads, trek in the rain forest, lunch at a plantation, take a swim, and skirt the capital. The full-day tour costs $65 for adults, $40 for children, and includes lunch. EkoTrek, based at Grand Anse Beach, offers adventurous tours to the rain forest, snorkeling trips, and tours of Carib caves and plantation houses. Dennis Henry of Henry's Safari Tours knows Grenada like the back of his hand. He leads adventurous hikes and four-wheel-drive vehicle safaris, or you can design your own tour. A full-day island tour, including lunch, costs about $55 per person; a six-hour hike to Concord Falls is $30–$45 per person. Spiceland Tours has several five- and seven-hour island tours, from the Urban/Suburban tour of St. George's and the south coast to the Emerald Forest tour, highlighting Grenada's natural beauty. Sunsation Tours offers customized and private island tours to all the usual sites and "as far off the beaten track as you want to go." From garden tours or a challenging hike to a day sail on a catamaran, it's all possible. Tours Mandoo offers half- or full-day tours following northern, southern, or eastern routes, as well as hikes to Concord Falls and the mountains.

Grenada taxi drivers will take visitors on island sightseeing tours for $25 to $55 per person, depending on the destinations selected. Carriacou minibus drivers will take up to four people on a four-hour island tour for about $65; extra people, $15 each.

➤ CONTACTS: **Adventure Jeep Tours** (☎ 473/444–5337, FAX 473/444–5681, WEB www.grenadajeeptours.com); **EkoTrek** (☎ 473/444–7777, FAX 473/444–4808, WEB www.scubadivegrenada.com); **Henry's Safari Tours** (☎ 473/444–5313, FAX 473/444–4460); **Spiceland Tours** (☎

473/440–5127 or 473/440–5180, ℻ 473/440–5466); **Sunsation Tours**
(☎ 473/444–1594, ℻ 473/444–1103), 🕸 www.grenadasunsation.
com); **Tours Mandoo** (☎ ℻ 473/440–1428, 🕸 www.grenada-
tours.com).

TAXES
DEPARTURE TAX
The departure tax, collected at the airport, is $19 (EC$50) for adults
and $10 (EC$25) for children ages 5–11, payable in either currency.
A $4 (EC$10) departure tax is collected when departing Carriacou.

SALES TAX
An 8% government tax is added to all hotel and restaurant bills.

TAXIS
Taxis are plentiful, and rates are set by the government. The trip between Grand Anse and St. George's costs $8–$10; between Point
Salines and St. George's, $15. A $4 surcharge is added for rides taken
between 6 PM and 6 AM. Taxis often wait for fares at hotels, at the cruise-
ship welcome center, and on the north side of The Carenage. They can
be hired at an hourly rate of $20.

Water taxis are available along The Carenage. For $4 (EC$10) a motor
boat will transport you on a lovely cruise between St. George's and
the jetty at Grand Anse Beach. Water taxis are privately owned, un-
regulated, and don't follow any particular schedule—so make arrangements for a pickup time if you expect a return trip.

In Carriacou the taxi fare from Hillsborough to Belair is $4; to Prospect,
$6; and to Tyrrel Bay or Windward, $8.

TELEPHONES
COUNTRY AND AREA CODES
The area code is 473.

INTERNATIONAL CALLS
Grenada has a fully digital telecommunications service. From Grenada
you can place direct-dial calls to anywhere in the world from pay
phones, card phones, and most hotel room phones. For international
calls using a major credit card, dial 111; there's no surcharge. Pay phones
are available at the airport, the cruise-ship welcome center, or the
Cable & Wireless office on The Carenage in St. George's, shopping
centers, and other convenient locations. Pay phones accept EC25¢ and
EC$1 coins, as well as U.S. quarters.

LOCAL CALLS
Local calls are free from private phones and most hotels; for directory
assistance, dial 411. Prepaid phone cards, which can be used in special cardphones throughout Grenada and other Caribbean islands, are
sold at shops, attractions, transportation centers, and other convenient
outlets. (The phone card can be used for local or international calls.)

TIPPING
Many hotels and restaurants add a 10% service charge to your bill. If
a service charge is not included, a 10% gratuity should be added. Additional tipping is unnecessary except for extraordinary service.

VISITOR INFORMATION
➤ BEFORE YOU LEAVE: **Grenada Board of Tourism** in the U.S.: (✉ c/o
Richartz Fliss Clark & Pope, 317 Madison Ave., New York, NY
10017, ☎ 212/687–9554, ℻ 212/573–9731); in Canada: (✉ 439
University Ave., Suite 930, Toronto, Ontario M5G 1Y8, Canada, ☎

416/595–1343, FAX 416/595–8278); in the United Kingdom: (✉ c/o CIB Communications, 1 Battersea Church Road, London SW11 3LY, U.K., ☎ 020/7771–7016, FAX 020/7771–7181). **Grenada Hotel Association** (☎ 473/444–1353 or 800/322–1753 in the U.S. and Canada, FAX 473/444–4847, WEB www.grenadahotelsinfo.com).

➤ IN GRENADA: **Grenada Board of Tourism** (☎ 473/440–2001 or 473/440–2279, FAX 473/440–6637, WEB www.grenada.org).

12 GUADELOUPE

To step through the anteroom at the banana plantation in Belair is to go back 40 years to the Guadeloupe of wooden gingerbread houses with cane
planters chairs and vintage photos of creole women
in madras costume. In the country kitchen is a laudable display of local products—confitures and fruit
liqueurs (punches). Sweet, young shop girls try out
their English and offer dark, rich coffee and banana
flan with passion fruit couli. A French group, come
for the tour, is offered rum and "chiquita" bananas.
The dance music is cranked up. Outside the shuttered
windows is exuberant, tropical foliage and rows of
banana trees with hanging fruit. Beyond is Le Soufrire,
its volcanic peak haloed by white clouds.

Sprawling and changing by the mile—from jungle highlands to seaside
resorts, from mall shopping to rustic dining—Guadeloupe is richly varied. At 629 square mi (1,629 square km), it looks like a giant butterfly resting on the sea between Antigua and Dominica. Its wings—
Basse-Terre and Grande-Terre—are the two largest islands in the
Guadeloupe archipelago. The Rivière Salée, a 4-mi (6½-km) channel
flowing between the Caribbean and the Atlantic, forms the spine of
the butterfly. Smaller, flatter Grande-Terre, at 218 square mi (565
square km), is dry and sandy. It has Guadeloupe's best beaches, restaurants, casinos, resorts, and clubs. Basse-Terre (Low Land) is wild, wet,
and mountainous. It once lagged behind Grande-Terre, but today is
popular with those who love hiking, whale-watching, diving, or deep-
sea fishing. Its lush, west coast is as beautiful as any other place in the
Caribbean. On Les Saintes, La Désirade, Marie-Galante, and the other
islands of the archipelago, you'll find places have remained largely untouched by the world.

Guadeloupe was annexed by France in 1674. During the French Revolution, battles broke out between royalists and revolutionaries on the
island. In 1794 Britain aided Guadeloupe royalists, and that same
year France dispatched Victor Hugues to sort things out. (In virtually
every town and village you'll run across a Victor Hugues street, boule-

vard, or park.) After his troops banished the British, Hugues abolished slavery and guillotined recalcitrant planters. Those who managed to keep their heads fled to Louisiana or hid in the hills of Grande-Terre, where their descendants now live. Hugues—"the Robespierre of the Isles"—was soon relieved of his command, slavery was reestablished by Napoléon, and the French and English continued to battle over the island. The 1815 Treaty of Paris restored Guadeloupe to France, and in 1848, thanks to Alsatian Victor Schoelcher, slavery was abolished. The island was made a *département* of France in 1946, and in 1974 was elevated to a *région*, administered by a prefect appointed from Paris. With Martinique, St. Barths, and St. Martin, it is in *les Antilles Françaises,* or the French West Indies.

An old saying of the French Caribbean refers to *"les grands seigneurs de la Martinique et les bonnes gens de la Guadeloupe* (the lords of Martinique and the bourgeoisie of Guadeloupe)." Though there are few aristocrats left on Martinique, the saying still holds some truth in Guadeloupe. Middle-class French tourists come (most on package tours) to swim and sunbathe, scuba dive, or hike. But sugar is still Guadeloupe's primary source of income. Only 10% of the workforce is employed in the tourism industry—which thrives from mid-November through May and is quiet the rest of the year. At harvest time, in February, the fields teem with workers cutting cane, and the roads are clogged with trucks taking the harvest to factories or distilleries.

Everything about Guadeloupe—from the *franglais* (*le topless, le snack-bar*) to the zippy little cars and ubiquitous *vendeuses de la plage* (women who model bathing suits on *le beach* and do a strip-tease show in the process)—is French. And whether in hotel corridors or on the beach, at breakfast or on a dive boat, cigarette smoke is as much a part of the ambience as the tropical breeze. The prices are Parisian, and unlike on St. Martin, there are stiff taxes on most goods. To really feel at home here, some *français* is indispensable, though you may receive a bewildering response in Creole patois. Still you'll be welcomed in this land of volcanoes, French food, and 'ti punch (white rum, sugarcane syrup, and a lime).

Lodging

On Guadeloupe you can opt for a splashy hotel with a full complement of activities or a small *relais* (inn) for more personal attention or a more authentic island experience. Many of the island's chain hotels cater to French package groups. Gosier, St-François, and Bas-du-Fort are generally considered resort areas, as is Ste-Anne. There are small hotels on Iles des Saintes and Marie-Galante. More, and better, hotels are opening in Basse-Terre. Most hotels include buffet breakfast in their rates. As tourism to the French islands has slipped in recent years, hotel prices have fallen. Prices decline 25%–40% in the off-season.

CATEGORY	COST*
$$$$	over $300
$$$	$225–$300
$$	$150–$225
$	under $150

All prices are for a standard double room, excluding taxe de séjour, which varies from hotel to hotel, and 10%–15% service charge.

Hotels

GRANDE-TERRE

$$$$ 🖼 **La Cocoteraie.** Although technically part of Le Méridien St-François, this classy, boutique hotel is its own entity. Consisting of spacious suites

Guadeloupe

Lodging

Auberge de l'Arbre
à Pain 41
Auberge de la
Vieille Tour 3
L'Auberge les
Petits Saints
aux Anarcadiers . . . 34
Bois Joli 33
Canella Beach
Hotel Residence . . . 9
Cap Sud
Caraïbes 8
Le Clipper 5
Club Méditerranée
La Caravelle 13
La Cocoteraie 17
La Créole Beach
Hotel 6
Domaine de
Malendure 31
Domaine de
Petite-Anse 30
Habitation
Grande Anse 27
Hôtel Cohoba 40
Hôtel Hajo 42
Hôtel Saint-John 1
Hôtel la Toubana . . 14
Le Jardin
Malanga 32
Le Méridien
St-François 18
Le Mirage 45
L'Oasis 46
Les Pavillons
Ti Ta'Anse 28
Novotel/
Fleur d'Épée 7
La Plantation
Ste-Marthe 21
Résidence Soleil
Le Vant 43
La Sucrerie
du Comté 25
Au Village
de Ménard 44

Dining

Auberge de la
Vieille Tour 3
Auberge de
St-François 16
L'Auberge les
Petits Saints aux
Anacardiers 34
Le Bananier 4
Château de
Feuilles 23
Chez Clara 24
Chez Jackye 29
Coté Jardin 2
El Dorado 37
Le Flibustier 12
Le Genois 39
Iguane Café 20
Le Karacoli 26
La Maison du
Pecheur 11
La Louisiane 22
Nilce's Bar 38
La Nouvelle
Table Créole 10
Les Oiseaux 19

KEY

⛴ Cruise Ship Terminal

◥ Dive Sites

❶ Exploring Sights

⛴ Ferry

① Hotels and Restaurants

Guadeloupe Passage

Anse Laborde
Anse Bertrand
Souffleur
Port Louis
Beauport
Anse du Vieux Fort
Pte. Allègre
Ilet à Fajou
Anse du Canal
Petit-Canal
La Grande-Anse
Ste-Rose
Vieux-Bourg
Grand Cul-de-Sac Marin
Deshaies
Lamentin
Destrelan
Aéroport International Pôle Caraïbes
Abyr
Pointe-Noire
Anse Caraïbe
PARC NATIONAL DE LA GUADELOUPE
Bas-du-Fort
Pointe-à-Pitre
Jabrun du Suc
Mahaut
La Traversée
Petit Cul-de-Sac Marin
Malendure
Pigeon Island
Bouillante
Vernou
Petit-Bourg
Goyave
BASSE-TERRE
Marigot
Vieux-Habitants
Matouba
La Soufrière
Ste-Marie
Capesterre-Belle-Eau
Plage de Rocroy
St-Claude
St-Sauveur
Bananier
Caribbean Sea
Basse-Terre
Gourbeyre
Trois-Rivières
Anse Turlet
Vieux Fort
Iles des Saintes (Les Saint⋯
Terre-de-Haut
Plage Crawen
Terre-de-Bas
La Coche
Grand Ilet

Les Pavillions
Restaurant **28**
Le P'tit Patron **35**
La Saladerie **36**
La Varangue **15**

Exploring
Anse Bertrand **10**
Aquarium de la
Guadeloupe **3**
Bas-du-Fort **2**
Basse-Terre **26**
Bouillante **23**
Cascade aux
Ecrevisses **19**
Chutes du
Carbet **29**
La Désirade **32**
Gosier **4**
Ilet de Pigeon **22**
Les Mamelles **17**
Maison de la
Forêt **18**
Marie-Galante **31**
Morne-à-l'Eau **12**
Le Moule **8**
Parc Archéologique
des Roches
Gravées **28**
Parc National de la
Guadeloupe **16**
Petit-Bourg **21**
Pointe des
Châteaux **7**
Pointe-Noire **15**
Pointe-à-Pitre **1**
Porte d'Enfer **9**
Port Louis **11**
Ste-Anne **5**
St-Claude **25**
St-François **6**
Ste-Rose **14**
Station Thermale
de Ravine Chaude
René Toribio **13**
Terre-de-Haut **30**
Vernou **20**
Vieux Fort **27**
Vieux-Habitants **24**

housed in blue and white colonial buildings, 20 are directly on the "private" beach, and the rest have views (second floors are best) of the marina or the glorious pool embellished with blue and white Oriental urns. Suites have two bathrooms and Hermès octagonal tubs, set in the curve of sunny bow windows. Mahogany beds are clothed in expensive French bed ensembles. The pool is traversed by a white, covered footbridge and is adjacent to the circular Indigo Bar. Many guests sipping rum cocktails relive their day spent on the acclaimed public, 18-hole Robert Trent Jones course, across from the hotel, which provides clubs and lessons. The La Varangue restaurant is renowned for its imaginative cuisine. A lobby and room renovation that will upgrade and further enhance this refined property is underway for 2001. ⊠ *Av. de l'Europe, St-François 97118*, ☎ *590/88–79–81 or 800/322–2223*, FAX *590/88–78–33*, WEB *www.lemeridien.com. 50 suites. Restaurant, bar, in-room safes, minibars, pool, 2 tennis courts, gym, beach, baby-sitting, car rental. AE, DC, MC, V. CP, MAP.*

$$$$ ⊡ **Club Méditerranée La Caravelle.** Dating from the 1970s, this Club Med sits on 50 secluded acres on Caravelle beach, widely considered the island's best white-sand beach. Simple rooms have A/C and twin beds, some balconies, and are acceptable to the clientele that is 80% European, mostly French. Americans may want to pay the 20% extra for the Marie Galante wing. Nonguests can call for day passes (about $60), which include all sports and either lunch or dinner, with complimentary wine and beer. The club's high-energy *gentils employés* make sure everyone is having fun, especially at the new animation theater and huge pool. Bar bills are paid for with coupons—no more beads. Family-oriented, the resort is great for children, who love the kids' club. ⊠ *Quartier Caravelle, Ste-Anne 97180*, ☎ *590/85–49–50 or 800/258–2633*, FAX *590/85–49–70*, WEB *www.clubmed.com. 340 rooms. 2 restaurants, pub, air-conditioning, pool, 6 tennis courts, aerobics, archery, volleyball, beach, windsurfing, boating, nightclub, children's programs. AE, MC, V. All-inclusive.*

$$$ ⊡ **Auberge de la Vieille Tour.** One of the island's first hotels, this
★   property grew from six rooms fashioned around a 200-year-old stone sugar mill, to a luxury resort under the Sofitel brand. Guests love coming here, from the time they are welcomed by pretty, local girls in white eyelet and madras, dispensing moist, heated towels and fresh juice, to each night when they return "home" to their split-level suite with a glass-walled bathroom looking out to a winking lighthouse. Clever landscaping conceals the three large, apartment-style buildings housing the lowest-priced rooms. Blue and white, with a nautical decor, and tiled floors, they, too, look out to sea. Auberge de la Vieille Tour restaurant is unquestionably one of the island's finest. A fabulous breakfast buffet, lunch, and a weekly buffet (at which there is a traditional dance and music show) are served at the poolside *ajoupa*, an open-sided structure. A snack bar, and an infinity pool surrounded by wooden decking, should be finished by the time you get there. Free shuttles run to the larger, seaside resort, Novotel, which has a long beach, a host of water sports and catamaran excursions. ⊠ *Rte. de Montauban, Gosier 97190*, ☎ *590/84–23–23 or 800/322–2223*, FAX *590/84–33–43*, WEB *www.sofitel.com. 77 rooms, 102 suites. 2 restaurants, bar, pool, 2 tennis courts, beach, shops. AE, MC, V. EP, MAP.*

$$$ ⊡ **Le Méridien St-François.** Adjacent to La Cocoteraie, this 150-acre resort puts strong emphasis on its animation program and wide range of activities that might include a volleyball game, fashion show, circus, or Caribbean night on the beach with lobster and fireworks. Check the hotel's own broadcast on Télé Méridien for the latest events. Although the hotel's facade is dated and the public areas are best de-

scribed as shabby chic, the hotel underwent a serious renovation in spring 2001. Most of the guest rooms already have new tile floors and attractive mint and mango tropical fabrics. A children's club opens during the French school holidays; the boutique sells resort wear with élan. ⊠ *Av. de l'Europe, St-François 97118,* ☎ *590/88–51–00 or 800/543–4300,* FAX *590/88–40–71,* WEB *www.lemeridien.com. 253 rooms, 10 suites. 2 restaurants, 2 bars, air-conditioning, refrigerators, pool, spa, 2 tennis courts, beach, snorkeling, boating, shops, car rental. AE, MC, V. CP, MAP, EP.*

$$ 🖬 **Hôtel La Toubana.** Talk about a view: the solarium terrace, perched on a cliff that drops to the sea, has the kind of Caribbean views "that movies are made of." Adjacent to its fine restaurant, Le Grand Bleu, the magnificent infinity pool looks as if it flows into the sea below. Twelve bungalows have ocean views, 20 are admidst luxuriant gardens. All have terraces and are furnished with inexpensive, blond rattan pieces, including armoires. ⊠ *Fonds Thezan,, Ste-Anne 97180,* ☎ *590/88–25–57,* FAX *590/88–38–90,* WEB *www.toubana.gp/us/index-us.htm. 32 bungalows. 2 restaurants, bar, kitchenettes, tennis court, beach, snorkeling, jet skiing. MC, V. CP, MAP, AP.*

$$ 🖬 **La Créole Beach Hotel.** Part of a larger complex, also housing a residential development and the upscale Mahogany Hotel, this resort spans 10 acres of tropical greenery and two beaches. There is a nice expanse of wooden terrace and teak chaise longues for sunbathing, topless or otherwise. The oversized rooms are akin to a fine wooden yacht. The Le Créole sailboat logo has been worked into the marine blue and gold drapes. Palm fronds, painted blue, are under glass and hung over the beds. Expensive white bedspreads carry on the crisp, minimalistic look. An international buffeteria, named Route des Espaces (Road of Spices), is an impressive all-you-can-eat dining room offering everything from columbos (curries) to prime rib. ⊠ *Pointe de la Verdure (Box 61), Gosier 97190,* ☎ *590/90–46–46 or 800/322–2223,* FAX *590/90–46–66,* WEB *www.creole-beach.gp. 156 rooms. 2 restaurants, bar, air-conditioning, pool, volleyball, snorkeling, boating, meeting rooms, car rental. AE, DC, MC, V. CP, EP, MAP.*

$$ 🖬 **La Plantation Ste-Marthe.** A few miles inland, among gently rolling
★ hills and fields, the grounds are lovely, with old sugar-refining machinery cleverly incorporated into the landscaping. You can see the ocean from some rooms, and there's shuttle service to the beach. The whole place is sumptuous; the august reception area has columns of pale blue and mango, vast murals, a winding double staircase of polished wood, and marble floors. The large rooms are in four three-story buildings with ornate, iron grillwork. Spacious terraces overlook the large pool. Duplex suites have loft-style bedrooms above salons. Mahogany beds and aquamarine and coral tile work contribute to the refined aura. There are horses and ATVs (all-terrain vehicles) for traveling to secluded beaches that you cannot reach by car. ⊠ *St-François 97118,* ☎ *590/93–11–11 or 800/322–2223,* FAX *590/88–72–47. 96 rooms, 24 duplexes. Restaurant, bar, air-conditioning, in-room safes, minibars, pool, horseback riding, meeting rooms. AE, MC, V. CP, MAP.*

$$ 🖬 **Novotel/Fleur d'Épée.** Two hotels merged to make this sprawling, water sports–oriented resort. Most guests arrive from France on package deals; there are none for Americans. Rooms at the Fleur d'Épée are rather cramped, but the powder-blue fabrics and white tiles give them a pleasant, fresh look; equally pleasant are those in its "better half" (the former Novotel). All rooms have terraces, most with sea views; prices include full-day cruises to the Iles de Saintes on a large catamaran— an ideal way to pass a Sunday. The spacious grounds look magical when lit at night. ⊠ *Gosier 97190,* ☎ *590/90–40–00 or 800/221–4542,*

FAX *590/90–99–07. 400 rooms. 4 restaurants, bar, air-conditioning, minibars, pool, beach, snorkeling, boating. AE, D, DC, MC, V. CP, MAP.*

$ ⊞ **Canella Beach Hotel Residence.** Designed to look like a creole village, all fretwork and pastels, this is one resort where people actually do move in for a while because the monthly rates for the studios and duplex apartments are doable, particularly in low season. Weekly and even daily rates are also available. The complex has its own semiprivate cove, a beach bar, and water-sports shack. The Veranda Restaurant, looking like a white gingerbread house, features creole, French, and lobster specialties and has a prix-fixe menu for 75F. More important, it has personality. Live music, great bar concoctions, and a fun crowd make it a happening nightspot. ⊠ *Pointe de la Verdure, Gosier 97190,* ☎ *590/90–44–00 or 800/322–2223,* FAX *590/90–44–44. 145 rooms. Restaurant, bar, kitchenettes, pool, beach, snorkeling, windsurfing, boating, jet skiing, waterskiing, fishing. AE, DC, MC, V. EP, MAP.*

$ ⊞ **Cap Sud Caraïbes.** This tiny relais is on a country road between Gosier and Ste. Anne and just a five-minute walk from a quiet beach. It's homey and simple and a good value for the money. The staff does its best to make you feel comfortable. Each individually decorated room is equipped with a double bed and has only a shower in the bathroom. It has a sizable pool that overlooks a beautiful garden and a fun bar with tropical rum drinks. Special rates are given to honeymooners and guests who stay more than seven nights. ⊠ *Chemin de la Plage, Gosier 97190,* ☎ *590/85–96–02,* FAX *590/85–80–39. 12 rooms. Bar, air-conditioning, pool, snorkeling, laundry service, airport shuttle. MC, V. CP.*

$ ⊞ **Hôtel Saint-John.** This simple hotel next to the port is your best bet if you need to stay over in Pointe-à-Pitre. Small rooms are clean, comfortable, and decorated with Mediterranean colors—a number of them overlook the water. Popular with businesspeople, the hotel lies within easy walking distance of the tourist office and is near the cruise-ship debarkation. Don't expect luxury—and be alert after dark—but this is the city's best option. ⊠ *Quai des Croisières, Pointe-à-Pitre 97110,* ☎ *590/82–51–57,* FAX *590/82–52–61. 44 rooms. Restaurant, air-conditioning. AE, MC, V.*

BASSE-TERRE

$$$ ⊞ **Le Jardin Malanga.** A quiet hideaway for nature-lovers and hon-
★ eymooners, this *hotel de charme* is surrounded by gardens of buttercup blossoms, bougainvillea, birds of paradise, orchids, chenille plants, hibiscus, periwinkles, and tropical fruits. Accommodations are in traditional creole buildings of courbaril wood from French Guinea; the antique-filled main house was built in 1927. A cliff-side pool looks to the sea, and the property is close to Guadeloupe's national park and Iles des Saintes. Each room's white-tile bathroom gleams; next to its tub is a one-way picture window that looks out to the lush surroundings. There are no TVs or radios here, so quiet is inevitable. French-creole meals with produce from the gardens are served table de hôte in a small outdoor dining area for hotel guests only. You will need a car to get here. ⊠ *Hermitage, Trois-Rivières 97114,* ☎ *590/92–67–57 or 800/322–2223,* FAX *590/92–67–58. 8 rooms, 1 suite. Air-conditioning, fans, pool. AE, MC, V. CP, FAP, MAP.*

$ ⊞ **Le Clipper.** A three-star, beachfront property of the Karibéa Hotel Group, it has a good location, next to Le Créole Beach Hotel. Utilizing shiplike features, including porthole-style windows, the low-rise building (with elevators) is all blue and white. A friendly, helpful G.M. and staff, most of whom speak English, make the French tour groups and everyone else feel at home. A kids' club is available during French school holidays, and baby-sitters with 24 hours' notice. ⊠ *Pointe de la Verdure, Gosier 97190,* ☎ *590/84–01–75,* ﬁⁿ *590/84–38–15,* ᴡᴇʙ *www.karibea.com/hotelleclipper.htm. 87 rooms, 3 suites. Restaurant, bar, pool, 2 tennis courts, beach, snorkeling, windsurfing, boating, shop, laundry. AE, MC, V. CP, MAP, AP.*

$ ⚏ **Domaine de Malendure.** Perched in the hills above Bouillante with
★ a gorgeous view of Pigeon Island, this is the best location in Guadeloupe for scuba and snorkeling aficionados. Simple but well-equipped duplex- and studio-style rooms have air-conditioning, TVs, refrigerators, and phones, which can be hard to find in other similarly priced hotels. English is spoken, and Malendure Beach—with its numerous dive shops—is close by. ⊠ *Morne Tarare Pigeon, Bouillante 97132,* ☎ *590/98–92–12,* ﬁⁿ *590/98–92–10. 44 duplexes, 6 studios. Restaurant, bar, car rental. AE, MC, V. CP, EP, MAP.*

$ ⚏ **Domaine de Petite-Anse.** The ochre, red-roof buildings of this complex spill down lushly landscaped hills above the ocean, and there's a terrific pool overlooking the sea. Accommodations are either in simple and small—though well-equipped—rooms (ask for one with a sea view, which costs the same as one without) or bungalows with full baths, kitchenettes, and terraces. The decor consists of dark rattan furniture lightened by bright floral fabrics. The staff is friendly, but most speak only a little English. The resort, noted for its dive shop and nature tours of the national park, is very popular with young French couples and families. ⊠ *Plage de Petite-Anse, Monchy, Bouillante 97125,* ☎ *590/ 98–78–78,* ﬁⁿ *590/98–80–28. 135 rooms, 40 bungalows. Restaurant, bar, air-conditioning, in-room safes, refrigerators, pool, archery, hiking, volleyball, dive shop, snorkeling, boating, shops. AE, DC, MC, V. EP.*

$ ⚏ **Habitation Grande Anse.** With beautiful views of Baie Anse and the
★ surrounding hills, this lovely property offers a mix of bungalows, apartments, studios, and standard rooms. The youthful Italian owner, Fulvio, speaks English. The quality of the accommodations and service is in striking contrast to that of similarly priced hotels on the island. Rooms are decorated in Mediterranean colors; apartments house four to six people and share their own pools (apartments 16 and 17 have the best views). Across the road, Grande Anse Beach is a five-minute walk. The hotel will help arrange fishing and diving excursions, and rents Citroens at a reasonable price, full insurance included. ⊠ *Localité Ziotte 97126,* ☎ *590/28–45–36,* ﬁⁿ *590/28–51–17,* ᴡᴇʙ *www.grande-anse.com. 3 rooms, 20 studios, 6 apartments, 19 bungalows. Air-conditioning, kitchenettes, 3 pools. AE, MC, V. EP, MAP.*

$ ⚏ **Les Pavillions Ti Ta'Anse.** Recently built, this cluster of two-story bungalows makes its way up a verdant hillside, with the highest having views of the beach. The central complex houses a casual grill and a small nightclub on the ground floor; the recommendable Les Pavillons Restaurant is on the second. All of the facades and railed porches are of a beautiful hardwood. Buildings are capped with green, copper roofs detailed with fretwork. Interiors have the same dark, native mahogany and pine wood trim, Dutch doors and beams and rustic floor tiles. Surrounded by frangipani trees, lush gardens with aromatic plants like citronella grass and night lit by lanterns, this is one nice place, tucked into a gorgeous mountainous countryside. ⊠ *Baillargent, Pointe-Noire, 97116,* ☎ *590/99–97–51,* ﬁⁿ *590/99–97–57. 5 bungalows. Restaurant, air-conditioning, kitchenettes, beach, dance club. AE, MC, V. EP, MAP.*

$ ⚏ **La Sucrerie du Comté.** The ruins and rusting equipment of a 19th-century sugar factory punctuate the lawns and gardens. In fact, the historically significant grounds, along with the attractive public areas, are this resort's main attractions. The bar recreates a plantation setting, with wood beams, stone walls, and towering floral arrangements. The restaurant is built with a Brazilian wood roof and serves creole and international food. Small, simple rooms are housed in 26 bungalows that duplicate the gingerbread architecture of the turn of the 20th century. All have private verandas with tropical garden views. The nearest beach is a five-minute stroll through a tangle of greenery. Management recommends diving in the nearby "Grand Cul Sac Marin" and offers guests a free introductory lesson in the pool once a week. ✉ *Comté de Lohéac, Ste-Rose, 97115,* ☎ *590/28–60–17,* FAX *590/28–65–63,* WEB *www.prime-invest-hotels.com. 52 rooms. Restaurant, bar, air-conditioning, fans, pool. AE, DC, MC, V. CP, MAP.*

ILES DES SAINTES

$$ 🏨 **Bois Joli.** A beautiful bayside setting 3 km (2 mi) from the main town is the attraction here. Most rooms, in the inn or one of the bungalows, are air-conditioned but rather drab. Those cottages on the high hill at the hotel's entrance are the best bet: clean and stark but with magnificent sea views. The pool area is pleasant and looks down to a golden strip of beach. Americans may not feel the warmest welcome and will have trouble communicating. Half-board is obligatory during high season. Water sports can be arranged. ✉ *Terre-de-Haut 97137,* ☎ *590/ 99–50–38 or 800/322–2223,* FAX *590/99–55–05. 18 rooms, 8 bungalows. Restaurant, bar, pool, airport shuttle. MC, V. CP, MAP.*

$ 🏨 **L'Auberge les Petits Saints aux Anarcadiers.** This distinctive inn is
★ trimmed with trellises and topped by dormers, but do not come expecting an American brand of luxury. A wild-looking clutter greets you in the reception area, crammed with antiques, objets d'art, and attic treasures collected by owners. Room furnishings are a similarly odd assortment of antiques. Eight rooms have queen-size beds, and two have twin beds; all have private baths but no telephones. There's also a one-bedroom bungalow and a separate guest house with five large rooms suitable for families. Throughout the inn, windows open to a view of gardens, hills, and the bay (Room 2 has an extraordinary vista). L'Auberge les Petits Saints aux Anarcadiers opens for dinner and offers a prix-fixe (170F) menu. The pool area has an enviable hillside view of the bay. ✉ *La Savane, Terre-de-Haut 97137,* ☎ *590/99–50– 99 or 800/322–2223,* FAX *590/99–54–51,* WEB *www.petitssaints.com. 10 rooms, 2 bungalows. Restaurant, bar, air-conditioning, pool, sauna. AE, MC, V. CP, MAP.*

MARIE-GALANTE

$ 🏨 **Au Village de Ménard.** Care has gone into the gardens of this hotel, which sits on a cliff at the island's north end (the beach is 1 mi/1½ km away). Ask for one of the nine newer, brightly colored bungalows that are on a rise above the pool. The owner speaks English. ✉ *Vieux Fort, St-Louis 97134,* ☎ *590/97–09–45,* FAX *590/97–15–40. 9 bungalows. Air-conditioning, fans, kitchenettes, pool. MC, V. CP.*

$ 🏨 **Hôtel Cohoba.** Set on a sandy beach, this hotel is named for a plant whose hallucinogenic red pods gave the earliest Caribbean peoples prophetic powers. Half the suites are sky-blue and sea-green stucco bungalows; the rest are slightly larger studios. White walls and white tile floors lend an air of space; cool and warm fabrics add touches of cheer, and air-conditioning keeps things cool. In the dining room you can contemplate the past while studying the painstakingly reproduced cave paintings that decorate the walls. ✉ *Grand Bourg 97112,* ☎ *590/97–50– 50 or 800/322–2223,* FAX *590/97–97–96. 100 suites. Restaurant, bar,* *air-conditioning, 2 tennis courts, pool, beach, boating, shops. AE, MC, V. CP, MAP.*

There are several other small, simple lodgings on Marie-Galante. Consider the following: **Auberge de l'Arbre à Pain** (9 rooms; ✉ 32 Jeanne D'Arc du Docteur Marcel Enzol, ☎ 590/97–73–69), in Grand-Bourg; **Hôtel Hajo** (6 rooms; Section Bernard #140, Capesterre, ☎ 590/97–32–76), in Capesterre; or **Résidence Soleil Le Vant** (12 rooms; ✉ 42 rue de la Marine, ☎ 590/97–31–55, FAX 590/97–41–65).

LA DÉSIRADE

An even more remote island than Marie-Galante or Isle des Saintes, La Désirade has few lodging options. In Grande-Anse there's **L'Oasis** (☎ 590/20–02–12), a six-room hotel whose simple restaurant serves excellent seafood. **Le Mirage,** also in Grande-Anse, is a tiny eight-room establishment (☎ 590/20–01–08, FAX 590/20–07–45).

Villas

For information about villas, apartments, and private rooms in modest houses, contact one of the following agencies: **Gîtes de France** (✉ 5 Square de la Banque, Pointe-a-Pitre 97171, ☎ 590/91–64–33, FAX 590/91–45–40); or the **Association des Villas et Meublés de Tourisme** (✉ 12 Faubourg Alexandre Issac, Pointe-a-Pitre 97171, ☎ 590/82–02–62, FAX 590/82–56–65).

Dining

Guadeloupe's fine creole dishes feature local seafood and vegetables, such as christophenes (also known as chayote, like a squash) and plantains. Favorite appetizers are *accras* (codfish fritters), *boudin* (highly seasoned blood sausage), and *crabes farcis* (stuffed land crabs). *Blaff* is a spicy fish stew. *Langouste* (lobster) and *lambi* (conch) are widely available, as is *souchy,* a Tahitian version of sushi. The island boasts a diverse selection of dining options—including French, Italian, African, Indian, Vietnamese, and South American establishments—but they aren't cheap. The local libation is 'ti punch—a heady concoction of rum, lime juice, and sugarcane syrup.

What to Wear

Dining is casual at lunch, but beach attire is a no-no. Except at the more laid-back marina and beach eateries, dinner is slightly more formal. Long pants, collared shirts, and skirts or dresses are appreciated, although not required.

CATEGORY	COST*
$$$$	$30 or more
$$$	$20–$30
$$	$10–$20
$	under $10

* per person for a main course at dinner

Grande-Terre

CARIBBEAN

$$ ✕ **Le Bananier.** *Nouvelle cuisine creole,* creatively prepared food utilizing local produce, is the specialty at this well-established Gosier restaurant. Try les soupe aux crustacea—bisque with lobster and fish with a cheese-garlic crouton, or boiled red snapper with a passion-fruit banana sauce, and finish with a crêpe with coconut flambéed with rum and curaçao. Jean Clarus is one of the island's most experienced chefs. This little wooden gingerbread "house" could use a serious sprucing up, however. ✉ *Montauban, Gosier,* ☎ *590/84–34–85. MC, V. Closed Mon.*

$$ ✕ **La Maison du Pecheur.** American music and some wonderful French oldies play as twinkling lights surround the al fresco terrace dining room. Servers are dressed in French sailor jerseys and captain caps and pose for snapshots with guests. It's a fun place, offering a marriage of French and creole cooking, two prix fixes, and à la carte. Here, court bouillon does not mean soup but rather a creole sauce with tomatoes, peppers, and onions served over a local fish steak. Stuffed christophone, a squash puree, rice, and beans share the plate on the 95 F Menu Caraïbe. The Menu Langouste, a grilled half lobster preceded by conch sausage or stuffed crab, and followed by flambéd fruit, is a good value. A rum liqueur comes on the "maison." ⊠ *Pointe de la Verdure, Gosier,* ☎ *590/84–81–46. MC, V.*

$$ ✕ **Le P'tit Jardin Chez Lucile.** If you're in Le Moule, stop by this casual, friendly restaurant for rapid service and big portions. The prix-fixe lunch menu (70F) features grilled red snapper. There's also a 130F lobster menu, which is as cheap as the little red critters come on this island. ⊠ *Rue St-Jean Prolongée, Cité Cadenet, Le Moule,* ☎ *590/23–51–63. MC, V.*

$ ✕ **La Nouvelle Table Créole.** Carmélite Jeanne rules the kitchen of this
★ little terrace eatery, and she turns out dazzling, deceptively mild creole cuisine that can heat you up like the noonday sun. Sea urchin gratin and lobster fricassee are among her memorable dishes. Fresh flowers are everywhere, and Madame Jeanne usually dresses colorfully to match. ⊠ *Hotel Village Caraibes, St-Félix,* ☎ *590/84–28–28. MC, V. No dinner Sun.*

CONTEMPORARY

$$$ ✕ **Auberge de la Vieille Tour.** Tables at this restaurant in the Auberge de la Vieille Tour resort are grouped around a historic whitewashed sugar mill; the conservatory-style extension has views up into lighted trees. Without a doubt, some of the best, most contemporary food on the island is here, such as a delectable red snapper atop a layer of pureed pumpkin with an orange-ginger sauce. Dessert presentations are dazzling with lots of puff pastry, Napoléons, sauces, and glacés. ⊠ *Rte. de Montauban, Gosier,* ☎ *590/84–23–23. AE, MC, V. No lunch.*

$$$ ✕ **Château de Feuilles.** This restaurant is 9 mi (14½ km) from Le
★ Moule—on the Campêche road between Gros-Cap and Campêche— and it's worth a special trip. You'll be hard-pressed to find a finer luncheon than that served by Martine and Jean-Pierre Dubost. The country setting is relaxed and stylish. You can take a dip in the pool or stroll around the two-acre farm. For an aperitif, you can choose from about 20 punch concoctions. The changing menu is an imaginative utilization of fresh produce and seafood. ⊠ *Rte. Campêche, Anse Bertrand,* ☎ *590/22–30–30. V. Closed Mon. No dinner (except for groups of 10 or more by reservation).*

$$$ ✕ **Iguane Café.** Sylvan and Marie Seronait serve innovative food at this
★ excellent restaurant. Just beyond the reception area and bar, a group of chefs busily prepare such specialties as thin slices of lamb with mango and sweet potato or steamed five-spice fish. Hibiscus beignets make an unusual and delicious dessert. ⊠ *Rte. de la Pointe des Château (½ mi/¾ km from airport), St-François,* ☎ *590/88–61–37. AE, MC. Closed Sun. and Tues.*

$$$ ✕ **Les Oiseaux.** In a stucco-and-stone house set in a tangle of gardens that overlook the sea, owner-chefs Claudette and Arthur Rolle prepare creative fish dishes, unlikely combinations with clever names. Ask Claudette to show you her book of local remedies. If your French is *very* good, she might even prepare a special infusion for your particular complaint, but it's best to stick to remedies for external illnesses

only. If English is your only language, perhaps simply having a home-made *digestif* (after-dinner liqueur) will be enough to cure what ails you. ⊠ *Anse des Rochers,* ☎ *590/88–56–92. Reservations essential. MC, V. No lunch. Closed weekdays Sept.–Oct.*

$$$ ✕ **Le Flibustier.** This place is straight out of "Pirates of the Caribbean" with nautical trappings from the 1970s. That was when Chef/Owner Phillippe, who with ponytail, large moustache, and breeches, looks like a pirate, left France. He's learned to be a good man on the grill, and if you're hankering for a big slab of juicy steak or a grilled lobster with a couple of sauces on the side, this be *the* place. Start with foie gras, tip a bottle of Medoc, and finish with profiteroles. ⊠ *La Coline, Fonds Thézan (between Ste-Anne and St-Félix),* ☎ *590/88–23–36. MC, V. Closed June–July. Closed Mon. No dinner Sun.*

$$ ✕ **La Louisiane.** Daniel and Murielle Hugon have taken over this small
★ restaurant, known for its refined French cuisine and service, and did a major renovation in early 2001. Specialties include lamb chops grilled with garlic and served with pineapple and tomato chutney. The dozen or so tables here are on a terrace decorated with paintings and flower-filled hanging pots. ⊠ *On road to Ste-Marthe, near St-François,* ☎ *590/ 88–44–34. MC, V. Closed Mon.*

$$$ ✕ **Coté Jardin.** Fresh oysters arrive here each Thursday, and they are just some of the special treats that personable owner Jacques Bergerie offers. The food is innovative and beautifully presented, the wine list is solid. Air-conditioning, red-and-green tablecloths, and plenty of large plants make the surroundings comfortable and pleasant. ⊠ *La Marina, Pointe-à-Pitre,* ☎ *590/90–91–28. AE, MC, V. Closed Sun. No lunch Sat.*

$$$ ✕ **La Varangue.** In the beautiful surroundings of La Cocoteraie Hotel, La Varangue offers the most refined dining on the island. Open to hotel guests and the general public, this open-air restaurant overlooking the elegant hotel pool offers haute cuisine with a creole flair. The menu changes regularly, but the dishes are always imaginative and beauti-fully presented. Even a simple grilled lobster is perfection; the wine list is upscale. ⊠ *Av. de l'Europe, St-François,* ☎ *590/88–79–81. AE, MC, V.*

$$$ ✕ **Auberge de St-François.** Claude Simon's country home is in an or-chard, and his tables are set with Royal Doulton and fine crystal. Din-ing is indoors or on one of the flower-filled patios, with a superb view of Marie-Galante and Pointe des Châteaux. The house specialty is cray-fish: fricassee with bacon and scallops. The conch dishes are also good. A *menu touriste* (190F) of three courses, each with a choice of three dishes, is an alternative to the à la carte offerings. ⊠ *St-François,* ☎ *590/88–51–25. MC, V. Closed Sun.–Mon.*

Basse-Terre

$$$ ✕ **Le Karacoli.** With her flowing white dress and flamboyant style, Lu-cienne Salcede, the owner of this pleasant seaside restaurant, has her pictures hanging in the interior dining room, from when she began cheff-ing decades ago, when the place was decorated. Sit outside, instead, on the beachfront terrace and listen to the waves splash. The food is solid (and expensive) creole fare like boudin noir with a piquante sauce. The prix fixe is the best deal, but avoid the tough lambi. Do go with a fine French wine. Coconut flan is a nice finale with a rum

liqueur (punch). Then stretch out on a chaise longue and wake up and take a swim. ⊠ *La Grande-Anse, north of Deshaies,* ☎ *590/28–41–17. MC, V. No dinner.*

$$ ✕ **Chez Clara.** Clara Lesueur, who gave up a jazz-dancing career in Paris
★   to run her family's seaside restaurant with her mother, dishes out delicious creole meals. Seating is on the inviting terrace of a gorgeous house with lacy gingerbread trim. Clara takes the orders (her English is excellent), and the place is often so crowded with her friends and fans that you may have to wait at the octagonal wooden bar. Check the daily specials listed on the blackboard. ⊠ *Bd. Maritime, Ste-Rose,* ☎ *590/28–72–99. MC, V. Closed Wed. No dinner Sun.*

$$ ✕ **Les Pavillons Restaurant.** In the Les Pavillons Ti Ta'Anse Hotel, this
★   restaurant is on a terrace with views of Le Rouix beach. Traditional Antilles specialties like lambi in butter sauce are joined by innovations like avocado with hot roquefort cream sauce and lamb with pine nuts. Finish with Tourment d'amour, Guadeloupe's famous coconut cake, and choose a homemade rum liqueur (punch) from the fascinating display (the best is aged with raisins, pistachios, or sea grapes). Downstairs a simple grill menu from brochettes to lobster, is available for lunch. ⊠ *Baillargent, Pointe-Noire 97116,* ☎ *590/99–97–51. AE, MC, V.*

ECLECTIC

$ ✕ **Chez Jackye.** Jacqueline Cabrion serves creole and African dishes in her cheerful, plant-filled seaside restaurant. Boudin is a house specialty, as are lobster (grilled, vinaigrette, or fricassee), fried crayfish, clam blaff, and goat in port sauce. There's also a wide selection of omelets, sandwiches, and salads. For dessert try the peach Melba or banana flambé. The 120F menu will have you waddling out happily. ⊠ *Anse Guyonneau, rue de la Bataille, Pointe-Noire,* ☎ *590/98–06–98. DC, MC, V. Closed Sun.*

Îles des Saintes

ECLECTIC

$$$ ✕ **L'Auberge les Petits Saints aux Anarcadiers.** Hotel guests and a few
★   visitors have the privilege of dining at the veranda restaurant of L'Auberge les Petits Saints aux Anarcadiers. The set *tableau de jour* menu (170 F) constantly changes, but what's certain is meat is no longer served because proprietor Jean Paul Colas says he only wants what is fresh and available, i.e., seafood and produce. Dinner is consistently enjoyable, with the night sounds of the tropics and oldies like Bobby Darin's "Beyond the Sea." Didier Spindler, co-owner and pastry chef, makes a superb almond pastry with vanilla sauce with nuts from the overhanging trees. ⊠ *La Savane, Terre-de-Haut,* ☎ *590/99–50–99. AE, MC, V.*

$$ ✕ **La Saladerie.** This delightful seaside terrace restaurant serves a so-
★   phisticated mélange of creole and Continental dishes. You might begin with a warm crêpe filled with lobster, conch, octopus, and fish. Entrées include an assortment of smoked fish served cold and stuffed fish fillet in a white-wine sauce. The wine list is pleasantly varied. ⊠ *Anse Mirre, Terre-de-Haut,* ☎ *590/99–53–43. MC, V.*

$$ ✕ **El Dorado.** This plant-filled creole-style house with a double veranda—on Bourg's delightful main square—is the setting for tasty creole fare. Go with the cod fritters with dog sauce, the chicken Columbo, or the warm goat cheese on toast with salad and the fresh fish or lobster from the grill. The ice cream is the best—be it rum raisin or coffee. What makes this place special is that wife Roselle cooks and Guy, her husband, is the very personable, English-speaking host. Breakfast, lunch, and dinner are available. ⊠ *Bourg, Terre-de-Haut,* ☎ *590/99–54–31, VHF 68. AE, MC, V. Closed Sun.*

$ ✕ **Nilce's Bar.** A large creole-style house on the waterfront is the setting for this piano bar-restaurant. Owner Ghyslain Laps serves breakfast, lunch, and dinner, as well as a wide selection of ice cream, in the upstairs dining room. Downstairs, local musicians (including Laps's wife, Nilce) perform Brazilian, French, and creole music. Dogs and children wander about—it's very casual and informal. ⊠ *Bourg, Terre-de-Haut,* ☎ *590/99–56–80. AE, MC, V.*

FRENCH

$$ ✕ **Le Genois.** On the waterfront, to the left of the ferry dock, this one
★ has it all—location, creative French-island cuisine, cool music, an exceptional wine list, and personality endowed by its owners Philip, an English-speaking, French lawyer and his beautiful wife (and chef) Chantrelle. Begin with a smoked swordfish pâté with red peppers and chiles. Perfect soufflés of lobster, fish, or cheese can be had with a "real" salad (the usual is shredded root vegetables). Duck breast in a fruit and wine sauce with smashed green papaya is an example of the daily specials. Desserts, including black chocolate pie, banana tarte Tatin, and white chocolate fondant with caramel sauce, are incredible. A fun place with tapas at Happy Hour, it caters to yachters and sponsors the annual Genois regatta. Philip has started a Havana Club for the celebration of fine Cuban cigars. ⊠ *Terre-de-Haut,* ☎ *590/99–53–01, VHF 69. MC, V.*

Marie-Galante

SEAFOOD

$$ ✕ **Le Touloulou.** On the curve of Petite-Anse beach, this ultracasual eatery serves sumptuous seafood at down-to-earth prices. Chef José Viator's standouts include conch *feuilleté* (in puff pastry) with yams. There are set menus for 60F, 95F, 120F, and 150F. ⊠ *Petite-Anse,* ☎ *590/97–32–63. MC, V. Closed Mon. and mid-Sept.–mid-Oct.*

Beaches

Guadeloupe's beaches are generally narrow (particularly since the hurricanes of 1995) and tend to be cluttered with cafés and cars (when the parking spots fill up, folks create impromptu lots in the sand). But all beaches are free and open to the public; for a small fee, hotels allow nonguests to use changing facilities, towels, and beach chairs. On the southern coast of Grande-Terre, from Ste-Anne to Pointe des Châteaux, you'll find stretches of soft white sand. Along the western shore of Basse-Terre you'll see signposts to many small beaches. The sand starts turning gray as you reach Ilet de Pigeon (Pigeon Island); it becomes volcanic black farther south. There is one official nudist beach (noted below), and topless bathing is common. Note that the Atlantic waters on the northeast coast of Grande-Terre are too rough for swimming.

Anse de la Gourde is a beautiful stretch of sand that is popular on weekends. **Plage Caravelle,** southwest of Ste-Anne, is one of Grande-Terre's longest and (the occasional dilapidated shack aside) prettiest stretches of sand. Protected by reefs, it's also a fine snorkeling spot. Club Med occupies one end of this beach; nude bathing is no longer permitted. **Ilet du Gosier** is a little speck off the shore of Gosier where you can bathe in the buff. Take along a picnic for an all-day outing. The beach is closed on weekends. **Pointe Tarare,** a secluded sandy strip just before the tip of Pointe des Châteaux, is the island's only official nudist beach. There's a small bar-café in the parking area—a four-minute walk away. **Souffleur,** on the west coast of Grande-Terre and north of Port-Louis, has brilliant, flamboyant trees that bloom in the summer. There are no facilities on the beach, but you can buy picnic supplies from nearby shops.

La Grande-Anse, north of Deshaies on Basse-Terre's northwest coast, has soft beige sand sheltered by palms; it's probably the best on the island. There's a large parking area but no facilities other than those at a nearby restaurant. **Malendure** Beach lies on Basse-Terre's west coast, in Bouillante across from Pigeon Island.

Anse Crawen is a secluded ½-mi (¾-km) stretch of white sand on Terre-de-Haut (one of the Isles des Saintes) and is popular with families on Sunday. **Les Pompierres,** a palm-fringed stretch of tawny sand, is a popular beach on Terre-de-Haut.

Anse Carot, like all the beaches on Marie-Galante, is longer, wider, and less crowded than other beaches in Guadeloupe. **Anse de Vieux Fort,** on Marie-Galante, is known as a beach for lovers. **Petite-Anse,** on Marie-Galante, is a long beach with golden sand that is crowded with locals on weekends. The only facilities are at the little seafood restaurant nearby. Marie-Galante's **Plage de Folle Anse** is perfect for a sunset walk.

Outdoor Activities and Sports

BICYCLING

The French are mad about *le cyclisme,* so if you want to feel like a native, take to two wheels. Pedal fever hits the island in August every year, when hundreds of cyclists converge here for the 10-day Tour de Guadeloupe, which covers more than 800 mi (1,290 km). On Grande-Terre you can rent bikes in Grand Camp at **Eli Sport** (⊠ Rond Point de Grand-Camp, ☎ 590/90–37–50). In St-François you can rent from **Espace VTT** (☎ 590/88–79–91). On Iles des Saintes try **Localizes** (⊠ Place des Débarcadere, Terre-de-Haut, ☎ 590/99–51–99).

BOATING AND SAILING

If you plan to sail these waters, you should be aware that the winds and currents tend to be strong. There are excellent, well-equipped marinas in Pointe-à-Pitre, Bas-du-Fort, Deshaies, St-François, and Gourbeyre. You can rent a yacht (bareboat or crewed) from the following companies: **Cap Sud** (⊠ 3 pl. Creole, Bas-du-Fort, ☎ 590/90–76–70); **Stardust** (⊠ Lagon Bleu, Gosier, ☎ 590/90–92–02).

FISHING

You can fish for bonito, dolphinfish, captain fish, barracuda, kingfish, marlin, swordfish, and tuna. Expect to pay about 3,500F for a half day's boat charter and 4,500F for a full day (800F per person). **Michel** (⊠ Plage de Malendure, Basse-Terre, ☎ 590/85–42–17) is near Pigeon Island.

GOLF

Golf Municipal St-François (⊠ St-François, ☎ 590/88–41–87), across from the Le Méridien and Cocoteraie hotels, is an 18-hole, par-71, Robert Trent Jones–designed course; it has an English-speaking pro, a clubhouse, a pro shop, and electric carts for rental. The greens fees are $30 for nine holes and $50 for the day; carts rent for $27 and $40.

HIKING

With hundreds of trails and countless rivers and waterfalls, the **Parc National de la Guadeloupe,** on Basse-Terre, is a hiker's paradise. Some of the trails should be attempted only with an experienced guide. All tend to be muddy, so wear a good pair of boots. Trips for as many as 12 people are arranged by **Organisation des Guides de Montagnes de la Caraïbe** (⊠ Maison Forestière, Matouba, ☎ 590/99–28–92). A half-day guided tour costs $80; a full day, $150. The acknowledged private-sector pros are at **Parfum d'Aventure** (⊠ Roche Blonval, St-

François, Grande-Terre, ☎ 590/88–47–62). They offer everything from hiking to four-wheel-drive safaris, sea kayaking, and white-water canoeing. **Sport D'av** (✉ La Marina, Gosier, ☎ 590/32–58–41) is a reliable company that organizes both treks and canoe trips.

HORSEBACK RIDING

You can arrange lessons, beach rides, or trips with a picnic lunch through **Le Criolo** (✉ Vieux Bourg, Morne a L'eau, ☎ 590/20–99–34). The half- or full-day excursions offered by **La Manade** (✉ St-Claude, Basse-Terre, ☎ 590/81–52–21) utilize trails through the rain forest and are an interesting place to ride.

SCUBA DIVING

The main diving area, at the **Cousteau Underwater Park** just off Basse-Terre near Pigeon Island, offers routine dives to 60 ft (18 m). But the numerous glass-bottom boats and day-trippers make the site feel like a crowded marine parking lot. That said, the underwater sights are spectacular. Guides and instructors here are certified under the French CMAS (and some have PADI, but none have NAUI). Most operators offer two-hour dives three times per day for about $40–$50 per dive. Hotels and dive operators usually rent snorkeling gear.

Leading operations include the following: **Caraïbes Plongées** (✉ Gosier, Grande-Terre, ☎ 509/90–44–90); **Chez Guy et Christian** (✉ Plage de Malendure, Basse-Terre, ☎ 590/98–82–43); **Les Heures Saines** (✉ Plage de Malendure, Basse-Terre, ☎ 590/98–86–63); and **Aux Aquanautes Antillais** (✉ Plage de Malendure, Basse-Terre, ☎ 590/98–87–30). An all-day scuba-diving cruise on a catamaran to Iles des Saintes is offered by **Croisieres sous le vent** (✉ Plage de Malendure, Basse-Terre, ☎ 590/98–83–73).

On Iles des Saintes itself, you'll find two dive operators: the **Centre Nautique des Saintes** (✉ Plage de la Coline, Terre-de-Haut, ☎ 590/99–54–25) and **Espace Plongé Caraïbes** (✉ Quartier Fond de Curé, Terre-de-Haut, ☎ 590/99–51–84).

SEA EXCURSIONS

The *King Papyrus* (✉ Marina, Bas-du-Fort, Grande-Terre, ☎ 590/90–92–98) is a catamaran that's available for full-day snorkeling outings replete with rum, dances, and games; a moonlight sail is also a possibility. **Nautilus** (✉ Plage de Malendure, Basse-Terre, ☎ 590/98–89–08) offers (rather crowded) glass-bottom-boat tours and snorkeling.

TENNIS

Many hotels have courts (most lighted); if you're not a guest of a hotel with tennis facilities, call ahead for more information and to reserve a court. The **Auberge de la Vieille Tour** (✉ Rte. de Montauban, Gosier, Grande-Terre, ☎ 590/84–23–23) has two courts. **Club Méditerranée La Caravelle** (✉ Quart Carvelle, Ste-Anne, Grande-Terre, ☎ 590/85–49–50) has six courts. **Le Méridien St-François** (✉ Av. de l'Europe, St-François, ☎ 590/88–51–00) has two courts.

On Grande-Terre, you can play at the **Marina Club** (☎ 590/90–84–08) in Pointe-à-Pitre. The **Tennis League of Guadeloupe** (☎ 590/90–90–97) is in the Centre Lamby-Lambert Stadium in Gosier.

WINDSURFING

Most beachfront hotels can help you arrange lessons and rentals. Windsurfing buffs congregate at the **UCPA Hotel Club** (☎ 590/88–64–80) in St-François on Grande-Terre. You can rent a *planche-à-voile* (Windsurfer) through **Callinago** (✉ Gosier, Grande-Terre, ☎ 590/84–25–25).

Shopping

You can find good buys on anything French—perfume, crystal, china, cosmetics, fashions, scarves. Many stores offer a 20% discount on luxury items purchased with traveler's checks or, in some cases, major credit cards. As for local handicrafts, you'll find fine wood carvings, madras table linens, island dolls dressed in madras, woven straw baskets and hats, and *salako* hats made of split bamboo. Of course, there's the favorite Guadeloupean souvenir—rum.

Areas and Malls

Grande-Terre's largest shopping mall, **Destrelland,** has more than 70 stores and is just minutes from the Aéroport International Pôle Caraïbes, which, with its duty-free stores, is a shopping destination in its own right. It is open Monday–Saturday 8:30–8:30. In **Pointe-à-Pitre** you can enjoy browsing in the street stalls around the harbor quay and at the two markets (the best is the Marché de Frébault). The town's main shopping streets are rue Schoelcher, rue de Nozières, and the lively rue Frébault. At the St-John Perse Cruise Terminal there's an attractive mall with about two dozen shops. **Bas-du-Fort**'s two shopping areas are the Cora Shopping Center and the marina, where there are 20 or so boutiques and quite a few restaurants. In **St-François** there are several shops surrounding the marina.

Specialty Items

ART

Brigitte Boesch (☎ 590/88–48–94), a German-born painter who has exhibited all over the world, lives in St-François; her studio is worth a visit. Guadeloupean painter **Joel Nankin** (☎ 590/23–28–24) lives in Baie Mahault. He specializes in masks and acrylic and sand paintings.

CHINA, CRYSTAL, AND SILVER

Rosebleu (✉ 5 rue Frébault, Pointe-à-Pitre, Grande-Terre, ☎ 590/82–93–43; ✉ Aéroport International Pôle Caraïbes, ☎ no phone) sells china, crystal, and silver by top manufacturers, including Christoffle.

COSMETICS, LINGERIE, AND PERFUME

L'Artisan Parfumeur (✉ Centre St-John Perse, Pointe-à-Pitre, Grande-Terre, ☎ 590/83–80–25) sells top French and American brands as well as tropical scents. **Au Bonheur des Dames** (✉ 49 rue Frébault, Pointe-à-Pitre, Grande-Terre, ☎ 590/82–00–30) offers an array of cosmetics and skin-care products in addition to its perfumes. **Phoenicia** (✉ Bas-du-Fort, Grande-Terre, ☎ 590/90–85–56; ✉ 8 rue Frébault, Pointe-à-Pitre, Grande-Terre, ☎ 590/83–50–36; ✉ 121 bis rue Frébault, Pointe-à-Pitre, Grande-Terre, ☎ 590/82–25–75) sells various perfumes. **Vendôme** (✉ 8–10 rue Frébault, Pointe-à-Pitre, Grande-Terre, ☎ 590/83–42–84) is Guadeloupe's exclusive purveyor of Stendhal and Germaine Monteil cosmetics.

HANDICRAFTS

Boutique de la Plage (✉ Bd. Général de Gaulle, Gosier, Grande-Terre, ☎ 590/84–52–51) offers a mind-boggling jumble of items ranging from tacky tchotchkes ("fertility" sculptures, for example) to sublime art naïf canvases for as little as $20. **La Case à Soie** (✉ Ste-Anne, Grande-Terre, ☎ 590/88–11–31) sells flowing silk dresses and scarves in Caribbean colors. The **Centre d'Art Haitien** (✉ 65 Montauban, Gosier, Grande-Terre, ☎ 590/84–32–60) is the place to buy imaginative art. The **Centre Artisanat** (✉ Ste-Anne, Grande-Terre) offers a wide selection of local crafts.

On Basse-Terre, the **Centre de Broderie** (✉ Vieux Fort, ☎ 590/92–04–14) is renowned for its traditional lacework. The center is built into the ruins of Ft. L'Olive, and you can watch local ladies tat intricate tablecloths, napkins, and place mats. This kind of lacework is rare, so prices are *très cher* ($30 for a doily).

On the Iles des Saintes, head for **Mahogany Artisanat** (✉ Bourg, Terre-de-Haut, ☎ 590/99–50–12), which sells Yves Cohen's batik and hand-painted T-shirts in luminescent seashell shades. **Pascal Foy** (✉ Rte. à Pompierres, Bourg, Terre-de-Bas, ☎ 590/99–52–29) produces stunning homages to traditional Creole architecture: paintings of houses that incorporate collage and make marvelous wall hangings. Prices begin at $100. **Didier Spindler** (✉ Terre-de-Haut, ☎ 590/99–50–99) has opened his art gallery in the new row of shops between the dock and the church. His oils depict Caribbean life.

LIQUOR AND TOBACCO

Aéroport International Pôle Caraïbes (☎ 590/21–14–72) has a good selection of island rum and tobacco. **Délice Shop** (✉ 45 rue Achille René-Boisneuf, Pointe-à-Pitre, Grande-Terre, ☎ 590/82–98–24) is the spot for island rum and items from France—from cheese to chocolate.

Nightlife

Cole Porter notwithstanding, Guadeloupeans maintain that the beguine began here (the Martinicans and St. Lucians make the same claim for their islands). Discos come, discos go, and the current music craze is zouk (music with an African-influenced Caribbean rhythm), but the beat of the beguine remains steady. Many resorts have dinner dancing, as well as entertainment by steel bands and folk groups.

BARS AND NIGHTCLUBS

Join Fidel Castro and Che Guevara, whose photos hang proudly on the walls of **Lollapalooza** (✉ 122 Montauban, Gosier, Grande-Terre, ☎ 590/84–58–58) for hot Latin dancing and genuine Cuban rum. **Lele Bar** (✉ Le Méridien St-François, av. de l'Europe, St-François, ☎ 590/88–51–00) draws locals and visitors alike. If you're on Ile des Saintes, check out **Nilce's Bar** (✉ Terre-de-Haut, ☎ 590/99–56–80), at the pier in Bourg.

CASINOS

Both of the island's two casinos are on Grande-Terre, and both have American-style roulette, blackjack, and chemin de fer. Admission is free. The legal age is 18, and you'll need a photo ID. Jacket and tie aren't required, but "proper attire" means no shorts. **Casino de Gosier** (✉ Gosier, ☎ 590/84–79–69) has a bar, restaurant, and cinema next door. It is open Monday–Saturday 7:30 PM–dawn. Slot machines open at 10 AM. **Casino de St-François** (✉ Marina, St-François, ☎ 590/88–41–31) has a snack bar and nightclub and is open weekdays 9 PM–2 AM, weekends 9 PM–3 AM.

DISCOS

Night owls should note that carousing isn't cheap. Most discos charge a cover of at least $20, which includes one drink (drinks cost about $10 each). **Le Barracuda** (✉ Route du Club Méditerranée, Ste-Anne, ☎ 590/88–18–19) is really on fire with the hot dance rhythms of the tropics: zouk, funk, reggae, salsa, and soukouss.

On Grande-Terre, **Caraïbes 2** (✉ Carrefour de Blanchard, Bas-du-Fort, ☎ 590/90–85–27) features Brazilian dancing and erotic spectacles with charming girls from around the world; the ambience is like the Parisian music halls. On Basse-Terre try **La Plantation** (✉ Gourbeyre, ☎ 590/81–23–37), which is the area's top spot; couples dance to zouk, funk, and house on the immense mezzanine dance floor. Outside Gosier, there's **Shiva 1** (☎ 590/23–53–59), in Le Moule, a tri-level with the first floor like the loges in a theater; many local musicians often perform here. **Le Sans Tabou** (⊠ 153, av. Charles de Gaulle, Gosier, ☎ 590/84–31–15) is a high-tech, chrome-covered dance club that plays the music that's hot in New York, London, and Paris to a cosmopolitan clientele. **Zenith** (⊠ Rte. de la Riviera, Gosier, ☎ 590/90–72–04) is one of the island's most exclusive clubs, featuring local creole salsa and remarkable service; there is a view of the sea and a terrace with a pool.

Exploring Guadeloupe

To see each "wing" of the butterfly, you'll need to budget at least one day. Grande-Terre has pretty villages along its south coast and the spectacular Pointe des Châteaux. You can see the main sights in Pointe-à-Pitre in about a half day. Touring the rugged, mountainous Basse-Terre is a challenge. If time is a problem, head straight to the west coast; you could easily spend a day traveling its length, stopping for a bit of sightseeing, lunch, and a swim. For the outlying islands, budget more time and more money, as you'll probably have to stay overnight.

Numbers in the margin correspond to points of interest on the Guadeloupe map.

Grande-Terre

SIGHTS TO SEE

🔟 **Anse Bertrand.** The northernmost village in Guadeloupe lies 4 mi (6½ km) south of La Pointe de la Grande Vigie. It was the Caribs' last refuge and was prosperous in the days of sugar. Most excitement takes place in the St-Jacques Hippodrome, where horse races and cockfights are held. The beach at **Anse Laborde** is good for swimming.

③ **Aquarium de la Guadeloupe.** The Caribbean's largest aquarium is a good place to spend an hour. The well-planned facility is in the marina near Pointe-à-Pitre and features an assortment of tropical fish, crabs, lobsters, moray eels, dorsal spines, trunkfish, and coral. ⊠ *Pl. Créole, off rte. N4,* ☎ *590/90–92–38.* 🎫 *38F.* ⊙ *Daily 9–7.*

② **Bas-du-Fort.** The main attraction in this town is the **Fort Fleur d'Épée**, an 18th-century fortress that hunkers down on a hillside behind a deep moat. It was the scene of hard-fought battles between the French and the English in 1794. You can explore its well-preserved dungeons and battlements and take in a sweeping view of Iles des Saintes and Marie-Galante.

④ **Gosier.** With its red-roofed villas perched above the sea, this could be a small town on the Côte d'Azur. People stroll about with baguettes under their arms or sit at sidewalk cafés reading *Le Monde* and drinking *planteurs,* the local rum punch. It's the island's major tourist center, with hotels and inns, nightclubs, shops, a casino, and a long stretch of sand.

⑫ **Morne-à-l'Eau.** This agricultural city of about 16,000 people is home to an amphitheater-shape cemetery, with black-and-white-checkerboard tombs, elaborate epitaphs, and multicolor (plastic) flowers. On All Saints' Day (November 1) it's the scene of a moving (and photogenic) candlelight service.

⑧ **Le Moule.** Once the capital city of Guadeloupe, this port city of about 24,000 has had more than its share of troubles: it was bombarded by the British in 1794 and 1809 and by a hurricane in 1928. Canopies of flamboyant trees hang over its narrow streets, where colorful vegetable and fish markets do a brisk business. The town hall, with graceful balustrades, and a small 19th-century neoclassical church are on the main square. Le Moule also has a beach protected by a reef, perfect for windsurfing.

⑦ Pointe des Châteaux. The island's easternmost point offers a breathtaking (though windy) view of the Atlantic crashing against huge rocks, carving them into pyramidlike shapes. The majestic cliffs are reminiscent of the headlands of Brittany. There are spectacular views of Guadeloupe's south and east coasts and the island of La Désirade. On weekends locals come in large numbers to walk their dogs, surf, or look for romance.

❶ Pointe-à-Pitre. Although not the capital city, this is the largest commercial and industrial hub in the southwest of Grande-Terre. It's bustling, noisy, and hot—a place of honking horns and traffic jams. By day its pulse is fast, but at night its streets are almost deserted.

The city has suffered severe damage over the years from earthquakes, fires, and hurricanes. The most recent damage was done by Hurricanes Frederick (1979), David (1980), and Hugo (1989). On one side of rue Frébault you can see the remaining French colonial structures; on the other, the modern city. The downtown area has been rejuvenated. Completion of the Centre St-John Perse has transformed old warehouses into a cruise-terminal complex that consists of the Hotel St-John, restaurants, shops, and the port authority headquarters.

The heart of the old city is Place de la Victoire, surrounded by wooden buildings with balconies and shutters and many sidewalk cafés. Place de la Victoire was named in honor of Victor Hugues's 1794 victory over the British. The sandbox trees in the park are said to have been planted by Hugues the day after the victory. During the French Revolution Hugues ordered the guillotine to be set up in the square so the public could witness the bloody end of 300 recalcitrant royalists.

Even more colorful is the bustling marketplace, between rues St-John Perse, Frébault, Schoelcher, and Peynier. It's a cacophonous place, where housewives bargain for papayas, breadfruits, christophenes, tomatoes, and a bright assortment of other produce.

Anyone with an interest in French literature and culture won't want to miss the **Musée St-John Perse.** It's dedicated to Guadeloupe's most famous son and one of the giants of world literature, Alexis Léger, better known as St-John Perse, winner of the Nobel Prize for literature in 1960. Some of his finest poems are inspired by the history and landscape—particularly the sea—of his beloved Guadeloupe. The museum contains a complete collection of his poetry and some of his personal belongings. Before you go, look for his birthplace, at No. 54 rue Achille René-Boisneuf. ☒ *Corner of rues Noizières and Achille René-Boisneuf,* ☎ *590/90–01–92.* 🎫 *10F.* ☉ *Thurs.–Tues. 8:30–12:30 and 2:30–5:30.*

Guadeloupe's other famous son is celebrated at the **Musée Schoelcher.** Victor Schoelcher, a high-minded abolitionist from Alsace, fought against slavery in the French West Indies in the 19th century. The museum contains many of his personal effects, and exhibits trace his life and work. ☒ *24 rue Peynier,* ☎ *590/82–08–04.* 🎫 *10F.* ☉ *Weekdays 8:30–11:30 and 2–5.*

For fans of French ecclesiastical architecture, there's the imposing **Cathédrale de St-Pierre et St-Paul** (✉ rue Alexandre Isaac at rue de l'Eglise), built in 1807. Although battered by hurricanes, it is reinforced with iron pillars and ribs that look like leftovers from the Eiffel Tower. The fine stained-glass windows and creole-style balconies make it worth a look.

⑨ Porte d'Enfer. The Gate of Hell, 1½ mi (2½ km) north of Campêche, marks a dramatic point on the coast where two jagged cliffs are stormed by the wild Atlantic waters. Legend has it that a Madame Coco strolled out across the waves carrying a parasol and vanished without a trace.

⑪ Port Louis. This fishing village of about 7,000 is best known for the Souffleur Beach. It was once one of the island's prettiest, but it has become a little shabby. Still, the sand is fringed by flamboyant trees, and though the beach is crowded on weekends, it's blissfully quiet during the week. There are also spectacular views of Basse-Terre.

⑤ Ste-Anne. In the 18th century this town, 8 mi (13 km) east of Gosier, was a sugar-exporting center. Sand has replaced sugar as the town's most valuable asset. La Caravelle and the other beaches here are among the best in Guadeloupe. On a more spiritual note, Ste-Anne has a lovely cemetery with stark-white tombs.

⑥ St-François. This was once a simple little village primarily involved with fishing and harvesting tomatoes. Increasingly, though, St-François is overtaking Gosier as Guadeloupe's most fashionable tourist resort area (it also has a slightly better climate). The fish and tomatoes are still here, but so are some of the island's ritziest hotels. Avenue de l'Europe runs between the well-groomed 18-hole Robert Trent Jones–designed municipal golf course and the marina. On the marina side, a string of shops, hotels, and restaurants caters to tourists.

Basse-Terre

Yellow butterflies—clouds of them—are the first thing you see when you arrive on Basse-Terre. Rugged, green, and mysterious, this half of Guadeloupe is all mountain trails, lakes, waterfalls, and hot springs. It's the home of La Soufrière volcano, as well as of the capital city, also called Basse-Terre. The northwest coast, between Bouillante and Grande-Anse, is magnificent; the road twists and turns up steep hills smothered in vegetation and then drops down and skirts deep blue bays and colorful seaside towns. Constantly changing light, towering clouds, and frequent rainbows only add to the beauty. The Parc National is crisscrossed by numerous trails, many following the old *traces,* routes that porters once took across the mountains.

SIGHTS TO SEE

㉖ Basse-Terre. Because Pointe-à-Pitre is so much bigger, few people suspect that this little town of 15,000 inhabitants is the capital and administrative center of Guadeloupe. But if you have any doubts, walk up the hill to the state-of-the-art Théâtre Nationale, where some of France's finest theater and opera companies perform. Paid for by the French government, it's a symbol of the new Basse-Terre. The town has had a lot to overcome. Founded in 1640, it has endured not only foreign attacks and hurricanes but sputtering threats from La Soufrière as well. The last major eruption was in the 16th century, though the volcano seemed active enough to warrant evacuating more than 70,000 people in 1975.

Start exploring the city at the imposing 17th-century Fort Louis Delgrès. Its small museum gives a good outline of Basse-Terre's history. The Cathedral of Our Lady of Guadeloupe, to the north across the Rivière aux Herbes, is also worth a look. On boulevard Félix Eboué you can see the impressive colonial buildings housing government offices. Two main squares, both with gardens, Jardin Pichon and Champ d'Arbaud, give you a feel for how the city used to be. Not far from Champ d'Arbaud are the botanical gardens.

For shopping, walk down rue Dr. Cabre, with its brightly painted creole houses and imposing church, Ste-Marie de Guadeloupe. For a flavor of local life, check out the daily vegetable and fruit market on boulevard Basse-Terre, which runs parallel to the ocean. The other main street is rue St-François. For a guided tour climb aboard the **Pom, Pom** (☎ 590/81–24–83), a miniature train that does a circuit of the major sights. The ride costs 40F and lasts 2½ hours.

㉓ Bouillante. The name means "boiling," and so it's no surprise that hot springs were discovered here. However, today the biggest attraction is scuba diving on nearby Pigeon Island, which is accessed by boat from Plage de Malendure. There's an information office on the beach that can help you with diving and snorkeling arrangements.

⑲ Cascade aux Ecrevisses. Part of the Parc National de la Guadeloupe, Crayfish Falls is one of the island's loveliest (and most popular) spots. There's a marked trail (walk carefully—the rocks can be slippery) leading to this splendid waterfall that dashes down into the Corossol River—a good place for a dip. Come early, though, otherwise you probably won't have it to yourself.

㉙ Chutes du Carbet. You can reach three of the Carbet Falls (one drops from 65 ft/20 m, the second from 360 ft/110 m, the third from 410 ft/125 m) via a long, steep path from the village of Habituée. On the way up you'll pass the Grand Étang (Great Pond), a volcanic lake surrounded by interesting plant life. For horror fans there's also the curiously named Étang Zombi, a pond believed to house evil spirits.

㉒ Ilet de Pigeon. This tiny, rocky island, a few hundred yards off the coast, is the site of the Jacques Cousteau Marine Reserve, the best scuba and snorkeling site on Guadeloupe. Les Heures Saines and Chez Guy et Christian, both on the attractive Malendure Beach, conduct diving trips, and the glass-bottom *Aquarium* and *Nautilus* make daily trips to this spectacular site.

⑰ Les Mamelles. Two mountains—Mamelle de Petit-Bourg, at 2,350 ft (719 m), and Mamelle de Pigeon, at 2,500 ft (765 m)—rise in the Parc National de la Guadeloupe. *Mamelle* means "breast," and when you see the mountains, you'll understand why they are so named. Trails ranging from easy to arduous lace up into the surrounding mountains. There's a glorious view from the lookout point 1,969 ft (602 m) up Mamelle de Pigeon. If you're a climber, plan to spend several hours exploring this area.

㉘ Parc Archéologique des Roches Gravées. In the town of Trois-Rivières, this site contains rocks carved by the Arawaks. The park—set in a lovely botanical garden full of moss-covered boulders, stairways cut into the rock, and lush plants—is a haven of tranquillity. ✉ Bord de la Mer, Trois-Rivières, ☎ 590/92–91–88. 🎫 4F. ☉ Daily 9–5.

⑯ Parc National de la Guadeloupe. This 74,100-acre park has been recognized by UNESCO as a Biosphere Reserve. Before going, pick up a *Guide to the National Park* from the tourist office; it rates the hiking trails according to difficulty (note: most mountain trails are in the southern half of the park). The park is bisected by the Route de la Traversée, a 16-mi (26-km) paved road lined with masses of tree ferns, shrubs, flowers, tall trees, and green plantains. It's the ideal point of entry to the park. Wear rubber-soled shoes and take along a swimsuit, a sweater, and perhaps food for a picnic. Try to get an early start to stay ahead of the hordes of cruise-ship passengers who are making a day of it. ⊠ *Administrative Headquarters, rte. de la Traversée, Saint-Claude,* ☎ *590/ 80–86–00.*

⑱ Maison de la Forêt. This part of the Parc National de la Guadeloupe is where you can park and explore various nature trails. The Habitation Beausoleil has a variety of displays that describe (in French) the flora, fauna, and topography of the national park. It's open daily 9– 4:30; admission is free. There are three marked botanical trails and picnic tables.

㉑ Petit-Bourg. The highlight of this town is the **Domaine de Valombreuse,** a nearby floral park. Three hundred species of flowers, spice gardens, and numerous bird species make this a pleasant place for a stroll. There's also a restaurant in the gardens. ⊠ *Petit-Bourg,* ☎ *590/95– 50–50.* 🎫 *38F.* ☉ *Daily 9–5.*

⑮ Pointe-Noire. This town has two small museums devoted to local products. **La Maison du Bois** (☎ 590/98–17–09) offers a glimpse into the traditional use of wood on the island. Superbly crafted musical instruments and furnishings are on sale. It's open Tuesday–Sunday 9:30– 5:30 and charges a 5F admission. Just across the road is **La Maison du Cacao** (☎ 590/98–21–23), at which daily 9–5 for a 25F admission, you can see a working cocoa plantation. Pointe-Noire is a good jumping-off point from which to explore Basse-Terre's little-visited northwest coast. A road skirts magnificent cliffs and tiny coves, dances in and out of thick stands of mahogany and gommier trees, and weaves through unspoiled fishing villages with boats and ramshackle houses as brightly colored as a child's finger painting. One of the most attractive villages is Deshaies (pronounced day).

㉕ St-Claude. Head for the **Le Musée Volcanologique** (⊠ Rue Victor Hugo, St-Claude, ☎ 596/78–15–16), a museum that will tell you everything you need to know about volcanoes. It's open daily 9–5, and admission is 15F.

⑭ Ste-Rose. In addition to a sulfur bath, there are two good beaches (Amandiers and Clugny) and several interesting small museums in Ste-Rose. **Le Domaine de Séverin** (☎ 590/28–91–86), free and open daily 8:30–12:30, is a historic rum distillery with a working waterwheel; the restaurant in a colonial house is known for its accras and colombos.

⑬ Station Thermale de Ravine Chaude René Toribio. It's not Vichy, but this spa is a good place to soak after tackling the trails. It draws upon the area's healthful geothermal waters. Massage, sauna, algae masks, and hydrotherapy are some of the available treatments. The surrounding landscape in the foothills of Grosse Montagne—with its cane fields, country lanes, and colorful little villages—is very pleasant. ⊠ *Le Lamentin,* ☎ *590/25–75–92.* 🎫 *20F.* ☉ *Daily 8–8.*

⑳ Vernou. Many of the old mansions in this area remain in the hands of the original aristocratic families, the *bekés* (Créole for "whites"), who trace their lineage to before the French Revolution. Traipsing along a path that leads beyond the village through the lush forest, you'll come to the waterfall at Saut de la Lézarde (Lizard's Leap).

② **Vieux Fort.** In 1980, 40 local lace makers united to preserve—and display—the ancient tradition of lace making. At the Centre de Broderie you can always see one of them at work. There are handkerchiefs, tablecloths, doilies, and even negligees for sale.

② **Vieux-Habitants.** This was the island's first colony, established in 1635. Beaches, a restored coffee plantation, and the oldest church on the island (1666) make this village worth a stop.

Iles des Saintes

The eight-island archipelago of Iles des Saintes, usually referred to as Les Saintes, dots the waters off the south coast of Guadeloupe. The islands are Terre-de-Haut, Terre-de-Bas, Ilet à Cabrit, Grand Ilet, La Redonde, La Coche, Le Pâté, and Les Augustins. Columbus discovered them on November 4, 1493, and christened them Los Santos in honor of All Saints' Day.

Only Terre-de-Haut and Terre-de-Bas are inhabited, with a combined population of 3,260. Many of les Saintois, as the islanders are called, are fair-haired, blue-eyed descendants of Breton and Norman sailors. Fishing is their main source of income, and the shores are lined with their boats and *filets bleus* (blue nets dotted with burnt-orange buoys). The fishermen wear hats called *salakos,* which look like inverted saucers. They're patterned after a hat said to have been brought here by a seafarer from China or Indonesia.

③ **Terre-de-Haut.** With 5 square mi (13 square km) and a population of about 1,500, Terre-de-Haut is the largest and most developed of Les Saintes. Its "big city" is Bourg, with one street and a few bistros, cafés, and shops. Clutching the hillside are trim white houses with bright red or blue doors, balconies, and gingerbread frills.

Terre-de-Haut's ragged coastline is scalloped with lovely coves and beaches, including the semi-nudist beach at Anse Crawen. The beautiful bay, complete with a "sugarloaf" mountain, has been called a mini Rio. To get around, it's a good idea to rent a motorbike—although Terre-de-Haut is tiny, it's also very hilly. Take your time on these rutted roads because around nearly every bend you're apt to find a herd of goats chomping on a fallen palm frond. This island makes a great day trip, but you'll really get a feel for Les Saintes if you stay over.

Fort Napoléon. This gallery holds a collection of 250 modern paintings, influenced by cubism and surrealism. However, this museum is noted for their exhaustive exhibit of the greatest sea battles ever fought. You can also visit the well-preserved barracks and prison cells, or admire the botanical gardens, which specialize in cacti of all sizes and descriptions. ⊠ *Bourg,* ☎ *590/37–99–59.* 🎟 *20F.* ☉ *Daily 9–12:30.*

Marie-Galante

③ Columbus sighted this 60-square-mi (155-square-km) island on November 3, 1493, the day before he landed at Ste-Marie on Basse-Terre. He named it for his flagship, the *Maria Galanda,* and sailed on. It's dotted with ruined 19th-century sugar mills, and sugar is still its major product. With its rolling hills of green cane still worked by oxen and men with broad-brim straw hats, this island is a journey back to a time when all of Guadeloupe was an agrarian place. Only an hour by high-speed boat from Pointe-à-Pitre, this is where Guadeloupeans come for day trips; it has only just become a tourist destination. The country folk are still a bit shy and have a gentle sense of humor. There are yellow butterflies, pigs tethered by the side of the road, and some of the archipelago's best beaches. Ox-pulling contests, visits to distilleries, days at the beach, or country hikes await you. The dramatic coast is also worth exploring. There are soaring cliffs—such as the Gueule Grand Gouffre (Mouth of the Giant Chasm) and Les Galeries (where the sea has sculpted a natural arcade)—and enormous sun-dappled grottoes, such as Le Trou à Diable, whose underground river can be explored with a guide. After sunset no-see-ums can be a nuisance, especially near beaches.

The **Château Murat** (⊠ Grand-Bourg, ☎ 590/97–94–41) is a restored 17th-century sugar plantation and rum distillery housing exhibits on the history of rum making and sugarcane production and an admirable *ecomusée,* whose displays celebrate local crafts and customs. The château is open daily 9:15–5; admission is 10F.

Le Moulin de Bézard (⊠ Chemin de Nesmond, off D202) is the only rebuilt windmill in the Caribbean. There's a café here and two gift shops. They're housed in replicated slave quarters: tiny cabins (with wattle walls) of a type found only on this island. Admission is 15F; it's open daily 10–2.

You should also make it a point to see the distilleries, especially **Père Labat** (⊠ Heritiers E. Rameau, Marie-Galante, ☎ 590/97–03–44), whose rum is considered one of the finest in the Caribbean and whose atelier turns out lovely pottery; admission is free, and it's open daily 9–5.

An entertainment complex in Grand-Bourg, called **El Rancho,** has a 400-seat movie theater, a restaurant, a terrace grill, a snack bar, a disco, and a few double rooms.

La Désirade

㉜ According to legend, this is the "desired land" of Columbus's second voyage. Like Marie-Galante, it was spotted on November 3, 1493. The 8-square-mi (21-square-km) island, 5 mi (8 km) east of St-François, was a leper colony for many years. Most of today's 1,700 inhabitants are fishermen and boatbuilders. The main settlement is Grande-Anse, which has a pretty church and a couple of lodgings. There are good beaches here and there's little to do but loll around on them.

GUADELOUPE A TO Z

To research prices, get advice from other travelers, and book travel arrangements, visit www.fodors.com.

AIR TRAVEL
Most airlines fly into Aéroport International Pôle Caraïbes.

American has many flights from U.S. cities direct to San Juan, Puerto Rico, with seasonal connections to Guadeloupe on American Eagle. Air Canada has direct flights from Montréal on Saturday. Air France flies nonstop from Paris to Guadeloupe and to Fort-de-France on Martinique and has direct service from Miami and San Juan. Air Caraïbes flies in daily from Martinique, San Juan, St. Martin/St. Maarten, St. Barths, and Santo Domingo in the Dominican Republic. LIAT flies from St. Croix, Antigua, and St. Maarten in the north and is your best bet from Dominica, Martinique, St. Lucia, Grenada, Barbados, and Trinidad.

➤ AIRLINES AND CONTACTS: **American/American Eagle** (☎ 590/87–70–40 or 590/21–11–80); **Air Canada** (☎ 590/21–12–77); **Air Caraïbes** (☎ 590/82–47–00 or 590/21–12–88); **Air France** (☎ 590/82–62–74); **LIAT** (☎ 590/21–13–93).

AIRPORTS

Cabs meet flights at the airport, 3 mi (5 km) from Pointe-à-Pitre. The metered fare is about 60F to Pointe-à-Pitre, 150F to Gosier, and 250F to St-François. Fares go up 40% on Sunday and holidays and from 9 PM to 7 AM. For 6F you can take a bus from the airport to downtown Pointe-à-Pitre.

➤ AIRPORT INFORMATION: **Aéroport International Pôle Caraïbes** (☎ 590/21–14–32).

BIKE AND MOPED RENTALS

You can rent a Vespa (motorbike) at Eli Sport and Equator Moto. A motorbike generally costs 200F per day, including insurance. You'll need to put down a 1,000F deposit. On Terre-de-Haut mopeds start at about 120F a day. There are numerous vendors by the ferry dock; shop around for the best price. On Marie-Galante try Loca Sol.

➤ BIKE AND MOPED RENTALS: **Eli Sport** (✉ Grand Camp, Grande-Terre, ☎ 590/90–37–50); **Equator Moto** (✉ Gosier, Grande-Terre, ☎ 590/90–36–77); **Loca Sol** (✉ rue du Fort, Grand-Bourg, ☎ 590/97–76–58).

BOAT AND FERRY TRAVEL

Express des Isles and Transport Maritime Brudey Frères provide ferry service to Les Saintes and Marie-Galante. Schedules often change, especially on weekends, so check them at the tourist or harbor offices.

FARES AND SCHEDULES

It's a choppy 45-minute crossing to Terre-de-Haut from Trois-Rivières on Basse-Terre; ferries leave at about 8:30 AM (7:30 AM on Sunday) and return about 3 PM. From Pointe-à-Pitre on Grande-Terre it's a 60-minute ride. Departure time is 8 AM, with return at 4 PM, the round-trip fare is 170F.

The ferry to Grand-Bourg on Marie-Galante departs from Pointe-à-Pitre at 8 AM, 2 PM, and 5 PM, with returns at 6 AM, 9 AM, and 3:45 PM. It takes one hour, is 170F round-trip. The *Sotramade Bateau L'Impériale* runs between La Désirade and St-François on Grande-Terre, departing daily at 8 AM and 4 PM. Return ferries depart daily at 3:30 PM.

The *Express des Isles* has service to Dominica (470F, 2½ hours) and Martinique (490F, four hours) from Pointe-à-Pitre. The ferry departs at 8 AM four days a week; check schedules for changes. If you are not prone to seasickness, this can be the most direct and least costly way to get to Martinique.

➤ BOAT AND FERRY INFORMATION: *Express des Isles* (☎ 590/83–12–45 or 590/83–04–43); *Sotramade Bateau L'Impériale* (☎ 590/88–58–06); **Transport Maritime Brudey Frères** (☎ 590/90–04–48).

BUSINESS HOURS

BANKS

Banks are open weekdays 8–noon and 2–4. Crédit Agricole, Banque Populaire, and Société Générale de Banque aux Antilles have branches that are open Saturday. In summer most banks are open 8–3. Banks close at noon the day before a legal holiday that falls during the week.

POST OFFICES

Post offices are open weekdays 8–noon and 2–4.

SHOPS

Shops are open weekdays 8 or 8:30–noon and 2:30–6.

CAR RENTALS

There are rental offices at Aéroport International Pôle Caraïbes and the major resorts. Count on spending about $60 a day for a small car. Note: allow yourself an extra 30 minutes to drop off your car at the end of your stay—the rental return sites are still at the old airport, Le Raizet, 2 mi (3 km) away.

➤ Major Agencies: **Avis** (☎ 590/21–13–54 or 590/85–00–11); **Budget** (☎ 590/21–13–48); **Europcar** (☎ 590/21–13–52); **Hertz** (☎ 590/21–13–46); **Jumbo Car** (☎ 590/91–42–17).

CAR TRAVEL

If you are based in Gosier or at a larger resort, you will probably not need a car for your entire stay. Most visitors rent a car for a day or two of sightseeing. But if driving isn't your thing, taxis are always available.

GASOLINE

Gas is expensive, at about 7F per liter (roughly $4 per gallon).

ROAD CONDITIONS

Guadeloupe has 1,225 mi (1,976 km) of roads (marked as in Europe), and driving around Grande-Terre is relatively easy. On Basse-Terre it will take more effort to navigate the hairpin bends on the mountains and around the eastern shore. Guadeloupeans are skillful (and fast) drivers. At night these roads are poorly lit and treacherous.

RULES OF THE ROAD

Driving is on the right, as in the U.S. and Europe. Your valid driver's license will suffice for up to 20 days, after which you'll need an international driver's permit.

ELECTRICITY

Electricity is 220 volts (though some hotels have 110 volts), so if you're visiting from North America, you'll need to pack an adapter and a converter to use any appliances you bring with you.

EMERGENCIES

Pharmacies alternate in staying open around the clock. The tourist offices or your hotel can help you locate the pharmacist that's on duty and/or find an English-speaking doctor.

➤ Ambulance and Fire: Dial (☎ 15) for an ambulance. Dial ☎ 18 for a fire truck. **SAMU** (☎ 590/89–11–00). **SOS Taxi ambulance** (☎ 590/82–89–33).

➤ Hospitals: **Centre Hôpitalier de Pointe-à-Pitre** (✉ Abymes, ☎ 590/89–10–10).

➤ Police: Dial (☎ 17) in an emergency. On Grande-Terre (☎ 590/82–13–17). On Basse-Terre (☎ 590/81–11–55).

ETIQUETTE AND BEHAVIOR

Ask permission before taking a picture of an islander, and don't be surprised if the answer is a firm "No." Guadeloupeans are also deeply religious and traditional. Don't offend them by wearing short-shorts or swimwear off the beach.

FESTIVALS AND SEASONAL EVENTS

Carnival starts in early January and continues until Lent, finishing with a parade of floats and costumes on Mardi Gras (Fat Tuesday) and a huge bash on Ash Wednesday. On a Sunday in early August, Point-à-Pitre on Grande-Terre holds the Fête des Cuisinières, which celebrates the masters of creole cuisine with a five-hour banquet that's open to the public. The festival was started in 1916 by a guild of female cooks who wanted to honor the patron saint of cooks, St. Laurent. August also sees the Tour Cycliste de la Guadeloupe, a highly competitive bike race that begins in Point-à-Pitre and covers more than 800 mi (1,290 km) on both Grande-Terre and Basse-Terre.

HEALTH

Water is safe to drink, though most people drink bottled water anyway. Beware of the manchineel tree, whose green fruit, which looks like an apple, is poisonous; even standing under the tree during a rainstorm is inadvisable since residue from the leaves can burn your skin. However, most trees are labeled as such.

HOLIDAYS

Public holidays for 2002 are: New Year's Day, Ash Wednesday (Feb. 28), Good Friday (Apr. 13), Easter Monday (Apr. 18), Labor Day (May 1), Bastille Day (July 14), Assumption Day (August 15), All Saints' Day (Nov. 1), Armistice Day (Nov. 11), and Christmas.

LANGUAGE

The official language is French. Everyone also speaks a Creole patois, which you won't be able to understand even if you're fluent in French. In the major hotels most of the staff knows some English, but communicating may be more difficult in the countryside and in stores. Some taxi drivers speak a little English. Arm yourself with a phrase book, a dictionary, patience, and a sense of humor.

MAIL AND SHIPPING

Postcards to the United States cost 3.80F and to Canada 4.40F; letters up to 20 grams, 5.20F. Postcards and letters to Europe cost 3F. Stamps can be purchased at post offices, *café-tabacs*, hotel newsstands, and souvenir shops. When writing to Guadeloupe, be sure to include the name of the specific island in the archipelago (e.g., Grande-Terre, Basse-Terre, etc.) as well as the postal code, Guadeloupe, and the French West Indies.

MONEY MATTERS

Prices quoted throughout the chapter are in U.S. dollars unless otherwise noted.

ATMS

There are ATMs that accept Visa and MasterCard at Aéroport International Pôle Caraïbes and at some banks—such as Crédit Agricole, Banque Populaire, and Société Générale de Banque aux Antilles, and BDAF; they dole out francs, though they don't always work with foreign ATM cards.

CURRENCY

Legal tender is the French franc until June 2002, when the euro will replace it permanently. Some places accept U.S. dollars, but it's best to change your money into the local currency. You can exchange your money at a bank or at your hotel, but you tend to get better rates at a bureau de change, such as Change Caraïbe, which is near both the tourist office and market in Point-à-Pitre.

➤ CONTACTS: **Change Caraïbe** (✉ 21 rue de Rene Frebault, Point-à-Pitre).

PASSPORTS AND VISAS

All visitors from the United States, Canada, and the United Kingdom need a passport and a return or ongoing ticket.

SAFETY

Put your valuables in the hotel safe. Don't leave them unattended in your room or on the beach. It isn't a good idea to walk around Pointe-à-Pitre at night, since it's almost deserted after dark. If you rent a car, always lock it with luggage and valuables stashed out of sight.

SIGHTSEEING TOURS

Guides de Montagne de la Caraïbe provides guides for hiking tours in the mountains. Emeraude Guadeloupe offers everything from hikes up the volcano to botanical tours and visits to creole homes. Guides are certified by the state, but you'll probably need some French to understand them. For those who really want a challenge, Parfum d'Aventure offers adventure trips on Basse-Terre, including canoeing on the Lézarde, sea kayaking, four-wheel driving, and hiking. Sport D'av can set you up with adventures on Basse-Terre, including mountain climbing, sea kayaking, hiking, and diving.

➤ CONTACTS: **Guides de Montagne de la Caraïbe** (✉ Maison Forestière, Matouba, Basse-Terre, ☎ 590/99–28–92 or 590/92–06–10); **Emeraude Guadeloupe** (✉ St-Claude, ☎ 590/81–98–28); **Parfum d'Aventure** (✉ Roche Blonval, St-François, Grande-Terre, ☎ 590/88–47–62); **Sport D'av** (✉ Jarry, ☎ 590/32–58–41) .

TAXES

DEPARTURE TAX

A departure tax is built into your airline ticket.

SALES TAX

The *taxe de séjour* (room tax) varies from hotel to hotel but never exceeds 12F per person, per day. Most hotel prices include a 10%–15% service charge; if not, it will be added to your bill.

TAXIS

Taxis are metered and fairly pricey, and on Sunday, holidays, and between 9 PM and 7 AM, fares increase by 40%. If your French is in working order, you can call for a radio cab. For an English-speaking, professional taxi driver and tour guide, call Narcisse Taxi. Tourist offices or your hotel can arrange for an English-speaking taxi driver and even organize a small group for you to share the cost of a tour.

➤ TAXI CONTACTS: **Narcisse Taxi** (☎ 590/35–27–29 or 590/83–24–79; on Basse-Terre ☎ 590/81–79–70); **radio cabs** (☎ 590/82–00–00, 590/83–09–55, and 590/20–74–74).

TELEPHONES

Coin-operated phones are rare. If you need to make many calls outside of your hotel, purchase a *télécarte* at the post office or other outlets marked TÉLÉCARTE EN VENTE ICI. Télécartes look like credit cards and are used in special booths labeled TÉLÉCOM. Local and international calls made with these cards are cheaper than operator-assisted calls. (Note: you can't place collect or credit-card calls to the United States from Guadeloupe.)

COUNTRY AND AREA CODES

To call direct from the U. S., dial 011–590, then the local number.

LOCAL CALLS

To make on-island calls, simply dial the six-digit phone number.

TIPPING

Restaurants are legally required to include a 15% gratuity in the menu price, and no additional gratuity is necessary (although appreciated if service is exceptional). Tip skycaps and porters about 7F. Many cab drivers own their own cabs and don't expect a tip. You won't have any trouble ascertaining if a 10% tip is expected.

VISITOR INFORMATION

➤ BEFORE YOU LEAVE: **French Government Tourist Office In the U.S.:** (✉ 444 Madison Ave., New York, NY 10022, ☎ 212/659–7779; ✉ 9454 Wilshire Blvd., Beverly Hills, CA 90212, ☎ 310/276–2835; ✉ 645 N. Michigan Ave., Chicago, IL 60611, ☎ 312/337–6339; WEB www.francetourism.com). **In Canada:** (✉ 1981 McGill College Ave., Suite 490, Montréal, Québec H3A 2W9, Canada, ☎ 514/288–4264; ✉ 30 St. Patrick St., Suite 700, Toronto, Ontario M5T 3A3, Canada, ☎ 416/593–6427). **In the U.K.:** (✉ 178 Piccadilly, London W1V 0AL, U.K., ☎ 0171/499–6911).

➤ IN GUADELOUPE: **Office Départemental du Tourisme** (✉ 5 sq. de la Banque [Box 1099], Pointe-à-Pitre, 97181, ☎ 590/82–09–30); **Syndicats d'Initiatives** (✉ Av. de l'Europe, St-François, 97118, ☎ 590/88–48–74; Marie-Galante ☎ 590/97–56–51).

Updated by
Paris Permenter
and John
Bigley

Around one bend of the winding North Coast Highway lies a palatial home; around another, a shanty without doors or windows. The towns are frenetic centers of activity, filled with pedestrians, street vendors, and neighbors visiting. Roads are crammed with vehicles and full of honking—not a chorus of hostility but notes of greeting or of friendly caution or just for the heck of it. Drivers wait patiently while groups of uniformed schoolchildren and women bearing loads on their heads cross the street, and a spirit of cooperation prevails amid chaos.

The cultural life of Jamaica is a wealthy one; its music, art, and cuisine have a spirit that's as hard to describe as the rhythms of reggae or an outburst of streetwise patois. Although 95% of the population traces its bloodlines to Africa, Jamaica is a stockpot of cultures, including those of other Caribbean islands, Great Britain, the Middle East, India, China, Germany, Portugal, and South America. The third-largest island in the Caribbean (after Cuba and Hispaniola), Jamaica enjoys a considerable self-sufficiency based on tourism, agriculture, and mining.

The island's physical attractions include jungle mountaintops, clear waterfalls, and unforgettable beaches, and its tourist areas are grouped around the northern and western coastlines. Ocho Rios (often just Ochi) is a major cruise port, resort center, and the home of Dunn's River Falls, probably the most photographed spot in the nation. Montego Bay (or MoBay, as it's affectionately known), destination of most tourist flights, is a sprawling blend of opulent beach resorts and commerce. At the island's western tip lies Negril, once a sleepy hangout for bohemian travelers; though now bigger and glitzier, it's still a haven for the hip and the hedonistic. In addition to these pleasure capitals, Jamaica has a real capital in Kingston. For all its congestion—and for all the disparity between city life and the bikinis and parasails to the north—Kingston is the true heart and head of the island. This is where politics, literature, music, and art wrestle for acceptance in the largest (800,000 people) English-speaking city in the Western hemisphere south of Miami.

The first group known to have reached Jamaica were the Arawak Indians, who paddled their canoes from the Orinoco region of South America around AD 1000. In 1494 Christopher Columbus stepped ashore at what is now called Discovery Bay. Having spent four centuries on the island, the Arawaks had little notion that his footsteps on their sand would mean their extinction within 50 years thanks to overwork, cruelty, and European diseases. When the indigenous population died out, the Spanish brought African slaves to the island.

What is now St. Ann's Bay was established as New Seville in 1509 and served as the Spanish capital until the local government crossed the island to Santiago de la Vega (now Spanish Town). The Spaniards were never impressed with Jamaica; they found no precious metals, and they let the island fester in poverty for 161 years. When 5,000 British soldiers and sailors appeared in Kingston Harbor in 1655, the Spaniards didn't put up a fight.

The arrival of the English and the three centuries of rule that followed provided Jamaica with the genteel underpinnings of its present life—and a period of history enlivened by a rousing pirate tradition that was fueled by rum. The very British 18th century was a time of prosperity for Jamaican landholders. This was the age of the sugar baron, who ruled his plantation great house—and his slaves—and made the island the largest sugar-producing colony in the world.

The British were challenged soon after their arrival, however, by the Maroons, former slaves the Spanish had freed and armed to harass the island's new rulers. (Other accounts say the Maroons were actually escaped slaves, named for the Spanish word *cimarrón*: wild.) The Maroons took to the most rugged regions of the island, led by the runaway slave and head of an Ashanti freedom-fighting family, Cudjoe. The First Maroon War (1690–1739) was played out across the island using guerrilla warfare. The island then remained quiet until 1760, when a slave rebellion broke out; later that century the Second Maroon War began. Tensions reached a peak in 1832 with the hanging of a Baptist minister, Sam Sharpe, in Montego Bay—punishment for his role as ringleader in an island-wide slave rebellion. Three years later slavery was abolished. Today the hanging is remembered at Sam Sharpe Square in the midst of bustling MoBay with a statue of the fallen leader; nearby "the Cage," once used to imprison runaways, is another solemn reminder of this period in Jamaican history.

The second half of the 20th century brought independence to Jamaica. On August 6, 1962, the island became an independent nation, although still a member of the British Commonwealth. The government is headed by a freely elected prime minister. Two political parties, the People's National Party (PNP) and the Jamaica Labour Party (JLP), vie for this position, and elections can become heated, even violent, events. Elections in 1980 resulted in many deaths, mostly in Kingston's ghettos. The late 1997 election was carefully monitored by a contingent that included Jimmy Carter and Colin Powell. But the mood remained peaceful throughout most of the island, in spite of an economy marked by high unemployment, low wages, and high interest rates. In April 1999 the island experienced brief riots over an increase in the gasoline tax.

Today's Jamaica is a place where poverty is rampant, and many citizens must work at the fringes of the tourist industry as unlicensed taxi drivers, hair braiders, and vendors who walk the beaches in search of a vacationer. Being hassled is one of the most common complaints by travelers to Jamaica, and the government has increased fines and even penalties of jail time for hassling tourists. Many problems involve attempts to sell marijuana, or *ganja,* an illegal product.

Smoking of sacramental ganja and flowing dreadlocks are the most recognized aspects of Rastafarianism, a religion that believes in the divinity of Haile Selassie, former emperor of Ethiopia. The Rastas gained strength in the 1960s, inspired in part by the 1930s movement led by Jamaican Marcus Garvey, founder of the U.S.–based Universal Negro Improvement Association. Garvey advocated black pride, which, along with his "back to Africa" message, was picked up by the Rastas, who embraced Ethiopia as their homeland. Today the Rastas are a small sector of the Jamaican population, but they are known internationally because of prominent Rastas such as the late reggae singer Bob Marley.

The reggae rhythms and lyrics for which Marley is known provide a peek at the Jamaican culture, but music is just one aspect of this rich island. Travelers here find a multitude of melodies—from the sizzle of jerk pork on a roadside grill to the lap of waves on a sandy beach, the call of the magnificent doctor bird flitting through the trees, or the quiet whistle of a breeze through the Blue Mountains.

Lodging

Jamaica was the birthplace of the Caribbean all-inclusive resort, a concept that took the Club Med idea and gave it an excess-in-the-tropics spin. The all-inclusive is the most popular vacation option here, offering incredible values, with rates from $145 to $350 per person per night. Prices usually include airport transfers, accommodations, three meals a day plus snacks, all bar drinks (often including premium liquors) and soft drinks, a plethora of sports options (from scuba diving to golf), nightly entertainment, and all gratuities and taxes. Usually the only surcharges are for such luxuries as massages, tours, and weddings or vow-renewal ceremonies (though even these are often included at high-end establishments). The all-inclusives have branched out, some of them courting families, others going after an upper crust that wouldn't even have picked up a brochure a few years ago.

If you like to get out and explore, you may prefer an EP property. Many places offer MAP or FAP packages that include such extras as airport transfers and tours. Even if you don't want to be tied down to a meal plan, it pays to inquire because the savings can be considerable.

Jamaica's resorts and hotels have varying policies about children; some don't accept children under 16 or 18 years old, but those that do often allow up to two to stay in their parents' room at no additional charge. Others allow kids to stay free in the off-season or offer discounted meal plans. Baby-sitting is readily available at properties that accept children, and several offer fully supervised kids' programs. If you plan to bring the kids, ask lots of questions before making a reservation, or have your travel agent find the best deal. In addition, some resorts are for male-female couples only. If you're a same-sex couple or a single parent traveling with one child, ask lots of questions before booking a room in a couples-only establishment.

Please note that the price categories listed below are based on winter rates. As a rule, rates are reduced anywhere from 10% to 30% from April 30 to December 15. All price categories are based on standard double rooms at the most comprehensive (and most expensive) meal-plan rate. Opting for a less comprehensive plan (if it's available in winter) can save you 20%–40%. The **Jamaica Reservations Service** (☎ 800/526–2422 in the U.S. and Canada) can book resorts, hotels, villas, and guest houses throughout the country.

CATEGORY	COST EP/CP*	COST MAP*	COST AI*
$$$$	over $245	over $250	over $275
$$$	$175–$245	$190–$250	$225–$275
$$	$105–$175	$130–$190	$175–$225
$	under $105	under $130	under $175

*EP prices are for a standard double room for two in winter, excluding 15% tax and any service charge. Many hotels either include breakfast in the tariff or offer a CP price, which includes breakfast as their minimum plan.
**MAP prices include daily breakfast and dinner for two in winter. Often, MAP packages include use of nonmotorized water sports and other benefits.
***All-inclusive (AI) winter prices are per person, double occupancy, and include tax, service, gratuities, all meals, drinks, facilities, lessons, and airport transfers. Motorized water sports and scuba diving are sometimes included; if it's important to you, ask.

Kingston

Some of the island's finest business hotels are in Kingston, and these high towers are filled with rooftop restaurants, English pubs, theater and dance presentations, art museums and galleries, jazz clubs, upscale supper clubs, and disco dives.

$$$$ ⊡ **Strawberry Hill.** One of many island properties owned by Chris
★ Blackwell, formerly the head of Island Records (the late Bob Marley's label), this Blue Mountains retreat 45 minutes north of Kingston offers refined luxury and absolute peace. Authors, musicians, and screenwriters come here for extended periods to relax, rejuvenate the creative juices (perhaps in the Aveda spa), and work. The food is top-notch, as are the staff and the accommodations—elegant Georgian-style villas with mahogany furnishings and private balconies with grand vistas. There's no air-conditioning here, simply because it's not needed at 3,100 ft (948 m) above sea level. Sunday brunch, with an enormous Jamaican buffet, is an affair to remember, but reserve a spot early—it's a favored event among Kingston's movers and shakers. ⊠ *New Castle Rd., Irishtown, St. Andrew,* ☎ *876/944–8400 or 800/688–7678,* FAX *876/944–8408,* WEB *www.islandoutpost.com/StrawberryHill. 12 1-, 2-, and 3-bedroom villas. Restaurant, bar, refrigerators, room service, pool, sauna, spa, croquet, airport shuttle. AE, MC, V. CP.*

$$$ ⊡ **Hilton Kingston.** This high-rise is the best of Kingston's business hotels. The expansive marble lobby leads to attractive, well-appointed guest rooms. The concierge floors include complimentary cocktails, hors d'oeuvres, and Continental breakfast. There are lots of extras throughout: secured-access elevators, an American Airlines service desk, and in-room coffee and tea setups. Rates include admission to Jonkanoo, the hotel's hot nightclub; there's also an art gallery. A meal in the Palm Court will surely make your day (or night). ⊠ *77 Knutsford Blvd. (Box 112),* ☎ *876/926–5430 or 800/445–8667,* FAX *876/929–7439,* WEB *www.caribehilton.com. 284 rooms, 13 suites, 6 1- and 2-bedroom units. 2 restaurants, 3 bars, in-room data ports, in-room safes, pool, massage, sauna, 2 tennis courts, health club, shops, nightclub, recreation room, concierge. AE, DC, MC, V. EP, MAP.*

$$$ ⊡ **Le Méridien Pegasus.** You'll find an efficient, accommodating staff and Old World decor at this 17-story complex near downtown. All rooms have balconies and large windows that face the Blue Mountains, the pool, or the Caribbean. There's also an excellent business center, duty-free shops, and 24-hour room service. ⊠ *81 Knutsford Blvd. (Box 333),* ☎ *876/926–3690 or 800/225–5843,* FAX *876/929–5855,* WEB *www.meridienjamaica.com. 325 rooms, 16 suites. Restaurant, 2 bars, coffee shop, in-room safes, minibars, room service, pool, wading pool, hair salon, 2 tennis courts, basketball, gym, jogging, shops, playground, concierge, business services. AE, DC, MC, V. EP, MAP.*

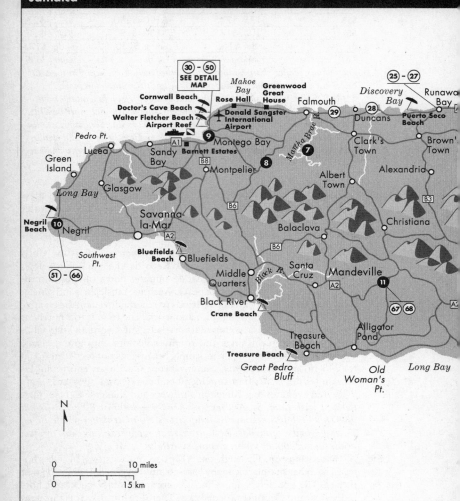

N

0		10 miles
0		15 km

Lodging

Astra Country
Inn & Restaurant . . . **67**

Breezes
Runaway Bay **25**

Charela Inn **55**

Coco La Palm . . . **65**

Comfort Suites **22**

Couples Negril . . **66**

Couples
Ocho Rios **21**

Couples Swept
Away Negril **57**

Crowne Plaza
Kingston **4**

Dragon Bay **11**

Enchanted
Garden **17**

FDR, Franklyn
D. Resort **26**

Goblin Hill **10**

Grand Lido
Braco **28**

Grand Lido
Negril **60**

Grand Lido
Sans Souci **15**

Hedonism II **59**

Hedonism III . . **27**

Hilton Kingston **3**

Hotel Mocking
Bird Hill **9**

Jamaica Inn **14**

Jamaica Palace . . **13**

Mandeville
Hotel **68**

Le Méridien
Pegasus **7**

Morgan's Harbour
Hotel, Beach
Club, and
Yacht Marina **69**

Negril Cabins
Resort **62**

Point Village **63**

Renaissance
Jamaica
Grande **20**

Rockhouse **53**

Sandals Dunn's
River Golf Resort
and Spa **24**

Sandals Negril
Beach Resort
and Spa **61**

Starfish Trelawny . . **29**

Strawberry Hill **8**

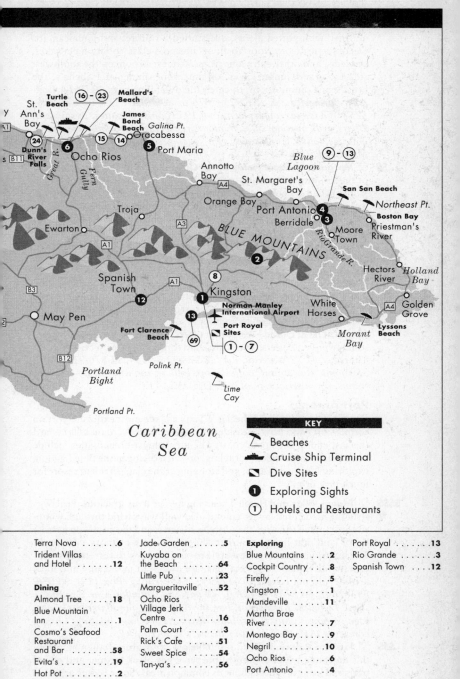

KEY

Beaches
Cruise Ship Terminal
Dive Sites
1 Exploring Sights
① Hotels and Restaurants

Terra Nova 6
Trident Villas
and Hotel 12

Dining

Almond Tree 18
Blue Mountain
Inn 1
Cosmo's Seafood
Restaurant
and Bar 58
Evita's 19
Hot Pot 2

Jade Garden 5
Kuyaba on
the Beach 64
Little Pub 23
Margueritaville . . .52
Ocho Rios
Village Jerk
Centre 16
Palm Court 3
Rick's Cafe 51
Sweet Spice 54
Tan-ya's 56

Exploring

Blue Mountains 2
Cockpit Country . . .8
Firefly 5
Kingston 1
Mandeville 11
Martha Brae
River 7
Montego Bay 9
Negril 10
Ocho Rios 6
Port Antonio 4

Port Royal 13
Rio Grande 3
Spanish Town 12

$$ ⊡ **Crowne Plaza Kingston.** On a hill in Constant Spring, a classy Kingston suburb, this ocher-color high-rise has sophisticated public areas adorned with potted plants, overstuffed furniture, and Jamaican art. Decor varies from floor to floor. Business-class rooms have faxes, modems, and other extra amenities. Request a room on the southwest side for grand sunset views, or time your dinner at Isabella's, the hotel's fine dining room, to catch the dwindling rays. ⊠ *211A Constant Spring Rd.,* ☎ *876/925–7676 or 800/618–6534,* FAX *876/925–5757,* WEB *www.crowneplaza.com. 193 rooms, 26 suites. Restaurant, 2 bars, grill, in-room safes, minibars,refrigerators, room service, pool, massage, sauna, tennis court, gym, jogging, squash, concierge. AE, DC, MC, V. EP.*

$$ ⊡ **Morgan's Harbour Hotel, Beach Club, and Yacht Marina.** A favorite of the sail-into-Jamaica set, this small property has 22 acres of beachfront at the very entrance to the old pirates' town. Done in light tropical prints, the rooms are very basic, but many have a balcony and a mini-refrigerator; the suites with loft bedrooms are the nicest. Ask for one in the newer wing. ⊠ *Port Royal,* ☎ *876/967–8030 or 876/967–8040,* FAX *876/967–8073. 45 rooms, 6 suites. Restaurant, bar, room service, pool, volleyball, dive shop, snorkeling, boating, fishing, billiards, dance club, airport shuttle. AE, MC, V. EP.*

$$ ⊡ **Terra Nova.** This intimate hotel is in a quieter part of New Kingston, 1 mi (1½ km) from the commercial district and within walking distance of Devon House, a historic home surrounded by boutiques and fine restaurants. Rooms are decked out in classic mahogany furniture and fine art. The El Dorado restaurant offers international cuisine and reasonably priced buffets. You'll also find formal high-tea service here on Thursday. ⊠ *17 Waterloo Rd.,* ☎ *876/926–9334,* FAX *876/929–4933. 35 rooms. Restaurant, coffee shop, grill, in-room safes, no-smoking rooms, room service, pool. AE, DC, MC,V. EP.*

Port Antonio

Described by poet Ella Wheeler Wilcox as "the most exquisite port on earth," Port Antonio is a seaside town at the foot of verdant hills toward the east end of the north coast. The area's must-do activities include rafting the Rio Grande, snorkeling, or scuba diving in the Blue Lagoon, exploring Nonsuch Caves, and stopping at the classy Trident resort for lunch or a drink.

$$$$ ⊡ **Trident Villas and Hotel.** The living here is truly gracious. Peacocks
  ★ strut the manicured lawns, colonnaded walkways wind through whimsically sculpted topiaries that dot the 14 acres, and the pool—on a rocky bit of land that juts out into crashing surf—is a memory unto itself. The luxurious Laura Ashley–style rooms, many with turrets, bay windows, and balconies or verandas, are awash in mahogany and local art; they do not have TVs or clocks. ⊠ *Anchovy (Box 119),* ☎ *876/993–2602,* FAX *876/993–2960,* WEB *www.tridentvillas.com. 8 rooms, 1 suite, 14 villas. Restaurant, bar, in-room safes, minibars, pool, massage, 2 tennis courts, aerobics, beach, snorkeling, boating, library, concierge. AE, MC, V. All-inclusive, CP, FAP, MAP.*

$$$ ⊡ **Jamaica Palace.** Built to resemble a 17th-century Italian mansion, this imposing white-columned property has black lacquer and gilded oversized furniture throughout its common areas. Some rooms are more lavish than others, though each has a semicircular bed, European objets d'art, and Asian rugs; none is equipped with TV (you can, however, rent one). Although the hotel isn't on the beach, there's a 114-ft swimming pool that's shaped like Jamaica. ⊠ *Williamsfield (Box 277),* ☎ *876/993–7720 or 800/423–4095,* FAX *876/993–7759,* WEB *www.insite.com/jampal. 24 rooms, 56 suites. 2 restaurants, 2 bars, in-room safes, room service, pool, laundry service. AE, MC, V. CP, EP, MAP.*

$$$ 🏨 **Dragon Bay.** Set on a private cove, Dragon Bay is an idyllic grouping of individually decorated villas surrounded by tropical gardens. Villa 35 has a private pool, a large living room, and two bedrooms with separate sitting rooms that have sofa beds. This place is popular with German and Italian tour groups. ⊠ *Dragon Bay (Box 176)*, ☎ *876/993–8514 or 800/633–3284*, FAX *876/993–8971*, WEB *www.dragonbay.com. 30 1-, 2-, and 3-bedroom villas. 2 restaurants, 3 bars, refrigerators, room service, pool, massage, tennis court, aerobics, gym, volleyball, beach, dive shop, snorkeling. AE, MC, V. All-inclusive, EP, FAP, MAP.*

$$ 🏨 **Goblin Hill.** This lush 12-acre estate is atop a hill overlooking San San Bay. Each attractively appointed villa comes with its own dramatic view, plus a staff member to do the grocery shopping, cleaning, and cooking for you. The rooms and villas aren't equipped with phones or TVs, but they do have ceiling fans, air-conditioners, and a tropical decor. The beach is a 10-minute walk away. Excellent car-rental packages are available. ⊠ *San San (Box 26)*, ☎ *876/925–8108 or 800/472–1148*, FAX *876/925–6248. 12 rooms, 28 1- and 2-bedroom villas. Bar, kitchenettes, pool, 2 tennis courts, beach, library. AE, MC, V. EP.*

$$ 🏨 **Hotel Mocking Bird Hill.** With only 10 rooms, all overlooking the sea and the Blue Mountains, Mocking Bird Hill feels more like a cozy B&B than a hotel. Owners Barbara Walker and Shireen Aga run an environmentally sensitive operation: you'll find bamboo instead of hardwood furniture, solar-heated water, ceiling fans instead of ozone-depleting air-conditioning systems, meals made with local produce in the Mille Fleurs dining terrace, locally produced toiletries and stationery sets, and seven naturally landscaped acres. The tasteful blue-and-white rooms do not have phones or TVs, and most are designated no-smoking. There's also an array of ecotour options. ⊠ *East of Port Antonio on North Coast Hwy. (Box 254, Port Antonio)*, ☎ *876/993–7267*, FAX *876/993–7133*, WEB *www.hotelmockingbirdhill.com. 10 rooms. Restaurant, bar, in-room safes, no-smoking rooms, pool, massage. AE, MC, V. CP, EP, MAP.*

Ocho Rios

On the northeast coast halfway between Port Antonio and MoBay, Ocho Rios is hilly and lush. Its resorts, hotels, and villas are all a short drive from a bustling crafts market, boutiques, duty-free shops, restaurants, and several scenic attractions.

$$$$ 🏨 **Couples Ocho Rios.** The emphasis here is on romantic adventures for two. Each one-bedroom suite has a two-person hot tub in its bathroom that peeks through a window at the four-poster king-size bed. There's a lovely white beach for relaxation or water sports, and a private island where you can sunbathe in the buff. Weddings are included in the package as are five off-site excursions. If you plan to visit for seven nights, you can split your stay between this resort and the new Couples Negril (both establishments are exclusively for male-female couples). ⊠ *Tower Isle, St. Mary*, ☎ *876/975–4271 or 800/268–7537*, FAX *876/975–4439*, WEB *www.couples.com. 201 rooms, 11 suites. 4 restaurants, 4 bars, in-room safes, room service, pool, 5 outdoor hot tubs, massage, sauna, 5 tennis courts, horseback riding, squash, beach, dive shop, snorkeling, windsurfing. 3-night minimum stay. AE, MC, V. All-inclusive.*

$$$$ 🏨 **Grand Lido Sans Souci.** A stay at this pastel-pink cliff-side resort is a
★ wonderfully luxurious experience. Romantic oceanfront suites have oversize whirlpool tubs. Throughout, blond-wood furniture, cool tile floors, and sheer curtains are accented by pastel watercolors and Jamaican prints on the walls. A highlight is Charlie's Spa, which offers complimentary pampering massages, body scrubs, reflexology sessions, facials, and manicures and pedicures (book treatments as soon as you

arrive, if not before). Weddings are part of the all-inclusive package, as is room service, a unique feature for all-inclusives. ⊠ *2 mi (3 km) east of Ocho Rios (Box 103),* ☎ *876/994–1353 or 800/467–8737,* FAX *876/994–1544,* WEB *www.superclubs.com. 146 suites. 6 restaurants, 4 bars, grill, in-room safes, minibars, room service, 4 pools, 2 hot tubs, massage, spa, 2 tennis courts, beach, library, complimentary weddings, laundry service, concierge, airport shuttle. 2-night minimum stay. AE, D, DC, MC, V. All-inclusive.*

$$$$ ⭐ 🏨 **Jamaica Inn.** A combination of class and quiet attracts a discerning crowd, including such celebrities as Kate Moss and I. M. Pei, to this vintage property that was once a favorite of Winston Churchill. Each room has its own veranda (larger than most hotel rooms) on the private cove's powdery champagne-colored beach. The colonial decor is accented by blue-and-white touches, including Wedgwood china, and by Jamaican antique furniture and terrazzo floors (there are no TVs or radios). The requirement for ties has been dropped, although jackets are still de rigueur after 7 PM during high season (December–April); off-season a collared shirt and long pants are required for men during dinner. Note that the Full American Plan is available during summer months only. ⊠ *East of Ocho Rios on North Coast Hwy. (Box 1),* ☎ *876/974–2514 or 800/837–4670,* FAX *876/974–2449,* WEB *www.jamaicainn.com. 49 rooms, 4 suites. Restaurant, 2 bars, room service, pool, croquet, gym, beach, snorkeling, boating, library. AE, MC, V. FAP, MAP.*

$$$$ 🏨 **Sandals Dunn's River Golf Resort and Spa.** Twenty-five acres of lush, manicured grounds surround this luxury all-inclusive resort. Set on a wide, sugary beach, with courteous service and posh rooms, it's the finest of Sandals's Jamaican properties. Rooms are decorated in light pink, blue, turquoise, and cream, and most have a balcony or patio that overlooks the sea or the grounds. The resort is exclusively for male-female couples—most of whom are in their thirties and forties—and prides itself on catering to guests' every whim. Guests here have access to two nearby golf courses at other Sandals resorts, with a free shuttle service. ⊠ *2 mi (3 km) east of Ocho Rios on North Coast Hwy. (Box 51),* ☎ *876/972–1610 or 800/726–3257,* FAX *876/972–1611,* WEB *www.sandals.com. 256 rooms, 10 suites. 4 restaurants, 7 bars, in-room safes, 2 pools, 3 outdoor hot tubs, sauna, steam room, putting green, 2 tennis courts, racquetball, beach, concierge. 2-night minimum stay. AE, MC, V. All-inclusive.*

$$ 🏨 **Comfort Suites.** Families on a budget planning an extended stay should consider a suite here; the fully stocked kitchens can help keep the dining bills down. This is also one of the few places where you'll find no-smoking rooms (be sure to request one when booking). Each spacious, immaculate unit has white tile floors, rattan furniture, and tropical floral prints. The two-bedroom suite has an open bathroom (it's divided from the main room by only a screen), as well as a whirlpool tub in its master-bedroom loft. This hotel is not on the beach (though it's close enough to walk to and a shuttle is provided), but suites in the "A" block do have a partial ocean view. ⊠ *17 Da Costa Dr.,* ☎ *876/974–8050 or 800/221–2222,* FAX *876/974–8070,* WEB *www.choicehotels.com. 87 suites. Restaurant, bar, in-room safes, kitchenettes, no-smoking rooms, refrigerators, room service, outdoor hot tub, tennis court, airport shuttle. AE, MC, V. EP, FAP, MAP.*

$$ 🏨 **Renaissance Jamaica Grande.** The Renaissance, one of the largest conference hotels in Jamaica, attracts all types of travelers: families, couples, singles (there are special singles activities and no supplementary fee for singles), and conference attendees. Even though it's a beachfront resort, the focal point is definitely the tiered and winding pool, which has a waterfall, a swaying bridge, and a swim-up bar. Rooms in the south

building are the largest, but those in the north building have slightly better views. Kids are kept busy in the daily Club Mongoose activity program (included in the all-inclusive package). The hotel's disco, Jamaic'N Me Crazy, is *very* popular. ✉ *Main St. (Box 100),* ☎ *876/974–2201 or 800/468–3571,* FAX *876/974–5378,* WEB *www.renaissancehotels. com. 706 rooms, 15 suites. 5 restaurants, 8 bars, in-room safes, 3 pools, 2 outdoor hot tubs, massage, 2 tennis courts, beach, dive shop, snorkeling, windsurfing, boating, children's programs, nursery, playground, concierge, convention center. AE, DC, MC, V. All-inclusive, EP.*

$ 🏨 **Enchanted Garden.** The 20-acre gardens here are filled with tropical plants and flowers and punctuated by streams and waterfalls. You'll also find an aviary and an aquarium, where you can enjoy a deli lunch or tea surrounded by tanks of fish and hanging orchids. The futuristic cream-color villas (some with private plunge pools) seem somewhat out of place amid the natural splendor, but the rooms (on the small side) are comfortable, and you're never far from the soothing sound of rushing water. Don't miss the guided garden tour, just one of dozens of activities here. There's a free shuttle to the beach, several minutes away. ✉ *Eden Bower Rd. (Box 284),* ☎ *876/974–1400 or 800/847–2535,* FAX *876/974–5823. 60 rooms, 53 suites. 5 restaurants, 4 bars, 2 pools, outdoor hot tub, sauna, spa, Turkish baths, 2 tennis courts, croquet, beach, snorkeling, airport shuttle. AE, DC, MC, V. All-inclusive.*

Runaway Bay

The smallest of the resort areas, Runaway Bay, west of Ocho Rios, has a handful of modern hotels, a few new all-inclusive resorts, and an 18-hole golf course.

$$$$ 🏨 **FDR, Franklyn D. Resort.** Jamaica's first all-inclusive family resort
★ 🐣 is the answer to parents' prayers. Upscale yet unpretentious, the beachside complex has spacious, well-planned one-, two-, and three-bedroom suites in pink villas set in a horseshoe around a pool. Best of all, a staff member is assigned to each suite, filling the role of nanny and housekeeper. Children and teens are kept busy with supervised activities and sports. Parents can join in or just lounge by the pool, golf, or scuba dive. Children age 16 and under stay and eat free when staying in a room with their parents. ✉ *Runaway Bay (Box 201),* ☎ *876/973–4591 or 800/654–1337(reservations service),* FAX *876/973–3071,* WEB *www.fdrholidays.com. 76 suites. 2 restaurants, 3 bars, kitchenettes, pool, tennis court, beach, dive shop, snorkeling, baby-sitting, children's programs. AE, MC, V. All-inclusive.*

$$$$ 🏨 **Grand Lido Braco.** Just a 15-minute drive west of Runaway Bay, this
★ all-inclusive, adults-only, gingerbread- and Georgian-style village (a member of the SuperClubs family) focuses on the culture, crafts, music, and food of Jamaica. Boutiques, an art shop, and several restaurants—including a jerk grill, a pastry shop, and a sidewalk café—fan out from a central fountain in the "town square." The meandering pool next to the white-sand beach is one of the largest in the country. Rooms, done in bright tropical colors, are generously sized, and all but a few (which have garden views) are steps from the 2,000-ft (612-m) beach, including a nude beach with nearby nude pool, bar, and snack bar, or have a great view of the ocean from a patio. ✉ *Trelawny between Duncans and Rio Bueno,* ☎ *876/954–0000 or 800/467–8737,* FAX *876/954–0020,* WEB *www.superclubs.com. 232 rooms. 5 restaurants, 8 bars, café, in-room safes, 2 pools, 2 hot tubs, driving range, 9-hole golf course, 3 tennis courts, health club, hiking, soccer, beach, dive shop, snorkeling, windsurfing, fishing, shops, dance club, complimentary weddings, concierge, meeting rooms, airport shuttle. 3-night minimum stay. AE, DC, MC, V. All-inclusive, EP, FAP, MAP.*

$$$$ ⊞ **Hedonism III.** Like its more spartan cousin in Negril, Hedonism is
★ an adult all-inclusive hotel for travelers looking for physical fun that
ranges from a circus clinic and waterslide (through the disco, no less)
to nude beach body painting. Unlike its Negril equivalent, however,
the newly opened Hedonism III offers luxurious rooms and Jamaica's
first swim-up rooms. The guest rooms, each with mirrored ceilings, have
Jacuzzi tubs, TVs, and CD players. The beach is divided into "nude"
and "prude" sides, although a quick look shows that most guests
choose to leave the suits at home. Scheduled activities include nude body
painting and volleyball; there's even shuffleboard in the buff. Weddings,
including Jamaica's only nude weddings, are complimentary. ⊠ *Main
Road (Box 250), Runaway Bay,* ☎ *876/973–5029 or 800/467–8737,* FAX
876/973–5402, WEB *www.superclubs.com. 225 rooms. 4 restaurants,
5 bars, 2 grills, in-room safes, 3 pools, 2 outdoor hot tubs, 3 tennis
courts, health club, beach, dive shop, snorkeling, windsurfing, boating, dance club, complimentary weddings, airport shuttle. 2-night minimum stay. AE, DC, MC, V. All-inclusive.*

$$ ⊞ **Breezes Runaway Bay.** This moderately priced SuperClubs resort em-
★ phasizes an active, sports-oriented vacation—from golf (at the resort's
18-hole course), tennis, and horse and carriage rides to an array of water
sports. Expert instruction and top-rate equipment are part of the pack-
age. Rooms have white tile floors, cozy love seats, TVs, carved wooden
headboards, and big marble bathrooms. Guests—often Germans, Ital-
ians, and Japanese—flock here for the reef just off the beach, as well
as for the superb golf school. Free weddings are also part of the pack-
age. ⊠ *North Coast Hwy. at Runaway Bay (Box 58),* ☎ *876/973–2436
or 800/467–8737,* FAX *876/973–2352,* WEB *www.superclubs.com. 234
rooms. 2 restaurants, 4 bars, 2 grills, in-room safes, pool, 3 outdoor
hot tubs, 4 tennis courts, driving range, 18-hole golf course, beach, dive
shop, snorkeling, windsurfing, complimentary weddings, airport shut-
tle. 2-night minimum stay. AE, DC, MC, V. All-inclusive.*

Montego Bay

MoBay has miles of hotels, villas, apartments, and duty-free shops. Al-
though lacking much in the way of cultural stimuli, it presents a com-
fortable island backdrop for the many conventions it hosts.

$$$$ ⊞ **Half Moon Golf, Tennis, and Beach Club.** For more than 40 years,
this 400-acre resort has been a destination unto itself. Although it has
mushroomed from 30 to more than 400 units, it has maintained an
intimate, luxurious feel. With its black-and-white decor, the rooms, suites,
and villas are exquisitely decorated with such flourishes as Asian rugs
and antique radios. Several villas (which come with a cook, a butler,
a housekeeper, and a rental car or golf cart) have private pools, and
the 1-mi-long (1½-km-long) stretch of beach is just steps from every
room. On the grounds there's an upscale shopping mall as well as a
nature reserve, a croquet lawn (considered one of the Caribbean's
best), and a hospital. The Sugar Mill restaurant is sure to please. ⊠ *7
mi (11 km) east of MoBay (Box 80),* ☎ *876/953–2211 or 800/237–
3237,* FAX *876/953–2731,* WEB *www.halfmoon.com.jm. 44 rooms, 176
suites, 197 villas. 7 restaurants, 3 bars, 2 pools, outdoor hot tub, sauna,
spa, 18-hole golf course, 13 tennis courts, aerobics, badminton, cro-
quet, gym, horseback riding, Ping-Pong, squash, beach, dive shop,
snorkeling, windsurfing, bicycles, shops, theater, concierge. AE, DC,
MC, V. All-inclusive, EP, FAP, MAP.*

$$$$ ⊞ **Ritz-Carlton Rose Hall, Jamaica.** Across the road from the historic
★ Rose Hall estate, this expansive property is the newest addition to Ja-
maica's luxury hotels. The beige buildings span a large swath of beach-
front east of Montego Bay, although most beach and water-sports
action takes place at the nearby Rose Hall Beach Club (transportation

is provided for guests). Rooms here are subtly Caribbean with under-stated tropical florals and mahogany and rattan furniture. Along with a full-service spa, the resort offers a fully supervised children's club, making it a popular choice for families, especially those bringing along the kids while attending a meeting at the resort's convention center. ✉ *1 Ritz Carlton Dr., Rose Hall, St. James,* ☎ *876/953–2800 or 800/ 241–3333,* FAX *876/953–2501,* WEB *www.ritzcarlton.com. 428 rooms. 4 restaurants, 3 bars, in-room safes, pool, 18-hole golf course, spa, health club, beach, dive shop, snorkeling, windsurfing, shops, concierge, meeting rooms. AE, DC, MC, V. EP, FAP, MAP.*

$$$$ ★ 🏨 **Round Hill Hotel and Villas.** The Hollywood set frequents this peace-ful resort, 8 mi (13 km) west of town on a hilly peninsula. Twenty-seven villas are set on 98 acres, and the Pineapple House, a building that over-looks the sea, houses 36 hotel rooms. Rooms are done in a refined Ralph Lauren style, with mahogany furnishings and terra-cotta floors. Vil-las are leased back to the resort by private owners and vary in decor, but jungle motifs are a favorite. All come with a personal maid and a cook (for an extra charge) to make your breakfast, and several have private pools. The restaurant's good food and elegant presentation make for a memorable meal in the dining room, or better yet, on the seaside terrace. ✉ *8 mi (13 km) west of Montego Bay on North Coast Hwy. (Box 64),* ☎ *876/956–7050 or 800/237–3237,* FAX *876/956–7505,* WEB *www.roundhilljamaica.com. 36 rooms, 27 villas. Restaurant, room service, pool, hair salon, massage, 5 tennis courts, aerobics, gym, jog-ging, beach, dive shop, snorkeling, windsurfing, shops, concierge, he-lipad. AE, DC, MC, V. All-inclusive, EP, FAP, MAP.*

$$$$ 🏨 **Sandals Montego Bay.** The largest private beach in MoBay is the spark that lights this Sandals—one of the most popular upscale resorts exclusively for male-female couples in the Caribbean. Its all-inclusive rate, nonstop activities, and rooms overlooking the bay make it a bit like a cruise ship that remains in port. The atmosphere here is one of a great big party, despite the planes that zoom overhead (the airport is nearby). The crowd here tends to be younger (under 35 mostly) than at other Sandals resorts in Jamaica. Rooms are done in tropical col-ors and have four-poster beds. The Oleander Room may well be the best fine-dining establishment in the Sandals chain. ✉ *Kent Ave. (Box 100),* ☎ *876/952–5510 or 800/726–3257,* FAX *876/952–0816,* WEB *www.sandals.com. 244 rooms. 5 restaurants, 4 bars, snack bar, in-room safes, 4 pools, 4 outdoor hot tubs, sauna, 4 tennis courts, racquetball, beach, dive shop, dock, snorkeling, windsurfing, boating, library, con-cierge. 2-night minimum stay. AE, MC, V. All-inclusive.*

$$$$ 🏨 **Sandals Royal Caribbean.** Formerly Sandals Royal Jamaican, this upscale, all-inclusive resort exclusively for male-female couples is made up of Jamaican-style buildings arranged in a semicircle around at-tractive gardens. Although there are plenty of activities here, the re-sort is quieter and more genteel than Sandals Montego Bay and draws something of an international crowd. Oceanfront rooms and suites are elegant and inviting, with floral-print fabrics and mahogany four-poster beds. A colorful "dragon boat" transports you to Sandals's pri-vate island for meals at an Indonesian restaurant. ✉ *4 mi (6½ km) east of airport on North Coast Hwy. (Box 167),* ☎ *876/953–2231 or 800/ 726–3257,* FAX *876/953–2788,* WEB *www.sandals.com. 176 rooms, 14 suites. 4 restaurants, 5 bars, in-room safes, 4 pools, hair salon, 5 out-door hot tubs, sauna, 3 tennis courts, aerobics, beach, dive shop, snorkeling, windsurfing, concierge, airport shuttle. 2-night minimum stay. AE, MC, V. All-inclusive.*

$$$$ 🏨 **Tryall Golf, Tennis, and Beach Club.** Part of a posh residential de-velopment 15 mi (24 km) west of MoBay, Tryall clings to a hilltop that overlooks a golf course and the Caribbean. Here you'll stay in one of

Lodging
Breezes Montego Bay 42
Coyaba Beach Resort and Club . . . 49
Half Moon Golf, Tennis, and Beach Club . . 45
Holiday Inn Sunspree Resort 46
Lethe Estate 32
Richmond Hill Inn 39
Ritz-Carlton Rose Hall . . 50
Round Hill Hotel and Villas 31
Sandals Inn . 43
Sandals Montego Bay 44
Sandals Royal Caribbean . . 48
Tryall Golf, Tennis, and Beach Club 30
Wyndham Rose Hall . . . 47

Dining
Le Chalet . . . 41
Day-O Plantation Restaurant . . 33
Julia's Italian Restaurant . . 40
Margueritaville Caribbean Bar and Grill . . . 37
Marguerites . . 38
The Native . . 36
Pier 1 35
Sugar Mill . . 45
Town House 34

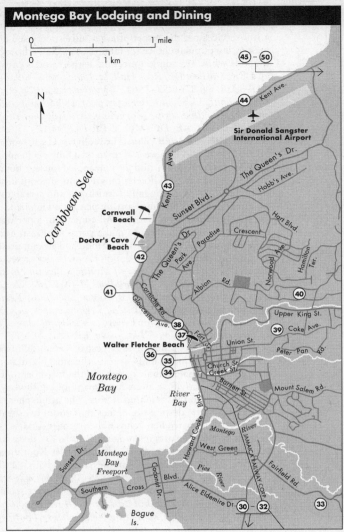

Montego Bay Lodging and Dining

the many villas—each with its own pool, full staff (butler, cook, maid, and gardener), and golf cart—that dot the 2,200-acre island plantation. All accommodations are individually and plushly decorated. The elegant fine dining room in the great house serves Continental and Jamaican cuisine. The beautiful seaside golf course is one of this resort's more memorable features; it's also one of the meanest courses in the world and, as such, hosts big-money tournaments. ⊠ *15 mi (24 km) west of MoBay on North Coast Hwy. (Box 1206),* ☎ *876/956–5660, 876/956–5667, or 800/238–5290;* FAX *876/956–5658,* WEB *www.tryall-club.com. 57 villas. Restaurant, 4 bars, refrigerators, pool, massage, driving range, 18-hole golf course, 9 tennis courts, jogging, beach, dive shop, snorkeling, windsurfing. AE, DC, MC, V. EP.*

$$$ 🏨 **Coyaba Beach Resort and Club.** Owners Joanne and Kevin Robert-
★ son live on the property, interacting with guests and giving this ocean-front retreat the feel of an intimate country inn. Coyaba is also very family friendly. The plantation-style great house, just east of MoBay, successfully blends modern amenities with Old World grace. Rooms

are decorated with lovely colonial prints and hand-carved mahogany furniture, and sunshine pours through tall windows and over terra-cotta floors and potted plants. A basket with bottled spring water and freshly baked banana bread greets you upon check-in; regular rates include afternoon tea and evening cocktail parties as well as tennis. ⊠ *Mahoe Bay, Little River,* ☎ *876/953–9150 or 800/237–3237,* FAX *876/953–2244,* WEB *www.coyabajamaica.com. 50 rooms. 2 restaurants, 3 bars, pool, outdoor hot tub, massage, tennis court, gym, volleyball, beach, dive shop, snorkeling, windsurfing, library, recreation room, playground, airport shuttle. AE, MC, V. All-inclusive, EP, MAP.*

$$$ 🏨 **Sandals Inn.** If you can forgo a private beach (there's a public one across the street), you can stay here for much less than at the other Sandals. Managed more as a small hotel than a large resort, this hotel is intimate and relatively quiet. Rooms are compact, and most have balconies that face the pool. Dark carpet contrasts with white-lacquered furniture and tropical-print fabrics. There's plenty to do here, and you can get in on the action at the other two MoBay Sandals by hopping on the free hourly shuttle. The in-town location puts you close to shops and sights. (Note that this establishment is exclusively for male-female couples.) ⊠ *Gloucester Ave. (Box 412),* ☎ *876/952–4140 or 800/726–3257,* FAX *876/952–6913,* WEB *www.sandals.com. 52 rooms. 2 restaurants, 2 bars, in-room safes, pool, hair salon, outdoor hot tub, tennis court, concierge, airport shuttle. 2-night minimum stay. AE, MC, V. All-inclusive.*

$$$ 🏨 **Wyndham Rose Hall.** This self-contained resort, on the 400-acre Rose
🦢 Hall Plantation, is a bustling business hotel that's popular with large groups. It has plenty of amenities, including a 110,000-sq-ft water complex, Sugar Mill Falls, complete with lagoons and a towering water slide. You can enjoy lazy river rafting among waterfalls scattered throughout the park. Rooms—done in tropical florals in shades of deep peach—are comfortable though somewhat sterile. The waters off the thin crescent beach are good for sailing and snorkeling. ⊠ *4 mi (6½ km) east of airport on North Coast Hwy. (Box 999),* ☎ *876/953–2650 or 800/996–3426,* FAX *876/953–2617,* WEB *www.wyndham.com. 470 rooms, 19 suites. 5 restaurants, 3 bars, in-room safes, room service, 3 pools, massage, 6 tennis courts, golf, aerobics, basketball, gym, volleyball, beach, dive shop, snorkeling, water park, windsurfing, nightclub, children's programs, playground. AE, DC, MC, V. All-inclusive, EP, MAP.*

$$ 🏨 **Breezes Montego Bay.** Like its cousin in Runaway Bay, this Super-Clubs resort for guests age 16 and up emphasizes moderate prices and plenty of around-the-clock activities. Located on the portion of Gloucester Avenue known as the "Hip Strip," this small property's rooms have white tile floors, cozy love seats, TVs, carved wooden headboards, and big marble bathrooms. The resort doesn't have its own private beach but uses the adjacent Doctor's Cave Beach. Free weddings are also part of the package. ⊠ *Gloucester Ave.,* ☎ *876/940–1150 or 800/467–8737,* FAX *876/940–1160,* WEB *www.superclubs.com. 124 rooms. 2 restaurants, 4 bars, 1 grill, in-room safes, pool, 2 tennis courts, beach, dive shop, snorkeling, windsurfing, complimentary weddings, airport shuttle. 2-night minimum stay. AE, DC, MC, V. All-inclusive.*

$$ 🏨 **Holiday Inn Sunspree Resort.** There are activities day and night at this recently renovated family-oriented resort. Although the rooms—spread out in seven buildings—are cheerful enough, the hotel is big and can be noisy (rooms farthest from the pool and central dining-entertainment area are the quietest). However, adults can take a break in the new quiet pool with a swim-up bar on the resort's west side. On the east end, the resort now features a miniature golf course. Room ser-

vice is available for breakfast. ⊠ *6 mi (9½ km) east of airport on North Coast Hwy. (Box480),* ☎ *876/953–2485 or 800/465–4329,* FAX *876/ 953–2840,* WEB *www.holiday-inn.com. 521 rooms, 23 suites. 3 restaurants, 4 bars, 2 snack bars, in-room safes, no-smoking rooms, room service, 3 pools, 4 tennis courts, beach, dive shop, snorkeling, windsurfing, children's programs, playground, concierge, airport shuttle. AE, DC, MC, V. All-inclusive, EP.*

$$ 🏨 **Lethe Estate.** Tucked on the bank of the Great River near the village of Lethe, this quiet mountainside inn is a far cry from the bustling beach resorts for which MoBay is known. Interruptions come not from reggae music or dance contests but from the sounds of birds. You don't have the sea nearby, but you can take a dip in the river (or float down it on a bamboo raft), take a jitney through the nearby Lethe Estate plantation, or fish in freshwater ponds. ⊠ *Reading Rd. (Box 23), 20 mins west of MoBay,* ☎ *876/956–4920,* FAX *876/956–4927,* WEB *www.lethejamaica.com. 15 rooms. Restaurant, pool, tennis court, horseback riding, fishing, airport shuttle. AE, MC, V. CP, FAP, MAP.*

$$ 🏨 **Richmond Hill Inn.** This hilltop inn—a quaint 200-year-old great house originally owned by the Dewars clan—has spectacular views of the Caribbean and a great deal of peace. Decor tends toward the dainty: frilly lace curtains and doilies, lots of lavenders and mauves, and crushed-velvet furniture here and there. A free shuttle will take you to shops and beaches, about 10–15 minutes away. ⊠ *Union St. (Box 362),* ☎ *876/952–3859,* FAX *876/952–6106. 15 rooms, 5 suites. Bar, coffee shop, dining room, pool, laundry service. AE, MC, V. EP, FAP, MAP.*

$$ 🏨 **Starfish Trelawny.** This moderately priced all-inclusive hotel catering
☺ to families, singles, and couples, opens in December 2001 after a $5-million renovation. A supervised children's program plans activities for younger visitors from 8AM–9PM daily. Rooms have white tile floors and overlook the pool area, the sea, or the surrounding countryside. Several cottages are especially popular with larger family groups. Nightly entertainment at poolside is for the whole family; a late-night disco is aimed at the adult set. The resort is all-inclusive, but some motorized sports such as waterskiing, the banana boat ride, and scuba diving are offered on à la carte. ⊠ *North Coast Hwy. 23 miles east of Montego Bay,* ☎ *876/ 954–2450 or 800/659–5436,* FAX *876/954–2173,* WEB *www.superclubs.com. 350 rooms. 2 restaurants, 4 bars, grill, pool, 4 tennis courts, badminton, beach, dive shop, snorkeling, windsurfing, waterskiing, dance club, baby-sitting, children's programs, meeting rooms, airport shuttle. 2-night minimum stay. AE, DC, MC, V. All-inclusive.*

Negril

Some 50 mi (80 km) west of MoBay, Negril was long a sleepy bohemian retreat. In the last decade the town has blossomed and added a number of classy all-inclusive resorts, with several more on the drawing board for Bloody Bay (northeast of Negril Beach). Negril itself is only a small village with little of historic significance. But such sights are not what draws the sybaritic singles and couples. The young, hip crowd here comes for sun, sand, and sea.

$$$$ 🏨 **Couples Negril.** The emphasis here is on romance and relaxation, and you will find neither hard to come by. The property's 18 acres are set along Bloody Bay. Negril's bohemian nature is reflected throughout the nine low-rise buildings, where a rainbow of colors and lively art by local craftspeople pepper public spaces. All land and water activities, selected excursions, and weddings are included in the all-inclusive rates. The resort is exclusively for male-female couples. ⊠ *Norman Manley Blvd.,* ☎ *876/957–5960 or 800/268–7537,* FAX *876/957– 5858,* WEB *www.couples.com. 216 rooms, 18 suites. 3 restaurants, 5 bars, in-room safes, room service, 2 pools, 2 outdoor hot tubs, spa, 4 tennis* *courts, aerobics, health club, beach, dive shop, snorkeling, windsurfing, complimentary weddings, concierge, airport shuttle. 3-night minimum stay. AE, MC, V. All-inclusive.*

$$$$ ★ 🏨 **Couples Swept Away Negril.** This adults-only resort, with its emphasis on sports and healthful cuisine, primarily attracts fitness-minded male-female couples. The suites are in 26 two-story, tropical villas—each with a private garden atrium—spread out along a ½-mi (¾-km) stretch of gorgeous beach. There's an outstanding 10-acre sports complex across the road. At the Feathers Continental restaurant, the chefs prepare dishes designed to keep you fit and trim, with lots of fish, white meat, fresh fruits, and vegetables. Complimentary weddings are part of the all-inclusive package. ✉ *Norman Manley Blvd., Long Bay,* ☎ *876/957–4061 or 800/545–7937,* FAX *876/957–4060,* WEB *www.sweptaway.com. 134 suites. 2 restaurants, 4 bars, in-room safes, 2 pools, 2 outdoor hot tubs, massage, spa, 2 saunas, 2 steam rooms, 10 tennis courts, aerobics, health club, jogging, racquetball, squash, dive shop, beach, snorkeling, windsurfing, complimentary weddings, concierge, airport shuttle. 3-night minimum stay. AE, DC, MC, V. All-inclusive.*

$$$$ ★ 🏨 **Grand Lido Negril.** The dramatic entrance of marble floors and columns, filled with Jamaican artwork, sets an elegant tone at this SuperClubs all-inclusive property for ages 16 and over. It's geared to folks with some money in their pockets, and it attracts mature, settled couples and singles. The well-appointed split-level oceanfront and garden suites are spacious and stylish. For some guests, the pièce de résistance is a sunset cruise on the resort's 147-ft yacht, *M/Y Zein,* which was a wedding gift from Aristotle Onassis to Prince Rainier and Princess Grace of Monaco. The Piacere restaurant is superb. The sprawling resort sits on Bloody Bay and one of Jamaica's top stretches of white-sand beach including a clothing-optional beach. ✉ *Norman Manley Blvd. (Box 88),* ☎ *876/957–5010 or 800/467–8737,* FAX *876/957–5517,* WEB *www.superclubs.com. 210 suites. 4 restaurants, 9 bars, in-room safes, room service, 2 pools, 5 outdoor hot tubs, massage, spa, 4 tennis courts, health club, beach, dive shop, snorkeling, windsurfing, shops, library, laundry service, complimentary weddings, concierge, airport shuttle. 2-night minimum stay. AE, DC, MC, V. All-inclusive.*

$$$$ 🏨 **Hedonism II.** Hedonism appeals mostly to uninhibited vacationers age 18 and over who like a robust mix of physical activities (you can try everything from scuba diving to a trampoline-trapeze clinic). Public areas are filled with potted plants and scantily clad guests. Handsome guest rooms, which do not include TVs, have mirrored ceilings above king-size or twin beds (solo guests either pay a hefty supplement or are assigned a roommate of the same sex). You'll find a skinny-dipping pool and hot tubs, and with both "nude" and "prude" beaches, the atmosphere here is lively around the clock. Most guests prefer the nude beach, with its new pool and swim-up bar. Scheduled activities include nude body painting and volleyball; there's even shuffleboard in the buff. Weddings are complimentary. ✉ *Norman Manley Blvd., Ruthland Point (Box 25),* ☎ *876/957–5200 or 800/467–8737,* FAX *876/957–5289,* WEB *www.superclubs.com. 280 rooms. 2 restaurants, 5 bars, 2 grills, in-room safes, 2 pools, 2 outdoor hot tubs, 6 tennis courts, squash, beach, dive shop, snorkeling, windsurfing, boating, shops, dance club, complimentary weddings, airport shuttle. 2-night minimum stay. AE, DC, MC, V. All-inclusive.*

$$$$ 🏨 **Sandals Negril Beach Resort and Spa.** Male-female couples looking for an upscale, sports-oriented getaway and a casual atmosphere (you can wear dressy shorts to dinner) flock to this resort on one of the best stretches of Negril Beach. Water sports, particularly scuba diving, are popular; the capable staff is happy to work with neophytes (one pool is designated for scuba training) as well as certified veterans. There's a nearby island, a huge swim-up pool bar, and a range of spacious accommodations. Both rooms and staff are sunny and appealing. ⊠ *Norman Manley Blvd. (Box 12),* ☎ *876/957–5216 or 800/726–3257,* 🅵🅰🆇 *876/957–5338,* 🆆🅴🅱 *www.sandals.com. 137 rooms, 86 suites. 4 restaurants, 4 bars, in-room safes, 2 pools, 2 outdoor hot tubs, sauna, 4 tennis courts, racquetball, squash, beach, dive shop, snorkeling, windsurfing, concierge. 2-night minimum stay. AE, MC, V. All-inclusive.*

$$$ 🏨 **Negril Cabins Resort.** These elevated timber cottages are amid lush vegetation and towering royal palms. Rooms are open and airy, with floral bedspreads, gauzy curtains, natural-wood floors, and high ceilings. The most popular rooms have TVs and air-conditioning; others have no TV and are cooled by ceiling fans and breezes that come through slatted windows. The gleaming beach across the road is filled with sunbathers and water-sports enthusiasts; for shopping you can take the shuttle into town. A most convivial place, this property is popular with young Europeans. Reasonably priced dive packages are available, and children under 12 stay in their parents' room at no additional charge. ⊠ *Norman Manley Blvd. (Box 118),* ☎ *876/957–5350 or 800/ 382–3444,* 🅵🅰🆇 *876/957–5381,* 🆆🅴🅱 *www.negril-cabins.com. 80 rooms, 2 suites. 2 restaurants, 2 bars, in-room safes, room service, pool, outdoor hot tub, tennis court, gym, beach, dive shop, snorkeling, recreation room, baby-sitting, playground. AE, MC, V. EP, MAP.*

$$ 🏨 **Charela Inn.** Each quiet, elegantly appointed room here has a private balcony or a covered patio. The owners' French-Jamaican roots find daily expression in La Vendôme restaurant, where you can dine on local produce and seafood dressed up with French sauces; there's also an excellent selection of wines. The small beach is part of the glorious 7-mi (11-km) Negril crescent. On Saturday night many guests staying at other resorts come here to watch a folkloric show. ⊠ *Norman Manley Blvd. (Box 3033),* ☎ *876/957–4277,* 🅵🅰🆇 *876/957–4414,* 🆆🅴🅱 *www.charela.com. 49 rooms. Restaurant, bar, pool, beach, windsurfing, boating, laundry service. 5-night minimum stay in high season, 3-night minimum stay in summer. MC, V. EP, MAP.*

$$ 🏨 **Coco La Palm.** This quiet seaside hotel features oversized rooms (junior suites average 525 sq ft) in octagonal buildings set in a U-shape around the pool. Amenities include direct-dial phones, color TVs, coffeemakers, and private patios or terraces—most overlooking gardens (only seven rooms have ocean views). On Negril Beach, the sandy shoreline of Coco La Palm is dotted with palm trees. The beachside restaurant is open-air and casual. ⊠ *Norman Manley Blvd.,* ☎ *876/957–4227 or 800/896– 0987 for reservations,* 🅵🅰🆇 *876/957–3460,* 🆆🅴🅱 *www.cocolapalm.com. 41 rooms. Restaurant, bar, grill, air-conditioning, fans, refrigerators, pool, outdoor hot tub, beach. AE, DC, MC, V. EP, MAP.*

$$ 🏨 **Point Village.** This moderately priced resort is family friendly. Rooms have tile floors and basic furnishings, and each is individually decorated. Popular with tour groups, the sprawling property has two small crescent beaches, rocky grottoes to explore, and fine snorkeling offshore. If you don't opt for the all-inclusive plan, the one- and two-bedroom suites with kitchens are a good choice. ⊠ *Norman Manley Blvd. (Box 105),* ☎ *876/957–5170; 877/764–6852 for reservations,* 🅵🅰🆇 *876/957– 5113,* 🆆🅴🅱 *www.pointvillage.com. 99 rooms, 66 1-, 2-, and 3-bedroom suites. 3 restaurants, 4 bars, 2 grills, grocery, pool, outdoor hot tub, massage, tennis court, beach, snorkeling, windsurfing, children's programs, playground. AE, MC, V. All-inclusive, EP, FAP, MAP.*

$ 🏨 **Rockhouse.** You're side-by-side with nature at this stylish resort on Negril's rugged cliffs. Accommodations are built from rough-hewn timber, thatch, and stone, and are filled with furniture that echoes the nature theme. All rooms have private, indoor baths, but even these seem pleasantly rustic; villa rooms have private, enclosed, outdoor showers. There's a thatch-roof Jamaican restaurant and a cliff-top pool and bar. Because of the steep cliffs, parents traveling with children under 12 are well advised to rule out a stay here. ☒ *West End Rd. (Box 24)*, ☎ *876/957–4373,* FAX *876/957–0557,* WEB *www.rockhousehotel.com. 16 rooms, 12 villas. Restaurant, 2 bars, in-room safes, minibars, pool, snorkeling. AE, MC, V. EP.*

Mandeville

At 2,000 ft above the sea, Mandeville is noted for its cool climate and proximity to secluded south-coast beaches. Most accommodations don't have air-conditioning (you really don't need it). Many are close to golf, tennis, horseback riding, and bird-watching areas.

$ 🏨 **Astra Country Inn & Restaurant.** "Country" is the key word in the name of this mountain retreat. The low price reflects the nature of the very basic rooms: they're spartan but immaculately clean. The small restaurant is open from 7 AM to 9 PM and serves snacks in addition to breakfast, lunch, and dinner. The food is billed as "home cooking" and emphasizes fresh produce—lots of vegetables and fruit juices. The rates here include breakfast. ☒ *62 Ward Ave. (Box60),* ☎ *876/962–3725. 20 rooms, 1 suite. Restaurant, bar, kitchenettes, pool, sauna, laundry service. MC, V. CP.*

$ 🏨 **Mandeville Hotel.** Tropical gardens wrap around the building, and flowers spill onto the terrace restaurant, where breakfast and lunch are served. Rooms are simple and breeze-cooled; suites have full kitchens. You'll need a car to get around town, go out for dinner, and get to the beach, an hour away. ☒ *4 Hotel St. (Box 78),* ☎ *876/962–2460,* FAX *876/962–0700,* WEB *www.mandevillehotel.com. 46 rooms, 17 1-, 2-, and 3-bedroom suites. Restaurant, bar, coffee shop, refrigerators, pool, golf, baby-sitting, laundry service, meeting rooms, travel services. AE, MC, V. EP.*

Dining

Although many cultures have contributed to Jamaica's cuisine, it has become a true cuisine in its own right. It would be a shame to travel to the heart of this complex culture without having at least one typical island meal.

Probably the most famous Jamaican dish is jerk pork—the ultimate island barbecue. The pork (purists cook a whole pig) is covered with a paste of Scotch bonnet peppers, pimento berries (also known as allspice), and other herbs and cooked slowly over a coal fire. Many aficionados believe the best jerk comes from Boston Beach, near Port Antonio. Jerk chicken and fish are also seen on many menus. The ever-so-traditional rice and peas, also known as "coat of arms," is similar to the *moros y christianos* of Spanish-speaking islands: white rice cooked with red kidney beans, coconut milk, scallions, and seasonings.

The island's most famous soup—the fiery pepper pot—is a spicy mixture of salt pork, salt beef, okra, and the island green known as callaloo. Patties (spicy meat pies) elevate street food to new heights. Although they actually originated in Haiti, Jamaicans excel at making them. Curry goat is another island standout: young goat is cooked with spices and is more tender and has a gentler flavor than the lamb for which it was substituted by immigrants from India. Salted fish was once the best that islanders could do between catches. Out of necessity, a breakfast staple (and the national dish of Jamaica) was invented. It joins seasonings with salt fish and ackee, a red fruit that grows on trees throughout the island. When cooked in this dish, ackee reminds most people of scrambled eggs.

Where restaurants are concerned, Kingston has the widest selection, with establishments that serve Italian, French, Cantonese, German, Thai, Indian, Korean, and Continental fare as well as Rasta natural foods, also known as *I-tal*. There are also fine restaurants in all the resort areas, many in the resorts themselves. Most restaurants outside the hotels in MoBay and Ocho Rios will provide complimentary transportation.

What to Wear

Dress is usually casual chic (or just plain casual at many local hangouts). There are a few exceptions in Kingston and at the top resorts, some require semiformal wear in the evening during high season. People tend to dress up for dinner; men might be more comfortable in nice slacks, women in a sundress.

CATEGORY	COST*
$$$$	over $30
$$$	$20–$30
$$	$10–$20
$	under $10

per person for a main course at dinner

Kingston

ASIAN

$$ ✕ **Jade Garden.** On the third floor of the Sovereign Centre shopping mall, this establishment, with its shiny black-lacquer chairs and views of the Blue Mountains, garners rave reviews for its Cantonese and Thai menu. Favorites include steamed fish in black-bean sauce, black mushrooms stuffed with shrimp, and shrimp with lychee. Dim sum is served every Sunday afternoon. ⊠ *106 Hope Rd.,* ☎ *876/978–3476 or 876/ 978–3476. AE, MC, V.*

CONTINENTAL

$$$ ✕ **Blue Mountain Inn.** The elegant Blue Mountain Inn is a 30-minute
★ taxi ride from New Kingston and worth every penny of the fare. On a former coffee plantation, the antiques-laden inn complements its English colonial atmosphere with Continental cuisine. All the classic beef and seafood dishes are here, including chateaubriand béarnaise and lobster thermidor. ⊠ *Gordon Town Rd.,* ☎ *876/927–1700 or 876/927– 2606. Reservations essential. Jacket required. AE, MC, V. Closed Sun. No lunch.*

$$$ ✕ **Palm Court.** On the mezzanine floor of the Hilton Kingston, the elegant Palm Court is open for lunch and dinner. The menu is Continental; the rack of lamb, sautéed snapper almandine, and grilled salmon are delicious. ⊠ *77 Knutsford Blvd.,* ☎ *876/926–5430. AE, DC, MC, V.*

JAMAICAN

$ ✕ **Hot Pot.** Jamaicans love the Hot Pot for breakfast, lunch, and din-
★ ner. Fricassee chicken is the specialty, along with other local dishes, such as mackerel rundown (salted mackerel cooked with coconut milk and spices), and ackee and salted cod. The restaurant's fresh juices in season are the best—tamarind, sorrel, coconut water, soursop, and cucumber. ⊠ *2 Altamont Terr.,* ☎ *876/929–3906. MC, V.*

Ocho Rios

ECLECTIC

$$$ ✕ **Almond Tree.** One of the most popular restaurants in Ocho Rios, the
★ Almond Tree has a menu of Jamaican and Continental favorites: pumpkin soup, pepper pot, and wonderful preparations of fresh fish, veal *piccata,* and fondue. The swinging rope chairs of the terrace bar and the tables perched above a Caribbean cove are great fun. ⊠ *83 Main St.,* ☎ *876/974–2813. Reservations essential. AE, DC, MC, V.*

When you pack your MCI Calling Card, it's like packing your loved ones along too.

Your MCI Calling Card is the easy way to stay in touch when you travel. Use it to call to and from over 125 countries. Plus, every time you call, you can earn frequent flier miles. So wherever your travels take you, call home with your MCI Calling Card. It's even easy to get one. Just visit **www.mci.com/worldphone.**

EASY TO CALL WORLDWIDE

1. Just enter the WorldPhone® access number of the country you're calling from.
2. Enter or give the operator your MCI Calling Card number.
3. Enter or give the number you're calling.

Aruba ⁜	800-888-8
Bahamas ⁜	1-800-888-8000
Barbados ⁜	1-800-888-8000
Bermuda ⁜	1-800-888-8000
British Virgin Islands ⁜	1-800-888-8000
Canada	1-800-888-8000
Mexico	01-800-021-8000
Puerto Rico	1-800-888-8000
United States	1-800-888-8000
U.S. Virgin Islands	1-800-888-8000

⁜ Limited availability.

EARN FREQUENT FLIER MILES

MCI®

SEE THE WORLD
IN FULL COLOR

Fodor's Exploring Guides bring all the great sights vividly to life with hundreds of photographs, fascinating historical background, and colorful anecdotes. Detailed maps and practical information keep you headed in the right direction.

Pair a **Fodor's** Exploring Guide with your trusted Gold Guide for a complete planning package.

$$ ✕ **Evita's.** The setting here is a hilltop 1860s gingerbread house. Large
★ windows open to cooling mountain breezes and stunning views of city
and sea. More than 30 kinds of pasta are served, ranging from lasagna
Rastafari (vegetarian) and fiery jerk spaghetti to *rotelle colombo* (crab-
meat with white sauce and noodles). There are also excellent fish
dishes—sautéed fillet of red snapper with orange sauce, scampi and
lobster in basil cream sauce, red snapper stuffed with crabmeat—and
several meat dishes, among them a tasty grilled sirloin with mushroom
sauce. Kids under 12 eat for half price, and light eaters will appreci-
ate half-portion orders. ✉ *Mantalent Inn, Eden Bower Rd.,* ☎ *876/
974–2333. AE, MC, V.*

$$ ✕ **Little Pub.** Alfresco dining in a village-square setting awaits you at
this charming restaurant. It also has a bustling sports bar and an en-
ergetic Caribbean revue several nights a week. Jamaican standards (jerk
or curried chicken, baked crab, sautéed snapper) accompany surf-and-
turf, lobster thermidor, pasta primavera, seafood stir-fry, crêpes suzette,
and bananas flambé. Burgers and other standard pub fare are also available. ✉ *59 Main St.,* ☎ *876/974–2324. AE, MC,V.*

JAMAICAN

$ ✕ **Ocho Rios Village Jerk Centre.** This blue-canopied open-air eatery
★ is a good place to park yourself for frosty Red Stripe beer and fiery jerk
pork, chicken, or seafood. Milder barbecued meats, also sold by weight
(typically, ¼ or ½ pound makes a good serving), turn up on the fresh
daily chalkboard menu posted on the wall. It's lively at lunch, especially when passengers from cruise ships swamp the place. ✉ *DaCosta
Dr.,* ☎ *876/974–2549. MC, V.*

Montego Bay

ECLECTIC

$$ ✕ **Day-O Plantation Restaurant.** Transport yourself back in time with
a fine meal served on the garden terrace of this Georgian-style plan-
tation house. You might start with smoked marlin and then segue into
seafood ragoût, broiled rock lobster with lemon butter, or beef fillet
with béarnaise sauce. Sweeten things up with one of the traditional Ja-
maican desserts (rum pudding, sweet cakes, or fruit salad). After din-
ner, tour the house. ✉ *Beside Barnett Estate Plantation, Fairfield,* ☎
876/952–1825. AE, MC, V. Closed Mon.

$$$ ✕ **Sugar Mill.** Seafood is served with flair at this terrace restaurant on
★ the golf course of the Half Moon Golf, Tennis, and Beach Club.
Caribbean specialties, steak, and lobster are usually offered in a pungent sauce that blends Dijon mustard with Jamaica's own Pickapeppa
sauce. Otherwise, choices are the daily à la carte specials and anything
flame-grilled. Live music and a well-stocked wine cellar round out the
experience. ✉ *7 mi (11 km) east of MoBay,* ☎ *876/953–2228. Reservations essential. AE, MC, V.*

$ ✕ **Margueritaville Caribbean Bar and Grill.** This brightly painted bar-
restaurant is tough to miss: just look for the slide that connects it with
the water. You'll find plenty of casual dishes on the menu, including
burgers, chicken sandwiches, tuna melts, pizzas, and the like. ✉
Gloucester Ave., ☎ *876/952–4777. AE, MC,V.*

$ ✕ **The Native.** Shaded by a large poinciana tree and overlooking Glouces-
ter Avenue, this open-air stone terrace serves Jamaican and international dishes. To go native, start with smoked marlin, move on to the
boonoonoonoos platter (a sampler of local dishes), and round out with
coconut pie or *duckanoo* (a sweet dumpling of cornmeal, coconut, and
banana wrapped in a banana leaf and steamed). Caesar salad, seafood
linguine, and shrimp kabobs are fine alternatives. Live entertainment
and candlelit tables make this a romantic choice for dinner on weekends. The popular afternoon buffets on Friday and Sunday are family

affairs. ⊠ *29 Gloucester Ave.,* ☎ *876/979–2769. Reservations essential. AE, MC, V.*

$$$ ✕ **Town House.** Most of the rich and famous who have visited Jamaica over the decades have eaten here. You'll find daily specials, delicious variations of standard dishes (red snapper *papillote* is a specialty, with lobster, cheese, and wine sauce), and many Jamaican favorites (curried chicken with breadfruit and ackee). The 18th-century Georgian house is adorned with original Jamaican and Haitian art. There's alfresco dining on the stone patio. ⊠ *16 Church St.,* ☎ *876/952–2660. Reservations essential. AE, DC, MC, V. No lunch Sun.*

$$ ✕ **Le Chalet.** Don't let the French name fool you. This Denny's look-
★   alike, set in a nondescript shopping mall, serves heaping helpings of some of the best Chinese and Jamaican food in MoBay. Tasty lobster Cantonese costs only $15. ⊠ *32 Gloucester Ave.,* ☎ *876/952–6063. AE, MC, V. No lunch Sun.*

ITALIAN

$$$$ ✕ **Julia's Italian Restaurant.** Couples flock to this romantic Italian restaurant in the hills overlooking MoBay. You can choose from an à la carte menu or order a five-course prix-fixe meal ($33–$45 per person) that includes homemade soups and pastas, entrées of fish, chicken, and veal, and scrumptious desserts. Don't expect the meal to equal the stupendous view, and you won't be disappointed. ⊠ *Bogue Hill,* ☎ *876/952–1772. Reservations essential. AE, MC, V.*

SEAFOOD

$$ ✕ **Marguerites.** At this romantic pier-side dining room, "flambé" is the operative word. Lobster, shrimp, fish, and several desserts are prepared in dancing flames as you sip an exotic cocktail. The Caesar salad, prepared table-side, is also a treat. ⊠ *Gloucester Ave.,* ☎ *876/952–4777. Reservations essential. AE, MC, V. No lunch.*

$$ ✕ **Pier 1.** After tropical drinks at the deck bar, you'll be ready to dig into the international variations on fresh seafood; the best are the grilled lobster and any preparation of island snapper. Several party cruises leave from the marina here, and on Friday night the restaurant is mobbed by locals, who come to dance. ⊠ *Off Howard Cooke Blvd.,* ☎ *876/952–2452. AE, MC, V.*

Negril

CARIBBEAN

$ ✕ **Sweet Spice.** This mom-and-pop diner run by the Whytes serves inexpensive, generous plates of conch, fried or curried chicken, freshly caught fish, oxtail in brown stew sauce, and other down-home specialties. The fresh juices are quite satisfying. Drop by for breakfast, lunch, or dinner. ⊠ *1 White Hall Rd.,* ☎ *876/957–4621. MC, V.*

ECLECTIC

$$ ✕ **Margueritaville.** Set on a beautiful stretch of Negril Beach, this op-
★   eration, a sibling of the wildly popular Margueritaville Caribbean Bar and Grill in MoBay, is a sports bar, a disco, a beach club, and a restaurant. You'll also find an art gallery, a gift shop, a five-star PADI dive shop, volleyball and basketball courts, and changing rooms so that you can slip out of your wet suit. Lobster is the house specialty. Far less expensive are the fish, chicken, and sandwich platters. There are also more than 50 varieties of margaritas. ⊠ *Norman Manley Blvd.,* ☎ *876/957–9326. MC, V.*

$$ ✕ **Tan-ya's.** This alfresco restaurant overlooks the pool and hot tub at Sea Splash Resort, an intimate 15-suite property surrounded by palm trees on lovely Negril Beach. Jamaican delicacies with an international flavor are served for breakfast, lunch, and dinner. Try the excellent deviled crab backs or the smoked marlin. ✉ *Norman Manley Blvd.,* ☎ *876/957–4041. AE, DC, MC, V.*

$$ ✕ **Rick's Café.** Here it is—the local landmark complete with cliffs, cliff divers, and powerful sunsets, all perfectly choreographed. Most folks come for the drinks and the renowned sunset party, since the standard pub menu is overpriced. In the sundown ritual the crowd toasts Mother Nature with rum drinks amid shouts, laughter, and ever-shifting meeting and greeting. When the sun slips below the horizon, there are more shouts, more cheers, and more rounds of rum. ✉ *West End Rd.,* ☎ *876/957–0380. MC, V.*

$ ✕ **Kuyaba on the Beach.** This charming thatch-roof eatery features an international menu—including curried conch, kingfish steak, grilled lamb with sautéed mushrooms, and an array of pasta dishes—and a lively ambience, especially at the bar. There's a crafts shop on the premises, and chaise longues line the beach; come prepared to spend some time, and don't forget a towel and bathing suit. ✉ *Norman Manley Blvd.,* ☎ *876/957–4318. AE, MC, V.*

SEAFOOD

$$ ✕ **Cosmo's Seafood Restaurant and Bar.** Owner Cosmo Brown has made
★ this seaside open-air bistro a pleasant place to spend the afternoon—and maybe stay on for dinner. Fish is the main attraction, and the conch soup—a house specialty—is a meal in itself. You'll also find lobster (grilled or curried), fish-and-chips, and the catch of the morning. Customers often drop cover-ups to take a dip before coffee and dessert and return to lounge in chairs scattered under almond and sea grape trees (there's a small entrance fee for the beach). ✉ *Norman Manley Blvd.,* ☎ *876/957–4330. AE, MC, V.*

Beaches

Jamaica has 200 mi (325 km) of beaches, some of them relatively deserted. Generally, the farther west you go, the lighter and finer the sand. The beaches listed below are public (though there's usually a small admission charge) and are among the best Jamaica has to offer. In addition, nearly every resort has its own private beach, complete with towels and water sports. Some of the larger resorts sell day passes to nonguests.

KINGSTON AREA

As a rule, the beaches near Kingston are not as beautiful as those in the resort areas. **Fort Clarence,** in the Hellshire Hills region southwest of the city, has changing facilities and entertainment. You can reach **Lime Cay** by boat (which you can hire at Morgan's Harbor Marina in Port Royal for a small fee). This island, just beyond Kingston Harbor, is perfect for picnicking, sunning, and swimming. **Lyssons Beach,** in Morant Bay, sometimes lures Kingstonians 32 mi (52 km) east of the city to its lovely golden sand.

PORT ANTONIO

Boston Bay, approximately 11 mi (18 km) east of Port Antonio, beyond the Blue Lagoon, is a small, intimate beach. It's a good place to buy the famous peppery delicacy jerk pork, available at any of the shacks spewing scented smoke along the beach. **San San Beach,** about 5 mi (8 km) east of Port Antonio, has beautiful blue waters and is used mainly by area villa or hotel owners and their guests.

OCHO RIOS

Turtle Beach, stretching behind the Renaissance Jamaica Grande, is the busiest beach in Ocho Rios (where the islanders come to swim). **James**

Bond Beach, east of Ocho Rios in the quaint village of Oracabessa, is popular because of the live reggae performances on its bandstand.

DISCOVERY BAY

Puerto Seco Beach is a stretch of sand that's frequented primarily by locals. There's an admission charge of $5 for the beach, which is open daily 9–5. You'll find plenty of water-sports activities and some concessions that sell local foods.

MONTEGO BAY

Cornwall Beach is a lively beach with lots of places that sell food and drink as well as a water-sports concession. The 5-mi (8-km) **Doctor's Cave Beach** has been spotlighted in so many travel articles and brochures that it often resembles Fort Lauderdale during spring break. On the bright side, it has much to offer admirers beyond just sugary sand, including changing rooms, colorful if overly insistent vendors, and plenty of places to grab a snack. **Walter Fletcher Beach,** near the center of town, offers protection from the surf on a windy day and therefore unusually fine swimming; the calm waters make it a good bet for children.

NEGRIL

Not too long ago, **Negril Beach** was a beachcomber's Eden. Today much of its 7 mi of white sand is fronted by resorts, although some stretches along Bloody Bay remain relatively untouched. A few resorts have built accommodations overlooking their nude beaches, adding a new twist to the notion of "ocean view."

THE SOUTHWEST COAST

To find a beach off the main tourist routes, head for Jamaica's unexploited southwest coast. These isolated beaches are some of the island's safest because the population in this region is sparse, and hasslers are practically nonexistent. You should, however, use common sense; never leave valuables unattended on the beach. **Bluefields Beach,** near Savanna-La-Mar (or just Sav-La-Mar to locals), south of Negril, is the south coast beach nearest to "civilization." **Crane Beach,** at Black River, has retained its natural beauty and has—so far—remained undiscovered by most tourists. **Treasure Beach** has to be the best that the south shore has to offer. By a quaint fishing village, this undeveloped beach has coves that are ideal for snorkeling explorations.

Outdoor Activities and Sports

The tourist board licenses all recreational activity operators and outfitters, which should ensure you of fair business practices as long as you deal with companies that display its decals.

BIRD-WATCHING

Many bird-watchers flock here for the chance to see the vervian hummingbird (the second-smallest bird in the world, larger only than Cuba's bee hummingbird), the Jamaican tody (which nests underground), or another of the island's 27 unique species. A great place to spot birds is the **Rocklands Feeding Station** (⊠ Anchovy, south of Montego Bay, ☎ 876/952–2009). It costs about $9 for an afternoon's visit. In Mandeville, tours of the bird sanctuary at **Marshall's Penn Great House** (☎ 876/904–54545) are by appointment only and are led by owner Robert Sutton, one of Jamaica's leading ornithologists. A full-day of bird-watching costs $150 for as many as three people.

FISHING

Port Antonio makes deep-sea fishing headlines with its annual Blue Marlin Tournament, and MoBay and Ocho Rios have devotees who exchange tales (tall and otherwise) about sailfish, yellowfin tuna, wahoo, dolphinfish, and bonito. Licenses aren't required, and you can arrange to charter a boat at your hotel. A boat (with captain, crew, and equipment) that accommodates four to six passengers costs about $400 for a half day.

GOLF

Golfers appreciate both the beauty and the challenges offered by Jamaica's courses. Caddies are almost always mandatory throughout the island, and rates are $5–$15. Cart rentals are available at all courses except Constant Spring and Manchester Country Club; costs are $20–$35.

The Runaway Bay golf course is found at **Breezes Runaway Bay** (✉ North Coast Hwy., ☎ 876/973–7319). This 18-hole course has hosted many championship events (greens fee is $80 for nonguests; guests play for free). In Kingston, **Caymanas** (✉ 6 mi (9½ km) west of Kingston, ☎ 876/922–3386) was Jamaica's first major championship 18-hole course (greens fee is $53).

Ocho Rios has the **Sandals Golf and Country Club** (✉ 2 mi (3 km) east of Ocho Rios, ☎ 876/975–0119), whose adjacent 18-hole course is 700 ft (214 m) above sea level (greens fee is $70 for nonguests). In Trelawny east of Falmouth, try **Grand Lido Braco Golf Club** (✉ Trelawny, between Duncans and Rio Bueno, ☎ 876/954–0010), a 9-hole course with lush vegetation (nonguests should call for fee information). Caddies are not mandatory on this course. The **Prospect Plantation** (✉ A-3, 5 mi (8 km) east of Ocho Rios, ☎ 876/994–1373) has miniature golf.

Some of the best courses are found near MoBay. **Half Moon Golf, Tennis, and Beach Club** (✉ 7 mi (11 km) east of MoBay, ☎ 876/953–3105), a Robert Trent Jones–designed 18-hole course, is the home of the Red Stripe Pro Am (greens fee is $130 for guests, $130 for nonguests). **Ironshore** (✉ 3 mi (5 km) east of airport, ☎ 876/953–2800) is an 18-hole links-style course (the greens fee is $50). **Tryall Golf, Tennis, and Beach Club** (✉ 15 mi (24 km) west of MoBay on North Coast Hwy., ☎ 876/956–5681) has an 18-hole championship course on the site of a 19th-century sugar plantation (greens fee is $40 for guests, $150 for nonguests). The **Wyndham Rose Hall** resort (✉ 4 mi (6½ km) east of airport on North Coast Hwy., ☎ 876/953–2650) hosts several invitational tournaments (greens fee runs $70 for guests, $80 for nonguests). The newest course in Jamaica is the Ritz Carlton's **White Witch course** (✉ 1 Ritz Carlton Dr., Rose Hall, St. James, ☎ 876/518–0174). The greens fees at this 18-hole championship course is $180 for guests of the resort, $225 for nonguests.

Great golf, rolling hills, and a "liquor mobile" go hand in hand at the 18-hole **Negril Hills Golf Club** (✉ East of Negril on Sheffield Rd.,☎ 876/957–4638); the greens fee is $58. In the hills of Mandeville, the 9-hole **Manchester Club** (✉ Caledonia Rd., ☎ 876/962–2403) is the Caribbean's oldest golf course and has a greens fee of about $22.

HORSEBACK RIDING

Jamaica is fortunate to have an outstanding equestrian facility in **Chukka Cove** (☎ 876/972–2506), near Ocho Rios. This resort offers riding, polo, and jumping (starting at $50), as well as hour-long trail rides ($30) and three-hour beach rides ($55). During in-season weekends this is the place for polo (and social) action. In Montego Bay, you can saddle up at the **Rocky Point Riding Stables at Half Moon** (☎ 876/953–2286), which is east of the Half Moon Club. **Prospect Plantation** (☎ 876/994–1373), in Ocho Rios, offers horseback riding for $20 per hour, but travelers must call first to make reservations.

SCUBA DIVING AND SNORKELING

You'll find good scuba diving off the the coasts of Ocho Rios, Port Antonio, and Negril. MoBay, known for its wall dives, has **Airport Reef** at its southwestern edge. The site is known for its coral caves, tunnels, and canyons. Near the Kingston airport is **Port Royal,** filled with sunken ships that are home to a variety of tropical fish. Prices on the island range from $30 to $60 for a single dive. All the large resorts rent equipment, and the all-inclusive places sometimes include scuba diving in their rates.

To scuba dive, you need to show a certification card. The following operators are licensed by the tourist board and offer certification courses, dive trips, and snorkel gear rentals: **Dolphin Divers** (✉ Beach Rd., Negril, ☎ 876/957–4944) offers scuba facilities for sites in western Jamaica. **Garfield Diving Station** (✉ Shop 13, Santa Maria, west of Renaissance Jamaica Grande, Ocho Rios, ☎ 876/974–5749) offers guided dives near Ocho Rios. **Negril Scuba Centre** (✉ Negril Beach Club, Norman Manley Blvd., Negril, ☎ 876/957–4425) offers one-tank dives in the western end of Jamaica for $50. **North Coast Marine Sports** (✉ Several locations in Montego Bay, ☎ 876/953–2211), with a location at Half Moon, offers dives to numerous north coast sites. **Resort Divers** (✉ Gloucester Ave., Montego Bay, ☎ 876/952–4285 or 876/940–1183; ✉ Island Plaza, Ocho Rios, ☎ 876/974–5338) offers dives in both Montego Bay and Ocho Rios.

TENNIS
Many hotels have tennis facilities that are free to their guests, but some will allow nonguests to play for a fee. Court fees generally run $5–$8 per hour for nonguests; lessons start at $12 an hour. In Kingston, the **Crowne Plaza Kingston** (✉ 211A Constant Spring Rd., ☎ 876/925–7676) has tennis courts for guest use only. The **Hilton Kingston** (✉ 77 Knutsford Blvd., ☎ 876/926–5430) has two tennis courts for guest use only. **Le Méridien Pegasus** (✉ 81Knutsford Blvd., ☎ 876/926–3690) has three courts for guest use only.

Grand Lido Sans Souci (✉ North Coast Hwy., 2 mi (3 km) east of Ocho Rios, ☎ 876/974–2353) has two lighted tennis courts and a pro. **Sandals Dunn's River Golf Resort and Spa** (✉ North Coast Hwy., ☎ 876/972–1610) has two courts lit for night play as well as the services of a pro. In Runaway Bay, **Breezes Runaway Bay** (✉ North Coast Hwy., ☎ 876/973–2436) has four tennis courts.

In MoBay tennis is a highlight at **Sandals Montego Bay** (✉ Kent Ave., ☎ 876/952–5510), with four courts lit for night play and a tennis pro. **Half Moon Golf, Tennis, and Beach Club** (✉ 7mi (1 km) east of MoBay, ☎ 876/953–2211) offers tennis buffs the use of 13 Laykold courts (7 lit for night play) along with a resident pro and a pro shop. **Tryall Golf, Tennis, and Beach Club** (✉ 15 mi/4 km) west of MoBay on North Coast Hwy., ☎ 876/956–5660) has nine courts.

In Negril you'll find five hard courts and five clay courts, all lit for night play, at **Swept Away Negril** (✉ Norman Manley Blvd., ☎ 876/957–4040).

Shopping

Jamaican crafts are made with style and skill and take the form of resort wear, hand-loomed fabrics, silk-screened items, wood carvings, paintings, and other fine arts. Jamaican rum is a great take-home gift. So is Tia Maria, Jamaica's world-famous coffee liqueur. The same goes for the island's prized Blue Mountain and High Mountain coffees and its jams, jellies, and marmalades. If you shop around, you'll find good deals on such duty-free luxury items as jewelry, cameras, china, Swiss watches, and Irish crystal. The top-selling French perfumes are sold alongside Jamaica's own fragrances.

Areas and Malls

A shopping tour of the **Kingston** area should begin at Constant Spring Road or King Street. The city's ever-growing roster of malls includes Twin Gates Plaza, New Lane Plaza, the New Kingston Shopping Centre, Tropical Plaza, Manor Park Plaza, the Village, the Springs, and the newest (and some say nicest), Sovereign Shopping Centre. Devon House is the place to find things old and new made in Jamaica. The great house is now a museum with antiques and furniture reproductions; boutiques and an ice cream shop—try one of the tropical flavors (mango, guava, pineapple, and passion fruit)—now fill what were once the stables.

The crafts markets in **Port Antonio** and—unless there's a cruise ship in port—**Ocho Rios** are less hectic than the one in MoBay. Ocho Rios shopping plazas are Pineapple Place, Ocean Village, the Taj Mahal, Coconut Grove, and Island Plaza.

In **MoBay** you should visit the crafts market on Market Street; just be prepared for haggling over prices in the midst of pandemonium. If you want to spend serious money, head for City Centre Plaza; Half Moon Village; Holiday Inn Shopping Centre; St. James's Place; Westgate Plaza; and Montego Bay Shopping Centre, a favorite with locals. At **Negril**'s crafts market you'll find a plethora of T-shirts, straw hats, baskets, and place mats, carved wood statues, colorful Rasta berets, and cheap jewelry. The newest shopping area in Negril is Time Square, filled with luxury items, from jewelry to watches to leather goods.

Specialty Items

COFFEE

In Kingston you'll find Blue Mountain coffee at **John R. Wong's Supermarket** (⊠ 1–5 Tobago Ave., ☎ 876/926–4811). **Magic Kitchen Ltd.** (⊠ Village Plaza, ☎ 876/926–6877) sells the magic beans. The **Sovereign Supermarket** (⊠ Sovereign Center, 106 Hope Rd., ☎ 876/978–1254) has a wide selection of coffee and other goods.

In Negril, java lovers will find beans and ground coffee at **Hi-Lo Supermarket** (⊠ West End Rd., ☎ 876/957–4546). If the stores are out of Blue Mountain, you may have to settle for High Mountain coffee, the locals' second-favorite brand.

HANDICRAFTS

Gallery of West Indian Art (⊠ 11 Fairfield Rd., Montego Bay, ☎ 876/952–4547) is the place to find Jamaican and Haitian paintings. A corner of the gallery is devoted to hand-turned pottery (some painted) and beautifully carved and painted birds and animals.

Harmony Hall (⊠ 8-min drive east on A–1 from Ocho Rios, ☎ 876/975–4222), a restored great house, is where Annabella Proudlock sells her unique wooden boxes (their covers are decorated with reproductions of Jamaican paintings). Also on sale—and magnificently displayed—are larger reproductions of paintings, lithographs, and signed prints of Jamaican scenes and hand-carved wooden combs. In addition, Harmony Hall is well known for its shows by local artists.

Ital-Craft (⊠ Upper Manor ParkShopping Plaza, 184C Spring Rd., Kingston, ☎ 876/931–2812) sells belts, bangles, and beads. Although Ital-Craft's handmade treasures are sold in boutiques throughout Jamaica, this, the factory location, has an outstanding selection of belts made of spectacular shells, as well as leather, feathers, or fur (the most ornate creations sell for about $75). You'll also find some intriguing jewelry and purses here.

Things Jamaican (⊠ Devon House, 26 Hope Rd., Kingston, ☎ 876/929–6602; ⊠ Sangster International Airport, Montego Bay,☎ 876/952–1936) sells some of the best Jamaican crafts—from carved wooden bowls and trays to reproductions of silver and brass period pieces.

LIQUOR AND TOBACCO

As a rule, only rum distilleries, such as Sangster's, have better deals than the airport stores. Best of all, if you buy your rum or Tia Maria at either the Kingston or the MoBay airport before you leave, you don't have to tote all those heavy, breakable bottles to your hotel and then to the airport. Fine handmade **Macanudo** (☎ 876/925–1082) cigars make great easy-to-pack gifts; why not pick some up at Montego Bay airport on your way home? If you get the urge to puff during your stay, call the company to find out where to buy them in Jamaica.

RECORDS AND CDS

Kingston has several good music stores. If you like reggae by world famous Jamaican artists—Bob Marley, Peter Tosh, and Third World, to name a few—a pilgrimage to **Randy's Record Mart** (⊠ 17 N. Parade, Kingston, ☎ 876/922–4859) is a must. **Record Plaza** (⊠ Tropical Plaza, Kingston, ☎ 876/926–7645) is a good place to stop for Jamaican tunes.

Outside the capital are a wide selection of stores. In Negril, music buffs should check out **Countryside** (⊠ Hi-Lo Shopping Centre, Negril, ☎ 876/957–4538). **De Muzik Shop** (⊠ Island Plaza, Ocho Rios, ☎ 876/974–9500) showcases Jamaican recording artists. **Record City** (⊠ 1 William St., Port Antonio, ☎ 876/993–2836) has many new sounds as well as popular favorites. You'll find the works of Jamaican musical stars at **Top Ranking Records** (⊠ Westgate Plaza, Montego Bay, ☎ 876/952–1216).

SHOES

Cheap sandals are good buys in shopping centers throughout Jamaica. Although workmanship and leathers don't rival the craftsmanship of those found in Italy or Spain, neither do the prices (about $20 a pair). In Kingston, **Jacaranda** (⊠ DevonHouse, ☎ 876/929–6602) is a good place to sandal shop. **Lee's Fifth Avenue Shoes** (⊠ Tropical Plaza, ☎ 876/926–7486) is a good store in the capital. In Ocho Rios, the **Pretty Feet Shoe Shop** (⊠ Ocean Village Shopping Centre ☎ 876/974–5040) is a good bet. In MoBay try **Best Ever Footwear** (⊠ 5 E. Street, ☎ 876/979–5095) if you find yourself in need of footwear during your trip.

Nightlife and the Arts

Nightlife

Jamaica—especially Kingston—supports a lively community of musicians. For starters there's reggae, popularized by the late Bob Marley and the Wailers and performed today by son Ziggy Marley, Jimmy Tosh (the late Peter Tosh's son), Gregory Isaacs, Jimmy Cliff, and many others. If your experience of Caribbean music has been limited to steel drums and Harry Belafonte, then the political, racial, and religious messages of reggae may set you on your ear; listen closely and you just might hear the heartbeat of the people.

Those who know and love reggae should visit between mid-July and August for the Reggae Sunsplash. This four-night concert—at the Bob Marley Performing Center (a field set up with a temporary stage), in the Freeport area of MoBay—showcases local talent and attracts such big-name performers as Third World and Ziggy Marley and the Melody Makers.

DANCE AND MUSIC CLUBS

For the most part, the liveliest late-night happenings throughout Jamaica are in the major resort hotels. Some of the all-inclusives offer a dinner and disco pass from about $50. Pick up a copy of the *Daily Gleaner,* the *Jamaica Observer,* or the *Star* (available at newsstands throughout the island) for listings on who's playing when and where.

One of the most popular spots in Kingston is **Jonkanoo** (✉ Hilton Kingston, 77 Knutsford Blvd., ☎ 876/929–3390). The trendy disco **Mirage** (✉ Sovereign Centre, ☎ 876/978–8557) is a favorite with both Kingstonians and travelers.

Port Antonio has several hot spots. If you have but one night to dance, do it at the **Roof Club** (✉ 11 West St., ☎ 876/993–3817). On weekends from 11PM on, this is where it's all happening. Dancers often head to **Shadows** (✉ 40 West St., ☎ 876/993–3823). Live jazz performances are offered on Saturday evenings at the **Blue Lagoon Restaurant** (✉ San San Beach, ☎ 876/993–8491).

Ocho Rios also has nightlife to satisfy most. One of the top dance clubs is **Jamaic'N Me Crazy** (✉ Renaissance Jamaica Grande, Main St., ☎ 876/974–2201); the popular club is a favorite with both guests and local residents who pay a hefty cover charge. **Silks** (✉ Shaw Park Beach Hotel, Shaw Park Ridge Rd., 1½ mi/2½ km south of Ocho Rios, ☎ 876/974–2552) has long been a favorite on the dance scene. The **Little Pub** (✉ Main St., ☎ 876/974–2324) produces Caribbean revues several nights a week.

The widest variety of nightlife is probably found in Montego Bay. With its location right on what's deemed the "Hip Strip," **Hurricanes Disco** (✉ Breezes Montego Bay Resort, Gloucester Ave., ☎ 876/940–1150) is packed with both guests and travelers and locals from other hotels willing to pay a hefty cover charge. The **Rhythm Nightclub** (✉ Holiday Inn Sunspree Resort, 6 mi (9½ km) east of airport on North Coast Hwy., ☎ 876/953–2485) rocks with a Jamaican beat nightly. **Walter's** (✉ 39 Gloucester Ave., ☎ 876/952–9391) is a downtown favorite. After 10 PM on Friday night, the crowd gathers at **Pier 1** (✉ Howard Cooke Blvd., ☎ 876/952–2452), opposite the straw market. **Brewery** (✉ Shop 4, Miranda Ridge, Gloucester Ave., ☎ 876/940–2433) is a popular sports bar. The colorful **Margueritaville** (✉ NormanManley Blvd., ☎ 876/952–4777) throbs with a spring-break crowd during the season and with a fun-loving atmosphere any night of the year.

Negril also has its fair share of happening nightspots. You'll find the best live music at **Alfred's Ocean Palace** (✉ Norman Manley Blvd., ☎ 876/957–4735) with live performances right on thebeach. **De Buss** (✉ Norman Manley Blvd., ☎ 876/957–4405) pulsates with a Jamaican sound, and it's impossible to miss; this joint is in a former double decker bus. The sexy, always packed disco at **Hedonism II** (✉ Norman Manley Blvd., ☎ 876/957–5200) is the wildest dance spot on the island; Tuesday (pajama night) and Thursday (toga night) are tops.

The Arts

Although many resorts offer a "native night" with dances and limbo shows, for true Jamaican culture you should see a stage show in Kingston. Recommended are performances by the Jamaica Philharmonic, the National Chorale, the Jamaica Folk Singers, and the National Dance Theater Company. For schedules check with the tourist board.

Exploring Jamaica

Touring Jamaica can be both thrilling and frustrating. Rugged (albeit beautiful) terrain and winding—often potholed—roads make for slow going. (In the rainy season from June through October, roads can easily be washed out; *always* check conditions prior to heading out.) Primary roads that loop around and across the island are two-lane, and signs are not prevalent. Numbered addresses are seldom used outside major townships, locals drive aggressively, and people and animals seem to have a knack for appearing on the street out of nowhere. That said, Jamaica's scenery shouldn't be missed. The solution? Stick to guided tours and licensed taxis—to be safe and avoid frustration.

If you're staying in Kingston or Port Antonio, set aside at least one day for the capital's highlights and another for a guided excursion to the Blue Mountains. If you have more time, head for Mandeville. You'll find at least three days' worth of activity right along MoBay's boundaries; you should also consider a trip to Cockpit Country or Ocho Rios. If you're based in Ocho Rios, be sure to visit Dunn's River Falls; you may also want to stop by Firefly or Port Antonio. If Negril is your hub, take in the south shore, including Y. S. Falls and the Black River.

Numbers in the margin correspond to points of interest on the Jamaica map.

SIGHTS TO SEE

❷ Blue Mountains. These lush mountains rise to the north of Kingston. If you admire Jamaica's coffee, be sure to visit **Pine Grove** (☎ 876/977–8009), a working coffee farm that doubles as an inn. It also has a restaurant that serves owner Marcia Thwaites's Jamaican cuisine. Another place worth a visit is **Mavis Bank** (☎ 876/977–8005) and its Jablum coffee plant. A half-hour guided tour is available for $5; inquire when you arrive at the main office. **Appleton Rum Factory** (☎ 876/963–9215) is open Monday through Saturday 9–3:30. Visitors tour this expansive South Coast factory; samples are part of the tour.

Unless you're traveling with a local, don't rent a car and go to the Blue Mountains on your own; the roads wind and dip, hand-lettered signs blow away, and you could easily get lost—not just for hours but for days. It's best to hire a taxi (look for red PPV license plates to identify a licensed taxi) or to take a guided tour.

❽ Cockpit Country. Fifteen miles (24 km) inland from MoBay is one of the most untouched areas in the West Indies: a terrain of pitfalls and potholescarved by nature in limestone. For nearly a century after 1655 it was known as the Land of Look Behind because British soldiers nervously rode their horses through here, on the lookout for the guerrilla freedom fighters known as Maroons. Former slaves who refused to surrender to the invading English, the Maroons eventually won their independence. Today their descendents live in this area, untaxed and virtually ungoverned by outside authorities. Most visitors stop in Accompong, a small community in St. Elizabeth Parish. You can stroll through town, take in the historic structures, and learn more about the Maroons—considered Jamaica's greatest herbalists.

❺ Firefly. About 20 mi (32 km) east of Ocho Rios in Port Maria, Firefly was once Sir Noël Coward's vacation home and is now maintained by the Jamaican National Heritage Trust. Although the setting is Eden-like, the house is surprisingly spartan, considering that he often entertained jet-setters and royalty. He wrote *High Spirits, Quadrille,* and other plays here, and his simple grave is on the grounds next to a small stage where his works are occasionally performed. Recordings of Coward singing about mad dogs and Englishmen echo over the lawns. Tours include time in the photo gallery and a walk through the house and grounds, the viewing of a video on Coward, and a drink in the gift shop. ✉ *Port Maria,* ☎ *876/725–0920.* 🎟 *$10.* ☉ *Mon.–Sat. 8:30–5:00.*

❶ Kingston. The reaction of most newcomers to the capital is far from love at first sight. Yet the islanders themselves can't seem to let the city go. Everybody talks about it, about their homes or relatives there, about their childhood memories. Indeed, Kingston seems to reflect more of the true Jamaica—a wonderful cultural mix—than do the sunny havens of the north coast. As one Jamaican put it, "You don't really know Jamaica until you know Kingston." Parts of the city may be dirty, crowded, and raucous, yet it's still where international and local movers and shakers come to move and shake, where the arts flourish, and where the shopping is superb. It's also home to the University of the West Indies, one of the Caribbean's largest universities.

Sprawling Kingston spills over into communities in every direction. To the west, coming in from Spanish Town, lie some of the city's worst slums, in the neighborhoods of Six Miles and Riverton City. Farther south, Spanish Town Road skirts through a high-crime district that many Kingstonians avoid. In the heart of the business district, along the water, the pace is more peaceful, with a lovely walk and parks on Ocean Boulevard. Also here is the Jamaica Convention Centre, home of the UN body that creates all laws for the world's seas. From the waterfront you can look across Kingston Harbour to the Palisadoes Peninsula. This narrow strip is home to Norman Manley International Airport and, farther west, Port Royal, the island's former capital, which was destroyed by an earthquake. (A few words of caution: downtown Kingston is considered unsafe, particularly at night. Be careful.)

New Kingston, north of downtown, is bordered by Old Hope Road on the east and Half Way Tree Road (which changes to Constant Spring Road) on the west. The area is sliced by Hope Road, a major thoroughfare that connects this region with the University of the West Indies, about 15 minutes east of New Kingston. You may feel most comfortable in New Kingston, which glistens with hotels, office towers, apartments, and boutiques. But don't let your trip to the capital end here; away from the high-rises of the new city, Kingston's colonial history is recalled at many well-preserved sites.

North of New Kingston, the city gives way to steep hills and magnificent homes. East of here, the views are even grander as the road winds into the Blue Mountains. Hope Road, just after the University of the West Indies, becomes Gordon Town Road and starts twisting up through the mountains—it's a route that leaves no room for error.

Devon House, built in 1881 and bought and restored by the government in the1960s, is filled with period furnishings, such as Venetian crystal chandeliers, and period reproductions. You can see the inside of the two-story mansion (built with a South American gold miner's fortune) only on a guided tour. On the grounds you'll find some of the island's best crafts shops as well as one of the few mahogany trees to have survived Kingston's ambitious, but not always careful, development. ⊠ *26 Hope Rd.,* ☎ *876/929–7029 or 876/929–6602.* ☞ *$3 for house tour.* ☉ *Devon House Tues.–Sat. 9:30–5, shops Mon.–Sat. 10–6.*

The **Institute of Jamaica,** near the waterfront, is a natural-history museum and library that traces the island's past from the Arawaks to today. The charts and almanacs here are fascinating. The famed Shark Papers, for example, contain evidence of wrongdoing by a sea captain. In an attempt to destroy this evidence, the guilty captain tossed it overboard his ship, but it was later recovered from the belly of a shark. ⊠ *12 East St.,* ☎ *876/922–0620.* ☞ *Free.* ☉ *Weekdays 9–5.*

The artists represented at the **National Gallery** may not be household names in other countries, but their paintings are sensitive and moving. You'll find works by such Jamaican masters as intuitive painter John Dunkley and Edna Manley, a sculptor who worked in a cubist style.

Among other highlights from the 1920s through the 1980s are works by the artist Kapo, a self-taught painter whose creations portray religious images. Reggae fans should look for Christopher Gonzalez's controversial statue of Bob Marley (it was slated to be displayed near the National Arena but was placed here because many Jamaicans felt it didn't resemble Marley). ⌧ *12 Ocean Blvd. (Kingston Mall, near the waterfront),* ☎ *876/922–1561.* ➤ *$1.* ⊙ *Weekdays 10–4.*

At the height of his career, Bob Marley built a recording studio. Today the structure—painted Rastafarian red, yellow, and green—houses the **Bob Marley Museum.** The guided tour takes you through the medicinal herb garden, his bedroom, and other rooms wallpapered with magazine and newspaper articles that chronicle his rise to stardom. The tour includes a 20-minute biographical film on him; there's also a reference library if you want to learn more. Certainly there's much here that will help you to understand Marley, reggae, and Jamaica itself. A striking mural by Jah Bobby, *The Journey of Superstar Bob Marley,* depicts the hero's life from its beginnings, in a womb shaped like a coconut, to enshrinement in the hearts of the Jamaican people. ⌧ *56 Hope Rd.,* ☎ *876/927–9152.* ➤ *$9.75.* ⊙ *Mon.–Sat. 9:30–4.*

⓫ Mandeville. At 2,000 ft (612 m) above sea level, Mandeville is considerably cooler than the coastal areas 25 mi (40 km) to the south. Its vegetation is also more lush, thanks to the mists that drift through the mountains. But climate and flora aren't all that separate it from the steamy coast: Mandeville seems a hilly tribute to all that is genteel in the British character. The people here live in tidy cottages with gardens around a village green; there's even a Georgian courthouse and a parish church. The entire scene could be set down in Devonshire, were it not for the occasional poinciana blossom or citrus grove.

The **Manchester Club** (☎ 876/962–2403) has tennis courts and a well-manicured 9-hole golf course, the first golf course in the Caribbean. At the **Bird Sanctuary** (☎ 876/975–7158), you may spot some of the more than 25 species of unique birds. Tours (by appointment only) are led by owner Robert Sutton, one of the island's leading ornithologists. At **Lovers' Leap,** legend has it that two slave lovers chose to jump off the 1,700-ft-high (520-m-high) cliff rather than be recaptured by their master. At the **High Mountain Coffee Plantation** (☎ 876/963–4211), in Williamsfield, free tours (by appointment only) show how coffee beans are turned into one of the world's favorite morning drinks.

❼ Martha Brae River. The gentle waterway takes its name from an Arawak Indian who killed herself because she refused to reveal the whereabouts of a local gold mine to the Spanish. According to legend, she agreed to take them there and, on reaching the river, used magic to change its course, drowning herself and the greedy Spaniards with her. Her *duppy* (ghost) is said to guard the mine's entrance. Rafting on this river is a very popular activity. Martha Brae River Rafting arranges trips downriver. Near the rafting company ticket office you'll find gift shops, a bar-restaurant, and a swimming pool.

❾ Montego Bay. Today many explorations of MoBay are conducted from a reclining chair—frothy drink in hand—on Doctor's Cave Beach. Believe it or not, the area had a history before all the resorts went up. If you can pull yourself away from the water's edge and brush the sand off your toes, you'll find some very interesting colonial sights.

The outstanding free tour of **Barnett Estates** is led by a charming guide in period costume who recites period poetry and sings period songs. The Kerr-Jarrett family has held the land here for 11 generations, and they still grow coconuts, mangoes, and sugarcane on 3,000 acres. ⌧

Granville Main Rd., ☎ *876/952–2382.* ⌨ *Free, but open only for diners at the Day-O Plantation Restaurant, next door.* ☉ *Great house 9:30 AM–10 PM; tours daily 6:30 PM–11 PM.*

In the 1700s, **Rose Hall** may well have been the greatest of great houses in the West Indies. Today it's popular less for its architecture than for the legend surrounding its second mistress: Annie Palmer was credited with murdering three husbands and a *busha* (plantation overseer) who was her lover. The story is told in a novel that's sold everywhere in Jamaica: *The White Witch of Rose Hall.* There's a pub on site. ✉ *East of Montego Bay, across highway from Rose Hall resorts,* ☎ *876/953–2323.* ⌨ *$15.* ☉ *Daily 9–6.*

The **Greenwood Great House** has no spooky legend to titillate, but it's much better than Rose Hall at evoking the atmosphere of life on a sugar plantation. The Barrett family, from whom the English poet Elizabeth Barrett Browning descended, once owned all the land from Rose Hall to Falmouth, and built this and several other great houses on it. (The poet's father, Edward Moulton Barrett, "the Tyrant of Wimpole Street," was born at nearby Cinnamon Hill, currently the estate of country singer Johnny Cash.) Highlights of Greenwood include oil paintings of the Barretts, china made for the family by Wedgwood, a library filled with rare books from as early as 1697, fine antique furniture, and a collection of exotic musical instruments. There's a pub on-site as well. ✉ *15 mi (24 km) east of Montego Bay,* ☎ *876/953–1077.* ⌨ *$12.* ☉ *Daily 9–6.*

⑩ **Negril.** In the 18th century English ships assembled here in convoys for dangerous ocean crossings. The infamous pirate Calico Jack and his crew were captured right here while they guzzled rum. All but two of them were hanged on the spot; Mary Read and Anne Bonney were pregnant at the time, so their executions were delayed.

On the winding coast road 55 mi (89 km) southwest of MoBay, Negril was once Jamaica's best-kept secret. Recently, however, it has begun to shed some of its bohemian, ramshackle atmosphere for the attractions and activities traditionally associated with MoBay. One thing that hasn't changed around this west-coast center (whose only true claim to fame is a 7-mi [11-km] beach) is a casual approach to life. As you wander from lunch in the sun to shopping in the sun to sports in the sun, you'll find that swimsuits and cover-ups are common attire. Want to dress for a special meal? Slip on a caftan over your swimsuit.

Negril stretches along the coast south from horseshoe-shape Bloody Bay (named when it was a whale-processing center) along the calm waters of Long Bay to the Lighthouse section and landmark Rick's Cafe. Sunset at Rick's is a Negril tradition. Divers spiral downward off 50-ft-high cliffs into the deep green depths as the sun turns into a ball of fire and sets the clouds ablaze with color. Sunset is also the time when Norman Manley Boulevard, which intersects with West End Road, comes to life with bustling bistros and ear-splitting discos.

Even nonguests can romp at **Hedonism II.** The resort beach is divided into "prude" and "nude" sides; a quick look around reveals where most guests pull their chaise longues. Nude volleyball, body-painting contests, and shuffleboard keep daytime hours lively; at night most action occurs in the high-tech disco or in the hot tub. Your day pass (10:30–5; $65) includes food and drink and participation in water sports, tennis, squash, and other activities. Night passes ($75) cover dinner, drinks, and entrance to the disco. Day or night, reservations are a must; bring a photo ID as well.

West End Road leads to Negril's only structure of historical significance, the **Lighthouse,** which has guided ships past Jamaica's rocky western coast since 1895. You can stop by the adjacent caretaker's cottage 11–7 (except Tuesday) and, for the price of a tip, climb the spiral steps to the best view in town.

❻ **Ocho Rios.** Although Ocho Rios isn't near eight rivers as its name would seem to indicate, it does have a seemingly endless series of cascades that sparkle from limestone rocks along the coast. (The name Ocho Rios came about because the English misunderstood the Spanish *laschorreras*—"the waterfalls.")

Today Ocho Rios can be a traffic-clogged community, but a visit is worthwhile, if only to enjoy its two chief attractions—Dunn's River Falls and Prospect Plantation. A few steps from the main road in Ocho Rios are some of the most charming inns and oceanfront restaurants in the Caribbean. Lying on the sand of what seems to be your very own cove or swinging gently in a hammock while sipping a tropical drink, you'll soon forget the traffic that's just a stroll away.

Dunn's River Falls is an eye-catching sight: 600 ft (184 m) of cold, clear mountain water splashing over a series of stone steps to the warm Caribbean. The best way to enjoy the falls is to climb the slippery steps: don a swimsuit, take the hand of the person ahead of you, and trust that the chain of hands and bodies leads to an experienced guide. The leaders of the climbs are personable fellows who reel off bits of local lore while telling you where to step; you can hire a guide's service for a tip of a few dollars. ⊠ *Off A–1, between St. Ann's and Ocho Rios,* ☎ *876/974–2857.* ≊ *$6.* ☉ *Daily 8:30–5.*

To learn about Jamaica's former agricultural lifestyle, a trip to **Prospect Plantation** is a must. But it's not just a place for history lovers or farming aficionados; everyone seems to enjoy the views over the White River Gorge and the tour by jitney (a canopied open-air cart pulled by a tractor). The grounds are full of exotic fruits and tropical trees, some planted over the years by such celebrities as Winston Churchill and Charlie Chaplin. You can also go horseback riding on the plantation's 900 acres or play miniature golf, grab a drink in the bar, or buy souvenirs in the gift shop. If you want more time to really explore, you can rent one of the on-site villas. ⊠ *Hwy. A–1, west of downtown Ocho Rios,* ☎ *876/994–1058.* ≊ *$12.* ☉ *Daily 8–5. Tours Mon.–Sat. 10:30, 2, and 3:30; Sun. 11, 1:30, and 3.*

The original "defenders" stationed at the Old Fort, built in 1777, spent much of their time sacking and plundering as far afield as St. Augustine, Florida, and sharing their booty with the local plantation owners who financed their missions. Fifteen miles (24 kilometers) west is Discovery Bay, site of Columbus's landing, with a small museum of artifacts and such local memorabilia as ships' bells and cannons and iron pots used for boiling sugarcane.

Jamaica's national motto is "Out of Many, One People," and at the **Coyaba River Garden and Museum** you'll see exhibits on the many cultural influences that have contributed to the creation of the one. The museum covers the island's history from the time of the Arawak Indians up to the present day. A guided 45-minute tour through the lush 3-acre garden introduces you to the flora and fauna of the island. The complex includes a crafts and gift shop and a snack bar. ⊠ *Shaw Park Estate, Shaw Park Ridge Rd., 1½ mi (2½ km) south of Ocho Rios,* ☎ *876/974–6235.* ≊ *$4.50.* ☉ *Daily 8:30–5.*

Other excursions of note include Runaway Bay's Green Grotto Caves (and the boat ride on an underground lake); a ramble through the Shaw Park Botanical Gardens; a visit to Sun Valley, a working plantation with banana, coconut, and citrus trees; and a drive through Fern Gully, a natural canopy of vegetation filtered by sunlight (Jamaica has the world's largest number of fern species, more than 570).

④ **Port Antonio.** Early in the 20th century the first tourists seeking a respite from New York winters arrived on the northeast coast, drawn by the exoticism of the island's banana trade. In time the area became fashionable among a fast-moving crowd and has counted J. P. Morgan, Rudyard Kipling, William Randolph Hearst, Clara Bow, Bette Davis, and Ginger Rogers among its admirers. Its most passionate devotee was the actor Errol Flynn, whose spirit still seems to haunt the docks, and you can almost imagine him devouring raw dolphinfish and swigging gin at 10 AM. Although the action has moved elsewhere, the area can still weave a spell. Robin Moore wrote *The French Connection* here, and Broadway's tall and talented Tommy Tune found inspiration for the musical *Nine* while being pampered at Trident.

Port Antonio has also long been a center for some of the Caribbean's finest deep-sea fishing. Dolphins (the delectable fish, not the lovable mammal) are the likely catch here, along with tuna, kingfish, and wahoo. In October the weeklong Blue Marlin Tournament attracts anglers from around the world. By the time they've all had their fill of beer, it's the fish stories—rather than the fish—that carry the day.

A good way to spend a day in Port Antonio is to laze in the deep azure water of the **Blue Lagoon.** Although there's not much beach to speak of, you'll find a water-sports center, changing rooms, and a soothing mineral pool. Good, inexpensive Jamaican fare is served at a charming waterside terrace restaurant; it's open daily for lunch and dinner and has live jazz music on Saturday night. ⊠ *1 mi (1½ km) east of San San Beach,* ☎ *876/993–8491.*

Queen Street, in the residential Titchfield area, a couple of miles north of downtown Port Antonio, has several fine examples of Georgian architecture. **DeMontevin Lodge** (⊠ 21 Fort George St., on Titchfield Hill, ☎ 876/993–2604) is owned by the Mullings family. The late Gladys Mullings was Errol Flynn's cook, and you can still get great food here. The lodge, and a number of structures on nearby Musgrave Street (the crafts market is here), are built in a traditional seaside style that's reminiscent of New England.

③ **Rio Grande.** The Rio Grande (yes, Jamaica has a Rio Grande, too) is a granddaddy of river-rafting attractions: an 8-mi-long (13-km-long) swift, green waterway from Berrydale to Rafter's Rest (it flows into the Caribbean at St. Margaret's Bay). The trip of about three hours is made on bamboo rafts pushed along by a raftsman who is likely to be a character. You can pack a picnic lunch and eat it on the raft or on the riverbank; wherever you lunch, a vendor of Red Stripe beer will appear at your elbow. A restaurant, a bar, and souvenir shops are at Rafter's Rest. The trip costs about $40 per two-person raft.

A short drive east from Port Antonio puts you at Boston Bay, which is popular with swimmers and has been enshrined by lovers of jerk pork. The spicy barbecue was originated by the Arawaks and perfected by the Maroons. Eating almost nothing but wild hog preserved over smoking coals enabled them to survive years of fierce guerrilla warfare with the English.

Some 6 mi (9½ km) northeast of Port Antonio in the village of Nonsuch are the **Athenry Gardens,** a 3-acre tropical wonderland, and the Nonsuch Caves, whose underground beauty has been made accessible by concrete walkways, railed stairways, and careful lighting. ⊠ *First*

right after Dragon Bay, east of Port Antonio, ☎ *876/993–3740.* 🖃
$6. ☉ *Daily 10–4.*

⑬ **Port Royal.** Just south of Kingston, Port Royal was called "the wickedest
city in the world" until an earthquake tumbled much of it into the sea
in 1692. The spirits of Henry Morgan and other buccaneers add energy to what remains. The proudest possession of St. Peter's Church,
rebuilt in 1726 to replace Christ's Church, is a silver communion set
said to have been donated by Morgan himself (who probably obtained
it during a raid on Panama).

Port Royal is slated for a massive redevelopment project that will ren-
ovate existing historical sites and introduce new museums, shops,
restaurants, and perhaps even a cruise-ship pier if funding for these ambitious plans can be secured.

A ferry from the square in downtown Kingston goes to Port Royal at
least twice a day, and the town is small enough to see on foot. If you
drive out to Port Royal from Kingston, you'll pass several other sights,
including remains of old forts virtually overgrown with vegetation, an
old naval cemetery (which has some intriguing headstones), and a
monument commemorating Jamaica's first coconut tree, planted in 1863
(there's no tree there now, just plenty of cactus and scrub brush).

You can no longer down rum in Port Royal's legendary 40 taverns,
but two small pubs still remain in operation. You can explore the impressive remains of **Ft. Charles,** once the area's major garrison. Built
in 1662, this is the oldest surviving monument from the British occupation of Jamaica. On the grounds are a maritime museum and the
old artillery storehouse, Giddy House, that gained its name after being
tilted by the earthquake of 1907: locals say its slant makes you giddy.
☎ *876/967–8438.* 🖃 *$4.* ☉ *Daily 9–5.*

⑫ **Spanish Town.** Twelve miles (19 kilometers) west of Kingston on A–
1, Spanish Town was the island's capital when it was ruled by Spain.
The town has a Georgian Antique Square, the Jamaican People's Museum of Crafts and Technology (in the Old King's House stables), and
St. James, the oldest cathedral in the Western Hemisphere. Spanish
Town's original name was Santiago de la Vega, meaning St. James of
the Plains. Contact the Institute of Jamaica (☎ 876/922–0620) for further information on this heritage town.

JAMAICA A TO Z

*To research prices, get advice from other travelers, and book travel ar-
rangements, visit www.fodors.com.*

AIR TRAVEL

Air Canada offers daily service from Toronto, Halifax, Winnipeg, and
Montréal in conjunction with Air Jamaica. Air Jamaica provides the
most frequent service from U.S. cities, including Atlanta, Baltimore,
Chicago, Fort Lauderdale, Los Angeles, Miami, New York, Orlando,
Philadelphia, Phoenix, and San Francisco; flights are also available from
London. American Airlines flies nonstop daily from New York and
Miami. British Airways connects Kingston with London. The Pana-
manian carrier Copa offers service between Miami and Kingston.
Cubana flies in from Havana. Northwest Airlines has daily direct ser-
vice to MoBay from Tampa. USAirways flies in from Philadelphia.
➤ AIRLINES AND CONTACTS: **AirCanada** (☎ 876/952–5160 in Montego
Bay; 876/942–8211 in Kingston); **Air Jamaica** (☎ 876/952–4300 in
Montego Bay; 876/922–4661 in Kingston); **American Airlines** (☎

876/952–5950 in Montego Bay; 876/920–8887 in Kingston); **British Airways** (☎ 876/929–9020 in Kingston); **Copa** (☎ 876/926–1762); **Cubana** (☎ 876/978–3410); **Northwest Airlines** (☎ 876/952–9740); **USAirways** (☎ 876/940–0171).

AIRPORTS

Donald Sangster International Airport, in MoBay, is the most efficient point of entry for visitors destined for MoBay, Ocho Rios, Runaway Bay, and Negril. Norman Manley International Airport, in Kingston, is the best arrival point for visitors to the capital or Port Antonio.

➤ AIRPORT INFORMATION: **Donald Sangster International Airport** (☎ 876/952–3124); **Norman Manley International Airport** (☎ 876/924–8452).

BIKE AND MOPED TRAVEL

Although the front desks of most major hotels can arrange the rental of bicycles, mopeds, and motorcycles, we recommend that you *don't* rent a moped or motorcycle; the strangeness of driving on the left, the less-than-cautious driving style that prevails on the island, the abundance of potholes, and the prevalence of vendors who will approach you at every traffic light are just a few reasons why.

BUSINESS HOURS

BANKS

Banks are generally open Monday–Thursday 9–2, Friday 9–4.

POST OFFICES

Post office hours are weekdays 9–5.

SHOPS

Normal business hours for stores are weekdays 8:30–4:30, Saturday 8–1.

CAR RENTALS

Although Jamaica has dozens of car-rental companies (you'll find branches at the airports and the resorts among other places), rentals can be difficult to arrange once you've arrived. Make reservations and send a deposit before your trip. (Cars are scarce, and without either a confirmation number or a receipt, you may have to walk.) You must be at least 21 years old to rent a car (at least 25 at several agencies), have a valid driver's license (from any country), and have a valid credit card. You may be required to post a security of several hundred dollars before taking possession of your car; ask about it when you make the reservation. Rates average $65–$120 a day, after the addition of the compulsory CDW coverage, which you must purchase even if your credit card offers it.

Avis offers rental cars for both the north coast and capital city. Budget has a variety of car types and price ranges. Hertz has several types of rental cars in various price ranges. In both the capital city and in Montego Bay, vehicles are available at Island Car Rentals. For north coast rentals, Jamaica Car Rental has several different rental plans. For rentals in Montego Bay, United Car Rentals offers several types of vehicles.

➤ MAJOR AGENCIES: **Avis** (☎ 876/952–4543 in Montego Bay; 876/924–8013 in Kingston); **Budget** (☎ 876/952–3838 in Montego Bay; 876/924–8762 in Kingston); **Hertz** (☎ 800/654–3131; 876/979–0438 in Montego Bay; 876/924–8028 in Kingston); **Island Car Rentals** (☎ 876/952–5771 in Montego Bay; 876/926–5991 in Kingston); **Jamaica Car Rental** (☎ 876/952–5586 in Montego Bay; 876/974–2505 in Ocho Rios); **United Car Rentals** (☎ 876/952–3077 in Montego Bay).

CAR TRAVEL

GASOLINE

Gas stations are open daily but accept cash only. Gas costs roughly $1.35–$1.60 a gallon.

ROAD CONDITIONS

Driving is a chore and can be extremely frustrating. You must constantly be on guard—for enormous potholes, people, and animals darting out into the street, as well as aggressive drivers.

RULES OF THE ROAD

Traffic keeps to the left in Jamaica.

ELECTRICITY

Like the electrical current in North America, the current in Jamaica is 110 volts but only 50 cycles, with outlets that take two flat prongs. Some hotels provide 220-volt plugs as well as special shaver outlets. If you plan to bring electrical appliances with you, it's best to ask when making your reservation.

EMBASSIES

➤ CANADA: **Canadian High Commission** (✉ 30 Knutsford Blvd., Kingston, ☎ 876/926–1500).

➤ UNITED KINGDOM: **British High Commission** (✉ Trafalgar Rd., Kingston, ☎ 876/926–9050).

➤ UNITED STATES: **U.S. Embassy** (✉ 32 Oxford Rd., Kingston, ☎ 876/929–4850 or 876/926–9565).

EMERGENCIES

➤ AIR RESCUE: Dial ☎ 119.

➤ AMBULANCE AND FIRE: Dial ☎ 110.

➤ HOSPITALS: **Cornwall Regional Hospital** (✉ Mt. Salem, Montego Bay, ☎ 876/952–6683); **Mo Bay Hope** (✉ Half Moon Resort, Montego Bay, ☎ 876/853–3981) has dialysis services; **Port Antonio Hospital** (✉ Naylor's Hill, Port Antonio, ☎ 876/993–2646); **St. Ann's Bay Hospital** (✉ St. Ann's Bay, ☎ 876/972–2272); **University Hospital** (✉ Mona, Kingston, ☎ 876/927–1620).

➤ PHARMACIES: **Great House Pharmacy** (✉ Brown's Plaza, Ocho Rios, ☎ 876/974–2352); **Le Méridien Pegasus** (✉ 81 Knutsford Blvd., Kingston, ☎ 876/926–3690).

➤ POLICE: Dial ☎ 119.

➤ SCUBA DIVING EMERGENCIES: **St. Ann's Bay Hospital** (✉ St. Ann's Bay, ☎ 876/972–2272), has a hyperbaric chamber.

ETIQUETTE AND BEHAVIOR

As you travel the island, you'll see Rastafarians, with their flowing dreadlocks (although some prefer to wear their hair beneath knitted caps). Rastas smoke marijuana as part of their religious rites, do not eat salt or pork (many are vegetarians), and often sell crafts. Always ask for permission before taking a photograph.

FESTIVALS AND SEASONAL EVENTS

The biggest festival is Carnival, an event filled with lots of music and dancing in the streets. It's held in Kingston, Ocho Rios, and MoBay every April and in Negril every May. Music lovers also fill the island for the August Reggae Sunsplash International Music Festival, which is getting hotter every year, because the best, brightest, and newest of the reggae stars gather to perform in open-air concerts in MoBay. Anglers come to Port Antonio to compete in the annual Blue Marlin Tournament, which is usually held in October.

➤ CONTACTS: **Reggae Sunsplash International Music Festival** (☎ 800/526–2422).

HEALTH

Carry along insect repellent and a strong sunscreen to avoid Jamaica's natural hazards. Water is generally safe to drink, especially in large resorts, but many people prefer to drink bottled water when they are in a new environment.

HOLIDAYS

Public holidays for 2002 are: New Year's Day, Ash Wednesday (Feb. 13), Good Friday (March 29), Easter Monday (Apr. 1), Labor Day (May 23), Independence Day (first Mon. in Aug.), National Heroes Day (Oct. 15), Christmas, and Boxing Day (Dec. 26).

LANGUAGE

The official language of Jamaica is English. Islanders usually speak a patois among themselves, a lyrical mixture of English, Spanish, and various African languages. Some examples of patois are *me diyah* (I'm here; pronounced mee *de*-ya); *nyam* (eat; pronounced yam); and, if someone asks how your vacation is going, just say *irie* (pronounced *eye*-ree), which means "great."

MAIL AND SHIPPING

Postcards may be mailed anywhere in the world for J$25. Letters to the United States and Canada cost J$25, to Europe J$12.50, to Australia J$40, and to New Zealand J$30.

➤ CONTACTS: **Kingston Post Office** (✉ 13 King Street, ☎ 876/922–2120); **Montego Bay Post Office** (✉ 122 Barnett Street, ☎ 876/952–7389).

MONEY MATTERS

Note that prices quoted throughout this chapter are in U.S. dollars unless otherwise noted.

ATMS

ATM machines do not accept American bank cards, although cash advances can be made using credit cards.

CREDIT CARDS

Major credit cards are widely accepted throughout the island, although cash is required at gas stations, in markets, and in many small stores. Discover and Diner's Club are accepted at many resorts.

CURRENCY

The official currency is the Jamaican dollar. At press time the exchange rate was about J$45 to US$1. U.S. money (currency only, no coins) is accepted at most establishments, although you'll often be given change in Jamaican money.

CURRENCY EXCHANGE

Currency can be exchanged at airport bank counters, exchange bureaus, or commercial banks. Throughout the island you'll find branches of the Bank of Nova Scotia.

➤ CONTACTS: **Bank of Nova Scotia** (✉ Sam Sharpe Square, Montego Bay, ☎ 876/952–4440; ✉ Main St., Ocho Rios, ☎ 876/974–2689; ✉ Negril Square, Negril, ☎ 876/957–3040; ✉ 35 King St., Kingston, ☎ 876/922–1420).

PASSPORTS AND VISAS

U.S. and Canadian citizens must have apassport (not expired beyond one year). Or, to prove citizenship, bring an original birth certificate (with a raised seal) or a naturalization certificate along with a government-issued photo ID (all documents must bear the same name). British, Australian, and New Zealand visitors need passports. Everyone must have a return or ongoing ticket. Declaration forms are usually distributed in flight to keep customs formalities to a minimum.

SAFETY

Don't let the beauty of Jamaica cause you to abandon the caution you would practice in any unfamiliar place. Never leave valuables in your room; use the safe-deposit boxes that most hotels make available. Carry your funds in traveler's checks, and keep a record of the check numbers in a secure place. Never leave a rental car unlocked, and never leave valuables in a locked car. Ignore efforts, however persistent, to sell you ganja (marijuana). Independent travelers, especially those renting cars, need to take special precautions. Some travelers have been harassed by locals offering to "guard" cars and have experienced vandalism when requests for money were denied.

SIGHTSEEING TOURS

Half-day tours are offered by a variety of operators in the important areas of Jamaica. The best great-house tours include Rose Hall, Greenwood, and Devon House. Plantations to tour are Prospect, Barnett Estates, and Sun Valley. The Appleton Estate Tour uses a bus to visit villages, plantations, and a rum distillery. The increasingly popular waterside folklore feasts are offered on the Dunn's, Great, and White rivers. The significant city tours are in Kingston, MoBay, and Ocho Rios.

Caribic Tours offers various tours to Jamaica as well as excursions to Cuba. CS Tours has island sightseeing tours to major attractions. Glamour Tours offers guided tours to many top sightseeing spots on the north coast. Safari Tours schedules guided jeep tours, downhill biking tours, and horseback tours. Sun Holiday Tours offers sightseeing tours across Jamaica; you can sign up for one-day or multiday tours. Tourwise offers guided tours of top attractions including Dunn's River Falls, Black River Safari, rafting, Cockpit Country, Kingston, Mayfield Falls, Blue Lagoon, and more; tours are available in English, French, Spanish, German, Italian, and Dutch.

➤ CONTACTS: **Caribic Tours** (✉ 1310 Providence Dr., Montego Bay, ☎ 876/953–9895); **CS Tours** (✉ 66 Claude Clarke Ave., Montego Bay, ☎ 876/952–6260); **Glamour Tours** (✉ Montego Freeport, Montego Bay, ☎ 876/979–8207); **Safari Tours** (✉ Mammee Bay, Montego Bay, ☎ 876/972–2639); **Sun Holiday Tours** (✉ Donald Sangster International Airport, Montego Bay, ☎ 876/979–1061); **Tourwise** (✉ 103 Main St., Ocho Rios, ☎ 876/974–2323).

BOAT

Calico Sailing offers snorkeling trips and sunset cruises on the waters of MoBay; costs are $35 and $25, respectively. Martha Brae River Rafting leads trips down the Martha Brae River, about 25 mi (40 km) from most hotels in MoBay. The cost is just under $42 (two per raft) for the 1½-hour river run. Mountain Valley Rafting runs trips down the River Lethe, approximately 12 mi (19 km) (a 50-minute trip) southwest of MoBay; the trip is about $36 per raft (two per raft) and takes you through unspoiled hill country. Bookings can also be made through hotel tour desks.

Rio Grande Attractions Ltd. guides raft trips down the Rio Grande; the cost is $45 per raft. South Coast Safaris Ltd. has guided excursions up the Black River for some 10 mi (16 km) (round-trip), into the mangroves and marshlands to see alligators, birds, and plant life. The trip on the 25-passenger *Safari Queen* or *Safari Princess* costs around $15.
➤ BOAT: **Calico Sailing** (✉ North Coast Highway, Montego Bay, ☎ 876/952–5860); **Martha Brae River Rafting** (✉ Claude Clarke Ave.,

Montego Bay, ☎ 876/952–0889); **Mountain Valley Rafting** (✉ Lethe, ☎ 876/956–4920); **Rio Grande Attractions Ltd.** (✉ St. Margaret's Bay, ☎ 876/993–5778); **South Coast Safaris Ltd.** (✉ 1 Crane Rd., Black River, ☎ 876/965–2513).

HELICOPTER

Helitours Jamaica Ltd., 1 mi (1½ km) west of Ocho Rios, offers helicopter tours of Jamaica, ranging from 20 minutes to an hour, at prices from $65 to $225.
➤ CONTACTS: **Helitours Jamaica Ltd.** (✉ North Coast Hwy., ☎ 876/974–2265 or 876/974–1108).

SPECIAL-INTEREST

Countrystyle offers unique, personalized tours of island communities. You're linked with community residents based on your interests; there are tours that include anything from bird-watching in Mandeville to nightlife in Kingston. **Maroon Attraction Tours Co.** leads full-day tours from MoBay to Maroon headquarters at Accompong, giving you a glimpse of the society of Maroons who live in Cockpit Country. The cost is $50 per person.
➤ CONTACTS: **Countrystyle** (✉ 62 Ward Ave., Mandeville, ☎ 876/962–7979 or 800/526–2422); **Maroon Attraction Tours Co.** (✉ North Coast Hwy., Montego Bay, ☎ 876/952–4546).

TAXES

DEPARTURE TAX

The departure tax is $27, although many ticket prices now include the departure tax.

SALES TAX

Jamaica has replaced the room occupancy tax with a general consumption tax of 15% on most goods and services.

TAXIS

Some but not all of Jamaica's taxis are metered. If you accept a driver's offer of his services as a tour guide, be sure to agree on a price before the vehicle is put into gear. (Note that a one-day tour should run about $100–$180, depending on distance traveled.) All licensed taxis display red Public Passenger Vehicle (PPV) plates. Cabs can be summoned by phone or flagged down on the street. Rates are per car, not per passenger, and 25% is added to the metered rate between midnight and 5 AM. Licensed minivans are also available and bear the red PPV plates. JUTA is the largest taxi franchise and has offices in all resort areas.
➤ CONTACTS: **JUTA** (☎ 876/974–2292 in Ocho Rios; 876/957–9197 in Negril; 876/952–0813 in Montego Bay; 876/927–4534 in Kingston).

TELEPHONES

Most hotels offer direct-dial telephone services; local businesses provide telegraph and fax services for a fee. Pay phones are available in most communities.

COUNTRY AND AREA CODES

To dial Jamaica from the United States, just dial 1 + the area code 876.

INTERNATIONAL CALLS

Some U.S. phone companies, such as MCI, won't permit credit-card calls to be placed from Jamaica because they have been victims of fraud. The best option is to purchase Jamaican phone cards, sold in most stores across the island.

LOCAL CALLS

While on the island, calls from town to town are long distance.

TIPPING

Most hotels and restaurants add a 10% service charge to your bill. When a service charge isn't included, a 10% to 20% tip is appreciated. Tips of 10% to 20% are customary for taxi drivers as well.

TRANSPORTATION AROUND JAMAICA

Air Jamaica Express, a subsidiary of Air Jamaica, provides shuttle services on the island. Be sure to reconfirm your departing flight a full 72 hours in advance. Tropical Airlines offers service between Kingston and MoBay as well as flights to Cuba. Tim Air offers quick flights between resort areas as well as to Kingston.

➤ CONTACTS: **Air Jamaica Express** (☎ 876/952–5401 in Montego Bay; 876/923–8680 in Kingston, WEB www.airjamaica.com); **Tropical Airlines** (☎ 876/920–3770 in Kingston; 876/940–5917 in Montego Bay); **Tim Air** (☎ 876/952–2516).

VISITOR INFORMATION

➤ BEFORE YOU LEAVE: **Jamaica Tourist Board** (✉ 801 2nd Ave., 20th floor, New York, NY 10017, ☎ 212/856–9727 or 800/233–4582; ✉ 500 N. Michigan Ave., Suite 1030, Chicago, IL 60611, ☎ 312/527–1296; ✉ 1320 S. Dixie Hwy., Suite 1101, Coral Gables, FL 33146, ☎ 305/665–0557; ✉ 3440 Wilshire Blvd., Suite 1207, Los Angeles, CA 90010, ☎ 213/384–1123; ✉ 1 Eglinton Ave. E, Suite 616, Toronto, Ontario M4P 3A1, Canada, ☎ 416/482–7850; ✉ 1–2 Prince Consort Rd., London SW7 2BZ, U.K., ☎ 0171/224–0505, WEB www.jamaicatravel.com).

➤ IN JAMAICA: **Jamaica Tourist Board** (✉ 2 St. Lucia Ave., Kingston, ☎ 876/929–9200 or 888/995–9999 for the on-island help line; ✉ Hendriks Bldg., 2 High St., Black River, ☎ 876/965–2074); ✉ Cornwall Beach, Montego Bay, ☎ 876/952–4425; ✉ Coral Seas Plaza, Negril, ☎ 876/957–4243; ✉ Ocean Village Shopping Centre, Ocho Rios, ☎ 876/974–2570; ✉ City Centre Plaza, Port Antonio, ☎ 876/993–3051).

14 MARTINIQUE

Updated by
Eileen
Robinson Smith

On a hilltop at Leyritz Plantation, a brisk *alizé* rustles palm fronds. A vast banana plantation rolls out below and does more than suggest the Old World—it is the past. The Atlantic stretches beyond to the horizon. Reaching this vantage point requires travel up serpentine roads etched into Mont Pelée, an active volcano that earlier in this century erased St-Pierre, the former capital, leaving only one survivor: a prisoner locked in his underground cell. The breeze smells of earth and sea. From this singular spot the New World—out there—is all but forgotten.

The Arawak Indians named Martinique *Madinina* (Island of Flowers). Exotic wild orchids, frangipani, anthurium, jade vines, flamingo flowers, and hundreds of vivid varieties of hibiscus still grow on the island. But these days the scent of flowers competes with those of French perfume and espresso.

Martinique is like a tropical suburb of Paris; it has a definite sense of style, from the snappy new airport to the old plantation houses. Even the women working at the rental-car desks look as if they are straight from the Champs Elysées. It's no surprise, then, the island has one of the highest standards of living in the Caribbean. In their dealings with foreigners, Martinicans are polite and self-assured—qualities anchored in the privileged position the island has enjoyed historically.

Martinique was the administrative, social, and cultural center of the French Antilles. Guadeloupe was an island of merchants and shopkeepers. Martinique was a rich, aristocratic island, famous for its beautiful women and gracious living, which gave birth to an empress, Napoléon's Josephine, and saw the full flowering of plantation-house society with its servants and soirées, wine cellars and snobbery.

This 425-square-mi (1,101-square-km) island, the largest of the Windwards, has landscapes as varied as its culture and history. In the south, which holds most of the development and the best beaches, there are rolling hills and sugarcane fields. In the north look for lush, tropical vegetation, fields of bananas and pineapples, deep gorges, towering cliffs, and one of the Caribbean's most impressive volcanoes, Mont Pelée. Fort-de-France is the island's capital city as well as its cultural and commercial hub. Most of the other towns—such as Ste-Anne and Vauclin, to the south, and Carbet and Marigot, to the north—are either small resorts or fishing villages.

Britain and France squabbled over Martinique until 1815, when the island was ceded by treaty to Paris. Today the French connection means French-influenced food from the motherland and wine, a wonderful elán, superb roads, Franco-Caribbean pop music, relatively high prices, and plenty of culture and arts (Martinique has one of the finest jazz festivals in the Caribbean, and in Patrick Chamoiseau it has a world-class novelist). However, the island's tourism industry has suffered in recent years. The chic upper-crust French are not as prevalent as in decades past. Women in long dresses and men in dinner jackets are no longer the norm. French package tours have reduced the incentive for hotels to provide high-quality service and have made it difficult for free-standing restaurants to remain in business. The upshot is prices have fallen and the island is generally more affordable than years past, what with the dollar strong and the franc low, so most Americans who come are Francophiles.

You'll need some French to feel truly at home, though the locals are more forthcoming with English here than in other places in the French-speaking world. Franglais is universal. This island is not *like* France—it *is* France. Most everything shuts down at midday and reopens sometime after 2:30. Topless bathing is almost de rigueur, the driving is frenetic, and poodles are the pedigree pooch of choice. High season runs mid-November through May, and the island can be very quiet the rest of the year, with some hotels closing down for months, others discounting tarifs significantly.

Lodging

Martinique's accommodations range from tiny inns called *relais créoles* to splashy tourist resorts and restored plantation houses. The majority of hotels are clustered in Le Diamant, Ste-Anne, Pointe du Bout, and Anse-Mitan on Les Trois-Illets Peninsula across the bay from Fort-de-France. In recent years the big resorts have worked at attracting a mass-market, package-tour clientele mainly from France. There are only several deluxe properties on the island. A number that lack mega-stellar ratings make up for it with charisma, hospitality, and French style. Most hotels have the busy, slightly frenetic feel that the French seem to like. The major establishments usually include a large buffet breakfast of fresh fruit, cheese, croissants, baguettes, jam, and café au lait. Many hotels can accommodate wheelchairs.

CATEGORY	COST*
$$$$	over $240
$$$	$150–$240
$$	$85–$150
$	under $85

All prices are for a standard double room, excluding $1.50 per-person, per-night tax and 10% service charge.

Hotels

BASSE-POINTE

$$ ☷ **Leyritz Plantation.** Sleeping on a former sugar plantation in one of
★ the antiques-furnished rooms of the manor house, cottages, or renovated slave cabins is a novelty. The isolated Leyritz sits on 16 lush acres with stunning views of Mont Pelée. Cottage rooms feature rough wood beams and mahogany four-poster beds, secretaries, and other antiques. The former slave quarters, which are undergoing extensive renovation and expansion, have eaves, stone-and-stucco walls, more contemporary furnishings, and madras linens. Ironically, it's the 20 newer bungalows that are smaller and lack individuality, but these have views of the sea. The former masters' wing is also being fashioned into guest

rooms. Except when the tours from the hotels in the south come through, it's very quiet here—a sharp contrast to the frenzied level of activity at the hotels in Pointe du Bout. Le Ruisseau Restaurant and some rooms are accessible to people with disabilities. A taxi will charge about $70 from the airport, so most guests pick up a rent-a-car on arrival. However, if the sun has set, stay closer to the airport and chart your course in the morning. ✉ *Bourg 97218,* ☎ *596/78–53–92,* FAX *596/78–92–44. 72 rooms. Restaurant, bar, air-conditioning, pool, tennis court. AE, DC, MC, V. CP, MAP.*

FORT-DE-FRANCE

$$ ⊞ **Valmenière.** This is the closest hotel to the airport and is also ideal for first-night stays when your flight arrives too late to navigate a long drive to a remote hotel. Perched on a hilltop overlooking Fort-de-France, it has blue-tinted windows, a high-tech elevator, and white tubular steel walkways—squeaky clean, efficient, and wired for work. The suites are large, with a separate entrance to the living room, and have desks. Three *chambres de bureau* (business rooms) have beds you can fold away, turning the room into a flexible office space; the hotel also offers a full range of business services, including translation. There's also a good restaurant, a pool, and a sun roof on the top floor. ✉ *Av. des Arawaks, 97200,* ☎ *596/75–75–75 or 800/528–1234,* FAX *596/75–69–70,* WEB *www.karibea.com. 116 rooms, 4 suites. Restaurant, bar, pool, gym, business services, meeting rooms. AE, DC, MC, V. CP.*

$ ⊞ **Squash Hotel** This accommodating three-star hotel is a good base in the city for business or for touring the capital, especially if you need to stay the night in the capital after arriving at the airport (just 10 minutes away) before heading out to your hotel in the country. Near the center of town, it is just a short walk from Savannah Park. A major renovation is to be completed by October 2001. ✉ *3 Boulevard Marne, Fort-de-France, 97200,* ☎ *596/72–80–80,* FAX *596/63–00–74,* WEB *www. karibea.com. 105 rooms, 3 suites. Restaurant, bar, air-conditioning, pool, spa, health club, squash, meeting rooms, car rental. AE, DC, MC, V. EP.*

LA TRINITÉ

$ ⊞ **La Caravelle.** This is a simple two-star lodging, built in 1985 and lovingly maintained by the Combaluziers, the hands-on owners, who will make you feel like family. Jean Luc, a Frenchman with the king's English, knows everything about everything and willingly helps you plot your course. The lack of a pool is compensated by extra special food at the restaurant and vistas of the sandy beach of L'Anse L'Etang, which is many-steps down (coming back up the hill is for the agile). Most guests rent through Eurocar, which gives special rates to La Caravelle, but Jean Luc can arrange a taxi for the initial transfer from the airport, a wise decision since first-day driving is more than a challenge, especially if arriving at night. ✉ *L'Anse L'Etang, Trinité Route de Chateau Dubuc 97220,* ☎ *596/58–07–32;* FAX *596/58–07–90. 14 studio apartments. Restaurant, air-conditioning, kitchenettes. AE, MC, V. CP.*

$ ⊞ **Residence Oceane.** The view here of the Caravelle Peninsula is one of the best. These fanciful creole bungalows overlook the Atlantic surf, with an unobstructed panorama of cliffs that meet blue ocean; some are many steps down a hillside. Built in 1998, they are enjoying excellent repeat business, especially from surfers. This patch of ocean is the wild side of the peninsula, and there is a professional surfing school here. Fishing can also be arranged. Each bungalow has five rooms, decorated with yellow and blue fabrics, have blonde rattan furniture (there are a few bunk beds), and attractive tile work in the bathrooms. Televisions are available on request, and air-conditioning has an extra

Lodging

Anse Caritan 36
La Caravelle 10
Club des Trois-Ilets . . 27
Club Med/
Buccaneer's Creek . . 35
Diamant
Les Bains 32
Diamant-Novotel . . . 31
Fregate Bleue 15
L'Habitation de l'Ilet
de Thierry 16
Habitation
Lagrange 9
Hôtel Amyris 34
Leyritz Plantation 7
Manoir de
Beauregard 37
Le Méridien
Trois-Ilets 21
La Pagerie 18
Le Plein Soleil 14
Relais Caraïbes 33
Résidence Oceane . . 11
La Résidence
Village Créole 24
Rivage Hôtel 19
Sofitel Bakoua
Coralia 22
Squash Hôtel 30
Valmenière 4

Dining

L'Abordage 25
La Belle Epoque 1
La Canne á Sucre . . . 3
La Caravelle 10
Chez Titine 12
Le Colibri 8
Fatzo 29
Habitation Céron . . . 5
La Maison de l'Ilet
Oscar 17
Le Marie Sainte 2
Les Passages
du Vent 28
La Plantation
Pays Mêlé 13
Le Plein Soleil 14
Poï et Virginie 38
Pointe-Nord 6
Le Regal de la Mer . 26
Le Ruisseau
Restaurant 7
Sapori d'Italia 23
La Villa Creole 20

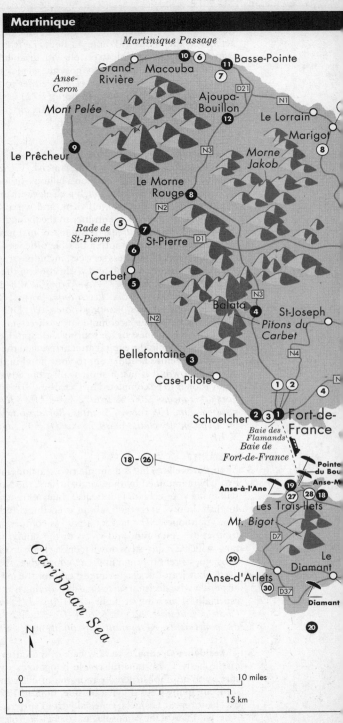

Martinique

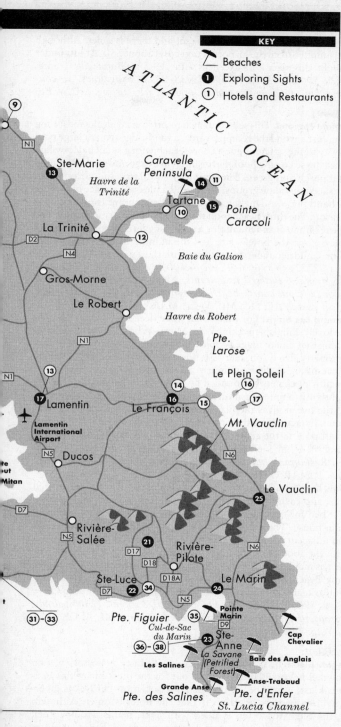

443

KEY

🔱 Beaches

❶ Exploring Sights

① Hotels and Restaurants

Exploring

Ajoupa-Bouillon 12
Balata 4
Basse-Pointe 11
Bellefontaine 3
Diamond Rock 20
Dubuc Castle 15
Forêt de
Montravail 21
Fort-de-France 1
Habitation Anse
Latouche 5
Le François 16
Lamentin 17
Macouba 10
Le Marin 24
Le Morne Rouge . . . 8
Musée Gauguin . . . 6
Pointe du Bout 19
Le Prêcheur 9
Presqu'île du
Caravelle 14
Ste-Anne 23
Ste-Luce 22
Ste-Marie 13
St-Pierre 7
Schoelcher 2
Les Trois-Ilets 18
Le Vauclin 25

ATLANTIC OCEAN

Caravelle Peninsula

Ste-Marie

Havre de la Trinité

Tartane

Pointe Caracoli

La Trinité

Baie du Galion

Gros-Morne

Le Robert

Havre du Robert

Pte. Larose

Le Plein Soleil

Lamentin

Le François

Mt. Vauclin

Lamentin International Airport

Ducos

Le Vauclin

Rivière-Salée

Rivière-Pilote

Ste-Luce

Le Marin

Pte. Figuier

Cul-de-Sac du Marin

Pointe Marin

Cap Chevalier

Ste-Anne

Baie des Anglais

Les Salines

La Savane (Petrified Forest)

Anse-Trabaud

Grande Anse

Pte. d'Enfer

Pte. des Salines

St. Lucia Channel

charge of about $5 a day. However, with the ocean winds and ceiling fans, it is usually not a necessity. Corner rooms, which have the largest terraces, are the best. English is spoken, and there is quiet. Although only 20 minutes from the airport, a taxi costs about $50. At just under $60 a night, this place is an excellent value. ⊠ *Anse Bonneville Trinité, 97220,* ☎ *596/25–85–93,* ℻ *596/58–33–95. 24 bungalows. Air-conditioning, fans, kitchenettes (some), pool, beach, surfing. MC, V. EP.*

LE DIAMANT

$$$$ 🏨 **Diamant-Novotel.** This self-contained resort is in an ideal windsurfing location. Just beyond the reception area, a footbridge spans a large pool on the way to the spacious guest rooms, each with a small balcony facing either the sea or the pool. Furnishings are cane and wicker painted in pastel peach and green. The dining room is large and unromantic, set up to accommodate groups, but there's a pleasant terrace bar where a local band plays. A smaller, more formal restaurant is open during peak season. The three beaches on the five-acre property are small. The staff speaks English and maintains a surprising level of enthusiasm and efficiency, given the hotel's size and the number of tour groups that stay here. Children under 16 stay free with their parents. ⊠ *Pointe de la Chery 97223,* ☎ *596/76–42–42 or 800/322–2223,* ℻ *596/76–22–87. 175 rooms, 6 suites. 2 restaurants, 3 bars, air-conditioning, pool, hair salon, 2 tennis courts, beach, dive shop, snorkeling, windsurfing, shops, car rental. AE, DC, MC, V. CP, MAP.*

$$ 🏨 **Diamant Les Bains.** For more than three decades, Hubert Andrieu and his lovely, English-speaking wife, Marie-Yvonne, have been doing everything they can to make people feel at home at this intimate beachfront property. Their son, Herve, is now taken over the creole kitchen. A few rooms are in the main house, above the restaurant, but opt for the beachfront chalets surrounded by flowers and palm trees. The tile floors, brightly painted furniture, white ceilings, and light breeze playing off the ocean gives the place the feeling of an old-fashioned seaside hotel. In fact, it was the first hotel in Diamant in the 1940s. There is a small pool in the center of the property. ⊠ *Bourg du Diamant, Diamant 97223,* ☎ *596/76–40–14,* ℻ *596/76–27–00. 7 rooms, 20 bungalows. Restaurant, bar, air-conditioning, refrigerators, pool, beach. MC, V. CP, MAP. Closed Sept.*

$$ 🏨 **Relais Caraïbes.** Twelve bungalows are spread over the manicured grounds, and each has a hammock, a bedroom, a small salon with a pull-out bed for two, and a bathroom; there are also three rooms in the main house. The pool is on the edge of a cliff that overlooks the sea and adjacent to the appealing terrace restaurant. Even nonguests come for the good French food, wine, and music. The new owner, Eric Bordiere, is maintaining the inn's charisma while making improvements. The tiny beach is a short walk, and there's scuba and boating instruction available at the nearby Diamant-Novotel. ⊠ *Pointe de la Chery 97223,* ☎ *596/76–44–65,* ℻ *596/76–21–20. 3 rooms, 12 bungalows. Restaurant, bar, refrigerators (some), pool, boating. MC, V. CP, MAP. Closed Aug.–Oct.*

LE FRANÇOIS

$$$ 🏨 **Fregate Bleue.** In 1991 Madame Yveline de Lucy de Fossarieu, who once owned Leyritz Plantation, sold out for the quiet life at this bed-and-breakfast, a member of the French association Les Relais du Silence, whose primary criterion is that the hotel is quiet. Although dated, the blue stucco inn is filled with light, plants, trompe l'oeil paintings, and hand-carved parrots. The spacious rooms have four-poster beds, Persian rugs, and the occasional antique; most balconies overlook Les Ilets de l'Impératrice. All rooms have a small kitchenette and a modern bathroom. *Le petit déjeuner* (breakfast) is served on the upstairs veranda. The nearest restaurants are a 10-minute drive, and you must negotiate a rutted road to get to the highway. The on-site pool is small, but the beaches of Le François and Le Vauclin are only five minutes away. The hotel is 5 mi (8 km) south of Le François on Vauclin Rd. ⊠ *Quartier Frégate 97240,* ☎ *596/54–54–66 or 800/633–7411,* FAX *596/54–78–48. 7 rooms. Air-conditioning, kitchenettes, pool. AE, MC, V. CP.*

$$$ ⊞ **L'Habitation de L'Ilet Thierry.** From a boat, at first all you see is a dock with a palapa and a single palm tree attached to a long pier that dead-ends at a steep, stone staircase. The staircase leads to this primitive hotel on a remote, windswept island. The white stucco, colonial-style, two-story edifice, which made its first debut at the turn-of-the-twentieth-century, is 10 minutes away from François, and five minutes from the island of Oscar. It might as well be two days from nowhere because there is nothing else on this island, fronted by a coral reef surrounded by turquoise water. The rooms are large but stark, so forget about plush creature comforts. Although rooms have basic bathrooms, you must shower on the first floor due to lack of water pressure. On the first floor is the salon-dining room that looks like something from the movie *Key Largo*. Some come just for the prix-fixe lunch—190 to 320 F (that's lobster) with a swing in a hammock thrown it; boat transportation, however, is not and costs $43 round trip. Because of its island-off-an-island location, prices are not inexpensive. Rates include breakfast and dinner (MAP) and boat transportation to and from the Club Nautique du François. ⊠ *Ilet Thierry, 97240, 10 min by boat from François,* ☎ *596/65–88–54 or 596/27–66–07, 5 rooms. Kitchenettes. No credit cards. AP, MAP.*

$$ ⊞ **Le Plein Soleil.** This hotel is chic, contemporary creole at its unex-
★ pected best. The scattering of new gingerbread cottages, with fretwork and facades painted in Caribbean pastels, clings to the hillside, overlooking the sea below. As attractive as these terraced suites are—minimalistic, with blue and white bedding and contemporary French armoires—it is the inn's "great house" that captivates. Trés chic, it is a study in white, with classy, tropical furnishings, objets d'nature and art, including a wild-looking nude, and up the wooden stairs, a loft—the designated TV room. The salon flows into the terrace-restaurant, which affords a panoramic view of verdent, rolling hills dropping to the sea. The teak furniture is subtly impressive. Creative lighting plays up the artistic vignettes of pods, berries, and palm fronds. Some of the island's best cuisine is served here—contemporary French utilizing tropical ingredients. The great-looking pool is on its own plateau, with views down the coastline. This is one of Martinique's special finds, and owner Jean Christophe (former creative talent for a Parisian ad agency) a most caring host. ⊠ *Villa Lagon Sarc, Pointe Thalemont, Le François 97240,* ☎ *596/38–07–77,* FAX *596/65–58–13. 12 bungalows. Restaurant, air-conditioning, kitchenettes, pool. MC, V. EP, MAP.*

LES TROIS-ILETS

$$$$ ⊞ **Sofitel Bakoua Coralia.** Once a family estate overlooking the bay
★ of Fort-de-France, the Bakoua today is probably Martinique's finest hotel. Its impressive canopied entrance with international flags hoisted, could be an embassy's. Accommodations are in three hillside buildings, with a fourth on the beautiful white-sand beach. Beach rooms, while small, are modern, light, quiet, and comfortable. All have a balcony or patio, a bathroom with hand-painted tiles, and a marble vanity with a hair dryer and deluxe amenities. The rooms in the original residence are the largest and most charismatic. There is always an animated scene at the circular bar near the gorgeous infinity pool. The beach grill has been redone and enlarged; there is a new "computer corner" for check-

ing e-mail. Entertainment consists of live music and nightly shows. ⊠ *Pointe du Bout 97229,* ☎ *596/66–02–02 or 800/322–2223,* FAX *596/ 66–00–41. 138 rooms, 6 suites. 2 restaurants, 2 bars, air-conditioning, minibars, pool, 2 tennis courts, beach, snorkeling, boating, shops. AE, DC, MC, V. CP, MAP.*

$$$ 🏨 **Hotel Amyris.** In the south, some 20 minutes from the airport, this resort from the Karibéa group is a stand out. The newest in this developing tourist area on the Caribbean side, it has a panoramic view of a natural cove, protected by a lush garden. Four three-story buildings (sans elevators), housing the guest rooms, are situated within the park-like gardens and the beautifully designed pool. Each junior suite has two bathrooms, either his and hers, or one for the parents, one for the kids. There are convertible couches in the living rooms, balconies, nice rattan and ceruse wood furniture, and hair dryers. The garden rooms have full kitchenettes. Also, the food served is of a high caliber for a three-star resort. The management is professional; the front-desk crew have young, smiling faces and are English-speaking. ⊠ *Sainte-Luce 97228,* ☎ *596/62–12–00,* FAX *596/62–12–10,* WEB *www.karibea.com. 110 Jr. suites. Restaurant, in-room safes, kitchenettes (some), refrigerators, pool, tennis court, children's programs, meeting rooms, car rental. AE, MC, V CP.*

$$$ 🏨 **Le Méridien Trois-Ilets.** There's a great deal of activity here, even in the low season, much of it revolving around the beautifully designed pool and man-made beach. Also, the jetty is the delightful setting for special theme nights. The ferry to Fort de France is just a walk-in-the-sand away. The exterior of this mega-hotel may still say mid-1970s, but the guest rooms have been completely renovated. The rose-colored lamps coordinate perfectly with the madras chairs and the tropical floral bedspreads and drapes. Solidly built, the rooms are soundproof; tile floors have replaced worn carpet. Some have balconies with a splendid view of the bay and Fort-de-France or the marina. Two luxury and four one-bedroom suites are also available. The aerobic and aqua-aerobic classes are exceptional. The 60-ft catamaran cruise with lobster lunch is a must do. The sailing club promotes an excellent boating atmosphere. The hotel's ambience is the island's most convivial, and there's live entertainment nightly, including folkloric dinners. Fifty new suites are planned for 2002. ⊠ *Pointe du Bout 97229,* ☎ *596/ 66–00–00; 212/245–2920 in NY,* FAX *596/66–00–74,* WEB *www.lemeridien.com. 295 rooms, 6 suites. 2 restaurants, bar, air-conditioning, minibars, pool, spa, 2 tennis courts, beach, dive shop, snorkeling, boating, casino, car rental. AE, DC, MC, V. CP, MAP.*

$$$ 🏨 **La Pagerie.** La Pagerie looks as if it were plucked out of the Côte d'Azur and planted near the marina in Pointe du Bout. Now a member of the Karibéa Group, the hotel has small, air-conditioned rooms and studios, each with a bath and a trim little balcony. The decor is attractive throughout, with light rattan furnishings, planters, tropical floral curtains, and floral bedspreads. Although there's no beach or water sports, you're only a short stroll from resort hotels, restaurants, the marina, and many activities. ⊠ *Pointe du Bout 97229,* ☎ *596/66–05– 30 or 212/757–6500 in NY,* FAX *596/66–00–99. 95 rooms. Restaurant, bar, air-conditioning, pool, hair salon. AE, MC, V. CP, MAP.*

$$ 🏨 **Club Des Trois-Ilets.** Actually a 15-minute drive from Trois-Ilets, 10 from the touristic area of Pointe du Bout, this modest, seafront resort is more in the country. The low-rise buildings (no elevators) housing the guest rooms are sequestered in a tropical garden. This three-star property managed by the French Accor Group, appeals to a young, sporty crowd (including some with children) since there is a dive club on site. Kids go for the Ping-Pong, pedal boats, and volleyball. The staff is pleasant; front-desk receptionists always try to be helpful, and some speak

English. In general, neither service nor food are strong points, but the restaurant, bar, and dance floor are right on the water. ⊠ *Anse d' l'Anse, Trois-Illets 97229,* ☎ *596/68–31–67,* FAX *596/68–37–65. 77 rooms. Restaurant, bar, air-conditioning, pool, Ping-Pong, volleyball, beach, snorkeling, dive shop, boating, shop. AE, MC, V. CP, AP, MAP.*

$ ⊞ **Rivage Hotel.** You get good value for your money at Maryelle and Jean Claude Riveti's small hotel. The place does have the air of a motor inn of the 1950s, but it's immaculately maintained, and the studios are much larger than comparable rooms at neighboring hotels— for about a third of the cost. Each pool-view unit has a private bath and either a kitchenette or a minirefrigerator. You should have no trouble communicating: English, Spanish, and French are spoken. The beach is across the road. ⊠ *Anse-Mitan 97229,* ☎ *596/66–00–53,* FAX *596/66–06–56,* WEB *pro.wanadoo.fr/rivagehotel/index.html. 4 rooms, 12 studios. Snack bar, air-conditioning, pool, beach, car rental. MC, V. EP.*

$ ⊞ **La Résidence Village Créole.** New vacation rentals from studios to two-bedroom apartments have opened on the second floor (no elevator) of this fun, attractive, nouveau creole complex. Simple, modern, tropical furniture and bright, floral fabrics give these units a clean, uncluttered look. Each has fully equipped kitchen facilities. With convertible couches, it is ideal for families. Travel packages are available with charter flights out of Boston. The complex is a few minutes from Anse Mitan. ⊠ *Pointe du Bout, Les Trois Ilets 97229,* ☎ *596/66–03–19,* FAX *596/66–07–35,* WEB *www.villagecreole.com. 35 apartments. Air-conditioning, kitchenettes. AE, DC, MC, V.*

MARIGOT

$$$$ ⊞ **Habitation Lagrange.** Nowhere on the island do you feel the style, romance, and elegance of the old plantation-house society more than in this 19th-century manor house, set in a rain forest on the northeast coast. Everything—from the dual antique shaving mirrors to the flowered commodes in the "water closets," bespeak of another era. A huge entrance hall with fascinating murals that depict Martinique's history opens onto a bar with antique sailing ships. A small library, where you can browse or play solitaire or backgammon, is a delight—a step back into gracious living. Rooms in the main building have four-poster beds, mahogany floors, and tall French windows that open onto a wraparound veranda. The Écurie, which once were stables, houses two more rooms. The original stone walls have been incorporated into the decor; parquet floors, huge windows, and two canopy beds in each room complete the picture. A 1990s pink-and-white creole-style building houses another six rooms with gabled ceilings, mahogany armoires, wicker chaise lounges, and chintz curtains. Breakfast is served outdoors overlooking the curvaceous pool. Lunch, which is like a complete dinner, is served in the formal dining room. However, the food under the elegant silver domes is nothing exceptional, especially for the high prices. The wine list is one of the most extensive on the island. Giant ficus trees and a profusion of flowers make wandering the grounds a delight. However, the "bush" and its critters threaten to take over. Some serious capital needs to be injected into the property to return it to its former glory circa 1994, when it became a hotel. The road to La Grange, off the main highway, is like something out of Indiana Jones; do not attempt it after dark. ⊠ *Marigot 97225,* ☎ *596/53–60–60 or 800/322–2223,* FAX *596/53–50–58,* WEB *www.habitation-lagrange.com. 14 rooms, 1 suite. Bar, dining room, pool, tennis court, library. AE, DC, MC, V. CP, MAP.*

STE-ANNE

$$$ 🏨 **Club Med/Buccaneer's Creek.** Built in 1969 and occupying 48 land-scaped acres, this older Club Med is an all-inclusive village with plazas, cafés, restaurants, a boutique, and a small marina. Air-conditioned pastel rooms contain twin beds and a private shower. The only money you need to spend here is for bar drinks, personal expenses, and excursions. There's a white-sand beach, a plethora of water sports, and plenty of nightlife. In fact, it is one 24-hour-a-day party, appealing to singles from their 20s to 40s, mainly from France. Excursion tours are narrated in French. Children are welcome, but there is no kids' club. Although well-maintained, the club and rooms are not plush and have never had a full renovation. Prices quoted are usually air-inclusive, which is generally the most cost-effective way to go. ✉ *Pointe du Marin 97227,* ☎ *596/76–72–72 or 800/258–2633,* 🅵🅰🆇 *596/76–83–36,* 🆆🅴🅱 *www. clubmed.com. 308 rooms. 2 restaurants, 2 bars, air-conditioning, 7 tennis courts, basketball, gym, volleyball, beach, dive shop, dock, snorkeling, boating, waterskiing, dance club, nightclub. AE, MC, V. All-inclusive.*

$$$ 🏨 **Manoir de Beauregard.** Built in the early 18th century, this impos-
★ ing plantation house was made into a hotel in 1928. The main building, with its 2-ft-thick stone walls and mullioned windows, feels like a medieval abbey church. Where the nave would be is a drawing room with bentwood rockers, chandeliers, and checkerboard marble floors. It is flanked by "aisles" with sloping roofs; one serves as the bar, which leads out onto a sunny terrace and a small L-shape pool. The three rooms upstairs in the main building have high wood-beam ceilings, antique furniture, four-poster beds, brocade, table linens, and curtains. Other rooms are in a modern annex at the other side of the property. Most are not very nice, but one is a gem, a circular tower room in the former sugar mill, and is favored by honeymooners. However, the bathroom is on the ground floor, down the circular staircase. All rooms have phones and TVs. This property has history and personality, as does its Cornell-educated owner, Christian Saint-Cyr, but it would benefit greatly from a redecoration. ✉ *Chemin des Salines 97227,* ☎ *596/76–73–40,* 🅵🅰🆇 *596/76–93–24. 11 rooms. Bar, air-conditioning, pool. AE, MC, V. EP. Closed Sept–Dec.*

$$ 🏨 **Anse Caritan.** This appealing property combines the amenities of a large hotel with the service and ambience of a more intimate one. It's amid exquisite gardens fronting a ribbon of champagne-colored sand. With your reading material, you can take shade under the frangipani trees. Management does its best to give the hotel an "island" feel. All rooms are done in soft colors (periwinkle, mauve, and gray) and have phones, hair dryers, and rough-wood terraces or balconies, most with a sea view. The restaurant is known for its innovative creole fare; breakfast is good, and the beachfront restaurant serves everything from pizza and calzones to shrimp flambéed in aged rum and grilled lobster. Sepia posters depict island life of centuries past. A guitarist-singer often entertains. The staff is remarkably friendly and diligent. ✉ *Pointe des Salines 97227,* ☎ *596/76–74–12,* 🅵🅰🆇 *596/76–72–59. 228 rooms. 2 restaurants, bar, snack bar, air-conditioning, in-room safes, pool, beach, dive shop, snorkeling, boating, fishing, dance club. AE, MC, V. CP, MAP.*

Villas and Condominiums

The **Villa Rental Service** (☎ 596/71–56–11, 🅵🅰🆇 596/63–11–64) can help you find a home, a villa, or an apartment to rent. Most properties are in the south of the island near good beaches, and you can rent for a week or a month.

Dining

Martinique's restaurants serve classic French, contemporary, and creole cuisines, though their cellars are generally filled with fine French wines. Increasing numbers of package tours, which limit dining to certain hotels, have threatened the island's distinguished freestanding restaurants, but you can still find excellent spots in the countryside. The farther you venture from tourist hotels, the less likely you are to discover English-speaking folk. But that shouldn't stop you.

The local creole specialties are *colombo* (curry), *accras* (cod or vegetable fritters), *crabes farcis* (stuffed land crab), *écrevisses* (freshwater crayfish), *boudin* (creole blood sausage), *lambi* (conch), *langouste* (clawless Caribbean lobster), *soudons* (sweet clams), *blaff* (fish or shellfish plunged into seasoned stock), and *oursin* (sea urchin). And, if you like your *poisson* (fish) or any other dish with a little tang, try the *chien* sauce; it literally means "dog" sauce. It's made from onions, shallots, peppers, oil, and vinegar. Don't confuse chien sauce with the local pepper, which is sometimes served in oil and has an atomic kick. The favorite local libation is 'ti punch, concocted of four parts white rum and one part sugarcane syrup.

Most restaurants offer a prix-fixe menu, often with several choices of entrées and wine. Finding a cheap American-style bite at lunch is almost impossible. For additional savings pick up a copy of the *Ti Gourmet* booklet at the tourist office and larger hotels; most restaurants listed offer a free drink or discount upon presentation.

What to Wear

For dinner, casual resort wear is appropriate. Generally, men do not wear jackets and ties, as they did in decades past, but they do wear collared shirts. Women typically wear light cotton sundresses, short or long. At dinnertime, beach attire is too casual for most restaurants. Nice shorts are okay for lunch, depending on the venue. Dresses and skirts are more appropriate in a formal setting or a city restaurant frequented by business people. Keep in mind, in Martinque lunch is usually a three-course, two-hour affair.

CATEGORY	COST*
$$$$	over $30
$$$	$20–$30
$$	$10–$20
$	under $10

per person for a main course at dinner

Anse-d'Arlets

FRENCH CUISINE

$$ **✕ Fatzo.** Despite the connotations of its name, this is one Grand Dame
★ that has it all: food, ambience, service, hospitality, history, decor, and a good crowd of interesting types, from fun locals to yachters. A former 1890 residence, it is decorated with vintage straw hats, old island lithographs, and vintage photos of Martinique plantation houses. For starters, consider escargot in garlic butter sauce, and perfect avocados with two fresh shrimp dressed with pink mayonnaise sauce. As a main course, go for a thick slab of grilled duck with two sauces—curry and honey, accompanied by perfect pommes frites, christophene gratin, and garlicky haricots verts. Finish with a crêpe Fatzo with bananas, chocolate, coco rape, and chantilly cream. Alain, the man in charge, is wonderfully hospitable, a true pro, from the service he gives to the incredible piña coladas he makes with fresh pineapple juice. There are two prix-fixe menus, as well as a celebratory Couscous Royal night on Friday

that draws a crowd (make reservations). Located between Trois Ilets and Diamant. ⊠ *11 Rue Felix Eboue, Anses-D'Arlet,* ☎ *596/68–62–79. V. Closed Sun. No lunch Mon.*

Basse-Pointe

CARIBBEAN

$$ ✕ **Le Ruisseau Restaurant.** Located within the restored 17th-century plantation inn, Leyritz Plantation, the pride of Martinque, the restaurant serves a full lunch and dinner. It is a pleasant respite after a tour of the grounds and is wheelchair-accessible. The bar, crafted from local stone, serves a mean Planters Punch. The restaurant has exquisite stone walls, luxuriant vines and hanging plants, and is alfresco. The calming music helps drown the din if a tour group is in. The servers are in creole costume and are pleasant but stressed when large groups dominate the dining room. The fare is mostly creole: boudin, chicken with coconut, curry dishes, stewed octopus, and steaks. Leyritz is an ancient, rural estate, and a visit here is a must-do when touring the north. ⊠ *Bourg,* ☎ *596/78–53–92. MC, V.*

Fort-de-France

CONTEMPORARY

$$$ ✕ **La Belle Epoque.** High above Fort-de-France in the wealthy suburb
★ of Didier is this restaurant in a white colonial house with beautiful tile floors. Crystal glasses, proper silver cutlery, and white linens adorn tables in the small antiques-filled dining room and on the garden-view terrace. The specialty is a delectable bisque served in the shell of an Atlantic king crab. The wine selection here is as good as any in Paris. ⊠ *97 rte. de Didier,* ☎ *596/64–41–19. AE, MC, V. Closed Sun.*

ECLECTIC

$$ ✕ **Le Marie Sainte.** Warm wood paneling, exposed beams, colorfully
★ tiled tables, and bright napery create a homey ambience in this wildly popular lunchtime spot. It's worth waiting on the occasional line for the scrumptious *daube des poissons* (braised fish), crayfish, and banana beignets. The prix-fixe menu gets you all that you need and then some. This typical creole eatery is also open for breakfast and serves macadamia, saltfish with rice and fish sauce, originally the morning protein dish slaves were fed. ⊠ *160 rue Victor Hugo,* ☎ *596/70–00–30. AE, MC, V. Closed Sun. No dinner.*

Lamentin

CARIBBEAN

$$$ ✕ **La Canne á Sucre.** Gerard Virginus moved to Martinique and opened
★ this restaurant, which has the same name and excellent reputation as the one he ran on Guadeloupe years ago. Three tiny rooms seat only 40 people. Haute nouvelle creole cuisine is served at lunch and dinner. Sea urchin mousse, flying fish in chive sauce, and such desserts as crème brûlée with passion fruit are presented with artistry. The wine list is good and the ambience welcoming. ⊠ *Patio de Cluny, on road to Schoelcher,* ☎ *596/63–33–95. Reservations essential. AE, DC, MC, V. Closed Sun.*

ECLECTIC

$$$ ✕ **La Plantation Pays Mêlé.** Don't be discouraged by the difficulty of
★ finding this place, the *dernier cri* in Martinique's best restaurants (it's on the grounds of the Martinique Cottages hotel). There's a vaguely Asian design to the bridge that arches over a lily pond and broad staircased entranceway into the restaurant's dark, wood-paneled interior. Chef Eric Voiron combines his classical French training with a passion for local creole traditions and ingredients. He enthusiastically creates such treats as mahimahi mousse with rare sea urchin sauce, crayfish

salad with orange nectar and wisps of ginger, or fish of the day grilled in a sauce of crushed lobster, butter, spices, and saffron. ⊠ *Jeanne d'Arc section of Lamentin,* ☎ 596/50–16–08. AE, MC, V. Closed Sun. No lunch Sat.

La Trinité
FRENCH CUISINE

$ ✕ **La Caravelle.** This is a gastronomic find in Tartane, a fishing village cum resort area on the gorgeous peninsula called Caravelle. A French twist on local produce and creole dishes are done by the amicable Jean Luc Combaluizer, owner of the restaurant and hotel La Caravelle. His British English is impeccable, and his wife, Nicole, gives the warmest welcome. Menus are in French and English. Breakfast and dinner are served. Choose redfish papillote with stuffed sea urchins or a wonderful roasted duck with tamarind sauce. Local callalou soup with crab could precede the freshest shrimp with aioli, followed by a frozen soufflé glace with Schrubb, an orange-flavored rum. A creole table d'hote is another good option. Enjoy the panoramic sea view from the terrace or call for a take-out order. Lunch is served topside on the roadside with hill to sea views. Simple and delicious crêpes, pizza, and salads are offered. ⊠ *Route du Château Dubuc, L'Anse, L'Etang, Trinité,* ☎ 596/58–07–32. MC, V.

SEAFOOD

$$ ✕ **Chez Titine.** There's a view of the water and a little rocky island from this simple, cheerful restaurant with bright tablecloths and wooden chairs. Owner Emile is very welcoming and serves fresh big salads, accras, boudin creole, *steak frites,* fried chicken, and lobster that you can pick yourself from a lobster tank. Simply, it is the best creole food on Tartane's waterfront. The tropical sorbets hit the spot after a morning on the beach. ⊠ *Rte. du Tartane, Tartane,* ☎ 596/58–27–28. MC. No dinner Sun.

Le François
FRENCH

$$ ✕ **Le Plein Soleil.** At this lovely spot, a girl named "Fred," a cute, bub-
★ bly Parisian, creates one memorable meal after another, all offered in a single prix-fixe menu. Fish pâtés, like terrine aux deux saumons, are often a first course. Laudable main courses include lamb with prunes, pork à la citronnelle with honey and confits d'oignons and dried fruit, local fish with a sauce of petites pois, white vermouth, fish broth, and crème frâiche. Mashed breadfruit is an excellent accompaniment. Desserts include tatin à la banane, Neige (merengue) des Antilles, with coulis of white chocolate and coconut cream perfumed with orange. José, the gregarious "front-of-the-house" man, sets a beautiful table, utilizing palm reeds and tropical flowers, and gives both professional and enthusiastic service. Getting here means a drive up a sketchy road, but it is well worth every shift of the gears.⊠ *Villa Lagon Sarc, Pointe Thalemont, Le François, 97240,* ☎ 596/38–07–77. *Reservations essential, 24 hours in advance. MC, V, CB.*

SEAFOOD

$$$$ ✕ **La Maison de l'Ilet Oscar.** To get to this Robinson Crusoe bistro, you have to be fetched by yawl from François. (The boat trip is included in the price of the two prix-fixe menus offered.) One menu features grilled fish and lambi (conch) pie, the other grilled lobster. Some nice bottles of French wine are available as well. The vintage creole house cum hotel resort was won by the grand-uncle of the current owner in 1935 in a poker game. The tables are laid out under shade palms at the water's edge. Before lunch you will probably be taken to La Baignoir de Joséphine, a gorgeous shallow area with emerald-color water

and white sand where, according to legend, Napoléon's ill-fated wife would swim. You'll be served a glass of 'ti punch and some accras as you stand in the water. ✉ *Baie de François,* ☎ *596/65–82–30. Reservations essential. AE, MC, V.*

Les Trois-Ilets

ECLECTIC

$$$ ✕ **La Villa Créole.** The setting at this bistro is romantic, but the real draw is the entertainment and the ambience it creates. For nearly 20 years, owner Guy Brére-Dawson, the man in black, has been singing and playing his guitar, as guests dance the floor in front of his gazebo stage. His understudy is a handsome Frenchman, who might first appear as your waiter. On the down side, tables are small, and the restaurant may be living on its laurels as far as its food goes. Choose some basics like warm goat cheese in puff pastry, grilled lobster, and profiteroles, and you should have an enjoyable night out. ✉ *Anse-Mitan,* ☎ *596/66–05–53. Reservations essential. AE, MC, V. Closed Sun. No lunch Mon.*

$$ ✕ **L'Abordage.** This is a fun, happening place in the Village Créole, with a good bar scene downstairs and live entertainment some nights. Tuesdays there is a French wine, cheese, and music party. Happy Hour is a daily occurrence. Some memorable food is put out by day and by night. For lunch, you can have a couple of starters, such as camembert gratin with cumin, or a country terrine with cornichons and a sweet onion compôte. Or you can have the typical two-hour French lunch and go on to a meat course such as a perfect veal chop with a wild mushroom cream sauce, or lamb coated with bread crumbs and herbs de Provence. To complement, there is a laudatory wine list. The music is great and waiters, who are friendly, professional, and often English-speaking, wear French sailor jerseys. ✉ *Village Créole, Pointe du Bout,* ☎ *596/66–64–40. Reservations not accepted. MC, V.*

$$ ✕ **Les Passages du Vent.** In a pretty brick building on the main street, this bistro has art naïf murals, shuttered windows, and a wooden ceiling and floors that give it a warm character. There's a terrace for alfresco dining. The menu has changed and upgraded since its days of offering simple grills and pizzas. The "new food" has such creative dishes as potatoes stuffed with smoked salmon and a memorable seafood carpaccio. It represents good value for the money. The crowd is lively and young. There's jazz and blues on Saturday. ✉ *27 rue de l'Impératrice Joséphine,* ☎ *596/68–42–11. MC, V. Closed Sun. No lunch Sat.*

ITALIAN

$$ ✕ **Sapori d'Italia.** This outdoor terrace restaurant in Village Créole,
★ has some of the island's best food. The owner, from Milan, is confident that his Italian food is the island's most authentic. Pasta offerings include homemade gnocchi al gorgonzola; ravioli stuffed with walnut cream sauce; penne with broccoli, garlic, and anchovies. Shrimp with a white bean sautée is a laudable main course. The long wine list focuses on Italian vintages. Desserts are special, like the strawberry ice cream with a balsamic sauce. Finish with a perfect espresso and a grappa or a Barolo Chinato Cocchi. ✉ *Village créole, Pointe du Bout,* ☎ *596/ 66–15–85. AE, MC, V. Closed Wed. Apr. 15–May 31. Closed June– mid. Oct.*

SEAFOOD

$$$ ✕ **Le Regal de la Mer.** This casual seafood restaurant opens to the street, with its lobster tank a focal point. Lobster is a big seller, both à la carte and the prix-fixe Menu Langouste, along with codfish fritters and soufflé glace. They carpaccio everything here, from duck to beef to salmon. Beef—good quality beef, from tournedos to tartare—is offered, as is duck, but most guests come for the seafood from the pêche du jour to the écrivesses (crabs) l'Armoricaine. The menu has an entire page of desserts. Lunch and dinner are served. Live piano nightly, from December through May. ⊠ *23 rue des Anthuriums, Anse Mitan,* ☎ *596/66–11–44. AE, MC. Closed Tues. June–Nov.*

Macouba

SEAFOOD

$$$ ✕ **Pointe-Nord.** If you're driving around the northern end of the island, this is one of the few watering holes in the area, which means it's busy, especially on the weekend. Built among the ruins of the Perpigna rum distillery, with fine views of Dominica in the distance, it serves only lunch seven days a week. Seafood is the specialty here; try the poached *thazar,* a local fish, marinated with red beans, onions, and tomatoes. ⊠ *On road to Grand' Rivière,* ☎ *596/78–56–56. Reservations essential on weekends. MC, V. No dinner.*

Morne-des-Esses

CONTEMPORARY

$$$$ ✕ **Le Colibri.** Gregarious Joel Palladino is lovingly continuing a fam-
★   ily culinary tradition with this little spot in the island's northeastern reaches. Dishes—such as *tarte aux lambis,* a quiche made with conch paste, and *buisson d'écrevisses,* a pyramid of six giant freshwater cray-fish decorated with flowers and accompanied by a tomato sauce sea-soned with thyme, scallions, and tiny bits of crayfish—involve hours of work in the kitchen. Some of the traditional creole dishes, like stuffed pigeon and *cochon au lait* (suckling pig), are also offered here. There's an excellent wine list. The view, across the ocean, is spectac-ular: if you're lucky, you'll see a rainbow. ⊠ *4 rue des Colibris,* ☎ *596/ 69–91–95. AE, MC, V. Closed Mon.*

Ste-Anne

ECLECTIC

$$$ ✕ **Poï et Virginie.** Facing the jetty in the center of Ste-Anne is this pop-ular restaurant with bamboo walls, bright art naïf, ceiling fans, and fresh-cut flowers. The menu is extensive—from meats to fish—but the specialties are blaff, lobster, and crayfish fricassee. Other noteworthy dishes are a zesty seviche, smothered in garlic and lime, and crayfish in saffron. Lunchtime is busy, especially on weekends; get here soon after noon if you want a table with views of the bay and St. Lucia in the distance. ⊠ *Pl. de l'Eglise,* ☎ *596/76–72–22. AE, DC, MC, V. Closed Mon. No lunch Tues.*

St-Pierre

ECLECTIC

$$$ ✕ **Habitation Céron.** In a tropical forest on the grounds of a 17th-cen-
★   tury sugar plantation, this popular outdoor lunch spot serves a multi-course prix-fixe creole menu. After eating, wander through the estate where you might find Madeira hummingbirds and red partridges, green and blue lizards, and trapdoor spiders. There's a river running through the property, with some of the island's oldest trees surround-ing it. Saint-Pierre is a 15-minute drive away. ⊠ *Anse Céron,* ☎ *596/ 52–94–53. AE, MC, V. No dinner.*

Beaches

All of Martinique's beaches are open to the public, but hotels charge a fee for nonguests to use changing rooms and facilities. There are no official nudist beaches, but topless bathing is prevalent. Unless you're an expert swimmer, steer clear of the Atlantic waters, except in the area of Cap Chevalier and the Caravelle Peninsula. The soft white-sand beaches are south of Fort-de-France; to the north, the beaches are hard-packed gray volcanic sand. Some of the most pleasant beaches are around Ste-Anne and Ste-Luce.

Anse-à-l'Ane has picnic tables and a nearby shell museum. Cool off in the bar of Le Calalou hotel. **Anse-Mitan** has golden sand and excellent snorkeling. Small, family-owned bistros are half hidden among palm trees nearby. **Anse-Trabaud** is on the Atlantic side, across the southern tip of the island from Ste-Anne. There's nothing here but white sand and the sea. Drive through a plantation in Ste-Anne and pay the owner 15 francs to get to huge, quiet **Baie des Anglais,** a sandy beach with a bit of surf. **Diamant,** the island's longest beach (2½ mi), has a splendid view of Diamond Rock, but the waters are rough.

Les Salines is a 1½-mi (2½-km) cove of soft white sand lined with coconut palms. A short drive south of Ste-Anne, Les Salines is awash with families and children during holidays and on weekends but quiet and uncrowded during the week—even at the height of the winter season. This beach, especially the far end, is the most beautiful. **Pointe du Bout**'s beaches are small, man-made, and lined with luxury resorts, among them the Méridien and the Bakoua. **Pointe Marin** stretches north from Ste-Anne. A good windsurfing and waterskiing spot, it has restaurants, campsites, sanitary facilities, and a 20F charge. Club Med is on the northern edge.

Outdoor Activities and Sports

BOATING AND SAILING

Only people very familiar with handling marine craft should consider striking out on the rough Atlantic side. The Caribbean side is much calmer—more like a vast lagoon rather than an actual sea. If you are unsure of your nautical prowess, cruises can be arranged through several companies: **Caraïbes Evasion** (⊠ Pointe du Bout Marina, ☎ 596/66–02–85); **Moorings Antilles Françaises** (⊠ Port de Plaisance du Marin, ☎ 596/74–75–39); **Stardust** (⊠ Port de Plaisance du Marin, ☎ 596/74–98–17, 909/678–2250, or 800/227–5317 in the U.S.); **Star Voyages** (⊠ Pointe du Bout Marina, ☎ 596/66–00–72); or **Tropic Yachting** (⊠ Pointe du Bout Marina, ☎ 596/66–03–85).

You can rent Hobie Cats, Sunfish, and Sailfish by the hour from hotel beach shacks. Also check with **Alphamar** (⊠ Les Trois-Ilets, ☎ 596/66–00–89) and **Club Nautique du Marin** (⊠ Le François, ☎ 596/74–92–48).

CYCLING

Mountain biking is popular in mainland France, and now it has reached Martinique. You can rent a VTT (Vélo Tout Terrain), a bike specially designed with 18 speeds to handle all terrains, from **V.T.Tilt** (⊠ Les Trois-Ilets, ☎ 596/66–01–01), which also does some fun day tours that include lunch.

FISHING

Fish cruising these waters include tuna, barracuda, dolphinfish, kingfish, and bonito. For a day's outing on the 37-ft *Egg Harbor,* with gear and breakfast included, contact **Bathy's Club** (⊠ Méridien, Pointe de Bout, ☎ 596/66–00–00). **Bleu Marine Evasion** (⊠ Le Diamant, ☎ 596/76–46–00) also offers excursions. Charters of up to five days can be arranged on Captain René Alaric's 37-ft **Rayon Vert** (⊠ Auberge du Vare, Case-Pilote, ☎ 596/78–80–56).

GOLF

At **Golf Country Club de la Martinique** (✉ Les Trois-Ilets, ☎ 596/68–32–81, FAX 596/68–38–97) there's a par-71, 18-hole Robert Trent Jones course with an English-speaking pro, a fully equipped pro shop, a bar, and a restaurant. A mile (1½ km) from Pointe du Bout, the club offers special greens fees to guests of some hotels and cruise-ship passengers. Normal greens fees are $40; an electric cart costs another $40.

HIKING

The island has 31 marked hiking trails. At the beginning of each, a notice is posted advising on the level of difficulty, the duration of a hike, and any interesting points to note. The **Parc Naturel Régional de la Martinique** (✉ 9 bd. Général de Gaulle, Fort-de-France, ☎ 596/73–19–30) organizes inexpensive guided excursions year-round.

HORSEBACK RIDING

Excursions and lessons are available at several places on the island: **Black Horse Ranch** (✉ Les Trois-Ilets, ☎ 596/68–37–80); **La Cavale** (✉ Pointe de la Chery, ☎ 596/76–22–94); **Ranch Jack** (✉ Near Anse-d'Arlets, ☎ 596/68–37–69); and **Ranch Val d'Or** (✉ Ste-Anne, ☎ 596/66–03–46).

SCUBA DIVING AND SNORKELING

To explore the old shipwrecks, coral gardens, and other undersea sites, you must have a medical certificate and insurance papers. Martinique has several dive operators: **Atout Plongee** (✉ 46 Plateau Roy, Schoelcher, ☎ 596/70–29–33); **Le Marine Hotel** (✉ Le Diamant, ☎ 596/76–46–00); **Méridien Plongée** (✉ Hotel Méridien, Pointe du Bout, ☎ 596/66–00–00); **Okeanos Club** (✉ Le Diamant, ☎ 596/62–52–36); **Planète Bleue** (✉ La Marina, Les Trois-Ilets, ☎ 596/66–08–79); and **Plongée Passion** (✉ Anse-d'Arlets, ☎ 596/76–27–39).

For details on sailing, swimming, and snorkeling and beach picnic trips, contact **Affaires Maritimes** (☎ 596/60–79–90).

SPORTS CENTERS

The **La Basse de Plein Air et Loisirs** (☎ 596/58–24–32), on the Caravelle Peninsula, is an open-air sports and leisure center offering tennis, windsurfing, waterskiing, and other activities.

TENNIS AND SQUASH

In addition to its links, the **Golf Country Club de la Martinique** (✉ Les Trois-Ilets, ☎ 596/68–32–81) has three lighted tennis courts. There are also seven courts (six lighted) at **Club Med/Buccaneer's Creek** (✉ Pointe du Marin, ☎ 596/76–74–52) **Diamant-Novotel** (✉ Pointe de la Chery, Le Diamant, ☎ 596/76–42–42) has two tennis courts. There are six excellent courts at **Framissima** (✉ La Batelière, Schoelcher, ☎ 596/61–64–52). There are two courts at **Le Bakoua** (✉ Pointe du Bout, ☎ 596/66–02–02). **Le Méridien Trois-Ilets** (✉ Pointe du Bout, Les Trois-Ilets, ☎ 596/66–00–00) has two courts. There is one court at the **Leyritz Plantation** (✉ Bourg, Basse-Pointe, ☎ 596/78–53–92).

Several other hotels have tennis courts that are available to nonguests when empty: **Anchorage Hotel** (✉ Domaine de Belfond, Ste-Anne, ☎ 596/76–92–32); **Le Mercure Diamant** (✉ Pointe de la Chery, Le Diamant, ☎ 596/76–46–00); and **Primerêve Hotel** (✉ Ste-Marie, ☎ 596/69–40–40). For additional information about tennis on the island, contact **La Ligue Régionale de Tennis** (✉ Petit Manoir, Lamentin, ☎ 596/51–08–00), a tennis club where an hour's court time averages 50F for nonguests.

There are three squash courts at the aptly named **Squash Hotel** (✉ 3 bd. de la Marine, ☎ 596/72–80–80), Fort-de-France.

Shopping

French fragrances and designer scarves, fine china and crystal, leather goods, and liquors and liqueurs are all good buys in Fort-de-France. Purchases are further sweetened by the 20% discount on luxury items when paid for with travelers checks or certain major credit cards. Among local items, look for creole gold jewelry, such as hoop earrings and heavy bead necklaces; white and dark rum; and handcrafted straw goods, pottery, and tapestries.

Areas and Malls

The area around the cathedral in Fort-de-France has a number of small shops that carry luxury items. Of particular note are the shops on **rue Victor Hugo, rue Moreau de Jones, rue Antoine Siger,** and **rue Lamartine.** The **Galleries Lafayette** department store on rue Schoelcher in downtown Fort-de-France sells everything from perfume to crockery. On the outskirts of Fort-de-France, the **Centre Commercial de Cluny, Centre Commercial de Dillon, Centre Commercial de Bellevue, Centre Commercial la Rond Point,** and more than 100 boutiques at **La Galleria** in Le Lamentin are among the major shopping malls. In Pointe du Bout there are a number of appealing tourist shops, both in Village Créole and on the surrounding streets. One stand-out is **Cannelle** (☎ 596/66–05–33) with smashing French maillots and bikinis, name-brand resort wear for women and men, sandals, watches, and backpacks.

Specialty Items

CHINA AND CRYSTAL

Cadet Daniel (⊠ 72 rue Antoine Siger, Fort-de-France, ☎ 596/71–41–48) sells Lalique, Limoges, and Baccarat. **Roger Albert** (⊠ 7 rue Victor Hugo, Fort-de-France, ☎ 596/71–71–71) carries designer crystal.

HANDICRAFTS

Following the roadside signs advertising ATELIERS ARTISANALES (art studios) can yield unexpected treasures, many of them reasonably priced. **Art et Nature** (⊠ Ste-Luce, ☎ 596/62–59–19) features Joel Gilbert's unique wood paintings, daubed with 20–30 shades of earth and sand. **Artisanat & Poterie des Trois-Ilets** (⊠ Les Trois-Ilets, ☎ 596/68–18–01) allows you to watch the creation of Arawak- and Carib-style pots, vases, and jars. **Galerie de Sophen,** ☎ 596/66–13–64 also in Trois-Ilets, is a combination of Sophie and Henry, both in name and content. This art gallery showcases the work of a French husband and wife team, who live aboard their sailboat and paint the beauty of the sea and the island. **Atelier Céramique** (⊠ Just outside Le Diamant, ☎ 596/76–42–65) displays the ceramics, paintings, and miscellaneous souvenirs of owners and talented artists David and Jeannine England, members of the island's small British expat community. **Centre des Métiers d'Art** (⊠ Rue Ernest Deproge, Fort-de-France, ☎ 596/70–25–01) exhibits authentic local arts and crafts. **Galerie Arti-Bijoux** (⊠ 89 rue Victor Hugo, Fort-de-France, ☎ 596/63–10–62) has some unusual and excellent Haitian art—paintings, sculptures, ceramics, and intricate jewelry cases.

L'Éclat de Verre (⊠ Hwy. N4, outside Gros Morne, ☎ 596/58–34–03) specializes in all manner of glittering glasswork. **La Paille Caraibe** (⊠ Morne des Esses, ☎ 596/69–83–74) is where you can watch artisans weave straw baskets, mats, and hats. **Victor Anicet** (⊠ Monésie, ☎ 596/68–25–42) fashions lovely ceramic masks and vases.

LIQUOR

One of the best rums on the island is the *vieux rhum* from **JM Distillery** (⊠ Macouba, ☎ 596/78–92–55). You can get some great rum and also tour the grounds of the bucolic 32-acre **Habitation Clément** (⊠ Le

François, ☎ 596/54–62–07, ⨳ 596/54–63–50). There are other distilleries on Martinique, including the following: **Duquesnes** (✉ Fort-de-France, ☎ 596/71–91–68); **St. James** (✉ Ste-Marie, ☎ 596/69–30–02); and **Trois Rivières** (✉ Ste-Luce, ☎ 596/62–51–78).

PERFUMES

Roger Albert (✉ 7 rue Victor Hugo, Fort-de-France, ☎ 596/71–71–71) stocks such popular scents as those by Dior, Chanel, and Guerlain.

Nightlife and the Arts

Although Martinique is dotted with lively discos and nightclubs, nightlife isn't confined to partying. Most leading hotels offer nightly entertainment in season, including the marvelous **Les Grands Ballets de Martinique,** one of the finest folkloric dance troupes in the Caribbean. Consisting of about 30 musicians and dancers dressed in traditional costume, the ballet revives the Martinique of yesteryear through dance rhythms such as the beguine or the mazurka. This folkloric group appears once a week at Le Meredien. The price includes a lavish buffet dinner. In addition, many restaurants offer live entertainment, usually on weekends. A prime example is in Village Créole's Havana Café (☎ 596/66–15–93). The Village Créole complex itself has a good line-up of entertainment in season that includes music, theater, and art expos.

CASINOS

The **Casino Batelière Plaza,** (✉ Schoelcher, ☎ 596/61–91–51) on the outskirts of Fort-de-France, is divided into two areas: to the left are more than 100 slot machines; to the right you'll need 70F, a passport (you must be 18 to play), and the proper attire (jacket and tie for men, dresses for women) to play blackjack, roulette, or baccarat. Fine dining is offered in an area about the size of a boxing ring. The slots are open Monday–Saturday noon–3 AM; for the other games things start rolling at 8 PM and continue until 3 AM.

You must be at least 18 (with a picture ID) to enter the **Casino Trois-Ilets** and play American roulette or blackjack. This casino is adjacent to and a part of Le Meridien Hotel, and houses a restaurant. Admission to the slot-machine room is free. ✉ *Le Méridien,* ☎ *596/66–00–30.* ⨳ *70F.* ⏰ *Mon.–Sat. 9 PM–3 AM.*

DANCE AND MUSIC CLUBS

Your hotel or the tourist office can put you in touch with the current "in" places. It's also wise to check on opening and closing times and cover charges. For the most part, the discos draw a mixed crowd. There are several hot spots: **L'Alibi** (✉ Morne Tartenson, Fort-de-France, ☎ 596/63–45–15); **Le Cheyenne,** (✉ 6/8 rue Joseph Compere, Fort-de-France, ☎ 596/70–31–19; **Crazy Nights,** (✉ Ste-Luce, ☎ 596/68–56–68; **Le Top 50** (✉ Zone Artisanale, La Trinité, ☎ 596/58–61–43); and **New Hippo** (✉ 24 bd. Allègre, Fort-de-France, ☎ 596/60–20–22).

Jazz musicians, like their music, tend to be informal and independent. They rarely hold regular gigs. Zouk music mixes Caribbean rhythm and an Occidental tempo with Créole words. Jacob Devarieux is the leading exponent of this style and is occasionally on the island. You'll hear zouk played by one of his followers at the hotels and clubs.

Le Molokoi (✉ Le Diamant, ☎ 596/76–48–63) is a hot spot for zouk and pop music. In season you'll find one or two combos playing at clubs and hotels, but it's only at **West Indies** (✉ Bd. Alfassa, Fort-de-France, ☎ 596/63–63–77), next to the tourist office, that there are regular jazz sessions.

Les Soirees de l'Amphore (⊠ Anse Mitan, ☎ 596/66–03–03) piano bar is a mini-restaurant, too. It features everything from funk, soul, and disco, to international music from the 1970s and 80s. Wednesdays there are live soirees and Thursday is karaoke night. **Las Tapas** (⊠ 7 rue Garnier Pages, Fort-de-France, ☎ 596/63–71–23) presents flamenco or salsa and merengue bands and attracts a mixed crowd. **La Villa Créole** (⊠ Anse-Mitan, ☎ 596/66–05–53) is a charming bistro whose owner, Guy Dawson, strums nightly on the guitar—everything from Piaf to Sting, and some original ditties.

ISLAND CULTURE

L'Atrium. Martinique's cultural center in Fort-de-France is where large-scale theater, dance, and musical performances take place. ⊠ Bd. Général de Gaulle, ☎ 596/70–79–29 or 596/60–78–78.

Exploring Martinique

The north of the island will appeal to nature lovers, hikers, and mountain climbers. The drive from Fort-de-France to St-Pierre is particularly impressive, as is the one across the island, via Morne Rouge, from the Caribbean to the Atlantic. This is Martinique's wild side—a place of waterfalls, rain forest, and mountains. The highlight is Mont Pelée. The south is the more developed half of the island, where the resorts and restaurants are, as well as the beaches.

Numbers in the margin correspond to points of interest on the Martinique map.

SIGHTS TO SEE

⑫ Ajoupa-Bouillon. This flower-filled 17th-century village amid pineapple fields is the jumping-off point for several sights. The Saut Babin is a 40-ft-high (12-m-high) waterfall, half an hour's walk from Ajoupa-Bouillon. The Gorges de la Falaise is a river gorge where you can swim. **Les Ombrages** botanical gardens has marked trails through the rain forest. ☎ 15F. ☉ Daily 9–5:30.

④ Balata. This quiet little town has two sights worth visiting. Built in 1923 to commemorate those who died in World War I, **Balata Church** is an exact replica of Paris's Sacré-Coeur Basilica. The **Jardin de Balata** (Balata Gardens), created more than 20 years by Jean-Philippe Thoze, a professional landscaper and horticulturist, has thousands of varieties of tropical flowers and plants. There are shaded benches from which to take in the mountain view. You can order anthuriums and other tropical flowers to be delivered to the airport. ⊠ Rte. de Balata, ☎ 596/64–48–73. ☎ 40F. ☉ Daily 9–5.

⑪ Basse-Pointe. On the route (and there's really only one) to this village on the Atlantic coast at the island's northern end, you pass many banana and pineapple plantations—agriculture for as far as the eye can see. Just south of Basse-Pointe is a **Hindu temple** built by descendants of the East Indians who settled in this area in the 19th century. The view of the eastern slope of Mont Pelée is terrific. The highlight of Basse-Pointe is the estimable **Leyritz Plantation,** which has been a hotel for several years. When tour groups aren't a-swarming, the rustic setting, complete with sugarcane factory and gardens, is delightful and includes Musée des Figurines Végétales. Local artisan Will Fenton has used bananas, *balisier* (a tall grass), and other local plants to make dolls of famous French women—from Marie Antoinette to Madame Curie—in period costumes. ⊠ Leyritz Plantation, ☎ 596/78–53–92. ☎ 15F. ☉ Daily 10–6.

❸ **Bellefontaine.** This colorful fishing village has pastel houses on the hillsides and beautifully painted *gommiers* (fishing boats) bobbing in the water. Look for the restaurant built in the shape of a boat.

⓴ **Diamond Rock.** This volcanic mound is 1 mi (1½ km) offshore from the small, friendly village of Le Diamant and is one of the island's best diving spots. In 1804, during the squabbles over possession of the island between the French and the English, the latter commandeered the rock, armed it with cannons, and proceeded to use it as a warship. For almost 1½ years, the British held the rock, attacking any French ships that came along. The French got wind that the British were getting cabin fever on their isolated ship-island and arranged a supply of barrels of rum for those on the rock. The French easily overpowered the inebriated sailors, ending one of the most curious engagements in naval history.

⓯ **Dubuc Castle.** At the eastern tip of the Presqu'île du Caravelle are the ruins of this castle, once the home of the Dubuc de Rivery family, who owned the Caravelle Peninsula in the 18th century. According to legend, young Aimée Dubuc de Rivery was captured by Barbary pirates, sold to the Ottoman Empire, became a favorite of the sultan, and gave birth to Mahmud II.

⓴ **Forêt de Montravail.** A few miles north of Ste-Luce, this tropical rain forest is ideal for a short hike. Look for the interesting group of Carib rock drawings.

❶ **Fort-de-France.** With its historic fort and superb setting beneath the towering Pitons du Carbet on the Baie des Flamands, Martinique's capital and home to about one-third of the island's 360,000 inhabitants should be a grand place. It isn't. The most pleasant districts, such as Bellevue and Schoelcher, are on the hillside, and you need a car to reach them. But if you come here by car, you may find yourself trapped in gridlock in the warren of narrow streets in the center of town. True, there are some good shops with Parisian wares (at Parisian prices) and lively street markets that sell, among other things, human hair for wigs (starting price: 200F). But the heat, exhaust fumes, and litter tend to make exploring here a chore. At night the city feels dark and gloomy, with little street life except for the extravagantly dressed prostitutes who openly parade the streets from 10 PM. If you plan to go out, it is best to go with a group.

The heart of Fort-de-France is **La Savane**, a 12½-acre park filled with trees, fountains, and benches. It's a popular gathering place and the scene of promenades, parades, and impromptu soccer matches. Along the east side are numerous snack wagons. A statue of Pierre Belain d'Esnambuc, leader of the island's first settlers, is unintentionally upstaged by Vital Dubray's vandalized white Carrara marble statue of the empress Joséphine, Napoléon's first wife. The most imposing historic site is **Fort St-Louis**, which runs along the east side of La Savane. It is open Monday–Saturday 9–3, and admission is 25F. Near the harbor is a marketplace where local crafts and souvenirs are sold. Across from La Savane, you can catch the ferry *La Vedette* for the beaches at Anse-Mitan and Anse-à-l'Ane and for the 20-minute run across the bay to the resort hotels of Pointe du Bout. It's much faster than the journey round the bay by car and costs $5.

The **Bibliothèque Schoelcher** is the wildly elaborate Romanesque public library. It was named after Victor Schoelcher, who led the fight to free the slaves in the French West Indies in the 19th century. The eye-popping structure was built for the 1889 Paris Exposition, after which it was dismantled, shipped to Martinique, and reassembled piece by ornate piece. ✉ *Corner of rue de la Liberté (runs along west side of*

La Savane) and rue Perrinon, ☎ *596/70–26–67.* ⊙ *Mon. 1–5:30, Tues.–Thurs. 8:30–5:30, Fri. 8:30–5:30, Sat. 8:30–noon.*

Rue Victor Schoelcher runs through the center of the capital's primary shopping district, a six-block area bounded by rue de la République, rue de la Liberté, rue de Victor Severe, and rue Victor Hugo. Stores feature Paris fashions and French perfume, china, crystal, and liqueurs, as well as local handicrafts. The Romanesque **St-Louis Cathedral** (⊠ Rue Victor Schoelcher) with its lovely stained-glass windows was the sixth to be built 1878 on this site (the others were destroyed by fire, hurricane, or earthquake.

The Galerie de Biologie et de Géologie at the **Parc Floral et Culturel,** in the northeastern corner of the city center, will acquaint you with the island's exotic flora. There's also an aquarium. The park contains the island's official cultural center, where there are sometimes free evening concerts. ⊠ *Pl. José-Marti, Sermac,* ☎ *596/71–66–25.* 🖼 *Grounds free, aquarium 35F, botanical and geological gallery 5F.* ⊙ *Park daily dawn–10* PM; *aquarium daily 9–7; gallery Tues.–Fri. 9:30–12:30 and 3:30–5:30, Sat. 9–1 and 3–5.*

The **Rivière Madame** meanders through the park and joins the bay at Pointe Simon. The river divides the downtown area from the ritzy residential district of Didier in the hills. Fronting the river, on avenue Paul Nardal, are the vibrantly noisy, messy, smelly vegetable and fish markets. One of the best shows in town occurs around 4 PM, when fishermen return with their catch, effortlessly tossing 100-pound bundles of rainbow-hued fish.

⑯ Le François. With some 16,000 inhabitants, this is the main city on the Atlantic coast. Sadly, the old wooden buildings are being replaced by concrete structures. But the classic West Indian cemetery, with its black-and-white tiles, is still here. The **Habitation Clément** is Martinique's Williamsburg, complete with Creole ladies in traditional dresses moving about the grounds. It was built with the wealth generated by its rum distillery, and its 18th-century splendor has been lovingly preserved, providing a glimpse into the elegance and privilege of plantation society. Framed vintage labels from rum bottles track the changes in Martinique over the decades. President George Bush and François Mitterrand had a summit meeting here. The rum distillery is operational and offers free tastings. New is a top-of-the-line rum, Canne Bleu, made from a special cane. Call first to inquire about the caleche rides. An antique carriage pulled by an impressive, black steed traverses the cane fields and returns through the tropical gardens and trees. ⊠ *Domaine de l'Acajou,* ☎ *596/54–62–07,* WEB *www.rhum-clement.com.* 🖼 *50F.* ⊙ *Daily 9–6.*

Le François is also noted for its snorkeling. Offshore are the privately owned Les Ilets de l'Impératrice. The islands received that name because, according to legend, this is where Empress Joséphine came to bathe in the shallow basins known as *fonds blancs* because of their white-sand bottoms. Group boat tours leave from the harbor ($30 per person includes lunch and drinks). You can also haggle with a fisherman to take you out for a while on his boat to indulge in the uniquely Martinican custom of standing waist-deep in warm water, sipping a 'ti punch, eating accras, and smoking. There's a fine bay 6 mi (9½ km) farther along the coast at Le Robert, though the lacklaster town.

❺ Habitation Anse Latouche. Tour the ruins of this former cane plantation, see its great house, distillery, and modern-day botanical gardens. ⊠ *Habitation Anse Latouche in Carbet (near Musée Gauguin),* ☎ *596/ 78–19–19.* 🖼 *15F, 10F for children.* ⊙ *10–4 Sundays.*

⑰ Lamentin. There's nothing pretty about Lamentin; the multibillion-franc airport is its most notable landmark. The rest of the town is a sprawling industrial and commercial zone. But you come here for shopping in the big, fancy shopping mall Euromarché. La Galleria, a megamall of roughly 100 shops and boutiques, offers everything from pâté de foie gras and Camembert to CDs and sunglasses.

⑩ Macouba. Named after the Carib word for "fish," this village was a prosperous tobacco town in the 17th century. Today its cliff-top location affords magnificent views of the sea, the mountains, and—on clear days—the neighboring island of Dominica. The **JM Distillery** produces the best *rhum vieux* on the island here. A tour and samples are free. Macouba is the starting point for a spectacular drive, the 6-mi (9½-km) **route to Grand' Rivière** on the northernmost point. This is Martinique at its greenest: groves of giant bamboo, cliffs hung with curtains of vines, and 7-ft (2-m) tree ferns that seem to grow as you watch them. Literally, at the end of the road, is Grand' Rivière, a colorful sprawling fishing village at the foot of high cliffs.

㉔ Le Marin. The yachting capital of Martinique is also known for its colorful August carnival and its Jesuit church, circa 1766. From Le Marin a narrow road leads to picturesque Cap Chevalier (Cape Knight), about 1 mi (1½ km) from town.

⑧ Le Morne Rouge. This town sits on the southern slopes of the volcano that destroyed it in 1902. Today it's a popular resort spot and offers hikers some fantastic mountain scenery. From Le Morne Rouge you can start the climb up the 4,600-ft (1,406-m) **Mont Pelée** volcano. But don't try it without a guide unless you want to get buried alive under pumice stones. Instead, drive up to the Refuge de l'Aileron. From the parking lot it's a mile (1½ km) up a well-marked trail to the summit. Bring a sweatshirt because there's often a mist that makes the air damp and chilly. From the summit follow the route de la Trace (Route N3), which winds south of Le Morne Rouge to St-Pierre. It's steep and winding, but that didn't stop the *porteuses* of old: balancing a tray, these women would carry up to 100 pounds of provisions on their heads for the 15-hour trek to the Atlantic coast.

⑥ Musée Gauguin. Martinique was a brief station in Paul Gauguin's wanderings but a decisive moment in the evolution of his art. He arrived from Panama in 1887 with friend and fellow painter Charles Laval and, having pawned his watch at the docks, rented a wooden shack on a hill above the village of Carbet. Dazzled by the tropical colors and vegetation, Gauguin developed a style, his Martinique period, that directly anticipated his Tahitian paintings. Although this modest museum has no originals, it does have a set of reproductions. There are also interesting exhibits of letters and documents relating to the painter, and an exhibition of local costumes. Also remembered here is the Writer Lafcadio Hearn. In his endearing book *Two Years in the West Indies,* he provides the most extensive description of the island before St-Pierre was buried in ash and lava. ✉ *Anse-Turin, Carbet,* ☎ *596/78–22–66.* ☞ *20F.* ☉ *Daily 9–5:30.*

⑲ Pointe du Bout. This area is filled with resort hotels, among them the Sofitel Bakoua, the Méridien, and a marina. The ferry to Fort-de-France leaves from here. A cluster of boutiques, ice-cream parlors, and rental-car agencies forms the hub from which restaurants and hotels of varying caliber radiate. The beach at Anse-Mitan is one of the best on the island. At Anse-à-l'Ane, a little to the west, is a pretty white-sand beach with picnic tables. There are also numerous small restaurants and inexpensive guest-house hotels here. Ten miles (16 kilometers) south is Anse-d'Arlets, a quiet backwater fishing village.

9 **Le Prêcheur.** This quaint town, the last on the northern Caribbean coast, is surrounded by volcanic hot springs. The village itself was the childhood home of Françoise d'Aubigné, who later became the Marquise de Maintenon and the second wife of Louis XIV. At her request, the Sun King donated a handsome bronze bell to the village, which you can see hanging outside the church. The Tomb of the Carib Indians, on the way from St-Pierre, commemorates a sadder event. The site is actually a formation of limestone cliffs from which the last of the Caribs are said to have flung themselves to avoid capture by the Marquise's forebears.

14 **Presqu'île du Caravelle.** Much of the Caravelle Peninsula, which juts 8 mi (13 km) into the Atlantic Ocean, is under the protection of the Regional Nature Reserve and offers places for trekking, swimming, and sailing. This is also the site of Anse-Spoutourne, an open-air sports and leisure center operated by the reserve. Tartane has a popular beach with cool Atlantic breezes.

23 **Ste-Anne.** A lovely white-sand beach and a Roman Catholic church are the highlights of this town on the island's southern tip. To the south of Ste-Anne is Pointe des Salines, the southernmost tip of the island and site of Martinique's best beach. Near Ste-Anne is **La Savane des Pétrifications,** the Petrified Forest. This desert-like stretch was once swampland and is a veritable geological museum where a few specimens of petrified wood can still be found.

22 **Ste-Luce.** This quaint fishing village has a sleepy main street that's deserted at midday, panoramic views across to the island of St. Lucia, and excellent beaches. To the east is Pointe Figuier, an excellent spot for scuba diving. On the way from Ste-Luce to Pointe Figuier, is **Ecomusée de Martinique.** Showcasing artifacts from Arawak and Carib settlements through the plantation years. ⊠ *Anse Figuier,* ☎ *596/62–79–14.* 🎫 *20F.* ☉ *Tues.–Sun. 9–1:30 and 2:30–5.*

13 **Ste-Marie.** This town is home to about 20,000 and is the commercial capital of the island's north. There's a lovely mid-19th-century church here. The **Musée du Rhum,** operated by the St. James Rum Distillery, is housed in a graceful, galleried creole house. Guided tours take in displays of the tools of the trade and include a visit and tasting at the distillery. ⊠ *Ste-Marie,* ☎ *596/69–30–02.* 🎫 *Free.* ☉ *Weekdays 9–5, weekends 9–1, except during the harvest period, Feb.–June (call first).*

Le Musée de la Banane. You probably won't find more cordial hosts than those at the Banana Museum in Ste-Marie. After navigating the extremely narrow road, you'll arrive at the compound. Four different stops with excellent graphics and beautiful prints tell the story of the banana (Martinique's primary export) as it makes its way from the fields to your table. ⊠ *Habitation Limbé,* ☎ *596/69–45–52.* 🎫 *30F.* ☉ *Daily 9–5.*

7 **St-Pierre.** The rise and fall of St-Pierre is one of the most remarkable stories in the Caribbean. Martinique's modern history began here in 1635. By the turn of this century, St-Pierre was a flourishing city of 30,000, known as the Paris of the West Indies. As many as 30 ships at a time stood at anchor. By 1902 it was the most modern town in the Caribbean, with electricity, phones, and a tram. On May 8, 1902, two thunderous explosions rent the air. As the nearby volcano erupted, Mont Pelée split in half, belching forth a cloud of burning ash, poisonous gas, and lava that raced down the mountain at 250 mph. At 3,600°F, it instantly vaporized everything in its path; 30,000 people were killed in two minutes. One man survived. His name was Cyparis, and he was a prisoner in an underground cell in the town's jail. He was later pardoned and afterward was a sideshow attraction in the Barnum & Bailey Circus.

For those interested in the eruption of 1902, the **Musée Vulcanologique** is a must. Established in 1932, it houses photographs of the old town, documents, and a number of relics—some gruesome—excavated from the ruins, including molten glass, melted iron, and contorted clocks stopped at 8 A.M. ☎ *596/78–15–16.* ✉ *10F.* ☽ *Daily 9–5.*

Today St-Pierre is trying to reinvent itself. A snappy new Office du Tourisme has been built, as well as a seafront promenade. There are plenty of sidewalk cafés, some of which have live music, and you can also see the ruins of the island's first church (built in 1640), the theater, the toppled statues, and Cyparis's cell. The *Cyparis Express* is a small tourist train that runs through the city, hitting the important sights with a running narrative (in French). ✉ *Pl. des Ruines du Figuier,* ☎ *596/55–50–92.* ✉ *50F.* ☽ *Departs hourly, weekdays 9:30–1 and 2:30–5:30.*

❷ Schoelcher. Pronounced "shell-*share*," this suburb of Fort-de-France is home of the University of the French West Indies and Guyana and the site of Martinique's largest convention center, Madiana.

⑱ Les Trois-Ilets. Named after the three rocky islands nearby, this lovely little village (population 3,000) has unusual brick and wood buildings roofed with antique tiles. It's known for its pottery, straw, and woodwork, but above all as the birthplace of Napoléon's empress Joséphine. In the square, where there's also a market and a fine *mairie* (town hall), you can visit the simple church where she was baptized Marie-Joseph Tascher de la Pagerie. The Martinicans have always been enormously proud of Joséphine, even though she reintroduced slavery on the island and most historians consider her to have been rather shallow. A stone building that held the kitchen of the estate where she grew up is home to the **Musée de la Pagerie** (the main house blew down in the hurricane of 1766, when Joséphine was three). It contains an assortment of memorabilia pertaining to her life and rather unfortunate loves. At 16 she was wed (an arranged marriage) to Alexandre de Beauharnais. When he died, she married Napoléon, but he divorced her because she didn't produce any children. There are family portraits; documents, including a marriage certificate; a love letter written to her in 1796 by Napoléon; and various antiques. ☎ *596/68–34–55.* ✉ *20F.* ☽ *Tues.–Fri. 9–5, weekends 9–1 and 1:30–5:30.*

The **Maison de la Canne** will teach you everything you ever wanted to know about sugarcane. Exhibits take you through three centuries of cane production, with displays of tools, scale models, engravings, and photographs. ✉ *Les Trois-Ilets,* ☎ *596/68–32–04.* ✉ *15F.* ☽ *Tues.–Sun. 9–5.*

㉕ Le Vauclin. The return of the fishermen at noon is the big event in this important fishing port on the Atlantic. There's also an 18th-century church here, the Chapel of the Holy Virgin. Nearby is the highest point in the south, Mont Vauclin (1,654 ft). A hike to the top rewards you with one of the best views on the island.

MARTINIQUE A TO Z

To research prices, get advice from other travelers, and book travel arrangements, visit www.fodors.com.

AIR TRAVEL

Air France is the only airline with direct connections between the U.S. and Martinique (it flies daily from Miami), and you can purchase a code-share ticket with Delta or Continental Airlines to make the Miami connection. Alternatively, you can fly BWIA International Airways from Miami to Bridgetown, Barbados, and then take LIAT to Fort-de-France. LIAT flies in from Antigua, Barbados, Dominica, Grenada, Guadeloupe, St. Lucia, St. Maarten, and Trinidad and Tobago. The new Air Caraïbes offers interisland service to Guadeloupe, San Juan, St. Martin/St. Maarten, St. Barths. You can fly US Airways to San Juan or Santo Domingo, and connect with Air Caraïbes.

➤ AIRLINES AND CONTACTS: **Air France** (☎ 596/55–33–33 or 800/237–2747); **BWIA International Airways** (☎ 800/538–2942); **LIAT** (☎ 596/42–16–02); **Air Caraïbes** (☎ 596/42–16–58); **US Airways** (☎ 800/428–4322).

AIRPORTS

There are no U.S. or Canadian airlines serving Martinique's new Lamentin International Airport, so you will have to do some island-hopping. The airport is about a 15-minute taxi ride from Fort-de-France and about 40 minutes from Les Trois-Ilets peninsula.

➤ AIRPORT INFORMATION: **Lamentin International Airport** (☎ 596/42–19–95 or 596/42–19–96).

BIKE AND MOPED RENTALS

Bikes, scooters, and motorbikes are all popular, and you can rent them from Discount, Funny, or Grabin's Rental. In Ste-Anne try Huet, and in Ste-Luce check out Vespa Marquis.

➤ BIKE AND MOPED RENTALS: **Discount** (✉ Pointe du Bout Marina, Les Trois Ilets, ☎ 596/66–05–34); **Funny** (✉ 80 rue Ernest Deprage, Fort-de-France, ☎ 596/63–33–05); **Grabin's Rental** (✉ Morne Calbasse, Fort-de-France, ☎ 596/71–51–61); **Huet** (☎ 596/76–79–66); **Vespa Marquis** (☎ 596/60–02–84).

BOAT AND FERRY TRAVEL

Weather permitting, *vedettes* (ferries) operate daily between Fort-de-France and the Marina Méridien, in Pointe du Bout, as well as between Fort-de-France and Anse-Mitan and Anse-à-l'Ane and take 15 minutes. The Quai d'Esnambuc is the arrival and departure point in Fort-de-France.

The *Express des Isles* offers scheduled interisland service aboard a 128-ft, 227-passenger motorized catamaran, linking Martinique with Dominica, Guadeloupe, Les Saintes, and St. Lucia. For those who don't get seasick, it's an enormously pleasurable way to travel, with great views of the islands.

FARES AND SCHEDULES

The round-trip fare between Fort-de-France and the Marina Méridien, in Pointe du Bout, as well as between Fort-de-France and Anse-Mitan and Anse-à-l'Ane is 40F.

The *Express des Isles* fares run approximately 25% below economy airfares. Sailings are not every day of the week for all destinations; check the schedule.

➤ BOAT AND FERRY INFORMATION: *Express des Isles* (☎ 596/63–12–11).

BUSINESS HOURS

BANKS

Banks are open weekdays 7:30–noon and 2:30–4.

Post offices are generally open Mon.–Sat. 7 AM–6 PM, though many close on Wed. at 1 PM.

Stores that cater to tourists are generally open weekdays 8:30–6, Sat. 8:30–1. Many stores in Fort de France close 12:30–2 for lunch.

CAR RENTALS
A valid U.S. driver's license is needed to rent a car for up to 20 days. After that, you'll need an International Driver's Permit. U.K. visitors can use their EU licenses (Martinique is still a part of France).

Rates are about $60 per day (unlimited mileage) in "season," but always question agents thoroughly about possible discounts. Although the rent-a-car companies have some automatics, they are substantially more expensive than the more common manuals. If you book from the U.S. at least 48 hours in advance, you can qualify for a hefty discount. If you wait until you arrive, you may be able to negotiate a weekly rate discount. A hefty deposit will be put on your credit card until the car is returned safely. Lowest prices are 1,400F per week ($200) in low season, 2,100F ($300) in high season. Among the many agencies in Fort-de-France are Avis, Budget, Hertz, Jumbo Car, and Europcar.
➤ MAJOR AGENCIES: **Avis** (☎ 596/42–11–00 or 800/331–1212); **Budget** (☎ 596/51–22–88 or 800/472–3325); **Hertz** (☎ 596/42–16–90 or 800/654–3131); **Jumbo Car** (☎ 596/42–22–22); **Europcar** ☎ (596/42–42–42)).

CAR TRAVEL
Unless you're at an all-inclusive resort, you may want a car. Almost everyone on the island drives a small car with a manual shift. Why? Because many of the roads are narrow in the small towns and in mountainous areas. It helps to have a stick shift to climb those hills. If you have questions, ask the rental agent to explain the gears and operation of the car to you. For those who haven't driven a stick in years, be aware that traffic jams often occur on steep inclines that will necessitate the deft use of clutch, gas pedal, and emergency brake. And then it will inevitably rain.

Martinique, especially around Fort-de-France and its environs, has become a place with heavy traffic. Streets in the city itself are narrow and choked with traffic during the day. The capital is tough driving, and it is wise to tour it on the weekends, certainly not when cruise ships are in. Absolutely avoid the Lametin airport area and Fort-de-France during weekday rush hours, roughly 7–10 AM and 4–7:30 PM. Even the smaller towns like Trinité have rush hours that could cause you to spend two hours getting to Trois-des-Ilets instead of 30 minutes.

Watch out, too, for *dos d'ânes* (literally, donkey backs), speed bumps that are extremely hard to spot—particularly at night—though if you hit one, you'll know it. If you want a detailed map, the *Carte Routière et Touristique* is available at bookstores.

Gas is costly (about 7F per liter, or roughly $4 per gallon).

The main highways, about 175 mi (280 km) of well-paved and well-marked roads are excellent, but only in certain areas are they illuminated at night. Many of the hotels are off the beaten path on roads that should be condemned. Get wherever you are going by nightfall, or prepare to be lost.

Pay attention round-a-bouts, a good source of collision possibilities. And drive defensively: Martinicans drive with aggressive abandon.

ELECTRICITY
Most tourist locations are equipped with 220-volt electrical outlets. If you're coming from North America and plan to use your own appliances, bring a converter kit with a variety of adapters.

EMERGENCIES
➤ AMBULANCE AND FIRE: Dial ☎ 596/70–36–48 or 596/71–59–48 for an ambulance. Dial ☎ 18 for fire.
➤ HOSPITALS: There's a 24-hour emergency room at SAMU (✉ At Hôpital Pierre Zabla Quitman in Lamentin, just outside Fort-de-France, ☎ 596/55–20–00).
➤ PHARMACIES: **Pharmacie Cypria** (✉ Bd. Général de Gaulle, Fort-de-France, ☎ 596/63–22–25); **Pharmacie de la Paix** (✉ Corner rue Victor Schoelcher and rue Perrinon, Fort-de-France, ☎ 596/71–94–83).
➤ POLICE: Dial ☎ 17.

FESTIVALS AND SEASONAL EVENTS
Martinique's Carnival begins in early January and runs through the first day of Lent. About 20 days into Lent, there's a mini-Carnival called Mi-carême. This one-day hiatus from what is traditionally 40 days of abstinence brings parties, dances, and the like; after it, however, everyone returns to the somber (and often sober) business of penance until Easter. Early August sees the Tour des Yoles Rondes point-to-point yawl race. In early December the island hosts the Caribbean's premier jazz festival, Jazz à la Martinique. In addition to showcasing the best musical talent of the islands, it has attracted such top American performers as Branford Marsalis.

HEALTH
Beware of the *mancenillier* (manchineel) trees. These pretty trees with green fruits that look like apples are poisonous. Sap and even raindrops falling from the trees can cause painful, scarring blisters. The trees have red warning signs posted by the forestry commission. If you plan to ramble through the rain forest, be careful where you step. There are fer-de-lances and other poisonous snakes on Martinique. A medical warning, just to be on the safe side, slather yourself with insect repellent, particularly at night and during the rainy season. There have been incidents of dengue fever. Dengue is caused by viruses carried by mosquitoes. It can bring headaches, eye aches, pains in the muscles and joints, and a skin rash. The fever subsides and then it rises again. It is more dangerous for children. Dengue is certainly not epidemic here, but if you go to a pharmacy for aspirin, you will be advised to buy ibuprofen instead, just on the remote chance that if you get bitten by a disease-bearing mosquito, it can be dangerous to have aspirin in your system.

HOLIDAYS
Public holidays for 2002 are: New Year's Day, Ash Wednesday (Feb. 28), Good Friday (Apr. 13), Easter Monday (Apr. 18), Labor Day (May 1), Bastille Day (July 14), Assumption Day (August 15), All Saints' Day (Nov. 1), Armistice Day (Nov. 11), and Christmas.

LANGUAGE
Many Martinicans speak Créole, a mixture of Spanish and French. Even if you do speak fluent French, you may have a problem understanding the accent. Try *sa ou fe* for "hello." In major tourist areas you'll

find someone who speaks English, but using a few French words—even if it's only to say, *"Parlez-vous anglais?"*—will be appreciated. Most menus are written in French. But rest assured that these people are typically courteous and will work with you on your French—or lack thereof.

MAIL AND SHIPPING

Airmail letters to the U.S. and Canada cost 4.60F for up to 20 grams; postcards, 3.70F. For Great Britain the costs are 4.40F and 3.60F, respectively. Stamps may be purchased from post offices, café-tabacs, and hotel newsstands. Letters to Martinique should include the name of the business, street (if available), town, postal code, the island, and French West Indies. Be forewarned, however, that mail is extremely slow both coming and going.

MONEY MATTERS

Prices quoted here are in U.S. dollars unless otherwise indicated.

ATMS

There are ATMs at the airport and at branches of the Crédit Agricole Bank, which is on the Cirrus system and also accepts Visa and MasterCard. If the change bureau at the airport is closed when you arrive, and you need francs for a taxi, you can use the ATM machine and put in your American debit or credit card to withdraw francs.

CREDIT CARDS

Major credit cards are accepted in hotels and restaurants in Fort-de-France and the Pointe du Bout areas, and you will generally get a favorable exchange rate on purchases; few establishments in the countryside accept them. Many establishments are no longer accepting American Express because its fees are too high. There's generally a 20% discount on luxury items paid for with traveler's checks or with certain credit cards.

CURRENCY

The currency is the French franc until June 2002, when the euro will replace it. U.S. dollars are accepted in some hotels, but it's better to convert your money. Banks give a more favorable rate than hotels. A currency exchange service that also offers a favorable rate is Change Caraïbes. If you are cashing less than a $100, it is usually better to go to the exchange or to use your ATM card.

➤ CONTACTS: **Change Caraïbes** (✉ Lamentin International Airport, ☎ 596/42–17–11; ✉ Rue Ernest Deproge, Fort-de-France, across from tourist office, ☎ 596/60–28–40).

PASSPORTS AND VISAS

All visitors must have a valid passport and a return or ongoing ticket.

SAFETY

Exercise the same safety precautions you would in any large city. Don't leave jewelry or money unattended on the beach. Except for the area around Cap Chevalier and the Tartane Peninsula, the Atlantic waters are rough and should be avoided by all but expert swimmers.

SIGHTSEEING TOURS

The terrific staff at the tourist office can help you arrange a personalized island tour with an English-speaking driver. There are set rates for certain tours, and if you share the ride with others, the per-person price will be whittled down.

Madinina Tours offers half- and full-day jaunts (lunch included). Boat tours are also available, as are air excursions to the Grenadines and

St. Lucia. Madinina has tour desks in most of the major hotels. Parc Naturel Régional de la Martinique organizes inexpensive guided hiking tours. Descriptive folders are available at the tourist office.

The semi-submersible *Aquascape* conducts 45- to 60-minute excursions so that riders can see the flora and fauna beneath the sea.
➤ CONTACTS: *Aquascope* (✉ Pointe du Bout Marina, ☎ 596/68–36–09; ✉ Ste-Anne, ☎ 596/74–87–41); **Madinina Tours** (✉ 111–113 rue Ernest Deproge, Fort-de-France, ☎ 596/70–65–25); **Parc Naturel Régional de la Martinique** (✉ 9 bd. Général de Gaulle, Fort-de-France, ☎ 596/73–19–30).

TAXES
DEPARTURE TAX
A departure tax of 260F is included in the cost of your airline ticket.

SALES TAX
A resort tax varies from hotel to hotel; the maximum is $2 per person per day. Rates quoted by hotels usually include a 10% service charge; some hotels add 10% to your bill.

TAXIS
Taxis are expensive. From the airport to Fort-de-France is about 100F; from the airport to Pointe du Bout, about 225F, and to Trois Ilets, 200F. A 40% surcharge is levied between 8 PM and 6 AM and on Sunday. This means that if you arrive at night, depending on where your hotel is, it may be cheaper (although not safer) to rent a car from the airport and keep it for 24 hours than to take a taxi to your hotel.
➤ CONTACTS: Dial (☎ 596/63–63–62 or 596/63–10–10) to request a cab. **M. Morital** (☎ 596/45–69–07 or mobile 596/45–69–07) for Mercedes taxi for a few francs more.

TELEPHONES
There are no coin-operated phone booths. Public phones now use a *télécarte,* which you can buy at post offices, *café-tabacs,* hotels, and at *bureaux de change.*

COUNTRY AND AREA CODES
To call Martinique from the U.S., dial 011 + 596 + the local six-digit number.

INTERNATIONAL CALLS
To call the U.S. from Martinique, dial 00 + 1, the area code, and the local number. You can now make collect calls to the states by dialing the Bell operator at 0 800/99–00–16; you can get the ATT operator at 0–800/99–00–11, or MCI at 0–800/99–00–19, from special service phones at the cruise ports and in town. These phones are blue, and one such is at the Super Sumo snack bar, on Rue de la Liberté, near the library. To call Great Britain from Martinique, dial 00 + 44, the area code (without the first zero), and the number.

INTERNET SERVICE
In Fort-de-France there is the Cyber Café Blénac open Mon.–Fri. 10–1 and Sat. 6 PM–1 AM, and there is also Internet service at the main post office.
➤ CONTACTS: **Cyber Café Blénac** (✉ rue Blénac, Fort de France, ☎ 596/70–31–62).

LOCAL CALLS
To place a local or inter-island call, dial the local six-digit number.

TIPPING

All restaurants include a 15% service charge in their menu prices. You can always add to this if you feel that service was exceptional.

VISITOR INFORMATION

➤ BEFORE YOU LEAVE: **Martinique Promotion Bureau** (✉ 444 Madison Ave., New York, NY 10022, ☎ 800/391–4909; ✉ 9454 Wilshire Blvd., Beverly Hills, CA 90212, ☎ 310/271–6665; ✉ 676 N. Michigan Ave., Chicago, IL 60611, ☎ 312/751–7800; ✉ 1981 McGill College Ave., Suite 490, Montréal, Québec H3A 2W9, Canada, ☎ 514/288–4264; ✉ 1 Dundas St. W, Suite 2405, Toronto, Ontario M5G 1Z3, Canada, ☎ 416/593–4723 or 800/361–9099; ✉ 178 Piccadilly, London W1V 0AL, U.K., ☎ 0181/124–4123; WEB www.martinique.org).

➤ IN MARTINIQUE: **Martinique Tourist Office** (✉ Bd. Alfassa, Fort-de-France, ☎ 596/63–79–60, FAX 596/73–66–93).

15 PUERTO RICO

Updated by
Delinda Karle

The pigeons have made Old San Juan their own. They flutter through plazas, rushing for scraps dropped by office workers lunching on the run. Old men sit on shaded benches, enveloped by the scent of roasting coffee from a nearby kiosk, talking quietly about long lives, and holding crumbling paper bags of stale bread. The birds dance for that bread, their gray wings buffing arms and shoulders. It's an ancient, symbiotic moment—a gentle touch for morsels of food.

Few Caribbean cities are as steeped in Spanish tradition as Puerto Rico's Old San Juan. Originally built as a fortress, the old city's myriad attractions include restored 16th-century buildings and 200-year-old houses with balustraded balconies of filigreed wrought iron that overlook narrow cobblestone streets. Spanish traditions are also apparent in the countryside—from the festivals celebrated in honor of small-town patron saints to the *paradores,* inexpensive but accommodating inns whose concept originated in Spain.

Puerto Rico, 110 mi (177 km) long and 35 mi (56 km) wide, was populated by several tribes of Indians (primarily the Taíno) when Columbus landed during his second voyage in 1493. In 1508 Juan Ponce de León, the frustrated seeker of the Fountain of Youth, established a settlement on the island and became its first governor; in 1521 he founded what would become known as Old San Juan. For three centuries the French, Dutch, and English tried unsuccessfully to wrest the island from Spain. In 1897 Spain granted the island dominion status and a year later—as a result of the Spanish-American War—Spain ceded the island to the United States. In 1917 Puerto Ricans became U.S. citizens, and in 1952 Puerto Rico became a semiautonomous commonwealth.

The years since have brought several referenda to determine whether the island should remain a commonwealth, become a state, or gain independence. As recently as 1998, statehood received 47% of the vote. With such a narrow majority of voters choosing to remain a commonwealth, statehood advocates contend the tide is turning in their favor. Or perhaps not. It may be true that all the latest American TV programs are broadcast here, that *el béisbol* (baseball) is a major pastime, that San Juan has the trappings of any American city, and that many islanders have family stateside. But life *en la isla* (on the island) is far more traditional. A strong Latin sense of community and family prevails, and *puertorriqueños* are fiercely proud of both their Spanish and African heritages.

Music is another source of Puerto Rican pride, and increasingly it seems that everyone wants to live *la vida loca* espoused by Puerto Rican pop star Ricky Martin. The brash Latin sound is best characterized by the music/dance form salsa, which shares not only its name with the Spanish word for "sauce" but also has a zesty, hot flavor. This fusion of West African percussion, jazz (especially swing and big band) and other Latin beats (mambo, merengue, flamenco, cha-cha, rumba) is sexy and primal. Dancing to it is a chance to let go of inhibitions.

Moving to the beat of salsa isn't your only nightlife option here. In San Juan's sophisticated Condado and Isla Verde areas you'll find flashy cabaret shows and casinos. By day you can step into the Old World—in Old San Juan, in a quiet colonial town, or on a coffee plantation. If you're the athletic type, you'll appreciate the island's many acres of golf courses, its abundant tennis courts, and its hundreds of beaches that offer every imaginable water sport. In the extraordinary 28,000-acre Caribbean National Forest (known as El Yunque) you'll find 100-ft-high trees and dramatic mountain ranges. If all this isn't enough, you can head to the outlying islets of Culebra, Vieques, and Mona, where the snorkeling and scuba diving are fine.

Lodging

San Juan's high-rise beachfront hotels cater primarily to the cruise-ship and casino crowd, though several target business travelers. Outside San Juan, particularly on the east coast, you'll find self-contained luxury resorts that cover hundreds of acres. In the west, southwest, and south—as well as on the islands of Vieques and Culebra—smaller inns, villas, condominiums for short-term rentals, and government-sponsored paradores are the norm.

Some paradores are rural inns, some offer no-frills apartments, and some are large hotels, but all must meet certain standards, such as proximity to an attraction or beach. Most have a small restaurant that serves local cuisine. They're great bargains (prices range from $60 to $125 for a double room) but can get noisy on weekends when local families descend for minivacations. For information on the paradores, contact the **Puerto Rico Tourism Company** (⊠ Box 9023960, San Juan, Puerto Rico 00902-3960, ☎ 800/866–7827).

Most hotels in Puerto Rico operate on the EP, although larger establishments often offer other meal plans or even all-inclusive packages. In the off-season, or summer months, rates at some hotels can drop 20% or more. For hotels outside of San Juan rates most often do not include airport transfers. Be sure to ask when you book. If you're traveling with several people, villas and condominiums are an affordable option. Call the tourist information office in the area where you want to stay, or try the options below.

Investigate rates at higher-end properties in San Juan's Isla Verde area through **Condo World** (⊠ 4230 Orchard Lake Rd., Suite 5, Orchard Lake, MI 48323, ☎ 800/521–2980, FAX 248/683–5076). **Puerto Rico Vacation Apartments** (⊠ Marabella del Caribe Oeste S-5, Isla Verde, San Juan 00979, ☎ 787/727–1591 or 800/266–3639, FAX 787/268–3604) represents some 200 properties in the Condado and Isla Verde areas. **Island West Properties** (⊠ Rte. 413, Km 0.7, Box 700, Rincón 00677, ☎ 787/823–2323, FAX 787/823–3254) has weekly and monthly rentals in Rincón. For properties on Vieques, the person to talk to is Jane Sabin

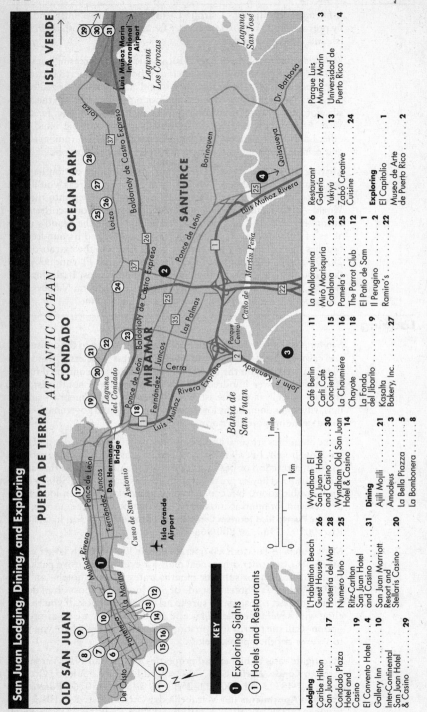

San Juan Lodging, Dining, and Exploring

at **Connections** (✉ Box 358, Esperanza, Vieques 00765, ☎ 787/741–0023). You can try **Acacia Apartments** (✉ 236 Calle Acacia, Box 1211, Esperanza, Vieques 00765, ☎ 787/741–1856).

CATEGORY	COST*
$$$$	over $225
$$$	$150–$225
$$	$75–$150
$	under $75

All prices are for a double room, high season, excluding 9% tax (11% for hotels with casinos, 7% for paradores) and 10%–15% service charge.

Hotels

OLD SAN JUAN

$$$$ 🏨 **El Convento Hotel.** Once a Carmelite convent, this 350-year-old
★ pastel-yellow building epitomizes Old World gentility enhanced by modern luxury. Much of its original architecture is intact, including a colonial interior courtyard. Rooms have a Spanish deco look, with dark woods, wrought-iron lamps, ornate furniture, and unusual antique details. Complimentary wine and hors d'oeuvres are served before dinner, and the third-floor honor bar is open around the clock. Shaded by a giant *nispero* tree, the courtyard's Café de Nispero has one of the best settings in the Old City. At night locals and visitors crowd the second-floor terrace restaurant, El Picoteo, as much for the tapas as for the sangria. The street-side Café Bohemio is a great spot for lunch or a quick coffee; it takes on a club-type atmosphere Tuesday through Friday nights with live music. ✉ *100 Calle Cristo (Box 1048), 00902,* ☎ *787/723–9020; 800/468–2779 direct to hotel,* FAX *787/721–2877,* WEB *www.elconvento.com. 54 rooms, 4 suites. 3 restaurants, bar, air-conditioning, in-room safes, minibars, pool, massage, gym, shops, library, meeting rooms, parking (fee). AE, D, DC, MC, V. CP.*

$$$ 🏨 **Gallery Inn.** Owners Jan D'Esopo and Manuco Gandia transformed
★ this rambling, classically Spanish house—one of the city's oldest residences—into an inn of "bohemian opulence," as some describe it. It's full of comforts and quirky details: winding, uneven stairs; balconies; a music room with a Steinway grand piano. The lush courtyard gardens, where Jan's pet macaws and cockatoos hang out, reach for the sunlight. Each room has a decor all its own as well as a phone and air-conditioning. Several rooms have whirlpool baths, but not one room has a TV. From the rooftop deck the spectacular panorama is of El Morro and San Cristóbal forts and the Atlantic. Galería San Juan, a small gallery and studio gives the hotel its name. A dining room is the sight for group banquets only, but dozens of restaurants are within walking distance in Old San Juan. The inn has no sign in front, so tell your taxi driver it's on the corner of Calles Norzagaray and San Justo. ✉ *204–206 Calle Norzagaray, 00901,* ☎ *787/722–1808,* FAX *787/724–7360,* WEB *www.thegalleryinn.com. 19 rooms, 3 suites. Air-conditioning, free parking. AE, DC, MC, V. CP.*

$$$ 🏨 **Wyndham Old San Juan Hotel & Casino.** The gleaming Wyndham has a triangular structure that subtly echoes the cruise ships docked nearby yet also has classic neo–Spanish colonial lines. The lobby, adjacent to the casino, shines with multicolored tiles and mahogany. Each standard room has a two-line phone, cable TV, an ironing board, a coffeemaker, and a hair dryer. Spacious suites also have sitting rooms, extra TVs, and minibars. On the ninth floor you'll find a small patio swimming pool and whirlpool bath; the seventh-floor concierge level provides hassle-free check-ins, Continental breakfast, and evening hors d'oeuvres. In the second-floor Dársena restaurant, spices from around the world are blended into Caribbean and Puerto Rican dishes, and

the hotel's Chips Lounge features a large drop-down screen for viewing sports events. ⊠ *100 Calle Brumbaugh, 00901,* ☎ *787/721–5100 or 800/996–3426,* ℻ *787/721–1111,* ⓦⓔⓑ *www.wyndham.com. 200 rooms, 40 suites. Restaurant, 2 bars, pool, hot tub, gym, casino, concierge floor, business services, meeting rooms, parking (fee). AE, D, DC, MC, V. EP.*

SAN JUAN

$$$$ 🏨 **Caribe Hilton San Juan.** This mainstay hotel in San Juan reopened after $50 million in renovations at the end of 1999. The rooms and halls are vibrant with bright paint and furniture all around; the three-level pool has gentle cascades as well as an attached wading pool and (cold water) whirlpool tubs. The hotel's exclusive beach has been expanded with imported sand. Room balconies feature ocean or lagoon views, the higher the floor, the better the view. An executive floor pampers business travelers. The spacious open-air lobby has a sunken bar looking out over the pool area. Restaurants include Morton's of Chicago and Olas Health Bar, which serves healthy cuisine near the spa and fitness center. The hotel reopened without a casino, but a new one was slated to open in late 2001. ⊠ *Calle Los Rosales, San Gerónimo Grounds, Puerta de Tierra, 00901,* ☎ *787/721–0303; 800/468–8585 direct to hotel;* ℻ *787/725–8849,* ⓦⓔⓑ *www.caribe.hilton.com. 604 rooms, 41 suites. 4 restaurants, 3 bars, air-conditioning, pool, spa, health club, 3 tennis courts, beach, shops, children's programs, meeting rooms, business services, parking (fee). AE, D, DC, MC, V. EP, CP, FAP, MAP.*

$$$$ 🏨 **Condado Plaza Hotel and Casino.** The Atlantic and the Condado Lagoon border this property. Two wings, appropriately named Ocean and Lagoon, are connected by an enclosed, elevated walkway. Standard rooms have walk-in closets and separate dressing areas. There's a variety of suites, including spa suites with oversized hot tubs. The Plaza Club floor has 24-hour concierge service and a private lounge. The Ocean wing sits on a small strip of a public beach, and there are four pools to choose from. Kids can find plenty to do at their own activity center, Camp Taíno. Dining options include Tony Roma's (a branch of the American barbecue chain), an informal poolside restaurant, and Max's Grill, open 24 hours for late-night noshing and a 24-hour casino for late-night gambling. ⊠ *999 Av. Ashford, 00902,* ☎ *787/721–1000, 800/468–8588, or 800/468–5228;* ℻ *787/728–1260,* ⓦⓔⓑ *condadoplaza.com. 570 rooms, 62 suites. 6 restaurants, 2 lounges, air-conditioning, 3 pools, 3 hot tubs, 2 tennis courts, shops, health club, beach, dock, boating, casino, children's programs, concierge floor, business services, parking (fee). AE, D, DC, MC, V. CP, EP, FAP, MAP.*

$$$$ 🏨 **Inter-Continental San Juan Resort and Casino.** Formerly the San Juan Grand Beach Resort and Casino, this hotel became an Inter-Continental in 2000. The 16-story monolith sits on one of the city's most popular beaches, and the theme of understated luxury carries from the large cream- and brown-tiled lobby, with its blue-sky ceiling motif, to the spacious rooms, decorated in somber brown and green hues. Suites of the upscale Club Inter-Continental, have their own private concierge and check-in and overlook the pool area, but the views from the standard rooms—either over the ocean or toward the city and the San José Lagoon—are pleasant. Off the lobby is the jangling casino, and on-site restaurants include a branch of Ruth's Chris Steak House and Momoyama, for Japanese cuisine. ⊠ *5961 Av. Isla Verde, (Box 6676), 00976,* ☎ *787/791–6100; 800/443–2009 direct to hotel,* ℻ *787/253–2510,* ⓦⓔⓑ *www.interconti.com. 400 rooms, 19 suites. 6 restaurants, 3 bars, air-conditioning, in-room safes, no-smoking rooms, pool, hot tub, spa, health club, boating, beach, shops, casino, nightclub, video games,* *children's programs, concierge floor, business services, meeting rooms, parking (fee). AE, D, MC, V. EP.*

$$$$ 🏨 **Ritz-Carlton San Juan Hotel and Casino.** San Juan has been puttin' on the ritz since this resort opened in late 1997. The large, multi-story hotel on Isla Verde beach is just about everything you think a Ritz should be, with some qualifications. The wide, beige-tinted lobby, with imported Italian marble and regal columns, is elegant if somewhat severe. Island art is displayed throughout the hotel. The standard rooms are decorated in light Caribbean florals, with muted carpets, dark-wood armoires, and marble sinks in the smallish bathrooms. They all come with cable TV, in-room movies, phones with data ports, and terry-cloth robes. The windows are not geared for the pleasant sea breeze—they're sealed shut for hurricane protection and presumably to muffle noise from the nearby international airport. But the beach is lovely, as is the large free-form pool, and the hotel spa is one of the island's largest. A Ritz Kids program and a well-equipped business center should meet all needs. ⊠ *6961 Av. Los Gobernadores, 00979,* ☎ *787/253–1700 or 800/241–3333,* FAX *787/253–0700,* WEB *www.ritzcarlton.com. 403 rooms, 11 suites. 3 restaurants, 3 bars, sushi bar, air-conditioning, minibars, no-smoking floors, pool, hair salon, hot tub, spa, 2 tennis courts, gym, casino, shop, concierge floor, children's programs, business services, parking (fee). AE, D, DC, MC, V. EP.*

$$$$ 🏨 **San Juan Marriott Resort and Stellaris Casino.** The red neon sign
★ atop this hotel is a beacon to its excellent Condado location. Rooms have soothing pastel carpeting, floral spreads, attractive tropical artwork on the walls, and balconies that overlook the ocean, the pool, or both. Restaurants include the Tuscany, for northern Italian cuisine, and the more casual La Vista, which is popular for dining alfresco. On weekends live entertainment in the lobby draws many locals, making it a lively and, when combined with the ringing of the slot machines from the casino, noisy spot (rooms are soundproof, though). Gorgeous Condado Beach is right outside, as is a large pool area. ⊠ *1309 Av. Ashford, 00907,* ☎ *787/722–7000, 800/644–5005, or 800/228–9290* FAX *787/722–7955,* WEB *www.marriott.com. 525 rooms, 15 suites. 4 restaurants, 1 lounge, 1 bar, air-conditioning, no-smoking rooms, 2 pools, hair salon, hot tub, 2 tennis courts, spa, gym, beach, casino, shops, children's programs, business services, meeting rooms, parking (fee). AE, D, DC, MC, V. EP, FAP, MAP.*

$$$$ 🏨 **Wyndham El San Juan Hotel and Casino.** An immense antique chan-
★ delier illuminates the hand-carved mahogany paneling, Italian rose marble, and 250-year-old French tapestries in the 13,000-square-ft lobby of this resort on the Isla Verde Beach. You'll be hard pressed to decide whether you want a main tower suite with a whirlpool bath and wet bar, a garden room with a patio and whirlpool bath, or a *casita* with a sunken Roman bath. All guest quarters have CD players, VCRs, and walk-in closets with irons and ironing boards; dark rattan furnishings are complemented by rich carpets and tropical-print spreads and drapes throughout. Relax at the lobby's Cigar Bar and sample some of Puerto Rico's finest cigars, or take dinner at The Ranch, a rooftop country-and-western bar and grill. The hotel's Palm Court lobby is the place to see and be seen on a Friday or Saturday night. ⊠ *Av. Isla Verde (Box 2872), 00902,* ☎ *787/791–1000, 800/468–2818, or 800/996–3426;* FAX *787/791–0390,* WEB *www.wyndham.com. 332 rooms, 57 suites. 8 restaurants, 14 bars, air-conditioning, in-room data ports, minibars, no-smoking room, 2 pools, 5 hot tubs, 3 tennis courts, spa, gym, beach, shops, casino, nightclub, children's programs, business services, parking (fee). AE, DC, MC, V. EP, MAP.*

Puerto Rico

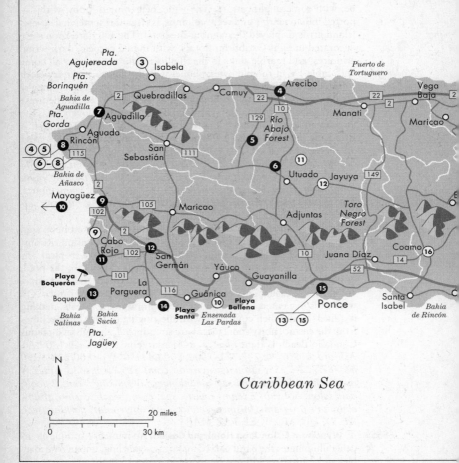

Lodging
Baños de Coamo . . . **16**
Copamarina
Beach Resort **10**
Doral Resort at
Palmas del Mar . . . **17**
Hacienda
Tamarindo **19**
Horned Dorset
Primavera **6**
Hotel La Casa
Grande **11**

Hotel Meliá **13**
Hyatt Dorado
Beach Resort &
Country Club **2**
Hyatt Regency
Cerromar Beach . . . **1**
Inn on the Blue
Horizon **18**
Lemontree Waterfront
Cottages **8**
Martineau Bay **20**

Parador Hacienda
Gripiñas **12**
Parador Villas
del Mar Hau **3**
Ponce Hilton
and Casino **14**
Westin Rio Mar
Beach Resort and
Country Club **23**
Wyndham
El Conquistador
Resort &
Country Club . . . **22**

Dining
Anchor's Inn **21**
El Bohio **9**
Horned Dorset
Primavera **6**
Larry B's
Black Eagle **5**

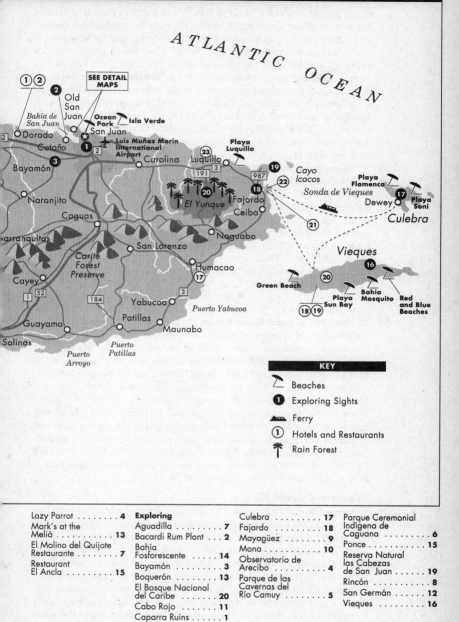

ATLANTIC OCEAN

SEE DETAIL MAPS

① ②

Old San Juan

② Old San Juan

Bahía de San Juan

② Dorado

Cataño

③

Bayamón

Ocean Park

San Juan

Isla Verde

★ Luis Muñoz Marín International Airport

① ② ③

Naranjito

Caguas

arranquitas

Carite Forest Preserve

Cayey

① 52

Guayama

Salinas

184

Yabucoa

Patillas

Maunabo

Puerto Yabucoa

Puerto Arroyo

Puerto Patillas

Carolina

Luquillo ②③

191 3

El Yunque

②⓪

Fajardo

Ceiba

Naguabo

San Lorenzo

Humacao

⑰

3

Playa Luquillo

⑲

②②

⑱

Cayo Icacos

Sonda de Vieques

Dewey ⑰

Playa Flamenco

Playa Soni

Culebra

②①

Vieques

⑯

Green Beach

②⓪

⑱ ⑲

Playa Sun Bay

Bahía Mosquito

Red and Blue Beaches

KEY

Beaches

❶ Exploring Sights

Ferry

① Hotels and Restaurants

Rain Forest

Lazy Parrot **4**

Mark's at the Meliá **13**

El Molino del Quijote Restaurante **7**

Restaurant El Ancla **15**

Exploring

Aguadilla **7**

Bacardi Rum Plant . . . **2**

Bahía Fosforescente **14**

Bayamón **3**

Boquerón **13**

El Bosque Nacional del Caribe **20**

Cabo Rojo **11**

Caparra Ruins **1**

Culebra **17**

Fajardo **18**

Mayagüez **9**

Mona **10**

Observatorio de Arecibo **4**

Parque de las Cavernas del Río Camuy **5**

Parque Ceremonial Indígena de Caguana **6**

Ponce **15**

Reserva Natural las Cabezas de San Juan **19**

Rincón **8**

San Germán **12**

Vieques **16**

$$$ 🏨 **Numero Uno.** Former New Yorker Esther Feliciano bought this three-story, red-roofed guest house on the beach, spruced it up, and made it a very pleasant place to stay. It's in a quiet residential area in the middle of San Juan's nicest beach. The rooms offer double-, queen-, or king-size beds. Three rooms have ocean views, and the apartments come with kitchenettes and televisions. A walled-in patio provides privacy for sunning or hanging out by the small pool, the bar, and its Pamela's restaurant is a popular spot for lunch and dinner for both guests and nonguests of the hotel. On the other side of the wall, the wide, sandy beach beckons; if you're a guest here, you're provided with beach chairs, umbrellas, and towels. ✉ *1 Calle Santa Ana, Ocean Park, 00911,* ☎ *787/726–5010,* 𝖥𝖠𝖷 *787/727–5482. 12 rooms, 2 apartments. Restaurant, bar, air-conditioning, minibars, fans, pool, beach, free parking. AE, MC, V. CP.*

$$ 🏨 **Hostería del Mar.** This small white inn's location on the beach in
★ Ocean Park, a residential neighborhood, is a wonderful alternative to the bustle of the Condado or Old San Juan—you have to go down to the beach and look west to see the high-rises of the Condado looming in the distance. Rooms are attractive and simple, with tropical prints and rattan furniture, and many have ocean views. Four apartments have kitchenettes with microwaves and two-burner stoves. The staff is courteous and helpful. The restaurant serves many vegetarian dishes, faces the trade winds, and offers fabulous views of the wide beach. ✉ *1 Calle Tapia, Ocean Park, 00911,* ☎ *787/727–3302 or 800/742–4276,* 𝖥𝖠𝖷 *787/268–0772. 8 rooms, 4 apartments, 1 minisuite. Restaurant, air-conditioning, beach, free parking. AE, D, DC, MC, V. EP.*

$$ 🏨 **L'Habitation Beach Guest House.** On the beach in Ocean Park is this guest house with a definite French atmosphere and a primarily gay clientele. You'll be on a first-name basis with owners Marie and Michel, both from France by way of Guadeloupe. They keep a very relaxed ambience in this 10-room accommodation. Rooms are simple and comfortable; numbers 8 and 9 are the largest and have ocean views. There is a reading library for guests. A bar/snack bar sits in a corner of a palm-shaded patio between the guest house and the beach. Beach chairs and towels are provided; get your beach gear together before you have one of Michel's margaritas, which will knock your sandals off. Pets are welcome. ✉ *1957 Calle Italia, Ocean Park, 00911,* ☎ *787/727–2499,* 𝖥𝖠𝖷 *787/727–2599. 10 rooms. Bar, snack bar, air-conditioning, fans, beach, library, coin laundry, free parking. AE, D, MC, V. CP.*

Western Puerto Rico

$$$$ 🏨 **Horned Dorset Primavera.** The Spanish colonial-style resort is tucked
★ away amid lush landscaping overlooking the sea and is hardly noticeable from the road; it's the only Relais & Chateaux property in Puerto Rico. The only sounds you're likely to hear as you lounge on the long, secluded beach are the crash of the surf and an occasional squawk from Pompidou, the enormous *guacamayo* (parrot) in the lounge. Suites have balconies and are exquisitely furnished with antiques, including mahogany four-poster beds, dressers, and nightstands. Casa Escondida has eight rooms—four with their own plunge pools and hot tubs—and is designed as a turn-of-the-20th-century Puerto Rican hacienda, with tile or wooden floors, mahogany furnishings, terraces, and black-marble baths. There are no radios, TVs, or phones in any of the rooms. The Horned Dorset Primavera restaurant is popular with nonguests. (Parents take note: young children won't feel comfortable at this hotel.) ✉ *Rte. 429, Km 3 (Box 1132), Rincón, 00677,* ☎ *787/823–4030, 787/823–4050, or 800/633–1857 (direct to hotel),* 𝖥𝖠𝖷 *787/823–5580,* 𝖶𝖤𝖡 *www.horneddorset.com. 31 rooms. Restaurant, air-conditioning, fans, 2 pools, beach, tennis, gym, library. AE, MC, V. EP, MAP.*

$$$$ ☷ **Ponce Hilton and Casino.** The biggest resort on the south coast—a cream-and-turquoise complex on 80 acres of landscaped grounds—is completely self-contained and caters to a corporate clientele. You'll find a casino, a shopping arcade, a pool, a spa, and a disco. You'll also find several restaurants, including the intimate and romantic La Cava, built as if it were a wine cellar. The casual La Terraza is in an atrium with cascading waterfalls and serves buffet breakfasts as well as lunch and dinner. The hotel's new owners, Hoteles Serrallés, have redecorated all the rooms in tropical style and at press time were planning to break ground for two new golf courses. New villas near the golf courses are on the drawing board. A practice golf range is currently available for guests. The hotel has a black-sand beach and is a five-minute cab ride from downtown Ponce. ⊠ *Rte. 14, 1150 Av. Caribe (Box 7419), Ponce, 00732,* ☎ *787/259–7676 or 800/981–3232 (direct to hotel), or 800/445–8667,* ℻ *787/259–7674,* ⠧⠑⠃ *www.ponce.hilton.com. 148 rooms, 5 suites. 4 restaurants, 5 bars, in-room safes, minibars, pool, hot tub, spa, driving range, 4 tennis courts, basketball, gym, Ping-Pong, volleyball, beach, bicycles, shops, casino, dance club, baby-sitting, playground, children's program, business services, meeting rooms, parking (fee). AE, D, MC, V. EP, FAP MAP.*

$$$ ☷ **Copamarina Beach Resort.** This resort is a nature-lovers' paradise.
★ Set on 16 acres between the sea and the Guánica Dry Forest, it has dozens of different kinds of palm and fruit trees and flowering plants. The open-air reception center leads out to the pool, Las Palmas Café, and the building wings. The resort fronts a beach and is minutes from some of the best stretches of sand in the Guánica area. Guests are given a guide book to the trails of the dry forest, and guided tours with forest rangers can be arranged. There's an on-site PADI dive shop and all kinds of toys for the water—from kayaks to water bicycles. Trips to the offshore Gilligan's Island ($4) can be arranged. The spotless rooms have small terraces with water views and one queen-size or two double beds. Two spanking-new three-bedroom apartments are to one side of the property in a hacienda-style building with sweeping balconies. Chef Mark French of Mark's at the Meliá consults at the Coastal Cuisine dining room, where chef Julio Martínez (who has won cooking awards of his own) rules the roost. ⊠ *Rte. 333, Km 6.5, Caña Gorda (Box 805), Guánica, 00653,* ☎ *787/821–0505, 800/468–4553 (direct to hotel), or 800/207–6900,* ℻ *787/821–0070,* ⠧⠑⠃ *www.copamarina.com. 106 rooms. 2 restaurants, 2 bars, air-conditioning, 2 pools, 2 wading pools, 2 hot tubs, spa, 2 tennis courts, gym, volleyball, dive shop, windsurfing, shop, meeting rooms. AE, MC, V. CP, EP, MAP.*

$$ ☷ **Baños de Coamo.** This historic mountain inn is at the hot sulfur springs purported to be the Fountain of Youth of Ponce de León's dreams. Rooms, in four modern two-story buildings, open onto latticed wooden verandas and have a lodge-like atmosphere. All come with TVs, phones, and private baths. The restaurant, in part of the inn that dates from the 19th century, serves large portions of Puerto Rican cuisine, and on weekend afternoons there are often live musicians playing near the outdoor bar. The hotel's spring-fed hot bath, said to have been used by Franklin D. Roosevelt, shows signs of aging but is extremely popular with guests and residents alike. The 18-hole Coamo Springs Golf Course is nearby. ⊠ *Rte. 546 (Box 540), Coamo, 00769,* ☎ *787/825–2186 or 787/825–2239,* ℻ *787/825–4739. 48 rooms. Restaurant, bar, air-conditioning, pool, AE, DC, MC, V. EP.*

$$ ☷ **Hotel La Casa Grande.** Surrounded by lakes, lush green vegetation and mountain peaks, it's not hard to imagine Tarzan swinging in for dinner at this quaint inn. Built in 1947 on a sugar, tobacco, coffee, and cattle plantation, the main house contains a restaurant, bar, and reception area. Five wooden buildings surrounding the main house hold

20 guest rooms with peaked ceilings and fans. The grounds cover 107 acres, a swimming pool, and beautiful gardens lovingly planted and marked by owner Steven Weingarten. The hotel captures mountain water for use in the hotel, recycles its trash, and strives to be as energy efficient as possible. There are no TVs, phones, or radios in the rooms, but a chorus of tiny tree frogs provides symphonies at night. Dining is on an outdoor patio at Jungle Jane's restaurant, which serves breakfast, lunch, and dinner. The inn is near two lakes, including Lago Dos Bocas (where you can rent kayaks), and forest reserves; it is convenient for day trips to the Arecibo Observatory and the Río Camuy Cave Park; horseback riding is nearby. ✉ *Rte. 612, Km 0.3 (Box 1499), 00641,* ☎ *787/894–3939 or 888/343–2272,* 𝖥𝖠𝖷 *787/894–3900,* 𝖶𝖤𝖡 *www.hotelcasagrande.com. 20 rooms. Restaurant, fans, pool, conference center. AE, MC, V. EP.*

$$ ⊡ **Hotel Meliá.** Set in the heart of Ponce and facing the Parque de Bombas and the Ponce Cathedral, this family-owned hotel provides a wonderful, low-key base for exploring the marvelous turn-of-the-20th-century architecture, museums, and landmarks of downtown. The lobby has an Old World feel, with high ceilings, blue-and-beige tile floors, and well-worn but charming decor. Room furnishings are standard and have a distinct European feel. Six suites have balconies with terrific views of Ponce's historic district. Breakfast is served on the rooftop terrace, which offers pretty views of the city and mountains. The hotel's restaurant, owned by Mark French, is justly popular. A pool is planned. ✉ *2 Calle Cristina (Box 1431), Ponce, 00733,* ☎ *787/842–0260 or 800/742–4276,* 𝖥𝖠𝖷 *787/841–3602,* 𝖶𝖤𝖡 *home.coqui.net/melia. 77 rooms, 6 suites. Restaurant, air-conditioning, parking (fee). AE, MC, V. CP.*

$$ ⊡ **Lemontree Waterfront Cottages.** These sparkling, large apartments
★ sit right on the beach. The owner-managers, Mary Jeanne and Paul Hellings, have put their own personal touches on the apartments (Paul created all the detailed woodwork, and Mary Jeanne designed the interiors). The bright tropical decor includes local artwork. There are one three-bedroom unit with two baths, one two-bedroom unit, two one-bedroom units, and two newer studios. The one-bedroom units have wooden cathedral ceilings and picture windows. All the apartments have kitchens; the studios have kitchenettes. Each unit also has a TV, and a deck with a wet bar and a grill. There's weekly maid service, and phones are available on request. The beach is small, but larger ones are close by. Downtown Rincón is a 10-minute drive away. (The Lemontree was up for sale at the time this book went to press.) ✉ *Rte. 429 (Box 200), Rincón, 00677,* ☎ *787/823–6452,* 𝖥𝖠𝖷 *787/823–5821,* 𝖶𝖤𝖡 *www.lemontreepr.com. 6 units. Air-conditioning, kitchenettes, beach, laundry service MC, V. EP.*

$$ ⊡ **Parador Hacienda Gripiñas.** The sea is more than 30 mi (48 km) from this white hacienda, so come if you're really looking for a romantic mountain hideaway. Polished wooden ceilings warm the interior. Large, airy rooms are decorated with native crafts. Relaxation beckons at every turn: rocking chairs nod in the spacious lounge, hammocks swing on the porch, and splendid gardens invite a leisurely stroll. Your morning coffee is grown on the adjacent plantation, and its aroma fills the air, as does the joyful chirp of the *coquís* (small tree frogs that blend in well with their surroundings; if you see one, local lore has it you'll be blessed with good fortune). ✉ *Rte. 527, km 2.5 (Box 387), Jayuya, 00664,* ☎ *787/828–1717,* 𝖥𝖠𝖷 *787/828–1718,* 𝖶𝖤𝖡 *www.haciendagripinas.com. 19 rooms. Restaurant, bar, pool, hiking. AE, MC, V. MAP.*

$$ ⊡ **Parador Villas del Mar Hau.** This secluded escape has a fanciful row of pastel-colored cottages and newer concrete buildings overlooking Montones Beach on the north coast. The one-, two-, and three-bedroom cot-

tages are linked with a boardwalk—some have a TV, some have air-conditioning in the bedrooms, and others have fans. All have balconies with an ocean view. Sheets and kitchen equipment are supplied, and the interiors are simply and tastefully decorated. The larger concrete buildings contain studios, some with a kitchen and some without. Maid service is available every two days. The grounds include a barbecue area and sand volleyball court. Horses are also available to ride, and tours can be arranged on-site. Olas y Arena restaurant is known for its fish dishes and its paella. ✉ *Rte. 466, Km 8.2 (Box 510), 00622, ☎ 787/872-2045, FAX 787/872-2627, WEB www.villahau.com. 38 units. Restaurant, air-conditioning (some), fans, pool, massage, tennis court, basketball, horseback riding, volleyball, coin laundry. AE, MC, V. EP.*

Eastern Puerto Rico

$$$$ 🏨 **Doral Resort at Palmas del Mar.** The sprawling Palmas del Mar complex—some might say too big and too isolated—is a 2,750-acre resort community that was once a coconut plantation. At the resort itself, recently renamed the Doral Resort at Palmas del Mar, it's easy to relax on one of the open-air lobby's plushly cushioned rattan couches, listening to the fountain (and the friendly staffers greeting guests). Large rooms have tile floors, white and pastel stucco walls with cheery prints, and abstract-pattern fabrics in bold colors. Some rooms have balconies or cathedral ceilings that keep them from feeling too boxy. Many of the privately owned villas are also for rent through the hotel. Horseback riding on the beach, diving offshore, and matches at the large tennis center are among the activities here. Most people, however, come for the golf, on the Rees Jones–designed Flamboyán course or the older Gary Player–designed Palmas course. As you're never sure if you're walking on grounds or greens here, it's best to rent a cart or hop the free shuttle to get around. ✉ *170 Candelero Dr. (Box 2020), Humacao, 00791, ☎ 787/852-6000 or 800/725-6273 (direct to hotel), FAX 787/852-6320, WEB www.palmasdelmar.com. 101 rooms, 135 villas. 9 restaurants, 2 bars, lobby lounge, air-conditioning, in-room safes, refrigerators, room service, pool, 2 18-hole golf courses, driving range, putting green, 20 tennis courts, health club, horseback riding, beach, dive shop, dock, boating, fishing, bicycles, shops, casino, children's programs. AE, DC, MC, V. EP, MAP.*

$$$$ 🏨 **Hyatt Dorado Beach Resort & Country Club.** The ambience is more subdued here than at its sister hotel, the Hyatt Regency Cerromar Beach, where you can also take advantage of the facilities. A variety of accommodations are in low-rise buildings on 1,000 landscaped acres. Most rooms have patios or balconies, and all have polished terra-cotta floors and marble baths. Upper-level rooms in the Oceanview Houses have a vista of the two beaches. The resort's two golf courses have recently been renovated, and a new clubhouse has been added. Restaurants include the romantic Su Casa, which serves dinner on the terrace of an old plantation home. ✉ *Rte. 693, Km 10.8 (Box 1351), Dorado, 00646, ☎ 787/796-1234 or 800/233-1234, FAX 787/796-2022 or 787/796-6560, WEB www.hyatt.com. 298 rooms. 5 restaurants, air-conditioning, minibars, 2 pools, wading pool, spa, 2 18-hole golf courses, 7 tennis courts, health club, hiking, jogging, beach, snorkeling, windsurfing, boating, bicycles, children's programs. AE, D, DC, MC, V. EP, MAP (compulsory from Dec. 15–Feb. 28).*

$$$$ 🏨 **Hyatt Regency Cerromar Beach.** The family- and sports-oriented Cerromar has two Robert Trent Jones golf courses, tennis courts, a spa and fitness center, jogging and biking trails, a pool that's more than 900 ft long, a hot tub in a man-made cavern, a swim-up bar, and a three-story water slide. The modern seven-story hotel is done up in tropical style. Rooms have tile floors, marble baths, and a king-size bed or

two double beds. You'll find quieter rooms on the west side, away from the pool. Guests at the Cerromar and its sister facility, the Hyatt Dorado Beach, less than a mile (1½ km) down the road, have access to the facilities of both resorts, and trolleys make frequent runs between the two. The Steak Company serves prime cuts of beef, and Zen Garden serves Japanese and Chinese cuisine and features a Sushi bar. ⊠ *Rte. 693, Km 11.8 (Box 1351), Dorado, 00646,* ☎ *787/796–1234 or 800/233–1234,* FAX *787/796–4647,* WEB *www.hyatt.com. 506 rooms. 4 restaurants, 3 bars, air-conditioning, minibars, pool, hot tub, spa, 2 18-hole golf courses, 8 tennis courts, gym, hiking, jogging, beach, snorkeling, water slide, bicycles, shops, casino, children's programs, dance club. AE, D, DC, MC, V. EP.*

$$$$ ⬚ **Wyndham El Conquistador Resort & Country Club.** Divided into four
★   different areas, including the main hotel and Las Olas Village, built on the side of a cliff, this complex is a world unto itself. It's perched dramatically atop a 300-ft bluff with views of the ocean, offshore islets, and El Yunque. The architecture is a blend of Moorish and Spanish colonial: cobblestone streets, white stucco and terra-cotta buildings, open-air plazas with tinkling fountains, tiled benches, and gas lamps. Plants and caged parrots decorate many of the open spaces. Rooms are tropical and modern with entertainment centers and well-stocked minibars. An array of different units is available throughout the complex, from standard rooms to three-bedroom suites with fully equipped kitchens. In the secluded Las Casitas Village, built to resemble a Spanish-colonial city, the Golden Door Spa has opened its first Caribbean location. The resort is one of the few on the island to provide motorcoach transfers from LMM International Airport (for $58 per person round-trip). The ride is a little more than an hour. The hotel's beach is the offshore Palomino Island, which you reach by ferry (free to guests). ⊠ *1000 Av. El Conquistador (Box 70001), Fajardo, 00738,* ☎ *787/ 863–1000, 800/468–8365 (direct to hotel), or 800/996–3426,* FAX *787/ 863–6500,* WEB *www.wyndham.com. 918 units. 10 restaurants, 8 bars, air-conditioning, minibars, 6 pools, spa, 18-hole golf course, 6 tennis courts, spa, health club, beach, dive shop, dock, snorkeling, windsurfing, boating, jet skiing, shops, casino, nightclub, children's programs, business services, meeting rooms. AE, D, DC, MC, V. EP, MAP.*

$$$ ⬚ **Westin Río Mar Beach Resort, Country Club & Ocean Villas** Set on
★   481 acres (the grounds of a former country club), this resort, anchored by a contemporary version of a Caribbean manor house, has red-tile roofs and a massive lobby with ocher floor tiles, ornate stairways, potted plants, and shimmering chandeliers. Rooms and suites are spacious and have dark-grained wood and floral patterns, in-room video games, and balconies; the suites also have large desks. In 2000, 58 new one-, two-, and three-bedroom villas opened on the resort near the ocean, with an oceanside restaurant catering to guests there. The resort has two 18-hole golf courses and 13 Har-Tru tennis courts. In addition to the beach, kids have their own activities centers, indoors and out, and a large pool with a winding slide. The resort is about an hour from San Juan, and El Yunque is just minutes away. ⊠ *6000 Río Mar Blvd. (Box 6100), Río Grande, 00745,* ☎ *787/888–6000 or 800/474–6627 (direct to hotel),* FAX *787/888–6235,* WEB *www.westinriomar.com. 600 rooms, 72 suites, 52 villas. 9 restaurants, 3 bars, 1 lounge, air-conditioning, in-room safes, minibars, no-smoking rooms, 2 pools, hair salon, spa, 2 18-hole golf courses, 13 tennis courts, health club, beach, dive shop, snorkeling, water slide, windsurfing, boating, jet skiing, casino, business services, meeting rooms. AE, D, DC, MC, V. EP, FAP, MAP.*

Vieques Island

$$$$ 🏨 **Inn on the Blue Horizon.** Known for its restaurant, Café Blu, and
★ its octagonal Blu bar, this small, popular hotel is owned by former New
Yorkers James Weis and Billy Knight. It sits on 20 windswept acres
fronting the Caribbean, and its rooms—furnished with antiques—are
sumptuous and lovely, as is the patio-lounge area. Two rooms have air-
conditioning; all have fans. The pool is gorgeous, although you'll have
to drive to a good beach. (Note to parents, children under 14 won't
feel comfortable here). ✉ *Rte. 996 (Box 1556), 00765,* ☎ *787/741–
3318,* FAX *787/741–0522,* WEB *www.enchanted-isle.com/bluehorizon. 9
rooms. Restaurant, bar, fans, pool, gym, massage. MC, V. CP.*

$$$$ 🏨 **Martineau Bay** The first large-scale resort to open on Vieques and
the first resort in Puerto Rico managed by Rosewood Hotels & Resorts, this brand-new property skirts the ocean near Isabel Segunda and
opened in Spring 2001. The reception area and restaurants are in a hacienda-style great house with a sweeping wrap-around veranda. All
rooms are in low-rise tin-roofed guesthouses and all have air-conditioning, TVs, and three telephones. The one-bedroom suites have
Jacuzzi tubs. Many of the rooms are furnished like traditional Spanish villas, with patterned tile and wrought-iron fixtures. There's a
pool, a restaurant overlooking the sea, a poolside grill serving seafood,
a spa, and children's and teen's programs. ✉ *Rte., 200 Km 3.4, (Box
9368), 00765,* ☎ *787/741–4100 or 800/767–3966,* FAX *787/741–4105,*
WEB *www.rosewood-hotels.com. 136 rooms, 20 suites. 2 restaurants,
bar, pool, beach, spa, 2 tennis courts, children's programs, business services. EP, FAP, MAP.*

$$$ 🏨 **Hacienda Tamarindo.** Owners Burr and Linda Vail left Vermont to
★ build this extraordinary hotel—with a huge tamarind tree right in the
middle and sweeping Caribbean views from its windswept location atop
a hill. Rooms are individually decorated but have such details as ma-
hogany louvered doors and terra-cotta tile floors. Some rooms have
terraces, and half the rooms have air-conditioning; the rest face the trade
winds. All have ceiling fans and are furnished with eclectic art and an-
tiques shipped from Vermont. A full breakfast is served on the second-
floor terrace. You can walk down the hill to the Inn on the Blue
Horizon for dinner. Box lunches are available on request. (Children
under 15 won't feel comfortable here; best to leave the kids at home.)
✉ *Rte. 996 (Box 1569), 00765,* ☎ *787/741–8525,* FAX *787/741–3215,*
WEB *www.enchanted-isle.com/tamarindo. 16 rooms. Fans, pool. AE, MC,
V. CP.*

Dining

In San Juan you'll find everything from Italian to Thai, as well as su-
perb local eateries serving *comida criolla* (traditional Caribbean cre-
ole food). All of San Juan's large hotels have fine restaurants, but
some of the city's best eateries are stand-alone, and smaller hotels also
often present good options. There is also a mind-boggling array of U.S.
chain restaurants. No matter your price range or taste, San Juan is a
great place to eat.

Mesónes gastronómicos are restaurants recognized by the government
for preserving culinary traditions. There are more than 30 island-wide.
(Although there are fine restaurants in the system, the *mesón gas-
tronómico* label is not an automatic symbol of quality.) Wherever you
go, it's *always* good to make reservations in the busy season, mid-Novem-
ber–April, in restaurants where they are accepted.

Puerto Rican cooking uses a lot of local vegetables: plantains are
cooked a hundred different ways—as *tostones* (fried green), *amarillos*

(baked ripe), and chips. Rice and beans with tostones or amarillos are accompaniments to every dish. Locals cook white rice with *habichuelas* (red beans), *achiote* (annatto seeds), or saffron; brown rice with *gandules* (pigeon peas); and *morro* (black rice) with *frijoles negros* (black beans). Yams and other root vegetables, such as yucca and yautía, are served baked, fried, stuffed, boiled, and mashed. *Sofrito*—a garlic, onion, sweet pepper, coriander, oregano, and tomato puree—is used as a base for practically everything.

Beef, chicken, pork, and seafood are rubbed with *adobo,* a garlic-oregano marinade, before cooking. *Arroz con pollo* (chicken with rice), *sancocho* (beef or chicken and tuber soup), *asopao* (a soupy rice gumbo with chicken or seafood), and *encebollado* (steak smothered in onions) are all typical plates. Also look for fritters served along highways and beaches. You may find *empanadillas* (stuffed fried turnovers), *surrullitos* (cheese-stuffed corn sticks), *alcapurias* (stuffed green banana croquettes), and *bacalaitos* (codfish fritters).

Puerto Rican cuisine, naturally, also relies on local catches. Caribbean lobster, available mainly at coastal restaurants, is sweeter and easier to eat than Maine lobster, and there is always plentiful fresh dolphinfish and red snapper. Conch is prepared in a chilled ceviche salad or stuffed with tomato sauce inside fritters.

Puerto Rican coffee is excellent black or cut *con leche* (with hot milk). The origin of the piña colada is attributed to numerous places, from the Caribe Hilton to Gran Hotel El Convento to a La Fortaleza Street bar. Puerto Rican rums range from light mixers to dark, aged liqueurs. Look for Bacardi, Don Q, Ron Rico, Palo Viejo, and Barrilito.

What to Wear
Dress codes vary greatly, though a restaurant's price category is a good indicator of its formality. For less-expensive places, anything but beachwear is fine. You can always head straight from the beach to a Pollo Tropical (a local fast-food chain) for a satisfying sandwich with a side of amarillos. There are many casual family-owned restaurants where dress is unimportant. Ritzier eateries will expect collared shirts for men and chic attire for women (jacket and tie requirements are rare). However, Puerto Ricans enjoy dressing up for dinner, so chances are you'll never feel overdressed.

CATEGORY	COST*
$$$$	over 30
$$$	$20–$30
$$	$10–$20
$	under $10

*per person for a main course at dinner

Old San Juan
ASIAN
$$$ ✕ **Yukiyú.** The only Japanese restaurant in Old San Juan serves some of the best Japanese food in Puerto Rico. If you crave a sushi bar, you should beeline for this establishment; non-sushi diners will find satisfaction in the selection of cooked dishes as well. For dinner, there's also a teppan yaki menu. ⊠ *311 Recinto Sur,* ☎ *787/721–0653. AE, D, MC, V.*

CAFÉS
$ ✕ **Café Berlin.** This casual café, bakery, and delicatessen overlooks the Plaza Colón. Tasty vegetarian fare prevails—try one of the creative salads—but nonvegetarian dishes are also available. The café's pastries, desserts, fresh juices, and Puerto Rican coffees are the perfect elixir after

a day of touring Old San Juan. ⊠ *407 Calle San Francisco,* ☎ *787/ 722–5205. AE, MC, V.*

$ ✕ **La Bombonera.** This landmark restaurant, with its ornate street-side facade, was established in 1903 and is known for its strong Puerto Rican coffee and excellent pastries. It's open every day from 7:30 AM until early evening, and full breakfasts are served until 11. It's a favorite Sunday-morning gathering place. The grumpy uniformed waiters give the appearance of having worked here since day one. ⊠ *259 Calle San Francisco,* ☎ *787/722–0658. AE, MC, V.*

CONTEMPORARY

$$$ ✕ **Amadeus.** A trendy crowd enjoys the nouvelle Caribbean menu here. The front dining room is attractive—whitewashed walls, dark wood, white tablecloths—but go through the outside passage to the romantic back room with printed cloths, candles, and exposed brick. The roster of appetizers includes dumplings with guava sauce, and plantain mousse with shrimp. Chicken stuffed with escargot, and Cajun-grilled mahimahi are a few of the delectable entrées. ⊠ *106 Calle San Sebastián,* ☎ *787/722–8635. AE, MC, V. No lunch Mon.*

$$ ✕ **Carli Café Concierto.** This intimate, hip bistro, with rust-hued walls
★ and black-marble tables, sits under the Banco Popular building, which dominates the Old San Juan skyline. You can dine—inside or on the street-side patio—on international savories such as juicy, seared loin of lamb or a light spinach and ricotta ravioli in pesto sauce. The genial owner and host, Carli Muñoz, is a pianist (he's toured with the Beach Boys—note the gold album on the wall) who plays his Steinway grand each evening. Visiting singers and musicians often join in the fun. ⊠ *Plazoleta Rafael Carrión, Calle Recinto Sur (corner of Calle San Justo),* ☎ *787/725–4927. AE, MC, V.* ☉ *Closed Sun.*

ECLECTIC

$$ ✕ **El Patio de Sam.** A large selection of blended fruit drinks makes this a popular stop during the day, and a wide selection of beers makes it a hoppin' late-night spot. You can grab a hamburger or sandwich or enjoy a steak, seafood, or local dish. The flan melts in your mouth. There's live music Friday and Saturday nights. ⊠ *102 Calle San Sebastián,* ☎ *787/723–1149. AE, D, DC, MC, V.*

$$ ✕ **Restaurant Galería.** This stylish, airy restaurant, with marble floors, white walls, and dark-wood accents, is lighted by a central atrium. The menu features Italian and international cuisine, including fresh pastas (try the signature pasta *galería,* with alfredo sauce and calamari), risottos, and seafood dishes as well as delicious local desserts such as flan, *arroz con dulce* (rice pudding), and fruit tarts. ⊠ *205 Calle San Justo,* ☎ *787/725–0478. AE, MC, V. Closed Mon.*

FRENCH

$$$$ ✕ **La Chaumière.** Reminiscent of a provincial French inn, this intimate restaurant with black-and-white-tile floors and heavy wood beams serves onion soup, snails in garlic butter, rack of lamb, filet mignon with peppercorn, and poached salmon in vermouth, in addition to daily specials. Behind the Teatro Tapia, this restaurant has been under the same management since 1969 and is one of the island's best French eateries. ⊠ *367 Calle Tetuan,* ☎ *787/722–3330. AE, DC, MC, V. Closed Sun. No lunch.*

ITALIAN

$$$$ ✕ **Il Perugino.** This intimate restaurant set in a 200-year-old building has been visited by the likes of Ruben Blades, Andy Garcia, and Luciano Pavorotti. Classic carpaccio; scallops with porcini mushrooms, and other exotic salads; homemade pastas such as black fettuccine with crayfish and baby eels; hearty main courses including rack of lamb with red wine sauce and aromatic herbs; and desserts like a killer tiramisu make it a must for serious gourmets. ⊠ *105 Calle Cristo,* ☎ *787/722–5481. Reservations essential. MC, V. No lunch.*

$$$
★ ✕ **La Bella Piazza.** La Bella Piazza's a great place to gather with friends and family and was the winner in 2000 of the "Tenedor de Honor" for best Italian trattoria. In an old Spanish building, the restaurant consists of a bar area, a long dining room, and an outdoor courtyard with tables. Try the delicious antipastas, pastas, and main courses like lamb chops baked with sage and white wine, and shrimp in a carrot, celery, onion, tomato, cream, and brandy sauce. The staff is friendly, and owner Stefano Conenna is often on hand to welcome clientele. ⊠ *355 Calle San Francisco,* ☎ *787/721–0396. AE, M, V. Closed Wed.*

LATIN

$$$ ✕ **The Parrot Club.** This spacious, colorful place serves up inventive nuevo Latino cuisine—variations of Cuban and Puerto Rican classics—in a casual yet efficient manner. Enjoy one of its 12 different martinis at the bar before moving to the adjacent dining room or back courtyard. Appetizers include mouthwatering crab cakes and tamarind-barbecued ribs, while main courses range from seared blackened tuna in a dark rum sauce to *churrasco* (barbecued steak) with tomato chimichurri. The Parrot Club's presence on the east end of La Fortaleza street has prompted other restaurants to open around it, a testament to its well-deserved popularity. ⊠ *363 Calle Fortaleza,* ☎ *787/725–7370. Reservations not accepted. AE, DC, MC, V.*

$$ ✕ **La Mallorquina.** The food here is basic Puerto Rican and Spanish fare (such as asopao and paella), the decor consists of peach walls and whirring ceiling fans, and the staff is nattily attired and friendly. But the atmosphere is what recommends this spot. Dated from 1848, it's considered Puerto Rico's oldest restaurant. ⊠ *207 Calle San Justo,* ☎ *787/722–3261. AE, MC, V. Closed Sun.*

$ ✕ **La Fonda del Jibarito.** This family-run restaurant has been a favorite with *sanjuaneros* for years, serving freshly prepared Puerto Rican specialties in a casual setting. The walls are replicas of Calle Sol, and there is a back porch filled with plants and fresh fruit. The conch ceviche and chicken fricassee are two of the menu's highlights. ⊠ *280 Calle Sol,* ☎ *787/725–8375. Reservations not accepted. MC, V.*

San Juan

CAFÉ

$ ✕ **Kasalta Bakery, Inc.** Make your selection from display cases full of tempting treats. Walk up to the counter and order from an assortment of sandwiches (try the Cubano), tender octopus salad, savory *caldo gallego* (a soup of fresh vegetables, sausage, and potatoes), cold drinks, strong café con leche, and luscious pastries. ⊠ *1966 Calle McLeary, Ocean Park,* ☎ *787/727–7340. AE, MC, V.*

CARIBBEAN

$$$ ✕ **Ajili Mojili.** This is traditional Puerto Rican food prepared with a flourish and served in an attractive plantation setting. Sample the fried cheese and yautia dumplings with the house sauce, a tomato, herb, garlic, and shaved-almond concoction. The *mofongo,* a mashed plantain casserole with a seafood or meat stuffing, is wonderful, as are the plantain-encrusted shrimp in white-wine herb sauce. ⊠ *1052 Ashford Av., Condado,* ☎ *787/725–9195. AE, DC, MC, V.*

ECLECTIC

$$$ ✕ **Zabó Creative Cuisine.** This inventive restaurant is in a restored plantation home set back from bustling Ashford Avenue. The large, pastoral front yard is enough to make you feel far from San Juan. "Grazing" from the appetizer menu is one of the main pastimes here, with pop-

ular choices including breaded calamari in a tomato-basil sauce and lobster pancakes in beurre blanc. Notable main courses are the veal chop stuffed with provolone, pancetta, and herbs, and the fresh fish of the day over a yellow raisin couscous with curry and mango rosemary sauce. ⊠ *14 Calle Candida, Condado,* ☎ *787/725–9494. AE, D, DC, MC, V. Closed Mon.*

$$$ ✕ **Chayote.** Slightly off the beaten path, this chic eatery, in the Hotel Olimpo Court, done in earth tones and decorated with contemporary Puerto Rican art, is an "in" spot to eat. The chef blends haute international cuisine with tropical panache. Appetizers include *sopa del día* (soup of the day) made with local produce, chayote salad with shrimp and avocado, and corn tamales with shrimp in coconut sauce. Half the menu's entrées are seafood dishes, including an excellent green pepper- and coriander-crusted tuna filet. ⊠ *603 Av. Miramar, Miramar,* ☎ *787/722–9385. AE, MC, V. Closed Sun. No lunch Sat.*

$$$ ✕ **Pamela's.** Facing the beach at the Numero Uno guest house in
★ Ocean Park, this restaurant draws people from all walks of life for a casual lunch or romantic dinner. The innovative menu includes barbecued shrimp on coconut corn arepas and seared cornish hen over caramelized pumpkin. The salads, such as endive and baby spinach with a smoked bacon dressing, or grilled chicken tossed with baby spinach topped with dried cranberries and feta cheese, are exceptional. You can sit in a greenhouse-like room facing the ocean or, at night, ask for a candlelit table on the beach. The service leaves nothing to be desired. ⊠ *1 Calle Santa Anna, Ocean Park,* ☎ *787/725–5010. AE, MC, V.*

SEAFOOD

$$ ✕ **Miró Marisquería Catalana.** Seafood Catalan-style is in the spotlight at this brightly colored restaurant in the heart of the Condado. An extensive appetizer list allows you to make a meal by selecting several choices; main courses include grilled halibut with fresh basil and prosciutto, grilled tuna with anchoviews and capter butter, and sautéed salmon with tomatoes, oregano, and fresh clams. There are also chicken and steak dishes. ⊠ *74 Av. Condado, Condado,* ☎ *787/723–9593. AE, MC, V.*

SPANISH

$$$$ ✕ **Ramiro's.** Step into a soft sea-green dining room for some imaginative Castillian cuisine. Chef-owner Jesus Ramiro is known for his artistic presentations and unique combinations. The menu includes peppers filled with lamb, halibut with banana chutney, and roast duckling with guava and kumquat sauce. If you can stand more, there's a lucious kiwi dessert sculpted to resemble twin palms. ⊠ *1106 Av. Magdalena, Condado,* ☎ *787/721–9049. AE, DC, MC, V. No lunch Sat.*

Western Puerto Rico

CONTEMPORARY

$$ ✕ **Larry B's Black Eagle.** Formerly located in the Beside the Pointe inn, Larry B's now offers steaks, shrimp, pasta, salads, and fresh fish in the former Black Eagle restaurant near the marina in Rincón. You can dine indoors or outside on a waterfront patio. The food is simply prepared and served in generous helpings and is quite popular among the locals. ⊠ *685 Black Eagle Rd., Rincón,* ☎ *787/823–3510. MC, V. Closed Tues. No lunch Mon., Wed.–Fri.*

$$ ✕ **Lazy Parrot.** Highly regarded for its fresh mahimahi, filet mignon, and homemade desserts, this little restaurant is part of the Lazy Parrot guest house. Perched in the hills, with mountain and ocean views, it's a great place to kick back and listen to the coquís. It's also where the local surfer contingent shares a beer or two after sundown. ⊠ *Rte. 413, Km 4.1, Barrio Puntas, Rincón,* ☎ *787/823–5654. AE, D, MC, V. Closed Mon.*

ECLECTIC

$$$ ✕ **Mark's at the Meliá.** One of the best restaurants on the island, this
★ eatery is tucked off the lobby of the Meliá hotel on Ponce's town square.
Chef Mark French, formerly of the Hilton Ponce, was named Caribbean
Chef of the Year in 2000 by the Caribbean Chefs Association, and his
menu lives up to that honor. You'll find a long list of appetizers, from
a three-cheese onion soup to a wonderful bacon, lettuce, and tomato
salad. You can also get "Mark's Sampler" as an appetizer, including tos-
tones with caviar, croquets, chorizo yuca, and sautéed shrimp. Entrées
range from plantain-crusted dorado with congri to medallions of ten-
derloin with a shrimp and bernaise sauce. The chocolate truffle cake
alone draws diners all the way from San Juan. ✉ *75 Calle Cristina, Ponce,*
☎ *787/284–6275. AE, MC, V. Closed Mon.–Tues.*

FRENCH

$$$$ ✕ **Horned Dorset Primavera.** Tucked away on the west coast of the is-
★ land in the posh Horned Dorset Primavera hotel, this is the finest food
you'll encounter outside San Juan. Although tropical accents appear here
and there, the cuisine is heavily Cordon Bleu–influenced: filet mignon
in a mushroom sauce, grilled squab in a black currant sauce, and grilled
fish du jour are de rigueur here. A five-course prix-fixe menu is avail-
able for $64 per person, and a chef's tasting menu for $88. ✉ *Rte. 429,*
Km 3, Rincón, ☎ *787/823–4030 or 787/823–4050. AE, MC, V.*

LATIN

$$ ✕ **Restaurant El Ancla.** The seafood and Puerto Rican specialties of this
mesón gastronómico are served with tostones, *papas fritas* (french
fries), and garlic bread. The menu ranges from lobster and shrimp to
chicken, beef, and asopao. The salmon filet with capers is one of the
most popular dishes, and the piña coladas—with or without rum—and
the flan are exceptional. ✉ *Av. Hostos Final 9, Playa Ponce, Ponce,*
☎ *787/840–2450. AE, MC, V.*

SEAFOOD

$$ ✕ **El Bohio.** A local favorite, this informal restaurant 15 minutes south
of Mayagüez is known for its seafood—cooked just about any way you
want. There are also some steak and chicken dishes and Puerto Rican
side dishes such as yuca and mofongo, or mashed plantains. You can
dine on the enclosed wooden deck that juts out over the sea (and
watch fish play in the water) or in the dining room. ✉ *Rte. 102, Km*
13.9, Playa Joyuda, Cabo Rojo, ☎ *787/851–2755. AE, DC, MC, V.*

SPANISH

$$ ✕ **El Molino del Quijote Restaurante.** Amid beautifully landscaped
gardens just off the beach, this colorful restaurant with tile-topped ta-
bles and local artwork serves Spanish and Puerto Rican cuisine. Try
the *bolas de pescado* (fish balls) appetizer with one of the paellas as
an entrée, or combine several appetizers for a meal. The sangria is terrific. Two two-bedroom cabanas are available to rent. ✉ *Rte. 429, Km*
3.3, Rincón, ☎ *787/823–4010. AE, MC, V. Closed Mon.–Thurs.*

Eastern Puerto Rico

SEAFOOD

$$ ✕ **Anchor's Inn.** This mesón gastronómico is a perfect example that good
things come in simple packages. The fishermen pull their boats into the
nearby Fajardo Harbor, with flotillas of brightly colored yachts, and
must head straight for the restaurant with their catch, for the seafood
is as fresh and succulent as it gets. It shows up in such Puerto Rican
dishes as surrullitos, asopao, and lobster mofongo. For carnivores,
prime cuts of meat also are available. There are also 14 guest rooms
upstairs. ✉ *Rte. 987, Km 2.4, Fajardo,* ☎ *787/863–7200. AE, MC, V.*

Beaches

By law, all Puerto Rican *playas* (beaches) are open to the public. The government runs 13 *balnearios* (public beaches), which have dressing rooms, lifeguards, parking, and in some cases picnic tables, playgrounds, and camping facilities. Admission is free, parking is $2. Most balneario facilities are open 9–5 daily in summer and Tuesday–Sunday the rest of the year. You can use the beaches anytime. Listed below are some major balnearios. For complete information about Puerto Rico's beaches, you can contact the **Department of Recreation and Sports** (☎ 787/721–2800).

SAN JUAN AREA

Balneario de Carolina, a few miles east of Isla Verde and so close to the airport the palms rustle when planes take off, is a long stretch of beach shaded by palms and almond trees, with an often rough surf. There's space to spread out and loads of parking. **Isla Verde,** a white-sand beach bordered by huge resort hotels, is good for swimming, and there are chair rentals along the beach. **Ocean Park,** a residential neighborhood east of the Condado, is home to a wide mile-long stretch of fine golden sand. The water is often choppy but very swimmable. On weekends it fills up with local college students; it's also one of the city's two beaches that are popular with the gay community. (The other is in front of the Atlantic Beach Hotel.) The **Parque de Tercer Milenio** (Third Millennium Park) in Puerta de Tierra at the entrance to Old San Juan encompasses Balneario Escambrón, a patch of honey-color beach with shade from coconut palms and a mostly gentle surf. There are showers available, and several restaurants; parking is $2, and the park is open daily 7–7. Kids will like **Playita Condado,** marked CONDADO PUBLIC BEACH on its sign. The small beach has an even surf and some shade from trees and is adjacent to the Condado Plaza Hotel off busy Avenida Ashford.

WEST COAST

Balneario Boquerón, on the southwest coast, is a broad beach of hard-packed sand fringed with coconut palms. Nearby, Playa Santa and Ballena beaches are often deserted.

EAST COAST AND THE OFFSHORE ISLANDS

Crescent-shaped **Playa Luquillo** comes complete with coconut palms (it was once a coconut plantation), changing rooms, lockers, showers, picnic tables, tent sites, and stands that sell Puerto Rican savories and tropical cocktails. Coral reefs protect its crystal-clear lagoon from the Atlantic waters, making it an ideal place to swim. It's one of the island's largest and best-known beaches and is crowded on weekends. It also has a *Mar Sin Barreras* (Sea Without Barriers) ramp that allows wheelchair users water access. The beach is a family favorite because of the shallow, calm waters.

The spectacularly beautiful **Playa Flamenco** is on the north shore of Culebra Island. The 3-mi-long crescent has shade trees, clear, shallow water, picnic tables, and rest rooms, and is popular on weekends with day-trippers from Fajardo. In winter, storms in the Atlantic often create great waves for bodysurfing. **Playa Soni,** on the eastern end of Culebra, is a wide strand of sparkling white sand on a protected bay with calm waters. The views of the islets of Culebrita, Cayo Norte, and St. Thomas are stunning. Snorkeling here is popular, too. As there are no facilities and little shade, bring lots of water and an umbrella. **Playa Sun Bay,** a white-sand beach on Vieques Island, has shade trees, picnic tables, and tent sites.

Outdoor Activities and Sports

Participant Sports

BOATING AND SAILING

Virtually all the resort hotels on San Juan's Condado and Isla Verda strips rent paddleboats, Sunfish, kayaks, and the like. The waves here can be strong, but the constant wind makes for good sailing. In San Juan **San Juan Water Fun** (⊠ Isla Verde Beach behind the Wyndham El San Juan Hotel and Casino, Av. Isla Verde, ☎ 787/644–2585) has all kinds of water sport equipment, including kayaks. **Sun Riders Watersports** (⊠ Condado Plaza Hotel and Casino, 999 Av. Ashford, ☎ 787/721–1000 ext. 2699) rents kayaks and offers windsurfing lessons.

Iguana Water Sports (⊠ Westin Río Mar Beach Resort and Country Club, 6000 Río Mar Blvd., Río Grande, ☎ 787/888–6000) has a particularly good selection of small boats. Sailing instruction is available on the east coast at **Karolette Charter** (⊠ Palmas del Mar, AB-12 St., Rd. 3, Km 86.4, Humacao, ☎ 787/850–7442 or 787/637–7992).

CYCLING

In general, you'll want to stay away from the main highways and streets of San Juan and Old San Juan for biking—the traffic is too heavy and the automobile fumes too thick. However, in the countryside biking is a great way to get around. An especially nice trip is along the new Paseo Piñones, an 11-mi bike path that skirts the ocean and meanders through mangrove forests east of San Juan on Route 187. **Condado Bikes** (⊠ 1106 Av. Ashford, Condado, ☎ 787/722–6288), offers daily and weekly bicycle rentals. **Pulpo Loco** (⊠ Rte. 187, Km 4.5, Piñones, ☎ 787/791–8382), rents bikes on an hourly or daily basis and is next to the new Paseo Piñones bicycle path.

FISHING

Puerto Rico's waters are home to large game fish such as marlin, wahoo, dorado, tuna, and barracuda; as many as 30 world records for catches have been set off the island's shores. Half-day, full-day, split charters, and big- and small-game fishing can be arranged through **Benítez Deep-Sea Fishing** (⊠ Club Náutico de San Juan, Miramar, San Juan, ☎ 787/723–2292). **Caribe Aquatic Adventures** in the Radisson Normandie Hotel (⊠ Corner of Av. Roisales and Av. Muñoz Rivera, Puerta de Tierra, ☎ 787/724–1882) offers a number of different deep-sea fishing trips.

Grand Illusion Charters (⊠ San Juan Bay Marina, ☎ 787/796–4645) offers charters and split charters off the north coast. Mickey Amador at **Parguera Fishing Charters** (⊠ Rte. 304, Km 3.8, La Parguera, ☎ 787/899–4698 or 787/382–4698), takes anglers on half-day and full-day outings on the Caribbean. **Tropical Fishing Charters** (⊠ 1000 Av. El Conquistador, Piers 15–16, Fajardo, ☎ 787/863–6594) has fishing charters off the east coast.

GOLF

For aficionados, Puerto Rico is known as the birthplace of golf legend Chi Chi Rodríguez—and he had to hone his craft somewhere. Currently, you'll find 18 courses on the island, including many championship links. Be sure to call ahead for tee times; hours vary, and several hotel courses give preference to guests. Greens fees start at about $30 and go up as high as $150.

One of the newer courses is the 18-hole Flamboyán at **Palmas del Mar** (⊠ Rte. 906, Humacao, ☎ 787/285–2221 or 787/285–2256). A Rees Jones design, the course has a view of the island of Vieques from its 12th hole. If you can't get a tee time, try the property's older but revitalized Gary Player–designed Palmas course or book time at the immense driving range. The four Robert Trent Jones–designed 18-hole courses shared by the **Hyatt Dorado Beach** and the **Hyatt Regency Cerromar Beach** hotels (☒ Rte. 693, Km 10.8 and Km 11.8, Dorado, ☎ 787/796–1234 ext. 3238 or 3016) have long been considered the island's top golf jewels and all have recently been renovated. The Chrysler Senior Match Play Challenge is held each November on the East course.

The **Westin Río Mar Beach Resort and Country Club** (☒ 6000 Río Mar Blvd., Río Grande, ☎ 787/888–6000 ext. 1401) has two 18-hole courses, the newer River Course designed by Greg Norman and the George and Tom Fazio–designed Ocean Course. The **Wyndham El Conquistador**'s 18-hole course (☒ 1000 Av. Conquistador, Las Croabas, ☎ 787/863–1000) is known for its striking elevation changes and scenic views. The island's newest course, the 18-hole **Coamo Springs Golf Course** (☒ Rte. 546, Km 1, Coamo, ☎ 787/825–1370), has a more rugged feeling than other island courses. **Dorado del Mar** (☒ Rte. 693, Dorado, ☎ 787/796–3065) has an 18-hole Chi Chi Rodríguez signature course. The **Bahia Beach Plantation** (☒ Rte. 187, Km 4.2, Río Grande, ☎ 787/256–5600 or 787/648–7400) has an 18-hole course with three beachfront finishing holes.

HIKING

Trails lace the rain forests of **El Bosque Nacional del Caribe (El Yunque)**; stop by the El Portal Tropical Forest Information Center (☒ Rte. 191, ☎ 787/888–1810) for trail information or go on one of many guided trips to the rain forest. Trails wind through picnic areas and lakes in **Bosque de Río Abajo** (Río Abajo Forest; ☒ Rte. 621, Utuado, ☎ 787/880–6557). The dry **Bosque de Guánica** (Guánica State Forest, is a United Nations Biosphere Reserve; ☒ Rte. 116, Guánica, ☎ 787/821–5706). **Bosque de Toro Negro** (Toro Negro Forest; ☒ Rte. 143, Jayuya, ☎ 787/867–3040) has hiking trails, picnic areas, and waterfalls. For information on hiking in forest reserves contact the **Department of Natural Resources** (☎ 787/724–3647 or 787/724–3724).

HORSEBACK RIDING

Puerto Rico's unique *paso fino* horses, with their distinct gait, are often used for riding. **Hacienda Campo Alegre** (☒ Rte. 127, Km 5.1, Yauco, ☎ 787/856–2609) offers rides on the trails of its 200-acre ranch, where you will also find playgrounds and a restaurant. **Hacienda Carabali** (☒ Rte. 992, Km 6, Luquillo, ☎ 787/889–5820) offers beach and rain forest trail rides. Beach and trail rides can be arranged for all skill levels at **Palmas del Mar Equestrian Center** (☒ 170 Candelero Dr., Rd. 3, Km 86.4, Humacao, ☎ 787/852–6000 ext. 10310).

SCUBA DIVING AND SNORKELING

The diving is excellent off Puerto Rico's south, east, and west coasts as well as its offshore islands. Particularly striking are dramatic walls created by a continental shelf off the south coast between La Parguera and Guanica. It's best to choose specific locations with the help of a guide or outfitter, who will know current conditions and safety concerns.

Some outfitters offer package deals combining accommodations with daily diving trips. Escorted half-day dives range from $45 to $90 for one or two tanks, including equipment. Packages including lunch and other extras start at $100. Night dives are often available at close to double the price. Snorkeling excursions, which include transportation (most often a sailboat filled with snorkelers), equipment rental, and sometimes lunch, start at $55. Snorkel equipment rents at beaches for about $5–$7. (Caution: coral-reef waters and mangrove areas can be dangerous. Unless you're an expert or have an expert guide, avoid unsupervised areas and stick to the water-sports centers of hotels.)

Snorkeling and scuba instruction, equipment rentals, and tours are available at **Caribbean School of Aquatics** (✉ Taft St. No. 1, Suite 10F, ☎ 787/728–6606) has certification courses, and diving and snorkeling trips. **Caribe Aquatic Adventures** in the Radisson Normandie Hotel (✉ Corner of Av. Roisales and Av. Muñoz Rivera, Puerta de Tierra, ☎ 787/724–1882) offers scuba instruction, equipment rental, and scuba and snorkeling trips. **Coral Head Divers** (✉ Palmas del Mar, Rte. 906, Humacao, ☎ 787/850–7208 or 800/635–4529) has boat dives to more than 30 sites. **Dive Copamarina** (✉ Copamarina Beach Resort, Rte. 333, Km 6.5, Guánica, ☎ 787/821–0505 ext. 729), has hotel-dive packages and dive trips to points along the wall off the south coast. **La Cueva Submarina Dive Shop** (✉ Rte. 466, Km 6.3, Isabela, ☎ 787/872–1390) offers guided snorkeling and diving tours through underground caves on the north coast and also provides certification courses. **Parguera Divers Training Center** in the Hotel Posada Prlamar (✉ Rte. 304, Km 3.3, La Parguera, ☎ 787/899–4171) offers scuba training and dive trips. **Puerto Rican Diver Supply** (✉ A-E6 Santa Isidra 111, Fajardo, ☎ 787/863–4300) offers courses and dive trips. In Vieques, **Blue Caribe Dive Center** (✉ Waterfront, Esperanza, ☎ 787/741–2522) gives scuba classes and offers dive trips.

Several catamarans leave from marinas in the Fajardo area and take passengers on day-long trips to off-shore cays for snorkeling and swimming excursions. Rates, which include lunch, run around $55 a person and operators normally make arrangements to pick up guests at hotels in San Juan for a nominal fee. **The Traveler** (✉ Villa Marina, Rte. 987, Km 1.3, ☎ 787/863–2821) takes guests to snorkeling areas off the east coast and makes a stop at a deserted beach. **The Fun Cat** (✉ Villa Marina, Rte. 987, Km 1.3, ☎ 787/728–6606) takes snorkelers to cays such as Icacos and Lobos off the Fajardo area in a 51-ft catamaran. **East Wind** (✉ Marina Puerto del Rey, Rte. 3, Km 51.4, ☎ 787/860–3434) takes snorkelers in a catamaran with underwater windows and a waterslide.

SURFING

Surfing is best from November to April. Aviones, in Pinones near the airport, has summer surfing. The very best surfing beaches are along the western coast from Isabela south to Rincón. For surfing gear, try **West Coast Surf Shop** (✉ 2 E. Muñoz Rivera St., Rincón, ☎ 787/823–3935).

TENNIS

If you'd like to use courts at a property where you aren't a guest, call in advance for information. Hotel guests usually get first priority, and you are likely to have to pay a fee. Courts at the following hotels are open to non-guests: Caribe Hilton, Condado Plaza, Copamarina Beach Resort, Hilton Ponce, Hyatt Dorado Beach, Hyatt Regency Cerromar Beach, Palmas del Mar, San Juan Marriott, Westin Río Mar Beach Resort, Wyndham El Conquistador, and Wyndham El San Juan. The four lighted courts of the **Isla Verde Tennis Club** (✉ Ema and Delta Rodríguez sts., ☎ 787/727–6490) are open for nonmember use at $4 per person per hour, daily 8 AM–10 PM. Your best bets in San Juan are the 23 lighted courts at **San Juan Central Municipal Park** (✉ Calle Cerra, exit on Rte. 2, ☎ 787/722–1646). Fees run $1.50 per person per hour 8–6, $2 per person per hour 6 PM–10 PM.

Spectator Sports

BASEBALL

The late, great Roberto Clemente is just one of many Puerto Rican ballplayers to find success in the U.S. major leagues after honing their skills at home. The island's pro season runs from October to February. Santurce, Ponce, Carolina Caguas, Arecibo, and Mayagüez all have teams. Contact the tourist office for schedules and locations of parks or call **Professional Baseball of Puerto Rico** (☎ 787/765–6285).

HORSE RACING

Thoroughbred races are run year-round at **El Comandante Racetrack,** about 20 minutes east of San Juan. Races are at 2:45 PM Monday, Wednesday, Saturday, and Sunday; and at 4:45 PM Friday. The Terrace Dining Room opens at noon the day of the races, and there's also a sports bar. ⊠ *Rte. 3, Km 15.3, Canóvanas,* ☎ 787/724–6060. ☉ *Mon., Wed., Sat., Sun. noon–6.*

Shopping

San Juan isn't a free port, so you won't find bargains on electronics and perfumes. You can, however, find excellent prices on china, crystal, fashions, and jewelry. Shopping for local crafts can also be gratifying: you'll run across a lot that's tacky, but you can also find treasures, and in many cases you can watch the artisans at work. For guidance on finding genuine craftspeople, contact the **Puerto Rico Tourism Company's Asuntos Culturales** (Cultural Affairs Office, ☎ 787/723–0692).

Popular items include *santos* (small carved figures of saints or religious scenes), hand-rolled cigars, handmade *mundillo* lace from Aguadilla, *vejigantes* (colorful masks used during Carnival and local festivals) from Loíza and Ponce, and fancy men's shirts called guayaberas.

Areas and Malls

Old San Juan is full of shops, especially on Cristo, Fortaleza, and San Francisco streets. The stores are all within walking distance of each other, and trolleys are at your beck and call. There are also several malls in San Juan. **Plaza Las Américas** (⊠ 525 Av. Franklin Delano Roosevelt, Hato Rey, ☎ 787/767–1525), south of San Juan, has almost 300 shops, restaurants, and movie theaters, including a new Macy's. **Prime Outlets Puerto Rico** (⊠ Rte. 22, Exit 55, Barceloneta, ☎ 787/845–9001) has more than 40 outlet stores, including Liz Claiborne and Reebok.

Specialty Items

ART

Atlas Art (⊠ 209 Calle Cristo, Old San Juan, ☎ 787/723–9987) has paintings, sculptures, and antique santos. **DMR Gallery** (⊠ 204 Calle Luna, Old San Juan, ☎ 787/722–4181) has handmade furniture by Nick Quijano. **Galería Fosil Arte** (⊠ 200 Calle Cristo, Old San Juan, ☎ 787/725–4252) features art pieces by Radamés Rivera made from coral and limestone more than 30 million years old, as well as paintings by Yolanda Velásquez. **Galería San Juan** (⊠ Gallery Inn, 204–206 Calle Norzagaray, Old San Juan, ☎ 787/722–1808) has the sculptures of artist Jan D'Esopo. Take advantage of the Old San Juan's **Gallery Night** (☎ 787/723–7080), when the galleries and select museums open their doors after hours for viewing, accompanied by refreshments and music. Gallery Night is held the first Tuesday of the month, September to December and February to May, from 6 to 9 PM.

CLOTHES

Big Planet (⊠ 205 Calle Cristo, Old San Juan, ☎ 787/725–1204) sells shorts, knit shirts, and active-wear clothing. **Latimer** (⊠ 53 Calle Palmeras, Puerta de Tierra, ☎ 787/724–1500), has top-of-the-line bathing suits. The **Mrs. & Miss Boutique** (⊠ 154 Calle Fortaleza, Old San Juan, ☎ 787/724–8571) has cool, flowing skirts, dresses, and beach wraps. You can buy high-end men's and women's original designs at **Nono Maldonado** (⊠ 1051 Av. Ashford, Condado, ☎ 787/721–0456). **Speedo Authentic Fitness** (⊠ 65 Calle Fortaleza at Calle Cristo, ☎ 787/724–3089) sells swimsuits, warm-up jackets, sandals, and swimming goggles. **Wet** (⊠ 150 Calle Cruz, Old San Juan, ☎ 787/722–2052) carries linen dresses, shorts, and tops.

HANDICRAFTS

At the **Convento de los Dominicos** (⊠ 98 Calle Norzagaray, Old San Juan, ☎ 787/721–6866), the Dominican Convent on the north side of the Old City, which houses offices of the Instituto de Cultura Puertorriqueña, you'll find baskets, masks, *cuatro* guitars, santos, books and tapes, and Indian artifacts. The **Haitian Gallery**'s two stores (⊠ 367 Calle Fortaleza, Old San Juan, ☎ 787/725–0986; ⊠ 206 Calle Fortaleza, Old San Juan, ☎ 787/721–4362) carry Puerto Rican crafts and folksy paintings from around the Caribbean. **La Calle Shopping Mall** (⊠ 105 Calle Fortaleza, Old San Juan, ☎ 787/725–1306) displays a myriad of island masks. **Puerto Rican Art & Crafts** (⊠ 204 Calle Fortaleza, Old San Juan, ☎ 787/725–5596) is considered one of the best places to buy Puerto Rican goods. **Puerto Rican Handmade Crafts & Mask Center** (⊠ 1035 Av. Ashford, Condado, ☎ 787/724–3840) has a wide selection of masks and other local crafts. In Ponce, **Mi Coqui** (⊠ 9227 Calle Marina, Ponce, ☎ 787/841–0216) has rum, carnival masks, domino sets, and more.

JEWELRY

For a wide array of watches and jewelry, visit **Bared Jewelers** (⊠ Calles Fortaleza and San Justo, Old San Juan, ☎ 787/724–4811). Diamonds and gold are found at **Joseph Manchini** (⊠ 101 Calle Fortaleza, Old San Juan, ☎ 787/722–7698).

Nightlife and the Arts

Qué Pasa, the official visitor's guide, has listings of events in San Juan and out on the island. For up-to-the-minute listings, pick up a copy of the English-language edition of the *San Juan Star,* the island's oldest daily. The Thursday edition's weekend section is especially useful. You can also check with the local tourist offices and the concierge at your hotel to find out what's doing.

Nightlife

From Thursday through Sunday it sometimes feels like there's a celebration going on nearly everywhere in San Juan. If you're going out, dress to party: bars are usually casual, but if you're wearing jeans, sneakers, and a T-shirt, you'll probably be refused entry at most nightclubs or discos, unless you look like a model.

Old San Juan's Calle San Sebastián has been the scene of nightlife revelry for decades now. Bars and restaurants line the street from San Justo to Cristo. At the Plaza San José, the young and beautiful gather to flaunt and socialize. Pool halls blaring salsa compete for space with top-flight restaurants and nightspots presenting live jazz and tropical music.

An eclectic crowd—including office workers, college students, and tourists—heads to the Plaza Del Mercado off Av. Ponce de León at Calle Canals after work to hang out in the plaza or enjoy drinks and food in one of the small establishments skirting the farmers market. Thursday and Friday nights are particularly lively; the action starts about 5 PM.

El Batey (✉ 101 Calle Cristo, Old San Juan, ☎ 787/725–1787) is a hole-in-the-wall run by crusty New Yorker Davydd Gwilym Jones III; it looks like a military bunker, but it has the best oldies juke box in the city and is wildly popular.

The **Reef Bar & Grill** (✉ First turn after bridge when you enter Piñones, ☎ 787/791–1374) is in rustic Piñones, the undeveloped beachfront east of the airport. It has stunning sunsets and a priceless view, from the hotels of Isla Verde to the distant fortresses of Old San Juan. You can drink tasty piña coladas, snack on local specialties, and shoot pool. At night there's often live music, from salsa to reggae.

Rumba (✉ 152 San Sebastián, Old San Juan, ☎ 787/725–4407) has live salsa and Afro-Cuban music Wednesday–Saturday, plus special engagements. It's an attractive place, with local art on the walls. There's a big open stage and dance area, with the main bar set apart in a front room. The air-conditioner blasts, the crowd is hip, and the house bands smoke. Often the best party in town.

CASINOS

By law, all casinos are in hotels, primarily in San Juan. The government keeps a close eye on them. Dress for the larger casinos is on the formal side, and the atmosphere is refined. Casinos set their own hours but are generally open from noon to 4 AM. The casino at the Condado Plaza Hotel is open 24 hours a day. In addition to slot machines, typical games include blackjack, roulette, craps, Caribbean stud (a five-card poker game), and *pai gow* poker (a combination of American poker and the Chinese game pai gow). Hotels with casinos have live entertainment most weekends, restaurants, and bars. The minimum age to gamble is 18.

Among the San Juan hotels that have casinos are the Condado Plaza Hotel, Ritz-Carlton San Juan, Inter-Continental San Juan Resort and Casino, San Juan Marriott, Wyndham El San Juan Hotel, and Wyndham Old San Juan Hotel. Elsewhere on the island, there are casinos at the Hyatt Regency Cerromar, the Doral Resort at Palmas del Mar, Hilton Ponce and Casino, Westin Río Mar Beach Resort and Country Club, and Wyndham El Conquistador Resort & Country Club.

DANCE AND MUSIC CLUBS

Nightclubs have a short shelf life; they come and go with the whims of the hip crowd. The crowd dresses up at **Babylon** in the Wyndham El San Juan (✉ Av. Isla Verde, Isla Verde, ☎ 787/766–7700), which is open to those 23 and older. **Café Bohemio** (✉ El Convento Hotel, 100 Calle Cristo, Old San Juan, ☎ 787/723–9200), a Latin restaurant, turns into a live jazz and Bohemian music club from 11 PM to 2 AM Tuesday through Friday (after the kitchen closes); Tuesday night is best. The multilevel **Club Lazer** (✉ 251 Calle Cruz, ☎ 787/725–7581) has a landscaped roof deck overlooking San Juan and attracts different crowds on different nights; Saturday is ladies night. **Eros** (✉ 1257 Av. Ponce de León, Santurce, San Juan, ☎ 787/722–1390) plays terrific dance music and is popular with the gay community. **The Lobby Lounge** at the San Juan Marriott (✉ 1309 Av. Ashford, Condado, ☎ 787/722–7000) has live Latin music daily starting at 9 PM and is popular with the local crowd. Friday is particularly hot. The Wyndham El San Juan's **Palm Court Lobby** (✉ Av. Isla Verde, Isla Verde, ☎ 787/791–1000) is where everyone goes to see and be seen, especially on Friday and Saturday nights, when the crowd dresses to the nines as they mingle at the Oval Bar, the Cigar Bar, or the nearby casino. The former hot-spot Egipto the Club is now **Stargate** (✉ 1 R. H. Todd Ave., Santurce, ☎ 787/725–4664), a futuristic club with Latin and 1970s music pounding Thursdays through Sunday nights.

The Arts

The **Luis A. Ferré Center for the Performing Arts** (✉ Stop 22, corner of Av. Ponce De León and Av. José De Diego, Santurce, ☎ 787/724–4747 information; 787/725–7334 tickets) has something going nearly every night, from visiting Caribbean and Latin American singers to opera and ballet to jazz concerts. It's home base for the San Juan Symphony Orchestra.

Exploring Puerto Rico

Old San Juan

Old San Juan, the original city, founded in 1521, contains carefully preserved examples of 16th- and 17th-century Spanish colonial architecture. More than 400 buildings have been beautifully restored. Graceful wrought-iron balconies with lush hanging plants extend over narrow streets paved with *adoquines* (blue-gray stones originally used as ballast for Spanish ships). The old city is partially enclosed by walls that date from 1633 and once completely surrounded it. Designated a U.S. National Historic Zone in 1950, Old San Juan is chockablock with shops, open-air cafés, homes, tree-shaded squares, monuments, pigeons, and people. The traffic is awful. You can get an overview on a morning's stroll (bear in mind that this "stroll" includes some steep climbs). However, if you plan to immerse yourself in history or to shop, you'll need two or three days. You may want to set aside extra time to see El Morro and Fort San Cristóbal, especially if you're an aficionado of military history. UNESCO has designated each fortress a World Heritage Site; each is also a National Historic Site.

SIGHTS TO SEE

Numbers in the margin correspond to points of interest on the Old San Juan Exploring map.

⓫ Alcaldía. The city hall was built between 1604 and 1789. In 1841 extensive renovations were done to make it resemble Madrid's city hall, with arcades, towers, balconies, and a lovely inner courtyard. A tourist information center and an art gallery are on the first floor. ✉ *North side of Plaza de Armas,* ☎ 787/724–7171. ☞ *Free.* ◷ *Weekdays 8–4.*

❽ Capilla del Cristo. According to legend, in 1753 a young horseman named Baltazar Montañez, carried away during festivities in honor of San Juan Bautista (St. John the Baptist), raced down the street and plunged over the steep precipice. A witness to the tragedy promised to build a chapel if the young man's life could be saved. Historical records maintain the man died, though legend contends he lived. Regardless, this chapel was built, and inside it is a small silver altar dedicated to the Christ of Miracles. ✉ *Calle Cristo.* ☞ *Free.* ◷ *Tues. 10–3:30.*

❹ Casa Blanca. The original structure on this site, not far from the ramparts of El Morro, was a frame house built in 1521 as a home for Ponce de León. But Ponce de León died in Cuba without ever having lived in it, and it was virtually destroyed by a hurricane in 1523, after which his son-in-law had the present masonry home built. His descendants occupied it for 250 years. From the end of the Spanish-American War in 1898 to 1966, it was the home of the U.S. Army commander in Puerto Rico. The home now contains several rooms decorated in colonial-era furnishings and an archaeology exhibit. The lush garden, cooled by spraying fountains, is a tranquil spot. ✉ *1 Calle San Sebastián,* ☎ 787/724–4102. ☞ *$2.* ◷ *Tues.–Sat. 9–noon and 1–4:30.*

Alcaldía 11
Capilla del
Cristo 8
Casa Blanca . . . 4
La Casa
del Libro 9
Catedral de
San Juan 5
Convento de los
Dominicos 3
La Fortaleza . . . 7
Fuerte San Felipe
del Morro
(El Morro) 1
Museo Pablo
Casals 2
Paseo de la
Princesa 15
Plaza de
Armas 10
Plaza
de Colón 12
Plazuela de
la Rogativa 6
San
Cristóbal 13
Teatro Tapia . . . 14

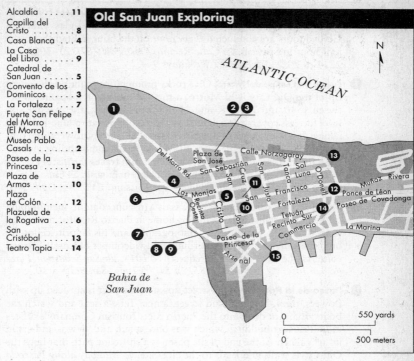

Old San Juan Exploring

❾ La Casa del Libro. This 18th-century building contains exhibits devoted to books and bookbinding. The museum's 6,000 books, sketches, and illustrations include some 200 rare volumes written before 1501. ✉ *255 Calle Cristo,* ☎ *787/723–0354,* WEB *www.lacasadellibro.org.* ✉ *$2 donation suggested.* ⊙ *Tues.–Sat. 11–4:30.*

❺ Catedral de San Juan. The Catholic shrine of Puerto Rico had humble beginnings in the early 1520s as a thatch-topped wooden structure. Hurricane winds tore off the thatch and destroyed the church. It was reconstructed in 1540, when the graceful circular staircase and vaulted Gothic ceilings were added, but most of the work was done in the 19th century. The remains of Ponce de León are in a marble tomb near the transept. ✉ *153 Calle Cristo,* ☎ *787/722–0861.* ⊙ *Daily 8:30–4; masses Sat. 7 PM, Sun. 9 AM and 11 AM, weekdays 12:15 PM.*

❸ Convento de los Dominicos. Built by Dominican friars in 1523, this convent often served as a shelter during Carib Indian attacks and, more recently, as headquarters for the Antilles command of the U.S. Army. Now home to some offices of the Institute of Puerto Rican Culture, the beautifully restored building contains religious manuscripts, artifacts, and art. The institute also maintains a craft store and bookstore here, and occasionally classical concerts are held. The convent is connected to the Iglesia de San José, built in 1532 under the supervision of Dominican friars. The church is closed indefinitely for repairs. ✉ *98 Calle Norzagaray,* ☎ *787/721–6866.* ✉ *Free.* ⊙ *Mon.–Sat. 9–5.*

❼ La Fortaleza. Sitting on a hill overlooking the harbor, La Fortaleza, the western hemisphere's oldest executive mansion in continuous use and official residence of the governor of Puerto Rico, was built as a fortress. The original primitive structure, constructed in 1540, has seen numerous changes over the past four centuries, resulting in the present collection of marble and mahogany, medieval towers, and stained-glass galleries. Guided tours are conducted every hour on the hour in English, on the half hour in Spanish. ⊠ *Calle Recinto Oeste,* ☎ *787/721–7000 ext. 2211 or 2358.* ☞ *Free.* ⊙ *Weekdays 9–4.*

① **Fuerte San Felipe del Morro.** On a rocky promontory on the northwestern tip of the Old City is El Morro, a fortress built by the Spaniards between 1540 and 1783. Rising 140 ft above the sea, the massive six-level fortress covers enough territory to accommodate a nine-hole golf course. It is a labyrinth of dungeons, barracks, turrets, towers, and tunnels. Built to protect the port, El Morro has a commanding view of the harbor. Its small, air-conditioned museum traces the history of the fortress. Tours and a video show are available in English. ⊠ *Calle Norzagaray,* ☎ *787/729–6960,* WEB *www.nps.gov.saju.* ☞ *$2.* ⊙ *Daily 9–5.*

② **Museo Pablo Casals.** The Pablo Casals Museum contains memorabilia of the famed cellist, who made his home in Puerto Rico for the last 16 years of his life. Manuscripts, photographs, and his favorite cellos are on display, in addition to recordings and videotapes of Casals Festival concerts (the latter shown on request). ⊠ *101 Calle San Sebastián, Plaza de San José,* ☎ *787/723–9185.* ☞ *$1.* ⊙ *Tues.–Sat. 9:30–5:30.*

⑮ **Paseo de la Princesa.** This street down at the port is spruced up with flowers, trees, benches, and street lamps. Take a seat and watch the boats zip by, or duck into the Puerto Rico Tourism Company's offices in La Princesa building, which was once a jail, and view island art in its art gallery. At the end of the paseo is a shoreline path that hugs the Old City's walls and leads to the city gate. ⊠ *Midway along Paseo la Princesa,* ☎ *787/721–2400.* ☞ *Free.* ⊙ *Mon.–Fri. 9–noon, 1–4.*

⑩ **Plaza de Armas.** This is the original main square of Old San Juan. The plaza, bordered by Calles San Francisco, Fortaleza, San José, and Cruz, has a lovely fountain with 19th-century statues representing the four seasons.

⑫ **Plaza de Colón.** A statue of Christopher Columbus is atop a high pedestal in this bustling square. Originally called St. James Square, it was renamed in honor of Columbus on the 400th anniversary of the discovery of Puerto Rico. On the plaza's north side is a terminal for buses to and from San Juan. ⊠ *East of Calle O'Donell between calles San Francisco and Fortaleza.*

⑥ **Plazuela de la Rogativa.** According to legend, the British, while laying siege to the city in 1797, mistook the torches of a *rogativa* (religious procession) for Spanish reinforcements and beat a hasty retreat. In this little plaza, statues of a bishop and three women commemorate the legend. The monument was donated to the city in 1971 on its 450th anniversary. ⊠ *Caleta de las Monjas.*

⑬ **San Cristóbal.** This 18th-century fortress guarded the city from land attacks. Even larger than El Morro, San Cristóbal was known in its heyday as the Gibraltar of the West Indies. ⊠ *Calle Norzagaray,* ☎ *787/729–6960,* WEB *www.nps.gov/saju.* ☞ *$2.* ⊙ *Daily 9–5.*

⑭ **Teatro Tapia.** This municipal theater was named after Puerto Rican playwright Alejandro Tapia y Rivera. Built in 1832 and remodeled in 1949 and again in 1987, it's the site of ballets, plays, and operettas. ⊠ *Calle Fortaleza at Plaza de Colón,* ☎ *787/722–0407.*

San Juan

You'll need to resort to taxis, buses, *públicos* (public cars), or a rental car to reach the points of interest in "new" San Juan. Avenida Muñoz

Rivera, Avenida Ponce de León, and Avenida Fernández Juncos are the main thoroughfares that cross Puerta de Tierra, east of Old San Juan, to the business and tourist districts of Santurce, Condado, and Isla Verde. Dos Hermanos Bridge connects Puerta de Tierra with Miramar, Condado, and Isla Grande. Isla Grande Airport, from which you can take short hops, is on the bay side of the bridge. On the other side, the Condado Lagoon is bordered by Avenida Ashford, which threads past the high-rise Condado hotels and Avenida Baldorioty de Castro Expreso, which barrels east to the airport and beyond. Due south of the lagoon is Miramar, a residential area with fashionable turn-of-the-century homes and a few hotels and restaurants. South of Santurce is the Golden Mile—Hato Rey, the financial hub. Isla Verde, with its glittering beachfront hotels, casinos, discos, and public beach, is to the east, near the airport.

Numbers in the margin correspond to points of interest on the San Juan Exploring, Dining, and Lodging map.

SIGHTS TO SEE

❶ **El Capitolio.** In Puerta de Tierra, Puerto Rico's capitol is a white marble building that dates from the 1920s. The grand rotunda, with mosaics and friezes, was completed a few years ago. The seat of the island's bicameral legislature, the capitol contains Puerto Rico's constitution and is flanked by the modern buildings of the Senate and the House of Representatives. There are spectacular views from the observation plaza on the sea side of the capitol. Pick up a booklet about the building from the House Secretariat on the second floor. Guided tours are by appointment only. ⊠ *Av. Ponce de León, Puerta de Tierra,* ☎ *787/724–2030 ext. 2472.* ⊒ *Free.* ☼ *Weekdays 8:30–5.*

❷ **Museo de Arte de Puerto Rico** This museum opened in mid-2000 as the largest museum in Puerto Rico. Covering 130,000 square ft, it consists of a renovated neoclassical building dating from the 1920s and a newer wing with an atrium leading to gardens and outdoor sculptures. The museum is building a collection of Puerto Rican art, and normally has several special exhibits on display. It also hosts concerts and other events and has a restaurant, Pikayo, and a gift shop. ⊠ *299 Av. De Diego, Santurce, Santurce* ☎ *787/977–6277,* WEB *www.mapr.org.* ⊒ *$5.* ☼ *Tues. and Thurs.–Sun. 10–5, Wed. 10–8, Sun. 11–6.*

☾ ❸ **Parque Luis Muñoz Marín.** This idyllic 90-acre tree-shaded park is dotted with gardens, lakes, playgrounds, and picnic areas. An aerial gondola connects it with the parking area and provides a 6½-minute tour of the grounds. An outdoor amphitheater is the venue for plays, concerts, and folk performances. ⊠ *Next to Las Américas Expressway, west on Av. Jesús Piñero, Hato Rey,* ☎ *787/751–3353.* ⊒ *Free; parking $1 per vehicle.* ☼ *Wed.–Sun. 8–6.*

❹ **Universidad de Puerto Rico.** Río Piedras, a southern suburb, is home to the University of Puerto Rico, between Avenida Ponce de León and Avenida Barbosa. The campus is one of the two performance venues for the Puerto Rico Symphony Orchestra. Theatrical productions and other concerts are also scheduled here. The **Museo de Historia, Antropología y Arte** (Museum of History, Anthropology and Art) is home to one of the island's best-treasured works of art, Francisco Oller's "El Velorio," an oversized painting of a countryside wake for a child. The museum has other works of art and archaeological exhibits. ⊠ *Next to main entrance on Av. Ponce de León, Río Piedras,* ☎ *787/764–0000 ext. 2452.* ⊒ *Free.* ☼ *Mon., Wed.–Sat. 9–4:30, Sun. 11–4:30.*

The university's main attraction is the **Jardín Botánico** (Botanical Garden), a lush 75-acre forest of more than 200 species of tropical and subtropical vegetation. Gravel footpaths lead to a graceful lotus lagoon, a bamboo promenade, an orchid garden with some 30,000 plants, and a palm garden. Signs are in Spanish and English. Trail maps are available at the entrance gate, and guided tours can be arranged in advance between 8 and 3:30 on weekdays for $25. ⊠ *Intersection of Rtes. 1 and 847 at entrance to Barrio Venezuela, Río Piedras,* ☎ *787/767– 1710.* ☞ *Free.* ⊙ *Daily 8–6.*

San Juan Environs

Numbers in the margin correspond to points of interest on the Puerto Rico map.

SIGHTS TO SEE

❷ **Bacardi Rum Plant.** You can take a 45-minute tour of the bottling plant, museum (called the Cathedral of Rum), and distillery. The facility can produce 100,000 gallons of spirits a day. There is a gift shop (yes, you'll be offered a sample). ⊠ *Bay View Industrial Park, Rte. 888, Km 2.6, Cataño,* ☎ *787/788–8400,* WEB *www.bacardi.com.* ☞ *Free.* ⊙ *Tours every 30 mins Mon.–Sat. 9–10:30 and noon–4.*

❸ **Bayamón.** In the central park, across from Bayamón's city hall, there are some historical buildings. Outside of the city center, the **Luis A. Ferré Science Park** on Rte. 167 features several museums, a zoo, and a planetarium. Admission is $5 for adults and $3 for children, and it is open Wednesday through Friday from 9 to 4, weekends from 10 to 6.

❶ **Caparra Ruins.** In 1508 Ponce de León established the island's first settlement here. The ruins are what remain of an ancient fort. the tiny **Museo de la Conquista y Colonización de Puerto Rico** (Museum of the Conquest and Colonization of Puerto Rico) contains historical documents, exhibits, and excavated artifacts. ⊠ *Rte. 2, Km 6.6, Guaynabo,* ☎ *787/781–4795.* ☞ *Free.* ⊙ *Tues.–Sat. 8:30–4:30.*

Western Puerto Rico

Puerto Rico's 3,500 square mi (9,065 square km) are a lot of land to explore. Although you can get from town to town via público, it's not the best way to travel unless your Spanish is good and you know exactly where you're going. The public cars stop in each town's main square, leaving you on your own to reach the beaches, restaurants, paradores, and attractions. You'll do much better if you rent a car. Most roads are excellent. However, there's a tangle of routes through the mountains, and they're not always well marked; buy a good road map.

Numbers in the margin correspond to points of interest on the Puerto Rico map.

❼ **Aguadilla.** Somewhere between Aguadilla and Añasco, south of Rincón, Columbus is said to have dropped anchor on his second voyage in 1493. Both Aguadilla and Aguada, a few miles to the south, claim to be the spot where his foot first hit ground, and both towns have parks to commemorate the occasion. ⊠ *Rte. 111.*

⑭ **Bahía Fosforescente.** The fishing village of La Parguera, an area of simple seafood restaurants, mangrove cays, and small islands, lies south of San Germán at the end of Route 304, off Route 116. This is an excellent scuba-diving area, but the main attraction is Phosphorescent Bay. Boats tour the bay, where microscopic dinoflagellates (marine plankton) light up like Christmas trees when disturbed by any kind of movement. The phenomenon can be seen best on moonless nights. Boats leave for the hour-long trip nightly from dusk until midnight, depending on demand, and the trip costs about $5 per person. You can also rent or charter a small boat to explore the cays.

⑬ **Boquerón.** This tiny, funky, pastel village has sidewalk oyster vendors, bars, restaurants serving fresh seafood, and the standard T-shirt shops. In addition, you can arrange diving and snorkeling tours at the Boquerón Dive Shop on Main Street. Boquerón's balneario is one of the best beaches on the island. Parking is $2 per car, and two-room rustic cabins are available for rent (☎ 787/851–1900). ✉ *Rte. 101.*

⑪ **Cabo Rojo.** Once a pirates' hangout, this town is now a favorite resort area of Puerto Ricans. It has long stretches of white-sand beaches on the clear, calm Caribbean Sea and is home to a lighthouse with a breathtaking view over rough cliffs. South of town, the **Cabo Rojo Wildlife Refuge** (✉ Rte. 310, Km 5.1, ☎ 787/851–7258) has a visitor's center and bird-watching trails. Admission is free, and it's open Monday to Friday, 7 to 3:30. There are also many seafood restaurants (especially along the waterfront of the Jayuya area), bars, hotels, and several paradores in the region. ✉ *Rte. 102.*

⑨ **Mayagüez.** With a population of slightly more than 100,000, this is the largest city on Puerto Rico's west coast. Although bypassed by the mania for restoration that has spruced up Ponce and Old San Juan, Mayagüez is graced by some lovely turn-of-the-twentieth-century architecture, such as the landmark Art Deco Teatro Yagüez and the Plaza de Colón. Just north of town, visit the **Tropical Research Station,** an agriculture experiment station run by the U.S. Department of Agriculture with more than 2,000 plant species from all over the world. ✉ *Intersection of Rte. 2 and Rte. 108,* ☎ *787/831–3435.* 🎟 *Free.* ◷ *Weekdays 7–4.*

⑩ **Mona.** Fifty mi (80 km) west of Mayagüez in the turbulent, shark-infested Mona Passage, Mona Island is nicknamed the Galápagos of the Caribbean thanks to the many unique indigenous species that call it home. The variety of marine and bird life is especially breathtaking. The coastline is rimmed with imposing limestone cliffs up to 200 ft high pocked with caves that are said to contain buried treasure; the many perfectly preserved Taíno hieroglyphs and rock paintings here are of great archaeological value. Access to the island is only via private plane or boat. Very limited camping facilities are available on the pristine beaches. Call the **Department of Natural Resources** (☎ 787/724–3724) for information and camping reservations. Some tour companies arrange trips, including AdvenTours in Mayagüez.

④ **Observatorio de Arecibo.** Hidden in lush fields and rolling hills outside of Arecibo is one of the world's largest radar-radio telescopes. A 20-acre dish, with a 600-ton suspended platform hovering over it, sits in a 565-ft-deep sinkhole. (Karst fields, an alien landscape of collapsed limestone sinkholes, are the prevalent geology throughout this part of the island.) This facility is part of the National Astronomy and Ionosphere Center of Cornell University and has become known for its work in programs to look for extraterrestrial life (some scenes for the movie *Contact* were filmed here). Visitors can walk around the platform and view the huge dish and also visit the Angel Ramos Foundation Visitor Center with two levels of interactive exhibits on planetary systems, meteors, and weather phenomenons. ✉ *Rte. 625,* ☎ *787/878–2612,* 🖥 *www.naic.edu.* 🎟 *$3.50.* ◷ *Wed.–Fri. noon–4, weekends 9–4.*

⑤ **Parque de las Cavernas del Río Camuy.** The 250-acre Río Camuy reserve contains one of the world's largest cave networks. Tours take you on a tram down through dense tropical vegetation to the cave entrance, where you continue on foot over underground trails, ramps, and bridges. The caves, sinkholes, and subterranean streams are all spectacular (the world's third-largest underground river runs through here).

Tours are given on a first-come, first-served basis, so it's best to arrive early. The newly opened Cathedral Cave, open only on weekends by appointment, is for more adventurous guests—accessing it involves rappelling down the side of a cave. ✉ *Rte. 129, Km 19.8,* ☎ *787/898–3100 or 787/898–3136.* ☜ *$10, parking $1; cathedral cave $30.* ⊙ *Wed.–Sun. 8:30–4. Last tour starts at 3:45.*

6 **Parque Ceremonial Indígena de Caguana.** The area that is now the Caguana Indian Ceremonial Park was used 800 years ago by the Taíno for recreation and worship. Mountains surround a 13-acre site planted with royal palms and guava. According to historians, the Taíno played a game similar to soccer, and in this park there are 10 *bateyes* (courts) bordered by cobbled walkways. There are also stone monoliths—some with colorful petroglyphs—a small museum, and a souvenir shop. ✉ *Rte. 111, Km 12.4,* ☎ *787/894–7325.* ☜ *$2.* ⊙ *Daily 8:30–4.*

⓯ **Ponce.** From San Germán, Route 2 traverses splendid peaks and valleys; pastel houses cling to steep, green hillsides. The Cordillera Central Mountains run parallel to Route 2 here and provide a stunning backdrop. East of the picturesque town of Yauco, the road dips and sweeps right along the Caribbean and into Ponce.

Puerto Rico's second-largest urban area (population 194,000) underwent a massive restoration starting in 1985 under former Governor Rafael Hernádez Colón. Today, the city shines in 19th-century style with pink-marble-bordered sidewalks, gas lamps, painted trolleys, and horse-drawn carriages. You haven't seen a firehouse until you've seen the **Parque de Bombas,** a structure built in 1882 for an exposition and converted to a firehouse the following year. Today it is a museum tracing the history—and glorious feats—of Ponce's fire brigade ✉ *Plaza Las Delicias,* ☎ *787/284–3338 ext. 342.* ☜ *Free.* ⊙ *Wed.–Mon. 9:30–6.*

Ponce's charm stems from a combination of neoclassical, Ponce Creole, and Art Deco styles. The tiny streets lined with wrought-iron balconies are reminiscent of New Orleans's French Quarter. Stop in and pick up historical information about this seaside city at the columned **Casa Armstrong-Poventud** (☎ 787/844–2540), the home of the Institute of Puerto Rican Culture, open weekdays 8–noon and 1–4:30. Stroll around the Plaza Las Delicias, with its perfectly pruned India-laurel fig trees, graceful fountains, gardens, and park benches. View the Catedral de Nuestra Señora de Guadalupe (Our Lady of Guadalupe Cathedral), perhaps even attend the 6 AM mass, and walk down calles Isabel and Cristina to see turn-of-the-20th-century wooden houses with wrought-iron balconies.

Two superlative examples of early 20th-century architecture house the **Museo de la Historia de Ponce** (Ponce History Museum), where 10 rooms of exhibits vividly re-create Ponce's golden years, providing fascinating glimpses into the worlds of culture, high finance, and journalism in the 19th century. Hour-long tours in English and Spanish are available, but there is no set time when they start. ✉ *53 Calle Isabel,* ☎ *787/844–7071.* ☜ *$3.* ⊙ *Wed.–Mon. 9–5.*

Continue as far as calles Mayor and Cristina to the white stucco **Teatro La Perla** (La Perla Theater; ☎ 787/843–4322), with its Corinthian columns and wonderful acoustics; it's open daily with no admission charge. Be sure to allow time to visit the **Museo de Arte de Ponce** (Ponce Museum of Art). The architecture alone is worth seeing: the modern two-story building designed by Edward Durrell Stone (who designed New York's Museum of Modern Art) has seven interconnected hexagons, glass cupolas, and a pair of curved staircases. The collection includes late Renaissance and Baroque works from Italy, France, and Spain, as well as contemporary art by Puerto Ricans. ⊠ *2325 Av. Las Américas,* ☎ *787/848–0505 or 787/848–0511,* WEB *www.museoarteponce.org.* ▱ *$4.* ☉ *Daily 10–5.*

The **Castillo Serrallés** is a splendid Spanish Revival mansion perched on El Vigía Hill. This former residence of the owners of the Don Q rum distillery has been restored with a mix of original furnishings and antiques that recall the era of the sugar barons. A short film details the history of the sugar and rum industries; tours are given every half hour in English and Spanish. The 100-ft-tall cross (La Cruceta del Vigía) behind the museum has a windowed elevator; you can ascend for views of Ponce and the coast for $1. ⊠ *17 El Vigía Hill,* ☎ *787/259–1770,* WEB *www.castilloserralles.com.* ▱ *$3.* ☉ *Tues.–Thurs. 9–5, Fri.–Sun. 10–5:30.*

There are two intriguing sights just outside the city. **Hacienda Buena Vista** is a 19th-century coffee plantation, restored by the Conservation Trust of Puerto Rico, with authentic machinery and furnishings intact. Reservations are required for the 90-minute Spanish-language tours (at 8:30, 10:30, 1:30, and 3:30). Tours in English are available at 1:30, also by reservation only. ⊠ *Rte. 10, Km 16.8, north of Ponce,* ☎ *787/722–5882 weekdays; 787/284–7020 weekends,* WEB *www.fideicomiso.org.* ▱ *$5.* ☉ *Wed.–Fri. morning open to tour groups; Fri. afternoon–Sun. open to public.*

At the **Centro Ceremonial Indígena de Tibes** (Tibes Indian Ceremonial Center), you'll find pre-Taíno ruins and burials dating from AD 300 to AD 700. Some archaeologists, noting the symmetrical arrangement of stone pillars, surmise the cemetery may have been of great religious significance. The complex includes a detailed re-creation of a Taíno village and a museum. ⊠ *Rte. 503, Km 2.5,* ☎ *787/840–2255 or 787/840–5685.* ▱ *$2.* ☉ *Tues.–Sun. 9–4.*

❽ Rincón. On scenic Route 115, Rincón is perched on a hill and overlooks its beach, the site of the World Surfing Championship in 1968. Skilled surfers flock here in winter, when the water is rough and challenging. The town is also increasingly popular with divers. Locals boast that the best diving and snorkeling in Puerto Rico (and some even say the Caribbean) is off the Rincón coast, particularly around the island of Desecheo, a federal wildlife preserve. Whale-watching is another draw for this town; humpback whales winter off the coast from December to March.

⓬ San Germán. This quiet, colorful Old World town is home to the oldest chapel in Puerto Rico. Built in 1606, the mission-style Porta Coeli (Heaven's Gate) is now a museum of religious art, housing 18th- and 19th-century paintings, and wooden statues. ⊠ *Rte. 102,* ☎ *787/892–5845.* ▱ *$1.* ☉ *Tues.–Sun. 9–noon and 1–4:45.*

Eastern Puerto Rico

🐾 ⓴ **El Bosque Nacional del Caribe.** To take full advantage of the 28,000-acre Caribbean National Forest—or El Yunque, as it's commonly known—go with a tour. Dozens of trails lead through the thick rain forest (it sheltered the Carib Indians for 200 years), and guides take you to the best observation points, bathing spots, and waterfalls. Some of the trails are slippery, and there are occasional washouts. However, if you'd like to drive here yourself, take Route 3 east from San Juan and turn right (south) on Route 191, about 25 mi (40 km) from the city. Stop in at the **Centro de Información El Portal** (El Portal Tropical Forest Information Center; ☎ *787/888–1810*), on Route 191 at the entrance to the park. Nature talks, programs, and displays at the center are in Spanish and English. The center is open daily 9 to 5; admission is $3.

El Yunque, named after the good Indian spirit Yuquiyu, is in the Luquillo mountain range. The rain forest is verdant with feathery ferns, thick ropelike vines, white tuberoses, miniature orchids, and some 240 species of trees. More than 100 billion gallons of rainwater fall on it annually. Rain-battered, wind-ravaged dwarf vegetation clings to the top peaks. (El Toro, the highest peak in the forest, is 3,532 ft) El Yunque is also a bird sanctuary and the home of the rare Puerto Rican parrot. Millions of inch-long coquís can be heard singing (or squawking, depending on your sensibilities). The **visitors' centers** at Palo Colorado and Sierra Palm (☎ 787/888–1880) are open daily 8–5. Call in advance and take advantage of the park's Rent-a-Ranger program (you'll pay a fee) for guided tours. For further information write: ⊠ *Caribbean National Forest, Box B, Palmer 00721,* ☎ *787/888–1810 or 787/888–1880,* WEB *www.r8web.com/caribbean.*

⑰ Culebra. This island off Puerto Rico's east coast has lovely white-sand beaches, coral reefs, and a wildlife refuge. In the sleepy town of Dewey (called "town" by everyone on the island), on Culebra's southwestern side, check at the **visitor information center** at city hall (☎ 787/742–3291) about boat, bike, or car rentals. Don't miss the very pretty Playa Flamenco, 3 mi (5 km) north of town, or Playa Soni on the island's eastern end.

⑱ Fajardo. This is a major fishing and sailing center with thousands of boats tied and stacked in tiers at its three large marinas. You can rent or charter a boat here, or you can have catamarans take you out for a day of snorkeling, swimming, and sunning for about $55 per person. Fajardo is also the embarkation point for ferries to the islands of Culebra (a $2.25 fare) and Vieques ($2). ⊠ *Rte. 987,* ☎ *787/863–4560.*

⑲ Reserva Natural las Cabezas de San Juan. Most of Puerto Rico's natural habitats—mangrove swamps, coral reefs, beaches, and a dry forest—are rolled into Las Cabezas reserve's 316 acres. Nineteenth-century El Faro, one of the island's oldest lighthouses, is restored and still functioning; its first floor contains a small nature center that has an aquarium and other exhibits. The wide variety of birds, including mockingbirds, laughing gulls, and yellow warblers, makes this a favorite spot for bird-watchers. The reserve is open, by reservation only, to the public Friday afternoon–Sunday and to tour groups Wednesday–Friday morning. Tours are given on request (in advance, by phone) three times a day—in Spanish at 9:30 AM, 10:30 AM, and 2 PM; in English at 2 PM. ⊠ *Rte. 987, Km 5.8,* ☎ *787/722–5882 or 787/860–2560,* WEB *www.fideicomiso.org.* 🎫 *$5.*

⑯ Vieques. This island off Puerto Rico's east coast is famed for its Playa Sun Bay, a gorgeous stretch of sand with picnic facilities and shade trees. Bahía Mosquito (Mosquito Bay) is best experienced on moonless nights, when millions of bioluminescent organisms glow when disturbed—it's like swimming in a cloud of fireflies. Seventy percent of Vieques is owned by the U.S. Navy, although negotiations are expected to reduce the military presence—and open the way for more tourism development. The deserted beaches—such as Green, Red, and Blue—are among the Caribbean's loveliest; at press time access was limited to beaches on the naval reserve due to occasional demonstrations; your hotel or tourism officials will be able to give you the latest status. A **visitor information center** (☎ 787/741–5000) is in Isabel Segunda. Both Vieques and Culebra, parched in contrast to the lush eastern end of Puerto Rico, are havens for colorful "expatriates" escaping the rat race stateside. This is pure old-time Caribbean: fun, funky, and unspoiled—the kind of getaway that's fast disappearing.

PUERTO RICO A TO Z

To research prices, get advice from other travelers, and book travel arrangements, visit www.fodors.com.

AIR TRAVEL

Luis Muñoz Marín is the Caribbean hub for American Airlines, which has nonstop flights from New York, Boston, Newark, Miami, St. Louis, and many other North American cities. American Trans Air (ATA) operates nonstop from Orlando, Indianapolis, and Chicago. Continental has daily nonstop service from Newark, Houston, and Cleveland. Delta operates daily nonstop service from Atlanta and Cincinnati. Northwest has daily nonstop flights from Detroit and weekend nonstop service from Memphis and Minneapolis. United flies daily nonstop from Chicago and weekends from New York and Washington, D.C. US Airways offers daily nonstop flights from Pittsburgh, Philadelphia, and Charlotte. Continental has daily service to the Rafael Hernández Airport in Aguadilla.

Foreign carriers include Air Canada, which has flights from Montreal and Toronto, connecting in Chicago. British Airways has flights to San Juan through New York and Miami. Lufthansa's Condor has a weekly flight from Frankfurt. Martinair has weekly flights between Amsterdam and San Juan. Iberia services San Juan via Madrid. LACSA flies from several Central American countries, including San José and Panama. Copa flies to Panama, Costa Rica, Guatemala, and other Central American countries from San Juan.

Connections between Caribbean islands can be made through American Eagle, which has flights to other Caribbean islands and also flies to Ponce's Mercedita Airport and to Vieques's Aeropuerto Antonio Rivera Rodríguez. Air ALM flies to the Dutch islands, including Aruba and Bonaire. LIAT flies to Antigua and other Caribbean islands either directly or through connections. Cape Air connects San Juan to Ponce, Tortola, St. Thomas, and St. Croix.

➤ AIRLINES AND CONTACTS: **Air ALM** (☎ 800/327–7230); **Air Canada** (☎ 888/247–2262); **American Airlines/American Eagle** (☎ 787/749–1747); **American Trans Air (ATA)** (☎ 787/791–3135); **British Airways** (☎ 787/723–4327); **Cape Air** (☎ 508/771–6944 or 800/352–0714); **Condor** (☎ 800/645–3880); **Continental** (☎ 787/793–7373); **Copa** (☎ 787/722–6969); **Delta** (☎ 787/754–3333); **Iberia** (☎ 787/721–5630); **LACSA** (☎ 787/724–3444 or 800/225–2272); **LIAT** (☎ 787/791–0800); **Martinair** (☎ 800/366–3734); **Northwest** (☎ 787/253–0206); **United** (☎ 787/253–2776); **US Airways** (☎ 787/725–4895).

AIRPORTS

The Luis Muñoz Marín International Airport east of downtown San Juan, is one of the easiest and cheapest destinations to reach in the Caribbean. Smaller planes service Ponce through the Aeropuerto Mercedita just minutes from downtown Ponce. Aguadilla is served through the Rafael Hernández Airport in the old Ramey Air Force Base just north of town. Aeropuerto Antonio Rivera Rodríguez in Isabel Segunda, Vieques, is being expanded to accommodate larger planes.

Taxis Turisticos charge set rates from the airports based on zones, so the fare depends on the destination. Uniformed and badged officials help you find a cab at the airport (look for the tourism company booth) and hand you a slip with your fare, which you can present to your driver. To Isla Verde, the fare is $8; to Condado, it's $12; to Old San Juan, it's $16. If you don't hail one of these cabs, you're at the mercy of the meter and the driver.

Another option is the Airport Limousine Service, which provides minibuses to hotels in the Isla Verde, Condado, and Old San Juan areas at basic fares of $2.50, $3, and $3.50, respectively; fares do vary, depending on the time of day and number of passengers, and you may have to wait until the van fills before leaving the airport. Limousines of Dorado Transport Co-op serve hotels and villas in the Dorado area for $20 per person.

➤ AIRPORT INFORMATION: **Aeropuerto Antonio Rivera Rodríguez** (in Vieques, ☎ 787/722–3736); **Luis Muñoz Marín International Airport** (in San Juan, ☎ 787/791–4670); **Mercedita Airport** (in Ponce, ☎ 787/842–6292); **Rafael Hernández Airport** (in Aguadilla, ☎ 787/891–2286).
➤ AIRPORT TRANSPORTATION CONTACTS: **Airport Limousine Service** (☎ 787/791–4745); **Dorado Transport Co-op** (☎ 787/796–1214).

BOAT AND FERRY TRAVEL
FARES AND SCHEDULES
The ferry between Old San Juan (Pier 2) and Cataño costs a mere 50¢ one-way. It runs every half hour from 6 AM to 10 PM. The 400-passenger ferries of the Fajardo Port Authority, which carry cargo as well as passengers, make the 90-minute trip between Fajardo and Vieques three times daily ($2 one-way). They make the 90-minute run from Fajardo to Culebra twice a day weekdays and twice (with three runs from Culebra to Fajardo) on weekends ($2.25 one-way).
➤ BOAT AND FERRY INFORMATION: **Old San Juan (Pier 2) to Cataño Ferry** (☎ 787/788–1155); **Fajardo Port Authority** (☎ 787/863–4560).

BUSINESS HOURS
BANKS
Banks are open weekdays 8:30–2:30 (some branches stay open to 4 PM) and Saturday 9:45–noon.

POST OFFICES
Post offices are open weekdays 7:30–4:30 and Saturday 8–noon.

SHOPS
Independent shops are open Monday–Saturday 9–6 (9–9 during Christmas holidays); mall stores tend to stay open later, until 8 or 9 in most cases. On Sunday, stores are open from 11 AM–5 PM.

CAR RENTALS
If you rent a car, a good road map will be helpful in remote areas. Some car-rental agencies give you an island map when you pick up your car, but these lack detail and are usually out-of-date. Head to the nearest gas station and buy a better map, or you can buy maps at Cronopios book store in Old San Juan.

A valid driver's license from your country of origin can be used in Puerto Rico for three months. Rental rates can start as low as $30 a day (plus insurance), with unlimited mileage. Discounts are offered for long-term rentals, and insurance can be waived for those who rent with credit cards that offer insurance. (Be sure to check with your credit-card company before renting.) Some discounts are offered for AAA or 72-hour advance bookings. Most car rentals have shuttle service between the airport and the pickup/drop-off point.

All major U.S. car-rental agencies are represented on the island, including Avis. Budget has numerous offices on the island, including an airport location. Hertz operates at the airport and in other locations throughout the island. Local rental companies, sometimes less expensive, include Charlie Car Rental. L & M Car Rental also has numerous locations on the island.

➤ MAJOR AGENCIES: **Avis** (☎ 787/721–3600); **Budget** (☎ 787/791–3685); **Hertz** (☎ 787/791–0840); **Charlie Car Rental** (☎ 787/791–1101 or 800/289–1227); **L & M Car Rental** (☎ 787/791–1160 or 800/666–0807).

➤ MAPS: **Cronopios** (✉ 255 Calle San José, Old San Juan, ☎ 787/724–1815).

CAR TRAVEL

If you are staying in San Juan, then you may not need to rent a car. If you venture out on the island, a rental car is your best option. Roads in Puerto Rico are generally well marked (just keep in mind that distances are posted in kilometers and speed limits in miles per hour).

GASOLINE

Gasoline prices are roughly the same as in the U.S. and in some cases a little lower (depending on where you are coming from). Gas prices are about 36.9 ¢ per liter. Many service stations in the central mountains don't take credit cards.

ROAD CONDITIONS

Roads are in generally good condition although you may want to keep an eye out for potholes, especially after heavy rains. Some roads in the mountains are very curvy and take longer to cover than the distance on a map might suggest. Not every road is marked, but most Puerto Ricans are happy to help with directions.

ELECTRICITY

Puerto Rico uses the same electrical current as the U.S. mainland, namely 110 volts.

EMERGENCIES

➤ AMBULANCE AND FIRE: Dial ☎ 911.

➤ HOSPITALS: **Ashford Memorial Community Hospital** (✉ 1451 Av. Ashford, Condado, San Juan, ☎ 787/721–2160); **Bella Vista Hospital** (✉ Cerro las Mesas, Mayagüez, ☎ 787/834–2350), serves the west coast; **Eastern Medical Associates** (✉ 261 Av. Valero, Fajardo, ☎ 787/863–0669).

➤ PHARMACIES: **Puerto Rico Drug** (✉ 157 Calle San Francisco, Old San Juan, ☎ 787/725–2202). **Walgreens** (✉ 1130 Av. Ashford, Condado, ☎ (787/725–1510).

➤ POLICE: Dial ☎ 911.

ETIQUETTE AND BEHAVIOR

Puerto Ricans have, in general, a strong sense of religion—as evidenced by the numerous Catholic patron-saint festivals held throughout the year. Many islanders are somewhat conservative in dress and manners despite a penchant for frenetic music and sexually charged dance. There's also a strong sense of island identity, marked by often-ferocious debates over Puerto Rico's political destiny.

FESTIVALS AND SEASONAL EVENTS

Puerto Rico's festivals are colorful and inclined toward lots of music and feasting. The towns and villages are particularly fond of their patron saints, and every year each of the island's 78 municipalities celebrate *fiestas patronales* (patron saints' festivals). The festivities are religious in origin and feature processions, sports events, folklore shows, feasts, music, and dance. They last about 10 days, with more activities on weekends than on weekdays. San Juan's *fiesta patronal* honors San Juan Bautista in late June; Ponce honors Nuestra Señora de la Guadalupe in mid-December. Several towns and regions also have pre-Lenten Carnivales, complete with parades, folk music, local dishes, a Carnival Queen pageant, and music competitions. Ponce's carnival, celebrated the week before Ash Wednesday, is the most famous. Contact the tourist office for a complete list of fiestas patronales and other events.

In addition to the patron saints' festivals, Old San Juan holds an annual San Sebastián Street Festival in January. Emancipation Day on March 22 honors the abolition of slavery. Mid-April's Sugar Harvest Festival, in San Germán, celebrates the crop with exhibitions, music, and feasts. The Casals Festival, held at the Luis A. Ferré Performing Arts Center in San Juan in early June, honors the late, great cellist with 10 days of classical music. In mid-November you can find the annual Festival of Puerto Rican Music in San Juan and other venues, celebrating the vibrancy of Puerto Rico's *plena* and *bomba* folk music, highlighted by a contest featuring the cuatro, a traditional guitar. During Christmas week you can join the residents of Hatillo for the Hatillo Masks Festival, when they retell the Biblical tale of King Herod's attempt to find and kill the infant Jesus. Men in masks move about town all day, representing Herod's soldiers, and the town brings out music and crafts.

HEALTH
Tap water is generally fine on the island. Thoroughly wash or peel produce you buy in markets before eating it.

HOLIDAYS
Public holidays for 2002 are: New Year's Day, Three Kings Day (Jan. 6), Eugenio María de Hostos Day (first Monday in January), Dr. Martin Luther King Jr. Day (third Mon. in Jan.), Presidents' Day (third Mon. in Feb.), Palm Sunday (March 24), Good Friday (March 29), Easter Sunday (March 31), Memorial Day (last Mon. in June), Independence Day (July 4), Luis Muñoz Rivera Day (July 17), Constitution Day (July 25), José Celso Barbosa Day (July 27), Labor Day (first Mon. in Sept.), Columbus Day (second Mon. in Oct.), Veterans' Day (Nov. 11), Puerto Rico Discovery Day (Nov. 19), Thanksgiving Day (Nov. 25), and Christmas.

LANGUAGE
Puerto Rico is officially bilingual, but Spanish predominates. Although English is widely spoken, you'll probably want to take a Spanish phrase book along on your travels about the island.

MAIL AND SHIPPING
The island uses U.S. postage stamps and has standard U.S. mail rates for both domestic and international destinations. Post offices in major Puerto Rican cities offer Express Mail next-day service to the U.S. mainland and to Puerto Rican destinations. Major post office branches are at 153 Calle Fortaleza in Old San Juan, 163 Avenida Fernández Juncos in San Juan, 60 Calle McKinley in Mayagüez, and 102 Calle Garrido Morales in Fajardo.

MONEY MATTERS
Prices quoted in this chapter are in U.S. dollars.

ATMS
ATMs are numerous and easy to find, at most banks and casinos and in some stores and supermarkets.

CREDIT CARDS

Credit cards, including Diner's Club and Discover, are widely accepted, especially in tourist areas. Some stateside gasoline credit cards may not be accepted at gas stations here.

CURRENCY

Puerto Rico, as a commonwealth of the United States, uses the U.S. dollar as its official currency.

➤ CONTACTS: **Banco Popular** (✉ 1060 Ashford Ave., Condado, ☎ 787/725–4197; ✉ 206 Calle Tetuán, Old San Juan, ☎ 787/725–2636); **Scotiabank de Puerto Rico** (✉ 273 Ponce de León Ave., Hato Rey, ☎ 787/766–8039).

PASSPORTS AND VISAS

Puerto Rico is a commonwealth of the United States, so U.S. citizens don't need passports to visit the island (they must have a valid photo ID, however). Canadians need proof of citizenship (preferably a valid passport; otherwise bring a birth certificate with a raised seal along with a government-issued photo ID). Citizens of Australia, New Zealand, and the United Kingdom must have passports.

SAFETY

San Juan, like any other big city, has its share of crime, so guard your wallet or purse on the city streets. Puerto Rico's beaches are open to the public, and muggings can occur at night even on the beaches of the posh Condado and Isla Verde tourist hotels. Although you certainly can, and should, explore the city and its beaches, use common sense. Don't leave anything unattended on the beach. Leave your valuables in the hotel safe, and stick to the fenced-in beach areas of your hotel. Always lock your car and stash valuables and luggage out of sight. Avoid deserted beaches at night.

SIGHTSEEING TOURS

You can see Old San Juan on the free trolley or on a self-guided walking tour. (Look for tours in a copy of *Qué Pasa!* available at all tourist offices and hotels).

To explore the rest of the city and the island, rent a car and head out on your own. (You should, however, consider taking a guided tour of the vast El Yunque rain forest.) If you'd rather not do your own driving, there are several tour companies you can call. Most San Juan hotels have a tour desk that can make arrangements for you. The three standard half-day tours ($30–$35) are of Old and "new" San Juan; Old San Juan and the Bacardi Rum Plant; and Playa Luquillo and El Yunque rain forest. All-day tours ($45–$60) can include a trip to Ponce, a day at El Comandante Racetrack, El Parque de las Cavernas del Río Camuy, or a combined tour of San Juan and El Yunque rain forest.

Leading tour companies include Castillo Tours. Sunshine Tours offers a range of outings, from rain forest tours to Old San Juan tours. Aventuras Tierra Adentro specializes in adventure tours, such as rock climbing and rafting. Encantos Ecotours has nature-oriented tours across the island, including kayaking tours and biking tours. Cordero Caribbean Tours runs tours in air-conditioned limousines for an hourly rate. Wheelchair Getaway offers wheelchair transport from airports and cruise-ship docks to San Juan hotels, as well as city sightseeing trips.

AdvenTours in Mayagües and Tour Marine in Cabo Rojo arrange trips to Mona Island, off Puerto Rico's west coast, known as the "Galapagos of the Caribbean."

➤ CONTACTS: **AdvenTours** (✉ 17 Uroyán St., Mayagües, ☎ 787/831–6447); **Aventuras Tierra Adentro** (☎ 787/766–0470); **Castillo Tours**

(☎ 787/791–6195); **Cordero Caribbean Tours** (☎ 787/786–9114; 787/780–2442 evenings); **Encantos Ecotours** (☎ 787/272–0005); **Sunshine Tours** (☎ 787/721–7300); **Tour Marine** (✉ Rte. 101, Km 14.1, Cabo Rojo, ☎ 787/851–9259); **Wheelchair Getaway** (☎ 787/883–0131 or 800/868–8028).

TAXES
SALES TAX
There is no sales tax in Puerto Rico. Some hotels automatically add a 10%–15% service charge to your bill. Check ahead to confirm whether this charge is built into the room rate or will be tacked on at checkout. Some smaller hotels might charge extra (as much as $5 per day) for use of air-conditioning, called an "energy tax." The government tax on rooms is 9% (11% in hotels with casinos, 7% in paradores). As with service charges, you'll need to confirm whether or not the tax is built into the room rate.

TAXIS
The Puerto Rico Tourism Company has instituted a well-organized taxi program. Taxis painted white and sporting the *garita* (sentry box) logo and Taxi Turistico label charge set rates depending on the destination; they run from the airport or the cruise-ship piers to Isla Verde, Condado/Ocean Park, and Old San Juan, with rates ranging from $6 to $16. City tours start at $30 per hour. Metered cabs authorized by the Public Service Commission start at $1 and charge 10¢ for every additional ⅓ mile, 50¢ for every suitcase. Waiting time is 10¢ for each 45 seconds. The minimum charge is $3 and there is an extra $1 night charge between 10 PM and 6 AM. Be sure the driver starts the meter. For cab service, you can call Major Taxicabs in San Juan. You can call Ponce Taxi for cab service in Ponce.

LINÉAS
Linéas are private taxis you share with three to five other passengers. There are more than 20 companies, each usually specializing in a certain region. Most will arrange door-to-door service. Check local Yellow Pages listings under *Linéas de Carros*. They're affordable and are a great way to meet people, but be prepared to wait: they usually don't leave until they have a full load.

PÚBLICOS
Públicos (public cars), with yellow license plates ending in *P* or *PD*, scoot to towns throughout the island, stopping in each town's main plaza. These 17-passenger vans operate primarily during the day, with routes and fares fixed by the Public Service Commission. In San Juan the main terminals are at the airport and at Plaza Colón, on the waterfront in Old San Juan.
➤ CONTACTS: **Major Taxicabs** (☎ 787/723–2460); **Ponce Taxi** (☎ 787/840–0088); **Public Service Commission** (☎ 787/751–5050).

TELEPHONES
COUNTRY AND AREA CODES
Puerto Rico's area codes are 787 and 939. For North Americans, dialing Puerto Rico is the same as dialing another U.S. state or a Canadian province.

INTERNATIONAL CALLS
Dial 011, the country code, the city code, and the number. Dial 00 for an international long-distance operator. Phone cards are not required, but can be useful and are widely available (most drug stores carry them). Hotels can add substantial surcharges for calls to the U.S. mainland and international calls, so check with your hotel before calling.

LOCAL CALLS

To make a local call in Puerto Rico you must dial 1, the area code, and the seven-digit number.

TIPPING

Tips are expected, and appreciated, by restaurant waitstaff (15%–20% if a service charge isn't included), hotel porters ($1 per bag), maids ($1–$2 a day), and taxi drivers (15%–18%).

TRANSPORTATION AROUND PUERTO RICO
AIRPLANES

The Isla Grande Airport (officially Aeropuerto Fernando L. Rivas Dominici), facilitates smaller planes. From Isla Grande, you can take a Vieques Air-Link flight to Vieques ($43 one-way) or to Culebra for $50 one-way.

➤ CONTACTS: **Isla Grande Airport** (☎ 787/729–8711); **Vieques Air-Link** (☎ 787/722–3736).

BUSES

The Metropolitan Bus Authority (AMA) operates *guaguas* (buses) that thread through San Juan. The fare is 25¢–50¢, depending on the route, and the buses run in exclusive lanes on major thoroughfares, stopping at signs marked PARADA or PARADA DE GUAGUAS. The main terminals are Covadonga parking lot in Old San Juan, and Capetillo Terminal in Río Piedras, next to the central business district. Buses marked A5 and B21 cover the popular beach and hotel areas of Isla Verde, Condado, and Old San Juan.

➤ CONTACTS: **Metropolitan Bus Authority** (☎ 787/767–7979).

TRAINS

A $1.6-billion urban train system connecting San Juan and major suburbs is slated to go online beginning in 2002, when it will connect Bayamón, Guaynabo, and Santurce. For the latest information, call the Department of Transportation.

➤ CONTACTS: **Department of Transportation** (☎ 787/722–2929).

TROLLEYS

If your feet fail you in Old San Juan, climb aboard the free open-air trolleys that rumble and coast through the narrow streets. Departures are from La Puntilla and from the marina, but you can board anywhere along the route. Ponce has free trolleys that leave from Plaza Las Delicias and stop at major tourist attractions.

VISITOR INFORMATION
➤ BEFORE YOU LEAVE: **Puerto Rico Tourism Company** (✉ Box 902–3960, Old San Juan Station, San Juan, PR 00902-3960, ☎ 787/721–2400 or 800/866–7827, WEB www.prtourism.com); ✉ 3575 W. Cahuenga Blvd., Ste. 405, Los Angeles, CA 90068, ☎ 213/874–5991; ✉ 901 Ponce de León Blvd., Ste. 101, Coral Gables, FL 33134, ☎ 305/445–9112.
➤ IN PUERTO RICO: **Puerto Rico Tourism Company** (✉ Paseo de la Princesa, Old San Juan 00901, ☎ 787/721–2400); ✉ Luis Muñoz Marín International Airport, (☎ 787/791–1014 ; ✉ La Casita (☎ 787/722–1709); in Ponce (✉ 209 Av. Los Caobos, Paseo del Sur Plaza, ☎ 787/843–0465); in Aguadilla (✉ Rafael Hernández Airport, ☎ 787/890–3315); Cabo Rojo (✉ Rte. 100, Km 13.7, ☎ 787/851–7070).

16 SABA

Updated by
Suzanne
Gordon

Just after daybreak, the street sweepers begin their task, brooms in hand, up and down the winding roads that zig zag around the mountains—steep and dramatic. Every day they follow these concrete ribbons that twist and turn—connecting the villages on the island—sweeping them all by hand until no dirt or litter remains. This tradition of cleanliness makes Saba special, and by nightfall the streets are pristine again, a testimony to what makes the islanders proud.

Tiny Saba (pronounced *say*-ba) has some of the Caribbean's most dramatic scenery, with sweeping, steep mountainsides and sheer cliffs. The breeze is always pleasant, the 1,200 friendly Sabans more so. Everyone knows everyone—indeed, there are fewer than a dozen family names on the island, so many people are also related—and unemployment and crime are virtually nonexistent. The island is a perfect hideaway, a challenge for hikers (Mt. Scenery rises to 2,855 ft/871 m), a haven for seasoned divers, and heaven on water. It's no wonder Sabans call their island "the unspoiled queen."

Despite all its glories, however, this 5-sq-mi (13-sq-km) fairy-tale isle isn't for everybody. If you want exciting nightlife or lots of shopping, forget Saba (or make it a one-day excursion from St. Maarten). There are only a handful of shops, a few inns and eateries, and cable TV has replaced the movie theater. Sun worshipers should note that Saba is an essentially beachless volcanic island: steep cliffs ring the island and plummet sharply to the sea. Saba's famous disappearing black-sand beach at Well's Bay, on the northwestern coast, is usually only around for a few months in summer (the sand is washed in and out by rough winter surf). And because of precarious overhanging rocks above, it's no longer recommended as a place to swim.

The capital of Saba is The Bottom, which sits at the bottom of an extinct volcano. In Windwardside, the island's second-largest village, the streets have no names. On the Road (and there's really only one), meandering goats have right of way, though chickens cross at their own risk. In toylike villages, flower-draped walls and neat picket fences border narrow paths. Tidy, sturdy white houses with gingerbread trim, green shutters, and red roofs are planted on the mountainsides among the bromeliads, palms, hibiscus, orchids, and Norwegian pines. Despite such modern additions as TVs (since 1965) and electricity (since 1970), this immaculate, picturesque island's uncomplicated lifestyle has persevered, giving it a make-believe air. Saban ladies still produce handmade lace—a genteel art that has flourished since the 1870s—and brew a potent rum-based liquor, Saba Spice, that's flavored with herbs and spices. Families still follow the generations-old tradition of burying their dead in their neatly tended gardens.

Saba is part of the Netherlands Antilles' Windward Islands and is 28 mi (45 km)—a 12-minute flight with a hair-raising landing on a teeny airstrip (with a 100% safety record)—from St. Maarten. The island is a volcano that has been extinct for 5,000 years. Columbus spotted the little speck in 1493, but except for the Carib Indians who may have lived here around AD 800, Saba remained uninhabited until Dutch settlers arrived from St. Eustatius (Statia) in 1640. From that time on, until the early 19th century, the French, Dutch, English, and Spanish vied for control, and Saba changed hands 12 times before permanently raising the Dutch flag in 1816. Today the Kingdom of the Netherlands comprises three entities: Holland, the Netherlands Antilles (Saba, St. Maarten, St. Eustatius, Bonaire, and Curaçao), and Aruba. Saba's local administration supervises internal affairs, and the island elects representatives and sends them to the capital of the Netherlands Antilles, Willemstad in Curaçao, to attend to regional issues.

Sabans are a hardy lot. To get from Fort Bay to The Bottom, early settlers carved 900 steps out of the mountainside. Everything that arrived on the island, from a pin to a piano, had to be hauled up. Those rugged steps were the only way to travel until the Road was built by Josephus Lambert Hassell (a carpenter who took correspondence courses in engineering) in the 1940s. An extraordinary feat, the Road—known as the "road that couldn't be built"—took 25 years to construct. If you like roller coasters, you'll love the 9-mi (14½-km) white-knuckle route, which begins at sea level in Fort Bay, zigs up to 1,968 ft (600 m), and zags down to 131 ft (40 m) above sea level at the airport, constructed on the island's only flat point, called (what else?) Flat Point.

Lodging

Saba's stock of hotel rooms is rebounding from serious hits by Hurricanes Georges in 1998 and Lenny in 1999, but at press time, the well-known Captain's Quarters still had not been rebuilt. The remaining accommodations are tidy inns or guest houses perched on ledges or tucked into tropical gardens. You'll also find more than a dozen apartments, cottages, and villas—all with hot water and modern conveniences—for daily, weekly, and monthly rental.

For a list of properties contact the **Saba Tourist Office. WIMCO** (⌧ Box 1461, Newport, RI 02840,☎ 800/932–3222) rents the fabulous and palatial Haiku House ($2,000–$4,500 a week) and other villas.

CATEGORY	COST*
$$$$	over $200
$$$	$125–$200
$$	$75–$125
$	under $75

All prices are for a standard double room in high season, excluding 5% room tax and 3% turnover tax, and 10%–15% service charge.

$$$$ 🏨 **Queens Garden Resort.** This classy resort is an elegant addition to
★ Saba's collection of intimate inns. Three four-story buildings hug the mountain and house 12 suites with antique Dutch colonial and Indonesian furnishings, four-poster beds, TVs, kitchens, and hot tubs on hidden verandas that have breathtaking ocean views. Sit inside the Mango Royale Restaurant or on the patio beside the island's largest pool—particularly nice when the torches are lighted and soft music plays in the background.

Saba

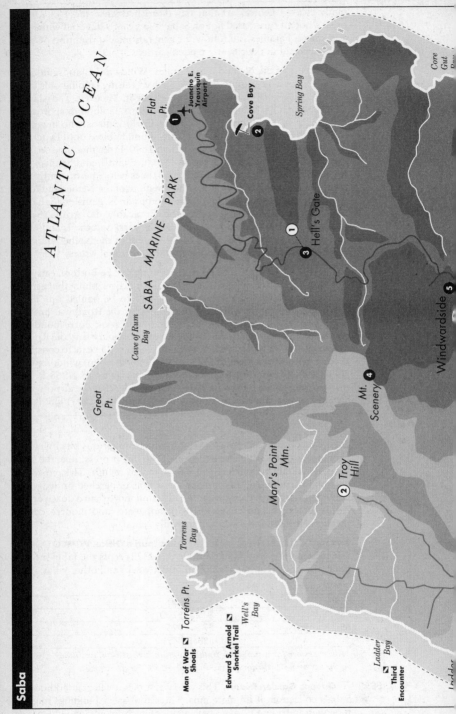

ATLANTIC OCEAN

Flat Pt.

Juancho E. Yrausquin Airport

Cove Bay

Spring Bay

Core Gut

SABA MARINE PARK

Cave of Rum Bay

Hell's Gate

Great Pt.

Windwardside

Mt. Scenery

Mary's Point Mtn.

Torrens Bay

Troy Hill

Torrens Pt.

Man of War Shoals

Well's Bay

Edward S. Arnold Snorkel Trail

Ladder Bay

Third Encounter

Ladder

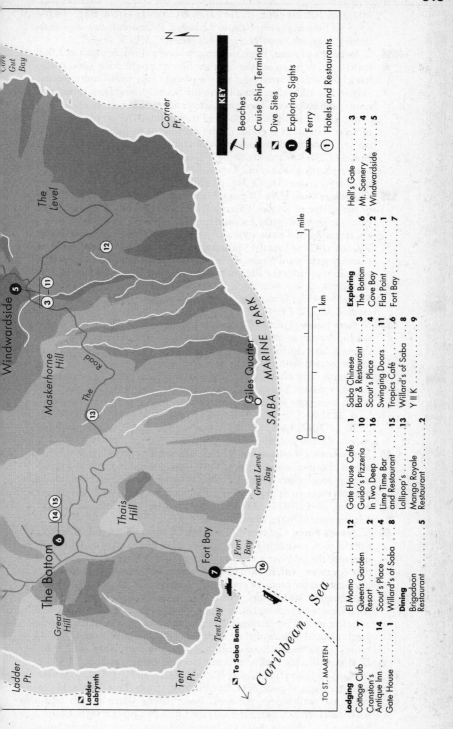

KEY

↙ Beaches

⚓ Cruise Ship Terminal

◨ Dive Sites

① Exploring Sights

⛴ Ferry

① Hotels and Restaurants

N

Lodging

Cottage Club **7**
Cranston's
Antique Inn **14**
Gate House **1**
El Momo **12**
Queens Garden
Resort **2**
Scout's Place **4**
Willard's of Saba . . . **8**

Dining

Brigadoon
Restaurant **5**
Gate House Café **1**
Guido's Pizzeria **10**
In Two Deep **16**
Lime Time Bar
and Restaurant **15**
Lollipop's **13**
Mango Royale
Restaurant **2**
Saba Chinese
Bar & Restaurant . . . **3**
Scout's Place **4**
Swinging Doors **11**
Tropics Café **6**
Willard's of Saba . . . **8**
Y II K **9**

Exploring

The Bottom **6**
Cove Bay **2**
Flat Point **1**
Fort Bay **7**
Hell's Gate **3**
Mt. Scenery **4**
Windwardside **5**

Corner Pt.

The Level

Windwardside

Maskerhorne Hill

The Road

The Road

Giles Quarter

SABA MARINE PARK

Great Level Bay

Fort Bay

Fort Bay

Thais Hill

The Bottom

Great Hill

Ladder Pt.

Ladder Labrynth

Tent Bay

Tent Pt.

Caribbean Sea

◨ To Saba Bank

TO ST. MAARTEN

Cove Gut Bay

0   1 km

0   1 mile

✉ *1 Troy Hill Dr. (Box 4), Troy Hill,* ☎ *599/416–3494,* 𝔽𝔸𝕏 *599/416–3495,* 𝕎𝔼𝔹 *www.queensaba.com.12 suites. Restaurant, bar, air-conditioning, fans, kitchenettes, pool, hot tub. AE, MC, V, D. EP.*

$$$$ ▦ **Willard's of Saba.** From this luxury hotel's cliff-side perch at 2,000
  ★   ft (610 m), you can see the faint profiles of neighboring isles. It also has a large solar-heated pool and the island's only tennis court. Rooms vary in size and decor, but all have tile floors, ceiling fans, rattan furniture, and balconies. Though isolated and inconvenient to get to from town, this hotel offers privacy and tranquillity. The on-site Willard's of Saba restaurant is good. (Note: because of its location, this hotel isn't recommended for families with children under 12 years old.) ✉ *Box 515, Windwardside,*☎ *599/416–2498,* 𝔽𝔸𝕏 *599/416–2482,* 𝕎𝔼𝔹 *www.willardsofsaba.com. 7 rooms.Restaurant, bar, fans, pool, hot tub, tennis court. AE, D, MC, V. EP, MAP.*

$$$ ▦ **Cottage Club.** Here 10 gingerbread bungalows overlooking the sea or the village of English Quarter (Numbers 1, 2, and 6 have the best views) are owned by the Johnson brothers. Spacious and breezy, rooms are furnished in a basic style and have beamed ceilings, phones, cable TV, and kitchens that the Johnsons will stock for you. Below the stone colonial-style main house, there's a lovely secluded pool area, where you can just catch the edge of the runway and see planes landing and taking off. ✉ *Windwardside,*☎ *599/416–2486 or 599/416–2386,* 𝔽𝔸𝕏 *599/416–2476,* 𝕎𝔼𝔹 *www.turq.com/cottage-club. 10 units. Pool, kitchenettes. MC, V. EP.*

$$$ ▦ **Gate House.** Former Chicagoan Jim Siegel has created this whimsical hideaway in the tiny village of Hell's Gate. Here he paints and displays his colorful work on whitewashed walls. The cheery rooms are decorated with tile floors and crisp pinstripe or checked fabrics. Two units have kitchenettes. The pool is a great place to relax as the sun goes down. You can eat indoors or out at the Gate House Café, which overlooks the sea and has created an admiring buzz on the island. ✉ *Hell's Gate,* ☎ *599/416–2416 or 708/354–9641,* 𝔽𝔸𝕏 *599/416–2550 or 708/352–1390,* 𝕎𝔼𝔹 *www.members.aol.com/travelsaba. 6 rooms. Restaurant, pool. MC, V. CP.*

$$ ▦ **Cranston's Antique Inn.** Recent renovations have made the five rooms of this reasonably priced inn good values indeed. They have mahogany four-poster beds and other antiques, baths (one even has an original stone oven in it), cable TV, air-conditioning, and fans. ✉ *The Bottom,* ☎ *599/416–3203,* 𝔽𝔸𝕏 *599/416–3469. 5 rooms. Restaurant, bar, air-conditioning, fans. D, MC, V. EP.*

$$ ▦ **Scout's Place.** German dive masters Wolfgang Tooten and Barbara Schafer took over Scout's in late 1999 (after Hurricane Lenny severely damaged the property), and began to transform it into the island's first dive operation with its own accommodations. You can take initial dive instruction at the property's pool and take advantage of special dive packages through Saba Divers, which Wolfgang and Barbara operate here. All rooms have private baths; 11 rooms have four-poster beds as well as balconies and refrigerators. The Scout's Place restaurant serves three meals daily. ✉ *Windwardside,*☎ *599/416–2740,* 𝔽𝔸𝕏 *599/416–2741. 15 rooms, 1 apartment. Restaurant, bar, pool, pro shop, shop. MC, V. BP.*

$ ▦ **El Momo.** This funky inn amid tropical gardens is about 1,500 ft (458 m) up Jimmy's Hill, near Windwardside, and is a 70-step climb—a good reason to pack light. But the views from the gingerbread cottages are well worth the trek. Four rooms share a bath and a solar-powered hot-water shower; the fifth has a private bath. Claim a hammock or chair in the snack bar (with honor bar) in the main house to watch the sunset. The property has the only bridge on Saba—a footbridge across its pool. Breakfast is available for about $6. ✉ *Jimmy's*

Hill *(Box 542, Windwardside),* ☎ FAX *599/416–2265,* WEB *www. elmomo.com. 5 cottages. Snack bar, pool, shop. D, MC, V. EP.*

Dining

The caliber of Saban restaurants is definitely improving, so it's easy to find an appealing meal every night of a weeklong stay. Several restaurants serve wonderfully fresh seafood and such Caribbean dishes as stuffed crabs, goat stew, and grilled lobster. A decent selection of wines is available at the better restaurants. Reservations aren't usually necessary, but it wouldn't hurt to call ahead to confirm hours and stake your claim to a table (some of the restaurants are quite small). In addition, some places provide transportation.

What to Wear

Restaurants are informal. Shorts are fine during the day, but for dinner you may want to put on pants or a casual sundress. Just remember that nights in Windwardside can be cool due to the elevation.

CATEGORY	COST*
$$$$	over $35
$$$	$25–$35
$$	$15–$25
$	under $15

per person for a main course at dinner

ASIAN

$ ✕ **Saba Chinese Bar & Restaurant.** In this plain little house with plastic cloths on its tables you can get, among other things, sweet-and-sour pork or chicken, cashew chicken, and curried dishes. ⊠ *Windwardside,* ☎ *599/416–2268. MC, V. Closed Mon.*

CARIBBEAN

$$ ✕ **Gate House Café.** Slightly out of the way, on the road to the airport, this delightful restaurant in the Gate House hotel features Caribbean cuisine. Chef Beverly changes the menu daily, making use of the freshest seafood, meats, and local produce and herbs. Don't bypass dessert, especially the chocolate mousse. The prix-fixe dinner is $25. There are only eight tables here, and they're often filled by Sabans—meaning reservations are a good idea. When you call to reserve a spot, you can also arrange transportation to and from the restaurant. ⊠ *Hell's Gate,* ☎ *599/416–2416. MC, V. No lunch. Closed Wed.*

$$ ✕ **Lollipop's.** Owner Carmen Caines was nicknamed Lollipop in honor
★ of her sweet disposition. She and her husband, Will, prepare land crab, goat, and fresh grilled fish. Meals are served in a down-home-style dining room overlooking the sea, and there's a room for playing pool as well. No reservations are necessary, but if you call, Lollipop will pick you up and drop you off after dinner—a sweet touch, indeed. ⊠ *St. John's,* ☎ *599/416–3330. MC, V.*

$ ✕ **Lime Time Bar and Restaurant.** A Saban house has been spruced up to create this lively bar-eatery. You can eat on the front porch with a view of the Governor's House. Sample such local favorites as spare ribs, burgers, garlic shrimp, and conch chowder. The music is cheeky. ⊠ *The Bottom,* ☎ *599/416–3351. AE, MC, V.*

CONTEMPORARY

$$$$ ✕ **Willard's of Saba.** Set on a cliff high above Windwardside, Saba's most expensive restaurant in the Willard's of Saba hotel has views of the sea at a dizzying 2,000 ft (610 m) below. Chef Corazon de Johnson, an enthusiastic, charming cook, fuses international and Asian cuisine to offer such dishes as drunken pork loin (tender pork baked in a vegetable wine sauce), Shanghai rolls, and fresh lobster; Corazon also

prepares kosher, vegetarian, and will fill requests to fit most any dietary need. Order one of the Bava wines from Italy; Willard's is the only restaurant in the Caribbean that offers them. Access to the restaurant is up a steep drive; only a few taxis will make the climb, but you can call the restaurant to arrange transport. ✉ *Windwardside,* ☎ *599/416–2498. AE, D, MC, V.*

$$$$ ✕ **YIIK.** Latticework, plants, tiny lights, and wind chimes add consid-
★ erable charm to this rooftop restaurant in the heart of town. Folks are drawn by the relaxed ambience, the pastries, and the coffee. Local chefs Rudolph Hassell and Carl Buncamper also offer tasty shrimp and lobster dishes for dinner and lunch specials such as curried goat. ✉ *Windwardside,* ☎ *599/416–2539. MC, V. Closed Sun.*

$ ✕ **Tropics Cafe.** A black-and-white-checked tile floor, crisp black-and-white napery, and gleaming silver flatware create a chic atmosphere at this poolside restaurant of Juliana's hotel. Run by British-trained chef Caroline Willcock, the restaurant has a menu that features contemporary bistro-style dishes such as penne with crab in a mango sauce. The restaurant serves three meals most days. ✉ *Windwardside,* ☎ *599/416–2469. MC, V. No dinner Mon.*

ECLECTIC

$$ ✕ **Brigadoon Restaurant.** A local favorite, this restaurant on the first
★ floor of a colonial house lets you take in the passing action on the street—which may not mean a whole lot on Saba, but it's still a nice thought. Fresh fish grilled and served with a light creole sauce is the specialty, but there are also chicken and steak dishes, lobster, and flavorful creations such as shrimp encrusted with salt and pepper. ✉ *Windwardside,* ☎ *599/416–2380. AE, DC, MC, V. No lunch. Closed Tues.*

$ ✕ **In Two Deep.** The owners of the Saba Deep dive shop run this lively harborside spot, with its stained-glass window and mahogany bar. The soups and sandwiches (especially the Reuben) are excellent, and the customers are usually high-spirited—most have just come from a dive. ✉ *Fort Bay,* ☎ *599/416–3438. MC, V. No dinner, except on some holidays.*

$ ✕ **Scout's Place.** At this restaurant in the Scout's Place hotel chef/dive master Wolfgang Tooten is in charge of the kitchen. Tables on the porch offer stunning views of the water. Cuisine runs the gamut from local goat stew to Italian pasta dishes to German specialties. Wednesday breakfast is when expatriates gather for their unofficial town meeting. ✉ *Windwardside,* ☎ *599/416–2740. Reservations essential. MC, V.*

$ ✕ **Swinging Doors.** A cross between an English pub and an Old West saloon (yes, there are swinging doors), this lively watering hole serves good, ample burgers, jalapeño poppers (a deep-fried flour puff ball seasoned with hot peppers), parrotfish sandwiches, and plenty of brew daily from 9 AM until late at night. You'll also find plenty of conversation, including some local gossip. ✉ *Windwardside,* ☎ *599/416–2506. No credit cards.*

FRENCH

$$ ✕ **Mango Royale Restaurant.** This elegant spot in the Queens Garden
★ Resort serves the creative cuisine of chef Bruno Lize and his wife Camille, who previously owned a well-known restaurant in a small village in the south west of France. They blend French techniques and Caribbean ingredients, focusing on freshly caught seafood, local vegetables, and meats. Camille is the wine expert, and delights in introducing guests to new varieties. Don't miss Bruno's wonderful pastries. In these magical hillside surroundings you can dine poolside or inside. The couple plans dance evenings, poolside barbecues, musical events, and theme nights with international flavors. ✉ *1 Troy Hill Dr. (Box 4), Troy Hill,* ☎ *599/416–3494. AE, D, MC, V.*

ITALIAN

$ ✕ **Guido's Pizzeria.** Students at the Saba University School of Medicine love this place. And what's not to love? In addition to pizza and lasagna, there are a pool table, a few rooms to rent, the Mountain High Club nightspot, and a fitness center. The restaurant is gaining a second story, too, so you'll soon get a view with that pie. ⊠ *Windwardside,* ☎ *599/416–2230. No credit cards. Closed Sun.*

Outdoor Activities and Sports

FISHING

This island is not a big fishing destination, but a few Sabans will take you out on their boats. Keep in mind that these are not big, fancy vessels. If you want to arrange a fishing trip, contact **Saba Deep** (☎ 599/416–3347 or 888/348–3722), or the tourist office, or ask your hotel to arrange it for you.

HIKING

On Saba you can't avoid some hiking, even if you just go to mail a postcard. The big deal, of course, is Mt. Scenery, with 1,064 steps leading to its top. Many of the trails, including the Mt. Scenery trail, have signs that describe the flora. For information about Saba's 18 recommended botanical hikes, check with the **Saba Conservation Foundation** (⊠ Behind tourist office, Windwardside, ☎ 599/416–2630), which maintains trails, or the foundation's **trail shop** (☎ 599/416–2630 or 599/416–3307) across the street. Botanical tours are available upon request. A guided, strenuous full-day hike through the undeveloped back side of Mt. Scenery costs about $50. At the shop you can book a hike with island native Crocodile James (James Johnson), who will explain the local flora and fauna.

SCUBA DIVING AND SNORKELING

Saba has long been recognized as one of the world's premier scuba-diving destinations. Within ½ mi (¾ km) from shore, sea walls drop to depths of more than 1,000 ft (305 m). Visibility is extraordinary, and the dive sites administered by the Saba Marine Park include shoals, reefs, and sea walls, all with a variety of corals and sea life. As other islands become "dived out," Saba is dedicated to preserving its marine life, despite hosting 22,000 dives each year.

Divers have a pick of 26 sites, including **Third Encounter,** a top-rated pinnacle dive (usually to about 110 ft/34 m) for advanced divers, with plentiful fish and spectacular coral; **Man of War Shoals,** another hot pinnacle dive 70 ft (21 m) with outstanding fish and coral varieties; and **Ladder Labyrinth,** a formation of ridges and alleys (down to 80 ft/24 m) where likely sightings include groupers, sea turtles, and sharks. **Saba Bank** is a fertile fishing ground 3 mi (5 km) southwest of Saba. It's also an excellent dive spot because of its coral gardens and undersea mountains.

Snorkelers need not feel left out: the marine park has several marked spots where reefs or rocks sit in shallow water. Among these sites are **Torrens Point,** on the northwest side of the island, and the new **Edward S. Arnold Snorkel Trail**—a self-guided underwater tour (off the northwest coast near Well's Bay) with 11 numbered and marked sites. Waterproof maps are available from the marine park, the Saba Conservation Foundation, or dive shops.

Expect to pay about $50 for a one-tank dive, and around $90 for a two-tank dive. Here are some dive operators that can help get you started: **Caradonna Caribbean Tours** (⊠ 435 Douglas Ave., Suite 2205, Altamonte Springs, FL 32714, ☎ 407/774–9000 or 800/328–2288, WEB www.caradonna.com) will put together packages at the hotel of your choice. **Saba Deep** (✉ Fort Bay, ☎ 599/416–3347 or 888/348–3722, WEB www.sabadeep.com) offers both PADI- and/or NAUI-certified instructors, directed by owner Mike Myers. **Saba Divers** (✉ Windwardside, ☎ 599/416–2740, WEB www.sabadivers.com) is the newest dive operation on the island, founded by a German-state registered instructor. It offers multi-lingual instruction. **Sea Saba** (✉ Windwardside, ☎ 599/416–2246) will take you to all of Saba's dive sites. Packages that include accommodations anywhere on the island are available. **Unique Destinations** (✉ 120 Elmdale Rd., North Scituate, RI 02857, ☎ FAX 401/934–3398, WEB www.unique-destinations.com) will arrange and recommend activities for your trip.

Shopping

Lace is one of the island's most popular purchases. The history of Saba lace goes back more than a century to Saban Gertrude Johnson, who attended a Caracas convent school where she learned the arts of drawing and tying threads to adorn fine linens. When she returned home to Saba in the 1870s, she taught lace-making, and the art has endured since. Every weekday Saban ladies display and sell their creations at the community center in Hell's Gate. Many also sell their wares from their houses; just follow the signs. Collars, tea towels, napkins, and other small items are relatively inexpensive; larger items, such as tablecloths, can be pricey. You should know that the fabric requires some care—it's not drip-dry. Saba Spice is another island buy. Although it *sounds* as delicate as Saba lace and the aroma is as sweet as can be, the base for this liqueur is 151-proof rum.

You'll find a variety of souvenirs and gifts in almost every shop. Look for the superlative book *Saban Cottages: A Book of Watercolors,* sold in several stores. In The Bottom, the **Saba Artisan Foundation** (☎ 599/416–3260) turns out hand-screened fabrics that you can buy by the yard or that is already made into resort clothing. It also sells T-shirts and spices.

In Windwardside, stop in at **Around the Bend** (☎ 599/416–2259), which carries souvenirs and clothing as well as "gifts, oddments, and pretties." The **Breadfruit Gallery** (☎ 599/416–2509) showcases and sells local artists' work. **El Momo Folk Art** (☎ 599/416–2518) has silk-screened T-shirts and souvenirs. **Jobean Designs** (☎ 599/416–2490) features intricate, handmade glass-bead jewelry as well as sterling silver and gold pieces by artist-owner Jo Bean. She also offers bead-making workshops. **Katherine's Windwardside Gallery** (☎ 599/416–2360) was Saba's first gallery for works by local artist Katherine Maeder, who now works out of Meadowview Cottage on Park Lane. The **Lynn Gallery** (☎ 599/416–2435), which is open by appointment or by chance, displays and sells artwork by the multitalented Lynn family, which also has a gallery in St. Martin's Grand Case. **Sea Saba** (☎ 599/416–2246) carries T-shirts, diving equipment, clothing, and books. The **Yellow House** (☎ 599/416–2334) sells local books, souvenirs, and lace.

Nightlife

On weekends Guido's Pizzeria is transformed into the **Mountain High Club** (☎ 599/416–2230)—there's even a mirrored disco ball suspended from the ceiling, and you can dance 'til 2 AM. **Scout's Place** (☎ 599/416–2740) is a good place to hang out. For other options, check the bulletin board in each village for a list of events, which often include parties.

Exploring Saba

Getting around the island means negotiating the narrow, twisting roadway that clings to the mountainside and rises from sea level to almost 2,000 ft (612 m). Although driving isn't difficult, just be sure to go slowly and cautiously. If in doubt, leave the driving to a cabbie so you can enjoy the scenery. You won't need long to tour the island by car—if you don't stop, you can cover the entire circuitous length of the Road in the space of a morning. If you want to shop, have lunch, and do some sightseeing, plan on a full day.

Numbers in the margin correspond to points of interest on the Saba map.

SIGHTS TO SEE

❻ The Bottom. Sitting in a bowl-shape valley 820 ft (251 m) above the sea, this town is the seat of government and the home of the lieutenant governor. The gubernatorial mansion, next to Wilhelmina Park, has fancy fretwork, a high-pitched roof, and wraparound double galleries. In 1993 Saba University opened a **medical school** (WEB www.saba.org) in The Bottom, at which about 200 students are enrolled.

On the other side of town is the Wesleyan Holiness Church, a small stone building with white fretwork. It dates from 1919, and although it's no longer used, you can go inside and look around. Stroll by the church, beyond a place called the Gap, to a lookout point where you can see the 400 rough-hewn steps leading down to Ladder Bay. This and Fort Bay were the two landing sites from which Saba's first settlers had to haul themselves and their possessions. Sabans sometimes walk down to Ladder Bay to picnic. Think long and hard before you do: going back requires 400 steps *up* to the Road.

❷ Cove Bay. Near the airport on the island's northeastern side, a 20-ft-long (6-m-long) strip of rocks and pebbles laced with gray sand is really the only place for sunning. There's also a small tidal pool here for swimming.

❶ Flat Point. This is the only place on the island where planes can land. The runway here is one of the world's shortest, with a length of 1,200 ft (366 m). Only STOL (short takeoff and landing) prop planes dare land here, as each end of the runway drops off more than 100 ft (31 m) into the crashing surf below.

❼ Fort Bay. The end of the Road is also the jumping-off place for all of Saba's dive operations and the location of the St. Maarten ferry dock. The island's only gas station is here, as is a 277-ft (84-m) deep-water pier that accommodates the tenders from ships. On the quay are a decompression chamber, one of the few in the Caribbean, and three dive shops. Saba Deep's restaurant, In Two Deep, is a good place to catch your breath while enjoying some refreshments and the view of the water.

❸ Hell's Gate. The Road makes 20 hairpin turns up more than 1,000 vertical ft (305 m) to Hell's Gate. Holy Rosary Church, on Hell's Gate's Hill, is a stone structure that looks medieval but was built in 1962. In the community center behind the church, village ladies sell blouses, handkerchiefs, and tablecloths embellished with the delicate and unique Saba lace. The same ladies make the potent rum-based Saba Spice, each according to her old family recipe. The intrepid can venture to Lower Hell's Gate, where the Old Sulphur Mine Walk leads to bat caves (with a sulfuric stench) that can—with caution—be explored.

❹ Mt. Scenery. Stone and concrete steps—1,064 of them—rise to the top of Mt. Scenery. En route to the mahogany grove at the summit, the steps pass giant elephant ears, ferns, begonias, mangoes, palms, and orchids; there are six identifiable ecosystems in all. Signs name the trees, plants, and shrubs, and the staff at the trail shop in Windwardside can provide a field guide. Have your hotel pack a picnic lunch, wear nonslip shoes, and take along a jacket and a canteen of water. The round-trip excursion will take about three hours and is best begun in the early morning.

Saba Marine Park. Established in 1987 to preserve and manage the island's marine resources, the park circles the entire island, dipping down to 200 ft (61 m), and is zoned for diving, swimming, fishing, boating, and anchorage. One of the unique features of Saba's diving is the submerged pinnacles of land at about the 70-ft (21-m) depth mark. Here all forms of sea creatures rendezvous. The information center offers talks and slide shows for divers and snorkelers and provides literature on marine life. (Divers are requested to contribute $3 a dive to help maintain the park facilities.) Before you go, call first to see if anyone is around. ⊠ *Harbor Office, Fort Bay,*☎ *599/416–3295.* ☉ *Weekdays 8–5.*

❺ **Windwardside.** The island's second-largest village, perched at 1,968 ft (602 m), commands magnificent views of the Caribbean. Here amid the oleander bushes you'll find rambling lanes and narrow alleyways winding through the hills, and clusters of tiny, neat houses and shops. At the village's northern end is the Church of St. Paul's Conversion, a colonial building with a red-and-white steeple. Just down the road is the Saba Tourist Office, where you can pick up books about Saba. You may also want to browse through the town's shops.

Small signs mark the way to the **Saba Museum.** This 150-year-old house, surrounded by lemongrass and clover, replicates a sea captain's home. Period pieces on display include a handsome mahogany four-poster bed, an antique organ, and, in the kitchen, a rock oven. You can also look at old documents, such as a letter a Saban wrote after the hurricane of 1772, in which he sadly says, "We have lost our little all." Don't miss the delightful stroll to the museum down the stone-walled Park Lane, one of the prettiest walks in the Caribbean. ⊠ *Windwardside,* ☎ *No phone.* ☎ *$1 (suggested donation).* ☉ *Weekdays 10–4.*

SABA A TO Z

To research prices, get advice from other travelers, and book travel arrangements, visit www.fodors.com.

AIR TRAVEL
The approach to Saba's tiny airstrip is as thrilling as a roller coaster ride. The strip is only ¼-mi (½-km) long, but the STOL aircraft are built for it, and the pilot needs only half of that length to land properly. Try not to panic; remember that the pilot knows what he's doing and wants to live just as much as you do. (If you're nervous, don't sit on the right. The wing just misses grazing the cliff side on the approach.) Once you've touched down on the airstrip, the pilot taxis an inch or two, turns, and deposits you just outside a little shoe box called the Juancho E. Yrausquin Airport.

➤ AIRLINES AND CONTACTS: **Windward Islands Airways** (☎ 599/416–2255 or 800/634–4907).

AIRPORTS
Saba's Juancho E. Yrausquin Airport is being expanded into a full-fledged airport—the runway has been widened to increase safety and a new terminal is underway. Taxi fare from the airport to Hell's Gate is $6; to Windwardside it's $8, and to The Bottom it's $12.50.

➤ Airport Information: **Juancho E. Yrausquin Airport** (☎ 599/416–2255).

BOAT AND FERRY TRAVEL
FARES AND SCHEDULES

The Edge, a high-speed ferry, leaves St. Maarten's Pelican Marina in Simpson Bay for Fort Bay on Saba daily, except Monday, at 9 AM and boards for the return trip at about 4 PM. The trip, which can be rough, takes just over an hour each way, and the round-trip fare is $60, plus 5% additional if you pay by credit card.

Other options for a trip to or from St. Maarten are the *Voyager I,* a large catamaran that holds 150 people and runs on Tuesdays and Thursdays between Marigot or Philipsburg and Fort Bay, and the *Voyager II,* a large powerboat that can take 100 people and runs on Tuesdays and Thursdays between Marigot and Philipsburg and Fort Bay. The fare on either Voyager boat is $60, plus $2 port fees from Marigot.
➤ Boat and Ferry Information: The following boats and ferries are in San Maarten: *The Edge* (☎ 599/544–2640); *Voyager I and II* (☎ 599/54–4096).

BUSINESS HOURS
BANKS

The island's two banks are open 8:30–2 (Barclays) or 8:30–3, and until 4 on Fridays (Antilles).

POST OFFICES
Post offices are open weekdays 8–5.

SHOPS
Shops are open weekdays and Saturday 8–5.

CAR RENTALS
The Road—Saba's one and only—is serpentine, with many a hairpin (read: hair-raising) curve. However, if you dare to drive, you can rent a car (about $45 a day with a full tank of gas and unlimited mileage).
➤ Major Agencies: **Caralfan Rent-A-Car** (✉ Windwardside, ☎ 599/416–2575 or 599/416–2296). **Johnson's Rent A Car** (✉ Juliana's Cottages, Windwardside, ☎ 599/416–2269).

GASOLINE
If you run out of gas, call the island's only gas station (☎ 599/416–3272), down at Fort Bay; note that it closes at 3 PM. Gas costs roughly NAf1.32 per liter ($3 per gallon).

ELECTRICITY
Saba's current is 110 volts, 60 cycles, and visitors from North America should have no trouble using their travel appliances.

EMERGENCIES
➤ Ambulance and Fire: For an ambulance, dial ☎ 5995/416–3289. To report a fire, dial ☎ 5995/416–2410.
➤ Hospitals: The **A. M. Edwards Medical Center** (✉ The Bottom, ☎ 599/416–3288) is a 10-bed hospital with a full-time physician.
➤ Pharmacies: The **Pharmacy** (✉ A. M. Edwards Medical Center, The Bottom, ☎ 599/416–3289).
➤ Police: **Police** (The Bottom, ☎ 599/416–3237).
➤ Scuba Diving Emergencies: **Saba Marine Park Hyperbaric Facility** (✉ Fort Bay, ☎ 599/416–4395).

FESTIVALS AND SEASONAL EVENTS
Saba's Carnival might not be as big as those of other Caribbean islands, but it *is* energetic. This weeklong celebration, which starts in late July

and runs 'til early August, features many special events, local and imported steel-pan bands, food booths, and parades (including the final Grand Carnival Parade). And just so Sabans don't forget what fun is, they hold a Saba Day the first weekend in December—three days of band contests, food tastings, and other events.

HOLIDAYS
Public holidays for 2002 are: New Year's Day, Good Friday (Mar. 29), Easter Monday (Apr. 1), Coronation Day and the Queen's Birthday (Apr. 30, celebrating the birthday and coronation of Holland's Queen Beatrix), Labor Day (May 1), Ascension Day (May 24), Christmas, and Boxing Day (Dec. 26).

LANGUAGE
Saba's official language is Dutch, but everyone on the island speaks English. Sabans are always willing to help, and they enjoy conversation. If you're open to chatting, you may get some good local advice.

MAIL AND SHIPPING
An airmail letter to North America or Europe costs NAf2.25; a postcard, NAf1.10. Book reservations through a travel agent or over the phone; mail can take a week or two to reach the island. The main branch of the post office is in The Bottom in the government administration building; a second office is in Windwardside, near Scout's Place. Both branches offer express mail service. When writing to Saba, don't worry about addresses without post office box numbers or street locations—on an island this size, all mail finds its owner. However, do make sure to include "Netherlands Antilles" and "Caribbean" in the address.

MONEY MATTERS
Prices quoted throughout the chapter are in U.S. dollars unless otherwise noted.

ATMS
There are no ATMs on the island.

CURRENCY
U.S. dollars are accepted everywhere, but Saba's official currency is the Netherlands Antilles florin (NAf; also called the guilder). The exchange rate fluctuates slightly but was around NAf1.77 to US$1 at press time. The island's two banks provide foreign-exchange services.
➤ BANKS: **Antilles Bank** (✉ Windwardside, ☎ 599/416–2631). **Barclays Bank** (✉ Windwardside, ☎ 599/416–2216).

PASSPORTS AND VISAS
U.S. and Canadian citizens need proof of citizenship. A valid passport is preferred, but a birth certificate with a raised seal along with a government-issued photo ID will do. British citizens must have a British passport. All visitors must have an ongoing or return ticket.

SAFETY
Take along insect repellent, sunscreen, and sturdy, no-nonsense shoes that get a good grip on the ground. Also you may encounter the harmless racer snake while hiking. Don't be alarmed; these snakes lie on rocks to sun themselves, but skitter off when people approach.

SIGHTSEEING TOURS
The taxi drivers who meet the planes at the airport or the boats at Fort Bay conduct tours of the island. Tours can also be arranged by dive shops or hotels. A full-day trek costs $40 for one to four passengers and $10 per person for groups larger than four. If you're in from St. Maarten for a day trip, you can do a full morning of sightseeing, stop

off for lunch (have your driver make reservations before starting), complete the tour afterward, and return to the airport in time to make the last flight back to St. Maarten. Guides are available for hiking; arrangements may be made through the tourist office or the trail shop in Windwardside.

TAXES
DEPARTURE TAX
You must pay a $5 departure tax when leaving Saba by plane for either St. Maarten or St. Eustatius, or $20 when continuing on an international flight. (Note: when flying home through St. Maarten from here, list yourself as "in transit" and avoid repaying the tax in St. Maarten, which is $20.) There's no departure tax when you leave by boat.

SALES TAX
Several of the larger hotels will tack on a 10%–15% service charge, others will build it into the rates. Call ahead to inquire about service charges. Hotels add a 5% government tax plus a 3% turnover tax to the cost of a room (sometimes it's tacked on to your bill, other times it's built into the room rate). Restaurants on Saba add service charges of 10%–15%.

TAXIS
Taxis meet planes, the ferry, and *Voyager* boats and take you to your destination. They charge a set rate for up to four people per taxi, with an additional cost for each person more than four. The fare from the airport to Hell's Gate is $6; to Windwardside it's $8, and to The Bottom it's $12.50. The fare from the Fort Bay ferry docks to Windwardside is $9.50. A taxi from Windwardside to The Bottom is $6.50.

TELEPHONES
Telephone communications are excellent on the island, and you can dial direct long-distance. You'll find public phone booths in The Bottom and Windwardside. They take prepaid phone cards, which can be bought at stores throughout the island, or local coins.

COUNTRY AND AREA CODES
To call Saba from the United States, dial 011/599/416, followed by the four-digit number.

TIPPING
Even if service charges have been added into your bill, it's customary to tip hotel personnel and restaurant waitstaff; you should tip taxi drivers, as well. About 10%–15% should do it.

TRANSPORTATION AROUND SABA
Carless Sabans get around the old-fashioned ways—walking and hitchhiking (very popular and safe). If you choose to thumb rides, you'll need to know the rules of the Road. To get a lift from The Bottom (which actually is near the top of the island), sit on the wall opposite the Anglican church; to catch one in Fort Bay, sit on the wall opposite the Saba Deep dive center, where the road begins to twist upward.

VISITOR INFORMATION
➤ IN SABA: **Saba Tourist Office** (✉ Box 527, Windwardside, ☎ 599/416–2231 or 599/416–2322, WEB www.turg.com/saba).

Updated by
Elise Meyer

It's 3:30 PM. Sun-kissed youngsters tumble into the tanned arms of their *mamans* after a twirl on the brightly painted school yard carousel. Traffic along the narrow road stops while the children hop into waiting cars. Nobody cares much about the delay, preferring instead to enjoy the afternoon air perfumed by sea spray and jasmine. The red-tiled roofs along the hillsides glitter in the sun and seem to tumble into the sapphire water. It feels more like a small town in the south of France than an island in the Caribbean.

St. Barthélemy blends the essence of the Caribbean with the essence of France. This island has a feeling of organized calm and barefoot chic that quickly puts visitors into a state of bliss. A sophisticated but unstudied approach to relaxation and respite prevails: you can spend the day on a deserted beach under a palm tree, enjoy a massage at your hotel or villa, try on the latest in causal-wear trends, and watch the sun set while nibbling tapas over Gustavia Harbor, then choose from nearly 100 excellent restaurants for an elegant evening meal. When you tire of the sun, you can putter all over the island, explore the fabulous shops, or just admire the lovely views.

A mere 8 square mi (21 square km), St. Barths has lots of hills and sheltered inlets. Gustavia, the only town, wraps itself neatly around a lilliputian harbor lined with sizable yachts and rustic fishing boats. Red-roof bungalows dot the hillsides, and beaches run the gamut from calm to "surfable," from deserted to packed. The French cuisine here is tops in the Caribbean, part of the French *savoir vivre* that prevails throughout the island. It's definitely a place for the style-conscious—casual but always chic.

Longtime visitors speak wistfully of the old, quiet St. Barths. Development has quickened the pace of life here, but the island hasn't yet been overbuilt—although vacation villas are under construction everywhere. Still, the largest hotel has fewer than 100 rooms, and the remaining accommodations are divided among about 40 small hotels. The tiny planes that arrive with regularity still land at the lonely airport only during daylight hours. And "nightlife" usually means a delicious dinner and a stargazing walk on the beach.

Christopher Columbus discovered the island—called "Ouanalao" by its native Carib Indians—in 1493; he named it for his brother Bartholomé. The first group of French colonists arrived in 1648, drawn by the ideal location on the West Indian Trade Route, but they were wiped out by the Carib Indians who dominated the area. A new group from Normandy and Brittany arrived in 1694. This time the settlers prospered—with the help of French buccaneers, who took advantage of the island's strategic location and protected harbor. In 1784 the French traded the island to King Gustav III of Sweden in exchange for port rights in Göteborg. The king dubbed the capital Gustavia, laid out and paved streets, built three forts, and turned the community into a prosperous free port. The island thrived as a shipping and commercial center until the 19th century, when earthquakes, fire, and hurricanes brought financial ruin. Many residents fled for newer lands of opportunity, and Oscar II of Sweden decided to return the island to France. After briefly considering selling it to America, Saint-Barthélemy became French once again on August 10, 1877.

Today the island is still a free port and, as a dependency of Guadeloupe, is part of an overseas department of France. Arid, hilly, and rocky, St. Barths was unsuited to sugar production and thus never developed an extensive slave base. Most of the 3,000 current residents are descendants of the tough Norman and Breton settlers of three centuries ago. They are feisty, industrious, and friendly—but insular. However, you will find many new, young French arrivals, predominantly from northwestern France and Provence, who speak English well.

Lodging

There is no denying that hotel rooms carry high prices. You're paying for the privilege of staying on the island, and even at $500 a night the bedrooms tend to be small. Still, if you're flexible—in terms of timing and in your choice of lodgings—you can enjoy a holiday in St. Barths and still afford to send the kids to college.

The most expensive season falls during the holidays (mid-December to early January), and hotels are booked far in advance for this period. (Rates in listings below are for the second-highest period, early January through April, which is still in season but not the holiday peak.) Although more hotels and restaurants here have seasonal closings (from August to September or October) than on other islands, some places are still open in August. If you're on a budget, look into an off-season stay, when rates can drop by as much as 50%. Most top hotels are on four northern beaches: Anse des Flamands, Anse des Cayes, Baie de St-Jean, and Grand Cul de Sac. In the hills away from the beaches are a number of surprisingly reasonable small hotels, guest houses, rental villas, and bungalows that significantly broaden your options. And regardless of the lodgings you choose, you'll want a car to explore the island.

On St. Barths, the term *villa* is used to describe anything from a small cottage to a sprawling manor. Today almost half of St. Barths's visitor accommodations are in villas, and rentals make a lot of sense, especially for longer stays or if more than one or two people are traveling together. Most houses include a small private swimming pool and maid service daily except Sunday. Houses are well equipped with linens, kitchen tools, and such electronic playthings as CD players, TVs, and VCRs. In-season rates range from $700 to $25,000 a week. If you get a group of friends together, you can rent a villa for significantly less than it would cost for each person to stay in an expensive hotel. Peak periods are usually booked solid by the previous summer. Though cancellations do occur, it's best to *reserve a villa as far in advance as possible.*

CATEGORY	COST*
$$$$	over $500
$$$	$350–$500
$$	$200–$350
$	under $200

*All prices are for a standard double room during the second-highest rate period: January through mid-April. Christmas through New Year rates are close to double, but summer rates are about half. In most cases prices include tax and service.

Hotels

$$$$ ★ **Carl Gustaf.** Emmanuelle and Christophe Bourgueil's hotel superbly embodies what St. Barths offers to visitors: beautifully designed spaces that feel elegant and private. The red-tile-roof buildings of this small, very expensive luxury resort spill down a hill. Each one- and two-bedroom suite looks out across a deck (with a small plunge pool) to lovely views of quaint Gustavia, its harbor, and the island's coastline. Each suite has high ceilings and spacious gleaming white bedrooms. Living rooms are stylishly decorated with nautical and tropical prints, rough marble floors, marble baths, tiny but state-of-the-art kitchens, and such welcome extras as a fax machine, two TVs, and two stereos. Summer package rates and an excellent honeymoon package are available. Carl Gustaf restaurant, known for its classic French cuisine, is spectacular. ⊠ *Rue des Normands (Box 700), Gustavia 97133,* ☎ 590/29–79–00, FAX 590/27–82–37, WEB *www.hotelcarlgustaf.com. 14 suites. Restaurant, air-conditioning, kitchenettes, minibars, refrigerator, in-room VCRs, pool, sauna, health club. AE, DC, MC, V. CP.*

$$$$ **Eden Rock.** Set on a craggy bluff that splits Baie de St-Jean is St. Barths' first hotel, originally opened in the 1950s by Rémy de Haenen. Comfortable rooms have four-poster beds, mosquito netting, sparkling silver fixtures, terra-cotta floors, and stunning bay views. The hotel's beach features comfortable chaises, umbrellas, and a sea-water whirlpool. The price includes a terrific breakfast buffet. The Rock, Michael's, and the Sand Bar restaurants are all first rate. ⊠ *Baie de St-Jean 97133,* ☎ 590/29–79–99, FAX 590/27–88–37, WEB *www.edenrockhotel.com. 15 rooms. 2 restaurants, 2 bars, minibars, pool, snorkeling, windsurfing, library. AE, MC, V. CP.*

$$$$ ★ **Guanahani.** The Guanahani is the largest full-service resort on the island, and it offers everything from private beaches to the most up-to-date gym. Rooms and one-bedroom suites (some with private pools) are in tightly clustered, high-ceilinged bungalows called *cases.* All units have comfortable bathrooms, and, depending on when they were refurbished, are decorated in pretty island pastel fabrics with stylish rattan furnishings, or luxurious fabrics in deep tropical colors, which are complemented by dark, plantation-style wood furniture. Note that units vary in terms of privacy, view, and distance from activities; make your preferences known when reserving. The poolside restaurant is open for breakfast and lunch. The more formal Bartolomeo serves classic French dinners in an indoor dining room and a tropical garden. Service throughout the resort is impeccable. ⊠ *Grand Cul de Sac (Box 609) 97098,* ☎ 590/27–66–60, FAX 590/27–70–70, WEB *www.guanahani-hotel.com. 47 rooms, 31 suites. 2 restaurants, piano bar, 2 pools, hair salon, 2 tennis courts, windsurfing, meeting rooms. AE, MC, V. CP.*

$$$$ ★ **Hôtel Isle de France.** Everything at this intimate resort, set on a white sandy beach, says casual elegance. Enormous rooms and suites are either in a two-story beachfront clubhouse or across the street in bungalows that face gardens and a pool. All units have a patio or a balcony, mahogany furniture, authentic 19th-century island prints, and white cotton bedspreads; some garden bungalows have kitchenettes. The

restaurant serves breakfast (in its dining area or in your room) and lunch. Summer packages are available. ✉ *Baie des Flamands (Box 612) 97098,* ☎ *590/27–61–81,* FAX *590/27–86–83,* WEB *www.isle-de-france. com. 24 rooms, 5 suites. Restaurant, bar, refrigerators, 2 pools, tennis court, gym, squash. AE, MC, V. CP.*

$$$$ 🏨 **Le Toiny.** When you only have eyes for each other, and privacy is
★ more important than cost, Le Toiny is for you. Each spacious green-roofed villa has a patio and pool. Rooms are elegantly appointed, each with a massive four-poster mahogany bed and armoire, with yards of red toile upholstery. Phones, a fax, satellite TV, a VCR, and a stereo are standard, and you can request either a stair-stepper or a stationary bike. The bathroom has a walk-in shower as well as a tub. Many returning visitors make a tradition of the Sunday Brunch buffet at the alfresco restaurant, Le Gaiac, which overlooks the Italian-tiled communal pool and beyond to the ocean. A wonderful beach, Saline, is a 10-minute drive. ✉ *Anse de Toiny 97133,* ☎ *590/27–88–88,* FAX *590/ 27–89–30,* WEB *www.letoiny.com. 12 villa-suites. Restaurant, bar, air-conditioning, in-room safes, in-room VCRs, minibars, pool, laundry service. AE, DC, MC, V. CP.*

$$$ 🏨 **Filao Beach.** Excellent service and a location on one of St. Barths' most popular and centrally located beaches keep guests coming back to this casual Relais & Châteaux resort. Rooms are in two-unit bungalows set back from the beach amid gardens. (Quarters closer to the beach are the most expensive, but note that the more affordable garden rooms are only steps from the sand.) Each simple, smallish room has rattan furniture, pastel-print fabrics, a compact but tidy bath, and a patio. You'll find the restaurant (open for breakfast and lunch) on a raised wooden deck that surrounds the pool; the bartender is well known for his killer cocktails. ✉ *Baie de St-Jean (Box 667) 97099,* ☎ *590/27–64–84,* FAX *590/27–62– 24,* WEB *www.filaobeach.com. 30 rooms. Restaurant, bar, air-conditioning, refrigerators, pool, beach. AE, MC, V. CP.*

$$$ 🏨 **François Plantation.** A colonial-era graciousness pervades this inti-
★ mate, exquisite hillside complex of West Indian–style cottages. The charming owner, longtime island habitué François Beret, is a passionate gardener, discriminating gourmand, and oenophile. A hint of shared interest may result in a tour of the grounds, or of the exceptional wine cellar. The grounds are an intense display of tropical flowers and greenery. The small but pristinely maintained rooms (four with garden views, eight with sea views) have queen-size mahogany four-poster beds that are brightened by colorful fabrics. Two larger rooms can accommodate an extra bed. The pool is atop a very steep hill, with magnificent views of nearby islets. You'll need a car (some packages include one) to get down to the sand and out and about for lunch. The La Route Des Epices restaurant, one of the best on the island, serves dinner on a romantic veranda. ✉ *Colombier 97133,* ☎ *590/29–80–22,* FAX *590/27–61–26,* WEB *www.francois-plantation.com. 12 rooms. Restaurant, air-conditioning, refrigerators, pool, gym. AE, MC, V. CP.*

$$$ 🏨 **Hôtel Christopher.** The Christopher, a Sofitel hotel, has oversized rooms and a gracious, attentive staff, which make it one of the island's best deals. Four two-story colonial-style buildings house beautifully furnished suites, a sitting area, colonial reproduction furnishings, delightful island artwork, American country fabrics, and a contemporary marble bath. (Note that some baths have a little garden; if seeing a small lizard is the kind of thing that would ruin your vacation, ask for a bath sans greenhouse.) Each also has a balcony or terrace from which you can see St. Maarten and nearby islets. The hotel's swimming pool is the largest on the island, with a wading area. L'Orchidée restaurant serves superb French-creole cuisine. ✉ *Pointe Milou 97133,* ☎ *590/27–63–*

St. Barthélemy

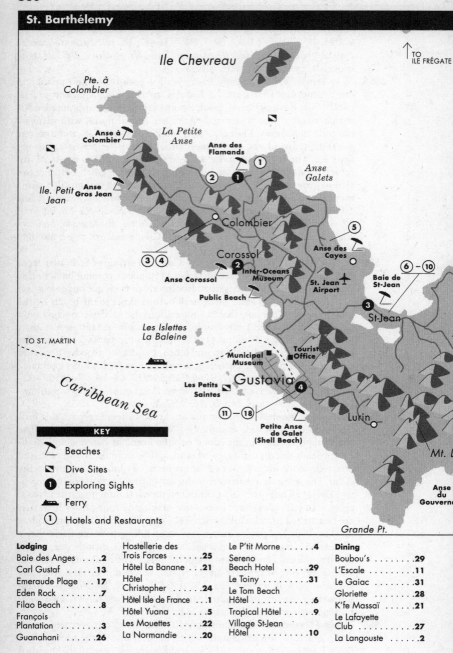

Ile Chevreau

↑ TO
ILE FRÉGATE

*Pte. à
Colombier*

*La Petite
Anse*

Anse des
Flamands

**Anse à
Colombier**

*Anse
Galets*

① ②

**Anse
Gros Jean**

*Ile. Petit
Jean*

⑤

Colombier

Anse des
Cayes

③ ④

Corossol

② **Inter-Oceans
Museum**

⑥ — ⑩

Anse Corossol

St. Jean
Airport

Baie de
St-Jean

Public Beach

③

St-Jean

*Les Islettes
La Baleine*

TO ST. MARTIN

**Municipal
Museum**

**Tourist
Office**

Caribbean Sea

Gustavia

④

**Les Petits
Saintes**

Lurin

⑪ — ⑱

**Petite Anse
de Galet
(Shell Beach)**

Mt. L

*Anse
du
Gouverne*

Grande Pt.

KEY

⌐ Beaches

◥ Dive Sites

❶ Exploring Sights

🚢 Ferry

① Hotels and Restaurants

Lodging		
Baie des Anges **2**	Hostellerie des Trois Forces **25**	Le P'tit Morne **4**
Carl Gustaf **13**	Hôtel La Banane ..**21**	Sereno Beach Hotel **29**
Emeraude Plage .. **17**	Hôtel Christopher **24**	Le Toiny **31**
Eden Rock **7**	Hôtel Isle de France ..**1**	Le Tom Beach Hôtel **6**
Filao Beach **8**	Hôtel Yuana **5**	Tropical Hôtel **9**
François Plantation **3**	Les Mouettes **22**	Village St-Jean Hôtel **10**
Guanahani **26**	La Normandie ...**20**	

Dining	
Boubou's **29**	
L'Escale **11**	
Le Gaiac **31**	
Gloriette **28**	
K'fe Massaï **21**	
Le Lafayette Club **27**	
La Langouste **2**	

↑ TO
ILE TOC VERS

A T L A N T I C   O C E A N

Les Grenadiers

La Tortue

Pte. Milou

㉔
㉓

㉑ ㉒

**Anse de
Lorient**

**Anse de
Marigot**

**Anse
Marechal**

㉖

Marigot

**Ansé de Grand
Cul de Sac**

㉗ — ㉚

Lorient

**Anse de Petit
Cul de Sac**

➐

㉕

Vitet

20

*Mt. du
Grand Fond*

Toiny

*Toiny
Coast*

Morne Vitet

㉛

➑

*Anse
Toiny*

⑲

*Grande
Saline*

*Grand
Fond*

*Anse de
Grand Fond*

Pt. à Toiny

➏

**Anse de
Grande
Saline**

N ↑

urin

*Morne
Rouge*

➎

0 ————————— 1 mile

ur

Pt. Gouverneur

0 ————————— 1 km

La Mandala **16**	Le Sapotillier **14**
La Marine **15**	Le Tamarin **19**
L'Orchidée **24**	Le Ti St. Barth
Le Repaire **12**	Caribbean
Restaurant des	Tavern **23**
Trois Forces. **25**	
Le Rivage **30**	
La Route des Epices . **3**	
La Saladerie **18**	

Exploring
Anse des Flamands . . **1**
Anse du
  Gouverneur **5**
Corossol **2**

Grande Saline **6**
Gustavia **4**
Lorient **7**
St-Jean **3**
Toiny coast **8**

63, FAX 590/27–92–92. *42 suites. 2 restaurants, air-conditioning, room service, pool, gym. AE, DC, MC, V. CP, EP, FAP, MAP.*

$$$ ⊡ **Le Tom Beach Hôtel.** Carole Gruson worked wonders in bringing this pretty, compact hotel on Plage St-Jean, the island's in-town beach, up to its current level of chic. The main building houses the reception area and breezy upstairs rooms with sea views. A path surrounded by flowers and greenery winds around the brightly painted garden suites, over the pool via a small footbridge, and into the hopping open-air restaurant, La Plage. The plantation-style rooms have high ceilings, blue beams, white wooden walls, four-poster beds with mosquito nets, and tile floors. All rooms have kitchenettes and patios. ⊠ *Plage St-Jean 97133,* ☎ *590/27–53–13,* FAX *590/27–53–15,* WEB *www.tombeach.com. 12 rooms. Restaurant, bar, refrigerators, pool, beach AE, MC, V. CP.*

$$ ⊡ **Emeraude Plage.** Right on St. Jean beach, the modern and clean bungalows, with outdoor kitchenette-patios that are convenient, well located, and pleasant. Nice new bathrooms add to the comfort. Guests gather to socialize in the comfortable library-lounge. ⊠ *Baie de Saint Jean, 97113,* ☎ *590/27–64–78,* FAX *590/27–83–08,* WEB *www.emeraudeplage.com. 24 bungalows, 3 suites, 1 villa. Air-conditioning, fans, beach. MC, V. EP.*

$$ ⊡ **Hostellerie des Trois Forces.** Set atop the highest island peak, this
★   charming "holistic New Age inn" is an idiosyncratic delight. Each of its tiny, gingerbread-trim cottages is done in an astrological color scheme (Libra is soft blue, Leo is bright red, etc.). The very personable owner and astrologer, Hubert de la Motte (a Gemini), has matched handcrafted furnishings to suit each sign. All units have air-conditioning or a ceiling fan as well as a terrace with a breathtaking ocean view; most have four-poster beds. When Hubert, who recently won the coveted international cooking prize *La Marmite D'Or,* isn't in the kitchen, he might do your chart or lead an early-morning yoga session beside the pool. Don't miss a leisurely lunch or dinner at the superb Restaurant des Trois Forces. Note: a four-wheel-drive vehicle is imperative for reaching the property. ⊠ *Morne Vitet, 97133,* ☎ *590/27–61–25,* FAX *590/ 27–81–38,* WEB *www.st-barths.com/3forces. 7 rooms. Restaurant, bar, air-conditioning, fans, minibars, pool. AE, MC, V. EP.*

$$ ⊡ **Hotel La Banane.** A totally new and modern spirit has transformed
★   this intimate hideaway set in a tropical garden. The nine completely redone bungalows are decorated in a surprisingly successful combination of island chic and high style. The rooms are relaxing and cool. Breakfast is included in the price and is served around the pretty pool; the beach is just a three-minute walk. The new K'fe Massaï African-theme restaurant is very popular. ⊠ *Quartier Lorient, 97133,* ☎ *590/52–03– 00,* FAX *590/27–68–44. 9 rooms. Restaurant, bar, air-conditioning, in-room VCR, 2 pools. AE, MC, V. CP.*

$$ ⊡ **Hôtel Yuana.** West Indian–style cottages are strung along a flowery hillside overlooking Anse De Cayes, the island's most popular surfing beach. Appealing rooms have white tile floors, colorful tile baths, blue- or peach-painted wicker furniture, floral-print fabrics, kitchenettes, and wide terraces overlooking the ocean. You can rent the hotel's 30-ft boat. A three-night package for two people, which includes breakfast and car rental, runs about $900. Children under 12 stay free. ⊠ *Anse des Cayes, 97133,* ☎ *590/27–80–84,* FAX *590/27–78–45,* WEB *www.yuana.com. 12 rooms. Bar, breakfast room, air-conditioning, fans, kitchenettes, in-room VCRs, pool, airport shuttle. AE, MC, V. EP.*

$$ ⊡ **Sereno Beach Hotel.** This hotel has changed from a quiet beach getaway into a funky resort for attractive twenty- and thirtysomethings. Large suites with private solariums look out to the hotel's private beach, but the small garden rooms are half the price. Continental breakfast is included. Highlights of the beach rooms include oversize

wooden chairs, an open-air, four-poster bed, and views of the Moroccan tents of Boubou's restaurant. Also here are Raffia's boutique and the well-equipped Forma Form fitness studio, is open to the sea. Honeymoon and summer packages are available. ⊠ *Grand Cul de Sac (Box 19), 97133,* ☎ *590/27–64–80,* FAX *590/27–75–47,* WEB *www.serenobeach. com. 18 rooms, 14 suites. 2 restaurants, bar, air-conditioning, refrigerators, pool, health club, beach, snorkeling, boating. AE, MC, V. EP.*

$$ 🏨 **Tropical Hôtel.** Straight up the hill from Baie de St-Jean is a classic example of what the French affectionately call a *hôtel bourgeois*: a simple, stylish place that's also a good value. You'll find well-maintained rooms (those with lower numbers are the best) in a one-story L-shape building. All open onto patios with views of either the ocean or thick tropical foliage and have pristine white walls, linens, and furnishings, beam ceilings, and beds swathed in mosquito netting. Continental breakfast is included in the price. ⊠ *Baie de St-Jean (Box 147), 97133,* ☎ *590/27–64–87,* FAX *590/27–81–74,* WEB *www.st-barths.com/tropical-hotel. 21 rooms. Bar, snack bar, air-conditioning, refrigerators, pool, recreation room. AE, MC, V. CP.*

$ ✕🏨 **Baie des Anges.** Ten clean, fresh, and nicely decorated rooms are right on the serene Flamands Beach. Guests are treated like family at this casual retreat. The food at La Langouste is tasty and reasonable. ⊠ *Flamands,* ☎ *590/27–63–61,* FAX *590/27–83–44. 10 rooms. Restaurant, pool, beach, car rental. AE, MC, V. EP*

$ 🏨 **Les Mouettes.** Six clean, simply furnished bungalows open directly ★ onto the beach. Each has a bathroom with shower, a kitchenette, a patio, two double beds, and a twin bed or fold-out sofa, making it a good bet for families. ⊠ *Quartier Lorient, 97133,* ☎ *590/27–77–91,* FAX *590/ 27–68–19. 7 rooms. Kitchenettes, beach, shops, car rental. No credit cards. EP.*

$ 🏨 **La Normandie.** This cozy family-run hotel offers modestly furnished rooms (some with a TV) for well under $100 a night, making it one of the best deals on St. Barths. There's a small pool here, and the beach is a five-minute walk. ⊠ *Quartier Lorient, 97133,* ☎ *590/27–73–78,* FAX *590/27–98–83. 8 rooms. Air-conditioning, pool. MC, V. EP.*

$ 🏨 **Le P'tit Morne.** Each of the modestly furnished mountainside stu- ★ dios has a private balcony and panoramic views of the coastline. The small kitchenettes are adequate for creating picnic lunches and other light meals. The snack bar serves breakfast. It's relatively isolated here, however: the beach is a 10-minute drive away. ⊠ *Colombier (Box 14) 97133,* ☎ *590/27–62–64,* FAX *590/27–84–63. 14 rooms. Snack bar, air-conditioning, kitchenettes, pool, library. AE, MC, V. CP.*

$ 🏨 **Village St-Jean Hôtel.** For two generations the Charneau family has ★ seen to it that the quality of the service here remains high and the rates reasonable. The handsome stone-and-redwood cottages are spacious, with high ceilings, dark wood, and airy fabrics. One has a patio Jacuzzi. Open-air kitchenettes and patios are also featured. The six hotel-style rooms have refrigerators, and most have king-size beds. There is also a three-bedroom villa available. The location is great—you can walk to the beach and town from here—and most accommodations have views. ⊠ *Baie de St-Jean (Box 623), 97098,* ☎ *590/27–61–39; 800/651– 8366 direct to hotel,* FAX *590/27–77–96,* WEB *www.villagestjeanhotel.com. 6 rooms, 20 cottages. Restaurant, bar, grocery, air-conditioning, kitchenettes (some), pool, hot tub, shops, library. AE, MC, V. EP.*

Villas and Condominiums

Professionalism and congeniality are the hallmarks of **St. Barth Properties, Inc.** (☎ 508/528–7727 or 800/421–3396, FAX 508/528–7789, www.stbarth.com). American owner Peg Walsh has been a regular on St. Barths since 1986 and represents properties only here. Peg and her staff are in tune with their clients' vacation rental desires, and they go to great lengths to fulfill them. With more than 100 properties, they can guide you to the perfect place to stay. Weekly peak-season rates range from $1,400 to $40,000 depending on the property's size, location, and amenities. Write for their *Dream Portfolio* booklet, which describes the villas they represent. The company also has an office in Gustavia, with their French affiliate **St. Barth Dream Vacations** (✉ Residence La Source, Gustavia, ☎ 590/29–72–03, WEB www.stbarth.com).

SiBarth Real Estate oversees more than 200 properties on St. Barths. Bookings are arranged through the company's representative, WIMCO (☎ 800/932–3222, FAX 401/847–6290, WEB www.wimcovillas.com), which is based in Newport, Rhode Island. Properties can be previewed and reserved over the Internet, or you can obtain the *Vendome Guide to St. Barthélemy* by mail. Rents range from $1,000 to $3,500 per week for one-bedroom villas and $1,800 to $7,000 for two- and three-bedroom villas. Larger villas rent for $7,000 per week and up.

Dining

Dining on the small island of St. Barths compares favorably to almost anywhere in the world. Varied and exquisite cuisine, breathtaking natural beauty, a French flair in decor and accoutrements, sensational wine, and attentive but unobtrusive service are combined for a wonderful epicurean experience. St. Barths' style is expressed in dozens of charming places to eat, running the gamut from beachfront grills to serious five-course meals. Freshly caught local seafood mingles on the plate with top-quality provisions that arrive every afternoon from Paris. Myth has it that St. Barths' restaurants are frightfully expensive—and, certainly, you can spend a small fortune in a number of restaurants by choosing rare vintages and luxury ingredients. However, you can also dine superbly on the island without breaking the bank.

Although à la carte prices at some restaurants are high, many offer a more reasonable prix-fixe menu. Lunch is usually a less costly meal than dinner, and many casual restaurants are inexpensive. Furthermore, the strength of the U.S. dollar has softened prices. Be sure to sample such local specialties as *accras* (salt cod fritters), usually served with one or more varieties of creole sauce (herbs and crushed, spicy peppers in oil); spiced *christophene* (similar to acorn squash, usually stuffed); *boudin créole* (blood sausage); and lusty *soupe de poissons* (fish soup). Available local fish include *dorade* (mahimahi) and tuna; also look for langouste (spiny lobster). Delicious and interesting variations on *Gazpacho,* (cold tomato soup) are common, and a refreshing starter at lunch. If you are concerned about the possibility of unsafe beef rest assured that most meat available in St. Barth comes from the U.S. or Argentina.

Reservations are always appreciated and, in high season, essential. If you enter a restaurant without a reservation and find there are empty tables, do not automatically assume the owner will seat you. Restaurant owners on St. Barths take great pride in their service as well as in their food, and they would rather turn you away than slight you on an understaffed evening. And don't think you're being ignored at the end of a leisurely meal; it is considered rude to present a bill too promptly. Linger at the table and enjoy the small complimentary glass of the restaurant's own vanilla rum. Check restaurant bills carefully. A service charge (*service compris*) is almost always added, but you may leave the server a bit extra (5–10%) if that person has been particularly attentive. It is generally advisable to charge restaurant meals on a credit card, as the issuer will offer a better exchange rate than the restaurant. As long as exchange rates remain favorable, have your check charged in francs for the best deal. Many restaurants serve locally caught lobster (*langoustine*); priced by weight, it is usually the most expensive item on a menu, and depending on its size and the restaurant, will range in price from $40 to $60. In noting menu prices below, it has been left out of the range.

What to Wear

A bathing suit and pareo (sarong) are suitable at lunch. Jackets are never required and rarely worn, but people dress fashionably for dinner. Casual chic is the idea; women wear whatever is hip and tight, such as mini skirts. Shorts at the dinner table may label a man *américain*, but many locals have adopted the habit, and nobody cares much. Pack a light sweater or shawl for an after-dinner beach stroll.

CATEGORY	COST*
$$$$	over $35
$$$	$25–$35
$$	$15–$25
$	under $15

per person for a main course at dinner

CARIBBEAN

$$$$ ✕ **L'Orchidée.** This elegant French-creole restaurant with coral stucco
★ walls and mahogany archways is in the Hôtel Christopher. Have a seat at the outdoor bar, the Mango, and ask the bartender to make you one of his first-rate piña coladas. Sunsets and moonlight vistas are spectacular from the restaurant. The staff is friendly and solicitous, the atmosphere romantic, and the food serious and beautifully presented. Try the Chef's Foie Gras in lemon sauce, roast duck in demi-glace, or grilled mahimahi with lime. A prix-fixe menu is also available for about $55. ⊠ *Pointe Milou,* ☎ *590/27–63–63. AE, MC, V.*

$$ ✕ **Gloriette.** This beachside spot serves delicious local creole dishes, such as crunchy accras and a cassoulet of local lobster, as well vegetarian dishes and light salads. ⊠ *Grand Cul de Sac,* ☎ *590/27–75–66. AE, MC, V.*

$$ ✕ **Le Ti St. Barth Caribbean Tavern.** As much house party as restau-
★ rant, chef-owner Carole Gruson captures the funky spirit of the island in her wildly popular hilltop hot spot. Lounge to loud music with the attractive crowd lingering at the bar; wander inside to relax on pillow-strewn banquettes drawn up to Indian silk–topped tables with elaborate silver candelabras; or chat on the torchlit outdoor terrace—by the time your appetizers arrive, you'll be best friends with the next table. The creative menu includes Thai beef salad, house-smoked fish on blinis, grilled duck fillet with cranberries, fish tartare with tropical fruits, or a superb Argentine beef filet. The extensive wine list features everything from the basic Beaujolais to a Pétrus '88 ($1,400). ⊠ *Pointe Milou,* ☎ *590/27–97–71. Reservations essential. MC, V.*

$ ✕ **Le Rivage.** This popular and surprisingly affordable restaurant in
★ the St. Barths Beach Hôtel serves wonderful gazpacho and huge salads. Tantalizing choices of the latter include the warm chèvre (goat cheese) with bacon, the cold seafood salad, and the classic *salade niçoise* (with tuna, olives, green beans, and hard boiled eggs). Grilled fresh seafood and steaks attend to those with heartier appetites—but save room for the warm chocolate cake with vanilla sauce. The restaurant also offers much more than food: come for lunch and spend the rest of the afternoon sunning or windsurfing on the beautiful beach. ⊠ *Grand Cul de Sac,* ☎ *590/27–82–42. AE, MC, V.*

CONTEMPORARY

$$$ ✕ **La Mandala.** Boubou, the owner, is in the process of establishing himself as the premier host on the island with his eponymous Boubou's, on the beach at Grand Cul de Sac. All his restaurants are excellent, fun, attractive, and reasonable in price, with cute servers who are friendly and efficient. Enjoy dinner on the sweeping terrace, which faces west for spectacular views across the harbor. The menu features such tasty Thai-influenced dishes as swordfish spring rolls wrapped in lettuce leaves with a tangy dipping sauce, green-curry shrimp, or filet mignon in a light sate sauce. ✉ *Rue de la Sous-Préfecture, Gustavia,* ☎ *590/27–96–96,* WEB *www.lamandala.com. AE, MC, V. No lunch June and Sept.*

$$ ✕ **K'fe Massaï.** Even first-time visitors are enchanted by this restaurant's stunning ethnotropical decor, but the main attractions are its inventive food and lively, romantic atmosphere. The theme is African, but the food is basically French. Starters include chilled tomato soup with ricotta sorbet, and a delicious tomato and caramelized onion tart. Main courses include thyme-roasted veal, and salmon with grilled potato skewers in green tea sauce. However, these fade into memory the minute your fork hits the decadent chocolate dessert medley. ✉ *Lorient,* ☎ *590/29–76–78. No credit cards.*

ECLECTIC

$$$$ ✕ **Le Lafayette Club.** Despite outrageous prices, this lunch-only surfside bistro is so popular that reservations are necessary. And it's the best spot on St. Barths for people-watching, as the daily fashion show of beachwear from the adjoining shop provides a great cover for having a good look at whichever celebrities are seated at the next table (don't worry—they're people-watching, too). Matching the ambience, the food is consistently exciting, with a variety of salads and grills. Drink champagne and be part of the fantasy. ✉ *Grand Cul de Sac,* ☎ *590/27–62–51. No credit cards.*

$$ ✕ **Boubou's.** On the beach of the Sereno Beach Hotel, you'll find con-
★ temporary cooking in a gorgeous setting. The restaurant's high-ceiling Moroccan tent with Indian-Berber decor is the ultimate in romantic. Salads, ribs, and grilled fish are on tap for lunch, and dinner includes delicious homemade pastas, such as goat cheese ravioli with wild mushrooms and artichokes, risotto, grilled shrimp, and fried calamari. The tropical sorbets are excellent. Stay to drink at the bar or dance the night away. ✉ *Grand Cul de Sac,* ☎ *590/29–83–01. Reservations essential. AE, MC, V.*

$$ ✕ **La Marine.** In-the-know islanders are always here to gobble down the mussels that arrive from France every Wednesday. Settled at the popular dockside picnic tables, the locals smother them in wine sauce with butter and cream. The menu also includes fish, oysters, hamburgers, steaks, and omelets. Many think that meals here are the best buys on the island. ✉ *Rue Jeanne d'Arc, Gustavia,* ☎ *590/27–68–91. AE, MC, V.*

$$ ✕ **Le Repaire.** This busy brasserie overlooks Gustavia's harbor and is a popular spot from 6 AM to 1 AM. Grab a cappuccino, pull a captain's chair up to the front window, and watch cruise-ship passengers descend upon the town. The menu includes everything from cheeseburgers and creole specialties to foie gras and grilled fish and lobster. The *assiette creole* (creole assortment platter) is a great introduction to this fine cuisine. Try your hand at the billiards table, or show up on weekends for live music. ✉ *Quai de la République, Gustavia,* ☎ *590/27–72–48. MC, V.*

FRENCH

$$$$ ✕ **Le Gaiac.** Cool breezes waft through this open-air restaurant at the elegant, out-of-the-way Le Toiny hotel. Pale blue napery and blue canvas chairs beautifully complement the blue bay view. Lunch includes chilled, spicy mango soup, club sandwiches, salads, and grilled seafood.

The dinner menu features such dishes as roast rack of lamb in a clay shell with thyme and honey, yellowtail snapper with lightly curried lentils and squash, and pigeon layered with red cabbage and sweet potato and spiced with local herbs. Tableside crêpes suzettes are de rigueur. There's a buffet lunch on Sunday. ⊠ *Anse de Toiny*, ☎ *590/29–77–47. AE, DC, MC, V. Closed Sept.–mid-Oct.*

$$$$ ✕ **La Route des Epices.** Follow the lanterns down the arbor way to this
★ elegant restaurant in the François Plantation complex considered by many to be the best restaurant on the island. Inside, sparkling white-wash, luxuriant greenery, and buffed mahogany combine to create a pristine atmosphere of elegance and professionalism. Owner François Beret is justifiably proud of his wine cellar, which is one of the best on the island. Either he or his superlative waitstaff will help choose wines to enhance the sublime and serious cuisine. Offerings include a magi-cal terrine of foie gras with caramel, served with a perfect sauternes, layered smoked salmon and leek "lasagna," and grilled sea bass served with wild rice risotto and roasted tomato. A vanilla soufflé with choco-late sauce elicited swooning. ⊠ *Colombier*, ☎ *590/29–80–22. Reser-vations essential. AE, DC, MC, V. Closed Sept.–Oct. No lunch.*

$$$ ✕ **Restaurant des Trois Forces.** Make your way to the top of the high-
★ est hilltop on the island for a memorable meal at the hands of owner-chef Hubert de la Motte. Sublime *émincés de veau*, homemade bread, chateaubriand, and exquisite desserts are complemented by rare vin-tages. ☎ *590/27–62–25. Reservations essential. AE, MC, V.*

$$$ ✕ **Le Sapotillier.** Dining inside this cozy boîte or in its courtyard under a grand old sapodilla tree, you may feel like a guest in the owners' house—a loving re-creation of a typical St. Barths *case* (Creole for cot-tage), down to the brick walls, hand-painted wooden chairs, exquisite white linen tablecloths, and vivid creole paintings. This is exactly the way Adam Rajner, the owner, wants you to feel. Yet the food is any-thing but down-home. This long-established French-creole restaurant serves such classic French cuisine as frogs legs, and turbot in potato crust. The sumptuous black-and-white-chocolate mousse is a house fa-vorite. ⊠ *Rue de Centenaire, Gustavia*, ☎ *590/27–60–28. Reserva-tions essential. MC, V. Closed May–mid-Oct. No lunch.*

$$ ✕ **Le Tamarin.** A leisurely lunch here en route to Saline Beach is a St.
★ Barths *must*. Delicious French and creole cuisine is served at this so-phisticated open-air restaurant, which comes complete with a terrific little boutique for shopping in between courses. Get to know the par-rot, or relax in a hammock after some of the house-special carpaccios of salmon, tuna, and beef. The lemon tart deserves its excellent repu-tation. ⊠ *Salines*, ☎ *590/27–72–12. AE, MC, V. Closed Mon. No din-ner weekdays.*

ITALIAN

$ ✕ **L'Escale.** Great food, ambience, and views draw locals and visitors alike to this open-air restaurant at the water's edge on the far side of Gustavia's harbor. The varied menu includes a wide range of pasta (lasagna, tortellini, ravioli, and spaghetti with marinara, Bolognese, and other sauces), as well as fresh local fish, veal scallopini in an assort-ment of sauces, steak tartare, chicken, and 12 kinds of pizza. Many dishes are cooked in a wood-burning oven. ⊠ *Rue Jeanne d'Arc, Gus-tavia*, ☎ *590/27–81–06. Reservations essential. MC, V. No lunch.*

$ ✕ **La Saladerie.** Another good casual choice on the far side of Gus-tavia, the crisp-crust pizzas are a popular choice for lunch or a light dinner. Watch the boats and sip a cold Domaine Ott rosé, which at $30 a bottle is a bargain by St. Barths standards. ⊠ *6, rue Jeanne d'Arc, Gustavia*, ☎ *590/27–52–48. MC.*

SEAFOOD

$ ✕ **La Langouste.** This tiny beachside restaurant in the pool-courtyard of newly renovated Hotel Baie des Anges lives up to its name by serving fantastic, fresh grilled lobster. Simple, well-prepared fish, pastas, and soups are also available. ✉ *Flamands Beach,* ☎ *590/27–63–61. Reservations essential. AE, MC, V. Closed Mon. in summer. Closed Sept.*

Beaches

There are many *anses* (coves) and nearly 20 *plages* (beaches) scattered around the island, each with a distinctive personality and each open to the general public. Even in season you can find a nearly empty beach. Topless sunbathing is common, but nudism is forbidden—although both Saline and Gouverneur are de facto nude beaches.

The beach at **Anse à Colombier** is the least accessible but the most private on the island; to reach it you must take either a rocky footpath from Petite Anse or brave the 30-minute climb down (and back up) a steep, cactus-bordered trail from the top of the mountain behind the beach. Boaters favor this beach and cove for its calm anchorage. **Anse Corossol** is a top boat- and sunset-watching spot. **Anse du Gouverneur** is secluded—hence the nude sunbathing—and truly beautiful, with good snorkeling, blissful swimming, and views of St. Kitts, Saba, and St. Eustatius. Next to the Guanahani Hotel is tiny **Anse Marechal,** which offers some of the island's best snorkeling. **Baie de St-Jean** is like a mini Côte d'Azur—beachside bistros, bungalow hotels, bronzed bodies, windsurfing, and lots of day-trippers. The reef-protected strip is divided by Eden Rock promontory, and there's good snorkeling west of the rock.

Flamands is the most beautiful of the hotel beaches—a roomy strip of silken sand. Shallow, reef-protected **Grand Cul de Sac** is especially nice for small children, fly fishermen, and windsurfers; it has excellent lunch spots and lots of pelicans. Secluded **Grande Saline,** with its sandy ocean bottom, is just about everyone's favorite beach and is great for swimmers. Despite the law, young and old alike go nude. It can get windy here, so go on a calm day.

Lorient is popular with St. Barths families and surfers, who like its rolling waves. Be aware of the level of the tide, which can come in very fast. **Marigot** is a tiny, calm beach with good snorkeling along the rocky far end. A five-minute walk from Gustavia is **Petite Anse de Galet** (Shell Beach), named after the tiny shells on its shore—it was totally destroyed by the 1999 hurricane and at this writing is being rebuilt through the efforts of several municipal organizations. Bear in mind that the windy, rocky beaches around **Anse á Toiny** are not swimmable.

Outdoor Activities and Sports

BOATING AND SAILING

St. Barths is a popular yachting and sailing center thanks to its location mid-way between Antigua and St. Thomas. Gustavia's harbor, 13 to 16 ft deep, has mooring and docking facilities for 40 yachts. There are also good anchorages available at Public, Corossol, and Colombier.

Marine Service (✉ Gustavia, ☎ 590/27–70–34) offers full-day outings on a 40-ft catamaran to the uninhabited Ile Fourchue for swimming, snorkeling, cocktails, and lunch; the cost is $100 per person. The company also arranges deep-sea-fishing trips, with a full-day charter of a 30-ft crewed cabin cruiser running $800; an unskippered motor rental runs about $260 a day. Marine Service can also arrange an hour's cruise ($32) on the glass-bottom boat *L'Aquascope.* **Nautica** (✉ Gustavia, ☎ 590/27–56–50) specializes in day sails and charters. **Océan Must Ma-**

rina (☎ 590/27–62–25), in Gustavia, offers all kinds of boat charters. **Ship Chandler du Port Franc** (✉ Gustavia, ☎ 590/27–89–27), a ship chandlery, is the place for yachting information and supplies.

FISHING

Most fishing is done in the waters north of Lorient, Flamands, and Corossol. Popular catches are tuna, marlin, wahoo, and barracuda. Deep-sea fishing can be arranged through **Marine Service** (✉ Gustavia, ☎ 590/27–70–34). **Océan Must Marina** (☎ 590/27–62–25), in Gustavia, arranges deep-sea-fishing expeditions as well as boat charters.

HORSEBACK RIDING

Laure Nicolas leads two-hour excursions in the morning and the afternoon for $40 per person from **Ranch des Flamands** (✉ Anse des Flamands, ☎ 590/27–80–72; 24-hr notice preferred).

SCUBA DIVING

Several dive shops arrange scuba excursions to local sites. Depending on the weather conditions you may dive at **Pain de Sucre, Coco Island,** or toward nearby **Saba Island.** There is also an underwater shipwreck to explore, plus sharks, rays, sea tortoises, coral, and the usual array of colorful fish. The waters on the island's leeward side are the calmest.

Marine Service operates the only five-star, PADI-certified diving center on the island, called **West Indies Dive** (☎ 590/27–70–34); scuba trips, packages, resort dives, and certifications start at $50, gear included. **Odysée Caraibe** (☎ FAX 590/27–55–94) is recommended for its up-to-the-minute equipment and boat.

TENNIS

If you wish to play tennis at a hotel at which you are not a guest, call ahead to inquire about fees and reservations. There are two lighted tennis courts at the **Guanahani** (✉ Grand Cul de Sac, ☎ 590/27–66–60). **Le Flamboyant Tennis Club** (✉ Anse de Toiny, ☎ 590/27–69–82) has available courts.

There's one lighted court at **Hôtel Isle de France** (✉ Baie des Flamands, ☎ 590/27–61–81). **Hôtel Manapany Cottages** (✉ Anse de Cayes, ☎ 590/27–66–55) has a lighted court, but the hotel was under reconstruction at press time.

WINDSURFING

Windsurfing fever has definitely caught on here. You can rent boards for about $20 an hour at water-sports centers along Baie de St-Jean and Grand Cul de Sac beaches. Lessons are offered for about $40 an hour at **Le Centre Nautique** (✉ Eden Rock at Baie de St-Jean, ☎ 590/27–74–77) rents boards and offers lessons. **Wind Wave Power** offers an extensive, six-hour training course (✉ St. Barth Beach Hotel at Grand Cul de Sac, ☎ 590/27–60–70).

Shopping

St. Barths is a duty-free port, and with its sophisticated crowd of visitors, shopping is a definite delight, especially for beachwear, accessories, jewelry, and casual wear. Note that stores often close from noon to 2, and many on Wednesday afternoon as well, so plan your shopping day accordingly. A popular afternoon pastime is strolling about the two major shopping areas in Gustavia and St. Jean.

Areas

In **Gustavia,** boutiques line the two major shopping streets, and the **Carré d'Or** plaza is great fun to explore. Shops are also clustered in **La Savane Commercial Center** (across from the airport), **La Villa Créole,** in St-Jean, and **Espace Neptune,** on the road to Lorient. It's worth working your way from one end to the other at both of these shopping complexes—just to see or maybe be seen. Boutiques in all three areas carry the latest in French and Italian sportswear and some haute-couture. Prices, although still on the high side, are often well below those for comparable merchandise in France.

Specialty Items

CLOTHES

Fans of Longchamp handbags and leather goods will find a good selection at about 20% off at Elysée Caraïbes stores in the Carré d'Or and Gustavia. **Stéphane & Bernard** (⊠ Rue de la Républic, Gustavia) stocks a large selection of French fashion designers, including Rykiel, Tarlazzi, Kenzo, Feraud, and Mugler. The **Hermès** (⊠ Gustavia) store in St. Barths is an independently owned franchise, and prices are about 20% below those in the States. **Laurent Effel** (⊠ Rue Général-de-Gaulle features beautiful leather belts, colorful linen shirts, and bags and shoes. **Dovani** (⊠ Rue de la République) has elegant leather goods and Baccarat jewelry.

In Gustavia and St-Jean you'll find clusters of clothing shops. **Black Swan** (⊠ Le Carre d'or, Gustavia, ☎ 590/27–65–16; ⊠ Villa Creole, St-Jean) has a good selection of bathing suits. Look to **St. Tropez KIWI** for resort wear. **Morgan's** has a line of popular and wearable casual wear in the trendy vein. Across from the St-Jean airport is **Samaly,** which features fashions and accessories. Don't miss the **Lolita Jaca** shops in St-Jean and Gustavia for their collections of exquisite raffia bags and hats from Madagascar. **Raffia,** at Boubou's and in St-Jean, has tiny handbags and such up-to-the-minute fashions as military-inspired khakis, pastel linen skirts, and embroidered accessories. **Calypso,** in Gustavia's Carré d'Or, has feminine resort wear by Chloé. **Quickssilver Boatriders Club** (⊠ Pelican Plage, St. Jean, ☎ 590/29–76–66) is the place for surfer-inspired fashions for all ages. Next door to Quickssilver Boatriders Club is **Terra** for pretty resort wear.

FOODSTUFFS

Match gourmet supermarket, across from the airport, has a wide selection of French cheeses, pâtés, cured meats, produce, and fresh bread. **A.M.C.** in Gustavia is a bit older than Match but able to supply anything you might need for housekeeping in a villa, or for a picnic. **JoJo Supermarché,** in Lorient is the well-stocked counterpart to Gustavia's two supermarkets and gets daily deliveries of bread and fresh produce. For exotic groceries or picnic fixings, stop by St. Barths's gourmet *traiteur* (take-out) **La Rotisserie** (⊠ Gustavia, ☎ 590/27–63–13; St-Jean, ☎ 590/29–75–69) for salads, prepared meats, groceries from Fauchon, and Iranian caviar.

HANDICRAFTS

The ladies of Corossol produce intricate straw work, wide-brim beach hats, and decorative ornaments by hand. Local works of art include paintings, and are sold in the bright **Made in St.-Barth La Boutique** (⊠ Villa Créole, ☎ 590/27–56–57) shop.

Call the tourist office, which can provide information about the studios of other island artists such as Christian Bretoneiche, Robert Danet, Nathalie Daniel, Patricia Guyot, Rose Lemen, and Marion Vinot.

Chez Pompi (⊠ On the road to Toiny, ☎ 590/27–75–67) is a cottage whose first room is a gallery for the naive paintings of Pompi (also known as Louis Ledee).

Look for Fabienne Miot's unique gold jewelry at **L'Atelier de Fabienne** (⊠ Rue de la République, Gustavia, ☎ 590/27–63–31). Superb skin-care products made on-site from local tropical plants by **Ligne de St. Barths** (⊠ Rte. de Saline, Lorient, ☎ 590/27–82–63) are worth buying.

JEWELRY

For fine jewelry visit **Cartier** (⊠ Quai de la République) on the harborside of Gustavia. Next door to Cartier, **Oro del Sol** (⊠ Quai de la République), features beautiful fine accessories by Bulgari, Ebel, and others. **Carat** (⊠ Quai de la République) has Chaumet and a large selection of watches including Breitling. More watches, including Patek Phillippe and Chanel, can be found at **Diamond Genesis** (⊠ Rue Général de Gaulle).

LIQUOR AND TOBACCO

Wine lovers will enjoy **La Cave du Port Franc** (⊠ Rue de la République, Gustavia, ☎ 590/27–65–27). **La Cave de Saint-Barths** (⊠ Marigot, ☎ 590/27–63–21) has an excellent collection of French vintages stored in temperature-controlled cellars. **Le Comptoir du Cigare** (⊠ Rue de Général-de-Gaulle, Gustavia, ☎ 590/27–50–62), run by Jannick and Patrick Gerthofer, is a top purveyor of cigars. The walk-in humidor has an extraordinary selection. Try the Cubans while you are on the island, and take home the Davidoffs. They will ship refills stateside. Be sure to try on the Panama hats.

Nightlife

In clubs change from season to season, so you might ask around for the hot spot of the moment. **Bar de l'Oubli** (⊠ Rue du Roi Oscar II, Gustavia, ☎ 590/27–70–06) is where young locals gather for drinks. **Carl Gustaf** (⊠ Rue des Normands, Gustavia, ☎ 590/27–82–83) lures those in search of quiet conversation and sunset watching. **New Feeling** (☎ 590/27–88–67) is a disco in the Lurin Hills that has special theme nights on Thursday.

Jungle Café (⊠ 6 rue Jeanne d'Arc, ☎ 590/27–67–29), overlooking the harbor in Gustavia, features live music and entertainment during and after dinner. **La Licorne** (☎ 590/27–83–94) in Lorient is hot with a local crowd and open only on Saturday night. **Le Petit Club** (☎ 590/27–66–33) in Gustavia is the place to head for late-night dancing. **Le Repaire** (⊠ Rue de la République, ☎ 590/27–72–48) in Gustavia lures a crowd for cocktail hour. **Le Select** (☎ 590/27–86–87) in Gustavia is St. Barths' original hangout, commemorated by Jimmy Buffet's "Cheeseburger in Paradise." The boisterous garden is where the barefoot boating set gathers for a brew.

Exploring St. Barthélemy

With a little practice, negotiating St. Barths' narrow, steep roads soon becomes fun. Free maps are everywhere, roads are well marked, and painted signs will point you where you want to be. Take along a towel, sandals, and a bottle of water on your explorations, and you will surely find a beach upon which to linger.

Numbers in the margin correspond to points of interest on the St. Barthélemy map.

SIGHTS TO SEE

❶ Anse des Flamands. From this wide, white-sand, hotel-lined beach, you can take a brisk hike to the top of the now-extinct volcano believed to have given birth to St. Barths.

⑤ Anse du Gouverneur. Legend has it that pirates' treasure is buried at this beautiful beach. The road here from Gustavia features spectacular vistas. If the weather is clear, you'll be able to see the islands of Saba, St. Eustatius, and St. Kitts from the beach.

❷ Corossol. The island's French provincial origins are most evident in this two-street fishing village with a little rocky beach. Residents speak an old Norman dialect, and a few of the older women still wear traditional garb—ankle-length dresses, bare feet, and starched white sunbonnets called *quichenottes* (kiss-me-not hats). The women don't like to be photographed, but they aren't shy about selling you some of their handmade straw work—handbags, baskets, broad-brim hats, and delicate strings of birds—made from lantana palms. The palms were introduced to the island 100 years ago by foresighted Father Morvan, who planted a grove in Corossol and Flamands, thus providing the country folk with a living that survives today. Here, too, is M. Ingenu Magras' **Inter Oceans Museum,** with more than 9,000 seashells from around the world. It also has a budding and intriguing collection of sand samples from around the world. ☎ *590/27–62–97. ☞ 20F. ☺ Tues.–Sun. 9–12:30 and 2–5.*

⑥ Grande Saline. The big salt ponds of Grande Saline are no longer in use, and the place looks a little desolate. Still, you should climb the short hillock behind the ponds for a surprise—the long arc of Anse de Grande Saline.

❹ Gustavia. You can easily explore all of Gustavia during a two-hour stroll. Street signs in both French and Swedish illustrate the island's history. Shops close from noon to 2, so plan lunch accordingly.

A good spot to park your car is rue de la République, where catamarans, yachts, and sailboats are moored. The **tourist office** (☎ 590/27–87–27) on the pier can provide maps and a wealth of information.

On the far side of the harbor known as La Pointe is the charming **Municipal Museum,** where you will find watercolors, portraits, photographs, and historic documents detailing the island's history as well as displays of the island's flowers, plants, and marine life. ☎ *599/29–71–55. ☞ 10F. ☺ Mon.–Thurs. 8:30–12:30 and 2:30–6, Fri. 8:30–12:30 and 3–6, Sat. 9–11.*

❼ Lorient. Site of the first French settlement, Lorient is one of the island's two parishes; a restored church, a school, and a post office mark the spot. Note the gaily decorated graves in the cemetery. One of St. Barths' treasured secrets is **Le Manoir** (☎ 590/27–79–27), a 1610 Norman manor that was painstakingly shipped from France and reconstructed here in 1984 by the charming Jeanne Audy Rowland in tribute to the island's Viking forebears. The tranquil surrounding courtyard and garden contain a waterfall and a lily-strewn pool. The Savoyard family, who purchased the property, graciously welcomes visitors. Look for the entrance by the Ligne St. Barth building.

❸ St-Jean. The ½-mi (¾-km) crescent of sand at St-Jean is the island's most popular beach. Windsurfers skim along the water here, catching the strong trade winds. A popular activity is watching and photographing the hair-raising airplane landings. You'll also find some of the best shopping on the island here, as well as several restaurants.

❽ Toiny coast. Over the hills beyond Grand Cul de Sac is this much-photographed coastline. Stone fences crisscross the steep slopes of Morne Vitet, one of many small mountains on St. Barths, along a rocky shore that resembles the rugged coast of Normandy.

ST. BARTHS A TO Z

To research prices, get advice from other travelers, and book travel arrangements, visit www.fodors.com.

AIR TRAVEL

The principal gateway from North America is St. Maarten's Juliana International Airport. Although it's only 10 minutes by air to St. Barths, the last two may take your breath away. Don't worry when you see those treetops out your window. You're just clearing a hill before dropping down to the runway of Aéroport de St-Jean (St-Jean Airport). Flights leave at least once an hour between 7:30 AM and 5:30 PM on Windward Islands Airways. St. Barth Commuter is another option.

Air Guadeloupe offers daily service from Espérance Airport, in St. Maarten, as well as direct flights to St. Barths from Guadeloupe and Puerto Rico. Air St. Thomas has daily flights to St. Barths from both St. Thomas and Puerto Rico.

You must reconfirm your return interisland flight, even during off-peak seasons, or you may very well lose your reservation. Be prepared to fly at a more convenient time for one of the airlines if it doesn't have enough passengers to justify a previously scheduled flight.
➤ AIRLINES AND CONTACTS: **Air Guadeloupe** (☎ 590/27–61–90); **Air St. Thomas** (☎ 590/27–71–76); **St. Barth Commuter** (☎ 590/27–54–54); **Windward Islands Airways** (☎ 590/27–61–01 or 800/634–4907).

AIRPORTS

Many hotels offer free airport shuttles. When you make your reservations, specify your arrival time. Hotels can be called from a free telephone in the arrivals building. Unmetered taxis cost $5–$20, depending on distance. Drivers set a fare before setting out, and it's usually not negotiable. The taxi dispatcher will help. If you have reserved a rental car, your name will be on a blackboard at the appropriate counter.
➤ AIRPORT INFORMATION: **Aéroport de St-Jean** (☎ 590/27–65–41); **Taxi dispatcher** (☎ 590/27–66–31).

BIKE AND AND MOPED TRAVEL

Several companies rent motorbikes, scooters, mopeds, and mountain bikes. Motorbikes go for about $30 per day and require a $100 deposit. Helmets are required.
➤ BIKE AND MOPED TRAVEL: **Boutique Harley Davidson** (☎ 590/27–70–59); **Duffau** (☎ 590/27–54–83); **St. Barths Motorbike** (☎ 590/27–67–89).

BOAT AND FERRY TRAVEL

Voyager offers ferry service for day trips between St. Barths, St. Maarten (both Phillipsburg and Marigot), and Saba. Round-trips for two are offered for $70. All service is from the Quai République.
➤ BOAT AND FERRY INFORMATION: *Voyager* (☎ 590/27–54–10).

BUSINESS HOURS

BANKS

Banks are generally open weekdays 8–noon and 2–3:30. There are 24-hour cash machines at most.

POST OFFICES

The main post office on rue Jeanne d'Arc in Gustavia is open Monday–Tuesday and Thursday–Friday 8–3, Wednesday and Saturday 8–noon. The branch in Lorient is open weekdays 7 AM–11 AM and Saturday 8 AM–10 AM. The post office in St-Jean opens Monday–Tuesday 8–2 and Wednesday and Saturday 8–noon.

SHOPS

Stores are generally open weekdays 8:30–noon and 2–5, Saturday 8:30–noon. Some of the shops across from the airport and in St-Jean stay open on Saturday afternoon and until 7 PM on weekdays. Although some shops are closed on Wednesday afternoon, most are open 8:30–noon and 3–6.

CAR RENTALS

In the last two years the dune-buggy-ish minimoke has largely been replaced with small four-wheel-drive vehicles, which provide a welcome increase of power and maneuverability on the steep, narrow roads. Be sure to check the brakes before you head out, and make a careful inventory of the existing dents and scrapes on the rental agreement.

You'll find major rental agencies at the airport, and all accept credit cards. Check with several counters for the best price. You must have a valid driver's license to rent, and in high season there may be a three-day minimum. Be sure to supply the licenses of all who might drive the car. During peak periods, such as Christmas week and February, be sure to arrange for your car rental ahead of time. Charges average about $55 a day; you may be able to bargain if you plan a stay longer than a week. When you make your hotel reservations, ask if the hotel has its own cars available to rent. Though the choice of vehicles may be limited, some hotels provide 24-hour emergency road service—something most rental companies don't offer.

Smart of St. Barth rent tiny, colorful vehicles (called "Smart Cars") that are the current rage.

➤ MAJOR AGENCIES: **Avis** (☎ 590/27–71–43); **Budget** (☎ 590/27–67–43); **Europcar** (☎ 590/27–73–33); **Gumbs** (☎ 590/27–75–32); **Hertz** (☎ 590/27–71–14); **Smart of St. Barth** (☎ 590/29–71–31).

CAR TRAVEL

Roads are sometimes unmarked, so be sure to get a map. Instead of road signs, look for signs pointing to a destination. These will be nailed to posts at all crossroads. Roads are narrow and sometimes very steep, so check the brakes and gears of your rental car before you drive away. Some hillside restaurants and hotels have steep entranceways and difficult steps that require a bit of climbing or negotiating.

GASOLINE

There are two gas stations on the island, one near the airport and one in Lorient. They aren't open after 5 PM or on Sunday, but you can use the one near the airport at any time with some credit cards, including JCB or Carte Blanche—but not Visa, MasterCard, or American Express. A full tank of gas runs $13–$15; considering the short distances, this should last you most of a week.

RULES OF THE ROAD

St. Barths drivers often seem to be in an unending grand prix and thus tend to keep their cars maxed out, especially and inexplicably when in reverse. Parking is an additional challenge.

ELECTRICITY

Voltage is 220 AC, 60 cycles, as in Europe. You can sometimes use American appliances with French plug converters and transformers. Most hotel rooms are conveniently supplied with hair dryers.

EMERGENCIES

The tourist office can provide an up-to-date list of local health professionals.

➤ AMBULANCE AND FIRE: Dial ☎ 18 or 590/27–62–31 for the ambulance.
➤ HOSPITALS: **Gustavia Clinic** (⊠ Rue Jean Bart, at rue Sadi Carnot, ☎ 590/27–60–35; 590/27–76–03 for the doctor on call).
➤ PHARMACIES: Pharmacies are located at ⊠ Quai République, Gustavia, ☎ 590/27–61–82 and ⊠ La Savane Commercial Center, St-Jean, ☎ 590/27–66–61.
➤ POLICE: Dial ☎ 17 or 590/27–66–66.

FESTIVALS AND SEASONAL EVENTS

In January, St. Barths hosts an international collection of musicians as part of the St. Barths Music Festival. February brings a flood of feasting, dancing, music, and parades during Carnival season. The Caribbean Film Festival takes place in early April. On July 14 Bastille Day is celebrated with a parade, a regatta, parties, and a fireworks display. In early December the annual St. Barths Marble Tournament attracts contestants of all ages.

HEALTH

The manchineel tree has poisonous green apples, and raindrops falling off its acidic leaves can cause painful blisters. Depending on the season, you might need insect repellent.

HOLIDAYS

Public holidays for 2002 are: New Year's Day, Easter weekend (Apr. 13–15), Labor Day (May 1), Pentecost (June 11), Bastille Day (July 14), Pitea Day (commemorates the joining of St. Barths with Pitea in Sweden, Aug. 15), All Saints' Day (Nov. 1), Armistice Day (Nov. 11), and Christmas.

LANGUAGE

French is the official language, so it can't hurt to pack a phrase book and/or a French dictionary. If you speak any French at all, don't be shy. You may also hear Creole, the regional French dialect called patois, and even the Creole of Guadeloupe. Most hotel and restaurant employees speak some English—at least enough to help you find what you need.

MAIL AND SHIPPING

Mail is slow. Correspondence between the U.S. and the island can take up to three weeks to arrive. Post offices are in Gustavia, St-Jean, and Lorient. It costs 3.10FF to mail a postcard to the United States, 3.90FF to mail a letter. When writing to an establishment on St. Barths, be sure to include "French West Indies" at the end of the address. Faxes are widely used.
➤ CONTACTS: **Main post office** (⊠ rue Jeanne d'Arc Gustavia, ☎ 590/ 27–62–00).

MONEY MATTERS

Prices quoted in this chapter are in U.S. dollars unless otherwise noted.

ATMS

There are 24-hour cash machines at most banks.

CREDIT CARDS

Credit cards are accepted at most shops, hotels, and restaurants. Paying with a credit card will generally yield a better exchange rate than what the individual restaurant or shop will offer.

CURRENCY

The French franc is legal tender until June 2001, when the euro will replace it, but U.S. dollars are accepted in most establishments (though you may receive change in francs). Figure about 7 francs to the U.S. dollar.

PASSPORTS AND VISAS
All foreign visitors need a passport and a return or ongoing ticket.

SAFETY
There is essentially no crime on St. Barth. Visitors can travel anywhere on the island with confidence.

SIGHTSEEING TOURS
You can arrange island tours by minibus or car at hotel desks, through the tourist office, or through any of the island's taxi operators in Gustavia or at the airport. Wish Agency can arrange customized tours, as well as take care of airline ticketing, event planning, maid service, and private party arrangements.
➤ CONTACTS: **Gustavia taxi dispatcher** (☎ 590/27–66–31); **St. Jean Airport taxi dispatcher** (☎ 590/27–75–81); **Wish Agency** (☎ 590/29–83–74, FAX 590/29–83–75).

TAXES
DEPARTURE TAX
The island charges a 10F departure tax when your next stop is another French island, 16F if you're off to anywhere else.

SALES TAX
Some hotels add a 10%–15% service charge to bills; others include it in their tariffs.

TAXIS
Taxis are expensive and not particularly easy to arrange, especially in the evening. There's a taxi station at the airport and another in Gustavia; from elsewhere you must contact a dispatcher in Gustavia or St. Jean. There's a flat rate of 25F for rides up to five minutes long. Each additional three minutes is 20F. Usually, however, cabbies name a fixed rate—and will not budge. Fares are 50% higher from 8 PM to 6 AM and on Sunday and holidays.
➤ CONTACTS: **Gustavia taxi dispatcher** (☎ 590/27–66–31); **St. Jean taxi dispatcher** (☎ 590/27–75–81).

TELEPHONES
MCI and AT&T services are available. Public telephones do not accept coins; they accept *télécartes,* prepaid calling cards that you can buy at the gas station next to the airport and at post offices in Lorient, St-Jean, and Gustavia. Making an international call using a télécarte is much less expensive than making it through your hotel.

If you would like to retrieve e-mail while you're on the island, the best bet is a visit to the Internet Service at Centre Alizes, which has fax service and 10 computers on line. They are open weekdays, 8:30–12:30 and 2:30–7, as well as Saturday morning. France Télécom can provide you with temporary Internet access that may let you connect your laptop. They can also arrange cellular phone service.

COUNTRY AND AREA CODES
To phone St. Barths from the U.S., dial 011–590 and the local six-digit number.

INTERNATIONAL CALLS
To call the U.S. from St. Barths, dial 001, the area code, and the local number.

LOCAL CALLS
For St. Barths and St. Martin dial just the six-digit number.
➤ E-MAIL SERVICE CONTACTS: **Centre Alizes** (✉ Rue de la République, Gustavia, ☎ 590/29–89–89, WEB centralizes@wanadoo.fr); **France Télé-com** (✉ Espace Neptune, St-Jean).

TIPPING
Restaurants include a 15% service charge in their published prices, but it is common French practice to leave 5–10% *pourboire* (literally: for a drink) and no more on top of this. Keep this in mind that when your credit-card receipt is presented to be signed, the tip space should be blank—just draw a line through it—or you could end up paying a 30% service charge. Most taxi drivers don't expect a tip.

TRANSPORTATION AROUND ST. BARTHS
HITCHHIKING
Hitching rides is a popular, legal, and interesting way to get around. It's widely practiced in the more heavily trafficked areas on the island. But there is more and more traffic, so be careful.

VISITOR INFORMATION
A daily news sheet called *NEWS* that lists local happenings like special dinners or music is available at markets and newsstands. You will also find free, weekly *Journal de Saint-Barth*—although mostly in French—is useful for current events. The small *Ti Gourmet Saint-Barth* is a free pocket-size guidebook that is invaluable for addresses and telephone numbers of restaurants and services; pick one up anywhere.
➤ BEFORE YOU LEAVE: **French West Indies Tourist Board** (✉ 610 5th Ave., New York, NY 10020, WEB www.fgtousa.org); **France-on-Call** (☎ 900/990–0040) charges a fee; **French Government Tourist Office** (✉ 444 Madison Ave., 16th Floor, New York, NY 10022; ✉ 9454 Wilshire Blvd., Suite 303, Beverly Hills, CA 90212, ☎ 213/272–2661; ✉ 645 N. Michigan Ave., Suite 3360, Chicago, IL 60611, ☎ 312/337–6301; in Canada: ✉ 1981 McGill College Ave., Suite 490, Montréal, Québec, H3A 2W9, Canada, ☎ 514/288–4264; ✉ 30 St. Patrick St., Suite 700, Toronto, Ontario, M5T 3A3, Canada, ☎ 416/593–4723; in the U.K.: ✉ 178 Piccadilly, London W1V OAL, U.K., ☎ 0171/629–9376).
➤ IN ST. BARTHS: **Office du Tourisme** (✉ Quai Général-de-Gaulle, ☎ 590/27–87–27, FAX 590/27–74–47).

18 ST. EUSTATIUS

Updated by
Suzanne
Gordon

Down a country road that seems to lead to nowhere, the rural dwelling of the Berkel family appears. Ismael Berkel wanders through, showing guests his family's heirlooms, photos of his ancestors from a century ago. It's easy to see why he's proud of this property, part of the 82-acre original plantation. The charming clapboard houses, each one room in size, hold the past: the family Bible, old glasses, even the old Singer that Pa gave Ma in 1944. Such was life in Statia's past, but the times here haven't changed all that much.

The tiny Dutch island of St. Eustatius, commonly called Statia (pronounced *stay*-sha), in the Netherlands Antilles, is ideal for those with a penchant for quiet times and strolls through history. It was once one of the most powerful merchant centers in the Caribbean; today it's home to remnants of those times—forts, narrow cobblestone streets, and historic buildings. Statians themselves are reason enough to visit. So is the landing approach: in the distance looms the Quill, an extinct volcano with a primeval rain forest in its crater.

This 12-square-mi (31-square-km) island that Columbus sailed past in 1493 prospered from the day the Dutch Zeelanders colonized it in 1636. In the 1700s a double row of warehouses crammed with goods stretched 1 mi (1½ km) along the bay, and there were sometimes as many as 200 ships tied up at the duty-free port. The island was called the Emporium of the Western World and Golden Rock. There were almost 8,000 Statians in the 1790s (today the population is about 2,700). Holland, England, and France fought over the island, which changed hands 22 times. It has been a Dutch possession, however, since 1816.

During the American War of Independence, when the British blockaded the North American coast, food, arms, and other supplies for the revolutionaries were diverted to the West Indies, notably to neutral Statia (Benjamin Franklin had his mail routed through the island to ensure its safe arrival in Europe). On November 16, 1776, the brig-of-war *Andrew Doria*, commanded by Captain Isaiah Robinson of the Continental Navy, sailed into Statia's port flying the Stars and Stripes. The ship fired a 13-gun salute to the Royal Netherlands standard, and Governor Johannes de Graaff ordered the cannons of Ft. Oranje to return the salute. That first official acknowledgment of the new American flag by a foreign power earned Statia the nickname America's Childhood

Friend. In retaliation, British admiral George Rodney attacked and destroyed much of the island in 1781. Statia has yet to recover its prosperity, which, ironically, ended partly because of the American Revolution's success: the island was no longer needed as a trans-shipment port, and its bustling economy gradually came to a stop.

Statia is in the Dutch Windward Triangle, 178 mi (287 km) east of Puerto Rico and 35 mi (56 km) south of St. Maarten. Oranjestad, the capital and only "city," is on the western side, facing the calm Caribbean. On the eastern side are the often-rough waters of the Atlantic. The island is anchored at the north and the south by extinct volcanoes separated by a central, dry plain. The higher elevations are alive with greenery and abloom with flowers—bougainvillea, oleander, and hibiscus.

Statia is a playground for divers and hikers. Colorful coral reefs and myriad ships rest on the ocean floor alongside 18th-century warehouses that were slowly absorbed by the sea. On land, much of the activity involves archaeology and restoration; students come here to study pre-Columbian artifacts, and the island's historical foundation restores local landmarks. Statia is also a way station for oil, with a 16-million-barrel storage bunker encased in the Boven, an extinct volcano on the island's northern end. On any given day there are several oil tankers at anchor waiting to give or receive the liquid gold.

Most visitors will be content with a day visit from nearby St. Maarten, exploring some of the historical sights and maybe enjoying a meal. Those who stay longer tend to be collectors of unspoiled islands with a need to relax and a taste for history. Statians are mindful of the potential gold mine of tourism, and, in addition to preserving many historical buildings and forts, they're expanding the island's pier and improving its infrastructure. But it may be the locals themselves who make coming here such a pleasure. Folks in these parts still say hello to strangers, and drivers wave or beep to one another.

Lodging

None of Statia's accommodations could be considered luxury. Cheerful, tidy, and homey are the best you can expect, and all (at press time, Statia had only three hotels) have 20 units or less; room decor and furnishing are eclectic but comfortable. If there's a philosophy to owning and running a hostelry on Statia, it's "do what you can with what you have."

Renting an apartment is another lodging alternative. Although Statia has only a handful of them, several new properties have gone up recently to meet demand. Figure on $50 or less per night, and don't expect much beyond a bathroom and kitchenette. **Country Inn** (☎ 599/318–2484), in Biesheuvelweg near the airport, is one of the newer apartment houses. Check with the tourist office for more options.

CATEGORY	COST*
$$$	over $125
$$	$90–$125
$	under $90

All prices are for a standard double room, excluding 7% room tax and 3% turnover tax, and 10%–15% service charge.

$$$ ⊞ **The Gin House.** This gracious old waterfront building—recently renovated by the same people who run the Holland House hotel on St. Maarten—is a wonderful addition to Statia's hotel scene. Rooms are simply decorated and face a courtyard with a pool. At press time, construction had begun on several new rooms across the street on the

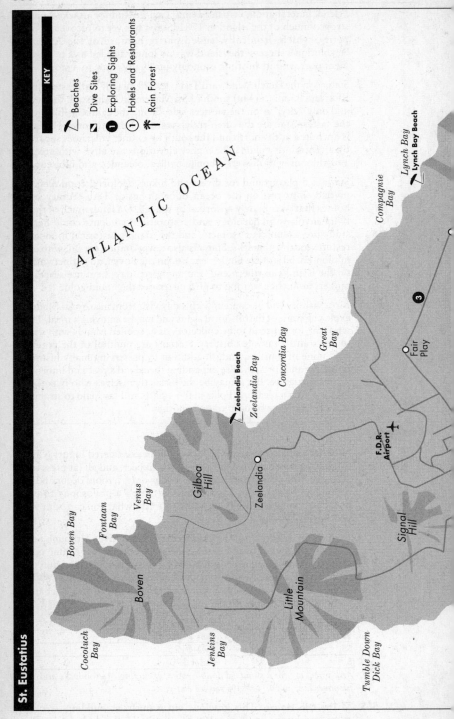

St. Eustatius

KEY

Beaches
Dive Sites
Exploring Sights
Hotels and Restaurants
Rain Forest

ATLANTIC OCEAN

Cocoluch Bay

Boven Bay

Fontaan Bay

Venus Bay

Boven

Jenkins Bay

Gilboa Hill

Zeelandia

Little Mountain

Tumble Down Dick Bay

Zeelandia Beach

Zeelandia Bay

Concordia Bay

Great Bay

Signal Hill

F.D.R. Airport

Fair Play

Compagnie Bay

Lynch Bay

Lynch Bay Beach

❸

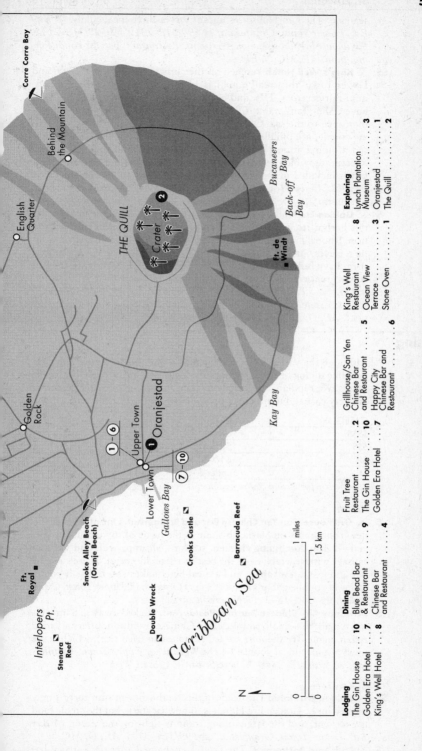

Lodging

The Gin House 10
Golden Era Hotel 7
King's Well Hotel 8

Dining

Blue Bead Bar
& Restaurant 9
Chinese Bar
and Restaurant 4

Fruit Tree
Restaurant 2
The Gin House 10
Golden Era Hotel 7

Grillhouse/San Yen
Chinese Bar
and Restaurant 5
Happy City
Chinese Bar and
Restaurant 6

King's Well
Restaurant 8
Ocean View
Terrace 3
Stone Oven 1

Exploring

Lynch Plantation
Museum 3
Oranjestad 1
The Quill 2

sea side. The Gin House restaurant serves three meals daily. ✉ *Bay Rd., Lower Town, Oranjestad,* ☎ *599/318–2319,* ℻ *599/318–2135,* 🌐 *www.oldginhouse.com. 14 rooms. Restaurant, bar, air-conditioning, pool. AE, MC, V. EP.*

$$ 🏨 **King's Well Hotel.** Perched on the cliffs between Upper Town and
★ Lower Town, this small hotel has 14 pleasant rooms with balconies, mini-refrigerators, TVs, and baths. The four large rooms at the back have ceiling fans, cable TV, queen-size waterbeds, and French doors that open to the sea. Owners Win and Laura Piechutzki, an expatriate couple, are building an exercise room and pool. The make-yourself-at-home atmosphere includes an honor bar in the King's Well Restaurant, which serves guests three meals a day (though only breakfast is included in the rates) and is open to the public for dinner. ✉ *Bay Rd., Lower Town, Oranjestad,* ☎ ℻ *599/318–2538. 14 rooms. Restaurant, bar, refrigerators. D, MC, V. BP.*

$ 🏨 **Golden Era Hotel.** Don't be put off by the 1960s-style motel look: this harbor-front hotel has a friendly staff and a central seaside location. Rooms have tile floors, mini-refrigerators, TVs, phones, and little terraces. Just be sure to ask for a room with a view; only half of them have full or partial sea vistas. The Golden Era Hotel restaurant serves great creole food. ✉ *Bay Rd., Lower Town (Box 109), Oranjestad,* ☎ *599/318–2345 or 800/223–9815,* ℻ *599/318–2445. 19 rooms, 1 suite. Restaurant, bar, air-conditioning, refrigerators, saltwater pool. AE, D, MC, V. EP, MAP.*

Dining

Although the variety of cuisine available may surprise you, don't expect fine dining or fancy restaurants. Your best bet is to eat local style; that is, West Indian, and keep your expectations simple. All restaurants are very casual, but do cover up your beachwear.

CATEGORY	COST*
$$$$	over $35
$$$	$25–$35
$$	$15–$25
$	under $15

per person for a main course at dinner

ASIAN

$ ✕ **Grillhouse/San Yen Chinese Bar and Restaurant.** One of several Chinese restaurants on Statia, this one in the heart of town touts its special—a dish combining chicken, scallops, shrimp, beef, and Chinese sausage with vegetables—as the best entrée on the menu. There's a small bar and just a few tables, and a meal here makes you feel as if you're eating at your neighbor's house. ✉ *Fort Oranjestad, Upper Town, Oranjestad,* ☎ *599/318–2915. No credit cards.*

$ ✕ **Happy City Chinese Bar and Restaurant.** Tucked away in a little intown mall, this small, simple, clean Chinese restaurant offers a varied Asian menu. Try the *nasi goreng* (Indonesian fried rice), which is the most popular local choice. ✉ *De Windtweg, Upper Town, Oranjestad,* ☎ *599/318–2540. No credit cards. Closed Wed.*

CARIBBEAN

$$ ✕ **Golden Era Hotel.** The decor of this establishment (not surprisingly located in the Golden Era Hotel) is somewhat stark, but the creole food is excellent, and the large dining room is right on the water. ✉ *Bay Rd., Lower Town, Oranjestad,* ☎ *599/318–2345. AE, D, MC, V.*

$ ✕ **Fruit Tree Restaurant.** The Fruit Tree, named after the papaya, ba-
★ nana, and soursop trees that grow on its grounds, serves heaping plates of West Indian specialties: bull-foot soup (a stew with vegetables and

beef), goat water, oxtail, and rice. Top it all off with johnnycakes and bush tea. There are only four tables on the patio, but you won't wait long, if at all. Next door is a small crafts shop. ⊠ *484 Prinsesweg, Upper Town, Oranjestad,* ☎ *599/318–2584. No credit cards. Closed Mon.*

$ ✕ **Stone Oven.** A Spanish couple runs this cozy eatery, offering such West Indian specialties as "goat water" (goat stew). You can eat inside the little house, which is in a residential neighborhood, or outside on the palm-fringed patio. ⊠ *16A Feaschweg, Upper Town, Oranjestad,* ☎ *599/318–2543. No credit cards.*

ECLECTIC

$$$$ ✕ **The Gin House.** A new chef, Tresa Soewondo, has brought unique food, blending cuisine from her native Surinam and the Caribbean to this charming, old-world style restaurant in The Gin House hotel. The result is something exotic for Statia, where most of the food is classic West Indian. Whether you eat inside or on the front porch, the ambience is casual yet elegant, and your fellow diners will no doubt include everyone from divers to government officials. Reservations are a good idea. ⊠ *Bay Rd., Lower Town,* ☎ *599/318–2319. AE, MC, V.*

$$$ ✕ **King's Well Restaurant.** It's like watching mom and dad make dinner to see owners Win and Laura Piechutzki scurry around their open kitchen preparing the night's meal in this breezy terrace eatery. And don't expect to eat alone, because a meal here makes you part of the family at the King's Well Hotel. Overlooking the sea, the restaurant is run by this fun-loving expatriate couple. The steaks are from Colorado, the lobster is fresh, and the *rostbraten* (roast beef) and schnitzels are authentic: Win is German. ⊠ *Bay Rd., Lower Town, Oranjestad,* ☎ *599/318–2538. D, MC, V.*

$$ ✕ **Blue Bead Bar & Restaurant.** Right on the waterfront, this attractive
★ eatery is the perfect spot for a sunset cocktail. Meals are served on a cheery, bright blue-and-yellow-trimmed veranda decked with potted plants; the fare runs the gamut of influences: West Indian, Indonesian, Dutch, Mexican, and American. The daily specials are recommended, as is anything served with the *saté* sauce—a spicy, peanutty heaven. Fridays are seafood nights; and Saturdays for families, when the kids (of any age) can enjoy the Blue Bead Baby Bimmer Burger. ⊠ *Bay Rd., Lower Town, Oranjestad,* ☎ *599/318–2873. AE, D, MC, V.*

$$ ✕ **Ocean View Terrace.** This patio spot in the courtyard next to the tourist office serves sandwiches and burgers at lunch, and local cuisine—baked snapper with shrimp sauce, spicy chicken, tenderloin steak—at dinner (you can get breakfast here, too). The courtyard is surrounded by the beautiful old stone fort and government buildings. ⊠ *Oranjestraat, Upper Town, Oranjestad,* ☎ *599/318–2934. No credit cards. No lunch Sun.*

$ ✕ **Chinese Bar and Restaurant.** Owner Kim Cheng serves up tasty Asian and Caribbean dishes—*bami goreng* (Indonesian noodles with bits of beef, pork, or shrimp as well as tomatoes, carrots, bean sprouts, cabbage, soy sauce, and spices) and Spanish pork chops, for example—in hearty portions at his unpretentious establishment. Dining indoors can be claustrophobic; just ask your waitress if you may tote your Formica-top table out onto the terrace. She'll probably be happy to lend a hand and then serve you under the stars. ⊠ *Prinsesweg, Upper Town, Oranjestad,* ☎ *599/318–2389. No credit cards.*

Beaches

Beachcombing on Statia is for the intrepid: the beaches are pristine but unmaintained and occasionally rocky. Sand is mainly volcanic black and gray. The nicest strands are on the Atlantic side, but the surf is generally too rough for swimming. You can (though it's not recommended) hike around the coast at low tide; but driving is the best way to reach remote Atlantic stretches. A big deal on the beaches here is searching for Statia's famed blue-glass beads. Manufactured in the 17th century by the Dutch West Indies Company, these beads were traded for rum, slaves, cotton, and tobacco. Although they're found only on Statia, some researchers believe that it was beads like these that were traded for Manhattan. They're best unearthed after a heavy rain, but as the locals chuckle, "If you find one, it's a miracle, man."

A 30-minute hike down an easy, marked trail behind the Mountain Road will bring you to **Corre Corre Bay** and its gold-sand cove. Two bends north of Corre Corre Bay, **Lynch Bay** is somewhat protected from the wild swells. On the Atlantic side, especially around Concordia Bay, the surf is rough, and there's sometimes an undertow, making beaches better for sunning than swimming. **Smoke Alley Beach** (also called Oranje Beach) is the nicest and most accessible. The beige-and-black-sand beach is on the Caribbean, off Lower Town, and is relatively deserted until late afternoon, when the locals arrive. **Zeelandia Beach** is a 2-mi (3-km) strip of black sand on the Atlantic side. A dangerous undertow runs here, but a small section is considered okay for swimming. It's a lovely, deserted stretch for sunning, walking, and wading.

Outdoor Activities and Sports

Participant Sports

FISHING

By and large, deep-sea fishing is not a major activity off Statia's shores. But it's nice to be out on the water. **Golden Rock Dive Center** (✉ Bay Rd., Lower Town, Oranjestad, ☎ FAX 599/318–2964) offers full- and half-day trips for $500 and $350, respectively, including gear and bait.

HIKING

Trails range from the easy to the "Watch out!" The big thrill here is the Quill, the 1,968-ft (602-m) extinct volcano with its crater full of rain forest. Give yourself two to three hours to make the climb and the return. The tourist office has a list of 12 marked trails and can put you in touch with a guide (whose fee will be about $20). On May 4, 1998, the Quill National Park was formed, and later that year a new trail into the crater was created: longer and windier but easier and safer. Maps are available at the Saba Marine Park headquarters on Bay Road. Wear layers: it can be cool on the summit and steamy in the interior.

SCUBA DIVING AND SNORKELING

Statia has more than 30 dive sites protected by the Saba Marine Park, which has an office on Bay Road in Lower Town. Both this park and Quill National Park are under the supervision of STENAPA (the St. Eustatius National Parks Foundation). You pay $3 per dive to help offset the costs of preserving the coral and other sea life here.

Barracudas swim around colorful coral walls at **Barracuda Reef,** off the island's southwest coast. At **Double Wreck,** just offshore from Lower Town, you'll find two tall-masted ships that date from the 1700s. The coral has taken on the shape of these two disintegrated vessels, and the site attracts large schools of fish, sting rays, and moray eels. Off the island's western shore, **Stenapa Reef** is an artificial reef created from the wrecks of barges, a harbor boat, and other ship parts. Large grouper and turtles are among the marine life you'll spot here. For snorkelers, **Crooks Castle** has several stands of pillar coral, giant yellow sea fans, and sea whips just southwest of Lower Town.

With 5,000 dives out of Statia each year—and the numbers are growing—the island's three dive shops along Bay Road in Lower Town are busy. They rent all types of gear (including snorkeling gear for about $20 a day), offer certification courses, and organize dive trips. The average cost of a one-tank dive is $35; two-tank dives run around $65. **Dive Statia** (✉ Bay Rd., Lower Town, Oranjestad, ☎ 599/318–2435), a fully equipped and PADI-certified dive shop (it has received PADI's five-star Gold Palm Designation), is operated by Rudy and Rinda Hees out of a warehouse. In addition to offering standard courses, Dive Statia also offers underwater photography courses and night and multi-level dives. They have recently added Nitrox diving. **Golden Rock Dive Center** (✉ Bay Rd., Lower Town, Oranjestad, ☎ FAX 599/318–2964 or 800/311–6658) is another of Statia's PADI facilities. The staff here specializes in custom dive trips. **Scubaqua** (✉ Golden Era Hotel, Bay Rd., Lower Town, Oranjestad, ☎ 599/318–2345, FAX 599/318–2160) has a variety of dive courses, which are offered in various languages.

WATERSKIING

Dive operators **Dive Statia** and **Scubaqua** will also take you waterskiing for $90 per hour. Scubaqua offers wake boarding (riding on a small, short surfboard, while kneeling or standing and being towed by a boat) for the same price.

Spectator Sports

Cricket and soccer matches are played at the sports complex in Upper Town. Statia hosts teams from other Caribbean islands on weekends; admission is free. Call the office of the **sports coordinator** (☎ 599/318–2330 or 599/318–2209) for schedules.

Shopping

Though shopping here is duty-free, it's also very limited. Other than the predictable souvenirs, there's not much to buy. Look for the wonderful new book by Saban artist Heleen Cornett *St. Eustatius: Echoes of the Past,* sold in several stores. **Mazinga Gift Shop** (☎ 599/318–2245), on Fort Oranjestraat in Upper Town, is a small department store of sorts, selling basic necessities. The **Paper Corner** (✉ Van Tonningenweg, Upper Town, ☎ 599/318–2208) sells magazines, a few books, and stationery supplies.

Nightlife

Statia's nightlife is far from brisk. Local bands play around the island on weekends, and the hotels are good places to have a few quiet drinks. Sometimes the **community center** (✉ Rosemary Laan, Upper Town, Oranjestad, ☎ 599/318–2249) holds a dance. **Cool Corner** (☎ 599/318–2523), a tiny corner bar in the heart of town, across from the St. Eustatius Historical Foundation Museum, is a lively after-work and weekend hangout.

Exploring St. Eustatius

Statia is an arid island consisting of a valley between two mountain peaks. Most sights lie in the valley, making touring the island easy. From the airport you can rent a car or take a taxi and be in historic Oranjestad in minutes; to hike the Quill, Statia's highest peak, you can drive to the trailhead in less than 15 minutes from just about anywhere.

Numbers in the margin correspond to points of interest on the St. Eustatius map.

SIGHTS TO SEE

❸ **Lynch Plantation Museum.** Also known as the Berkel Family Plantation, this museum consists of two one-room buildings, set up as they were almost 100 years ago. A remarkable collection preserves this family's history—pictures, Bibles, spectacles, original furniture, and farming and fishing implements give a detailed perspective of life on Statia. You'll need either a taxi or a car to visit, and it's well worth the trouble. ⊠ *Lynch Bay,* ☎ *599/318–2209 to arrange tour.* 🎫 *Free (donations accepted).*

❶ Oranjestad. Statia's capital and only town sits on the west coast facing the Caribbean. Both Upper Town and Lower Town are easy to explore on foot. History buffs will enjoy poking around the Dutch colonial buildings, which are being restored by the historical foundation. At the tourist office, right in the charming courtyard of the government offices, you can pick up maps, brochures, advice, and a listing of 12 marked trails. You can also arrange for guides and tours.

With its three bastions, **Ft. Oranje** has clutched these cliffs since 1636. In 1976 Statia participated in the U.S. bicentennial celebration by restoring the fort, and now the black cannons point out over the ramparts. In the parade grounds a plaque, presented in 1939 by Franklin D. Roosevelt, reads, HERE THE SOVEREIGNTY OF THE UNITED STATES OF AMERICA WAS FIRST FORMALLY ACKNOWLEDGED TO A NATIONAL VESSEL BY A FOREIGN OFFICIAL.

In the center of Upper Town is the award-winning **St. Eustatius Historical Foundation Museum.** It's in the Doncker House, where British admiral Rodney set up his headquarters during the American Revolution. While here, he confiscated everything from gunpowder to port in retaliation for Statia's gallant support of the fledgling country. The house, acquired by the foundation in 1983 and completely restored, is Statia's most important intact 18th-century dwelling. Exhibits trace the island's history from the 6th century to the present. The basement exhibit details Statia's pre-Columbian history with the results of archaeological digs. Statia is the only island thus far where ruins and artifacts of the Saladoid, a newly discovered tribe, have been excavated. ⊠ *3 Wilhelminaweg,* ☎ *599/318–2288.* 🎫 *$2.* ⊙ *Weekdays 9–5, weekends 9–noon.*

The Dutch Reformed Church, on Kerkweg (Church Way), was built in 1775. It has been partially restored and has lovely stone arches that face the sea. Ancient tales can be read on the gravestones in the adjacent 18th-century cemetery. On Synagogepad (Synagogue Path), off Kerkweg, is Honen Dalim ("She Who Is Charitable to the Poor"), one of the Caribbean's oldest synagogues. Dating from 1738, it's now in ruins but is slated for restoration.

Lower Town sits below Ft. Oranjestraat (Fort Orange Street) and some steep cliffs and is reached from Upper Town on foot via the zigzagging, cobblestone Fort Road or by car via Van Tonningenweg. Warehouses and shops that were piled high with European imports in the 18th century are either abandoned or simply used to store local fishermen's equipment. Along the waterfront is a lovely park with palms, flowering shrubs, and benches—the work of the historical foundation. Peeking out from the shallow waters are the crumbling ruins of 18th-century buildings, from Statia's days as the merchant hub of the Caribbean. The sea has slowly advanced since then, and it now surrounds many of the stone and brick ruins, making for fascinating snorkeling.

❷ The Quill. This extinct 1,968-ft-high (602-m-high) volcano has a primeval rain forest in its crater. If you like to hike, you'll want to head here to see giant elephant ears, ferns, flowers, wild orchids, fruit trees, and birds hiding in the trees. You might also encounter an endangered *iguana delicatissima* (a large—sometimes several feet long—greenish-gray creature with spines down its back). The volcanic cone rises 3 mi (5 km) south of Oranjestad on the main road. Local boys go up to the Quill by torchlight to catch delectable land crabs. The tourist board will help you make hiking arrangements.

ST. EUSTATIUS A TO Z

To research prices, get advice from other travelers, and book travel arrangements, visit www.fodors.com.

AIR TRAVEL

Windward Islands Airways makes the 20-minute flight from St. Maarten to Statia's Franklin Delano Roosevelt Airport several times a day, the 10-minute flight from Saba daily, and the 15-minute flight from St. Kitts twice a week in high season. Be sure to confirm your flight a day or two ahead; schedules change abruptly.

➤ AIRLINES AND CONTACTS: **Windward Islands Airways** (Winair; ☎ 599/318–2362).

➤ AIRPORT INFORMATION: **Franklin Delano Roosevelt Airport** (☎ 599/318–2362).

BUSINESS HOURS

BANKS

Banks have varying hours: Barclays Bank is open weekdays 8:30–3:30; Windward Islands Bank is open weekdays 8:30–noon and 1–3:30.

POST OFFICES

Post offices are open weekdays 8–noon and 1–4 or 5.

SHOPS

Shops are open 8–6, and grocery stores often stay open until 7.

CAR RENTALS

To explore the island (and there isn't very much of it), car rentals, which cost about $40 to $45 a day, do the job. Local agencies have a variety of rentals: Brown's rents Mazdas, Suzuki Altos, and sometimes has pick-ups; Walter's rent cars and Jeeps; Rainbow Car Rental has several Hyundais available.

➤ MAJOR AGENCIES: **Brown's** (✉ White Wall Rd. 8, Oranjestad, ☎ 599/318–2266); **Rainbow Car Rental** (✉ Statia Mall, Oranjestad, ☎ 599/318–2811);**Walter's** (✉ Chapel Piece, Oranjestad, ☎ 599/318–2719).

GASOLINE

The island's only gas station—at the south end of Lower Town on the waterfront—is open daily 7:30–7. Gas costs about $1 per liter ($4 per gallon).

ROAD CONDITIONS

Statia's roads are pocked with potholes, and the going is slow and bumpy.

ELECTRICITY

Statia, like the other islands of the Netherlands Antilles, uses a 110/120-volt system, the same as in North America.

EMERGENCIES

➤ AMBULANCE AND FIRE: Fire: dial ☎ 120; Ambulance: dial ☎ 140.

➤ HOSPITALS: **Queen Beatrix Medical Center** (✉ 25 Prinsesweg, ☎ 599/318–2211 or 599/318–2371) has a full-time licensed physician on duty.

➤ PHARMACIES: There's a pharmacy at the medical center. Dial ☎ 599/318–2211 or 599/318–2371.

➤ POLICE: Dial (☎ 599/318–2333 or ☎ 111).
➤ SCUBA DIVING EMERGENCIES: **Saba Marine Park Hyperbaric Facility**
(✉ Fort Bay, Saba, ☎ 599/416–4395).

ETIQUETTE AND BEHAVIOR

Statians tend to emphasize social niceties, and everyone seems to have
time for a "Good morning," or a "Hello." Do the same, and you'll
find it opens doors and hearts.

FESTIVALS AND SEASONAL EVENTS

Statia celebrates Carnival for a week in July, and the events include
parades (culminating in the Grand Carnival Parade), street parties
called "jump-ups," local and imported steel-pan bands, sports activities, and food tastings.

HOLIDAYS

Public holidays for the year 2002 are: New Year's Day, Good Friday
(Mar. 29), Easter Monday (Apr. 1), Coronation Day and the Queen's
Birthday (Apr. 30, celebrating the birthday and the coronation of Hol-
land's Queen Beatrix), Labor Day (May 1), Ascension Day (May 24),
Emancipation Day (July 1), Statia-America Day (Nov. 16, commem-
orating the events of 1776, when Statia became the first foreign gov-
ernment to salute the American flag), Christmas, and Boxing Day
(Dec. 26).

LANGUAGE

Statia's official language is Dutch (it's used in government documents),
but everyone speaks English. Dutch is taught as the primary language
in the schools, and street signs are in both Dutch and English.

MAIL AND SHIPPING

The post office is in Upper Town, near the police station on Cot-
tagewege. Airmail letters to North America and Europe are NAf2.25;
postcards, NAf1.10. When sending letters to the island, be sure to include "Netherlands Antilles" and "Caribbean" in the address.

MONEY MATTERS

Prices quoted throughout this chapter are in U.S. dollars unless noted
otherwise.

ATMS

There are no ATMs on the island.

CURRENCY

U.S. dollars are accepted everywhere, but legal tender is the Netherlands Antilles florin (NAf), also referred to as the guilder, and you should-
n't be surprised to receive change in them. The exchange rate fluctuates
slightly but was about NAf1.77 to US$1 at press time. The island's
two banks in Upper Town provide foreign-exchange services.
➤ BANKS: **Barclays Bank** (☎ 599/318–2392); **Windward Islands Bank**
(☎ 599/318–2846).

PASSPORTS AND VISAS

U.S. and Canadian visitors must have proof of citizenship. A valid passport is best, but a birth certificate with a raised seal along with a government-authorized photo ID will do. British citizens need a valid
passport. All visitors need a return or ongoing ticket.

SAFETY

Statia is relatively crime-free, but common sense should prevail. Lock
your rental car when leaving it, store valuables in the hotel safe, and
lock your hotel room door behind you. When driving, particularly at

night, be on the lookout for goats and other animals that have wandered onto the road. While hiking you might see the harmless racer snake sunning itself. These snakes are afraid of people and will promptly leave when you arrive.

SIGHTSEEING TOURS

All 10 of Statia's taxis are available for island tours. A two- to three-hour outing costs $40 per vehicle of four (extra persons are $5 each), usually including airport transfer. One of the better taxi tour operators is driver-historian Josser Daniel; ask him to show you his citation from President Clinton for rescuing an American tourist from drowning. The St. Eustatius Historical Foundation Museum sells a sightseeing package that includes a guided walking tour, a booklet detailing the sights, and museum admission. The tour begins in Lower Town at the marina and ends at the museum. You can take it on your own using the booklet (numbered blue signs on most of the sights correspond to signs in the booklet), but a guide may prove more illuminating.

➤ CONTACTS: **Josser Daniel** (☎ 599/318–2358); **The St. Eustatius Historical Foundation Museum** (✉ 3 Wilhelminaweg, Oranjestad, ☎ 599/318–2288).

TAXES

DEPARTURE TAX

The departure tax is $5.65 for flights to other islands of the Netherlands Antilles and $12 to foreign destinations. Note: when flying home through St. Maarten, list yourself as "in transit" and avoid paying the $20 tax levied in St. Maarten, if you are there for less than 24 hours.

SALES TAX

Hotels collect a 7% government tax and 3% turnover tax.

TAXIS

Taxis meet all flights from Franklin Delano Roosevelt Airport and charge about $3.50 for the drive into town.

TELEPHONES

Statia has microwave telephone service to all parts of the world. Direct dial is available. There are two pay phones on the island, one near the airport and one in Landsradio. They work with phone cards that you can buy at stores throughout the island.

COUNTRY AND AREA CODES

To call Statia from North America, dial 011/599/318, followed by the four-digit number.

TIPPING

Although your hotel or restaurant might add a 10%–15% service charge, it's customary to tip maids, waitstaff, and other service personnel, including taxi drivers. About 10% for taxi drivers should do it; hotel maids will appreciate about a dollar or two per day, and members of the waitstaff will be grateful for an extra 5%–10%.

VISITOR INFORMATION

➤ IN ST. EUSTATIUS: The **Tourist Office** (✉ Fort Oranjestraat, Oranjestad, ☎ FAX 599/318–2433).

19 ST. KITTS AND NEVIS

Updated by
Jordan Simon

Several couples—men in blazers and slacks, women in flowing cotton dresses—sip cocktails on the patio of a magnificently restored 18th-century plantation great house. A mountain carpeted in lush rain forest towers over the building, and a flawlessly green croquet lawn sweeps down to the sea. Some people sit quietly; others speak into cell phones, checking on stocks or tots back home. It's an incongruous, anachronistic, utterly delightful scene: a Gatsby-esque party transplanted to today's Caribbean.

The sister islands of St. Kitts and Nevis (pronounced *nee*-vis) have developed a sibling rivalry. They're competing for increasingly upscale visitors, and it's a tight race: both islands have uncrowded beaches, lush rain forests, historic ruins; charming if slightly dilapidated capitals in Basseterre (St. Kitts) and Charlestown (Nevis), and restored 18th-century plantation inns. And yet, despite their rivalry, both blissful islands have remained mellow. Though many of their guests are well-heeled sorts who enjoy playing dress-up, others prefer the comfort of sandals. They all know how to amuse themselves, and they genuinely seem to enjoy experiencing local culture.

Mountainous St. Kitts, the first English settlement in the Leeward Islands, crams some stunning scenery into its 65 square mi (168 square km). Its shape has been compared to a whale, a cricket bat, and a guitar; suffice it to say, it's roughly an oval, with a narrow peninsula trailing off toward Nevis, just 2 mi (3 km) southeast across the strait. Vast, brilliant green fields of sugarcane run to the shore. The fertile, lush island has some fascinating natural and historical attractions: a rain forest replete with waterfalls, thick vines, and secret trails; a central mountain range, dominated by the 3,792-ft (1,378-m) Mt. Liamuiga, whose crater has long been dormant; and Brimstone Hill, known in the 17th century as the Gibraltar of the West Indies.

St. Kitts is known as the mother colony of the West Indies because it was from here that English settlers sailed to Antigua, Barbuda, Tortola, and Montserrat and French settlers dispatched colonizing parties to Martinique, Guadeloupe, St. Martin, and St. Barths. The French, who inexplicably brought a bunch of green vervet monkeys—an African species—with them as pets (the creatures now outnumber the 35,000 residents), arrived on St. Kitts a few years after the British. As rich in history as it is fertile and lush, St. Kitts is still developing its tourism industry. It now hosts some 75,000 overnight visitors annually—no doubt drawn by the island's rare combination of natural and historic attractions and water-sports opportunities.

In 1493, when Columbus spied a cloud-crowned volcanic isle during his second voyage to the New World, he named it Nieves—the Spanish word for "snows"—because it reminded him of the snow-capped peaks of the Pyrénées. Nevis rises from the water in an almost perfect cone, the tip of its 3,232-ft (1,174-m) central mountain smothered in clouds. Even less developed than St. Kitts, Nevis is known for its long beaches with white and black sand, its lush greenery, and its restored sugar plantations that now house charming inns. In 1628 settlers from St. Kitts sailed across the 2-mi (3-km) channel that separates the two islands. At first they grew tobacco, cotton, ginger, and indigo, but with the introduction of sugarcane in 1640, Nevis became the island equivalent of a boomtown. As the mineral baths were drawing crowds, the island was producing an abundance of sugar. Slaves were brought from Africa to work on magnificent estates, many of them high in the mountains amid lavish tropical gardens.

Restored plantation homes that now operate as inns are true sybaritic lures. Though there's plenty of activity for the energetic—mountain climbing, swimming, tennis, horseback riding, snorkeling—the going is easy here, with hammocks for snoozing, lobster bakes on palm-lined beaches, and candlelight dinners in stately dining rooms and on romantic verandas. Each inn has its own ambience, thanks to the delightful, often eccentric owners—either British or American expatriates.

St. Kitts and Nevis, along with Anguilla, achieved self-government as an associated state of Great Britain in 1967. In 1983 St. Kitts and Nevis became an independent nation. Nevis papers sometimes run fiery articles advocating independence, and the sister islands may separate someday (they came close in a 1998 Nevis plebiscite that fell just short of the required two-thirds majority). However, it's unlikely that a shot will be fired: any war will probably be waged through ad campaigns.

ST. KITTS

Lodging

St. Kitts has an appealing variety of places to stay—beautifully restored plantation inns (where MAP is encouraged, if not mandatory), full-service hotels, simple beachfront cottages, and two all-inclusive resorts. There are also several guest houses and self-serve condos. Don't expect to find much more than the basic amenities (and reasonable prices) at the hotels: TVs, air-conditioning, and phones are standard (though not in the inns). Increasing development has been touted (or threatened) for years, including the only modern chain hotel: a much-delayed 250-room Hyatt in South Friar's Bay with a casino, water-sports and tennis complexes, and health club, which was slated to begin construction in summer 2001. Meanwhile, two projects have begun construction in Frigate Bay, with anticipated openings in late 2001. The Island Paradise Resort and Casino will feature 450 rooms and condo units (twice as many rooms as the current largest property). In an even more ambitious undertaking, Marriott is cofinancing and managing the Royal St. Kitts Condominium Beach Resort and Casino, which supposedly will mushroom to 900 units in three phases (the initial stage called for a 231-unit condominium complex and 200-room hotel). An-

562

Lodging

Allegro Jack Tar Village
Royal St. Kitts
Hotel and Casino **19**

Bird Rock
Beach Resort **12**

Fairview Inn **6**

Frigate Bay
Resort **16**

Golden Lemon **10**

Horizons Villas
Resort **18**

Ocean Terrace Inn . . .**2**

Ottley's
Plantation Inn **11**

Rawlins
Plantation Inn **9**

Rock Haven Bed
and Breakfast **15**

Timothy
Beach Resort **17**

Dining

Ballahoo **1**

Chef's Place **3**

Fisherman's Wharf . . .**2**

Golden Lemon **10**

Mango's **4**

Manhattan
Gardens **7**

Marshall's **18**

PJ's Pizza **13**

Rawlins Plantation . . .**9**

Royal Palm **11**

Sprat Net **8**

Stonewall's **5**

Turtle Beach
Bar and Grill **14**

Exploring

Basseterre **1**

Black Rocks **5**

Brimstone Hill **4**

Old Road Town **2**

Romney Manor **3**

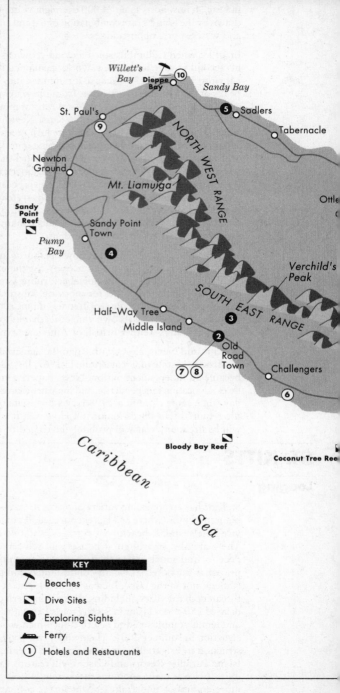

St. Kitts

Willett's Bay
Dieppe Bay
Sandy Bay
St. Paul's
Sandy Bay
Sadlers
Tabernacle
NORTH WEST RANGE
Newton Ground
Mt. Liamuiga
Ottle
Sandy Point Reef
Sandy Point Town
Pump Bay
Verchild's Peak
SOUTH EAST RANGE
Half–Way Tree
Middle Island
Old Road Town
Challengers
Bloody Bay Reef
Coconut Tree Ree
Caribbean
Sea

KEY

Beaches

Dive Sites

1 Exploring Sights

Ferry

1 Hotels and Restaurants

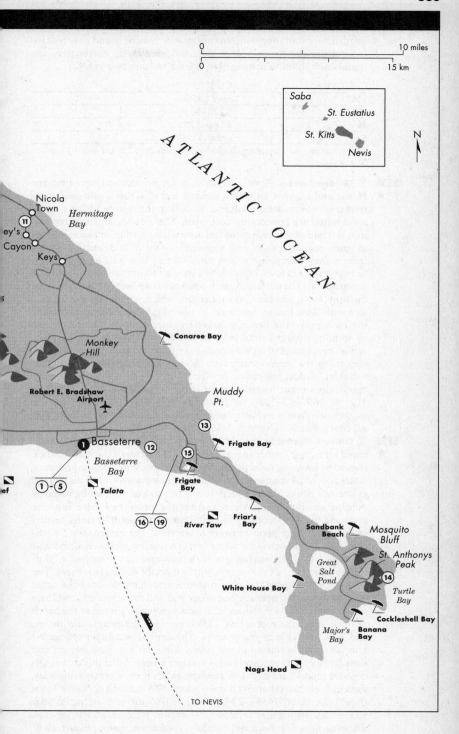

ATLANTIC OCEAN

Saba

St. Eustatius

St. Kitts

Nevis

N

Nicola Town

Hermitage Bay

ey's

Cayon

Keys

Conaree Bay

Monkey Hill

Robert E. Bradshaw Airport

Muddy Pt.

Basseterre

Basseterre Bay

13

Frigate Bay

12

15

Frigate Bay

ef

1 - 5

Talata

16 - 19

River Taw

Friar's Bay

Sandbank Beach

Mosquito Bluff

St. Anthonys Peak

Great Salt Pond

14

Turtle Bay

White House Bay

Cockleshell Bay

Major's Bay

Banana Bay

Nags Head

11

1

TO NEVIS

0 ——————— 10 miles

0 ——————— 15 km

other major development may be in the works in the island's north-west. Should all these projects materialize, the room base will easily quadruple, prompting concerns about whether the island's current infrastructure can support large-scale sudden growth. Fortunately, the islandscape shouldn't change for at least another two years.

CATEGORY	COST*
$$$$	over $350
$$$	$225–$350
$$	$150–$225
$	under $150

All prices are for a standard double room, excluding 7% tax and 10% service charge.

$$$$ ⊞ **Golden Lemon.** Arthur Leaman, a former decorating editor for
★ *House and Garden* magazine, created and runs this world-renowned retreat on the isolated north end. Rooms in the restored 17th-century great house are impeccably decorated. There are canopied, wrought-iron and four-poster beds swaddled in mosquito netting, armoires, chaises longues, rocking chairs, and a variety of fabrics in delectable shades from mango to raspberry. You can also stay in a fully equipped one- or two-bedroom town house (some have a wraparound terrace and/or private pool). The cool, dark, well-appointed bar-lounge is a haven from the bright sun, and the Golden Lemon, which serves Continental cuisine with West Indian flourishes, is one of the best restaurants on the island. A gray-sand beach, guarded by rusty cannonballs and shaded by spindly, elegant palms, has views of St. Maarten and St. Eustatia. A high percentage of repeat guests have returned punctually for years, cherishing the serene ambience (children under 18 won't feel comfortable), almost telepathic service from long-time staffers, and romantically remote location (a car is necessary). ⊠ *Dieppe Bay (Box 17),* ☎ *869/465–7260 or 800/633–7411,* FAX *869/465–4019,* WEB *www.goldenlemon.com. 9 rooms, 22 villas. Restaurant, fans, pool, tennis court, beach, shop. AE, MC, V. BP, MAP.*

$$$$ ⊞ **Ottley's Plantation Inn.** At the foot of Mt. Liamuiga, on 35 mani-
★ cured acres, this former sugar plantation has views of the wild Atlantic framed by towering royal palms. The 18th-century great house and stone cottages hold 24 spacious, high-ceilinged guest rooms with walls painted in luscious colors like raspberry sorbet or powder blue, white wood or polished oak floors, and wicker and antique furnishings. Nine Supreme units and five two-room Royal Suites are honeymoon heavens, featuring private plunge pools or oversize hot tubs. The gardens are a horticulturist's delight, while the adjacent rain forest includes such memorable sights as a vaulting banyan tree with bannister-like roots and a "butterfly singles bar," as the owners wittily describe one fragrant area. The 65-ft spring-fed pool stretches from the remaining walls of the sugar factory and has an open-air bar at one end and the alfresco Royal Palm restaurant to one side. Thoughtful extras include a shuttle to the beach or town, direct Internet access, a DVD player in the great house library, and TVs available in many units. The staff is warm yet efficient—knowing their business but not yours, while the engaging owners and their (grown) kids genuinely treat you like family. All of this makes Ottley's the model Caribbean inn: atmospherically historic yet contemporary, supremely elegant yet utterly unpretentious. ⊠ *Southwest of Nicola Town (Box 345),* ☎ *869/465–7234; 800/729–0709 direct to hotel,* FAX *869/ 465–4760,* WEB *www.ottleys.com. 24 rooms. Restaurant, bar, air-conditioning, fans, in-room safes, minibars, pool, tennis court, croquet, shop. AE, D, MC, V. BP, MAP.*

$$$$ ⊞ **Rawlins Plantation Inn.** This idyllic plantation inn occupies 25 iso-
★ lated acres at the end of a notoriously bumpy dirt road. The views are

spectacular: on one side, lush greenery climbs up Mt. Liamuiga; on the other, the Caribbean stretches out to the island of St. Eustatia. Ten rooms, each with a bath, are in restored estate buildings (including the original sugar mill) scattered amid the lavishly landscaped grounds. Hammocks are slung between pear or almond trees, and the plantation's original copper syrup vats pop up hither and yon. Guest quarters have mahogany four-poster or brass beds, wicker chairs, hardwood floors, grass mats, and fabrics in cheery pastel prints. The charming owners, Claire and Paul Rawson, admit they use their annual trips to London as excuses to redecorate. In proper British fashion, complimentary afternoon tea is offered. The Rawlins Plantation restaurant, well known for its Continental-Caribbean cuisine, is a faithful re-creation of the original great house, decorated with Claire and Paul's family antiques. You can also take a stroll to the studio of Kate Spencer (an expat Brit who has become the leading local artist), which sits on the estate. ⊠ *St. Paul's (Box 340),* ☎ *869/465–6221 or 800/346–5358,* FAX *869/465–4954,* WEB *www.rawlinsplantation.com. 10 rooms. Restaurant, fans, pool, tennis court, croquet, laundry service. AE, MC, V. MAP.*

$$$ 🖫 **Allegro Jack Tar Village Royal St. Kitts Hotel and Casino.** A lively atmosphere pervades this all-inclusive resort. Two pools are a nice touch: one is for the volleyball and water-aerobics crowd, the other for those who want a quiet, relaxing dip. Regular shuttle buses take you to the beach and golf course. Each day brings a schedule of recreational activities and contests. Live entertainment, a disco, and (for now at least) the island's only casino keep the place pulsating into the wee hours. Rooms are bright if spare, with pale aquamarine walls, white-tile floors, striped curtains, blond-wood furnishings, and hallucinogenic floral fabrics in mauve, cantaloupe, and lime. However, the party-hardy atmosphere means the noise carries to most rooms—your best bets for peace are the 100 block and those numbered higher than 350. Topaz restaurant is noted for its theme buffets; the dinner-only Caruso's serves competent Italian fare. If all you want is an occasionally rowdy, hassle-free week in the sun, the bill for billeting and bill-of-fare here is low indeed. ⊠ *Frigate Bay (Box 406),* ☎ *869/465–8651 or 800/858–2258,* FAX *869/465–1031,* WEB *www.allegroresorts.com. 267 rooms. 2 restaurants, 3 bars, 2 grills, air-conditioning, in-room safes, 2 pools, hair salon, 18-hole golf course, 2 tennis courts, health club, Ping-Pong, shuffleboard, volleyball, dive shop, snorkeling, windsurfing, boating, waterskiing, bicycles, shops, casino, baby-sitting, children's programs, car rental. AE, D, DC, MC, V. All-inclusive.*

$$$ 🖫 **Horizons Villa Resort.** These gleaming coral, white, and jade duplex villas, most with stunning Caribbean and/or Atlantic views, are meticulously maintained. The slightly cramped one-bedroom villas have enormous terraces; the larger three- and four-bedroom units (many occupied as longer-term rentals) have plunge pools. All have every conceivable amenity, from full kitchens to bathtubs fit for a Roman emperor to washer-dryers, VCRs, and CD players. The individually owned and decorated units favor soothing pink, olive, teal, and taupe tones, with rattan and blond-wood furnishings, vivid local artwork, and pristine white-tile floors. The pool area is uncommonly pleasant, Frigate Bay Beach is a two-minute walk down the hill, and the golf course is a short drive away. The standard hotel rooms are enormous, if spare, with immaculate white tile floors, frilly pink wicker furnishings, and floral fabrics; each has an oceanview balcony and cable TV. But Horizons is primarily recommended for its villas, which are ideal for families and groups. ⊠ *Fort Tyson (Box 1143), Frigate Bay,* ☎ *869/465–0584; 800/830–9069 direct to hotel,* FAX *869/465–0785. 24 rooms, 48 villas. Restaurant, air-conditioning, fans, pool, tennis court. AE, MC, V. EP.*

$$ ☷ **Bird Rock Beach Resort.** Perched on a bluff a few miles from the airport and downtown, this rather plain but well-maintained resort consists of several pastel two-story buildings snaking through a narrow garden. All have louvered windows, tile floors, rattan and wicker furnishings, balconies, and ocean views; suites also have kitchenettes and sofa beds. The newer units are more stylish, with throw rugs and mahogany two-poster beds. The pool, replete with swim-up bar, boasts sterling views of Basseterre, the sea, and the mountains. A complimentary shuttle whisks guests to Frigate Bay. The alfresco Sunburst turns out Continental favorites with local ingredients, while the more informal Tipsy Lobster Cafe sports a pubby ambience and nautical theme. The staff is hospitable, and the mix of young Europeans on a budget and divers from around the world gives Bird Rock an international flavor. ⊠ *Basseterre Bay (Box 227, Basseterre),* ☎ *869/465–8914 or 800/621–1270,* FAX *869/465–1675,* WEB *www.birdrockbeach.com. 31 rooms, 19 studios. 2 restaurants, 2 bars, air-conditioning, fans, 2 pools, tennis court, volleyball, dive shop, snorkeling, shops. AE, D, MC, V. EP, MAP.*

$$ ☷ **Frigate Bay Resort.** The third fairway of the island's golf course adjoins this property (a stay here gets you discounts on greens fees), and you can reach the two nearby beaches—Caribbean and Atlantic—by complimentary shuttle buses (you can also take a path from the far end of the pool to the Caribbean beach). The buildings, cheerful in canary yellow with lemon trim, house standard rooms as well as condos with full kitchens. There are hillside and poolside units; the latter have nicer views and have been more recently renovated but tend to be noisier. Ask for the higher numbered rooms in the blocks: they have partial ocean views at the same price. All accommodations have ceiling fans, beige- or navy-tile floors, and sliding glass doors that open onto a terrace or balcony; older rooms are more appealing and even larger. The pool has a swim-up bar. A thatched, split-level, octagonal restaurant overlooks the pool area; it's known for its raucous buffets with live entertainment in season but also serves an elegant fusion of Caribbean and Continental fare. ⊠ *Frigate Bay (Box 137, Basseterre),* ☎ *869/465–8935; 800/266–2185 direct to hotel,* FAX *869/465–7050,* WEB *www.frigatebay.com. 40 rooms, 24 studios. Restaurant, bar, air-conditioning, fans, refrigerators, pool, meeting rooms. AE, D, MC, V. EP, MAP.*

$$ ☷ **Ocean Terrace Inn.** OTI, as the locals call it, is a stylish hotel with
★ many amenities for business travelers (including newly installed Internet access)—a rarity on St. Kitts. The main building sits atop a hill overlooking the ocean and amid lovingly tended gardens, a spectacular courtyard, and a man-made lagoon that feeds the large free-form pool and its waterfall. One- and two-bedroom condos farther down the hill also have water views. Rooms are attractively decorated in rattan and bright fabrics, though there's huge variation in size and style. Twenty-three luxury junior suites are handsomely appointed with maple paneling, beige tile floors, walk-in closets, and bleached-wood patios or balconies. Several deluxe units have kitchenettes and whirlpool tubs. There are even two houses by the shore with charmingly colonial-style units that wouldn't seem out of place in a B&B. Fisherman's Wharf is a casual, waterfront restaurant. The Ocean Restaurant boasts superb water views and a fine Continental menu; its Friday-night buffets attract a festive crowd, and live entertainment of some sort is offered most nights. The on-site marina has a fleet of boats for rent or charter, and there's a shuttle to nearby beaches. ⊠ *Bay Rd. (Box 65), Basseterre,* ☎ *869/465–2754; 800/524–0512 direct to hotel,* FAX *869/465–1057,* WEB *www.oceanterraceinn.net. 64 rooms, 8 condominiums. 3 restaurants, 4 bars, air-conditioning, refrigerators, 3 pools, outdoor hot tub,*

health club, dock, windsurfing, boating, waterskiing, meeting rooms. AE, D, MC, V. EP, FAP, MAP.

$$ 🏨 **Timothy Beach Resort.** The management is attentive and friendly at this casual hotel, the only St, Kitts property directly on the Caribbean. Simple powder-blue stucco buildings hold comfortable rooms and suites. Larger units have kitchens and multiple bedrooms, which can be blocked off to form standard rooms. Opt to stay in one of the original buildings; they're right on the beach and are larger and airier and have better views than recent additions. Units are a hodgepodge of the usual wicker, rattan, and hardwood furnishings, but many have been freshened up with draperies, fabrics, and Caribelle Batik wall hangings favoring cool blue hues. The beachfront Sunset Café serves tasty Caribbean-Continental fare, and just steps away are a top watersports concession and lively beach bar (both unaffiliated with the resort). ✉ *Frigate Bay (Box 1198),* ☎ *869/465–8597 or 800/288–7991,* FAX *869/ 466–7085,* WEB *www.timothybeach.com. 18 rooms, 42 1-bedroom suites. Restaurant, bar, air-conditioning, pool, beach. AE, MC, V. EP.*

$ 🏨 **Fairview Inn.** The main building of this quiet, simple inn is an 18th-century French great house, with graceful white verandas and Asian rugs on hardwood floors. The cottages lack unimpeded ocean views, but Mt. Ottley's Level towers in the distance. Though the smallish rooms lack period flair, they're comfortable and motel-like, with TVs and minifridges. Each has a beamed wood ceiling, white-tile floors, wicker furnishings, and light pastel or floral fabrics. Some, like Room 11, are built into original foundations and have partial fieldstone walls and a little more atmosphere. The dining room serves authentic island fare. The management is always willing to lower rates for stays of three days or longer, and offers Internet specials. ✉ *Off Old Town Rd., 7 mi (11 km) northwest of Basseterre (Box 212, Basseterre),* ☎ *869/465–2472 or 800/223–9815,* FAX *869/465–1056. 30 rooms. Restaurant, bar, air-conditioning, fans, refrigerators, room service, pool. AE, D, DC, MC, V. EP, BP, MAP.*

$ 🏨 **Rock Haven Bed and Breakfast.** Judith and Keith Blake have converted their stylish gingerbread house, a two-minutes drive from Frigate Bay beaches, into a relaxing, homey B&B. The living and dining rooms have carved mahogany doors, crystal chandeliers, English rugs, straw mats, and hardwood floors. Two units have brass beds draped with mosquito netting, as well as ceiling fans. The larger one has a full kitchen, a private patio, and a separate entrance. The vast, breezy terrace is lovely, with a terra-cotta floor, white-wicker chaises longues, hammocks, and majestic sea views. Judith prepares sumptuous breakfasts of banana pancakes, Spanish omelets, fried plantains, and pumpkin fritters. Islanders also cherish her homemade ice creams. ✉ *Frigate Bay (Box 821),* ☎ FAX *869/465–5503. 2 rooms. Dining room, fans, laundry service. No credit cards. BP.*

Dining

St. Kitts restaurants range from funky beachfront bistros to elegant plantation dining rooms (most with prix-fixe menus), and there's a variety of cuisine to sample, most of it tinged with the flavors of the Caribbean. Many restaurants offer West Indian specialties such as curried mutton, pepper pot (a stew of vegetables, tubers, and meats), and Arawak chicken (seasoned and served with rice and almonds on breadfruit leaf).

What to Wear
Throughout the island, dress is casual at lunch (but no bathing suits). Dinner, although not necessarily formal, definitely calls for long pants and sundresses.

CATEGORY	COST*
$$$$	over $30
$$$	$20–$30
$$	$10–$20
$	under $10

*per person for a main course at dinner

CARIBBEAN

$$ ✕ **Manhattan Gardens.** Even the gingerbread exterior of this 17th-century creole house looks appetizing, painted as it is in tangerine, teal, and peach. Inside, it's homey, with batik hangings, lace tablecloths, and wood carvings. The garden in back overlooks the sea and comes alive for Saturday's Caribbean Food Fest and Sunday's brunch and barbecue. The regular menu includes lobster in lemon butter (the one pricey entrée), and wahoo in creole sauce; specials might consist of goat water (goat stew), souse (pickled pigs' trotters), jerk, and saltfish. ✉ *Old R. Town,* ☎ *869/465–9121. No credit cards. No dinner Sun.*

$ ✕ **Chef's Place.** Two things are the draw at this restaurant in a charmingly dilapidated 19th-century house: inexpensive West Indian meals and eavesdropping opportunities (the clientele runs toward local cops, cabbies, and mid-level government workers). Try the St. Kitts version of jerk chicken, the kingfish creole, or the goat stew. The best tables are outside on the wide, white veranda. ✉ *Upper Church St., Basseterre,* ☎ *869/465–6176. No credit cards. Closed Sun.*

CONTEMPORARY

$$$$ ✕ **Golden Lemon.** Arthur Leaman and his partner Martin Kreiner create the recipes for the West Indian, Continental, and American dishes served in the restaurant of their Golden Lemon hotel. The evening begins with cocktails and hors d'oeuvres on the flagstone patio amid bougainvillea and ferns and beneath a turquoise-and-yellow-stripe awning. Afterward, a set three-course dinner is served in a tasteful room with crystal chandeliers, white rattan furnishings, antiques, and arched doorways that welcome the breezes. The Kittitian chefs might tempt you with a breadfruit puff in a peanut sauce, grilled snapper with eggplant and sweet-pepper relish, or baked chicken in an orange and white-wine sauce. The patio is a popular spot for Sunday brunch, with such offerings as banana pancakes and beef stew made with rum; lunch is available the rest of the week. Arthur and Martin are usually about to hold clever court (do ask them for anecdotes of running a Caribbean hostelry). ✉ *Dieppe Bay,* ☎ *869/465–7260. Reservations essential. AE, MC, V.*

$$$$ ✕ **Rawlins Plantation.** The refined dining room at the Rawlins Plan-
★ tation Inn has fieldstone walls, lovely family antiques and period furnishings, and high vaulted ceilings. Owner Claire Rawson is one of the island's most sophisticated chefs, and meals here are well worth the long drive. The prix-fixe four-course dinner ($50 per person) changes nightly but always emphasizes local ingredients. Dishes may include home-smoked mahimahi with caper berries, conch ravioli in lobster sauce, shrimp ceviche with coriander and sour oranges, or pan-fried duck breast with honey and hot chilies. The banana puffs with lime sauce and chocolate terrine with passion-fruit sauce are delicious. The bountiful lunch buffet ($25) offers such classic West Indian items as breadfruit salad, shrimp fritters with mango salsa, lobster and spinach crêpes, and *bobote* (ground beef, eggplant, spices, curry, and homemade chutney). ✉ *St. Paul's,* ☎ *869/465–6221. Reservations essential. AE, MC, V.*

$$$$ ✕ **Royal Palm.** Beside the pool at Ottley's Plantation Inn, this is a restau-
★ rant best savored at night, under the latticed roof, gazing across manicured lawns to the lights of the elegant great house. Imaginative,

assured chef Pam Yahn—a graduate of the prestigious Culinary Institute of America—blends indigenous ingredients with Pacific Rim, Mediterranean, southwestern, and Latin touches. Your four-course feast might include roasted rack of lamb in *moutarde de Meaux* crust with mango chutney sauce, Caribbean lobster baked atop a chili-shrimp corn cake with passion-fruit butter, or South American vegetable soup atop pan-seared snapper with feta and cilantro. Even the "intermezzos" are artful: witness a roasted squab, toasted cashews, and balsamic-baked onion salad in organic greens. For dessert, beg Pam for banana fritters *l'antillaise* (spiced and fried in rum). The combination of superb food, artful presentation, and warm bonhomie here is unbeatable. ⊠ *Southwest of Nicola Town,* ☎ 869/465–7234. *Reservations essential. AE, D, MC, V.*

$$$ ✕ **Marshall's.** The pool area of Horizons Villa Resort is transformed into a romantic eatery thanks to smashing ocean views, huge potted plants, and elegantly appointed tables. (A future change in venue is possible because the owner is looking for another location with more parking.) Jamaican chef Verral Marshall, with the help of noted island chef-consultant, Janice Barber, fuses ultrafresh local ingredients with a United Nations of cuisines that is best described as Continental-creole. Delectable offerings include conch cutlets with white-rum lime sauce and black bean salad, portobello-stuffed tortellini with lobster and shrimp in creamy tomato basil sauce, and a classic saltfish with *ackee* (a local vegetable that when cooked resembles scrambled eggs). The menu could be even more daring in its unconventional pairings, but the execution is invariably excellent. ⊠ *Frigate Bay,* ☎ 869/466–8245. *Reservations essential. AE, MC, V.*

$$ ✕ **Stonewall's.** Affable owners Garry and Wendy Steckles practically built this lush tropical courtyard restaurant by hand. "Our sweat is varnished into the bar," Garry swears. Banana trees, bougainvillea, and bamboo grow everywhere. Selections are limited, depending on what's fresh and the cook's mood: it could be a proper roast beef and Yorkshire pudding, tapenade-crusted wahoo, or chicken breast in sun-dried tomato sauce. Be sure to try the house drink, Stone Against the Wall, concocted from Cavalier rum, amaretto, coconut rum, triple sec, pineapple and orange juices, and grenadine. ⊠ *5 Princes St., Basseterre,* ☎ 869/465–5248. *AE, MC, V. No lunch.*

ECLECTIC

$$ ✕ **Ballahoo.** This second-floor terrace restaurant, in the heart of downtown, draws a crowd for breakfast, lunch, and dinner. Lilting calypso and reggae on the sound system, whirring ceiling fans, potted palms, and colorful island prints create the appropriate tropical ambience. Specialties include marlin in lemon butter, chili shrimp, conch simmered in garlic butter, madras beef curry, lobster stir fry, and (it's true) a rum-and-banana toasted sandwich. Go at lunchtime when you can watch the bustle of the Circus and the prices for many dishes are slashed nearly in half. ⊠ *Fort St., Basseterre,* ☎ *869/465–4197. AE, MC, V. Closed Sun.*

$$ ✕ **Mango's.** This cheerful eatery is in the tranquil stone courtyard of the 18th-century Georgian House, and seemingly grows out of the luxuriant garden. The menu runs the gastronomic gamut from enchiladas to teriyaki chicken and rack of lamb in port and mint sauce. By all means, try the definitive conch fritters and chicken roti (a Trinadadian wrap spiced with curry). Though the lunch menu is simpler and cheaper, Mango's really comes alive weekend nights, when even the island's chefs repair here for a drink at the hopping bar and informal disco. The owners occasionally open the main house, with its glorious parquet floors, brick-and-fieldstone walls, and high-back mahogany chairs. ⊠ *Independence Sq., Basseterre,* ☎ *869/465–4049. AE, MC, V. Closed Sun.*

$$ ✕ **Turtle Beach Bar and Grill.** Simple but scrumptious cuisine has made this a popular daytime watering hole. Treats include honey-mustard ribs, coconut-shrimp salad, and grilled lobster. Business cards and pennants from around the world plaster the bar, and the room is decorated with colorful crusted bottles dredged from the deep, ships' lanterns, harpoons, conch shells, and painted wooden fish. You can snorkel here, spot hawksbill turtles, feed the tame families of monkeys that have been known to belly-up to the bar (they're partial to peaches and bananas), schedule a deep-sea fishing trip, laze in a hammock in the shade of an arching palm, or rent a kayak, Windsurfer, or mountain bike. On Sunday afternoon, locals come for dancing to live bands and volleyball. ✉ *Turtle Beach (South end of S. E. Peninsula Rd.; look for signs)*, ☎ *869/469–9086. AE, MC, V. No dinner Mon.–Sat.*

ITALIAN

$$ ✕ **PJ's Pizza.** "Garbage pizza" may not sound appetizing, but this pie—topped with everything but the kitchen sink—is a favorite. You can also choose from 10 other pizzas or create your own. Sandwiches and Italian standards are also served (leading island chef Janice Barber has upgraded the pasta selection). Finish your meal with delicious, moist rum cake. This casual spot, bordering the golf course and open to cooling breezes, is always boisterous, despite—or perhaps because of—its ironic location atop the Frigate Bay police station. ✉ *Frigate Bay*, ☎ *869/465–8373. AE, MC, V. Closed Mon. and Sept. No lunch.*

SEAFOOD

$$ ✕ **Fisherman's Wharf.** Part of the Ocean Terrace Inn, this extremely casual waterfront eatery is decorated in swaggering nautical style, with rustic wood beams, rusty anchors, cannons, and buoys. Try the excellent conch chowder, followed by fresh grilled lobster or other ship-shape seafood, and finish off your meal with a slice of the memorable banana cheesecake. The tables are long, wooden affairs, and the place is generally lively, especially on weekend nights. ✉ *Fortlands, Basseterre*, ☎ *869/465–2754. AE, D, MC, V. No lunch.*

$$ ✕ **Sprat Net.** This simple cluster of picnic tables, sheltered by a brilliant turquoise corrugated-tin roof and decorated with driftwood and fishnets, is on a strip of sand that barely qualifies as a beach. Nonetheless, it is one of the hottest spots on St. Kitts. There's nothing fancy on the menu: just grilled fish, lobster, and meats—served with mountains of coleslaw and peas and rice. But the fish is amazingly fresh: the fishermen-owners heap their catches on a center table, where you choose your own dinner, just as if you were at market, and then watch it grilled to your specification. ✉ *Old Road Town*, ☎ *No phone. No credit cards. Closed Sun. No lunch.*

Beaches

The powdery white-sand beaches, free and open to the public (even those occupied by hotels), are in the Frigate Bay area or on the lower peninsula. **Banana Bay** is one of the island's loveliest beaches, covering over a mile (1.5 km) at the southeastern tip of the island. Several large hotels, including Banana Bay and Casablanca, were abandoned in the early stages of development—their skeletal structures marring an otherwise idyllic scene. Reachable on foot is Banana Bay's twin beach, **Cockleshell Bay,** another eyebrow of glittering sand, backed by lush vegetation.

Conaree Bay, on the Atlantic side, is a narrow strip of gray-black sand where the water is good for bodysurfing. Snorkeling and windsurfing are good at **Dieppe Bay,** a black-sand beach on the north coast, home of the Golden Lemon Hotel.

Locals consider the Caribbean (southern) side of **Friar's Bay** the island's finest beach; it also boasts two hopping beach bars, Shipwreck and Sunset, which serve excellent inexpensive grilled and barbecued food. You can haggle with fishermen here to take you snorkeling off the eastern point. The waters on the Atlantic (northern) side are rougher, but the beach has a wild, desolate beauty. **Frigate Bay,** on the Caribbean, has talcum-powder-fine sand, while on the Atlantic side, its 4-mi-wide (6½-km) stretch is a favorite with horseback riders.

A tiny dirt road, nearly impassable after heavy rains, leads to **Sandbank Beach,** a long taupe crescent on the Atlantic. The shallow coves are protected here, making it ideal for families, and it's usually deserted. **White House Bay** is rocky, but the snorkeling, taking in several reefs surrounding a sunken tugboat, is superb.

Outdoor Activities and Sports

BOATING

Most operators are on Frigate Bay, known for its gentle currents. Turtle Bay offers stronger winds and stunning views of Nevis. **Mr. X Watersports** (✉ Frigate Bay, ☎ 869/465–0673) rents a variety of small craft, including motorboats (waterskiing and jetskiing are available). Paddleboats are $15 per hour, sailboats (with one free lesson) $20–$25 per hour. Mr. X and his cohorts are usually hanging out at the adjacent open-air Monkey Bar. **Tropical Surf** (also known as Turtle Tours) (✉ Turtle Bay, ☎ 869/469–9086) rents Sunfish, Hobie Cats, surfboards, kayaks, and boogie boards; the athletically inclined operators offer several soft adventure tours, as well as private snorkeling and fishing charters.

FISHING

The waters surrounding St. Kitts aren't renowned for their big game fish. Still, you can angle for yellowtail snapper, wahoo, mackerel, tuna, dolphinfish, shark, and barracuda. Rates are occasionally negotiable. Figure approximately $350 for a four-hour excursion with refreshments. Most of the large day-sail operators can arrange private charters, usually through the knowledgeable Todd Leypoldt of **Wahoo Water Tours** (✉ Basseterre, ☎ 869/465–2690, who takes you out on his Robalo, *No Problem.* He's also available for snorkeling charters, beach picnics, and sunset-moonlight cruises.

GOLF

The **Royal St. Kitts Golf Club** (✉ Frigate Bay, ☎ 869/465–8339) is an 18-hole, par-72, 6,918-yard championship course. Greens fees are $40 for 18 holes, $30 for nine; cart rentals are $35 for nine holes, $50 for 18. Despite some attractive palm-lined fairways and a few strategically placed water hazards and numerous sand traps, avid golfers may be disappointed. It's rarely challenging and has surprisingly undramatic water views, and the greens aren't always immaculate.

HIKING

Trails in the central mountains vary from easy to don't-try-it-by-yourself. Monkey Hill and Verchild's Peak aren't difficult, although the Verchild's climb will take the better part of a day. Don't attempt Mt. Liamuiga without a guide. You'll start at Belmont Estates on horseback, then proceed on foot to the lip of the crater, at 2,600 ft (944 m). You can go down into the crater—1,000 ft (363 m) deep and 1 mi (1½ km) wide, with a small freshwater lake—clinging to vines and roots. Tour rates range from $35 for a rain-forest walk to $65 for a volcano expedition and usually include round-trip transportation from your hotel and picnic lunch.

Addy of **Addy's Nature Tours** (☎ 869/465–8069) offers a picnic lunch and cold drinks during treks through the rain forest; she also discusses the history and folklore relating to native plants. **Greg Pereira** (☎ 869/465–4121), whose family has lived on St. Kitts for well over a century, takes groups on half-day trips into the rain forest and on full-day hikes up the volcano and through the grounds of a private 250-year-old great house, followed by excursions down canyons and past petroglyphs. He and his staff relate fascinating historical, folkloric, and botanical information. **Kriss Tours** (☎ 869/465–4042) takes small groups into the crater, through the rain forest, and to Dos d'Anse Pond, on Verchild's Mountain.

HORSEBACK RIDING

Wild North Frigate Bay and desolate Conaree Beach are great for riding. Guides from **Trinity Stable** (☎ 869/465–3226) offers beach rides ($35) and trips into the rain forest ($45).

SCUBA DIVING AND SNORKELING

St. Kitts has more than a dozen excellent dive sites. **Bloody Bay Reef** is noted for its network of underwater grottoes daubed with purple anemones, sienna bristle worms, and canary-yellow sea fans that seem to wave you in. **Coconut Tree Reef,** one of the largest in the area, includes sea fans, sponges, and anemones. Underwater shutterbugs will be in dive heaven. **Nags Head** features strong currents, but experienced divers might spot gliding rays, lobsters, turtles, and reef sharks. Since it sank just over a decade ago in 50 ft (18 m) of water, the *River Taw* makes a splendid site for less-experienced divers. **Sandy Point Reef** has been designated a National Marine Park, including Paradise Reef, with swim-through 90-ft (33-m) sloping canyons, and Anchors Away, where anchors have been encrusted with coral formations. The 1985 wreck of the *Talata* lies in 70 ft (25 m) of water; barracudas, rays, groupers, and grunts dart through its hull.

Auston MacLeod, a PADI-certified dive master-instructor and owner of **Pro-Divers** (☎ 869/465–3483), offers resort and certification courses. His prices are the lowest on the island: $50 less for an open-water certification course, and $10 less for individual dives. Kenneth Samuel of **Kenneth's Dive Centre** (☎ 869/465–2670) is a PADI-certified dive master who takes small groups of divers with C cards to nearby reefs. Rates average $50 for single-tank dives, $80 for double-tank dives; add $10 for equipment. Night dives, including lights, are $50, and snorkeling trips (4 person minimum) are $35, drinks included. **St. Kitts Scuba** (✉ Bird Rock Hotel, 2 mi east of Basseterre, ☎ 869/465–1189) offers competitive prices, friendly dive masters, and a more international clientele.

TENNIS

Unfortunately, options are quite limited unless you're staying at a hotel with a tennis court. The plantation inns all have one court each and will rent to nonguests on a space-available basis in low season, but it's not worth the long drive, unless you're planning to stay on for a meal or to explore other parts of the island. **Allegro Jack Tar Village Royal St. Kitts Hotel and Casino** (✉ Frigate Bay, ☎ 869/465–8651) has two lighted courts, but you must buy a day pass ($50) for the resort in order to play. The fee does include breakfast and lunch, drinks, and other activities (such as nonmotorized watersports).

WINDSURFING

Winds are usually calm on the Caribbean side, meaning beginners won't get into deep water. Turtle Bay, site of the prime outfitter, is particularly well protected. **Tropical Surf,** also known as Turtle Tours (✉

Turtle Bay, ☎ 869/469–9086), rents Windsurfers and offers the best lessons on island.

Shopping

St. Kitts has limited shopping, but there are a few small duty-free shops with good deals on jewelry, perfume, china, and crystal. Several galleries sell excellent paintings and sculptures. The batik fabrics, scarves, caftans, and wall hangings of Caribelle Batik are well known. British expat Kate Spencer is an artist who has lived on the islands for years, reproducing its vibrant colors on everything from silk pareu (beach wraps) to note cards to place mats. Other good island buys include crafts, jams, and herbal teas. Don't forget to pick up some CSR, a "new cane spirit drink" that's distilled from fresh sugarcane right on St. Kitts.

Areas and Malls

Most shopping plazas are in downtown Basseterre, on the streets radiating from the The Circus. The **Pelican Mall**—a shopping arcade designed to look like a traditional Caribbean street—has 26 stores, a restaurant, tourism offices, and a bandstand. Directly behind it, on the waterfront, is **Port Zante,** the deep-water cruise-ship pier; a much-delayed (by hurricane damage in 1998 and 1999) upscale shopping-dining complex is expected to include at least 25 stores by 2002. **Shoreline Plaza** is next to the Treasury Building, right on Basseterre's waterfront. **TDC Mall** is just off the Circus in downtown.

Specialty Items

ART AND ANTIQUES

Spencer Cameron Art Gallery (⊠ 10 N. Independence Sq., ☎ 869/465–1617) has historical reproductions of Caribbean island charts and prints, in addition to owner Rosey Cameron's popular Carnevale clown prints and a wide selection of exceptional artwork by Caribbean artists. They will mail anywhere. **Hidden Treasures Art and Antiques** (⊠ Cayon St., ☎ 869/465–5450) purveys colonial Caribbean furnishings, marvelous old Victorian costume jewelry and Venetian art glass, and exquisite Art Deco and Art Nouveau tea sets and stemware.

CDS AND TAPES

Music World (⊠ The Circus, ☎ 869/465–1998) offers a vast selection of island rhythms—lilting *soca* (a mix of soul and calypso) and *zouk* (a bopping beguine from Martinique and Guadeloupe), pulsating salsa and merengue, wicked hip-hop, and mellow reggae and calypso. You can also buy the CDs of some rocking local bands: hard-driving exponents of soca such as Nu-Vybes, Grand Masters, and Small Ave, and the "heavy dancehall" reggae group, House of Judah.

HANDICRAFTS

Caribelle Batik (⊠ Romney Manor, ☎ 869/465–6253) sells batik wraps, T-shirts, dresses, wall hangings, and the like. **Glass Island** (⊠ 4–5 Princes St., ☎ 869/466–6771) features frames, earrings, and blown-art glass vases, bowls, and plates in sinuous shapes and seductive colors. **Island Hopper** (⊠ The Circus, ☎ 869/465–2905) is a good place for island crafts, especially wood carvings, pottery, textiles, and colorful resort wear, as well as humorous T-shirts and trinkets. **Kate Designs** (⊠ Bank St., ☎ 869/465–5265) showcases the enchanting silk pareos, jewelry, hand-pressed notebooks, prints, greeting cards, and papier-mâché works of Kate Spencer, who also has a studio outside the Rawlins Plantation, and the fanciful, striking hats of Dale Isaacs. **The Potter's House** (⊠ West Bay Rd., ☎ 869/465–5947) is the atelier-home of Carla Astaphan, whose beautifully glazed ceramics and masks celebrate Afro-Caribbean heritage. The **Crafthouse** (⊠ Bay Rd., Southwell Industrial Site, ½ mi east of Shoreline Plaza, ☎ 869/465–7754) is one of the best sources for local dolls, woodcarvings, and straw work. **Stonewall's Tropical Boutique** (⊠ 7 Princes St., ☎ 869/466–9124) carries top-of-the-line products from around the Caribbean: hand-painted Jamaican pottery, West Indian photos and artworks, brass jewelry, hand-painted T-shirts, and flowing resort wear by leading Caribbean designer, John Warden.

Nightlife

Most nightlife revolves around the hotels, which host folkloric shows and calypso and steel bands of the usual limbo-rum-and-reggae variety. Check with your hotel or the tourist board for schedules.

BARS

Bayembi Cultural Entertainment Bar and Cafe (⊠ Bank St., off The Circus, ☎ 869/466–5280) looks like a UN garage sale, and the ambience is definitely Peace Corps hip, with jazz guitar sets Wednesday, karaoke Saturday, joyous happy hours daily, and even poetry readings. It also sells light snacks and local artwork. A favorite happy-hour watering hole is the **Circus Grill** (⊠ Bay Rd., ☎ 869/465–0143), a second-floor eatery whose veranda offers views of the harbor and the activity on The Circus.

CASINOS

The only game in town is the **Allegro Jack Tar Village Beach Royal St. Kitts Resort and Casino,** which offers slots and very limited low-stakes action in a space reminiscent of a low-rent, Las Vegas hole-in-the-wall.

DANCE AND MUSIC CLUBS

Doo-Wop Days (⊠ Memory La., Frigate Bay, ☎ 869/465–1960), owned by Americans Linda and Joe Pozzuolo, features old 45s, photos, velvet Elvis paintings, guitar-shape pillows, hula hoops, and *Look* magazine covers. There's live music some nights and the inevitable karaoke contests. Try Joe's authentic Philly cheese steaks.

Locals disco down at **Henry's Night Spot** (⊠ Dunn's Cottage, Lower Cayon St., Basseterre, ☎ 869/465–3508). **Mango's** (⊠ Independence Sq., Basseterre, ☎ 869/465–4049) parties down on Friday nights, when it seems half the island squeezes onto its minuscule dance floor.

Exploring St. Kitts

You can see the sights of Basseterre, the capital city, in half an hour or so; allow three to four hours for an island tour. Main Road traces the northwestern perimeter through seas of sugarcane and past breadfruit trees and stone walls. Villages with tiny pastel-color houses of stone and weathered wood are scattered across the island, and the drive back to Basseterre around the island's other side passes through several of them. The most spectacular stretch of scenery is on Dr. Kennedy Simmonds Highway to the tip of the Southeast Peninsula. Reminiscent of California's famed Highway 1, this ultrasleek modern road twists and turns through the undeveloped grassy hills that rise between the calm Caribbean and the windswept Atlantic, past the shimmering pink Great Salt Pond, a volcanic crater, and seductive beaches.

Numbers in the margin correspond to points of interest on the St. Kitts map.

SIGHTS TO SEE

❶ Basseterre. In the south of the island, St. Kitts's capital is a walkable town. It's graced with tall palms, and although many of the buildings appear run-down and in need of paint, there are interesting shops, excellent art galleries, and some beautifully maintained houses.

The octagonal Circus, built in the style of London's famous Piccadilly Circus, has duty-free shops along the streets and courtyards off from it. There are lovely gardens on the site of a former slave market at **Independence Square** (⊠ Off Bank St.). The square is surrounded on three sides by 18th-century Georgian buildings. **St. George's Anglican Church** (⊠ Cayon St.) is a handsome stone building with a crenellated tower originally built by the French in 1670 and called Nôtre-Dame. The British burned it down in 1706 and rebuilt it four years later, naming it after the patron saint of England. Since then it has suffered a fire, an earthquake, and hurricanes, and was once again rebuilt in 1869. **Port Zante** (⊠ Waterfront, behind The Circus) is an ambitious 27-acre cruise-ship pier-marina reclaimed from the sea. The domed welcome center sports an imposing neoclassical design, with columns and stone arches; when completed (construction will continue through 2002), it will feature walkways, fountains, and West Indian–style buildings housing luxury and crafts shops, restaurants, and perhaps even a hotel/casino.

⑤ **Black Rocks.** This series of lava deposits was spat into the sea ages ago when the island's volcano erupted. It has since been molded into fanciful shapes by centuries of pounding surf. ⊠ *Atlantic coast, outside town of Sadlers, in Sandy Bay.*

④ **Brimstone Hill.** The well-restored 38-acre fortress, declared a UNESCO World Heritage Site in 2000, is part of a national park dedicated by Queen Elizabeth in 1985. The steep walk up the hill from the parking lot is well worth it if military history and/or spectacular views interest you. After routing the French in 1690, the English erected a battery here, and by 1736 there were 49 guns in the fortress. In 1782, 8,000 French troops laid siege to the stronghold, which was defended by 350 militia and 600 regular troops of the Royal Scots and East Yorkshires. A plaque in the old stone wall marks the place where the fort was breached. When the English finally surrendered, the French allowed them to march from the fort in full formation out of respect for their bravery (the English afforded the French the same honor when they surrendered the fort a mere year later). A hurricane severely damaged the fortress in 1834, and in 1852 it was evacuated and dismantled. The beautiful stones were carted away to build houses.

The citadel has been partially reconstructed and its guns remounted. A seven-minute orientation film recounts the fort's history and restoration. You can see what remains of the officers' quarters, the redoubts, the barracks, the ordinance store, and the cemetery. Its museum collections, sadly, were scattered and depleted by recent hurricanes, but some pre-Columbian artifacts, objects pertaining to the African heritage of the island's slaves (masks, ceremonial tools, etc.), weaponry, uniforms, photographs, and old newspapers remain. The view from here includes Montserrat and Nevis, to the southeast; Saba and St. Eustatia, to the northwest; and St. Barths and St. Maarten, to the north. Nature trails snake through the tangle of surrounding hardwood forest and savanna (a fine spot to catch the green vervet monkeys skittering about). ⊠ *Main Rd., Brimstone Hill.* 🔊 *$5.* ⊙ *Daily 9:30–5:30.*

② **Old Road Town.** This site marks the first permanent English settlement in the West Indies, founded in 1624 by Thomas Warner. Take the side road toward the interior to find some Carib petroglyphs, testimony of even earlier habitation. The largest depicts a female figure on black volcanic rock, presumably a fertility goddess. Less than a mile east of Old Road Town along Main Road is **Bloody Point**, where French and

British soldiers joined forces in 1629 to repel a mass Carib attack; reputedly so many Caribs were massacred, the stream ran red for three days. ⊠ *Main Rd., west of Challengers.*

❸ **Romney Manor.** The ruins of this somewhat restored house (destroyed by fire in 1996) and surrounding cottages that duplicate the old chattel-house style are set in 6 acres of gardens, with exotic flowers, an old bell tower, and an enormous gnarled 350-year-old *saman* tree (sometimes called a rain tree). Inside, at **Caribelle Batik,** you can watch artisans hand-printing fabrics by the 2,500-year-old process known as batik. Look for signs indicating a turnoff for Romney Manor near Old Road Town.

NEVIS

Lodging

Most lodgings are in restored manor or plantation houses scattered throughout the island's five parishes (counties). The owners often live at these inns, and they receive you warmly. It's easy to feel as if you've been personally invited down for a visit. Before dinner you may find yourself in the drawing room having a cocktail and conversing with the family, other guests, and visitors who have come for a meal in the restaurant. Most inns operate on MAP and offer a free shuttle service to their private stretch on Pinney's Beach. If you require TVs and air-conditioning, you're better off staying at the hotels, and then dining with the engaging inn owners.

For approximate costs, *see* the lodging price chart *in* St. Kitts.

$$$$ 🏨 **Four Seasons Resort Nevis.** This resort, which has been practically
★   rebuilt after Hurricane Lenny, combines world-class elegance with West Indian ambience and hospitality. On 300 exquisitely landscaped acres along Pinney's Beach, the hotel offers a complete range of water sports, tennis, lap and free-form infinity pools (the latter spectacularly lit at night), a Robert Trent Jones Jr.–designed golf course, health club, and spa. A state-of-the-art business center and high-speed in-room Internet access have been added; the children's facilities, including a teen video center, were also expanded. Both service and services are irreproachable, including regular private ferry service to St. Kitts, an American Airlines pavilion where you can check luggage and pay departure tax, even a "beach concierge," dispensing everything from reading materials to CDs, for sunbathers. Spacious rooms (550 square ft) are furnished with mahogany armoires and headboards, marble bathrooms, dhurrie rugs, and cushioned rattan sofas and chairs in restrained pastels. Each room has large seating areas—indoors and on a veranda—where you can enjoy a private meal. The 43 individually designed and owned golf-course villas (more are being built) have cathedral ceilings, tile floors, open kitchens, and enormous verandas. Nouvelle Caribbean–Continental fare is served in the hotel's spectacularly ornate gourmet dining room amid gentle sea breezes and sweeping views. The less formal Grill Room offers a more standard meat-and-potatoes menu. Packages are available, even in high season. ⊠ *Pinney's Beach, 2½ mi (4 km) north of Charlestown (Box 565, Charlestown),* ☎ *869/469–1111 or 800/332–3442 in the U.S.; 800/ 268–6282 in Canada;* ℻ *869/469–1112,* 🌐 *www.fourseasons.com. 179 rooms, 17 suites, 43 villas. 2 restaurants, grill, 2 bars, air-conditioning, fans, in-room safes, in-room VCRs, minibars, room service, 2 pools, hair salon, hot tub, spa, 18-hole golf course, pro shop, 10 tennis courts, aerobics, health club, beach, dive shop, snorkeling, wind-*

surfing, boating, bicycles, shops, baby-sitting, children's programs, coin laundry, laundry service, meeting rooms, business services, car rental. AE, D, MC, V. EP, FAP, MAP.

$$$$ ★ 🔟 **Hermitage Plantation Inn.** A 250-year-old great house—said to be the oldest wooden house in the West Indies—is the heart of this hillside complex. The vivacious owners, Maureen and Richard "Loopy" Lupinacci, add to the charm and will no doubt introduce you to everyone who's anyone on Nevis. Guest quarters are in rooms or duplex cottages (the Blue Cottage and the Yellow Room are knockouts), furnished with antiques and four-poster canopy beds (mostly king-size) swaddled in mosquito netting and patios or balconies; some units also have full kitchens, TVs, and lovely views of the distant ocean. If you need more space, there's a two-bedroom replica of a manor house with a private pool. The beach is 15 minutes away; complimentary transportation will be arranged (you'll delight Richard, a keen horseman, if you request to saddle up or take a jaunt in an old-fashioned horse-drawn cottage). In the great house, you can feast on contemporary cuisine in the Hermitage Plantation Inn restaurant. The Hermitage bespeaks an appreciation of the finer things in life, from the simple elegance of the accommodations to the sparkling dialogue at the bar as everyone congregates for dinner. ✉ *St. John Fig Tree Parish,* ☎ *869/469–3477,* FAX *869/469–2481,* WEB *www.hermitagenevis.com. 8 rooms, 8 cottages, 1 house. Restaurant, bar, fans, in-room safes, refrigerators, pool, tennis court, horseback riding, shops. AE, MC, V. BP, MAP.*

$$$$ ★ 🔟 **Nisbet Plantation Beach Club.** From the manor house of this 18th-century plantation you can see the beach; from one of its bars you look out over an old sugar mill covered with hibiscus, cassia, frangipani, and flamboyants. There are three categories of accommodations in several pale yellow Bermudian-style cottages. All are well maintained and simply but tastefully appointed with patios, vaulted ceilings, gleaming tile floors, whitewashed wicker and rattan, grass mats and baskets, soothing sea-foam and peach fabrics, and abstract tropical prints. Among the in-room amenities are coffeemakers, irons, and hair dryers; higher-end rooms have air-conditioning. All units sit along an avenue lined with stately coconut palms that leads to the beach, where you'll find a deck bar (terrific sunset watching) and two casual beach restaurants. The Nisbet Plantation Beach Club, the restaurant in the great house, has varied five-course menus and the most elegant ambience on the island. ✉ *Newcastle Beach,* ☎ *869/469–9325 or 800/742–6008,* FAX *869/469–9864,* WEB *www.nisbetplantation.com. 38 rooms. 3 restaurants, 2 bars, fans, in-room safes, refrigerators, pool, tennis court, croquet, beach, snorkeling, laundry service. AE, MC, V. EP, MAP.*

$$$ ★ 🔟 **Montpelier Plantation Inn.** Iron gates provide a majestic entrance to this intimate inn on 60 acres, with 10 acres exquisitely landscaped by owner James Gaskell. The rusted remains of old machinery dot the grounds like abstract sculpture. Complimentary afternoon tea, evening cocktails, and dinner are at the great house—an imposing re-creation of an 18th-century fieldstone structure furnished with antiques (Horatio Nelson and Fanny Nisbet were married on the grounds). Accommodations are in spare but sparkling hillside cottages. Each has one or two rooms, two patios, Italian ceramic-tile floors, and large bathrooms with exquisite tracery; most rooms have four-poster or rattan beds and delicate floral or jade spreads that contrast with vivid yellow-and-white-striped curtains. A gorgeous mural decorates one of the walls around the large pool area; if you need saltwater and sand to enjoy the sun, you can take the free shuttle to Pinney's Beach, where the estate has a private 3-acre stretch and a pavilion. Guests come not so much for the amenities as for the incomparable quiet and unpretentious elegance. James and his wife, Celia, downplay their royal re-

Nevis

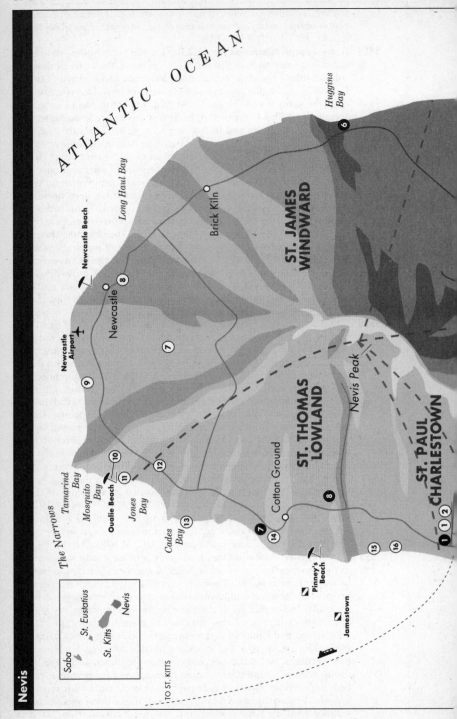

ATLANTIC OCEAN

Huggins
Bay

⑥

Long Haul Bay

Brick Kiln ○

ST. JAMES
WINDWARD

Newcastle Beach

⑧

Newcastle Airport ✈

Newcastle ○

⑦

⑨

Nevis Peak

ST. THOMAS
LOWLAND

ST. PAUL
CHARLESTOWN

Tamarind Bay

⑩

⑪

ᵒualie Beach

Jones Bay

Mosquito Bay

⑫

Cotton Ground ○

⑧

The Narrows

⑬

Cades Bay

⑦ ⑭

① ①②

⑮ ⑯

Pinney's Beach

Jamestown

Saba

St. Eustatius

St. Kitts

Nevis

TO ST. KITTS

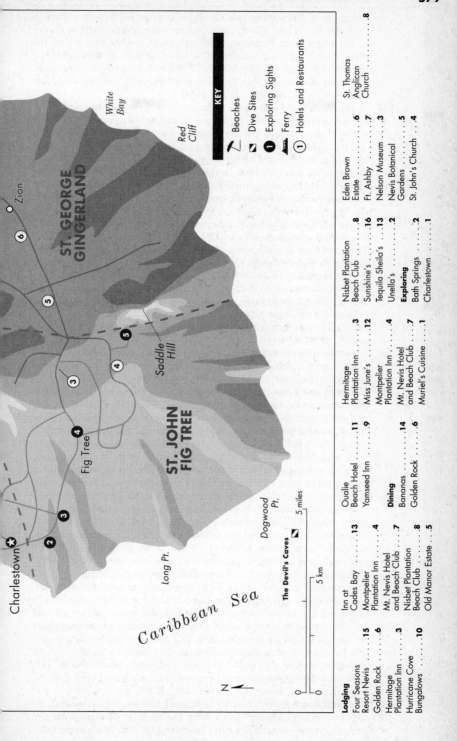

KEY

- Beaches
- Dive Sites
- **1** Exploring Sights
- Ferry
- **1** Hotels and Restaurants

Lodging

Four Seasons Resort Nevis	**15**
Golden Rock	**6**
Hermitage Plantation Inn	**3**
Hurricane Cove Bungalows	**10**
Inn at Cades Bay	**13**
Montpelier Plantation Inn	**4**
Mt. Nevis Hotel and Beach Club	**7**
Nisbet Plantation Beach Club	**8**
Old Manor Estate	**5**
Oualie Beach Hotel	**11**
Yamseed Inn	**9**

Dining

Bananas	**14**
Golden Rock	**6**
Hermitage Plantation Inn	**3**
Miss June's	**12**
Montpelier Plantation Inn	**4**
Mt. Nevis Hotel and Beach Club	**7**
Muriel's Cuisine	**1**
Nisbet Plantation Beach Club	**8**
Sunshine's	**16**
Tequila Sheila's	**13**
Unella's	**2**

Exploring

Bath Springs	**2**
Charlestown	**1**
Eden Brown Estate	**6**
Ft. Ashby	**7**
Nelson Museum	**3**
Nevis Botanical Gardens	**5**
St. John's Church	**4**
St. Thomas Anglican Church	**8**

lations; James prefers to talk about his organic gardens or engage in droll debates. The Gaskells' gracious presence, particularly at dinner in the Montpelier Plantation Inn restaurant, makes this a civilized place, indeed. ✉ *Pond Hill (Box 474, Charlestown),* ☎ *869/469–3462 or 800/223–9832,* ℻ *869/469–2932,* WEB *www.montpeliernevis.com. 17 rooms. Restaurant, bar, fans, pool, tennis court, beach. Closed late Aug.–early Oct. AE, MC, V. EP, MAP.*

$$$ 🏨 **Mt. Nevis Hotel and Beach Club.** Here you'll find reasonably priced,
★   contemporary accommodations and typical Nevisian warmth courtesy of the Maguid family. Deluxe rooms and suites have handsome white and natural-wicker furnishings, apricot, mint, and white fabrics, glass-top tables, and colorful island prints. Suites have full, modern kitchens, dining areas, and sofa beds, making them a decent value for families; all units have large balconies. You're best off with the junior suites, as the hotel rooms are comparatively cramped. The main building houses the Mt. Nevis Hotel and Beach Club restaurant and bar, which opens onto a terrace that overlooks the pool and distant St. Kitts. The hotel's beach club reopened and a small business center was added in 2001. The hotel's verdant site was once a lime plantation; the perfume of the wild trees wafts through the air. The grounds make for invigorating hiking, especially down to the 18th-century ruins of the Thomas Cottle Church, unusual in that owners and slaves worshiped side by side. A small fitness room inspires with its sea views. Three fully equipped hillside houses have two or three bedrooms, handsome individual decor, and spacious sea-view patios. ✉ *Shaw's Rd. (Box 494, Newcastle),* ☎ *869/469–9373 or 800/756–3847,* ℻ *869/469–9375,* WEB *www.mountnevishotel.com. 28 units, 3 houses. Restaurant, bar, air-conditioning, fans, in-room VCRs, refrigerators, pool, gym, meeting rooms, business services. AE, D, MC, V. EP, MAP.*

$$$ 🏨 **Old Manor Estate.** Vast tropical gardens surround this former sugar plantation set in the shadow of Mt. Nevis. The smokehouse, the jail, and other outbuildings have been imaginatively restored as public spaces used for barbecues, musical performances, and banquets; the old cistern is now the pool. The stone and wood buildings have been brightened with fresh coats of apricot and forest-green paint. Throughout, there's a striking blend of old and new, including rusting sugar-making equipment forming a virtual sculpture garden that's lit up at night, while old photos in the public rooms tell the estate's history. Many of the enormous guest rooms have high ceilings with exposed wood beams, gorgeous stone, polished hardwood, or tile floors, marble vanities, king-size four-poster beds, antique wardrobes, and colonial reproduction furnishings. Some rooms, however, are still a bit gloomy, with dowdy madras settees and soiled carpets. Welcome amenities such as coffeemakers, irons, and robes have been added. There's a pleasant game room-library where you can mingle with other guests or catch up on the latest scores on the satellite TV. The expanded terrace of the manor house's respected Cooperage restaurant has splendid views of the sea and Montserrat; the excellent nouvelle Continental menu has been thoroughly revamped. Of all the Nevisian inns, Old Manor probably best re-creates the old-time plantation atmosphere. ✉ *Charlestown, (Box 70),* ☎ *869/469–3445 or 800/892–7093 (direct to hotel),* ℻ *869/469–3388,* WEB *www.oldmanornevis.com. 14 rooms. 2 restaurants, 2 bars, fans, refrigerators, pool, library, shops. AE, MC, V. BP, MAP.*

$$$ 🏨 **Oualie Beach Hotel.** This cozy, congenial, activity-oriented resort con-
★   sists of white-and-hunter-green West Indian–style cottages with gingerbread trim—all on a beautiful beach and all with views of St. Kitts. Twelve new units opened in late 2000. Bright, airy rooms are tastefully furnished: deluxe rooms have mahogany four-poster canopy beds, all conceivable amenities (including VCRs in the premier categories),

and marble vanities; studios have full kitchens. Hammocks are casually slung throughout. The on-site dive shop (dive and windsurfing packages are available) offers NAUI-certified instruction, and you can rent Sunfish and Windsurfers, charter a sailboat, take a sea-kayaking or turtle-watching tour, or spend time on a Skimmer waterborne rowing machine. Breakfast, lunch, and dinner are served at the informal Oualie Beach Hotel restaurant, best known for its West Indian–themed Saturday nights. ⊠ *Oualie Beach,* ☎ *869/469–9735; 800/682–5431 direct to hotel,* FAX *869/469–9176,* WEB *www.oualie.com. 34 rooms. Restaurant, bar, air-conditioning, fans, in-room safes, refrigerators, beach, dive shop, snorkeling, windsurfing, boating, fishing. AE, D, MC, V. EP, MAP.*

$$ ⚇ **Golden Rock.** More than 200 years ago, Pam Barry's great-great-great-grandfather built this estate, which she now co-owns and runs as an inn. It's on 96 mountainous acres (25 of them have lavish tropical gardens) crisscrossed by trails. (An avid horticulturist, Pam organizes historical and nature hikes—just bring a machete.) Rusting cannons placed strategically about the grounds add to the historic ambience. The 16 guest units have four-poster beds of magnificently carved mahogany or bamboo, native grass mats, found-object or bamboo lamps, gingham, madras, cornflower blue, or floral-print fabrics, and patios, most with splendid sea views. The sugar mill has been transformed into a bi-level suite (with a glorious wood-and-bamboo staircase), the old cistern into a spring-fed swimming pool. Free transportation is provided to the inn's beach bar on Pinney's. The mahogany-and-bamboo bar is an oasis; be sure to admire the displays of Pam's family china and silver and the magnificent Eva Wilkin mural. The Saturday-night West Indian buffet in the Golden Rock restaurant is very popular from December to June. Green vervet monkeys skitter about the premises (usually showing up punctually at 4 PM), and anyone is a potential perch for La Rue, a gloriously colored (and doesn't he know it?) Amazona parrot. Pam swears she doesn't know how he learned to wolf-whistle at women. ⊠ *Gingerland (Box 493),* ☎ *869/469–3346,* FAX *869/469–2113,* WEB *www.golden-rock.com. 16 rooms, 1 suite. Restaurant, grill, bar, fans, pool, tennis court, hiking. Closed Sept.–early Oct. AE, MC, V. EP, MAP.*

$$ ⚇ **Hurricane Cove Bungalows.** Don't be deceived by the ramshackle exterior of these one-, two-, and three-bedroom bungalows clinging precariously to a cliff overlooking lovely Oualie Beach. The interiors are charmingly rustic, with gleaming terra-cotta floors, hand-carved wood furnishings, batik wall-hangings, and beds swaddled in mosquito netting. All have full kitchens and an enormous enclosed beached-wood patio with breathtaking ocean views (most in-demand, especially for honeymooners, are Sea Biscuit, Baobab, and Williwah). Several have private pools. The postage-stamp-size hotel pool is in the foundation of a 250-year-old fort, under the shade of a baobab tree. The beach is a five-minute walk. Fans cool these glorified tree houses on rare still days. ⊠ *Hurricane Hill, St. James Parish,* WEB *www.hurricanecove.com,* ☎ FAX *869/469–9462. 11 cottages. Fans, pool. AE, MC, V. EP. Closed Sept.*

$$ ⚇ **Inn at Cades Bay.** At this complex, each of the tidy peach-colored cottages with sage-green gabled roofs has its own tiny lawn. Sizable rooms have high ceilings, bleached-wood paneling, rattan beds, hand-carved Indonesian teak furnishings, smart, abstract Spanish fabrics, and terra-cotta patios that overlook the sea. The lovingly tended grounds include 10 varieties of palm trees and a cactus garden. The beach is lined with gazebos with hammocks; the activity on Pinney's Beach is a bit of a hike but doable. You can dine next door at Tequila Sheila's. Ask about special "low" high season rates in January and February. ⊠ *Cades Bay,* ☎ *869/469–8139,* FAX *869/469–8129,* WEB *www.cadesbayinn.com. 19*

rooms. Restaurant, bar, air-conditioning, fans, minibars, pool. AE, MC, V. EP, MAP.

$ ☷ **Yamseed Inn.** At the end of a very rough access road and away from other inns, this pale-yellow house's friendly innkeeper, Sybil Siegfried, receives guests (there's a three-night minimum). Hummingbirds on the B&B's beautiful grounds (Sybil is an avid gardener) welcome you to the stylish reception area. Each of four guest rooms has a private bath and is handsomely appointed with a mahogany bed, wood-paneled ceiling, throw rugs, white tile floors, and antiques. Breakfast includes homemade muffins and muesli with grated coconut. The B&B has a view of St. Kitts and its own patch of white sand. The only flaw in this paradise is its location in the flight path of the nearby airport (fortunately, air traffic is sparse). ⊠ *Newcastle Beach,* ☎ *869/469–9361. 4 rooms. Beach. No credit cards. CP.*

Dining

Dinner options include the elegance of the dining room at the Four Seasons Resort, intimate dinners at plantation guest houses (where the menu is often prix fixe), and a variety of casual eateries. Seafood is ubiquitous, and there are many places where you can sample West Indian fare.

What to Wear

Dress is casual at lunch, although beach attire is unacceptable. Dress pants and sundresses are appropriate for dinner; men may even want to put on a jacket in season at some inns and at the Four Seasons Resort.

For approximate costs, *see* the dining price chart *in* St. Kitts.

CARIBBEAN

$$$$ ✕ **Miss June's.** Dinner with Miss June Mestier, a lady from Trinidad,
★   could never be called ordinary. While she prepares the fare, her son serves drinks—from Miss June's secret rum punch to a very proper martini—to guests (limited to 20) on the veranda. Promptly at 8:30 everyone heads to the dining room, where tables are set with mismatched fine china and crystal. The first course is a soup, usually something spicy; the second course, fresh fish prepared in some exotic local style, followed by salad. "Now that you've had your dinner," Miss June announces, "it's time to have fun!" You and other guests will be directed to a buffet table laden with at least 18 dishes. Selections change nightly but always include curries, local vegetable dishes, seafood, and such meats as leg of lamb in champagne orange sauce, chicken simmered in coconut milk, or ribs in *mauby* (a bark distillation) and pineapple— all adapted from Trinidadian recipes. Wine flows freely. Later, Miss June will join you for coffee and brandy; she won't kick you out, but she may ask you to turn the lights out when you leave. ⊠ *Jones Bay,* ☎ *869/469–5330. Reservations essential. MC, V.*

$$$ ✕ **Golden Rock.** Tables are draped in pink and arranged in a romantic, dimly lighted room whose fieldstone walls date from when the Golden Rock inn was a plantation house. Enchanting Eva Wilkin originals grace the walls, copper sugar-boiling pots are used as planters, and straw mats and unglazed local pottery add to the island ambience. Local Nevisian cuisine is the specialty here. The prix-fixe menu might include house favorites like velvety pumpkin soup, chicken in a raisin curry, and grilled local snapper with *tania* (a type of tuber) fritters. Don't miss the homemade juices, like passion fruit, soursop, and ginger beer. ⊠ *Gingerland,* ☎ *869/469–3346. Reservations essential. AE, MC, V. Closed Sun.*

$$ ✕ **Sunshine's.** Everything about this palm-thatched beach shack is
★   colorful and larger than life, including the Rasta man Llewelyn "Sun-
shine" Caines himself. Flags from around the world drape the lean-to
and complement the international clientele (including many celebrities)
who wander over from the adjacent Four Seasons. Picnic tables are
splashed with bright sunrise-to-sunset colors; nothing has been left un-
painted, including the palm trees. Fishermen cruise up to the grill with
their catch—you might savor lobster rolls, conch fritters, or snapper
creole. Dinner is by reservation only, and only if there are enough book-
ings. Don't miss the lethal house specialty, Killer Bee rum punch. As
Sunshine boasts, "One and you're stung, two you're stunned, three it's
a knockout." ✉ *Pinney's Beach,* ☎ *869/469–1089. No credit cards.*

$$ ✕ **Unella's.** The atmosphere is nothing fancy—just tables on a second-
floor porch overlooking Charlestown's waterfront. Stop here for ex-
ceptional lobster (more expensive than the rest of the menu), curried
lamb, island-style spareribs, and steamed conch, all served with local
vegetables, rice, and peas. Unella opens shop around 9 AM, when locals and boaters appear waiting for their breakfast, and stays open all
day. ✉ *Waterfront, Charlestown,* ☎ *869/469–5574. No credit cards.*

$ ✕ **Muriel's Cuisine.** Hanging plants, local still lifes, and table vases dress
★   up this eatery. Three meals are served daily, except Sunday. Bountiful
entrées come with mounds of rice and peas as well as fresh vegetables,
a side salad, and garlic bread. The subtly spiced jerk chicken would
pass muster in many a Jamaican kitchen, and the goat water and beef
stews are fabulous: full-bodied and fragrant with garlic and coriander.
A popular West Indian lunch buffet packs 'em in on Wednesdays.
Muriel St. Jean is the gracious hostess. Her restaurant attracts a very
local clientele—women in hair curlers and young men who come to
flirt shyly with the waitresses. ✉ *Upper Happy Hill Dr., Charlestown,*
☎ *869/469–5920. AE, D, MC, V. Closed Sun.*

CONTEMPORARY

$$$$ ✕ **Hermitage Plantation Inn.** After cocktails in the antiques-filled parlor (incomparable bartender Shabba's rum punches are legendary, and
during a week's stay, you're likely to meet all Nevisian society, high
and low, at the postage-stamp-sized bar), dinner is served at tables on
the outside veranda of the Hermitage Plantation Inn. The four-course
prix-fixe menu might include lemongrass and pumpkin soup, papaya
with prosciutto and ginger aïoli, plantains with crème frâiche, black
beans, and caviar, tuna with guava and rosemary, and a rum soufflé—
all lovingly prepared by the local chef, Lovey. Expect an evening of bon
mots and bonhomie: the conversation is always lively, thanks to witty,
gregarious owners Maureen and Richard Lupinacci. ✉ *St. John Fig
Tree Parish,* ☎ *869/469–3477. Reservations essential. AE, MC, V.*

$$$$ ✕ **Montpelier Plantation Inn.** Genial owners James and Celia Gaskell
★   preside over an elegant evening. Cocktails and hors d'oeuvres are served
in the antiques-filled parlor of the Montpelier Plantation Inn great
house. Note the detail of the embroidered madras and pineapple-pat-
tern upholstery, all sewn by local ladies, and look for the circa-1880
portrait of James's relative, Lady Catherine Gaskell. Dinner is served
by candlelight on the west veranda. The inventive chef, Mark Roberts,
makes full use of the herb gardens and fruit trees on the property and
occasionally even hauls in the day's catch himself. The menu changes
nightly. House-smoked wahoo in butter infused with various herbs,
mahimahi salad with pesto dressing, a proper tournedos in red wine
and garlic sauce, and lobster marinated in passion fruit and coconut
milk are a few standouts. Lunches are served on the refreshing patio
and are much simpler affairs than dinner. ✉ *Pond Hill,* ☎ *869/469–
3462. Reservations essential. AE, MC, V. Closed late Aug.–early Oct.*

$$$$ × **Nisbet Plantation Beach Club.** The dining room in the great house
★   of the Nisbet Plantation Beach Club inn—an oasis of polished hard-
       wood floors, mahogany and cherry-wood furnishings, straw mats,
       wicker furnishings, and stone walls—has long been a popular place for
       lunch and dinner. There are also tables on the screened-in veranda, where
       there's a view down the palm-tree-lined fairway to the sea. Kevin
       Hall's five-course menu combines Continental, Pacific Rim, and
       Caribbean cuisines with local ingredients. Sumptuous choices include
       crepinette of lobster on sautéed butternut with black bean sauce and
       pineapple chutney, christophene and yam soup with lentils, fennel-roasted
       quail stuffed with pumpkin, coconut-crusted snapper with citrus pasta
       and charred pumpkin lemongrass sauce, and chocolate truffle torte.
       Enjoy your cocktail or coffee in the civilized front bar area, where a
       pianist or jazz combo plays nightly. Lighter fare (sandwiches, salads,
       hamburgers) is served at lunch at the beach restaurants. ⊠ *Newcastle
       Beach,* ☎ *869/469–9325. Reservations essential. AE, MC, V.*

$$$ × **Mt. Nevis Hotel and Beach Club.** White wicker tables are set with
       coral tablecloths, flickering candles, china, and silver in the airy din-
       ing room of the Mt. Nevis Hotel and Beach Club. It opens onto the
       terrace and pool, and there's a splendid view of St. Kitts in the distance.
       The creative menu deftly blends local ingredients with a cornucopia
       of cuisines, from Mexican to Thai. Starters include calamari tempura
       with red peppers and saffron aïoli, or Caribbean conch cake with mild
       basil-chili mayonnaise; excellent entrées include pan-seared salmon with
       garlic lime butter sauce. There are also flambé specials, with such su-
       perbly prepared and presented dishes as shrimp in annato chive sauce
       with a rum splash, roasted garlic couscous, and baby carrots; or pan-
       seared lamb chops in rosemary mint reduction with scalloped pota-
       toes and ratatouille. The service is attentive, the setting sublime (with
       some lovely Fauvist-hued artworks), and the food perfectly pitched to
       the climate: elegant yet light. The hotel's beach club serves scrumptious
       pizzas and rotisseries chicken. ⊠ *Shaws Rd.,* ☎ *869/469–9373. AE,
       D, MC, V.*

ECLECTIC

$$ × **Bananas.** British expat Gillian Smith, who once worked in various
       capacities for Disney and Relais et Châteaux, opened this delightful
       lean-to across from the water (with one four-burner stove in a cramped
       kitchen). The wooden patio is painted in mauve, turquoise, and peach;
       madras tablecloths complete the colorful look. Scrumptious starters in-
       clude zucchini cakes with yogurt sauce and crab quesadillas; follow
       with curry, meat loaf, moussaka, or lobster tails with pineapple and
       ginger salsa. Gillian throws the occasional theme night, according to
       whim, from Thai to Greek. Jazz, blues, or the Three Tenors play qui-
       etly on the sound system. A fine selection of Cuban cigars and single-
       malt Scotches in the adjacent lounge rounds out the evening. No
       wonder Gillian calls it, quite fittingly, a "Caribbean bistro." Call to
       ensure she's open off-season, as she keeps an irregular schedule. ⊠ *Cot-
       ton Ground,* ☎ *869/469–1891. MC, V. Closed Sun. No lunch.*

$$ × **Tequila Sheila's.** Right next door to the Inn at Cades Bay, this shack
       of corrugated tin and wood sits on a beach (there are even chaises
       longues). It has been gussied up with plant-filled baskets and colorful
       billowing windsocks, but the laid-back air remains. The Pacific Rim–
       California cuisine (with lighter fare and sauces) includes such entrees
       as blackened wahoo, fish quesadillas, coconut shrimp, and chicken in
       mango sauce. The rollicking Sunday Beach Party Brunch draws locals
       and tourists alike. ⊠ *Cades Bay,* ☎ *869/469–1633. MC, V. Closed Mon.
       No lunch Tues.*

Beaches

All the beaches are free to the public, but there are no changing facilities, so wear a swimsuit under your clothes. **Newcastle Beach,** by Nisbet Plantation, is popular among snorkelers. This broad swath of soft, ecru sand, shaded by coconut palms, sits at the northernmost tip of the island, on the channel between St. Kitts and Nevis. **Oualie Beach,** south of Mosquito Bay and north of Cades and Jones bays, is a beige-sand beach where the folks at Oualie Beach Hotel can mix you a drink and fix you up with water-sports equipment. The island's showpiece, **Pinney's Beach,** has almost 4 mi (6½ km) of soft, golden sand on the calm Caribbean, lined with a magnificent grove of palm trees. Alas, the effects of hurricane lashings the past few years have reduced it to a ghost of its former self in spots. The Four Seasons Resort is here, as are the private cabanas and pavilions of several mountain inns.

Outdoor Activities and Sports

Participant Sports

BOATING

The seas are usually uncommonly calm, with light breezes. The northwest side of Nevis is particularly delightful, thanks to the sterling views of St. Kitts. You can rent kayaks, Hobie Cats, and Sunfish from **Oualie Beach Club** (⊠ Oualie Beach, ☎ 869/469–9518), which also provides excellent instruction. **Nevis Water Sports** (⊠ Jones Estate, ☎ 869/469–9060) also rents everything from Sunfish ($20 per hour) to powerboats ($100 per hour).

FISHING

Fishing here includes kingfish, wahoo, grouper, tuna, and yellowtail snapper, with marlin occasionally spotted. The best areas are Monkey Shoals and around Redonda. Charters are $350 per half day. **Nevis Water Sports** (⊠ Jones Estate, ☎ 869/469–9060) offers sport fishing aboard its tournament-winning boats, the 31-ft *Sea Brat* and *Sea Troll,* under the supervision of Captain Julian Rigby. If you want local expertise, call **Captain Valentine Glasgow** (☎ 869/469–1989), who has a 31-ft Ocean Master, *Lady James,* to take you in search of the big ones.

GOLF

Duffers doff their hats to the beautiful, impeccably maintained Robert Trent Jones Jr.–designed 18-hole, par-72, 6,766-yard championship course at the **Four Seasons Resort Nevis** (⊠ Pinney's Beach, ☎ 869/469–1111). The signature hole is the 15th, a 660-yard monster that encompasses a deep ravine; other holes include bridges, steep drops, rolling pitches, and fierce doglegs. The virtual botanical gardens surrounding the fairways almost qualify as a hazard themselves. Greens fees are $100 per person for nine holes, $150 for 18.

HIKING

The center of the island is Nevis Peak, which soars 3,232 ft (967 m) and is flanked by Hurricane Hill on the north and Saddle Hill on the south. If you plan to scale Nevis Peak, a day-long affair, it is highly recommended that you go with a guide. Your hotel can arrange it (and a picnic lunch) for you.

Eco-Tours Nevis (☎ 869/469–2091), headed by David Rollinson, rambles through 18th-century estates and explores what remains of Nevis's last working sugar factory as well as archaeological evidence of pre-Columbian settlements. David also offers treks up Mountravers, a spectacular great-house ruin, and historical walks through Charlestown. The fee is $20 per person, $10 for the Charleston walk. **Michael Herbert** (☎ 869/469–2856) leads four-hour nature hikes up to Herbert

Heights, where he offers fresh local juices as you drink in the views of Montserrat; his powerful telescope makes you feel as if you're staring right into that island's simmering volcano. The price is $20; for $25 you can ride one of Herbert's donkeys. Michael also brings people up by appointment to Saddle Hill Battery and Nelson's Lookout, where he constructed a thatched hut. The festive atmosphere includes crab races, refreshments, rock climbing, and whale-watching in season through a telescope donated by Greenpeace. **Upper Round Road Trail** is a 9-mi (14½-km) road constructed in the late 1600s and recently cleared and restored by the **Nevis Historical and Conservation Society** (NHCS; ☎ 869/469–5786). Now a heritage trail, it connects the Golden Rock Hotel, on the east side of the island, with Nisbet Plantation Beach Club, on the northern tip. The trail encompasses numerous vegetation zones, including pristine rain forest, and impressive plantation ruins. The original cobblestones are still evident in many places. The NHCS sells an informational guidebook on the trail at various shops and the island museums. **Top to Bottom** (☎ 869/469–9080), run by Jim and Nikki Johnston, offers ecorambles (slower tours) and hikes that emphasize Nevis's volcanic and horticultural heritage (including pointing out folkloric herbal medicines). The Johnstons are also keen bird-watchers. Three-hour rambles or hikes are $20 per person (snacks and juice included); it's $30 for a more strenuous climb up Mt. Nevis.

HORSEBACK RIDING
You can arrange for leisurely beach rides or tackle more demanding trail rides through the lush hills ($50 per person) and lessons ($20 per hour) through **Nevis Equestrian Centre** (✉ Pinney's Beach at Clifton Estate, ☎ 869/469–8118). Kids will love the petting zoo, with donkeys, goats, peacocks, and tortoises.

SCUBA DIVING AND SNORKELING
The Devil's Caves are a series of grottoes where divers can navigate tunnels, canyons, and underwater hot springs while viewing lobsters, sea fans, sponges, squirrel fish, and much more. The village of Jamestown was washed into the sea around Fort Ashby, just south of Cades Bay, making the area a popular spot for snorkeling and diving. Reef-protected Pinney's Beach offers especially good snorkeling. Single-tank dives are usually $50, two-tank dives $80.

Under the Sea (✉ Tamarind Bay, ☎ 869/469–1291) is the inventive brainchild of Barbara Whitman, a marine biologist from Connecticut. It doubles as a restaurant-bar and snorkeling center, where Barbara gives comprehensive snorkeling lessons and tours, stressing both comprehensive knowledge and ecological awareness. She has painted a detailed mural of Nevisian marine life on one wall, which she uses for initial familiarization with the various underwater environments, followed by hands-on demonstrations in the plexiglass "touch-tanks" teeming with over 50 species. The lessons, held twice daily except Mondays, and tours (in sleek trimarans on the small dark-sand beach) are $20 ($35 with snorkel tour included), and profits go to educating local school children. Try **Dive Nevis** (✉ Pinney's Beach, ☎ 869/469–9373) for excellent, affordable dives and packages. **Scuba Safaris** (✉ Oualie Beach, ☎ 869/469–9518) is a PADI five-star facility, NAUI Dream Resort, and NASDS Examining Station, whose experienced dive masters offer everything from a resort course to full certification. They also provide a snorkeling-learning experience that enables you to not only see but listen to sealife, including whales and dolphins.

TENNIS
There are 10 tennis courts (3 lighted), 6 clay and 4 all-weather hardcourts, at the **Four Seasons Resort Nevis** (✉ Pinney's Beach, ☎ 869/

469–1111), which also offers instruction by Peter Burwash International pros. The court at **Hermitage Plantation** (✉ St. John Fig Tree Parish, ☎ 869/469–3477) is often graciously rented for nominal fees to nonguests. The court at **Golden Rock** (✉ Gingerland, ☎ 869/469–3346) can be rented by nonguests.

WINDSURFING

Waters are generally calm and winds steady yet gentle, making Nevis an excellent spot for beginners and intermediates. **Windsurfing Nevis** (✉ Oualie Beach Hotel, ☎ 869/469–9682) offers top-notch instructors (Winston Crooke is one of the best in the islands) and equipment for $25 per half hour.

Spectator Sports

One of the Caribbean's most unusual events is the occasional "Day at the Races," sponsored by the **Nevis Turf and Jockey Club** (☎ 869/469–3477). The races, which attract a "pan-Caribbean field" (as the club likes to boast), are held on a windswept course called Indian Castle, overlooking the "white horses" of the Atlantic. Last-minute changes and scratches are common; a party atmosphere prevails, with local ladies dispensing heavenly fried chicken and gossip.

Shopping

Nevis is certainly not the place for a shopping spree, but there are some unique and wonderful surprises, notably the island's stamps, batik, and hand-embroidered clothing.

Areas and Malls

Other than a few hotel boutiques and isolated galleries, virtually all shopping is concentrated on or just off Main Street in Charlestown. The lovely old stonework and wood floors of the waterfront Cotton Ginnery Complex make an appropriate setting for stalls of local artisans.

Specialty Items

ART

Nevis has produced one artist of some international repute, the late Dame Eva Wilkin, who for more than 50 years painted island people, flowers, and landscapes in an evocative art naïf style (an Eva Wilkin mural hangs over the bar at the Golden Rock). Her originals sell for $100 and up, and prints are available in some local shops. The **Eva Wilkin Gallery** (✉ Clay Ghaut, Gingerland, ☎ 869/469–2673) occupies her former atelier. If the paintings, drawings, and prints are out of your price range, consider buying the lovely note cards based on her designs. The front rooms of **Café des Arts** (✉ Main St., ☎ 869/469–7098) carry Kate Spencer's marvelous hand-painted silk scarves and pareos, prints, notebooks, and place mats; still more island paintings (many from Haiti) and pottery are displayed in the charming interior courtyard, where light lunches and superb croissants and espresso are served. **Robert Humphreys** sells his paintings, flowing bronze sculptures of pirouetting marlins, and clay renderings of local fauna from his studio (✉ Palm Hill, Brazier Estate, ☎ 869/469–2421). You must call ahead for an appointment.

CLOTHING

Beach Works (✉ Pinney's Beach, inside Beachcomber restaurant, ☎ 869/469–0620) has become the island's classiest boutique, with an excellent selection of everything from bathing suits to Balinese batik and puppets. The adjoining restaurant also exhibits works by island artists on its walls. You'll find Caribelle Batik caftans, scarves, shorts, and blouses, as well as caps, T-shirts, jewelry, steel drums, straw hats, painted fish, and anything conceivable emblazoned with the name Nevis in the **Island Hopper** (⊠ Main St., ☎ 869/469–5430). **Fanny's Closet,** in The Hermitage, sells John Warden's line of flowing, breathable linen resortwear in eggshell to earth tones, as well as hand-painted baubles and bibelots. **Jerveren's Fashions** (⊠ Cotton Ginnery, ☎ 869/469–0062) carries still more batik resort wear and light cotton sundresses in pastel colors.

FOOD & WINE

Beekeeping is a buzzing biz, and you'll find beeswax candles (which burn longer than those made of regular wax) and fragrant, tropically flavored honey at many stores. Quentin Henderson, the amiable head of the **Nevis Beekeeping Cooperative,** will even arrange trips by appointment to various hives for demonstrations of beekeeping procedures (⊠ Gingerbread, ☎ 869/469–5521). At **Caribbean Wine** (⊠ Prospect Rd., ☎ 869/469–3908), Dominique Nelson Ashley, a chemist by trade, produces surprisingly tasty wines by traditional methods from local plants such as soursop, white sorrel, ginger, guava, red plum, passion fruit, cane, mango, and star apple. He then corks and seals them in recycled bottles.

HANDICRAFTS

Caribco Gifts (⊠ Main St., ☎ 869/469–1432) sells affordable T-shirts, candles, and pottery emblazoned with Nevis logos. **Knick Knacks** (⊠ Between Waterfront and Main sts., next to Unella's Restaurant, ☎ 869/469–5784) showcases top local artisans, including Marvin Chapman (stone and wood carvings) and Jeannie Rigby (exquisite dolls). The **Nevis Handicraft Co-op Society** (⊠ Main St., ☎ 869/469–1746), next to the tourist office, offers work by local artisans (clothing, ceramic ware, woven goods) and locally produced honey, hot sauces, and jellies. **AAAC** (⊠ Main St., ☎ 869/469–0657) is the acronym for Adams Afro-Caribbean Art & Craft; the name's promise is fulfilled with such striking pieces as drums from Mozambique, hand-carved elephant and lion walking sticks, Nigerian warri boards, Guyanese painted gourds, and various masks and straw mats. **Bocane Ceramics** (⊠ Main St., ☎ no phone) stocks beautifully designed and glazed local pottery, such as platters painted with marine life. Stamp collectors should head for the **Philatelic Bureau** (☎ 869/469–0617), off Main Street opposite the tourist office. St. Kitts and Nevis are famous for their decorative, and sometimes valuable, stamps. Real beauties include the butterfly, hummingbird, and marine life series. An early Kittitian stamp recently brought in $7,000.

Nightlife

In season it is usually easy to find a local calypso singer or a steel or string band performing at one of the hotels (one combo, Carib Roots, plays nightly on the Ocean Terrace at the **Four Seasons Resort Nevis** (⊠ Pinney's Beach, ☎ 869/469–1111). Such performances are often in tandem with a special buffet dinner. Scan the posters plastered on doorways announcing informal jump-ups.

BARS

Beachcomber (⊠ Pinney's Beach, ☎ 869/469–1192) offers huge barbecues, happy hours, and occasional live bands in addition to a simple menu of burgers and grilled meats. The Charlestown lunchtime staple, **Eddy's Bar and Restaurant** (⊠ Main St., Memorial Sq., ☎ 869/469–5958), opens Wednesday nights for a raucous West Indian happy hour featuring half-price snacks, including tannia and conch fritters served with terrific hot sauce made by Eddy's mom, Eulalie Williams (you can buy a bottle down the block at the Main Street Supermarket) and dancing, usually to a live string band. **The Pump House** (⊠ Pump St., by the cemetery, ☎ No phone) is the informal name for a lively Friday-night jump-up that's run by two fellows from the local water department. Cars line the streets and the guys dish up fabulous BBQ ribs and chicken—as certain customers lobby to get their water pressure adjusted. It's a classic Caribbean scene. **Under the Sea** (⊠ Tamarind Bay, ☎ 869/469–1291) features not only sterling sunset views overlooking St. Kitts, but a fine menu, dancing to live bands into the wee hours on weekends, and owner Barbara Whitman's cool aquariums and hand-painted murals of marine life.

DANCE AND MUSIC CLUBS

Apart from the hotel scene, there are a few places where young locals go for late-night calypso, reggae, and other island music. **Dick's Bar** (⊠ Brickiln, ☎ No phone) has live music or a DJ on Friday and Saturday evenings. **Sand Dollar** (⊠ Pinney's Beach, ☎ no phone), an informal beach hangout, is the hopping happening spot on Friday nights for boogieing barefoot in the sand.

Exploring Nevis

Nevis's main road makes a 20-mi (32-km) circuit through the five parishes; various offshoots of the road wind into the mountains. You can tour Charlestown, the capital, in a half hour or so, but you'll need three to four hours to explore the entire island. Part of the island's charm is its rusticity: there are no traffic lights, goats still amble through the streets of Charlestown, and local grocers announce whatever's in stock on a blackboard (anything from pig snouts to beer).

Numbers in the margin correspond to points of interest on the Nevis map.

SIGHTS TO SEE

② Bath Springs. The springs and the ruins of the Bath Hotel, built by John Huggins in 1778, sustained hurricane damage in 1995 and 1998, and reopening has been delayed while the government lobbies the private sector to create a modernized spa (well, that's the official story, anyway; the full story is a complex web of Caribbean politics). The springs, with temperatures of 104–108°F, bubble out of the hillside. Huggins' 50-room hotel, the first hotel in the Caribbean (and allegedly a notorious brothel), was next to the waters. Eighteenth-century accounts reported that a few days of imbibing and soaking in these waters resulted in miraculous cures. It would take a minor miracle to restore the decayed hotel to anything like grandeur—it closed down in the late 19th century—but the spring house has been partially restored. Although locals still romp in the waters, you should think twice about it (not only are the springs dirty, but they're closed, making such a romp technically illegal). Still, this is a fascinating sight. ⊠ *Follow Main St. south from Charlestown, past Caribbean Cove.* ⊑ *Free.* ☺ *Weekdays 8–noon and 1–3:30, Sat. 8–noon.*

① Charlestown. About 1,200 of the island's 9,300 inhabitants live in the capital of Nevis. The town faces the Caribbean, about 12½ mi (20 km) south of Basseterre on St. Kitts. If you arrive by ferry, as most people do, you'll walk smack onto Main Street from the pier. Although it's true that tiny Charlestown, founded in 1660, has seen better times, it's easy to imagine how it must have looked in its heyday. The weathered buildings still have their fanciful galleries, elaborate gingerbread fretwork, wooden shutters, and hanging plants. The stonework building with the clock tower houses the 1825 courthouse and the second-floor library, open Monday to Saturday, 9 to 6. A fire in 1873 damaged the building and destroyed valuable records; much of the present building dates from the turn of the 20th century. You're welcome to poke around the library, one of the coolest places on the island. The little park next to it is Memorial Square, dedicated to the fallen of World Wars I and II. Down the street from the square, archaeologists have discovered the remains of a Jewish cemetery and synagogue (Nevis reputedly had the Caribbean's second-oldest congregation), but though the tourist board makes a big deal out of it, there's nothing to see.

The **Alexander Hamilton Birthplace,** which contains the Museum of Nevis History, is on the waterfront, covered in bougainvillea and hibiscus. This Georgian-style house is a reconstruction of the statesman's original home, built in 1680 and thought to have been destroyed during an earthquake in the mid-19th century. Hamilton was born here in 1755. He left for the American colonies 17 years later to continue his education; he became secretary of the Treasury to George Washington and died in a duel with political rival Aaron Burr. The Nevis House of Assembly occupies the second floor of this building, and the museum downstairs contains Hamilton memorabilia, documents pertaining to the island's history, and displays on island geology, politics, architecture, and cuisine. ⊠ *Low St.,* ☎ *869/469–5786,* WEB *www. nevis-nhcs.com.* ☞ *$2 ($1 if admission already paid to affiliated Nelson Museum).* ⊙ *Weekdays 9–4, Sat. 9–noon.*

6 Eden Brown Estate. This government-owned mansion, built around 1740, is known as Nevis's haunted house or, rather, haunted ruins. In 1822 a Miss Julia Huggins was to marry a fellow named Maynard. However, on the day of the wedding, the groom and his best man had a duel and killed each other. The bride-to-be became a recluse, and the mansion was closed down. Local residents claim they can feel the presence of "someone" whenever they go near the eerie old house with its shroud of weeds and wildflowers. You're welcome to drop by; it's always open, and it's free. ⊠ *East Coast Rd., between Lime Kiln and Mannings,* ☎ *No phone.*

7 Ft. Ashby. Overgrown with tropical vegetation, this site overlooks the place where the settlement of Jamestown fell into the sea after a tidal wave hit the coast in 1680. Needless to say, this is a favorite scuba-diving site. ⊠ *1½ mi (2½ km) southwest of Hurricane Hill, on Main Rd.*

3 Nelson Museum. This collection merits a visit for its memorabilia of Lord Nelson, including letters, documents, paintings, and even furniture from his flagship. Nelson was based in Antigua but came to Nevis often to court, and eventually to marry, Frances Nisbet, who lived on a 64-acre plantation here. ⊠ *Bath Rd.,* ☎ *869/469–0408.* ☞ *$2 ($1 if admission already paid to affiliated Museum of Nevis History).* ⊙ *Weekdays 9–4, Sat. 9–noon.*

5 Nevis Botanical Gardens. In addition to terraced gardens and arbors, this remarkable 7.8-acre site, in the glowering shadow of Mt. Nevis, has natural lagoons, streams, and waterfalls, as well as superlative bronze mermaids, egrets and herons, old copper pots used as floral centerpieces, and extravagant fountains. You'll find a proper rose garden, sections devoted to orchids and bromeliads, cacti, and flowering trees and shrubs—even a bamboo garden. The entrance to the Rain Forest Conservatory—which attempts to include every conceivable Caribbean ecosystem and then some—duplicates an imposing Mayan temple. A splendid re-creation of a plantation-style great house contains a tea room with sweeping sea views and a souvenir shop that sells teas, teapots, jams, botanical oils, candles, Caribbean cookbooks, and the like. ⊠ *Montpelier Estate,* ☎ *869/469–3399 or 869/469–3509.* ☞ *$8.* ⊙ *Daily 10–6.*

❹ **St. John's Church.** Among the records of this church built in 1680 is a tattered, prominently displayed marriage certificate that reads: HORATIO NELSON, ESQUIRE, TO FRANCES NISBET, WIDOW, ON MARCH 11, 1787. ✉ *Fig Tree Parish*, ☎ *No phone.*

❽ **St. Thomas Anglican Church.** The island's oldest church was built in 1643 and has been altered many times over the years. The gravestones in the old churchyard have stories to tell, and the church itself contains memorials to Nevis's early settlers. ✉ *Along the main west coast road, just south of Cotton Ground*, ☎ *No phone.*

ST. KITTS AND NEVIS A TO Z

To research prices, get advice from other travelers, and book travel arrangements, visit www.fodors.com.

AIR TRAVEL

American flies into San Juan, Puerto Rico, where its commuter arm, American Eagle, flies twice daily to St. Kitts. Other major domestic airlines fly from their eastern hubs either into Antigua, St. Thomas, or St. Maarten, where connections to St. Kitts (and, less frequently, to Nevis) can be made on American Eagle, LIAT, and Windward Island Airways. British Airways flies daily from London to Antigua; Air Canada, daily in season from Toronto to Antigua.

➤ AIRLINES AND CONTACTS: **Air Canada** (☎ 800/776–3000); **American/American Eagle** (☎ 869/465–0500); **British Airways** (☎ 800/247–9297); **LIAT** (☎ 869/465–8613); **Windward Island Airways** (☎ 869/465–8010).

AIRPORTS

Taxis meet every flight at the newly expanded and modernized Robert L. Bradshaw Golden Rock Airport on St. Kitts and Newcastle Airport on Nevis. The taxis are unmetered, but fixed rates, in EC dollars, are posted at the airport and at the jetty. Note that rates are the same for one to four passengers. On St. Kitts the fare from the airport to the closest hotel in Basseterre is EC$18; to the farthest point, EC$72. From the airport on Nevis it costs EC$20 to Nisbet Plantation, EC$37 to the Four Seasons, and EC$45 to Golden Rock. Before setting off in a cab, be sure to clarify whether the rate quoted is in EC or U.S. dollars. There's a 50% surcharge for trips made between 10 PM and 6 AM.

➤ AIRPORT INFORMATION: **Robert L. Bradshaw Golden Rock Airport** (☎ No phone) is located just north of Basseterre, outside the village of Golden Rock. **Newcastle Airport** (☎ No phone) on Nevis is located at the northern tip of the island in Newcastle.

BOAT AND FERRY TRAVEL

There are three services between St. Kitts and Nevis, all with byzantine schedules that are subject to change. Call the ferry information lines for the most up-to-date schedules. The 150-passenger government-operated ferry M/V *Caribe Queen* makes the 45-minute crossing from Nevis to St. Kitts twice daily except Thursday and Sunday. Round-trip fare is $8. The former cargo ship, *Sea Hustler* is larger and makes the trip twice daily. Nevis Cruise Lines runs an air-conditioned, 110-passenger ferry, the M/V *Spirit of Mount Nevis,* which makes the run twice daily Thursday and Sunday. The fare is $12 ($15 first class) round-trip.

Sea-taxi service between the two islands is operated by Kenneth Samuel, Todd Leypoldt of Wahoo Water Tours, Nevis Water Sports, Leeward Island Charters, and Auston MacLeod of Pro-Divers for $20 one-way in summer, $25 in winter; discounts can be negotiated for small groups.

Sample taxi fares from the ferry dock in Charlestown are EC$18 to the Four Seasons and EC$27 to Hermitage.

FARES AND SCHEDULES

➤ BOAT FERRY INFORMATION: **Ferry information** (☎ 869/466–INFO); **Kenneth Samuel** (☎ 869/465–2670); **Leeward Island Charters** (☎ 869/465–7474); **Nevis Cruise Lines** (☎ 869/469–9373); **Nevis Water Sports** (☎ 869/469–9060); **Pro-Divers** (☎ 869/465–3223); *Sea Hustler* (☎ 869/467–9702 or 869/467–9826); **Wahoo Water Tours** (☎ 869/465–2690).

BUSINESS HOURS

BANKS

Hours vary somewhat for banks but are typically Monday–Thursday 8–3 and Friday 8–5. St. Kitts & Nevis National Bank is also open Saturday 8:30 AM–11 AM.

POST OFFICES

Post offices are open Monday–Wednesday and Friday 8–3, Thursday and Saturday 8–noon.

SHOPS

Although shops used to close for lunch from noon–1, more and more establishments are remaining open Monday–Saturday 8–4. Some shops close earlier on Thursday.

CAR RENTALS

You'll need a local driver's license, which you can get by presenting yourself, your valid driver's license, and $20 at the police station on Cayon Street in Basseterre (on Nevis the car-rental agency will help you obtain a local license at the police station). The license is valid for one year. Car rentals start at about $35 per day for a compact; expect to pay a few extra bucks for air-conditioning. Most agencies offer substantial discounts when you rent by the week.

Agencies include Avis, which has the best selection of Suzuki and Daihatsu four-wheel-drive vehicles. Delise Walwyn also provides an excellent selection and the option of a replacement car for one day on Nevis if you rent for three days or more on St. Kitts. TDC Rentals has a wide selection of vehicles and outstanding service; it offers a three-day rental that includes a car on both islands.

➤ MAJOR AGENCIES: **Avis** (✉ S. Independence Sq., ☎ 869/465–6507); **Delise Walwyn** (☎ 869/465–8449, WEB www.delisleco.com); **TDC Rentals** (✉ W. Independence Sq., Basseterre, St. Kitts, ☎ 869/465–2991; ✉ Bay Rd., Charlestown, Nevis, ☎ 869/469–5690, WEB www.cp-scaribnet.com/tdc/rental.html).

CAR TRAVEL

One well-kept main road circumnavigates St. Kitts, and signs are usually clearly marked, making it difficult to get lost. If you'd like to dine at the various inns and sightsee for more than one day, a car is advisable. If you plan to stay in the Frigate Bay–Basseterre area on St. Kitts, you can get by using taxis and doing a half-day island tour. You may not want to drive in Nevis. The island's roads are not in good shape; driving is on the left; and to make it more difficult, you may be given a right-drive vehicle. And if you deviate from Main Street in Charlestown, you're likely to have trouble finding your way.

GASOLINE

Gasoline is expensive, about $2.75 per gallon.

ROAD CONDITIONS

The main roads on St. Kitts are in admirable condition, especially in the more developed southwestern part, though the northeast can get a bit bumpy and the access roads to the plantation inns are notoriously rough. The roads on Nevis are pocked with crater-size potholes, and pigs, goats, and cattle amble along the road.

RULES OF THE ROAD

Driving is on the left.

ELECTRICITY

St. Kitts and Nevis hotels function on 110 volts, 60 cycles, making all North American appliances safe to use.

EMERGENCIES

➤ AMBULANCE AND FIRE: Dial ☎ 911 for an ambulance. On St. Kitts, dial ☎ 869/465–2333 to report a fire. On Nevis, dial ☎ 869/469–5391 to report a fire.

➤ HOSPITALS: **Joseph N. France General Hospital** (⊠ Cayon St., Basseterre, St. Kitts, ☎ 869/465–2551); **Alexandra Hospital** (⊠ Government Rd., Charlestown, Nevis, ☎ 869/469–5473).

PHARMACIES

There are no 24-hour pharmacies on St. Kitts or Nevis, but several are open seven days a week, usually until at least 5 PM. Call ahead if it's late in the afternoon, though.

➤ CONTACTS: **City Drug** (⊠ Fort St., Basseterre, St. Kitts, ☎ 869/465–2156; ⊠ Sun 'n' Sand Beach Resort, Frigate Bay, St. Kitts, ☎ 869/465–1803); **Claxton Medical Centre Pharmacy** (⊠ Main St., Charlestown, Nevis, ☎ 869/469–5357); **Evelyn's Drugstore** (⊠ Main St., Charlestown, Nevis, ☎ 869/469–5278) ; **Parris Pharmacy** (⊠ Central St., Basseterre, St. Kitts, ☎ 869/465–8569).

➤ POLICE: Dial ☎ 911.

ETIQUETTE AND BEHAVIOR

People are friendly but shy; always ask before you take photographs. Also, be sure to wear wraps or shorts over beach attire when you're in public places.

FESTIVALS AND SEASONAL EVENTS

ST. KITTS

Carnival is held for 10 days immediately following Christmas Eve and is the usual riot of color and noise, with steel-band and Calypso Monarch competitions and flamboyant parades of the various troupes. The St. Kitts Music Festival, held the last week of June, celebrates everything from R&B to reggae. Among the top international acts to perform have been Chaka Khan, Earl Klugh, Kool and the Gang, and Peabo Bryson. Much of September is devoted to various Independence Celebrations (contact the Government Information Service for information), ranging from beach picnic to military parades and theatrical events.
➤ CONTACTS: **Carnival** (☎ 869/465–4151); **Independence Celebrations** (☎ 869/465–2521); **St. Kitts Music Festival** (☎ 869/465–4040).

NEVIS

As on St. Kitts, Carnival is held for 10 days immediately following Christmas Eve. A special Tourism Week is usually held in mid-February and includes horse races, bartender competitions, and jump-ups. Early August's Culturama and mid-September's Heritage Week include pageants, jump-ups, and celebrations of local culture, from food fairs to craft exhibitions.

➤ CONTACTS: **Carnival** (☎ 869/469–1042); **Culturama** (☎ 869/469–1992); **Heritage Week** (☎ 869/469–1992); **Tourism Week** (☎ 869/469–1042).

HEALTH
The water in St. Kitts and Nevis is safe to drink, and there are no other health concerns of note on either island.

HOLIDAYS
Public holidays for 2002 are: New Year's Day, Ash Wednesday (Feb. 13), Easter Monday (April 1), Labour Day (May 7), Whit Monday (June 10), Emancipation Day (Aug. 6), Independence Day (Sept. 19), Christmas Day, and Boxing Day (Dec. 26).

LANGUAGE
The official language of St. Kitts and Nevis is English, which is spoken with a strong West Indian lilt.

MAIL AND SHIPPING
Airmail letters to the United States and Canada cost EC90¢ per half ounce; postcards require EC80¢; to the United Kingdom letters cost EC$1.20, postcards EC$1; to Australia and New Zealand, letters cost EC$1.60, postcards EC$1.20. Mail takes at least 7 to 10 days to reach the United States. St. Kitts and Nevis issue separate stamps, but each honors the other's. The beautiful stamps are collector's items, and you may have a hard time pasting them on postcards.

MONEY MATTERS
Prices quoted throughout this chapter are in U.S. dollars unless otherwise noted.

ATMS
The Royal Bank of St. Kitts has an ATM that accepts CIRRUS and PLUS cards. There are no ATMs on Nevis.
➤ CONTACTS: **Royal Bank of St. Kitts** (✉ Independence Sq., Basseterre).

CREDIT CARDS
Most large hotels, restaurants, and shops accept major credit cards, but small inns and shops often do not.

CURRENCY
Legal tender is the Eastern Caribbean (EC) dollar. The rate of exchange was EC$2.70 to US$1. U.S. dollars are accepted practically everywhere, but you'll usually get change in EC currency.

CURRENCY EXCHANGE
Exchanging currency is usually not necessary.

PASSPORTS AND VISAS
U.S. and Canadian citizens need a valid passport or must prove citizenship with a birth certificate (with a raised seal) accompanied by a government-issued photo ID. British citizens must have a passport. A return or ongoing ticket is mandatory.

SAFETY
Visitors, especially women, should not jog on long, lonely roads.

SIGHTSEEING TOURS
The taxi driver who picks you up will probably offer to act as your guide to the island. Each driver is knowledgeable and does a three-hour tour of Nevis for $50 and a four-hour tour of St. Kitts for $60. He can

also make a lunch reservation at one of the plantation restaurants, and you can incorporate this into your tour.

BOAT

In addition to the usual snorkeling, sunset, and party cruises (ranging in price from $35 to $65), nearly all the companies listed below are beginning to offer humpback whale-watching excursions during the winter migrating season, January to April. On St. Kitts, Blue Water Safaris offers half-day snorkeling trips or beach barbecues on deserted cays, as well as sunset and moonlight cruises on its 65-ft catamaran *Irie Lime*. Leeward Island Charters offers day and overnight charters on three catamarans—the 47-ft *Caona*, and two 70-footers *Eagle* and *Spirit of St. Kitts*. Day sails are from 9:30 to 4:30 and include a barbecue, an open bar, and use of snorkeling equipment. Banana Boat Tours provides snorkeling and sunset cruises from Turtle Beach on its 34-ft inflatable, Coast Guard-certified Scarib boat. Private charters, Nevis–St. Kitts shuttles, and deep sea fishing can be arranged. Turtle Tours offers sea kayaking along the Nevis coast, stopping at an otherwise inaccessible beach underneath a towering cliff for snorkeling and at Pinney's for refreshments and a refreshing view of St. Kitts. Tropical Tours offers moonlight cruises on the 52-ft catamaran *Cileca III* as well as glass-bottom-boat tours. On Nevis, Sea Nevis Charters offers its 44-ft *Sea Dreamer* for snorkeling and island sunset cruises.

➤ CONTACTS: **Banana Boat Tours** (☎ 869/469–9086); **Blue Water Safaris** (☎ 869/466–4933); **Leeward Island Charters** (☎ 869/465–7474); **Sea Nevis Charters** (✉ Cades Bay, ☎ 869/469–9239); **Turtle Tours** (☎ 869/469–8503); **Tropical Tours** (☎ 869/465–4167).

ORIENTATION

Kantours offers general island tours. Tropical Tours can run you around St. Kitts and take you to the rain forest for $45 per person. Norris Martin's Paradise Tours offers a variety of options and will customize tours as well. On Nevis, All Seasons Streamline Tours has a fleet of air-conditioned 14-seat vans—operated by uniformed drivers—to take you around the island at a cost of $75 for three hours. Fitzroy "Teach" Williams is recommended: he's the former president of the taxi association—even older cabbies call him "the Dean." Jan's Travel Agency arranges half- and full-day tours of the island. You can also stop by the Nevis Tourist Office for the historical society's self-guided island tour.

➤ ST. KITTS CONTACTS: **Kantours** (☎ 869/465–2098); **Paradise Tours** (☎ 869/466–6999 or 869/465–4128); **Tropical Tours** (✉ Cayon St., Basseterre, ☎ 869/465–4167).

➤ NEVIS CONTACTS: **All Seasons Streamline Tours** (☎ 869/469–1138); **Fitzroy "Teach" Williams** (✉ Main St., Charlestown, ☎ 869/469–1140); **Jan's Travel Agency** (✉ Arcade, Charlestown, ☎ 869/469–5578); **Nevis Tourist Office** (✉ Main St., Charlestown, ☎ 869/469–1042).

SPECIAL-INTEREST

Mountain-biking is growing in popularity on both islands. On St. Kitts, Fun Bikes provides three 3-hour excursions daily on all-terrain quad bikes that hold two people. You'll wind through cane fields, rain forest, abandoned plantation ruins, and local villages. Free taxi transfers from Frigate Bay and Basseterre and a complimentary drink are included in the $65 rate. On Nevis, Windsurfing Nevis offers rentals as well as specially tailored tours on its state-of-the-art Gary Fisher, Trek, and Specialised bikes. The tours encompass lush rain forest, majestic ruins, and spectacular views. Rates vary according to itinerary and ability level. Wheel World is run by master windsurfer Winston Crooke, who has also won several bike competitions. Though the

shop primarily rents top-notch equipment, Winston and his associates also provide exhilarating tours, generally for experienced riders. Addy's Nature Tours, Greg's Safari, and Kriss Tours specialize in rain-forest and volcano tours on St. Kitts. David Rollinson of Eco-Tours Nevis and the folks at Top to Bottom organize hiking adventures on Nevis.
➤ CONTACTS: **Addy's Nature Tours** (☎ 869/465–8069); **Eco-Tours Nevis** (☎ 869/469–2091); **Fun Bikes** (☎ 869/466–3202 or 869/662–2088); **Greg's Safari** (☎ 869/465–4121); **Kriss Tours** (☎ 869/465–4042); **Top to Bottom** (☎ 869/469–5371); **Wheel World** (Main St., ☎ 869/469–7137); **Windsurfing Nevis** (☎ 869/469–9682).

TAXES

DEPARTURE TAX
The departure tax is $16.50. There's no departure tax when you depart from St. Kitts for Nevis, or vice versa.

SALES TAX
There is no sales tax on either St. Kitts or Nevis. Hotels collect a 7% government tax (8.5% on Nevis).

TAXIS
Taxi rates are government regulated and are posted at the airport, the dock, and in the free visitor tourist guide. There are fixed rates to and from all the hotels and to and from major points of interest. In St. Kitts you can call the St. Kitts Taxi Association. In Nevis, taxi service is available at the airport, by the dock in Charlestown, and through arrangements made at your hotel. Sample fares from the dock: EC40 to Nisbet Plantation, EC18 to the Four Seasons, and EC30 to Golden Rock.
➤ CONTACTS: **St. Kitts Taxi Association** (☎ 869/465–8487, 869/465–4253, or 869/465–7818 after hrs); **Nevis taxi service** (☎ 869/469–5621, 869/469–9790, or 869/469–5515 after dark).

TELEPHONES
Phone cards, which you can buy in denominations of $5, $10, and $20, are handy for making local phone calls, calling other islands, and accessing U.S. direct lines.

COUNTRY AND AREA CODES
To call St. Kitts and Nevis from the United States, dial the area code 869, then access code 465, 466, 468, or 469 and the local four-digit number.

INTERNATIONAL CALLS
A warning for both islands: many private lines and hotels charge access rates if you use your ATT, Sprint, or MCI calling card; there's no regularity, so phoning can be frustrating. Avoid using the widely advertised Skantel, which allows you to make credit-card calls; rates are usurious, and they freeze an outrageous amount of your available credit for up to a week until they put through the exact bill. Pay phones, usually found in major town squares, take EC coins or phone cards.

LOCAL CALLS
To make a local call, dial the seven-digit number.

TIPPING
Hotels add a 10% service charge to your bill. Restaurants occasionally do the same; to be on the safe side, ask if it is isn't printed on the menu. In restaurants, where there's no service charge included in the bill, a tip of 15% is appropriate. Taxi drivers typically receive a 10% tip, porters and bellmen $1 per bag; if you feel the service was exemplary, leave $3–$4 per night for the housekeeping staff.

TRANSPORTATION AROUND ST. KITTS AND NEVIS

AIRPLANES

LIAT, Carib Aviation, and Nevis Express are reliable charter operations providing service between St. Kitts and Nevis and to other islands. Nevis Express is currently the only carrier with regularly scheduled flights between St. Kitts and Nevis.

➤ CONTACTS: **Carib Aviation** (☎ 869/469–9295 in St. Kitts; 869/465–3055 in Nevis); **LIAT** (☎ 869/465–8613); **Nevis Express** (☎ 869/469–9755).

BUSES

A privately owned minibus circles St. Kitts. Check with the tourist office about schedules and fares.

VISITOR INFORMATION

➤ BEFORE YOU LEAVE: **St. Kitts & Nevis Tourist Board** (In the U.S.: ✉ 414 E. 75th St., New York, NY 10021, ☎ 212/535–1234 or 800/582–6208, WEB www.stkitts-nevis.com or www.nevisisland.com; in Canada: ✉ 365 Bay St., Suite 806, Toronto, Ontario M5H 2V1, Canada, ☎ 416/368–6707 or 888/395–4887; in the U.K. ✉ 10 Kensington Ct., London W8 5DL, U.K., ☎ 0171/376–0881).

➤ IN ST. KITTS AND NEVIS: **St. Kitts/Nevis Department of Tourism** (✉ Pelican Mall, Bay Rd., (Box 132), Basseterre, ☎ 869/465–2620 or 869/465–4040); **St. Kitts–Nevis Hotel Association** (✉ Liverpool Row (Box 438), Basseterre, ☎ 869/465–5304); **Nevis Tourist Office** (✉ Main St., Charlestown, ☎ 869/469–1042).

Updated by
Jane E. Zarem

Watching the festivities from the porch of the corner bar, the lady seems disappointed with the Friday-night street party. The pounding beat sounds more disco than Caribbean. "Where's the reggae, the calypso?" she wonders aloud. "It's down there, Miss," offers a wiry young man with a broad smile and smooth moves. "You have to be dancing, near the speakers. Come on." Taking her hand, he leads her to the middle of the street, where the melody is loud and clear, the rhythm, definitely Caribbean. To really enjoy the Gros Islet jump-up, you must first jump in.

Historians feel certain that the intrepid Christopher Columbus never set foot on St. Lucia. That was his loss. Today the eye-popping scenery and pristine beaches that Columbus missed are sprinkled with sprawling resorts, small hideaways, and friendly villages—all of which draw more and more visitors to this lush, tropical paradise.

Settled between Martinique and St. Vincent, and 100 mi (160 km) due west of Barbados, the 27 mi (43½ km) by 14 mi (22½ km) island of St. Lucia (pronounced *loo*-sha) occupies a prime position in the Caribbean, its natural beauty easily earning it the moniker of "the Helen of the West Indies." The capital city of Castries and surrounding villages in the north are home to 40% of the population; they are also the destination of most vacationers, who stay at posh resorts and play on honey-colored beaches. The south, on the other hand, is dominated by striking natural beauty. Thick jungle and vast banana plantations cover the hills, but a torturously winding road follows the coastline, cutting through mountains, rain forest, and fertile valleys. On the southwest coast, Petit Piton and Gros Piton, the island's unusual twin peaks, rise from the sea to more than 2,600 ft (795 m) and are familiar navigational landmarks to sailors and aviators alike. Divers are attracted to the reefs, found just offshore north of Soufrière, the picturesque French colonial capital of St. Lucia. Most of the natural tourist attractions are, in fact, situated in this area. "If you haven't been to Soufrière," the local people will tell you, "you haven't been to St. Lucia."

The Arawaks were St. Lucia's first inhabitants. They paddled up from South America sometime before AD 200. The aggressive Caribs followed, conquering the Arawaks around AD 800. The Caribs called the island Hewanorra (Land Where the Iguana Is Found) after the island's oldest and most unusual inhabitants. Having been hunted for their meat over the centuries, the iguanas are now on St. Lucia's endangered species list.

Caribs still lived on the island when Europeans attempted to establish a settlement. François Le Clerc, a pirate nicknamed Jambe de Bois (Wooden Leg), was actually the first European settler. In the late 16th century he holed up on Pigeon Island, just off St. Lucia's northernmost point, and attacked passing ships. In 1605, 67 English settlers bound for Guiana aboard the *Olive Branch* were blown off course and landed at the island's southern tip, near Vieux Fort. Within a few weeks, the Caribs had killed all but 19, who escaped in a canoe. Another group of English settlers came by 30 years later and were met with a similar lack of hospitality. The French arrived in 1651 after the French West India Company purchased the island.

For the next 150 years there were battles between the French and the English for possession of the island, with a dizzying 14 changes in power before the British took possession in 1814. During this time Europeans established sugar plantations, using slaves from West Africa to work the fields. By 1838, when the slaves were emancipated, more than 90% of the population was of African descent, and this is still the approximate racial mix of today's 150,000 St. Lucians. Beginning in 1863, the island developed a coal industry that flourished until about 1920. Indentured East Indian laborers were brought over in 1882 to help bail out the dying sugar industry, which suffered when slavery was abolished. Sugar all but died in the 1960s, when bananas (called "figs") became the major crop. On February 22, 1979, St. Lucia became an independent state within the British Commonwealth of Nations, with a resident governor-general appointed by the queen. Still, there are many relics of French occupation, notably the island patois (spoken in addition to English), the cuisine, the place names, and surnames.

Lodging

Virtually all St. Lucia's lodgings are along the calm Caribbean coast, either around Soufrière, to the south, or between Castries and Cap Estate, in the north. Low-rise resorts are tucked into lush surroundings on secluded coves, along unspoiled beaches, or in forested hillsides.

A group of 32 small hotels and inns, called Inns of St. Lucia, is represented by a central reservations service. Participating establishments are found all over the island; they have between 3 and 62 rooms, with rents starting at just $15 per room. For more information contact the **St. Lucia Tourist Board** (⊠ Pointe Seraphine, Castries, ☎ 758/452–4094, ℻ 758/453–1121). For villa rentals contact **Tropical Villas** (⊠ Box 189, Castries, ☎ 758/452–8240, ℻ 758/450–8089).

CATEGORY	COST*
$$$$	over $300
$$$	$200–$300
$$	$100–$200
$	under $100

All prices are for a standard double room, excluding 8% tax and 10% service charge. When comparing rates, remember that the price categories for all-inclusive resorts reflect the inclusion of all meals, beverages, and activities.

Castries and the North

$$$$ 🏨 **Hyatt Regency St. Lucia.** Strategically constructed on the narrow causeway that links the northern tip of St. Lucia with Pigeon Island, this ex-

Lodging

Anse Chastanet
Beach Hotel 5
Auberge
Seraphine 27
Bay Gardens 20
Club St. Lucia 12
Hummingbird
Beach Resort 6
Hyatt Regency
St. Lucia 13
Jalousie Hilton
Resort & Spa 8
Ladera Resort 9
LeSPORT 10
Marigot
Beach Club 3
Orange Grove
Hotel 23
Papillon St. Lucia . . . 19
Rendezvous 26
Royal St. Lucian 17
St. Lucian 18
Sandals Halcyon
St. Lucia 25
Sandals St. Lucia
Golf Resort & Spa . . 1
Still Plantation
& Beach Resort 7
Windjammer
Landing Villa
Beach Resort 22
Wyndham
Morgan
Bay Resort 24

Dining

Anse Chastanet
Beach Restaurant
and Bar 5
Capone's 15
The Coal Pot 29
La Creole 14
Dasheene
Restaurant
and Bar 9
The French
Restaurant 21
Great House 11
Green Parrot 2
Hummingbird
Restaurant 6
J.J.'s Paradise 4
Jimmie's 28
The Lime 16
The Still 7
Tao 10

St. Lucia

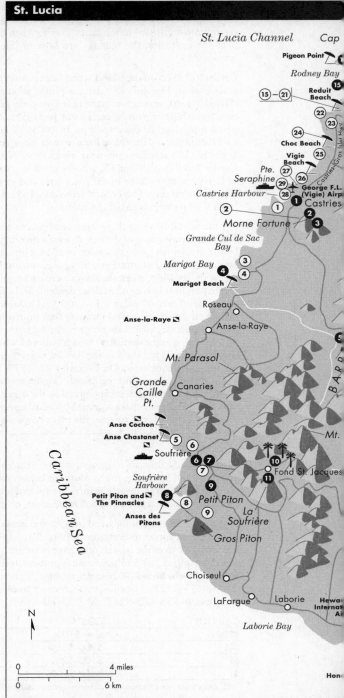

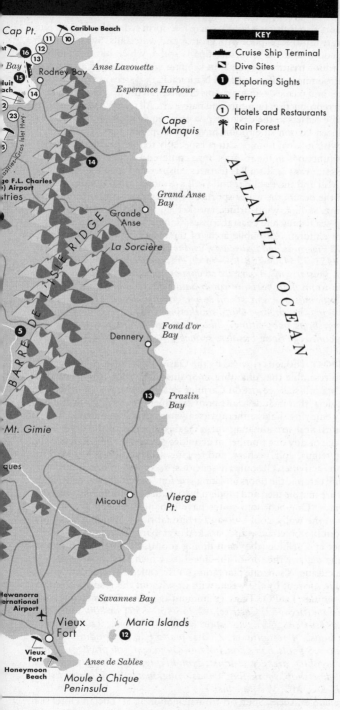

Exploring

Barre de l'Isle
Forest Reserve 5
Castries 1
Diamond
Botanical
Gardens 7
Ft. Charlotte 2
Fregate Island
Nature Reserve 13
Maria Islands
Nature Reserve 12
Marigot Bay 4
Marquis Estate 14
Morne Coubaril
Estate 9
Morne Fortune 3
Pigeon Island 16
The Pitons 8
Rodney Bay 15
St. Lucia
National
Rain Forest 10
Soufrière 6
La Soufrière
Drive-in
Volcano 11

KEY

🚢 Cruise Ship Terminal
🐚 Dive Sites
❶ Exploring Sights
⛴ Ferry
① Hotels and Restaurants
🌴 Rain Forest

travagant resort offers guest rooms with panoramic views of Rodney Bay and the Caribbean on one side or the Atlantic Ocean on the other. The resort also features a lavish 3-acre free-form swimming lagoon plus a separate multi-level pool with grottos and waterfalls. Sybaritic souls can be soothed at the luxurious Spa Coyaba, which has both indoor and outdoor treatment rooms. In keeping with its historical and natural surroundings—Pigeon Island National Park is steps away (and great for hikes and picnics)—guest rooms are decorated with plantation-style antique reproduction furniture and native art. All rooms have data ports and 110v outlets at the desk for powering equipment and appliances. Two dozen lagoon-side rooms have swim-up verandas. The Regency Club, with its own lounge, caters especially to guests attending meetings or functions in the resort's huge conference space. Admiral Rodney's Restaurant & Rum Bar features cuisines that span the globe. The Sugar Mill and the Pool Bar and Grill are more casual dining options. And at the beach, the water-sports pier offers guests opportunities for kayaking, sailing, windsurfing, snorkeling, and scuba diving, as well as deep-sea fishing and coastal cruises. Camp Hyatt activities are available for children. All public areas of the resort are wheelchair-accessible. ⊠ *Pigeon Island Causeway, Rodney Bay (Box 2247, Gros Islet),* ☎ *758/451–1234,* F̄A̅X̄ *758/450–9450,* W̄E̅B̄ *www.hyatt.com. 280 rooms, 4 villas. 3 restaurants, 4 bars, ice cream parlor, pizzeria, air-conditioning, fans, in-room data ports, in-room data safes, room service, 2 pools, hair salon, massage, spa, steam room, golf privileges, 2 tennis courts, gym, hiking, beach, dive shop, snorkeling, windsurfing, boating, waterskiing, shops, baby-sitting, children's programs, laundry service, concierge, concierge floor, business services, meeting rooms. AE, D, DC, MC, V. EP.*

$$$$ ⊞ **LeSPORT.** Though crowned by the Oasis—a "temple to well being"
★   built to resemble the Alhambra in Spain—LeSPORT is not exactly a spa. It's a full-scale resort on Cariblue Beach, at the very northern tip of St. Lucia, that includes daily body treatments in its rates. Spend half the day enjoying thalassotherapy (seawater beauty treatments), fitness programs, and stress-management classes; the rest of the time, enjoy the beach or any of a number of activities—scuba diving, waterskiing, sailing, tennis, golf, archery, and fencing. (Instruction is included for all sports activities.) Rooms are spacious, decorated in soft, muted pastels, with ceramic tile floors and king-size four-poster or twin beds. Bathrooms are marble tiled and modern but small. Each room has a balcony or terrace. One-bedroom suites have a hand-stenciled gingerbread motif on the walls, cool blue-and-white fabrics, white marble floors, huge double balconies, and stocked wet bars. Dining is excellent, whether at Cariblue (the main dining room), a casual buffet restaurant, the deli, or the top-of-the-line Tao, which serves pan-Asian, or fusion, cuisine. A separate plantation house, called "Manderley," is also available for rent by the week, with or without the resort's all-inclusive amenities. LeSPORT has a minimum age of 16. ⊠ *Cariblue Beach, Cap Estate (Box 437, Castries),* ☎ *758/450–8551 or 800/544–2883,* F̄A̅X̄ *758/450–0368,* W̄E̅B̄ *www.lesport.com.lc. 147 rooms, 9 suites, 1 plantation house. 4 restaurants, 2 bars, piano bar, air-conditioning, refrigerators, 3 pools, hair salon, hot tub, sauna, spa, golf privileges, tennis court, aerobics, archery, croquet, gym, hiking, Ping-Pong, volleyball, beach, dive shop, snorkeling, windsurfing, waterskiing, airport shuttle. AE, DC, MC, V. All-inclusive.*

$$$$ ⊞ **Papillon St. Lucia.** Spun off from neighboring St. Lucian Hotel several years ago, this 10-acre property on Reduit Beach is an all-inclusive resort. Rooms are furnished with one king-size or two twin beds, rattan furniture, tile floors, and tropical-print fabrics in blue and peach. Deluxe and superior quarters have air-conditioning, full baths,

sitting areas, minibars, and ocean views; standard rooms have ceiling fans and a shower only. Meals are served at The Monarch, the main restaurant, or The Clipper Bar, the informal beachside snack bar. Evening entertainment is presented at Tropigala lounge. ✉ *Box 512, Castries,* ☎ *758/452–0984 or 800/255–5859,* FAX *758/452–9332,* WEB *www.rexcaribbean.com. 140 rooms. Restaurant, bar, snack bar, air-conditioning, pool, golf privileges, 2 tennis courts, gym, shuffleboard, volleyball, beach, snorkeling, windsurfing, boating, waterskiing, shops, baby-sitting, children's club, laundry service. AE, DC, MC, V. All-inclusive.*

$$$$ 🏨 **Rendezvous.** This couples-only resort (under the same ownership as LeSPORT) sprawls along 2-mi (3-km) Malabar Beach amid 7 acres of gardens. The entrance is directly opposite the end of the George F. L. Charles Airport runway, so planes can be a distraction. Since the airport only accommodates small-propeller aircraft, however, the effect is almost charming—in a retro, B-movie kind of way. Accommodations have ginger-colored marble floors, king-size four-poster beds, large marble baths, and balconies or terraces—but no TVs. Meals are served buffet style at the beachfront terrace restaurant. There's also an air-conditioned dining room, the Trysting Place. (This resort caters only to male-female couples.) ✉ *Malabar Beach (Box 190, Castries),* ☎ *758/452–4211 or 800/544–2883,* FAX *758/452–7419,* WEB *www.rendezvous.com.lc. 84 rooms, 8 suites, 8 cottages. 2 restaurants, 2 bars, piano bar, air-conditioning, fans, 2 pools, 2 hot tubs, sauna, 2 tennis courts, aerobics, archery, gym, volleyball, beach, dive shop, boating, waterskiing, bicycles, shops, airport shuttle. AE, MC, V. All-inclusive.*

$$$$ 🏨 **Royal St. Lucian.** This classy resort, facing beautiful Reduit Beach,
★ caters to your every whim. The stunning colonnaded reception area greets you with a vaulted atrium, cool marble walls, a fountain, and a sweeping grand staircase. The russet-roofed white buildings form a *U* on the pristine grounds, so each guest room has an ocean view. The large, rambling pool has Japanese-style bridges, a waterfall, and a swim-up bar. The split-level suites are sumptuous, with sitting areas, luxurious bathrooms, large patios or balconies, soothing pastel color schemes, background music systems, cable TVs, three phones, and jet showers. Massages, hydrotherapy, and other treatments can be arranged at the Royal Spa. Dining is a pleasure at the elegant L'Epicure at dinner. La Nautique, a casual restaurant, serves all meals; La Mirage, which overlooks the pool, serves lunch alfresco. A stay here allows you to use the tennis and water-sports facilities at the adjacent sister property, the St. Lucian. ✉ *Reduit Beach, Rodney Bay (Box 977, Castries),* ☎ *758/452–9999 or 800/255–5859,* FAX *758/452–9639,* WEB *www. rexcaribbean.com. 96 suites. 3 restaurants, 2 bars, air-conditioning, in-room safes, minibars, room service, pool, massage, spa, health club, golf privileges, 2 tennis courts, beach, snorkeling, shops, baby-sitting, children's programs, laundry service, business services, meeting rooms. AE, DC, MC, V. EP, MAP.*

$$$$ 🏨 **Sandals Halcyon St. Lucia.** This resort for male-female couples only is 10 minutes north of Castries. All rooms are surrounded by gardens and have cable TV, attractive mahogany furniture (including king-size four-poster beds with bright print spreads), and white-tile floors. Although it's more low-key than its sister resort, the Sandals St. Lucia Golf Resort & Spa, the Halcyon is still fairly busy, and its guests and staff are enthusiastic. The sea here is generally calm, and you can enjoy a wide range of water sports and other activities—exercise equipment, nightly entertainment, and more. A shuttle runs hourly between the two Sandals resorts, so you can "stay at one, play at two." Three restaurants serve sumptuous buffet breakfasts and lunches, Italian, Caribbean, and international cuisine at dinner; and a snack bar serves

light food all day long. Seaside weddings are frequent. No tipping is allowed. ⊠ *Choc Bay (Box GM 910, Castries),* ☎ *758/453–0222 or 800/223–6510,* ℻ *758/451–8435,* WEB *www.sandals.com. 170 rooms. 3 restaurants, 2 bars, piano bar, snack bar, air-conditioning, 3 pools, hair salon, golf privileges, 2 tennis courts, basketball, gym, Ping-Pong, shuffleboard, volleyball, beach, snorkeling, windsurfing, boating, waterskiing, billiards, nightclub, airport shuttle. AE, DC, MC, V. All-inclusive.*

$$$$ 🖭 **Sandals St. Lucia Golf Resort & Spa.** This secluded 210-acre, all-inclusive resort for male-female couples only is a 15-minute drive south of Castries. Each room has rich mahogany furnishings and king-size four-poster beds, hair dryers, direct-dial phones, and cable TV. Several suites have concierge service, and many have their own plunge pools. Most important, guests seem to have a blast—thanks in part to a young, fun-loving staff. Resort facilities include a communal pool with a waterfall and bridges and a long crescent beach. Massages (single or duet), therapies, scrubs, and wraps are available at the full-service spa (for an additional charge). There's no shortage of restaurants either; choose Asian, Continental, French, Mediterranean, Southwestern, or Caribbean cuisine. For a change of scene you can also use the facilities and restaurants at sister resort Sandals Halcyon St. Lucia, just 20 minutes north. No tipping is allowed. ⊠ *La Toc Rd. (Box 399, Castries),* ☎ *758/452–3081 or 800/223–6510,* ℻ *758/453–7089,* WEB *www.sandals.com. 212 rooms, 116 suites. 6 restaurants, 9 bars, piano bar, air-conditioning, in-room safes, room service, 3 pools, hair salon, 2 hot tubs, spa, 9-hole golf course, 5 tennis courts, basketball, boccie, croquet, gym, horseshoes, Ping-Pong, shuffleboard, volleyball, beach, dive shop, snorkeling, windsurfing, boating, waterskiing, shops, billiards, nightclub, recreation room, laundry service, complimentary weddings, concierge floor, business services, meeting rooms, airport shuttle. AE, DC, MC, V. All-inclusive.*

$$$ 🖭 **Club St. Lucia.** Set on 65 acres at the island's northernmost point, this huge all-inclusive family resort has a village concept, with activities and amenities that appeal to people of all ages and interests. Tennis enthusiasts come to be close to the adjacent St. Lucia Racquet Club—free for guests—and golfers enjoy privileges at the Cap Estate course just across the road. Rooms and suites (called family rooms) sprawl on the hillside in buildings that are color-coordinated by village; each group has its own concierge, or "mayor." Accommodations are spacious, with one king-size or two queen-size beds, tile floors, patios, and air-conditioning in all but some standard rooms, which have ceiling fans. The children's club is separated by age group—nursery (infant–3), tiny tykes (4–9), and "older" kids (9–12). Teenagers have their "Jump" Club, complete with a juke box, a roller-blade track, and an e-mail system for keeping in touch with their parents. Live entertainment is scheduled nightly. In addition to being able to dine at several on-site restaurants and grab all-day snacks at pool-side food carts, a stay here gets you a discount at the Great House restaurant. ⊠ *Cap Estate (Box 915, Castries),* ☎ *758/450–0551, 800/777–1250, or 800/223–9815;* ℻ *758/450–0281,* WEB *www.splashresorts.htm. 297 rooms, 72 suites. 2 restaurants, 8 bars, pizzeria, 5 pools, hair salon, hot tub, spa, golf privileges, 9 tennis courts, gym, beach, snorkeling, windsurfing, boating, waterskiing, shops, dance club, children's programs, laundry service, travel services, car rental. AE, DC, MC, V. All-inclusive.*

$$$ 🖭 **St. Lucian Hotel.** The broad, white, informal lobby—with potted plants and upholstered sofas—leads to 10 acres of gardens, a pool, and beautiful Reduit Beach. Rooms are attractively decorated in rattan and tropical prints and have two double beds, TVs, and patios or balconies. Deluxe rooms have minibars, hair dryers, and ocean views. You can enjoy dining at the Oriental restaurant or stroll to any of several dining and nightspots in the Rodney Bay Marina area. ✉ *Reduit Beach, Rodney Bay (Box 512, Castries),* ☎ *758/452–8351, 800/255–5859, or 800/223–9868;* FAX *758/452–8331,* WEB *www.rexcaribbean.com. 120 rooms. 2 restaurants, 2 bars, ice cream parlor, air-conditioning, minibars, pool, golf privileges, 2 tennis courts, gym, beach, dive shop, snorkeling, windsurfing, boating, waterskiing, shops, baby-sitting, children's club, laundry service, business services, meeting rooms. AE, DC, MC, V. EP, MAP.*

$$$ 🏨 **Windjammer Landing Villa Beach Resort.** Beachcombers will love this sun-kissed resort village with sweeping views of one of St. Lucia's prettiest bays. Brilliant white stucco villas crowned with tile roofs climb the hillside; a porticoed reception area opens to shops, restaurants, and one of two pools that stretch along the beachfront. Villas are huge and stylishly decorated, with painted wood timbers, tile floors, and wicker furniture loaded with pillows in rich colors; two- and three-bedroom villas have plunge pools. You can eat at various on-site restaurants, make your own meals, or arrange to have dinner prepared for you and served in your villa. Electric carts whoosh you up and down the steep hill from the villas to the main activity area and two hillside pools connected by a waterfall. This hotel is good both for families and for couples seeking a romantic getaway. There's lots to do yet plenty of privacy if that's what you want. ✉ *Labrelotte Bay (Box 1504, Castries),* ☎ *758/452–0913 or 800/223–6510,* FAX *758/452–9454,* WEB *www.wlv-resort.com. 131 villas. 3 restaurants, 3 bars, grocery, air-conditioning, fans, kitchenettes, 3 pools, hair salon, massage, 2 tennis courts, gym, beach, dive shop, snorkeling, windsurfing, boating, waterskiing, shops, children's programs, laundry service, concierge, car rental. AE, MC, V. EP, MAP.*

$$$ 🏨 **Wyndham Morgan Bay Resort.** Eight three-story buildings fan out from a central pool-restaurant area at this all-inclusive resort on Choc Bay. Rooms, decorated in tropical pastel florals and peach wicker, are furnished with comfortable king-size beds. Each has a TV, a radio, a coffeemaker, a hair dryer, and a small veranda with either a garden or partial sea view. To the delight of the mostly European crowd, drinks flow freely, and there's plenty to do—from early morning aerobics to midnight pizza at the beachside Palm Grill. ✉ *Choc Bay, Gros Islet (Box 2167, Castries),* ☎ *758/450–2511 or 800/996–3426,* FAX *758/450–1050,* WEB *www.wyndham.com. 238 rooms. 2 restaurants, 2 bars, air-conditioning, pool, hot tub, sauna, 4 tennis courts, aerobics, archery, gym, Ping-Pong, beach, snorkeling, windsurfing, boating, waterskiing, shops, recreation room, children's programs, meeting rooms, airport shuttle. AE, D, MC, V. All-inclusive.*

$$ 🏨 **Bay Gardens.** Set on the south side of Rodney Bay and 7 mi (11
★ km) north of Castries, this small boutique resort is an easy walk to beautiful Reduit Beach, several popular restaurants and nightclubs, and shops at Rodney Bay Marina. In addition to vacationing guests, quite a few business travelers are attracted by the hotel's new conference center, business services, and in-room amenities. Bay Gardens is modern and colorful—the lime-green building is studded with flower gardens. Rooms surround a courtyard with a serpentine pool and a Jacuzzi. All are furnished with white wicker furniture and colorful print spreads in tropical colors, and each has cable TV and a balcony or patio. Executive rooms also have a trouser press and a whirlpool bath. Eight self-contained apartments with kitchenettes and sitting rooms are perfect for families. Spices restaurant offers a varied menu, along with a weekly barbecue, Caribbean buffet, and Sunday brunch. One child (to age 12) stays free when sharing a room with two adults. Guests recognize the value Bay Gardens offers, as 75% are repeat visitors. ✉ *Rod-*

ney Bay (Box 1892, Castries), ☏ *758/452–8060 or 800/223–9815,* FAX
758/452–8059, WEB *www.baygardenshotel.com. 63 rooms, 8 apartments.
Restaurant, bar, ice cream parlor, air-conditioning, in-room data ports,
refrigerators, 2 pools, hot tub, shops, recreation room, library, business services, meeting rooms. AE, MC, V. EP, MAP.*

$$ 🖼 **Marigot Beach Club.** On beautiful Marigot Bay, this quiet resort is
9 mi (14½ km) south of Castries and close to the mountains and sights
around Soufrière. The Firefly Suites climb the steep hillside that forms
a backdrop for the resort, and a tram transports you up and down. Stu-
dios and one-bedroom suites have kitchenettes, pickled-wood furniture,
and patios that overlook the water. Marigot Bay is a favorite of yacht-
owners, so the boating activity adds atmosphere. The resort has an ex-
cellent water-sports center, and the beach, shaded by coconut palms,
looks like one you'd find in the South Seas. Club Paradis, the open-air
waterfront bar and restaurant, offers a wide selection of Caribbean and
Continental fare. ⌗ *Marigot Bay (Box 101, Castries),* ☏ *758/451–4974
or 800/223–9815,* FAX *758/451–4973,* WEB *www.marigotdiveresort.com.
9 studios, 23 suites. Restaurant, bar, kitchenettes, pool, hair salon,
gym, beach, dive shop, snorkeling, windsurfing, boating, shops. MC,
V. EP, MAP.*

$ 🖼 **Auberge Seraphine.** This small, impressive hotel overlooks Vigie Cove
and is minutes from George F. L. Charles Airport, Pointe Seraphine,
and downtown Castries. It's popular among business travelers but cer-
tainly a pleasant, attractive choice for vacationers who don't require
a beachfront location—a refreshing dip in the pool is enough—nor the
breadth of activities found at a resort. Accommodations are spacious,
cheerful, and bright. Most have a view of the cove and Vigie Yacht Ma-
rina; all have cable TV and direct-dial phones. A broad tiled sun-
deck—the center of activity—surrounds a small pool. A shuttle service
transports you to and from a nearby beach. The popular restaurant
offers fine Caribbean, French, and Continental cuisine; the manage-
ment is proud of its well-stocked wine cellar. One child (to age 12) stays
free when sharing a room with two adults. ⌗ *Vigie Cove (Box 390,
Castries),* ☏ *758/453–2073,* FAX *758/451–7001,* WEB *www.sluonestop.
com/auberge. 22 rooms. Restaurant, bar, air-conditioning, pool, shops,
meeting rooms. AE, MC, V. EP, MAP.*

$ 🖼 **Orange Grove Hotel.** Up a long hill, off the road to Windjammer
★   Landing, you'll find a lovely surprise: an intimate country inn and one
of the best values on St. Lucia. The restored French colonial building
dates back a century, and service is Orange Grove's hallmark. The rooms
are large, bright, attractively decorated, and packed with the conve-
niences you'd expect at a larger resort—TVs, hair dryers, phones.
Standard rooms have showers; superior rooms and suites also have tubs.
All rooms are decorated in contemporary tropical prints, with Caribbean-
style rattan furniture, tile floors, king-size beds, a sitting area and a
balcony or patio with a panoramic view. Although you're not on the
beach, there's a large pool and free shuttle service to Waves Beach Club
at Choc Beach, five minutes away. Café Clementine serves West Indian
and international cuisine; meal plans are an option. ⌗ *Bois d'Orange,
Gros Islet (Box GM 702, Castries),* ☏ *758/452–0021, 800/223–6510,
or 800/223–9815;* FAX *758/452–8094,* WEB *www.stluciatravel.com.lc/
orangegrove.htm. 51 rooms, 11 suites. Restaurant, bar, room service,
air-conditioning, fans, pool, golf privileges, billiards, shops, meeting
rooms. AE, MC, V. EP, MAP, all-inclusive.*

Soufrière

$$$$ 🖼 **Anse Chastanet Beach Hotel.** If you invest in one of the deluxe hill-
★   side rooms, you're in for a slice of heaven. Nick Troubetzkoy, the Cana-
dian owner-architect, designed them to blend into the mountainside,

with louvered wooden walls that open to stunning Piton and Caribbean vistas or to the deep green forest. Each has a balcony, terra-cotta tile floor, madras cotton fabrics, chunky handmade wooden furniture, and truly covetable artwork. Large rooms have have irresistible quirks: a tree growing in the bathroom or a shower completely open to the panorama of the Pitons. Standard rooms are mostly octagonal gazebos, with the same decor but far less drama. Rooms do not have a phone or TV, but each has a hair dryer, refrigerator, and coffeemaker. The Kai Belte (in patois, House of Beauty) has four therapists that provide professional beauty and body treatments. This resort has a magical setting, as long as you're fit to climb the 100 steps from the gray-sand beach up to the Piton Restaurant and Bar, followed by another steep climb to your room. Great diving is one of the premier draws here, and divers come from the earth's four corners to peep at the nearby reefs and take a break at the Anse Chastanet Beach Restaurant and Bar. Rates include breakfast and dinner during peak season. ⊠ *Anse Chastanet (Box 7000),* ☎ *758/459–7000 or 800/223–1108,* FAX *758/459–7700,* WEB *www.ansechastanet.com. 48 rooms. 2 restaurants, 2 bars, fans, refrigerators, spa, tennis court, gym, hiking, 2 beaches, dive shop, snorkeling, windsurfing, boating, bicycling, shops, airport shuttle. AE, DC, MC, V. EP, MAP.*

$$$$ 🏨 **Jalousie Hilton Resort & Spa.** This 325-acre property has a dramatic
★ location directly between the Pitons. It was built on the remains of an 18th-century sugar plantation, and the foliage is so lush that hillside villas are all but hidden from view—the ultimate in privacy. Sugar Mill Suites are large, luxurious, and close to the main buildings and beach. Villas have elegant furnishings, king-size beds, huge bathrooms, tile floors, and plenty of closet space. Villa suites also have sitting rooms and plunge pools for a romantic dip. All quarters accommodate up to three adults or a family of four. A 24-hour shuttle service transports you around the grounds, a blessing given the steep hillside. Meals range from fine dining to beach buffet at four on-site restaurants. The spa offers massage, aromatherapy, and beauty treatments; the health club has aerobics, weight-training sessions, and exercise classes. There's an executive three-hole, par-3 golf course, tennis, a marina, and a private beach with a picturesque view. ⊠ *Anse des Pitons (Box 251), 2 mi (3 km) south of Soufrière,* ☎ *758/459–7666, 888/744–5256 (direct to hotel), 800/445–8667, or 800/223–9868;* FAX *758/459–7667,* WEB *www.hilton.com. 12 suites, 64 villas, 36 villa suites. 4 restaurants, 4 bars, air-conditioning, fans, in-room safes, minibars, no-smoking rooms, pool, hair salon, massage, sauna, spa, 3-hole golf course, 4 tennis courts, aerobics, basketball, health club, hiking, racquetball, squash, beach, dive shop, dock, snorkeling, windsurfing, boating, marina, waterskiing, fishing, shops, nightclub, baby-sitting, children's programs, business services, meeting rooms, airport shuttle, car rental, helipad. AE, D, DC, MC, V. EP, FAP, MAP.*

$$$$ 🏨 **Ladera Resort.** Nestled in lush botanical gardens high in the moun-
★ tains 2 mi (3 km) south of Soufrière, this elegantly rustic hideaway overlooks the Pitons and the Caribbean. It's one of the most sophisticated and unusual small resorts in the Caribbean—a home away from home for rock stars, TV celebs, corporate VIPs, and honeymooners. Each villa or suite is stylishly furnished with a blend of French colonial antiques and local crafts and has a completely open west wall with a dazzling view of the Pitons. Six deluxe villas have private pools fed by waterfalls; eight suites have smaller plunge pools. Daily shuttle service to Soufrière and Anse Chastanet Beach is provided. The view of the Pitons from the Dasheene Restaurant and Bar, 1,000 ft (305 m) above Jalousie Bay, is breathtaking—probably the best on the island. Room rates include breakfast, and transfers to Hewanorra International Air-

port are complimentary if you stay at least three nights. Although children 8–15 stay free when sharing a room with an adult, the resort's mountainside location and many private pools make it unsuitable for really young children. ⊠ *Above the Pitons, 2 mi (3 km) south of town (Box 225),* ☎ *758/459–7323, 800/223–9868, or 800/738–4752;* 𝖥𝖠𝖷 *758/459–5156,* 𝖶𝖤𝖡 *www.ladera-stlucia.com. 18 suites, 6 villas. Restaurant, 2 bars, pool, shops, library, airport shuttle. AE, MC, V. BP, MAP.*

$ 🏠 **Hummingbird Beach Resort.** This delightful little resort is on the bay at the northern edge of Soufrière. Rooms are in small seaside cabins joined by a maze of wooden decking; most have magnificent views of the Pitons. The decor is attractive but simple; a primitive motif is emphasized by African wood sculptures. Two rooms each have a dark mahogany four-poster bed hung with a sheer mosquito netting; the cool trade winds and the sound of the sea will lull you to sleep. Most rooms have modern baths; two rooms and a suite share a bath. The two-bedroom country cottage—with a sitting room, kitchenette, and spectacular Piton view—is suitable for a family or two couples vacationing together. The Hummingbird Restaurant is a favorite lunch stop for locals and visitors touring Soufrière. ⊠ *Anse Chastanet Rd. (Box 280, Soufrière),* ☎ *758/459–7232 or 800/223–9815,* 𝖥𝖠𝖷 *758/459–7033,* 𝖶𝖤𝖡 *www.nvo.com/pitonresort. 9 rooms, 1 suite, 1 cottage. Restaurant, bar, pool, beach, shops. D, MC, V. EP, MAP.*

$ 🏠 **Still Plantation & Beach Resort.** About a five-minute walk inland from Soufrière are these simple but modern one- and two-bedroom apartments with sitting rooms and kitchenettes, as well as studios with no kitchens. On the grounds here you'll find a swimming pool, a boutique, and the Still restaurant, well known for its Caribbean cuisine. The separate Still Beach Resort is on a black-sand beach at the northern end of Soufrière Bay and has a commanding view of the Pitons. The beachfront property is clean and comfortable but small, with just three one-bedroom apartments and two studios—all of which share a common veranda with a partial sea view. Only the bedrooms have air-conditioning; sitting rooms have fans, and most units have a kitchenette. If hiking and nature walks are more important than a beach, the Plantation is the better choice. If you prefer sand and sea to pool and gardens, choose the Beach Resort. A stay at one allows you to use the facilities of the other. Rates are the same year-round. ⊠ *Lewis St. and Anse Chastanet Rd. (Box 246), Soufrière),* ☎ *758/459–7224 or 800/ 223–9815,* 𝖥𝖠𝖷 *758/459–7301. 13 apartments, 6 studios. 2 restaurants, 2 bars, pool, beach, shops, laundry service. MC, V. EP.*

Dining

Mangoes, plantains, breadfruit, avocados, limes, pumpkins, cucumbers, papaya (pawpaw), yams, christophenes (a squash-like vegetable), and coconuts are among the fresh local produce that grace St. Lucian menus. The French influence is strong, and most chefs cook with a creole flair. Resort buffets and restaurant fare run the gamut, offering steaks and chops, pasta and pizza, and everything in between. Every menu lists fresh fish along with the ever-popular lobster. Caribbean standards include callaloo, stuffed crab back, pepper-pot stew, curried chicken or goat, and *lambi* (conch). The national dish of salt fish and green fig—a stew of dried, salted codfish, and boiled green banana—is, let's say, an acquired taste. Soups and stews are traditionally prepared in a coal pot, a rustic clay casserole on a matching clay stand that holds the hot coals. Chicken and pork dishes and barbecues are also popular here. As they do throughout the Caribbean, local vendors who set up barbecues along the roadside, at street fairs, and at Friday night "jump ups," do a land-office business selling grilled chicken legs, bakes (biscuits), and beer—all for about $3. Most other meats are imported—beef from Argentina and Iowa, lamb from New Zealand. Piton is the local brew, and Bounty is the local rum.

With so many all-inclusive resorts, guests take most meals at hotel restaurants—which are generally quite good and, in some cases, exceptional. It's fun when vacationing, however, to try some of the local restaurants, as well—for lunch when sightseeing or for a special night out.

What to Wear

Dress on St. Lucia is casual but conservative. Shorts are usually fine during the day, but bathing suits and immodest clothing are frowned on anywhere but at the beach. In the evening the mood is casually elegant, but even the fanciest places generally expect only a collared shirt and long pants for men and a sundress or slacks for women.

CATEGORY	COST*
$$$$	over $30
$$$	$20–$30
$$	$10–$20
$	under $10

per person for a main course at dinner

Castries and the North

CARIBBEAN

$$ ✕ **The French Restaurant.** French West Indian cuisine—direct from St. Lucia's neighbor island, Martinique—is the specialty at this Rodney Bay establishment. Choices include wonderful pumpkin or fish soup to start; curried goat, conch, fresh lobster you select from the tank; and exotic seafood such as octopus and shark. Everything has a hot, spicy sauce, but a delicious French pastry or homemade ice cream will quell the fire on your tongue. A creole buffet is the special at lunch. ⊠ *Rodney Bay,* ☎ *758/450–0022. D, MC, V. No lunch.*

$ ✕ **J. J.'s Paradise.** Not only are the prices right, but the local fare is among the best on the island. Superbly grilled fish with fresh vegetables gets top honors. The welcome is friendly, and the atmosphere is casual; tables are set on a terrace overlooking the road to Marigot Bay. Wednesday is Seafood Night, when owner-chef J. J. prepares an enormous selection of local fish and shellfish. On Friday night the music blares, and the locals come to lime (hang out), eat barbecue, and dance inside or on the street. ⊠ *Marigot Bay Rd. (3 mi before the bay), Marigot,* ☎ *758/451–4076. No credit cards.*

CONTEMPORARY

$$$ ✕ **Tao.** For truly exquisite dining, this small restaurant at the all-inclusive resort LeSPORT welcomes nonguests for dinner. Perched on a second-floor balcony at the edge of Cariblue Beach, you're guaranteed a pleasant breeze and a starry sky while you enjoy fusion cuisine—a marriage of various Asian tastes (borrowed from China, Japan, Indonesia, the Philippines) with a Caribbean touch. Tender slices of pork loin satay accompanied by *nasi goreng* rice, scallops steamed in rice paper, hibachi-grilled strip steak—the menu choices are mouth-watering. Fine wines accompany the meal, desserts are extravagant, and the service is superb. Be sure to reserve ahead, as the seating is limited and hotel guests are given priority. ⊠ *Cap Estate,* ☎ *758/450–8551. Reservations essential. AE, DC, MC, V. No lunch.*

ECLECTIC

$$$ ✕ **Green Parrot.** Situated atop the Morne, this is the restaurant where chef Harry Edwards (who trained at London's prestigious Claridge's hotel) prepares a menu of West Indian, creole, and international dishes. There's lively entertainment—a floor show with a belly dancer on

Wednesday night and limbo dancing on Saturday—but the best reasons to dine here are the seafood specialties and the romantic view of the twinkling lights in Castries and the harbor. On Monday night, if a lady wears a flower in her hair and is accompanied by a "well-dressed" gentleman, she receives a free dinner. ⊠ *Morne Fortune, south of Castries,* ☎ *758/452–3399. Reservations essential. Jacket required. AE, MC, V.*

$$ ✕ **The Lime.** A casual bistro with lime-color gingham curtains, straw hats decorating the ceiling, and hanging plants, the Lime is one of the most popular of the many restaurants at Rodney Bay. The menu includes char-grilled steaks and fresh-caught fish, along with spicy jerk chicken or pork. The meals are well prepared, the portions are plentiful, and prices are reasonable, which is perhaps why the restaurant is popular among local St. Lucians and visitors alike. Next door is the Late Lime, a club where the crowd gathers as night turns to morning. ⊠ *Rodney Bay,* ☎ *758/452–0761. MC, V.*

FRENCH

$$$ ✕ **Great House.** Elegant, gracious, and romantic are all perfect de-
★ scriptions of the atmosphere at the Great House. The building was reconstructed on the foundation of the original Cap Estate plantation house, and the grandeur of those early days has been revived, as well, in the restaurant's ambience. The waitstaff all wear traditional St. Lucian costumes, and the French chef adds a piquant creole touch to traditional French cuisine, which includes pumpkin-and-potato soup, local crab back with lime vinaigrette, sautéed Antillean shrimp in a creole sauce, and broiled sirloin with thyme butter and sweet-potato chips. The menu changes nightly and always includes vegetarian dishes. You won't mind waiting for your table for a few minutes at the open-air bar—especially if you arrive in time to watch the sunset. Operated by the owners of the Club St. Lucia, resort guests receive a discount and free transportation. The Derek Walcott Theatre is next door. ⊠ *Cap Estate,* ☎ *758/450–0450 or 758/450–0211. Reservations essential. AE, DC, MC, V. No lunch.*

$$ ✕ **The Coal Pot.** Established in 1967, this popular restaurant overlooking
★ the waterfront is now managed by Michelle Elliott, daughter of the original owner, and her French husband, Chef Xavier. For a light lunch opt for Greek or shrimp salad, or broiled fresh fish with creole sauce. Dinner might start with coquilles St. Jacques or divine pumpkin soup, followed by a range of seafood accompanied by one (or more) of the chef's fabulous sauces—ginger, coconut curry, lemon-garlic butter, or wild mushroom. Hearty eaters may prefer duck, lamb, beef, or chicken laced with peppercorns, red wine and onion, or Roquefort cheese sauce. There are only 10 tables, so be sure to reserve ahead. ⊠ *Vigie Marina, Castries,* ☎ *758/452–5566. Reservations essential. AE, D, MC, V. Closed Sun. No lunch Sat.*

ITALIAN

$$ ✕ **Capone's.** The tropics meet art deco in this two-in-one restaurant. Dinner is served in the bistro, where the French chef lends a Gallic twist and Caribbean spice to some of your favorite Italian dishes. Paper-thin carpaccio is drizzled with olive oil and lime, before being treated to shavings of parmesan cheese. Polenta and local vegetables accompany delicate slices of calves liver that have been gently sautéed with onions. And fresh Caribbean snapper is blessed with ginger and rum en route to your plate. Other selections from the extensive menu include pasta dishes, seafood, and Black Angus beef. At the informal La Piazza, next door, diners enjoy casual meals of burgers, sandwiches, and pizza from noon to midnight. ⊠ *Rodney Bay, across from St. Lucian hotel,* ☎ *758/452–0284. AE, MC, V. Closed Mon.*

SEAFOOD

$$ ✕ Jimmie's. This open-air mom-and-pop restaurant-bar overlooking Vigie Bay is a relaxing daytime stop and a romantic dinner spot. The seafood-dominated menu includes a great creole-style stuffed crab appetizer and a seafood platter with samplings of all the different fish in the day's catch. The national dish—salt fish and green fig—is the lunch special on Friday and Saturday. All entrées come with several local vegetables (pumpkin, black beans, christophenes, greens) and garlic bread. Dessert lovers had better be in a banana mood: the menu lists about 10 options, from warm fritters to ice cream. ⊠ *Vigie Marina, Castries,* ☎ *758/452–5142. Reservations not accepted. AE, MC, V.*

Soufrière

CARIBBEAN

$$ ✕ The Hummingbird. The chef at this cheerful restaurant-bar in the Hummingbird Beach Resort specializes in French creole cuisine, starting with fresh seafood or chicken seasoned with local herbs and accompanied by a medley of fresh vegetables. Sandwiches and salads are also available. If you stop for lunch, be sure to visit the batik studio of proprietor Joan Alexander, adjacent to the dining room. ⊠ *Anse Chastanet Rd., Soufrière,* ☎ *758/459–7232. AE, D, MC, V.*

$$ ✕ The Still. If you're visiting Diamond Waterfall, this is a good lunch spot. The two dining rooms of the Still Plantation & Beach Resort seat up to 400 people, so it's a popular stop for tour groups and cruise passengers. The emphasis is on creole cuisine using local vegetables—christophenes, breadfruits, yams, callaloo—and seafood, but there are also pork and beef dishes. All fruits and vegetables used in the restaurant are organically grown on the estate. ⊠ *Bay St.,* ☎ *758/459–7224 or 758/459–7060. MC, V.*

$ ✕ Anse Chastanet Beach Restaurant and Bar. This open-air lunch spot at the Anse Chastanet Beach Hotel is the perfect place to take a break from a day of diving, boating, or sunbathing. The West Indian cuisine is delicious, and many specialties are grilled right before your eyes. The outstanding *rotis* (turnovers filled with curried meat and/or vegetables) are served with homemade mango chutney you could eat by the jar. Also try the pepper pot—pork, beef, or lamb simmered for hours with local veggies and spices; or have a good old tuna melt in case you're homesick. Dessert always features an unusual flavor of ice cream. There's a young and lively crowd here, and although the restaurant caters mostly to resort guests, everyone is welcome. Lunch is served daily; dinner—a very popular beach barbecue and creole buffet—is Tuesday and Friday only. ⊠ *Anse Chastanet, 1 mi (1½ km) north of town,* ☎ *758/459–7000. AE, DC, MC, V.*

CONTEMPORARY

$$$ ✕ Dasheene Restaurant and Bar.
★ Part of the striking Ladera Resort, this casual terrace restaurant has breathtaking views of the Pitons and the sea between them (try to arrive in time to watch the sun set). The food—among St. Lucia's best—consists of Caribbean specialties with international accents. Appetizers on the changing menu may include smoked kingfish crêpes and spicy seafood gazpacho. Typical entrées are tuna steak with coconut-avocado cream sauce and chicken breast with a mango or a pecan-and-peanut sauce. For dessert, the chocolate crème brûlée flambé takes five minutes to cool but is worth the wait. There's live entertainment many nights, and soft, jazzy background music otherwise. ⊠ *2 mi (3 km) south of Soufrière,* ☎ *758/459–7323. AE, DC, MC, V.*

Beaches

Beaches are all public, and many on the west coast are flanked by hotels where you can rent water-sports equipment and have a rum punch or a snack. A few secluded stretches of beach are accessible only by water; hotels can arrange boat trips. Don't swim along the windward (east) coast; the Atlantic Ocean is too rough—but the views are spectacular.

In front of the resort of the same name, just north of Soufrière, **Anse Chastanet** is a palm-studded dark-sand beach with a backdrop of green hills, brightly painted fishing skiffs bobbing at anchor, and the island's best reefs for snorkeling and diving. The resort's wooden gazebos are nestled among the palms; its dive shop, restaurant, and bar are on the beach. **Anse Cochon** is a remote black-sand beach 3 mi (5 km) south of Marigot Bay and accessible only by boat. The waters and adjacent reef are superb for swimming, diving, and snorkeling, but there are no facilities. South of Soufrière, between the Pitons on Jalousie Bay, **Anse des Pitons** is a crescent of white sand that was imported by Jalousie Hilton Resort and spread over the original black sand. The beach, accessible from the resort or by boat, offers good snorkeling, diving, and a magnificent setting. At the southeastern tip of St. Lucia, **Anse de Sables,** at Vieux Fort, is a long stretch of white sand with crystal-clear waters protected by reefs.

In the north, just below Rodney Bay, **Choc Beach** is easily accessible from the road. Windsurfers and Sunfish can be rented and waterskiing arranged at Waves restaurant on the beach. The finger of sand studded with palm trees on **Marigot Bay** is a postcard-pretty scene; dive trips can be arranged nearby, and refreshments are available at adjacent restaurants. **Pigeon Point,** part of the Pigeon Island National Historic Park, is a small beach; there's a restaurant, but it's a perfect spot for picnicking. **Reduit Beach** is a long stretch of beige sand next to Rodney Bay. The St. Lucian Hotel, which faces the beach, has a water-sports center. Many feel that Reduit (pronounced red-*wee*) is the island's finest beach. **Vigie Beach** is a 2-mi (3-km) stretch of white sand that runs parallel to the George F. L. Charles Airport runway, in Castries, and continues on to become Malabar Beach, the beachfront for the Rendezvous resort.

Outdoor Activities and Sports

Participant Sports

BOATING AND SAILING

Rodney Bay and Marigot Bay are centers for bareboat and crewed yacht charters. Their marinas offer safe anchorage, shower facilities, restaurants, groceries, and maintenance for yachts sailing the waters of the eastern Caribbean. **Destination St. Lucia (DSL) Ltd.** (✉ Rodney Bay, ☎ 758/453–8531) offers bareboat yacht charters; vessels range in length from 38 ft to 51 ft. The **Moorings Yacht Charters** (✉ Marigot Bay, ☎ 758/451–4357 or 800/535–7289) rents bareboat or crewed yachts ranging from Beneteau 39s to Morgan 60s.

CAMPING

St. Lucia's only campsite is administered by the St. Lucia National Trust (☎ 758/452–5005) and located at the **Environmental Educational Centre** at Anse La Liberté, on the west coast near the village of Canaries. Rough campsites and platformed tent huts are available, along with communal toilets and showers, a cooking center, a beautiful beach, and hiking trails. Camping fees are inexpensive, particularly if you bring your own tent, and reservations are required.

FISHING

Among the deep-sea creatures you'll find in St. Lucia's waters are dolphin (dorado), king mackerel, barracuda, kingfish, and white marlin. Sportfishing is done on a catch-and-release basis. Neither spearfishing nor collecting live fish in coastal waters is permitted. Half- or full-day deep-sea fishing excursions can be arranged at Vigie Cove or Rodney Bay Marina. Rates for a half-day fishing trip are about $100. Beginners are welcome. **Captain Mike's** (⊠ Vigie Cove, ☎ 758/452–1216 or 758/452–7044) has a fleet of Bertram fishing boats (up to 38-ft long) that accommodates as many as eight passengers; all equipment and cold drinks are supplied. **Mako Watersports** (⊠ Rodney Bay Marina, ☎ 758/452–0412 or 758/452–0778) takes fishing enthusiasts out on the well-equipped six-passenger *Annie Baby.*

GOLF

Courses on St. Lucia are scenic and enjoyable, but they're not championship quality. **Sandals St. Lucia Golf Resort & Spa** (⊠ La Toc Rd., Castries, ☎ 758/452–3081) has a nine-hole course for Sandals guests only. **St. Lucia Golf and Country Club** (⊠ Cap Estate, ☎ 758/452–8523), the island's only public course, is at the island's northern tip and boasts panoramic views of both the Atlantic and Caribbean. With a new "back nine," the course now has 18 holes (6,815 yards, par 71). The clubhouse has a bar and a pro shop where you can rent clubs and shoes and arrange lessons. Greens fees are $65 for nine holes or $85 for 18 holes; carts are included. Reservations are essential.

HIKING

The island is laced with trails, but you shouldn't attempt the challenging peaks on your own. The **Forest and Land Department** (☎ 758/450–2231 or 758/450–2078) manages trails throughout the rain forest and provides guides for a small fee—about $10 per person. The **St. Lucia National Trust** (☎ 758/452–5005) maintains two trails: one is at Anse La Liberté, near Canaries on the Caribbean coast; the other is on the Atlantic coast, from Mandélé to the Fregate Islands Nature Reserve. Full-day excursions with lunch cost about $50–$60 per person and can be arranged through hotels or tour operators.

HORSEBACK RIDING

Riding is popular on St. Lucia. Creole horses, an indigenous breed, are fairly small, fast, sturdy, and even-tempered animals suitable for beginners. Established stables can accommodate all skill levels and offer countryside trail rides, beach rides with picnic lunches, plantation tours, carriage rides, and lengthy treks. Prices run about $35 for one hour, $45 for two hours, and $60 for a three-hour beach ride with picnic. Transportation is usually provided between the stables and nearby hotels. Local people sometimes appear on beaches with their steeds and offer 30-minute rides for $10; ride at your own risk.

Country Saddles (⊠ Marquis Estate, Babonneau, ☎ 758/450–5467), 45 minutes east of Castries, guides beginners and advanced riders through banana plantations, forest trails, and along the Atlantic coast. **International Riding Stables** (⊠ Beauséjour Estate, Gros Islet, ☎ 758/452–8139) offers either English- or Western-style riding. Their beach picnic ride includes time for a swim—with or without your horse. **North Point Riding Stable** (⊠ Cap Estate, ☎ 758/450–8853) offers one-hour trail rides, three-hour early morning or two-hour sunset rides. **Trekkers** (⊠ Morne Coubaril Estate, Soufrière, ☎ 758/459–7340) will escort you to a variety of trails around the estate as well as to the nearby Sulphur Springs. Both English- and Western-style saddles are available. For real adventurers, week-long treks can be arranged. **Trim's National Riding Stable** (⊠ Cas-en-Bas, Gros Islet, ☎ 758/452–8273), the island's oldest establishment, offers four riding sessions per day, plus beach tours, trail rides, and carriage tours to Pigeon Island.

SCUBA DIVING AND SNORKELING

Anse Chastanet, near the Pitons on the southwest coast, is the best beach-entry dive site. The underwater reef drops off from 20 ft to nearly 140 ft (6–42 m) in a stunning coral wall. A 165-ft freighter, *Lesleen M,* was deliberately sunk in 60 ft (18 m) of water near **Anse Cochon** to create an artificial reef where divers can explore the ship in its entirety and view huge gorgonians, black coral trees, gigantic barrel sponges, lace corals, schooling fish, angel fish, sea horses, spotted eels, stingrays, nurse sharks, and sea turtles. **Anse La Raye,** midway up the west coast, is one of St. Lucia's finest wall and drift dives and a great place for snorkeling. At the base of the **Petit Piton,** a spectacular wall drops to 200 ft (61 m). You can view an impressive collection of huge barrel sponges and black coral trees; strong currents ensure good visibility. **The Pinnacles** is impressive: here four coral-encrusted stone piers rise to within 10 ft (3 m) of the surface.

Buddies (⊠ Rodney Bay Marina, ☎ 758/450–8406) offers wall, wreck, reef, and deep dives; resort courses and open-water certification with advanced and specialty courses are taught by PADI-certified instructors. **Frogs** (⊠ Windjammer Landing, Labrelotte Bay, ☎ 758/452–0913; ⊠ Jalousie Hilton, 2 mi south of Soufrière, ☎ 758/452–0913 or 758/459–7666 ext. 4024) provides resort courses and open-water certification. Two-tank and night dives are also offered, and rental equipment is available. **Rosemond's Trench Divers** (⊠ Marigot Bay, ☎ 758/451–4761) offers PADI training, wreck dives, night dives, and special dive packages for yachties. **Scuba St. Lucia** is a PADI five-star training facility, with a dive shop at Anse Chastanet (⊠ Soufrière, ☎ 758/459–7755). Daily beach and boat dives and resort and certification courses are offered; underwater photography and snorkeling equipment are available. Day trips from the north of the island include round-trip speedboat transportation.

SEA EXCURSIONS

A day sail or sea cruise to Soufrière and the Pitons is a wonderful way to see St. Lucia and, perhaps, the perfect way to get to the island's distinctive natural sites. Prices for a full-day sailing excursion to Soufrière run about $70–$85 per person and include a land tour to the Sulphur Springs and the Botanical Gardens, lunch, a stop at Anse Cochon for swimming and snorkeling, and a visit to pretty Marigot Bay. Two-hour sunset cruises along the northwest coast cost about $40 per person. Most boats leave from either Vigie Cove, Castries or Rodney Bay. The 140-ft tall ship *Brig Unicorn* (⊠ Vigie Cove, ☎ 758/452–6811), used in the filming of the TV miniseries *Roots,* is a replica of a 19th-century brig. Several nights each week, a sunset cruise, with drinks and a live steel band, sails to Pigeon Point and back. On either *Endless Summer I* or *Endless Summer II* (⊠ Rodney Bay Marina, ☎ 758/450–8651), both 56-ft "party" catamarans, you can take a day trip to Soufrière or a half-day swimming and snorkeling trip. For romantics, there's a weekly sunset cruise, with dinner and entertainment. *Surf Queen* (Vigie Cove, ☎ 758/452–8232), a trimaran, offers a fast, sleek sail and has a special tour for German-speaking passengers. From Pigeon Island, north of Rodney Bay, you can take a more intimate cruise to the Pitons aboard the 57-ft luxury cruiser MV *Vigie* (☎ 758/452–8232). Customized sea and snorkeling charters can be arranged for small groups (four to six people) through **Captain Mike's** (⊠ Vigie Cove, Castries, ☎ 758/452–0216 or 758/452–7044).

TENNIS AND SQUASH

All large resorts have their own tennis courts; most are lit for night play and often have pros who offer lessons. Anyone staying at a smaller hotel without tennis courts or who wants to play squash can try: the **St. Lucian** hotel (⊠ Reduit Beach, Rodney Bay, ☎ 758/452–8351) has two tennis courts open to the public at $20 per half hour or $30 per hour; reservations are required. **St. Lucia Racquet Club** (⊠ Club St. Lucia, Cap Estate, ☎ 758/450–0106), the site of the St. Lucia Open each December, has seven lit courts, a pro shop, and restaurant-bar, and a squash court. The club charges $10 per person per hour for use of the facilities; reservations are required. **St. Lucia Yacht Club** (⊠ Rodney Bay, ☎ 758/452–8350), at the north end of the island, has two air-conditioned, wooden-floored, glass-backed squash courts; rackets can be rented. The club charges $10 per hour, and you'll need to make reservations. **Windjammer Landing** (⊠ Labrelotte Bay, ☎ 758/452–0913) permits nonguests to use its tennis courts for $10 per hour; reservations are required.

WINDSURFING

Major resorts generally offer Windsurfers and instruction; some will accommodate nonguests for a fee. Cas-en-Bas, on the northeast coast, and Vieux Fort, on the southeast, are the most popular windsurfing locations for advanced and intermediate windsurfers. Reduit Beach, near Rodney Bay, and elsewhere along the calmer west coast are the best areas for beginners. Note that from August to October the wind loses strength island-wide. **Island Windsurfing Ltd.** (⊠ Anse de Sables Beach, Vieux Fort, ☎ 758/454–7400) offers board rentals and instruction; it's open daily from 10 AM until dusk. **Waves** (⊠ Choc Beach, Castries, ☎ 758/451–3000) has a windsurfing center attached to the restaurant and beach club of the same name.

Spectator Sports

CRICKET AND SOCCER

These two national pastimes are played at Mindoo Philip Park in Marchand, 2 mi (3 km) east of Castries. Contact the tourist board for details on schedules and tickets.

Shopping

The island's best-known products are artwork and wood carvings; clothing and household items made from batik and silk-screened fabrics, designed and printed in island workshops; and clay pottery. You can also take home straw hats and baskets and locally grown cocoa, coffee, and spices.

Areas and Malls

Along the harbor in Castries you may notice structures with bright-orange roofs; these house several markets, which are open from 6 AM to 5 PM Monday through Saturday. Saturday morning is the busiest and most colorful time to shop. For more than a century, farmers' wives have gathered at the **Castries Market** to sell produce, which, alas, you can't import to the United States. But you can bring back spices, such as cocoa, turmeric, cloves, bay leaves, ginger, peppercorns, cinnamon sticks, nutmeg, mace, and vanilla essence, as well as bottled hot pepper sauces, all of which cost a fraction of what you'd pay back home. The **Craft Market,** which backs up to the produce market, has aisles and aisles of baskets and other handmade straw items, rustic brooms made from palm fronds, wood carvings and leather work, clay pottery, and souvenirs— all at affordable prices. The **Vendor's Arcade,** across the street from the Castries Craft Market, is a maze of stalls and booths where you'll find handicrafts among the T-shirts and costume jewelry.

Gablewoods Mall, on the Gros Islet Highway a couple of miles north of downtown Castries, has about 35 shops that sell groceries, wines and spirits, jewelry, clothing, crafts, books and foreign newspapers, music, souvenirs, household goods, and snacks. At the grocery or liquor store at Gablewoods, you might pick up a bottle of Bounty Rum, the local firewater made at a distillery in Roseau, just south of Castries. Along with 54 boutiques, restaurants, and other businesses that sell services and supplies, a large supermarket is the focal point of each **J. Q.'s Shopping Mall;** one is at Rodney Bay and the other's at Vieux Fort. If you're a die-hard shopper, be sure to visit **Pointe Seraphine,** an attractive Spanish-style complex on Castries Harbour with more than 20 shops that sell duty-free goods, clothing, and local artwork. **La Place Carenage,** on the opposite side of the harbor, is another duty-free complex with many of the same stores as at Pointe Seraphine. The waterfront site originally got its French name because it was the part of the harbor where ships were "careened" to clean, repair, and paint the bottom of their hulls. What was once an old cargo shed is now two floors of inviting boutiques. **William Peter Boulevard,** the capital's main shopping street, is primarily where locals shop for household items.

Most shops in **Soufrière** provide goods for local consumption; the few that might be of interest to visitors are just steps from the boat jetty. The market faces the town square, and there's a small crafts center right on the waterfront where local women sell sticks of fresh cocoa and handmade dolls and doilies.

Specialty Items

ART

Artsibit Gallery (⊠ Brazil and Mongiraud sts., Castries, ☎ 758/452–7865) exhibits and sells moderately priced pieces by St. Lucian painters and sculptors. **Modern Art Gallery** (⊠ Gros Islet Highway, Bois d'Orange, ☎ 758/452–9079) is a home studio, open by appointment only, where you can buy contemporary and avant-garde Caribbean art. **Snooty Agouti** (⊠ Rodney Bay, ☎ 758/452–0321) sells original Caribbean artwork, wood carvings, prints, and maps; it's adjacent to bar and restaurant of the same name. **St. Lucia Fine Art** (⊠ Pointe Seraphine, Castries, ☎ 758/459–0891) has original artwork by world-renowned artists, including local painter Llewellyn Xavier.

BOOKS AND MAGAZINES

Sunshine Bookshop (⊠ Gablewoods Mall, Castries, ☎ 758/452–3222) has novels and titles of regional interest, including books by Caribbean authors—among them the works of the St. Lucian Nobel laureate, poet Derek Walcott. You'll also find current newspapers and magazines. At **Valmont Books** (⊠ Corner of Jeremie and Laborie sts., Castries; ☎ 758/452–3817), you'll find West Indian literature and picture books, as well as stationery items.

CLOTHES AND TEXTILES

Bagshaw Studios (⊠ La Toc Rd., La Toc Bay, Castries, ☎ 758/452–2139 or 758/451–9249) sells clothing and table linens with colorful tropical patterns; the fabric is designed and silk-screened by hand in the adjacent workroom. You'll also find Bagshaw boutiques at Pointe Seraphine, La Place Carenage, and Rodney Bay, and select items are sold in gift shops at Hewanorra Airport. **Batik Studio** (⊠ Hummingbird Beach Resort, on the bayfront, north of wharf, Soufrière, ☎ 758/459–7232) offers superb batik sarongs, scarves, and wall panels designed and created on site by Joan Alexander and her son, David. At **Caribelle Batik** (⊠ Howelton House, Morne Fortune, Castries, ☎ 758/452–3785), craftsmen demonstrate the art of batik and silk-screen printing. Meanwhile, seamstresses are creating clothing and wall hangings, which you can purchase in the shop. The studio is in an old Victorian mansion, high atop the Morne overlooking Castries. There's a terrace where you can have a cool drink and there's a garden full of tropical orchids and lilies. Caribelle Batik creations are featured in many gift shops throughout St. Lucia. **Sea Island Cotton Shop** (⊠ Bridge St., Castries, ☎ 758/452–3674; ⊠ Gablewoods Mall, ☎ 758/451–6946) sells quality T-shirts, Caribelle Batik clothing and other resort wear, and colorful souvenirs.

DUTY-FREE GOODS

Pointe Seraphine and La Place Carenage in Castries, the arcade at the St. Lucian Hotel in Rodney Bay, and Hewanorra International Airport are the only places where duty-free goods are sold. You must present your passport and airline ticket to get the duty-free price. If you can forget for a moment that you're in the tropics, try on beautiful wool sweaters at **Benetton** (⊠ Pointe Seraphine, ☎ 758/452–7685). **Colombian Emeralds** (⊠ Pointe Seraphine, ☎ 758/453–7721; ⊠ La Place Carenage, ☎ 758/452–4288; ⊠ Hewanorra Airport, ☎ 758/454–7774) has fine-quality gems set in beautiful pieces of jewelry. **Images** (⊠ Pointe Seraphine, ☎ 758/452–6883; ⊠ La Place Carenage, ☎ 758/452–0887; ⊠ Hewanorra Airport, ☎ 758/454–7884) sells designer fragrances; they also stock watches, cameras, sunglasses, electronics, and gifts. **Little Switzerland** (⊠ Pointe Seraphine, ☎ 758/452–7587; ⊠ La Place Carenage, ☎ 758/451–6785) specializes in imported china and crystal, jewelry, and leather goods.

GIFTS AND SOUVENIRS

Caribbean Perfumes (⊠ Green Parrot, Morne Fortune, Castries, ☎ 758/453–7249) blends a half dozen lovely scents for women and two aftershaves for men from exotic flowers, fruits, tropical woods, and spices. Fragrances are all made in St. Lucia, reasonably priced, and available at the perfumery and at many hotel gift shops. **Noah's Arkade** (⊠ Jeremie St., Castries, ☎ 758/452–2523; ⊠ Pointe Seraphine, 758/452–7488) has hammocks, wood carvings, straw mats, T-shirts, books, and other regional items. Take home a cassette recording or CD by a local band, which you can find at **Sights 'n Sounds** (⊠ 46 Micoud St., Castries, ☎ 758/451–9600; ⊠ Gablewoods Mall, Castries, ☎ 758/451–7300). The **St. Lucia Philatelic Bureau,** at the General Post Office (⊠ Bridge St., Castries, ☎ 758/452–3774), supplies collectors and stamp dealers throughout the world with beautiful St. Lucian commemoratives.

HANDICRAFTS

On the southwest coast, halfway between Soufrière and Vieux Fort, you'll find locally made clay and straw items at the **Choiseul Arts & Crafts Centre** (⊠ La Fargue, ☎ 758/454–3226). Many of St. Lucia's artisans come from this area. At Marigot Bay, **Cinnamon Batiks** (⊠ Marigot Bay Beach Club, Marigot Bay, ☎ 758/451–4974) has colorful handmade batik wall hangings and pillow covers depicting island themes, such as fish, parrots, and flowers, which are reasonably priced. **Eudovic Art Studio** (⊠ Morne Fortune, Castries, ☎ 758/452–2747) is a workshop and studio where you can buy trays, masks, and figures sculpted from local mahogany, red cedar, and eucalyptus wood. As its name suggests, **Made in St. Lucia** (⊠ Gablewoods Mall, Castries, ☎ 758/453–2788) sells only items that are made on the island. You'll find sandals, shirts, dolls, sauces and jams, costume jewelry, carved wooden objects, steel drums, coal pots for cooking, original art, and other quality items at fair prices. At **Zaka** (⊠ Rodney Bay, ☎ 758/452–0946), next to Shamrock's Pub, you'll find contemporary Caribbean masks and totems carved from local driftwood and painted in brilliant colors. All items are created in a home studio, just down the road, by London-born woodcarver Simon Gajadhar and his wife, St. Lucian artist Sophie Barnard Gajadhar.

Nightlife and the Arts

Nightlife

The large, all-inclusive resort hotels have nightly entertainment—island music, calypso singers, and steel bands, as well as disco, karaoke, and even talent shows and toga parties. Many offer entertainment packages, including dinner, to nonguests. Otherwise, Rodney Bay is a best bet for nightlife. The many restaurants and bars there attract a crowd most any night.

BARS

Banana Split (⊠ St. George's St., Castries, ☎ 758/450–8125) has live entertainment and a perpetual spring-break atmosphere. The **Captain's Cellar** (⊠ Pigeon Island, ☎ 758/450–0253) is a cozy Old English pub with live jazz on weekends. **Shamrocks Pub** (⊠ Rodney Bay, ☎ 758/452–8725) is an Irish-style pub with pool tables and darts, lots of beer, and music. **Waves** (⊠ Choc Bay, Castries, ☎ 758/451–3000) is a popular hangout day and night, with happy hours, karaoke nights, and occasional live music performances.

DANCE CLUBS

Most dance clubs with live bands have a cover charge of $6–$8 (EC$15–EC$20), and the music usually starts at 11 PM. **Foly's** (⊠ Rodney Bay, ☎ 758/450–0022), attached to The French Restaurant, next to the Rodney Bay Marina, is a disco with music ranging from salsa and zouk to oldies and love songs; you must be at least 21 years old to enter. At **Indies** (⊠ Rodney Bay, ☎ 758/452–0727) you can dance to the hottest rhythms Wednesday, Friday, and Saturday; dress is casual though smart—no hats or sandals, no shorts or sleeveless shirts for men. There's shuttle bus service to and from most major hotels. The **Late Lime** (⊠ Reduit Beach, Rodney Bay, ☎ 758/452–0761) is a particular favorite of St. Lucians; it's air-conditioned and intimate, with DJ dance music every night but Tuesday.

THEME NIGHTS

For a taste of St. Lucian village life, head south from Castries to the **Anse La Raye "Fish Feast"** on a Friday night. Beginning at 6:30 PM, streets in this tiny fishing village are closed to vehicles, and the residents prepare what they know best: fish cakes for about 40¢ each, fried or stewed fish for $3 a portion, even a whole lobster for $10–$15, depending on size. Walk around, eat, chat with the local people, and listen to live music in the village square until the wee hours of the morning. The **Green Parrot** (⊠ Morne Fortune, ☎ 758/452–3399) is in a class all by itself. On Wednesday and Saturday, chef Harry Edwards hosts the floor show—singing, dancing, and shimmying under the limbo pole himself. Dress semiformally for these evenings of frolic. The **Gros Islet Jump Up** is legendary. Every Friday night, starting at about 9 PM, the sleepy fishing village a mile or so north of Rodney Bay becomes a huge street party. A mammoth sound system facing the central intersection beats out pulsating Caribbean rhythms; vendors sell barbecued chicken, conch, and local beverages; and everyone lets their hair down and dances until about 1 AM. It's very crowded and can get rowdy, so it's best to travel in a group—women shouldn't carry a purse. **J. J.'s Friday Night Street Jam** (⊠ Marigot Bay, ☎ 758/451–4076) is the south-side alternative to Gros Islet; barbecues are set up along the street, and a band plays island music.

The Arts

St. Lucian artist **Llewellyn Xavier** (☎ 758/450–9155) creates modern art, ranging from vigorous oil abstracts that take up half a wall to small objects made from beaten silver and gold. Much of his work has an environmental theme, created from recycled materials. Xavier exhibits his work at his studio in Cap Estate; call to arrange a visit.

THEATER

Derek Walcott Center Theatre. This small, open-air theater, built on the foundation of an 18th-century Cap Estate plantation house next to the Great House Restaurant, seats just 200 people for monthly productions of music, dance, and drama, as well as Sunday brunch programs. The Trinidad Theatre Workshop also presents an annual performance here. For schedule and ticket information contact the Great House (✉ Cap Estate, ☎ 758/450–0551 or 758/450–0450).

Exploring St. Lucia

One main route rings all of St. Lucia, except for a small portion in the extreme northeast. The road snakes along the coast, cuts across mountains, makes hairpin turns and sheer drops, and reaches dizzying heights. It takes four or five hours to drive the whole loop. Even when taken at a leisurely pace with frequent sightseeing stops, it's a tiring drive.

The West Coast Road from Castries to Soufrière has steep hills and sharp turns, but it's well marked and incredibly scenic. South of Castries, the road climbs Morne Fortune, cuts through the island's largest banana plantation (more than 127 varieties of bananas, called "figs" in this part of the Caribbean, are grown on the island), and passes through fishing villages. The area north of Soufrière is the island's fruit basket, where most of the mangoes, breadfruit, tomatoes, limes, and oranges are grown. In the mountainous region that forms a backdrop for Soufrière, you'll see Mt. Parasol and 3,118-ft (954-m) Mt. Gimie (pronounced Jimmy), St. Lucia's highest peak. As you approach Soufrière, you'll have several opportunities for spectacular views of the Pitons.

The landscape changes dramatically between the Pitons and Vieux Fort, on the island's southeastern tip. Along the South Coast Road, the terrain starts as steep mountainside with dense vegetation, progresses to undulating hills that form a backdrop for sleepy fishing villages, and finally becomes rather flat and comparatively arid. Anyone arriving at Hewanorra International Airport and staying at a resort near Soufrière will travel along this route, a journey of just over an hour. From Vieux Fort to Castries, the East Coast Road twists through Micoud, Dennery, and other villages; winds up, down, and around mountains; crosses Barre de l'Isle Ridge; and slices through the rain forest. The scenery is breathtaking. The Atlantic pounds against rocky cliffs, and acres and acres of bananas and coconut palms cover the hillsides. If you arrive at Hewanorra and stay at a resort near Castries, you'll travel along the East Coast Road—a 1¼-hour ride.

Numbers in the margin correspond to points of interest on the St. Lucia map.

Castries and the North

Castries, the capital, and the area north of it are the island's most developed areas. The roads are straight, flat, and easy to navigate. The beaches are some of the island's best. This area is the location of most of the resorts and busy Rodney Bay Marina. One of the island's important historical sites, Pigeon Island, is off the northwestern tip.

❺ Barre de l'Isle Forest Reserve. St. Lucia is divided into eastern and western halves by Barre de L'Isle Ridge. A mile-long (1½-km-long) trail cuts through the reserve, and four lookout points provide panoramic views. Visible in the distance are Mt. Gimie, immense green valleys, the Caribbean and the Atlantic, and coastal communities. The reserve is about a half-hour drive from Castries; it takes about an hour to walk the trail and another hour to climb Mt. La Combe Ridge. Permission from the **Forest and Lands Department** (☎ 758/450–2231 or 758/450–2078) is required to access the trail in Barre de L'Isle; a naturalist or forest officer guide will accompany you.

❶ Castries. The capital, a busy commercial city of about 65,000 people, wraps around a sheltered bay. Morne Fortune rises sharply to the south of town, creating a dramatic green backdrop. The charm of Castries lies almost entirely in its liveliness, since practically all the colorful colonial buildings were destroyed by four fires that occurred between 1796 and 1948. Freighters (exporting bananas, coconut, cocoa, mace, nutmeg, and citrus fruits) and cruise ships come and go daily, making Castries Harbour one of the Caribbean's busiest ports.

Pointe Seraphine is a duty-free shopping complex on the north side of the harbor, about a 20-minute walk or two-minute cab ride from the city center; a launch shuttles passengers across the harbor when ships are in port. Pointe Seraphine's attractive Spanish-style architecture houses more than 20 upscale duty-free shops, a tourist information kiosk, a taxi stand, and car-rental agencies. The St. Lucia Tourist Board has its main office on the upper level.

Derek Walcott Square is a green oasis bordered by Brazil, Laborie, Micoud, and Bourbon streets. Formerly Columbus Square, it was renamed in 1993 to honor the hometown poet who won the 1992 Nobel prize in literature—one of two Nobel laureates from St. Lucia (the late Sir W. Arthur Lewis won the 1979 Nobel prize in economics). Some of the 19th-century buildings that have survived fire, wind, and rain can be seen on Brazil Street, the southern border of the square. On the Laborie Street side there's a huge, 400-year-old *samaan* tree with leafy branches that shade a good portion of the square.

Directly across Laborie Street from Derek Walcott Square is the Roman Catholic **Cathedral of the Immaculate Conception,** which was built in 1897. Though rather somber on the outside, its interior walls are decorated with colorful murals reworked by St. Lucian artist Dunstan St. Omer in 1985, just prior to the pope's visit. This church has an active parish and is open daily for both public viewing and religious services.

At the corner of Jeremie and Peynier streets, spreading beyond its brilliant-orange roof, is the **Castries Market.** Full of excitement and bustle, the market is open every day except Sunday, but it is most lively on Saturday morning, when farmers bring their fresh produce and spices to town as they have for more than a century. Next door to the produce market is the **Craft Market,** where you can buy pottery, wood carvings, and handwoven straw items. Across Peynier Street from the Craft Market, at the **Vendor's Arcade,** you'll find still more handicrafts and souvenirs.

❷ Ft. Charlotte. Begun in 1764 by the French as the Citadelle du Morne Fortune, Ft. Charlotte was completed after 20 years of battling and changing hands. Its old barracks and batteries are now government buildings and local educational facilities, but you can drive around and look at the remains, including redoubts, a guardroom, stables, and cells. You can also walk up to the Inniskilling Monument, a tribute to the battle fought in 1796, when the 27th Foot Royal Inniskilling Fusiliers wrested the Morne from the French. At the military cemetery, which was first used in 1782, faint inscriptions on the tombstones tell the tales of French and English soldiers who died here. Six former governors of the island are buried here as well. From this point atop Morne Fortune you can view Martinique to the north and the twin peaks of the Pitons to the south.

④ Marigot Bay. This is one of the prettiest natural harbors in the Caribbean. In 1778 British Admiral Samuel Barrington sailed into this secluded bay-within-a-bay and covered his ships with palm fronds to hide them from the French. Today this picturesque community—where parts of the original movie *Doctor Doolittle* were filmed more than 30 years ago—is a favorite anchorage. You can charter a yacht, swim, snorkel, or mingle with the yachting crowd at one of the bars. There are several small inns and restaurants here. A 24-hour ferry connects the bay's two shores.

⑭ Marquis Estate. If you want a close-up view of a working plantation and are willing to get a little wet and muddy in the process, you can tour the island's largest one. The 600-acre Marquis Estate, situated on the north Atlantic coast, began as a sugar plantation. Now it produces bananas and copra (dried coconut processed for oil) for export, as well as a number of other tropical fruits and vegetables for local consumption. St. Lucia Representative Services Ltd. conducts the tour and will pick you up at your hotel in an air-conditioned bus. You can see the estate by bus or on horseback; a river ride to the coast and lunch at the plantation house are included. Self-drive or private taxi tours aren't permitted. Wear your most casual clothes, and be prepared to rough it. ⊠ *Marquis Bay,* ☎ *758/452–3762.*

③ Morne Fortune. Morne Fortune forms a striking backdrop for the capital. With a name that translates to "Hill of Good Luck," this mountain has, ironically, seen more than its share of bad luck over the years—including devastating hurricanes and four fires that leveled Castries. The drive to Morne Fortune from Castries will take you past **Government House,** on Government House Road, the official residence of the governor-general of St. Lucia and one of the island's few remaining examples of Victorian architecture.

⑯ Pigeon Island. Jutting out of the northwest coast, Pigeon Island is connected to the mainland by a causeway. Tales are told of the pirate Jambe de Bois (Wooden Leg), who once hid out here. This 44-acre hilltop islet, a strategic point during the struggles for control of St. Lucia, is now a national landmark. It's also a venue for concerts, festivals, and family gatherings. There are two small beaches with calm waters for swimming and snorkeling, a restaurant, and picnic areas. Scattered around the grounds are ruins of barracks, batteries, and garrisons that date from 18th-century French and English battles. In the Museum and Interpretative Centre, housed in the restored British officers' mess, a multimedia display explains the island's ecological and historical significance. ⊠ *Pigeon Island, St. Lucia National Trust,* ☎ *758/452–5005.* ☜ *$4.* ☉ *Daily 9–5.*

⑮ Rodney Bay. About 15 minutes north of Castries, the 80-acre man-made lagoon—surrounded by hotels and many popular restaurants—is named for British admiral George Rodney, who sailed the English Navy out of Gros Islet Bay in 1780 to attack and ultimately decimate the French fleet. Rodney Bay Marina is one of the Caribbean's premier water-sports centers and the destination of the Atlantic Rally for Cruisers (trans-Atlantic yacht crossing) each December. Yacht charters and sightseeing day trips can be arranged at the marina. The Rodney Bay Ferry makes hourly crossings between the marina and the shopping complex, as well as daily excursions to Pigeon Island.

Soufrière and the South

The southwest coast is the destination of most sightseeing trips. This is where you'll find the landmark Pitons and the French colonial town of Soufrière, with its drive-in volcano, botanical gardens, working plantations, and countless other examples of the natural beauty for which St. Lucia is deservedly famous.

SIGHTS TO SEE

⑦ Diamond Botanical Gardens. These splendid gardens are part of Soufrière Estate, a 2,000-acre land grant made in 1713 by Louis XIV to three Devaux brothers from Normandy in recognition of their services to France. The estate is still owned by their descendants; the gardens are maintained by Joan Du Bouley Devaux. Bushes and shrubs bursting with brilliant flowers grow beneath towering trees and line pathways that lead to a natural gorge. Vapor steaming up from La Soufrière volcano and water bubbling up from sulfur springs stream downhill in rivulets to become Diamond Waterfall, deep within the botanical gardens. Through the centuries the rocks over which the cascade spills have become encrusted with minerals and tinted yellow, green, and purple. Adjacent to the falls, curative mineral baths are fed by underground springs. For $2.50 you can slip into your swimsuit and bathe for 30 minutes in one of the outside pools; a private bath costs $3.75. King Louis XVI of France provided funds in 1784 for the construction of a building with a dozen large stone baths to fortify his troops against the St. Lucian climate. It is claimed that Joséphine Bonaparte bathed here as a young girl while visiting her father's plantation nearby. During the Brigand's War, just after the French Revolution, the bathhouse was destroyed. In 1930 the site was excavated by André Du Boulay, and two of the baths were restored for his use. The outside baths were added later. ⊠ *Soufrière Estate, Soufrière,* ☎ *758/452–4759 or 758/454–7565.* ☞ *$2.75.* ☉ *Mon.–Sat. 10–5, Sun. and holidays 10–3.*

⑬ Fregate Island Nature Reserve. A mile-long (1½-km) trail encircles the preserve, which you reach from the East Coast Road near the fishing village of **Praslin,** where boat builders still fashion traditional fishing canoes, called *gommiers* for the trees from which the hulls are made; the ancient design was used by the original Amerindian people who populated the Caribbean. A natural promontory at Praslin provides a lookout where you can view the two small islets, Fregate Major and Fregate Minor, and—with luck—the frigate birds that nest here in summer. Guided tours of Fregate Island Nature Reserve, which include a ride in a *gommier* to Fregate Minor for a picnic lunch and swim, are arranged through the **St. Lucia National Trust** (⊠ Box 595, Castries, ☎ 758/452–5005). All visitors must be accompanied by a guide. The cost is $18 per person (minimum of two), and trips are by appointment only.

⑫ Maria Islands Nature Reserve. Two tiny islands in the Atlantic, off the southeast coast, comprise the reserve, which has its own interpretive center. The 25-acre Maria Major and the 4-acre Maria Minor, its little sister, are inhabited by two rare species of reptiles (the colorful Maria Island ground lizard and the harmless grass snake) that share their home with frigate birds, terns, doves, and other wildlife. There's a small beach for swimming and snorkeling, as well as an undisturbed forest, a vertical cliff covered with cacti, and a coral reef for snorkeling or diving. Tours, including the boat trip, cost $35 per person and are arranged by the St. Lucia National Trust; bring a picnic lunch. ⊠ *St. Lucia Na-*

tional Trust, Box 595, ☎ *758/452–5005.* ☉ *Aug.–mid-May, Wed.–Sun. 9:30–5.*

🐾 ❾ **Morne Coubaril Estate.** This 250-acre coconut and cocoa plantation in Soufrière, the first major estate established on St. Lucia, has a rich French history that dates from 1713, when Crown land was granted by King Louis IV to three St. Lucian brothers. Authentic 18th-century plantation life is explained, as a guide escorts you along an original mule-carriage pathway and through a reconstructed typical village. On the fascinating 90-minute tour you'll see how cocoa, copra, and manioc were processed in the days before mechanization. The foliage is thick and green, and the tropical flowers are beautiful. The plantation house has been renovated and furnished according to the original plans. You can purchase freshly made cocoa, straw items, and hand-carved wooden items. If you wish to have lunch, a delicious creole buffet is available by reservation for $10 per person. ✉ *Soufrière,* ☎ *758/459–7340.* 🎫 *$6.* ☉ *Daily 9–5.*

❽ **The Pitons.** These incredible mountains have become the symbol of St. Lucia. The road south out of Soufrière offers a magnificent view of the twin peaks, which rise precipitously from the cobalt blue Caribbean. The two pyramidal cones, covered with thick tropical vegetation, were formed by lava from a volcanic eruption 30 to 40 million years ago. They are not identical twins since—confusingly—2,619-ft (801-m) Petit Piton is taller than 2,461-ft (753-m) Gros Piton, though Gros is, as the word translates, broader. Gros Piton is currently the only one where climbing is permitted, though the trail up even this shorter Piton is one very tough trek and requires the permission of the **Forest and Lands Department** (☎ 758/450–2231 or 758/450–2078) and a knowledgeable guide—whose services cost about $45.

❿ **St. Lucia National Rain Forest.** Dense tropical rain forest stretches from one side of the island to the other, sprawling over 19,000 acres of mountains and valleys. It's home to a multitude of exotic flowers and plants, as well as rare birds—including the brightly feathered Jacquot parrot. The Edmund Forest Reserve, on the island's western side, is most easily accessible from just east of Soufrière, on the road to Fond St. Jacques. A trek through the lush landscape, with spectacular views of mountains, valleys, and the sea beyond, can take a full day. It takes an hour or so just to reach the reserve from the north end of the island. You'll also need plenty of stamina and sturdy hiking shoes. Permission from the **Forest and Lands Department** (☎ 758/450–2231 or 758/450–2078) is required to access reserve trails, and the department requires a naturalist or forest officer guide ($10 per person) because the vegetation is so dense.

❻ **Soufrière.** The oldest town in St. Lucia, the picturesque fishing village of Soufrière, was founded by the French in 1746 and named for the nearby volcano. The former French colonial capital currently has a population of about 9,000. Its harbor accommodates boats that dock at the wharf and cruise ships that tie up at moorings in the bay. On a nearby jetty there's a small crafts center. French colonial influences can be noticed in the architecture of the wooden buildings around the market square, with their second-story verandas and gingerbread trim. The market building is decorated with colorful murals. The **Soufrière Tourist Information Centre** (✉ Bay St., ☎ 758/459–7200) provides information about area attractions.

🐾 ⓫ **La Soufrière Drive-In Volcano.** Here your nose will pick up the strong scent of the sulfur springs—more than 20 belching pools of muddy water, multicolored sulfur deposits, and other assorted minerals baking and steaming on the surface. Actually, you don't drive in. You drive up within a few hundred feet of the gurgling, steaming mass, then walk behind your guide—whose service is included in the admission price—around a fault in the substratum rock. It's a fascinating, educational half hour that can also be pretty stinky on a hot day. ✉ *Bay St.,* ☎ *758/459–5500.* ⬛ *$1.25.* ⊙ *Daily 9–5.*

ST. LUCIA A TO Z

To research prices, get advice from other travelers, and book travel arrangements, visit www.fodors.com.

AIR TRAVEL

Air Canada has direct weekend service to Hewanorra from Toronto and Montréal. Air Jamaica flies direct to Hewanorra via Grenada from New York twice weekly and also offers connecting service to Hewanorra via Montego Bay, Jamaica; there's connecting service to George F. L. Charles Airport via Barbados. American Airlines/American Eagle has daily service to George F. L. Charles via San Juan from New York and other major U.S. cities. British Airways has direct service to Hewanorra from London via Barbados. BWIA has direct service to George F. L. Charles via either Barbados or Trinidad from Miami, New York, Washington, D.C., and London. Virgin Atlantic has a weekly nonstop flight to Hewanorra from London. From other parts of the world, connections must be made through U.S. cities, San Juan, Toronto, or London.

Air Caraïbes flies into George F. L. Charles Airport from Martinique and other islands in the French West Indies. Caribbean Star connects George F. L. Charles with Antigua. HelenAir flies charter service between Barbados and George F. L. Charles. LIAT operates at Hewanorra, as well as at George F. L. Charles, linking St. Lucia with Barbados, Trinidad, Antigua, Martinique, Dominica, Guadeloupe, and other islands.

➤ AIRLINES AND CONTACTS: **Air Canada** (☎ 758/452–3051 or 758/452–2550); **Air Caraïbes** (☎ 758/452–2463 or 758/453–6660); **Air Jamaica** (☎ 758/453–6611 or 758/454–8870); **American Airlines/American Eagle** (☎ 758/452–1820); **British Airways** (☎ 758/452–3951); **BWIA** (☎ 758/452–3778, 758/451–7700, or 758/454–5075); **Caribbean Star** (☎ 758/461–7827); **HelenAir** (☎ 758/452–7196); **LIAT** (☎ 758/452–3051 or 758/452–2348); **Virgin Atlantic** (☎ 800/744–7477).

AIRPORTS

There are two airports on St. Lucia. Hewanorra International Airport, at Vieux Fort on the southern tip of the island, is a modern airport with a long runway capable of handling wide-body jets. George F. L. Charles Airport, in Castries, is a short airstrip that accommodates small, propeller-driven aircraft used for interisland and charter flights.

The drive from Hewanorra to Castries takes about 1¼ hours; to Soufrière, just over an hour. Although both are long rides, either route follows a picturesque coastline and traverses lush rain forest. George F. L. Charles Airport is only 10 to 20 minutes from resorts in or near Castries; it's about 30 minutes to Marigot and 1¼ hours to Soufrière. Another option is to take a boat from George F. L. Charles Airport (Vigie Cove) to Soufrière, which shortens the trip to about 40 minutes.

Many resorts include airport transfers in their rates. Taxis are always available at the airports. If you take one, be sure to agree on the fare (and in which currency it's being quoted) before you get in. Between Hewanorra and the resorts near Castries, expect to pay $60–$70 each way; between George F. L. Charles Airport and nearby resorts, $15–$20.

➤ AIRPORT INFORMATION: **George F. L. Charles Airport** (☎ 758/452–1156); **Hewanorra International Airport** (☎ 758/454–6355).

BOAT AND FERRY TRAVEL

Cruise ships from major lines call at Castries and Soufrière. At Port Castries ships tie up at berths right in town and are convenient to duty-free shops, the market, and transportation for sightseeing excursions. In Soufrière ships anchor offshore, and passengers are transferred ashore by tenders.

Visitors arriving on private or chartered yachts will find full-service facilities—including duty-free fuel, ship's chandlery, sail and engine repair, telecommunications, groceries, and other services—at the island's two main yachting centers, Port Castries (including Vigie Creek) and Rodney Bay, or at picturesque Marigot Bay. All are official ports of entry to St. Lucia.

FARES AND SCHEDULES

The Rodney Bay Ferry makes the trip between the marina and the shopping complex daily on the hour from 9 to 4 for $4 round-trip. Ferry service to Pigeon Island from Rodney Bay (adjacent to the Lime restaurant) is available twice daily for $50 round-trip, including the entrance fee to Pigeon Island and lunch; snorkel equipment can be rented for $12.

➤ BOAT AND FERRY INFORMATION: **Port Castries** (☎ 758/452–3036); **St. Lucia Yacht Services** (☎ 758/452–5057); **Castries Yacht Centre** (☎ 758/452–6234); **Rodney Bay Ferry** (✉ Box 672, Gros Islet, ☎ 758/452–8816); **Rodney Bay Marina Boatyard** (☎ 758/452–0324); **The Moorings Yacht Charters** (☎ 758/451–4357).

BUSINESS HOURS

BANKS

Banks are open Monday–Thursday 8–3, Friday 8–5; a few branches in Rodney Bay are also open Saturday 9–noon.

POST OFFICES

Post offices are open weekdays 8:30–4:30.

SHOPS

Most stores are open weekdays 8:30–12:30 and 1:30–4:30, Saturday 8–12:30; Gablewoods Mall shops are open Monday–Saturday 9–7; Pointe Seraphine shops are open weekdays 9–5, Saturday 9–2. Stores, with rare exceptions (such as hotel gift shops), and banks are closed on Sunday.

CAR RENTALS

To rent a car, you must be 25 years or older and hold a valid driver's license and a credit card. If you don't have an international driver's license, you must buy a temporary St. Lucian driving permit at car-rental firms, the immigration office at either airport, or the Gros Islet police station. The permit costs $20 (EC$54) and is valid for three months. Car-rental rates are usually quoted in U.S. dollars and range from $45 to $80 per day or $250–$400 per week, depending on the car.

Car-rental agencies generally include free pickup at your hotel and unlimited mileage. Many major U.S. car-rental firms have agencies in St. Lucia. Avis has a main office in Castries and desks at both airports, at the Pointe Seraphine transportation center, and at Rodney Bay Marina. Budget has its main office in Castries and a desk at Hewanorra International Airport. Hertz has desks at both airports.

Local agencies offer competitive service and rates. C. T. L. Rent-a-Car is convenient for people staying at resorts near Rodney Bay or who arrive in St. Lucia by private yacht. Cool Breeze Jeep/Car Rental is convenient for people staying at resorts in the southwest near Soufrière. Courtesy Car Rental has an office north of Rodney Bay and a rental desk at the Bay Gardens Hotel in Rodney Bay. Gibin Rent A Car is convenient for people staying in the north, near Gros Islet. St. Lucia National Car Rental has desks at both airports, at the Pointe Seraphine transportation center, and a desk at LeSPORT and a few other hotels.

➤ MAJOR AGENCIES: **Avis** (⊠ Castries, ☎ 758/452–2700; ⊠ Rodney Bay, ☎ 758/452–0782; ⊠ Vieux Fort, ☎ 758/454–6325; ⊠ Vigie, ☎ 758/452–2046); **Budget** (⊠ Castries, ☎ 758/452–0233; ⊠ Vieux Fort, ☎ 758/454–5311); **Cool Breeze Jeep/Car Rental** (⊠ Soufrière, ☎ 758/459–7729); **Courtesy Car Rental** (⊠ Bois d'Orange, Gros Islet, ☎ 758/452–8140); **C. T. L. Rent-a-Car** (⊠ Rodney Bay Marina, ☎ 758/452–0732); **Gibin Rent A Car** (⊠ Beausejour, Gros Islet, ☎ 758/452–9528); **Hertz** (⊠ Castries, ☎ 758/452–0679; ⊠ Vieux Fort, ☎ 758/454–9636; ⊠ Vigie, ☎ 758/451–7351); **St. Lucia National Car Rental** (⊠ Castries, ☎ 758/450–8721; ⊠ Vieux Fort, ☎ 758/454–6699; ⊠ Vigie, ☎ 758/452–3050; ⊠ Pointe Seraphine, ☎ 758/453–0085).

CAR TRAVEL

Driving yourself is a fine idea if you want to do a lot of exploring and try lots of restaurants during your stay. If you're staying at an all-inclusive resort and plan limited excursions off the property, however, taxis would be a better bet. The drive from Castries to Soufrière is magnificent, but the winding roads can be exhausting for the uninitiated; local drivers are accustomed to the trek. You might even prefer to make that trip by boat, which is a popular option.

GASOLINE

Gasoline is expensive: about EC$2 per liter (the equivalent of $2.75 per gallon).

ROAD CONDITIONS

St. Lucia has about 500 mi (800 km) of roads, but only about half (281 mi) are paved. All towns and villages are connected by major routes. The highways on both coasts are winding and steep—and often scarred by potholes.

RULES OF THE ROAD

Driving in St. Lucia is on the left, British style. Observe speed limits, particularly the 30-mph limit within Castries. Respect no-parking zones; police issue tickets, and penalties start at about $15 (EC$40). Wear your seat belts.

ELECTRICITY

The electric current on St. Lucia is 220 volts, 50 cycles, with a square three-pin plug. A few large hotels have 110-volt outlets—at least for shavers. To use most North American appliances, however, you'll need a transformer to convert voltage and a plug adapter; dual-voltage computers or appliances will still need a plug adapter. Hotels will sometimes lend you one for use during your stay.

EMBASSIES

➤ UNITED KINGDOM: **British High Commission** (⊠ N.I.S. Building, Waterfront Second Floor, Castries, ☎ 758/452–2482).

EMERGENCIES

➤ AMBULANCE AND FIRE: For an ambulance dial ☎ 999. For a fire emergency dial ☎ 911. For sea-air rescue dial ☎ 758/452–2894, 758/452–1182, or 758/453–6664.

➤ HOSPITALS: **Dennery Hospital** (✉ Main Rd. Dennery, ☎ 758/453–3310) is on the east coast; **St. Jude's Hospital** (✉ Airport Rd. Vieux Fort, ☎ 758/454–6684 or 758/454–6051) is near Hewanorra International Airport; **Soufrière Hospital** (✉ West Quinlan St., Soufrière, ☎ 758/459–7258); **Victoria Hospital** (✉ Hospital Rd., Castries, ☎ 758/452–2421 or 758/453–7059) is St. Lucia's main hospital, located on the southwest side of Castries Harbour heading toward La Toc.

➤ PHARMACIES: **M & C Drugstore** (✉ Bridge St., Castries, ☎ 758/452–2811; ✉ J.Q. Shopping Mall, Rodney Bay, ☎ 758/458–0178; ✉ Gablewoods Mall, Gros Islet Hwy., Choc, ☎ 758/451–7808; ✉ New Dock Rd., Vieux Fort, ☎ 758/454–3760); **Williams Pharmacy** (✉ Bridge St., Castries, ☎ 758/452–2797).

➤ POLICE: Dial ☎ 999. For marine police dial ☎ 758/453–0770 or 758/452–2595.

ETIQUETTE AND BEHAVIOR

Dress conservatively in town and in restaurants. In St. Lucia, as well as throughout the Caribbean, beachwear should be reserved for the beach. If you wish to take photographs of local people or their property, be sure to ask permission first and offer a small gratuity in appreciation. Note that souvenir vendors can be persistent, particularly outside some of the popular attractions in and around Soufrière. Be polite but firm if you're not interested.

FESTIVALS AND SEASONAL EVENTS

For two days in May, the St. Lucia National Trust holds its annual fundraiser, the Festival of Comedy; adult comedy shows are held at the Cultural Centre in Castries, and there's a day of family entertainment, with storytellers and comedians, at Pigeon Island. In early May the weeklong St. Lucia Jazz Festival, one of the premier events of its kind in the Caribbean, sees international jazz greats entertain at outdoor venues on Pigeon Island and at various hotels, restaurants, and nightspots throughout the island; free concerts are also held at Derek Walcott Square in downtown Castries. In June, the St. Lucia Golf Open, a two-day tournament held at the St. Lucia Golf and Country Club in Cap Estate, is open to amateurs; it's a handicap event, and prizes are awarded. St. Lucia's Carnival, the most extravagant two days of the year, is held on the third Monday and Tuesday in July; a costume parade winds through Castries, prizes are awarded for the best band, the calypso king and queen are crowned, and there are endless music and dancing in the streets. The St. Lucia Billfishing Tournament, held in late September or early October, attracts anglers from all over the Caribbean, with prizes awarded for the biggest fish and the largest catch; the blue marlin is the most sought-after fish, and everyone hopes to find one that beats the 1,000-lb mark. The last Sunday in October marks Jounen Kweyol Etenasyonnal (International Creole Day), the grand finale of Creole Heritage month; festivities are held in several communities, but musicians always do their stuff at Pigeon Point Park and in the streets in Castries; vendors set up stalls and sell food and handicrafts. The annual Atlantic Rally for Cruisers, or ARC, is the world's largest ocean-crossing race. It starts in Las Palmas, Canary Islands, and ends in early December at Rodney Bay; the event is marked by a week of festivities and parties.

HEALTH

Tap water is perfectly safe to drink throughout the island, but you should be sure that fruit is peeled or washed thoroughly before eating it. Insects can be a real bother during the wet season (July–November), particularly in the rain forest; bring along repellent to ward off mosquitoes and sand flies. Manchineel trees have poisonous fruits that look like small green apples and leaves that can cause skin blisters on contact. Even raindrops falling off the trees can cause blisters. Manchineels grow near the water; those on hotel property or populated areas are usually marked with a sign or a band of red paint.

HOLIDAYS
Public holidays for 2002 are: New Year's Day, Independence Day (Feb. 22), Good Friday (Mar. 29), Easter Monday (Apr. 1), Labour Day (May 1), Whit Monday (May 20), Corpus Christi (May 30), Emancipation Day (1st Mon. in Aug.), Carnival (July 16–17), Thanksgiving Day (Oct. 25), National Day (Dec. 13), Christmas, and Boxing Day (Dec. 26).

LANGUAGE
English is the official language and is spoken everywhere, but you'll often hear local people speaking a French Creole patois (Kweyol) among themselves. If you're interested in learning some patois words and phrases, pick up a copy of *A Visitor's Guide to St. Lucia Patois,* a small paperback book sold in local bookstores for $4.

As in many of the Caribbean islands, to "lime" is to hang out and a "jump-up" is a big party with lots of dance music (often in the street, as in the village of Gros Islet every Friday night). Don't be surprised if people in St. Lucia call you "darling" instead of "ma'am" or "sir"— they're being friendly not forward.

MAIL AND SHIPPING
The General Post Office is on Bridge Street in Castries and is open weekdays 8:30–4:30; all towns and villages have branches. Postage for airmail letters to the U.S., Canada, and the U.K. is EC95¢ per ½ ounce; postcards are EC65¢. Airmail letters to Australia and New Zealand cost EC$1.35; postcards, EC70¢. Airmail can take two or three weeks to be delivered—even longer to Australia and New Zealand.

MONEY MATTERS
Prices quoted in this chapter are in U.S. dollars unless otherwise indicated.

The international Bank of Nova Scotia, or Scotiabank, has its head office in central Castries and branch offices at Rodney Bay and Vieux Fort. Barclays Bank offers international banking services from its two offices in Castries and branches in major towns. National Commercial Bank of St. Lucia is a large regional bank, with two offices in Castries and branches at Hewanorra Airport, Gros Islet, and Soufrière. Royal Bank of Canada has its main office in downtown Castries and a branch at Rodney Bay Marina.
➤ CONTACTS: **Bank of Nova Scotia** (✉ Wm. Peter Blvd., Castries, ☎ 758/452–2292; ✉ Rodney Bay; ☎ 758/452–8805; ✉ Vieux Fort, ☎ 758/454–6314); **Barclays Bank** (✉ Jeremie St., Castries, ☎ 758/452–4041; ✉ Bridge St., Castries, ☎ 758/452–3306; ✉ Rodney Bay Marina, Rodney Bay, ☎ 758/452–9384; ✉ Hewanorra Airport, Vieux Fort, ☎ 758/454–6255; ✉ Soufrière, ☎ 758/459–7255); **National Commercial Bank of St. Lucia** (✉ Bridge St., Castries, ☎ 758/456–6000; ✉ Pointe Seraphine, Castries, ☎ 758/452–4787; ✉ Hewanorra Airport, ☎ 758/454–7780; ✉ Gros Islet, ☎ 758/450–0928; ✉ Soufrière, ☎ 758/459–7450); **Royal Bank of Canada** (✉ William Peter Blvd., Castries, ☎ 758/452–2245; ✉ Rodney Bay Marina, Rodney Bay, ☎ 758/452–9921).

ATMS

Automated teller machines (ATMs) are available 24 hours a day at bank branches, transportation centers, and shopping malls, where you can use major credit cards to obtain cash (in local currency only).

CREDIT CARDS

Major credit cards and traveler's checks are widely accepted.

CURRENCY

The official currency is the Eastern Caribbean dollar (EC$). It's linked to the U.S. dollar at EC$2.67, but stores and hotels often exchange at EC$2.50 or EC$2.60. U.S. currency is readily accepted, but you'll probably get change in EC dollars.

PASSPORTS AND VISAS

U.S., Canadian, and British citizens whose stay does not exceed six months must have a valid passport or prove citizenship with a birth certificate (with a raised seal) and a government-issued photo ID. Visitors from other countries must present a valid passport. All visitors must have a return or ongoing ticket.

SAFETY

Although crime isn't a significant problem, take the same precautions you would at home—lock your door, secure your valuables, and don't carry too much money or flaunt expensive jewelry on the street.

Coastal waters surrounding the island of St. Lucia are protected areas. Spearfishing and collecting live fish are prohibited. Be aware that sea urchins live among the rocks on the coastline; should one's long black spines lodge under your skin, don't try to pull them out. Apply an ammonia-based liquid (such as urine!), and the spine will retreat, allowing you to ease it out. Swimming on the rough Atlantic side of the island is dangerous.

SIGHTSEEING TOURS

A variety of guided half- and full-day land and/or sea tours depart from the Castries area (Pointe Seraphine and Vigie Cove) or Rodney Bay and head north to Pigeon Island or south along the picturesque west coast to the Pitons and the sights in and around Soufrière. Half-day land tours range in price from $35 to $40 per person; full-day land tours, from $120 to $140 for 1–4 people. Cruises include refreshments and range in price from $40 per person at sunset to $80 for a full day.

BOAT

Board the 140-ft *Brig Unicorn* for a full-day sail to Soufrière or a sunset cruise under full sail, accompanied by champagne, snacks, and live music. Endless Summer Cruises (Cats Inc., offers full-day tours and champagne sunset cruises aboard one of their huge 56-ft catamaran party boats, *Endless Summer I* or *Sunkist*. The 56-ft motor cruiser MV *Vigie* takes passengers for half-day cruises to Pigeon Island or full-day tours to the Pitons and the sights around Soufrière, with lunch, swimming, and snorkeling at Anse Cochon included.
➤ CONTACTS: **Brig Unicorn** (✉ Vigie Cove, Castries, ☎ 758/452–8811); **Endless Summer Cruises** Cats Inc., (✉ Rodney Bay, ☎ 758/450–8651); **MV *Vigie*** (✉ Rodney Bay Marina, ☎ 758/452–9423 or 758/452–8232).

HELICOPTER

Helicopter sightseeing tours are fascinating ways to get a bird's-eye view of the island. A 10-minute North Island tour ($45 per person) leaves from Pointe Seraphine, in Castries, continues up the west coast to Pigeon Island, then flies along the rugged Atlantic coastline before returning inland over Castries. The 20-minute South Island tour ($120 per person) starts at Pointe Seraphine and follows the western coastline, circling picturesque Marigot Bay, Soufrière, and the majestic Pitons before returning inland over the volcanic hot springs and tropical rain forest. To arrange a helicopter sightseeing trip, contact St. Lucia Helicopters.

➤ CONTACTS: **St. Lucia Helicopters** (✉ Pointe Seraphine, ☎ 758/453–6950, FAX 758/452–1553).

BICYCLE

Although the terrain can get pretty rugged, several tour operators have put together fascinating bicycle and combination bicycle-hiking tours that appeal to novice riders as well as those who enjoy a good workout. It's a marvelous way to enjoy the spectacular scenery throughout the St. Lucia countryside. Prices range from $60–$100 per person.

Bike St. Lucia takes small groups of bikers on Jungle Biking™ tours along trails that meander through the remnants of an 18th-century plantation near Soufrière. Stops are made to explore the French Colonial ruins, study the beautiful tropical plants and fruit trees, enjoy a picnic lunch, and take dip in a river swimming hole or a swim at the beach. For those staying in the north, transportation to and from the facility is provided by land taxi and boat from Vigie Marina, in Castries.

Island Bike Hikes is suitable for all fitness levels. Jeep or bus transportation is provided across the central mountains to Dennery, on the east coast. After a 3-mi ride through the countryside, bikes are exchanged for shoe leather. The short hike into the rain forest ends with a picnic and a refreshing swim next to a sparkling waterfall—then the return leg back to Dennery. All gear is supplied.

St. Lucia Mountain Bike Tour is a four-hour excursion that begins at Morne Fortune, south of downtown Castries, winds north and east through banana plantations to Babonneau, finally ending up at Waves, the beach club at Choc Bay. The group is limited to 20 participants, and several water and refreshment stops are made along the way.

➤ CONTACTS: **Bike St. Lucia** (✉ Anse Chastanet, Soufrière, ☎ 758/451–2453); **Island Bike Hikes** (✉ Rodney Bay, Gros Islet, ☎ 758/458–0908); **St. Lucia Mountain Bike Tour** (✉ Choc Bay, Castries, ☎ 758/452–4049).

ORIENTATION

Taxi drivers are well informed and can give you a full tour—and often an excellent one, thanks to government-sponsored training programs. From the Castries area, full-day island tours cost $140 for up to four people; sightseeing trips to Soufrière, $120. If you plan your own day, expect to pay the driver $20 per hour plus tip.

St. Lucia Heritage Tourism has put together what they term an "authentic St. Lucia experience"; they specialize in the local culture and traditions. Groups are small, and some of the off-the-beaten-track sites visited are a 19th-century plantation house surrounded by nature trails, a 20-ft waterfall hidden away on private property, and a living museum where creole practices and traditions are experienced. Plan on paying $65 per person for a full-day tour.

Jungle Tours specializes in rain forest hiking tours for all levels of ability. Prices range from $80 to $90 and include lunch, fees, and transportation via open Landrover truck.

Sunlink Tours offers dozens of land, sea, and combination sightseeing tours, as well as shopping tours, plantation, and rain forest adventures via Jeep safari, deep-sea fishing excursions, and day trips to other islands. Prices range from $20 for a half-day shopping tour to $120 for a full-day land-and-sea Jeep safari to Soufrière.

➤ CONTACTS: **Jungle Tours** (✉ Cas en Bas, Gros Islet, ☎ 758/450–0434); **St. Lucia Heritage Tours** (✉ Pointe Seraphine, Castries, ☎ 758/451–6058); **Sunlink Tours** (✉ Reduit Beach Ave., Rodney Bay, ☎ 758/452–8232 or 800/SUNLINK, 🌐 www.stluciareps.com).

TAXES

DEPARTURE TAX

The departure tax is $20 (EC$54), payable in cash only (either Eastern Caribbean or U.S. dollars).

SALES TAX

A government tax of 8% is added to all hotel and restaurant bills. There is no sales tax on items purchased in shops.

TAXIS

Taxis are always available at the airports, the harbor, and in front of major hotels. They're unmetered, although nearly all drivers belong to a taxi cooperative and adhere to standard fares. Sample fares for up to four passengers are: Castries to Rodney Bay, $16; Rodney Bay to Cap Estate, $10; Castries to Cap Estate, $20; Castries to Marigot Bay, $24; Castries to Soufrière, $64. Always ask the driver to quote the price *before* you get in, and be sure that you both understand whether it's in EC or U.S. dollars. Drivers are knowledgeable and courteous.

TELEPHONES

COUNTRY AND AREA CODES

The area code for St. Lucia is 758.

INTERNATIONAL CALLS

You can make direct-dial overseas and interisland calls from St. Lucia, and the connections are excellent. To charge an overseas call to a major credit card, dial 811; there is no surcharge. From public phones and many hotels, you can dial AT&T Direct Service 1–800/USA–2881 or MCI Worldcom at 1–800/888–8000 and charge the call to your calling card to avoid expensive rates or hotel surcharges. Phonecards can be purchased at many retail outlets and used from any touch-tone telephone (including pay phones) in St. Lucia.

LOCAL CALLS

You can dial local calls throughout St. Lucia directly from your hotel room by connecting to an outside line and dialing the seven-digit number. Some hotels charge a small fee (usually about EC50¢) for local calls. Pay phones accept EC25¢ and EC$1 coins. Phone cards can be used for local calls, as well as for international calls.

TIPPING

Most restaurants add a 10% service charge to your bill in lieu of tipping; if one has not been added, a 10%–12% tip is appropriate for good service. Tip porters and bellhops $1 per bag, although many of the all-inclusive resorts have a no-tipping policy. Taxi drivers also appreciate a 10%–12% tip.

TRANSPORTATION AROUND ST. LUCIA

Privately owned and operated minivans constitute St. Lucia's bus system, an inexpensive and efficient means of transportation used primarily by local people. Minivan routes cover the entire island and run from early morning until approximately 10 PM. You'll find this method of getting around most useful for short distances, between Castries and the Rodney Bay area, for example; longer hauls can be uncomfortable. The fare between Castries and Gablewoods Mall is EC$1; Castries and

Rodney Bay, EC$1.50; Castries and Vieux Fort (a trip that takes more than two hours), EC$7. Minivans follow designated routes (signs are displayed on the front window); ask at your hotel for the appropriate route number for your destination. Wait at a marked bus stop or hail a passing minivan from the roadside. You can also catch one in Castries, at the corner of Micoud and Bridge streets.

Each minivan has a driver and a conductor, a young man whose job it is to collect fares, open the door, and generally take charge of the passenger area. If you're sure of where you're going, simply knock twice on the metal window frame to signal the conductor when you want to get off at the next stop. Otherwise, just let him know where you're going, and he'll make sure the bus stops to let you out.

Some visitors to St. Lucia opt for helicopter transportation—a more expensive mode but much quicker. The cost for the 15-minute flight from Hewanorra to Castries is $100 per person, including luggage; for the 10-minute flight to Soufrière, $85 per person. There are helipads at Pointe Seraphine, Windjammer Landing, the Jalousie Hilton, and Rodney Bay. Contact St. Lucia Helicopters.
➤ CONTACTS: **St. Lucia Helicopters** (⌧ Pointe Seraphine, ☎ 758/453–6950, FAX 758/452–1553).

VISITOR INFORMATION
➤ BEFORE YOU LEAVE: **St. Lucia Tourist Board** (In the U.S.: ⌧ 800 2nd Ave., Suite 400-J, New York, NY 10017, ☎ 212/867–2950 or 888/478–5824, FAX 212/867–2795; In Canada: ⌧ 8 King St. E, Suite 700, Toronto, Ontario M5C 1B5, Canada, ☎ 416/362–4242, FAX 416/362–7832; In the U.K.: ⌧ 421A Finchley Rd., London NW3 6HJ, U.K., ☎ 0171/431–3675, FAX 0171/431–7920, WEB www.st-lucia.com).
➤ IN ST. LUCIA: **St. Lucia Tourist Board** (⌧ Box 221, Castries, ☎ 758/452–4094 or 758/452–5968, FAX 758/453–1121, WEB slutour@candw.lc; ⌧ Jeremie St., Castries, ☎ 758/452–2479; ⌧ Bay St., Soufrière, ☎ 758/459–7200); at George F. L. Charles Airport ⌧ Vigie, Castries, ☎ 758/452–2596; at Hewanorra International Airport ⌧ Vieux Fort, ☎ 758/454–6644.

21 ST. MAARTEN/ ST. MARTIN

Updated by
Karl Luntta

A warm breeze gently caresses the dining room, while lights dance off the water in the canal. A young couple dressed in black, their foreheads almost touching, whisper in French; a Dutch family gathers around a large table for a festive reunion; and four animated Americans just off a charter boat recap the day's adventures. On this island, such multicultural scenes regularly unfold.

There are several advantages to visiting St. Maarten/St. Martin. Airline service is good, so you don't have to spend half your vacation getting here. The 37-square-mi (96-square-km) island is home to two cultures—St. Maarten is Dutch and St. Martin is French—and you can experience both for the price of one. And the island is ideal if you like to have lots of things to do.

Whatever can be done in or on the water—snorkeling, windsurfing, waterskiing—is available here; golf and tennis are also options. Serious diners will find a different top-class restaurant each night. The duty-free shopping is as good as anywhere in the Caribbean. There's an active nightlife, with discos and casinos. Day trips can be taken by ship or plane to the nearby islands of Anguilla, Saba, St. Eustatius, and St. Barthélemy. There are hotels for every budget—from motel-type units to some of the Caribbean's most exclusive resort accommodations. The standard of living is one of the highest in the Caribbean, so islanders can afford to be honest and treat visitors as welcome guests. Corruption and crime, which had been on the rise, decreased dramatically in the 1990s, thanks to an exemplary cooperative effort between the two governments.

On the negative side, St. Maarten/St. Martin has been thoroughly discovered and exploited; unless you stay in an exclusive resort, you may well end up sharing beachfronts with tour groups (the exception being some of the beaches in Terres Basses, on the French side). Yes, there's gambling, but the table limits are so low that hard-core gamblers have a better time gamboling on the beach. As is often the case in the Caribbean, the island infrastructure has not kept pace with development. The governments, however, have upgraded the port area and the airport, and improved the roads—both to better accommodate visitors and to make things more comfortable for islanders.

Lodging

On the Dutch side the main resort areas are along beaches such as Maho Bay, where the swimming is great and the restaurants are abundant;

at Simpson Bay, south of the airport where traffic can be heavy; and along Front Street in downtown Philipsburg, where shops and eateries abound. The casinos are still found exclusively on the Dutch side (gambling is illegal on the French side). Note that most signs and publications on the Dutch side are in English, the lingua franca. Most newspapers are also in English (although there are Dutch papers imported from Holland), as are place names on maps.

The French side's attractive Baie Nettlé (Nettlé Bay area, whose pretty beach offers a variety of water-sports opportunities) and busy, popular Baie Orientale (Orient Bay, with its sports outfitters and beachside bistros) are two resort areas. Others include secluded Anse Marcel (Marcel Cove); Mont Vernon, which has a nice beach a bit removed from the crowds; and the town of Marigot, with shops, an open-air market, and fine dining (you'll find restaurants in town and south along a strip called Sandy Ground). All hotels on the French side have English-speaking staff members, but French is used by most citizens and on street signs and maps.

There are small inns and Mediterranean-style facilities on both sides. Many hotels offer enticing packages, and you'll save substantially if you travel off-season. In general, the French resorts are more intimate, but what the Dutch properties lack in ambience they compensate for in clean, comfortable rooms with all the extras. Most large Dutch resorts feature time-share annexes; the units are often available for rental to those who prefer the condo lifestyle. Most properties are EP or CP (the latter usually only in season), though meal plans are sometimes available.

The island has recovered from the thrashing it took when 1999's Hurricane Lenny (dubbed "Wrong-Way Lenny" because it came in from the west rather than the east) hovered over the island for 36 hours. The hotels are back in business, in several cases with major improvements, the beaches are back on track—Philipsburg's Great Bay Beach has been widened—and services are back to normal.

CATEGORY	COST*
$$$$	over $350
$$$	$250–$350
$$	$150–$250
$	under $150

All prices are for a standard double room in high season, excluding a 15% service/energy tax and 5% government tax (Dutch side), a taxe de séjour (set by individual hotels on the French side), and a 10%–15% service charge.

Hotels

DUTCH SIDE

$$$ **Divi Little Bay Beach Resort.** This resort sits on a beach that's clean but rocky and thin in places. There's a light-blue-and-cream, Dutch colonial motif throughout the hotel, and the large rooms have king-size beds, wide balconies with sea views, and small but adequate kitchens. Bathrooms have luxurious whirlpool baths and separate showers. The poolside Sea Breeze Bar hosts weekly barbecues and live music. ⊠ *Little Bay Rd., Little Bay (Box 961), Philipsburg,* ☎ *599/54–22333 or 800/367–3484,* 📠 *599/54–37725,* 🌐 *www.divire-sorts.com. 235 units. Restaurant, bar, grocery, refrigerators, 3 pools, tennis court, beach, snorkeling, boating, coin laundry. AE, MC, V. EP, FAP, MAP.*

$$$ **La Vista.** At this intimate property Antillean buildings are connected by brick walkways lined with riotous hibiscus and bougainvillea. All suites have small stoves, cable TV, mini-refrigerators, and

balconies. A stay here gets you use of the pool, tennis courts, and spa facilities at the adjacent Pelican Resort & Casino. ✉ *Pelican Key (Box 2086), Simpson Bay,* ☎ *599/54–43005,* FAX *599/54–43010,* WEB *www.lavistaresort.com. 32 suites. Restaurant, air-conditioning, refrigerators. AE, MC, V. EP.*

$$$ 🏨 **Maho Beach Resort & Casino.** This megaresort took the opportunity during its post-Hurricane Lenny repairs to expand and refurbish. The infrastructure has been touched up with new room furniture and decor, a brightened lobby, added walkways, and expanded meeting facilities. Also new is the Q Disco, for late night dancing. The spacious rooms have cathedral ceilings and sea or garden views. The trick is to get a room far enough from the airport's landing strip (those behind the main lobby are the quietest). Dining options include Italian fare at Dolce Vita and beachside American fare at Harbor Point. The hotel is home to the island's largest casino, the Casino Royal, and its largest pool. The people at the on-site activities desk can arrange all manner of water sports. ✉ *Airport Rd. (Box 834), Maho Bay,* ☎ *599/54–52115 or 800/ 223–0757,* FAX *599/54–53180,* WEB *www.mahobeachresort.com. 570 rooms, 25 suites. 10 restaurants, 3 bars, air-conditioning, 2 pools, spa, 4 tennis courts, health club, beach, shops, casino, dance club, babysitting, business services, car rental. AE, D, MC, V. EP.*

$$$ 🏨 **Mary's Boon Beach Plantation.** This St. Martin fixture was hard hit by Hurricane Lenny; indeed, the main building was so severely damaged it was completely rebuilt. The rooms retain a comfortable plantation style, with imported Indonesian mahogany furniture and four-poster beds, and have air-conditioning, fans, cable TV, and patios overlooking the long beach. There's an honor bar, and a traditional family-style dinner is served nightly, featuring both island cuisine (lobster Creole, shrimp provencale) and international selections (roast duck, beef tenderloin). ✉ *17 Simpson Bay Rd., Simpson Bay,* ☎ *599/ 54–54235,* FAX *599/54–53403,* WEB *www.marysboon.com. 20 rooms. Restaurant, bar, kitchenettes, minibars, pool, beach. MC, V. EP.*

$$$ 🏨 **Pelican Resort & Casino.** The white stucco buildings here house apartments, suites, and deluxe studios—all with sweeping Caribbean views. Gaming tables greet you in the reception area, and a lower-level sales office entices you to buy into this hotel-condo complex. Sadly, the resort hasn't kept pace with all the refurbishing that swept the island after recent hurricanes, and the staff seems more interested in selling timeshare units than attending to guests. Still the location is central, and there are 1,400 ft (428 m) of beach. ✉ *Off Airport Rd., Simpson Bay (Box 431, Pelican Key),* ☎ *599/54–42503 or 800/550–7088,* FAX *599/ 54–42133,* WEB *www.pelicanresort.com. 210 suites, 132 apartments. 2 restaurants, 4 bars, grocery, kitchenettes, 5 pools, spa, 4 tennis courts, beach, dive shop, dock, snorkeling, windsurfing, boating, jet skiing, waterskiing, casino, playground, car rental. AE, D, MC, V. EP.*

$$$ 🏨 **Radisson Vacation Villas at Oyster Bay.** The Radisson group took over this island hotel and time-share resort in 2001, but not much has changed. Its refined elegance is immediately evident in the architecture: two towers with Moorish arches and stone walls surround a courtyard. Split-level suites and standard rooms all have terra-cotta floors, balconies or terraces, and pastel French cottons. An ongoing expansion, unaffected by the takeover, will enlarge the pool, which overlooks the sea, and add 190 more time-share units. The work will continue through 2002. The hotel is a one-minute walk from Dawn Beach. The Radisson Vacation Villas restaurant opens onto the Atlantic. ✉ *North of Dawn Beach, Oyster Pond (Box 239, Philipsburg),* ☎ *599/54–36040 or 877/478–6669,* FAX *599/54–36695,* WEB *www.radisson.com. 124 units. Restaurant, bar, air-conditioning, fans, pool, hot tub, car rental. AE, D, MC, V. BP, EP.*

Lodging

Alizéa **17**
Anse Margot **39**
Blue Bay Club
Mont Vernon **15**
Captain Oliver's . . . **12**
Divi Little Bay
Beach Resort **51**
Esmeralda Resort . . . **16**
Grand Case
Beach Club **23**
Great Bay Beach
Hotel & Casino **52**
Green Cay
Village **14**
Hévéa **24**
Holland House
Beach Hotel **8**
Hôtel l'Atlantide . . . **26**
Hôtel L'Esplanade
Caraïbes **27**
Maho Beach
Resort & Casino . . . **41**
Mary's Boon
Beach Plantation . . . **42**
Mercure Simson
Beach Coralia **38**
Le Méridien **19**
Nettlé Bay
Beach Club **37**
Pasanggrahan
Royal Inn **9**
Pavillon Beach
Hotel **25**
Pelican Resort
& Casino **46**
Le Privilege
Resort & Spa **18**
Radisson Vacation
Villas at
Oyster Bay **11**
La Résidence **30**
Le Royale
Louisiana **33**
La Samanna **40**
Sunterra Royal
Palm Beach Club . . . **43**
La Vista **47**

Dining

Antoine **1**
Le Bec Fin **5**
Bistrot Nu **28**
Chesterfield's **2**
Claude
Mini-Club **29**
L'Escargot **3**
Indiana Beach **48**
Kangaroo Court
Caffé **4**
Maison sur
le Port **32**
Le Mango **17**
Mario's Bistro **35**
Le Perroquet **44**
La Plaisance **34**
Le Pressoir **20**
Radisson
Vacation Villas
at Oyster Bay **11**
The Rainbow **22**
Ric's Place **10**

St. Maarten/St. Martin

TO ANGUILLA

KEY

Beaches

Cruise Ship Terminal

Dive Sites

1 Exploring Sights

Ferry

① Hotels and Restaurants

Pt. Arago

Pte. du Bluff

Pt. du Plum

Baie de la Potence

Baie Rouge

Pte. des Pierres à Chaux

Terres Basses

Baie de Marigot

Baie Nettlé

Marigot

Musée de Saint-Martin

Baie Longue

Simpson Bay Lagoon

Cupecoy Beach

Sentry Hill

Mullet Bay

S T.

Juliana International Airport

Maho Bay

Simpson Bay

Koolbaai

Annie

Cole Bay

Caribbean Sea

N

0   2 miles
0   3 km

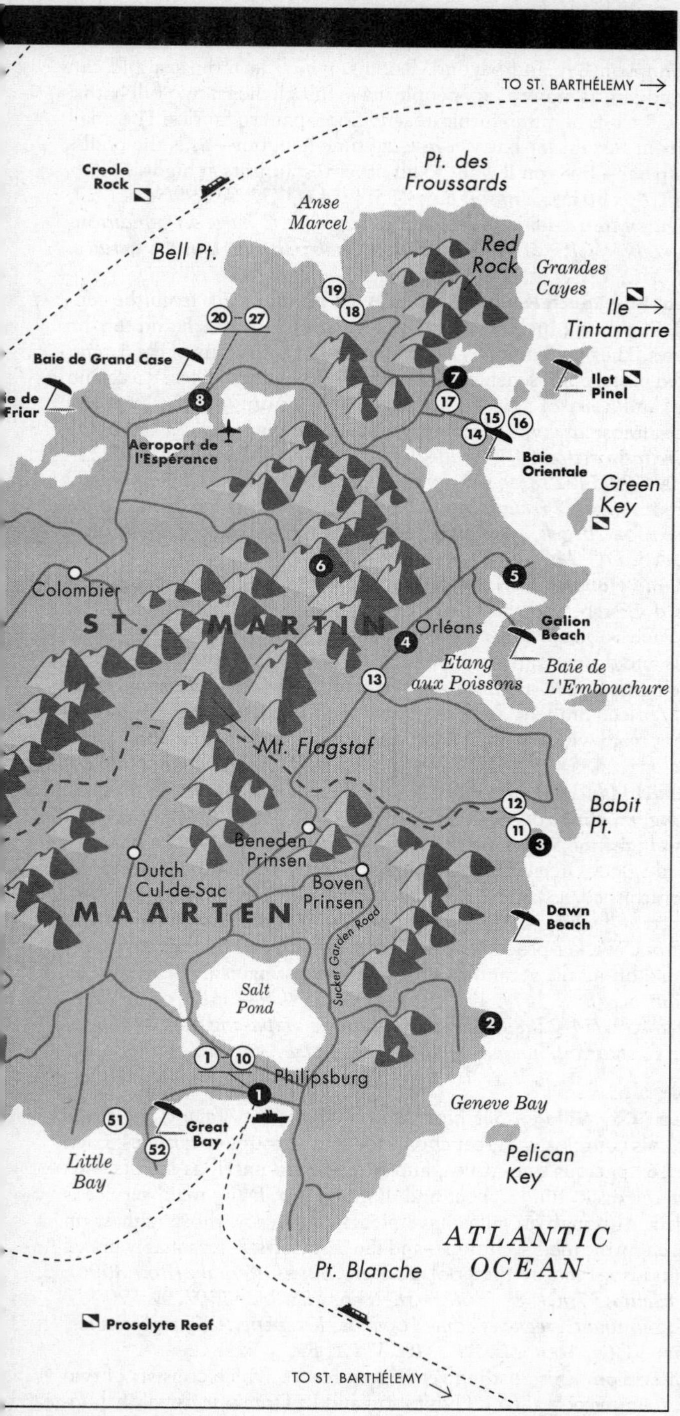
TO ST. BARTHÉLEMY
Creole Rock
Pt. des Froussards
Anse Marcel
Bell Pt.
Red Rock
Grandes Cayes
Ile Tintamarre
Baie de Grand Case
ie de Friar
Ilet Pinel
Aeroport de l'Espérance
Baie Orientale
Green Key
Colombier
ST. MARTIN
Orléans
Galion Beach
Etang aux Poissons
Baie de L'Embouchure
Mt. Flagstaf
Babit Pt.
Beneden Prinsen
Boven Prinsen
Dutch Cul-de-Sac
MAARTEN
Dawn Beach
Sucker Garden Road
Salt Pond
Philipsburg
Geneve Bay
Great Bay
Little Bay
Pelican Key
ATLANTIC OCEAN
Pt. Blanche
Proselyte Reef
TO ST. BARTHÉLEMY

Le Santal	36
Saratoga	49
Shiv Sagar	6
Spartaco	50
Le Tastevin	21
Turtle Pier Bar & Restaurant	45
La Vie En Rose	31
Wajang Doll	7
Yvette's	13

Exploring

Butterfly Farm	5
French Cul de Sac	7
Grand Case	8
Guana Bay Point	2
Marigot	9
Orléans	4
Oyster Pond	3
Philipsburg	1
Pic du Paradis	6

$$$ 🏨 **Sunterra Royal Palm Beach Club.** A complex of suites and shops on Kimsha Beach, the Royal Palm is an excellent place from which to explore Simpson Bay and beyond. Rooms, which face the sea and can accommodate as many as six people, have full kitchens, two full baths, TVs, VCRs, lots of rattan furniture, and floral-pattern fabrics. The small beachfront restaurant-bar is a fine daytime hangout—as is the pool's swim-up bar—but you'll want to hit other restaurants at night. ⊠ *Airport Rd. (Box 3035), Simpson Bay,* ☎ *599/54–43732,* FAX *599/54–43727,* WEB *www.sunterra.com. 142 suites. Restaurant, 2 bars, air-conditioning, in-room VCRs, pool, beach, shops, baby-sitting, laundry service. AE, D, MC, V. EP.*

$$ 🏨 **Great Bay Beach Hotel & Casino.** A 10-minute walk from the center of Philipsburg, this resort has its own stretch of beach and terrific bay views. The open-air lobby overlooks the sea, and many of the rooms, in muted pastel color schemes, have views of the ocean. There's a casino on site, and a list of activities is posted each morning. The staff can arrange almost any type of excursion or sporting pursuit. ⊠ *Little Bay Rd., Great Bay (Box 910, Philipsburg),* ☎ *599/54–22446 or 800/223–0757,* FAX *599/54–23859,* WEB *www.greatbayhotel.com. 275 rooms, 10 1-bedroom suites. 2 restaurants, 2 bars, 2 pools, hair salon, tennis court, exercise room, beach, snorkeling, boating, shops, casino, nightclub, car rental. AE, DC, MC, V. All-inclusive, EP.*

$$ 🏨 **Holland House Beach Hotel.** The shops of Front Street are at this hotel's doorstep, and the mile-long (1½-km) Great Bay Beach is out back. Each room (ask for one with a beach view) has muted-pastel spreads and drapes and a balcony; most rooms also have kitchenettes. The delightful open-air restaurant overlooking the water serves reasonably priced dinners, and the indoor-outdoor patio lounge is a popular spot from which to watch the sunset. ⊠ *43-A Front St. (Box 393), Philipsburg,* ☎ *599/54–22572 or 800/223–9815,* FAX *599/54–24673,* WEB *www.hhbh.com. 48 rooms, 6 suites. Restaurant, lounge, air-conditioning, meeting room. AE, D, DC, MC, V. BP, FAP, MAP.*

$$ 🏨 **Pasanggrahan Royal Inn.** It's entirely appropriate that the bar here ★ is named Sidney Greenstreet. Although the island's oldest inn has recently been refurbished, it still looks like a set for an old Bogie-Greenstreet film. The green-and-white building was formerly the guest house for royal Danish visitors. Wicker peacock chairs, balconies shaded by tropical greenery, and a broad tile veranda are some of its distinguishing features. ⊠ *15 Front St. (Box 151), Philipsburg,* ☎ *599/54–23588 or 599/54–22743,* FAX *599/54–22885,* WEB *www.gobeach.com/pasang.htm. 27 rooms, 1 suite. Restaurant, bar, air-conditioning, beach. AE, MC, V. EP.*

FRENCH SIDE

$$$$ 🏨 **Green Cay Village.** Set high above Orient Bay facing the trade ★ winds, this complex is a great choice for small groups or families. Each of the 16 spacious one-, two-, and three-bedroom villas has its own pool, large deck, full kitchen, and dining patio. Daily maid service is included. Although all villas have plenty of privacy, those highest on the hill enjoy the most seclusion—and the best views. A reasonably priced breakfast is served by the pool. ⊠ *Parc Baie Orientale (Box 3006), Baie Oriental 97064,* ☎ *590/87–38–63 or 888/832–2302,* FAX *590/87–39–27,* WEB *www.greencay.com. 16 villas. Kitchenettes, room service, in-room VCRs, 16 pools. AE, MC, V. CP, EP.*

$$$$ 🏨 **Le Méridien.** This bustling yet elegant resort, which consists of two smaller complexes called L'Habitation and Le Domaine, is wildly popular with tour groups and families. There are 1,600 ft (489 m) of white-sand beach and a slew of sports facilities. The service is polite and the setting—amid beautifully landscaped gardens on enchanting but windless Marcel Cove—pleasant. All rooms and suites have balconies, and suites on the marina have fully equipped kitchens and patios. A stay here gets you free access to the facilities at Le Privilege Resort & Spa. La Belle France is a typically solid and *très cher* restaurant. ⊠ *Bear north at French Cul de Sac, follow signs to Anse Marcel (Box 581), Anse Marcel 97150,* ☎ *590/87–67–00 or 800/543–4300,* ℻ *590/87–30–38,* WEB *www.lemeridien-hotels.com. 396 rooms, 84 suites. 4 restaurants, 4 bars, air-conditioning, refrigerator, 2 pools, miniature golf, 6 tennis courts, aerobics, gym, racquetball, squash, beach, dive shop, dock, snorkeling, boating, jet skiing, waterskiing, shops, dance club, car rental. AE, DC, MC, V. EP.*

$$$$ 🏨 **Le Privilege Resort & Spa.** At this resort, perched above Marcel Cove and Le Méridien, those into the spa life can take advantage of all kinds of treatments. Rooms and suites are spacious and comfortably furnished, with tile floors, marble baths, and such touches as CD players and in-room safes. There's a free shuttle to the beach and the resort's marina. ⊠ *Bear left at French Cul de Sac, follow signs, Anse Marcel 97150,* ☎ *590/87–38–38 or 800/874–8541,* ℻ *590/87–44–12,* WEB *www. privilege-spa.com. 16 rooms, 18 suites. 2 restaurants, bar, in-room safes, in-room VCRs, 3 pools, hair salon, massage, spa, 6 tennis courts, health club, racquetball, squash, dive shop, dock, windsurfing, boating, fishing, nightclub. AE, MC, V. CP.*

$$$$ 🏨 **La Samanna.** Overlooking a perfect white beach and set on 55 acres of lush gardens, this Mediterranean-style retreat is pure luxury. The designer rooms are furnished with mahogany and teak imports, and there are a variety of ultraluxurious penthouses and suites for the chic set. And, if you want, you can just drop in via the hotel's new nearby helicopter pad. The service is impeccable, the food exquisite. ⊠ *Baie Longue(Box 4007), Marigot 97064),* ☎ *590/87–64–00 or 800/854–2252,* ℻ *590/87–87–86,* WEB *lasamanna.orient-express.com. 81 units. Restaurant, bar, pool, massage, 3 tennis courts, aerobics, health club, beach, windsurfing, waterskiing, shops, library. AE, MC, V. CP, MAP. Closed Sept.–Oct.*

$$$ 🏨 **Blue Bay Club Mont Vernon.** Gingerbread fretwork decorates this rambling hotel, which sits on a bluff over Orient Bay, but its multicolor veneer makes it an eyesore when seen from the beach. Looking out is another story: rooms in the buildings that face the ocean have the best views and are slightly larger than the others. Other choice rooms are in buildings by the pool and beach. All rooms have balconies. This is a big resort that lures package-tour groups and business seminars. ⊠ *On French Cul de Sac (Box 1174), Baie Orientale 97062,* ☎ *590/87–62–40 or 800/258–3229,* ℻ *590/87–37–27,* WEB *www.bluebayresorts.com. 394 rooms. 3 restaurants, 2 bars, 2 pools, 2 tennis courts, gym, beach, snorkeling, windsurfing, shops, children's program, car rental. AE, DC, MC, V. All-inclusive.*

$$$ 🏨 **Esmeralda Resort.** The green roofs and stacked configuration make this villa complex look like a Sun Belt development, but the interiors are tastefully decorated. The 65 rooms and suites in 18 villas can be combined any way you like, from studios to five-bedroom palatial digs. Each villa has a private pool, and all rooms have terraces. The restaurant, L'Astrolabe, serves excellent French cuisine. Five other restaurants on the nearby beach let you charge meals to your room. ⊠ *Box 5141, Baie Orientale 97064,* ☎ *590/87–36–36 or 800/622–7836,* ℻ *590/87–35–18,* WEB *www.esmeralda-resort.com. 65 rooms in 18 villas. 6 restaurants, in-room safes, kitchenettes, 17 pools, 2 tennis courts, shops. AE, MC, V. EP.*

$$$ 🏨 **Grand Case Beach Club.** This informal condo complex is on a crescent beach, and there's another "secret" strand of sand a short walk away. Although the hotel underwent a major renovation several years ago, the management continues to upgrade the facilities here. The

tastefully furnished studios and one- and two-bedroom apartments have balconies or patios; the 62 oceanfront units are in demand. The aptly named Sunset Café sits over the beach, facing west. ✉ *Petit Plage, north end of bd. de Grand Case (Box 339), Grande Case 97150,* ☎ *590/ 87–51–87 or 800/223–1588,* FAX *590/87–59–93. 77 units. Restaurant, lounge, air-conditioning, kitchenettes, tennis court, beach, car rental. AE, D, MC, V. CP.*

$$$ ⊡ **Hôtel L'Esplanade Caraïbes.** This complex is on a hillside over-
★   looking Grand Case Bay and is a three-minute walk from the beach. Two curved stone staircases with inlaid tile and brick lead up to the open-air reception area. Standard suites are large, and duplexes have cathedral ceilings and mahogany staircases as well as an extra half bath and a loft bedroom; upholstery throughout is striped with muted pinks and corals. There's no on-site restaurant, but Grand Case's roster of gourmet spots is just a short walk away. ✉ *Box 5007, Grande Case, 97150,* ☎ *590/87–06–55,* FAX *590/87–29–15,* WEB *www.esplanade-caraibes.com. 24 units. Kitchenettes (some), 2 pools, car rental. AE, MC, V. EP. Closed Sept.*

$$$ ⊡ **Nettlé Bay Beach Club.** The units of this large resort, about five minutes from Marigot, are spread across the sands of striking Nettlé Bay. Four sets of villa suites (one- or two-bedroom) and a set of garden bungalows, each with its own pool, face the waterfront and Dutch St. Maarten across the bay. Rooms and suites are furnished simply but comfortably and have kitchens, TVs, and patios or balconies. The on-site restaurants offer South American and French cuisine. There's also a beach bar, Le Grand Bleu. This is an excellent location from which to explore Marigot and the island's south side. ✉ *Sandy Ground Rd., Baie Nettlé (Box 4081, Marigot 97064),* ☎ *590/87–68–68 or 800/999–3543,* FAX *590/87–21–51. 150 units. 2 restaurants, bar, air-conditioning, kitchenettes, 4 pools, 3 tennis courts, beach, snorkeling, jet skiing, shops. AE, MC, V. CP, EP.*

$$ ⊡ **Alizéa.** The view of Orient Bay from this Mont Vernon hill setting is stunning. An open-air feeling pervades the hotel, from the Le Mango restaurant—where the food is superb—to the 26 guest apartments with their contemporary light-wood furnishings. Rooms vary in style and design, but all are tasteful and have large balconies. There's a path to the beach, a 10-minute walk away. ✉ *Bear right on road to French Cul de Sac, Mont Vernon 97150,* ☎ *590/87–33–42,* FAX *590/87–41–15,* WEB *www.alizeahotel.com. 8 1-bedroom bungalows, 18 studios. Restaurant, bar, kitchenettes (some), pool. AE, D, MC, V. CP.*

$$ ⊡ **Anse Margot.** This quiet, thoroughly French property is one of the many hotels that line Nettlé Bay. Rooms here are in eight three-story town houses. All units have balconies with either a garden or lagoon view. Upholstery, drapes, and spreads are a brown-and-coral geometric print. There's a stretch of beach along the Simpson Bay lagoon that's good for sunbathing but not swimming; you may prefer the Nettlé Beach across the street. A complimentary breakfast buffet is served in the open-air Playa Margo, one of the better hotel restaurants. It's about a five-minute drive to Marigot. ✉ *Sandy Ground Rd. (Box 979), Baie Nettlé 97150,* ☎ *590/87–92–01 or 800/622–7836,* FAX *590/87–92–13,* WEB *www.hotels-anchorage.com. 80 units. Restaurant, bar, kitchenettes, 2 pools, 2 hot tubs, beach, snorkeling, boating, jet skiing, waterskiing, shops, business services, meeting rooms. AE, MC, V. BP.*

$$ ⊡ **Captain Oliver's.** This property straddles the St. Maarten–St. Martin border: stay in France, and dine in the Netherlands—there's even
★   a small "International Bridge" to cross from side to side. The suites, all in bungalows, are a good bargain and a good way to avoid the hustle and bustle of St. Maarten. The main hotel building faces a beautiful horseshoe-shape bay; outlying bungalows have views of the marina

or garden. If you're interested in a sail-and-stay package, the friendly, helpful staff can arrange it. The hotel's dinghy will transport guests to nearby Dawn Beach. ✉ *East side of Oyster Pond, Oyster Pond 97150,* ☎ *590/87–40–26,* FAX *590/87–40–84,* WEB *www.captainolivers.com. 50 suites. Restaurant, snack bar, air-conditioning, kitchenettes, minibars, pool, dive shop, shops. AE, MC, V. CP.*

$$ 🏨 **Hôtel l'Atlantide.** The 10 sun-drenched units here range in size from a studio to a two-bedroom suite. The decor is airy, with gleaming white-tile floors, crisp pastel-striped or floral upholstery, and balconies that overlook Grand Case Bay and the beach. There's no restaurant or bar, but the village of Grand Case is known for its lively restaurant scene. ✉ *Bd. de Grand Case (Box 5140), Grand Case 97150,* ☎ *590/87–09–80,* FAX *590/87–12–36. 9 apartments, 1 suite. Kitchenettes, beach. MC, V. EP.*

$$ ★ 🏨 **Mercure Simson Beach Coralia.** Budget-conscious Europeans love this place because of such extras as a huge breakfast buffet and nightly local entertainment. Rooms and suites are cheerfully decorated; most have water views, and all have kitchenettes on the balconies. There are shuttles (not free) to Marigot, Philipsburg, and beaches. ✉ *Sandy Ground Rd. (Box 172), Baie Nettlé 97150,* ☎ *590/87–54–54 or 800/ 221–4542,* FAX *590/87–92–11,* WEB *www.mercure-simson-beach.com. 132 studios, 46 1-bedroom duplexes. Restaurant, bar, grocery, kitchenettes, 2 pools, tennis court, beach, dive shop, snorkeling, windsurfing, boating, jet skiing, waterskiing, bicycles, shops, coin laundry, car rental. AE, DC, MC, V. BP.*

$$ 🏨 **Pavillon Beach Hotel.** Every room and suite here faces the sea and has a balcony. The spacious studios and one-bedroom suites are done in warm pastel colors and have tile floors and elegant rattan furniture. Bathrooms have hair dryers and showers but no tubs. Ground-level rooms have sliding shuttered doors opening right onto the beach. ✉ *Plage de Grand Case, RN 7 (Box 5133), Grand Case 97070,* ☎ *590/ 87–96–46 or 800/223–9815,* FAX *590/87–71–04,* WEB *www.pavillonbeach. com. 6 rooms, 11 suites. Kitchenettes, beach. AE, MC, V. CP.*

$ ★ 🏨 **Hévéa.** This small white guest house with smart striped awnings is across the street from the beach in the heart of Grand Case. Rooms are dollhouse small but will appeal to romantics. There are beam ceilings, washstands, and carved-wood beds with lovely white coverlets and mosquito nets. Several rooms and studios and one apartment are on the terrace level; two studios and one apartment are on the garden level. As a guest here you're entitled to a special "house" dinner at the delightful gourmet restaurant for about $30. ✉ *163 bd. de Grand Case, Grand Case 97150,* ☎ *590/87–56–85,* FAX *590/87–83–88. 10 units. Restaurant, air-conditioning, kitchenettes (some). AE, MC, V. EP.*

$ ★ 🏨 **La Résidence.** The downtown location and soundproof rooms of this Marigot hotel make it a popular place for business travelers. All rooms have phones, TVs, balconies, dark rattan furniture, and tile floors. You have a choice between single or double rooms, some with loft beds. The intimate restaurant offers a good $28 three-course menu. You'll have to take a cab or drive to the beach. ✉ *Rue du Général de Gaulle (Box 679), Marigot 97150,* ☎ *590/87–70–37 or 800/223–9815,* FAX *590/87–90–44. 22 rooms. Restaurant, lounge, minibars, shops. AE, D, MC, V. CP, MAP.*

$ 🏨 **Le Royale Louisiana.** This hotel's white and pale green galleries overlook a flower-filled courtyard. There's a selection of twin, double, and triple duplexes. Although you may want to take a taxi to the beach (the nearest one is a 20-minute walk away), you'll find plenty of shopping just steps from your door in downtown Marigot's boutique area. ✉ *Rue du Général de Gaulle (Box 476), Marigot 97055,* ☎ *590/87–86–51,* FAX *590/87–96–49. 58 rooms. Restaurant, snack bar, air-conditioning, hair salon. AE, D, MC, V. CP.*

Villas

Both sides of the island have a variety of houses. In the United States you can get information on villa rentals through **Caribbean Concepts** (⊠ 575 Underhill Blvd., Suite 140, Syosset, NY 11791, ☎ 800/423–4433). **French Caribbean International** (⊠ 5662 Calle Real, #333, Santa Barbara, CA 93117-2317, ☎ 805/967–9850 or 800/322–2223) offers island condos and villas. **Villas of Distinction** (⊠ Box 55, Armonk, NY 10504, ☎ 914/273–3331 or 800/289–0900) is one of the oldest villa rental companies serving the island. **WIMCO** (⊠ Box 1461, Newport, RI 02840, ☎ 401/849–8012 or 800/932–3222) has more villa, apartment, and condo listings in the Caribbean than just about anyone else. On the island contact **Carimo** (⊠ Rue du Général de Gaulle [Box 220], Marigot 97150, ☎ 590/87–57–58), which has fabulous villas for rent in the tony Terres Basses area. **St. Martin Rentals** (⊠ Box 10300, St. Martin, ☎ 599/54–54330; Box 10300, Bedford, NH 03110, ☎ 800/308–8455) also carries a range of rental properties.

Dining

It may seem that this island has no monuments, but they're here—all are dedicated to gastronomy. You'll scarcely find a touch of Dutch; the major influences are French and Italian. This season's "in" eatery may be next season's remembrance of things past, as things do have a way of changing rapidly. The steep prices reflect both the island's high culinary reputation and the difficulty of obtaining fresh ingredients. In high season *make reservations,* and call to cancel if you can't make it. Many restaurants close completely or just for lunch during August, September, and into October; in the off-season call ahead to check hours.

What to Wear

Appropriate dining attire on this island ranges from swimsuits to sport jackets. For men, a jacket and khakis or jeans take you anywhere; for women, dressy pants, a skirt, or even fancy shorts are usually acceptable. Jeans are de rigueur in the less formal and trendier eateries. In the listings below dress is casual (and chic) unless otherwise noted, but ask when making reservations if you're unsure.

CATEGORY	COST*
$$$$	over $35
$$$	$25–$35
$$	$15–$25
$	under $15

*per person for a main course at dinner

Dutch Side

AMERICAN

$$ ✕ **Turtle Pier Bar & Restaurant.** Monkeys and parrots greet you at the
★ entrance to this classic Caribbean hangout, teetering over the lagoon and festooned with creeping vines. There are 200 animals in this informal zoo, but that's nothing compared to the menagerie hanging out at the bar during happy hour. The genial owner, Sid Wathey, whose family is one of the island's oldest, and his American wife, Lorraine, have fashioned one of the funkiest, most endearing places in the Caribbean, with cheap draft beer, huge American breakfasts, all-you-can-eat rib dinners, and live music several nights a week. ⊠ *114 Airport Rd., Simpson Bay,* ☎ *599/54–52562. No credit cards.*

$ ✕ **Ric's Place.** This Front Street sports bar is popular with Americans who need a dose of home and with just about anyone who wants to drool over one of the biggest burgers in town. College and pro sports banners and caps hang all over the place, and seating is indoors at the bar or over the water of Great Bay. The fare is American and Tex-Mex;

try the nachos *grande* with a couple of friends. ✉ *69 Front St., Philipsburg,* ☎ *599/54–26050. No credit cards.*

ASIAN

$$ ✕ Wajang Doll. Indonesian dishes are served in the garden of this West Indian–style house. *Nasi goreng* (fried rice) and red snapper in a sweet soy glaze are standouts, as is rijsttafel, a traditional Indonesian meal of rice accompanied by 15 to 20 dishes. A *wajang* doll is used in Indonesian shadow plays, a traditional art form. ✉ *167 Front St., Philipsburg,* ☎ *599/54–22687. AE, MC, V. Closed Sun. No lunch Sat.*

CAFÉ

$ ✕ Kangaroo Court Caffè. The Kangaroo might just serve the island's best cup of coffee. Decorated in a whimsical West Indian style with potted plants and colorful tiles and umbrellas, it's in an old salt warehouse off Front Street. Come for breakfast or a lunch of salads, pastas, and sandwiches. The pastries are fresh, and there's a wide array of coffees—cappuccinos, mocha lattes, caramel lattes, and espressos. ✉ *6 Hendrickstraat, Philipsburg,* ☎ *599/54–24278. MC, V. No dinner.*

CONTEMPORARY

$$$$ ✕ Le Perroquet. A cool green-and-white West Indian–style house overlooking a lagoon is the peaceful, romantic setting for this restaurant. Chef Pierre Castagna prepares exotic specialties, such as grilled breast of ostrich in a bordelaise sauce, as well as savory dishes featuring duck, veal, and beef. ✉ *Airport Rd., Simpson Bay,* ☎ *599/54–54339. AE, MC, V. No lunch. Closed Mon., June, and Sept.*

CONTINENTAL

$$ ✕ Chesterfield's. Casual lunches of burgers and salads and more elaborate Continental dinners are served at this informal, nautically themed marina restaurant. The dinner menu includes French onion soup, roast duckling with fresh pineapple and banana sauce, and several different preparations of shrimp. The Mermaid Bar is popular with yachties. ✉ *Great Bay Marina, Philipsburg,* ☎ *599/54–23484. D, MC, V.*

ECLECTIC

$$$ ✕ Saratoga.
★ The handsome mahogany-outfitted dining room in the yacht club's stucco and red-tile building has views of the Simpson Bay Marina. The menu changes daily, borrowing from various influences, including Asian and Southwestern. You might start with Malpeque oysters with balsamic-horseradish sauce or seven-seaweed salad with beans, daikon, and sesame, then segue into crispy fried roundhead snapper in fermented black bean sauce or grilled chicken breast in a cumin-Gouda crust. The wine list is admirably balanced and reasonably priced, with 10–12 wines offered by the glass. ✉ *Simpson Bay Yacht Club, Airport Rd., Simpson Bay,* ☎ *599/54–42421. Reservations essential. AE, MC, V. No lunch. Closed Sun. and Aug.–Sept.*

$$ ✕ Indiana Beach. This quirky restaurant-bar is fronted by Kimsha Beach at Simpson Bay. The motif is pure adventure and jungle exotic. Terracotta walls and tables are painted with designs based on Indian petroglyphs, and you'll find caged monkeys, snakes, parrots, and Wally the alligator on the lush grounds. The big night here is Thursday, when happy hour runs until the wee hours. You can swim at Kimsha or at the restaurant's own pool, and although the fare is mainly sandwiches, steaks, and seafood, don't be surprised to find wild boar or alligator ribs on the menu. ✉ *Pelican Key, Simpson Bay,* ☎ *599/54–42797. AE, MC, V.*

FRENCH

$$$ ✕ Antoine. The setting is romantic at this elegant spot overlooking Great Bay. Candles glow on tables set with crisp blue-and-white tablecloths and gleaming silver, and the sound of the surf drifts up from the beach. You might start your meal with French onion soup or lobster bisque, then move on to steak au poivre, duck in brandy sauce with cherries, or lobster thermidor. Pastas and creole specials are also available. For dessert try the sublime Grand Marnier soufflé. ☒ *103 Front St., Philipsburg,* ☏ *599/54–22964. Reservations essential. AE, MC, V. Closed Sun. off-season.*

$$$ ✕ **Le Bec Fin.** You stroll through a flowery courtyard to reach this well-known upstairs restaurant. The rotation of chefs has unfortunately led to inconsistency in the quality of the classical French cuisine, but it's always pleasant for its ambience and views of Great Bay. Starters include *vol-au-vent* (pastry) bursting with escargots and served in a fennel cream sauce. Fish, such as red snapper fillet in rum butter sauce, is your best bet for a main course. The meringue with mint ice cream is delightful to the eye and the palate. The breezy downstairs café serves breakfast and lunch with great crepes and salads. ☒ *141 Front St., Philipsburg,* ☏ *599/54–22976. AE, MC, V.*

$$$ ✕ **L'Escargot.** A 19th-century house wrapped in verandas is home to one of St. Maarten's oldest French restaurants. Starters include frogs' legs in garlic sauce and crêpes filled with caviar and sour cream. There's also, of course, a variety of snail dishes. For an entrée try grilled red snapper with red wine and shallot sauce or *canard de l'escargot* (duck in pineapple and banana sauce). There's often a cabaret Wednesday night; you don't have to pay the cover charge if you come for dinner. ☒ *84 Front St., Philipsburg,* ☏ *599/54–22483. AE, MC, V.*

$$$ ✕ **Radisson Vacation Villas at Oyster Bay.** Tables on a terrace over-
★   looking the sea are decked with fresh flowers at this Radisson resort's family-friendly restaurant. Lobster in a mushroom sauce; fillet of red snapper in sauce piquant; and sweet, billowy, dessert soufflés, prepared by the resident pastry chefs, are specialties. Hotel guests have priority here, so reserve well in advance. ☒ *East side of Oyster Pond, Oyster Pond,* ☏ *599/54–36040 or 877/478–6669. Reservations essential. AE, D, MC, V.*

INDIAN

$ ✕ **Shiv Sagar.** Authentic East Indian cuisine, emphasizing Kashmiri and
★   Mogul specialties, is served in this small mirrored room fragrant with cumin and coriander. Marvelous tandooris and curries are offered, but try one of the less familiar preparations, such as *madrasi machi* (red snapper with hot spices). A large selection of vegetarian dishes is also offered. There's a friendly open-air bar out front. ☒ *20 Front St., Philipsburg,* ☏ *599/54–22299. AE, D, DC, MC, V. Closed Sun.*

ITALIAN

$$$ ✕ **Spartaco.** Every element of the Northern Italian cuisine served in this 200-year-old stone plantation house is either homemade or imported from Italy. Some of the specialties are black angel-hair pasta with shrimp and garlic, swordfish baked with pink peppercorns and rosemary and served over linguine, and veal Vesuviana with mozzarella, oregano, and tomato sauce. ☒ *Almond Grove, Cole Bay,* ☏ *599/54–45379. AE, MC, V. No lunch. Closed Mon. and May.*

French Side

CAFÉ

$ ✕ **Bistrot Nu.** It's hard to top the simple, unadorned fare and reason-
★   able prices you'll find here. Traditional brasserie-style food—coq au vin, fish soup, snails, and pizza—is served in a friendly atmosphere. The place is enormously popular; its tables are packed until it closes at 2 AM. ☒ *Rue de Hollande, Marigot,* ☏ *590/87–97–09. MC, V. Closed Sun.*

CARIBBEAN

$$ ★ **✕ Claude Mini-Club.** This brightly decorated upstairs restaurant on the harbor serves terrific creole and French cuisine. The chairs and madras tablecloths are a mélange of sun-yellow and orange, and the whole place is built (tree house–like) around the trunks of coconut trees. It's the place to be on Wednesday and Saturday nights, when the dinner buffet features roast pig, lobster, roast beef, and all the trimmings. ⊠ *Front de Mer, Marigot,* ☎ *590/87–50–69. AE, MC, V. No lunch Sun.*

$$ ★ **✕ Yvette's.** The attempts at romance couldn't be more endearing: classical music plays softly, and the tiny eight-table room is surrounded in yellow decor. Yvette passed away in August 1999, but husband Andre has continued on with her traditional food, which includes creole specialties, such as *accras* (spicy fish fritters), stewed chicken with rice and beans, and conch and dumplings. ⊠ *Off the Orléans road, Orléans,* ☎ *590/87–32–03. No credit cards. Closed Wed.*

CONTEMPORARY

$$$ **✕ Le Tastevin.** A chic pavilion, with tropical plants, ceiling fans, and water views, provides an elegant dining setting. Owner Daniel Passeri, a native of Burgundy, also founded the homey Auberge Gourmande across the street. The menu here is more ambitious, including foie gras in Armagnac sauce, duck breast in banana-lime sauce, and red snapper fillet with curry and wild-mushroom sauce. ⊠ *86 bd. de Grand Case, Grand Case,* ☎ *590/87–55–45. Reservations essential. AE, MC, V.*

ECLECTIC

$$$ ★ **✕ Le Pressoir.** Many say that presentation is everything. Combine that with excellent food and a setting in a charming West Indies house, where the bill won't break the bank, and you have a great restaurant. French and creole fusion cuisine reigns; go for the fresh local fish prepared with tropical fruit glazes and sauces. The crème brûlée is superb. ⊠ *30 bd. de Grand Case, Grand Case,* ☎ *590/87–76–62. AE, MC, V. No lunch. Closed Sun.*

$$$ ★ **✕ The Rainbow.** In a town of splendid seaside boîtes, this is one of the best. The cobalt-blue-and-white decor of the split-level dining room is strikingly simple, and the atmosphere, created by lapping waves and murmuring guests, is highly romantic. Fleur and David are the stylish, energetic hosts. Specialties include shrimp and scallop fricassee with Caribbean chutney, and dishes are dressed with such fanciful touches as red cabbage crisps. ⊠ *176 bd. de Grand Case, Grand Case,* ☎ *590/ 87–55–80. AE, MC, V. Closed Sun.*

$$ **✕ Maison sur le Port.** Watching the sunset from the palm-fringed terrace isn't the least of the pleasures in this old West Indian house surrounded by romantically lighted garden fountains. Try the sautéed duck fillet in passion-fruit sauce or red snapper with beurre blanc. Chef Jean-Paul Fahrner's imaginative salads are lunchtime treats. There's a children's menu with burgers and chicken sandwiches. ⊠ *Front de Mer, Marigot,* ☎ *590/87–56–38. AE, D, MC, V. Closed Sun.*

FRENCH

$$$$ ★ **✕ Le Santal.** The approach to this dazzler, through a working-class suburb of Marigot, is forbidding. The exterior appears ramshackle, but the interior is transformed by soft lighting, china, and crystal. Specialties include lobster soufflé on a bed of spinach and eggplant, foie gras sautéed in cassis, and lacquered duck. Reservations aren't required, but they're highly recommended if you want to eat at one of the five tables by the water. ⊠ *Sandy Ground Rd., Sandy Ground,* ☎ *590/87–53–48. AE, MC, V. No lunch.*

$$$ ★ **✕ Le Mango.** Many claim that this elegant terrace restaurant at the Alizéa hotel offers the island's best cuisine. The menu features a tanta-

lizing blend of French creole and traditional French specialties, with appetizers like homemade foie gras with red-wine jelly or roasted sea scallops. For the main course, take your pick from a range of fresh seafood, including mahimahi and tuna, or try the beef tenderloin with stewed shallots in red wine sauce. There are also several vegetarian selections. ⊠ *Bear right on road to French Cul de Sac, Mont Vernon,* ☎ *590/87–41–20. AE, D, MC, V.*

$$$ ✕ **Mario's Bistro.** From Mario Tardif, formerly with The Rainbow in Grand Case, comes this fabulous eatery. His wife, Martyne, and partner, Didier Gonnon, are out front, while Mario is in the kitchen creating dishes such as baked salmon in a caramelized onion crust. The open-air country French–style restaurant is on the canal as you enter Marigot from Sandy Ground, and if you didn't know better, you'd think you were in Venice. ⊠ *Sandy Ground,* ☎ *590/87–06–36. Reservations essential. AE, MC, V. Closed Sun.*

$$$ ✕ **La Vie En Rose.** This bustling restaurant is right off the pier, about a 30-second stroll from the tourist office. The menu is classic French with an occasional Caribbean twist—fillet of swordfish sautéed in a passion-fruit butter sauce, freshwater crayfish in puff pastry. Appetizers include a warm smoked salmon with potatoes and chives and lobster salad with a touch of ginger. Save room for chocolate mousse cake topped with vanilla sauce. The ground-floor tearoom and pastry shop serve an excellent luncheon with wine for about $20. In season you may make dinner reservations up to one month in advance. ⊠ *Rue de la République and bd. de France, Marigot,* ☎ *590/87–54–42. Reservations essential. AE, D, DC, MC, V. No lunch Sun.*

SEAFOOD
$$ ✕ **La Plaisance.** Cool strains of jazz waft through this lively open-air brasserie as you sample terrific salads (try the Niçoise or *landaine*—duck, smoked ham, croutons, and fried egg), pizzas (wonderful lobster), pastas (garlic and basil *pistou*), and grilled seafood at unbeatable prices. This is one of several ultracasual eateries at Port La Royale, all offering simple, appetizing food, fixed-price menus, and happy hours. ⊠ *La Marina Port la Royale, Marigot,* ☎ *590/87–85–00. AE, MC, V.*

Beaches

The island's 10 mi (16 km) of beaches are all open to the public. Those occupied by resorts may charge a fee (about $3) for changing facilities. You can't, however, enter the beach via a hotel unless you're a paying guest or are renting water-sports equipment there. Some of the 37 beaches are secluded, and some are in the thick of things, but on several, vendors rent beach umbrellas and chairs for $5 each per day. Topless bathing is virtually de rigueur on the French side, where the beaches are generally better than on the Dutch side. If you take a cab to more remote sands, be sure to arrange a specific time for your driver to pick you up. Don't leave valuables unattended on the beach or in your rental car—even in the trunk.

Dutch Side
Cupecoy Beach. Near the Dutch-French border and south of Baie Longue, this small, shifting arc of white sand is fringed by eroded limestone cliffs. You'll also find vendors who sell cold sodas and beers and rent chairs and umbrellas. There are two parking spots: one is near the Cupecoy and Sapphire beach clubs; the other (where you can park for about $2) is a few yards west. At one time there were sections where folks wore suits and sections where folks went without. These days, however, the entire strip seems to have gone clothing-optional. The beach also attracts the island's gay crowd.

Dawn Beach–Oyster Pond. The approach to this long stretch of white sand is through the grounds of the Dawn Beach Hotel. The long beach is partly protected by reefs (good for snorkeling), but the water isn't always calm. When the waves come rolling in, this is the island's best bodysurfing spot.

Great Bay. Narrow in some places, wide in others, this long stretch runs behind the shops, restaurants, and hotels of Philipsburg's Front Street. There are numerous beachside bistros; some even offer showers and toilets (for a fee) and rent water-sports equipment. The bay is a favorite with cruise-ship passengers, but its east end, near the marinas, can be dirty with detritus from boats.

Maho Bay. Ecru-color sand, palm and sea-grape trees, calm waters, and the roar of jets lowering to nearby Juliana International Airport distinguish this beach.

Mullet Bay. The powdery white sands of this beach are always crowded: people come to bask in its wide spaces and enjoy its great surf. Concession stands offer refreshments.

Simpson Bay. This long half-moon of white sand is near Simpson Bay Village, one of the island's last undiscovered hamlets. In this small fishing village you'll find refreshments, a dive shop, and neat little ultra-Caribbean town homes.

French Side

Baie de Friar. The beach at Friar's Bay is on a small, picturesque cove between Marigot and Grand Case. It attracts a casual crowd of locals and has a small snack bar, Kali's, that's owned by a welcoming gentleman with dreadlocks.

Baie de Grande Case. A gentle surf and plenty of fine restaurants are the draws of the thin beach at Grand Case Bay. You'll find water-sports activities, and, at the north end, small coves. The snorkeling is best at the south end. The north end is home to *lolos,* barbecue huts that serve inexpensive local fare.

Baie Longue. Long Bay's beach is a beautiful 1-mi-long (1½-km-long) curve of white sand on the island's westernmost tip. It's a good place for snorkeling and swimming, but beware of a strong undertow when the waters are rough. You can sunbathe in the buff, though only a few do. There are no facilities.

Baie Orientale. The beach at Orient Bay, the island's best-known clothing-optional beach, is at the top of the agenda for voyeurs from cruise ships. You can enter from one of two parking areas—one at the southern end and one at the northern end—which put you in the middle of the beach. The nude section is to the right on the southern end. Farther down, toward the middle of the beach, is a resort with several restaurants, bars, and chaises (with food and beverage service) for rent. This is windsurfing heaven, with a couple of on-site rental shops that can help you take advantage of the steady trade winds.

Baie Rouge. Red Bay is right off the main road past Prune Bay. Some consider it the prettiest beach on the island, though the waves here can be rough. You'll find refreshment stands and places to rent beach chairs and umbrellas.

Ilet Pinel. This little speck of land off the northeast coast has about 500 yards of beach that offer a great deal of privacy. Boats can transport you here from French Cul de Sac and the beach at Orient Bay (about $5 per person round-trip). A couple of small beachside restaurants offer refreshments.

Outdoor Activities and Sports

The island's waters and winds make it ideal for exploring or relaxing by boat. It'll cost you around $500 per day to rent a 20-ft power boat, less for smaller boats. A 35-ft sailboat runs about $700 per day. You can rent motorboats, speedboats, and sailboats at **Aquamania Watersports** (⊠ Pelican Marina, Simpson Bay, ☎ 599/54–42640). **Bobby's Marina** (⊠ Yrausquin Blvd., Philipsburg, ☎ 599/54–22366) has numerous watersports options. **Caraïbes Sport Boats** (⊠ Marina Port la Royale, Marigot, ☎ 590/87–89–38), is a good contact for boat rentals. For the best full-service yacht and watersports rentals on the French side, contact **Marine Time** (☎ 590/87–20–28), behind the tourist office at the port in Marigot. The **Moorings** (⊠ Captain Oliver's Marina, Oyster Pond, ☎ 590/87–32–54 or 800/521–1126) has a fleet of Beneteau yachts as well as bareboat and crewed catamarans. **Sunsail** (⊠ Captain Oliver's Marina, ☎ 590/27–42–85 or 800/327–2276), in Oyster Pond, has a fleet of sailboats for hire. For the thrill of a lifetime, you can join the **St. Maarten America's Cup Challenge** at Bobby's Marina (☎ 599/54–22366). Participants are put on teams and compete using such one-time 36-ft racing machines as Dennis Connor's *Stars and Stripes* and the *Canada II* (yes, the actual boats). The cost to participate in the two-plus hour races, which are held daily, is $65.

You can angle for yellowtail snapper, grouper, marlin, tuna, and wahoo on deep-sea excursions. Costs (for four people) range from $400 for a half day to $650 for a full day. Prices usually include bait and tackle, instruction for novices, and an open bar. Contact **Lee Deepsea Fishing** (⊠ Airport Rd., Simpson Bay, ☎ 599/54–44233, 599/54–44234), which is convenient for hotels in that area. **Rudy's Deep Sea Fishing** (⊠ Airport Rd., Simpson Bay, ☎ 599/54–52177) has been around for years, and is one of the more experienced sport angling outfits. **Sailfish Caraïbes** (⊠ Anse Marcel, ☎ 590/87–31–94 or 590/27–40–90) is your best bet on the north side of the island.

Mullet Bay Resort (⊠ Airport Rd., north of airport, ☎ 599/54–52801 or 599/54–53069), which has been closed since 1995, has an 18-hole course—the island's *only* course. Greens fees start at $52 for 9 holes, and $93 for 18 holes. Club and cart rentals are also available. If you happen to be in the area, stop in to book a tee time–the phone never sems to be manned.

You can arrange rides through most hotels or by contacting **Bayside Riding Club** (⊠ On Galion Beach road, Baie Orientale, ☎ 590/87–36–64). **Caid & Isa** (⊠ French Cul de Sac–Anse Marcel road, Anse Marcel, ☎ 590/87–45–70) has been offering guided rides for years. **Crazy Acres Riding Center** (⊠ Wathey Estate, Cole Bay, ☎ 599/54–42793) is your best bet for guided rides in the Philpsburg area. **O.K. Corral** (⊠ Coralita Beach Hotel, Baie Lucas, Oyster Pond, ☎ 590/87–40–72) features rides for people of all skill levels. All the outfitters above can accommodate novices and experts alike; costs start at $50 for a two-hour ride.

On the French side, **Orient Bay Watersports** (⊠ North entrance to the bay, Baie Orientale, ☎ 590/87–40–75) offers parasailing rides.

SCUBA DIVING AND SNORKELING

The water temperature here is rarely below 70°F (21°C), and visibility is usually excellent, averaging about 100 ft (30 m). There are many diving attractions, both around the island and close to several nearby islands. Beginners and night divers will appreciate the tugboat **Annie,** which lies in 25 ft–30 ft (6 m–9 m) of water in Simpson Bay. Fish and other marine life make the tug their home. Off the north coast, in the protected and mostly current-free Grand Case Bay, is **Creole Rock.** The water here ranges in depth from 10 ft–25 ft (3 m–8 m), visibility is excellent, and plenty of colorful marine life inhabits the waters—great underwater photo ops. Other sites off the north coast include Ilet Pinel, for its good shallow diving; Green Key, with its vibrant barrier reef; and Tintamarre (Flat Island), for its sheltered coves and geologic faults. One of the most popular sites is **Proselyte Reef,** named for the British frigate HMS *Proselyte.* The ship, initially a Dutch frigate, was captured by the British in 1796 and sank about 1 mi (1½ km) south of Great Bay in 1801. Today the hulk lies 15 ft–45 ft (5 m–14 m) below the surface and is almost completely covered with coral. Cannons and anchors are scattered around the wreck, and a variety of vibrant marine animals scoot about searching for food. There are mooring buoys at the site.

On the Dutch side, SSI- (Scuba Schools International) and PADI-certified dive centers include the following. **Leeward Island Divers** (⊠ Airport Rd., Simpson Bay, ☎ FAX 599/54–42268) offers day and night dives. **Ocean Explorers Dive Shop** (⊠ 113 E. Walfare Rd., Simpson Bay, ☎ 599/54–45252) is a complete dive shop and dive operation. **Pelican Dive Adventures** (⊠ Pelican Resort Marina, Pelican Key, Simpson Bay, ☎ 599/54–42503 ext. 1553) is convenient to airport area hotels. **Trade Winds Dive Center** (⊠ Great Bay Marina, Philipsburg, ☎ 599/54–75176) is one of the island's oldest dive operations, and a good choice in the Philipsburg area.

On the French side, **Blue Ocean** (⊠ Sandy Ground Rd., Baie Nettlé, ☎ 590/87–66–89 or 590/87–89–73) is PADI- and CMAS-certified. **Lou Scuba** (⊠ Mercure Simson Beach Coralia, Sandy Ground Rd., Baie Nettlé, ☎ 590/87–16–61) is a PADI-certified dive center. **Octoplus** (⊠ Bd. de Grand Case, Grand Case, ☎ 590/87–20–62) is a complete PADI-certified dive center. On average, one-tank dives start at $50, two-tank dives start at $80, and certification courses start at $350.

Some of the best snorkeling on the Dutch side can be found around the rocks below Fort Amsterdam off Little Bay Beach, in the west end of Maho Bay, off Pelican Key, and around the reefs off Dawn Beach and Oyster Pond. On the French side, the area around Orient Bay, Caye Verte (Green Key), Ilet Pinel, and Flat Island is especially lovely and is officially classified, and protected, as a regional underwater nature reserve. **Dive Safairs** (⊠ Bobby's Marina, Yrausquin Blvd., Philipsburg, ☎ 599/54–44056) is a full-service outfit for snorkelers and divers. Arrange rentals and snorkeling trips through **Kontiki Watersports** (⊠ Northern beach entrance, Baie Orientale, ☎ 590/87–28–75). **Ocean Explorers** (⊠ 113 E. Walfare Rd., Simpson Bay, ☎ 599/54–45252) offers diving and snorkeling excursions. **Orient Bay Watersports** (⊠ Southern beach entrance, Baie Orientale, ☎ 590/87–40–75) runs trips to the outlying Green Cay for picnics and snorkeling. The average cost of an afternoon snorkeling trip is $25 per person.

SEA EXCURSIONS

The 50-ft catamaran **Bluebeard II** (☎ 599/54–52898), moored in Simpson Bay, sails around Anguilla's south and northwest coasts to Prickly Pear, where there are excellent coral reefs for snorkeling and powdery white sands for sunning. These excursions cost $45–$65 per person. You can take a daylong picnic sail to nearby islands or secluded coves aboard the 45-ft ketch *Gabrielle* (☎ 599/54–23170). The sleek 76-ft catamaran *Golden Eagle* (☎ 599/54–30068) takes day sailors to outlying islets and reefs for snorkeling and partying. The *Laura Rose* (☎ 599/54–70710) offers a variety of half- and full-day sails, ranging from $25 to $65 per person.

A cross between a submarine and a glass-bottom boat, the 34-passenger *Seaworld Explorer* (✉ Bd. de Grand Case, Grand Case, ☎ 599/54–24078), crawls along the water's surface while you, submerged in a lower chamber, view marine life and coral through large windows. Divers jump off the boat and feed the fish and eels. The cost is $30 for adults, $20 for kids; transport to and from your hotel costs an extra $10 per adult, $7 per child.

The 100-passenger motor boat *Voyager I* (☎ 599/54–24096 or 599/54–23170) and its sister craft, the luxurious 82-ft motor catamaran *Voyager II,* make runs to St. Barths, departing Wednesday, Thursday, and Friday at 8:30 AM from Bobby's Marina (☎ 599/54–22366) or daily at 9 AM from the marketplace on the Marigot waterfront. Return trips are at 5 PM. The cost is $57 per adult, which includes port fees, open bar, snacks, and snorkel equipment.

In St. Martin, sailing, snorkeling, and picnic excursions to nearby islands can be arranged through **Kontiki Watersports** (✉ Northern beach entrance, Baie Orientale, ☎ 590/87–28–75). **Le Méridien's L'Habitation** (✉ Anse Marcel, ☎ 590/87–33–33) is a good choice for those staying in the north. **Orient Bay Watersports** (✉ Southern beach entrance, Baie Orientale, ☎ 590/87–40–75) arranges snorkeling, windsurfing, and excursions to outlying islands.

TENNIS

If you want to play tennis at a hotel at which you aren't a guest, be sure to call ahead to find out whether it allows visitors. You'll probably need to make reservations, and there's usually an hourly fee. There are two lighted courts at the **Blue BayClub Mont Vernon** (✉ East off road to French Cul de Sac, Baie Orientale, ☎ 590/87–62–00). You'll find four lighted courts at the **Maho Beach Resort & Casino** (✉ Airport Rd., Maho Bay, ☎ 599/54–52115). You can use the four lighted courts at the **Pelican Resort & Casino** (✉ Airport Rd., Pelican Key, Simpson Bay, ☎ 599/54–42503). The six lighted courts at **Le Privilège Resort & Spa** (✉ Anse Marcel, ☎ 590/87–38–38) are available to nonguests, as are its four squash and two racquetball courts.

WATERSKIING

On the Dutch side rent waterskiing and jet-skiing equipment through **Aquamania** (✉ Pelican Marina, Simpson Bay, ☎ 599/54–42640), a water-sports activity center. At Simpson Bay's Kimsha Beach, contact **Westport Watersports** (☎ 599/54–42557). On the French side, **Kontiki Watersports** (✉ Northern beach entrance, Baie Orientale, ☎ 590/87–28–75) rents wind boards, takes water skiers out, and provides instruction. **Laguna Watersports** (✉ Laguna Beach Hotel, Sandy Ground Rd., Baie Nettlé, ☎ 590/87–91–75) provides instruction. Try **Orient Bay Watersports** (✉ Southern beach entrance, Baie Orientale, ☎ 590/87–40–75) for water skiing; instruction is also available. Expect to pay $50 per half-hour for waterskiing, and $40–$45 per half hour for jet-skiing.

WINDSURFING

The **Nathalie Simon Windsurfing Club** (✉ Northern beach entrance, Baie Oriental, ☎ 590/87–48–16) offers rentals and lessons. Lessons are $25–$30 per hour. Rental and instruction are available at **Orient**

Bay Watersports (⊠ Southern beach entrance, Baie Orientale, ☎ 590/87–40–75).

Shopping

Nearly 200 cruise ships call at St. Maarten each year, and they do so for about 500 reasons. That's roughly the number of duty-free shops on the island. Prices can be 25%–50% below those in the United States and Canada on French perfumes, liquor, cognac and fine liqueurs, cigarettes and cigars, Swedish crystal, Irish linen, Italian leather, cameras, designer fashions, Swiss watches, plus thousands of other things you never knew you wanted. If you're shopping for electronics in Philipsburg, try negotiating for a lower price. Competition is fierce, and some stores will bargain if you pay cash. You'll find more fashion on the French side in Marigot, although stalwarts such as Polo Ralph Lauren, Tommy Hilfiger, and Benetton have Philipsburg outlets. You'll also find Marigot to be a much more pleasant place to shop and stroll.

If you're looking for local crafts, you may be disappointed. Although you can find carvings, painting, basketry, and some jewelry that have been produced locally mixed in with the T-shirts at the crafts stalls on the Marigot harbor, these tend to be of the cheesy type. St. Maarten's best-known local product is its guavaberry liqueur, made from rum and the wild berries (not to be confused with guavas) that grow only on this island's central mountains.

Prices are quoted in florins, francs, and dollars; shops take credit cards and traveler's checks. Most shopkeepers, especially on the Dutch side, speak English. Although most merchants are reputable, there are occasional reports of inferior or fake merchandise passed off as the real thing. As a rule of thumb, if you can bargain excessively, it's probably not worth it.

Areas

Front Street, Philipsburg, is one long strip lined with sleek boutiques and colorful shops, including, oddly, a Harley-Davidson outlet. Note that if more than one cruise ship is in port, it's best to avoid this street as you won't be able to move. **Old Street,** near the end of Front Street, has 22 stores, boutiques, and open-air cafés. There's a slew of boutiques in the **Maho** shopping plaza as well as at the **Plaza del Lago,** at the Simpson Bay Yacht Club complex. Wrought-iron balconies, colorful awnings, and gingerbread trim decorate Marigot's smart shops, tiny boutiques, and bistros in the **Marina Port La Royale** complex and on the main streets, **rue de la Liberté** and **rue de la République.** You're likely to find more creative and fashionable buys in Marigot than in Philipsburg.

Specialty Items

DUTY-FREE GOODS

Carat (⊠ 16 rue de la République, Marigot, ☎ 590/87–73–40; ⊠ 73 Front St., Philipsburg, ☎ 599/54–22180) sells china and jewelry. **Havane** (⊠ Marina Port la Royale, Marigot, ☎ 590/87–70–39) is a good place for designer fashions. **Lipstick** (⊠ Plaza Caraïbes, rue du Général de Gaulle, Marigot, ☎ 590/87–53–92; ⊠ 31 Front St., Philipsburg, ☎ 599/54–26051) has an enormous selection of perfume and cosmetics.

Little Europe (⊠ 80 Front St., Philipsburg, ☎ 599/54–24371; ⊠ 1 rue de Général de Gaulle, Marigot, ☎ 590/87–92–64) sells fine jewelry, crystal, and china. **Little Switzerland** (⊠ 6 rue de la Liberté, Marigot, ☎ 590/87–09–02; ⊠ 52 Front St., Philipsburg, ☎ 599/54–23530) purveys fine crystal and china as well as perfume and jewelry. **Oro Diamante** (⊠ 62 Front St., Philipsburg ☎ 599/54–30343) carries loose diamonds, jewelry, watches, perfume, and cosmetics. **Manek's** (⊠ rue de la République, Marigot, ☎ 590/87–54–91) sells, on two floors, a range of luggage, perfume, jewelry, Cuban cigars, duty-free liquors, and tobacco products.

HANDICRAFTS

Galerie Lynn (⊠ 83 bd. de Grand Case, Grand Case, ☎ 590/87–77–24) sells stunning paintings and sculptures. **Gingerbread Galerie** (⊠ Marina Port La Royale, Marigot, ☎ 590/87–73–21) specializes in Haitian art. **Greenwith Galleries** (⊠ 33 Front St., Philipsburg, ☎ 599/54–23842) has Caribbean art.

The **Guavaberry Company Shop** (⊠ 8 Front St., Philipsburg, ☎ 599/54–22965) is the small factory where the famous guavaberry liqueur is made by the Sint Maarten Guavaberry Company; on sale are myriad versions of the liqueur (including one made with jalapeño peppers), as well as spices and batiks.

Minguet (⊠ Rambaud Hill, ☎ 590/87–76–06) carries richly hued paintings, lithographs, posters, and postcards, all depicting island flora and landscapes by the artist Alexandre Minguet. **Roland Richardson Paintings and Prints** (⊠ 6 rue de la République, Marigot, ☎ 590/87–84–08) sells oil and watercolor paintings by the well-known local artist Roland Richardson. Richardson, who also works in monoprints, copper etchings, and woodcuts, is famous for his elaborate depictions of the flamboyant, or royal poinciana, tree. **Shipwreck Shop** (⊠ 42 Front St., Philipsburg, ☎ 599/54–22962; ⊠ Marina Port La Royale, Marigot, ☎ 590/87–27–37) stocks Caribelle batiks, hammocks, handmade jewelry, the local guavaberry liqueur, and herbs and spices.

Nightlife

To find out what's doing on the island, pick up any of the following publications: *St. Maarten Nights, St. Maarten Events,* or *St. Maarten Holiday*—all distributed free in the tourist office and hotels. The glossy *Discover St. Martin/St. Maarten* magazine, also free, has articles on island history and on the newest shops, discos, and restaurants.

Most resorts have a Caribbean spectacular—replete with limbo and fire dancers and steel bands—one night a week. Casinos are the main focus on the Dutch side, but there are discos that usually start late and keep on 'til the fat lady sings.

BARS

Axum Café (⊠ 7L Front St., Philipsburg, ☎ No phone), a bar and 1960s-style coffee shop, offers cultural activities, dancing, open-mike night, and art exhibits. It's open daily, 11:30 AM until the wee hours. **Le Bar de la Mer** (⊠ Market Sq., Marigot, ☎ 590/87–81–79), on the harbor, is a popular gathering spot in the evening (it's open until 2). **Cheri's Café** (⊠ Across from Maho Beach Hotel & Casino, Airport Rd., Simpson Bay, ☎ 599/54–53361) is a local institution, with cheap food and great live bands.

Road signs from the New Jersey Turnpike posted at the entrance of the **Surf Club South** (⊠ East of Grand Case, ☎ 590/87–50–40) are dead giveaways that the bar is owned by Americans. **Turtle Pier Bar & Restaurant** (⊠ Airport Rd., Simpson Bay, ☎ 599/54–52230) always hops with a lively crowd.

CASINOS

All the island's casinos—found only on the Dutch side—have craps, blackjack, roulette, and slot machines. You must be 18 years or older to gamble. Dress is casual (most anything goes except bathing suits or skimpy beachwear). Many casinos are in hotels such as Great Bay Beach Hotel, Pelican Resort, and Casino Royal at Maho Beach (which produces the splashy Paris Revue Show). You'll also find independent casinos: **Coliseum** (⊠ Front St., Philipsburg, ☎ 599/54–32101) is small, but you can win or lose as much as you'd like. The **Lightning Casino** (⊠ Airport Rd., Cole Bay, ☎ 599/54–43290) easily recognized by its gaudy, flashing sign. The **Rouge et Noir Casino** (⊠ Front St., Philipsburg, ☎ 599/54–22952) is another Front Street casino, small but busy.

DANCE CLUBS

Club One (⊠ Marina Port Royale, Marigot Bay, ☎ 590/87–98–41) is a late-night (really, all-night every night but Sunday and Monday) happening spot on the marina. **Footsteps** (⊠ Cole Bay, ☎ 599/54–42156) is particularly popular with young people Friday–Sunday nights. **Greenhouse** (⊠ Front St., Philipsburg, ☎ 599/54–22941) features canned DJ music and a two-for-one happy hour that lasts all night Tuesday. **L'Atmo** (⊠ Marina Port la Royale, Marigot, ☎ 590/87–98–41) is where French nationals and locals flock for salsa and soca on Friday. It's open every night but Monday. **Liquid** (⊠ Airport Rd., Simpson Bay, ☎ 599/54–52632) is a sophisticated place above a restaurant. **Pink Mango** (⊠ Sandy Ground Rd., Baie Nettlé Bay, ☎ 590/87–91–75) at the Hotel Laguna is a popular spot for gays and a young, mixed crowd.

Exploring St. Maarten/St. Martin

St. Maarten–St. Martin's roads are very good and are generally well marked, although many of the main routes outside Marigot and Philipsburg don't have official names. Traffic signs tend to be in Dutch (IN-HALEN VERBODEN for no passing, for example) or French on the respective sides. However, international symbols—such as the inverted triangle for a stop sign—are used as well. With the exception of some annoying congestion, especially in and around Philipsburg and Marigot, the island is easy to traverse (it's best to rent a car, motorcycle, or scooter).

If you're looking for scenic routes on the Dutch side, try the road that leads to Oyster Pond, north of Philipsburg. It winds past soaring hills, turquoise waters, quaint West Indian houses, and wonderful views of St. Barths, and it eventually leads down to Dawn Beach, one of the island's best snorkeling spots. Terres Basses is a western coastal area that runs from Sandy Ground, just south of Marigot, to Cupecoy Beach, on the Dutch side—a short, beautiful stretch of sandstone cliffs and coves. Beaches here also include Baie Rouge and Baie Longue.

Numbers in the margin correspond to points of interest on the St. Maarten/St. Martin map.

Sights to See

⑤ Butterfly Farm. Run by Karin and Willy Slayter, British lovers of lepidoptera, the Butterfly Farm showcases dozens of varieties of colorful insects in various stages of development. At any given time, some 40 species of butterfly, numbering as many as 600, are fluttering around in a garden under a tented net. ⊠ *Rte. de Le Galion*, ☎ 590/87–31–21, WEB *www.thebutterflyfarm.com.* 🎟 *$10.* ☉ *Daily 9–4.*

⑦ French Cul de Sac. North of Orient Bay Beach, you'll find the French colonial mansion of St. Martin's mayor nestled in the hills. Little red-roof houses look like open umbrellas tumbling down the green hillside. The scenery here is glorious, and the area is great for hiking. There's a lot of construction, however, as the surroundings are slowly being developed. From the beach here shuttle boats make the five-minute trip to Ilet Pinel, an uninhabited island that's fine for picnicking, sunning, and swimming.

❽ Grand Case. The island's most picturesque town is set in the heart of the French side on a beach at the foot of green hills and pastures. Though it has only a 1-mi-long (1½-km-long) main street, it's known as the "restaurant capital of the Caribbean": More than 27 restaurants serve French, Italian, Indonesian, and Vietnamese fare here. The budget-minded love the half dozen lolos—kiosks at the far end of town that sell savory barbecue and seafood. Grand Case Beach Club is at the end of this road and has two beaches where you can take a dip.

❷ Guana Bay Point. North of Philipsburg, Guana Bay Point offers a splendid view of the island's east coast, tiny deserted islets, and petite St. Barths, which is anything but deserted.

❾ Marigot. This town is a wonderful place to tarry awhile if you are a shopper, a gourmet, or just a Francophile. Marina Port La Royale is the shopping complex at the port, but rue de la République and rue de la Liberté, which border the bay, are also filled with duty-free shops, boutiques, and bistros. The harbor area has a pavilion that sells everything from handmade crafts to fish so fresh they're still mad. There's less bustle here than in Philipsburg, and the open-air cafés are tempting places in which to stop for a rest. Marigot doesn't die at night, so you might wish to stay here into the evening—particularly on Wednesdays, when the market opens its art, crafts, and souvenir stalls, and on Thursdays, when the shops of Marina Port La Royale remain open until 10 and shoppers enjoy live music. In the harbor's main parking lot you'll find the kiosk for the Anguilla ferry as well as several crafts stalls. Across the parking lot, near the small traffic circle, is the helpful French tourist office. North of town there's a shopping complex on the inland side of the main road. At the back of it is **Match** (☎ 590/87–92–36), the largest supermarket on the French side. It carries tempting picnic makings—from country pâté to foie gras—and a vast selection of wines.

The small, ambitious **Musée de Saint-Martin** (St. Martin Museum), south of town, has artifacts from the island's pre-Columbian days. Included are pottery exhibits, rock carvings, and petroglyphs, as well as displays from the colonial and sugar plantation days. Upstairs is a small art gallery, where you'll find locally produced art, including lithographs and posters. ✉ *Sandy Ground Rd.,* ☎ *590/29–22–84.* 🎟 *$5.* ✆ *Mon.–Sat. 9–1 and 3–6.*

❹ Orléans. North of Oyster Pond and the Étang aux Poissons (Fish Lake) is the island's oldest settlement, also known as the French Quarter. You'll find classic, vibrantly painted West Indian–style homes with elaborate gingerbread fretwork.

❸ Oyster Pond. North of Dawn Beach is the point where two early settlers, a Frenchman and a Dutchman, allegedly began to pace in opposite directions around the island to divide it between their respective countries. Local legend maintains that the obese, sweaty Hollander stopped frequently to refresh himself with gin—the reason the French side is nearly twice the size of the Dutch (the official boundary marker is on the other side of the island).

❶ Philipsburg. The capital of Dutch St. Maarten stretches about a mile (1½ km) along an isthmus between Great Bay and the Salt Pond and has five parallel streets: Front, Back, C. A. Cannegieter, Walter Nisbeth, and Pondfill. Front Street has been recobbled, cars are discouraged from using it, and the pedestrian area has been widened. Shops, restaurants, and casinos vie for the hordes coming off cruise ships. Little lanes called *steegjes* connect Front Street with Back Street, which has fewer shops and is considerably less congested.

Wathey Square (pronounced watty), in the middle of the isthmus on which Philipsburg sits, bustles with souvenir shops and visitors. Directly across from the square are the town hall and the courthouse, in the striking white building with the cupola. The structure was built in 1793 and has served as the commander's home, a fire station, a jail, and a post office. The streets surrounding the square are lined with hotels, duty-free shops, fine restaurants, and cafés—most of them in West Indian cottages gussied up with gingerbread trim. Alleys lead to arcades and flower-filled courtyards where there are yet more boutiques and eateries. The **Captain Hodge Pier,** just off the square, is a good spot to view Great Bay and the beach that stretches alongside.

The **Sint Maarten Museum** hosts rotating cultural exhibits and a permanent historical display called Forts of St. Maarten/St. Martin. The artifacts range from Arawak pottery shards to articles salvaged from the wreck of the HMS *Proselyte.* ⊠ *7 Front St.,* ☎ *599/54–24917.* ⊑ *$1 (suggested donation).* ⊘ *Weekdays 10–4, Sat. 10–2.*

❻ Pic du Paradis. From Friar's Bay Beach, a bumpy, tree-canopied road leads inland to this peak. At 1,278 ft (390 m), it's the island's highest point and the Caribbean vistas from it are breathtaking.

Loterie Farms is a peaceful 150-acre peaceful oasis run by American expat B. J. Welch to preserve farm, forest, and mountain land. He's renovated an old farmhouse and welcomes visitors, who can participate in a variety of activities—horseback riding, hiking, mountain biking—or such inactivities as meditation. ⊠ *Route de Pic du Paradis,* ☎ *590/ 87–86–16.* ⊑ *$5 entry fee; 1½-hr tour, $15; 4-hr tour, $35.* ⊘ *Daily sunrise–sunset.*

ST. MARTIN A TO Z

To research prices, get advice from other travelers, and book travel arrangements, visit www.fodors.com.

AIR TRAVEL
Air ALM has daily service from Curaçao, with connections from Aruba, Bonaire, and Caracas, and from Miami via Curaçao. The airline also works with KLM to carry passengers from numerous European cities. Air France offers daily nonstop flights from Paris, with connections from other European cities, as well as connections to and from Martinique and Antigua. Air Caraïbes, formed when the local airlines Air St. Barthélemy, Air Guadeloupe, and Air Martinique combined some services and routes, offers daily flights St. Barths, as well as frequent service to Martinique and Guadeloupe. The airline flies mainly out of L'Espérance, on the French side.

The most convenient carrier from the United States is American Airlines, with daily nonstop flights from New York and Miami, as well as connections from more than 100 U.S. cities via its San Juan hub. BWIA offers service from Trinidad, Jamaica, and Antigua. Continental Airlines has daily nonstop flights from Newark and connections from San Juan. LIAT has daily service from San Juan and several Caribbean islands, including Antigua, the USVI, the BVI, and St. Kitts–Nevis. US Airways has nonstop service from Philadelphia on Saturday and Sunday and from Charlotte on Saturday. Windward Islands Airways, based on St. Maarten, has daily service to Anguilla, Saba, St. Barths, St. Eustatius, and St. Kitts–Nevis, as well as several weekly flights to Tortola. The company also offers tour and charter services.

➤ AIRLINES AND CONTACTS: **Air ALM** (☎ 599/54–54240); **KLM** (☎ 599/54–54344); **Air France** (☎ 599/54–54212); **Air Caraïbes** (☎ 599/

54–53651 or 590/87–53–74); **American Airlines** (☎ 599/54–52040);
BWIA (☎ 599/54–54646); **Continental Airlines** (☎ 599/54–53444);
LIAT (☎ 599/54–54203); **US Airways** (☎ 599/54–54344); **Windward
Islands Airways** (☎ 599/54–54230).

AIRPORTS
Aeroport de L'Espérance, on the French side, is small and handles only
island hoppers. Jumbo jets fly into Princess Juliana International Air-
port, on the Dutch side.
➤ AIRPORT INFORMATION: **Aeroport de L'Espérance** (☎ 590/87–53–03);
Princess Juliana International Airport (☎ 599/54–54211).

BIKE AND MOPED TRAVEL
Although roads are crowded and there are some spots where people
drive too fast, a motorbike is a great way get around. Parking is easy,
filling the tank with gas is affordable, and you've got that sea breeze
in your hair. Scooters rent for $22–$32 a day at Eugene Moto, on the
French side. If you're in the mood for a more substantial bike, contact
the Harley-Davidson dealer, on the Dutch side, where you can rent a
big hog for $90 a day.
➤ BIKE AND MOPED RENTALS: **Eugene Moto** (✉ Sandy Ground Rd., ☎
590/87–13–97); **Harley-Davidson** (✉ Cole Bay, ☎ 599/54–42779).

BOAT AND FERRY TRAVEL
FARES AND SCHEDULES
The *Voyager I* and *Voyager II* offer daily service from Marigot to St.
Barths. Both boats also carry passengers from Bobby's Marina (at the
east end of Front Street in Philipsburg) to St. Barths on Wednesday, Thursday, and Friday. The cost for the 75-minute trip is $57 per person, in-
cluding an open bar, snacks, and port fees. Both boats also make
Tuesday (from Marigot) and Thursday (from Philipsburg) runs to Saba,
also for $57 per person. Children under 12 are roughly half price, and
children under five travel for free. The high-speed 50-passenger ferry
Edge motors from Simpson Bay's Pelican Marina to Saba on Wednesday, Friday, and Sunday (70 minutes, $60 round-trip) and to St. Barths
on Tuesday, Thursday, and Saturday (45 minutes, $50 round-trip). The
trips depart at 9 and return by 5 the same day. A ferry makes the 20-
minute trip between the Marigot piers and Blowing Point, on Anguilla,
departing and returning every half hour from 8 AM until 7 PM daily. The
fare is $10 one-way plus $2 departure tax, or $24 round-trip; accord-
ing to ferry authorities, this fee is due to rise to $15 one-way plus $4
departure tax, or $38 round-trip, in the near but undetermined future.
➤ BOAT AND FERRY INFORMATION: *Voyager I* and *Voyager II* (☎ 599/
54–24096 or 599/54–23170, WEB www.voyager-st-barths.com); *Edge*
(☎ 599/54–42640).

BUSINESS HOURS
BANKS
Banks on the Dutch side are open Monday–Thursday 8:30–3:30 and
Friday 8:30–4:40. French banks are open weekdays 8:30–12:30 and
2:30–4 and close afternoons preceding holidays.

POST OFFICES
Dutch-side post offices are open Monday–Thursday 7:30–5 and Friday 7:30–4:30. The branch at the Food Center at Cul de Sac keeps Saturday hours 9–1. On the French side post offices are open weekdays
7:30–4:45 and Saturday 7:30–11:30.

SHOPS
Shops on the Dutch side are open Monday–Saturday 8–noon and 2–
6; on the French side, Monday–Saturday 9–noon or 12:30 and 2–6.

(Note that many shops on both sides now remain open during lunch; others set their own capricious hours.) Some of the larger shops open on Sunday and holidays when cruise ships are in port.

CAR RENTALS

You can book a car at Juliana International Airport, where all major rental companies have booths. If you don't have a reservation and aren't exactly sure from whom to rent, there are nearly 50 companies on the island. Check the various vendors at the airport to get the best price. There are also rentals at every hotel area. Rates, in general, are low—approximately $40–$50 a day for a subcompact car. All foreign driver's licenses are honored, and major credit cards are accepted. Avis, Budget, Dollar, Hertz, and National (Eurocar) all have cars for rent.

➤ MAJOR AGENCIES: **Avis** (☎ 800/331–1084); **Budget** (☎ 800/472–3325); **Dollar** (☎ 800/800–4000); **Hertz** (☎ 800/654–3131); **National (Eurocar)** (☎ 800/328–4567).

CAR TRAVEL

GASOLINE

Gas costs about $1.10 per liter ($3.85 per gallon).

ROAD CONDITIONS

Most roads are paved and generally well-marked on both sides of the island. In many cases signs will be in either French or Dutch, but they're easy to figure out, and international symbols are used. Roads in and around Marigot and Philipsburg are likely to be crowded and parking will be a problem. Try the side streets for parking, and don't forget to lock your rental car. There are occasional and short-lived traffic back-ups in town and at major intersections such as the Cole Bay traffic light.

ELECTRICITY

Generally, the Dutch side operates on 110 volts AC (60-cycle) and has outlets that accept flat-prong plugs—the same as in North America. The French side operates on 220 volts AC (60-cycle), with round-prong plugs; you'll need an adapter and a converter for North American appliances. Note: some Dutch-side hotels are 220 volts, and some French hotels are 110 volts, so call ahead to confirm.

EMERGENCIES

➤ AMBULANCE AND FIRE: Dial ☎ 911 or 599/54–22111 Dutch side; 15 or 590/87–86–25 (day) French side; 590/87–72–00 (night) French side.

➤ HOSPITALS: Dutch side: **St. Maarten Medical Center** (⊠ Cay Hill, ☎ 599/54–31111); French side: **Hospital de Marigot** (⊠ Rue de l'Hôpital Marigot, ☎ 590/29–57–57).

➤ PHARMACIES: **Central Drug Store** (⊠ Walter Nisbeth St., Philipsburg ☎ 599/54–22321); **Pharmacie du Port** (⊠ Rue de la Liberté, Marigot, ☎ 590/87–50–79).

➤ POLICE: Dial ☎ 911 or 599/54–22222 Dutch side; 17 or 590/87–50–06 French side.

ETIQUETTE AND BEHAVIOR

Religion plays an important part in island life, and churches are packed on Sunday, their roofs lifted by the energetic and exalted voices of the faithful. Sunday, too, is a day of rest, and islanders like to head to the beaches for picnics and a splash. That's about the only time you'll see them in any state of undress—on the streets and in shops, conservative dress is the norm. Take the cue. In addition, a smile and a simple greeting go a long way toward establishing good relations with locals.

FESTIVALS AND SEASONAL EVENTS
The French side's Carnival is a pre-Lenten bash of costume parades, music competitions, and feasts. On the Dutch side, Carnival takes place after Easter, usually in early May. On the French side the Calypso Festival is held in early July. The Caribbean Quest Musical Awards, a festival of regional music with guests from around the islands, is held in early August on the French side. On the Dutch side early March sees the Heineken Regatta, an international sailing regatta around the island.

HEALTH
Mosquitos come out in the early evening, but the gentle sea winds are enough to keep them to a minimum in most places. The biggest problem might be sun exposure. Even on seemingly cloudy days the sun can cause painful burns, so make sure to use sunscreen, and limit your sunbathing to about 15 min at a stretch. Drinking water is generally safe, except immediately following a hurricane or storm. If in doubt, buy bottled drinking water, which is plentiful at shops throughout the island.

HOLIDAYS
Both sides of the island celebrate specific holidays related to their government and culture, and some, such as New Year's, the Easter holidays (Apr. 13–15), Labor Day (May 1), Christmas, and Boxing Day (Dec. 26) are celebrated together.

Other French-side holidays are: Ascension Day (May 25), Bastille Day (July 14), Schoelcher Day (July 21), All Saints' Day (Nov. 1), and the Feast of St. Martin (Nov. 11). Dutch-side holidays are: Antillean Day (Oct. 21) and St. Maarten Day (Nov. 11; this coincides with Feast of St. Martin on the French side).

LANGUAGE
Dutch is the official language of St. Maarten, and French is the official language of St. Martin, but almost everyone speaks English. If you hear a language you can't quite place, it's Papiamento—a mix of Spanish, Portuguese, Dutch, French, and English—spoken throughout the Netherlands Antilles.

MAIL AND SHIPPING
The main Dutch-side post office is on Walter Nisbeth Road in Philipsburg. Other branches are at the Food Center Mall in Cul de Sac and at Princess Juliana Airport. The main post office on the French side is in Marigot, on rue de la Liberté. Letters from the Dutch side to North America, Europe, and New Zealand cost NAf2.25; postcards NAf1.10. A standard letter to Australia is NAf2.75, a postcard is NAf1.30. From the French side, letters up to 20 grams and postcards are 3.80F to North America and 5.20F to Europe, New Zealand, and Australia. When writing to Dutch St. Maarten, call it "Sint Maarten" and make sure to add "Netherlands Antilles" to the address. When writing to the French side the proper spelling is "St-Martin," and you add "French West Indies" to the address. Postal codes are only used on the French side.

MONEY MATTERS
Note: prices quoted in this chapter are in U.S. dollars unless otherwise noted.

ATMS
All banks now have automatic teller machines (ATMs) that accept international cards. On the Dutch side try ABN-Amro. Windward Islands Bank has several branches on the island. On the French side, try Banque des Antilles Françaises or Banque Française Commerciale. Both are found on rue de la République in Marigot.

➤ CONTACTS: **ABN-Amro** (✉ Emnaplein, Philipsburg, ☎ 599/54–23344; ✉ Union Rd., Cole Bay, ☎ 599/54–43078, WEB www.abnamro.com); **Windward Islands Bank** (✉ Wathey Sq., Front St., Philipsburg, ☎ 599/54–22313, WEB www.wib-bank.net); **Banque des Antilles Françaises** (☎ 590/29–13–30); **Banque Française Commerciale** (BFC; ☎ 590/87–53–80).

CREDIT CARDS
Credit cards are accepted all over the island.

CURRENCY
Legal tender on the Dutch side is the Netherlands Antilles florin (guilder), written NAf; on the French side, the French franc (F). The exchange rates fluctuate, but in general they're about NAf1.80 to US$1 and about 7F to US$1. On the Dutch side prices are usually given in both NAf and U.S. dollars, which are accepted all over the island.

PASSPORTS AND VISAS
U.S. and Canadian citizens need proof of citizenship. A passport (valid or not expired more than five years) is always the best document with which to travel, particularly for children. Barring a passport, an original birth certificate with raised seal (or a photocopy with notary seal) *plus* a government-issued photo ID, such as a driver's license, is also acceptable. This is why children are best served by passports, since they are unlikely to have other types of photo ID. British citizens need a valid passport or a national ID card. Citizens of Australia and New Zealand require a valid passport. All visitors must have a confirmed room reservation and an ongoing or return ticket.

˙SAFETY
Always lock your valuables and travel documents in your room safe or your hotel's front desk safe. When sightseeing in a rental car, keep valuables locked in the trunk or car, and never leave your things unattended at the beach. Despite the romantic imagery of the Caribbean, it's not good policy to take long walks along the beach at night.

SIGHTSEEING TOURS
HELICOPTER
You can arrange island tours and charters through Heli-Inter Caraïbes in Anse Marcel. St. Martin Helicopters also offers transport and tours by helicopter. Tours run upward of $400 for six people.
➤ CONTACTS: **Heli-Inter Caraïbes** (☎ 590/87–35–88); **St. Martin Helicopters** (☎ 599/54–54287).

ORIENTATION
A 2½-hour taxi tour of the island costs $30 for one or two people, $10 for each additional person. Your hotel or the tourist office can arrange it for you. On the Dutch side Calypso Tours has, among other things, three-hour island tours for $20 per person. Elle Si Belle offers tours by van or bus. You can also contact St. Maarten Sightseeing Tours. On the French side R&J Tours will show you the island; a three-hour tour (minimum of five people) is $15 per person.
➤ CONTACTS: **Elle Si Belle** (✉ Airport Blvd., Simpson Bay, ☎ 599/54–52271); **St. Maarten Sightseeing Tours** (✉ Maho Plaza at Maho Beach Hotel & Casino, Airport Rd., Simpson Bay, ☎ 599/54–52115); **R&J Tours** (✉ North of Marigot, Colombier, ☎ 590/87–56–20).

TAXES
DEPARTURE TAX
Departure tax from Juliana Airport is $6 to destinations within the Netherlands Antilles and $20 to all other destinations. Note that if you

arrive on the island by plane and depart within 24 hours, you will be considered "in transit" and won't be required to pay the $20 departure tax. It will cost you 15F (about $3, usually included in the ticket price) to depart by plane from L'Espérance Airport, and $4 by ferry to Anguilla from Marigot's pier.

SALES TAX
Hotels on the Dutch side add a 15% service-energy charge to the bill as well as a 5% government tax, for a total of 20%. Hotels on the French side add 10%–15% for service and a *taxe de séjour*; the amount of this visitor's tax differs from hotel to hotel, and can be as high as 5%.

TAXIS
The government regulates taxi rates. You can hail cabs on the street, or call the Dutch taxi dispatch on the Dutch side. On the French side of the island, contact the French taxi dispatch for pickups. There's a taxi service at the Marigot port near the tourist information bureau. Fixed fares apply from Juliana International Airport and the Marigot ferry to the various hotels around the island. Fares are 25% higher between 10 PM and midnight, 50% higher between midnight and 6 AM.
➤ CONTACTS: **Dutch taxi dispatch** (☎ 147); **French taxi dispatch** (☎ 590/87–56–54).

TELEPHONES
COUNTRY AND AREA CODES
To call the Dutch side from the United States, dial 011–599/54 plus local number; for the French side, 011–590 plus local number.

INTERNATIONAL CALLS
At the Landsradio in Philipsburg, there are facilities for overseas calls and an ATT USADirect phone, where you are directly in touch with an ATT operator who will accept collect or credit-card calls. On the French side you can't make collect calls to the United States, and there are no coin phones. If you need to use public phones, go to the special desk at Marigot's post office and buy a Telecarte, which gives you 40 units (it takes 120 units to cover a five-minute call to the United States) for around 31F or 120 units for 93F. There's a public phone at the tourist office in Marigot where you can make credit-card calls: the operator takes your card number (any major card) and assigns you a PIN (Personal Identification Number), which you then use to charge calls to your card.

LOCAL CALLS
To phone from the Dutch side to the French, dial 00–590 plus local number; from the French side to the Dutch, 00–599/54 plus local number. Keep in mind that a call from one side to the other is considered an overseas call, not a local one.

TIPPING
Service charges are added to hotel and restaurant bills all over the island. These are often included in all menu prices on the French side; on the Dutch side most restaurants add 10%–15% to the bill. Still, you should tip as you would at home; taxi drivers, porters, chambermaids, and restaurant waitstaff all expect a tip, even when a service charge is included in the bill. Think about 10%–15% for waitstaff, a couple of dollars for cabbies, a dollar per bag for porters, and $1–$5 per night for chambermaids.

TRANSPORTATION AROUND ST. MARTIN
At a flat rate of $1.50 ($2 after 8 PM), buses are the island's best bargains. They operate frequently between 7 AM and midnight from Philipsburg through Cole Bay to Marigot and on to Grand Case. There

are no official stops: you just stand by the side of the road and flag the bus down. Exact change is preferred though not required, and drivers accept both U.S. and local currency.

VISITOR INFORMATION

➤ BEFORE YOU LEAVE: **St. Maarten Tourist Office** (✉ 675 3rd Ave., Suite 1806, New York, NY 10017, ☎ 800/786–2278 or 212/953–2084, WEB www.st-maarten.com); **St. Maarten Tourist Information** (✉ 703 Evans Ave., Suite 106, Toronto, Ontario M9C 5E9, Canada, ☎ 416/622–4300); **St. Martin Office of Tourism** (✉ 675 3rd Ave., Suite 1807, New York, NY 10017, ☎ 212/475–8970, WEB www.st-martin.org). (✉ 9454 Wilshire Blvd., Suite 715, Beverly Hills, CA 90212, ☎ 310/271–6665); (✉ 676 N. Michigan Ave., Suite 3360, Chicago, IL 60611, ☎ 312/751–7800); (✉ 1981 McGill College Ave., Suite 490, Montréal, Québec H3A 2W9, Canada, ☎ 514/288–4264); (✉ 30 St. Patrick St., Suite 700, Toronto, Ontario M5T 3A3, Canada, ☎ 416/593–6427).
➤ IN ST. MARTIN: **Dutch-side tourist information bureau** (✉ Cyrus Wathey Sq., Philipsburg, ☎ 599/54–22337); **Dutch-side tourist bureau administrative office** (✉ 33 W. G. Buncamper Rd., in the Vineyard Park Bldg., Philipsburg, ☎ 599/54–22337). **French-side tourist information office** (☎ 590/87–57–21).

22 ST. VINCENT AND THE GRENADINES

Updated by
Jane E. Zarem

Standing on Dorsetshire Hill, above Kingstown, the wily old gentleman points to an island just offshore. On it is a large white cross that glimmers in the sun. "Know what that's about?" he asks. The grin on his weathered face fades to a wry smile as, without pause, he tells the tale. A local land developer, it seems, bought the island and put up the cross. Later, when he died, his body was placed upright inside it so that he could always face his life's work. "You see," says the gent with a shrug, "Vincentians love their country with a passion."

The island of St. Vincent and the string of 32 islands and cays that make up the Grenadines are a single nation—one that's loved passionately by its inhabitants as much for its interesting history as for its natural beauty. SVG, as it's abbreviated, is in the Windward Islands chain in the southern Caribbean. Mountainous St. Vincent, only 18 mi (29 km) by 11 mi (18 km) and just 13° north of the equator, is the largest and the northernmost in the group; the Grenadines extend in a 45-mi (73-km) arc southwest to Grenada. Each island is, in its own way, a refuge for escapists. You will be hard pressed to find glitzy resorts, flashy discos, or shopping malls. Rather, these islands dazzle you with their getaway-from-it-all atmosphere, sleepy villages, secluded white-sand beaches, and fine sailing waters.

St. Vincent's major export is bananas, and these plants, along with coconut palms and breadfruit trees, crowd more of the island than the 110,500 inhabitants (another 10,000 live on the Grenadines). This has obvious charm for nature lovers, who can spend days walking or hiking St. Vincent's well-defined trails, catching a glimpse of the rare St. Vincent parrot in the Vermont Valley, or climbing the active volcano La Soufrière, which last erupted in 1979. Below sea level, snorkeling and scuba landscapes are similarly intriguing.

Historians believe that the Ciboney Indians were the first to journey from South America to St. Vincent, which they called Hairoun (Land of the Blessed). The Ciboney ultimately moved on to Cuba and Haiti, leaving St. Vincent to the agrarian Arawak tribes, who journeyed from coastal South America to islands throughout the Lesser Antilles. Not long before Columbus sailed by in 1492, the Arawaks succumbed to the powerful Carib Indians, who had also paddled their way north from South America, conquering one island after another.

St. Vincent's mountains and forests thwarted European settlement. As colonization advanced elsewhere in the Caribbean, many Caribs fled to St. Vincent—making it even more of a Carib stronghold. In 1626 the French managed to settle on the island, but their success was short-lived; England took over a year later. Although "possession" of the island seesawed between France and England for years, the Caribs continued to make complete European colonization impossible. Ironically it was a rift in the Carib community itself that enabled the Europeans to gain a foothold.

In 1675 African slaves who had survived a Dutch shipwreck were welcomed into the Carib community. Over time the Carib nation became, for all intents and purposes, two nations—one composed of the so-called Yellow Caribs, the other of the so-called Black Caribs. Relations between the two groups were often strained. In 1719 tensions rose so high the Yellow Caribs united with the French (who were the colonizers that year) against the Black Caribs in what is called the First Carib War. The Black Caribs ultimately retreated to the hills, but they continued to resist the Europeans.

The French went on to establish plantations, importing African slaves to work the fertile land. In 1763 the British claimed the island yet again, and a wave of Scottish slave masters and indentured servants from India and Portugal arrived. Although the ethnic groups have mixed over the years to give Vincentians their unique heritage, communities of direct descendents of the Scots live near St. Vincent's Dorsetshire Hill and on Bequia. In 1779 the French surprised the British and reclaimed the island without a struggle; but four years later St. Vincent was back in the British grip. The determined French backed the Black Caribs against the British in 1795's Second Carib War (also known as the Brigands War). British plantations were ravaged and burned on the island's windward coast, and Black Carib chief Chatoyer pushed British troops down the leeward coast to Kingstown. On Dorsetshire Hill, high above the town, Chatoyer subsequently lost a duel with a British officer. The 5,000 remaining Black Caribs were rounded up and shipped off to Honduras and present-day Belize, where their descendents (the Garifuna people) remain to this day. The few remaining Yellow Caribs retreated to the remote northern tip of St. Vincent, near Sandy Bay, where many of their descendents now live. A monument to Chatoyer has been erected on Dorsetshire Hill, where there's a magnificent view over Kingstown and the Caribbean Sea toward Central America.

The Grenadines were historically as free from war and politics as their pristine beaches are today free from crowds. Just south of St. Vincent is Bequia, the largest of the Grenadines. Its Admiralty Bay is one of the most popular anchorages in the Caribbean. With superb views, snorkeling, hiking, and swimming, the island has much to offer the international mix of backpackers and luxury-yacht owners who frequent its shores.

South of Bequia, on the exclusive, private island of Mustique, posh villas are tucked into lush hillsides. Mustique does not encourage wholesale tourism, least of all to those hoping for a glimpse of the rich and famous (Princess Margaret, Mick Jagger, and Tommy Hilfiger, for example) who own villas here. The appeal of Mustique is its seclusion.

Boot-shape Canouan, just over 3 square mi (8 square km) in area, is an unspoiled island where you can relax on the beach, snorkel, or hike. Its 1,000 residents earn their living from farming and fishing. Tiny Mayreau has fewer than 200 residents and one of the area's most beautiful beaches—where the Caribbean Sea is often mirror calm, and just yards away the rolling Atlantic surf washes the northern end of this narrow island.

Union Island is the transportation center of the southern Grenadines, with a busy airport for landlubbers and yacht services for sailors. It took decades to turn the 100-acre, mosquito-infested mangrove swamp called Prune Island into the private paradise of Palm Island; now resort guests lounge on the island's five palm-fringed white-sand beaches. Petit St. Vincent is another private island, reclaimed from the overgrowth by owner-manager Hazen K. Richardson II. The luxury resort's stone houses are far enough apart that you could spend your vacation without ever seeing another human being.

Although SVG has its share of the poor and unemployed, the super-fertile soil allows everyone to grow enough food to eat and trade for necessities. Villages are busy and clean, concrete-block homes are painted in tropical colors, and colorful flowers and bright green foliage grow in profusion. The issue of possession of St. Vincent has long since been resolved; fully independent since 1979 (but still a part of the British Commonwealth), it belongs to a diverse, culturally rich people now known only as Vincentians—who truly have good reason to love their homeland with a passion.

ST. VINCENT

Lodging

With few exceptions, tourist accommodations and facilities on St. Vincent are located in either Kingstown or the Villa Beach area. Luxury resorts may require advance booking, but most SVG hotels can squeeze you in on short notice. There's also a lull in January—after Christmas week and before the February rush—when rooms may be available with little advance notice. Most hotels offer the MAP; at resorts in the Grenadines, the FAP is common. All guest rooms have TV and telephone, unless stated otherwise.

CATEGORY	COST*
$$$$	over $250
$$$	$175–$250
$$	$100–$175
$	under $100

All prices are for a standard double room, excluding 7% tax and 10% service charge. Note when comparing rates: The price categories for all-inclusive resorts reflect the inclusion of all meals, beverages, and activities.

KINGSTOWN

$$ ☆ **Camelot Inn.** Snuggled in the hills of Kingstown Park, five minutes
★ from downtown and 10 minutes from the airport, this lovely inn was rebuilt on the site of the island's oldest guest house (1781), which was itself the former residence of St. Vincent's first French governor. The atmosphere is stylish and elegant; the service is impeccable; and the location offers magnificent views of the capital, the hills, and the sea. Owner Audrey Ballantyne decorated each guest room in a soothing white and deep green color scheme, with gray-green Spanish rattan furniture, antique mirrors and prints, and parquet floors. Each spacious room has a patio. Porcelain hand-painted sinks imported from France are the centerpieces of each bathroom. The King Arthur dining room is excellent; there's an outdoor dining terrace (with entertainment in season), and afternoon tea is served in the garden. Guests receive complimentary airport pickup, a city tour, and one massage, as well as access to Young Island Resort's beach and water-sports facilities

(transportation included). ✉ *Kingstown Park (Box 787),* ☎ *784/456–2100 or 800/223–6510,* 𝔽𝔸𝕏 *784/456–2233. 19 rooms, 3 suites. 2 restaurants, 2 bars, air-conditioning, fans, in-room safes, pool, beauty salon, massage, sauna, tennis court, exercise room, library, laundry service, meeting rooms, airport shuttle. AE, DC, MC, V. EP.*

$ 🏨 **Cobblestone Inn.** On the waterfront in "the city," as Vincentians call Kingstown, this small hotel occupies a former sugar and arrowroot warehouse, built in 1814 of local stone and renovated in recent years to expose its original Georgian architecture, sunny interior courtyard, and winding cobblestone walkways and arches. Rooms are tiny, but each has stone walls, rattan furniture, and a private bath. Number 5, at the front, is lighter and bigger than most of the other rooms—but noisier, too. A rooftop bar-restaurant serves breakfast and light lunches. The popular Basil's Bar and Restaurant is located at ground level. ✉ *Upper Bay St. (Box 867),* ☎ *784/456–1937,* 𝔽𝔸𝕏 *784/456–1938. 19 rooms. Restaurant, bar, air-conditioning, shops, baby-sitting, laundry service, meeting room. AE, D, MC, V. EP.*

VILLA BEACH AREA

$$$$ 🏨 **Young Island Resort.** St. Vincent's premier resort is on a 35-acre pri-
★ vate island 200 yards off Villa Beach. A hotel launch is on call to take you across the channel (a five-minute ride) to the island, where you're handed a rum punch crowned with a hibiscus blossom and then escorted to one of 30 hillside cottages. Rooms are huge, airy, and decorated in natural colors (ecru, ochre, and green) with bamboo and rattan furniture, walls of stone and glass, a sitting area (no TV), ceiling fans and louvred windows to maximize the cooling trade winds (no air-conditioning), patio, and a bathroom with an open-air shower. Two luxury beachfront cottages have their own plunge pools. All accommodations have ocean views despite being hidden in lush tropical vegetation. Superior cottages are nearest the beach; the deluxe ones are higher on the hillside. Watch hummingbirds flutter among the flowers as you enjoy breakfast on your terrace; sip a cool drink at the swim-up bar, anchored several feet off the white-sand beach; laze away the day in a hammock; or dine in one of the private thatched-roof gazebos adjacent to the Young Island dining room. Sailaway packages include five nights at the hotel and two nights touring the Grenadines on the resort's 44-ft sailboat. ✉ *Young Island (Box 211),* ☎ *784/458–4826 or 800/223–1108,* 𝔽𝔸𝕏 *784/457–4567,* 𝕎𝔼𝔹 *www.youngisland.com. 30 cottages. Restaurant, 2 bars, fans, in-room safes, refrigerator, room service, pool, tennis court, beach, snorkeling, windsurfing, boating, baby-sitting, laundry service, meeting room, airport shuttle. AE, MC, V. MAP.*

$$$ 🏨 **Grand View Beach Hotel.** The Sardine family's turn-of-the-20th-cen-
★ tury cotton-plantation great house is now Tony and Heather Sardine's grand hotel, perched on a point just above Indian Bay. It has both extensive facilities and intimate charm—all set on 8 acres of grounds that beckon you to explore. The decor is attractive but not fussy; rooms have plain white walls and hardwood floors, and most offer sweeping vistas of Villa Beach, Young Island, and the Grenadines. Luxury-level rooms have broad terraces with ocean views; two honeymoon suites have king-size beds and whirlpool tubs. Wilkie's restaurant serves good West Indian and Continental-style cuisine. Sailboats, Windsurfers, and snorkeling equipment are complimentary, but you have to hike down a rather steep hill to the beach. ✉ *Villa Point,* ☎ *784/458–4811; 800/633–7411; 800/223–6510; 800/424–5500 in Canada;* 𝔽𝔸𝕏 *784/457–4174,* 𝕎𝔼𝔹 *www.grandviewhotel.com. 17 rooms, 2 suites. 2 restaurants, 3 bars, air-conditioning, fans, pool, massage, sauna, tennis court, beach, health club, squash, snorkeling, library, baby-sitting, laundry service, meeting room. AE, MC, V. CP, EP, MAP.*

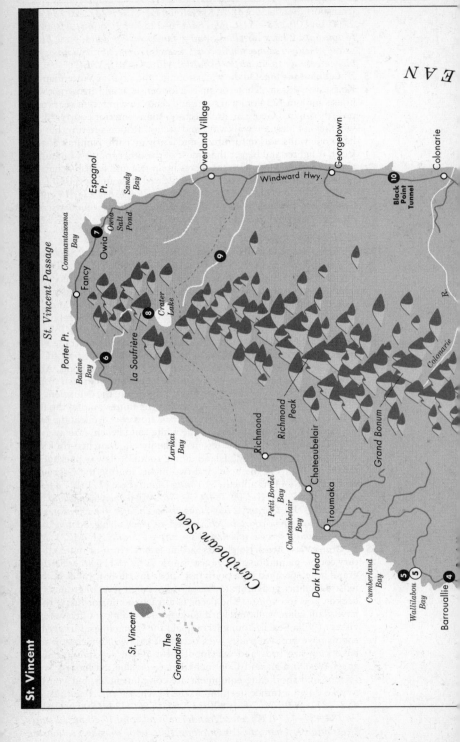

St. Vincent

666

St. Vincent Passage

Commantawana Bay

Porter Pt.

Baleine Bay

Fancy

Espagnol Pt.

Sandy Bay

Owia

Owia Salt Pond

Overland Village

Windward Hwy.

Georgetown

Colonarie

Black Point Tunnel

⑩

⑦

⑧

⑥

Crater Lake

La Soufrière

⑨

Larikai Bay

Richmond

Richmond Peak

Grand Bonum

Colonarie

R.

Chateaubelair

Petit Bordel Bay

Chateaubelair Bay

Troumaka

Dark Head

Caribbean Sea

Cumberland Bay

Wallilabou Bay

⑤ ⑤

④

Barroualie

St. Vincent

The Grenadines

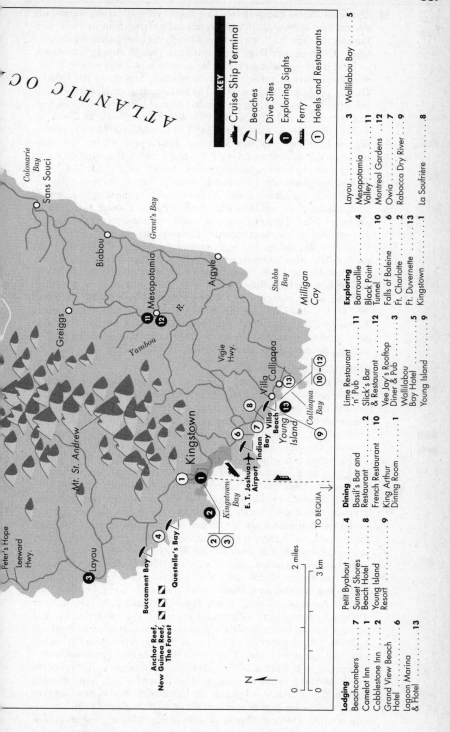

ATLANTIC OC

Colonarie Bay

Sans Souci

Biabou

Grant's Bay

Greggs

Mesopotamia

Argyle

Yambou

R.

Stubbs Bay

Milligan Cay

Peter's Hope

Mt. St. Andrew

Vigie Hwy.

Kingstown

Leeward Hwy.

Layou

Buccament Bay

Questelle's Bay

Kingstown Bay

E. T. Joshua Airport

Indian Bay
Villa Beach

Villa

Young Island

Calliaqua

Calliaqua Bay

TO BEQUIA

KEY

🚢 Cruise Ship Terminal

⚓ Beaches

▨ Dive Sites

① Exploring Sights

⛴ Ferry

① Hotels and Restaurants

N

| 0 | 2 miles |
| 0 | 3 km |

Lodging
Beachcombers 7
Camelot Inn 1
Cobblestone Inn 2
Grand View Beach
Hotel 6
Lagoon Marina
& Hotel 13
Petit Byahaut 4
Sunset Shores
Beach Hotel 8
Young Island
Resort 9

Dining
Basil's Bar and
Restaurant 2
French Restaurant . . . 10
King Arthur
Dining Room 1
Lime Restaurant
'n' Pub 11
Slick's Bar
& Restaurant 12
Vee Jay's Rooftop
Diner & Pub 3
Walliabou
Bay Hotel 5
Young Island 9

Exploring
Barrouallie 4
Black Point
Tunnel 10
Falls of Baleine 6
Ft. Charlotte 2
Ft. Duvernette 13
Kingstown 1
Layou 3
Mesopotamia
Valley 11
Montreal Gardens . . 12
Owia 7
Rabacca Dry River . . . 9
La Soufrière 8
Wallilabou Bay 5

Anchor Reef,
New Guinea Reef,
The Forest

$$ ☷ **Sunset Shores Beach Hotel.** This lemon-yellow low-rise surrounds a small pool and a gigantic and prolific mango tree (help yourself from January through July). It also faces a lovely curve of Indian Bay beach-front. All rooms are large and pleasantly, though simply, decorated; all have patios or balconies. Opt for a room with a water view; other-wise you'll have to amble over to the poolside Sunrunner Bar to get a glimpse of the gorgeous sunsets. The restaurant is good, with a small but varied menu featuring fresh local fish and lobster (in season); ser-vice is friendly and efficient. ✉ *Villa Beach (Box 849),* ☎ *784/458–4411; 800/223–6510; 800/424–5500 in Canada;* FAX *784/457–4800,* WEB *www.sunsetshores.com. 32 rooms. Restaurant, 3 bars, air-condi-tioning, room service, pool, Ping-Pong, beach, snorkeling, boating, baby-sitting, laundry service, meeting room. AE, D, MC, V. EP, MAP.*

$ ☷ **Beachcombers.** At Villa Beach, next to Sunset Shores, a pair of chalets on sloping lawns house the Beachcombers' guest rooms, restau-rant, outdoor bar, sundeck, and reception area. Though some rooms are better located than others, you could eat breakfast off the floor in any of them, such is the standard of housekeeping. In one building, half the rooms face the sea and half overlook the Mango Tree Lounge and garden. The other building, which faces the garden's frenzy of flowers, has a red-tile terrace in front. Rooms with air-conditioning cost extra, and bathrooms have showers only—insignificant privations when the welcome here is so warm and the rates so low. ✉ *Villa Beach (Box 126),* ☎ *784/458–4283,* FAX *784/458–4385. 18 rooms, 2 suites, 1 apartment. Restaurant, bar, air-conditioning, fans, kitchenettes, refrigerator, room service, pool, sauna, spa, steam room, Turkish baths, beach, library, baby-sitting, laundry service, meeting room. AE, MC, V. CP.*

ELSEWHERE ON ST. VINCENT

$$$$ ☷ **Petit Byahaut.** For those with Swiss Family Robinson fantasies, this 50-acre retreat 7 mi (11 km) north of Kingstown offers accommoda-tions in large deluxe tents, complete with wood floors, private decks, queen-size beds, hammocks, solar-powered lighting, and bathrooms with solar-heated alfresco showers. Each unit is unique in appearance and location. Gourmet meals, including dinners by candlelight, are served in the restaurant, which overlooks the bay. This adult camp is acces-sible only by a 20-minute boat ride from Kingstown (complimentary for guests). Once you've settled in, you'll find a selection of other boats with which to play, along with scuba and snorkeling equipment, a private black-sand beach, hammocks, a boutique, and some inter-esting Carib Indian finds. If you tire of the seclusion, excursions are easily arranged. A three-night minimum stay is required; weekly rates are available. ✉ *Petit Byahaut Bay,* ☎ FAX *784/457–7008. 6 tents. Restau-rant, bar, hiking, beach, dive shop, snorkeling, boating, shops, meet-ing room, airport shuttle. MC, V. Closed July–Oct. FAP.*

$$ ☷ **The Lagoon Marina & Hotel.** This hotel overlooking sheltered Blue Lagoon Bay may well be the island's busiest. Thanks to its marina, there are usually seafaring types liming (hanging out) in the terrace bar and plenty of yacht traffic to watch from one of two couches on your big balcony. Sliding patio doors lead onto these perches from the wood-ceilinged, carpeted rooms. Don't try it, but you could practically dive into the sea from Rooms 1–9, which hang over the wooden quay; Rooms 10–20 overlook a narrow crescent of black-sand beach. Basic wooden furniture, twin beds, dim lighting, tiled bathrooms, and ceiling fans pro-vide an adequate level of comfort; about half the rooms have air-con-ditioning (for a few extra bucks), but don't expect luxury. Sloping garden grounds contain a secluded two-level pool, and there's a pretty terrace restaurant. ✉ *Blue Lagoon, Ratho Mill (Box 133),* ☎ *784/458–4308 or 800/742–4246,* FAX *784/457–4308. 19 rooms, 2 apartments. Restau-*

rant, bar, grocery, air-conditioning, fans, kitchenettes, room service, pool, beach, dock, snorkeling, windsurfing, boating, marina, baby-sitting, laundry service, meeting room. AE, V. EP.

Dining

Nearly all the restaurants in St. Vincent specialize in West Indian cuisine. At posh resorts in the Grenadines, you're more likely to find chefs with a broad range of culinary experience and, therefore, more international selections appear on the menu. These wise chefs still use the local bounty—fresh seafood, tropical fruits and unique Caribbean vegetables—when preparing their specialties. Local dishes to try include *callaloo* (similar to spinach) soup, curried goat, *rotis* (turnovers filled with curried meat or vegetables), seasonal seafood (lobster, kingfish, snapper, and mahimahi), local vegetables (avocados, breadfruit, christophene, and pumpkin) and "provisions" (roots, such as yams, dasheen, and *eddoes*), and tropical fruit (from mangoes and soursop to pineapples and papaya). Fried or baked chicken is available everywhere, often accompanied by "rice 'n' peas," and you can get burgers and pizza at some restaurants. The local beer, Hairoun, is brewed according to a German recipe at Campden Park, just north of Kingstown.

What to Wear

Restaurants are casual. You may want to dress up a little, but none of the places listed below requires gentlemen to wear a jacket or tie. On the Grenadines ultracasual is fine nearly everywhere, although at pricey resorts, people tend to dress up a little in the evening—long pants and collared shirts for gents, summer dresses or dress pants for the ladies. Beachwear should always be reserved for the beach.

CATEGORY	COST*
$$$	over $25
$$	$15–$25
$	under $15

per person for a main course at dinner

Kingstown

CARIBBEAN

$ ✕ **Basil's Bar and Restaurant.** This refreshingly air-conditioned restaurant, downstairs at the Cobblestone Inn, is owned by Basil Charles, whose Basil's Beach Bar on Mustique is a hangout for the vacationing rich and famous. It's the Kingstown power-lunch venue, where local businesspeople gather for the daily buffet or a full menu of salads, sandwiches, barbecued chicken, or fresh seafood platters. Dinner entrées of pasta, local seafood, and chicken (try it poached in fresh ginger and coconut milk) are served at candlelit tables. There's a Chinese buffet on Friday, and takeout is available that night only. ⊠ *Upper Bay St.,* ☎ *784/457–2713. AE, MC, V.*

$ ✕ **Vee Jay's Rooftop Diner & Pub.** This eatery, above Roger's Photo Studios (have your pix developed while you eat) and opposite the Cobblestone Inn, offers downtown Kingstown's best harbor view from beneath a green corrugated-plastic roof. Among the "authentic Vincy cuisine" specials chalked on the blackboard are mutton or fish stew, chicken or vegetable rotis, curried goat, souse, and *buljol* (sautéed codfish, breadfruit, and vegetables). Not-so-Vincy sandwiches, fish and chips, and burgers can be authentically washed down with *mauby,* a bittersweet drink made from tree bark; linseed, peanut, passion fruit, or sorrel punch; local Hairoun beer or cocktails. Lunch is buffet style. ⊠ *Upper Bay St.,* ☎ *784/457–2845. Reservations essential. AE, MC, V. Closed Sun.*

CONTEMPORARY

$$ ✕ **King Arthur Dining Room.** Expect fine cuisine and elegant service when supping at this intimate dining room downstairs in the Camelot Inn. The chef's table d'hôte menu offers you a choice of two to three starters and entrées, which change daily. Dishes—fillet of beef, grilled fish with herb sauce, chicken sautéed in white wine—are served with local vegetables. The homemade soups are memorable, and so is the rum-raisin ice cream. There's entertainment in season and a weekly barbecue on the breezy Guinevere Terrace, which overlooks the harbor. ✉ *Kingstown Park,* ☎ *784/456–2100. Reservations essential. AE, D, MC, V.*

Villa Beach Area

CONTINENTAL

$$ ✕ **Young Island.** Even if you're not a guest at the Young Island Resort,
★ you can take the ferry (a 5-min ride from Villa Beach) over to the island for a picturesque lunch or a very special romantic evening. Stone paths lead through lush foliage to thatched huts with individual candlelit tables; the water laps against the shore, and a warm breeze rustles the leaves. Five-course table d'hôte, prix-fixe dinners of grilled seafood, roast pork, beef tenderloin, and sautéed chicken are accompanied by local vegetables; a board of wonderful fresh breads is offered for your selection. Two or three choices are offered for each course. Lunch is à la carte—with a choice of soups, salads, grilled meats or fish—and served on the beachfront terrace. ✉ *Young Island,* ☎ *784/ 458–4826. Reservations essential. AE, MC, V.*

ECLECTIC

$$ ✕ **Lime Restaurant 'n' Pub.** Although this sprawling, waterfront restaurant-bar is named after the *pursuit* of liming, its decor also features a great deal of green. A wide-ranging all-day menu caters to beachgoers and boaters, who drop by for a roti and a bottle of Hairoun—or burgers, curries, sandwiches, gourmet pizza or pasta, soups, and salads. Dinner choices include fresh seafood, volcano chicken (with a creole sauce that's as spicy as lava is hot), curried goat, and pepper steak. Casual and congenial during the day, the mood is all candlelight and romance at night—enhanced by the twinkling lights of boats at anchor and waves quietly breaking against the seawall. ✉ *Young Island Channel, Villa Harbour,* ☎ *784/458–4227. AE, D, DC, MC, V.*

$$ ✕ **Slick's Bar & Restaurant.** Located on the Villa Beach waterfront's "Restaurant Row," along with The Lime and The French, Slick's offers entrées culled from Italian, American, French, and West Indian cuisines. Whether you choose shrimp, lobster, steak, lamb chops, or chicken, the dish is ultimately determined that day by the chef's preparation and accompanying sauces. Dinner is by candlelight, and lunch affords a delightful view of Young Island, the harbor activity, and the distant Grenadines. The restaurant's small playground offers added pleasure for young children. ✉ *Young Island Channel, Villa Harbour,* ☎ *784/457–5783. AE, MC, V.*

FRENCH

$$$ ✕ **French Restaurant.** Referred to as "The French," this popular wa-
★ terfront bistro facing Young Island is where people go for a quiet waterfront breakfast or lunch—and also when they're in the mood for lobster. There's a lobster pool on the terrace, where you can watch the staff fish for your supper. As befits a bistro run by a couple from Orléans, France, most dishes are the Gallic version of local cuisine. Stuffed crab back, for instance, comes in a pastry shell, not a crab shell; steak—au poivre, with garlic butter or with béarnaise—is imported; the onion soup and lemon tart are French, the way they should be; and the warm, fresh bread is a genuine Parisienne-style baguette. At the in-

side bar, frothy cocktails and Martinique-style punch are served to yachties who hang out here in winter. ⊠ *Young Island Channel, Villa Harbour,* ☎ *784/458–4972. AE, V.*

Elsewhere on St. Vincent

CARIBBEAN

$ ✕ **Wallilabou Bay Hotel.** Halfway up the Caribbean coast of St. Vincent, this is a favorite anchorage for folks sailing the Grenadines as well as daytrippers returning from a visit to the Falls of Baleine. Pretty as a picture, it's open all day (from 8 AM), and it's a particularly perfect luncheon or sunset-viewing spot for landlubbers touring the leeward coast. The bar-and-restaurant serves snacks, sandwiches, tempting West Indian dishes, and lobster in season. Ice, telephone, business services, and shower facilities are available to boaters. ⊠ *Leeward Highway Wallilabou Bay,* ☎ *784/458–7270. AE, MC, V.*

Beaches

St. Vincent's origin is volcanic, so its beachfront ranges in color from golden-brown to black. Young Island has the only truly white-sand beach; but since the island is private, it's reserved for hotel guests. Otherwise, all beaches are public. On the windward coast dramatic swaths of broad black sand are strewn with huge black boulders, but the water is rough and unpredictable. Swimming is recommended only in the lagoons and bays along the leeward coast.

Buccament Bay, good for swimming, is a tiny black-sand beach 20 minutes north of Kingstown. **Indian Bay,** south of Kingstown, has golden sand but is slightly rocky—a good location for snorkeling. **Questelle's Bay** (pronounced keet-*ells*), north of Kingstown and next to Campden Park, has a black-sand beach. **Villa Beach,** opposite Young Island and 10 minutes south of Kingstown, is the island's main beach (although it's hardly big enough to merit such a title). Boats bob at anchor in the channel; dive shops and restaurants line the shore.

Outdoor Activities and Sports

BICYCLING

Although bicycles can be rented for about $10 per day, the roads are not particularly conducive to leisurely cycling. However, serious bicyclists will enjoy a day of mountain biking in wilderness areas. **Sailor's Wilderness Tours** (⊠ Middle St., ☎ 784/457–1712 or 784/457–9207 after hours) takes individuals or groups on half-day bike tours for $25 per person.

BOATING, FISHING, AND SAILING

From St. Vincent you can charter a monohull or catamaran (bareboat or complete with captain, crew, and cook) to weave you through the Grenadines for a day or a week of sailing—or a half-day, full-day, or overnight fishing trip. Boats of all sizes and degrees of luxury are available. **Barefoot Yacht Charters** (⊠ Ratho Mill, ☎ 784/456–9526, FAX 785/456–9238) has a fleet of yachts for charter, with or without crew. **Blue Water Charters** (⊠ Aquatic Club, Villa Beach, ☎ 784/456–1232, FAX 784/456–2382) will take you on full-day, half-day, or overnight fishing or sightseeing excursions on its modern 55-ft sportfishing boat. **Crystal Blue Charters** (⊠ Indian Bay, ☎ 784/457–4532, FAX 784/456–2232) offers sportfishing charters for amateur and serious fishermen. **Sunsail** (⊠ Blue Lagoon, ☎ FAX 784/458–4308) has 44-ft crewed sloops from $200 per day; 7- or 10-day packages are available. **TMM St. Vincent Ltd.** (⊠ Blue Lagoon, ☎ 784/456–9608, FAX 784/456–9917) charters catamarans and monohulls for weeklong cruises.

St. Vincent offers hikers and trekkers a choice of experiences: easy, picturesque walks near Kingstown; moderate-effort nature trails in the
central valleys; and exhilarating climbs through a rain forest to the rim
of an active volcano. Bring a hat, long pants, and insect repellent if
you plan to hike in the bush.

A hike up **Dorsetshire Hill,** about 3 mi (5 km) from Kingstown, rewards
you with a sweeping view of city and harbor. You can also see the monument to Black Carib chief Chatoyer, who lost his life in a duel at this
site.

La Soufrière, the queen of climbs, is St. Vincent's active volcano (which
last erupted, appropriately enough, on Friday the 13th, in April, 1979).
Approachable from either the windward or leeward coast, this is *not*
a casual excursion for inexperienced walkers—the massive mountain
covers nearly the entire northern third of the island. Climbs are
all-day excursions. You'll need stamina and sturdy shoes to reach the
top and peep into the mile-wide (1½-km) crater at just over 4,000 ft
(1,219 m). Be sure to check the weather before you leave; hikers have
been sorely disappointed to find a cloud-obscured view at the summit.
A guide ($25–$30) can be arranged through your hotel, the SVG Board
of Tourism, or tour operators. The eastern approach is more popular.
In a four-wheel-drive vehicle, you pass through Rabacca Dry River, north
of Georgetown, and the Bamboo Forest; then it's a two-hour, 3½-mi
(5½-km) hike to the summit. Approaching from the west, near
Châteaubelair, the climb is longer and rougher, but even more scenic.
If you hike up one side and down the other, arrangements must be made
in advance to pick you up at the end.

Trinity Falls, in the north, requires a trip by four-wheel-drive vehicle
from Richmond to the interior, then a steep two-hour climb to a crystal-clear river and three waterfalls, one of which forms a whirlpool where
you can take a refreshing swim. **Vermont Nature Trails** are two hiking
trails that start at the top of the Buccament Valley, 5 mi (8 km) north
of Kingstown. A network of 1½-mi (2½-km) loops passes through
bamboo, evergreen forest, and rain forest. In the late afternoon, you
may be lucky enough to see the rare St. Vincent parrot, *Amazona
guildingii.*

Novices and advanced divers alike will be impressed by the marine life
in SVG waters—brilliant sponges, huge deepwater coral trees, and shallow reefs teeming with colorful fish. Many sites are still virtually un-
explored.

You'll find dive shops on St. Vincent, Bequia, Mustique, Canouan, and
Union, as well as at private resorts on Mayreau, Petit St. Vincent, and
Palm Island. Most offer three-hour beginner "resort" courses, full certification courses, and excursions to reefs, walls, and wrecks found
throughout the Grenadines. A single-tank dive costs about $50; a two-
tank, $95; a 10-dive package, $400. All prices include equipment. It
can't be emphasized enough, however, that the coral reef is extremely
fragile, and you must only look and never touch.

The best dive spots on St. Vincent are in the small bays along the coast
between Kingstown and Layou; many are within 20 yards of shore and
only 20–30 ft (6–9 m) down. **Anchor Reef** has excellent visibility for viewing a deep-black coral garden, schools of squid, seahorses, and maybe
a small octopus. **The Forest,** a shallow dive, is still dramatic, with soft
corals in pastel colors and schools of small fish. **New Guinea Reef** slopes
to 90 ft (28 m) and can't be matched for its quantity of corals and sponges.

A snorkeling trip to **Tobago Cays,** in the southern Grenadines, will allow you to experience some of the best snorkeling in the world. A group of four islands surrounds a shallow reef studded with sponges and coral formations, and populated with countless colorful fish. **Young Island** is also a good place for snorkeling. If you're not a resort guest, phone for permission to take the ferry from Villa Beach over to the island and rent snorkeling equipment from the resort's water-sports center.

Dive St. Vincent (⊠ Young Island Dock, Villa Beach, ☎ 784/457–4928) is where NAUI- and PADI-certified instructor Bill Tewes and his staff offer beginner and certification courses and dive trips to the St. Vincent coast and the southern Grenadines. **Dive Fantasea** (⊠ Villa Beach, ☎ 784/457–4477 or 784/457–5555) offers dive and snorkeling trips to the St. Vincent coast and the Tobago Cays.

Shopping

The 12 blocks that hug the waterfront in downtown Kingstown comprise St. Vincent's main shopping district. Among the shops that sell goods to fulfill household needs are a few that sell local crafts, gifts, and souvenirs. Bargaining is neither expected nor appreciated.

CDS, TAPES, AND RECORDS
To bring back sounds of the islands, stop by **Music World** (⊠ Egmont St., ☎ 784/547–1884), where you'll find the latest reggae, soca, and calypso music on CD or tape.

DUTY-FREE GOODS
In Kingstown, the best place for duty-free shopping is at the **Cruise Ship Terminal** (⊠ Upper Bay St., ☎ 784/456–1830). Among its 26 shops are several that specialize in duty-free goods. A few stores in town also sell luxury goods at duty-free prices. A few shops at the airport sell handicrafts, sundries, and liquor at duty-free prices. At **Gonsalves Duty-Free Liquor** (⊠ Airport Departure Lounge, Arnos Vale, ☎ 784/456–4781), spirits and liqueurs are available at discounts of up to 40%.

HANDICRAFTS
Artisans Craft Shop (⊠ 2nd floor, Bonadie's Plaza, Bay St., ☎ 784/458–2306) sells local crafts, such as straw mats and baskets, woodcraft, pottery, macramé, and hand-painted and tie-dyed clothing. At **FranPaul's Selections** (⊠ 2nd floor, Bonadie's Plaza, Bay St., ☎ 784/456–2662), Francelia St. John fashions dresses, pants, and shirts from colorful fabrics she selects in Trinidad. The emphasis is on African, Afro-Caribbean, and casual wear. **Noah's Arkade** (⊠ Bay St., ☎ 784/457–1513) sells appealing crafts and gifts from all over the Caribbean, as well as T-shirts and a good selection of books on local customs and history. **Nzimbu Browne** (☎ 784/457–1677) creates original art from dried banana leaves, carefully selecting and snipping bits and arranging them on pieces of wood to depict local scenes. His creations are sold at Artisans Craft Shop, but he also sets up shop on Bay Street in front of the Cobblestone Inn. **St. Vincent Craftsmen's Centre** (⊠ Frenches St., ☎ 784/457–1288), three blocks from the wharf, sells locally made grass floor mats, place mats, and other straw items, as well as batik cloth, handmade West Indian dolls, hand-painted calabashes, and framed artwork. The large grass mats can be rolled and folded for easy transport home. No credit cards are accepted.

Nightlife

Nightlife here consists mostly of once-a-week hotel barbecue buffets with local music and jump-ups, so called because the lively steel-band and calypso music makes listeners jump up and dance. At nightspots in Kingstown and at Villa Beach, you can join Vincentians for late-night dancing to live or recorded reggae, hip-hop, and soca music.

CASINO

Emerald Valley Casino (⌧ Peniston Valley, ☎ 784/456–7824) combines the homey atmosphere of an English pub with the gaming of Vegas— roulette, blackjack, Caribbean stud poker, craps, and slots. It's generally open Wednesday–Monday 9 PM–3 AM, and until 4 AM on Saturday.

DANCE AND MUSIC CLUBS

Dance clubs generally charge a cover of $4 (EC$10), slightly more for headliners. At the **Aquatic Club** (⌧ Villa Beach, ☎ 784/458–4205), the rhythmic sounds of soca and reggae reverberate on the waterfront on Saturday night as locals and visitors dance to live music. The **Attic** (⌧ 1 Melville St., ☎ 784/457–2558), above the Kentucky Fried Chicken in Kingstown, features international jazz and blues on Thursday night; weekend parties begin at 10 PM. **Beachcombers** (⌧ Villa Beach, ☎ 784/ 458–4283) has an open-air terrace bar, where you can dance to live music on Friday nights. Kingstown's **Touch Entertainment Centre** (⌧ Grenville St., ☎ 784/457–1825) is a dance hall with disco music on Friday and live music on Saturday. It attracts a local crowd of mostly young people.

THEME NIGHTS

On Wednesday and Friday evenings at **Vee Jay's Rooftop Dining Club** (⌧ Bay St., Kingstown, ☎ 784/457–2845), karaoke accompanies dinner, drinks, and the open-air harbor view. **Young Island Resort** (⌧ Young Island, ☎ 784/458–4826) hosts sunset cocktail parties with hors d'oeuvres every Friday evening at adjacent Ft. Duvernette. Hotel guests and nonguests (with reservations) are ferried from Young Island Resort to the tiny island, where the 100 steps up the hill are lighted by flaming torches. The National String Band plays infectious music on guitars and instruments made of bamboo, bottles, and gourds.

Exploring St. Vincent

Kingstown's shopping and business district, historic churches and cathedrals, and other points of interest can easily be seen in a half day, with another half day for the Botanical Gardens. The coastal roads of St. Vincent offer spectacular panoramas and scenes of island life. The Leeward Highway follows the scenic Caribbean coastline; the Windward Highway follows the more dramatic Atlantic coast. A drive along the windward coast or a boat trip to the Falls of Baleine each requires a full day. Exploring La Soufrière and the Vermont Trails are also major undertakings, requiring a very early start and a full day's strenuous hiking.

Numbers in the margin correspond to points of interest on the St. Vincent map.

Sights to See

4 **Barrouallie.** This was once an important whaling village; now, however, the fishermen of Barrouallie (pronounced *bar*-relly) earn their livelihoods trawling for blackfish, which are actually small pilot whales. The one-hour drive north from Kingstown, on the Leeward Highway, takes you along ridges that drop to the sea, through small villages and lush valleys, and beside picturesque bays with black-sand beaches and safe bathing.

10 **Black Point Tunnel.** In 1815, under the supervision of British colonel Thomas Browne, Carib and African slaves drilled this 300-ft (90-m) tunnel through solid volcanic rock to facilitate the transportation of sugar from estates in the north to the port in Kingstown. The tunnel, an engineering marvel for the times, links Grand Sable with Byrea Bay, just north of Colonarie (pronounced con-a-*ree*).

6 **Falls of Baleine.** They're impossible to reach by car, so book an escorted, all-day boat trip from Villa Beach or the Lagoon Marina. The boat ride up the coast to the falls offers scenic island views. When you arrive, you have to wade through shallow water to get to the beach. Then local guides help you make the easy five-minute trek to the 60-ft (18-m) falls and their rock-enclosed freshwater pool—plan to take a dip.

2 **Ft. Charlotte.** Started by the French in 1786 and completed by the British in 1806, the fort sits on a dramatic promontory 636 ft (195 m) above sea level, with a stunning view of Kingstown and the Grenadines. Interestingly, cannons face inward—the fear of attack by native peoples was far greater than any threat approaching from the sea; though, truth be told, the fort saw no action. Nowadays the fort serves as a signal station for ships; its ancient cells house paintings depicting early island history.

13 **Ft. Duvernette.** The fort was built around 1800, on a massive rock behind Young Island, to defend the bay. Views from the 195-ft (60-m) summit are terrific, but you'll have to climb about 100 steps carved into the rock to get here. Two complete batteries of rusting armaments remain near the top. Arrange your visit at the Young Island Resort (☎ 784/458–4826)—their little ferry will transport you to the fort and bring you back.

1 **Kingstown.** The capital city of St. Vincent and the Grenadines is on the island's southwestern coast. The town of 25,000 residents, about a fourth of the nation's population, wraps around Kingstown Bay; a ring of green hills and ridges, studded with homes, forms a backdrop for the city. This is very much a working city, with a busy harbor and few concessions to tourists.

In fact, **Kingstown Harbour,** the only deepwater port on the island, was always more likely to host a freighter than a passenger ship. However, the island's $14 million Cruise Ship Berth, opened in 2000, has changed that.

What few gift shops there are can be found on and around **Bay Street,** near the harbor. Upper Bay Street, which stretches along the bay front, bustles with daytime activity—workers going about their business and housewives doing their shopping. Many of Kingstown's downtown buildings are built of stone or brick brought to the island in the holds of 18th-century ships as ballast (and replaced with sugar and spices for the return trip to Europe). The Georgian-style stone arches and second-floor overhangs on former warehouses create shelter from midday sun and the brief, cooling showers common to the tropics.

Grenadines Wharf, at the south end of Bay Street, is busy with schooners loading supplies and ferries loading people bound for the Grenadines. The **Cruise Ship Berth,** just south of the commercial wharf, has a duty-free mall with 26 shops, plus restaurants, a post office, communications facilities, and a taxi/minibus queue.

An almost infinite variety of produce fills the new indoor **Kingstown Produce Market,** a two-story building that takes up a whole city block on Upper Bay, Hillsboro, and Bedford Streets in the center of town. It's noisy, colorful, and open Monday–Saturday—but the busiest times (and the best times to go to see all the action) are Friday and Saturday mornings. Upstairs are shops that sell clothing, household items, gifts, and other products.

Little Tokyo, so called because funding for the project was a gift from Japan, is a waterfront shopping area with a bustling indoor fish market and dozens of stalls where you can buy inexpensive homemade meals, drinks, ice cream, bread and cookies, clothing, and trinkets, and even get a haircut.

St. George's Cathedral, on Grenville Street, is a pristine, creamy-yellow Anglican church built in 1820. The dignified Georgian architecture includes simple wooden pews, an ornate chandelier, and beautiful stained-glass windows; one was a gift from Queen Victoria, who actually commissioned it for London's St. Paul's Cathedral in honor of her first grandson. When the artist created an angel with a red robe, she was horrified and sent it abroad. The markers in the cathedral's graveyard recount the history of the island. Across the street is **St. Mary's Cathedral of the Assumption** (Roman Catholic), built in stages beginning in 1823. The strangely appealing design, a blend of Moorish, Georgian, and Romanesque styles applied to black brick, was built in stages beginning in 1823. Nearby, freed slaves built the **Kingstown Methodist Church** in 1841. The exterior is brick, simply decorated with quoins (solid blocks that form the corners), and the roof is held together by metal straps, bolts, and wooden pins. **Scots Kirk** (1839–80) was built by and for Scottish settlers but became a Seventh-Day Adventist church in 1952.

A few minutes north of downtown by taxi is St. Vincent's famous **Botanical Garden.** Founded in 1765, it is the oldest botanical garden in the western hemisphere. Captain Bligh—of *Bounty* fame—brought the first breadfruit tree to this island to feed the slaves. You can see a direct descendant of this tree among the specimen mahogany, rubber, teak, and other tropical trees and shrubs in the 20 acres of gardens. Several rare St. Vincent parrots live in the small aviary. Guides explain all the medicinal and ornamental trees and shrubs; they also appreciate a tip at the end of the tour. ⊠ *Off Leeward Hwy., Montrose,* ☎ *784/457-1003.* 🎫 *$3.* ⊙ *Daily 6–6.*

❸ Layou. Just beyond this small fishing village, about 45 minutes north of Kingstown, are petroglyphs (rock carvings) left by the Caribs 13 centuries ago. If you're seriously interested in archaeological mysteries, you'll want to arrange a visit (through the Tourist Board) with Victor Hendrickson, who owns the land. For $2 Hendrickson or his wife will meet you and escort you to the site.

⑪ Mesopotamia Valley. The rugged, ocean-lashed scenery along St. Vincent's windward coast is the perfect counterpoint to the lush, calm west coast. The fertile Mesopotamia Valley (called "Mespo," for short) offers a panoramic view of dense rainforests, streams, and endless banana plantations. Breadfruit, sweet corn, peanuts, and arrowroot also grow in the rich soil here. The valley is surrounded by mountain ridges, including 3,181-ft (973 m) Grand Bonhomme Mountain, and overlooks the Caribbean.

⑫ Montreal Gardens. Welsh-born landscape designer Timothy Vaughn renovated 7½ acres of neglected commercial flower beds and a falling-apart plantation house into a stunning, yet informal, garden spot. Anthuriums, ginger lilies, birds-of-paradise, and other tropical flowers are planted in raised beds; tree ferns create a canopy of shade along the walkways. The gardens are located in the shadow of majestic Grand Bon Homme mountain, deep in the Mesopotamia Valley, about 12 miles from Kingstown. ⊠ *Montreal St., Mesopotamia,* ☎ *784/458-1198.* 🎫 *$3.* ⊙ *Mon.–Fri. 9–4. Closed Sept.–Nov.*

❼ Owia. The Carib village of Owia, on the island's far northeast coast about two hours from Kingstown, is the home of many descendents of the Carib people of St. Vincent. It is also the location of the Owia Arrowroot Processing Factory. Used for generations to thicken sauces and flavor cookies, arrowroot is now in demand as a finish for computer paper. Close to the village is the **Owia Salt Pond,** where you can take a dip before the long, scenic ride back to Kingstown.

❾ Rabacca Dry River. This rocky gulch just beyond the village of Georgetown was carved out of the earth by the lava flow from the 1902 eruption of nearby **La Soufrière.** When it rains on La Soufrière, the river is no longer dry–and you can be stranded on one side or the other for an hour or two or, in rare cases, longer.

❽ The volcano **La Soufrière,** which last erupted in 1979, is so huge that it covers virtually the entire northern third of the island. The eastern trail to the rim of the crater, a two-hour ascent, begins at Rabacca Dry River.

❺ Wallilabou Bay. You can sunbathe, swim, picnic, or buy your lunch at Wallilabou (pronounced wally-la-*boo*) Anchorage, on the bay. This is a favorite stop for day-trippers returning from the Falls of Baleine, and boaters anchoring for the evening. Nearby there's a river with a small waterfall where you can take a freshwater plunge.

THE GRENADINES

The Grenadine Islands offer excellent sailing opportunities, fine diving and snorkeling, magnificent beaches, and unlimited chances to relax with a picnic, watch boats, and wait for the sun to set. Whether you're seeking peace and quiet or active water sports and informal socializing, you'll be happy in the Grenadines—though each island has a different appeal.

Bequia

Bequia (pronounced *beck*-way) is the Carib word for "island of the cloud." Hilly and green, with several sandy beaches, Bequia is just 9 mi (14½ km) south of St. Vincent's southwestern shore; with a population of 5,000, it's the largest of the Grenadines.

While boatbuilding, whaling, and fishing have been industries here for generations, sailing and Bequia have become almost synonymous. Bequia's picturesque Admiralty Bay is a favored anchorage for private or chartered yachts. The island's airport and regular, frequent ferry service from St. Vincent make this a favorite destination for day-trippers, as well. The ferry docks in Port Elizabeth, a tiny town with waterfront bars, restaurants, and shops where you can buy handmade souvenirs, including the exquisitely detailed model sailboats for which Bequia is famous.

Lodging

For approximate costs, *see* the lodging price chart *in* St. Vincent.

$$$$
★ **🏨 Plantation House.** Perhaps the most sophisticated hostelry on the island, the peach-pink Plantation House sits on 20 manicured acres of lawn and gardens facing Admiralty Bay. The property is punctuated by swaying palms, alabaster statuary, and strategically placed hammocks and lounge chairs. Standard rooms are in 17 garden cabanas; each has a dressing room, twin beds, and a veranda. Five deluxe rooms are on the second floor of the main building; two have verandas that overlook the bay. Five suites are in two beachfront cottages. Rooms are furnished

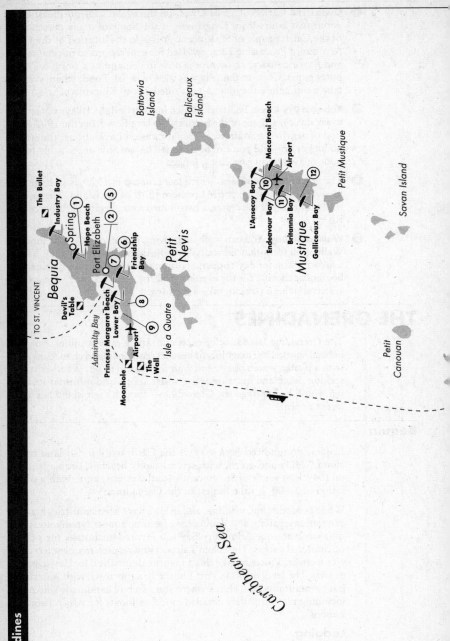

The Bullet
Industry Bay
① Spring
Hope Beach
② —⑤
Bequia
Devil's Table
Port Elizabeth
⑥
⑦ Friendship Bay
Petit Nevis
Princess Margaret Beach
Lower Bay
⑧
Admiralty Bay
Airport
⑨
Isle a Quatre
Moonhole
The Wall
Airport
TO ST. VINCENT

Battowia Island
Baliceaux Island

Macaroni Beach
Airport
⑩ L'Ansecoy Bay
Endeavour Bay
⑪ Britannia Bay
Mustique
Gelliceaux Bay
⑫
Petit Mustique
Savan Island

Petit Canouan

Caribbean Sea

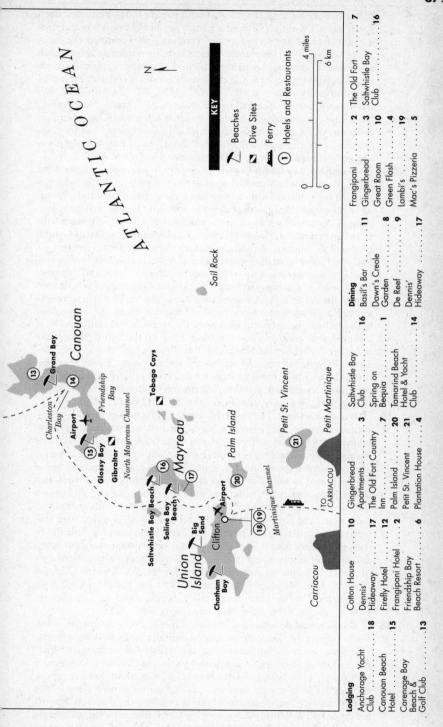

ATLANTIC OCEAN

N

Sail Rock

Canouan

Grand Bay

Charleston Bay

Airport

Friendship Bay

Glossy Bay

Gibraltar

North Mayreau Channel

Tobago Cays

Mayreau

Saltwhistle Bay Beach

Saline Bay Beach

Palm Island

Big Sand

Chatham Bay

Clifton

Airport

Union Island

Martinique Channel

Petit St. Vincent

Petit Martinique

Carriacou

TO CARRIACOU

KEY

↗ Beaches
◢ Dive Sites
⛴ Ferry
① Hotels and Restaurants

0 | 4 miles
0 | 6 km

Lodging

Anchorage Yacht Club 18
Canouan Beach Hotel 15
Carenage Bay Beach & Golf Club 13
Cotton House 10
Dennis' Hideaway 17
The Old Fort Country Inn 12
Firefly Hotel 2
Frangipani Hotel 20
Friendship Bay Beach Resort 6
Gingerbread Apartments 3
Palm Island 21
Petit St. Vincent 4
Plantation House 16
Saltwhistle Bay Club 1
Spring on Bequia 8
Tamarind Beach Hotel & Yacht Club 14

Dining

Basil's Bar 11
Dawn's Creole Garden 9
De Reef 19
Dennis' Hideaway 17
Frangipani 2
Gingerbread 3
Great Room 10
Green Flash 4
Lambi's 19
Mac's Pizzeria 5
The Old Fort 7
Saltwhistle Bay Club 16

with bamboo and textured fabrics in soft pastels and floral prints. Each room has a TV with VCR and a hair dryer. Buffet breakfast and candlelight dinners are served at the Verandah restaurant in the main house. The informal beachfront Green Flash bar-restaurant serves lunch and is also a convivial gathering place in the evening. Taxi-boat service to Princess Margaret Beach (a three-minute ride) is complimentary. ⊠ *Admiralty Bay (Box 16),* ☎ *784/458–3425,* F̅A̅X̅ *784/458–3612,* W̅E̅B̅ *www.hotel-plantation.com. 5 rooms, 5 suites, 17 cabanas. 2 restaurants, 2 bars, air-conditioning, fans, in-room safes, refrigerator, room service, in-room VCRs, pool, tennis court, beach, snorkeling, windsurfing, boating, waterskiing, mountain bikes, shops, piano, baby-sitting, laundry service, meeting room, airport shuttle. AE, MC, V. MAP.*

$$$ 🏨 **Friendship Bay Beach Resort.** This sprawling complex hugs a 1-mi (1½-km) arc of white sand. Rooms are in the main building, which is situated on a hillside with a sweeping view of the sea, and in a group of coral-stone cottages that dot the spacious landscaped grounds. Rooms, decorated with folk art, are small, but each has a terrace with an ocean panorama. Plan to relax, read, enjoy the sun, and surf—you'll find no TVs, phones, or radios to disturb the tranquillity. The open-air Spicy 'n' Herby beach bar and restaurant serves seafood and creole cuisine. On Saturday night there's a barbecue and jump-up, and the rope-swing seats at the bar will keep you upright even after a potent rum punch. Breakfast and occasional candlelight dinners (for special events and holidays) are served in the hotel's Oceanside restaurant, in the main house, where the morning view over the water is especially lovely. If sailing is your pleasure, you can book a trip on the 160-ft, three-mast schooner *Lady Ellen.* ⊠ *Friendship Bay (Box 9),* ☎ *784/458–3222,* F̅A̅X̅ *784/458–3840,* W̅E̅B̅ *www.friendshipbay.com. 27 rooms, 1 suite. 2 restaurants, 2 bars, fans, room service, tennis court, volleyball, beach, dive shop, dock, snorkeling, windsurfing, boating, waterskiing, shops, baby-sitting, laundry service, meeting room. AE, MC, V. CP, MAP.*

$$ 🏨 **Frangipani Hotel.** The venerable Frangipani is an institution—partly
★   because its owner, the Honorable James Mitchell, was the longtime prime minister of SVG and partly because its waterfront bar and its excellent Frangipani restaurant are hangouts for the yachting crowd. The five simple, inexpensive rooms in the original shingle-sided sea captain's home are decorated in old West Indian style, with painted-wood walls and floors, grass rugs, plain furniture, and no air-conditioning; all but one share a bath. The significantly more luxurious garden units are built of local stone and hardwoods and rise on a gentle slope filled with fragrant frangipani trees and bushes. Rooms in these units have tile floors with grass mats, louvered windows and doors, spacious modern baths and dressing rooms, and private verandas with spectacular sunset views of the yacht basin. ⊠ *Admiralty Bay (Box 1),* ☎ *784/458–3255,* F̅A̅X̅ *784/458–3824,* W̅E̅B̅ *www.frangipani.net. 15 rooms. Restaurant, bar, fans, room service, refrigerator, tennis court, beach, dive shop, snorkeling, boating, shops, baby-sitting, laundry service. MC, V. EP.*

$$ 🏨 **Gingerbread Apartments.** Identified by the decorative trellis work
★   on its facade, the Gingerbread faces Admiralty Bay's busy waterfront. The newer units are large, modern, and stylishly decorated, with bedroom alcoves, adjoining salons (with TV), and full kitchens. Downstairs rooms have twin beds and large porches that overlook the bay; upper rooms have king-size four-poster beds and verandas with views of the harbor activity. Each suite has a built-in bed for a third person. Rooms are decorated and furnished in a sophisticated tropical style, with terracotta tiles imported from Italy on the floors, blue-and-white geometric-print bed quilts, sheer mosquito netting gathered over beds, and natural wood and rattan furniture throughout. The bathrooms are large and modern. Weekly rates are available. The Gingerbread restaurant, up-

stairs in the main building, serves full meals; for snacks head to the café at the water's edge. ✉ *Admiralty Bay (Box 1),* ☎ *784/458–3800,* FAX *784/458–3907. 9 suites. Restaurant, bar, café, ice cream parlor, fans, in-room safes, kitchenettes, room service, tennis court, beach, 2 dive shops, snorkeling, boating, baby-sitting, travel services. MC, V. EP.*

$$ 🏨 **The Old Fort Country Inn.** Otmar Schaedle turned a stone sugar-estate manor house, built by the French more than 200 years ago, into a lovely, intimate inn. Surrounded by 30 acres of gardens and perched high on a seaside cliff, the setting is both remote and stunning. The overall decor of chunky hardwoods and exposed stone is a cross between Captain Bligh's cabin and a Provençal farmhouse. Each guest room has a panoramic Grenadine vista—you can see as far as Grenada on a clear day—as well as cooling trade-wind breezes (no need for air-conditioning here). There are six double rooms, all with kitchen facilities. The large Nature Cottage, suitable for 10–14 people, rents by the week. Because the nearest beach, Ravine, is nearly 450 ft (165 m) down a rather steep path and the water is too rough for swimming, the inn is a good choice for romantics and getaway purists who are content with a pool. The Old Fort restaurant is well worth the 10-minute trek from town by car. ✉ *Mt. Pleasant,* ☎ *784/458–3440,* FAX *784/457–3340,* WEB *www.oldfortbequia.com. 6 rooms. Restaurant, bar, kitchenettes, room service, pool, hiking, baby-sitting, laundry service, airport shuttle. MC, V. CP, EP, MAP.*

$$ 🏨 **Spring on Bequia.** Serenity and seclusion reign at Spring on Bequia. It's nestled on the 20 acres of green hills that belong to the 200-year-old Spring Plantation, about 1 mi (1½ km) north of Port Elizabeth. (It's a pretty walk into town, but you may want to take a taxi back uphill.) Two spacious guest rooms with balconies are in a stone-and-wood building called Fort, highest on the hill, with beautiful views of countless coconut palms and the sea. Four large units are in Gull, halfway up the hill, and have similar full or partial ocean views. Other rooms are on the remains of the plantation's original great house and are convenient to the pool, garden, open-air bar, and restaurant. Stroll down to the beach—a 10-minute walk—and you'll pass palm groves, grazing goats, and the ruins of a sugar mill (now overgrown with colorful flowers). ✉ *Spring Bay,* ☎ *784/458–3414,* FAX *784/457–3305; U.S. agent:* ✉ *Spring on Bequia (Box 19251), Minneapolis, MN 55419,* ☎ *612/823–1202. 10 rooms. Restaurant, bar, pool, tennis court, beach, snorkeling. Closed mid-June–Oct. AE, D, MC, V. EP, MAP.*

Dining

Dining on Bequia ranges from casual meals to gourmet cuisine, and the food and service are consistently good. Barbecues at Bequia's hotels mean spicy West Indian seafood, chicken, or beef, plus a buffet of side salads and vegetable dishes and sweet desserts.

For approximate costs, *see* the dining price chart *in* St. Vincent.

CARIBBEAN

$$ ✗ **Frangipani.** Just before sunset, sailors come ashore from yachts
★ bobbing in Admiralty Bay to relax and dine at what is arguably the most popular gathering spot in Bequia—the Frangipani Hotel waterfront bar. After a drink and a chat, the mood turns romantic, with candlelight and excellent Caribbean cuisine in the open-air dining room. The à la carte menu is extensive but emphasizes seafood and local dishes. Each night there's a three-course dinner special. On Monday nights in high season, a local string band plays catchy tunes on both usual (mandolin, guitar) and unusual instruments (bamboo, bottles, gourds); on Friday nights, folksingers entertain the crowd. The Thursday-evening Frangi barbecue buffet (about $30) is accompanied by steel-band

music and a jump-up. ✉ *Belmont Walkway, Admiralty Bay,* ☎ 784/ 458–3255. *Reservations essential. MC, V.*

$$ ✗ Old Fort. Otmar and Sonja Schaedle, owners of The Old Fort Country Inn, restored this mid-1700s estate to its current bougainvillea-shaded, stone-arched, candlelighted beauty and continue to serve food good enough to attract nonguests to its romantic atmosphere with one of the best views—and coolest breezes—on the island. At lunch feast on pumpkin or callaloo soup, crepes, sandwiches, salads, or pasta. At dinner the French creole cuisine focuses on entrées such as spring lamb, tuna steak, langouste Grenadines, or char-grilled whole snapper, accompanied by fresh, homemade bread and curried pigeon peas. ✉ *Mt. Pleasant,* ☎ 784/458–3440. *Reservations essential. MC, V.*

$ ✗ Dawn's Creole Garden. It's worth the walk uphill to the Creole Garden Hotel for the delicious West Indian food and the view. Lunch options include sandwiches, rotis, fresh mutton, "goat water" (a savory soup, with bits of goat meat and root vegetables), fresh fish, or conch. At dinner, the five-course creole seafood, lobster, or vegetarian specials feature the christophene and breadfruit accompaniments for which Dawn's is known. Barbecue is always available on request. The dinner menu changes daily. There's live guitar music most Saturday nights and a barbecue lunch, with live music, right on the beach on Sundays. ✉ *Lower Bay,* ☎ 784/458–3154. *Reservations essential. AE, MC, V.*

$ ✗ De Reef. This café-restaurant on Lower Bay is the primary feeding station for long, lazy beach days. When the café closes at dusk, the restaurant takes over—if you've made reservations, that is. For breakfast (from 7) or light lunch, the café bakes its own breads, croissants, coconut cake, and cookies—and blends fresh juices to accompany them. For a full lunch or dinner, conch, lobster, whelks, and shrimp are treated the West Indian way, and the mutton curry is famous. Every other Saturday in season, there's a seafood buffet dinner accompanied by live music. Sunday lunch is always popular. ✉ *Lower Bay,* ☎ 784/458–3484. *Reservations essential. No credit cards.*

CONTINENTAL

$$ ✗ Green Flash. The informal, waterfront restaurant at the posh Plantation House hotel has an à la carte menu that ranges from pizza and cold buffet at lunch to French, Italian, and local specialties (lobster and fresh grilled fish with regional vegetables) at dinner. On Tuesday evenings check out the creole buffet—a feast of barbecued meats and fish, side salads, vegetable dishes, and an excellent array of pastries— accompanied by live band music. ✉ *Belmont Beach, Admiralty Bay,* ☎ 784/458–3425. *AE, MC, V.*

ECLECTIC

$$ ✗ Gingerbread. The airy second-floor dining room at the Gingerbread Apartments overlooks Admiralty Bay and the waterfront activity. The lunch crowd can enjoy barbecued beef kebabs or chicken with fried potatoes or onions, grilled fish, homemade soups, salads, and sandwiches. In the evening, steaks, seafood, and curries are specialties of the house. Save some room for warm, fresh gingerbread—served here with lemon sauce. In season, dinner is often accompanied by music. ✉ *Belmont Walkway, Admiralty Bay,* ☎ 784/458–3800. *Reservations essential. MC, V.*

PIZZA

$ ✗ Mac's Pizzeria. Overheard at the dock in Mustique: "We're sailing over to Bequia for pizza." The two-hour sunset sail to Admiralty Bay is worth the trip for Mac's pizza. Choose from 14 mouthwatering toppings (including lobster), or select quiche, pita sandwiches, lasagna, or soups and salads. Mac's home-baked cookies and muffins are great for dessert or a snack. To complement your meal, the outdoor terrace offers fuchsia bougainvillea and water views. ⊠ *Belmont Walkway, Admiralty Bay, Port Elizabeth,* ☎ *784/458–3474. Reservations essential. No credit cards.*

Beaches

Bequia offers clean, uncrowded white-sand beaches. Some are within a short walk of the jetty at Port Elizabeth; others require transportation.

Friendship Bay can be reached by land taxi. You can rent windsurfing and snorkeling equipment at Friendship Bay Resort and also grab a bite to eat or a cool drink. Getting to **Hope Beach,** on the Atlantic side, involves a long taxi ride (about $7.50) and a mile-long (1½-km) walk downhill on a semipaved path. Your reward is a magnificent crescent of white sand, total seclusion, and—if you prefer—nude bathing. Be sure to ask your taxi driver to return at a prearranged time. Bring your own lunch and drinks; there are no facilities. Even though the surf is fairly shallow, swimming can be dangerous because of the undertow.

Industry Bay boasts towering palms and a nearly secluded beach. This is a good beach for snorkelers, but there could be a strong undertow. Industry Bay is on the northeast side of the island and requires transportation from Port Elizabeth. Bring a picnic; the nearest facilities are at Spring on Bequia resort, a 10- to 15-minute walk from the beach. **Lower Bay,** a wide, palm-fringed beach that can be reached by taxi or hiking beyond Princess Margaret Beach, is an excellent location for swimming and snorkeling. There are facilities to rent water-sports equipment here, as well as De Reef restaurant. **Princess Margaret Beach,** which is quiet and wide and has a natural stone arch at one end, is a half-hour walk over rocky bluffs from the Plantation House Hotel on Admiralty Bay. Though it has no facilities, it's a popular spot for swimming, snorkeling, or simply relaxing under palm and sea-grape trees.

Outdoor Activities and Sports

BOATING AND SAILING

With regular trade winds, visibility for 30 mi (48 km), and generally calm seas, Bequia is a center for some of the best blue-water sailing opportunities you'll find anywhere in the world. There are all kinds of options: day sails or weekly charters, bareboat or fully crewed, monohulls or catamarans—whatever's your pleasure. Prices for day trips run $60–$75 per person, depending on the destination.

Friendship Rose, an 80-ft schooner, retired after 25 years as a mail boat but was refitted in 1992 to take passengers on day trips from Bequia to Mustique and the Tobago Cays (for information: ☎ FAX 784/458–3373). The 60-ft catamaran **Passion** (⊠ Belmont, ☎ 784/458–3884), custom-built for day sailing, offers all-inclusive daylong snorkeling and/or sportfishing trips from Bequia to Mustique, the Tobago Cays, and St. Vincent's Falls of Baleine. It's also available for private charter. The Frangipani Hotel (☎ 784/458–3255) rents the **S. Y. Pelangi,** a 44-ft cutter, for day sails or longer charters; four guests can be accommodated comfortably, and the cost is $200 per day.

SCUBA DIVING AND SNORKELING

About 35 dive sites around Bequia and nearby islands are accessible within 15 minutes by boat. The leeward side of the 7-mi (11-km) reef that fringes Bequia has been designated a marine park. The best dive sites are **The Bullet,** off Bequia's north point, good for spotting rays, barracuda, and the occasional nurse shark; **Devil's Table,** a shallow dive that's rich in fish and coral and has a sailboat wreck nearby at 90 ft (28 m); **Moonhole,** shallow enough in places for snorkelers to enjoy; and **The Wall,** a 90-ft (28 m) drop off West Cay. Expect to pay dive operators $50 for a one-tank and $95 for a two-tank dive. Dive boats welcome snorkelers, but for the best snorkeling experience, take a water taxi to the bay at Moonhole and arrange a pickup time.

Dive Bequia (✉ Belmont Walkway, Admiralty Bay, ☎ 784/458–3504, FAX 784/458–3886), at the Gingerbread complex in Port Elizabeth, offers dive and snorkel tours, night dives, and full equipment rental. Resort and certification courses are available. **Dive Paradise** (✉ Friendship Bay, ☎ 784/458–3563, FAX 784/457–3115) has two modern dive boats and offers dive packages and certified instruction for beginners and advanced divers, equipment rental, night and wreck dives, and snorkeling packages (but they don't take credit cards).

TENNIS
Public tennis courts are located next to the Bequia airport and can be used by visitors at no charge on a first-come, first-served basis.

Shopping
Bequia's shops are on Front Street and Belmont Walkway, its waterfront extension, just steps from the jetty where the ferry arrives in Port Elizabeth. North of the jetty, there's an open-air market. Farther along the road are the model-boat builders' shops. Opposite the jetty, at Bayshore Mall, shops sell ice cream, baked goods, stationery, gifts, and clothing; a liquor store, pharmacy, travel agent, and bank are also on-site. On Belmont Walkway, south of the jetty, shops and studios showcase gifts and handmade items. Shops are open weekdays 8–5, Saturday 8–noon.

HANDICRAFTS
Long renowned for their boatbuilding skills, Bequians have translated that craftsmanship to model-boat building. In their workshops in Port Elizabeth you can watch as hair-thin lines are attached to delicate sails or individual strips of wood are glued together for decking. Other Bequian artisans work with fabric—designing or hand-painting it first, then creating clothing and gift items for sale.

Crab Hole (✉ Belmont Walkway, ☎ 784/458–3290) sells hand-printed and batik fabric, clothing, and household items. You can see the fabrics being created (and even request your own designs) in the workshop behind the boutique. **Local Color** (✉ Belmont Walkway, ☎ 784/458–3202), above the Porthole restaurant, has an excellent and unusual selection of handmade jewelry, wood carvings, and resort clothing. **Mauvin's Model Boat Shop** (✉ Front St., ☎ no phone) is where you can purchase the handmade model boats for which Bequia is known. You can even special-order a replica of your own yacht. They're incredibly detailed and quite expensive—from a few hundred to several thousand dollars. The simplest ones take about a week to make. **Sargeant's Model Boat Shop** (✉ Front St., ☎ 758/458–3312) is another location where you can buy a handmade model boat or commission one to be built for you.

You can visit the studio of French artist **Claude Victorine** (✉ Lower Bay, ☎ 784/458–3150) and admire her delicate hand-painted silk wall hangings and scarves. Large wall hangings cost $100, scarves $50. Her studio is open from noon to 7 PM; closed Fridays.

SOUVENIRS
Bequia Bookshop (✉ Belmont Walkway, ☎ 784/458–3905) has an exhaustive selection of Caribbean literature, plus cruising guides and charts, Caribbean flags, beach novels, souvenir maps, and exquisite scrimshaw and whalebone penknives hand-carved by Bequian scrimshander Sam McDowell. In the Frangipani Hotel, **Noah's Arkade** (✉ Belmont Walkway, ☎ 784/458–3424) has gifts, souvenirs, and contemporary arts and crafts from all over the Caribbean.

Exploring Bequia

To see the views, villages, beaches, and boatbuilding sites around Bequia, hire a taxi at the jetty in Port Elizabeth. Several usually line up to meet each ferry from St. Vincent. The driver will show you the sights in a couple of hours, point out a place for lunch, and drop you (if you wish) at a beach for swimming and snorkeling. (You can arrange to be picked up later on.) Negotiate the fare in advance; the established rate is $15 per hour.

Water taxis are available for transportation between the jetty in Port Elizabeth and the beaches. The cost is only a couple of dollars per person each way, but keep in mind that most of these operators are not insured: ride at your own risk.

SIGHTS TO SEE

Admiralty Bay. This huge, sheltered bay, on the leeward side of Bequia, is a favorite anchorage of yachtsmen. Throughout the year, it's filled with boats; in season they're moored, literally, cheek by jowl. It's the perfect spot for watching the sun dip over the horizon each evening—either from your boat or from the terrace bar of one of Port Elizabeth's bay-front hotels.

Hamilton Battery. Just north of Port Elizabeth, high above Admiralty Bay, the 18th-century battery was built to protect the harbor from marauders. Today it's a place to enjoy a magnificent view.

Mt. Pleasant. Bequia's highest point (881 ft/270 m) is a reasonable goal for a hiking trek. Alternatively, it's a pleasant drive. The reward is a stunning view of the island and surrounding Grenadines.

The Oldhegg Turtle Sanctuary (☎ 784/458–3245), in the far northeast of the island past Park Beach, is where Orton King, a retired fisherman, tends to endangered hawksbill turtles. He'll be glad to show you around and tell you how his project has increased the turtle population in Bequia. A contribution of $4 is requested.

Port Elizabeth. Bequia's capital is on the northeast side of Admiralty Bay. The ferry from St. Vincent docks at the jetty, in the center of the tiny town that's only a few blocks long and a couple of blocks deep. Walk north along Front Street, which faces the water, to the open-air market, where you can buy local fruits and vegetables and some handicrafts; farther along, you'll find the model-boat builders' workshops for which Bequia is renowned. Walk south along Belmont Walkway, which meanders along the bay front past shops, cafés, restaurants, bars, and hotels.

Whaling Museum. For a $2 admission, you can explore this one-room museum in the former home of the late whaler Athneal Olivierre, who passed away in 2000. The collection of whaling artifacts represents the lifetime career of this brave man, dubbed by locals as "the last of Bequia's harpooners." Even in his ninth decade, Olivierre would still hunt for whales from a sailboat with a handheld harpoon gun. Although a mainstay of the island economy in centuries past, whaling on Bequia is now more of a ritual. The Whaling Museum is in a tiny white-and-blue house on the waterfront in Paget Farm, on Bequia's south coast. Olivierre's son now runs the museum.

Whaling Station. From the front door of the Whaling Museum, you can see the whaling station on Petit Nevis, a small offshore island. This is where the kill is slaughtered, packed up, and shipped out. A limit of three whales per year can be caught in Bequia's waters, but catching even one is, in fact, rare nowadays.

Canouan

Goat herding is still a career choice here. Halfway down the Grenadines chain, this tiny boot-shape island—just 3½ mi (5½ km) long and 1¼ mi (2 km) wide—has only about 1,000 residents; however, it does have three resort hotels, a golf course, and a modern airstrip—with night-landing facilities and regularly scheduled flights from St. Vincent. Canouan (pronounced *can*-no-wan) also claims some of the finest, most pristine white-sand beaches in the Caribbean. Walk, swim, sail, dive, snorkel, or just relax—these are your options. Boats and shoe leather are the usual modes of transportation, so pack light.

Lodging

For approximate costs, *see* the lodging price chart *in* St. Vincent.

$$$$ 🏨 **Canouan Beach Hotel.** Perched on a lovely beach at the southwest end of the island, this all-inclusive hotel attracts French tourists most of the year. Simple white cottages with pastel roofs and trim have patios; most have ocean views. Included in the rates are soft drinks from the bar, rum punch each evening, and French wine with dinner—as well as all water sports, including a catamaran day sail to the Tobago Cays. Twice a week the hotel hosts live music and dancing. ⊠ *S. Glossy Bay (Box 520),* ☎ *784/458–8888,* ℻ *784/458–8875. 32 rooms. Restaurant, bar, grocery, air-conditioning, driving range, tennis court, Ping-Pong, volleyball, beach, dive shop, marina, snorkeling, windsurfing, boating, shops, airport shuttle. AE, MC, V. All-inclusive.*

$$$$ 🏨 **Carenage Bay Beach & Golf Club.** Opened in December 1999, this massive resort is set on 800 private acres surrounding Carenage Bay. Guest rooms are painted in bold colors—burnt orange, yellow, and amber—with terra-cotta tile floors, pale wood furniture, and oversize wicker sofas with large, bright cushions. Floor-to-ceiling louvered doors open to private patios and ocean views. La Piazza restaurant serves Italian cuisine; otherwise, you can dine in the relaxed Beach Club, Surfside Grill, or at the French-style Big Point Casino. Guests can enjoy a full range of water sports, scuba-diving excursions, and sailing opportunities; golfers are drawn to the resort's 18-hole championship course. ⊠ *Carenage Bay,* ☎ *784/458–8000; 800/336–4572; 800/567–4327 in Canada,* ℻ *784/458–8885,* 🕸 *www.canouan.com. 178 rooms. 4 restaurants, 4 bars, room service, air-conditioning, fans, in-room safes, minibars, pool, massage, golf, 3 tennis courts, exercise room, volleyball, windsurfing, boating, shops, casino, nightclub, baby-sitting, laundry service, concierge, meeting room, travel services airport shuttle, car rental. EP.*

$$$$ 🏨 **Tamarind Beach Hotel & Yacht Club.** Thatched roofs are a trademark of this attractive hostelry on reef-protected Grand Bay Beach. Accommodations are in three large two-story buildings that face the beach. Rooms have natural wood walls and are decorated with white wicker furniture (no TVs); louvered wooden doors open onto a spacious veranda with lounge chairs and a beautiful Caribbean vista. Ceiling fans join with the trade winds to keep you cool. The alfresco Palapa Restaurant serves Caribbean specialties, grilled meat or fish, pizzas, and pasta prepared by a European chef. Barbecues and themed dinners (Italian, French, and Caribbean menus) rotate throughout the week. Live Caribbean music is featured regularly at the Pirate Cove bar. The hotel also has a 55-ft catamaran available for day sails to the Tobago Cays. ⊠ *Charlestown,* ☎ *784/458–8044, 800/961–5006, or 800/223–1108;* ℻ *784/458–8851. 42 rooms. 2 restaurants, 2 bars, ice cream parlor, fans, in-room safes, beach, dive shop, marina, snorkeling, windsurfing, boating, fishing, bicycles, shops, baby-sitting, laun-*

dry service, meeting room, travel services, airport shuttle, car rental. AE, MC, V. MAP.

Beaches

Glossy Bay and other beaches along the southwest (windward) coast of Canouan are absolutely spectacular. To reach them, you cross a narrow ridge that runs the length of the island. **Grand Bay,** in the center of the island on the leeward side, is the main beach and the site of Charlestown, the largest settlement, where ferries dock.

Outdoor Activities and Sports

GOLF

Tiny Canouan boasts a challenging golf course. **Carenage Bay Golf Club** (⌂ Carenage Bay, ☎ 784/458–8000), opened in December 1999, is an 18-hole, par-72 course designed by Roy Case on 60 acres of seafront, with an on-site pro shop and bar. Greens fees are $120; club rental and instruction are available.

SCUBA DIVING AND SNORKELING

The mile-long (1½-km) reef and waters surrounding Canouan offer excellent snorkeling opportunities as well as spectacular dives for both novice and experienced divers. **Gibraltar,** a giant stone almost 30 ft (9 m) down, is a popular site; plenty of colorful fish and corals are visible. The crystalline waters surrounding the **Tobago Cays** offer marvelous diving and snorkeling opportunities.

Blueway International (⌂ Tamarind Beach Hotel, ☎ 784/458–8044, FAX 784/458–8851), a full-service dive facility, offers resort and certification courses and dive and snorkel trips to the Tobago Cays, Mayreau, and Palm Island.

Nightlife

Surprise! Canouan has a casino. At the Carenage Bay Beach & Golf Club, the French-style **Big Point Casino** (⌂ Carenage Bay, ☎ 784/458–8000) is open to resort guests and members. Besides the usual slots and tables, it has a nightclub, restaurant, and Club Privé facilities. And at **Villa Le Bijou** (⌂ Charlestown, ☎ 784/458–8025), a small guest house atop a hill overlooking Charlestown, 10 minutes (on foot) from Friendship Bay and 15 minutes from the airstrip, there's a bar with a disco on weekends.

Mayreau

Mayreau (pronounced *my*-ro) is minuscule—just 1½ square mi (4 square km). Farm animals outnumber the 200 or so residents who live in the hilltop village, and there are no proper roads. Guests at the picturesque resort on Saltwhistle Bay enjoy the natural surroundings in one of the prettiest locations in the Grenadines—one of the few spots where the calm Caribbean is separated from the Atlantic by only a narrow strip of beach. It's a favorite stop for boaters, as well. Except for water sports and hiking, there's not much to do–but everyone (locals and visitors alike) prefers it that way. For a day's excursion, you can hike up Mayreau's only hill (wear sturdy shoes) to a stunning view of the Tobago Cays. Then stop for a drink at Dennis' Hideaway and enjoy a swim at Saline Bay Beach, where you may be joined by a few boatloads of cruise-ship passengers. This pretty little island is a favorite stop for small ships that ply the waters of the Grenadines and anchor just offshore for the day. The only access to Mayreau is by boat (ferry, private, or hired), which you can arrange at Union Island.

Lodging

For approximate costs, *see* the lodging price chart *in* St. Vincent.

$$$$ ⊞ **Saltwhistle Bay Club.** This small resort is so cleverly hidden within
its 22 acres of manicured grounds that sailors need binoculars to be sure
it's there at all. Gorgeous Saltwhistle Bay is a half-moon of crystal-clear
water rimmed by ¾ mi (1¼ km) of sparkling white, sandy beach—a favorite anchorage of touring yachtsmen. Each roomy stone cottage has
a name, such as Oleander or Ivora, and is decked out with wooden shutters, ceiling fans, batiks on the walls, a selection of books (no TV), and
a circular stone shower. You can dry your hair on the breezy second-
story veranda atop each two-room bungalow. At the beachside dining
area—individual dining cabanas with stone tables, protected from sun
and the occasional raindrop by thatched roofs—you can enjoy turtle
steak, duckling, lobster, and à la carte lunches. ⊠ *Saltwhistle Bay,* ☎
784/458–8444, FAX *784/458–8944. 10 cottages. Restaurant, bar, fans,
Ping-Pong, volleyball, beach, dive shop, snorkeling, windsurfing, boating, baby-sitting. MC, V. FAP, MAP. Closed Oct.*

$ ⊞ **Dennis' Hideaway.** Dennis (who plays guitar two nights a week) is
a charmer, the seafood is great, the drinks are strong, and the view is
heaven. The rooms in the guest house are clean but very simple: a bed,
a nightstand, a chair, a private bath, and a place to hang some clothes.
⊠ *Saline Bay,* ☎ FAX *784/458–8594. 7 rooms. Restaurant, bar, air-conditioning. No credit cards. EP.*

Beaches

Saline Bay Beach, a beautiful 1-mi (1½-km) curve on the southwest coast,
has no facilities. The dock here is where the ferry from St. Vincent ties
up. **Saltwhistle Bay Beach,** in the north, takes top honors—it's an
exquisite half moon of powdery white sand, shaded by perfectly spaced
palms, seagrapes, and flowering bushes.

Outdoor Activities and Sports

BOATING, FISHING, AND SAILING

Yacht charters, drift fishing trips, and day sails on a 44-ft sailing yacht
can be arranged at Dennis' Hideaway (⊠ Saline Bay, ☎ 784/458–8594).
Expect to pay $40 per person for drift fishing for 1½ hours and $120–
$200 per person (depending on the number of passengers) for a full
day of sailing, swimming, and snorkeling–lunch included.

Mustique

This upscale hideaway, 18 mi (29 km) southeast of St. Vincent, is only
3 mi (5 km) by 1½ mi (2 km) at its widest point. The island is hilly and
has several valleys, each with a sparkling white-sand beach facing an
aquamarine sea. The permanent population is about 300.

Princess Margaret put this small, private island on the map after owner
Colin Tennant (Lord Glenconner) presented her with a 10-acre plot of
land as a wedding gift in 1960 (Tennant had purchased the entire 1,400-
acre island in 1958 for $67,500). The Mustique Company—which Ten-
nant formed in 1968 to develop the copra, sea-island cotton, and
sugarcane estate into the glamorous hideaway it has become—now manages 85 privately owned villas, provides housing for all island employees,
and operates a house-rentals department. Arrangements must be made
about a year in advance to rent the royal holiday home, Les Jolies Eaux,
or another of the 49 luxury villas available for rent that pepper the
northern half of the island.

Sooner or later, stargazers see the resident glitterati (e.g., Mick Jagger,
Elton John, David Bowie, Tommy Hilfiger) at Basil's Bar, the island's
social center. Basil also runs a boutique crammed with clothes and accessories specially commissioned from Bali. A pair of candy-color
buildings, the centerpiece of the tiny village, house a gift shop and cloth-

ing boutique. There's a delicatessen-grocery to stock yachts and supply residents with fresh Brie and Moët; an antiques shop is stocked with fabulous objets d'art for those fabulous villas.

Lodging

For approximate costs, *see* the lodging price chart *in* St. Vincent.

HOTELS

$$$$ ☒ **Cotton House.** The Mustique Company's world-class resort is built
★ around the island's 18th-century plantation house and stone sugar mill (now the boutique), the oldest structures on Mustique. The wraparound terrace on the main house functions as lounge, bar, tearoom, the Great Room restaurant, and social center. A fantastic oceanfront suite and four oceanfront rooms ooze charm. Walkways from private terraces lead to the beach. A quartet of spacious, deluxe ocean-view suites have sunken baths, king-size beds with mosquito nets, and individual terraces with beautiful views. Three charming private cottages, next to the pool, have balcony views of L'Ansecoy Bay. The remainder are deluxe terrace rooms with sweeping views of hillside and ocean. Stone walkways lead to the main house, which is decorated with original artwork and furnishings. The decor is sophisticated yet reflects Caribbean simplicity and light—white walls and ceiling fans, antiques, and rattan furniture. Rooms have dressing areas, French doors and windows, desks with a selection of books, bathrooms with marble fittings, your choice of bed pillows, and perfect peace. Airport transfers and an island tour are included, as are water sports, tennis, and a driver who will chauffeur you to Basil's restaurant or the beach. ⊠ *Endeavour Bay (Box 349)*, ☏ *784/456–4777 or 877/240–9945,* ⅁ᴇ *784/456–5887,* ᴡᴇʙ *www.cottonhouse.net. 12 rooms, 5 suites, 3 cottages. Restaurant, 2 bars, air-conditioning, fans, in-room safes, minibars, pool, massage, 2 tennis courts, horseback riding, 2 beaches, dive shop, snorkeling, windsurfing, boating, shops, library, baby-sitting, meeting room, airport shuttle. AE, D, MC, V. FAP.*

$$$$ ☒ **Firefly Hotel.** Tiny and charming, with just four guest rooms, this exclusive, reclusive three-story aerie is wedged into thick foliage on a hillside above Britannia Bay. One of the island's original villas, it has been transformed into a romantic hideaway with wonderful ocean views. Attractively appointed rooms have fabulous private baths—one with a bathtub protruding into the trees, another with an open-air shower. A full breakfast is included. The restaurant serves Caribbean cuisine, gourmet pizza, and pasta dishes; dinner is in an intimate, candlelit atmosphere. Swim in two pools connected by a waterfall or pack a picnic and spend a day at the beach, just down the (rather steep) garden path. Picnic equipment is provided in each room. Arrangements can be made for scuba-diving trips and other water sports or tennis or horseback riding nearby. Note: Because the inn is on the side of a very steep hill, it is not a suitable choice for people with disabilities or children under 12. ⊠ *Britannia Bay (Box 349)*, ☏ *784/456–3414,* ⅁ᴇ *784/456–3514,* ᴡᴇʙ *www.mustique.com. 4 rooms. Restaurant, 2 bars, minibars, room service, 2 pools, piano. AE, MC, V. CP.*

VILLAS

$$$$ ☒ **Mustique Company.** Villa rentals on Mustique are arranged solely through this company's house-rentals department, even though the villas are privately owned. Renting one of these magnificent homes is not as expensive as you may think, since rates are per villa, not per person—and they include a full staff (with a cook), laundry service, and a vehicle or two. Houses range from rustic (albeit with en-suite bathrooms for every bedroom, phones, pools, cable TVs, VCRs, CD players, and faxes) to extravagant, expansive, faux-Palladian follies with resident butler. All are designer-elegant and immaculately maintained. Villas accommodate up to 12 guests. Rentals run from $2,800 for a two-bedroom villa in the off-season to $25,000 per week for a palatial seven-bedroom, five-staff, two-jeep, one-whirlpool villa during winter. ✉ *House Rentals Dept., Mustique Company Ltd., Box 349, St. Vincent and the Grenadines,* ☎ *784/458–4621 or 800/225–4255,* FAX *784/456–4565 or 203/602–2265,* WEB *mustique-island.com. 50 villas. AE, DC, MC, V. FAP.*

Dining

For approximate costs, *see* the dining price chart *in* St. Vincent.

SEAFOOD

$$$ ✕ **Great Room.** Expect a world-class dining experience on the terrace ★ of the fine Cotton House resort. Executive chef Daniel Pochron and his staff whip up memorable dishes, pairing fresh island ingredients with excellent wines. Each evening a three-course menu du jour is offered, or you can select from the mouthwatering choices on the à la carte menu. Appetizers of conch Napoleon with potato crisps and cucumber or tuna carpaccio with cucumber slaw and candied ginger vinaigrette are every bit as tempting as the entrées—which might include grilled barracuda with thyme-braised potatoes or curry-rubbed chicken breast with coconut rice. A grilled vegetable plate is always available. Homemade ice cream or sorbet may be enough for dessert, if you can blink when the warm chocolate cake is offered. Lunch is served on the terrace, by the pool bar, or packed for you in a picnic basket. Pastas, sandwiches, and light fare are offered—the curried chicken salad in a whole wheat pita is both elegant and filling. ✉ *Endeavour Bay,* ☎ *784/ 456–4777. Reservations essential. AE, D, MC, V.*

$ ✕ **Basil's Bar.** Basil's is *the* place to be—and only partly because it is ★ the *only* place to be aside from the two hotel restaurants. This rustic eatery has a wooden deck built over the waves, a thatched roof, a congenial bar, and a dance floor that's open to the stars—in every sense. You never know what recognizable face may show up at the next table. The food is simple and good—mostly fish hauled from the water 100 yards away, homemade ice cream, burgers and salads, great French toast, the usual cocktails, and unusual wines. It's great to enjoy a quiet breakfast or brunch watching the morning sunshine dance on the water. Wednesday is barbecue and party night; on Monday there's live music. ✉ *Britannia Bay,* ☎ *784/458–4621. Reservations essential for dinner. AE, MC, V.*

Beaches

L'Ansecoy Bay, at the island's very northern tip, is a crescent of white sand with brilliant turquoise water. **Britannia Bay** is best for day-trippers, since it's next to the jetty, and Basil's Bar is convenient for lunch. **Endeavour Bay,** on the northwest coast, is the site of the Cotton House, as well as a dive shop and water-sports equipment rental. **Gelliceaux Bay,** on the southwest coast, is a good beach for snorkelers. **Macaroni Beach** is Mustique's most famous stretch of fine white sand—offering swimming (no lifeguards) in moderate surf that's several shades of blue, a few palm huts, and picnic tables in a shady grove of trees.

Outdoor Activities and Sports

Water-sports facilities are available at the Cotton House, and most villas have equipment of various sorts. Four floodlit tennis courts are near the airport for those whose villa lacks its own; there's a cricket field for the Brits (matches on Sunday afternoon); and motorbikes or "mules" (beach buggies) to ride around the bumpy roads rent for $45 per day.

HORSEBACK RIDING

Mustique is one of the few islands where you can rent a fine horse. Daily excursions leave from the **Equestrian Centre** (⊠ 1 block from airport, ☎ 784/458–4316). Rates are $50 per hour for an island trek, $60 per hour for a surf ride, and $45 per hour for lessons. All rides are accompanied, and children over five years are allowed to ride.

SCUBA DIVING AND SNORKELING

Basil's Bar (☎ 784/458–4621) arranges scuba-diving and snorkeling trips and rents equipment. You can also arrange scuba-diving excursions, instruction, and certification through **Mustique Watersports** (⊠ Cotton House, ☎ 784/456–4777). Rates are $60 for a one-tank dive, and multidive packages are available.

Palm Island

A private speck of land only 100 acres in area, Palm Island is surrounded by five white-sand beaches and is the location of an exquisite resort that was completely renovated in 1999. The views are marvelous—several neighboring islands are almost within spitting distance. Access is via Union Island, 1 mi (1½ km) to the west and a 10-minute boat ride on the resort's launch.

Lodging

For approximate costs, *see* the lodging price chart *in* St. Vincent.

$$$$ 🏨 **Palm Island.** This is a perfect spot for a honeymoon or a rendezvous. After being owned and operated for more than 25 years by the family that transformed uninhabited, swampy, mosquito-infested Prune Island into delightful Palm Island, new owner Rob Barrett (Antigua Resorts, Inc.) has poured millions of dollars into renovations, new buildings, a spectacular pool with a waterfall, along with major infrastructure improvements (e.g., its own desalinization plant) and staff training. Returning guests will notice the new sophistication and luxury, although the atmosphere remains casual and certainly comfortable. What hasn't changed at all are the island's pristine white-sand beaches, a calm aquamarine sea that's perfect for water sports, nature trails for quiet walks, and the peace and solitude you'd expect on a tiny speck of palm-studded sand in the southern Grenadines. A special treat is the snorkeling trip, with picnic lunch, to the nearby Tobago Cays. You can choose palm-view "Plantation" suites or beachfront rooms—or "Coconut Treehouses," which are private residences on stilts at the far side of the island. All guest rooms have custom-designed wicker and bamboo furniture, richly colored fabrics, walls with wooden louvers on three sides to catch every breeze, and original artwork created by a local artist who doubles as the resort's on-call physician should the need arise. The only TV is a 70-in model in the recreation lounge. Meals are well-prepared, and the table service is impeccable. The varied menu always includes fish, meat, and vegetarian entrées. The Sunset Bar & Grill, near the dock, has a light lunch and dinner menu for both guests and nonguests. ⊠ *Palm Island,* ☎ *784/458–8824 or 800/ 345–0356,* FAX *784/458–8804,* WEB *www.palmislandresorts.com. 36 rooms, 4 suites, 7 cottages. 2 restaurants, 2 bars, room service, air-conditioning, fans, in-room safes, refrigerator, pool, massage, tennis court, 5-hole golf course, hiking, 5 beaches, dock, snorkeling, windsurfing, boating, bicycles, recreation room, library, shop, recreation room, airport shuttle. AE, D, DC, MC, V. All-inclusive.*

Petit St. Vincent

The southernmost of St. Vincent's Grenadines, tiny PSV could also be dubbed "Private St. Vincent." It's ringed with white-sand beaches and covered with tropical foliage. Guests are treated royally at the one classy, secluded resort. To get here, you fly into Union Island, where the resort's motor launch meets you for the 30-minute trip.

Lodging

For approximate costs, *see* the lodging price chart *in* St. Vincent.

$$$$ **Petit St. Vincent.** On this very special 113-acre private island, you can indulge in shipwreck fantasies without foregoing the frozen mango daiquiri at sunset, room-service breakfast, and the skills of a great chef. Each of the 22 cottages has a bedroom, a sitting room, and one or two bathrooms—all surrounded by a large, partly covered wooden deck. Tile floors have grass mats. Walls are stone and—on two sides—glass, with patio doors that slide away entirely to take advantage of the breezy trade winds. Despite their rustic appearance, with copra-matting vanities and cobblestone shower stalls, bathrooms conceal fabulous toiletries, robes, beach bags, towels, and an iron—and they have American-style 110-volt, two-prong outlets, so you don't need transformers. No cottage is more than a five-minute walk from dinner, yet each is completely private, with a system of signal flags to convey whims to the staff (who outnumber guests two to one). Hoist your red flag, and nobody *dreams* of approaching; hoist the yellow, and you can promptly receive lunch or dinner, tea or drinks, a ride to the jetty, or a picnic for a day on the "West End." Some prefer the cottages that fringe the windward beach, others enjoy the distant trio high up on the bluff, and still others swear by the three perched above the Atlantic surf, with stone steps to the beach. ✉ *PSV, Box 12506, Cincinnati, OH 45212,* ☎ *784/458–8801, 513/242–1333, or 800/654–9326;* FAX *513/242–6951 or 784/458–8428. 22 cottages. Dining room, bar, room service, tennis court, jogging, beach, snorkeling, boating, shops. AE, MC, V. FAP. Closed Sept.–Oct.*

Union Island

The jagged peaks of Mt. Parnassus soar 900 ft (275 m) in the air, distinguishing Union Island from its neighbors. Union is a particularly popular anchorage for French vacationers sailing the Grenadines and a crossroads for others heading to surrounding islands (Palm, Mayreau, and Petit St. Vincent) just minutes away by speedboat. Clifton, the main town, is small and commercial, with a bustling harbor, three simple beachfront inns, a few restaurants, businesses that cater to yachts, and the regional airstrip—perhaps the busiest in the Eastern Caribbean. Taxis and minibuses are available.

Lodging

For approximate costs, *see* the lodging price chart *in* St. Vincent.

$$ **Anchorage Yacht Club.** Between the airstrip and the waterfront are comfortably furnished seaside rooms and beach bungalows with concealed outdoor showers and terraces that offer great bay views. Grounds are attractive, with flower gardens, palm trees, and a large fish pool. You'll find water-sports and yacht-chartering opportunities galore. The full-service marina creates a cosmopolitan buzz throughout the resort. Rates include breakfast at Les Pieds dans l'Eau, the adjoining restaurant, which also serves a barbecue lunch and French and creole cuisine at dinner. There's a pizza and sandwich counter as well. Each night guests and stranded sailors are serenaded by steel-band, reggae, or piano music in the bar. ⊠ *Clifton,* ☎ *784/458–8221,* FAX *784/458–8365. 10 rooms, 6 bungalows. Restaurant, bar, air-conditioning, beach, dock, snorkeling, boating, marina, fishing, shops. MC, V. CP, FAP, MAP.*

Dining

For approximate costs, *see* the dining price chart *in* St. Vincent.

CARIBBEAN

$ ✕ **Lambi's.** Overlooking the waterfront in Clifton, enjoy Lambi's specialty—delicious conch creole. Lambi is Creole patois for "conch," and the restaurant's walls are even constructed from conch shells. The menu also offers other local seafood and grilled meats. Yachts and dinghies can tie up at the wharf, and there's steel-band music every night in season. ⊠ *Clifton,* ☎ *784/458–8549. No credit cards.*

Beaches

Union has relatively few good beaches, but the trek to **Big Sand,** on the north shore, is worth the effort. The desolate but lovely **Chatham Bay** offers good swimming.

Outdoor Activities and Sports

BOATING AND SAILING

Union is a major base for yacht charters and sailing trips. At **Anchorage Yacht Club** (⊠ Clifton, ☎ 784/458–8221), you can arrange crewed yacht or sailboat charters for a day sail or longer treks around the Grenadines. For example, sailing out of Union to the nearby islands of Mayreau, Canouan, and the Tobago Cays for a full day of snorkeling, fishing, and swimming costs about $200 per person for two people or $120 per person for four or more—lunch and drinks included. The marina is also a good place to stock up on fresh-baked bread and croissants, ice, water, food, and other boat supplies.

SCUBA DIVING AND SNORKELING

Grenadines Dive (⊠ Sunny Grenadines Hotel, Clifton, ☎ 784/458–8138, FAX 784/458–8851), run by NAUI-certified instructor Glenroy Adams, offers Tobago Cays snorkeling trips and wreck dives at the *Purina,* a sunken World War I English gunboat. A single tank dive costs $60; multi-dive packages are discounted. Beginners can take a four-hour resort course, which includes a shallow dive, for $85. Certified divers can rent equipment by the day or week.

ST. VINCENT AND THE GRENADINES A TO Z

To research prices, get advice from other travelers, and book travel arrangements, visit www.fodors.com.

AIR TRAVEL

U.S. visitors fly into St. Vincent's E. T. Joshua Airport. You can take Air Jamaica nonstop from New York (or via Montego Bay from several other U.S. cities) to Barbados or Grenada, with connecting service for the 35-min flight to St. Vincent. Alternatively, take American Airlines/American Eagle from New York or Miami to San Juan, Puerto Rico, then connect with American Eagle to St. Vincent or Canouan. (Additional connections can be made through Barbados, Grenada, Martinique, St. Lucia, or Trinidad.) BWIA flies direct from New York to St. Vincent via St. Lucia and Barbados.

From other parts of the world, connections must be made through major U.S. cities, Toronto, or London and Caribbean hubs, such as San Juan or Barbados.

Regional carriers fly between neighboring islands and St. Vincent, Bequia, Mustique, Canouan, and Union. Air Caraïbe flies between Martinique and St. Vincent, Canouan, and Union islands. Caribbean Star flies to St. Vincent via Antigua, Dominica, Trinidad, and Grenada. LIAT connects St. Vincent and Union with Antigua, Grenada, and St. Lucia. Mustique Airways operates frequent shared-charter service linking St. Vincent with the four airports in the Grenadines, as well as with international connecting flights in Barbados. SVG Air has daily scheduled service between Barbados and Bequia and Mustique; between Grenada/Carriacou and Bequia, Canouan, and Union; and between St. Vincent and Mustique, Canouan, and Union. Other destinations in the Grenadines require a boat ride on either a scheduled ferry, a chartered boat, or a hotel launch.

➤ AIRLINES AND CONTACTS: **Air Jamaica** (☎ 758/453–6611 or 800/523–5585); **American Airlines/American Eagle** (☎ 784/456–5555); **Air Caraïbe** (☎ 784/458–4528 in St. Vincent; 784/458–8888 in Canouan; 784/458–8826 in Union); **BWIA** (☎ 784/627–2942); **Caribbean Star** (☎ 784/456–5800); **HelenAir** (☎ 784/458–4528); **LIAT** (☎ 784/458–4841 in St. Vincent; 784/458–8230 in Union); **Mustique Airways** (☎ 784/458–4380); **SVG Air** (☎ 784/457–5124 in St. Vincent; 784/458–3713 in Bequia; 784/458–8329 in Canouan; 784/458–8882 in Union).

AIRPORTS

St. Vincent's E.T. Joshua Airport is in Arnos Vale, about halfway between Kingstown and Villa Beach. It's a busy airport with night landing equipment, although it only services turboprop aircraft. The St. Vincent Department of Tourism has an information desk in the arrivals hall, where visitors can ask questions or collect maps, brochures, and other information. For departing passengers, there's a snack bar and a few shops that sell souvenirs, handicrafts, and sundry items. The departure lounge has a duty-free liquor shop.

In the Grenadines, Bequia has a small, modern airport with night landing equipment. Mustique, Canouan, and Union islands each have an airstrip with frequent commercial service.

Taxis and buses are readily available at the airport on St. Vincent. The taxi fare to hotels in either Kingstown or the Villa Beach area is about $10 (EC$25); bus fare is less than 50¢ (EC$1). If you have a lot of luggage, take a taxi—buses (minivans) are usually full of passengers. Taxi service is available from the airports on Bequia, Mustique, Canouan, and Union islands.

➤ AIRPORT INFORMATION: On St. Vincent: **E.T. Joshua Airport** (☎ 784/458–4011). On Bequia: **Hon. James F. Mitchell Airport** (☎ 784/458–3948). On Canouan: **Canouan Airport** (☎ 784/458–8049). On Mustique: **Mustique Airport** (☎ 784/458–4621). On Union: **Union Airport** (☎ 784/458–8750).

BOAT AND FERRY TRAVEL

St. Vincent is extremely proud of its new Cruise Ship Terminal, in Kingstown, which had been on the drawing board for several years and finally opened in January 2001 after recovering from severe water damage from Hurricane Lenny just weeks before its planned grand opening in November 1999. The berths can accommodate two or four ships, depending on their size, at one time. At the terminal building, arriving passengers will find a bank, post office, communications facility, tourism office, restaurant, food courts, and two dozen shops offering local goods (spices and seasonings, shellwork, leather goods, art and wood carvings, clothing, and straw mats) and duty-free items. Tour buses depart from the terminal, and visitors opting for a day in Bequia can board the ferry at an adjacent wharf.

FARES AND SCHEDULES

All scheduled ferries leave St. Vincent from Grenadines Wharf in Kingstown and from Port Elizabeth on Bequia. Hotels and the tourist information desk at the airport can provide current interisland schedules and fares. The one-way trip between St. Vincent and Bequia takes 60 minutes and costs $6 (EC$15) each way.

MV *Admiral I* and MV *Admiral II* make several round-trips between Bequia and Kingstown Monday–Saturday beginning at 6:30 AM in Bequia and 8 AM in St. Vincent; the latest departure each day is at 5 PM from Bequia and 7 PM from Kingstown. On Sunday the one round-trip leaves St. Vincent at 9 AM and returns from Bequia at 5 PM.

MV *Barracuda* leaves St. Vincent on Monday and Thursday mornings, stopping in Bequia, Canouan, Mayreau, and Union Island. It makes the return trip Tuesday and Friday. On Saturday it does the round-trip from St. Vincent to each island and returns in a day. Including stopover time, the trip takes 3¼ hours from St. Vincent to Canouan ($5), 4½ hours to Mayreau ($6), and 5¼ hours to Union Island ($8).

MV *Bequia Express* travels between Kingstown and Bequia, making two or three trips daily, including holidays.
➤ BOAT AND FERRY INFORMATION: **MV** *Admiral I* **and MV** *Admiral II* (☎ FAX 784/458–3348); **MV** *Barracuda* (☎ 784/456–5180); **MV** *Bequia Express* (☎ 784/458–3472).

BUSINESS HOURS

BANKS

Banks are open Monday–Thursday 8–1, 2, or 3, Friday until 5. The bank at the airport is open Monday–Saturday 7–5. Bank branches on Bequia, Canouan, and Union are open Monday–Thursday 8–1 and Friday 8–5.

POST OFFICES

The General Post Office, on Halifax Street in Kingstown, is open daily 8:30–3, Saturday 8:30–11:30.

SHOPS

Shops and businesses in Kingstown are open weekdays 8–4; many close for lunch noon–1. Saturday hours are 8–noon. Shops are closed on Sunday, but supermarkets in Kingstown and Arnos Vale are open Sunday mornings.

BUS TRAVEL

Public buses on St. Vincent are really privately owned, brightly painted minivans with colorful names like *Confidence, Mouse, Irie,* and *Who to Blame.* Bus fares range from 37¢–$2.25 (EC$1–EC $6) on St. Vincent; the 10-minute ride from Kingstown to Villa Beach, for example, costs 58¢ (EC$1.50). Buses operate from early morning until about midnight, and routes are indicated on a sign in the windshield. Just wave from the road or point your finger to the ground as a bus approaches, and the driver will stop. When you want to get out, signal by knocking twice on a window. A conductor rides along to open the door and collect fares; it's helpful to have the correct change in EC coins. In Kingstown, the bus terminal is near Market Square. Buses serve the entire island, although trips to remote villages are infrequent.

CAR RENTALS

Rental cars cost about $55 per day or $300 a week, with some free miles. Unless you already have an international driver's license, you'll need to buy a temporary local permit for $20 (EC$50), valid for six months. To get one, you'll need to present your valid driver's license at the police station on Bay Street or the Licensing Authority on Halifax Street in Kingstown.

Among the car-rental firms on St. Vincent are Avis Rent-A-Car–the one international agency represented on St. Vincent. Avis offers rates that are competitive with local firms. Ben's Auto Rental is located two minutes from the airport and offers all-terrain vehicles as well as cars. David's Auto Clinic, just south of Kingstown and not far from the airport, offers reliable vehicles at reasonable rates. Kim's Rentals, has been renting cars and jeeps on St. Vincent for nearly 40 years. Star Garage is right in town and rents minivans and buses, in addition to cars and four-wheel drive vehicles.

If you want to rent a four-wheel drive vehicle in Bequia, try B&G Jeep Rental. For a car during your stay on Bequia, check out Phil's Car Rental.

➤ MAJOR AGENCIES: **Avis Rent-A-Car** (✉ Airport, ☎ 784/456–2929); **B&G Jeep Rental** (✉ Port Elizabeth, ☎ 784/458–3760); **Ben's Auto Rental** (✉ Arnos Vale, ☎ 784/456–2907); **David's Auto Clinic** (✉ Sion Hill, ☎ 784/456–4026); **Kim's Rentals** (✉ Grenville St., Kingstown, ☎ 784/456–1884); **Phil's Car Rental** (✉ Port Elizabeth, ☎ 784/458–3304); **Star Garage** (✉ Grenville St., Kingstown, ☎ 784/456–1743).

CAR TRAVEL

About 300 mi (484 km) of paved road wind around St. Vincent's perimeter, except for a section in the far north with no road at all, precluding a circle tour of the island. A few roads jut into the interior a few miles, and only one east-west road (through the Mesopotamia Valley) bisects the island. It's virtually impossible to get lost.

GASOLINE

Gasoline costs about $2.50 per gallon.

ROAD CONDITIONS

Although major improvements are being made, roads are usually not marked and not always well maintained. Roads are narrow in the country, often not wide enough for two cars to pass, and people (including schoolchildren), dogs, goats, and chickens often share the roadway. Outside populated areas, they can be bumpy and potholed; be sure your rental car has proper tire-changing equipment and a spare in the trunk.

RULES OF THE ROAD

Be sure to drive on the left, and honk your horn before you enter blind curves out in the countryside—you'll encounter plenty of steep hills and hairpin turns.

ELECTRICITY

Electricity is generally 220/240 volts, 50 cycles; Petit St. Vincent has 110 volts/60 cycles (U.S. standard). Some resorts also have 110-volt current; most have 110-volt shaver outlets. Dual-voltage computers or small appliances will still require a plug adapter. Some hotels will lend transformers and/or plug adapters.

EMERGENCIES

ST. VINCENT

➤ AMBULANCE AND FIRE: Dial ☎ 999.

➤ COAST GUARD: Dial ☎ 784/457–4578.

➤ HOSPITALS: **Kingstown General Hospital** ☎ 784/456–1185.

➤ PHARMACIES: **Davis Drugmart** (✉ Tyrrell and McCoy Sts., Kingstown, ☎ 784/456–1174); **Deane's** (✉ Middle St., Kingstown, ☎ 784/457–2877); **People's Pharmacy** (✉ Bedford St., Kingstown, ☎ 784/456–1170).

➤ POLICE: Dial ☎ 999 for emergencies and (☎ 784/457–1211) for non-emergencies.

THE GRENADINES

➤ AMBULANCE AND FIRE: Dial ☎ 999.

➤ HOSPITALS: **Bequia Casualty Hospital** (✉ Port Elizabeth, ☎ 784/458–3294); **Canouan Clinic** (✉ Charlestown, ☎ 784/458–8305); **Mustique Company Island Clinic** (✉ Adjacent to Mustique Airport, ☎ 784/458–4621 ext. 353); **Union Island Health Centre** (✉ Clifton, ☎ 784/458–8339).

➤ PHARMACIES: On Bequia, **Imperial Pharmacy** (✉ Back St., Port Elizabeth, ☎ 784/458–3373); **People's Pharmacy** (✉ Port Elizabeth, ☎ 784/458–3936).

➤ POLICE: Dial ☎ 999.

ETIQUETTE AND BEHAVIOR

People are friendly, helpful, and photogenic. But if you wish to photograph them, their families, or their property, ask permission first—and offer a small tip as a gesture of appreciation.

Except in the evenings at the fanciest hotel restaurants, dress is extremely casual—particularly in the Grenadines. Keep in mind, however, that in St. Vincent, as throughout the Caribbean, local people dress modestly and expect visitors to do the same. Swimsuits and short-shorts are for beach and boat; cover up in town.

FESTIVALS AND SEASONAL EVENTS

The National Music Festival is held at Kingstown's Memorial Hall during March and April. The best in Vincentian music and song is presented—folk songs and calypso, solos and duets, choirs and group ensembles. Fisherman's Day (Labour Day, which falls on the first Monday in May) marks the end of a week's activities honoring the fisherman's contribution to the economy. All kinds of fishing competitions take place. Vincy Mas, St. Vincent's Carnival, is the biggest festival of the year, with street parades, costumes, calypso, steel bands, food and drink, and the crowning of Miss Carnival and the Soca Monarch. It begins in late June, builds in intensity through the first two weeks in July, and culminates in a calypso competition on the final Sunday (Dimanche Gras), a huge street party (Jouvert) on the final Monday, and a Parade of Bands on the final Tuesday. The National Dance Festival is held in September each year at Kingstown's Memorial Hall, with presentations of traditional, folk, ballroom, ballet, and tap dancing. Arts and crafts exhibitions, caroling, and street parties with music and dancing mark the Nine Mornings Festival, which occurs during the nine days immediately before Christmas.

On Bequia, the Easter Regatta is held during the four-day Easter weekend. Revelers gather to watch boat races and celebrate Bequia's seafaring traditions with food, music, dancing, and competitive games. The Bequia Carnival, with calypso music and revelry, is a four-day celebration held in late June, just prior to St. Vincent's Carnival. On Canouan, the Canouan Yacht Races are held in August. Besides competitive boat races and sailing events, there are fishing contests, calypso competitions, donkey and crab races, and a beauty pageant. On Union, Easterval occurs during the Easter weekend. Festivities include boat races, sports and games, a calypso competition, a beauty pageant, and a cultural show featuring the Big Drum Dance (derived from French and African traditions). Union is one of the few islands (along with Grenada's Carriacou) that perpetuates this festive dance.

HEALTH

Water from the tap is safe to drink, but bottled water is available. Fresh fruits and vegetables from the market are safe to eat, but (as at home) you should wash them first. Cooked food purchased at the market, in small shops, or at village snackettes is wholesome and safe for visitors to enjoy.

Insects can be a minor problem on the beach during the day–particularly in the southern Grenadines. When hiking and sitting outdoors in the evening, though, you'll be glad to have industrial-strength mosquito repellant. Sea urchins are spiny black sea creatures that sit on sand and in shallow water. If you step on one you can put away your dancing shoes. It's painful! Rubbing a little lime or an ammonia-based liquid (such as urine!) on the wound may help. The manchineel tree (found along the beachfront) has little green apples that look tempting but are toxic. Even touching the sap of the leaves will cause an uncomfortable rash, and you should not take shelter beneath one during a rainstorm. Most manchineels on hotel grounds are marked with signs; in remote areas, the bark may be painted with a red stripe. Hikers should watch for brazilwood trees and bushes, which can cause a reaction similar to poison ivy. And don't sit under a coconut tree—if a coconut should fall, and they do, you could get a nasty bump on the head.

HOLIDAYS
New Year's Day, National Heroes Day (Mar. 13), Good Friday (Mar. 29, 2002), Easter Monday (Apr. 1, 2002), May Day (first Monday in May), Whit Monday (May 20, 2002), Caricom Day (July 2), Carnival Tuesday (July 11, 2002), August Monday (first Mon. in Aug.), Independence Day (Oct. 27), Christmas, and Boxing Day (Dec. 26).

LANGUAGE
English is spoken throughout St. Vincent and the Grenadines. Although there's certainly a Caribbean lilt, you won't hear the Creole patois common on other islands that have a historical French presence. One term to listen for is "jump-up," in which case you can expect a party with music and dancing. And if you're going to "lime" at the next "gap," you'll be hanging out (probably at the bar) down the road.

MAIL AND SHIPPING
The General Post Office is on Halifax Street in Kingstown. Most villages have branch offices. Airmail postcards cost EC60¢ to the United States, Canada, the United Kingdom, Australia, and New Zealand; airmail letters cost EC90¢ per ounce to the United States and Canada; EC$1.10 to the United Kingdom, Australia, and New Zealand. When writing to a location in the Grenadines, the address on the envelope should always indicate the specific island name followed by "St. Vincent and the Grenadines, West Indies."

MONEY MATTERS
Prices quoted in this chapter are in U.S. dollars unless otherwise noted.

ATMS
ATMs are located at banks in Kingstown and at their branches.

BANKS
Several regional and international banks are located in Kingstown, with branches elsewhere on St. Vincent and in the Grenadines.
➤ IN ST. VINCENT: **Bank of Nova Scotia** (Scotiabank) (✉ Halifax St., Kingstown, ☎ 784/457–1601); **Barclays Bank** (✉ Halifax St., Kingstown, ☎ 784/456–1706); **National Commercial Bank of St. Vincent** (✉ Bedford St., Kingstown, ☎ 784/457–1844; ✉ E. T. Joshua Airport, ✉ Arnos Vale, Kingstown, ☎ 784/458–4943).
➤ IN THE GRENADINES: **Barclays Bank** on Bequia, (✉ Port Elizabeth, ☎ 784/458–3215); **National Commercial Bank of St. Vincent** (✉ Port

Elizabeth, ☎ 784/458–3700); Canouan, ✉ Charlestown, ☎ 784/458–8595; Union Island, ✉ Clifton, ☎ 784/458–8347).

Major credit cards—including Access, American Express, Diners Club, Discover, Eurocard, MasterCard, and Visa—and traveler's checks are accepted by hotels, car-rental agencies, and some shops and restaurants.

Although U.S. dollars are accepted nearly everywhere, Eastern Caribbean currency (EC$) is the official currency and preferred. The exchange rate is fixed at EC$2.67 to US$1. Price quotes in shops are often given in both currencies. Large U.S. bills may be difficult to change in small shops. U.S. coins are not accepted anywhere.

PASSPORTS AND VISAS
U.S., Canadian, and U.K. travelers need a valid passport or a birth certificate with a raised seal and a government-issued photo ID. Travelers from other countries must present a valid passport. All visitors must hold return or ongoing tickets.

SAFETY
There's relatively little crime here, but don't tempt fate by leaving your valuables lying around or your room or rental car unlocked. Also, be alert and mindful of your belongings around the wharf area in Kingstown; it's congested when passengers are disembarking from ferries or cruise ships.

SIGHTSEEING TOURS
Several operators offer sightseeing tours on land or by sea. Per-person prices range from $20 for a two-hour tour to St. Vincent's Botanical Gardens to $140 for a day sail to the Grenadines. A full day tour around Kingstown and either the leeward or windward coast, including lunch, will cost about $50 per person.

You can arrange informal land tours through taxi drivers, who double as knowledgeable guides. Expect to pay $25 per hour for up to four people.

On St. Vincent, Baleine Tours offers scenic coastal trips to the Falls of Baleine as well as charters to Bequia and Mustique, deep-sea fishing trips, and snorkeling excursions to the Tobago Cays. Calypso Tours has a 42-ft tour boat for trips to the Falls of Baleine, Bequia, Mustique, and the Tobago Cays. Fantasea Tours will take you by speedboat to the Falls of Baleine, Bequia and Mustique, or to the Tobago Cays for snorkeling. For bird-watchers, hikers, and ecotourists, HazECO Tours offers wilderness tours and hikes to enjoy the natural beauty and see historic sites throughout St. Vincent. Sailor's Wilderness Tours run the gamut, from a comfortable sightseeing drive (by day or by moonlight) to mountain biking on remote trails or a strenuous hike up the La Soufrière volcano. Sam's Taxi Tours offers half- or full-day tours of St. Vincent, as well as hiking tours to La Soufrière and scenic walks along the Vermont Nature Trails. Sam's also operates on Bequia, where a sightseeing tour includes snorkeling at Friendship Bay. SVG Tours has several hiking itineraries for St. Vincent and sailing day trips to the Grenadines.

➤ CONTACTS: **Baleine Tours** (✉ Villa Beach, ☎ 784/457–4089); **Calypso Tours** (✉ Blue Lagoon, ☎ 784/456–1746); **Fantasea Tours** (✉ Villa Beach, ☎ 784/457–4477); **HazECO Tours** (✉ Kingstown, ☎ 784/457–8634); **Sailor's Wilderness Tours** (✉ Middle St. Kingstown, ☎ 784/457–1712); **Sam's Taxi Tours** (✉ Cane Garden, ☎ 784/456–4338; or 784/458–3686 in Bequia); **SVG Tours** (✉ Kingstown, ☎ 784/458–4534).

TAXES

The departure tax from St. Vincent and the Grenadines is $12 (EC$30), payable in either currency; children under 12 are exempt.

SALES TAX
A government tax of 7% is added to hotel bills.

TAXIS

Fares are set by the government, but it's smart to settle on the price before entering the taxi—and be sure you know what currency is being quoted. Between Kingstown and the hotels and restaurants at Villa Beach, the one-way fare is about $10.

On some islands, most notably Bequia, water taxis can take you to and from the beaches for a couple of dollars each way. Keep in mind that these taxi operators aren't regulated or insured: travel at your own risk.

TELEPHONES

St. Vincent and the Grenadines has a fully digitized telephone system, with international direct dialing available throughout the entire area. Pay phones are readily available and best operated with the prepaid phone cards sold at many stores.

COUNTRY AND AREA CODES
The area code for St. Vincent and the Grenadines is 784.

E-MAIL
To check your E-mail, Internet access is available for a small fee at Office Essentials, Ltd. (✉ Bonadie's Plaza, Middle St., Kingstown, ☎ 784/457–2235).

INTERNATIONAL CALLS
For an international operator, dial ☎ 115; for international credit-card calls, dial ☎ 111.

LOCAL CALLS
Local calls are free from private phones and most hotels. For local directory assistance, dial ☎ 118. Prepaid phone cards, which can be used in special cardphones throughout St. Vincent and other Caribbean islands, are sold at shops, transportation centers, and other convenient outlets. (The phone cards can be used for local or international calls.)

TIPPING

Hotels and restaurants generally add a 10% service charge to the tab. If the charge hasn't been added, a gratuity at that rate is appropriate. Otherwise, tipping is expected only for special service.

VISITOR INFORMATION

➤ Before you leave: **St. Vincent and the Grenadines Tourist Office** (✉ 801 2nd Ave., 21st floor, New York, NY 10017, ☎ 212/687–4981 or 800/729–1726, FAX 212/949–5946; ✉ 6505 Cove Creek Pl., Dallas, TX 75240, ☎ 972/239–6451 or 800/235–3029, FAX 972/239–1002; ✉ 32 Park Rd., Toronto, Ontario M4W 2N4, Canada, ☎ 416/924–5796, FAX 416/924–5844; ✉ 10 Kensington Ct., London W8 5DL, U.K., ☎ 0207/937–6570, FAX 0207/937–3611). For St. Vincent and the Grenadines general information on the Internet, WEB www.svg-tourism.com. For St. Vincent and the Grenadines Hotel & Tourism Association information on the Internet, WEB www.svghotels.com.
➤ In St. Vincent and the Grenadines: The **St. Vincent and the Grenadines Department of Tourism** (✉ Box 834, Administrative Centre, Upper Bay St., Kingstown, ☎ 784/457–1502, FAX 784/456–2610, WEB

www.svgtourism.com; ✉ Port Elizabeth wharf, Port Elizabeth, Bequia, ☎ 784/458–3286; ✉ Union airport, Clifton, Union, ☎ 784/458–8350).

Tourist information desks are located in the arrivals area of St. Vincent's E. T. Joshua Airport (☎ 784/458–4685), at the Cruise Ship Terminal in Kingstown, (☎ 784/456–1830), and at the SVG Air/Mustique Airways desk in the arrivals hall at Grantley Adams International Airport on Barbados (☎ 246/428–0961).

23 TRINIDAD AND TOBAGO

Updated by
Vernon
O'Reilly-
Ramesar

The boat slides lazily through the brackish waters of the Caroni Bird Sanctuary. On either side of the channel the twisted fairytale roots of the mangrove trees seem locked in some eternal struggle. Curious caimans slice noiselessly through the water, and large snakes hang in the branches of the trees. In the distance the emerald-clad Northern Range rises imperiously toward an azure sky. All the world seems at peace. The small boat turns a corner and you are suddenly in a large lake surrounded by the mangrove forest. Then, as if on cue, the sky turns red—confusing the senses—the scarlet ibis have returned home in their thousands to settle in for the evening. Every tree is now cloaked with red birds—what was green is now red—squawking in appreciation of their own magnificent show. Thousands of performances behind them and no end in sight.

From the beat of calypso and *soca* to the steady tapping of raindrops accompanied by birdsong, Trinidad and Tobago offer cultural and natural diversions that are refreshing, vivid, and alive. This two-island republic—T&T, as it's commonly called—is the southernmost link in the Antillean island chain, lying some 9 mi (14½ km) off the coast of Venezuela and safely outside the path of all those devastating Caribbean hurricanes. Both Trinidad and Tobago are more geologically akin to continental South America than they are to other Caribbean islands: Tobago's Main Ridge and Trinidad's Northern Range are believed to represent the farthest reaches of the Andes Mountains. But although the two islands are linked geographically and politically, in some ways they could not be more dissimilar.

Trinidad's growth arose out of oil prosperity—it remains one of the largest petroleum producers in the western hemisphere—which made it a prime destination for business travelers. They enjoy the sophisticated shopping, restaurants, and hotels in the republic's lively capital,

Port-of-Spain, partying late into the night to the syncopated steel-band sounds that originated in Trinidad.

Port-of-Spain is still one of the most active commercial cities in the West Indies. The cultural scene is as vital as ever, especially during the country's riotous Carnival—a period of festivities, concerts, and shows that begins after Christmas and culminates in a two-day street parade that ends on Ash Wednesday. The capital is home to around 51,000 of Trinidad's 1.3 million residents—Africans, Indians, Americans, Europeans, and Asians, each culture with its own language and customs (though the official language is English). About a quarter of the population is Hindu, which is why there's an abundance of East Indian festivals, religious celebrations, and delicious East Indian food. Outside Port-of-Spain you'll find good beaches and many other natural attractions, though there are currently few hotels that offer more than bare-bones comfort.

On Tobago, 22 mi (35 km) away, the pace of life is slower, and seclusion is easier to find. Though a variety of seaside lodgings beckons, you can still lazily explore unspoiled rain forests, coral reefs, and a largely undeveloped coastline—for now, anyway. Tourism is a growing industry, and the number of hotel rooms has been growing dramatically. If this goes unchecked, Tobago could lose its idyllic quality.

Columbus reached these islands on his third voyage, in 1498. Three prominent peaks around the southern bay of Trinidad prompted him to name the land La Trinidad, after the Holy Trinity. Trinidad was captured by British forces in 1797, ending 300 years of Spanish rule. Tobago's history is more complicated. It was "discovered" by the British in 1508. The Spanish, Dutch, French, and British all fought for it until it was ceded to England under the Treaty of Paris in 1814. In 1962 both islands gained their independence within the British Commonwealth, finally becoming a republic in 1976.

TRINIDAD

Lodging

Trinidad accommodations range from charming guest houses to large business hotels; most acceptable establishments, however, are within the vicinity of Port-of-Spain, far from any beach. Most places offer breakfast and dinner for an additional flat rate (MAP). Port-of-Spain has a small downtown core—with a main shopping area along Frederick Street—and is surrounded by inner and outer suburbs. The inner areas include Belmont, Woodbrook, Newtown, St. Clair, St. Ann's, St. James, and Cascade. The number of private homes in Trinidad that offer bed-and-breakfast accommodations is growing each year. Contact the **Trinidad and Tobago Bed and Breakfast Co-Operative Society** (⊠ 1 Wrightson Rd., Port-of-Spain, ☎ FAX 868/627–2337) for a list of establishments. Regardless of the type of accommodation, be prepared to book far in advance (and to pay a good deal more) for stays during Carnival season.

CATEGORY	COST*
$$$$	over $175
$$$	$100–$175
$$	$60–$100
$	under $60

All prices are for a standard double room, excluding 15% tax and 10% service charge.

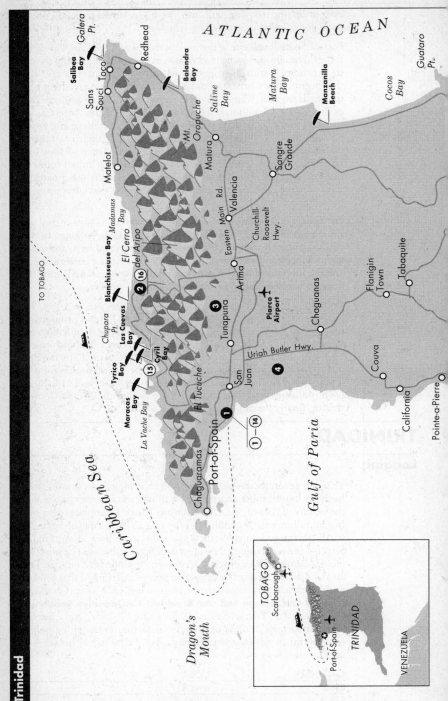

Trinidad

ATLANTIC OCEAN

Caribbean Sea

Gulf of Paria

Dragon's Mouth

Port-of-Spain

TO TOBAGO

TOBAGO
Scarborough
TRINIDAD
Port-of-Spain
VENEZUELA

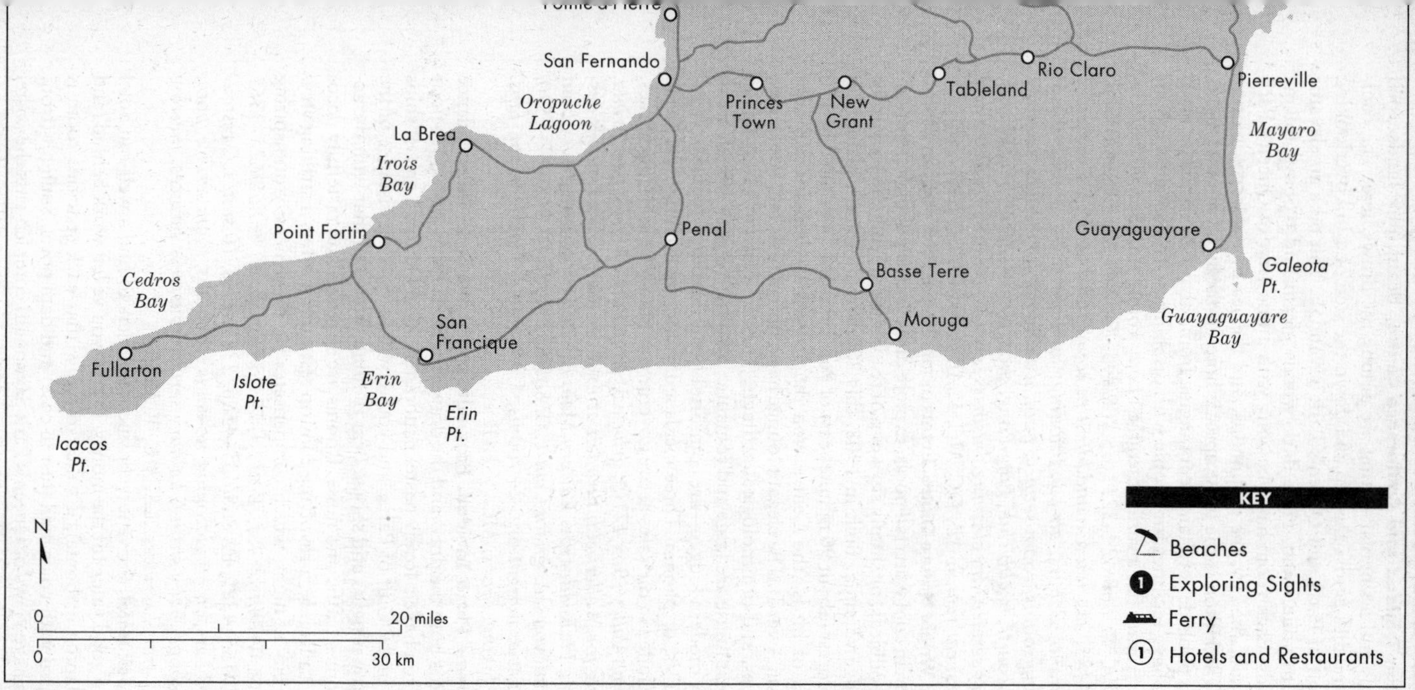

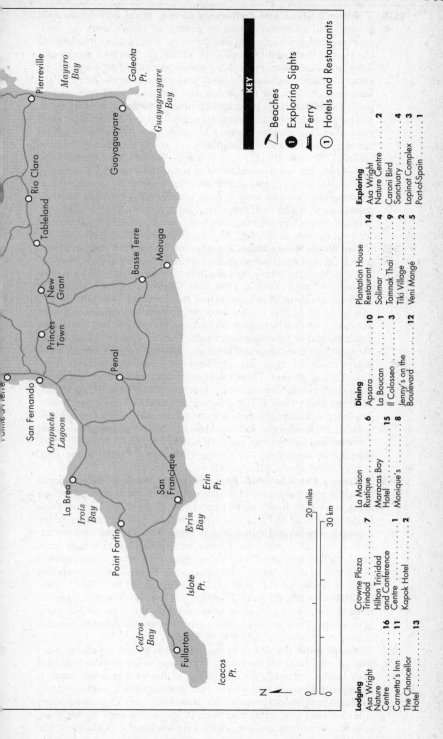

Lodging
- Asa Wright Nature Centre 16
- Carnetta's Inn 11
- The Chancellor Hotel 13
- Crowne Plaza Trindad 7
- Hilton Trinidad and Conference Centre 1
- Kapok Hotel 2
- La Maison Rustique 6
- Maracas Bay Hotel 15
- Monique's 8

Dining
- Apsara 10
- La Boucan 1
- Il Colosseo 3
- Jenny's on the Boulevard 12
- Plantation House Restaurant 14
- Solimar 4
- Tamnak Thai 9
- Tiki Village 2
- Veni Mangé 5

Exploring
- Asa Wright Nature Centre 2
- Caroni Bird Sanctuary 4
- Lopinot Complex 3
- Port-of-Spain 1

$$$$ 🏨 **Hilton Trinidad and Conference Centre.** Beautifully landscaped
★ grounds and a singular setting are among the draws here. The complex stretches across the top and down the side of a hill overlooking
the Gulf of Paria and Queen's Park Savannah. You take an elevator
down to your room. Here dark woods gleam and tropical foliage
abounds. Each room has a balcony with a fine view of Queen's Park
Savannah, the city, the mountains, and the sea or the large, inviting
pool. The Hilton is the most upscale hotel in the city. On most nights
there is poolside entertainment ranging from calypso to Latin jazz. Two
rooms have facilities for people with disabilities. The on-site La Boucan restaurant has a varied menu. ⊠ *Lady Young Rd. (Box 442), Port-
of-Spain,* ☎ *868/624–3211 or 800/445–8667 in the U.S.,* FAX *868/
624–4485,* WEB *www.trinidadhilton.com. 369 rooms, 25 suites. 2
restaurants, 3 bars, air-conditioning, in-room safes, minibars, no-
smoking rooms, room service, pool, wading pool, massage, sauna, 2
tennis courts, health club, Ping-Pong, shops, baby-sitting, playground,
laundry service, dry cleaning, business services, meeting rooms, travel
services, car rental. AE, DC, MC, V. All-inclusive, EP, FAP.*

$$$ 🏨 **Asa Wright Nature Centre.** In this mountain paradise you can choose
★ to swim in cool waterfall pools, explore dim caverns populated by noc-
turnal oilbirds, or simply sip a cup of tea while enjoying the view from
the lodge veranda. Built in 1908, this 200-acre mountain estate is in
a rain forest (about 90 minutes east of Port-of-Spain) populated by 170
species of birds (the Centre won the 1998 *Islands* magazine Eco-
Tourism Award). The elegant lounge has mahogany floors, bookcases,
antiques, and ornithological artifacts. The two original bedrooms in
the great house are large and romantic; all other rooms—which are in
nearby modern lodges—are comfortably outfitted but do not have ra-
dios, TVs, or phones. Three meals a day and the evening rum punch
are included in the rates as are government taxes and services charges.
⊠ *Arima Valley (Box 4710), drive east from Port-of-Spain past Arima,
heading for Wallerfield; turn left at Emmaus Centre after pillars des-
ignating Ft. Read; cross Eastern Main Rd. and bear right; drive about
½ hr until you see sign for Centre,* ☎ *868/667–4655,* FAX *868/667–4540,*
WEB *www.asawright.org. 24 rooms, 1 bungalow. Dining room, fans,
pond, hiking, shops. MC, V. FAP.*

$$$ 🏨 **Crowne Plaza Trinidad.** Proximity to the port and Independence
Square is both the draw and the drawback here. From any upper-floor
room you have a lovely pastel panorama of the old town and of ships
idling in the Gulf of Paria, and you're within walking distance of the
downtown sights and shops. Bear in mind, however, that with the action comes traffic and noise. Rooms are spacious and tastefully decorated. La Ronde, a revolving rooftop restaurant, offers a striking view
of the city at night, which compensates for the generally uninspiring
food. ⊠ *Wrightson Rd. (Box 1017), Port-of-Spain,* ☎ *868/625–3361
or 800/465–4329,* FAX *868/625–4166. 235 rooms, 10 suites. 2 restaurants, 3 bars, air-conditioning, no-smoking rooms, room service, pool,
gym, shops, baby-sitting, laundry service, business services, meeting
rooms, travel services. AE, MC, V. MAP.*

$$$ 🏨 **Kapok Hotel.** Leave it to business travelers to find a well-run hotel
★ that's a good value for the money. Even if you've left work behind (and
your laptop at home), it's nice to know that each spacious room is
equipped with voice mail (just in case) and data ports. Sunlight (front
rooms have views of Queen's Park Savannah) complements the pastel
color schemes and rattan furniture. If you're into cooking for your-
self, take one of the studios, which have kitchenettes. Otherwise, the
Tiki Village Asian restaurant has terrific views of the city and is pop-
ular with locals. On the second floor, the alfresco coffee and wine bar,

Bois Cano, has a lovely and relaxed atmosphere. ⊠ *16–18 Cotton Hill, St. Clair, Port-of-Spain,* ☎ *868/622–5765 or 800/344–1212,* FAX *868/ 622–9677,* WEB *www.kapok.co.tt. 75 rooms, 12 suites, 9 studios. Restaurant, air-conditioning, no-smoking rooms, room service, pool, gym, shops, coin laundry, dry cleaning, laundry service, business services, meeting rooms. MC, V. EP, FAP, MAP.*

$$$ 🏨 **Maracas Bay Hotel.** This is the only beachside hotel in Trinidad, sit-
★ ting on the island's most popular beach about ½ hour outside Port-of-Spain. Rooms are simple and clean, with bright, white-painted wood walls, firm double beds, and cool maroon tile floors (but no TVs, radios, or phones). All have spectacular bay views. In-house fresh fish and vegetarian dishes are well prepared, but other menu items may be a bit disappointing. The slow-paced beachside ambience also means you may have a long wait for your food, so be patient. During the day you may choose to eat from one of the many food huts on the beach serving a variety of local specialties. ⊠ *Maracas Bay,* ☎ *868/669–1914,* FAX *868/669–1643. 39 rooms, 1 suite. Dining room, lounge, air-conditioning, beach, meeting rooms. AE, MC, V. EP, MAP.*

$$ 🏨 **The Chancellor Hotel.** Billing itself as "the first true businessman's hotel in the Caribbean," this beautiful small hotel has Internet access in all rooms and full business services. Rooms are large and well appointed (each with cable TV) and are decorated with original batik hangings. The waterfall cascading into the nearby swimming pool adds a relaxing air to the bar and restaurant area. ⊠ *5 St. Ann's Ave., St. Ann's, Port-of-Spain,* ☎ FAX *868/623–0883,* WEB *www.thechancellorhotel.com. 15 rooms, 7 suites. Restaurant, bar, air-conditioning, in-room data ports, pool, business services, meeting rooms. AE, MC, V. EP.*

$$ 🏨 **La Maison Rustique.** You'll find plenty to charm you at this B&B, with its gingerbread detail, its setting amid other wonderful Victorian homes, and its proximity to Queen's Park Savannah. Rooms in the garden cottage are the nicest, but all are clean and presentable. Some have air-conditioning, and a few have private baths. The proprietor, Maureen Chin-Asiong, is a hotel-school graduate who also studied at the Wilton School of Cake Decorating in Chicago, among other places. She not only serves good breakfasts—popovers, croissants, quiche— but also whips up afternoon tea, snacks, and picnic baskets. ⊠ *16 Rust St., St. Clair, Port-of-Spain,* ☎ FAX *868/622–1512. 7 rooms, 3 with bath. Air-conditioning (some). MC, V. CP.*

$ 🏨 **Carnetta's Inn.** When Winston Borrell retired as director of tourism
★ for T&T, he and his wife, Carnetta, opened this inn on their suburban property in Maraval. All rooms have a bath (with shower), a phone, a radio, and cable TV; most have kitchenettes. Although there's air-conditioning, cool breezes usually do the trick. Carnetta uses her garden-grown herbs in her cooking and prepares excellent dinners. ⊠ *99 Saddle Rd., Maraval,* ☎ *868/628–2732,* FAX *868/628–7717. 14 rooms. Restaurant, bar, lounge, air-conditioning, laundry service, airport shuttle, car rental. AE, DC, MC, V. EP, MAP.*

$ 🏨 **Monique's.** Members of the Charbonné family really *like* having guests, as they've been proving for more than two decades. Rooms here are large and spotless, with solid teak floors and furniture as well as cable TV and phones. Ask for a room in the newer house, as each one has a kitchenette and a sizable balcony. One room is fully equipped for disabled guests, and all rooms are equipped with data ports. ⊠ *114– 116 Saddle Rd., Maraval,* ☎ *868/628–3334 or 868/628–2351,* FAX *868/622–3232,* WEB *www.best-caribbean.com/moniques. 20 rooms. Dining room, bar, air-conditioning, in-room data ports, laundry service, travel services, airport shuttle. AE, DC, MC, V. EP, MAP.*

Dining

The food on T&T is a delight to the senses and has a distinctively creole touch, though everyone has a different idea about what creole seasoning is (just ask around, and you'll see). Bountiful herbs and spices include bay, *chadon beni* (similar to cilantro), nutmeg, saffron, and a variety of peppers. The cooking also involves a lot of brown sugar, rum, plantain, and local fish and meat. If there's fresh juice on the menu, be sure to try it. You'll taste Asian, Indian, African, French, and Spanish influences, among others, often in a single meal. Indian-inspired food is a favorite: *rotis* (sandwiches of soft dough with a filling, similar to a burrito) are served as a fast food; a mélange of curried meat or fish and vegetables frequently makes an appearance as do *pelau*—a slow-stewed chicken with peas and rice—and a wide selection of *vindaloos* (spicy meat, vegetable, and seafood dishes). Crab lovers will find large blue-backs curried, peppered, or in callaloo made with green dasheen leaves, okra, and coconut milk. Shark-and-bake (lightly seasoned, fried shark meat) is the sandwich of choice.

No Trinidadian or Tobagonian dining experience is complete without a rum punch with fresh fruit and the legendary Angostura bitters, made by the same local company that produces the excellent Old Oak rum (just watch out for the fiendish sugar content). Light, refreshing Carib beer is the local lager; Stag is an even stronger lager, and dark-beer aficionados can try Royal Extra Stout (R. E.).

What to Wear

Restaurants are informal: you won't find any jacket-and-tie requirements. Beachwear, however, is a little too casual for most places. A nice pair of shorts is appropriate for lunch; for dinner you'll probably feel most comfortable in a pair of slacks or a casual sundress.

CATEGORY	COST*
$$$$	over $30
$$$	$20–$30
$$	$10–$20
$	under $10

per person for a main course at dinner

ASIAN

$$$ ✕ **Tamnak Thai.** In a beautifully renovated former colonial house around Queen's Park Savannah, this upscale restaurant offers the best Thai cuisine on Trinidad. You may choose to sit outside on the patio surrounded by flowing water and lush foliage or pick the elegant inside dining room for a more intimate (and cooler) dining experience. You might well start with the *hors d'oeuvres Tamnak Thai*, a delightful selection of Thai appetizers, and, if you can stand the heat move on to *gai pad med manuang, prik tod* (chicken with cashew nuts and fiery chilies). ✉ *13 Queen's Park East, Port-of-Spain,* ☎ *868/623–7510,* FAX *868/628–4783. AE, MC, V.*

$$ ✕ **Tiki Village.** Port-of-Spainers in the know flock to this upscale rooftop restaurant on the eighth floor of the Kapok Hotel, where the views of the city day and night are simply spectacular. The decor is a nonkitsch version of Trader Vic's and the menu features the best of Polynesian and Chinese fare. The dim sum—with tasting-size portions of dishes such as pepper squid and tofu-stuffed fish—is very popular. ✉ *16–18 Cotton Hill, St. Clair, Port-of-Spain,* ☎ *868/622–5765. AE, MC, V.*

CARIBBEAN

$$$$ ✕ **Plantation House Restaurant.** Fine dining and an elegant setting are hallmarks of this gem in a late 19th-century building and furnished in

colonial style with wrought iron and chintz. The menu features a variety of game and seafood dishes, all beautifully presented and served. Beware of the massive portions. The truly adventurous can order alligator tails (creole style, of course) or stewed agouti (a large local rodent). The conch-souse appetizer (conch strips marinated in a spicy lime-juice mixture) is a must-try. ☒ *38 Ariapita Avenue, Woodbrook,* ☎ *868/628–5551. AE, DC, MC, V. Closed Sun.*

$$ ✕ **Veni Mangé.** The best lunches in town are served upstairs in this
★ traditional West Indian house. Credit Allyson Hennessy—a Cordon Bleu–trained chef and local television celebrity—and her friendly, flamboyant sister-partner, Rosemary Hezekiah (Roses). The creative creole menu changes regularly; starters might include chip chip (a local clam) cocktail, and for a main course you could find a heavenly fillet of flying fish with a mango salsa. There's always a unique and delicious vegetarian entrée, too. If you can tear yourself away from the food, be sure to examine the huge collection of local art that adorns the restaurant's walls. This place is popular, and reservations are advised; dinner is served only on Wednesday from 7:30 to 10. The bar area is a fun hangout on a Friday evening (5 to midnight) when Allyson and Roses hold court. ☒ *67A Ariapita Ave., Woodbrook, Port-of-Spain,* ☎ *868/624–4597. AE, MC, V. Closed weekends. No dinner except Wed.*

ECLECTIC

$$$$ ✕ **Jenny's on the Boulevard.** Jenny's is in a beautifully restored grand old art nouveau-style home near Port-of-Spain's Queen's Park Savannah. The antique decor is decidedly eclectic (almost dizzying), ranging from the "Princess Diana tribute corner" to a stuffed buffalo head, but the excellent American steak-house food and true Cantonese cuisine shine. The Cellar Pub, a blend of British tradition and Hollywood kitsch, is fun, raucous, and upscale—but also tends to be smoke-filled and congested. A no-smoking room and a private dining room are available. ☒ *6 Cipriani Blvd., Port-of-Spain,* ☎ *868/625–1807. Reservations essential. AE, MC, V. Closed Sun.*

$$$$ ✕ **La Boucan.** Trinidadian dancer Geoffrey Holder painted the large mural of a social idyll in Queen's Park Savannah that dominates one wall of this room at the Hilton Trinidad and Conference Centre. A more leisurely Trinidad is also reflected in the old-fashioned charm of silver service, uniformed waiters, soft lighting, and pink tablecloths. The menu is international, including steaks, seafood grills, and other simple preparations, but you can also find such local specialties as callaloo soup, shrimp creole, and West Indian chicken curry. ☒ *Lady Young Rd., Port-of-Spain,* ☎ *868/624–3211. AE, DC, MC, V.*

$$$ ✕ **Solimar.** In a series of dimly lit, plant-filled dining areas, chef Joe Brown offers a menu that travels the world in one meal: you might enjoy a Malaysian seafood curry, Irish smoked salmon, Hawaiian barbecued mahimahi, Greek salad, or Zwiebelschnitzel—all the while listening to a guitarist gently strumming 1970s classics. Solimar is popular with expats and has a relaxed and informal atmosphere. Valet parking is available. ☒ *6 Nook Ave., St. Ann's, Port-of-Spain,* ☎ *868/624–6267. AE, MC, V.*

INDIAN

$$ ✕ **Apsara.** The name means "celestial dancer," and both the decor and food are heavenly. The elegant maroon interior is decorated with modern interpretations of Moghul art by local artist Sarah Beckett. Choosing dishes from the comprehensive menu is a bit daunting, so don't be afraid to ask for help. Your sari-clad waitress might suggest *murgh tikka makhani* (cubes of tender chicken in an intriguingly spiced sauce) with *Nav rattan korma* (a mixture of vegetables in a tongue-thrilling cashew paste) and a side of garlic *nan.* There are many vegetarian dishes avail-

able, as well as fish, shrimp, and lobster curries. Owner Marie Kavanagh is a delightful hostess and would be thrilled to give you the history of the restaurant. ⊠ *13 Queen's Park East Port-of-Spain,* ☏ *868/627–7364 or 868/623–7659. AE, MC, V. Closed Sun.*

ITALIAN

$$$ ✕ **Il Colosseo.** Calabrian chef Angelo Cofone married a Trinidadian and soon found himself co-owning the island's best Italian restaurant. In the heart of Port-of-Spain—in a remodeled 1940s home—it's popular with locals and visiting businesspeople alike. Waiters dressed in traditional black and white glide through the gray-and-turquoise dining room carrying delicacies such as *arragosta alla dario* (medallions of lobster in a spicy chili and brandy sauce) or *legumi alla griglia* (char-grilled local vegetables with a side of pasta). Manager Deborah Rees is the consummate hostess, overseeing her customers' needs. ⊠ *47 Ariapita Ave., Port-of-Spain,* ☏ *868/623–3654. AE, MC, V. Closed Sun.*

Beaches

Although Trinidad is not the beach destination Tobago is, it has its share of fine shoreline along the North Coast Road within an hour's drive of Port-of-Spain. To reach the east coast beaches, you must drive several hours and take the detour road to Arima. But "goin' behind God's back," as the Trinis say, rewards the persistent traveler with gorgeous vistas and secluded stretches of sand.

Balandra Bay, on the northeast coast, is sheltered by a rocky outcropping and is popular with bodysurfers.

Blanchisseuse Bay, on the North Coast Road, is a narrow, palm-fringed beach. Facilities are nonexistent, but it's an ideal spot for a romantic picnic. You can haggle with local fishermen to take you out in their boats to explore the coast.

Las Cuevas Bay is a narrow, picturesque strip on North Coast Road named for the series of partially submerged and explorable caves that ring the beach. A food stand offers tasty snacks, and vendors hawk fresh fruit across the road. You can also buy fresh fish and lobster from the fishing depot near the beach. There are basic changing and toilet facilities. It's less crowded here than at nearby Maracas Bay and seemingly serene, although, as at Maracas, the current can be treacherous.

Manzanilla Beach has picnic facilities and a pretty view of the Atlantic, though its water is occasionally muddied by the Orinoco River, which flows in from South America. The Cocal road running the length of this beautiful beach is lined with stately palms whose fronds vault like the arches at Chartres. This is where many well-heeled Trinis have vacation homes.

Maracas Bay is a long stretch of sand with a cove and a fishing village at one end. It's *the* local favorite, so it can get crowded on weekends. Watch out for the strong current. Parking sites are ample, and there are snack bars and rest rooms. Try a shark-and-bake (which you can choose to top with any of dozens of choices—such as tamarind sauce and coleslaw) at one of the huts (Patsy's is considered the best) on the beach or in the nearby carpark.

Salibea Bay, past Galera Point, which juts toward Tobago, is a gentle beach with shallows and plenty of shade—perfect for swimming. Snack vendors abound in the vicinity.

Tyrico Bay is a small beach made lively by the surfers who flock here. The strong undertow may be too much for some swimmers. Be sure to pack insect repellent as the sand flies and mosquitoes can be a nuisance in the rainy season.

Outdoor Activities and Sports

BIRD-WATCHING

Trinidad and Tobago are among the top 10 spots in the world in terms of the number of species of birds per square mile—more than 600 altogether, many living within pristine rain forests, lowlands and savannas, and fresh- and saltwater swamps. If you're lucky, you might spot the collared trogon, blue-backed manakin, or rare white-tailed Sabrewing hummingbird. Restaurants often hang feeders outside their porches, as much to keep the birds away from your food as to provide a chance to see them.

You can fill up your books with notes on the variety of species in Trinidad at two major bird sanctuaries. **Asa Wright Nature Centre** (☎ 868/667–4655), a half-hour drive from Blanchisseuse, has over 170 bird species in residence. **The Caroni Bird Sanctuary** (☎ 868/645–1305), a half-hour from Port-of-Spain, is home to the scarlet ibis, Trinidad's national bird. The **Point a Pierre Wildfowl Trust** (✉ 42 Sandown Rd., Point Cumana, ☎ 868/637–5145) is a haven for rare bird species on 26 acres within the unlikely confines of a petrochemical complex; you must call in advance for a reservation. **Winston Nanan** (☎ 868/645–1305) runs the highly regarded Nanan's Bird Sanctuary Tours to nearby Guyana and Venezuela.

FISHING

The islands off the northwest coast of Trinidad have excellent waters for deep-sea fishing; you'll find wahoo, king fish, and marlin, to name a few. The ocean here was a favorite angling spot of Franklin D. Roosevelt. Through **Bayshore Charters** (✉ 29 Sunset Dr., Bayshore, ☎ 868/637–8711) you can fish for an afternoon or hire a boat for a weekend; the *Melissa Ann* is fully equipped for comfortable cruising, sleeps six, and has an air-conditioned cabin, refrigerator, cooking facilities, and, of course, fishing equipment. Captain Sa Gomes is one of the most experienced charter captains on the islands. Members of the **Trinidad and Tobago Yacht Club** (✉ Bayshore, ☎ 868/637–4260) may be willing to arrange a fishing trip for you.

GOLF

The best course in Trinidad is the 18-hole **St. Andrew's Golf Club** (✉ Moka, Maraval, ☎ 868/629–2314), just outside Port-of-Spain. Greens fees are approximately $35 for 18 holes. Convenient tee times are available weekdays.

TENNIS

Several establishments allow nonmembers or nonguests to play tennis on their courts. The **Hilton Trinidad and Conference Centre** (✉ Lady Young Rd., Port-of-Spain, ☎ 868/624–3211) has 2 asphalt courts. The **Trinidad Country Club** (✉ Long Circular Rd., Maraval, ☎ 868/622–3470) has 6 asphalt courts. The **Tranquility Square Lawn Tennis Club** (✉ Victoria Ave., Port-of-Spain, ☎ 868/625–4182) has 4 asphalt courts.

Shopping

Good buys in Trinidad include duty-free items such as Angostura bitters and Old Oak or Vat 19 rum, all widely available throughout the country. Thanks in large part to Carnival costumery, there's no shortage of fabric shops. The best bargains for Asian and East Indian silks and cottons can be found in downtown Port-of-Spain, on Frederick Street, and around Independence Square. Recordings of local calypsonians and steel-pan performances are available throughout the islands and make great gifts.

Areas and Malls

Downtown Port-of-Spain, specifically **Frederick, Queen,** and **Henry** streets, is full of fabrics and shoes. **Ellerslie Plaza** (⊠ Bossiere Village, Maraval., Port-of-Spain, ☎ No phone) is an attractive outdoor mall well worth a browse. **Excellent City Centre** (⊠ 3–5 Frederick St., Port-of-Spain, ☎ 868/623–6503) is set in an old-style oasis under the lantern roofs of three of downtown's oldest commercial buildings. Look for cleverly designed keepsakes, trendy cotton garments, and original artwork. The upstairs food court overlooks bustling Frederick Street. **Long Circular Mall** (⊠ 51–53 Long Circular Rd., St. James, ☎ 868/622–4925) has upscale boutiques great for window-shopping. **The Market** (⊠ Nook Ave., adjoining Hotel Normandie, St. Ann's, Port-of-Spain, ☎ 868/624–1181) is a small collection of shops that specialize in indigenous fashions, crafts, jewelry, basketwork, and ceramics. You can also have afternoon tea in the elegant little café.

Specialty Items

CLOTHING

A fine designer clothing shop, **Meiling** (⊠ Kapok Hotel, Maraval, and Coco Reef Hotel, Tobago, ☎ 868/628–6205), features cottons in ecru or white and smart little girls' dresses with shirred tops. The designer will also create custom pieces. **Radical** (⊠ West Mall, ☎ 868/628–5693; ⊠ Long Circular Mall, ☎ 868/632–5800; ⊠ Excellent City Centre, ☎ 868/627–4425), which carries T-shirts and original men's and women's clothing, is something like the Gap of the Caribbean.

DUTY-FREE GOODS

De Lima's of Frederick Street (⊠ Corner of Queen and Frederick Sts., Port-of-Spain, ☎ 868/655–8872; ⊠ West Mall, Western Main Rd., St. James, ☎ 868/622–7050) sells traditional duty-free luxury items. **Stecher's** (⊠ Ellerslie Plaza, Port-of-Spain, ☎ 868/622–8870; ⊠ Long Circular Mall, ☎ 868/622–0017) is a familiar name for those seeking to avoid taxes on fine perfumes, china, crystal, handcrafted items, and jewelry; you can arrange to have your purchases delivered to the airport the day of your departure.

HANDICRAFTS

The tourism office can provide a list of local artisans who specialize in everything from straw and cane work to miniature steel pans. The **101 Art Gallery** (⊠ 101 Tragarete Rd., Port-of-Spain, ☎ 868/628–4081) is Trinidad's foremost gallery, which showcases local artists such as Sarah Beckett (semi-abstracts in oil, some of which are featured on local stamps); Jackie Hinkson (figurative watercolors); Peter Sheppard (stylized realist local landscapes in acrylic); and Carlisle Chang (colorful abstracts) in a faithfully restored pink gingerbread house. Openings are usually held Tuesday evenings year-round; the gallery is closed Sunday and Monday. For painted plates, ceramics, aromatic candles, wind chimes, and carved wood pieces and instruments, check out **Cockey** (⊠ Level 3, Long Circular Mall, ☎ 868/628–6546). **Poui Boutique** (⊠ Ellerslie Plaza, ☎ 868/622–5597) has stylish handmade batik items, Ajoupa ware (an attractive, local terra-cotta pottery) and many other gift items. The miniature ceramic houses and local scenes are astoundingly realistic, and are all handcrafted by owner Bunty O'Connor.

JEWELRY

The design duo of Barbara Jardine and Rachel Ross create handmade works of art with sterling silver, 18K gold, and precious and semiprecious

stones, for sale at **Alchemy** (✉ Precious Little, West Mall, ☎ 868/
632–1077).

Just CDs and Accessories (✉ Level 1, Long Circular Mall, ☎ 868/622–
7516) has a good selection of popular local musicians as well as other
music genres. **Rhyner's Record Shop** (✉ 54 Prince St., ☎ 868/625–2476;
✉ Piarco International Airport, ☎ 868/669–3064) has a decent (and
duty-free) selection of calypso and *soca* (a blend of Caribbean soul and
calypso) music.

Nightlife and the Arts

Nightlife

There's no lack of nightlife in Port-of-Spain, and spontaneity plays a
big role—around carnival time look for the handwritten signs announcing the PANYARD, where the next informal gathering of steel-drum
bands is going to be.

Three of the island's top nightspots are on a former American Armed
Forces base in Chaguaramas. **The Anchorage** (✉ Point Gourde Rd.,
Chaguaramas, ☎ 868/634–4334) is a good spot for early evening
cocktails and snacks. At **The Base** ☎ (✉ Western Main Rd., Chaguaramas, opposite Pier 1, ☎ No phone) you can party until the wee
hours in a hi-tech former hangar. **Pier 1** (✉ Western Main Rd., Chaguaramas, ☎ 868/634–4426) is *the* place for lively late-night action. You
can dance through the night on a large wooden deck jutting into the
ocean with gentle sea breezes to cool you down. It's about 20 minutes
west of Port-of-Spain, so get a party together from your hotel and hire
a cab. It opens at 9 PM, Wednesday–Sunday.

Mas Camp Pub (✉ Corner of Ariapata Ave. and French St., Woodbrook,
Port-of-Spain, ☎ 868/623–3745) is Port-of-Spain's most comfortable
and dependable nightspot. Along with a bar and a large stage where
a DJ or live band reigns, the kitchen dishes up hearty, reasonably
priced creole lunches, and if one of the live bands strikes your fancy,
chances are you can also buy their tape here. **Pelican** (✉ 2–4 Coblentz
Ave., St. Ann's, Port-of-Spain, ☎ 868/624–7486), an English-style
pub, gets increasingly frenetic as the week closes, with a (gay-friendly)
singles-bar atmosphere. The biggest nights are Wednesday, Friday, and
Sunday, when the crowd overflows into the parking lot. There is also
seasonal entertainment with calypso at carnival time and *parang* (Spanish influenced music) at Christmas time.

OFF THE
BEATEN PATH

HiRpm (✉ Gulf City Mall, 2nd floor, La Romain, ☎ 868/652–3760) is
a great alternative if you want something out of town. Just take the main
highway south to the end of the line and then follow South Trunk Road to
the mall. This lively establishment offers great pop music and a laid-back
atmosphere, where you can hear live local pop/rock bands on Wednesday nights performing a variety of cover songs. The large oval bar (it
takes up half the room) is a great place to meet talkative southerners.
The owner Selwyn "Bunny" Persad is a race car driver and enthusiast
and will be happy to talk to you about his favorite sport.

The Arts

Trinidad always seems to be either anticipating, celebrating, or recovering
from a festival. Visitors are welcome at these events, which are a great
way to explore the island's rich cultural traditions.

CARNIVAL

Trinidad's version of the pre-Lenten bacchanal is reputedly the oldest in the western hemisphere; there are festivities all over the country, but the most lavish are in Port-of-Spain. Not as overwhelming as its rival in Rio or as debauched as Mardi Gras in New Orleans, Trinidad's Carnival has the warmth and character of a massive family reunion.

The season begins right after Christmas, and the parties, called fêtes, don't stop till Ash Wednesday. Listen to a radio station for five minutes, and you'll find out where the action is. The Carnival event itself officially lasts only two days, from J'ouvert (2am) on Monday to midnight the following day, Carnival Tuesday. It's best to arrive in Trinidad a week or two early to enjoy the preliminary events. (Hotels fill up quickly, so be sure to make reservations months in advance, and be prepared to pay premium prices for a minimum five-night stay. Even private homes have been known to rent bedrooms for as much as $225 per night.)

Carnival is about extravagant costumes. Colorfully attired *mas* (troupes), whose membership sometimes numbers in the thousands, march to the beat set by massive music trucks and steel bands. You can visit the various mas "camps" around Port-of-Spain where these elaborate getups are put together—the addresses are listed in the newspapers—and perhaps join one that strikes your fancy. Fees run anywhere from $35 to $200; you get to keep the costume. You can also buy your costume online at the tourist board's Web site, which has links to all the major camps. Children can parade in a kiddie carnival that takes place on the Saturday morning before the official events.

Carnival is also a showcase for performers of calypso, music that mixes dance rhythms with social commentary—sung by characters with such evocative names as Shadow, the Mighty Sparrow, and Black Stalin—and soca, which fuses calypso with a driving dance beat. As Carnival approaches, many of these singers perform nightly in calypso tents around the city. Many hotels also have special concerts by popular local musicians. You can also visit the city's "panyards," where steel orchestras, such as the Renegades, Desperadoes, Neal and Massy All-Stars, Invaders, and Phase II, rehearse their musical arrangements (most can also be heard during the winter season).

For several nights before Carnival, costume makers display their work, and the steel bands and calypso singers perform in competitions at Queen's Park Savannah. Here the Calypso Monarch is crowned on the Sunday night before Carnival (Dimanche Gras). The city starts to fill with metal-frame carts carrying steel bands, trucks hauling sound systems, and revelers who squeeze into the narrow streets. At midnight on "Carnival Tuesday," Port-of-Spain's exhausted merrymakers go to bed. The next day feet are sore, but spirits have been refreshed. Lent (and theoretical sobriety) takes over for a while.

MUSIC

Trinidadian culture doesn't end with music, but it definitely begins with it. Although both calypso and steel bands are at their best during Carnival, steel bands play at clubs, dances, and fêtes throughout the year. At Christmastime the music of the moment is a Venezuelan-derived folk music called *parang,* sung in Spanish to the strains of a stringed instrument called a *quattro.* The Lopinot Complex in Arouca is a parang center. If you can stomach the steep uphill drive, Paramin, near Port-of-Spain (take Maracas Road and turn off on Paramin Road), is another spectacular location to hear this music.

THEATER
When Nobel prize–winning, St. Lucian–born poet Derek Walcott—who has called Trinidad home for many years—is on the island, he often gives readings or gets involved in one of the productions of the thriving local theater. Consult local newspapers for listings.

Exploring Trinidad

The intensely urban atmosphere of Port-of-Spain belies the tropical beauty of the countryside surrounding it. You'll need a car and three to eight hours to see all there is to see. Begin by circling the Queen's Park Savannah to Saddle Road, in the residential district of Maraval. After a few miles the road begins to narrow and curve sharply as it climbs into the Northern Range and its undulating hills of dense foliage. Stop at the lookout on North Coast Road; a camera is a must-have here. You'll pass a series of lovely beaches starting with Maracas. From the town of Blanchisseuse there's a winding route to the Asa Wright Nature Centre that takes you through canyons of towering palms, mossy grottoes, and imposing bamboo. In this rain forest keep an eye out for vultures, parakeets, hummingbirds, toucans, and if you're lucky, maybe red-bellied, yellow-and-blue macaws.

Numbers in the margin correspond to points of interest on the Trinidad map.

Sights to See

② Asa Wright Nature Centre. Nearly 500 acres here are covered with plants, trees, and multi-hued flowers, and the surrounding acreage is atwitter with more than 170 species of birds, from the gorgeous blue-green motmot to the rare, nocturnal oilbird. If you stay at the center's inn for two nights or more, take one of the center's guided hikes (included in your room price) to the oilbirds' breeding grounds in Dunston Cave. Those who don't want to hike can relax on the inn's veranda and watch birds swoop about the porch feeders—an armchair bird-watcher's nirvana. This stunning plantation house looks out onto the lush, untouched Arima Valley. Even if you're not staying over, book ahead for lunch (TT$37.50) Monday–Saturday or for the noontime Sunday buffet (TT$62.50). ⊠ *Arima Valley (Box 4710), ½ hr outside Blanchisseuse; take right at fork in road (signposted to Arima) and drive another ½ hr (sign for the center is at milepost 7¾) on Blanchisseuse Rd.; turn right there (for directions from Port-of-Spain, ☞ Lodging, above),* ☎ 868/667–4655, WEB *www.asawright.org.* ⊠ *$6.* ☺ *Daily 9–5. Guided tours at 10:30 and 1:30; reservations essential.*

④ Caroni Bird Sanctuary. This large swamp with maze-like waterways is bordered by mangrove trees, some plumed with huge termite nests. If you are lucky, you may see lazy caimans idling in the water and large snakes hanging from branches on the banks taking in the sun. In the middle of the sanctuary are several islets that are home to Trinidad's national bird, the scarlet ibis. Just before sunset the ibis arrive by the thousands, their richly colored feathers brilliant in the gathering dusk, and as more flocks alight, they turn the mangrove foliage a brilliant scarlet. Bring a sweater and insect repellent.

Across from the sanctuary's parking lot lies a sleepy canal with several boats with guides for hire; the smaller boats are best. The only official tour operator is Winston Nanan ($10, children over 5 years half price and under 5 free); phone or write him in advance for reservations. ⊠ *½ hr from Port-of-Spain; take Churchill Roosevelt Hwy. east to Uriah Butler south; turn right and in about 2 mins, after passing Caroni River Bridge, follow sign for sanctuary,* ☎ 868/645–1305. ⊠ *Free.*

❸ Lopinot Complex. It's said that the ghost of the French count Charles Joseph de Lopinot prowls his former home on stormy nights. Lopinot came to Trinidad in 1800 and chose this magnificent site to plant cocoa. His restored estate house has been turned into a museum—a guide is available from 10 to 6—and a center for parang, the Venezuelan folk music. ✉ *Take Eastern Main Rd. from Port-of-Spain to Arouca; look for sign that points north,* ☎ *No phone.* 🎫 *Free.*☉ *Daily 6–6.*

❶ Port-of-Spain. Most tours begin at the port. If you're planning to explore on foot, which will take two to four hours, start early in the day; by midday the port area can be hot and as packed as Calcutta. You'll want to end up on a bench in the Queen's Park Savannah, sipping a cool coconut water bought from one of the vendors operating out of flatbed trucks. For about 30¢ he'll lop the top off a green coconut with a deft swing of the machete and, when you've finished drinking, lop again, making a bowl and spoon of coconut shell for you to eat the young pulp. As in most cities, take extra care at night; women should not walk alone.

King's Wharf. Though it's no longer as frenetic as it was during the oil boom of the 1970s, the town's main dock entertains a steady parade of cruise and cargo ships, a reminder that the city started from this strategic harbor. It's on Wrightson Road, the main street along the water on the southwest side of town.

Independence Square. Across Wrightson Road and a few minutes' walk from the south side of King's Wharf, this busy thoroughfare has been the focus of the downtown area's major gentrification. Flanked by government buildings and the familiar twin towers of the Financial Complex (they adorn all T&T dollar bills), the square was formerly a dusty and noisy area where peddlers hawked their wares. It's been completely renovated and is now a lovely park with trees, flagstone walkways, chess tables, and the Brian Lara Promenade (named after Trinidad's world-famous cricketer). On its south side the Cruise Ship Complex, full of duty-free shops, forms an enclave of international anonymity with the Crowne Plaza Trinidad. On the eastern end of the square is the Cathedral of the Immaculate Conception; it was by the sea when it was built in 1832, but subsequent landfill around the port gave it an inland location. The imposing Roman Catholic structure is made of stone from nearby Laventille.

Frederick Street. Port-of-Spain's main shopping drag, starting north from the midpoint of Independence Square, is a market street of scents and sounds—perfumed oils sold by sidewalk vendors and music tapes being played from vending carts—and crowded shops.

Woodford Square. At Prince and Frederick streets, this square has served as the site of political meetings, speeches, public protests, and occasional violence. It's dominated by the magnificent Red House, a Renaissance-style building that takes up an entire city block. Trinidad's House of Parliament takes its name from a paint job done in anticipation of Queen Victoria's Diamond Jubilee in 1897. The original Red House was burned to the ground in a 1903 riot, and the present structure was built four years later. The chambers are open to the public.

The view of the south side of the square is framed by the Gothic spires of Trinity, the city's Anglican cathedral, consecrated in 1823; its mahogany-beam roof is modeled after that of Westminster Hall in London. On the north are the impressive public library building, the Hall of Justice, and City Hall.

Queen's Park Savannah. If the downtown port area is the pulse of Port-of-Spain, the great green expanse roughly bounded by Maraval Road, Queen's Park West, Charlotte Street, and Saddle Road is the city's soul. You can walk straight north on Frederick Street and get there within 20 minutes. Its 2-mi (3-km) circumference is a popular jogger's track. On the west side of the Savannah you'll see a garden of architectural delights: the elegant lantern-roof George Brown House and the Magnificent Seven. The Grandstand on the southern end is a popular venue for Calypso and cultural shows. The northern end of the Savannah is devoted to plants. A rock garden, known as the The Hollows, and a fishpond add to the rusticity.

Magnificent Seven. A series of astonishing buildings constructed in a variety of 19th-century styles flanks the western side of the Savannah. Notable are Killarney, patterned (loosely) after Balmoral Castle in Scotland, with an Italian-marble gallery surrounding the ground floor; Whitehall, constructed in the style of a Venetian palace by a cacao-plantation magnate and currently the office of the prime minister; Roomor, a flamboyantly Baroque colonial house with a preponderance of towers, pinnacles, and wrought-iron trim that suggests an elaborate French pastry; and the Queen's Royal College, in German Renaissance style, with a prominent tower clock that chimes on the hour.

National Museum and Art Gallery. Head over to the southeast corner of the Savannah to see the Carnival exhibitions, the Amerindian collection and historical re-creations, and the fine 19th-century paintings of Trinidadian artist Cazabon. ⊠ *117 Upper Frederick St.,* ☎ *868/623-5941.* ⊠ *Free.*⊙ *Tues.–Sat. 10–6.*

Emperor Valley Zoo and the Botanical Gardens. The cultivated expanse of parkland north of the Savannah is the site of the president's and prime minister's official residences. A meticulous lattice of walkways and local flora, the parkland was first laid out in 1820 for Governor Ralph Woodford. In the midst of the serene wonderland is the 8-acre zoo, which primarily features birds and animals of the region—from the brilliantly plumed scarlet ibis to slithering anacondas and pythons; you'll also see (and hear) the wild parrots that breed in the surrounding foliage. The zoo draws a quarter of a million visitors a year, and more than half of them are children, so admission is priced accordingly—a mere TT$2 for folks under 12. ⊠ *Botanical Gardens,* ☎ *868/622-3530 or 868/622-5343.* ⊠ *TT$4 for the zoo, gardens free.* ⊙ *Daily 9:30–5:30.*

TOBAGO

Lodging

On Tobago there are a few modest lodgings in the towns, but the trend is toward seaside resorts, many of them appealingly low-key. If you're staying on the east side of Tobago, accommodations with meal plans are almost essential owing to the dearth of restaurants.

The **Trinidad and Tobago Bed and Breakfast Co-operative Society** (⊠ 1 Wrightson Rd., Port-of-Spain, ☎ FAX 868/627-2337) maintains a list of B&B establishments in the entire country. **Tobago Bed and Breakfast Association** (⊠ Federal Villa, 1–3 Crooks River, Scarborough, ☎ 868/639-3926, FAX 868/639-3566) has information about B&Bs on Tobago.

For approximate costs, *see* the lodging price chart *in* Trinidad.

Tobago

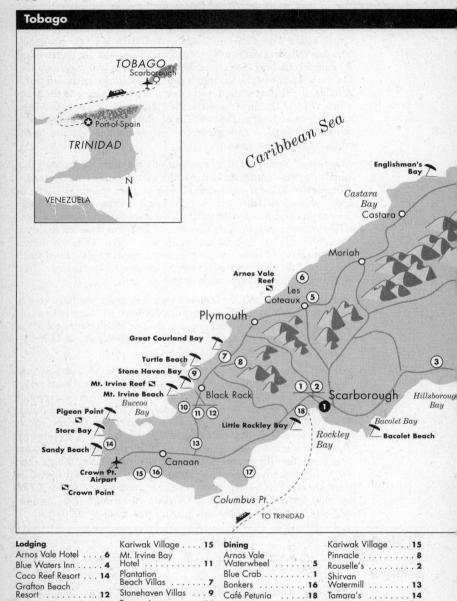

TOBAGO
Scarborough

TRINIDAD

Port-of-Spain

VENEZUELA

N

Caribbean Sea

Englishman's
Bay

*Castara
Bay*
Castara

Moriah

Arnos Vale
Reef
⑥
Les
Coteaux ⑤

Plymouth

Great Courland Bay
⑦
Turtle Beach ⑧
⑨
Stone Haven Bay
Mt. Irvine Reef
Mt. Irvine Beach
*Buccoo
Bay*
Black Rock
⑩ ⑪ ⑫
Pigeon Point
Store Bay
Little Rockley Bay
⑱
Sandy Beach
⑭
⑬
Canaan
Crown Pt.
Airport
⑮ ⑯
Crown Point
⑰

① ②
Scarborough
❶

*Hillsboroug
Bay*

③

Bacolet Bay
Bacolet Beach

*Rockley
Bay*

Columbus Pt.

TO TRINIDAD

Lodging
Arnos Vale Hotel **6**
Blue Waters Inn **4**
Coco Reef Resort . . . **14**
Grafton Beach
Resort **12**
Hilton Tobago **17**
Le Grand Courlan
Resort and Spa **8**

Kariwak Village **15**
Mt. Irvine Bay
Hotel **11**
Plantation
Beach Villas **7**
Stonehaven Villas . . . **9**
Toucan Inn **16**

Dining
Arnos Vale
Waterwheel **5**
Blue Crab **1**
Bonkers **16**
Café Petunia **18**
First Historical
Café/Bar **3**

Kariwak Village **15**
Pinnacle **8**
Rouselle's **2**
Shirvan
Watermill **13**
Tamara's **14**
La Tartaruga **10**

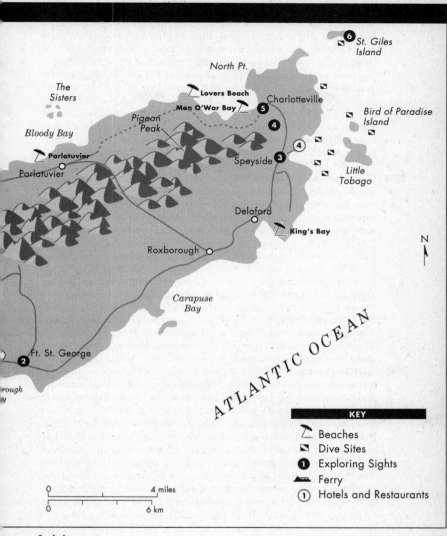

The Sisters

Bloody Bay

North Pt.

Lovers Beach

Man O'War Bay

Pigeon Peak

Parlatuvier

Parlatuvier

Charlotteville

Speyside

Delaford

King's Bay

Roxborough

Carapuse Bay

Ft. St. George

St. Giles Island

Bird of Paradise Island

Little Tobago

ATLANTIC OCEAN

N

KEY

Beaches
Dive Sites
Exploring Sights
Ferry
Hotels and Restaurants

0   4 miles
0   6 km

Exploring
Charlotteville **5**
Flagstaff Hill **4**
Ft. King George **2**
St. Giles Island **6**
Scarborough **1**
Speyside **3**

$$$$ ⊡ **Coco Reef Resort.** Service and luxury are the twin pillars of this resort. Elements of Caribbean, colonial, and Mediterranean architecture blend in an abundance of arches, tiles, and fretwork flourishes; harsh angles have been eliminated to create soothing spaces. Rooms have cool, calming tiles, pretty wall stencils, and handcrafted wicker furniture. If you want to venture off the resort's small beach, Coco Bay, Pigeon Point and Store Bay are both nearby. ⊠ *Coconut Bay (Box 434), Scarborough,* ☎ *868/639–8571 or 800/221–1294,* FAX *868/639–8574 or 305/ 639–2717,* WEB *www.cocoreef.com. 96 rooms, 39 suites. 2 restaurants, 2 bars, air-conditioning, room service, pool, hair salon, spa, 2 tennis courts, gym, beach, dive shop, snorkeling, windsurfing, baby-sitting, business services, meeting rooms, travel services, car rental. AE, D, DC, MC, V. CP, FAP, MAP.*

$$$$ ⊡ **Grafton Beach Resort.** This complex stretches out languidly along
★   the shore under tall palms. The hotel sports a huge lobby-bar-restaurant-pool area and the in-room amenities and decor (solid-teak furniture and terra-cotta floors) are all first class. The Neptune seafood restaurant and the bar, where local folkloric shows and bands perform nightly, are above and around a pool; the main restaurant is off to one side. A walkway leads directly to a fine beach, where you'll find another bar. You can learn to dive, play squash, work out in Le Grand Courlan Resort and Spa's gym next door, or go canoeing and sailing, among other things—all included in the rates. Guests here can also use the spa facilities at Le Grand Courlan for a fee. ⊠ *Black Rock,* ☎ *868/ 639–0191,* FAX *868/639–0030,* WEB *www.grafton-resort.com. 99 rooms, 4 suites. 2 restaurants, 3 bars, air-conditioning, pool, squash, beach, dive shop, snorkeling, surfing, windsurfing, boating, shops, dance club, meeting rooms, business services. AE, MC, V. All-inclusive.*

$$$$ ⊡ **Hilton Tobago.** This dazzling new property, which opened in 2000, sets a high standard for Tobago. The hotel occupies 20 beachfront acres and boasts, among other things, 200 rooms, an 18-hole championship par-72 golf course, and a massive pool. The huge atrium lobby has floor to ceiling windows that manage to blur the line between hotel and ocean. Rooms are spacious and comfortable, offering amenities that you would expect from any world-class hotel. All rooms have an ocean view; ground floor rooms have a small patio that opens onto the gardens. The three-story hotel also has the largest ballroom on the island and excellent meeting rooms. Art lovers will be thrilled by the collection of local art that decorates all areas of the hotel. ⊠ *Box 633 Scarborough,* ☎ *868/660–8500,* FAX *868/660–8503,* WEB *www.hilton.com. 178 rooms, 22 suites. 2 restaurants, 3 bars, air-conditioning, no-smoking rooms, pool, hair salon, sauna, health club, 18-hole golf course, 2 tennis courts, beach, snorkeling, windsurfing, waterskiing, fishing, shops, meeting rooms. AE, MC, V. All-inclusive, EP, MAP.*

$$$$ ⊡ **Le Grand Courlan Resort and Spa.** This hotel, under the same ownership as—and right next door to—the Grafton Beach Resort, is aiming for a *very* upscale clientele. The spacious rooms have pink-tile floors, oak furniture, and large balconies with fantastic views; the beach is one of the best on the island; and the staff is gracious. The Pinnacle dining room serves lovely dinners in a relaxed setting. The spa offers a variety of services, from aromatherapy with essential oil extracts to Swedish massage. Several packages are available including scuba, spa, and golf. ⊠ *Shirvan Rd., Black Rock,* ☎ *868/639–9667; 800/468–3750; or 800/424–5500 in Canada;* FAX *868/639–9292. 68 rooms, 10 suites. 3 restaurants, 2 bars, air-conditioning, in-room safes, minibars, no-smoking rooms, room service, pool, hair salon, hot tub, massage, sauna, spa, steam room, golf privileges, 2 tennis courts, health club, squash, beach, dive shop, windsurfing, boating, fishing, bicycles, shops, laundry ser-*

vice, business services, meeting rooms, travel services, car rental. AE, MC, V. EP, MAP.

$$$$ 🏨 **Mt. Irvine Bay Hotel.** The advantage of this low-key establishment is golf—guests get special rates on the 18-hole, par-72, 127-acre championship course. Since opening in 1972, this resort has had many, many repeat customers (who rave about the staff). For a romantic setting the cottages are worth the extra cost; they have private patios and are set in an arc around the main building. The main restaurant, the Sugar Mill, is set inside a 17th-century mill, and there are two more restaurants—a dressy French one, Le Beau Rivage, and the Jacaranda, which serves true Caribbean dishes. You can swim in the large pool, play tennis on the floodlit courts, or take the private trail across the road to the beach and its bar. The grounds are lovely, and the golf is great. ⊠ *Mt. Irvine Bay (Box 222),* ☎ *868/639–8871,* 𝔽𝔸𝕏 *868/639–8800,* 𝚆𝙴𝙱 *www.mtirvine.com. 105 rooms, 6 suites, 46 cottages. 3 restaurants, 6 bars, air-conditioning, no-smoking rooms, pool, hair salon, sauna, 18-hole golf course, 2 tennis courts, beach, snorkeling, windsurfing, waterskiing, fishing, shops, meeting rooms. AE, MC, V. CP, EP, MAP.*

$$$$ 🏨 **Plantation Beach Villas.** Nestled on a hillside above a palm-fringed beach, these pink-and-white villas are comfortably furnished in plantation style—four-poster beds, rocking chairs, louvered doors, and lots of West Indian fretwork. The accommodations (and the price) are perfect for large families or other groups: each two-story villa has three bedrooms, three baths, and a teak veranda with a view of the sea. Cleaning service and linens are included, and a housekeeper prepares your breakfast and lunch and will return (for an additional fee) to make dinner; baby-sitting is also available. ⊠ *Box 434, Scarborough,* ☎ 𝔽𝔸𝕏 *868/639–9377. 6 villas. Bar, air-conditioning, kitchenettes, pool, baby-sitting, laundry service. AE, MC, V. EP.*

$$$$ 🏨 **Stonehaven Villas.** If privacy, luxury and exclusivity are what you crave—and you have the money to spend—then Stonehaven Villas should suit the bill. The property perches on a hillside adjacent to a bird sanctuary and commands an impressive view of the Caribbean. The complex consists of 14 French-style villas and a club house, which serves as the restaurant and social gathering area. Each villa has three large bedrooms with ensuite bathrooms. Have no fear about cleaning, cooking, or ironing because each villa comes complete with all-day maid service. That leaves you lots of time to relax by your private vanishing-edge pool or perhaps to call for an in-villa massage and beauty treatment. ⊠ *Bon Accord (Box 1079), Grafton Estate,* ☎ *868/639–9887,* 𝔽𝔸𝕏 *868/639–0102. 14 villas. Restaurant, bar, air-conditioning, kitchenettes, pool, laundry service, meeting rooms. AE, MC, V. EP.*

$$$ 🏨 **Arnos Vale Hotel.** Romance isn't hard to find at this Mediterranean-style complex on 400 lush acres (Princess Margaret honeymooned here 40 years ago). Rooms are in white-stucco cottages on a hill; from your quarters you can take a winding path down to a secluded beach, a pool, and a bar. The hilltop restaurant—with antique pieces, iron-lattice tables, and chandelier—has a magnificent patio with sweeping sea views. ⊠ *Arnos Vale and Franklin rds. (Box 208), Scarborough,* ☎ *868/639–2881,* 𝔽𝔸𝕏 *868/639–4629. 35 rooms, 3 suites. Restaurant, bar, air-conditioning, pool, tennis court, beach, snorkeling, shops. AE, DC, MC, V. EP, MAP.*

$$$ 🏨 **Blue Waters Inn.** A 90-minute drive from Scarborough and a trek
★   down a bumpy driveway brings you to this beach hotel, with villas set amid 46 acres of greenery on the northeast Atlantic coast. Little Tobago and Bird of Paradise islands are across the turquoise bay. So lush is the location that the massive gnarled beach trees here seem to hold up the entire complex. You're guaranteed the sound of waves all night

in each room. The bungalows have one or two bedrooms, a living room, and a kitchen. There are only small stores in the area; if you don't want to shop in Scarborough before you set out, you can fax in an order for provisions and have the staff stock your room. The restaurant serves the freshest of fish, and the lively bar has an array of exotic drinks. Barbeque dinners are cooked up on the beach patio. ✉ *Bateaux Bay, Speyside,* ☎ 868/660–4077 or 800/742–4276, FAX 868/660–5195, WEB *www.bluewatersinn.com. 28 rooms, 3 suites, 4 bungalows. Restaurant, bar, tennis court, beach, dive shop, snorkeling, boating, baby-sitting, meeting rooms, car rental. AE, MC, V. CP, EP, FAP, MAP.*

$$$ 🏨 **Kariwak Village.** Guests tend to return to Allan and Cynthia Clo-
★   vis's charming, reasonably priced cabana village, which they describe as the "holistic haven and hotel." In this peaceful atmosphere you'll find all-natural cuisine (vegetarians love this place), an outdoor hot tub, and weekly yoga classes in the open-air conference area (nothing like a good stretch on a gleaming teak floor under a thatched roof). A bamboo pavilion houses the highly respected Kariwak Village restaurant. You can stroll through Cynthia's herb-and-vegetable garden or Allan's beautifully landscaped acre, drink terrific rum punches, and maybe listen to local bands in the lobby bar (all done up in bamboo, raw teak, and coral stone), or you can make the 10-minute walk to the beach. All accommodations are in nicely appointed cabanas featuring high ceilings (designed to maximize your energy potential). The complex is near the airport, Store Bay, and Pigeon Point. ✉ *Crown Point (Box 27), Scarborough,* ☎ 868/639–8442, FAX 868/639–8441, WEB *www.kariwak. co.tt. 24 rooms. Restaurant, bar, air-conditioning, pool. AE, DC, MC, V. EP, MAP.*

$$ 🏨 **Toucan Inn.** This charming 20-room hotel (it was voted Tobago's small hotel of the year for 2000 by the Trinidad and Tobago Hoteliers Association) is set in a beautiful garden setting. You may choose from garden rooms or the less private cabanas around the pool. Immaculate rooms are well appointed with beautiful local teak furniture. The rates, excellent service, and proximity to the airport make this hotel an unbeatable value. One of the main advantages of staying here is that the hotel's restaurant and bar, Bonkers, is one of Tobago's most popular hangouts. ✉ *Store Bay Local Rd., Crown Point,* ☎ 868/639–7173, FAX 868/639–8933, WEB *www.toucan-inn.com. 20 rooms. Restaurant, bar, air-conditioning, pool. AE, MC, V. CP, MAP.*

Dining

Macaroni pie and chicken is Tobago's Sunday dinner favorite, perhaps with fried plantain or potatoes. Oildown—a local dish—tastes better than it sounds: it's a gently seasoned mixture of boiled breadfruit and salt beef or pork flavored with coconut milk. Mango ice cream or a sweet and sour tamarind ball makes a tasty finish. You may want to take home some hot-pepper sauce or chutney to a spice-loving friend or relative.

For approximate costs, *see* the dining price chart *in* Trinidad.

CARIBBEAN

$$$ ✕ **Shirvan Watermill.** For a quiet, romantic dinner, this elegant alfresco restaurant surrounded by lush foliage and a winding fishpond filled with carp is an essential dining experience. The daily changing menu, the bouquets of anthuriums, and the starched navy tablecloths and white napkins add even more charm. A regular specialty is "river lobster" (crayfish) with garlic butter (a mess is expected). Owner and manager David Ford is an amiable host and will bring out samples of his "raw mate-

rials" so you can familiarize yourself with the local ingredients. ⊠ *Shirvan Rd., Mt. Pleasant,* ☎ *868/639–0000. AE, MC, V. No lunch.*

$$ ✕ **Blue Crab.** Alison Sardinha is Tobago's most ebullient and kindest
★   hostess, and her husband, Ken, one of its best chefs. The fresh ingredients on the menu may include kingfish, *katchowrie* (spiced split-pea patties, a little like falafel), curried chicken, or suckling pig. You'll always find callaloo, rotis, and coo-coo; sometimes you'll find a "cookup"—a pelau-type rice dish with *everything* in it. The place is officially open only on Wednesday and Friday nights, but Miss Alison will open up on other evenings and for weekend lunches if you call in the morning. The setting, on a wide, shady terrace overlooking the bay, is just about perfect. ⊠ *Robinson and Main sts., Scarborough,* ☎ *868/639–2737. AE, MC, V. Dinner Wed. and Fri. only. Closed weekends.*

$$ ✕ **Kariwak Village.** Recorded steel-band music plays gently in the
★   background at this romantic candlelit spot in the Kariwak Village complex. In a bamboo pavilion that resembles an Amerindian round hut, Cynthia Clovis orchestrates a very original four-course menu. Changing daily, the choices may include christophene (a squash-like fruit) soup, curried green figs, kingfish with shrimp sauce, and coconut cake. Whatever the dish, it will be full of herbs and vegetables picked from Cynthia's organic garden. The nonalcoholic drinks are wonderful. Saturday buffets, with live jazz or calypso, are a Tobagonian highlight. ⊠ *Crown Point, Scarborough,* ☎ *868/639–8442. AE, DC, MC, V.*

$ ✕ **Café Petunia.** This little gem is a true delight—the sort of place that you will brag to your friends that you "discovered." On a little hill and simply decorated in what can only be described as "mauve retro," it's a great place to while away the hours sipping on cappuccino or wine. Owner Petunia Thomas offers a variety of light snacks, salads, and fresh juices that she prepares herself. Friday evenings are lively with a band performing jazz, pop, and calypso standards and featuring the song stylings of Petunia herself. ⊠ *Old Milford Rd., near the Signal Hill turnoff between Crown Point and Scarborough,* ☎ *868/639–6878. No credit cards.*

$ ✕ **First Historical Café/Bar.** This funky little roadside eatery owned by the Washington family is in a traditional West Indian building. The back-porch dining area overlooking the sea has a crushed-rock-and-coral floor, brightly painted yellow, green, and red bamboo walls, time-line posters that present historical tidbits on Tobago, and a thatched roof. The food is simple but good, featuring such island delights as fruit plates, coconut bread, and fish sandwiches. ⊠ *Mile Marker 8, Windward Main Rd., in Studley Park area en route to Charlotteville,* ☎ *868/660–2233. No credit cards.*

CONTEMPORARY

$$$$ ✕ **Tamara's.** Here, at the elegant Coco Reef Resort, you dine on contemporary cuisine with an island twist while musicians play upbeat island songs on stringed instruments. The peach decor and whitewashed wooden ceiling give the place a light feel, and island breezes waft through the palm-tree-lined terrace. You might start with the homemade chicken-liver pâté with pear chutney and char-grilled brioche, followed by the grilled barracuda set on a bed of black-olive puree and dressed with pepper sauce. A full tropical buffet breakfast is served daily; dinner is served nightly. ⊠ *Pigeon Point, Scarborough,* ☎ *868/639–8571. AE, MC, V.*

$$$ ✕ **Arnos Vale Waterwheel Restaurant.** You'll find this popular eatery on landscaped grounds in a rain-forest nature park, where gleaming hardwood walkways take you past remnants of an old sugar mill. There's a roof overhead, but otherwise you're completely outdoors (insect repellent is a good idea). The decor is naturally elegant, with green

wrought-iron tables and chairs and lights fashioned in the shape of large pineapples. The menu changes but has an Italian flair: shaved pear and Parmesan salad, focaccia with grilled goat cheese, seviche of kingfish, or caramelized breast of chicken on moist polenta with a callaloo sauce. When you arrive at the park entrance, let the attendants know you're dining here to save the park admission fee. The restaurant also offers complimentary pick-up from the airport and all major hotels. ⊠ *Arnos Vale Estate, Franklyn Rd.,* ☎ *868/660–0815. MC, V.*

ITALIAN

$$$$ ✕ **La Tartaruga.** Milanese owner Gabriele de Gaetano is easily the most
★ colorful restaurateur in Tobago and his food the most unforgettable. Sitting on the large patio surrounded by lush foliage with Gabriele rushing from table to table chatting in Italian-laced English is all the entertainment you will need. Dishes are prepared with loving care and come as close to Italian perfection as is conceivably possible. The carpaccio with bruscetta and the tagliatelli with lobster and capers in wine and cream will give your tastebuds fond memories to last for years to come. The restaurant boasts an impressive wine cellar stocked with only Italian wines—be sure to ask for a tour. If you arrive before 6PM you can even shop for your own vintage wine in his charming wine and antique shop upstairs. ⊠ *Buccoo Rd., Buccoo,* ☎ *868/639–0940. Reservations essential. AE, MC, V. Closed Sun.*

ECLECTIC

$$$$ ✕ **Bonkers.** Despite the rather odd name, this restaurant at the Toucan Inn is atmospheric and excellent. Designed by expatriate British co-owner Chris James, the architecture is a blend of Kenyan and Caribbean styles, executed entirely in local teak and open on all sides. The menu is huge; Chris claims it pains him to remove any items, so he just keeps adding more. Once you unroll your pirate scroll menu, you might consider the smoked pork salad appetizer followed by a mouthwatering, aromatic sweet curried lamb. Afterward, move poolside or to the bar to enjoy the popular local entertainment featured on most nights. The restaurant is also open for breakfast and lunch 7 days a week; this is probably the busiest eatery on the island. ⊠ *Store Bay Local Rd., Crown Point,* ☎ *868/639–7173,* FAX *868/639–8933. AE, MC, V.*

$$$$ ✕ **Pinnacle.** The main dining room at Le Grand Courlan Resort and Spa serves a pleasing array of local dishes and international favorites in a large, open, airy space facing the beach. Light dinner music is performed nightly, starting at 8, and service is friendly. For a starter, the crab cake Castara (made with grated sweet potato) is tasty; and for an entrée, the mahimahi seasoned with coconut milk and wrapped in banana leaves with a side of plantain is excellent. ⊠ *Shirvan Rd., Black Rock,* ☎ *868/639–9667. AE, MC, V.*

$$$ ✕ **Rouselle's.** An enchanting terrace high above Scarborough Bay with
★ a big, congenial bar, Rouselle's has a menu that dons different accessories rather than changing completely, so you may find grouper, broiled and served with a fresh creole sauce and several vegetables (garlicky green beans, carrots with ginger, a raw bok choy salad, and potato croquette with spices and celery); mahimahi with white wine sauce; or lobster steamed just so. Whatever is being served, you can trust it will be delicious. An appetizer, hot garlic bread, and dessert (save room for pineapple pie or homemade ice cream) are included in the entrée price. Don't forego the Rouselle's punch: the recipe is supposed to be a secret, but the lovely, welcoming co-owners, Bobbie and Charlene, may let you in on it. ⊠ *Old Windward Rd., Bacolet,* ☎ *868/639–4738. AE, MC, V.*

Beaches

You won't find manicured country-club sand here. But those who enjoy feeling as though they've landed on a desert island will relish the untouched quality of these shores.

Bacolet Beach is a dark-sand beach that was the setting for the films *Swiss Family Robinson* and *Heaven Knows, Mr. Allison*.

Englishman's Bay is a charming beach; what's more, it's usually completely deserted.

Great Courland Bay, near Fort Bennett, has clear, tranquil waters. Its sandy beach—one of Tobago's longest—is home to several glitzy hotels. A marina attracts the yachting crowd.

King's Bay, surrounded by steep green hills, is the most visually satisfying of the swimming sites off the road from Scarborough to Speyside—the bay hooks around so severely you'll feel like you're in a lake. The crescent-shape beach is easy to find because it's marked by a sign about halfway between Roxborough and Speyside. Just before you reach the bay, there's a bridge with an unmarked turnoff that leads to a gravel parking lot; beyond that, a landscaped path leads to a waterfall with a rocky pool. You may meet locals who will offer to guide you to the top of the falls; however, you may find the climb not worth the effort.

Little Rockley Bay is west of Scarborough (take Milford Road off the main highway). The beach is craggy and not much good for swimming or sunbathing, but it's quiet and offers a pleasing view of Tobago's capital across the water.

Lovers Beach is so called because of its pink sand and its seclusion: you have to hire a local to bring you here by boat.

Man O' War Bay is in the pretty little fishing village of Charlotteville (just northwest of Speyside). You can lounge on the sand and purchase the day's catch for your dinner.

Mt. Irvine Beach, across the street from the Mt. Irvine Bay Hotel, is an unremarkable setting, but it has great surfing in July and August; the snorkeling is excellent, too. It's also ideal for windsurfing in January and April. There are picnic tables surrounded by painted concrete pagodas and a snack bar.

Parlatuvier, on the north side of the island, is best approached via the road from Roxborough. The beach here is a classic Caribbean crescent, a scene peopled by villagers and fishermen.

Pigeon Point is the stunning locale displayed on Tobago travel brochures. Although the beach is public, it abuts part of what was once a large coconut estate, and you must pay a token admission (about TT$10) to enter the grounds and use the facilities. The beach is lined with towering royal palms, and there are food stands, gift shops, a diving concession, and paddleboats for rent. The waters are calm.

Sandy Beach, along Crown Point, is abutted by several hotels. You won't lack for amenities around here.

Stone Haven Bay is a gorgeous stretch of sand that's across the street from the luxurious Grafton Beach Resort.

Store Bay, where boats depart for Buccoo Reef, is a very convivial setting. The beach is little more than a small sandy cove between two rocky breakwaters, but the food stands here are divine: six huts licensed by the tourist board to local ladies who sell roti, pelau, and the world's messiest dish—crab and dumplings. Miss Jean's (☎ 868/639–0563) is the most popular; but you should try Miss Esmie's crab.

Turtle Beach is named for the leatherback turtles that lay their eggs here at night between February and June. (If you're very quiet, you can watch; the turtles don't seem to mind.) It's set on Great Courland Bay.

Outdoor Activities and Sports

BIRD-WATCHING

Some 200 varieties of birds have been documented on Tobago: look for the yellow oriole, scarlet ibis, and the comical motmot—the male of the species clears sticks and stones from an area and then does a dance complete with snapping sounds to attract a mate. The flora is as vivid as the birds. Purple and yellow *poui* trees and spectacular orange immortelles splash color over the countryside, and something is blooming virtually every season. Naturalist and ornithologist **David Rooks** (☎ 868/639–4276) offers bird-watching walks inland and trips to offshore bird colonies. Call Pat Turpin (☎ 868/660–4327) or Renson Jack (☎ 868/660–5175) at **Pioneer Journeys** for information about their bird-watching tours of Bloody Bay rain forest and Louis D'Or River valley wetlands.

BOATING

Hew's Glass Bottom Boat Tours (✉ Pigeon Point, ☎ 868/639–9058) are perfect excursions for those who neither snorkel nor dive. Boats leave daily at 11:30 AM. **Kalina Kats** (✉ Scarborough, ☎ 868/639–6304) has a 50-ft catamaran on which you can sail around the Tobago coastline with stops for snorkeling and exploring the rain forest. The romantic sunset cruise with cocktails is a great way to end the day.

FISHING

Dillon's Fishing Charter (✉ Crown Point, ☎ 868/639–8765) is excellent for full- and half-day trips for kingfish, barracuda, wahoo, mahimahi, blue marlin, and others. Trips start at $165 for four hours, including equipment.

GOLF

The 18-hole course at the **Mt. Irvine Golf Club** (✉ Mt. Irvine Bay Hotel, ☎ 868/639–8871) has been ranked among the top five in the Caribbean and among the top 100 in the world. Greens fees are $30 for 9 holes; $48 for 18 holes (note that these rates are subject to 15% VAT tax).

HIKING

Eco-consciousness is strong on both islands and especially on Tobago, where the rain forests of the Main Ridge were set aside for protection in 1764, creating the first such preserve in the western hemisphere. Natural areas include Little Tobago and St. Giles islands, both major seabird sanctuaries. In addition, the endangered leatherback turtles maintain breeding grounds on some of Tobago's leeward beaches.

They groomed some of the rain forest around the **Arnos Vale Waterwheel** (✉ Arnos Vale Estate, Franklyn Rd., ☎ 868/660–0815) to insert a series of shiny wooden walkways that take you past the remnants of an old sugar factory. The walkways allow you to see much of the ruins without disturbing nature. There's also a small museum, an excellent restaurant, and several hiking trails around the property, including a 2½-mi (4-km) loop. The remnants of the Buckra Estate house are on a hilltop that has spectacular views of Tobago. There are also two Amerindian sights, remains of a slave village, and a tomb. Guides are available and can make your nature-history walk truly come alive. There's a TT$10 admission charge unless you're dining at the restaurant, so let the attendants know if you plan to have a meal here. Private-tour guide **AJM Tours** (⊠ Crown Point Airport, ☎ 868/639–0610, WEB www.ajmtours.com) offers tours of the Arnos Vale Waterwheel complex as well as guided tours of Tobago and even nearby Venezuela.

SCUBA DIVING

An abundance of fish and coral thrives on the nutrients of South America's Orinoco River, which are brought to Tobago by the Guyana current. **Crown Point,** on the island's southwest tip, is a good place for exploring the Shallows—a plateau at about 50–100 ft (15–30½ m) that's favored by turtles, dolphin, angelfish, and nurse sharks. Just north of Crown Point on the southwest coast, **Pigeon Point** is a good spot to submerge. North of Pigeon Point, long sandy beaches line the calm western coast; it has a gradual offshore slope and the popular **Mt. Irvine Wall,** which goes down to about 60 ft (18 m). Off the west coast is **Arnos Vale Reef,** with a depth of 40 ft (12 m) and several reefs that run parallel to the shore. Here you can spot French and queen angelfish, moray eels, southern stingrays, and even the Atlantic torpedo ray. Much of the diving is drift diving in the mostly gentle current.

A short trip from Charlotteville, off the northeast tip of the island, is **St. Giles Island.** Here you'll find natural rock bridges—London Bridge, Marble Island, and Fishbowl—and underwater cliffs. The **waters off Speyside** on the east coast draw scuba-diving aficionados for the many manta rays in the area. Exciting sites in this area include Batteaux Reef, Angel Reef, Bookends, Blackjack Hole, and Japanese Gardens—one of the loveliest reefs, with depths of 20–85 ft (6–26 m) and lots of sponges.

There are several places in Tobago to get information, supplies, and instruction. **AquaMarine Dive Ltd.** (⊠ Blue Waters Inn, Batteaux Bay, Speyside, ☎ 868/660–4341) is on the northeast coast. **Black Rock Divers** (⊠ La Grand Courlan Resort and Spa, Shirvan Rd., Black Rock, ☎ 868/639–0191) is on the west coast. **Man Friday Diving** (⊠ Charlotteville, ☎ 868/660–4676) is on the northwest coast. **Tobago Dive Experience** (⊠ Turtle Beach Hotel, Black Rock, ☎ 868/639–7034) is a west coast operation. **Tobago Dive Masters** (⊠ Speyside, ☎ 868/639–4697) is on the northeastern end of the island.

SNORKELING

Tobago offers many wonderful spots for snorkeling. Although the reefs around Speyside in the northeast are becoming better known, **Buccoo Reef,** off the island's southwest coast, is still the most popular—perhaps too popular. Over the years the reef has been damaged by the ceaseless boat traffic and by the thoughtless visitors who take pieces of coral for souvenirs. Still, it's worth experiencing, particularly if you have children. Daily 2½-hour tours by flat glass-bottom boats let you snorkel at the reef, swim in a lagoon, and gaze at Coral Gardens—where fish and coral are as yet untouched. The trip usually costs about $8, and masks, snorkeling equipment, and reef shoes are provided. Departure is at 11 AM from Pigeon Point. Most dive companies in the Black Rock area also arrange snorkeling tours. There is also good snorkeling near the **Arnos Vale Hotel** and the **Mt. Irvine Bay Hotel.**

TENNIS

Guests and nonguests can play on one of **Rex Turtle Beach**'s (⊠ Courland Bay, Black Rock, ☎ 868/639–2851) two lighted, all-weather courts. Lessons are available for $30 per hour. If you are in the Mt. Irvine area, the **Mt. Irvine Hotel** (⊠ Mt. Irvine Bay, ☎ 868/639–8871) has great lighted courts and a splendid view (if you can take your eye of the ball). The remote enclave of **Blue Waters Inn** (⊠ Batteaux Bay,

Speyside, ☎ 868/660–4341) on the northeast Atlantic coast has two of the best courts on the island and also allows nonresidents to play.

Shopping

The souvenir-bound will do better in Trinidad than in Tobago, but determined shoppers should manage to ferret out some things to take home. Scarborough has the largest collection of shops, and Burnett Street, which slopes sharply from the port to St. James Park, is a good place to browse.

FOODSTUFFS

Forro's Homemade Delicacies (✉ The Andrew's Rectory, Bacolet Street–opposite the fire station, Scarborough, ☎ 868/639–2485) sells its own fine line of homemade tamarind chutney, lemon or lime marmalade, hot sauce, and guava or golden apple jelly. Eileen Forrester, wife of the Anglican Archdeacon of Trinidad and Tobago, supervises a kitchen full of good cooks who boil and bottle the condiments and pack them in little straw baskets—or even in bamboo. Most jars are small, easy to carry, and inexpensive.

HANDICRAFTS

Cotton House (✉ Bacolet St., Scarborough, ☎ 868/639–2727) is a good bet for jewelry and imaginative batik work. Paula Young runs her shop like an art school. You can visit the upstairs studio; if it's not too busy, you can even make a batik square at no charge. **Souvenir and Gift Shop** (✉ Port Mall, Scarborough, ☎ 868/639–5632) stocks straw baskets and other crafts.

Nightlife

Tobago is not the liveliest island after dark but there is usually some form of nightlife to be found. Whatever you do the rest of the week, don't miss the huge impromptu party, affectionately dubbed Sunday School, that gears up after midnight on all the street corners of Buccoo and breaks up around dawn. Pick your band, hang out for a while, then move on. In downtown Scarborough on weekend nights you can also find competing sound systems blaring at informal parties that welcome extra guests. In addition, "blockos" (spontaneous block parties) spring up all over the island; look for the hand-painted signs. Tobago also has harvest parties on Sunday throughout the year, when a particular village extends its hospitality and opens its doors to visitors.

Bonkers (✉ Store Bay Local Rd., ☎ 868/639–7173) is lively on most evenings with live entertainment every night except Sunday. **The Deep** (✉ at Sandy Point Hotel in Crown Point, ☎ 868/639–8533) is a basement pub/disco that features an unusual blend of pop, rock and soca on their sound system. **Grafton Beach Resort** (✉ Black Rock, ☎ 868/639–0191) has some kind of organized cabaret-style event every night. Even if you hate that touristy stuff, check out Les Couteaux Cultural Group, which does a high-octane dance version of Tobagonian history. **Kariwak Village** (✉ Crown Point, ☎ 868/639–8442) has hip hotel entertainment and is frequented as much by locals as visitors on Friday and Saturday nights—one of the better local jazz-calypso bands almost always plays.

Exploring Tobago

A driving tour of Tobago, from Scarborough to Charlotteville and back, can be done in about four hours, but you'd never want to undertake this spectacular, and very hilly, ride in that time. The switchbacks can make you wish you had motion-sickness pills (take some along if you're prone). Plan to spend at least one night at the Speyside end of the island, and give yourself a chance to enjoy this largely untouched country and seaside at leisure.

Numbers in the margin correspond to points of interest on the Tobago map.

SIGHTS TO SEE

❺ Charlotteville. This delightful fishing village in the northeast is enfolded in a series of steep hills. Fishermen here announce the day's catch by sounding their conch shells. A view of Man O' War Bay with Pigeon Peak (Tobago's highest mountain) behind it at sunset is an exquisite treat.

❻ The underwater cliffs and canyons at **St. Giles Island,** off the northeastern tip of Tobago, draw divers to this spot where the Atlantic meets the Caribbean. ⊠ *Take Windward Rd. inland across mountains from Speyside.*

❹ Flagstaff Hill. One of the highest points of the island sits at the northern tip of Tobago. Surrounded by ocean on three sides and with a view of other hills, Charlotteville, and St. Giles Island, this was the site of an American military lookout and radio tower during World War II. It's an ideal spot for a sunset picnic.

❷ Ft. King George. On Mt. St. George, a short drive up the hill from Scarborough, Tobago's best-preserved historic monument clings to a cliff high above the ocean. Ft. King George was built in the 1770s and operated until 1854. It's hard to imagine that this lovely, tranquil spot commanding sweeping views of the bay and landscaped with lush tropical foliage was ever the site of any military action, but the prison, officers' mess, and several stabilized cannons attest otherwise. Just to the left of the tall wooden figures dancing a traditional Tobagonian jig is the former barrack guardhouse, now home to the small **Tobago Museum.** Exhibits include a variety of weapons along with pre-Columbian artifacts found in the area; the fertility figures are especially interesting. Upstairs are maps and photographs of Tobago's past. Be sure to check out the gift display cases for the perversely fascinating jewelry made from embalmed and painted lizards and sea creatures; you might find it hard to resist a pair of bright-yellow shrimp earrings. ⊠ *84 Fort St., Scarborough,* ☎ *868/639–3970.* 🖅 *TT$5.* ☺ *Weekdays 9–5.*

The **Fine Arts Centre** at the foot of the Ft. King George complex features the work of local artists.

❶ Scarborough. Around Rockley Bay on the island's leeward hilly side, this town is both the capital of Tobago and a popular cruise-ship port, but it conveys the feeling that not much has changed since the area was settled two centuries ago. It may not be one of the delightful pastel-color cities of the Caribbean, but Scarborough does have its charms, including an array of interesting little shops. Whatever you do be sure to check out the busy Scarborough Market, an indoor and outdoor affair featuring everything from fresh vegetables to live chickens and clothing. Note the red-and-yellow Methodist church on the hill, one of Tobago's oldest churches.

❸ Speyside. At the far reach of the windward coast of Tobago, this small fishing village has a few lodgings and restaurants. Divers are drawn to the unspoiled reefs in the area and to the strong possibility of spotting giant manta rays. The approach to Speyside from the south affords one of the most spectacular vistas of the island. Glass-bottom boats operate between Speyside and **Little Tobago Island,** one of the most important seabird sanctuaries in the Caribbean.

TRINIDAD AND TOBAGO A TO Z

To research prices, get advice from other travelers, and book travel arrangements, visit www.fodors.com.

AIR TRAVEL

American Airlines offers daily direct flights from both New York and Miami to Trinidad. The national carrier, BWIA West Indies Airways, offers direct flights to Trinidad from Atlanta, Miami, New York, and Washington, DC, in the U.S.; from Toronto in Canada; and from London in the U.K.; and many Caribbean islands; it also offers at least six connections to Tobago daily from Trinidad. Air Canada flies nonstop from Toronto to Trinidad; British Airways offers weekly flights to Tobago from London (the number of lights increases in peak season). LIAT offers numerous flights to Trinidad from other Caribbean islands; it also has service from the eastern Caribbean islands to Tobago. Air ALM has direct flights from Curaçao to Trinidad on Tuesday, Thursday, and Sunday; flights from Aruba and Bonaire connect with this Curaçao flight.

➤ AIRLINES AND CONTACTS: **Air ALM** (☎ 868/623–6522); **Air Canada** (☎ 868/664–4065); **American Airlines** (☎ 868/664–4661); **British Airways** (☎ 800/744–2997); **BWIA West Indies Airways** (☎ 868/625–1010 or 868/669–3000); **LIAT** (☎ 868/627–2942 or 868/623–1838).

AIRPORTS

Trinidad's Piarco International Airport, located about 30 minutes east of Port-of-Spain (take Golden Grove Road north to Arouca and then follow Eastern Main Road west for about 10 mi (16 km) to Port-of-Spain, is a spanking new structure that claims to be the most modern airport in the Caribbean. Tobago's Crown Point Airport is the gateway to the island. Taxis are readily available at Piarco Airport; the fare to Port-of-Spain is set at $20 ($30 after 10 PM) and $24 to the Hilton. In Tobago the fare from Crown Point Airport to Scarborough is fixed at $8, to Speyside at $36.

➤ AIRPORT INFORMATION: **Piarco International Airport** (☎ 868/669–4101, WEB www.airporttnt.com); **Crown Point Airport** (☎ 868/639–0509, WEB www.airporttnt.com).

BOAT AND FERRY TRAVEL

FARES AND SCHEDULES

The Port Authority maintains ferry service every day except Saturday between Trinidad and Tobago, although flying is preferable because the seas can be very rough. The ferry leaves once a day (from St. Vincent Street Jetty in Port-of-Spain and from the cruise-ship complex in Scarborough); the trip takes about five hours. The round-trip fare is TT$60. Cabins, when available, run TT$160 (round trip, double occupancy).

➤ BOAT AND FERRY INFORMATION: In Port-of-Spain, Trinidad (☎ 868/625–3055, WEB www.patnt.com/ferry.htm); in Scarborough, Tobago (☎ 868/639–2181, WEB www.patnt.com/ferry.htm).

BUSINESS HOURS

BANKS

Banks are open Monday–Thursday 8–3, on Friday 8–noon and 3–5.

POST OFFICES

Post offices are open 8–noon and 1–4:30 on weekdays.

SHOPS
Most shops are open weekdays 8–4:30, Saturday 8–noon; malls stay open later during the week and operate all day Saturday.

CAR RENTALS
All agencies require a credit card deposit, and in peak season you must make reservations well in advance of your arrival. Figure on paying $40–$60 per day in both Trinidad and Tobago. In addition to Thrifty, an international company, there are several local agencies operating on either Trinidad or Tobago or both; Auto Rentals is a local company with many locations on Trinidad.

➤ MAJOR AGENCIES IN TRINIDAD: **Auto Rentals** (☒ Piarco International Airport, ☎ 868/669–2277); **Econo-Car Rentals** (☒ Piarco International Airport, ☎ 868/669–2342); **Southern Sales Car Rentals** (☒ Piarco International Airport and other locations, ☎ 868/669–2424; dial ☎ 269 from a courtesy phone in airport baggage area); **Thrifty** (☒ Piarco International Airport, ☎ 868/669–0602).

➤ MAJOR AGENCIES IN TOBAGO: **Rattan's Car Rentals** (☒ Crown Point Airport, ☎ 868/639–8271); **Rollock's Car Rentals** (☒ Crown Point International Airport ☎ 868/639–0328); **Singh's Auto Rentals** (☒ Grafton Beach Resort, ☎ 868/639–0191 ext. 53); **Thrifty** (☒ Rex Turtle Beach Hotel, Courland Bay, Black Rock, ☎ 868/639–8507).

CAR TRAVEL
It's not worth renting a car if you're staying in Port-of-Spain, where the streets are often jammed with drivers who routinely play chicken with one another; taxis are your best bet. If you're planning to tour Trinidad, you'll need some wheels. In Tobago you're better off renting a four-wheel-drive vehicle than relying on expensive taxi service.

GASOLINE
Gas runs about TT$2.45 per liter. There are plenty of gas stations in Trinidad, but in Tobago, don't let your tank get low because there aren't many gas stations on the island.

ROAD CONDITIONS
Despite being one of the world's largest exporters of natural asphalt, Trinidad can't seem to get its roads smooth. Holes tend to pop up in unexpected places; keep your eyes peeled. Be especially careful when driving during the rainy season, as roads often flood. Never drive into downtown Port-of-Spain during afternoon rush hour.

In Tobago, many roads, particularly in the interior or on the coast near Speyside and Charlotteville, are bumpy, pitted, winding, and/or steep (though the main highways are smooth and fast).

RULES OF THE ROAD
Driving is on the left, in the British style, so remember to look to your right when pulling out into traffic.

ELECTRICITY
Electric current is usually 110 volts, but some establishments provide 220-volt outlets.

EMBASSIES
➤ CANADA: **Canadian High Commission** (3-3A Sweet Briar Rd., St. Clair, Port of Spain, ☎ 868/622–6232).
➤ UNITED KINGDOM: **British High Commission** (19 St. Clair Ave., St. Clair, Port of Spain, ☎ 868/622–2748).
➤ UNITED STATES: **U.S. Embassy** (15 Queen's Park West, Port of Spain, ☎ 868/622–6371).

EMERGENCIES

➤ AMBULANCE AND FIRE: Dial ☎ 990.

➤ HOSPITALS: **Port-of-Spain General Hospital** (✉ 169 Charlotte St., ☎ 868/623–2951); **St. Clair Medical Centre** (✉ 18 Elizabeth St., St. Clair, Port-of-Spain, ☎ 868/628–1451); **Scarborough Hospital** (✉ Fort St., Scarborough, ☎ 868/639–2551).

➤ PHARMACIES: **Kappa Drugs** (Roxy Round-a-bout, St. James, ☎ 868/622–2728); **Bhaggan's** (Charlotte and Oxford sts., Port-of-Spain, ☎ 868/627–4657); **Scarborough Drugs** (✉ Carrington St. and Wilson Rd., Tobago, ☎ 868/639–4161).

➤ POLICE: Dial ☎ 999.

Etiquette and Behavior

Religious and racial tolerance are important to the people of Trinidad and Tobago. You may hear a word used in public that elsewhere might constitute a slur; on these islands, chances are it's being used in jest—but only by locals who know one another well. Many islanders are well educated and well traveled; don't assume they're unfamiliar with international politics and customs. As in many British-influenced Caribbean nations, beach attire isn't appreciated in stores, restaurants, or hotel lobbies.

FESTIVALS AND SEASONAL EVENTS

In addition to the incomparable Trinidad Carnival, there are a number of celebrations throughout the year. During the Tobago Heritage Festival (July 16–Aug. 1) villages throughout the island hold events and activities that portray one aspect (music, dance, drama, cooking, costuming) of island arts or culture. October's Divali, known as the festival of lights, is the climax of long spiritual preparation in the Hindu community. Small lamps beautifully illuminate the night, and there are events involving music, dancing, gift exchanges, and much hospitality.

HEALTH

Insect repellent is a must during the rainy season (June–December) and is worth having around anytime. Trinidad is only 11 degrees north of the equator, and the sun here can be intense; bring a strong sun block. If you have a sensitive stomach, you're better off drinking bottled water, though tap water on the islands is generally safe.

HOLIDAYS

Public holidays for 2002 are: New Year's Day, Good Friday, Easter Monday, Indian Arrival Day (May 30), Labor Day (June 19), Emancipation Day (Aug. 1), Independence Day (Aug. 31), Spiritual Baptist Liberation Day (March 30), Divali (date is announced by government a few months before, but it is usually in October or November), Eid (a Muslim festival whose actual date late in the year varies), Christmas, and Boxing Day (Dec. 26). Carnival Monday and Tuesday are not official holidays, but don't expect anything to be open (in 2002 February 11th and 12th, in 2003 March 3rd and 4th).

LANGUAGE

The official language of Trinidad & Tobago is English, although there's no end of idiomatic expressions used by the loquacious locals. If the sun shines while it rains, folks here say the devil and his wife are fighting over a ham bone. If someone invites you for a "lime," by all means go—you're being invited to a party; "limin' " means relaxing and having a good time. To "beat pan" is to play the steel drum; "wine" is a sexy dance style done by rotating the hips. You'll also hear smatterings of French, Spanish, Chinese, and Hindi (Trinidad's population is about 40% Indian).

MAIL AND SHIPPING

Postage to the United States and Canada is TT$2.25 for first-class letters and TT$2 for postcards; prices are slightly higher for other destinations. The main post offices are on Wrightson Road (opposite the Crowne Plaza), in Port-of-Spain, and in the NIB Mall on Wilson Street (near the docks), in Scarborough. There are no zip codes on the islands. To write to an establishment here, you simply need its address, town, and "Trinidad and Tobago, West Indies."

MONEY MATTERS

Prices quoted in this chapter are in U.S. dollars unless otherwise noted.

ATMS

Banks (many with ATMs that accept international cards) are plentiful in the towns and cities (branches of the Republic Bank and the Royal Bank are a common sight) but much less so in the countryside. In addition to the banks in Scarborough and Tobago's airport, a couple of grocery stores in the southwest part of Tobago have ATMs.

CREDIT CARDS

Credit cards and ATM cards are almost universally accepted for payment by businesses, hotels, and restaurants. VISA and Mastercard are ubiquitous, American Express much less so, and Diner's Club and Discover rarely accepted. Cash is necessary only in the smallest neighborhood convenience shops and roadside stalls.

CURRENCY

The current exchange rate for the Trinidadian dollar (TT$) is about TT$6.30 to US$1. Most businesses on the island will accept U.S. currency if you're in a pinch.

PASSPORTS AND VISAS

Citizens of the United States, the United Kingdom, and Canada who expect to stay for less than six weeks may enter the country with a valid passport. Citizens of Australia and New Zealand must also obtain a visa before entering the country.

SAFETY

Travelers should exercise reasonable caution in Trinidad, especially in Port of Spain, where walking on the streets at night is not recommended. As a general rule, Tobago is safer than its larger sister island, though this should not lure you into a false sense of security. Petty theft occurs on both islands, so don't leave cash in bags that you check at the airport, and use hotel safes for valuables.

SIGHTSEEING TOURS

IN TRINIDAD

Almost any taxi driver in Port-of-Spain will take you around town and to beaches on the north coast. It costs around $70 for up to four people to go Maracas Bay beach, plus $20 per hour extra if you decide to go farther; but you should haggle for a cheaper rate. For a complete list of tour operators and sea cruises, contact the tourism office. The Travel Centre is one of Trinidad's best tour operators; its office is also American Express's card-member services office. Winston Nanan is the only official tour operator at the Caroni Bird Sanctuary; phone or write him in advance for reservations.

➤ CONTACTS: **The Travel Centre** (✉ 44–58 Edward St., Port-of-Spain, ☎ 868/623–5096, WEB www.the-travel-centre.com); **Winston Nanan** (✉ Nanan Bird Sanctuary Tours, 38 Bamboo Grove, No. 1, Uriah Butler Hwy., Valsayn, ☎ 868/645–1305).

Frank's Glass Bottom Boat and Birdwatching Tours offers glass-bottom-boat and snorkeling tours of the shores of Speyside; Frank also conducts guided tours of the rain forest and Little Tobago. As a native of Speyside, he's extremely knowledgeable about the island's flora, fauna, and folklore. Rooks Nature Tours offers a variety of tours, including rain-forest hikes and bird-watching expeditions, all with ornithologist David Rooks. Tobago Travel is the island's most experienced tour operator, offering a wide array of services and tours.

➤ CONTACTS: **Frank's Glass Bottom Boat and Birdwatching Tours** (✉ Speyside, Tobago, ☎ FAX 868/660–5438); **Rooks Nature Tours** (✉ 462 Moses Hill, Lambeau, ☎ 868/639–4276, WEB www.pariasprings.com/rookstours/tours.html); **Tobago Travel** (✉ Scarborough, ☎ 868/639–8778).

TAXES

DEPARTURE TAX
Departure tax, payable at the airport, is TT$100.

SALES TAX
All hotels will add a 15% government tax.

VALUE ADDED TAX (V.A.T.)
Restaurants charge a 15% V.A.T.

TAXIS
Taxis in Trinidad & Tobago are easily identified by their license plates, which begin with the letter H. Passenger vans, called Maxi Taxis, pick up and drop off passengers as they travel and are color-coded according to which of the six areas they cover. Rates are generally less than $1 per trip. (Yellow is for Port-of-Spain, red for eastern Trinidad, green for south Trinidad, and black for Princes Town. Brown operates from San Fernando to the southeast—Erin, Penal, Point Fortin. The only color for Tobago is blue.) They're easy to hail day or night along most of the main roads near Port-of-Spain. For longer trips you will need to hire a private taxi. Cabs aren't metered; many routes have fixed rates, though they aren't always observed, particularly at Carnival. Pick up a rate sheet from the tourism office. On the whole, drivers are honest, friendly, and informative, and the experience of riding in a Maxi Taxi with a souped-up sound system during Carnival is worth whatever fare you pay.

TELEPHONES
A digital phone system is now in place, bringing with it direct-dial service, a comprehensive cell-phone network, and easy Internet access. Pay phones take phone cards, which you can buy in different denominations at gift shops and newsagents.

COUNTRY AND AREA CODES
The area code for both islands is 868 ("TNT" if you forget). This is also the country code if you are calling to Trinidad & Tobago from another country.

INTERNATIONAL CALLS
Most hotels and guest houses will allow you to dial a direct international call. To dial a number in North America or the Caribbean simply dial "1" and the area code before the number you are calling, but be warned that most hotels add a hefty surcharge for overseas calls. Calls to Europe and elsewhere can be made by checking for the appropriate direct dial codes in the telephone directory. To make an international call from a pay phone you must first purchase a "companion card," which is readily available from most convenience shops—then

simply follow the instructions on the card. Cards are available in various denominations.

LOCAL CALLS

To make a local call to any point in the country simply dial the seven-digit local number.

TIPPING

Almost all hotels will add a 10%–15% service charge to your bill. Most restaurants include a 10% service charge, which is considered standard on these islands. If it isn't on the bill, tip according to service: 10%–15% is fine. Cabbies expect a token tip of around 10%. At drinking establishments tipping is optional, and the staff at smaller bars may tell you on your way out that you forgot your change.

VISITOR INFORMATION

➤ BEFORE YOU LEAVE: In the U.S., call Trinidad and Tobago's **Tourism Hotline** (☎ 888/595–4TNT). Or you can contact the **Trinidad and Tobago Tourism Office** (✉ 331 Almeria Ave., Coral Gables, Florida 33134, ☎ 800/748–4224; ✉ Mitre House, 66 Abbey Rd. Bush Park Hill, Enfield, Middlesex, England, EN1 2RQ, ☎ 011–44–208/350–1000; ✉ Taurus House, 512 Duplex Ave., Toronto, Ontario, Canada, M4R 2E3, ☎ 416/535–5617 or 416/485–8724, WEB www.visitTNT.com).

➤ IN TRINIDAD: Contact **TIDCO** (✉ 10–14 Phillips St., Port-of-Spain, ☎ 868/623–6023 or 868/623–1932; ✉ Piarco Airport, ☎ 868/669–5196, WEB www.visitTNT.com).

➤ IN TOBAGO: Contact the **Tobago Division of Tourism** (✉ N.I.B. Mall, Level 3, Scarborough, ☎ 868/639–2125), or drop in at its information booth at Crown Point Airport (☎ 868/639–0509, WEB www. visitTNT.com).

24 TURKS AND CAICOS ISLANDS

Updated by
Kathy Borsuk

"Everything cool, man?" Shadow asks with a laugh as he cuts the speedboat through Crocodile Pass en route to Middle Caicos. A Caribbean renaissance man, Shadow took his nickname from an uncanny ability to sneak up on bonefish. He also bats .500 for the local all-star team, fishes for trophy-size blue marlin in the annual rodeo, plays a mean guitar, and tells a great story. When he reaches the shore, he plans to whip up a batch of seviche using fresh conch, onion, sweet peppers, lime juice, and Tabasco—thus adding "cook" to an impressive, island-style resume.

Sportfishermen, scuba divers, and beach aficionados have long known about the Turks and Caicos (pronounced *kay*-kos). To them this British Crown colony of more than 40 islands and small cays (only eight of which are inhabited) is a gem that offers priceless stretches of sand and offshore reefs rich in marine life. Whether you're swimming with the fishes or attempting to catch them from the surface, the Turks and Caicos won't disappoint. In an archipelago 575 mi (927 km) southeast of Miami and 90 mi (145 km) north of Haiti, the total landmass of these two groups of islands is 193 square mi (500 square km); the total population is less than 25,000.

The Turks Islands include Grand Turk, which is the capital and seat of government, and Salt Cay. It's claimed that Columbus's first landfall was on Grand Turk. Legend also has it that these islands were named by early settlers who thought the scarlet blossoms on the local cactus resembled the Turkish fez.

Approximately 22 mi (35½ km) west of Grand Turk, across the 7,000-ft-deep (2,141-m-deep) Columbus Passage, is the Caicos group: South, East, West, Middle, and North Caicos and Providenciales (nicknamed Provo). South Caicos, Middle Caicos, North Caicos, and Provo are the only inhabited islands in this group; Pine Cay and Parrot Cay are the only inhabited cays. "Caicos" is derived from *cayos*, the Spanish word for "cay" and is believed to mean, appropriately, "string of islands."

In the mid-1600s, Bermudians began to rake salt from the flats on the Turks Islands, returning to Bermuda to sell their crop. Despite French and Spanish attacks and pirate raids, the Bermudians persisted and established a trade that became the bedrock of the islands' economy. In

1766 Andrew Symmers settled here to hold the islands for England. The American Declaration of Independence left British loyalists from South Carolina and Georgia without a country, causing many to take advantage of British Crown land grants in the Turks and Caicos. Cotton plantations were established and prospered for nearly 25 years until the boll weevil, soil exhaustion, and a terrible hurricane in 1813 devastated the land. Left behind to make their living off the land and sea were the former slaves, who remained to shape the culture of today.

Today the Turks and Caicos are known as a reputable offshore tax haven whose company formation, banking, trusts, and insurance institutions lure investors from the United States, Canada, and beyond. Provo, in particular, is on its way to becoming a popular Caribbean tourist destination. Mass tourism, however, shouldn't be in the cards; government guidelines promote a quality, not quantity policy, including conservation awareness. And without a port for cruise ships, the islands remain uncrowded and peaceful.

THE TURKS

Grand Turk

Bermudian colonial architecture abounds on this string bean of an island (just 7 mi/11 km long and 1½ mi/2½ km wide). Buildings have walled-in courtyards to keep wandering horses from nibbling on the foliage. The island caters to divers, and it's no wonder: the wall, a slice of vertical coral mountain, is less than 300 yards from the beach.

Lodging

Throughout the islands accommodations range from small (sometimes non-air-conditioned) inns to splashy resorts and hotels that are the ultimate in luxury. Most medium and large hotels offer a choice of EP and MAP. Almost all hotels offer dive packages.

Another popular option, especially on Provo, is renting a self-contained villa or private home. **Elliot Holdings and Management Company** (⊠ Box 235, Providenciales, ☎ 649/946–5355, WEB www.provo.net/elliot) offers a wide selection of modest to magnificent villas in the Leeward, Grace Bay, and Turtle Cove areas of Providenciales. **T C Safari** (⊠ Box 64, Providenciales, ☎ 649/941–5043, WEB www.tcsafari.tc) has exclusive oceanfront properties in the beautiful and tranquil Sapodilla Bay/Chalk Sound neighborhood on Provo's southwest shores. For the best villa selection, plan to make your reservations three to six months in advance.

CATEGORY	COST*
$$$$	over $250
$$$	$170–$250
$$	$110–$170
$	under $110

All prices are for a standard double room in winter, excluding 9% tax and 10%–15% service charge. Note that the government hotel tax doesn't apply to guest houses with fewer than four rooms.

$$$$ 🏠 **The Arches of Grand Turk.** If you're looking for a home away from home, these immaculate vacation town houses will more than satisfy. Newly built by on-site owners Wally and Cecile Wennick, each of the four two-story units offers space, privacy, and a loving touch. Suites are fully furnished and decor is clean-cut country style. Kitchen/dining areas are on the lower levels, with two huge bedrooms upstairs. Arched balconies front and back promise breathtaking sunrises and

Turks and Caicos Islands

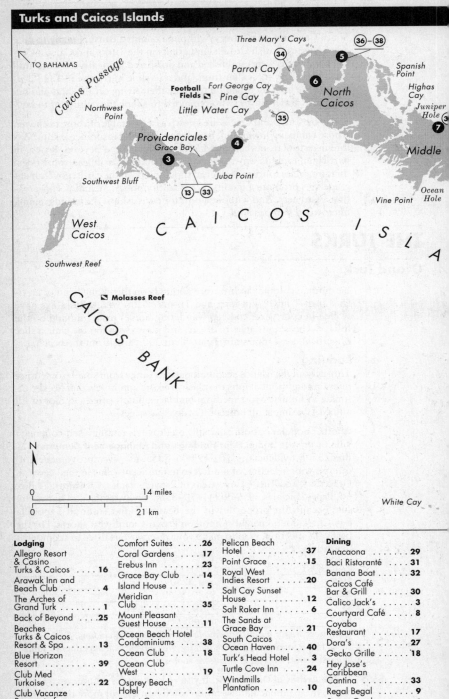

Lodging

Allegro Resort
& Casino
Turks & Caicos **16**
Arawak Inn and
Beach Club **4**
The Arches of
Grand Turk **1**
Back of Beyond **25**
Beaches
Turks & Caicos
Resort & Spa **13**
Blue Horizon
Resort **39**
Club Med
Turkoise **22**
Club Vacanze
Prospect of
Whitby Hotel **36**

Comfort Suites **26**
Coral Gardens **17**
Erebus Inn **23**
Grace Bay Club . . . **14**
Island House **5**
Meridian
Club **35**
Mount Pleasant
Guest House **11**
Ocean Beach Hotel
Condominiums . . . **38**
Ocean Club **18**
Ocean Club
West **19**
Osprey Beach
Hotel **2**
Parrot Cay
Resort **34**

Pelican Beach
Hotel **37**
Point Grace **15**
Royal West
Indies Resort **20**
Salt Cay Sunset
House **12**
Salt Raker Inn **6**
The Sands at
Grace Bay **21**
South Caicos
Ocean Haven **40**
Turk's Head Hotel . . **3**
Turtle Cove Inn **24**
Windmills
Plantation **10**

Dining

Anacaona **29**
Baci Ristoranté **31**
Banana Boat **32**
Caicos Café
Bar & Grill **30**
Calico Jack's **3**
Courtyard Café **8**
Coyaba
Restaurant **17**
Dora's **27**
Gecko Grille **18**
Hey Jose's
Caribbean
Cantina **33**
Regal Begal **9**
Secret Garden **6**

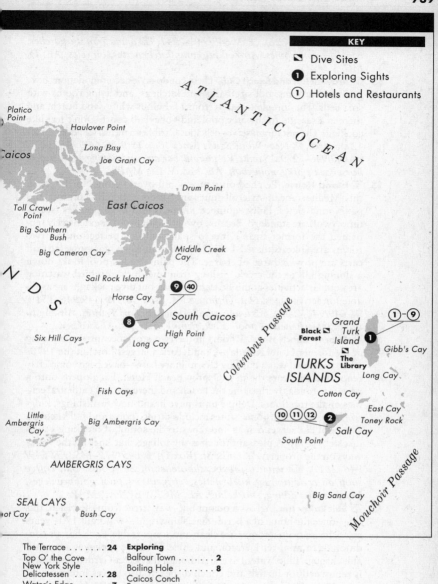

KEY

◈ Dive Sites

❶ Exploring Sights

① Hotels and Restaurants

ATLANTIC OCEAN

Platico
Point

Haulover Point

Caicos

Long Bay

Joe Grant Cay

Drum Point

Toll Crawl
Point

East Caicos

Big Southern
Bush

Big Cameron Cay

Middle Creek
Cay

Sail Rock Island

❾ **④⓪**

N D S

Horse Cay

❽

South Caicos

Six Hill Cays

High Point

Long Cay

Columbus Passage

Black
Forest

Grand
Turk
Island

Gibb's Cay

①–**❾**

①

TURKS
ISLANDS

The
Library

Long Cay

Fish Cays

Cotton Cay

East Cay

Little
Ambergris
Cay

Big Ambergris Cay

❿ **⑪** **⑫**

❷

Toney Rock

Salt Cay

South Point

AMBERGRIS CAYS

SEAL CAYS

ot Cay

Bush Cay

Big Sand Cay

Mouchoir Passage

The Terrace **24**

Top O' the Cove
New York Style
Delicatessen **28**

Water's Edge **7**

Exploring

Balfour Town **2**

Boiling Hole **8**

Caicos Conch
Farm **4**

Cockburn
Harbour **9**

Cockburn Town **1**

Conch Bar Caves . . . **7**

Downtown Provo **3**

Flamingo Pond **5**

Kew **6**

sunsets. Atop the ridge northeast of town, steady breezes keep insects away, and you can expect an eagle's-eye view of the island. ✉ *Lighthouse Rd. (Box 226),* ☎ 🖷 *649/946–2941,* 🌐 *www.grandturkarches. com. 4 town homes. Air-conditioning, kitchenettes, bicycles. AE, D, MC, V.*

$$ 🏠 **Arawak Inn and Beach Club.** These condo-style accommodations have private bedrooms, full-size baths and kitchens, and living rooms with sofa beds. The complex is steps from a fabulous white-sand beach, and there is a seaside freshwater pool and volleyball court. Don't feel like cooking? The restaurant serves delicious Caribbean meals. Children under 12 stay free. ✉ *Near White Sands Beach (Box 190),* ☎ *649/946–2277,* 🖷 *649/946–2279. 15 units. Restaurant, bar, air-conditioning, pool, beach, horseback riding, volleyball. AE, MC, V. CP, MAP.*

$$ 🏠 **Island House.** Perched on a breezy hill overlooking North Creek, this Mediterranean-style all-suites inn offers romantic comfort and panoramic views. Fully equipped kitchens and large porches (sometimes two!) are standard. Because owner Colin Brooker extensively renovated the former Evan's Inn to spanking new perfection, no two rooms are alike. Situated 1 mi (1½ km) from town, gas-powered golf carts are provided free of charge. The palm-shaded pool looks down a sloping hill to the creek. Fishing from the dock and bird-watching are popular activities at this peaceful retreat, but dive packages are available for active types. ✉ *Lighthouse Rd. (Box 36),* ☎ *649/946–1519,* 🖷 *649/946–2646,* 🌐 *www.islandhouse-tci.com. 8 suites. Air-conditioning, kitchenettes, pool, dock, fishing, bicycles. AE, MC, V.*

$$ 🏠 **Osprey Beach Hotel.** Rooms in the two-story oceanfront building at the former Hotel Kittina—Grand Turk's largest hotel in the 1970s when the island was a bustling U.S. military base—have been completely renovated to create the new Osprey Beach Hotel. Each opens onto a private veranda overlooking the beach and there are airy cathedral ceilings on the top floors. Deluxe units have brand-new furnishings, king-size beds, and bathrooms; suites include sitting rooms and full kitchens. The pool bar serves drinks and tapas to the sound of breaking waves just steps away. A pleasant touch is the foliage that lines all the walkways on the property. ✉ *Duke St. (Box 1),* ☎ *649/946–1453,* 🖷 *649/ 946–2817,* 🌐 *www.ospreybeachhotel.com. 28 rooms. Bar, coffee shop, air-conditioning, kitchenettes, refrigerators, pool, golf privileges, beach, scuba diving, snorkeling. AE, MC, V. EP, FAP, MAP.*

$$ 🏠 **Salt Raker Inn.** Across a quaint one-way street from the beach, this inn—once the home of a Bermudian shipwright—was built 170+ years ago. The renovated rooms are clean and comfortable. Each has air-conditioning, a mini-refrigerator, and cable TV. Dive packages are available through Blue Water Divers. Although the Secret Garden restaurant is renowned for its fish and conch dishes, it also serves international fare. ✉ *Duke St. (Box 1),* ☎ *649/946–2260,* 🖷 *649/946–2817,* 🌐 *www.microplan.com. 10 rooms, 3 suites. Restaurant, bar, air-conditioning, refrigerators, bicycles. AE, MC, V. EP, FAP, MAP.*

$$ 🏠 **Turks Head Hotel.** Although thoroughly modernized several years ago, the historical Turks Head Hotel has maintained its romantic charm and tranquil ambience. The two-story structure was built in 1840 as the home of a prosperous salt miner, and has also served as the American consulate and the governor's guest house. Today, rooms are equipped with air-conditioning, antique bedroom furnishings, and mini-refrigerators. The hotel bar and Calico Jack's Restaurant bustle at night; the beach is only a few strides away, and dive packages are available. Children under 12 stay free. ✉ *Duke St. (Box 58),* ☎ *649/ 946–2466,* 🖷 *649/946–1716,* 🌐 *www.grand-turk.com. 8 rooms. Restaurant, bar, air-conditioning, refrigerators, beach, bicycles. MC, V. EP, CP, FAP, MAP.*

Dining

Like everything else on these islands, dining out is a very laid-back affair, which is not to say it's cheap. Because of the high cost of importing all edibles, the price of a meal is usually higher than in the United States. Reservations are generally not required, and dress tends to be casual.

CATEGORY	COST*
$$$	over $25
$$	$15–$25
$	under $15

*per person for a main course at dinner

AMERICAN

$$ ✗ **Water's Edge.** Also known as Jan and Dave's Conch Café, this pleasantly rustic eatery would have to float to be any closer to the ocean. Although Jan and Dave have since left the island, new proprietor Seamus Day is still committed to serving conch in any way, shape, or form—conch salad, cracked conch, conch creole, curried conch, and even conch po' boys. Other choices include giant, juicy "Goo Burgers," made-from-scratch pizza, and homemade pies. ⊠ *Duke St.,* ☎ *649/946–1680. MC, V. Closed Sun.*

CAFÉS

$ ✗ **Courtyard Café.** Homemade waffles with fresh fruit and whipped cream? Huge omelets and oversized muffins? Submarine sandwiches and pasta salad? You'll find it all at this casual café, and you can enjoy your meal in the cool shade of the garden courtyard. Full breakfasts and light lunches are served from 6:45 AM to 4 PM daily. Prices are reasonable and daily specials range from lasagna and quiche to island-style beef patties. ⊠ *Duke St.,* ☎ *649/946–1453. AE, MC, V.*

ECLECTIC

$$ ✗ **Calico Jack's.** The menu changes daily at the lively restaurant—touted by many residents as the best on the island—in the Turks Head Hotel. Among the staples are conch fritters, stone crab claws (flown in from Miami), and local grouper fingers perfectly fried for fish-and-chips. Look for lobster, steaks, chicken curry, lamb shanks, pizza, and homemade soups on the menu, as well as an excellent selection of wines. On Friday nights there's a courtyard barbecue, with live music by local bands. You may not want to leave after your meal—come nightfall, the bar is abuzz with local gossip and mirthful chatter. ⊠ *Duke St.,* ☎ *649/946–2466. MC, V.*

SEAFOOD

$$ ✗ **Secret Garden.** Menu highlights at the Salt Raker Inn's restaurant include local conch and fish (grouper and snapper) dishes and grilled lobster tail. For dessert try the Caribbean bread pudding or Key Lime pie. Morning offerings include a full English breakfast and an island favorite, fish-and-grits. The Wednesday- and Sunday-night sing-alongs, featuring local guitarist/divemaster Mitch Rolling, are popular, as are the Wednesday- and Saturday-night steak, ribs, chicken, and seafood barbecues. ⊠ *Duke St.,* ☎ *649/946–2260. AE, MC, V.*

$ ✗ **Regal Begal.** Drop by this popular local eatery for island specialties such as cracked conch, minced lobster, and fish-and-chips. The atmosphere is casual and the decor unmemorable, but the portions are large and the prices easy on your wallet. ⊠ *Hospital Rd.,* ☎ *649/946–2274. No credit cards.*

Beaches

There are more than 230 mi (370 km) of beaches in the Turks and Caicos Islands, ranging from secluded coves to miles-long stretches, and most beaches are soft coralline sand. Tiny cays offer complete isolation for nude sunbathing and skinny-dipping. Many are accessible only by boat. **Governor's Beach,** a long white strip on the west coast of Grand Turk, is one of the nicest, with plenty of sparkling, powder-soft sand on which to stroll.

Outdoor Activities and Sports

CYCLING

The island's flat terrain isn't very taxing, and most roads have hard surfaces. Take water with you: there are few places to stop for refreshment. Most hotels in Cockburn Town have bicycles available, but you can also rent them for $10–$15 a day from **Sea Eye Diving** (☎ FAX 649/946–1407).

SCUBA DIVING AND SNORKELING

In these waters you'll find undersea cathedrals, coral gardens, and countless tunnels, but note that you must carry and present a valid certificate card before you'll be allowed to dive. As its name suggests, the **Black Forest** offers staggering black-coral formations as well as the occasional black-tip shark. In the **Library** you can study fish galore, including large numbers of yellowtail snapper. At the Columbus Passage separating South Caicos from Grand Turk, each side of a 22-mi-wide (35-km-wide) channel drops more than 7,000 ft (2,141 m). From January through March, thousands of Atlantic humpback whales swim through en route to their winter breeding grounds.

Dive outfitters are all located in Cockburn Town. **Blue Water Divers** (✉ Salt Raker Inn, Front St., ☎ FAX 649/946–1226) has been in operation on Grand Turk since 1983. **Oasis Divers** (✉ Duke St., ☎ FAX 649/946–1128) was ranked top dive operator in the world by readers of Rodale's *Scuba Diving* and offers complete gear handling and pampering treatment. It also supplies NITROX. Besides daily dive trips to the wall, **Sea Eye Diving** (✉ Duke St.,☎ FAX 649/946–1407) offers encounters with friendly stingrays. Two-tank boat dives cost $50–$65.

Nightlife

A fun crowd gathers at **Turk's Head Hotel** almost every night. There's folk and pop music at the **Salt Raker Inn** on Wednesday and Sunday nights. On weekends and holidays the younger crowd heads over to the **Nookie Hill Club** (✉ Nookie Hill, ☎ no phone) for late-night "wining" and dancing.

Exploring Grand Turk

Pristine beaches with vistas of turquoise waters, small local settlements, historic ruins, and native flora and fauna are among the sights on Grand Turk. Fewer than 5,000 people live on this 7½-square-mi (19-square-km) island, and it's hard to get lost as there aren't many roads.

Numbers in the margin correspond to points of interest on the Turks and Caicos Islands map.

① **Cockburn Town.** The buildings in the colony's capital and seat of government reflect a 19th-century Bermudian style of architecture. Narrow streets are lined with low stone walls and old street lamps, now powered by electricity. The once-vital salinas have been restored, and covered benches along the sluices offer shady spots for observing a variety of wading birds, including flamingos, herons, egrets, and plovers that frequent the shallows. In one of the oldest stone buildings on the islands, the **Turks & Caicos National Museum** houses the Molasses Reef wreck of 1513, the earliest shipwreck discovered in the Americas. The natural history exhibits include artifacts left by Taíno, African, North American, Bermudian, French, and Latin American settlers. An impressive addition to the museum is the coral-reef and sea-life exhibit, faithfully modeled on a popular dive site just off the island. ⊠ *Duke St.,* ☎ *649/946–2160,* WEB *www.tcmuseum.org.* 🖭 *$5.* ☉ *Mon.–Tues. and Thurs.–Fri. 9–4, Wed. 9–6, Sat. 9–1.*

Salt Cay

Fewer than 100 people live on this 2½-square-mi (6-square-km) dot of land, maintaining an unassuming lifestyle against a backdrop of quaint stucco cottages, stone ruins, and weathered wooden windmills standing sentry in the abandoned salinas. There's not much in the way of development, but there are splendid beaches on the north coast. As on the other Turks and Caicos islands, the land is arid, with mostly cactus and scrub brush growth. The most spectacular sites are beneath the waves: 10 dive sites are just minutes from shore.

Lodging

For approximate costs, *see* the lodging price chart *in* Grand Turk.

$$$$
★   🏨 **Windmills Plantation.** The attraction here is the lack of distraction: no nightlife, cruise ships, or shopping. The hotel resembles a romantic's version of a colonial-era plantation. The great house has four suites, each with a sitting area, a four-poster bed, ceiling fans, and a veranda or balcony with a sea view. All are furnished in a mix of antique English and wicker furniture. Four other rooms are housed in two adjacent buildings. Note: at press time, the hotel was up for sale. ⊠ *North Beach Rd.,* ☎ *649/946–6962 or 800/822–7715,* FAX *649/946–6930,* WEB *www.saltcaysite.com. 4 rooms, 4 suites. Restaurant, bar, pool, hiking, horseback riding, beach, snorkeling, fishing, library. AE, MC, V. BP.*

$ 🏨 **Mount Pleasant Guest House.** This simple, somewhat rustic hotel was a former salt-plantation home built around 1859, which Bryan Sheedy opened as a guest house catering to divers in the early 1990s. The premises are filled with memorabilia and artifacts, and his gazebo bar overlooks a cut-stone cistern pit that has been converted into a palm-laden grove for hammocks. Meals are superb, with dinners including whelk soup, grilled fresh fish and lobster, buttery cracked conch, and New York strip steaks. Dive packages are coordinated with Salt Cay Divers. ⊠ *Balfour Town,* ☎ FAX *649/946–6927,* WEB *www.turksandcaicos. tc/mtpleasant. 8 rooms, 2 with bath. Restaurant, bar, fans, horseback riding, bicycles, library. MC, V. FAP, MAP.*

$ 🏨 **Salt Cay Sunset House.** Built in 1832 by shipwright-turned-salt baron "Skipper" Harriott, this historic bed-and-breakfast and ocean-front café is housed in the oldest salt-plantation home on Salt Cay. Enthusiastic owners Michele Wells and Paul Dinsmore lovingly restored the rare mortise- and tenon-joined, rough-hewn cypress planking construction that has survived for almost two centuries. All three bedrooms have en suite baths; there is a shared living room. Period furnishings complete the ambience. Michelle serves hearty local and Continental fare for breakfast, lunch, and dinner on the breezy veranda at the Blue Mermaid Café. ⊠ *Balfour Town,* ☎ FAX *649/946–6942,* WEB *www.seaone.org. 3 rooms. Restaurant, fans, horseback riding, beach, scuba diving, snorkeling. BP, MAP. MC, V.*

Beaches

There are superb beaches on the north coast of **Salt Cay. Big Sand Cay,** 7 mi (11 km) south of Salt Cay, is also known for its long, unspoiled stretches of open sand.

Outdoor Activities and Sports

SCUBA DIVING AND SNORKELING

Scuba divers can explore the *Endymion,* a recently discovered 140-ft wooden-hull British warship that sank in 1790. It's off the southern point of Salt Cay. **Salt Cay Divers** (☎ 649/946–6906) conducts daily trips and rents all the necessary equipment. You'll pay around $60 for a two-tank dive.

Exploring Salt Cay

Salt sheds and salinas are silent reminders of the days when the island was a leading producer of salt. Island tours are often conducted by motorized golf cart. From January through March whales pass by on the way to their winter breeding grounds.

❷ **Balfour Town.** What little development there is on Salt Cay is found here. It's home to a variety of small hotels and a few stores that sell handwoven baskets, T-shirts, convenience foods, and beach items.

THE CAICOS

West Caicos

Accessible only by boat, this uninhabited, untamed island has no facilities whatsoever. A glorious white beach stretches for 1 mi (1½ km) along the northwest point, and the offshore diving here is among the most exotic in the islands. The "Wilds of West Caicos" encompass a pristine wall, about ¼ mi (½ km) from shore, which starts at 35–45 ft (11–14 m) and cascades to 7,000 ft (2,141 m). Here, sharks, eagle rays, and turtles are commonly seen on the many dive sites. It's about a 1½-hour boat ride from Provo but well worth the trip. Most dive operators depart from satellite locations on the south side of Provo for the journey.

The interior of West Caicos holds the remains of a sisal plantation that operated from 1890 to 1920 at Yankee Town. Flocks of migratory birds, including flamingos, congregate at Lake Catherine. If you plan to roam West Caicos, take along insect repellent.

Off the southeastern shore, **Molasses Reef** is rumored to be the final resting place of the *Pinta,* which is thought to have been wrecked here in the early 1500s. Over the past several centuries numerous wrecks have occurred in the area between West Caicos and Provo, and author Peter Benchley is among the treasure seekers who have been lured to this island.

Providenciales

In the mid-18th century, so the story goes, a French ship was wrecked near here, and the survivors were washed ashore on an island they gratefully christened La Providentielle. Under the Spanish, the name was changed to Providenciales. Today about 20,000 people live on Provo (as everybody calls it); a considerable number are expatriate British, Canadian, and U.S. businesspeople and retirees, or refugees from nearby Haiti. The island's 44 square mi (114 square km) are by far the most developed in the Turks and Caicos.

A development boom in the late 1990s brought tremendous advances in the island's infrastructure. The last several years have seen nearly a dozen new condominium-hotel projects, major renovations of the three all-inclusive resorts, several new shopping plazas and food stores, two new banks, a new airport terminal, piped water available to most of the island, a new movie theater, and the ongoing construction of several residential developments and countless new homes.

Lodging

For approximate costs, *see* the lodging price chart *in* Grand Turk.

$$$$ ★ ☍ 🏨 **Beaches Turks & Caicos Resort & Spa.** There's plenty to satisfy families at this member of the Sandals chain, including a Robinson Crusoe-themed children's park complete with a video game center, two water slides, a swim-up soda bar, a miniature golf course, a 1950s-style diner, and a teen disco. Luxurious accommodations, extravagant meals, and a full range of water sports make this all-inclusive resort an indulgent experience. A 4,000-sq-ft pool is encircled by the new 166-room French Village, a themed area reminiscent of a movie set, complete with French café and bistro. The spa offers body wraps, massages, and facials. Passes are available for nonguests to use the facilities. ✉ *Lower Bight Rd., Grace Bay,* ☎ *649/946–8000 or 800/726–3257,* 𝖥𝖠𝖷 *649/946–8001,* 𝖶𝖤𝖡 *www.beaches.com. 296 rooms, 84 suites. 9 restaurants, 6 bars, 6 pools, air-conditioning, in-room safes, hair salon, massage, hot tub, spa, 2 tennis courts, health club, beach, dive shop, snorkeling, water park, windsurfing, boating, fishing, shops, cinema, nightclub, recreation room, theater, video games, children's programs, concierge, meeting rooms, car rental. AE, MC, V. All-inclusive.*

$$$$ ★ 🏨 **Grace Bay Club.** Staying at this Swiss-owned, Mediterranean-style resort is a little like being the guest of honor of a very gracious host with unbeatable taste. Suites have breathtaking views of stunning Grace Bay and are furnished with rattan and pickled wood, with Mexican-tile floors and elegant Turkish and Indian throw rugs. Activities range from diving to golf to catered picnics on surrounding islands, but relaxing is the major pastime. French Caribbean meals are served in the Anacaona restaurant. ✉ *Grace Bay (Box 128),* ☎ *649/946–5757; 800/946–5757 direct to hotel,* 𝖥𝖠𝖷 *649/946–5758 or 800/946–5758,* 𝖶𝖤𝖡 *www.gracebayclub.com. 21 suites. Restaurant, bar, air-conditioning, in-room data ports, in-room fax, in-room safes, in-room VCRs, kitchenettes, room service, pool, hot tub, massage, 2 tennis courts, beach, windsurfing, boating, bicycles. Closed Sept. AE, MC, V. CP, MAP.*

$$$$ ★ 🏨 **Ocean Club.** These luxury all-suite condominiums are on a 12-mi (19-km) stretch of pristine beach, a short walk from Provo's only golf course. Units range from efficiency studios to three-bedroom suites with living rooms, dining rooms, kitchens, and screened balconies. Third-floor units have cathedral ceilings. You can take a free shuttle to use the facilities of sister property, Ocean Club West. The on-site Gecko Grille serves creative island dishes. ✉ *Grace Bay (Box 240),* ☎ *649/946–5880 or 800/457–8787,* 𝖥𝖠𝖷 *649/946–5845,* 𝖶𝖤𝖡 *www.oceanclubresorts.com. 101 suites. 2 restaurants, bar, air-conditioning, in-room data ports, kitchenettes, 2 pools, massage, golf, tennis court, gym, beach, dive shop, shops, concierge, car rental. AE, MC, V. EP.*

$$$$ ★ 🏨 **Ocean Club West.** This new sister property to Ocean Club maintains many signature features of the original—breathtaking seascapes, large balconies, and exquisite landscaping—while expanding the oceanfront central courtyard area to include a gazebo-capped island, winding free-form pool, and a seaside café and swim-up bar. Interiors are decorated in subdued sophistication, utilizing whites, light woods, and wicker. Condominium suites range in size from efficiencies to three bedrooms and are fully furnished. Junior one-bedrooms are an especially good value. ✉ *Grace Bay (Box 640),* ☎ *649/946–5880 or 800/457–8787,* 𝖥𝖠𝖷 *649/946–5845,* 𝖶𝖤𝖡 *www.oceanclubresorts.com. 90 suites. Restaurant, bar, air-conditioning, in-room data ports, kitchenettes, 2 pools, massage, golf, 2 tennis courts, gym, beach, dive shop, concierge. AE, MC, V. EP.*

$$$$ ★ 🏨 **Point Grace.** This new boutique hotel raises the bar for luxury resorts on the islands. Majestically designed in British Colonial style, two oceanfront buildings house magnificent two- and three-bedroom suites with a variety of floor plans. All feature expansive terraces overlooking Grace Bay and are furnished with Indonesian hardwood and teak.

Hand-painted tiles line the bathrooms and Frette linens cover the king-size, four-poster beds. Two four-bedroom penthouse suites each have two floors, with separate massage rooms and rooftop Jacuzzis. The one-bedroom cottages surround the courtyard pool-patio area. Private chefs are available for en-suite dining and you can enjoy gourmet dinners at Grace's Cottage, a private restaurant on the resort grounds. Point Grace also rents two four-bedroom luxury villas within a gated estate on the secluded end of the beach. ⊠ *Grace Bay (Box 700),* ☎ *888/682–3705 or 649/946–5096,* FAX *649/946–5097,* WEB *www.pointgrace.tc. 23 suites, 9 cottages, 2 villas. Restaurant, bar, air-conditioning, in-room fax, in-room safes, kitchenettes, room service, pool, beach, snorkeling, wind-surfing, boating, bicycles, recreation room, library, laundry service, concierge, car rental, free parking. Closed Sept. AE, D, MC, V.CP.*

$$$$ 🏨 **Royal West Indies Resort.** Distinctive British Colonial architecture and extensive gardens with nearly 200 different species of plants high-light Grace Bay's newest luxury condominium resort. Smartly de-signed to allow two-bedroom suites to be divided into self-sufficient studio and one-bedroom units; each suite faces the glorious turquoise ocean. Private balconies front all units to make the most of the sea view, and the interior decor is an eclectic blend of wood and fabrics from Central and South America. All suites are fully furnished, including washer-dryers. Deluxe studios have kitchenettes. Although the beach is steps away, the 80-ft-long pool surrounded by tropical fruit trees is a peaceful place to relax and sip a drink from the on-site Mango Reef restaurant and bar, serving dishes from around the Caribbean and Latin America. ⊠ *Grace Bay, (Box 482),* ☎ *649/946–5004,* FAX *649/946–5008,* WEB *www.royalwestindies.com. 99 suites. Restaurant, bar, air-conditioning, fans, in-room data ports, in-room safes, kitchenettes, re-frigerators, 2 pools, beach, snorkeling, laundry service. AE, MC, V. EP.*

$$$$ 🏨 **The Sands at Grace Bay.** "Simply breathtaking" describes the sparkling
★   ocean views from the huge screened patios and floor-to-ceiling windows adorning units at this new beach lover's haven. The upscale condominium resort offers units ranging from studios to three bedrooms; larger suites have two TVs, extra sleeper sofas, and washer-dryers. Efficiencies offer mini-refrigerators, microwaves, and coffeemakers. Contemporary decor combines Indonesian wood, wrought iron, and wicker with seaside-tone fabrics to emphasize the resort's theme of sophisticated simplicity. Amenities include a beachfront pool and the free use of windsurfers, ocean kayaks, a sailboat, and snorkeling equipment. An excellent ocean-front cabana restaurant and bar is on site as well. ⊠ *Grace Bay (Box 681),* ☎ *649/941–5199 or 877/777–2637,* FAX *649/946–5198,* WEB *www.thesandsresort.com. 116 suites. Restaurant, bar, air-conditioning, kitchenettes, refrigerators, in-room data ports, in-room safes, 3 pools, massage, tennis court, beach, boating, bicycles, baby-sitting, laundry service, concierge, car rental. AE, MC, V. EP.*

$$$ 🏨 **Allegro Resort and Casino Turks & Caicos.** Formerly the Turquoise Reef Resort, this sprawling beachfront property has been converted to an all-inclusive resort that caters primarily to adults (though still wel-comes children). The oversized oceanfront rooms have rattan furniture, a rich Caribbean color scheme, and private balcony or terrace. A pool-patio area and a PADI five-star dive facility are on site. Meals range from Caribbean fare to Italian specialties, with unlimited beverages. The American Casino, the island's only gaming facility, is here. ⊠ *Grace Bay (Box 205),* ☎ *649/946–5555 or 800/858–2258,* FAX *649/946–5522,* WEB *www.allegroresorts.com. 186 rooms. 3 restaurants, 3 bars, air-con-ditioning, pool, hot tub, 3 tennis courts, gym, beach, dive shop, snorkel-ing, windsurfing, shops, casino, theater, children's programs, concierge, travel services, car rental. AE, MC, V. All-inclusive.*

$$$ 🏨 **Club Med Turkoise.** This village is a water-sports paradise, with scuba diving, windsurfing, sailing, and waterskiing on the turquoise waters at the doorstep. Two- and three-story bungalows line a 1-mi (1½-km) beach, and all the usual sybaritic pleasures are here. This all-inclusive (except drinks) club is geared toward couples, singles age 18 and over, and divers. There are also a flying trapeze, nightly entertainment, and excursions offered to sites in the Turks and Caicos. Dive packages are available. Day ($40), dinner ($40) and disco ($30) passes can be purchased by nonguests to use the facilities. ⌧ *Grace Bay,* ☎ *649/946–5491 or 800/258–2633,* FAX *649/946–5500,* WEB *www.clubmed.com. 298 rooms. 2 restaurants, 3 bars, air-conditioning, pool, 8 tennis courts, gym, beach, dive shop, snorkeling, windsurfing, boating, fishing, bicycles, shops, dance club, theater. AE, MC, V. All-inclusive.*

$$$ 🏨 **Coral Gardens.** This intimate beachfront resort fronts one of Provo's
★ best snorkeling reefs and is in a tranquil area well west of bustling Grace Bay. The deluxe two-bedroom suites have huge terraces and floor-to-ceiling walls of sliding glass that face Provo's north shore. Gourmet kitchens open into the dining areas, and bedrooms and baths overlook the luxurious gardens. The beachfront area is accented by two dramatic waterfalls cascading down the face of each building. There's on-site scuba diving led by the resort's concierge. Hungry? Fine dining al fresco is offered at Coyaba Restaurant. The original "White House" villa, a large beachfront home around which Coral Gardens was built, is also available for group rental. ⌧ *Penn's Road (Box 281),* ☎ *649/941–3713 or 800/532–8536,* FAX *649/941–5171,* WEB *www.coralgardens.com. 30 suites. Restaurant, bar, air-conditioning, kitchenettes, pool, aerobics, beach, dive shop, snorkeling. AE, MC, V. EP.*

$$$ 🏨 **Erebus Inn.** The views are fabulous from this resort's cliff-side setting above Turtle Cove. The higher-priced cottages atop the cliff are more private than the rooms in the hotel proper; most rooms have private patios. The lively restaurant and bar has a menu of Asian/Pacific and Caribbean cuisine. Six affordable restaurants are within walking distance, as are snorkeling sites, several dive operations, and sailing and sportfishing charters. ⌧ *Turtle Cove (Box 238),* ☎ *649/946–4240 or 800/323–5655,* FAX *649/946–4704,* WEB *www.erebus.tc. 21 rooms, 4 cottages. Restaurant, bar, air-conditioning, in-room data ports, pool, 2 tennis courts, aerobics, gym, dive shop. AE, MC, V. EP, MAP.*

$$ 🏨 **Back of Beyond.** As the name suggests, this out-of-the-ordinary retreat is set apart from Provo's hustle and bustle on the quiet south shore. A burnished-orange stucco, pueblo-style inn houses the nine rooms, each charmingly decorated by proprietress Coleen Darragh, who with husband Ed designed and built the distinctive building to complement the surrounding cactus-dotted terrain. Rooms and the dining patio overlook the Discovery Bay canals and turquoise-green hues of the ocean beyond; a secluded white sand beach is just a stroll away. Coleen's mothering hospitality extends to the on-site restaurant and bar, where she cooks and serves home-style "comfort" fare like pancakes and muffins for breakfast and roast turkey for dinner. Fridays are folk music get-togethers, drawing people from across the island for an evening of music and poetry. If peace and quiet in an unpretentious atmosphere appeals to you, this is an affordable and comfortable spot to stay. ⌧ *Venetian Road,* ☎ *649/941–4555. 9 rooms. Restaurant, bar, fans, pool. No credit cards. BP.*

$$ 🏨 **Comfort Suites.** Although Comfort Suites is the island's only "franchise" hotel, the property's exceptional hospitality and superior performance are anything but standard. Suites are housed in two three-story buildings built around an Olympic-size pool and landscaped patio area; frosty drinks are served at the tiki bar. Like the rest of the hotel, rooms

are spotless and furnished in bright Caribbean decor. Each includes a small sitting area with sleeper sofa, mini-refrigerator, coffeemaker, and cable TV. Grace Bay's long swath of pearly white beach is just across the street, readily accessed via a designated lane. The hotel flanks the Ports of Call shopping village. The on-site tour desk helps guests with arrangements for diving, snorkeling, sailing, and fishing charters (with free hotel transfers). ✉ *Grace Bay (Box 590)*, ☎ *649/946–8888 or 888/678–3483*, ℻ *649/946–5444*, WEB *www.comfortsuitesci.com. 100 junior suites. Bar, air-conditioning, fans, in-room data ports, in-room safes, refrigerators, pool, travel services. AE, MC, V. CP.*

$$ 🏨 **Turtle Cove Inn.** Once known as the Turtle Cove Yacht and Tennis Club, this pleasant, two-story inn has kept up with the times and now offers affordable, comfortable lodging much in favor with scuba, boating and fishing enthusiasts. All rooms include a private balcony or patio overlooking either the courtyard's lush tropical gardens and pool or Turtle Cove Marina. Dockside is the Tiki Hut Cabana Bar and Grill, a popular local watering hole and restaurant specializing in Black Angus beef, pizza, fresh fish and pasta. In another corner is the more upscale Terrace Restaurant. You can readily stroll to the snorkeling trail at Smith's Reef, and access the remaining miles of north shore beach from there. There's a selection of deep-sea fishing and sailing charters at the marina, and a dive shop, car, scooter, and bicycle rental outlet, and liquor store on the premises, too. Within short walking distance is another diving operation, four additional restaurant-bars, a fitness club and tennis courts. Children under age 12 are free. ✉ *The Bight (Box 131)*, ☎ *649/946–4203 or 800/887–0477*, ℻ *649/946–4141*, WEB *www.Provo.net/TurtleCoveInn. 30 rooms, 2 suites. 2 restaurants, 2 bars, air-conditioning, pool, dive shop, marina, fishing, bicycles, car rental. AE, MC, V. EP.*

Dining

There are more than 50 restaurants on Provo, ranging from casual to elegant, with cuisine from Continental to Asian (and everything in between). You can spot the islands' own Caribbean influence no matter where you go, exhibited in fresh seafood specials, colorfulpresentations, and a tangy dose of spice.

For approximate costs, *see* the dining price chart *in* Grand Turk.

CARIBBEAN

$ ✗ **Dora's.** This popular local eatery serves island fare—stewed turtle, conch fritters, minced lobster, spicy conch chowder and fried fish—seven days a week, from 7 AM until the last person leaves the bar. Plastic print-and-lace tablecloths, hanging plants, and Haitian art add to the island ambience. Soups come with homemade bread; entrées such as steamed fish, cracked conch, and stewed pork are typically served with peas 'n' rice and a vegetable. Be sure to come early for the packed Monday- and Thursday-night all-you-can-eat $22 seafood buffets. The price includes transportation to and from your hotel and live music by a local band. ✉ *Leeward Hwy.*, ☎ *649/946–4558. AE, MC, V.*

DELI

$ ✗ **Top O' the Cove New York Style Delicatessen.** You can walk to this tiny café on Leeward Highway from Turtle Cove (don't be put off by the location in the Napa Auto Parts plaza). Order breakfast, deli sandwiches, salads, and enticingly rich desserts and freshly baked goods. From the deli case you can buy the fixings for a picnic; the shop's shelves are stocked with an eclectic array of gourmet foodstuffs. Open from 6:30 AM on weekdays and Saturday, from 8 to 2 on Sunday. ✉ *Leeward Hwy.*, ☎ ℻ *649/946–4694. No credit cards.*

ECLECTIC

$$$ ✕ **Anacaona.** At the impressive Grace Bay Club, this exquisitely de-
★ signed palapa-style restaurant offers a truly memorable dining expe-
rience minus the tie, the air-conditioning, and the attitude. Start with
a bottle of fine wine from the extensive cellar and then enjoy a three-
or four-course meal of the chef's light but flavorful cooking, which com-
bines traditional European recipes with Caribbean fare. Oil lamps on
the tables, gently circulating ceiling fans, and the sounds of the trade
winds add to the Eden-like environment. ✉ *Grace Bay,* ☎ *649/946–
5050. AE, MC, V.*

$$$ ✕ **Coyaba Restaurant.** As founding member of the local chapter of the
Chaîne des Rôtísseurs, chef Paul Newman lets his talent soar at Coral
Gardens' elegantly appointed, terrace-style restaurant. A typical meal
(served on Royal Doulton china, no less) might start with truffle
mousse with sherry, follow with one of many daily specials from
French trimmed rack of lamb to tamarind and chipotle glazed maple
leaf duck breast, and finish with upside down apple pie, served with
Jamaican Blue Mountain coffee. The lovely atmosphere, careful attention
to detail and hospitality of owners Tracey and Gianni Caporuscio all
make an evening here live up to its name's translation from the Arawak
Indian tongue, "heavenly." ✉ *Penn's Rd.,* ☎ *649/946–5186. Reservations essential. AE, MC, V. Closed Tues.*

$$ ✕ **Caicos Café Bar and Grill.** There's a pervasive air of celebration in
the tree-shaded outdoor dining terrace of this popular eatery. Choose
from fresh grilled seafood, steak, lamb, and chicken served hot off the
outdoor barbecue. Owner-chef Pierrik Marziou adds a French accent
to his appetizers, salads, and homemade desserts. ✉ *Across from Al-
legro Resort, Grace Bay,* ☎ *649/946–5278. AE, MC, V.*

$$ ✕ **Gecko Grille.** At this Ocean Club resort restaurant you can eat indoors surrounded by tropical murals or out on the garden patio, where
the trees are interwoven with tiny twinkling lights. Creative "Floribbean"
fare includes macadamia nut–encrusted grouper with a mango beurre
blanc and tropical salsa and grilled pork chops marinated in papaya
juice. Enjoy live music on Sunday evenings. ✉ *Grace Bay,* ☎ *649/946–
5885. AE, MC, V. Closed Mon. and Tues.*

$$ ✕ **The Terrace.** The cuisine at one of the most popular dining spots on
Provo has a Euro-Caribbean flair, specializing in creative dishes such as
conch ravioli, conch fillets encrusted with ground pecans, and a conch
roulade. Other main courses include grilled lobster tail (in season) and
roast rack of lamb. The house salad, sprinkled with pine nuts and shaved,
aged Parmesan, is excellent, as are the hot bread pockets served with your
meal. Top it all off with a classic crème brûlée or scoop of homemade
ice cream. ✉ *Turtle Cove,* ☎ *649/946–4763. AE, MC, V. Closed Sun.*

ITALIAN

$$ ✕ **Baci Ristoranté.** Aromas redolent of the Mediterranean waft from
the open kitchen as you walk into this intimate eatery east of Turtle
Cove. Outdoor seating is on a romantic canal-front patio. The menu
offers a small, varied selection of Italian delights. Main courses focus
on veal, specially imported and prepared five ways, but also include
pasta, chicken, and fresh fish dishes. House wines are personally selected by the owners and complement the tasteful wine list. Plate presentations are works of art, and service is careful and gracious. Try the
tiramisu for dessert with a flavored coffee drink. ✉ *Harbour Town,
Turtle Cove,* ☎ *649/941–3044. AE, MC, V. Closed Mon.*

SEAFOOD

$$ ✕ **Banana Boat.** Buoys and other sea relics deck the walls of this
brightly painted casual restaurant on the wharf. Grilled grouper, lob-
ster salad sandwiches, conch fritters, and conch salad are among the

options. Tropical drinks include the rum-filled Banana Breeze—a house specialty. ⊠ *Turtle Cove,* ☎ *649/941–5706. AE, MC, V.*

$ ✕ **Hey Jose's Caribbean Cantina.** Frequented by locals, this restaurant claims to serve the island's best margaritas. Customers also return for the tasty Tex-Mex treats: tacos, tostados, nachos, burritos, fajitas, and Jose's special-recipe hot chicken wings. Thick, hearty pizzas are another favorite—especially the "Kitchen Sink," with a little bit of everything thrown in! ⊠ *Central Sq.,* ☎ *649/946–4812. MC, V. Closed Sun.*

Beaches

A fine white-sand beach stretches 12 mi (19 km) along Provo's **north coast,** where most of the hotels are. There are also good beaches at **Sapodilla Bay** and **Malcolm Roads,** at North West Point, which is accessible only by four-wheel-drive vehicles.

Outdoor Activities and Sports

BICYCLING

Provo has a few steep grades to conquer, but they're short. Unfortunately, traffic on Leeward Highway and rugged road edges make pedaling here a less-than-relaxing experience. Instead, try the less-traveled roads through the native settlements of Blue Hills, the Bight, and Five Cays. Most hotels have bikes available. You can rent mountain bikes at **Provo Fun Cycles** (⊠ Ports of Call, Grace Bay, ☎ 649/946–5868) for $15 a day.

BOATING AND SAILING

Provo's calm, reef-protected turquoise seas combine with constant easterly trade winds for excellent sailing conditions. A variety of multihulled vessels offer charters with snorkeling stops, food and beverage service, and sunset vistas. Prices range from $39 for group trips to $600 or more for private charters. **Atabeyra** (☎ 649/941–5363) is a retired rum runner and the choice of residents for special events. **Sail Provo** (☎ 649/946–4783) runs 57-ft and 48-ft catamarans on scheduled half-day, full-day and sunset cruises.

FISHING

The island's fertile waters boast abundant angling opportunities ranging from bottom- and reef fishing (most likely to produce plenty of bites and a large catch) to bonefishing and deep-sea fishing (among the finest in the Caribbean). You are required to purchase a $15 visitor's fishing license; operators generally furnish all equipment, drinks, and snacks. You can rent a boat with a captain for a half or full day of bottom- or bonefishing through **J&B Tours** (⊠ Leeward Marina, ☎ 649/946–5047). Captain Arthur Dean at **Silver Deep** (⊠ Leeward Marina, ☎ 649/946–5612) is said to be among the Caribbean's finest bonefishing guides. Prices range from $100 to $375, depending on the length of trip and size of boat. For deep-sea fishing trips in search of marlin, sailfish, wahoo, tuna, barracuda, and shark, look up *Sakitumi* (⊠ Turtle Cove Marina, ☎ 649/946–4065).

GOLF

Provo Golf and Country Club's (☎ 649/946–5991) par-72, 18-hole championship course, designed by Karl Litten, is a combination of lush greens and fairways, rugged limestone outcroppings and freshwater lakes. Fees are $120 for 18 holes with shared cart.

PARASAILING

A 15-minute parasailing flight over Grace Bay is available for $60 (single) or $110 (tandem) at **Turtle Parasail** (☎ 649/231–0643).

For excellent close-to-shore snorkeling, try the **White House Reef,** off Penn's Road in the Bight, and **Smith's Reef,** over Bridge Road east of Turtle Cove. Both offer marked underwater snorkeling trails.

Scuba diving in the crystalline waters surrounding the islands ranks among the best in the Caribbean. The reef and wall drop-offs thrive with bright, unbroken coral formations and lavish numbers of fish and marine life. Mimicking the idyllic climate, waters are warm all year, averaging 76–78°F in the winter and 82–84°F during the summer. With minimal rainfall and soil runoff, visibility is naturally good and frequently superb, ranging from 60 to 150 ft (18 to 46 m) plus. An extensive system of marine national parks and boat moorings, combined with an ecoconscious mindset among dive operators, contributes to an underwater environment little changed in centuries.

Dive operators in Provo regularly visit sites at **Grace Bay** and **Pine Cay** for spur-and-groove coral formations and bustling reef diving. They make the longer journey to the dramatic walls at **North West Point** and **West Caicos,** depending on weather conditions. Instruction from the major diving agencies is available for all levels and certifications.

Art Pickering's Provo Turtle Divers (⊠ Ocean Club, Ocean Club West, Turtle Cove, ☎ 649/946–4232 or 800/833–1341) has been on Provo for more than 30 years. The staff is friendly, knowledgeable, and unpretentious. **Big Blue Unlimited** (⊠ Leeward Marina, ☎ 649/946–5034) specializes in eco-diving adventures, with a certified marine biologist on staff. It also offers Nitrox, Trimix and rebreathers. **Caicos Adventures** (⊠ Caicos Cafe Plaza,☎ FAX 649/946–3346) is run by friendly Frenchman Fifi Kuntz, and offers daily West Caicos trips with night dives on the West Caicos wall. **Dive Provo** (⊠ Allegro Resort, Ports of Call, ☎ 649/946–5040 or 800/234–7768) is a resort-based, PADI 5-Star operation that runs daily one- and two-tank dives to popular Grace Bay sites. **Flamingo Divers** (⊠ Turtle Cove Landing, ☎ 649/946–4193 or 800/204–9282) focuses on small groups and personalized service.

The following hotels have courts open to nonguests. Prices vary, so call before you go: **Club Med Turkoise** (☎ 649/946–5491). **Erebus Inn** (☎ 649/946–4240). **Grace Bay Club** (☎ 649/946–5754). **Ocean Club and Ocean Club West** (☎ 649/946–5880). **Provo Golf and Country Club** (☎ 649/946–5991).

Windsurfers will find the calm turquoise water ideal. **Windsurfing Provo** (⊠ Ocean Club, Ocean Club West, ☎ 649/946–5649) rents windsurfers, kayaks, motorboats and Hobie Cats and offers windsurfing instruction.

Shopping

Don't expect the variety of goods offered on more developed Caribbean destinations. You'll find several main shopping areas: Market Place and Central Square, on the Leeward Highway, and the Old World–style shopping village Ports of Call, in Grace Bay. Delicate woven baskets, polished conch shells, paintings, wood carvings, handmade dolls, and small metalwork are the only crafts native to the area.

The **Bamboo Gallery** (⊠ Market Place, ☎ FAX 649/946–4748) sells Caribbean art, from vivid Haitian paintings to wood carvings and local metal sculptures. For a large selection of duty-free liquors, visit **Carib West** (⊠ Airport Rd., ☎ 649/946–4215). **Greensleeves** (⊠ Central Sq.,

☎ FAX 649/946–4147) offers paintings by local artists, island-made rag rugs, baskets, jewelry, and sisal mats and bags. **Marilyn's Craft** (✉ Ports of Call, ☎ no phone) sells handmade dolls, rag rugs, and wood carvings, plus tropical clothing and knickknacks. **Paradise Gifts** (✉ Central Sq., ☎ 649/941–3828) offers a creative selection of decorated T-shirts, handmade jewelry, and paintings by local artists.

From outlets at the Provo airport, Allegro Resort, Arch Plaza, Beaches, Club Med, and Ocean Club Plaza, **Royal Jewels** (☎ 649/946–4699) sells gold and jewelry, designer watches, cameras, and perfumes—all duty-free.

Nightlife

Casablanca (✉ Next to Club Med, Grace Bay, ☎ no phone) is a Monte Carlo–style nightclub with a decked-out local crowd. Residents and tourists flock to **Lattitudes** (✉ Ports of Call, ☎ 649/946–5832) on Friday nights to let their hair down. On Thursday nights you can find a local band and lively crowd at **Sharkbite Bar & Grill** (✉ Harbour Town, Turtle Cove, ☎ 649/941–5090).

The only casino on the island is the **American Casino** (✉ Allegro Resort, Grace Bay, ☎ 649/946–5508). It's open to all visitors and includes 80 slot machines and a variety of table games including blackjack, Caribbean stud poker, and roulette. Drinks are free for all players.

Exploring Providenciales

Numbers in the margin correspond to points of interest on the Turks and Caicos Island map.

❸ **Downtown Provo.** Near Providenciales International Airport, downtown is really an extended strip mall that houses a grocery store, car-rental and travel agencies, law offices, banks, and other businesses.

❹ On the northeast tip of Provo you'll find the **Caicos Conch Farm,** a major mariculture operation where mollusks are farmed commercially (more than 3 million conch are here). Guided tours are available; call to confirm times. ✉ *Leeward-Going-Through (Box 286),* ☎ 649/946–5330. ☞ *$6.*☉ *Mon.–Sat. 9–4.*

Little Water Cay

This small, uninhabited cay is a protected area under the National Trust of the Turks and Caicos. On these 150 acres are two trails, small lakes, red mangroves, and an abundance of native plants. Boardwalks protect the ground and interpretive signs explain the habitat. The cay is home to about 2,000 rare, endangered rock iguanas. They say the iguanas are shy, but these creatures actually seem rather curious. They waddle right up to you, as if posing for a picture; you can usually get within a foot of them before they move.

Parrot Cay

Once said to be a hideout for pirate Calico Jack Rackham and his lady cohorts Mary Reid and Anne Bonny, the 1,000-acre cay, between Fort George Cay and North Caicos, is now the site of an ultra-exclusive hideaway resort, a holistic health spa, and upscale homesites. Bordered by a wild stretch of pristine beach to the north and mangrove-lined wetlands to the south, tiny Parrot Cay is a natural wonder.

Lodging

For approximate costs, *see* the lodging price chart *in* Grand Turk.

$$$$ ⚷ **Parrot Cay Resort.** Frequented by celebrities and the international
★   ultrachic, this exclusive resort combines natural beauty and elegant sim-

plicity to create a rarified atmosphere of tranquility. Mediterranean-style hillside structures house one- and two-bedroom suites, all with private terraces looking toward the ocean, with five stand-alone villas directly on the beach. Furnishings rely on white backdrops, natural materials, and distinct Asian touches, with four-poster beds and teak furniture. Seaside villas include some private pools, butler service, and gourmet kitchens, complete with chef and waitstaff on request. Guests congregate around the rimless infinity pool and patio bar. Meals are served on starched white linen and English bone china and favor Asia-meets-Islands cuisine. The resort can only be accessed by private boat from Leeward Marina. ⌧ *Box 164, Providenciales,* ☎ *649/946–7788,* FAX *649/946–7789,* WEB *www.parrot-cay.com. 60 rooms, 5 beach villas. 3 restaurants, 2 bars, air-conditioning, in-room safes, kitchenettes, minibars, room service, pool, hot tub, massage, mineral baths, sauna, spa, steam room, 2 tennis courts, gym, beach, snorkeling, windsurfing, boating, fishing, mountain bikes, library, baby-sitting, laundry service. AE, MC, V. BP, FAP.*

Pine Cay

One of a chain of small cays linking North Caicos and Provo, 800-acre Pine Cay is home to the Meridian Club—a retreat for people seeking peaceful seclusion. Its 2½-mi (4-km) beach is among the most beautiful in the archipelago. The island has a 3,800-ft (1,162-m) airstrip and electric golf carts for getting around. Offshore is the **Football Fields** dive site, which has been called the Grand Central Station of the fish world.

Lodging

For approximate costs, *see* the lodging price chart *in* Grand Turk.

$$$$ 🏨 **Meridian Club.** Here you can enjoy an unspoiled cay with vast
★ stretches of soft, white sand and a 500-acre nature reserve with tropical flora, freshwater ponds, and trails that lure bird-watchers and botanists. A stay here is truly getting away from it all, as there are no air-conditioners, phones, or TVs. A variety of accommodations includes spacious rooms with king-size beds and patios, as well as cottages that range from rustic to well appointed. Meals and activities are included in the room rate, as is your boat or air-taxi trip from Provo to the cay. Cottages start at $4,400 a week and are available with or without a meal plan. ⌧ *Pine Cay,* FAX *649/941–7010. 456 Glenbrook Rd., Stamford, CT 06906),* ☎ *800/331–9154 or 203/602–0300,* FAX *203/ 602–2265,* WEB *www.meridianclub.com. 12 rooms, 38 cottages. Restaurant, bar, pool, tennis court, hiking, beach, snorkeling, windsurfing, boating, bicycles, private airstrip. No credit cards. All-inclusive, EP, FAP.*

North Caicos

Thanks to abundant rainfall, this 41-square-mi (106-square-km) island is the garden center of the Turks and Caicos. Bird lovers will see a large flock of flamingos here, and fishermen will find creeks full of bonefish and tarpon. Bring all your own gear; this quiet island has no watersports shops. Although there is no traffic, almost all the roads are paved, so bicycling is an excellent way to sightsee.

Lodging

For approximate costs, *see* the lodging price chart *in* Grand Turk.

$$$$ 🏨 **Club Vacanze Prospect of Whitby Hotel.** This secluded, all-inclusive
★ retreat is run by an Italian resort chain, Club Vacanze. Miles of beach are yours for sunbathing, windsurfing, or snorkeling. Spacious guest rooms have elegant Tuscan floor tiles and pastel pink paneling; in true

getaway fashion, rooms lack TVs but include minibars. The restaurant, on a veranda overlooking the sea, is excellent, with a selection of local, Italian, and international dishes served buffet style for breakfast, lunch, and a three-course dinner in the evening. Scuba diving and daily excursions to nearby natural wonders are included in the rate. ⊠ *Whitby,* ☎ *649/946–7119,* FAX *649/946–7114,* WEB *www.clubvacanze.com. 23 rooms, 4 suites. Restaurant, bar, air-conditioning, in-room safes, minibars, pool, tennis court, beach, dive shop, windsurfing, boating, fishing, bicycles. AE, MC, V. All-inclusive.*

$$$ 🏨 **Pelican Beach Hotel.** Built and operated by Clifford Gardiner (the Islands' first licensed solo pilot) and his family, this laid-back hotel fronts beautiful expanses of deserted, windswept beach. Large rooms are done in pastels and dark-wood trim; suites have kitchens and living rooms. Second-floor rooms have high ceilings and fabulous ocean views; the sound of breaking waves will soothe you in the first-floor beachfront units. Excellent local conch, lobster, grouper, and snapper dishes and homemade bread and desserts are served in the airy dining room shaded by a grove of whispering casuarina pines. Room rates include breakfast and dinner. ⊠ *Whitby,* ☎ *649/946–7112,* FAX *649/946–7139. 14 rooms, 2 suites. Restaurant, bar, air-conditioning, beach, fishing. MAP.*

$$ 🏨 **Ocean Beach Hotel Condominiums.** This unpretentious place provides family-style accommodations on a 10-mi (16-km) stretch of sheltered beach. The spacious units, some with kitchenettes, face the ocean. (Who needs air-conditioning when there are constant trade winds passing through large sliding glass doors?) The hotel offers an intimate lifestyle away from the fray. You can learn about local plants from the botanical walk encircling the premises. Diving, snorkeling, and exploring trips are arranged through Beach Cruiser Charters, at the hotel. ⊠ *Whitby,* ☎ *649/946–7113, 800/710–5204, or 905/690–3817 in Canada;* FAX *649/946–7386,* WEB *www.turksandcaicos.tc/oceanbeach. 3 rooms, 7 suites. Restaurant, bar, pool, beach, dive shop, snorkeling, boating, fishing, bicycles, car rental. AE, MC, V. BP, FAP, MAP.*

Beaches
The beaches of North Caicos are superb for shelling and lolling, and the waters offshore present excellent opportunities for snorkeling, bonefishing, and scuba diving.

Exploring North Caicos
❺ **Flamingo Pond.** This is a regular nesting place for the beautiful pink birds. They tend to wander out in the middle of the pond, so bring binoculars.

❻ **Kew.** This settlement has a small post office, school, church, and ruins of old plantations—all set among lush tropical trees bearing limes, papayas, and custard apples. Visiting Kew will give you a better understanding of the daily life of many islanders.

Middle Caicos

At 48 square mi (124 square km), this is the largest and least-developed of the inhabited Turks and Caicos, with fewer than 300 residents. A limestone ridge runs to about 125 ft (38 m) above sea level, creating dramatic cliffs on the north shore and a cave system farther inland. Middle Caicos is best suited to those looking to unwind in a natural setting.

Lodging
For approximate costs, *see* the lodging price chart *in* Grand Turk.

$$$ 🏨 **Blue Horizon Resort.** Breathtaking scenery and sweet seclusion abound in this 50-acre retreat. Cottages (and one larger house) have screened-in porches, off-white tile floors, bleached wood furniture, comfortable beds, ceiling fans, and full kitchens. The slatted windows

open up to let in the nearly constant breeze. You'll think you're in your very own paradise during a stay in this resort, above a spectacular beachfront cliff with a hillside cave and private ocean swimming cove. Fax a (basic) grocery list ahead of time, and management will be happy to stock your refrigerator. Activities by request include spelunking, fishing, and snorkeling with local guides. ⊠ *Mudjin Harbor,* ☎ *649/946–6141,* FAX *649/946–6139. 5 cottages, 1 house. Fans, kitchenettes, refrigerators, hiking, snorkeling, fishing. AE, MC, V.*

Exploring Middle Caicos

❼ **Conch Bar Caves.** These limestone caves have eerie underground lakes and milky white stalactites and stalagmites. Archaeologists have discovered Lucayan Indian artifacts in the caves and the surrounding area. It's an easy walk through the main part of the cave, but wear sturdy shoes to avoid slipping. You'll hear, see, and smell some bats, but they don't bother visitors. **J&B Tours** (⊠ Leeward Marina, Provo, ☎ 649/946–5047, WEB www.jbtours.com) offers boat trips from Provo to the caves.

South Caicos

This 8½-square-mi (21-square-km) island was once an important salt producer; today it's the heart of the fishing industry. Nature prevails, with long, white beaches, jagged bluffs, quiet backwater bays and salt flats with pink flamingos. Diving and snorkeling on the pristine wall and reefs are a treat enjoyed by only a few.

Lodging

For approximate costs, *see* the lodging price chart *in* Grand Turk.

$ 🏨 **South Caicos Ocean Haven.** On Cockburn Harbour, a protected marine sanctuary, this hotel operates as the base from which divers can discover a pristine paradise minutes from the dock. Comfortable, air-conditioned rooms have ocean and pool or town views; evenings bring spectacular sunsets overlooking the harbor. The restaurant emphasizes local seafood. Instructors on staff offer a full range of PADI courses, with economical dive packages available. ⊠ *West St., Cockburn Harbour,* ☎ *649/946–3444,* FAX *649/946–3446,* WEB *www.oceanhaven.tc. 22 rooms. Restaurant, bar, air-conditioning, beach, dive shop, windsurfing, boating, fishing. MC, V. EP, FAP.*

Beaches

Due south is **Big Ambergris Cay,** an uninhabited cay about 14 mi (23 km) beyond the Fish Cays, with a magnificent beach at Long Bay. To the north, uninhabited **East Caicos** has a beautiful 17-mi (27-km) beach on its north coast. The island was once a cattle range and the site of a major sisal-growing industry. Both these cays are accessible only by boat.

Exploring South Caicos

Spiny lobster and queen conch are found in the shallow Caicos Bank to the west, and are harvested for export by local processing plants. The bonefishing here is some of the best in the West Indies. **Beyond the Blue** (⊠ Cockburn Harbour, ☎ 649/231–1703, WEB www.beyondtheblue.com) offers bonefishing charters on a specialized airboat, which can operate in less than a foot of water. At the northern end of the island are fine white-sand beaches; the south coast is great for scuba diving along the drop-off; and there's excellent snorkeling off the windward (east) coast, where large stands of elkhorn and staghorn coral shelter a variety of small tropical fish.

Abandoned salinas make up the center of the island—the largest, across from the downtown ball park, receives its water directly from **❽** an underground source connected to the ocean through the **Boiling Hole.**

❾ Cockburn Harbour. The best natural harbor in the Caicos chain is home to the South Caicos Regatta, held each year in May.

TURKS AND CAICOS A TO Z

To research prices, get advice from other travelers, and book travel arrangements, visit www.fodors.com.

AIR TRAVEL

American Airlines flies three times daily between Miami and Provo, with a fourth flight on Saturdays between New York/JFK and Provo. Delta Air Lines offers daily service between Atlanta and Provo. Bahamasair offers twice-weekly connections to Miami via Nassau. In season there are weekly charter flights from a number of North American cities, including Boston, Detroit, New York, Philadelphia, Montréal, and Toronto. Turks & Caicos Airways, the national flag carrier, offers regularly scheduled flights between Provo, Grand Turk, and the outer Turks and Caicos Islands. SkyKing connects Provo with Grand Turk and South Caicos several times daily and also offers flights to Cuba, the Dominican Republic, and Haiti.

➤ AIRLINES AND CONTACTS: **American Airlines** (☎ 649/946–4948 in Turks and Caicos; 800/433–7300); **Delta Air Lines** (☎ 800/241–4141); **Bahamasair** (☎ 800/222–4262); **Turks & Caicos Airways** (☎ 649/946–4255); **SkyKing** (☎ 649/941–5464).

AIRPORTS

All international flights currently arrive at Providenciales International Airport, which was expanded and modernized in late 1999 to include welcome air-conditioning inside the terminal. Visitors use domestic carriers to fly on to airports in Grand Turk and the out islands of North Caicos, Middle Caicos, South Caicos, and Salt Cay. All have paved runways in good condition and small buildings serving as terminals. You'll find taxis at the airports, and most resorts provide pickup service for guests. A trip between Provo's airport and most major hotels runs about $15. On Grand Turk a trip from the airport to Cockburn Town is about $8; it's $8–$12 to hotels outside town.

➤ AIRPORT INFORMATION: **Grand Turk International Airport** (☎ 649/946–2233); **Providenciales International Airport** (☎ 649/941–5670).

BIKE AND MOPED TRAVEL

You can scoot around Provo by contacting Provo Fun Cycles and Autos, which offers everything from single- and double-seater Honda scooters to sporty Honda 250 or 125 cc motorcycles. In Turtle Cove, go to Scooter Bob's to rent scooters and bicycles, as well as skiffs and canoes. Rates generally start at $30 per day for a one-seater and $40 a day for a two-seater, plus a one-time $5 government tax and gas expense.

➤ BIKE AND MOPED RENTALS: **Provo Fun Cycles and Autos** (☎ 649/946–5658); **Scooter Bob's** (☎ 649/946–4684).

BOAT AND FERRY TRAVEL

Sea Dancer offers live-aboard diving with weekly trips out of Provo. The *Turks and Caicos Aggressor* live-aboard dive boat plies the islands' pristine sites with weekly charters from Turtle Cove Marina.

➤ BOAT AND FERRY INFORMATION: *Sea Dancer* (✉ c/o Peter Hughes Diving, ☎ 800/932–6237); *Turks and Caicos Aggressor* (✉ c/o Aggressor Fleet, ☎ 800/348–2628).

BUSINESS HOURS

BANKS

Banks are open Monday–Thursday 8:30–2:30, Friday 8:30–4:30.

POST OFFICES

Post offices are open weekdays from 8 or 8:30 'til 4 or 4:30.

SHOPS

Shops are open weekdays from 8 or 8:30 'til 4 or 4:30.

CAR RENTALS

Car and jeep rental rates average $50–$80 per day, plus a $10-per-rental-agreement government tax. On Grand Turk try Tony's Car Rental. There are a number of rental agencies on Provo. Reserve well ahead of time during the peak winter season. Most offer free mileage and airport pick-up service. Avis offers corporate rates and specializes in Daihatsu and Toyota vehicles. Budget features Ford and Suzuki four-door sedans, vans and four-wheel-drive jeeps. Provo Rent-a-Car is steps away from the airport and is the island's largest agency. Rent a Buggy specializes in Suzuki Samurai and Sidekick jeeps. Tropical Auto Rentals has a large, modern fleet of Kia and Mazda vehicles, all in their trademark white color.
➤ MAJOR AGENCIES: On Grand Turk: **Tony's Car Rental** (☎ 649/946–1879). On Provo: **Avis** (☎ 649/946–4705); **Budget** (☎ 649/946–4079); **Provo Rent-a-Car** (☎ 649/946–4404); **Rent a Buggy** (☎ 649/946–4158); **Tropical Auto Rentals** (☎ 649/946–5300).

CAR TRAVEL

GASOLINE

Because it must be imported, gasoline runs around $3.00 per gallon.

ROAD CONDITIONS

There are paved, two-lane roads connecting the resort areas, airport, and major settlements on Providenciales. However, they are often pocked with potholes and have steep shoulder drop-offs. A major road rehabilitation project was in the planning stages in early 2001. Dusty, rutted side roads are in worse condition. Ironically, the little-traveled roads in Grand Turk and the out islands are, in general, smooth and paved.

RULES OF THE ROAD

Driving here is on the left side of the road; when pulling out into traffic, remember to look to your right.

ELECTRICITY

Electricity is fairly stable throughout the islands, and the current is the same as in North America (110 volts).

EMERGENCIES

➤ AMBULANCE AND FIRE: Dial ☎ 911 to summon an ambulance or report a fire.
➤ HOSPITALS: **Grand Turk Hospital** (✉ Hospital Rd.,☎ 649/946–2333). On Provo: **M.B.S. Group Medical Practices** (✉ Leeward Hwy., ☎ 649/946–4242).
➤ PHARMACIES: In Grand Turk: **Government Clinic** (✉ Grand Turk Hospital, ☎ 649/946–2040). On Provo: **Super Value Pharmacy,** (✉ South Winds Plaza, ☎ 649/941–3779).
➤ POLICE: Dial (☎ 649/946–2499 in Grand Turk; 649/946–7116 in North Caicos; 649/946–4259 in Provo; 649/946–3299 in South Caicos).
➤ SCUBA DIVING EMERGENCIES: **M.B.S. Group Medical Practice,** on Provo, (✉ Leeward Hwy., ☎ 649/946–4242) has a hyperbaric chamber.

ETIQUETTE AND BEHAVIOR

The Turks and Caicos are extremely visitor-friendly; the atmosphere is laid-back. Don't be afraid to greet people and smile.

HOLIDAYS

Public holidays for 2002 are: New Year's Day, Commonwealth Day (Mar. 11), Maundy Thursday (April 18), Good Friday (April 19), Easter Monday (April 21), National Heroes Day (May 27), Queen's Birthday (June 17), Emancipation Day (August 5), National Youth Day (September 30), Columbus Day (October 14), International Human Rights Day (October 28), Christmas Day, and Boxing Day (Dec. 26).

LANGUAGE

The official language of the Turks and Caicos is English. Native islanders (termed "Belongers") are of African descent, though the population—especially on cosmopolitan Provo—also consists of Canadian, British, American, European, Haitian, and Dominican expats.

MAIL AND SHIPPING

The main branch of the post office is in downtown Provo at the corner of Airport Road. It costs 50¢ to send a postcard to the United States, 60¢ to Canada and the United Kingdom, and $1.25 to Australia and New Zealand; letters, per ounce, cost 60¢ to the United States, 80¢ to Canada and the United Kingdom, and $1.40 to Australia and New Zealand. When writing to the Turks and Caicos Islands, be sure to include the specific island and "Turks and Caicos, BWI" (British West Indies). Delivery service is provided by FedEx, with offices in Provo and Grand Turk.

➤ CONTACTS: **FedEx** On Provo: (☎ 649/946–4682); in Grand Turk: (☎ 649/946–2542).

MONEY MATTERS

Prices quoted in this chapter are in U.S. dollars. Barclays, Scotiabank, and CIBC have offices on Provo, with branches on Grand Turk. Many larger hotels and the casino can take care of your money requests. Bring small denominations to the less-populated islands.

ATMS

There are few ATMs on the islands.

CREDIT CARDS

Major credit cards and traveler's checks are accepted at many establishments.

CURRENCY

The unit of currency is the U.S. dollar.

PASSPORTS AND VISAS

U.S. and Canadian citizens need some proof of citizenship, such as a birth certificate (original or certified copy), plus a photo ID or a current passport. All other travelers, including those from the United Kingdom, Australia, and New Zealand, require a current passport. All visitors must have an ongoing or return ticket.

SAFETY

Petty crime does occur here, and you're advised to leave your valuables in the hotel safe-deposit box and lock doors in cars and rooms when unattended. Bring along a can of insect repellent: the mosquitoes and no-see-ums can be vicious after rain.

In some hotels on Grand Turk, Salt Cay, and South Caicos, there are signs that read PLEASE HELP US CONSERVE OUR PRECIOUS WATER. These islands have no water supply other than rainwater collected in cisterns, and rainfall is scant. Drink only from the decanter of fresh water your hotel provides.

SIGHTSEEING TOURS

A taxi tour of the islands costs between $25 and $30 for the first hour and $25 for each additional hour. On Provo, contact Island's Choice for an entertaining and informative trip by a local tour guide.

J&B Tours offers a variety of sea and land tours, including trips to Middle Caicos, the largest of the islands, for a visit to the caves, or to North Caicos to see flamingos and plantation ruins.

If you want to island-hop on your own schedule, air charters are available through Inter-Island Airways. Global Airways specializes in trips to North Caicos. Aerial photo safaris are provided by Provo Air Charter.
➤ CONTACTS: **Global Airways** (☎ 649/941–3222); **Inter-Island Airways** (☎ 649/941–5481); **Island's Choice** (☎ 649/231–0409); **J&B Tours** (☎ 649/946–5047, WEB www.jbtours.com); **Provo Air Charter** (☎ 649/ 941–0685).

TAXES

DEPARTURE TAX
The departure tax is $15, payable only in cash or traveler's checks.

SALES TAX
Hotels add 10%–15% to your bill for service, and restaurants and hotels add a 9% government tax.

TAXIS

Cabs are now metered, and rates are regulated by the government. In Provo call the Provo Taxi Association for more information.
➤ CONTACTS: **Provo Taxi Association** (☎ 649/946–5481).

TELEPHONES

To place credit-card calls, dial 810 (English). Cellular phones can be rented through Cable & Wireless. Internet access is available via hotel room phone connections or Internet kiosks on Provo and Grand Turk. Although rates have dropped nearly 60% recently, calls from the islands are very expensive, and many hotels add steep surcharges for long-distance. Talk fast.

AREA CODE
The area code for the Turks and Caicos is 649.

INTERNATIONAL CALLS
To make calls from Turks and Caicos, dial 0, then 1, the area code, and the number.

LOCAL CALLS
To make local calls, dial the seven-digit number.
➤ CONTACTS: **Cable & Wireless** (☎ 649/946–2200, WEB www.tci-mall.tc).

TIPPING

At restaurants, tip 15% if service isn't included in the bill. Taxi drivers also expect a token tip, about 10% of your fare.

VISITOR INFORMATION

➤ BEFORE YOU LEAVE: **Turks and Caicos Islands Tourist Board** (☎ 649/ 946–2321 or 800/241–0824, WEB www.turksandcaicostourism.com);

Morris-Kevan International Ltd. (✉ Mitre House, 66 Abbey Rd., Bush Hill Park, Enfield, Middlesex EN1 2RQ, U.K., ☎ 0181/350–1000). ➤ IN TURKS AND CAICOS ISLANDS: **Government Tourist Office** In Grand Turk: (✉ Front St., Cockburn Town, Grand Turk, ☎ 649/946–2321. In Provo: ✉ Stubbs Diamond Plaza, Provo, ☎ 649/946–4970); **Times Publications** (✉ Caribbean Pl., Box 234, Provo, ☎ 649/946–4788, WEB www.timespub.tc).

25 UNITED STATES VIRGIN ISLANDS

Updated by
Carol
Bareuther
and Lynda Lohr

Mornings at the Squirrel Cage coffee shop on St. Thomas aren't much different from those in coffee shops back home. A cop stops by to joke with the waitress and collect his first cup of coffee; a high-heeled secretary runs in for the paper and some toast; a store clerk lingers over a cup of tea to discuss politics with the cook. But is the coffee shop back home in a bright-pink hole-in-the-wall of a 19th-century building, steps from a park abloom with frangipani—in January? Are bush tea and johnnycake served alongside oatmeal and omelets?

It's the combination of the familiar and the exotic found in St. Thomas, St. Croix, and St. John—the United States Virgin Islands (USVI)—that defines this "American paradise" and explains much of its appeal. The effort to be all things to all people—while remaining true to the best of itself—has created a sometimes paradoxical blend of island serenity and American practicality in this U.S. territory 1,000 mi (1,600 km) from the southern tip of the U.S. mainland.

The images you'd expect from a tropical paradise are here: Stretches of beach arc into the distance, and white sails skim across water so blue and clear it stuns the senses. Red-roof houses color the green hillsides as do the orange of the flamboyant tree, the red of the hibiscus, the magenta of the bougainvillea, and the blue stone ruins of old sugar mills. Towns of pastel-tone villas, decorated with filigree wrought-iron terraces, line narrow streets that climb from the harbor. Amid all the images you can find moments—sometimes whole days—of exquisite tranquillity: an egret standing in a pond at dawn, palm trees backlighted by a full moon, sunrises and sunsets that send your spirits soaring with the frigate bird flying overhead.

Chances are that on one of the three islands you'll find your own idea of paradise. Check into a beachfront condo on the east end of St. Thomas, eat burgers, and watch football at a beachfront bar and grill. Or stay at an 18th-century plantation great house on St. Croix, dine on Danish delicacies, and go horseback riding at sunrise. Rent a tent or a cottage in the pristine national park on St. John, take a hike, kayak off the coast, read a book, or just listen to the sounds of the forest. Or dive deep into "island time" and learn the art of limin' (hanging out, Caribbean-style) on all three islands.

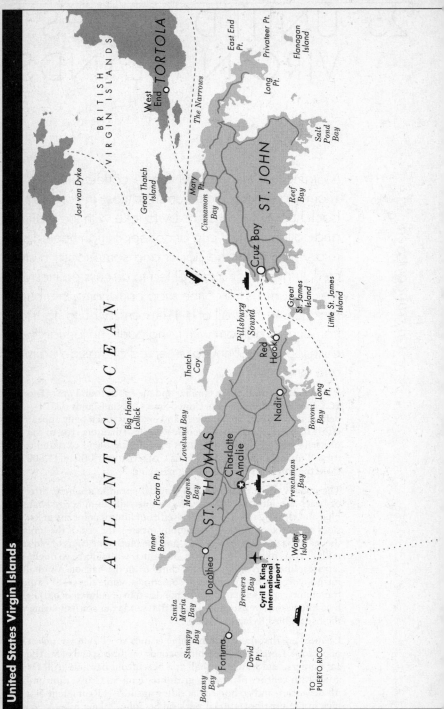

ATLANTIC OCEAN

BRITISH VIRGIN ISLANDS

TORTOLA

West End

Jost van Dyke

Great Thatch Island

Mary Pt.

The Narrows

East End Pt.

Privateer Pt.

Flanagan Island

Long Pt.

Salt Pond Bay

Cinnamon Bay

Cruz Bay

ST. JOHN

Reef Bay

Pillsbury Sound

Great St. James Island

Little St. James Island

Red Hook

Thatch Cay

Big Hans Lollick

Loveland Bay

Nadir

Bonomi Bay

Long Pt.

Picara Pt.

Magens Bay

ST. THOMAS

Charlotte Amalie

Frenchman Bay

Inner Brass

Santa Maria Bay

Dorothea

Water Island

Stumpy Bay

Brewers Bay

Cyril E. King International Airport

Fortuna

David Pt.

Botany Bay

TO PUERTO RICO

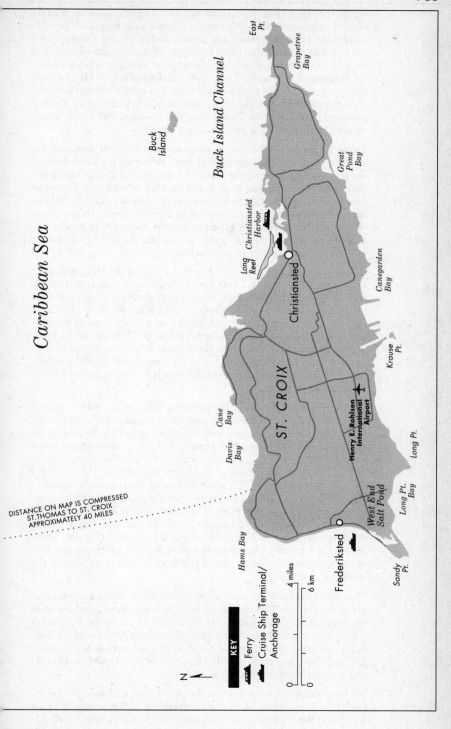

Caribbean Sea

East Pt.

Grapetree Bay

Buck Island Channel

Buck Island

Great Pond Bay

Christiansted Harbor

Long Reef

Canegarden Bay

Christiansted

ST. CROIX

Krause Pt.

Cane Bay

Davis Bay

Henry E. Rohlsen International Airport

Long Pt.

DISTANCE ON MAP IS COMPRESSED
ST. THOMAS TO ST. CROIX
APPROXIMATELY 40 MILES

Long Pt. Bay

West End Salt Pond

Hams Bay

4 miles

6 km

Frederiksted

Sandy Pt.

N

KEY

Ferry

Cruise Ship Terminal/Anchorage

Idyllic though they may be, these bits of volcanic rock in the middle of the Caribbean Sea haven't entirely escaped such worries of overdevelopment as trash, crime, and traffic. Isolation and limited space have, in fact, accentuated these problems. What, for example, do you do with 76 million cans and bottles imported annually when the nearest recycling plant is across 1,000 mi (1,600 km) of ocean? Despite these dilemmas wildlife has found refuge here. The brown pelican is on the endangered list worldwide but is a common sight in the USVI. The endangered native boa tree is protected, as is the hawksbill turtle, whose females lumber onto the beaches to lay eggs.

Preserving its own culture while progressing as a tourist destination is another problem. The islands have been inhabited by Taíno Indians (on St. John and St. Thomas); Carib Indians (on St. Croix); Danish settlers and Spanish pirates; traders and invaders from all the European powers; Africans brought in as slaves; migrants from other Caribbean islands; and, finally, Americans, first as administrators, then as businesspeople and tourists. All these influences are creating a more homogeneous culture, and with each passing year the USVI lose more of their rich, spicy, Caribbean personality.

Sailing into the Caribbean on his second voyage in 1493, Christopher Columbus came upon St. Croix before the group of islands that would later be known as St. Thomas, St. John, and the British Virgin Islands (BVI). He named St. Croix "Santa Cruz" (called Ay Ay by the Carib Indians already living there) but moved on quickly after he encountered the fierce residents. As he approached St. Thomas and St. John, he was impressed enough with the shapely silhouettes of the numerous islands and cays (including the BVI) to name them after Ursula and her 11,000 virgins, but he found the islands barren and moved on to explore Puerto Rico.

Over the next century, as it became clear that Spain couldn't defend the entire Caribbean, other European powers began to settle the islands. In the 1600s the French were joined by the Dutch and the English on St. Croix, and St. Thomas had a mixture of European residents in the early 1700s. By 1695 St. Croix was under the control of the French, but the colonists had moved on to what is today Haiti. The island lay virtually dormant until 1733, when the Danish government bought it—along with St. Thomas and St. John—from the Danish West India Company. At that time settlers from St. Thomas and St. John moved to St. Croix to cultivate the island's gentler terrain. St. Croix developed a plantation economy, but St. Thomas's soil was ill suited to agriculture. There the harbor became internationally known because of its size and ease of entry; it's still hailed as one of the most beautiful seaports in the world.

Plantations depended on slave labor, of which there was a plentiful supply in the Danish West Indies. As early as 1665, agreements between the Brandenburger Company (which needed a base in the West Indies from which to ship the slaves it had imported from Africa) and the West India Company (which needed the kind of quick cash it could collect in duties, fees, and rents from the slave trade) established St. Thomas as a primary slave market.

It's from the slaves who worked the plantations that most Virgin Islanders are descended. More than likely the salesclerk who sells you a watch and the waitress who serves your rum punch can trace their lineage to ancestors captured in Africa some 300 years ago and brought to the West Indies, where they were sold on the block, priced according to their comeliness and strength. Most were captured along Africa's

Gold Coast, from the tribes of Asante, Ibo, Mandika, Amina, and Wolof. They brought with them African rhythms in music and language, herbal medicine, and such crafts as basketry and wood carving. The West Indian–African culture comes to full bloom at Carnival time, when playing *mas* (with abandon) takes precedence over all else.

Yet you can still see the influence of the early Danish settlers here, too. It's reflected in the language and architecture; in common surnames such as Petersen, Jeppesen, and Lawaetz; and in street names such as Kongen's Gade (King Street) and Kronprindsen's Gade (Prince Street). The town of Charlotte Amalie was named after a Danish queen. The Lutheran Church is the state church of Denmark, and Frederick Lutheran Church on St. Thomas dates from 1666. Other peoples have left their marks on the USVI as well. Jewish settlers came to the territory as early as 1665; they were shipowners, chandlers, and brokers in the slave trade. Today their descendants coexist with nearly 1,500 Arabs—95% of whom are Palestinian. You'll also find many East Indians, who are active members of the business community. Immigrants from Puerto Rico and the Dominican Republic make up close to half of St. Croix's population. Transplants from Caribbean countries to the south continue to arrive, seeking better economic opportunities.

St. Thomas, St. Croix, and St. John were known collectively as the Danish West Indies until the United States bought the territory in 1917 during World War I, prompted by fears that Germany would establish a U-boat base in the western hemisphere. The name was changed to the United States Virgin Islands, and almost immediately thereafter British-held Tortola and Virgin Gorda—previously known simply as the Virgin Islands—hastily inserted "British" on the front of their name.

In the 1960s, Pineapple Beach Resort (today Renaissance Grand Beach Resort) was built on St. Thomas, and the Caneel Bay Resort on St. John, built in 1956, was expanded; and with direct flights from the U.S. mainland, the tourism industry was born. In 1960 the total population of all three islands was 32,000. By 1970 it had more than doubled to 75,000, as workers from throughout the Caribbean came to man the building boom. When the boom waned, the people stayed, bringing additional diversity to the territory but also putting a tremendous burden on its infrastructure. Today there are about 50,000 people living on 32-square-mi (83-square-km) St. Thomas (about the same size as Manhattan), 51,000 on the 84 square mi (216 square km) of pastoral St. Croix, and about 5,000 on 20-square-mi (52-square-km) St. John, two-thirds of which is a national park. The per capita income in the USVI is the highest in the West Indies. Just over 25% of the total labor force is employed by the government, and about 10% work in tourism.

Agriculture hasn't been a major economic factor since the last sugarcane plantation on St. Croix ceased operating in the 1960s, but a few farmers on St. Croix, St. Thomas, and St. John still produce some of the mangoes, pineapples, and herbs you'll find on your plate. The islands' cuisine reflects a dependency on a land that gives grudgingly of its bounty. Root vegetables such as sweet potato, hardy vegetables like okra, and stick-to-your-ribs breads were staples 200 years ago, and their influence is still evident in the sweet potato stuffing (mashed potatoes, spices, and raisins), *fungi* (cornmeal and okra), and johnnycakes (deep-fried dough rounds made of cornmeal and white flour) that are ever-present on menus today. The fruits are sweet (slaves got energy to cut sugarcane from a sugar-water drink made from sugar apples). Beverages include not only rum but coconut water, fruit juices, and *maubi,* made from tree bark, and reputedly a virility enhancer.

The backbone of the economy is tourism, but at the heart of the islands is an independent, separate being: a rollicking hodgepodge of West Indian culture with a sense of humor that puts sex and politics in almost every conversation. Lacking a major-league sports team, Virgin Islanders follow the activities and antics of their 15 elected senators with the rabidity of Washingtonians following the Redskins. Loyalty to country and faith in God are the rules in the USVI not the exceptions. Prayer is a way of life, and ROTC is one of the most popular high-school extracurricular activities.

The struggle to preserve the predominantly black Caribbean-influenced culture is heating up in America's paradise. Native Virgin Islanders say they want access to more than just the beach when big money brings in big development. But the three islands are far from united in their goals, especially in light of a $1 billion deficit that threatens the autonomy of the local government and protection of the territory's number-one resource—scenic beauty. The ongoing conflict between progress and preservation here is no mere philosophical exercise, and attempts at resolutions display yet another aspect of the islands' unique blend of character.

ST. THOMAS

Updated by
Carol
Bareuther

If you fly to the 32-square-mi (83-square-km) island of St. Thomas, you land at its western end; if you arrive by cruise ship, you come into one of the world's most beautiful harbors. Either way, one of your first sights is the town of Charlotte Amalie. From the harbor you see an idyllic-looking village that spreads into the lower hills. If you were expecting a quiet hamlet with its inhabitants hanging out under palm trees, you've missed that era by about 300 years. Although other islands in the USVI developed plantation economies, St. Thomas cultivated its harbor, and it became a thriving seaport soon after it was settled by the Danish in the 1600s.

The success of the naturally perfect harbor was enhanced by the fact that the Danes—who ruled St. Thomas with only a couple of short interruptions from 1666 to 1917—avoided involvement in some 100 years' worth of European wars. Denmark was the only European country with colonies in the Caribbean to stay neutral during the war of the Spanish succession in the early 1700s. Thus, products of the Dutch, English, and French islands—sugar, cotton, and indigo—were traded through Charlotte Amalie, along with the regular shipments of slaves. When the Spanish wars ended, trade fell off, but by the end of the 1700s Europe was at war again, Denmark again remained neutral, and St. Thomas continued to prosper. Even into the 1800s, while the economies of St. Croix and St. John foundered with the market for sugarcane, St. Thomas's economy remained strong. This prosperity led to the development of shipyards, a well-organized banking system, and a large merchant class. In 1845 Charlotte Amalie had 101 large importing houses owned by the English, French, Germans, Haitians, Spaniards, Americans, Sephardim, and Danes.

Charlotte Amalie is still one of the most active cruise-ship ports in the world. On almost any day at least one and sometimes as many as eight cruise ships are tied to the dock or anchored outside the harbor. Gently rocking in the shadows of these giant floating hotels are just about every other kind of vessel imaginable: sleek sailing mono- and multi-hulls that will take you on a sunset cruise complete with rum punch and a Jimmy Buffett soundtrack, private megayachts that spirit busy executives away, and barnacle-bottom sloops—with laundry draped to dry over the lifelines—that are home to world-cruising gypsies. Huge container ships pull up in Sub Base, west of the harbor, bringing in everything from cornflakes to tires. Anchored right along the waterfront are the picturesque down-island sloops of the type that has plied the waters between the Greater Antilles and the Leeward Islands for hundreds of years. The sloops still deliver produce, but today they also return down-island with refrigerators, VCRs, and disposable diapers.

The waterfront road through Charlotte Amalie was once part of the harbor. Before it was filled to build the highway, the beach came right up to the back door of the warehouses that now line the thoroughfare. Two hundred years ago those warehouses contained indigo, tobacco, and cotton. Today the stone buildings house silk, crystal, linens, and leather. Exotic fragrances are still traded—but by island beauty queens in air-conditioned perfume palaces instead of through open market stalls. The pirates of old used St. Thomas as a base from which to raid merchant ships of every nation, though they were particularly fond of the gold- and silver-laden treasure ships heading to Spain. Pirates are still around, but today's versions use St. Thomas as a drop-off for their contraband: illegal immigrants and drugs.

With the exception of some private homes, the island's western end is still relatively wild. If you stay on the quiet north side, you'll go up the mountain along roads lined with giant ferns and philodendron, banana trees, and flamboyant trees that thrive in the cooler, wetter climate. The lush vegetation muffles the sound of all but the birds, and it's here you'll find many private villas for rent. In the drier areas to the south and east, the roads are lined with colossal cacti and succulents, punctuated by the bright colors of the hardy bougainvillea and hibiscus. The southeastern and far eastern ends of the island are flat, and this is where you'll find the beachfront hotels and condominiums. At the eastern tip is Red Hook, a friendly village anchored by the marine community nestled at Red Hook harbor.

Lodging

Of the USVI, St. Thomas has the most rooms and the greatest variety of accommodations. You can let yourself be pampered at a luxurious south shore, east end, or west end resort—albeit at a price of $300 to more than $900 per night, not including meals. If your means are more modest, you will find fine hotels (often with rooms that have a kitchen and a living area) in lovely settings throughout the island. There are also guest houses and inns with great views (if not a beach at your door) and great service at about half the cost of the beachfront pleasure palaces. Many of these are east and north of Charlotte Amalie, in the Frenchtown area or overlooking hills—ideal if you plan to get out and mingle with the locals. There are also inexpensive lodgings (most right in town) that are perfect if you just want a clean room to return to after a day of exploring or beach-bumming.

Families often stay at an east end condominium complex. Although condos are pricey (winter rates average $240 per night for a two-bedroom unit, which usually sleeps six), they have full kitchens, and you can definitely save money by cooking for yourself—especially if you bring your own nonperishable foodstuffs. (Virtually everything on St. Thomas is imported, and restaurants and shops pass shipping costs on to you.) Though you may spend some time laboring in the kitchen, many condos ease your burden with daily maid service and on-site restaurants; a few also have resort amenities, including pools and tennis courts. The east end is convenient to St. John, and it's home to the boating crowd and some good restaurants. The prices below reflect rates in high

St. Thomas

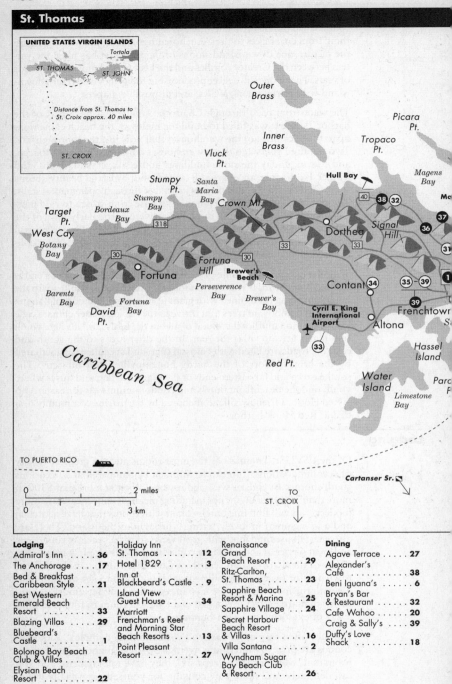

UNITED STATES VIRGIN ISLANDS

Tortola

ST. THOMAS ST. JOHN

· Distance from St. Thomas to
St. Croix approx. 40 miles ·

ST. CROIX

Outer
Brass

Picara
Pt.

Inner
Brass

Tropaco
Pt.

Vluck
Pt.

Hull Bay

Magens
Bay

Stumpy
Pt.

Santa
Maria
Bay

Crown Mt.

40 38 32

Stumpy
Bay

Target
Pt.

Bordeaux
Bay

37

West Cay

318

Dorthea

Signal
Hill

36

Botany
Bay

30

Fortuna
Hill

30

33

33

31

Fortuna

Brewer's
Beach

1

Barents
Bay

Perseverence
Bay

Contant

34

35 39

David
Pt.

Fortuna
Bay

Brewer's
Bay

Cyril E. King
International
Airport

39

Frenchtown

Altona

Caribbean Sea

33

Red Pt.

Hassel
Island

Water
Island

Parc

Limestone
Bay

TO PUERTO RICO

Cartanser Sr.

0   2 miles
0   3 km

TO
ST. CROIX

Lodging
Admiral's Inn 36
The Anchorage 17
Bed & Breakfast
Caribbean Style . . . 21
Best Western
Emerald Beach
Resort 33
Blazing Villas 29
Bluebeard's
Castle 1
Bolongo Bay Beach
Club & Villas 14
Elysian Beach
Resort 22

Holiday Inn
St. Thomas 12
Hotel 1829 3
Inn at
Blackbeard's Castle . 9
Island View
Guest House 34
Marriott
Frenchman's Reef
and Morning Star
Beach Resorts 13
Point Pleasant
Resort 27

Renaissance
Grand
Beach Resort 29
Ritz-Carlton,
St. Thomas 23
Sapphire Beach
Resort & Marina . . 25
Sapphire Village . . 24
Secret Harbour
Beach Resort
& Villas 16
Villa Santana 2
Wyndham Sugar
Bay Beach Club
& Resort 26

Dining
Agave Terrace 27
Alexander's
Café 38
Beni Iguana's 6
Bryan's Bar
& Restaurant 32
Cafe Wahoo 20
Craig & Sally's . . . 39
Duffy's Love
Shack 18

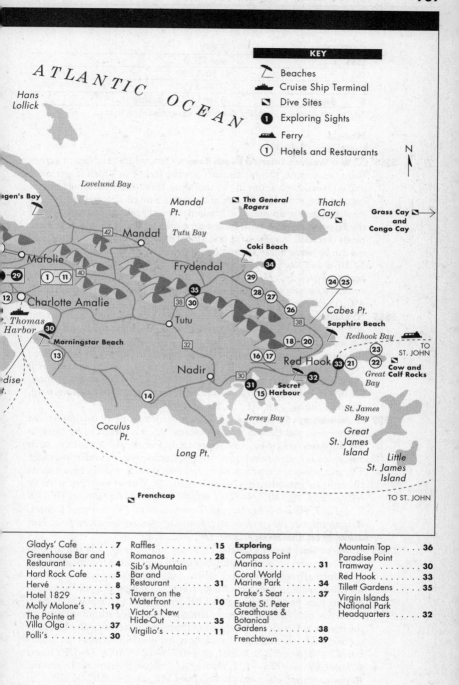

KEY

- Beaches
- Cruise Ship Terminal
- Dive Sites
- ❶ Exploring Sights
- ① Hotels and Restaurants

N

ATLANTIC OCEAN

Hans Lollick

Lovelund Bay

...gen's Bay

Mandal Pt.

Tutu Bay

The *General Rogers*

Thatch Cay

Grass Cay and Congo Cay

Coki Beach

Mafolie

42 Mandal

Frydendal

34

29

❷❾

①—⑪ 40

12 Charlotte Amalie

35

38 30

28 27

26

24 25

Cabes Pt.

38

Sapphire Beach

...t. Thomas Harbor

Tutu

Redhook Bay

TO ST. JOHN

30

Morningstar Beach

32

18—20

23

13

16 17

Red Hook

33 21 22

Cow and Calf Rocks

Nadir

30

32

...dise ...t.

14

31

15

Secret Harbour

Great Bay

St. James Bay

Coculus Pt.

Jersey Bay

Great St. James Island

Long Pt.

Little St. James Island

TO ST. JOHN

Frenchcap

		Exploring	
Gladys' Cafe 7	Raffles 15	**Exploring**	Mountain Top 36
Greenhouse Bar and Restaurant 4	Romanos 28	Compass Point Marina 31	Paradise Point Tramway 30
Hard Rock Cafe 5	Sib's Mountain Bar and Restaurant 31	Coral World Marine Park 34	Red Hook 33
Hervé 8	Tavern on the Waterfront 10	Drake's Seat 37	Tillett Gardens 35
Hotel 1829 3	Victor's New Hide-Out 35	Estate St. Peter Greathouse & Botanical Gardens 38	Virgin Islands National Park Headquarters 32
Molly Molone's 19	Virgilio's 11	Frenchtown 39	
The Pointe at Villa Olga 37			
Polli's 30			

season, which runs from December 15 to April 15. Rates are 25% to 50% lower the rest of the year.

CATEGORY	COST*
$$$$	over $200
$$$	$150–$200
$$	$100–$150
$	under $100

All prices are for a standard double room, excluding 8% tax.

Hotels

CHARLOTTE AMALIE

$$$$ 🏨 **Best Western Emerald Beach Resort.** On a white-sand beach across from the airport, this mini-resort has the feel of its much larger east-end cousins. Each room in the four pink three-story buildings has its own terrace or balcony, palms, and colorful flowers that frame an ocean view. Rooms are decorated in modern tropical prints and rattan. A plus: the resort is popular with business people, so the pool and beach are rarely crowded. A minus: the noise from nearby jets taking off and landing can be heard intermittently over a three-hour period each afternoon. ✉ *8070 Lindberg Bay, 00802,* ☎ *340/777–8800; 800/233–4936 direct to hotel,* FAX *340/776–3426,* WEB *www.emeraldbeach.com. 90 rooms. Restaurant, air-conditioning, pool, tennis court, beach. AE, D, MC, V. EP.*

$$$$ 🏨 **Bluebeard's Castle.** Though not exactly a castle, this large red-roof complex offers kingly comforts on a steep hill above town. All rooms are air-conditioned and have terraces. The hotel is a short ride from the shops of Charlotte Amalie and Havensight Mall, and there's free transportation to Magens Bay Beach and to town. ✉ *Bluebeard's Hill (Box 7480), 00801,* ☎ *340/774–1600; 800/524–6599 direct to hotel,* FAX *340/774–5134. 170 rooms. 3 restaurants, bar, air-conditioning, pool, 2 tennis courts, gym. AE, D, DC, MC, V. EP.*

$$$ 🏨 **Holiday Inn St. Thomas.** This harbor-front property is comfortable for business travelers as well as vacationers who want to be close to the duty-free shopping. Contemporary furnished rooms have such amenities as coffeemakers, hair dryers, ironing boards and irons, cable TV, and phones. Complimentary features include a daily beach shuttle and an introductory dive lesson. ✉ *Waterfront Hwy. (Box 640),00804,* ☎ *340/774–5200; 800/524–7389 direct to hotel,* FAX *340/774–1231,* WEB *www.holidayinn.st-thomas.com. 140 rooms, 11 suites. Restaurant, bar, air-conditioning, in-room safes, refrigerators, pool, hair salon, gym, dive shop. AE, D, DC, MC, V. EP.*

$$$ 🏨 **Inn at Blackbeard's Castle.** This cozy hilltop inn is laid out around a tower from which, it's said, Blackbeard kept watch for invaders. It's an informally elegant place, where you can while away a Sunday morning reading the *New York Times*. Mahogany furnishings, including four-poster beds, lend a 17th-century feel to the place, yet each room has many modern conveniences. You can see stunning views of the harbor at Charlotte Amalie from the tower as well as from the open-air bar, the fresh-water pool, and the many outdoor terraces. ✉ *Blackbeard's Hill (Box 6227), 00804,* ☎ *340/776–1234; 800/334–5771 direct to hotel,* FAX *340/776–4521,* WEB *www.blackbeardscastle.vi. 16 rooms. Restaurant, bar, air-conditioning, pool. AE, D, DC, MC, V. CP.*

$$ 🏨 **Hotel 1829.** This historic Spanish-style inn is popular with visiting
★   government officials and people with business at Government House down the street. Rooms, on several levels (no elevator), range from elegant and roomy to quite small but are priced accordingly, so there's one for every budget. Author Graham Greene is said to have stayed here, and it's easy to imagine him musing over a drink in the small,

dark bar. The second-floor botanical gardens and open-air champagne bar make a romantic spot for sunset viewing before dinner in the gourmet Hotel 1829 restaurant. Rooms count phones and TVs in their list of amenities. There's a tiny, tiny pool for cooling off, and the shops of Charlotte Amalie are close by. ⊠ *Government Hill (Box 1567), 00804,* ☎ *340/776–1829; 800/524–2002 direct to hotel,* FAX *340/776–4313,* WEB *www.hotel1829.com. 14 rooms. Restaurant, air-conditioning, refrigerators, pool. AE, D, MC, V, CP.*

$$ ★ 🛏 **Villa Santana.** Built by General Santa Anna of Mexico, the villa (circa 1857) still provides a panoramic view of the harbor and plenty of West Indian charm. This landmark, close to town, has six villa-style rooms. Dark-wood furniture, plaster-and-stone walls, shuttered windows, cathedral ceilings, and interesting nooks contribute to the sense of romance and history. All units have full kitchens, TVs, and either four-poster or cradle beds; ceiling fans and natural trade winds keep things cool. Villas La Torre and La Mansion are split-level quarters with spiral staircases. ⊠ *2D Denmark Hill, 00802,* ☎ *340/776–1311,* FAX *340/776–1311,* WEB *www.st-thomas.com/villasantana. 6 rooms. Kitchenettes, fans, pool, croquet. AE. CP.*

EAST END

$$$$ 🛏 **Elysian Beach Resort.** The coral-color villas here are situated along a hill all the way to the edge of Cowpet Bay. Rooms are decorated in muted tropical floral prints and have terraces, TVs, and phones; some have full kitchens. Activity centers on a kidney-shape pool with a waterfall and thatch-roofed pool bar. The Palm Court restaurant has a strong local following for the Sunday buffet brunch. ⊠ *Estate Nazareth (Box 51), Red Hook 00802,* ☎ *340/775–1000; 800/753–2554 direct to hotel,* FAX *340/776–0910. 175 rooms. 2 restaurants, 2 bars, air-conditioning, fans, pool, tennis court, health club, beach. AE, MC, V. EP.*

$$$$ 🛏 **Point Pleasant Resort.** Stretching up a steep, tree-covered hill and affording a great view of Drake's Channel, this resort offers a choice of accommodations from simple bedrooms to multi-room suites. Units are in buildings hidden among the trees. All have striking views, balconies, and fully equipped kitchens. Although the "beach" is almost nonexistent, three good-size pools surrounded by decks are placed at different levels on the hill. The property also has a labyrinth of well-marked nature trails to explore. Every guest gets four hours free use of a car daily (you do need to pay the $20, per use, fuel and maintenance fee). If you like seafood, don't miss dinner at the Agave Terrace restaurant. ⊠ *6600 Estate Smith Bay, No. 4, 00802,* ☎ *340/775–7200; 800/524–2300 direct to hotel,* FAX *340/776–5694,* WEB *www. pointpleasantresort.com. 95 suites. 2 restaurants, bar, kitchenettes, 3 pools, tennis court, gym, beach. AE, D, DC, MC, V. EP.*

$$$$ ★ 🛏 **Renaissance Grand Beach Resort.** The zigzag architectural angles spell luxury, and that's what you'll find everywhere, from the marble atrium lobby to the one-bedroom suites with whirlpool baths. The beach is excellent, and there's a fitness center with Nautilus machines. The lobby is often populated by those lucky business types whose companies favor the resort as a convention-and-conference center. Daily activities for children include iguana hunts, T-shirt painting, and sand-castle building. This tends to be a very busy hotel, with lots of people in the restaurants and on the beach. ⊠ *Smith Bay Rd. (Box 8267), 00801,* ☎ *340/775–1510 or 800/468–3571,* FAX *340/775–3757,* WEB *www. renaissancehotels.com/sttsr. 290 rooms, 36 suites. 2 restaurants, snack bar, air-conditioning, 2 pools, barbershop, hair salon, 6 tennis courts, health club, beach, children's programs, business services. AE, D, DC, MC, V. EP, MAP.*

$$$$ 🏨 **Ritz-Carlton, St. Thomas.** This premier luxury resort resembles a villa
★ in Venice and offers stunning ocean views through the lobby's glass
doors. Guest rooms, in six buildings that fan out from the main villa,
are spacious and tropically furnished. Elegance is everywhere, from the
beautiful pool that appears to become one with the sea to the gourmet
restaurant and casual alfresco lunch area. A multilingual staff and 24-
hour room service enhance the sophisticated atmosphere. A $75-mil-
lion renovation and expansion project, which should be completed by
the end of 2001, will add 48 additional rooms, a full-service spa and
fitness center, and 80 two- and three-bedroom private club residences.
✉ *6900 Great Bay Estate, 00802,* ☎ *340/775–3333 or 800/241–
3333,* 𝖥𝖠𝖷 *340/775–4444,* 𝖶𝖤𝖡 *www.ritzcarlton.com. 148 rooms. 3
restaurants, 3 bars, air-conditioning, room service, pool, 3 tennis
courts, health club, beach, children's programs, business services. AE,
D, DC, MC, V. EP.*

$$$$ 🏨 **Sapphire Beach Resort & Marina.** On a clear day the lush, green
mountains of the neighboring British Virgin Islands seem close enough
to touch from this picturesque, red-roofed resort. Room interiors, from
the tropical bold-pattern rugs and comforters to full kitchenettes,
were renovated in early 2000. A new five-building area in the center
of the property will open in fall of 2001 with retail shops, a meeting
area, and deli dining. The good news is that this construction doesn't
obscure the beautiful beachside view. The fun family-oriented atmosphere here is highlighted by a Sunday beach party that thumps with
rock and reggae and MeriStar's Fun Factory™ Kids Klub program,
where 4- to 12-year-olds can enjoy such activities as arts and crafts,
sing-alongs, and sand-castle building. Children under 12 eat free,
while teens up to 18 also can sleep in their parents' room at no additional charge. ✉ *Sapphire Bay (Box 8088), 00801,* ☎ *340/775–6100;
800/524–2090 direct to hotel,* 𝖥𝖠𝖷 *340/775–2403,* 𝖶𝖤𝖡 *www.
sapphirebeachstthomas.com. 171 suites. 4 restaurants, 2 bars, air-
conditioning, 4 tennis courts, health club, beach, children's programs.
AE, MC, V. EP, MAP.*

$$$$ 🏨 **Secret Harbour Beach Resort & Villas.** These beige buildings, which
contain low-rise studios and suites, are tucked into the hillsides and
along an inviting sandy cove. Watch marvelous sunsets from the balconies or the casual restaurant. All units have air-conditioning and maid
service. Children under age 13 stay free, making this a family-friendly
resort. ✉ *6280 Estate Nazareth, 00802-1104,* ☎ *340/775–6550; 800/
524–2250 direct to hotel,* 𝖥𝖠𝖷 *340/775–1501,* 𝖶𝖤𝖡 *www.st-
thomas.com/shb.vi. 49 suites, 15 studios. Restaurant, bar, air-conditioning, fans, kitchenettes, pool, 4 tennis courts, health club, beach,
dive shop, snorkeling, windsurfing. AE, MC, V. CP.*

$$$$ 🏨 **Wyndham Sugar Bay Beach Club & Resort.** This warm, terra-cotta
hillside resort is one of the island's most attractive. Most rooms overlook water; some have views of the British Virgin Islands. All are spacious and comfortable and have balconies, hair dryers, and coffeemakers.
The beach is small, but there's a giant pool with waterfalls. ✉ *6500
Estate Smith Bay, 00802,* ☎ *340/777–7100; 800/927–7100 direct to
hotel,* 𝖥𝖠𝖷 *340/777–7200,* 𝖶𝖤𝖡 *www.wyndham.com. 300 rooms, 9 suites.
Restaurant, bar, air-conditioning, 3 pools, 2 tennis courts, health club,
beach, snorkeling, windsurfing. AE, D, DC, MC, V. All-inclusive.*

FRENCHTOWN

$$ 🏨 **Admiral's Inn.** This charming inn sprawls down a hillside on the point
★ of land known as Frenchtown, just west of Charlotte Amalie. All
rooms have wonderful town, ocean, or harbor views; the four ocean-
view rooms have balconies and refrigerators. All units have rattan fur-
niture; cream- or teal-color bedspreads; vertical blinds; coral, teal, and

cream carpeting; and large, tiled vanity areas. The rocky shoreline is perfect for snorkeling, and the freshwater pool (there's bar service here) is surrounded by a large deck that's ideal for sunning. ✉ *Villa Olga, 00802,* ☎ *340/774–1376; 800/544–0493 direct to hotel,* FAX *340/774–8010,* WEB *www.admirals-inn.com.12 rooms. Restaurant, bar, kitchenettes (some), pool. AE, D, MC, V. CP.*

$$$$　🏨 **Bolongo Bay Beach Club & Villas.** This 75-room, beachfront resort also includes the 20-room Bolongo Villas next door and the six-room Bolongo Bayside Inn across the street. All rooms—which include minisuites and one- and two-bedroom units—have kitchens and balconies and are just steps from a strand of white-sand beach. The resort offers a choice of all-inclusive or semi-inclusive plans, which means you can pay less if you opt for fewer activities. The all-inclusive rate covers all meals and drinks, the use of tennis courts, and many water-sports activities—including an all-day sail and half-day snorkel trip on a yacht. There's a three-night minimum for the all-inclusive plan. ✉ *50 Estate Bolongo, 00802,* ☎ *340/775–1800; 800/524–4746 direct to hotel,* FAX *340/775–3208,* WEB *www.bolongo.com. 101 units. 2 restaurants, 2 bars, air-conditioning, kitchenettes, 3 pools, 2 tennis courts, health club, volleyball, beach, dive shop, dock, snorkeling, windsurfing, boating, jet skiing. AE, D, DC, MC, V. All-inclusive.*

$$$$　🏨 **Marriott Frenchman's Reef and Morning Star Beach Resorts.** On a
★　prime harbor promontory east of Charlotte Amalie, you'll find these two sprawling, luxurious, full-service superhotels. Frenchman's Reef has 128 suites—each with glorious ocean and harbor views. The more elegant Morning Star rooms are in buildings nestled surfside along the fine white sand of Morning Star Beach. Guests at both resorts can work out at the Reef Health Club & Spa, which offers state-of-the-art equipment, therapeutic massages, and skin-care therapies. Dining is alfresco on American or gourmet Caribbean fare or oceanfront at the Tavern on the Beach; there's also a lavish buffet served, overlooking the sparkling lights of Charlotte Amalie. Live entertainment and dancing, scheduled activities for all ages, and a shuttle boat to town make having fun easy. ✉ *Estate Bakkeroe (Box 7100), 00801,* ☎ *340/776–8500; 800/524–2000 direct to hotel,* FAX *340/776–3054,* WEB *www. marriott-fr.vi. 373 rooms, 128 suites. 6 restaurants, 6 bars, snack bar, air-conditioning, 2 pools, spa, 4 tennis courts, health club, beach. AE, D, DC, MC, V. EP.*

Guest Houses

$　🏨 **Island View Guest House.** In tropical foliage 545 ft (166 m) up on
★　the face of Crown Mountain, this simply furnished bed-and-breakfast offers sweeping views of Charlotte Amalie harbor from the pool and shaded terraces. Continental breakfast is served daily; however, six rooms have kitchenettes. All rooms have phones, ceiling fans, TVs, and baths. The friendly office staff can arrange tours. ✉ *Estate Contant (Box 1903), 00801,* ☎ *340/774–4270; 800/524–2023 direct to hotel,* FAX *340/774–6167,* WEB *www.st-thomas.com/islandviewguesthouse. 15 rooms. Fans, kitchenettes (some), pool. AE, MC, V. CP.*

Villas and Condominiums

$$$$　🏨 **The Anchorage.** Next to the St. Thomas Yacht Club and facing Cowpet Bay, these two- and three-bedroom villas are right on the beach. They have washing machines and dryers, and the complex has two lighted tennis courts, a freshwater pool, and an informal restaurant. ✉ *Estate Nazareth (Antilles Resorts, Box 8529, 00801),* ☎ *340/775–2600;*

800/874–7897 *direct to hotel,* FAX *340/775–5901,* WEB *www.antilleresorts.com. 30 rooms. Dining room, air-conditioning, kitchenettes, pool, 2 tennis courts. AE, D, MC, V. EP.*

$$$ 🏨 **Blazing Villas.** On the Renaissance Grand Beach Resort property,
★ these cool pastel yellow, pink, green, and blue villas have their own garden patios and can be combined with other villas to create a four-bedroom, four-bath unit. All quarters have refrigerators, microwaves, and phones. You can use all the resort's facilities. ✉ *Smith Bay Rd. (Box 502697), 00805,* ☎ *340/776–0760; 800/382–2002 direct to hotel,* FAX *340/776–3603,* WEB *www.blazingvillas.com. 19 rooms. 2 restaurants, snack bar, air-conditioning, refrigerators, 2 pools, 6 tennis courts, health club, beach, business services. AE, MC, V. EP.*

$$$ 🏨 **Sapphire Village.** A stay in these high-rise units may take you back to the swinging-singles days of apartment-house living since many of the units are rented out long-term to refugees from northern winters. The best units overlook the marina and St. John; the beach is in sight and just a short walk down the hill. ✉ *Sapphire Bay (Antilles Resorts, Box 8529, 00801),* ☎ *340/775–2600; 800/874–7897 direct to hotel,* FAX *340/775–5901,* WEB *www.antillesresorts.com. 35 units. Restaurant, pub, air-conditioning, kitchenettes, 2 pools. AE, D, MC, V. EP.*

$$ 🏨 **Bed & Breakfast Caribbean Style.** Honeymooners will enjoy the romantic feel of these private, elegantly decorated condos. Each unit has a king-size bed, a reading and video library, a porch with hammock, cable TV, and a phone. The kitchen comes stocked with a tempting variety of breakfast foods. There's a small pool on the property, and the beach and water sports are a five-minute walk away. Those seeking to tie the knot will find that making wedding arrangements, including professional photography, is a specialty of the owner. ✉ *Estate Vessup Bay (6501 Red Hook Plaza, Suite 96, 00802),* ☎ *340/775–6131,* WEB *www.cstyle.co.vi. 3 units. Air-conditioning, kitchenettes, pool. AE, MC, V. EP.*

Private Homes

You can arrange private-home rentals through various agents. **Calypso Realty** (✉ Box 12178, 00801, ☎ 340/774–1620 or 800/747–4858, WEB www.calypsorealty.com) specializes in rental properties in St. Thomas. **McLaughlin-Anderson Villas** (✉ 100 Blackbeard's Hill, Suite 3, 00802, ☎ 340/776–0635 or 800/537–6246, WEB www.mclaughlinanderson.com), handles rental villas throughout the U.S. Virgin Islands, British Virgin Islands, and Grenada. Both specialize in luxury residences, and have Web sites and brochures that show photos of the properties they represent. Some villas are suitable for travelers with disabilities.

Dining

The beauty of St. Thomas and its sister islands has attracted a cadre of professionally trained chefs who know their way around fresh fish and local fruits. You can dine on everything from terrific, cheap local dishes such as goat water (a spicy stew) and fungi, to imports such as hot pastrami sandwiches and raspberries in crème fraîche.

In large hotels you'll pay prices similar to those in New York City or Paris. Fancy restaurants may have a token chicken or pasta dish under $20, but otherwise, main courses are pricey. You can, however, find good inexpensive Caribbean restaurants. To snack on some local fare, order a johnnycake or a thick slice of dumb bread (a dense round loaf often cut into triangles and filled with cheddar cheese) from any of the mobile food vans parked all over the island. Familiar fast-food franchises also abound.

If your accommodations have a kitchen and you plan to cook, you'll find good variety in St. Thomas's mainland-style supermarkets. Note, however, that grocery prices are about 20% higher than those on the mainland United States. As for drinking, outside the hotels a beer in a bar will cost between $2 and $3 and a piña colada $4 or more.

What to Wear

Dining on St. Thomas is informal. Few restaurants require a jacket and tie. Still, at dinner in the snazzier places, shorts and T-shirts are inappropriate; men would do well to wear slacks and a shirt with buttons. Dress codes on St. Thomas rarely require women to wear skirts, but you'll never go wrong with something flowing.

CATEGORY	COST*
$$$$	over $30
$$$	$20–$30
$$	$10–$20
$	under $10

per person for a main course at dinner

Charlotte Amalie

AMERICAN

$$ ✕ **Greenhouse Bar and Restaurant.** Watch the waterfront wake up at this large, bustling open-air restaurant, whose wait staff looks like a bunch of all-American college kids on spring break. An eight-page menu features burgers, omelets, salads, sandwiches, and pizza that are served all day long, along with more upscale entrees like peel-'n'-eat shrimp, Maine lobster, and Certified black Angus prime rib that are reasonably priced. The atmosphere is family-friendly, though the Wednesday night live reggae band that starts thumping at 10 PM draws a lively young-adult crowd that enjoys partying into the early morning hours. ⊠ *Waterfront Hwy. at Storetvaer Gade,* ☎ *340/774–7998. AE, D, MC, V.*

$$ ✕ **Hard Rock Cafe.** A hot spot from the day it opened, this waterfront restaurant is pretty much like its namesakes around the world. Rock-and-roll memorabilia abound, and the menu offers hamburgers, sandwiches, salads, and great desserts. Jerk pork tenderloin is a delicious Caribbean addition. Doors are open from 11 AM until 2 AM; there's always a wait for a table during prime meal times. ⊠ *International Plaza on Waterfront,* ☎ *340/777–5555. AE, MC, V.*

ASIAN

$ ✕ **Beni Iguana's.** Here sushi is served as "edible art" in a charming Danish courtyard. Among the offerings are cucumber and avocado or scallop with scallion rolls, specialty big rolls such as the Kung Fooee (shiitake, cucumber, daikon, and flying-fish roe), and tuna or salmon sashimi. A pictorial menu board makes ordering by the piece, plate, or combination platter easy. ⊠ *Grand Hotel Court, Tolbod Gade at Norre Gade,* ☎ *340/777–8744. No credit cards. Closed Sun.*

CARIBBEAN

$ ✕ **Gladys' Cafe.** Even if the local specialties—conch in butter sauce, ★ salt fish and dumplings, hearty red bean soup—didn't make this a recommended café, it would be worth coming for Gladys's smile. While you're here, pick up some of her hot sauce for $6 a bottle. ⊠ *Waterfront at Royal Dane Mall,* ☎ *340/774–6604. AE. Closed Sun. No dinner.*

CONTINENTAL

$$$ ✕ **Hotel 1829.** You'll dine by candlelight flickering over stone walls ★ and pink table linens at this restaurant on the terrace of the Hotel 1829. The menu and award-winning wine list (325 varieties, 15 available by the glass) are extensive, from Caribbean rock lobster to rack of lamb.

Many items—including a warm spinach salad—are prepared table-side, and the restaurant is justly famous for its dessert soufflés: chocolate, Grand Marnier, raspberry, or coconut, to name a few. ⊠ *Government Hill near Main St.,* ☎ *340/776–1829. Reservations essential. AE, D, MC, V. Closed Sun.*

ECLECTIC

$$$ ✕ **Hervé.** French-trained Hervé Chassin's long experience in the St. Thomas restaurant industry has led to a menu that offers a delightful mix of Caribbean and Continental cuisine. In the warm glow of candlelight—at tables impeccably dressed with linen cloths, silver settings, and fine crystal—you can start off with crispy conch fritters served with a spicy-sweet mango chutney, and then choose from such entrées as fresh tuna encrusted with sesame seeds or succulent roast duck with a ginger and tamarind sauce. The passionfruit cheesecake is to die for. ⊠ *Government Hill,* ☎ *340/777–9703. AE, MC, V. Closed Sun.*

$$$ ✕ **Tavern on the Waterfront.** White linen tablecloths, silver and crystal table settings, and a rich mahogany decor set the scene for an elegant meal at this second-floor, air-conditioned restaurant that overlooks the harbor. Tiger Woods, Michael Jordan, and Walter Cronkite have all supped here. The menu offers flavors from every corner of the globe. Try the soft-shell crabs with mango salsa or the tuna sushi for lunch. Dinner offerings include a two-pound Caribbean lobster specialty. Sunday is Latin night. ⊠ *Waterfront at Royal Dane Mall,* ☎ *340/776–4328. AE, MC, V. Closed Sun.*

ITALIAN

$$$ ✕ **Virgilio's.** For the island's best Northern Italian cuisine, don't miss
★   this intimate, elegant hideaway tucked on a quiet side street. Eclectic art covers the two-story-high brick walls, and the sound of Italian opera music sets the stage for a memorable meal. Come here for more than 40 homemade pastas complemented by superb sauces—*cappellini* (very thin spaghetti) with fresh tomatoes and garlic, say, or spaghetti peasant style (in a rich tomato sauce with mushrooms and prosciutto). House specialties are osso buco and tiramisu for dessert, expertly prepared by chef Ernesto Garrigos. ⊠ *18 Main St.,* ☎ *340/776–4920. Reservations essential. AE, MC, V. Closed Sun.*

East End

ECLECTIC

$$$ ✕ **Raffles.** In a homey dining room, set in a quaint marina, owner-chef
★   Sandra Englesburger puts on a one-woman culinary show. Her from-scratch creations include a signature coconut shrimp appetizer, and entrées like beef Wellington, mahimahi in a rich lobster sauce, and a two-day Peking duck. There are fresh fish and vegetarian specials daily. For dessert, try the chocolate paté—Belgian chocolate melted and frozen into a decadent treat. ⊠ *41–6–1 Compass Point Marina,* ☎ *340/775–6004. Reservations essential. AE, MC, V. No lunch Apr.–Oct. Closed Mon.*

$ ✕ **Duffy's Love Shack.** If the floating bubbles don't attract you to this zany eatery, the lime-green shutters, loud rock music, and fun-loving wait staff sure will. It's billed as the "ultimate tropical drink shack," and the bartenders shake up such exotic concoctions as the Love Shack Volcano—a 50-ounce flaming extravaganza. Dining selections are just as trendy. Try the grilled mahimahi taco salad or jerk Caesar wrap. Thursday night features theme parties complete with giveaways. ⊠ *Red Hook Plaza parking lot,* ☎ *340/779–2080. No credit cards.*

IRISH

$$ ✕ **Molly Molone's.** This casual, alfresco restaurant has a devout following
★ of locals who live and work on boats docked nearby. You'll find such
traditional Irish dishes as stew, and bangers and mash (sausage and mashed
potatoes), as well as fresh fish, oversized deli sandwiches, and rich
soups. Beware: the iguanas like to beg for table scraps—bring your cam-
era. Upstairs, the same owners run A Whale of a Tale, a pricier seafood
eatery that also serves freshly made pasta and fine wines. ⊠ *American
Yacht Harbor, Bldg. D, Red Hook,* ☎ *340/775–1270. MC, V.*

ITALIAN

$$$$ ✕ **Romanos.** Inside this huge, old stucco house is a delightful surprise:
★ a spare yet elegant setting and superb Northern Italian cuisine. Owner
Tony Romano hasn't advertised since the restaurant opened in 1988,
yet it's always packed. Try the pastas, either with a classic sauce or
one of Tony's unique creations, such as a cream sauce with mushrooms,
prosciutto, pine nuts, and Parmesan. ⊠ *97 Smith Bay,* ☎ *340/775–
0045. Reservations essential. MC, V. No lunch. Closed Sun.*

SEAFOOD

$$$ ✕ **Agave Terrace.** At this dimly lit, open-air pavilion restaurant in the
Point Pleasant Resort, fresh fish is the specialty, served as steaks or fil-
lets, and the catch of the day is listed on the blackboard. There are more
than a dozen fish sauces to choose from, including teriyaki-mango and
lime ginger. Come early and have a drink at the Lookout Lounge, which
has breathtaking views of the British Virgins. The food enjoys as good
a reputation as the view. ⊠ *6600 Estate Smith Bay,* ☎ *340/775–4142.
AE, MC, V. No lunch.*

$$$ ✕ **Cafe Wahoo.** The fish is so fresh at this open-air eatery that you may
see it coming in from one of the boats tied up at the dock just steps
away. For starters, try the house-cured vodka salmon with mango
crème fraîche. Entrées include a rib-sticking wahoo bouillabaisse with
scallops, shrimp, and green tip mussels all in a lobster bisque. Steak,
poultry, and pasta lovers will find something to please on the menu,
too. ⊠ *American Yacht Harbor Marina, Red Hook,* ☎ *340/775–
6350. AE, MC, V. No lunch.*

TEX-MEX

$ ✕ **Polli's.** You'll feel as if you're sitting deep within a tropical jungle
at this open-air restaurant, where a parrot squawks a greeting to in-
coming diners. The menu is complete with jalapeño poppers (deep-fried
cheese-stuffed hot peppers), chicken- or seafood-stuffed fajitas, and apple
chimichangas for dessert. All entrées come vegetarian-style upon re-
quest. ⊠ *Tillett Gardens, Estate Tutu,* ☎ *340/775–4550. AE, MC, V.*

Frenchtown

AUSTRIAN

$$ ✕ **Alexander's Café.** This place is a favorite with the people in the restau-
★ rant business on St. Thomas—always a sign of quality. Alexander is
Austrian, and the schnitzels are delicious and reasonably priced; pasta
specials are fresh and tasty. Save room for strudel. Next door is Alexander's Bar & Grill, serving food from the same kitchen but in a more
casual setting and at lower prices. ⊠ *24-A Honduras,* ☎ *340/776–4211.
Reservations essential. AE, D, MC, V. Closed Sun.*

CARIBBEAN

$$ ✕ **Victor's New Hide-Out.** Although it's a little hard to find—it's up
the hill between the Nisky shopping center and the airport—this land-
mark restaurant is worth the search. Native food—steamed fish, mar-
inated pork chops, and local lobster—and native music are offered in
a casual, friendly West Indian atmosphere. ⊠ *Sub Base,* ☎ *340/776–
9379. AE, MC, V.*

ECLECTIC

$$$ ✕ **The Pointe at Villa Olga.** Set in the old Russian consulate great house at the tip of the Frenchtown peninsula, this restaurant offers superb views along with fresh fish, teriyaki dishes, lobster, and steaks grilled to order. A large salad bar, brimming with traditional salad fare, along with Mediterranean-style roasted vegetables and fresh-baked rustic breads, offers a meal in itself. ⊠ *Villa Olga,* ☎ *340/774–4262. AE, D, DC, MC, V.*

$$ ✕ **Craig & Sally's.** In the heart of Frenchtown, culinary wizard Sally
★ Darash creates menus with a passionate international flavor using fresh ingredients and a novel approach that makes for a delightful dining experience at this friendly casual eatery. Husband Craig maintains a 300-bottle wine list that's received *Wine Spectator*'s Award of Excellence. ⊠ *22 Honduras,* ☎ *340/777–9949. Reservations suggested. AE, MC, V. No lunch weekends. Closed Mon.–Tues.*

Northside

AMERICAN

$$ ✕ **Sib's Mountain Bar and Restaurant.** Here you'll find live music, football, burgers, barbecued ribs and chicken, and beer. This friendly two-fisted drinking bar, with a restaurant on the back porch, is a good place for a casual dinner after a day at the beach. Don't be surprised when the basil, tomatoes, or hot peppers you see the chef pick from the backyard garden wind up on your plate minutes later. ⊠ *Mafolie Hill,* ☎ *340/774–8967. AE, MC, V.*

ECLECTIC

$$ ✕ **Bryan's Bar & Restaurant.** Dramatic views of Hull Bay and Inner Brass Cay set the mood for your meal. Tuna, wahoo, and dolphinfish—caught daily by the island's French fishermen—are served grilled, fried, or broiled with a sauce that's a savory mix of garlic, onions, tomatoes, and fresh herbs. Baby-back ribs, 9-ounce beef burgers, and a kids' menu means there's something for everyone. Sunday brunch draws a big local crowd, who come for everything from the steak and eggs to salmon quesadillas. Live music and lively billiard games keep the place jumping on weekends. ⊠ *Hull Bay Road,* ☎ *340/777–1262. AE, MC, V. No lunch.*

Beaches

All 44 Street Thomas beaches are open to the public, although you can only reach some of them by walking through a resort. Hotel guests frequently have access to lounge chairs and floats that are off-limits to nonguests; for this reason you may feel more comfortable at one of the beaches not associated with a resort, such as Magens Bay (which charges an entrance fee to cover beach maintenance) or Coki. Whichever one you choose, remember to remove your valuables from the car and keep them out of sight when you go swimming.

On Route 30 near the airport, **Brewer's Beach** is a long stretch of powdery white sand. Trucks that sell lunch, snacks, and drinks often park along the road bordering the beach. **Coki Beach,** next to Coral World (turn north off Route 38), is a popular snorkeling spot for cruise-ship passengers; it's common to find a group of them among the reefs on the east and west ends of the beach. It's also a good place to dash in for a swim or just to do some people-watching. Don't leave valuables unattended in your car or on the beach.

On the north shore (Route 37), **Hull Bay** beach faces Inner and Outer Brass cays and attracts fishermen and beachcombers. With its rough Atlantic surf and relative isolation, Hull Bay is one of the island's best surfing spots. Take a break from the rigors of sightseeing at the Hull Bay Hideaway, a laid-back beach bar where a local band plays rock on Sunday afternoon.

On Route 35, **Magens Bay** is usually lively because of its spectacular crescent of white sand, more than ½ mi (¾ km) long, and its calm waters, which are protected by two peninsulas. It's often listed among the world's most beautiful beaches. (If you arrive between 8 AM and 5 PM, you'll have to pay an entrance fee of $3 per person.) The bottom is flat and sandy, so this is a place for sunning and swimming rather than snorkeling. On weekends and holidays the sounds of groups partying under the sheds fill the air. You'll also find a bar, bathhouses, a nature trail (unmarked and often overgrown), and a snack bar. East of the beach is Udder Delight, a one-room shop of the St. Thomas Dairies that serves a Virgin Islands tradition—a milk shake with a splash of Cruzan rum. Kids can enjoy virgin shakes, which have a touch of soursop, mango, or banana flavoring.

Close to Charlotte Amalie and fronting the Marriott Frenchman's Reef Hotel, the pretty curve of **Morning Star Beach** is where many young locals bodysurf or play volleyball. Snorkeling is good near the rocks when the current doesn't affect visibility.

At **Sapphire Beach** you'll find a fine view of St. John and other islands. The snorkeling is excellent at the reef to the right or east, near Pettyklip Point, and the Sapphire Beach Resort rents water-sports gear.

The condo resort at **Secret Harbor** doesn't at all detract from the attractiveness of the cove-like beach. Not only is this east end spot pretty, it also has superb snorkeling—head out to the left, near the rocks.

Outdoor Activities and Sports

Participant Sports

BOATING AND SAILING

Calm seas, crystal waters, and close-by islands (perfect for picnicking, snorkeling, and exploring) make St. Thomas a favorite jumping-off spot for day- or weeklong sails or powerboat adventures. With more than 100 vessels from which to choose, St. Thomas is the charter-boat mecca of the U.S. Virgin Islands. You can go through a broker to book a sailing vessel with a crew or contact a charter company directly. Crewed charters start at $1,200 per person per week, while bareboat charters are less expensive and can start at $600 to $800 per person on a weekly basis, not including provisioning.

Blue Water Cruises (⊠ Box 322, Islesboro, ME04848, ☎ 800/524–2020) is a brokerage with an excellent worldwide reputation. **Fan Fare Charters** (⊠ 6501 Red Hook Plaza, Suite 201, ☎ 340/715–1326), at the Vessup Bay Marina, is the only yacht rental business in the Virgin Islands to offer sailboats by the day as well as week. Day charter rates range from $220 to $450 for 30-ft to 50-ft yachts. In Red Hook, **Island Yachts** (⊠ 6100 Red Hook Quarter, 18B, ☎ 340/775–6666 or 800/524–2019), offers sail or power boats on either a bareboat or crewed basis. **Regency Yacht Vacations** (⊠ 5200 Long Bay Rd., ☎ 340/776–5950 or 800/524–7676), at the Yacht Haven Marina, is an outfitter that is expert at matching clients with yachts for a week-long crewed charter holiday. Bareboat sail and power boats, including a selection of stable trawlers, are available at **VIP Yacht Charters** (⊠ 6118 Estate Frydenhoj 58, ☎ 340/776–1510 or 800/524–2015), near Red Hook.

Nauti Nymph (⊠ 6501 Red Hook Plaza, Suite 201, ☎ FAX 340/775–5066 or ☎ 800/734–7345) has a large selection of powerboats for rent.

Rates range from $295 to $370 a day and include snorkel gear, water skis, and outriggers.

CYCLING

On St. Thomas, hills are steep and roads don't have shoulders, but you'll never ride too far from a beautiful beach and cool swim. **St. Thomas Mountain Bike Adventure** (⊠ Box 7037, 00801, ☎ 340/776–1727) takes you on a 1½-hour cycle out past Magens Bay to Peterborg Point using Trek 830 21-speed mountain bikes. There are lots of photo opportunities: flora, fauna, and a lesser-seen side of Magens Bay's picturesque beach. Helmets, water, and a guide are provided; the cost is $35. **Water Island Bike Tours** (⊠ Box 308262, 00803, ☎ 340/714–2186) is a cycling adventure to the USVI's "newest" Virgin. You'll take a 10-minute ferry ride from Crown Bay Marina to Water Island before jumping on a Cannondale M-200 18-speed mountain bike for a 3-hour tour over rolling hills on mostly paved roads. Helmets, water, a guide, and ferry fare are included in the $49 cost.

FISHING

Fishing here is synonymous with blue marlin angling—especially from June through October. Four 1,000-pound-plus blues, including three world records, have been caught on the famous North Drop, about 20 mi (32 km) north of St. Thomas. If you're not into marlin fishing, try hooking up sailfish in the winter, dolphinfish come spring, and wahoo in the fall.

At the **American Yacht Harbor** (⊠ 6100 Red Hook Plaza, ☎ 340/775–6454), you'll find charter boats *Blue Fin II, Marlin Prince,* and *Prowler.* The **Charter Boat Center** (⊠ 6300 Red Hook Plaza, ☎ 340/775–7990 or 800/866–5714) in Red Hook represents a wide range of sport fishing charters. Capt. Red Bailey's *Abigail III* bases out of the **Sapphire Beach Marina** (⊠ Sapphire Bay, ☎ 340/775–6100), along with several other charter operations. To really find the trip that will best suit you, walk down the docks at either American Yacht Harbor or Sapphire Beach Marina in the late afternoons and chat with the captains and crews.

GOLF

The **Mahogany Run Golf Course** (⊠ Rte. 42, ☎ 340/777–5000) is open daily and often hosts informal weekend tournaments. A spectacular view of the British Virgin Islands and the challenging three-hole Devil's Triangle attracts golfers to this Tom Fazio–designed par-70, 18-hole course.

HORSEBACK RIDING

Half Moon Stables (☎ 340/777–6088) offers hour-long rides along a secluded trail that winds through lush, green hills to a pebble-covered east end beach. Horses and ponies are available, and so are Western or English saddles. The cost is $55. There is a weight limit of 245 pounds. Children must be 8 years or older.

PARASAILING

The Caribbean waters are so clear here that the outlines of coral reefs are visible from high in the sky. Parasailers sit in a harness attached to a parachute that lifts them off a boat deck until they're sailing up in the air. Parasailing trips average a 10-minute ride in the sky that costs $55 per person. Friends who want to ride along and watch pay $10 for the boat trip. **Caribbean Parasail and Watersports** (⊠ 6501 Red Hook Plaza, ☎ 340/775–9360) makes parasailing pickups from every beachfront resort. They also rent jet skis, kayaks, and floating battery-powered chairs.

SCUBA DIVING AND SNORKELING

Dive sites feature wrecks such as the *Cartanser Sr.,* a beautifully encrusted World War II cargo ship sitting 35 ft deep (11 m deep), and the *General Rogers,* a 65-ft-deep (213-m-deep) Coast Guard cutter with a gigantic resident barracuda. Reef dives offer hidden caves and archways at **Cow and Calf Rocks,** coral-covered pinnacles at **Frenchcap,** and tunnels where you can explore undersea from the Caribbean to the Atlantic at **Thatch Cay, Grass Cay,** and **Congo Cay.** Many resorts and charter yachts offer dive packages. A one-tank dive starts at $40; two-tank dives are $55 or more. There are plenty of snorkeling possibilities, too. Nick Aquilar's *At-A-Glance Snorkeller's Guide To St. Thomas,* available at local souvenir shops, describes 15 idyllic spots in detail.

Aqua Action (✉ 6501 Red Hook Plaza, ☎ 340/775–6285) is a full-service, PADI five-star shop that offers all levels of instruction at Secret Harbour Beach Resort. **Blue Island Divers** (✉ Crown Bay Marina, Suite 505, ☎ 340/774–2001) is a full-service dive shop that offers both day and night dives to wrecks and reefs. **Chris Sawyer Diving Center** (☎ 340/777–7804 or 800/882–2965), at the American Yacht Harbor marina and the Renaissance Grand Beach Resort is a PADI five-star outfit that specializes in dives to the 310-ft-long RMS *Rhone,* in the British Virgin Islands. It also has a NAUI certification center that offers instruction up to dive master. **Snuba of St. Thomas** (✉ Coki Point, ☎ 340/693–8063) offers a cross between snorkeling and scuba diving: a 20-ft (6-m) air hose connects you to the surface.

SEA EXCURSIONS

Landlubbers and seafarers alike will enjoy the wind in their hair and salt spray in the air while exploring the waters surrounding St. Thomas. Several businesses can effortlessly book you on a half-day inshore light-tackle fishing trip for $300 to $400 for two anglers; a snorkel-and-sail to a deserted cay for the day that costs on the average $75 to $90 per person; or an excursion over to the British Virgin Islands starting at $100 per person plus $12 custom's fees. Contact the **Adventure Center** (✉ Marriott Frenchman's Reef Hotel, Estate Bakkeroe, ☎ 340/774–2990), for a soup-to-nuts choice of sea tours. The **Charter Boat Center** (✉ 6300 Red Hook Plaza, ☎ 340/775–7990 or 800/ 866–5714) specializes in day trips to the British Virgin Islands and day or weeklong sailing charters. **Limnos Charters** (✉ 6100 Red Hook Plaza, ☎ 340/775–3203) offers one of the most popular British Virgin Islands day trips, complete with lunch, open bar, and snorkel gear. Jimmy Loveland at **Treasure Isle Cruises** (✉ 6616 Estate Nadir 30–31, ☎ 340/775– 9500), can set you up with everything from a half-day sail to a 10-day multi-island sailing adventure that departs from St. Thomas.

SEA KAYAKING

Fish dart, birds sing, and iguanas lounge on the limbs of dense mangroves deep within a marine sanctuary on St. Thomas's southeast shore. Many resorts on St. Thomas's eastern end have kayaks. **Virgin Islands Ecotours** (✉ 2 Estate Nadir, on Rte. 32, ☎ 340/779–2155) offers 2½-hour guided trips on two-man sit-atop ocean kayaks; there are stops for swimming and snorkeling. The cost is $50 per person.

STARGAZING

Without the light pollution so prevalent in more densely populated areas, the heavens appear supernaturally bright. On a **Star Charters Astronomy Adventure** (✉ Nisky Mail Center, No. 693, ☎ 340/774–9211), you can peer into the Caribbean's largest telescope—an 18-inch Newtonian reflector—and learn the science and lore of the stars from a well-informed celestial guide.

SUBMARINING

Dive 90 ft (28 m) under the sea to one of St. Thomas's most beautiful reefs without getting wet. *Atlantis* **Submarines** (⊠ Havensight Shopping Mall, Bldg. VI, ☎ 340/776–5650) are 46-passenger, air-conditioned conduits to a watery world teeming with brightly colored fish, vibrant sea fans, and an occasional shark. A guide narrates the two-hour journey, while a diver makes a mid-tour appearance for a fish-feeding show. The cost is $75. No children less than 36 inches tall are allowed.

TENNIS

The Caribbean sun is hot, so be sure to hit the courts before 10 AM or after 5 PM (many courts are lighted). You can indulge in a set or two even if you're staying in a guest house without courts, since most hotels rent time to nonguests. **Marriott Frenchman's Reef Resort** (⊠ Estate Bakkeroe, ☎ 340/776–8500 Ext. 6818) has two courts, with nonguests charged $10 per hour per court. There are six courts at **Renaissance Grand Beach Resort** (⊠ Smith Bay Rd., ☎ 340/775–1510) that are lighted until 8 PM and rent for $8 per hour. Three courts are available at the **Ritz-Carlton, St. Thomas** (⊠ 6900 Great Bay Estate, ☎ 340/775–3333), where nonguests can reserve lessons for $60 per hour and $35 per ½ hour. Courts will be closed for part of 2002 as part of the property's building expansion and renovation. **Sapphire Beach Resort** (⊠ Sapphire Bay, ☎ 340/775–6100 ext. 2131) has four courts that fill up fast in the cool early morning hours. Tennis pro Cecil Phillips gives lessons to nonguests at **Wyndham Sugar Bay** (⊠ 6500 Estate Smith Bay, ☎ 340/777–7100) by appointment. Rates start at $40 for a half-hour lesson. **Lindberg Bay Park** has two courts that are open to the public; it's located opposite the Cyril E. King Airport. There are two public tennis courts at **Sub Base** (next to the Water and Power Authority), open on a first-come, first-served basis for no cost.

WINDSURFING

Expect some spills, anticipate the thrills, and try your luck clipping through the seas. Most beachfront resorts rent Windsurfers and offer one-hour lessons for about $60. One of the island's best-known independent windsurfing companies is **West Indies Windsurfing** (⊠ Vessup Beach, No. 9, Nazareth, ☎ 340/775–6530), which helped organize the U.S. Windsurfing Association National Championships on St. Thomas in 1997.

Spectator Sports

HORSE RACING

The **Clinton Phipps Racetrack** (⊠ Rte. 30 at Nadir 42, ☎ 340/775–4555) schedules races—especially on local holidays—with sanctioned betting. Be prepared for large crowds.

Shopping

St. Thomas lives up to its billing as a shopper's paradise. Even if shopping isn't your idea of how to spend a vacation, you still may want to slip in on a quiet day (check the cruise-ship listings—Monday and Saturday are usually the least crowded) to browse. Among the best buys are liquor, linens, china, crystal (most stores will ship), and jewelry. The amount of jewelry available makes this one of the few items for which comparison shopping is worth the effort. Local crafts include shell jewelry, carved calabash bowls, straw brooms, woven baskets, and dolls. Creations by local doll maker Gwendolyn Harley—like her costumed West Indian market woman—have been goodwill ambassadors bought by visitors from as far away as Asia. Spice mixes, hot sauces, and tropical jams and jellies are other native products.

There's no sales tax in the USVI, and you can take advantage of the $1,200 duty-free allowance per family member (remember to save your receipts). Although you'll find the occasional salesclerk who will make a deal, bartering isn't the norm.

Areas and Malls

The prime shopping area in **Charlotte Amalie** is between Post Office and Market squares; it consists of three parallel streets that run east–west (Waterfront Highway, Main Street, and Back Street) and the alleyways that connect them. Particularly attractive are the historic **Royal Dane Mall, A. H. Riise Alley,** and pastel-painted **International Plaza**—quaint alleys between Main Street and the Waterfront.

Vendors Plaza, on the waterfront side of Emancipation Gardens in Charlotte Amalie, is a central location for vendors selling handmade earrings, necklaces, and bracelets; straw baskets and handbags; T-shirts; fabrics; African artifacts; local foods; and fruit smoothies.

West of Charlotte Amalie, the pink-stucco **Nisky Center,** on Harwood Highway about ½ mi (¾ km) east of the airport, is more of a hometown shopping center than a tourist area, but there are a bank, a pharmacy, a record shop, and a Radio Shack.

Havensight Mall, next to the cruise-ship dock, may not be as charming as downtown Charlotte Amalie, but it does have more than 60 shops. You'll find an excellent bookstore, a bank, a pharmacy, a gourmet grocery, and smaller branches of many downtown stores. The shops at **Port of $ale,** which adjoins the Havensight Mall (its buildings are pink instead of the brown of the Havensight shops), feature discount items.

East of Charlotte Amalie, **Tillett Gardens** (⊠ Estate Tutu, ☎ 340/775–1405) is an oasis of artistic endeavor across from the Tutu Park Shopping Center. The late Jim Tillett and then-wife Rhoda converted this old Danish farm into an artists' retreat in 1959. Today you can watch artisans produce silk-screen fabrics, pottery, candles, watercolors, gold jewelry, stained glass, and other handicrafts. Something special is often happening in the gardens as well: the Classics in the Gardens program is a classical music series presented under the stars, and Arts Alive is a visual-arts and crafts festival held four times yearly.

Tutu Park Shopping Center, across from Tillett Gardens, is the island's one and only enclosed mall. The 47 stores and food court are anchored by a Kmart and the Plaza Extra grocery store. Archaeologists have discovered evidence that Arawak Indians once lived near the mall grounds.

Red Hook has **American Yacht Harbor,** a waterfront shopping area with a dive shop, a tackle store, clothing and jewelry boutique, and a few restaurants. Don't forget **St. John.** A ferry ride (an hour from Charlotte Amalie or 20 minutes from Red Hook) will take you to the charming shops of **Mongoose Junction** and **Wharfside Village,** which specialize in unique, often island-made items.

Specialty Items

ART

A. H. Riise Caribbean Print Gallery. Historic and contemporary prints, posters, and photo note cards depicting West Indian life are sold here. ⊠ *37 Main St., at Riise's Alley,* ☎ *340/776–2303.*
Camille Pissarro Art Gallery. This second-floor gallery, in the birthplace of St. Thomas's famous artist, offers a fine collection of original paintings and prints by local and regional artists. ⊠ *14 Main St.,* ☎ *340/ 774–4621.*
Jonna White Gallery. Vividly colored tropical images drawn on handmade paper have been White's trademark since 1978. You can buy etch-

ings, which run from small to large, framed or unframed. Shipping to the U.S. mainland is free. ⊠ *30 Main St.,* ☎ *340/774–1201.*

Mango Tango. Works by popular local artists—originals, prints, and note cards—are displayed (there's a one-person show at least one weekend a month) and sold here. You'll also find the island's largest humidor and a brand-name cigar gallery. ⊠ *Al Cohen's Plaza, atop Raphune Hill, ½ mi (¾ km) east of Charlotte Amalie,* ☎ *340/777–3060.*

BOOKS AND MAGAZINES

Dockside Bookshop. This place is packed with books for children, travelers, cooks, and historians, as well as a good selection of paperback mysteries, best-sellers, art books, calendars, and prints. It also carries a selection of books written in and about the Caribbean and the Virgin Islands. ⊠ *Havensight Mall,* ☎ *340/774–4937.*

Island Newsstand. This place has the largest selection of magazines and newspapers on St. Thomas. Expect to pay about 20% above stateside prices. ⊠ *Grand Hotel Court, Tolbod Gade at Norre Gade, Charlotte Amalie,* ☎ *340/774–0043.*

CAMERAS AND ELECTRONICS

Boolchand's. A variety of brand-name cameras, audio and video equipment, and binoculars is sold here. ⊠ *31 Main St.,* ☎ *340/776–0794;* ⊠ *Havensight Mall,* ☎ *340/776–0302.*

Royal Caribbean. Shop here for cameras, camcorders, stereos, watches, and clocks. ⊠ *33 Main St.,* ☎ *340/776–8166;* ⊠ *Havensight Mall,* ☎ *340/776–8890.*

CHINA AND CRYSTAL

A. H. Riise Gift Shops. A. H. Riise carries Waterford, Royal Crown, and Royal Doulton at good prices. For example, a five-piece place setting of Royal Crown Derby's Old Imari goes for less than $600. The branch at Riise's Alley also sells jewelry, pearls, perfumes, and watches—including an outstanding Rolex selection (Riise's is the exclusive retailer for Rolex in the USVI). ⊠ *37 Main St., at Riise's Alley,* ☎ *340/776–2303;* ⊠ *Havensight Mall,* ☎ *340/776–7713.*

The English Shop. This store offers figurines, cutlery, and china and crystal from major European and Japanese manufacturers, including Spode, Limoges, Royal Doulton, Portmeirion, Noritaki, and Wedgwood. You can choose what you like from the catalogs here, and shopkeepers will order and factory-ship it for you. (Be sure to keep your receipts in case something goes awry.) ⊠ *Havensight Mall,* ☎ *340/776–3776.*

Little Switzerland. All of this establishment's shops carry crystal from Baccarat, Waterford, Orrefors, and Riedel; china from Villeroy & Boch and Wedgwood, among others; and fine Swiss watches. There's also an assortment of cut-crystal animals, china and porcelain figurines, and many other affordable collectibles. They also do a booming mail-order business; ask for a catalog. ⊠ *Tolbod Gade, across from Emancipation Garden,* ☎ *340/776–2010;* ⊠ *3B Main St.,* ☎ *340/776–2010;* ⊠ *5 Main St., inside A. H. Riise Gift Mart,* ☎ *340/776–2010;* ⊠ *Dockside at Havensight Mall,* ☎ *340/776–2010.*

CLOTHING

Cosmopolitan. At this sophisticated clothing emporium, look for such top lines as Paul and Shark, Bally, Timberland, Sperry Topsider, Givenchy, and Nautica. ⊠ *Drake's Passage at the Waterfront,* ☎ *340/776–2040.*

Local Color. Men, women, and children will find something to choose from among brand name wear like Jams World, Urban Safari, and St. John artist Sloop Jones's colorful, hand-painted island designs on cool dresses, T-shirts, and sweaters. There are also tropically oriented accessories like big-brimmed straw hats, bold-color bags, and casual jewelry. (The Local Color Kids store in Hibiscus Alley has Fresh Produce T-shirts, shorts, and dresses along with toys, games and books.) ⊠ *Royal Dane Mall at the Waterfront,* ☎ *340/774–2280.*

Lover's Lane. With the motto "Couples that play together, stay together," this romantic second-floor shop sells sensuous lingerie, sexy menswear, and provocative swimwear. ⊠ *Waterfront Hwy. at Raadets Gade,* ☎ *340/777–9616.*

Nicole Miller Boutique. This world-renowned New York designer has created an exclusive motif for the USVI: a map of the islands, a cruise ship, and a tropical sunset. Find this print, and Miller's full line of other designs, on ties, scarves, boxer shorts, sarong skirts, and dresses at this chic boutique. ⊠ *24 Main St., at Palm Passage,* ☎ *340/774–8286.*

Pusser's Tropical & Nautical Co. Store. Here, tropical sports and travel clothing for men, women, and children all have a nautical theme. Look for bottles of Pusser's rum at the sales counter. ⊠ *Waterfront Hwy. at Riise's Alley,* ☎ *340/777–9281;* ⊠ *Across from Havensight Mall,* ☎ *340/774–9680.*

Tommy Hilfiger. Stop by this shop for classic American jeans and sportswear as well as trendy bags, belts, ties, socks, caps, and wallets. ⊠ *Waterfront Hwy. at Trompeter Gade,* ☎ *340/777–1189.*

FOODSTUFFS

Caribbean Chocolate. Everything at this confectionery tastes as good as it smells. A wide assortment of Godiva chocolates shares space with Caribbean rum balls, tropical-flavor saltwater taffy, colorful jelly beans, homemade fudge, and Caribbean coffees. ⊠ *Trompeter Gade,* ☎ *340/774–6675.*

Cost-U-Less. This store sells everything from soup to nuts, but in giant sizes and case lots. The meat and seafood department, however, has smaller, family-size portions. ⊠ *1 mi (1½ km) east of Charlotte Amalie on Rte. 38 (¼mi [½ km] west of Rte. 39 intersection),* ☎ *340/777–3588.*

Fruit Bowl. For fruits and vegetables, this is the place. ⊠ *Wheatley Center,* ☎ *340/774–8565.*

Gourmet Gallery. Visiting millionaires buy their caviar here. There's also an excellent and reasonably priced wine selection, as well as specialty ingredients for everything from tacos to curries to chow mein. A full-service deli offers imported meats, cheeses, and in-store prepared foods that are perfect for a gourmet picnic. ⊠ *Crown Bay Marina,* ☎ *340/776–8555;* ⊠ *Havensight Mall,* ☎ *340/774–4948.*

Marina Market. You won't find a better fresh-meat and seafood department anywhere on the island. ⊠ *Across from Red Hook ferry,* ☎ *340/779–2411.*

Plaza Extra. This supermarket has a large selection of Middle Eastern foods. ⊠ *Tutu Park Shopping Center,* ☎ *340/775–5646.*

Pueblo Supermarkets. You'll find stateside brands of most products at these large supermarkets—but at higher prices because of shipping costs. ⊠ *Four Winds Plaza, across from Tillett Gardens,* ☎ *340/775–4655;* ⊠ *Sub Base, 1 mi [1½ km] north of Havensight Mall,* ☎ *340/774–4200;* ⊠ *Estate Thomas, 1 mi (1½ km) north of Havensight Mall,* ☎ *340/774–2695.*

HANDICRAFTS

Arabella's. St. Croix artist Jan Mitchell displays her vibrantly colored fused-glass platters and ornaments in this cheery store. You'll also find pottery, batiks, baskets, and watercolors from Virgin Islands and Caribbean artists, not to mention hot sauces, jams and jellies too. ⊠ *Trompeter Gade,* ☎ *340/774–8041.*

Caribbean Marketplace. This is a great place to buy handicrafts from the Caribbean and elsewhere. Also look for Sunny Caribee spices, soaps, coffee, and teas from Tortola, and coffee from Trinidad. ⊠ *Havensight Mall,* ☎ *340/776–5400.*

Down Island Traders. These traders deal in hand-painted calabash bowls; finely printed Caribbean note cards; jams, jellies, spices, hot sauces, and herbs; teas made of lemongrass, passion fruit, and mango; coffee from Jamaica; and a variety of handicrafts from throughout the Caribbean. ⊠ *Waterfront Hwy. at Post Office Alley,* ☎ *340/776–4641.*

Native Arts and Crafts Cooperative. More than 40 local artists—including schoolchildren, senior citizens, and people with disabilities—create an ever-changing array of handcrafted items: African-style jewelry, quilts, calabash bowls, dolls, carved-wood figures, woven baskets, straw brooms, note cards, and cookbooks. ⊠ *Tolbod Gade, across from Emancipation Garden and next to visitors center,* ☎ *340/777–1153.*

Tropical Memories. The emphasis here is on Virgin Islands artists. There are prints, pottery, gorgeous glass trays, carved mahogany bowls, and scented soaps. ⊠ *Royal Dane Mall,* ☎ *340/776–7536.*

JEWELRY

Amsterdam Sauer. Many fine one-of-a-kind designs are displayed and this jeweler's three locations. ⊠ *14 Main St.,* ☎ *340/774–2222;* ⊠ *Havensight Mall,* ☎ *340/776–3828;* ⊠ *Ritz-Carlton Resort, 6900 Great Bay Estate,* ☎ *340/779–2308.*

Blue Carib Gems. At family-owned and -run Blue Carib Gems, watch Alan O'Hara, Sr., polish Caribbean amber and larimar, agate, and other gems and mount them into gold and silver settings. Visit Alan, Jr., at the Wharfside Village branch on St. John. ⊠ *2–3 Back St.,* ☎ *340/774–8525.*

Cardow's. An enormous "chain bar"—with gold chains in several lengths, widths, sizes and styles—awaits you here, along with diamonds, emeralds, and other precious gems. You're guaranteed 30%–50% savings off U.S. retail prices, or your money will be refunded within 30 days of purchase. ⊠ *33 Main St.,* ☎ *340/776–1140;* ⊠ *Havensight Mall,* ☎ *340/774–0530 or 340/774–5905;* ⊠ *Marriott Frenchman's Reef Resort, Estate Bakkeroe,* ☎ *340/774–0434.*

Colombian Emeralds. Well known in the Caribbean, this store offers set and unset emeralds as well as gems of every description. The watch boutique carries upscale Ebel, Tissot and Jaeger LeCoultre brands. ⊠ *30 Main St.,* ☎ *340/774–3400;* ⊠ *Havensight Mall,* ☎ *340/774–2442.*

Diamonds International. Choose a diamond, emerald, or tanzanite gem and a mounting, and you'll have your dream ring set in an hour. Famous for having the largest inventory of diamonds on the island, this shop welcomes trade-ins, has a U.S. service center, and offers free diamond earrings with every purchase. ⊠ *31 Main St.,* ☎ *340/774–3707;* ⊠ *3 Drakes Passage,* ☎ *340/775–2010;* ⊠ *7AB Drakes Passage,* ☎ *340/774–1516;* ⊠ *Havensight Mall,* ☎ *340/776–0040;* ⊠ *Wyndham Sugar Bay Beach Club & Resort.,* ☎ *340/777–7100.*

H. Stern. The World Collection of jewels set in modern, fashionable designs and an exclusive sapphire watch have earned this Brazilian jeweler a stellar name. ⊠ *12 Main St.,* ☎ *340/776–1939;* ⊠ *32AB Main St.,* ☎ *340/776–1146;* ⊠ *Havensight Mall,* ☎ *340/776–1223;* ⊠ *Marriott Frenchman's Reef Resort, Estate Bakkeroe,* ☎ *340/776–3550.*

LEATHER GOODS

Coach Boutique. A whole wall of high-fashion handbags leads deeper into the store, where lightweight Tumi luggage of nylon or leather is so strong you can sit on it. There are also sporty canvas Kipling bags, all under $100. ⊠ *34 Main St.,* ☎ *340/777–1469.*

Purses and Things. This "house of handbags" has a wide selection of sizes and great prices (you can buy a five-in-one leather clutch for only $20). Bargains are equally good on eel-skin goods. ⊠ *International Plaza,* ☎ *340/777–9713.*

Zora's. Fine leather sandals made to order are the specialty here. There's also selection of made-only-in-the-Virgin-Islands backpacks, purses, and briefcases in durable, brightly colored canvas. ⊠ *Norre Gade across from Roosevelt Park,* ☎ *340/774–2559.*

LINENS

Fabric in Motion. Fine Italian linens share space with Liberty's of London silky cottons, colorful batiks, cotton prints, ribbons, and accessories at this small shop. ⊠ *Storetvaer Gade,* ☎ *340/774–2006.*

Mr. Tablecloth. The friendly staff here will help you choose from the floor-to-ceiling array of linens, from Tuscany lace tablecloths to Irish linen pillowcases. The prices will please. ⊠ *6–7 Main St.,* ☎ *340/774–4343.*

LIQUOR AND TOBACCO

A. H. Riise Liquors. This Riise venture offers a large selection of tobacco (including imported cigars), as well as cordials, wines, and rare vintage Armagnacs, cognacs, ports, and Madeiras. It also stocks fruits in brandy and barware from England. ⊠ *37 Main St., at Riise's Alley,* ☎ *340/776–2303;* ⊠ *Havensight Mall,* ☎ *340/776–7713.*

Al Cohen's Discount Liquor. The wine selection at this warehouse-style store is very large. ⊠ *Across from Havensight Mall, Long Bay Rd.,* ☎ *340/774–3690.*

Rio Cigars. Find a wide selection of premium cigars and accessories, including A. Fuente, Romeo Y Juleta, Havana and more. ⊠ *Royal Dane Mall,* ☎ *340/774–5877.*

MUSIC

Modern Music. Shop for the latest stateside and Caribbean CD and cassette releases, plus oldies, classical, and New Age music. ⊠ *Across from Havensight Mall,* ☎ *340/774–3100;* ⊠ *Nisky Center,* ☎ *340/777–8787.*

Parrot Fish Records and Tapes. A stock of standard stateside tapes and CDs, plus a good selection of Caribbean artists, including local groups, can be found here. For a catalog of calypso, *soca* (up-tempo calypso), steel band, and reggae music, write to Parrot Fish, Box 9206, St. Thomas 00801. ⊠ *Back St.,* ☎ *340/776–4514.*

PERFUME

Tropicana Perfume Shoppes. Tropicana has the largest selection of fragrances for men and women in all of the Virgin Islands. ⊠ *2 Main St.,* ☎ *340/774–0010.*

SUNGLASSES

Davante. You'll find an enormous eyewear collection tucked into this glittering, glamorous store. Filling prescriptions is no problem. ⊠ *A. H. Riise Mall,* ☎ *340/714–1220.*

Tropical Optical. Take your pick from among name-brand eyewear. A real plus here is prescription sunglasses, copied from your present eyewear, ready in a 1/2-for $99. ⊠ *International Plaza.,* ☎ *340/777–5585.*

TOYS

Grandpa's Korner Emporium. Birds sing, dogs bark, and fish swim in this animated toyland. Adults have as much fun trying out the wares as do kids. ⊠ *International Plaza,* ☎ *340/777–4944;* ⊠ *Tutu Park Shopping Center,* ☎ *340/777–7533.*

Nightlife and the Arts

On any given night, especially in season, you'll find steel-pan orchestras, rock-and-roll, piano music, jazz, broken-bottle dancing (dancing atop broken glass), disco, and karaoke. Pick up a copy of the free, bright yellow *St. Thomas This Week* magazine when you arrive (you'll see it at the airport, in stores, and in hotel lobbies); the back pages list who's playing where. The Thursday edition of the *Daily News* carries complete listings for the upcoming weekend.

Nightlife

BARS

Epernay Bistro. This intimate night spot has small tables for easy chatting, wine by the glass, and a spacious dance floor. Mix and mingle with island celebrities. The action runs from 4 PM until the wee hours. ⌂ *24-A Honduras, Frenchtown,* ☎ *340/774–5348.*

The Greenhouse. Once this favorite eatery puts away the salt and pepper shakers at 10 PM, it becomes a rock-and-roll club with a DJ or live reggae bands raising the weary to their feet six nights a week. ⌂ *Waterfront Hwy. at Storetvaer Gade,* ☎ *340/774–7998.*

Iggies. Sing along karaoke-style to the sounds of the surf or the latest hits at this beachside lounge. There's often a DJ on weekends, when a buffet barbecue precedes the 9 PM music fest. Dance inside or kick up your heels under the stars. ⌂ *50 Estate Bolongo,* ☎ *340/775–1800.*

Old Mill Entertainment Complex. In—you guessed it—an old mill, this is a rock-'til-you-drop late-night spot Thursday through Sunday. There's also a tamer piano bar and jazz club in the complex, as well as billiards and foosball tables. ⌂ *193 Contant,* ☎ *340/776–3004.*

Island-style steel-pan bands are a treat that should not be missed. Pan music resonates after dinner on Thursdays, Fridays and Sundays at the **Agave Terrace** (⌂ Point Pleasant Resort, 6600 Estate Smith Bay, ☎ 340/775–4142). **Lord Rumbottoms Club** (⌂ Bolongo Bay Beach Club & Villas, ☎ 340/775–1800) hosts a Carnival night complete with steel pan music on Wednesdays. On Monday nights, catch pan music at the **Ritz-Carlton** (⌂ 6900 Great Bay Estate, ☎ 340/775–3333). **Raffles** (⌂ 41–6–1 Compass Point Marina, ☎ 340/775–6004) features open-mike night Thursdays, jazz and blues Fridays, and live guitar Saturdays. A live band and dancing under the stars is a big draw for locals and visitors alike at **Duffy's Love Shack** (⌂ Red Hook Plaza parking lot, ☎ 340/779–2080).

The Arts

THEATER

Reichhold Center for the Arts. This amphitheater has its more-expensive seats covered by a roof. Schedules vary, so check the paper to see what's on when you're in town. Throughout the year there's an entertaining mix of local plays, dance exhibitions, and music of all types. ⌂ *Rte. 30, across from Brewers Beach,* ☎ *340/693–1559.*

Exploring St. Thomas

St. Thomas is only 13 mi (21 km) long and less than 4 mi (6½ km) wide, but it's extremely hilly, and even an 8- or 10-mi (13- or 16-km) trip could take several hours. Don't let that discourage you, though; the mountain ridge that runs east to west through the middle and separates the island's Caribbean and Atlantic sides has spectacular vistas.

Charlotte Amalie

Look beyond the pricey shops, T-shirt vendors, and bustling crowds for a glimpse of the island's history. The city served as the capital of

Denmark's outpost in the Caribbean until 1917, an aspect of the island often lost in the glitz of the shopping district.

Emancipation Gardens, right next to the fort, is a good place to start a walking tour. Tackle the hilly part of town first: head north up Government Hill to the historic buildings that house government offices and have incredible views. Several regal churches line the route that runs west back to the town proper and the old-time market. Virtually all the alleyways that intersect Main Street lead to eateries that serve frosty drinks, sandwiches and burgers, and West Indian fare. You'll find public rest rooms in this area, too. Allow an hour for a quick view of the sights, two hours if you plan to tour Government House.

A note about the street names: in deference to the island's heritage, the streets downtown are labeled by their Danish names. Locals will use both the Danish name and the English name (such as Dronningens Gade and Norre Gade for Main Street), but most people refer to things by their location ("a block toward the Waterfront off Main Street" or "next to the Little Switzerland Shop"). It's best to ask for directions by shop names or landmarks.

Numbers in the margin correspond to points of interest on the Charlotte Amalie map.

SIGHTS TO SEE

⑰ All Saints Anglican Church. Built in 1848 from stone quarried on the island, the church has thick, arched window frames lined with the yellow brick that came to the islands as ballast aboard ships. Merchants left the brick on the waterfront when they filled their boats with molasses, sugar, mahogany, and rum for the return voyage. The church was built in celebration of the end of slavery in the USVI. ⊠ *Domini Gade,* ☎ *340/774–0217.* ☉ *Mon.–Sat. 6–3.*

㉖ American Caribbean Museum. Learn about the Virgin Islands intriguing past via life-sized replicas of historical figures and treasured artifacts. A 45-minute tour is led by knowledgable staff who encourage questions and delight in sharing true tales of the island's history from the days of the Amerindians to Danish transfer in 1917. Descriptive signs accompany each exhibit written in both English and Spanish. ⊠ *32 Raadets Gade,* ☎ *340/714–5150.* ☉ *Daily 9–3.*

㉕ Cathedral of St. Peter and St. Paul. This building was consecrated as a parish church in 1848 and serves as the seat of the territory's Roman Catholic diocese. The ceiling and walls are covered with murals painted in 1899 by two Belgian artists, Father Leo Servais and Brother Ildephonsus. The San Juan–marble altar and side walls were added in the 1960s. ⊠ *Lower Main St.,* ☎ *340/774–0201.* ☉ *Mon.–Sat. 8–5.*

⑳ Danish Consulate Building. Built in 1830, this structure housed the Danish Consulate until the Danish West India Company sold its properties to the local government in 1992. It now serves as home to the territory's governor. ⊠ *Take stairs north at corner of Bjerge Gade and Crystal Gade to Denmark Hill.*

⑯ Dutch Reformed Church. This church has an austere loveliness that's amazing considering all it has been through—founded in 1744, it burned down in 1804 and was rebuilt in 1844; it was then blown down by Hurricane Marilyn in 1995 and rebuilt in 1997. The unembellished cream-color hall gives you a sense of peace—albeit monochromatically. The only other color is the forest green of the shutters and the carpet. ⊠ *Nye Gade and Crystal Gade,* ☎ *340/776–8255.* ☉ *Weekdays 9–5. Call ahead; doors are sometimes locked.*

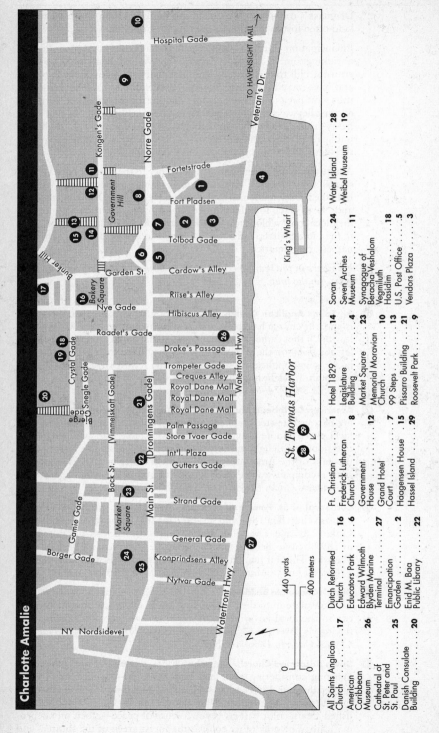

Charlotte Amalie

St. Thomas Harbor

Hospital Gade

TO HAVENSIGHT MALL →

Veteran's Dr.

King's Wharf

Fortetstrade

Fort Pladsen

Norre Gade

Kongen's Gade

Government Hill

Tolbod Gade

Cardow's Alley

Garden St.

Bakery Square

Riise's Alley

Nye Gade

Hibiscus Alley

Bunker Hill

Raadet's Gade

Drake's Passage

Crystal Gade

Trompeter Gade

Snegle Gade

Creques Alley

Royal Dane Mall

Bjerge Gade

Royal Dane Mall

(Vimmelskaft Gade)

Royal Dane Mall

(Dronningens Gade)

Palm Passage

Store Tvaer Gade

Int'l. Plaza

Gutters Gade

Back St.

Main St.

Strand Gade

Market Square

Gamle Gade

General Gade

Borger Gade

Kronprindsens Alley

Nytvar Gade

NY Nordsidevej

Waterfront Hwy.

Waterfront Hwy.

0 — 440 yards

0 — 400 meters

N

All Saints Anglican
Church 17
American
Caribbean
Museum 26
Cathedral of
St. Peter and
St. Paul 25
Danish Consulate
Building 20

Dutch Reformed
Church 16
Educators Park . . . 6
Edward Wilmoth
Blyden Marine
Terminal 27
Emancipation
Garden 2
Enid M. Baa
Public Library . . . 22

Ft. Christian 1
Frederick Lutheran
Church 8
Government
House 12
Grand Hotel
Court 7
Haagensen House . . 15
Hassel Island 22

Hotel 1829 14
Legislature
Building 4
Market Square . . . 23
Memorial Moravian
Church 10
99 Steps 13
Pissarro Building . . 21
Roosevelt Park . . . 9

Savan 24
Seven Arches
Museum 11
Synagogue of
Beracha Veshalom
Vegmiluth
Hasidim 18
U.S. Post Office . . . 5
Vendors Plaza 3

Water Island 28
Weibel Museum . . . 19

❻ Educators Park. A peaceful place amid the town's hustle and bustle, the park has memorials to three famous Virgin Islanders: educator Edith Williams, J. Antonio Jarvis (a founder of the *Daily News*), and educator and author Rothschild Francis. The latter gave many speeches from here. ⊠ *Main St. across from U.S. Post Office.*

㉗ Edward Wilmoth Blyden Marine Terminal. Locally called "Tortola Wharf," you can catch the *Native Son* and other ferries to the BVI from here. The restaurant upstairs is a good place to watch the Charlotte Amalie harbor traffic and sip an iced tea. Next door is the ramp for the *Seaborne* seaplane, which offers commuter service and flightseeing tours to St. Croix and the BVI. ⊠ *Waterfront Hwy.*

❷ Emancipation Garden. Built to honor the freeing of slaves in 1848, the garden was refurbished to mark the 150th anniversary of emancipation in 1998. A bronze bust of a freed slave blowing a symbolic conch shell commemorates this anniversary. The gazebo here is used for official ceremonies. Two other monuments show the island's Danish-American tie—a bust of Denmark's King Christian and a scaled-down model of the U.S. Liberty Bell. ⊠ *Between Tolbod Gade and Ft. Christian.*

㉒ Enid M. Baa Public Library. Like so many structures on the north side of Main Street, this large pink building is a typical 18th-century town house. Merchants built their houses (stores downstairs, living quarters above) across from the brick warehouses on the south side of the street. The library was once the home of merchant and landowner Baron von Bretton. It's the island's first recorded fireproof building, meaning it was built of ballast brick instead of wood. Its interior of high ceilings and cool stone floors is the perfect refuge from the afternoon sun. You can browse through historic papers or just sit in the breeze by an open window reading the paper. ⊠ *Main St.,* ☎ *340/774–0630.* ☉ *Weekdays 9–5, Sat. 9–3.*

🐾 ❶ Ft. Christian. St. Thomas's oldest standing structure, this monument anchors the shopping district. It was built in 1672–1680 and now has U.S. National Landmark status. The clock tower was added in the 19th century. This remarkable building has, over time, been used as a jail, governor's residence, town hall, courthouse, and church.

Ft. Christian now houses **The Virgin Islands Museum,** where you can see exhibits on USVI history, natural history, and turn-of-the-20th-century furnishings. Local artists display their works monthly in the gallery. A gift shop sells local crafts, books, and other souvenir items. This is also the site of the Chamber of Commerce's Hospitality Lounge where you'll find public rest rooms, brochures, and a place you can stash your luggage for some last-minute shopping on the way to the airport. ⊠ *Waterfront Hwy. just east of shopping district,* ☎ *340/776–4566.* 🎟 *Free.* ☉ *Weekdays 8:30–4:30.*

❽ Frederick Lutheran Church. This historic church has a massive mahogany altar, and its pews—each with its own door—were once rented to families of the congregation. Lutheranism is the state religion of Denmark, and when the territory was without a minister, the governor—who had his own elevated pew—filled in. ⊠ *Norre Gade,* ☎ *340/776–1315.* ☉ *Mon.–Sat. 9–4.*

⓬ Government House. Built as an elegant residence in 1867, today Government House serves as the governor's office, with the first floor open to the public. The staircases are of native mahogany, as are the plaques hand-lettered in gold with the names of the governors appointed and, since 1970, elected. Brochures detailing the history of the building are available, but you may have to ask for them.

The three murals at the back of the lobby were painted by Pepino Mangravatti in the 1930s as part of the U.S. government's Works Projects Administration. They depict Columbus's landing on St. Croix during his second voyage in 1493; the transfer of the islands from Denmark to the United States in 1917; and a sugar plantation on St. John.

A deputy administrator can take you on a tour of the second floor. You can call ahead for an appointment, or you can take a chance that an official will be in. It's worth the extra effort, if for no other reason than the terrace view. Imagine colonial affairs of state being conducted in the grandeur of the high-ceiling, chandeliered ballroom. In the reception room are four small paintings by Camille Pissarro, but unfortunately they're hard to appreciate because they're enclosed in frosted-glass cases. More interesting, and visible, is the large painting by an unknown artist that was found in Denmark and purchased by former governor Ralph M. Paiewonsky, who then gave it to Government House: it depicts a romanticized version of St. Croix. ⊠ *Government Hill,* ☎ *340/774–0001.* 🖾 *Free.* ⊙ *Weekdays 8–5.*

❼ Grand Hotel Court. This imposing building stands at the head of Main Street. Once the island's premier hotel, it has been converted into offices and shops. ⊠ *Tolbod Gade at Norre Gade,* ☎ *340/776–0100.* ⊙ *Weekdays 8–5, Sat. 9–noon.*

⓯ Haagensen House. Behind Hotel 1829, this lovingly restored home was built in the early 1800s by Danish entrepreneur Hans Haagensen and is surrounded by an equally impressive cookhouse, outbuildings, and terraced gardens. A lower-level banquet hall now showcases an antique-print and photo gallery. ⊠ *Government Hill,* ☎ *340/774–9605.* 🖾 *$8.* ⊙ *Daily 9–4.*

㉙ Hassel Island. East of Water Island in Charlotte Amalie harbor, Hassel Island is part of the Virgin Islands National Park, as it has the ruins of a British military garrison (built during a brief British occupation of the USVI during the 1800s) and the remains of a marine railway (where ships were hoisted into drydock for repairs). Also on Hassel Island is the shell of the hotel that writer Herman Wouk's fictitious character Norman Paperman tried to turn into his own paradise in the book *Don't Stop the Carnival.* There's a small ferry that runs from the Crown Bay Marina to the island; departure times are posted at Tickles Dockside Pub, and the fare is $3.

⓮ Hotel 1829. As its name implies, it was built in 1829, albeit as a residence of a prominent merchant named Lavalette rather than as a hotel. The building's bright coral-color exterior walls are accented with fancy black wrought iron, and the interior is paneled in a dark wood, which makes it feel delightfully cool. From the dining terrace there's an exquisite view of the harbor framed by tangerine-color bougainvillea. Be sure to visit Haagensen House, just behind the hotel, for a peek at another wonderfully restored 19th-century home. ⊠ *Government Hill,* ☎ *340/776–1829.*

❹ Legislature Building. Its pastoral-looking lime-green exterior conceals the vociferous political wrangling of the Virgin Islands Senate going on inside. Constructed originally by the Danish as a police barracks, the building was later used to billet U.S. Marines, and much later it housed a public school. You're welcome to sit in on sessions in the upstairs chambers. ⊠ *Waterfront Hwy. across from Ft. Christian,* ☎ *340/774–0880.* ⊙ *Daily 8–5.*

㉓ Market Square. Formally called Rothschild Francis Square, this is a good place to find produce. A cadre of old-timers sells mangoes and papayas, strange-looking root vegetables, and herbs; sidewalk vendors offer a variety of African fabrics and artifacts and tie-dyed cotton clothes at good prices. ⊠ *North side of Main St. at Strand Gade.*

🔟 **Memorial Moravian Church.** Built in 1884, it was named to commemorate the 150th anniversary of the Moravian Church in the VI. ⊠ *17 Norre Gade,*☎ *340/776–0066.* ⊘ *Weekdays 8–5.*

🅲 ⑬ **99 Steps.** This staircase "street," built by the Danes in the 1700s, leads to the residential area above Charlotte Amalie and Blackbeard's Castle. The castle's tower, built in 1679, was once used by the notorious pirate Edward Teach. Today this lookout serves at the backdrop for a trendy restaurant. If you count the stairs as you go up, you'll discover, as have thousands before you, that there are more than 99. ⊠ *Look for steps heading north from Government Hill.*

㉑ **Pissarro Building.** Home to several shops and an art gallery, this was the birthplace and childhood home of Camille Pissarro, who later moved to France and became an acclaimed impressionist painter. In the art gallery you'll find three original pages from Pissarro's sketchbook and two pastels by Pissarro's grandson, Claude.

🅲 ⑨ **Roosevelt Park.** You'll see members of the local legal community head to the nearby court buildings while you rest on a bench in this park—a good spot to people-watch. The small monument on the park's south side is dedicated to USVI war veterans. Kids enjoy the playground made of wood and tires. ⊠ *Norre Gade.*

㉔ **Savan.** A neighborhood of small streets and houses, it was first laid out in the 1700s as the residential area for a growing community of middle-class black artisans, clerks, and shopkeepers. You'll find a row of Rastafarian shops along the first block and restaurants that sell *pate*—a delicious turnover-type pastry stuffed with meat or vegetables. ⊠ *Turn north off lower Main St. onto General Gade.*

⑪ **Seven Arches Museum.** This restored 18th-century home is a striking example of classic Danish–West Indian architecture. There seem to be arches everywhere—seven to be exact—all supporting a "welcoming arms" staircase that leads to the second floor and the flower-framed front doorway. The Danish kitchen is a highlight: it's housed in a separate building just off the main house, as were all cooking facilities in the early days (in case of fire). Inside the house you'll find mahogany furnishings and gas lamps. ⊠ *Government Hill, 3 bldgs. east of Government House,* ☎ *340/774–9295.* ▣ *$5 (suggested donation).* ⊘ *10–4. By appointment only Aug.–Sept.*

⑱ **Synagogue of Beracha Veshalom Vegmiluth Hasidim.** The synagogue's Hebrew name translates to the Congregation of Blessing, Peace, and Loving Deeds. The small building's white pillars contrast with rough stone walls, as does the rich mahogany of the pews and altar. The sand on the floor symbolizes the exodus from Egypt. Since the synagogue first opened its doors in 1833, it has held a weekly Sabbath service, making it the oldest synagogue building in continuous use under the American flag and the second-oldest (after the one on Curaçao) in the western hemisphere. Next door, the Weibel Museum showcases Jewish history on St. Thomas. ⊠ *15 Crystal Gade,* ☎ *340/774–4312.* ⊘ *Weekdays 9–4.*

⑤ **U.S. Post Office.** While you buy your postcard stamps, contemplate the murals of waterfront scenes by *Saturday Evening Post* artist Stephen Dohanos. His art was commissioned as part of the Works Project Administration (WPA) in the 1930s. ⊠ *Tolbod Gade and Main St.*

③ Vendors Plaza. Here merchants sell everything from T-shirts to African attire to leather goods. Look for local art among the ever-changing selections at this busy market. ⊠ *West of Ft. Christian at the waterfront.* ⊘ *Weekdays 8–6, weekends 9–1.*

㉘ Water Island. This island, about ¼ mi (½ km) out in Charlotte Amalie Harbor, was once a peninsula of St. Thomas, but a channel was cut through so U.S. submarines could get to their base in a bay just to the west, known as Sub Base. On December 12, 1996, the U.S. Department of the Interior transferred 50 acres of the island, which included beaches and roads, to the territorial government, making it the fourth-largest of the USVI. A ferry goes between Crown Bay Marina and the island several times daily, at a cost of $3.

⑲ Weibel Museum. In this museum next to the synagogue, 300 years of Jewish history on St. Thomas are showcased. The small gift shop sells a commemorative silver coin celebrating the anniversary of the Hebrew congregation's establishment on the island in 1796. ⊠ *15 Crystal Gade,* ☎ *340/774–4312.* ☜ *Free.* ⊘ *Weekdays 9–4.*

Around the Island

To explore outside Charlotte Amalie, you'll need to rent a car or hire a taxi. Your rental car should come with a good map; if not, pick up the "St. Thomas–St. John Road Map" at a tourist information center. Roads are marked with route numbers, but they're confusing and seem to switch numbers suddenly. If you stop to ask for directions, it's best to have your map in hand because locals probably know the road you're looking for by another name. Allow yourself a day to explore, especially if you want to stop for picture taking or to enjoy a light bite or refreshing swim. Most gas stations are on the island's more populated eastern end, so fill up before heading to the north side. And remember to drive on the left.

Although the eastern end has many major resorts and spectacular beaches, don't be surprised if a cow or a herd of goats crosses your path as you drive through the relatively flat, dry terrain. The north side of the island is more lush and hush—fewer houses and less traffic. Here you'll find roller-coaster routes (made all the more scary because the roads have no shoulders) and incredible vistas. Leave time in the afternoon for a swim at the beach. Pick up some sandwiches from delis in the Red Hook area for a picnic lunch, or enjoy a slice of pizza at Magens Bay. A day in the country will reveal the tropical pleasures that have enticed more than one visitor to become a resident.

Numbers in the margin correspond to points of interest on the St. Thomas map.

SIGHTS TO SEE

㉛ Compass Point Marina. It's fun to park your car and walk around this marina. The boaters—many of whom have sailed here from points around the globe—are easy to engage in conversation. ⊠ *Turn south off Red Hook Rd. at well-marked entrance road just east of Independent Boat Yard.*

㉞ Coral World Marine Park. Coral World is home to an offshore underwater observatory that houses the Predator Tank, one of the world's largest coral-reef tanks, and an aquarium with more than 20 portholes providing close-ups of Caribbean sea life. *Sea Trekkin'* lets you tour the reef outside the park at a depth of 15 feet under the sea thanks to specialized high-tech headgear and a continuous air supply that's based on the surface. A guide leads the ½ hour tour and the narration is piped through a specialized microphone inside each trekker's helmet; the cost is $50 per person. The park also has several outdoor pools where you can touch starfish, pet a baby shark, feed stingrays, and view endangered sea turtles. In addition you'll find a mangrove lagoon and a nature trail full of lush tropical flora. Daily feedings and talks take place at most every exhibit. ⊠ *Coki Point, turn north off Rte. 38 at sign,* ☎ *340/775–1555,* WEB *www.coralworldvi.com.* ☞ *$18.* ☼ *Daily 9–5:30.*

🖑 ㊲ **Drake's Seat.** Sir Francis Drake was supposed to have kept watch over his fleet and looked for enemy ships from this vantage point. The panorama is especially breathtaking (and romantic) at dusk, and if you arrive late in the day you'll miss the hordes of day-trippers on taxi tours who stop here to take a picture and buy a T-shirt from one of the many vendors. ⊠ *Rte. 40.*

🖑 ㊳ **Estate St. Peter Greathouse & Botanical Gardens.** This unusual spot is perched on a mountainside 1,000 ft (306 m) above sea level, with views of more than 20 other islands and islets. You can wander through a gallery displaying local art, sip a complimentary rum or Virgin Punch while looking out at the view, or follow a nature trail that leads through nearly 200 varieties of trees and plants, including an orchid jungle. ⊠ *Rte. 40, St. Peter Mountain Rd.,* ☎ *340/774–4999,* WEB *www.greathouse-mountaintop.com.* ☞ *$8.* ☼ *Mon.–Sat. 9–4:30.*

㊴ **Frenchtown.** Popular for its several bars and restaurants, Frenchtown also serves as home to the descendants of immigrants from St. Barthélemy (St. Barths). You can watch them pull up their brightly painted boats and display their equally colorful catch of the day along the waterfront. If you chat with them, you'll hear speech patterns slightly different from those of other St. Thomians. Get a feel for the residential district of Frenchtown by walking west to some of the town's winding streets, where tiny wooden houses have been passed down from generation to generation. ⊠ *Turn south off Waterfront Hwy. at the U.S. Post Office.*

🖑 ㊱ **Mountain Top.** Stop here for a banana daiquiri and spectacular views from the observation deck more than 1,500 ft (459 m) above sea level. There are also shops that sell everything from Caribbean art to nautical antiques, ship models, and T-shirts. Kids will like talking to the parrots—and hearing them answer back. ⊠ *Head north off Rte. 33; look for signs.* WEB *www.greathouse-mountaintop.com.*

🖑 ㉚ **Paradise Point Tramway.** Fly skyward in a gondola to Paradise Point, an overlook with breathtaking views of Charlotte Amalie and the harbor. There are several shops, a bar, and a restaurant. A ¼-mi (½-km) hiking trail leads to spectacular sights of St. Croix to the south. Wear sturdy shoes; the trail is steep and rocky. ⊠ *Rte. 30 at Havensight,* ☎ *340/774–9809.* ☞ *$12.* ☼ *Daily 7:30–4:30.*

㉝ **Red Hook.** In this nautical mecca you'll find fishing and sailing charter boats, dive shops, and powerboat rental agencies at the American Yacht Harbor marina. There are also several bars and restaurants, including Molly Molone's, Duffy's Love Shack, and Cafe Wahoo. Two grocery stores and two delis offer picnic fixings—from sliced meats and cheeses to rotisserie-cooked chickens, gourmet salads, and fresh baked breads.

㉟ **Tillett Gardens.** Clustered in a booming shopping area, you'll find a colony where local artisans craft stained glass, pottery, gold jewelry, and ceramics. Tillett's paintings and silk-screened fabrics are also on display and for sale. The gardens encircle a shaded courtyard with fountains and Polli's Mexican restaurant. ⊠ *Rte. 38 across from Tutu Park Shopping Center,* ☎ *340/775–1929,* WEB *www.tillettgardens.com.* ☞ *Free.*

③ **Virgin Islands National Park Headquarters.** This facility consists of a dock, a small grassy area with picnic tables, and a visitor center where maps and brochures are available. Iguanas are common here. If you see one, hold out a hibiscus flower, which is this prehistoric-looking creature's favorite food. ⊠ *Turn east off Rte. 32 at sign,* ☎ *340/775– 6238.* ☉ *Weekdays 8–5.*

ST. CROIX

Updated by
Lynda Lohr

St. Croix, the largest of the three USVI at 84 square mi (218 square km), lies 40 mi (65 km) south of St. Thomas. But unlike the bustling island-city of St. Thomas, its harbor teeming with cruise ships and its shopping district crowded with bargain hunters, St. Croix has a slower pace and a more diverse economy, mixing tourism with light and heavy industry on rolling land that was once covered with waving carpets of sugarcane.

St. Croix's population has grown dramatically over the last 30 years, and its diversity reflects the island's varied history. The cultivation of sugarcane was more important here than on St. Thomas or St. John and continued as an economic force into the 1960s. After the end of slavery in 1848, the need for workers brought waves of immigrants from other Caribbean islands, particularly nearby Puerto Rico. St. Croix was divided into plantation estates, and the ruins of great houses and the more than 100 sugar mills that dot the land are evidence of an era when St. Croix was one of the greatest producers of sugar in the West Indies.

Tourism began and boomed in the 1960s, bringing visitors and migrants from the mainland United States (whom locals refer to as Continentals). In the late 1960s and early 1970s industrial development brought St. Croix yet another wave of immigrants. This time they came mostly from Trinidad and St. Lucia to seek work at the Hess oil refinery or at the south shore aluminum-processing plants.

St. Croix is a study in contrasting beauty. The island isn't as hilly as St. Thomas or St. John. A lush rain forest envelops the northwest, the eastern end is dry, and palm-lined beaches with startlingly clear aquamarine water ring the island. The capital, Christiansted, is a restored Danish port on a coral-bound northeastern bay. The tin-roof 18th-century buildings in both Christiansted and Frederiksted, on the island's western end, are either pale yellow, pink, or ocher—resplendent with bright blazes of bougainvillea and hibiscus. The prosperous Danes built well (and more than once, as both towns were devastated by fire in the 19th century), using imported bricks or blocks cut from coral, fashioning covered sidewalks (galleries) and stately colonnades, and leaving an enduring cosmopolitan air as their legacy.

Lodging

From plush resorts to simple beachfront digs, St. Croix's variety of accommodations is bound to suit every type of traveler. If you sleep in either the Christiansted or Frederiksted area, you'll be close to shopping, restaurants, and nightlife. Any of the island's other hotels will put you just steps from the beach. St. Croix has several small but special properties that offer personalized service. If you like all the comforts of home, you may prefer to stay in a condominium or villa. Room rates on St. Croix are competitive with those on other islands, and if you travel off-season, you'll find substantially reduced prices. Many properties offer honeymoon and dive packages that are also big money savers. Whether you stay in a hotel, a condominium, or a villa, you'll find up-to-date amenities, including cable TV.

Although a stay right in historic Christiansted may mean putting up with a little urban noise, you probably won't have trouble sleeping. Christiansted rolls up the sidewalks fairly early. The Frederiksted area is perfect for folks who want peace. A small, charming town—hardly more than a village—with a lovely waterfront, it has beaches within walking distance of its shops and restaurants. Solitude is guaranteed at hotels and inns outside the main towns. Old ruins dot the landscape where the green mountains meet the dark-blue and turquoise sea.

For approximate costs, *see* the lodging price chart *in* St. Thomas.

Hotels

CHRISTIANSTED

\$\$\$ ☒ **King's Alley Hotel.** In the center of Christiansted's hustle and bus-
★ tle, this small hotel (part of the King's Alley shopping and restaurant complex) mixes convenience with charm. The 12 premium rooms in the section across the courtyard have mahogany four-poster beds, Mexican tile floors, and Indonesian print fabrics. French doors open onto balconies with a view of the waterfront and the shopping arcade. The 23 standard rooms in the older section are a tad less interesting but still attractive. The staff can arrange all sorts of activities: water sports, tours, golf, tennis. ☒ *57 King St. (Box 4120), 00822,* ☎ *340/773–0103; 800/843–3574 direct to hotel,* FAX *340/773–4431,* WEB *www.kingsalley.com. 35 rooms. Air-conditioning, pool, dive shop, boating, fishing. AE, D, DC, MC, V. EP.*

\$\$ ☒ **Hilty House.** For an alternative to beach and in-town lodgings, try this tranquil hilltop bed-and-breakfast. Built on the ruins of an 18th-century rum factory, it has the feel of a Florentine villa. You can escape to a patio and while-away an afternoon in sun or shade, or mingle with others in the immense great room, where a prix-fixe dinner is served on Friday (reservations essential). Unless you want to spend your entire vacation reading or sunning at the large tiled pool, however, you'll need a rental car to venture forth from here. ☒ *Queste Verde Rd. (Box 26077), Gallows Bay, 00824,* ☎ FAX *340/773–2594. 4 rooms, 1 cottage. Dining room, pool. No credit cards. CP.*

\$\$ ☒ **Hotel Caravelle.** The fetching, three-story Caravelle offers moderately priced in-town lodgings. Rooms are done in tasteful dusky blues and have floral-print bedspreads and curtains, vaulted ceilings, phones, and TV with free HBO. Baths are clean and fresh, though the unique tile in the showers is a holdover from when the hotel was built in 1968. Most rooms have some sort of ocean view; the best overlook the harbor. Owners Sid and Amy Kalmans are friendly and helpful. The Rum Runners, a casual terrace eatery, serves local and Continental cuisine. ☒ *44A Queen Cross St., 00820,* ☎ *340/773–0687; 800/524–0410 direct to hotel,* FAX *340/778–7004,* WEB *www.hotelcaravelle.com. 43 rooms, 1 suite. Restaurant, bar, air-conditioning, refrigerators, pool, massage, gym, meeting room. AE, D, DC, MC, V. EP.*

\$ ☒ **Breakfast Club.** This rambling guest house is within walking distance of downtown. Rooms of various sizes and decors are clean, and each has a full kitchen and bath. Guests like to gather at the bar, and owner Toby Chapin includes gourmet breakfasts (featuring banana pancakes) in the room rates. ☒ *18 Queen Cross St., 00820,* ☎ *340/773–7383,* FAX *340/773–8642,* WEB *www.nav.to/thebreakfastclub. 7 rooms. Air-conditioning (some), fans, kitchenettes, hot tub. V, MC. BP.*

EAST END

\$\$\$\$ ☒ **The Buccaneer.** On the grounds of an old, 300-acre sugar plantation, this complex has it all: sandy beaches, swimming pools, golf, and many

St. Croix

↑
TO
ST. THOMAS

Salt River Bay

Cane Bay 25
North Star 26
80
5
24
4

Hams Bluff

Davis Bay

Hams Bay

27

Blue Mt.

75 *Northside R...*

7

Annaly

69

Christ...

Rain Forest

Rd.

6

Midland Rd.

72

Northside Rd.

West End Beaches

Mahogany

76

Sunny Isle

63

10

St. George Hill

Kingshill

Kingshill

Frederiksted

9

13

70

Frederiksted Pier

8

Centerline Rd.

69

Hess Oil Refinery

28 29

12

30 32

Melvin H. Evans Hwy.

Henry E. Rohlsen Airport

11

66

Krause Pt.

Long Pt. Bay

Long Pt.

KEY

⚲ Beaches

1 Exploring Sights

⛴ Cruise Ship Terminal

① Hotels and Restaurants

◣ Dive Sites

🌴 Rain Forest

Lodging
Breakfast Club **3**
Buccaneer **14**
Chenay Bay
Beach Resort **16**
Club St. Croix **21**
Colony Cove **23**
Divi Carina Bay
Resort **19**
Hibiscus Beach
Hotel **24**

Hilty House **11**
Hotel Caravelle **19**
King's Alley
Hotel **10**
Sandcastle on the
Beach **30**
Schooner Bay **13**
Seaview
Farm Inn **31**
Sugar Beach **22**

Sunterra
Carambola
Beach Resort **27**
Tamarind
Reef Hotel **15**
Villa Madeleine . . . **18**
Waves at Cane
Bay **25**

Dining
Bandana's **32**
Blue Moon **28**
Breezez **21**
The Galleon **17**
Great House at
Villa Madeleine **18**
Harvey's **4**
Indies **5**
Kendricks **12**

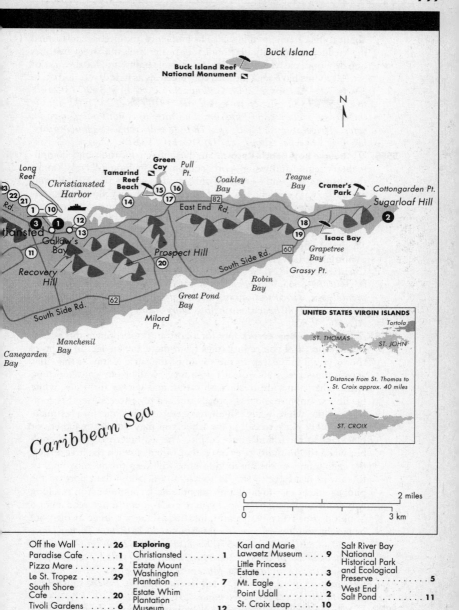

Buck Island

Buck Island Reef National Monument

N

Long Reef

Tamarind Reef Beach

Green Cay

Pull Pt.

Christiansted Harbor

Coakley Bay

Teague Bay

Cramer's Park

Cottongarden Pt.

Sugarloaf Hill

23 22 21
Rd.
1 10
3 1
12
13
Gallow's Bay
11
Recovery Hill

14

15 16
17

East End Rd. 82

18
19
Isaac Bay

2

Prospect Hill

20

South Side Rd. 60

Grapetree Bay

Grassy Pt.

Robin Bay

62

South Side Rd.

Milord Pt.

Great Pond Bay

Manchenil Bay

Canegarden Bay

Caribbean Sea

UNITED STATES VIRGIN ISLANDS

Tortola

ST. THOMAS

ST. JOHN

Distance from St. Thomas to St. Croix approx. 40 miles

ST. CROIX

0   2 miles
0   3 km

Off the Wall **26**
Paradise Cafe **1**
Pizza Mare **2**
Le St. Tropez **29**
South Shore Cafe **20**
Tivoli Gardens **6**
Top Hat **7**
Tutto Bene **8**

Exploring
Christiansted **1**
Estate Mount Washington Plantation **7**
Estate Whim Plantation Museum **12**
Frederiksted **8**
Judith's Fancy **4**

Karl and Marie Lawaetz Museum **9**
Little Princess Estate **3**
Mt. Eagle **6**
Point Udall **2**
St. Croix Leap **10**
St. George Village Botanical Gardens **13**

Salt River Bay National Historical Park and Ecological Preserve **5**
West End Salt Pond **11**

activities. A palm tree–lined main drive leads to the large, pink main building atop a hill; shops, restaurants, and guest quarters are scattered about rolling manicured lawns. The ambience and decor tend toward the Mediterranean, with tile floors, four-poster beds, massive wardrobes of pale wood, pastel fabrics, spacious marble baths, and local works of art. All rooms have such modern conveniences as hair dryers and cable TV. ⌂ *Rte. 82 (Box 25200), Gallows Bay, 00824,* ☎ *340/773–2100; 800/255–3881 direct to hotel,* FAX *340/778–8215,* WEB *www. thebuccaneer.com. 138 rooms. 4 restaurants, air-conditioning, in-room safes, refrigerators, 2 pools, spa, 18-hole golf course, 8 tennis courts, jogging, 3 beaches, shops. AE, D, DC, MC, V. BP.*

$$$$ ⊞ **Chenay Bay Beach Resort.** The beachfront location and complimentary tennis and water-sports equipment (including kayaks) make this resort a real find—especially for families with active kids. Rooms are basic, with ceramic-tile floors, bright peach or yellow walls, rattan furnishings, and front porches. Gravel paths connect the terraced wood or stucco cottages with the shore, where you'll find a large L-shape pool, a protected beach, a picnic area, and a casual restaurant. The hotel offers an inexpensive day camp for children ages 4–12 and a shuttle to grocery stores and shopping areas. ⌂ *Rte. 82 (Box 24600), Christiansted, 00824,* ☎ *340/773–2918; 800/548–4457 direct to hotel,* FAX *340/773–6665,* WEB *www.chenaybay.com. 50 rooms. Restaurant, bar, picnic area, air-conditioning, kitchenettes, pool, hot tub, 2 tennis courts, volleyball, beach, snorkeling, baby-sitting, children's programs. AE, MC, V. EP.*

$$$$ ⊞ **Divi Carina Bay Resort.** Opt for a bottom-floor room at this oceanfront resort, and you're just steps from the water's edge. In all hotel rooms you'll fall asleep to the sound of the surf. A stay at the villas across the street puts you a two-minute walk from your morning swim. The rooms are fresh, with rattan and wicker furniture, white tile floors, sapphire and teal spreads, and sea-tone accessories that compliment the white walls. Small refrigerators and microwaves make this a comfy place to call home while you play the slot machines or blackjack at the island's only casino. The sea breeze keeps you cool, but when the humidity rises or on that rare day when the breeze dies, the ceiling fans or the air-conditioning will keep the air moving. For folks who just have to stay in touch, a desk and a data port on the phone make it easy to hook up your notebook computer. You're a long way from anywhere here, so if you're not content to just read a good book on your balcony or patio, hit the casino, or lounge at the pool or beach, you'll need a car to get around. ⌂ *25 Estate Turner Hole, Rte. 60, 00820,* ☎ *340/773–9700 or 800/823–9352,* FAX *340/773–6802,* WEB *www.divicarina.com. 126 rooms, 2 suites, 20 villas. 2 restaurants, 3 bars, deli, air-conditioning, fans, in-room data ports, in-room safes, refrigerators, pool, hot tub, 2 tennis courts, gym, beach, snorkeling, dock, billiards, casino, video games. AE, D, DC, MC, V. EP.*

$$$$ ⊞ **Villa Madeleine.** A West Indian plantation great house is the centerpiece
★ of this exquisite resort complex. Richly upholstered furniture, Asian rugs, teal walls, and whimsically painted driftwood set the mood in the billiards room, the library, and the sitting room. The great house sits on a hill, and there are villas on both sides of it. Each has a full kitchen and a pool. The decor is modern tropical: rattan furniture with plush cushions, rocking chairs, and, in some villas, bamboo four-poster beds. Special touches include pink-marble showers and hand-painted floral wall borders. Enjoy fine dining on the terrace at the Great House at Villa Madeleine or steak at the Turf Club. ⌂ *52 Kings St., off Rte. 82 at Teague Bay, Christiansted, 00820,* ☎ *340/773–4850 or 800/237–1959,* FAX *340/773–8989,* WEB *www.teaguebayproperties.com. 43 villas. 1 restaurant, bar, air-conditioning, kitchenettes, tennis court. AE, MC, V. EP.*

$$$ ▥ **Tamarind Reef Hotel.** At this casual, motel-like seaside spot, you can sunbathe at the large pool and sandy beach or snorkel in the reef, which comes right to the shore (serious swimming here is difficult). The spacious, modern rooms have rattan furniture, tropical-print drapes and spreads, and either a terrace or a deck with views of the water and St. Croix's sister islands to the north. Many rooms have basic kitchenettes—handy for preparing light meals—and three rooms have facilities for guests with disabilities. There's a snack bar just off the beach and a restaurant at the adjacent Green Cay Marina. ⊠ *Off Rte. 82, 5001 Tamarind Reef, 00820,* ☎ *340/773–4455; 800/619–0014 direct to hotel,* FAX *340/773–3989,* WEB *www.usvi.net/hotel/tamarind. 46 rooms. Snack bar, air-conditioning, kitchenettes, pool. AE, DC, MC, V. EP.*

OUTSIDE FREDERIKSTED

$$ ▥ **Sandcastle on the Beach.** Right on a gorgeous strand of white beach, this resort caters mainly to gay and lesbian guests. Most are couples, but singles also enjoy the house-party atmosphere. There are several categories of rooms; some put you steps from the water, and most have sea views and kitchenettes. Room refurbishments are on-going; finished rooms have a modern look with Mexican tile floors; although the others are still a bit old-fashioned, all are comfortable. ⊠ *127 Smithfield, Rte. 71, 00840,* ☎ *340/772–1205; 800/524–2018 direct to hotel,* FAX *340/772–1757,* WEB *www.gaytraveling.com/onthebeach. 6 rooms, 11 suites, 4 villas. Air-conditioning, fans, in-room VCRs, kitchenettes, 2 pools, beach, snorkeling. AE, D, MC, V. CP.*

$ ▥ **Seaview Farm Inn.** Up on a hill overlooking the Frederiksted outskirts, a salt pond, and the sea, this inn is perfect for independent, romantic souls. All have a porch and most have a view—giving you something to look at each evening (there are no TVs). Each unit is different, but wicker furniture and iron four-poster beds give each a country look; showers are all large enough for two. Owners Dulcy and Roland Kushmore will serve you a candlelight dinner on your porch or you can enjoy dinner at the adjacent Bandana's Restaurant. You can stroll along the beach to Frederiksted (just be sure to take a cab if you return after dark). Families with children would be more comfortable elsewhere. ⊠ *180 Two Brothers, off Rte. 71, 00840,* ☎ *340/772–2950; 800/792–5060 direct to hotel,* FAX *340/772–5060,* WEB *www.seaviewfarm.net. 8 suites. Restaurant, bar, fans, kitchenettes.AE, MC, V. EP.*

NORTH SHORE

$$$ ▥ **Hibiscus Beach Hotel.** Rooms here are in five pink two-story buildings—each named for a tropical flower. Most rooms have ocean views, but those in the Hibiscus Building are closest to the water. All have such amenities as roomy balconies and cable TV, and all are tastefully decorated with white-tile floors, white walls, pink-stripe curtains, floral spreads, and fresh-cut hibiscus blossoms. Bathrooms are clean but nondescript—both the shower stalls and the vanity mirrors are on the small side. ⊠ *4131 Estate La Grande Princesse, off Rte. 752, 00820-4441,* ☎ *340/773–4042; 800/442–0121 direct to hotel,* FAX *340/773–7668,* WEB *www.1hibiscus.com. 37 rooms. Restaurant, air-conditioning, in-room safes, minibars, pool, beach, snorkeling. AE, D, MC, V. EP.*

$$$ ▥ **Sunterra Carambola Beach Resort.** The 25 quaint, two-story, red-
★ roof villas (including one that's wheelchair-accessible) are connected by lovely, lush arcades. Rooms are identical except for the view—ocean or garden. The decor is English country with a touch of Caribbean: terra-cotta floors, ceramic lamps, mahogany ceilings and furnishings, and rocking chairs and sofas upholstered in soothing floral fabrics. Each room has a patio and a huge bath (shower only). The two-bedroom suite, with its 3-ft-thick (1-m-thick) plantation walls and large patio, is the perfect Caribbean family dwelling. ⊠ *Rte. 80 (Box 3031), King-*

shill 00851, ☏ 340/778–3800 or 888/503–8760, 𝐅𝐀𝐗 340/778–1682. 150 rooms, 1 cottage. 2 restaurants, deli, air-conditioning, pool, golf, 4 tennis courts, gym, beach, dive shop, snorkeling, library. AE, D, DC, MC, V. CP.

$$$ 🖃 **Waves at Cane Bay.** Lapping waves lull you to sleep at this isolated inn. Although the beach here is rocky, Cane Bay Beach is next door, and the world-famous Cane Bay Reef is just 100 yards offshore (divers take note: this is a PADI resort). You can also sunbathe on a small patch of sand beside the very unusual pool: it's carved from the coral along the shore, and waves crash dramatically over its side, creating a foamy whirlpool on blustery days. Two peach and mint-green buildings house enormous, balconied guest rooms that are done in cream and soft pastel prints. ✉ Rte. 80 (Box 1749), Kingshill, 00851, ☏ 340/778– 1805; 800/545–0603 direct to hotel, 𝐅𝐀𝐗 340/778–4945, 𝐖𝐄𝐁 www.canebaystcroix.com.12 rooms, 1 suite. Restaurant, bar, air-conditioning, in-room safes, kitchenettes, pool, snorkeling. AE, MC, V. EP.

Cottages and Condominiums

$$$ 🖃 **Club St. Croix.** Popular with honeymooners, this complex's studio and one- and two-bedroom apartments are spacious and bright. Indian-print throw rugs and cushions complement the bamboo furniture and rough white-tile floors; glass-top tables and mirrored closet doors are lovely modern touches. Penthouses have loft bedrooms atop spiral staircases; studios have Murphy beds in their sitting rooms. All units have sundecks with waterfront views of Christiansted and Buck Island. On the beach you'll find the Breezez restaurant, a bar, and a dock. ✉ 3230 Estate Golden Rock, Rte. 752, 00820, ☏ 340/773–4800 or 800/524–2025, 𝐅𝐀𝐗 340/778–4009, 𝐖𝐄𝐁 www.antillesresorts.com. 54 apartments. Restaurant, bar, air-conditioning, kitchenettes, pool, 3 tennis courts, beach, dock. AE, D, MC, V. EP.

$$$ 🖃 **Colony Cove.** Next door to Sugar Beach, this condo-style resort has sunny apartments done up with pastel prints, white tile, and rattan furnishings. Each unit has two bedrooms, two baths, a balcony, a washer and dryer, and a kitchen so complete that it even has a lasagna pan. You'll find a large pool, a water-sports center, and tennis courts on the grounds, and you can walk along the beach to the restaurant next door. ✉ 3221 Golden Rock, Rte. 752, 00820, ☏ 340/773–1965 or 800/828– 0746 (direct to hotel), 𝐅𝐀𝐗 340/773–5397, 𝐖𝐄𝐁 www.usvi.net/hotel/colony. 60 apartments. Snack bar, air-conditioning, kitchenettes, pool, 2 tennis courts, beach, snorkeling. AE, MC, V. EP.

$$$ 🖃 **Schooner Bay.** This red-roof condo village climbs a hill above Gallows Bay and just outside Christiansted. Each modern two- or three-bedroom apartment has a balcony, a washer and dryer, and a full kitchen with a dishwasher and a microwave. Rattan furnishings are set on beige-tile floors; floral-print fabrics add splashes of color. Three-bedroom units have spiral staircases. Sun worshipers might be disappointed that the nearest beach is east, at the Buccaneer, but those with a yen to explore Christiansted will find the location ideal—within walking distance of downtown yet away from its bustle. ✉ 5002 Gallows Bay, 00820, ☏ 340/778–7670 or 888/868–7798, 𝐅𝐀𝐗 340/773–4740, 𝐖𝐄𝐁 www.stayinstcroix.com/schooner_bay.html. 40 apartments. Air-conditioning, fans, kitchenettes, 2 pools, tennis court. AE, MC, V. EP.

$$$ 🖃 **Sugar Beach.** A stay here puts you on the beach at the north side of the island and just five minutes from Christiansted. The apartments, which range from studios to units with four bedrooms, are immaculate and breezy. Each has a full kitchen and a large patio or balcony with an ocean view; larger units have washers and dryers. Though the exteriors of these condos are ordinary beige stucco, the interiors are lovely (white with tropical furnishings). The pool is amid the ruins of a 250-year-old sugar

mill. ✉ *3245 Estate Golden Rock, Rte. 752, 00820,* ☎ *340/773–5345;* *800/524–2049 direct to hotel,* FAX *340/773–1359,* WEB *www.* *sugarbeachstcroix.com. 46 apartments. Air-conditioning, kitchenettes,* *pool, 2 tennis courts, beach, meeting rooms. AE, D, MC, V. EP.*

Private Homes and Villas

Renting a house gives you the convenience of home as well as top-notch amenities. Many houses have pools, hot tubs, and deluxe furnishings. Most companies meet you at the airport, arrange for a rental car, and provide helpful information. **The Collection** (☎ 856/751–2413) specializes in villas at Carambola. **Island Villas** (☎ 340/773–8821 or 800-626- 4512, WEB www.stcroixislandvillas.com) rents villas across St. Croix. **Rent A Villa** (☎ 800/533–6863, WEB www.rentavillavacations.com) specializes in villas on the island's east end. **Richards & Ayer** (☎ 340/ 772–0420, WEB www.ayervirginislands.com) has villas on the island's west end. **Teague Bay Properties** (☎ 340/773–4850, WEB www.teague-bayproperties.com) specializes in villas on the eastern end of St. Croix.

Dining

Seven flags have flown over St. Croix, and each has left its legacy in the island's cuisine. You can feast on Italian, French, Danish, and American dishes; there are even Chinese and Mexican restaurants in Christiansted. Fresh local seafood is plentiful and always good; wahoo, mahimahi, and conch are popular. Island chefs often add Caribbean twists to familiar dishes. For a true island experience, stop at a local restaurant for goat stew, curry chicken, or fried pork chops. Regardless of where you eat, your meal will be an informal affair. But be forewarned, prices are a lot higher than you'd pay on the mainland.

For approximate costs, *see* the dining price chart *in* St. Thomas.

Christiansted

CARIBBEAN

$$ ✕ **Indies.** A historic courtyard full of tables covered with handmade
★ floral-print cloths is the setting for a wonderful dining experience. The menu of island-inspired dishes changes each day to take advantage of St. Croix's freshest bounties. Indulge in the crab cakes or the spicy Caribbean spring rolls to start, then the spice-rubbed chicken (every bite reveals a new, subtle flavor) or spiny lobster fresh from the sea. Enjoy live jazz Thursday, Friday, and Saturday evenings. ✉ *55–56 Company St.,* ☎ *340/692–9440. AE, D, MC, V. No lunch weekends.*

$ ✕ **Harvey's.** The plain, even dowdy dining room has just 14 tables, and plastic floral tablecloths constitute the sole attempt at decor. But who cares? The food is delicious. Daily specials, such as mouthwatering goat stew and tender whelks in butter, served with heaping helpings of rice, fungi, and vegetables, are listed on the blackboard. Genial owner Sarah Harvey takes great pride in her kitchen, bustling out from behind the stove to chat and urge you to eat up. ✉ *11B Company St.,* ☎ *340/773–3433. No credit cards. Closed Sun. No dinner.*

CONTEMPORARY

$$$ ✕ **Kendricks.** The chef at this open-air restaurant—a longtime favorite
★ with locals—conjures up creative, tasty cuisine. Try the Alaskan king crab cakes with lemon black pepper aïoli to start, or the warm *chipotle* pepper with garlic and onion soup. Move on to the house specialty: pecan-crusted roast pork loin with ginger mayonnaise. ✉ *21–32 Company St.,* ☎ *340/773–9199. AE, MC, V. Closed Sun. No lunch.*

CONTINENTAL

$$$ ✕ **Top Hat.** Owned by a delightful Danish couple, this restaurant has
★ been serving international cuisine (with Danish specialties, of course)

since 1970. Dishes include roast duck stuffed with apples and prunes, *frikadeller* (savory meatballs in a tangy cocktail sauce), conch beignets, and smoked eel. The signature dessert is a rum-ice-cream-filled chocolate windmill whose blades turn. ⊠ *52 Company St.,* ☎ *340/773–2346. AE, D, DC, MC, V. No lunch.*

$$ ✕ **Tivoli Gardens.** Fresh breezes and bowers of hanging plants virtu-
★ ally transform this restaurant in the heart of Christiansted into a garden. The menu features steak, lobster, and more lobster. To make it easy to eat, the chef takes all the succulent meat from a whole lobster, puts it into half the lobster's shell, and drips butter over the top. For dessert try the bittersweet chocolate velvet—a chocoholic's dream that's closer to candy than cake. ⊠ *39 Strand St.,* ☎ *340/773–6782. MC, V. No lunch weekends.*

ECLECTIC

$$ ✕ **Paradise Cafe.** The exposed brick walls of this tiny, lively spot are splashed with colorful island prints. Stop in for breakfast, lunch, or supper: sandwiches and burgers are the big draw, though steak and the daily seafood special, often wahoo or mahimahi, are also popular. ⊠ *Company and Queen Cross sts.,* ☎ *340/773–2985. No credit cards.*

ITALIAN

$$$ ✕ **Tutto Bene.** Its yellow walls, brightly striped cushions, and painted trompe l'oeil tables make Tutto Bene look more like a sophisticated Mexican cantina than an Italian cucina. One bite of the food, however, will clear up any confusion. Written on hanging mirrors is the daily menu, which includes such fare as veal Parmesan and seafood stew with a tasty fennel, cumin, tomato, and basil broth. Desserts are prepared by one of the island's finest pastry chefs. ⊠ *2 Company St.,* ☎ *340/773–5229. AE, MC, V.*

Outside Christiansted

ECLECTIC

$$ ✕ **Breezez.** This aptly named restaurant sits poolside at Club St. Croix condominiums. Visitors and locals are drawn by its reasonable prices, its very casual ambience, and its good food. This is *the* place to be for Sunday brunch, where the menu includes lobster rolls, burgers, and blackened prime rib with Cajun seasonings and horseradish sauce. For dessert, try the flourless chocolate torte—a wedge of rich chocolate served with a river of chocolate sauce. ⊠ *3220 Golden Rock, off Rte. 752,* ☎ *340/773–7077. AE, D, MC, V.*

ITALIAN

$ ✕ **Pizza Mare.** This trendy spot just may have the best pizza in all of
★ St. Croix. Residents gather for muffins in the morning as well as lasagna and meatball sandwiches for lunch or dinner. ⊠ *24 Estate Welcome, Rte. 82,* ☎ *340/773–3663. AE, D, MC, V. Closed Sun.*

East End

CONTEMPORARY

$$$ ✕ **Great House at Villa Madeleine.** The elegant restaurant at the Villa Madeleine resort serves such diverse cuisine as roasted ducking and macadamia-encrusted wahoo; there are also a number of fine beef dishes. The wine list is extensive. ⊠ *19A Teague Bay (Take Rte. 82 out of Christiansted, turn right at Reef Condominiums),* ☎ *340/778–7377. AE, D, MC, V. No lunch.*

ECLECTIC

$$$ ✕ **The Galleon.** Popular with locals and visitors, this dockside restaurant has something for everyone. Start with the Caesar salad or gravlax (fresh salmon with dill and pepper). Pasta lovers should sample the vegetable ravioli: the homemade pasta is filled not only with whatever grilled

vegetable the chef gets in that day (the eggplant is especially good) but also with Parmesan, ricotta, and mozzarella cheeses. The osso buco and rack of lamb are legendary. ⊠ *Teague Bay (Take Rte. 82 out of Christiansted, turn left at sign for Green Cay Marina)*, ☎ *340/773–9949. AE, MC, V. No lunch.*

$$ ✕ **South Shore Cafe.** This casual bistro sits near the Great Salt Pond on the island's south shore. Popular with locals for its good food and cozy ambience, the restaurant features dishes drawn from a variety of cuisines. Meat lovers and vegetarians can find common ground with a menu that runs from handmade pasta to prime rib. The selection isn't extensive, but the chef puts together a blackboard full of specials every day. ⊠ *Junction of Rtes. 62 and 624,* ☎ *340/773–9311. V. No lunch. Closed Mon.–Tues.*

Frederiksted

AMERICAN

$$$ ✕ **Bandana's.** Beef's the thing at this open-air spot overlooking Frederiksted Harbor. From a 20-ounce aged porterhouse to a six-ounce filet mignon, the beef comes cooked just the way you want it. If your fancy turns to seafood, you'll find yellow fin tuna, salmon, and the like on this extensive menu. Save room for a wedge of Roland's Rum Cake, a warm chocolate confection topped with vanilla ice cream and chocolate sauce. If you're around on Sunday, stop by for brunch. Lobster benedict and Alice's creamed chipped beef on an English muffin are the house specialties. ⊠ *180 Two Brothers,* ☎ *340/772–2950. AE, D, MC, V. Closed Mon.–Tues. No lunch. Brunch only Sun.*

ECLECTIC

$$ ✕ **Blue Moon.** This terrific little bistro, popular for its live jazz on Friday night, has a changing menu that draws on Asian, Cajun, and local flavors. Try the seafood chowder or crab cakes with a spicy aïoli as an appetizer; the roasted vegetables and shrimp over linguine as an entrée; and the Almond Joy sundae for dessert. ⊠ *17 Strand St.,* ☎ *340/772–2222. AE, D, DC, MC, V. Closed Mon.*

$$ ✕ **Le St. Tropez.** A ceramic-tile bar and soft lighting add to the Mediterranean atmosphere at this pleasant bistro, tucked into a courtyard off Frederiksted's main thoroughfare. Seated either inside or on the adjoining patio, you can enjoy such items as grilled meats in delicate French sauces. The menu changes daily, often taking advantage of local seafood. The fresh basil, tomato, and mozzarella salad is heavenly. ⊠ *227 King St.,* ☎ *340/772–3000. AE, MC, V. No lunch Sat. Closed Sun.*

Cane Bay

ECLECTIC

$ ✕ **Off the Wall.** Divers fresh from a plunge at the north shore's popular wall gather at this breezy spot right on the beach. If you want to sit a spell before you order, a hammock beckons. Burgers, fish sandwiches, quesadillas, and Philly steak sandwiches join pizza and hotdogs on the menu. The potato salad that comes with your sandwich is as good as you'd get at home. You might find blues and jazz on Friday, Saturday, and Sunday nights. ⊠ *Rte. 80,* ☎ *340/778–4771. AE, MC, V.*

Beaches

Buck Island. A visit to this island, part of the U.S. National Park system, is a must. The beach is beautiful, but its finest treasures are those you can see when you plop off the boat and adjust your mask, snorkel, and flippers. To get here, you'll have to charter a boat or go on an organized trip.

Cane Bay. The waters aren't always gentle at this breezy north shore beach, but there are never many people around and the scuba diving

and snorkeling are wondrous. You'll see elkhorn and brain corals, and less than 200 yards out is the drop-off called Cane Bay Wall.

Cramer's Park. This USVI territorial beach on the northeast coast (Route 82) is very popular with locals. It's a good spot for beach picnics and camping. Because of its isolation, though, it's not a good place to linger if you're traveling solo.

Isaac's Bay. This east-end beach is almost impossible to reach without a four-wheel-drive vehicle, but it's worth the effort. You'll find secluded sands for sunbathing, calm waters for swimming, and a barrier reef for snorkeling. You can also get here via footpaths from Jack's Bay.

Tamarind Reef Beach. Small but attractive Tamarind Reef Beach is east of Christiansted. Both Green Cay and Buck Island seem smack in front of you—an arresting view. The snorkeling is good.

West End Beaches. There are several unnamed beaches along the coast road north of Frederiksted. Just pull over at whatever piece of powdery sand catches your fancy. The beach at the Rainbow Beach Club, five-minute drive outside Frederiksted on Route 63, has a bar, a casual restaurant, water sports, and volleyball.

Outdoor Activities and Sports

CYCLING

A bike tour to some of the island's top sights adds a new dimension to your vacation and helps you stay in shape. **St. Croix Bike and Tours** (⊠ Strand Square Courtyard, Frederiksted, ☎ 340/772–1351) offers two tours; both cost $35. One heads through historic Frederiksted before cycling on a fairly flat road to Hamm's Bluff. The second, for heartier folks, takes you up and through the rain forest. Bikes rent for $7.50 for the first hour; $2.50 for each additional hour.

FISHING

In the past quarter century, some 20 world records—many for blue marlin—have been set in these waters. Sailfish, skipjack, bonito, tuna (allison, blackfin, and yellowfin), and wahoo are abundant. A charter runs about $100 an hour per person, with most boats going out for four-, six- or eight-hour trips. **Mile Mark Charters** (⊠ 59 King's Wharf, Christiansted,☎ 340/773–2628 or 800/523–3483) will take you out on a 38-ft powerboat, the *Fantasy.* **S.C.O.R.E./VI Divers** (⊠ 11–12 Strand St., Christiansted, ☎ 340/773–6045 or 877/773–60453) will take you fishing on either their 29-foot *Tarpon* or 36-ft *Tarpon Shark II.*

GOLF

St. Croix's courses welcome you with spectacular vistas and well-kept greens. Check with your hotel or the tourist board to determine when major celebrity tournaments will be held. There's often an opportunity to play with the pros. The **Buccaneer**'s (⊠ Off Rte. 82 at Teague Bay, ☎ 340/773–2100) 18-hole course is conveniently close to (east of) Christiansted. The **Reef Golf Course** (☎ 340/773–8844), in the northeastern part of the island, has 9 holes. The spectacular 18-hole course at **Sunterra Carambola Beach Resort** (⊠ Rte. 80,☎ 340/778–5638), in the northwest valley, was designed by Robert Trent Jones, Sr.

HIKING

Although you can set off by yourself on a hike through a rain forest or along a shore, a guide will point out what's important and tell you why. The **Nature Conservancy** (⊠ 52 Estate Little Princess [Box 1066], Christiansted, 00821, ☎ 340/773–5575) has two-hour hikes to Jack's and Isaac's bays, on the east end. The cost is $10 per person. The nonprofit **St. Croix Environmental Association** (⊠ Arawak Bldg., Suite 3, Gallows Bay, 00820, ☎ 340/773–1989) offers treks through several ecological treasures, including Estate Mt. Washington, Estate Caledonia, in the rain forest, and Salt River. The cost is $20 per person for a two-hour hike.

HORSEBACK RIDING

Well-kept roads and expert guides make horseback riding on St. Croix pleasurable. At Sprat Hall, near Frederiksted, Jill Hurd runs **Paul and Jill's Equestrian Stables** (⊠ Rte. 58, ☎ 340/772–2880 or 340/772–2627) and will take you clip-clopping through the rain forest, pastures, and hilltops (explaining the flora, fauna, and ruins on the way). A two-hour ride costs $50.

KAYAKING

Caribbean Adventure Tours takes you on trips through Salt River National Park and Ecological Preserve, one of the island's most pristine areas. A daytime ecotour runs $45, a moonlight trip is $40, and a combination kayaking and biking trip runs $50. (⊠ Columbus Cove Marina, Rte. 80, ☎ 340/773–4599).

SAILING

Day sail to Buck Island aboard a charter boat. Most leave from the Christiansted waterfront or from Green Cay Marina. They stop for a snorkel at the island's eastern end before dropping anchor off a gorgeous sandy beach for a swim, a hike, and lunch. A full-day sail runs about $65 with lunch included on most trips. A half-day sail costs about $50. **Big Beard's Adventure Tours** (☎ 340/773–4482) takes you on a catamaran, the *Renegade* or the *Flyer,* from the Christiansted Waterfront to Buck Island for snorkeling before dropping anchor at a private beach for a barbecue lunch. **Buck Island Charters** (☎ 340/773–3161) trimaran *Teroro II* leaves Green Cay Marina for full-or half-day sails. Bring your own lunch. **Mile Mark Charters** (☎ 340/773–2628 or 800/523–3483) departs from the Christiansted waterfront for half- and full-day sails on a variety of boats.

SCUBA DIVING AND SNORKELING

At **Buck Island,** a short boat ride from Christiansted or Green Cay Marina, the reef is so spectacular it's been named a national monument. You can dive right off the beach at **Cane Bay,** which has a spectacular drop-off. **Frederiksted Pier** is home to a colony of seahorses, creatures seldom seen in the waters off the Virgin Islands. At **Green Cay,** just outside Green Cay Marina in the east end, you'll see colorful fish swimming around the reefs and rocks. Two exceptional **north shore sites** are North Star and Salt River, which you can reach only by boat. You can float downward through a canyon filled with colorful fish and coral.

The island's dive shops take you out for one- or two-tank dives. Plan to pay about $50 for a one-tank dive and $70 for a two-tank dive, including equipment and an underwater tour. **Anchor Dive Center** (⊠ Salt River Marina, Rte. 801, ☎ 340/778–1522 or 800/532–3483; ⊠ Christiansted Wharf, ☎ 340/773–3307 or 800/532–3483) takes divers to 35 sites, including the wall at Salt River Canyon and Buck Island Reef National Monument. It also offers PADI certification. **Cane Bay Dive Shop** (⊠ Rte. 80, Cane Bay, ☎ 340/773–9913 or 800/338–3843) takes you on boat and beach dives along the north shore. The famed wall is just 150 yards from their shop. **Dive Experience** (⊠ Strand St., Christiansted, ☎ 340/773–3307 or 800/235-9047) is a five-star PADI training facility that offers everything from introductory dives to certification. It also runs trips to the north shore walls and reefs. **Scuba West** (☎ 340/772–3701 or 800/352–0107) operates out of Frederiksted. Although it runs trips to reefs and wrecks, its specialty is the seahorses that live around the Frederiksted Pier. **V. I. Divers Ltd.** (☎ 340/773–6045 or 877/

773–6045) is near the water at 11–12 Strand St. It's a PADI international outfit that will take you to your choice of 28 sites.

TENNIS

The public courts in Frederiksted and out east at Cramer Park are in questionable shape. It's better to pay a fee and play at one of the hotel courts. Costs vary by resort, but count on paying at least $10 an hour. **Buccaneer Hotel** (✉ Rte. 82, ☎ 340/773–2100) has eight courts (two lighted), plus a pro and a full tennis shop. **Chenay Bay Beach Resort** (✉ Rte. 82, ☎ 340/773–2918) has two courts (no lights). **Club St. Croix** (✉ Rte. 752, ☎ 340/773–4800) has three lighted courts. **Sunterra Carambola Beach Resort** (✉ Rte. 80, ☎ 340/778–3800) has four lighted courts.

WINDSURFING

St. Croix's trade winds make windsurfing a breeze. Most hotels rent Windsurfers and other water-sports equipment to nonguests. **St. Croix Watersports** (✉ Hotel on the Cay, ☎ 340/773–7060) offers Windsurfer rentals, sales, and rides; parasailing; and a wide range of water-sports equipment, such as Sea Doos and kayaks. Renting a windsurfer runs about $25 an hour.

Shopping

Areas and Malls

Although St. Croix doesn't offer as many shopping opportunities as St. Thomas, the island does have an array of small stores with unique merchandise. In Christiansted the best shopping areas are the **Pan Am Pavilion** and **Caravelle Arcade** off Strand Street, **Kings Alley Walk**, and along **King** and **Company streets.** These streets give way to arcades filled with boutiques. **Gallows Bay** has a blossoming shopping area in a quiet neighborhood. Stores are often closed on Sunday.

The best shopping in Frederiksted is along **Strand Street** and in the side streets and alleyways that connect it with **King Street.** Most stores close Sunday except when a cruise ship is in port.

Specialty Items

BOOKS

The Bookie. This shop carries paperback novels, stationery, newspapers, and cards. Stop in for the latest gossip and to find out about upcoming events. ✉ *1111 Strand St., Christiansted,* ☎ *340/773–2592.*
Undercover Books. For Caribbean books or the latest good read, try this bookstore across from the post office in the Gallows Bay shopping area. ✉ *5030 Anchor Way,* ☎ *340/719–1567.*

CLOTHING

From the Gecko. Come here for the hippest clothes on St. Croix, from superb batik sarongs to hand-painted silk scarves. ✉ *1233 Queen Cross St., Christiansted,* ☎ *340/778–9433.*
Coconut Vine. Pop into this store at the start of your vacation, and you'll leave with enough comfy cotton or rayon batik men's and women's clothes to make you look like a local. Although the tropical designs and colors originated in Indonesia, they're perfect for the Caribbean. ✉ *King's Alley, Christiansted,* ☎ *340/773–1991.*
Soul of Africa. The leopard- or zebra-trimmed clothing will catch your eye at this store. Elegant silk jackets and batik bedspreads in unique patterns also fill the shelves. ✉ *Kings Alley, Christiansted,* ☎ *340/773–3099.*
The White House/Black Market. This contemporary store sells clothes in all-white, black and natural colors. Look for exquisite lingerie, elegant evening wear, and unusual casual outfits. ✉ *8B Kings Alley Walk, Christiansted,* ☎ *340/773–9222.*

FOODSTUFFS

If you've rented a condominium or a villa, you'll appreciate that St. Croix offers excellent shopping at its stateside-style supermarkets. Fresh vegetables, fruits, and meats arrive frequently. Try the open-air stands strung out along Route 70 for island produce.

Plaza Extra sells Middle Eastern foods in addition to the usual grocery store items. ⊠ *United Shopping Plaza, Rte. 70, Frederiksted,* ☎ *340/778–6240.*

Pueblo is a stateside-style market with locations all over the island. ⊠ *Orange Grove Shopping Center, Rte. 75, Christiansted,* ☎ *340/773–0118; Sunny Isle Shopping Center, Rte. 70, mid-island,* ☎ *340/778–5005; Villa La Reine Shopping Center, Rte. 75, La Reine,* ☎ *340/778–1272.*

Schooner Bay Market is on the smallish side, but has good quality deli items. ⊠ *Rte. 82, outside Christiansted,* ☎ *340/773–3232.*

Cost-U-Less is a warehouse-type store across from Sunshine Mall. It does not charge a membership fee. ⊠ *Rte. 70, outside Frederiksted,* ☎ *340/692–2220.*

GIFTS

Gone Tropical. Whether you're looking for inexpensive souvenirs of your trip or a special, singular gift, you'll probably find it here. On her travels about the world, owner Margo Meacham keeps her eye out for items with which to stock her shop—from tablecloths and napkins in bright Caribbean colors to carefully crafted metal birds. ⊠ *5 Company St., Christiansted,* ☎ *340/773–4696.*

Island Webe. The coffees, jams, and spices—produced locally or elsewhere in the Caribbean—here will tempt your taste buds. Small *mocko jumbie* dolls depict an African tradition transported to the islands during slave days (they represent the souls of the ancestors of African slaves). The fabric dolls wearing Caribbean costumes will delight kids of all ages. Turn the double dolls upside down to see a white face on one side and a black one on the other. ⊠ *210 Strand St., Frederiksted,* ☎ *340/772–2555.*

Royal Poinciana. You'll find island seasonings and hot sauces, West Indian crafts, bath gels, and herbal teas at this attractive shop. Shop here for tablecloths and paper goods in tropical brights. ⊠ *1111 Strand St., Christiansted,* ☎ *340/773–9892.*

HANDICRAFTS

Folk Art Traders. Owners Patty and Charles Eitzen travel to Cuba as well as Haiti, Jamaica, and elsewhere in the Caribbean to find treasures for their shop. The baskets, ceramic masks, pottery, jewelry, and sculpture they find are unique examples of folk-art traditions. ⊠ *1B Queen Cross St., at Strand St., Christiansted,* ☎ *340/773–1900.*

HOUSEWARES

St. Croix Landmarks Museum Store. If a mahogany armoire or cane-backed rocker catches your fancy, the staff will arrange to have it shipped to your mainland store at no charge from its mainland warehouse. Furniture aside, this store has one of the largest selections of local art along with Caribbean-inspired bric-a-brac in all prices ranges. ⊠ *5A King St., Christiansted,* ☎ *340/713–8102.*

Textiles with a Story. Oriental rugs mingle with island-inspired batiks at this store that speaks of an Arabian souk. Comfy pillows in varied motifs and colors invite you to rest. ⊠ *52 King St., Christiansted,* ☎ *340/692–9867.*

JEWELRY

Colombian Emeralds. Specializing—of course—in emeralds, this store also carries diamonds, rubies, sapphires, and gold. A branch store, **Jewelers' Warehouse** (✉ 1 Queen Cross St., Christiansted, ☎ 340/773–5590), is across the street. The chain, the Caribbean's largest jeweler, offers certified appraisal and international guarantees. ✉ *43 Queen Cross St., Christiansted,* ☎ *340/773–1928 or 340/773–9189.*

Crucian Gold. This store, in a small courtyard of a West Indian–style cottage, carries the unique gold creations of St. Croix native Brian Bishop. His trademark piece is the Turk's Head ring (a knot of interwoven gold strands). ✉ *59 King's Wharf, Christiansted,* ☎ *340/773–5241.*

Karavan West Indies. The owner here designs her own jewelry and also sells an assortment of tchotchkes, including handmade Christmas ornaments. ✉ *5030 Anchor Way, Gallows Bay,* ☎ *340/773–9999.*

Sonya's. Sonya Hough opened this store in 1964 to showcase her jewelry creations; now she runs it with her daughter, Diana. Sonya invented the hook bracelet, popular among locals. With hurricanes hitting the island so frequently, she has added an interesting decoration to these bracelets: the swirling symbol used in weather forecasts to indicate these storms. ✉ *1 Company St., Christiansted,* ☎ *340/778–8605.*

LEATHER GOODS

Kicks. This upscale shop carries a good, if small, selection of shoes and leather goods. ✉ *57 Company St., Christiansted,* ☎ *340/773–7801.*

LIQUOR AND TOBACCO

Baci Duty Free Liquor and Tobacco. A walk-in humidor with a good selection of Arturo Fuente, Partagas, and Macanudo cigars is the centerpiece of this store. It also carries sleek Danish-made watches and Lladro Nao figurines. ✉ *55 Company St., Christiansted,* ☎ *340/773–5040.*

Cruzan Rum Distillery. A tour of the company's factory culminates in a tasting of its products, all sold here at bargain prices. ✉ *West Airport Rd.,* ☎ *340/692–2280.*

Kmart. The two branches of this discount department store—a large one in the Sunshine Mall and a smaller one mid-island at Sunny Isle Shopping Center—carry a huge line of discounted, duty-free liquor. ✉ *Sunshine Mall, Rte. 70, Frederiksted,* ☎ *340/692–5848;* ✉ *Sunny Isle Shopping Center, Rte. 70,* ☎ *340/719–9190.*

PERFUMES

Violette Boutique. Perfumes, cosmetics, and skin-care products are the draws here. ✉ *Caravelle Arcade, 38 Strand St., Christiansted,* ☎ *340/773–2148.*

Nightlife and the Arts

The island's nightlife is ever-changing, and its arts scene is eclectic—ranging from Christmastime performances of the *Nutcracker* to whatever local group got organized enough to put on a show. Folk-art traditions, such as quadrille dancers, are making a comeback. To find out what's happening, pick up the local newspapers—*V.I. Daily News* and *St. Croix Avis*—which are available at newsstands.

Nightlife

Christiansted has a lively and eminently casual club scene near the waterfront. **Hotel on the Cay** (✉ Protestant Cay, ☎ 340/773–2035) has a West Indian buffet on Tuesday night in the winter season that features a broken-bottle dancer (a dancer who braves a carpet of broken bottles) and mocko jumbie characters. Easy jazz flows from the courtyard bar at **Indies** (✉ 55–56 Company St., ☎ 340/692–9440) Thursday, Friday, and Saturday evenings. The **2 Plus 2 Disco** (✉ 17 La Grande Princesse, ☎ 340/773–3710) spins a great mix of calypso, soul, disco, and reggae; there's live music on weekends in the winter.

Frederiksted has a couple of restaurants and clubs with a variety of weekend entertainment. **Blue Moon** (✉ 17 Strand St., ☎ 340/772–2222), a waterfront restaurant, is the place to be for live jazz on Friday 9 PM– 1 AM.

Outside Frederiksted, **Off the Wall** (✉ Rte. 80, Cane Bay, ☎ 340/778– 4471), as blues or jazz every Friday, Saturday, and Sunday from 6 PM to 9 PM.

The Arts
The **Whim Greathouse** (✉ Rte. 70, ☎ 340/772–0598) hosts classical music concerts during the winter season.

Exploring St. Croix

Though there are things to see and do in St. Croix's two towns, Christiansted and Frederiksted (both named after Danish kings), there are lots of interesting spots in between them and to the east of Christiansted. Just be sure you have a map in hand (pick one up at rental-car agencies, or stop by the tourist office for an excellent one that's free). Many secondary roads remain unmarked; if you get confused, ask for help.

Numbers in the margin correspond to points of interest on the St. Croix map.

Christiansted and the East
Christiansted is a historic Danish-style town that always served as St. Croix's commercial center. Your best bet is to see the historic sights in the morning, when it's still cool. This two-hour endeavor won't tax your walking shoes and will leave you with energy to poke around the town's eclectic shops. Break for lunch at an open-air restaurant before spending as much time as you like shopping.

An easy drive (roads are flat and well marked) to St. Croix's eastern end takes you through some choice real estate. Ruins of old sugar estates dot the landscape. You can make the entire loop on the road that circles the island in about an hour, a good way to end the day. If you want to spend a full day exploring, you'll find some nice beaches and easy walks, with places to stop for lunch.

SIGHTS TO SEE

❶ Christiansted. In the 1700s and 1800s this town was a trading center for sugar, rum, and molasses. Today it's home to law offices, tourist shops, and restaurants, but many of the buildings, which start at the harbor and go up into the gentle hillsides, still date from the 18th century. You can't get lost. All streets lead gently downhill to the water. Still, if you want some friendly advice, stop by the **Visitors Center** (✉ 53A Company St., ☎ 340/773–0495) weekdays between 8 and 5 for maps and brochures.

Large, yellow **Ft. Christiansvaern** dominates the waterfront. Because it's so easy to spot, it makes a good place from which to begin a walking tour. In 1749 the Danish built the fort to protect the harbor, but the structure was repeatedly damaged by hurricane-force winds and was partially rebuilt in 1771. It's now a national historic site and the best preserved of the five remaining Danish-built forts in the Virgin Islands. ✉ *Hospital St.,* ☎ *340/773–1460.* ⌨ *$2 (includes admission to Steeple Bldg.).* ☉ *8–5.*

When you're tired of sightseeing, stop at D. Hamilton Jackson Park—on the street side of Ft. Christiansvaern—for a rest. It's named for a famed labor leader, judge, and journalist who started the first newspaper not under the thumb of the Danish crown. ⊠ *Between Ft. Christiansvaern and the Danish Customs House.*

Built in 1830 on foundations that date from 1734, the **Danish Customs House**—near Ft. Christiansvaern—originally served as both a customs house and a post office (second floor). In 1926 it became the Christiansted Library, and it has been a National Park Service office since 1972. ⊠ *King St.,* ☎ *340/773–1460.* ◷ *Weekdays 8–5.*

Constructed in 1856, the **Scale House** was once the spot where goods passing through the port were weighed and inspected. It now serves as the Christiansted Historic Site's visitors center. ⊠ *King St.,* ☎ *340/773–1460.* ◷ *Weekdays 8–4:30, weekends and holidays 8:30–4:30.*

Built by the Danes in 1753, the **Steeple Building** was the first Danish Lutheran church on St. Croix. It's now a national park museum and contains exhibits that document the island's Indian habitation. It's worth the block-long walk from Ft. Christiansvaern to see the building's collection of archaeological artifacts, displays on plantation life, and exhibits on the architectural development of Christiansted, the early history of the church, and Alexander Hamilton, the first secretary of the U.S. Treasury, who grew up in St. Croix. ⊠ *Church St.,* ☎ *340/773–1460.* ◩ *$2 (includes admission to Ft. Christiansvaern above).* ◷ *Daily 9–4:30.*

The **Post Office Building,** built in 1749, was once the Danish West India & Guinea Company warehouse. ⊠ *Church St.*

One of the town's most elegant structures, **Government House** was built as a home for a Danish merchant in 1747. Today it houses USVI government offices. If the building is open, slip into the peaceful inner courtyard to admire the still pools and gardens. A sweeping staircase leads you to a second-story ballroom, still the site of official government functions. ⊠ *King St.,* ☎ *340/773–1404.* ◷ *Weekdays 8–5.*

Around the corner and down a block from Government House, the tanks at the **St. Croix Aquarium** contain an ever-changing variety of local sea creatures. Children are invited to explore the discovery room, with its microscopes, interactive displays, and educational videos. Children will enjoy the petting tank, where they can feel starfish relax to their touch. ⊠ *Caravelle Arcade,* ☎ *340/773–8995.* ◩ *$5.* ◷ *Tues.–Sat. 11–4.*

Built in 1735 as a slave market, today **the market,** housed in a wood and galvanized aluminum structure, is where farmers and others sell their goods every Wednesday and Saturday from 8 to 5. The market is a three-block walk from the aquarium and is a great place to end a walking tour. ⊠ *Company St.*

The **Buck Island Reef National Monument,** off the northeast coast, has pristine beaches that are just right for sunbathing, but there's enough shade for those who don't want to fry. The spectacular snorkeling trail set in the reef allows close-up study of coral formations and tropical fish. After your arrival by charter boat, crew members give special attention to novice snorkelers and children. There's an easy hiking trail to the island's highest point, where you'll be rewarded for your efforts by spectacular views of the reef and St. John. Charter-boat trips leave daily from the Christiansted waterfront or from Green Cay Marina, about 2 mi (3 km) east of Christiansted. Check with your hotel for recommendations. ⊠ *North Shore,* ☎ *340/773–1460 (park headquarters),* WEB *www.nps.gov/buis.*

❷ **Point Udall.** This rocky promontory, the easternmost point in the
United States, is about a half-hour's drive from Christiansted. A paved
road takes you to an overlook with glorious views. More adventurous
folks can hike down to the pristine beach below. On the way back, look
for The Castle, an enormous mansion that can only be described as a
cross between a Moorish mosque and the Taj Mahal. It was built by
an extravagant recluse known only as the Contessa. ✉ *Rte. 82.*

Between Christiansted and Frederiksted

A drive through the countryside between these two towns will take you
past ruins of old plantations, many bearing whimsical names (Morningstar, Solitude, Upper Love) bestowed by early owners. The traffic
moves quickly—by island standards—on the main roads, but you can
pause and poke around if you head down some side lanes. It's easy to
find your way west, but driving from north to south requires good navigation. Don't leave your hotel without a map. Allow an entire day for
this trip so you'll have enough time for a swim at a north shore beach.
Although you'll find lots of casual eateries on the main roads, pick up
a picnic lunch if you plan to head off the beaten path.

SIGHTS TO SEE

❹ **Judith's Fancy.** In this upscale neighborhood you'll find the ruins of
an old great house and tower of the same name, both remnants of a
circa-1750 Danish sugar plantation. The "Judith" comes from the
first name of a woman buried on the property. From the guard house
at the neighborhood entrance, follow Hamilton Drive past some of St.
Croix's loveliest homes. At the end of Hamilton Drive the road overlooks Salt River Bay, where Christopher Columbus anchored in 1493.
A skirmish between members of Columbus's crew and a group of
Carib Indians resulted in the first bloody encounter between Europeans
and West Indians. The peninsula on the bay's east side is named for
the event: Cabo de las Flechas (Cape of the Arrows). On the way back,
make a detour left off Hamilton Drive onto Caribe Road for a close
look at the ruins. ✉ *Turn north onto Rte. 751, off Rte. 75.*

❸ **Little Princess Estate.** If the old plantation ruins decaying here and there
around St. Croix intrigue you, a visit to this Nature Conservancy project will give you even more of a glimpse into the past. The staff has
carved walking paths out of the bush that surrounds what's left of a
19th-century plantation. It's easy to stroll among well-labeled fruit trees
and see the ruins of the windmill, the sugar and rum factory, and the
laborers' village. This is the perfect place to reflect on St. Croix's
agrarian past fueled with labor from African slaves. The property also
has a community garden. ✉ *Just off Rte. 75 (turn north at the Five
Corners traffic light),* ☎ *340/773–5575.* ✉ *Free.* ☉ *9–2.*

❻ **Mt. Eagle.** This is St. Croix's highest peak (1,165 ft/356 m). Leaving
Cane Bay and passing North Star Beach, follow the coastal road that
dips briefly into a forest, then turn left on Rte. 69. Just after you make
the turn, the pavement is marked with the words THE BEAST and a set
of giant paw prints. The hill you're about to climb is the location of the
famous Beast of the St. Croix Half Ironman Triathlon, an annual event
during which participants must bike this intimidating slope. ✉ *Rte. 69.*

❺ **Salt River Bay National Historical Park and Ecological Preserve.** This
joint national and local park was dedicated in November 1993. In addition to sights with cultural significance, it encompasses a biodiverse
coastal estuary with the largest remaining mangrove forest in the USVI,
a submarine canyon, and several endangered species, including the
hawksbill turtle and the roseate tern. Plans are afoot to create a museum, interpretive walking trails, and a replica of a Carib village. A

ball court, used by the Caribs in worship ceremonies, was discovered at the spot where the taxis park. Take a short hike up the dirt road to the ruins of an old earthen fort for great views of Salt River Bay and the surrounding countryside. ⊠ *Rte. 75 to Rte. 80.*

Frederiksted and Environs

St. Croix's second-largest town, Frederiksted, was founded in 1751. A stroll around its historic sights will take you no more than an hour. Allow a little more time if you want to browse in the few small shops. The area just outside town has old plantations, some of which have been preserved as homes or historic structures that are open to the public.

SIGHTS TO SEE

❼ Estate Mount Washington Plantation. Several years ago, while surveying the property, the owners discovered the ruins of a sugar plantation beneath the rain-forest brush. The grounds have since been cleared and opened to the public. You can take a self-guided walking tour of the mill, the rum factory, and other ruins, and there's an antiques shop in what were once the stables. ⊠ *Rte. 63 (watch for antiques shop sign),* ☎ *340/772–1026.* ☉ *Ruins open daily; antiques shop open by appointment only.*

⓬ Estate Whim Plantation Museum. The lovingly restored estate, with a windmill, cook house, and other buildings, will give you a sense of what life was like on St. Croix's sugar plantations in the 1800s. The oval-shape great house has high ceilings and antique furniture, decor, and utensils. Notice its fresh, airy atmosphere—the waterless stone moat around the great house was used not for defense but for gathering cooling air. The apothecary exhibit is the largest in all the West Indies. If you have kids, the grounds are the perfect place for them to stretch their legs, perhaps while you browse in the museum gift shop. ⊠ *Rte. 70,* ☎ *340/772–0598,* WEB *www.stcroixlandmarks.com.* ✉ *$6.* ☉ *Mon.–Sat. 10–4.*

❽ Frederiksted. The town is noted less for its Danish than for its Victorian architecture, which dates from after the slave uprising and the great fire of 1878. One long cruise-ship pier juts into the sparkling sea. It's the perfect place to start a tour of this quaint city. The **Visitors Center** (⊠ Waterfront, ☎ 340/772–0357), right on the pier, was built in the late 1700s; the two-story gallery was added in the 1800s. The building once served as the customs house; today you can stop in weekdays from 8 to 5 and pick up brochures or view the exhibits on St. Croix.

On July 3, 1848, 8,000 slaves marched on the red-brick **Ft. Frederik** to demand their freedom. Danish governor Peter von Scholten, fearing they would burn the town to the ground, stood up in his carriage parked in front of the fort and granted them their freedom. The fort, completed in 1760, houses a number of interesting historical exhibits as well as an art gallery and a display of police memorabilia. It's within earshot of the Visitors Center. ⊠ *Waterfront,* ☎ *340/772–2021.* ✉ *Free.* ☉ *Weekdays 8:30–4:30.*

St. Patrick's Roman Catholic church, complete with three turrets, was built in 1843 of coral. Wander inside, and you'll find woodwork handcrafted by Frederiksted artisans. The churchyard is filled with 18th-century gravestones. ⊠ *Prince St.*

St. Paul's Anglican Church (circa 1812) is a mix of Georgian and Gothic Revival architecture. The bell tower of exposed sandstone was added later. The simple interior has gleaming woodwork and a tray ceiling (it looks like an upside-down tray) popular in Caribbean architecture. ⊠ *Prince St.*

Built in 1839, **Apothecary Hall** is a good example of 19th-century architecture; its facade has both Gothic and Greek Revival elements. ⊠ *King Cross St.*

Stop at the **market** for fresh fruits and vegetables (be sure to wash or peel this produce before eating it) sold each morning, just as they have been for more than 200 years. ⊠ *Queen St.*

➒ Karl and Marie Lawaetz Museum. For a trip back in time, tour this circa-1750 farm. Owned by the prominent Lawaetz family since 1899, just after Karl arrived from Denmark, the lovely two-story house is in a valley at La Grange. A Lawaetz family member shows you the four-poster mahogany bed Karl and Marie shared, the china Marie painted, the family portraits, and the fruit trees that fed the family for several generations. Initially a sugar plantation, it was subsequently used to raise cattle and produce. ⊠ *Estate Little La Grange, Rte. 76, Mahogany Rd.,* ☎ *340/772–1539.* ▱ *$6.* ☉ *Wed.–Sun. 10–4.*

➓ St. Croix Leap. This workshop sits in the heart of the rain forest, about a 15-minute drive from Frederiksted. It sells a wide range of articles, including mirrors, tables, bread boards, and mahogany jewelry boxes crafted by local artisans. ⊠ *Rte. 76,* ☎ *340/772–0421.* ☉ *Weekdays 8–5:30, Sat. 10–5.*

⓭ St. George Village Botanical Gardens. At this 17-acre estate you'll find lush, fragrant flora amid the ruins of a 19th-century sugarcane plantation village. There are miniature versions of each ecosystem on St. Croix, from a semiarid cactus grove to a verdant rain forest. ⊠ *Turn north off Rte. 70 at sign, Kingshill,* ☎ *340/692–2874,* WEB *www.sgvbg.com.* ▱ *$6.* ☉ *9–5.*

⓫ West End Salt Pond. A bird-watcher's delight, this salt pond attracts a vast variety of winged creatures, including flamingos. ⊠ *Veteran's Shore Dr.*

ST. JOHN

Updated by
Lynda Lohr

Beautiful and largely undisturbed St. John is 3 mi (5 km) east of St. Thomas across the Pillsbury Sound (a 20-minute ferry ride from Red Hook). In 1956 Laurance Rockefeller, who founded the Caneel Bay Resort, donated ⅔ of St. John's 20 square mi (53 square km) to the United States as a national park. Because of this, the island comes close to realizing that travel-brochure dream of "an unspoiled tropical paradise." It's covered with vegetation, including a bay-tree forest that once supplied St. Thomas with the raw material for its fragrant bay rum. Along St. John's north shore, clean, gleaming white-sand beaches fringe bay after bay, each full of iridescent water perfect for swimming, fishing, snorkeling, diving, and underwater photography.

In 1675 Jorgen Iverson claimed the unsettled island for Denmark. The British residents of nearby Tortola, however, considered St. John theirs, and when a small party of Danes from St. Thomas moved onto the uninhabited island, the British "invited" them to leave (which they did). Despite this, in 1717 a group of Danish planters founded the first permanent settlement at Coral Bay. The question of who owned St. John wasn't settled until 1762, when Britain decided that maintaining good relations with Denmark was more important than keeping St. John.

By 1728 St. John had 87 plantations and a population of 123 whites and 677 blacks. By 1733 there were more than 1,000 slaves working more than 100 plantations. In that year the island was hit by a drought, hurricanes, and a plague of insects that destroyed the summer crops.

Everyone felt the threat of famine, particularly the slaves, whose living and working conditions were already harsh. Sensing the growing desperation, the landowners enacted even more severe measures in a misguided attempt to keep control. On November 23 the slaves revolted. With great military prowess, they captured the fort at Coral Bay, took control of the island, and held on to it for six months. During this time nearly a quarter of the island's population—black and white—was killed. The rebellion was eventually put down by 100 Danish militia and 220 Creole troops brought in from Martinique. Slavery continued until 1848, when slaves in St. Croix marched on Frederiksted to demand their freedom from the Danish government. After emancipation, St. John fell into decline, with its inhabitants eking out a living on small farms. Life continued in much the same way until the national park was established in 1956 and tourism became an industry.

Today St. John may well be the most racially integrated of the three USVI. Its 5,000 residents, black and white, have a strong sense of community that seems rooted in a desire to protect the island's natural beauty. Cruz Bay, the administrative capital, is home to the Virgin Islands National Park Visitors Center and a few small shopping centers. It's more a small West Indian village (calm except when cruise ships arrive) than a major urban hub, and its residents want to keep it that way. When the government tried to install the island's first traffic light here, the citizens successfully opposed it, claiming it would change the character of the island and do little to help traffic. The consensus that the island's natural resources are sacrosanct may be curbing excesses on private land as well. Except for Cruz Bay, most of St. John—even areas outside the national park—still has a natural, undeveloped feel to it. Here you can truly escape the pressures of modern life for a day, a week—perhaps, forever.

Lodging

St. John doesn't have many beachfront hotels, but that's a small price to pay for all the pristine sand. However, the island's two world-class resorts—Caneel Bay Resort and the Westin Resort, St. John—*are* on the beach. Sandy, white beaches string out along the north coast, which is popular with sunbathers and snorkelers and is the home to the Caneel Bay Resort and Cinnamon and Maho Bay campgrounds. Most villas are in the residential south shore area, a 15-minute drive from the north shore beaches. If you head east you'll come to the laid-back community of Coral Bay, where you'll find a few villas and cottages. A stay outside of Coral Bay will be peaceful and quiet.

If you're looking for West Indian–village charm, there are a few inns in Cruz Bay. Just know that when bands play at any of the town's bars (some of which stay open till the wee hours), the noise can be a problem. Your choice of accommodations also includes condominiums and cottages near town; two campgrounds, both at the edges of beautiful beaches (bring bug repellent); ecoresorts; and luxurious villas, often with a pool or a hot tub (sometimes both), and a stunning view.

If your lodging comes with a fully equipped kitchen, you'll be happy to know that St. John's handful of grocery stores sells everything from the basics to sun-dried tomatoes and green chilies—though the prices will take your breath away. If you're on a budget, consider bringing some staples (pasta, canned goods, paper products) from home. Hotel rates throughout the island, though considered expensive by some, do include endless privacy and access to most water sports.

For approximate costs, *see* the lodging price chart *in* St. Thomas.

Hotels and Inns

$$$$ ⊞ **Caneel Bay Resort.** Set on 170 lush peninsular acres—originally part
★   of the Danish West India Company's Durloo plantation—Caneel Bay
Resort mixes a good bit of peace and quiet into its luxurious air. You
won't find crowds or glitz; your room won't have a TV, or even a phone
(though management will loan you a cellular). Instead, you'll discover
spacious, restful rooms that are open to the breezes and are tastefully
decorated with tropical furnishings; seven beaches, each more gorgeous
than the last; and an attentive staff that will fill your every need. ⊠
Rte. 20 (Box 720), Cruz Bay, 00830, ☎ *340/776–6111 or 888/767–
3966,* FAX *340/693–8280,* WEB *www.canelbay.com. 166 rooms. 4 restaurants, air-conditioning, 11 tennis courts, beach, dive shop, dock,
snorkeling, windsurfing, boating, children's programs, meeting rooms.
AE, DC, MC, V. EP, FAP, MAP.*

$$$$ ⊞ **Westin Resort, St. John.** Spread over 47 acres adjacent to Great Cruz
Bay, the Westin has lushly planted gardens, a pool, a beach (the swimming is good), and enough amenities to make stepping off the grounds
unnecessary. If you want to get out and about, though, taxi jaunts into
Cruz Bay are a breeze. Rooms have white spreads, rattan furniture,
and phones and computer ports for those who just *have* to keep in touch
with the world. Many rooms have views of boats bobbing in the
turquoise sea. You can keep very busy here if you like; perhaps play
some tennis in the morning, go windsurfing in the afternoon, and then
get a massage before heading to dinner in one of the restaurants.
Younger guests will appreciate the children's program. Guests at the
Westin Vacation Club, a condominium complex across the street, enjoy
all the hotel amenities. ⊠ *Rte. 104 (Box 8310), Cruz Bay, 00831,* ☎
340/693–8000 or 800/808–5020, FAX *340/693–8888,* WEB *www.thewest-
instjohnresort.com. 282 rooms. 3 restaurants, air-conditioning, in-
room data ports, refrigerators, pool, massage, 6 tennis courts, gym,
beach, dive shop, snorkeling, windsurfing, boating, fishing, shops,
children's programs, meeting rooms. AE, D, DC, MC, V. EP.*

$$$ ⊞ **Garden By the Sea Bed and Breakfast.** This cozy spot is an easy walk
from Cruz Bay. Its rooms are done in the hues of the sea and sky, and
white spreads and curtains provide pristine counterpoints. Enjoy views
of a salt pond and the sea as you enjoy your piña colada French toast
on the front porch. It's perfect for folks who enjoy peace and quiet–
there are no phones or TVs in the rooms, but each room does have a
small tabletop fountain. (If the gurgle of water over rocks annoys you,
the fountain has an off switch.) ⊠ *Enighed (Box 1469), Cruz Bay
00831,* ☎ FAX *340/779–4731,* WEB *www.gardenbythesea.com. 3 rooms.
Fans. No credit cards. BP.*

$$$ ⊞ **Harmony.** In the tree-covered hills adjacent to the Maho Bay Camps
is this Stanley Selengut ecotourism resort. The spacious two-story units
have the usual amenities—decks, sliding glass doors, living-dining
areas, great views. What makes this place unusual are the materials
used to build it. Though you can't tell when you look at them, the carpets are made of recycled milk cartons, the pristine white walls of old
newspapers. Energy for the low-wattage appliances is generated entirely by the wind and the sun, and each unit has a laptop computer
programmed to monitor energy consumption. Tile floors, undyed
cotton linens, and South American handicrafts create a decor that
seems in keeping with the ideals. There's a water-sports outfitter on
the beach. ⊠ *Maho Bay (Box 310), Cruz Bay, 00830,* ☎ *340/776–
6240, 212/472–9453, or 800/392–9004,* FAX *212/861–6210,* WEB
*www.mahobay.com. 12 units. Restaurant, beach, snorkeling, wind-
surfing. AE, D, MC, V. EP.*

St. John

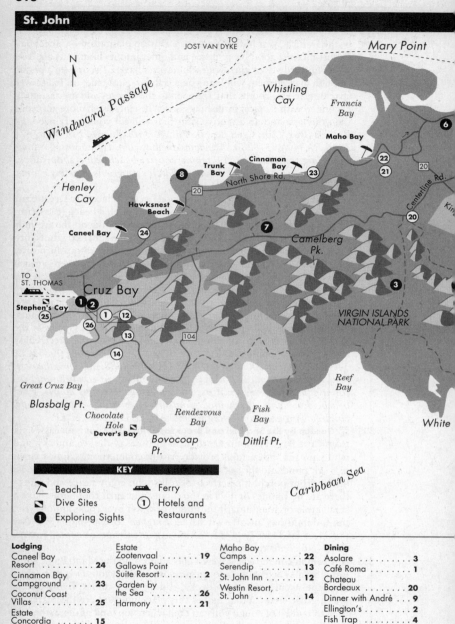

KEY

- ⟍ Beaches
- ◩ Dive Sites
- ❶ Exploring Sights
- 🚢 Ferry
- ① Hotels and Restaurants

Lodging
Caneel Bay Resort **24**
Cinnamon Bay Campground . . . **23**
Coconut Coast Villas **25**
Estate Concordia **15**
Estate Zootenvaal **19**
Gallows Point Suite Resort **2**
Garden by the Sea **26**
Harmony **21**

Maho Bay Camps **22**
Serendip **13**
St. John Inn **12**
Westin Resort, St. John **14**

Dining
Asolare **3**
Café Roma **1**
Chateau Bordeaux **20**
Dinner with André . . . **9**
Ellington's **2**
Fish Trap **4**
La Tapa **10**
Lime Inn **5**

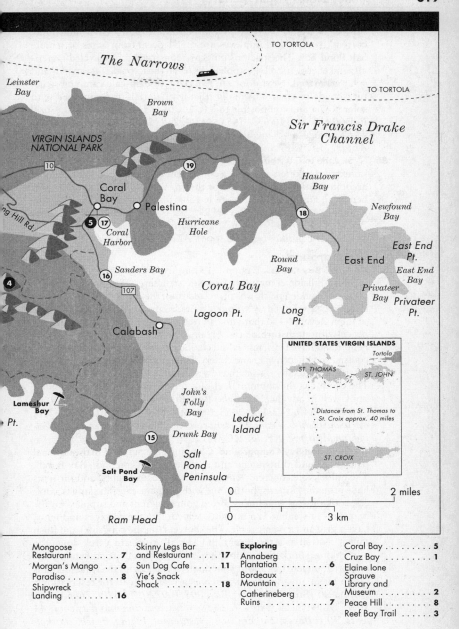

TO TORTOLA

The Narrows

Leinster Bay

TO TORTOLA

Brown Bay

VIRGIN ISLANDS NATIONAL PARK

10

Coral Bay

Palestina

Sir Francis Drake Channel

Haulover Bay

19

18

Newfound Bay

ng Hill Rd.

5   17

Coral Harbor

Hurricane Hole

East End Pt.

East End

East End Bay

4

Sanders Bay

16

107

Round Bay

Coral Bay

Privateer Bay

Privateer Pt.

Calabash

Lagoon Pt.

Long Pt.

UNITED STATES VIRGIN ISLANDS

Tortola

ST. THOMAS

ST. JOHN

John's Folly Bay

Leduck Island

Distance from St. Thomas to St. Croix approx. 40 miles

Lameshur Bay

15

Drunk Bay

ST. CROIX

Pt.

Salt Pond Peninsula

Salt Pond Bay

0   2 miles

Ram Head

0   3 km

Mongoose Restaurant 7	Skinny Legs Bar and Restaurant 17	**Exploring**
Morgan's Mango 6	Sun Dog Cafe 11	Annaberg Plantation 6
Paradiso 8	Vie's Snack Shack 18	Bordeaux Mountain 4
Shipwreck Landing 16		Catherineberg Ruins 7

Coral Bay 5
Cruz Bay 1
Elaine Ione Sprauve Library and Museum 2
Peace Hill 8
Reef Bay Trail 3

$$$ ⚐ **Estate Concordia.** The latest brainchild of Stanley Selengut, the developer of Maho Bay Camps and Harmony, these "environmentally correct" studios and duplexes are on 51 oceanfront acres of remote Salt Pond Bay. The spacious units are constructed of recycled materials, and energy for all the appliances (even the ice makers) is wind- and solar-generated. Next door are five eco-tents, upscale camping structures made of environmentally friendly materials and equipped with solar power and composting toilets. ⊠ *20–27 Estate Concordia, Coral Bay 00830,* ☎ *340/693–5855, 212/472–9453, or 800/392–9004,* FAX *212/861–6210,* WEB *www.mahobay.com. 20 units. Kitchenettes, pool. AE, D, MC, V. EP.*

$$ ⚐ **St. John Inn.** Within walking distance of Cruz Bay's shops and restaurants, this inn offers not only a convenient location but also affordable accommodations with a touch of charm. You might find a four-poster bed or an antique-style armoire in rooms painted in lush hues. ⊠ *Off Rte. 104 (Box 37), Cruz Bay, 00831,* ☎ *340/693–86888 or 800/666–7688,* FAX *340/693–9900,* WEB *www.stjohninn.com. 13 units. Kitchenettes, air-conditioning, fans, pool. AE, D, DC, MC, V. EP.*

Campgrounds

$$ ⚑ **Maho Bay Camps.** Eight mi (13 km) from Cruz Bay, this eco-camp is a lush hillside community of rustic structures. The 16×16-ft (5×5-m) tents (wooden platforms protected from the elements by canvas and screening) are linked by wooden stairs, ramps, and walkways—some of them elevated—so that you can trek around camp and down to the beach without disturbing the terrain. The tents sleep as many as four people and have beds, tables and chairs, electric lamps, propane stoves, coolers, and kitchenware and cutlery. Though all the units are surrounded by tropical greenery, some have spectacular views of the Caribbean. The camp has the chummy feel of a retreat, making it very popular; book well in advance. ⊠ *Maho Bay (Box 310), Cruz Bay, 00830,* ☎ *340/776–6240, 212/472–9453, or 800/392–9004;* FAX *212/861–6210,* WEB *www.mahobay.com. 114 tent cottages. Restaurant, beach, snorkeling, windsurfing. AE, D, MC, V. EP.*

$ ⚑ **Cinnamon Bay Campground.** Camping here puts you in the national park, surrounded by jungle and at the edge of Cinnamon Bay Beach. The unlockable concrete "cottages" have electric lights, and the tents have propane lanterns; both come with propane camping stoves, coolers, cooking gear, and linens. Bring your own tent and supplies for the bare sites (a steal at $25 a night), which, like the cottages and tents, have a grill and a picnic table. The showers (on the cool side) and flush toilets, as well as a restaurant and a small store, are a trek down the hill. Hiking, snorkeling, swimming, and evening environmental or history programs are free and at your doorstep. Spaces for the winter months fill up far in advance (by as much as a year), so call for reservations. ⊠ *Rte. 20 (Box 720), Cruz Bay, 00830-0720,* ☎ *340/776–6330 or 800/539–9998,* FAX *340/776–6458,* WEB *www.cinnamonbay.com. 44 tents, 40 cottages, 26 bare sites. Restaurant, hiking, beach, snorkeling, windsurfing. AE, MC, V. EP.*

Condominiums and Cottages

Most of the island's condos are just minutes from the hustle and bustle of Cruz Bay, but you'll find cottages in more far-flung locations.

$$$$ ⚐ **Estate Zootenvaal.** Set at the far reaches of the island, this small complex provides modest cottages right at the water or across the street. It's a quiet spot perfect for people who like to sit in the chaise and read. ⊠ *Rte. 10, Hurricane Hole, Coral Bay, 00830,* ☎ *340/776–6321,* WEB *www.usviguide.com/zootenvaal. 3 units. Fans, kitchenettes, beach. No credit cards. EP.*

$$$$ ⊞ **Gallows Point Suite Resort.** These soft-gray buildings are clustered on a peninsula south of the Cruz Bay ferry dock. The upper-level apartments have loft bedrooms and good views. There's air-conditioning only in the first-floor units; the harborside villas get better trade winds, but they're also noisier. The entranceway is bridged by Ellington's restaurant, which serves delicious contemporary cuisine. ✉ *Gallows Point (Box 58), Cruz Bay 00831,* ☎ *340/776–6434; 800/323–7229 direct to hotel,* FAX *340/776–6520,* WEB *www.gallowspointresort.com. 52 rooms. Restaurant, air-conditioning, pool, beach, snorkeling. AE, MC, V. EP.*

$$$$ ⊞ **Coconut Coast Villas.** Within walking distance of Cruz Bay's shops and restaurants, this small condominium complex sits so close to the water you'll fall asleep to the sound of waves. ✉ *Turner Bay (Box 618), Cruz Bay 00831,* ☎ *340/693–9100 or 800/858–7989,* FAX *340/779–4157,* WEB *www.coconutcoast.com. 9 units. Air-conditioning, kitchenettes, pool, beach. MC, V. EP.*

$$$ ⊞ **Serendip.** This complex offers modest units on lush grounds with lovely views. You definitely need a rental car if you stay here, though; it's about 1 mi (1½ km) up a killer hill out of Cruz Bay. If air-conditioning is important to you, be sure to mention it when booking, as some units have only ceiling fans. ✉ *Enighed (Box 273), Cruz Bay, 00831,* ☎ *340/776–6646 or 888/800–6445,* WEB *www.st-john.com/serendip. 10 units. Air-conditioning, fans, kitchenettes. MC, V. EP.*

Villas

Tucked here and there between Cruz Bay and Coral Bay are about 350 villas (prices range from $ to $$$$). With pools and/or hot tubs, full kitchens, and living areas, they provide a home away from home. They're perfect for couples and extended groups of families or friends. You'll need a car since most are up in the hills (very few are at the beach). Villa managers usually pick you up at the dock, arrange for your rental car, and answer questions you have upon arrival as well as during your stay.

To rent a luxury villa, contact one of the following rental agents:

Caribbean Villas and Resorts (✉ Box 458, 00831, ☎ 340/776–6152 or 800/338–0987, FAX 340/779–4044, WEB www.caribbeanvilla.com) handles condo rentals for Cruz Views, Lavender Hill, and Suite St. John as well as for private villas. **Catered To, Inc.** (✉ Box 704, 00830, ☎ 340/776–6641, FAX 340/693–8191, WEB www.cateredto.com) has luxury homes in Great Cruz Bay and Chocolate Hole areas. **Destination St. John** (✉ Box 8306, 00831, ☎ FAX 340/779–4647 or ☎ 800/562–1901, WEB www.destinationstjohn.com) manages villas within a 10-minute drive of Cruz Bay. **Park Isle Villas** (✉ Box 1263, 00831, ☎ FAX 340/693–8261 or ☎ 800/416–1205, WEB www.batteryhill.com) handles Battery Hill and Villa Caribe condos. **Private Homes for Private Vacations** (✉ Mamey Peak, 00830, ☎ FAX 340/776–6876, WEB www.privatehomesvi.com) has homes across the island. **Star Villa** (✉ Box 599, 00830, ☎ 340/776–6704, FAX 340/776–6183, WEB starvillas.com) has cozy villas just outside Cruz Bay. **Vacation Homes** (✉ Box 272, 00831, ☎ 340/776–6094, FAX 340/693–8455, WEB vacationstjohn.com) has luxury homes from outside Cruz Bay to mid-island. **Vacation Vistas** (✉ Box 476, 00831, ☎ 340/776–6462, WEB www.vacationvistas.com) manages villas in the Chocolate Hole and Great Cruz Bay area. **Windspree** (✉ 6-2-1A Estate Carolina,00830, ☎ 340/693–5423, FAX 340/693–5623, WEB www.windspree.com) handles villas mainly in the Coral Bay area.

Dining

The cuisine on St. John seems to get better every year, with culinary school–trained chefs vying to see who can come up with the most imaginative dishes. There are restaurants to suit every taste and budget—

from the elegant establishments at Caneel Bay Resort (where men may be required to wear a jacket at dinner) to the casual in-town eateries of Cruz Bay. For quick lunches try the West Indian food stands in Cruz Bay Park and across from the post office. The cooks prepare fried chicken legs, pates (meat- and fish-filled pastries), and callaloo.

For approximate costs, *see* the dining price chart *in* St. Thomas.

Bordeaux Mountain

CONTEMPORARY

$$$$ ✕ **Chateau Bordeaux.** This rustic restaurant with a to-die-for view is practically a tree house, albeit one that's made very elegant and romantic by wrought-iron chandeliers, lace tablecloths, and antiques. You might start with the ostrich stuffed with a roasted portabello mushrooms, sun-dried cherries, and roasted pine nuts; then segue into New Zealand rack of lamb with a honey-Dijon-pecan crust in a port wine cream sauce; or salmon crusted with black pepper and lemon zest and finished with a caviar and balsamic vinaigrette. Save room for dessert—the fresh berry cups with Chambord and caramel are to die for. The comprehensive, moderately priced wine list is predictably strong on Bordeaux reds. ⊠ *Rte. 10,* ☎ *340/776–6611. AE, MC, V. No lunch.*

Coral Bay and Environs

AMERICAN

$ ✕ **Skinny Legs Bar and Restaurant.** Sailors who live aboard boats an-
★ chored just off shore and an eclectic coterie of residents gather for lunch and dinner at this funky spot. If owners Doug Sica and Moe Chabuz are around, take a gander at their gams; you'll see where the restaurant got its name. It's a great place for burgers, fish sandwiches, and watching whatever sports event is on cable TV. ⊠ *Rte. 107 (near the Coral Bay dinghy dock),* ☎ *340/779–4982. AE, D, MC, V.*

CARIBBEAN

$ ✕ **Vie's Snack Shack.** Vie Mahabir conjures up what may well be the best conch fritters in all of St. John. They're crispy on the outside and creamy on the inside, with lots of conch. And they're not so spicy that you need a gallon of water to cool your throat. The coconut tarts, what mainlanders call a pie, add a sweet end to your alfresco meal. Take a swim afterward at Vie's gorgeous white strand just across the road. ⊠ *Rte. 10, Hansen Bay,* ☎ *340/693–5033. No credit cards.* ⊘ *Lunch only.*

ECLECTIC

$$ ✕ **Shipwreck Landing.** Start with one of the house drinks, perhaps a fresh-squeezed concoction of lime, coconut, and rum, then move on to hearty taco salads, fried shrimp, teriyaki chicken, and conch frit-ters. The birds keep up a lively chatter in the bougainvillea that sur-rounds you at this open-air restaurant, and there's live music on Wednesday and Sunday nights in season. ⊠ *Rte. 107,* ☎ *340/693–5640. AE, MC, V.*

Cruz Bay

CONTEMPORARY

$$$$ ✕ **Ellington's.** This peaceful, appealing spot extends out onto the sec-ond-story veranda of the Gallows Point Suite Resort's central build-ing. The outside tables are particularly quiet and romantic. You might start with the jumbo shrimp cooked in sweet coconut and served with mango sauce, or the seafood chowder. Entrées include sea scallops with garlic and olive oil, aïoli, parmesan cheese, and paprika; swordfish scampi; filet mignon; and fresh lobster. For dessert the banana–choco-late chip cake or the chocolate brownie are good bets. ⊠ *Gallows Point (5-min walk from Cruz Bay),* ☎ *340/693–8490. AE, MC, V. No lunch.*

$$$ ✕ **Lime Inn.** This open-air restaurant attracts mainland transplants who call St. John home as well as visitors who come for the congenial atmosphere and good food. There are shrimp and steak dishes and such specials as pistachio chicken breasts with plantains and Thai curry cream sauce. On Wednesday night there's an all-you-can-eat shrimp feast, and fresh lobster is the specialty every night. ✉ *Downtown, east of Chase Manhattan Bank,* ☎ *340/776–6425. AE, MC, V. Closed Sun.*

$$$ ✕ **Morgan's Mango.** A long flight of stairs leads you to this alfresco eatery, but good food awaits you. Although fish is the specialty—try the voodoo snapper topped with a many-fruit salsa—the chef also creates a vegetarian platter with black beans, fried plantains, salad, and even an ear of corn. ✉ *Across from V.I. National Park's Visitors Center,* ☎ *340/693–8141. AE, MC, V. No lunch.*

<u>ECLECTIC</u>

$$$ ✕ **Paradiso.** This popular spot is on the upper level of the island's largest
★ shopping complex. The menu is a mix of everything from beef sirloin with an herb-mustard crust to garlic rosemary-basted mahimahi. You can dine indoors, in the comfort of air-conditioning, or outdoors on a small terrace that overlooks the street. ✉ *Mongoose Junction shopping center,* ☎ *340/693–8899. AE, MC, V.*

$$$ ✕ **La Tapa.** Locals congregate here to feast on tapas and sip sangria. Although street-side tables let you watch the world go by, they're a little noisy; head inside for a quiet, bistrolike atmosphere. Owner Alex Ewald dishes up a changing menu of delicious soups, tapas as lighter fare or dinner, and yummy desserts. The buffalo mozzarella served with tomatoes and basil is made in her own tiny kitchen. ✉ *Across from Scotia Bank on unnamed street that heads inland from ferry dock,* ☎ *340/693–7755. AE, MC, V. No lunch.*

$$ ✕ **Fish Trap.** The rooms and terraces here all open to the breezes and buzz with a mix of locals and visitors. Chef Aaron Willis conjures up such tasty appetizers as conch fritters and Fish Trap chowder (a creamy soup of snapper, white wine, paprika, and secret spices). The menu also includes an interesting pasta of the day, steak and chicken dishes, and hamburgers. ✉ *Downtown, next to Our Lady of Mount Carmel Church,* ☎ *340/693–9994. AE, D, MC, V. No lunch. Closed Mon.*

$$ ✕ **Mongoose Restaurant.** Open to the breezes, this restaurant attracts an eclectic local crowd that tends to drop by for lunch at the bar. They aren't the only ones: tiny yellow birds peck at the wine glasses (full of sugar) that are used as feeders. For lunch there are hamburgers, sandwiches, and salads; for dinner, chicken, pork chops, and fish. ✉ *Mongoose Junction shopping center,* ☎ *340/693–8677. AE, MC, V.*

$ ✕ **Sun Dog Cafe.** You'll find an unusual assortment of dishes at this charming restaurant tucked into a courtyard in the upper reaches of the Mongoose Junction shopping center. Kudos to the white artichoke pizza with roasted garlic, artichoke hearts, mozzarella cheese, and capers. The Jamaican jerk chicken sub or the black bean quesadilla are also good choices. ✉ *Mongoose Junction shopping center,* ☎ *340/693–8340. AE, MC, V. ☉ Lunch only.*

<u>FRENCH</u>

$$$ ✕ **Dinner with Andre.** At night, this unassuming spot—it spends its days as Chilly Billy's sandwich joint—metamorphoses into a bistro with true French fare. If you aren't convinced, try the snails cooked in a sherry cream demi-glace or frog legs in a garlic cream sauce before moving on to the magret de canard, a breast of duck topped with Roquefort cheese and crushed walnuts. Desserts are just as rich (the profiteroles topped with Belgium chocolate sauce are yummy). ✉ *Lumberyard Shopping Complex,* ☎ *340/693–8708. MC, V. No lunch. Closed Sun.*

$$ ✕ **Café Roma.** This casual second-floor restaurant in the heart of Cruz Bay is *the* place for traditional Italian cuisine: lasagna, spaghetti and meatballs, chicken Parmesan. There is also a variety of excellent pizzas. Polenta cake with raspberry sauce is a dessert specialty. ✉ *Downtown on Vesta Gade,*☎ *340/776–6524. MC, V. No lunch.*

PAN-ASIAN

$$$$ ✕ **Asolare.** Contemporary Asian cuisine dominates the menu at this
★ elegant open-air eatery in an old St. John house. Come early and relax over drinks while you enjoy the sunset over the harbor. Start with an appetizer, say, pork spring rolls served with a cucumber salad. Entrées include such delights as grilled yellowfin tuna served with a sweet pepper and scallion rice cake and a bok choy and carrot salad. If you still have room for dessert, try the chocolate pyramid, a luscious cake with homemade ice cream melting in the middle. ✉ *Caneel Hill, Rte. 20,* ☎ *340/779–4747. AE, MC, V. No lunch.*

Beaches

St. John is blessed with many beaches, and all of them fall into the good, great, and don't-tell-anyone-else-about-this-place categories. Those along the north shore are all within the national park. Some are more developed than others—and all are crowded on weekends, holidays, and in high season—but by and large they're still pristine. Beaches along the south and eastern shores are quiet and isolated.

Caneel Bay. Caneel Bay is actually a catch-all name for seven white-sand north-shore beaches, six of which can be reached only by water if you aren't a guest at the Caneel Bay Resort. (Access to beaches is a civil right in the USVI, but access to land that leads to the beaches is not.) The seventh, **Caneel Beach,** is open to the public and is easy to reach from the main entrance of the resort; just ask for directions at the gatehouse. Nonguests can also dine at the three of the hotel's four restaurants and browse in its gift shop.

Cinnamon Bay. This long, sandy beach faces beautiful cays and abuts the national park campground. The facilities are open to the public and include cool showers, toilets, a commissary, and a restaurant. You can rent water-sports equipment here—a good thing because there's excellent snorkeling off the point to the right; look for the big angelfish and large schools of purple triggerfish. Afternoons on Cinnamon Bay can be windy, so arrive early to beat the gusts. The Cinnamon Bay hiking trail begins across the road from the beach parking lot; the ruins of a sugar mill mark the trailhead. There are actually two paths here: a level nature trail (signs along it identify the flora) that loops through the woods and passes an old Danish cemetery, and a steep trail that starts where the road bends past the ruins and heads straight up to Route 10.

Hawksnest Beach. Sea-grape trees line this narrow beach, and there are rest rooms, cooking grills, and a covered shed for picnicking. It's the closest beach to town, so it's often crowded.

Lameshur Bay. This nifty beach is toward the end of a very long dirt road on the southeast coast. It offers solitude, good snorkeling, and a chance to spy on some pelicans. The ruins of the old plantation are a five-minute walk down the road past the beach.

Maho Bay. This popular beach is below the Maho Bay Camps—a wonderful hillside enclave of tents. The campground offers informal talks and slide and film presentations on nature, environmentally friendly living, and whatever else crosses the manager's mind. In spring, jazz and jungle harmonize during a music series in the outdoor pavilion.

Salt Pond Bay. If you're adventurous, this somewhat rocky beach on the scenic southeastern coast—next to Coral Bay and rugged Drunk Bay—is worth exploring. It's a short hike down a hill from the parking lot, and the only facilities are an outhouse and a few picnic tables scattered about. There are interesting tidal pools, and the snorkeling is good. Take special care to leave nothing valuable in your car; reports of thefts are common.

Trunk Bay. St. John's most-photographed beach is also the preferred spot for beginning snorkelers because of its underwater trail. (Cruise-ship passengers interested in snorkeling for a day come here, so if you're looking for seclusion, check cruise-ship schedules in *St. Thomas This Week* before heading here.) Crowded or not, this stunning beach is sure to please. There are changing rooms, a snack bar, picnic tables, a gift shop, phones, lockers, and snorkeling equipment rentals.

Outdoor Activities and Sports

BOATING AND SAILING

For a speedy trip to offshore cays and remote beaches, a powerboat is a necessity. Rates start at around $300 per day with gas and oil charges depending on how much you use. More leisurely day sails to islands not far offshore or longer sails to points east are also possibilities. If you're boatless, book with one of the island's agents. Most day sails include lunch, beverages, and at least one stop to snorkel. A full-day sail with lunch runs around $90 per person.

Adventures in Paradise (☎ 340/779–4527), across from the post office in Cruz Bay, books fishing, sailing and scuba trips on most of the island's charter boats. **Connections** (✉ Cruz Bay, a block up from the ferry dock and catercorner from Chase Manhattan Bank, ☎ 340/776–6922) pairs you up with the sailboat that suits you. Have simple tastes? The smiling staff can help. If luxury is more your style, they can book that, too. **Ocean Runner** (☎ 340/693–8809), on the waterfront in Cruz Bay, rents one- and two-engine boats for fast trips around the island's seas. **Proper Yachts** (☎ 340/776–6256) books day sails and longer charters on its fleet of luxury yachts that depart from Caneel Bay Resort.

FISHING

Well-kept charter boats head out to the north and south drops or troll along the inshore reefs. The captains usually provide bait, drinks, and lunch, but you'll need your hat and sunscreen. Fishing charters run around $100 per hour per person. The **Charter Boat Center** (☎ 340/775–7990), in Red Hook on St. Thomas, also arranges fishing trips for folks in St. John. **Gone Ketchin'** (☎ 340/693–8657), in St. John, arranges trips with old salt Wally Leopold. **St. John World Class Anglers** (☎ 340/779–4281) offers light-tackle shore and offshore half- and full-day trips.

HIKING

Although it's fun to go hiking with a Virgin Islands National Park guide, don't be afraid to strike out on your own. To find a hike that suits your ability, stop by the park's visitors center in Cruz Bay and pick up the free trail guide; it details points of interest, dangers, trail lengths, and estimated hiking times. Although the park staff recommends pants to protect against thorns and insects, most people hike in shorts because pants are too hot. Wear sturdy shoes or hiking boots even if you're hiking to the beach. Don't forget to bring water and insect repellent.

The **Virgin Islands National Park** (☎ 340/776–6201) maintains more than 20 trails on the north and south shores and offers guided hikes along popular routes. A full-day trip to Reef Bay is a must; it's an easy hike through lush and dry forest, past the ruins of an old plantation, and to a sugar factory adjacent to the beach. Take the public Vitran bus or a taxi to the trailhead, where you'll meet a ranger who will serve as your guide. The park provides a boat ride back to Cruz Bay for $15 to save you the walk back up the mountain. The schedule changes from season to season; call for times and reservations, which are essential.

HORSEBACK RIDING

Clip-clop along the island's byways for a slower-pace tour of St. John. **Carolina Corral** (☎ 340/693–5778) offers horseback, donkey-back, and donkey-cart rides as well as riding lessons. Rates start at $45 for a 1-hour ride.

SCUBA DIVING AND SNORKELING

Although just about every beach has nice snorkeling—Trunk Bay, Cinnamon Bay, and Waterlemon Cay at Leinster Bay get the most praise—you'll need a boat to head out to the more remote snorkeling locations and the best scuba spots. Sign on with any of the island's water-sports operators to get to spots further from St. John. Their boats will take you to hot spots between St. John and St. Thomas, including the tunnels at **Thatch Cay,** the ledges at **Congo Cay,** and the wreck of the *General Rogers.* Dive off St. John at **Stephens Cay,** a short boat ride out of Cruz Bay, where fish swim around the reefs as you float downward. At **Devers Bay,** on St. John's south shore, fish dart about in colorful schools.

Count on paying $55 for a one-tank dive and $75 for a two-tank dive. Rates include equipment and a tour. **Cruz Bay Watersports** (☎ 340/776–6234) has three locations: in Cruz Bay, at the Westin Resort, and in the Palm Plaza Shopping Center. Owners Marcus and Patty Johnston offer regular reef, wreck, and night dives and USVI and BVI snorkel tours. **Low Key Watersports** (☎ 340/693–8999 or 800/835–7718), at Wharfside Village, offers PADI certification and resort courses, one- and two-tank dives, and specialty courses.

SEA KAYAKING

Poke around crystal bays and explore undersea life from a sea kayak. **Arawak Expeditions** (☎ 340/693–8312 or 800/238–8687) professional guides use traditional kayaks to ply coastal waters. Prices start at $40 for a half-day trip.

TENNIS

With hot weather the norm, tennis players take to the courts in the morning or late afternoon. The **Westin Resort, St. John** (⊠ Rte. 104, ☎ 340/693–8000), has six lighted courts. Nonguests are welcome to play here for a fee of $15 an hour. The **public courts,** near the fire station in Cruz Bay, are lit until 10 PM and are available on a first-come, first-served basis.

WINDSURFING

Steady breezes and expert instruction make learning to windsurf a snap. Try **Cinnamon Bay Campground** (⊠ Rte. 20, ☎ 340/776–6330), where rentals are available for $20–$30 per hour. Lessons are available right at the waterfront; just look for the Windsurfers stacked up on the beach. The cost for a 1-hour lesson is about $60.

Shopping

Areas and Malls

You'll find luxury items and handicrafts on St. John. Most shops carry a little of this and a bit of that, so it pays to poke around. The Cruz Bay shopping district runs from **Wharfside Village,** just around the corner from the ferry dock, through the streets of town to North Shore Road and **Mongoose Junction,** an inviting shopping center with stonework walls (its name is a holdover from a time when those furry island creatures gathered at a garbage bin that was here). Steps connect the two sections of the center, which has unique upscale shops. Out on Route 104, stop in at **Palm Plaza** to explore its handful of gift and crafts shops. At the island's other end, you'll find a few stores—selling clothes, jewelry, and artwork—here and there from the village of **Coral Bay** to the small complex at **Shipwreck Landing.**

Specialty Items

ART

Coconut Coast Studios. This waterside shop, a five-minute walk from Cruz Bay, showcases the work of Elaine Estern. She specializes in undersea scenes. ⊠ *Frank Bay,* ☎ *340/776–6944.*

Bajo el Sol. A cooperative gallery, Bajo el Sol features Aimee Trayser's expressionistic Caribbean scenes, Les Anderson's island scenes in oil, Kat Sowa's watercolors, and works by a handful of other artists. ⊠ *Mongoose Junction,* ☎ *340/693–7070.*

BOOKS

MAPes MONDe. Here you'll find a huge selection of books on the Caribbean, including the exquisite-looking publications that are the hallmark of Virgin Islands publisher MAPes MONDe. You'll also find many reproductions of old maps as well as contemporary prints and greeting cards. ⊠ *Mongoose Junction,* ☎ *340/779–4545.*

National Park Headquarters. The headquarters sells several good histories of St. John, including *St. John Back Time,* by Ruth Hull Low and Rafael Lito Valls, and for linguists, Valls's *What a Pistarckle!*—an explanation of the colloquialisms that make up the local version of English (*pistarckle* is a Dutch Creole word that means "noise" or "din," which pretty much sums up the language here). ⊠ *At the Creek,* ☎ *340/776–6201.*

CLOTHING

Big Planet Adventure Outfitters. You knew when you arrived that some place on St. John would cater to the outdoor enthusiasts that hike up and down the island's trails. Well, this outdoor-clothing store is where you'll find the popular Noats sandals, along with colorful and durable cotton clothing and accessories by Patagonia, the North Face, Columbia, and others. The nearby **Little Planet** sells children's clothes, often made from such unlikely materials as recycled plastic bottles. ⊠ *Mongoose Junction,* ☎ *340/776–6638.*

Bougainvillea Boutique. If you want to look like you stepped out of the pages of the resort-wear spread in an upscale travel magazine, try this store. Owner Susan Stair carries *very* chic men's and women's resort wear, straw hats, leather handbags, and fine gift items. ⊠ *Mongoose Junction,* ☎ *340/693–7190.*

The Clothing Studio. Several talented artists hand-paint original designs on clothing for all members of the family. You'll find T-shirts, beach cover-ups, pants, shorts, and even bathing suits with beautiful hand-painted creations. ⊠ *Mongoose Junction,* ☎ *340/776–6585.*

Jolly Dog. Stock up on the stuff you forgot to pack at this store. Sarongs in cotton and rayon, beach towels with tropical motifs, and hats and T-shirts sporting the Jolly Dog logs fill the shelves. ⊠ *Shipwreck Landing, Coral Bay,* ☎ *340/693–5333.*

St. John Editions. Shop here for nifty cotton shifts that go from beach to dinner with a change of shoes and accessories. Owner Ann Soper also carries attractive straw hats and inexpensive jewelry. ⊠ *North Shore Rd., Cruz Bay,* ☎ *340/693–8444.*

If you're renting a villa, condo, or cottage and doing your own cooking, there are several good places to shop for food; just be aware that prices are much higher than those at home.

Marina Market usually has the best prices, but its selection is small. ⊠ *Rte. 104, Cruz Bay,* ☎ *340/779–4401.*

Starfish Market is the island's largest store and usually has the best selection of meat, fish and produce. ⊠ *Marketplace Shopping Center, Rte 104, Cruz Bay,* ☎ *340/779–4949.*

Tropicale has great take-out meals in addition to its rather smallish selection of groceries. ⊠ *Palm Plaza, Rte. 104, Cruz Bay,* ☎ *340/693–7474.*

GIFTS

Bamboula. Owner Jo Sterling travels the Caribbean and the world to find unusual housewares, rugs, bedspreads, accessories, shoes, and men's and women's clothes for this multicultural boutique. ⊠ *Mongoose Junction,* ☎ *340/693–8699.*

The Canvas Factory. If you're a true shopper who needs an extra bag to carry all your treasures home, this store offers every kind of tote and carrier imaginable—from simple bags to suitcases with numerous zippered compartments—all made of canvas, naturally. It also sells great canvas hats. ⊠ *Mongoose Junction,* ☎ *340/776–6196.*

Donald Schnell Pottery. In addition to pottery, this place sells unique hand-blown glass, wind chimes, kaleidoscopes, fanciful water fountains, and more. Your purchases can be shipped worldwide. ⊠ *Mongoose Junction,* ☎ *340/776–6420.*

Fabric Mill. Shop here for handmade dolls, place mats, napkins, and batik wraps. Or take home a bolt of tropical brights from the upholstery-fabric selection. ⊠ *Mongoose Junction,* ☎ *340/776–6194.*

Pink Papaya. This store is the home of longtime Virgin Islands resident M. L. Etre's well-known artwork plus a huge collection of one-of-a-kind gift items, including bright tablecloths, unusual trays, dinnerware, and unique tropical jewelry. ⊠ *Lemon Tree Mall, Cruz Bay,* ☎ *340/693–8535.*

Wicker, Wood and Shells. Shop the second floor of this store for lovely sculptures and other objects d'art, all with a tropical theme. On the first floor, you'll find the island's best selection of greeting cards, notepaper, and other interesting items to tuck in your suitcase for friends back home. ⊠ *Mongoose Junction,* ☎ *340/776–6909.*

JEWELRY

Blue Carib Gems. Here you'll find custom-made jewelry, loose gemstones, and old coins as well as a small art gallery. ⊠ *Wharfside Village,* ☎ *340/693–8299.*

Caravan Gallery. Owner Radha Speer creates much of the unusual jewelry you'll find here. And the more you look, the more you see—folk art, tribal art, and masks for sale cover the walls and tables, making this a great place to browse. ⊠ *Mongoose Junction,* ☎ *340/779–4566.*

Colombian Emeralds. This branch of a St. Thomas store has high-quality emeralds and also sells rubies, diamonds, and other jewels set in attractive gold and silver settings. ⊠ *Mongoose Junction,* ☎ *340/776–6007.*

Free Bird Creations. Head here for the unique handcrafted jewelry—earrings, bracelets, pendants, chains—as well as the good selection of waterproof watches great for your excursions to the beach. ⊠ *Wharfside Village,* ☎ *340/693–8625.*

R&I Patton Goldsmiths. Rudy and Irene Patton design most of the unique silver and gold jewelry in this shop. The rest comes from various jeweler friends of theirs. Sea fans (those large, lacy plants that sway with the ocean's currents) in filigreed silver, lapis set in long drops of gold, starfish and hibiscus pendants in silver or gold, and gold sand dollar–shape charms and earrings are tempting choices. ⊠ *Mongoose Junction*, ☎ 340/776–6548.

Nightlife

St. John isn't the place to go for glitter and all-night partying. Still, after-hours Cruz Bay can be a lively little village in which to dine, drink, dance, chat, or flirt. Notices posted on the bulletin board outside the Connections telephone center—up the street from the ferry dock in Cruz Bay—or listings in the island's two small newspapers (the *St. John Times* and *Tradewinds*) will keep you apprised of special events, comedy nights, movies, and the like.

After a sunset drink at **Ellington's** (⊠ Gallows Point Suite Resort, ☎ 340/693–8490), up the hill from Cruz Bay, you can stroll here and there in town (much is clustered around the small waterfront park). Many of the young people from the U.S. mainland who live and work on St. John will be out sipping and socializing, too.

Outside town, **Caneel Bay Resort** (⊠ Rte. 20, ☎ 340/776–6111) usu-ally has entertainment (generally, of the quiet calypso variety) several nights a week in season. There's calypso and reggae on Wednesday and Friday at **Fred's** (⊠ Cruz Bay, ☎ 340/776–6363). The **Inn at Tamarind Court** (⊠ Rte. 104, ☎ 340/776–6378) serves up country rock on Fri-day. At Coral Bay, on the far side of the island, check out the action at **Skinny Legs Bar and Restaurant** (⊠ Rte. 107, ☎ 340/779–4982). Young folks like to gather at **Woody's** (⊠ Cruz Bay, ☎ 340/779–4625). Its sidewalk tables provide a close-up view of Cruz Bay's action.

Exploring St. John

St. John is an easy place to explore. One road runs along the north shore, another across the center of the mountains. There are a few roads that branch off here and there, but it's hard to get lost. Pick up a map at the visitor center before you start out, and you'll have no problems. Few residents remember the route numbers, so have your map in hand if you stop to ask for directions. Bring along a swimsuit for stops at some of the most beautiful beaches in the world. You can spend all day or just a couple of hours exploring, but be advised that the roads are narrow and wind up and down steep hills, so don't expect to get anywhere in a hurry. There are lunch spots at Cinnamon Bay and in Coral Bay, or you can do what the locals do—picnic. The grocery stores in Cruz Bay sell Styrofoam coolers just for this purpose.

If you plan to do a lot of touring, renting a car will be cheaper and will give you much more freedom than relying on taxis, which are re-luctant to go anywhere until they have a full load of passengers. Al-though you may be tempted by an open-air Suzuki or Jeep, a conventional car can get you just about everywhere on the paved roads, and you'll be able to lock up your valuables. You may be able to share a van or open-air vehicle (called a safari bus) with other passengers on a tour of scenic mountain trails, secret coves, and eerie bush-covered ruins.

Numbers in the margin correspond to points of interest on the St. John map.

Sights to See

❻ **Annaberg Plantation.** In the 18th-century sugar plantations dotted the steep hills of the USVI. Slaves and free Danes and Dutchmen toiled to harvest the cane that was used to create sugar, molasses, and rum for export. Built in the 1780s, the partially restored plantation at Leinster Bay was once an important sugar mill. Though there are no official visiting hours, the National Park Service has regular tours, and some well-informed taxi drivers will show you around. Occasionally you'll find a living-history demonstration—someone making johnnycake or weaving baskets. For information on tours and cultural events, contact the St. John National Park Service Visitors Center. ⊠ *Leinster Bay Rd.,* ☎ *340/776–6201.* ☞ *$4.*

❹ Bordeaux Mountain. St. John's highest peak rises to 1,277 ft (391 m). Route 10 passes near enough to the top to offer breathtaking views. Drive nearly to the end of the dirt road for spectacular views at Picture Point and for the trailhead of the hike downhill to Lameshur. Get a trail map from the park service before you start. ⊠ *Rte. 10.*

❼ Catherineberg Ruins. At this fine example of an 18th-century sugar and rum factory, there's a storage vault beneath the windmill. Across the road, look for the round mill, which was later used to hold water. In the 1733 slave revolt, Catherineberg served as headquarters for the Amina warriors, a tribe of Africans captured into slavery. ⊠ *Rte. 10.*

❺ Coral Bay. This laid-back community at the island's dry, eastern end is named for its shape rather than for its underwater life—the word *coral* comes from *krawl,* Danish for "corral." It's a small, quiet, neighborhoody settlement—a place to get away from it all. You'll need a Jeep if you plan to stay at this end of the island, as some of the rental houses are up unpaved roads that wind around the mountain. If you come just for lunch, a regular car will be fine.

❶ Cruz Bay. St. John's main town may be compact (it consists of only several blocks), but it's definitely a hub: the ferries from St. Thomas and the BVI pull in here, and it's where you can get a taxi or rent a car to travel around the island. There are plenty of shops in which to browse, a number of watering holes where you can stop for a breather, many restaurants, and a grassy square with benches where you can sit back and take everything in. Look for the current edition of the handy, amusing "St. John Map" featuring Max the Mongoose.

To pick up a handy guide to St. John's hiking trails, see various large maps of the island, and find out about current park service programs, including guided walks and cultural demonstrations, stop by the **V. I. National Park Visitors Center.** ⊠ *In an area known as the Creek, near Cruz Bay bulkhead and baseball field, Cruz Bay 00831,* ☎ *340/776–6201.* WEB *www.nps.gov/viis.* ☞ *Free.* ☉ *Daily 8–4:30.*

❷ Elaine Ione Sprauve Library and Museum. On the hill just above Cruz Bay is the **Enighed Estate Great House,** built in 1757. *Enighed* is the Danish word for "concord" (unity or peace). The great house and its outbuildings (a sugar-production factory and horse-driven mill) were destroyed by fire and hurricanes, and the house sat in ruins until 1982. Today it houses a library and museum that contains a dusty collection of Indian pottery and colonial artifacts. ⊠ *Rte. 104 (make a right past Texaco station),* ☎ *340/776–6359.* ☞ *Free.* ☉ *Weekdays 9–5.*

❽ Peace Hill. It's worth stopping at this spot just past the Hawksnest Bay overlook for great views of St. John, St. Thomas, and the BVI. The flat promontory features an old sugar mill. ⊠ *Off Rte. 20.*

❸ Reef Bay Trail. Although this is one of the most interesting hikes on St. John, unless you're a rugged individualist who wants a physical challenge (and that describes a lot of people who stay on St. John), you'll probably get the most out of the trip if you join a hike led by a park service ranger, who can identify the trees and plants on the hike down, fill you in on the history of the Reef Bay Plantation, and tell you about the petroglyphs on the rocks at the bottom of the trail. If you're without a car, take a taxi or the public Vitran bus from the Cruz Bay ferry dock to the trailhead on Route 10, where you'll meet a ranger for the hike downhill. A boat will take you to Cruz Bay ($15), saving you the uphill return climb.

The **Reef Bay Plantation,** according to architectural historian Frederik C. Gjessing, is the most architecturally ambitious structure of its kind on St. John. Though gutted, the great house is largely intact, and its classical beauty is still visible. It sits on a side trail to the north, off the trail to Lameshur Bay, and the sugar works are near the beach. Reef Bay was the last working plantation on St. John when it stopped production in 1920. ⊠ *Rte. 10 between Cruz Bay and Coral Bay; parking area is on the left, trail is to the right.*

U.S. VIRGIN ISLANDS A TO Z

To research prices, get advice from other travelers, and book travel arrangements, visit www.fodors.com.

AIR TRAVEL

One advantage to visiting the USVI is the abundance of nonstop and connecting flights to St. Thomas and St. Croix that can have you at the beach in three to four hours from most eastern United States departures. Small island-hopper planes and a seaplane connect St. Thomas and St. Croix, and a ferry takes you from St. Thomas to St. John.

American is the territory's major carrier with flights from Miami and New York. Continental flies from Newark. Delta flies from Atlanta. United flies from Chicago and Washington, D.C. US Airways flies from Philadelphia. American Eagle has frequent flights throughout the day from San Juan. Cape Air flies from San Juan to both St. Thomas and St. Croix. It has code-sharing arrangements with all major airlines so your luggage can transfer seamlessly. Seaborne Airlines flies between St. Thomas and St. Croix.

➤ AIRLINES AND CONTACTS: **American Airlines** (☎ 340/774–6464 or 340/778–1140); **American Eagle** (☎ 340/776–2560 or 340/778–2000); **Cape Air** (☎ 800/352–0714 or 340/774–2204); **Continental Airlines** (☎ 800/231–0856); **Delta Airlines** (☎ 340/777–4177); **Seaborne Airlines** (☎ 340/773–6442); **United Air Lines** (☎ 340/774–9190); **US Airways** (☎ 340/774–7885).

AIRPORTS

St. Thomas's Cyril E. King Airport sits at the western end of the island. There is no airport on St. John. St. Croix's Henry Rohlsen Airport sits outside Frederiksted, a 10-minute drive away. It takes about a half-hour to reach Christiansted from the airport.

Most hotels on St. Thomas do not have airport shuttles, but taxi vans at the airport are plentiful. From the airport, fees (set by the VI Taxi Commission) for two or more people sharing a cab are: $12 to the Ritz-Carlton, $9 to Renaissance Grand Beach Resort, $7.50 to Marriott Frenchman's Reef, and $5 to Bluebeard's Castle. Expect to be charged 50¢ per bag and to pay a higher fee if you're riding alone. During rush hour the trip to east end resorts can take up to 40 minutes, but but a half hour is typical. Driving time from the airport to Charlotte Amalie is 15 minutes.

Getting from the airport to St. Croix hotels by taxi costs about $10–$13. You'll spend a half-hour getting to the hotels in the Christiansted area, but those in the Frederiksted area are only about 10 minutes away. It takes about 45 minutes to get to the hotels on the East End.

Visitors to St. John fly into St. Thomas and take a taxi to either Charlotte Amalie or Red Hook, where they catch a ferry to Cruz Bay, St. John. The ferry from Charlotte Amalie makes the 45-minute trip several times a day and costs $7 a person. From Red Hook the ferry leaves on the hour; the 20-minute trip costs $3 a person.

➤ AIRPORT INFORMATION: **St. Croix's Henry Rohlsen Airport** (☎ 340/778–0589). **St. Thomas's Cyril E. King Airport** (☎ 340/774–5100).

BOAT AND FERRY TRAVEL

Virtually every type of ship and major cruise line calls at St. Thomas; only a few call at St. Croix. Many ships that call at St. Thomas also call in St. John or offer an excursion to that island.

Ferries are a great way to travel around the islands; there's service between St. Thomas and St. John and their neighbors, the BVI. There's something special about spending a day on St. John and then joining your fellow passengers—a mix of tourists, local families, and restaurant staffers en route to work—for a peaceful, sundown ride back to St. Thomas. Sometimes one of the St. John ferry services offers a special weekend trip to Fajardo, Puerto Rico. Such junkets depart from the waterfront in St. Thomas on a Friday evening and return to the same locale on Sunday afternoon.

FARES AND SCHEDULES

Ferries to Cruz Bay, St. John, leave St. Thomas from either the Charlotte Amalie waterfront west of the U.S. Coast Guard dock or from Red Hook. From Charlotte Amalie ferries depart at 9, 11, 1, 3, 4, and 5:30. To Charlotte Amalie from Cruz Bay, they leave at 7:15, 9:15, 11:15, 1:15, 2:15, and 3:45. The one-way fare for the 45-minute ride is $7 for adults, $3 for children. From Red Hook, ferries to Cruz Bay leave at 6:30 AM and 7:30 AM. Starting at 8 AM, they leave hourly until midnight. Returning from Cruz Bay, they leave hourly starting at 6 AM until 11 PM. The 15- to 20-minute ferry ride is $3 one-way for adults, $1 for children under 12.

Car ferries, called barges, run every half hour between Red Hook, St. Thomas, and Cruz Bay, St. John. The ride is 20 minutes (one way) and costs $25 (round-trip). Plan to check your vehicle in 15 minutes before departure.

Reefer is the name of both of the brightly colored 26-passenger skiffs that run between the Charlotte Amalie waterfront and Marriott Frenchman's Reef hotel daily every hour from 9 to 4, returning from the Reef from 9:30 until 4:30. It's a good way to beat the traffic (and is about the same price as a taxi) to Morning Star Beach, which adjoins the Reef. And you get a great view of the harbor as you bob along in the shadow of the giant cruise ships anchored in the harbor. The captain of the *Reefer* may also be persuaded to drop you at Yacht Haven, but check first. The fare is $4 one-way, and the trip takes about 15 minutes.

There's daily service between either Charlotte Amalie or Red Hook, on St. Thomas, and West End or Road Town, Tortola, BVI, by either Smiths Ferry or Native Son, Inc., and to Virgin Gorda, BVI, by Smiths Ferry. The times and days the ferries run change, so it's best to call for schedules once you're in the islands. The fare is $22 one-way or $40 round-trip, and the trip from Charlotte Amalie takes 45 minutes to an hour to West End, up to 1½ hours to Road Town; from Red Hook the trip is only half an hour. The twice-weekly 2¼-hour trip from Charlotte Amalie to Virgin Gorda costs $28 one-way and $40 round-trip. There's also daily service between Cruz Bay, St. John, and West End, Tortola, aboard the *Sundance*. The half-hour one-way trip is $21. You'll need to present proof of citizenship upon entering the BVI; a passport is best, but a birth certificate with a raised seal in addition to a government-issued photo ID will suffice.

➤ BOAT AND FERRY INFORMATION: **Native Son, Inc.** (☎ 340/774–8685); *Reefer* (☎ 340/776–8500 ext. 6814); **Smiths Ferry** (☎ 340/775–7292); *Sundance* (☎ 340/776–6597).

BUSINESS HOURS

BANKS

Bank hours are generally Monday–Thursday 9–3 and Friday 9–5; a handful have Saturday hours (9–noon). Walk-up windows open at 8:30 on weekdays.

POST OFFICES

Hours may vary slightly from branch to branch and island to island, but they are generally 7:30 or 8 to 4 or 5:30 weekdays and 7:30 or 8 to noon or 2:30 Saturday.

SHOPS

On St. Thomas, stores on Main Street in Charlotte Amalie are open weekdays and Saturday 9–5. The hours of the shops in the Havensight Mall (next to the cruise-ships dock) are the same, though occasionally some stay open until 9 on Friday, depending on how many cruise ships are at the dock. You may also find some shops open on Sunday if a lot of cruise ships are in port. Hotel shops are usually open evenings, as well.

St. Croix shop hours are usually Monday–Saturday 9–5, but you'll find some shops in Christiansted open in the evening. On St. John, store hours run from 9 or 10 to 5 or 6. Wharfside Village and Mongoose Junction shops in Cruz Bay are often open into the evening.

CAR RENTALS

Any U.S. driver's license is good for 90 days on the USVI, as are valid driver's licenses from other countries; the minimum age for drivers is 18, although many agencies won't rent to anyone under the age of 25. At the height of the winter season, it may be tough to find a car and occasionally, all rental companies run out of cars at once; reserve well in advance to ensure you get the vehicle of your choice.

ST. THOMAS

You can rent a car from several local and worldwide agencies.
➤ MAJOR AGENCIES: **ABC Rentals** (☎ 340/776–1222 or 800/524–2080); **Anchorage E-Z Car** (☎ 340/775–6255); **Avis** (☎ 340/774–1468 or 800/331–1084); **Budget** (☎ 340/776–5774 or 800/626–4516); **Cowpet Rent-a-Car** (☎ 340/775–7376); **Dependable Car Rental** (☎ 340/774–2253 or 800/522–3076); **Discount** (☎ 340/776–4858); **Hertz** (☎ 340/774–1879 or 800/654–3131).

ST. CROIX

Atlas is located outside Christiansted but provides pickups at hotels. Avis is located at the airport. Budget has locations at the airport and in the King Christian Hotel in Christiansted. Midwest is located outside Frederiksted, but picks up at hotels. Olympic and Thrifty are located outside Christiansted, but will pick up at hotels.
➤ CONTACTS: **Atlas** (☎ 340/773–2886 or 800/426–6009); **Avis** (☎ 340/778–9355 or 800/331–1084); **Budget** (☎ 340/778–9636 or 888/227–

3359); **Midwest** (☎ 340/772–0438); **Olympic** (☎ 340/773–2208 or 888/878–4227); **Thrifty** (☎ 340/773–7200 or 800/367–2277).

ST. JOHN

Best is just outside Cruz Bay near the public library off Route 10. Cool Breeze is in Cruz Bay across from the Creek. Delbert Hill Taxi Rental Service is in Cruz Bay around the corner from the ferry dock across from Wharfside Village. Denzil Clyne is across from the Creek. O'Connor Jeep is in Cruz Bay at the Texaco Station. St. John Car Rental is at the Creek in Cruz Bay. Spencer's Jeep is across from the Creek in Cruz Bay. V.I. Miscellaneous is in Cruz Bay across from the Creek.

➤ CONTACTS: **Best** (☎ 340/693–8177); **Cool Breeze** (☎ 340/776–6588); **Delbert Hill Taxi Rental Service** (☎ 340/776–6637); **Denzil Clyne** (☎ 340/776–6715); **O'Connor Jeep** (☎ 340/776–6343); **St. John Car Rental** (☎ 340/776–6103, WEB www.st-john.com/stjohncar-rental); **Spencer's Jeep** (☎ 340/693–8784 or 888/776–6628); **V.I. Miscellaneous** (☎ 340/776–6374).

CAR TRAVEL

Even at a sedate speed of 20 mph, driving can be an adventure—for example, you may find yourself in a stick-shift Jeep slogging behind a slow tourist-packed safari bus at a steep hairpin turn. Give a little beep at blind turns. Note that the general speed limit on these islands is only 25–35 mph, which will seem fast enough for you on most roads. If you don't think you'll need to lock up your valuables, a Jeep or open-air Suzuki with four-wheel drive will make it easier to navigate potholed dirt side roads and to get up slick hills when it rains. All main roads are paved.

GASOLINE

Gas is pricey: about $2 per gallon on St. Thomas, $1.25 on St. Croix, and $2.15 on St. John.

ROAD CONDITIONS

In St. Thomas, traffic can get pretty bad, especially in Charlotte Amalie at rush hour (7–9 and 4:30–6). Cars often line up bumper to bumper along the waterfront. If you need to get from an east end resort to the airport during these times, find the alternate route (starting from the east end, Route 38 to 42 to 40 to 33) that goes up the mountain and then drops you back onto Veterans Highway. If you plan to explore by car, be sure to pick up the "2002 Road Map St. Thomas–St. John" that includes the route numbers *and* the names of the roads that are used by locals. It's available anywhere you find maps and guidebooks.

St. Croix, unlike St. Thomas and St. John where narrow roads wind through hillsides, is relatively flat, and it even has a four-lane highway. The speed limit on the Melvin H. Evans Highway is 55 mph and ranges from 35–40 mph elsewhere. Roads are often unmarked, so be patient—sometimes getting lost is half the fun.

In St. John, use caution. The terrain is very hilly, the roads are wind-ing, and the blind curves numerous. You may suddenly come upon a huge safari bus careening around a corner or a couple of hikers strolling along the side of the road. Major roads are well paved, but once you get off a specific route, dirt roads filled with potholes are common. For such driving a four-wheel-drive vehicle is your best bet.

RULES OF THE ROAD

Driving is on the left side of the road (although your steering wheel will be on the left side of the car). The law requires *everyone* in a car to wear seat belts: many of the roads are narrow, and the islands are dotted with hills, so there's ample reason to put safety first.

ELECTRICITY

The USVI use the same current as the U.S. mainland—110 volts. Since power fluctuations occasionally occur, bring a heavy-duty surge protector (available at hardware stores) if you plan to use your computer.

EMERGENCIES

➤ AMBULANCE AND FIRE: Dial ☎ 911. The **Air Ambulance Network** (☎ 800/327–1966) serves the USVI area from Florida. **Medical Air Services** (☎ 340/777–8580 or 800/643–9023) has its Caribbean headquarters in St. Thomas.

➤ COAST GUARD: Call the **Marine Safety Detachment** (☎ 340/776–3497 in St. Thomas and St. John; 340/772–5557 in St. Croix) from 7 to 3:30 weekdays. If there's no answer at either number, call the **Rescue Coordination Center** (☎ 787/289–2040) in San Juan, Puerto Rico; it's open 24 hours a day.

➤ HOSPITALS ON ST. THOMAS: **Roy L. Schneider Hospital & Community Health Center** (✉ Sugar Estate, 1 mi [1½ km] east of Charlotte Amalie, ☎ 340/776–8311).

➤ HOSPITALS ON ST. CROIX: **Gov. Juan F. Luis Hospital and Health Center** (✉ 6 Diamond Ruby, north of Sunny Isle Shopping Center on Rte. 79, Christiansted, ☎ 340/778–6311); **Frederiksted Health Center** (✉ 516 Strand St., ☎ 340/772–1992).

➤ HOSPITALS ON ST. JOHN: **Myrah Keating Smith Community Health Center** (✉ Rte. 10, about 7 mins east of Cruz Bay, ☎ 340/693–8900).

➤ PHARMACIES ON ST. THOMAS: **Havensight Pharmacy** (✉ Havensight Mall, ☎ 340/776–1235); **Kmart Pharmacy** (✉ Tutu Park Mall, ☎ 340/777–3854); **Sunrise Pharmacy** (✉ Red Hook, ☎ 340/775–6600; Vitraco Park, near Havensight Mall, ☎ 340/776–7292).

➤ PHARMACIES ON ST. CROIX: **D&D Apothecary Hall** (✉ 501 Queen St., Frederiksted, ☎ 340/772–1890); **Kmart Pharmacy** (✉ Sunshine Mall, ☎ 340/692–2622); **People's Drug Store, Inc.,** (✉ Christiansted Wharf, ☎ 340/778–7355); (✉ Sunny Isle Shopping Center, Rte. 70, Christiansted, ☎ 340/778–5537).

➤ PHARMACIES ON ST. JOHN: **St. John Drug Center** (✉ Boulon Shopping Center, Rte. 10, Cruz Bay, ☎ 340/776–6353).

➤ POLICE: Dial ☎ 911.

➤ SCUBA-DIVING EMERGENCIES: The only hyperbaric chamber in the territory is at St. Thomas's Roy L. Schneider Hospital & Community Health Center (☎ 340/776–2686).

ETIQUETTE AND BEHAVIOR

A smile and a "good day" greeting will start any encounter off on the right foot. Dress is casual throughout the islands, but cover up when you're sightseeing or shopping in town; bare chests and bathing suit tops are frowned upon.

FESTIVALS AND SEASONAL EVENTS

ST. THOMAS

January–April sees Classics in the Garden, a chamber-music series at Tillett Gardens where young musicians from all over the world perform. Tillett Gardens hosts annual Arts Alive festivals in November, March, and August. During Easter weekend, St. Thomas Yacht Club hosts the Rolex Cup Regatta, which is part of the three-race Caribbean Ocean Racing Triangle (CORT) that pulls in yachties and their pals from all over. Carnival is a weeklong major-league blowout of parades, parties, and island-wide events. The dates change from year to year, following the Easter calendar. Marlin mania begins in May and so do the sportfishing tournaments. There are also several locally sponsored fishing events throughout summer and fall.

The St. Thomas Gamefishing Club hosts its July Open Tournament over the Fourth of July weekend. There are categories for serious marlin anglers, just-for-fun fishermen, and even kids who want to try their luck from docks and rocks. The mid-July celebration of Bastille Day—which commemorates the French Revolution—is marked by a mini-carnival in Frenchtown. During full moon in August, anglers compete for big-money prizes in the USVI Open/Atlantic Blue Marlin Tournament. September's Texas Society Chili Cook-Off is a party on Sapphire Beach—you'll find country music performances, dancing, games, and, of course, chili tasting. In November the St. Thomas–St. John Agricultural Fair showcases fresh produce, home-grown herbs, and local dishes, such as callaloo, salt fish and dumplings, and fresh fish simmered with green banana, pumpkin, and potatolike *tannia*.

➤ CONTACTS: **Arts Alive Festival** (☎ 340/775–1405); **Carnival** (☎ 340/776–3112); **Classics in the Garden** (☎ 340/775–1405); **July Open Tournament** (☎ 340/775–9144); **Rolex Cup Regatta** (☎ 340/775–6320); **St. Thomas–St. John Agricultural Fair** (☎ 340/693–1080); **Texas Society Chili Cook-Off** (☎ 340/776–3595); **USVI Open/Atlantic Blue Marlin Tournament** (☎ 340/775–9500).

ST. CROIX

The island celebrates Carnival with its Crucian Christmas Festival, which starts in late December. After weeks of beauty pageants, food fairs, and concerts, the festival wraps up with a parade in early January. In February and March the St. Croix Landmarks Society House Tours visit some of the island's most exclusive and historic homes and give you a chance to peek inside places you can usually view only from the road.

The St. Croix Half Ironman Triathlon attracts international-class athletes as well as amateurs every May for a 1-mi (2-km) swim, a 7-mi (12-km) run, and a 34-mi (55-km) bike ride; it includes a climb up The Beast, on Route 69. Serious swimmers should join island residents in early November for the Coral Reef Swim. Participants swim about 5 mi (8 km) from Buck Island to Christiansted. The event also includes an awards dinner. The International Regatta sets sail in February at the St. Croix Yacht Club. Sailors converge on Teague Bay for three days of sailing and parties.

➤ CONTACTS: **Coral Reef Swim** (☎ 340/773–2100); **International Regatta** (☎ 340/773–9531); **St. Croix Half Ironman Triathlon** (☎ 340/773–4470); **St. Croix Landmarks Society House Tours** (☎ 340/772–0598).

ST. JOHN

The island dishes up its own version of Carnival with the July 4th Celebration. Weeks of festivities—including beauty pageants and a food fair—culminate in a parade through the streets of Cruz Bay on July 4. On the two days after Thanksgiving an eclectic group of sailors takes to the waters of Coral Bay for the annual Coral Bay Thanksgiving Regatta. Some boats are "live-aboards," whose owners only pull up anchor for this one event; other boats belong to Sunday sailors; and a very few are owned by hotshot racers. If you'd like to crew, stop by Skinny Legs Bar and Restaurant.

➤ CONTACTS: **Coral Bay Thanksgiving Regatta Crew Information** (☎ 340/779–4982).

HEALTH

You should always wash produce before eating it. Also note that ciguatera, a toxin found in some reef fish (particularly kingfish), can be a problem at local restaurants.

HOLIDAYS

Public holidays, in addition to the U.S. federal holidays, for 2002 are: Three Kings Day (Jan. 6); Transfer Day (commemorates Denmark's

1917 sale of the territory to the United States, Mar. 31); Holy Thursday and Good Friday (Apr. 12–13); Emancipation Day (when slavery was abolished in the Danish West Indies in 1848, July 3); Columbus Day and USVI–Puerto Rico Friendship Day (Oct. 11); and Liberty Day (honoring Judge David Hamilton Jackson who secured freedom of the press and assembly from King Christian X of Denmark, Nov. 1).

Although the government closes down for 26 days a year, most of these holidays have no effect on shopping hours. Unless there's a cruise ship arrival, expect most stores to close for Christmas and a few other holidays in the slower summer months.

LANGUAGE
English is the official language, though island residents often speak it with a lilting Creole accent, so you might not recognize certain words at first. If you have trouble understanding someone, ask them to speak slowly.

MAIL AND SHIPPING
The main U.S. Post Office on St. Thomas is near the hospital, with branches in Charlotte Amalie, Frenchtown, Havensight, and Tutu Mall; there are post offices at Christiansted, Frederiksted, Gallows Bay, and Sunny Isle, on St. Croix, and at Cruz Bay, on St. John. The postal service offers Express Mail next-day service to major cities if you mail before noon; outlying areas may take two days. Letters to the United States are 34¢ and postcards are 21¢. Sending mail home to Canada you'll pay 46¢ for a letter and 40¢ for a postcard. To the United Kingdom and Australia, letters are 60¢, postcards 50¢.

On St. Thomas, FedEx offers overnight service if you get your package to the office before 5 PM. Parcel Plus, across from Havensight Mall, also has express mail service. The FedEx office on St. Croix is in Peter's Rest Commercial Center; try to drop off your packages before 5:30 PM. On St. John, Sprint Courier Service connects to all major couriers.
➤ CONTACTS: **FedEx** (✉ Cyril E. King Airport, St. Thomas, ☎ 340/777–4140; ✉ Peter's Rest Commercial Center, Rte. 708, St. Croix, ☎ 340/778–8180); **Parcel Plus** (✉ across from Havensight Mall on Rte. 30, St. Thomas, ☎ 340/776–9134); **Sprint Courier Service** (✉ just off Rte. 104 across from the basketball court St. John, ☎ 340/693–8130).

MONEY MATTERS
Prices quoted in this chapter are in U.S. dollars.

BANKS AND ATMS
Each of the islands has several banks. On St. Thomas, First Bank is near Market Square. There are waterfront locations for both Banco Popular and Chase Bank.

St. Croix has branches of Banco Popular in Orange Grove and Sunny Isle Shopping Centers. Chase Bank is located in Orange Grove Shopping Center and in downtown Christiansted. Scotia Bank has branches in Sunny Isle Frederiksted, Christiansted, and Sunshine Mall.

St. John's two banks are located near the ferry docks. Chase is one block up from the ferry dock, while Scotia Bank is located in a trailer about a block up from it.
➤ CONTACTS: **Banco Popular** (☎ 340/693–2777); **Chase Bank** (☎ 340/775–7777); **First Bank** (☎ 340/776–9494); **Scotia Bank** (St. Croix, ☎ 340/778–5350; St. John, ☎ 340/776–6552).

CREDIT CARDS

All major credit cards and traveler's checks are generally accepted. Some places will take Discover, though it is not as widely accepted as Visa, Mastercard, and American Express.

CURRENCY

The American dollar is used throughout the territory, as well as in the neighboring BVI. If you need to exchange foreign currency, you'll need to go to the main branch of major banks.

PASSPORTS AND VISAS

If you're a U.S. or Canadian citizen, you can prove citizenship with a current or expired (but not by more than five years) passport or with a birth certificate (with a raised seal) along with a government-issued photo ID. A valid passport, however, is best. Citizens of other countries need a passport.

SAFETY

Vacationers tend to assume that normal precautions aren't necessary in paradise. They are. Though there isn't quite as much crime here as in large U.S. mainland cities, it does exist. To be safe, stick to well-lighted streets at night and use the same kind of street sense (don't wander the back alleys of Charlotte Amalie or Christiansted after five rum punches, for example) that you would in any unfamiliar territory. If you plan to carry things around, rent a car—not a Jeep—and lock possessions in the trunk. Keep your rental car locked wherever you park. Don't leave cameras, purses, and other valuables lying on the beach while you snorkel for an hour (or even for a minute), whether you're on the deserted beaches of St. John or the more crowded Magens and Coki beaches on St. Thomas. St. Croix has several remote beaches outside Frederiksted and on the east end; it's best to visit them with a group rather than on your own.

SIGHTSEEING TOURS

AIR TOURS

Air Center Helicopters, on the Charlotte Amalie waterfront (next to Tortola Wharf) on St. Thomas, has 30-minute island tours priced at $375 (for up to 4 passengers) per trip. You can also arrange longer flights that loop over to the neighboring BVI, as well as photography tours. Seaborne Airlines offers narrated flightseeing tours of the USVI and the BVI from its Havensight base on St. Thomas. The 30-minute "Round-the-Island" tour is $89 per person.

➤ CONTACTS: **Air Center Helicopters** (✉ Waterfront, Charlotte Amalie, St. Thomas, ☎ 340/775–7335); **Seaborne Adventures** (✉ 5305 Long Bay Rd., Charlotte Amalie, St. Thomas, ☎ 340/773–5991).

BOAT TOURS

St. Thomas's *Kon Tiki* party boat is a kick. Put your sophistication aside, climb on this big palm-thatch raft, and dip into bottomless barrels of rum punch along with a couple of hundred of your soon-to-be closest friends. Dance to the steel-drum band, sun on the roof (watch out: you'll fry), and join the limbo dancing on the way home from an afternoon of swimming and beachcombing at Honeymoon Beach on Water Island. This popular 3½-hour afternoon excursion costs $29 for adults, $15 for children under 13 (although few come to this party).

Caribbean Pelican Rides offers a unique land and sea tour of Charlotte Amalie aboard an amphibious British Alvis Stalward vessel. Tours depart from the Coast Guard dock opposite Vendor's Plaza. The 55-minute excursions costs $55 for adults, $15 for children ages 12 and under.

➤ CONTACTS: **Caribbean Pelican Rides** (✉ Coast Guard Dock, opposite Vendor's Plaza, Charlotte Amalie, St. Thomas,☎ 340/774–7808); *Kon Tiki* (✉ Gregorie Channel East Dock, Frenchtown, St. Thomas, ☎ 340/775–5055).

BUS AND TAXI TOURS

V. I. Taxi Association St. Thomas City-Island Tour gives a two-hour $45 tour for two people in an open-air safari bus or enclosed van; aimed at cruise-ship passengers, this tour includes stops at Drake's Seat and Mountain Top. For just a bit more money (about $45–$50 for two) you can hire a taxi and ask the driver to take the opposite route so you'll avoid the crowds. But do see Mountain Top: the view is wonderful.

Tropic Tours offers half-day shopping and sightseeing tours of St. Thomas by bus six days a week ($25 per person). The company also has a full-day ferry tour to St. John that includes snorkeling and lunch. The cost is $70 per person.

St. Croix Safari Tours offers van tours of St. Croix. They depart from Christiansted, last about three hours, cost from $25 per person plus admission fees to attractions. St. Croix Transit offers van tours of St. Croix. They depart from Christiansted, last about three hours, cost from $25 per person plus admission fees to attractions.

In St. John, taxi drivers provide tours of the island, making stops at various sites including Trunk Bay and Annaberg Plantation. Prices run around $15 a person. The taxi drivers congregate near the ferry in Cruz Bay. The dispatcher will find you a driver for your tour.
➤ CONTACTS: **St. Croix Safari Tours** (☎ 340/773–6700); **St. Croix Transit** (☎ 340/772–3333); **Tropic Tours** (☎ 340/774–1855 or 800/524–4334); **V. I. Taxi Association St. Thomas City-Island Tour** (☎ 340/774–4550).

WALKING TOURS

The *St. Thomas–St. John Vacation Handbook,* available free at hotels and tourist centers, has an excellent self-guided walking tour of Charlotte Amalie on St. Thomas. The St. Thomas Historical Trust has published a self-guided tour of the historic district; it's available in book and souvenir shops for $1.95. A two-hour guided historic walking tour is available by reservation. It begins (at 9 AM) at the Emancipation Garden, covers all the in-town sights, and can be narrated in Spanish, Danish, German, and Japanese as well as in English. The cost is $35 per person; wear a hat and comfortable walking shoes.

Possible nature tours on St. Thomas include bird-watching, whale-watching, and waiting hidden on a beach while the magnificent hawksbill turtles come ashore to lay their eggs. Contact EAST (Environmental Association of St. Thomas–St. John.

St. Croix Heritage Tours leads walks through the historic towns of Christiansted and Frederiksted, detailing the history of the people and the buildings. Custom tours that cover the island are also available.

Along with providing trail maps and brochures about Virgin Islands National Park, the park service also gives a variety of guided tours on- and off-shore. Some are only offered during particular times of the year, and some require reservations. For more information, contact the National Park Service on St. John.
➤ CONTACTS: **EAST** (Environmental Association of St. Thomas–St. John); (✉ Box 12379, St. Thomas 00801, ☎ 340/776–1976); **St. Croix Heritage Tours** (✉ Box 7937, Sunny Isle, 00823, ☎ 340/778–6997); **St. Thomas Historical Trust** (☎ 340/776–2726)); **V. I. National Park Visitors Center** (✉ At the area known as the Creek; across from Cruz Bay

bulkhead and adjacent to the ball field, Cruz Bay, ☎ 340/776–6201; ✉ Cinnamon Bay, ☎ 340/776–6330, WEB www.nps.gov/viis).

TAXES

DEPARTURE TAX

Departure taxes ($10 for those leaving by air, $5 for those leaving by sea) are generally written into your ticket.

SALES TAX

There's no sales tax, but there is an 8% hotel-room tax in the USVI. The St. John Accommodations Council members ask that hotel and villa guests voluntarily pay a $1-a-day surcharge to help fund school and community projects and other good works.

TAXIS

USVI taxis don't have meters, but you needn't worry about fare gouging if you check a list of standard rates to popular destinations (required by law to be carried by each driver and often posted in hotel and airport lobbies and printed in free tourist periodicals, such as *St. Thomas This Week* and *St. Croix This Week*) and settle on the fare before you start out. Fares are per person, not per destination, but drivers taking multiple fares (which often happens, especially from the airport) will charge you a lower rate than if you're in the cab alone.

ST. THOMAS

On St. Thomas taxi vans line up along Havensight and Crown Bay docks when a cruise ship pulls in. If you booked a shore tour, the operator will lead you to a designated vehicle. Otherwise, there are plenty of air-conditioned vans and open-air safari buses to take you to Charlotte Amalie or the beach. The cab fare from Havensight to Charlotte Amalie is $2.50 per person; you can, however, make the 1½-mi (2½-km) walk into town in about 30 minutes along the beautiful waterfront. From Crown Bay to town the taxi fare is $2.50 per person whether you travel solo or you share; it's a 1-mi (1½-km) walk, but the route passes along a busy highway. Transportation from Havensight to Magens Bay for swimming is $6.50 per person ($4 if you share).

Additionally, taxis of all shapes and sizes are available at various ferry, shopping, resort, and airport areas, and they also respond to phone calls. There are taxi stands in Charlotte Amalie across from Emancipation Garden (in front of Little Switzerland, behind the post office) and along the waterfront. But you probably won't have to look for a stand, as taxis are plentiful and routinely cruise the streets. Walking down Main Street, you'll be asked "Back to ship?" often enough to make you never want to carry another shopping bag.

➤ CONTACTS: **East End Taxi** (☎ 340/775–6974); **Islander Taxi** (☎ 340/774–4077); **VI Taxi Association** (☎ 340/774–4550).

ST. CROIX

Taxis, generally station wagons or minivans, are a phone call away from most hotels and are available in downtown Christiansted, at the Alexander Hamilton Airport, and at the Frederiksted pier during cruise-ship arrivals.

In Frederiksted, all the shops are just a short walk away, and you can swim off the beach in Frederiksted. Most ship passengers visit Christiansted on a tour; a taxi will cost $20 for one or two people.

➤ CONTACTS: **Antilles Taxi Service** (☎ 340/773–5020); **Cruzan Taxi and Tours** (☎ 340/773–6388); **St. Croix Taxi Association** (☎ 340/778–1088).

ST. JOHN

Taxis meet ferries arriving in Cruz Bay. Most drivers use vans or open-air safari buses. You'll find them congregated at the dock and at hotel parking lots. You can also hail them anywhere on the road. You're likely to travel with other tourists en route to their destinations. It's very difficult to get taxis to respond to a phone call. If you need one to pick you up at your rental villa, ask the villa manager for suggestions on who to call or arrange a ride in advance.

Some cruise ships stop at St. John to let passengers disembark for a day. The main town of Cruz Bay is near the ship terminal. If you want to swim, the famous Trunk Bay is an $11 taxi ride (for two) from town.

TELEPHONES

On St. Thomas, AT&T has a state-of-the-art telecommunications center (it's across from the Havensight Mall) with 15 desk booths, fax and copy services, video phone, and TDD equipment (for people with hearing impairments). Islander Services and East End Secretarial Services offer long-distance dialing, copying, and fax services. Parcel Plus in St. Thomas has three computers available for accessing e-mail; the cost is $5 per half hour. Express mail service, international calling, and phone cards are also available here. On St. John, the place to go for phone or message needs is Connections.

➤ CONTACTS: **AT&T** (✉ Across from Havensight Mall, Charlotte Amalie, St. Thomas, ☎ 340/777–9201); **Connections** (✉ Cruz Bay, St. John, ☎ 340/776–6922; ✉ Coral Bay, St. John,☎ 340/779–4994); **East End Secretarial Services** (✉ Upstairs at Red Hook Plaza, Red Hook, St. Thomas, ☎ 340/775–5262); **Islander Services** (✉ 5302 Store Tvaer Gade, behind the Greenhouse Restaurant, Charlotte Amalie, St. Thomas, ☎ 340/774–8128); **Parcel Plus** (✉ Across from Havensight Mall, Charlotte Amalie, St. Thomas, ☎ 340/776–9134).

COUNTRY AND AREA CODES

The area code for all of the USVI is 340. If you are calling from within the U.S., you need only dial 1 plus the area code and number. If you are calling from outside the U.S., dial the U.S. country code 01.

INTERNATIONAL CALLS

You can dial direct to and from the mainland U.S., and to and from Australia, Canada, New Zealand, and the United Kingdom from most phones.

LOCAL CALLS

Local calls from a public phone cost up to 35¢ for each five minutes. If you have a cell phone, you can dial 6611 for information about how to use it locally.

TIPPING

Many hotels add a 10%–15% service charge to cover the room maid and other staff. However, some hotels may use part of that money to fund their operations, passing on only a portion of it to the staff. Check with your maid or bellboy to determine the hotel's policy. If you discover you need to tip, give bellmen and porters 50¢ to $1 per bag and maids $1 or $2 per day. Special errands or requests of hotel staff always require an additional tip. At restaurants bartenders and waiters expect a 10%–15% tip, but always check your tab to see whether service is included. Taxi drivers get a 15% tip.

TRANSPORTATION AROUND THE U.S. VIRGIN ISLANDS

AIRPLANE

American Eagle offers frequent flights daily from St. Thomas to St. Croix's Henry E. Rohlsen Airport. Cape Air flies from St. Thomas to

St. Croix, beginning its flight in Puerto Rico. Seaborne Airlines also flies between St. Thomas and St. Croix several times daily as well as to Beef Island Airport on Tortola, British Virgin Islands. LIAT has service from St. Thomas and St. Croix to Caribbean islands to the south.

➤ CONTACTS: **American Airlines/American Eagle** (☎ 340/778–0589, WEB www.aa.com); **Cape Air** (☎ 340/774–2204 or 800/352–0714, WEB www.capeair.com); **LIAT** (☎ 340/774–2313, WEB www.liatairline.com); **Seaborne Airlines** (☎ 340/773–6442, WEB www.seaborneairlines.com).

BUS

On St. Thomas, the island's 20 deluxe mainland-size buses make public transportation a very comfortable—though slow—way to get from east and west to Charlotte Amalie and back (service to the north is limited). Buses run about every 30 minutes from stops that are clearly marked with VITRAN signs. Fares are $1 between outlying areas and town and 75¢ in town.

Privately owned taxi vans crisscross St. Croix regularly, providing reliable service between Frederiksted and Christiansted along Route 70. This inexpensive ($1.50 one-way) mode of transportation is favored by locals, and though the many stops on the 20-mi (32-km) drive between the two main towns make the ride slow, it's never dull. The public Vitran buses aren't the quickest way to get around the island, but they're comfortable and affordable. The fare is $1 between Christiansted to Frederiksted or to places in between.

Modern Vitran buses on St. John run from the Cruz Bay ferry dock through Coral Bay to the far eastern end of the island at Salt Pond, making numerous stops in between. The fare is $1 to any point.

VISITOR INFORMATION

➤ BEFORE YOU LEAVE: **USVI Government Tourist Office** (✉ 245 Peachtree St., Center Ave. Marquis One Tower MB-05, Atlanta, GA 30303, ☎ 404/688–0906; ✉ 500 N. Michigan Ave., Suite 2030, Chicago, IL 60611, ☎ 312/670–8784; ✉ 3460 Wilshire Blvd., Suite 412, Los Angeles, CA 90010, ☎ 213/739–0138; ✉ 2655 Le Jeune Rd., Suite 907, Coral Gables, FL 33134, ☎ 305/442–7200; ✉ 1270 Ave. of the Americas, Room 2108, New York, NY 10020, ☎ 212/332–2222; ✉ Hall of Streets, #298, 444 N. Capital St. NW, Washington, DC 20006, ☎ 202/624–3590; ✉ 60 Washington St., San Juan, Puerto Rico 00907, ☎ 787/722–8023; ✉ 703 Evans Ave. Suite 106, Toronto, Ontario, Canada M9C 5E9, ☎ 416/233–1414; ✉ Molasses House, Clove Hitch Quay, Plantation Wharf, York Place, London SW11 3TW, U.K., ☎ 020/7978–5262; WEB www.usvi.net).

➤ IN THE U.S. VIRGIN ISLANDS: **USVI Division of Tourism** (✉ Box 6400, Charlotte Amalie, St. Thomas 00804, ☎ 340/774–8784 or 800/372–8784; ✉ Box 4538, Christiansted, St. Croix 00822, ☎ 340/773–0495); ✉ Strand St., Frederiksted, St. Croix 00840, ☎ 340/772–0357. St. John; ✉ Box 200, Cruz Bay, St. John 00830, ☎ 340/776–6450). **V.I. National Park** (✉ At the Creek in Cruz Bay, St. John, 00831, ☎ 340/776–6201, WEB www.nps.gov/viis).

26 BACKGROUND AND ESSENTIALS

Map of Caribbean

Island Finder Chart

Portrait of the Caribbean

Smart Travel Tips A to Z

The Caribbean

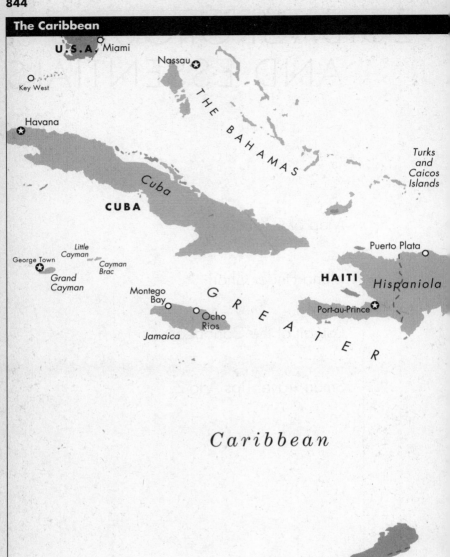

U.S.A. Miami

Key West

Nassau

THE BAHAMAS

Havana

Turks
and
Caicos
Islands

Cuba

CUBA

Little
Cayman

Cayman
Brac

George Town

Grand
Cayman

Montego
Bay

GREATER

Ocho
Rios

Jamaica

Puerto Plata

HAITI

Hispaniola

Port-au-Prince

T

E

R

Caribbean

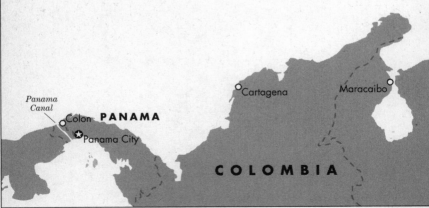

Panama
Canal

Colon

PANAMA

Panama City

Cartagena

Maracaibo

COLOMBIA

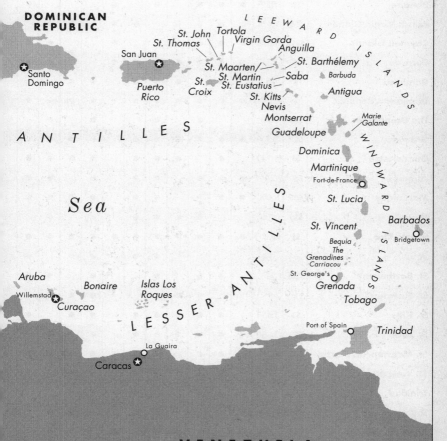

ATLANTIC OCEAN

N

DOMINICAN
REPUBLIC

*Santo
Domingo

San Juan

Puerto
Rico

St. Thomas
St. John
Tortola
Virgin Gorda

St. Maarten/
St. Martin
St. Eustatius

St.
Croix

Anguilla

St. Barthélemy

Saba

Barbuda

St. Kitts

Nevis

Montserrat

Antigua

LEEWARD ISLANDS

Marie
Galante

Guadeloupe

Dominica

Martinique

Fort-de-France

St. Lucia

WINDWARD ISLANDS

Barbados

Bridgetown

St. Vincent

Bequia
The
Grenadines
Carriacou

St. George's

Grenada

Tobago

A N T I L L E S

Sea

Aruba

Bonaire

Islas Los
Roques

Willemstad

Curaçao

L E S S E R   A N T I L L E S

La Guaira

Caracas

Port of Spain

Trinidad

VENEZUELA

0   200 miles
0   300 km

Island Finder

	Cost of Island	Number of rooms*	Nonstop flights	Cruise ship port	U.S. dollars accepted	Historic sites	Natural beauty	Lush	Arid	Mountainous	Rain forest	Beautiful beaches	Good roads
Anguilla	$$$	1,120			•				•			•	
Antigua & Barbuda	$$$$	4,000	•	•	•	•			•			•	•
Aruba	$$	7,500	•	•	•		•		•			•	•
Barbados	$$$	6,000	•	•	•	•						•	•
Bonaire	$$	989	•	•	•		•		•				•
British Virgin Islands	$$$	1,626		•	•	•	•	•		•	•	•	•
Cayman Islands	$$$$	4,318	•	•	•				•			•	•
Curaçao	$$	2,770	•	•	•	•			•			•	•
Dominica	$	857		•			•	•	•		•	•	
Dominican Republic	$	49,000	•	•	•	•	•	•		•		•	•
The Grenadines	$$$	500			•					•		•	
Grenada	$$$	2,300	•	•	•	•	•			•		•	•
Guadeloupe	$$	5,100		•			•	•		•		•	•
Jamaica	$$$	23,000	•	•	•		•	•		•		•	•
Martinique	$$$	6,000	•	•			•	•		•		•	•
Nevis	$$$	400		•	•	•	•	•		•		•	
Puerto Rico	$$	11,909	•	•	•	•	•	•	•	•	•	•	•
Saba	$	96		•			•	•		•	•		
St. Barthélemy	$$$$	715	•	•			•			•		•	•
St. Eustatius	$	95		•	•					•	•		
St. Kitts	$$	1,650		•	•	•	•	•		•	•		•
St. Lucia	$$$	3,300	•	•	•		•	•		•	•	•	
St. Maarten/St. Martin	$$$	6,146	•	•	•					•		•	
St. Vincent	$$	730		•	•	•	•	•		•	•		
Trinidad	$	1,462	•	•	•			•		•	•		
Tobago	$$	1,500	•		•	•	•	•			•	•	
Turks and Caicos	$$$	1,670	•		•	•	•		•			•	
U.S. Virgin Islands:													
St. Croix	$$	1,495		•	•	•	•					•	•
St. John	$$	1,003		•	•	•	•	•		•		•	•
St. Thomas	$$	3,038	•	•	•	•				•		•	•

* Figures based on 2000 estimates

Public transportation	Fine dining	Local cuisine	Shopping	Music	Casinos	Nightlife	Diving and Snorkeling	Sailing	Golf	Hiking	Ecotourism	Villa rentals	All-inclusives	Campgrounds	Luxury resorts	Secluded getaway	Good for families	Romantic hideaway
	•	•	•	•			•	•				•	•		•	•		•
•	•		•		•	•	•	•	•				•		•	•	•	
•	•	•	•	•	•	•	•	•		•	•	•			•		•	•
•	•	•	•		•		•	•		•	•	•			•	•		•
•	•	•	•	•			•	•		•	•	•			•	•		•
	•	•	•			•	•		•		•	•			•	•		
•	•	•	•	•		•	•	•	•		•	•			•	•	•	
•		•		•			•	•	•	•	•	•			•	•		•
	•	•					•	•		•	•	•			•	•		
•	•	•	•		•	•	•	•	•	•	•	•		•	•	•		•
•	•	•	•		•	•	•	•	•	•	•	•			•	•		•
•	•	•	•	•		•	•	•	•	•	•	•	•		•	•	•	
	•						•	•	•	•	•				•	•		•
•	•	•	•			•	•	•		•	•	•			•	•		•
		•					•	•							•	•		•
	•		•			•		•		•	•	•			•	•		•
							•			•	•					•		
	•	•	•		•		•	•	•	•	•	•			•	•		•
•	•	•	•	•		•	•	•	•	•	•	•			•	•		•
•	•	•		•	•	•	•	•	•		•				•		•	•
•	•	•	•		•	•	•	•			•	•			•	•		
•	•	•	•				•	•	•			•			•		•	
	•	•				•	•	•	•	•	•	•			•			•
		•			•		•								•			
•	•	•	•				•	•	•	•	•	•			•		•	
•	•	•	•			•	•	•	•	•	•	•		•	•	•	•	•
•	•	•	•			•	•	•	•			•	•		•		•	

THE MANY FACES
OF THE ISLANDS

If you have seen one island, you have by no means seen them all. The Caribbean has towering volcanic islands, such as Saba; islands with lush rain forests, such as Dominica, St. Lucia, Martinique, and Guadeloupe; and some islands, notably Puerto Rico, that have both jungle and arid climes. You'll find glittering discos, casinos, and dazzling nightlife on such islands as Aruba, the Dominican Republic, and Puerto Rico. There are also isolated cays with only sand, sea, sun, lizards, and mosquitoes. Some islands—Puerto Rico and St. Kitts among them—have ancient forts to view; others (Barbados and the Caicos Islands) have caverns and caves to explore. There are also places like Grand Turk and Little Cayman, where the only notable sights are beneath the translucent sea.

Different though they are in many ways, the islands are stylistically similar. The style-setter is the tropical climate. Year-round summertime temperatures and a plethora of beaches produce a pace known as "island time." Only the trade winds move swiftly. Operating on island time means "I'll get to it when the spirit moves me."

Similarities among the islands are also attributable to the region's history. The agrarian Arawaks paddled up from South America and populated the islands more than 1,000 years ago. In the early 14th century the mighty Caribs, for whom the area is named, arrived, probably from Brazil or Venezuela, gradually pushing the Arawaks up the spine of the Caribbean. (The actual name of the Caribs was Galibi, a word the Spanish corrupted to Canibal—the origin of the word *cannibal*.) Both tribes (as well as the peaceful Taíno people of Puerto Rico, Hispaniola, Cuba, and Jamaica) had remarkably sophisti-

cated cultures and elaborate sociological systems.

Christopher Columbus made four voyages through the region between 1492 and 1504, christening the islands while dodging Carib arrows. He landed on or sailed past all of the Greater Antilles and virtually all of the eastern Caribbean islands. From the 16th century until the early 19th century, the Dutch, Danes, Swedes, English, French, and Spanish fought bitterly for control of the islands. Some islands have almost as many battle sites as sand flies. After gaining control of the islands and annihilating the remaining Arawaks (mostly through diseases brought from Europe) and Caribs (mostly by sword and musket), the Europeans established vast sugar plantations and brought enslaved Africans to work the fields. With the abolition of slavery in the mid-19th century, people from Asia and India were brought to the region as indentured laborers.

Today the Caribbean is made up of individual countries, each with customs, immigration officials, and in a few instances, political difficulties. Most islands have opted for independence; others retain ties to a mother country. They're developing nations, and many have severe economic problems. Virtually all depend on tourism. And, human nature being what it is, some islanders resent their dependency on tourist dollars. Like as not, the person who serves you has stood in a long line, vying with other anxious applicants for the few available jobs. After serving your meals or cleaning your luxurious room, he or she returns to a tiny home, knowing full well that in less than a week you will have shelled out more than many islanders earn in a month.

Some visitors object to encountering resentment when all they seek is a pleasant vacation and have paid dearly for it. Some feel rather keenly that they'd always like hot water—or at least *some* water—when they turn on the shower. In even the most luxurious resorts there are times when things simply don't work: It's a fact of Caribbean life. No matter how diligent the upkeep, humidity and salt air take their toll, and cracked tiles and chipped paint are common everywhere. Many first-time visitors also forget that they're in the tropics and find it hard to get used to, say, a lizard scurrying away at the opening of a door. Still other visitors simply have no patience with island time. There are many, however, who travel to the Caribbean year after year. Some return to the same hotel on the same beach on the same island, while others try to sample as much as this vibrant region has to offer.

Finding Your Own Place in the Sun

GEOGRAPHY IN BRIEF

The Caribbean Sea, an area of more than a million square miles, stretches south of Florida down to the coast of Venezuela. The **Greater Antilles**—the islands closest to the United States—are composed of Cuba, Jamaica, Hispaniola (divided into Haiti and the Dominican Republic), and Puerto Rico (Haiti and Cuba are not covered in this book). The Cayman Islands lie south of Cuba, and the Turks and Caicos, which are in the Atlantic Ocean north of Hispaniola and technically part of the Bahamas, are included in this book because of their proximity to and affinity with the Caribbean islands.

The **Lesser Antilles**—greater in number but smaller in size than the Greater Antilles—are divided into three groups: the Leewards and the Windwards, in the eastern Caribbean, and the islands of the southern Caribbean. In the Leeward chain are the U.S. Virgin Islands (USVI), the British Virgin Islands (BVI), Anguilla, St. Martin/St. Maarten, St. Barthélemy, Saba, St. Eustatius, St. Kitts, Nevis, Barbuda, Antigua, Montserrat, and Guadeloupe. The Windwards are composed of Dominica, Martinique, St. Lucia,

St. Vincent and the Grenadines, and Grenada. Barbados is just east of this group. In the southern Caribbean, off the coast of Venezuela, Trinidad and Tobago are anchored in the east, and Aruba, Bonaire, and Curaçao (known as the ABC Islands) bathe in western waters.

A SAMPLING OF ISLAND CULTURE

The Caribbean population is a rich gumbo of nationalities, including Americans, British, Canadians who have retired to and invested in the islands. Little remains of the indigenous populations (there are Carib communities on Dominica and St. Vincent, as well as tantalizing, if sparse, archaeological remains), and many other groups have left their cultural imprint on the Caribbean.

Nowhere is **African** culture more noticeable than in island music. Calypso was born in Trinidad, and its catchy rhythms veil the barbed political satire of many of the lyrics. The island is also the stomping ground of a flat-out, freewheeling Carnival that rivals the pre-Lenten celebrations in Rio de Janeiro and New Orleans. Jamaica is the home of reggae, the Rastafarian sound that has racial, political, and religious undertones. The pulsating merengue, born in the Dominican Republic, is danced exuberantly everywhere on the island. On Puerto Rico you'll find the salsa, whose range encompasses unabashed hip-swiveling tunes and wailing ballads lamenting lost love. Martinique and Guadeloupe claim to be the cradle of the sinuous beguine, whose lilting rhythm sways like the palm trees. The music that animates Barbados ranges from *soca* (a catchy mix of soul and calypso) and calypso to the hottest jazz. St. Lucia is also proud of its annual jazz festival (held in May). On many islands with a French heritage, *zouk* (a syncopated beat, akin to Caribbean house) is now the rage.

It was from St. Kitts, known as the Mother Colony of the West Indies, that **British** colonists were dispatched in the 17th century to settle Antigua, Barbuda, Tortola, and Montserrat. If you're a history buff, you won't want to miss the beautifully restored Nelson's Dockyard (as in Horatio, Lord), at Antigua's English Harbour; Port Royal, outside Kingston, Jamaica, a pirate stronghold until an earthquake shook things up in 1692; or the hunkering fortress of Brimstone Hill on St. Kitts. Fans who understand the intricacies of cricket can watch matches between Nevis and St. Kitts teams. And the waters around Antigua and the BVI are a mecca for serious sailors. Barbados, which flew the British flag without interruption for 350 years, has cricket, horse racing at Garrison Savannah, polo, and rugby.

Saba, St. Eustatius, St. Maarten, Bonaire, and Curaçao all fly the **Dutch** flag, but they're laced with subtle differences. Saba is a tiny volcanic island known for its beauty, its friendly inhabitants, and its gingerbread-trim houses. Curaçao's colorful waterfront shops and restaurants are reminiscent of Amsterdam. Quiet St. Eustatius—affectionately called Statia—has well-preserved historical sites and is famed for being the first foreign nation to salute the new American flag in 1776. The streets of Philipsburg, the capi-

tal of St. Maarten, are lined with colorful Dutch colonial buildings replete with fretwork and verandas. Bonaire is best known for its excellent scuba diving.

Martinique, Guadeloupe, St. Martin, and St. Barthélemy (often called St. Barths or St. Barts) compose the **French** West Indies—actual *départements* (administrative regions) of France. The language, the currency, the culture, and the style are *très* French. St. Barths is the quietest (and chicest), Martinique the liveliest, St. Martin the friendliest, and Guadeloupe the lushest.

In the Dominican Republic, which occupies the eastern two-thirds of the island of Hispaniola, the language and culture are decidedly **Spanish.** The Colonial Zone of Santo Domingo is the site of the oldest city in the western hemisphere; its restored buildings reflect the 15th-century Columbus period. You also get a sense of the past in Puerto Rico's Old San Juan, with its narrow cobblestone streets and filigreed iron balconies.

ESSENTIAL INFORMATION

For island-specific information (including local phone numbers) see the A to Z sections in individual island chapters.

ADDRESSES

"Whimsical" might best describe Caribbean addresses. Street names change for no apparent reason, and most buildings have no numbers. Addresses throughout this guide may include cross streets, landmarks, and other directionals. But to find your destination, you might have to ask a local—and be prepared for such directions as, "Go down so, and take a right at the fish market. Stay on that road past the church and take a left after the river."

AIR TRAVEL

BOOKING

When you book, **look for nonstop flights** and **remember that "direct" flights stop at least once.** Try to avoid connecting flights, which require a change of plane. The more connections you make, the more likely your luggage won't keep up with you. For more booking tips and to check prices and make on-line flight reservations, log on to www.fodors.com.

CARRIERS

Air ALM serves the Dutch islands of Aruba, Bonaire, Curacao, and St. Maarten from Miami and San Juan. Air Jamaica flies from more than a dozen U.S. gateways to Jamaica, Barbados, Bonaire, Dominica, Grand Cayman, Grenada, St. Lucia, St. Vincent, Trinidad, and Turks and Caicos; some flights are nonstop, others connect through Montego Bay. American Airlines flies daily to and from about two dozen Caribbean destinations via American Eagle connecting flights through San Juan, Puerto Rico. BWIA International serves Trinidad and Tobago, as well as Antigua, Barbados, Grenada, Jamaica, St. Lucia, St. Maarten, and St. Vincent, from New York, Miami, Washington, D.C., Toronto, and London. Other major U.S. carriers with Caribbean code-share service through San Juan or Barbados include Continental, Delta, Northwest, United, and US Airways.

Air Canada flies from Toronto to Antigua, Barbados, Jamaica, St. Lucia, and Trinidad; from Montréal to Barbados, Guadeloupe, and Martinique.

Carriers that offer U.K. service include British Airways, JMC, and Virgin Atlantic, as well as Air Jamaica and BWIA. From Australia and New Zealand, British Airways will get you to London, where you can connect with nonstop Caribbean flights. Qantas will get you to Honolulu, with connections on American Airlines, or to London, with connections on British Airways. Air France and KLM fly from Paris or Amsterdam, respectively, to selected islands.

Several Caribbean flag carriers provide interisland service. Air Caraïbes serves the French West Indies (Guadeloupe, Martinique, St. Barths, and St. Martin), as well as Dominica, Saba, San Juan, St. Lucia, St. Maarten, and St. Vincent and the Grenadines. BWIA Express flies from Trinidad and Tobago to Antigua, Barbados, Grenada, Jamaica, St. Lucia, St. Maarten, and St. Vincent. Caribbean Star flies between its Antigua hub and Barbados, Dominica, Grenada, St. Vincent, Tortola, and Trinidad. LIAT flies to all the Lesser Antilles, using Puerto Rico, St. Maarten, Antigua, St. Thomas, and Barbados as its hubs. SVG Air flies from St. Vincent and the Grenadines to Barbados and Grenada. Winair (Windward Island Airways) is based on St. Maarten and flies to the neighboring islands of Saba, St. Eustatius, St. Kitts, Nevis, St. Barths, Anguilla, and Tortola.

➤ MAJOR AIRLINES: **American Airlines** (☎ 800/433–7300, WEB www.aa.com). **Continental** (☎ 800/231–0856, WEB www.continental.com). **Delta** (☎ 800/241–4141, WEB www.delta-airlines.com). **Northwest Airlines** (☎ 800/447–4747, WEB www.nwa.com). **United Airlines** (☎ 800/538–2929, WEB www.united.com). **US Airways** (☎ 800/428–4322, WEB www.usairways.com).

➤ SMALLER AIRLINES: **Air ALM** (☎ 800/327–7230, WEB www.airalm.com). **Air Jamaica** (☎ 800/523–5585, WEB www.airjamaica.com). **American Eagle** (☎ 800/433–7300, WEB www.aa.com). **BWIA** (☎ 800/538–2942, WEB www.bwee.com). **LIAT** (☎ 800/468–0482, WEB www.liatairline.com). **Winair** (☎ 800/634–4907, WEB www.windwardislandsairways.com).

➤ FROM THE U.K.: **Air Jamaica** (☎ 0181/570–9171, WEB www.airjamaica.com). **British Airways** (☎ 0345/222–111, WEB www.britishairways.com). **BWIA** (☎ 0171/745–1100, WEB www.bwee.com). **JMC** (☎ 0113/255–5222, WEB www.jmc-holidays.co.uk). **Virgin Atlantic** (☎ 0129/374–7747, WEB www.virginatlantic.com).

➤ FROM ELSEWHERE IN THE WORLD: **Air Canada** (☎ 800/776–3000 in the U.S.; 888/247–2262 in Canada, WEB www.aircanada.ca). **Air France** (☎ 0/802/802–802 in Paris, WEB www.airfrance.com). **British Airways** (☎ 02/9258–3399 in Sydney, 03/9603–1199 in Melbourne, and 07/3223–3133 in Brisbane, WEB www.britishairways.com). **KLM** (☎ 31/20–4–747–747 in Amsterdam, WEB www.klm.com), **Qantas** (☎ 13–13–13 in Australia or 0800/808–767 in New Zealand, WEB www.qantas.com).

CHECK-IN & BOARDING

Checking in, paying departure taxes (which are usually *not* included in your airfare in the Caribbean), clearing security, and boarding can take much longer than you expect at some island airports. Especially when heading home, **get to the airport at least 1½ hours ahead of time** (2 hours if you plan to squeeze in some duty-free shopping). From most islands there's often only one flight per day going in the direction you're headed.

Assuming that not everyone with a ticket will show up, airlines routinely overbook planes. When everyone does, airlines ask for volunteers to give up their seats. In return, these volunteers usually get a certificate for a free flight and are rebooked on the next flight out. If there are not enough volunteers, the airline must choose who will be denied boarding. The first to get bumped are passengers who checked in late and those flying on discounted tickets, so **get to the gate and check in as early as possible,** especially during peak periods.

Always **bring a government-issued photo I.D. to the airport;** a passport is best. You will be asked to show it before you are allowed to check in.

CUTTING COSTS

The least expensive airfares to the Caribbean must usually be purchased in advance and are nonrefundable. It's smart to **call a number of airlines, and when you are quoted a good price, book it on the spot**—the same fare may not be available the next day. Always **check different routings** and look into using different airports. Travel agents, especially low-fare specialists (☞ Discounts & Deals, *below*), are helpful.

Use the Internet to compare fares and schedules and buy tickets. Most airlines offer discounts or bonus frequent flyer miles if you purchase tickets on-line. General travel sites, such as www.expedia.com or www.travelocity.com, let you compare current fares for all airlines serving a particular destination and will also book your flights. In fact, many airline sites now show you competitive routings and fares. You can also **bid for cheaper fares over the Internet** through companies such as www.priceline.com, which are legitimate sources for seats on major airlines. The more flexible you are with your timing and destination, the better the deal you can make.

Ask about island-hopping passes. Air ALM's 30-day Caribbean Airpass, for example, may be used for five destinations, including Miami. If you stay over in Jamaica, Air Jamaica's island-hopping program allows you to fly round-trip to any of the airline's other Caribbean destinations for free. American Airlines and American Eagle offer a "Caribbean Explorer" fare to 23 Caribbean destinations out of San Juan. BWIA offers a 30-day "Caribbean Traveller" air pass for travel to its 12 Caribbean and South American destinations. LIAT has three categories of interisland "Explorer" passes for different durations.

Consolidators are another good source. They buy tickets for scheduled international flights at reduced rates from the airlines, then sell them at prices that beat the best fare available directly from the airlines, usually without restrictions. Sometimes you can even get your money back if you need to return the ticket. Carefully read the fine print detailing penalties for changes and cancellations, and **confirm your consolidator reservation with the airline.**

➤ CONSOLIDATORS: **Cheap Tickets** (☎ 800/377–1000, WEB www. cheaptickets.com). **Discount Airline Ticket Service** (☎ 800/576–1600). **Unitravel** (☎ 800/325–2222). **Up & Away Travel** (☎ 212/889–2345). **World Travel Network** (☎ 800/409–6753).

ENJOYING THE FLIGHT

For more legroom, **request an emergency-aisle seat.** Don't sit in the row in front of the emergency aisle or in front of a bulkhead, where seats may not recline. If you have dietary concerns, **ask for special meals when booking.** These can be vegetarian, low-cholesterol, lactose-free, or kosher, for example. On long flights, try to maintain a normal routine to help fight jet lag. At night, **get some sleep;** by day **eat light meals, drink water** (not alcohol), **do isometric exercises,** and **move around the cabin** to stretch your legs. For additional jet-lag tips consult *Fodor's FYI: Travel Fit & Healthy* (available at bookstores everywhere).

FLYING TIMES

The flight from New York to San Juan, Puerto Rico, takes 3½ hours; from Miami to San Juan it's 1½ hours. Flights from New York to Kingston or Montego Bay, Jamaica, take about 4 hours; those from Miami, about an hour. Nonstop flights from London to Antigua and Barbados and from Paris to Guadeloupe, Martinique, and St. Martin are about 7 hours. Once you've arrived in the Caribbean, hops between the islands range from 20 minutes to 2 hours.

HOW TO COMPLAIN

If your baggage goes astray or your flight goes awry, complain right away. Most carriers require that you **file a claim immediately** before leaving the baggage claim area. Be sure to get a receipt for your baggage check, which the airline may retain, and a phone number (not reservations) where you may inquire about the status of your bag. Although it's a special nuisance when you're en route to your vacation destination, it's good to know that lost bags are merely delayed and rarely lost forever.

➤ AIRLINE COMPLAINTS: U.S. Department of Transportation **Aviation Consumer Protection Division** (✉ C-75, Room 4107, Washington, DC 20590, ☎ 202/366–2220, WEB www. dot.gov/airconsumer). **Federal Aviation Administration Consumer Hotline** (☎ 800/322–7873).

RECONFIRMING

Be sure to **reconfirm your flights on interisland carriers.** You may be subject to a small carrier's whims: If no other passengers are booked on your flight, you may be requested (actually, told) to take another flight or departure time that's more convenient for the airline, or your plane may make unscheduled stops to pick up more clients or cargo. It's all part of the excitement—and unpredictability—of Caribbean travel. In addition, regional carriers use small aircraft with limited baggage space, and they often impose weight restrictions; **travel light,** or you could be subject to outrageous surcharges or delays in getting very large or heavy luggage, which may have to follow on another flight.

AIRPORTS

Airports on most of the islands are modern facilities, with comfortable waiting areas, restaurants, duty-free shops, and other services. The more remote destinations, of course, have tiny airfields and few services.

BIKE TRAVEL

Many Caribbean islands are mountainous, and their narrow, steep, winding roads already have difficulty accommodating cars, pedestrians, and occasional livestock. Serious bikers, of course, will take all this in stride. If you're more laid-back, however, good bets include: Antigua, Bonaire, Puerto Rico, Grand Turk and Providenciales (Turks and Caicos Islands), and St. Croix (USVI). Most islands have at least one bike-rental company (rates are usually reasonable), and some resorts offer guests the use of bikes at no additional charge.

BIKES IN FLIGHT

Most airlines accommodate bikes as luggage, provided they are dismantled and boxed. Airlines sell bike boxes, which are often free at bike shops, for about $5 (it's at least $100 for bike bags). International travelers can sometimes substitute a bike for a piece of checked luggage at no charge; otherwise, the cost is about $100. Domestic and Canadian airlines charge $25–$50.

BOAT & FERRY TRAVEL

Ferry travel is an inexpensive way to island-hop. Ferries ply the waters of the Grenadines, for example, and you can take a day trip or spend a week or more cruising from one lovely island to another. Cargo schooners and mail boats are even less expensive and more adventuresome modes of interisland travel, but you can't be in a hurry. High-speed ferries or catamarans link neighboring islands, such as Grenada with Carriacou; St. Maarten/St. Martin with St. Barths and Saba; and Martinique with Dominica, Guadeloupe, and St. Lucia. Reservations aren't usually necessary.

BUS TRAVEL

Some islands, such as Puerto Rico, St. Thomas, the Dominican Republic, Aruba, and Barbados have convenient, inexpensive bus service along regular routes—and with regular schedules. On smaller islands, "bus" service may be provided by privately owned vans that follow regular routes but not necessarily regular sched-

ules—they just keep coming, one after another, all day long. Fares are inexpensive (some buses require exact change in local currency), and this mode of transport is a good way to absorb the local culture.

BUSINESS HOURS

Though business hours vary from island to island, shops are generally closed Saturday afternoon and all day Sunday. Some shops close for an hour at lunchtime during the week, as well, although this practice is becoming increasingly rare. Farmers markets are often open daily (except Sunday), but Saturday morning is always the most colorful and exciting time to go.

CAMERAS & PHOTOGRAPHY

Frothy waves in a turquoise sea and palm-lined crescents of beach are relatively easy to capture on film if you **don't let the brightness of the sun on sand and water fool your light meter.** You must compensate or else work early or late in the day when the light isn't as brilliant and contrast isn't such a problem. Try to **capture expansive views** of waterfront, beach, or village scenes; consider shooting down onto the shore from a clearing on a hillside or from a rock on the beach. Or **zoom in on something colorful,** such as a delicate tropical flower or a craftsman at work—but always **ask permission to take pictures of locals or their property. Use a disposable underwater camera** to make your snorkeling and diving adventures more memorable. The *Kodak Guide to Shooting Great Travel Pictures* (available in bookstores or from Fodor's Travel Publications) is loaded with tips.

➤ PHOTO HELP: Kodak Information Center (☎ 800/242–2424).

EQUIPMENT PRECAUTIONS

Keep your film and tape out of the sun, and be advised that sand and sea water are no friends to most camera workings. Carry an extra supply of batteries, and **be prepared to turn on your camera or camcorder** to prove to airport security personnel that the device is real. **Keep all film, exposed or unexposed, in your hand luggage.** High-tech security scanners used on checked luggage in some airports can adversely affect film. Always **ask for hand inspection of film,** which becomes clouded after successive exposures to airport X-ray machines, and **keep videotapes away from metal detectors.** Although thievery isn't a major concern in the Caribbean, don't invite problems: **never leave your gear unattended on the beach or in a rental car,** and **lock up your camera or video equipment when you leave your hotel room.**

FILM & DEVELOPING

Film, batteries, and one-time-use cameras are available in camera stores, souvenir shops, hotel boutiques, and pharmacies—although such items can cost twice as much as at home. In all but the most remote areas, you can find 24-hour film-developing services, as well.

CAR RENTAL

Major firms, such as Avis, Hertz, and Budget, have agencies in many islands of the Caribbean. But **don't overlook local firms;** their cars are mechanically sound, and prices are competitive. Cars often have standard transmission, although automatic is usually an option. It's not crucial to reserve a rental car prior to your arrival. Many hotels, especially those far from the airport, include airport transfers, and taxis are always an option. Besides, you may only want a rental car for a day or two of on-your-own sightseeing. For exciting treks into remote areas where roads are hilly or unpaved, **rent a four-wheel-drive vehicle.**

➤ MAJOR AGENCIES: **Alamo** (☎ 800/522–9696; 020/8759–6200 in the U.K., WEB www.alamo.com). **Avis** (☎ 800/331–1084; 800/879–2847 in Canada; 02/9353–9000 in Australia; 09/525–1982 in New Zealand; 0870/606–0100 in the U.K., WEB www.avis.com). **Budget** (☎ 800/527–0700; 0870/607–5000 in the U.K., through affiliate Europcar, WEB www.budget.com). **Dollar** (☎ 800/800–6000; 0124/622–0111 in the U.K., through affiliate Sixt Kenning; 02/9223–1444 in Australia, WEB www.dollar.com). **Hertz** (☎ 800/654–3001; 800/263–0600 in Canada; 020/8897–2072 in the U.K.; 02/9669–2444 in Australia; 09/256–8690 in New Zealand, WEB

www.hertz.com). **National Car Rental** (☎ 800/227–7368; 020/8680–4800 in the U.K., where it is known as National Europe, WEB www.national-car.com).

CUTTING COSTS

Ask about required deposits and cancellation penalties. Plan to **pay by credit card to avoid a hefty cash deposit.** If you're traveling during a holiday period, **make sure that a confirmed reservation guarantees you a car.** To get the best deal, **book through a travel agent who will shop around.**

INSURANCE

When driving a rented car you are generally responsible for any damage to or loss of the vehicle as well as for any property damage or personal injury that you may cause. Before you rent, see what coverage your personal auto-insurance policy and credit cards provide.

REQUIREMENTS & RESTRICTIONS

An international driver's license or a temporary permit, which you can get at rental agencies or local police offices upon presentation of a valid license and a small fee, is often required.

SURCHARGES

Before you pick up a car in one city and leave it in another, **ask about drop-off charges or one-way service fees,** which can be substantial. This may be relevant in the larger islands with several large cities, such as Puerto Rico or the Dominican Republic. Note, too, that some rental agencies charge extra if you return the car before the time specified in your contract. To avoid a hefty refueling fee, **fill the tank just before you turn in the car.**

CAR TRAVEL

Although exploring on your own can give your sightseeing excursions a sense of adventure, tentative drivers should instead consider hiring a taxi for the day. Locals, who are familiar with the roads, often drive fast and take chances. You don't want to get in their way.

EMERGENCY SERVICES

Major-brand gas and service stations, where you can use your credit card, are found throughout the Caribbean but mainly in the larger towns. Before driving off into the countryside, **check your rental car for tire-changing equipment,** including an inflated spare.

ROAD CONDITIONS

Island roads, particularly in mountainous regions that experience heavy tropical rains, are often potholed and bumpy—as well as narrow, winding, and hilly. **Drive with extreme caution,** especially if you venture out at night. You won't see guardrails on every hill and curve, although the drops can be frighteningly steep. And pedestrians (including children and the elderly) and livestock often share the roadway with vehicles.

ROAD MAPS

Road maps are available from car-rental agencies and often at your hotel. Small islands have few roads—often one main road around the perimeter and a couple that cross the island. It's hard to get lost.

RULES OF THE ROAD

On islands with a British heritage, **be prepared to drive on the left.** Speed limits are low, because it's often hard to find a road long and straight enough to *safely* get up much speed. Drivers are generally courteous; for example, if someone flashes car headlights at you at an intersection, it means "after you."

CHILDREN IN THE CARIBBEAN

Kids of all ages love the beach and, therefore, love the Caribbean. Resorts are increasingly sensitive to families' needs, and many now have extensive children's programs and can arrange for a baby-sitter when parents need some time alone. On sightseeing days try to include some activities that will also interest them. Sights and attractions that children will particularly enjoy are indicated by a rubber-duckie icon (🦆) in the margin. For general advice about traveling with children, consult *Fodor's FYI: Travel with Your Baby* (available in bookstores everywhere).

If you are renting a car, don't forget to **arrange for a car seat** when you reserve.

FLYING

If your children are two or older, **ask about children's airfares.** As a general rule, infants under two not occupying a seat fly at greatly reduced fares or even for free. When booking, **confirm carry-on allowances** if you're traveling with infants. In general, for babies charged 10% of the adult fare you are allowed one carry-on bag and a collapsible stroller; if the flight is full, the stroller may have to be checked or you may be limited to less.

Experts agree that it's a good idea to use safety seats aloft for children weighing less than 40 pounds. Airlines set their own policies: U.S. carriers usually require that the child be ticketed, even if he or she is young enough to ride free, since the seats must be strapped into regular seats. Do **check your airline's policy about using safety seats during takeoff and landing.** And since safety seats are not allowed everywhere in the plane, get your seat assignments early.

When reserving, **request children's meals or a freestanding bassinet** if you need them. But note that bulkhead seats, where you must sit to use the bassinet, may lack an overhead bin or storage space on the floor.

FOOD

Even if your youngsters are picky eaters, meals in the Caribbean shouldn't be a problem. Baby food is easy to find (although often pricer than you might find at home, and brands may be limited), and hamburgers and hot dogs are available at many resorts. Restaurant menus offer pasta and vegetarian dishes, pizza, sandwiches, and ice cream—all of which appeal to kids. Supermarkets have cereal, snacks, and other packaged goods you'll recognize from home. At outdoor markets, a few dollars will buy you enough bananas, mangoes, and other fresh fruit to last your entire vacation. Just watch out for overly spicy food that may be upset children's sensitive stomachs.

LODGING

Children are welcome in most Caribbean resorts; exceptions are couples-only and adults-only establishments and the ultra-exclusive properties. Some places have only limited children's activities and may not welcome kids during peak season. Other properties offer fully supervised kids' programs, in-room babysitting, kids' menus and other family-friendly features. Children under 12 or 16 can often stay free in their parents' room (be sure to **find out the cutoff age for children's discounts** when booking).

Families should also **consider booking a condo or a villa**; a two-bedroom condo (and sometimes even a one-bedroom condo) is often suitable for two parents and two children traveling together and may also be cheaper than a larger room or suite in a hotel or resort for a similar time period. Meal preparation in the condo's kitchen can save substantially on the cost of meals. Some condo resorts even have children's programs. In some islands, such as Grand Cayman, condos and villas actually outnumber hotel rooms.

PRECAUTIONS

Don't underestimate the tropical sun. Throughout the day, even away from the beach, lather plenty of sunscreen—with a sun protection factor (SPF) of 15 or higher—on all exposed areas. Small children should also wear a hat. Mosquito bites can become infected when scratched, so **use bug spray** and avoid the problem. To prevent dehydration, **carry plenty of bottled water** at the beach and on sightseeing excursions.

To avoid immigration problems if your child carries a different last name, **bring identification that clarifies the family relationship** (e.g., a birth certificate identifying the parent or a joint passport). If a child is traveling without both birth parents, a notarized letter should accompany the child from the nonpresent parent(s) authorizing permission for the child to travel.

SIGHTS & ATTRACTIONS

Places that are especially appealing to children are indicated by a rubber-duckie icon (🐤) in the margin.

SUPPLIES & EQUIPMENT

Suites at many resorts and even small hotels have sofas suitable for children sharing a parent's room. High chairs and cribs are also generally available. Supermarkets sell common brands of disposable diapers, baby food, and other necessities. Bookstores and souvenir shops have activity books and toys that kids will enjoy on vacation and back at home.

COMPUTERS ON THE ROAD

Bring an adapter for your laptop plug. Adapters are inexpensive, and some models have several plugs suitable for different systems throughout the world. Some hotels lend adapters to guests to use during their stay.

At the airport, **be prepared to turn on your laptop** to prove to security personnel that the device is real. The security X-ray machines aren't damaging to a laptop, but **keep computer disks away from metal detectors.** In your hotel, **stow away and lock up your laptop when you're out of the room.** Although thievery isn't a major concern in the Caribbean, don't invite a problem.

CONSUMER PROTECTION

Whenever shopping or buying travel services in the Caribbean, **pay with a major credit card,** if possible, so you can cancel payment or get reimbursed if there's a problem. If you're doing business with a particular company for the first time, **contact your local Better Business Bureau and the attorney general's offices** in your state and (for U.S. businesses) the company's home state as well. Have any complaints been filed? Finally, if you're buying a package or tour, always **consider travel insurance** that includes default coverage (☞ Insurance).

➤ BBBs: **Council of Better Business Bureaus** (✉ 4200 Wilson Blvd., Suite 800, Arlington, VA 22203, ☎ 703/276–0100, ℻ 703/525–8277, ⓦⓔⓑ www.bbb.org).

CRUISE TRAVEL

Cruising is a relaxing and convenient way to tour this beautiful part of the world. You get all of the amenities of a luxury hotel and enough activities to guarantee fun, even on rainy days.

All your important decisions are made long before you board. Your itinerary is set, and you know the total cost of your vacation beforehand.

Ships usually call at several ports on a single voyage but are at each port for only one day. Thus, although you may be exposed to several islands, you don't get much of a feel for any one of them.

To learn how to plan, choose, and book a cruise-ship voyage, check out Cruise How-to's on www.fodors.com.

➤ CRUISE LINES: **American Canadian Caribbean Line** (✉ Box 368, Warren, RI 02885, ☎ 401/247–0955 or 800/556–7450, WEB www.accl-smallships.com). **Carnival Cruise Lines** (✉ 3655 N.W. 87th Ave., Miami, FL 33178, ☎ 305/599–2600 or 800/227–6482, WEB www.carnival.com). **Celebrity Cruises** (✉ 1050 Caribbean Way, Miami, FL 33122, ☎ 305/539–6000 or 800/437–3111, WEB www.celebrity-cruises.com). **Clipper Cruise Line** (✉ 7711 Bonhomme Ave., St. Louis, MO 63105, ☎ 314/727–2929 or 800/325–0010, WEB www.clippercruise.com). **Club Med** (✉ 75 Valencia Ave., Coral Gables, FL 33134, ☎ 800/258–2633 or 888/CLUBMED, WEB www.clubmed.com). **Costa Cruise Lines** (✉ World Trade Center Bldg., 80 S.W. 8th St., Miami, FL 33130, ☎ 305/358–7325 or 800/462–6782, WEB www.costacruises.com). **Crystal Cruises** (✉ 2049 Century Park E., Ste. 1400, Los Angeles, CA 90067, ☎ 310/783–9300 or 800/446–6620, WEB www.crystalcruises.com). **Cunard Line** (✉ 6100 Blue Lagoon Dr., Ste. 400, Miami, FL 33126, ☎ 305/463–3000 or 800/7–CUNARD, WEB www.cunardline.com). **Disney Cruise Line** (✉ 210 Celebration Pl., Ste. 400, Celebration, FL 34747, ☎ 407/566–3500, WEB www.disneycruise.com). **Holland America Line** (✉ 300 Elliott Ave. W, Seattle, WA 98119, ☎ 206/281–3465 or 800/426–6593, WEB www.hollandamerica.com). **Lindblad Expedition** (✉ 720 5th Ave., New York, NY 10019, ☎ 800/762–0003, WEB www.lindblad.com). **Norwegian Cruise Line** (✉ 7665 Corporate Center Dr., Miami, FL 33126, ☎ 305/436–4000 or 800/327–7030,

WEB www.ncl.com). **Princess Cruises** (✉ 10100 Santa Monica Blvd., Ste. 1800, Los Angeles, CA 90067, ☎ 310/553–1770 or 800/421–0522, WEB www.princesscruises.com). **Radisson Seven Seas Cruises** (✉ 600 Corporate Dr., Suite 410, Fort Lauderdale, FL 33334, ☎ 954/776–6123 or 800/477–7500, WEB www.rssc.com). **Regal Cruises** (✉ 300 Regal Cruises Way, Box 1329, Palmetto, FL 34221, ☎ 941/721–7300 or 800/270–7245, WEB www.regalcruises.com). **Renaissance Cruises** (✉ 350 Las Olas Blvd., Fort Lauderdale, FL 33302, ☎ 877/549–1124, WEB www.renaissancecruises.com). **Royal Caribbean Cruise Line** (✉ 1050 Caribbean Way, Miami, FL 33132, ☎ 305/539–6000 or 800/327–6700, WEB www.royalcaribbean.com). **Seabourn Cruise Line** (✉ 6100 Blue Lagoon Dr., Ste. 400, Miami, FL 33126, ☎ 305/463–3000 or 800/929–9391, WEB www.seabourn.com). **Silversea Cruises** (✉ 110 E. Broward Blvd., Fort Lauderdale, FL 33301, ☎ 954/522–4477 or 800/722–9055, WEB www.silverseacruises.com). **Star Clippers** (✉ 4101 Salzedo St., Coral Gables, FL 33146, ☎ 305/442–0550 or 800/442–0551, WEB www.star-clippers.com). **Windjammer Barefoot Cruises** (✉ 1759 Bay Rd., Miami Beach, FL 33139, ☎ 800/327–2602, WEB www.windjammer.com). **Windstar Cruises** (✉ 300 Elliott Ave. W, Seattle, WA 98119, ☎ 206/281–3535 or 800/258–7245, WEB www.windstarcruises.com).

➤ ORGANIZATIONS: **Cruise Lines International Association** (CLIA; ✉ 500 5th Ave., Ste. 1407, New York, NY 10110, ☎ 212/921–0066, WEB www.cruising.org).

CUSTOMS & DUTIES

When shopping, **keep receipts** for all purchases. Upon reentering the country, **be ready to show customs officials what you've bought.** If you feel a duty is incorrect or object to the way your clearance was handled, note the inspector's badge number and ask to see a supervisor. If the problem isn't resolved, write to the appropriate authorities, beginning with the port director at your point of entry.

IN AUSTRALIA

Australian residents who are 18 or older may bring home $A400 worth of souvenirs and gifts (including jewelry), 250 cigarettes or 250 grams of tobacco, and 1,125 ml of alcohol (including wine, beer, and spirits). Residents under 18 may bring back $A200 worth of goods. Prohibited items include meat products. Seeds, plants, and fruits need to be declared upon arrival.

➤ INFORMATION: **Australian Customs Service** (Regional Director, ✉ Box 8, Sydney, NSW 2001, Australia, ☎ 02/9213–2000, FAX 02/9213–4000, WEB www.customs.gov.au).

IN CANADA

Canadian residents who have been out of Canada for at least seven days may bring home C$500 worth of goods duty-free. If you've been away fewer than seven days but more than 48 hours, the duty-free allowance drops to C$200; if your trip lasts 24–48 hours, the allowance is C$50. You may not pool allowances with family members. Goods claimed under the C$500 exemption may follow you by mail; those claimed under the lesser exemptions must accompany you. Alcohol and tobacco products may be included in the seven-day and 48-hour exemptions but not in the 24-hour exemption. If you meet the age requirements of the province or territory through which you reenter Canada, you may bring in, duty-free, 1.14 liters (40 imperial ounces) of wine or liquor *or* 24 12-ounce cans or bottles of beer or ale. If you are 16 or older you may bring in, duty-free, 200 cigarettes and 50 cigars. Check ahead of time with Revenue Canada or the Department of Agriculture for policies regarding meat products, seeds, plants, and fruits.

You may send an unlimited number of gifts worth up to C$60 each duty-free to Canada. Label the package UNSOLICITED GIFT—VALUE UNDER $60. Alcohol and tobacco are excluded.

➤ INFORMATION: **Revenue Canada** (✉ 2265 St. Laurent Blvd. S, Ottawa, Ontario K1G 4K3, Canada, ☎ 613/993–0534 or 800/461–9999 in Canada, FAX 613/991–4126, WEB www.ccra-adrc.gc.ca).

IN THE CARIBBEAN

Most islands wave tourists through immigration and customs with only a cursory question or two. Exceptions include major hubs within the Caribbean, such as Jamaica, Puerto Rico, and Antigua. To allay their concerns about smuggling or drug running, some countries do inspect most baggage at customs. If you're yachting through the islands, note that harbor customs are often thorough, as well.

These rules generally apply throughout the Caribbean: you're limited to bringing *in* 2 liters of alcohol, 2 cartons of cigarettes, and a reasonable amount of duty-free goods for your personal use. More than that, and you'll be asked to pay a hefty import tax.

IN NEW ZEALAND

Homeward-bound residents 17 or older may bring back NZ$700 worth of souvenirs and gifts. Your duty-free allowance also includes 4.5 liters of wine or beer; one 1,125-ml bottle of spirits; and either 200 cigarettes, 250 grams of tobacco, 50 cigars, or a combination of the three up to 250 grams. Prohibited items include meat products, seeds, plants, and fruits.

➤ INFORMATION: **New Zealand Customs** (Custom House, ✉ 50 Anzac Ave., Box 29, Auckland, New Zealand, ☎ 09/300–5399, FAX 09/359–6730, WEB www.customs.govt.nz).

IN THE U.K.

Although some Caribbean nations are part of the British Commonwealth, they are not part of the European Union (EU) with regard to customs. If you're a U.K. resident, you may bring home from countries outside the European Union, duty-free, 200 cigarettes or 50 cigars; 1 liter of spirits or 2 liters of fortified or sparkling wine or liqueurs; 2 liters of still table wine; 60 ml of perfume; 250 ml of toilet water; plus £136 worth of other goods, including gifts and souvenirs. Prohibited items include meat products, seeds, plants, and fruits.

➤ INFORMATION: **HM Customs and Excise** (✉ Dorset House, Stamford St., Bromley, Kent BR1 1XX, U.K., ☎ 020/7202–4227, WEB www.hmce.gov.uk).

IN THE U.S.

U.S. residents who have been out of the country for at least 48 hours and who have not used the $600 allowance or any part of it in the past 30 days may bring home $600 worth of foreign goods duty-free. This allowance, higher than the standard $400 exemption, applies to the two dozen countries in the Caribbean Basin Initiative (CBI). If you visit a CBI country and a non-CBI country, such as Martinique, you may still bring in $600 worth of goods duty-free, but no more than $400 may be from the non-CBI country. If you're returning from the U.S. Virgin Islands (USVI), the duty-free allowance is $1,200. If your travel included the USVI and another country—say, the Dominican Republic—the $1,200 allowance still applies, but at least $600 worth of goods must be from the USVI.

U.S. residents 21 and older may bring back 1 liter of alcohol duty-free. In addition, regardless of your age, you are allowed 200 cigarettes and 100 non-Cuban cigars. Antiques, which the U.S. Customs Service defines as objects more than 100 years old, enter duty-free, as do original works of art done entirely by hand, including paintings, drawings, and sculptures.

You may also mail or ship packages home duty-free: up to $200 worth of goods for personal use, with a limit of one parcel per addressee per day (except alcohol or tobacco products or perfume worth more than $5); label the package PERSONAL USE and attach a list of its contents and their retail value. Do not label the package UNSOLICITED GIFT or your duty-free exemption will drop to $100. Mailed items do not affect your duty-free allowance on your return.

➤ INFORMATION: **U.S. Customs Service** (✉ 1300 Pennsylvania Ave. NW, Washington, DC 20229, WEB www.customs.gov; inquiries ☎ 202/354–1000; complaints c/o ✉ 1300 Pennsylvania Ave. NW, Room 5.4D, Washington, DC 20229; registration of equipment c/o ✉ Resource Management, ☎ 202/927–0540).

DINING

The Caribbean islands offer dining experiences that will delight any palate. You'll find French cuisine with exquisite service, lavish buffets, fresh seafood served by the waterfront, Italian pasta with a modern twist, Chinese cuisine to eat in or take out, vegetarian dishes of just-picked produce, and more. Fast-food restaurants usually feature fried chicken, not burgers, but pizza is everywhere. The restaurants we list are the cream of the crop in each price category.

MEALS & SPECIALTIES

Give your taste buds a vacation and try local cuisine, which could be Spanish-style in Puerto Rico and the Dominican Republic, French créole in St. Lucia and Dominica, Indian in Trinidad, Indonesian in Aruba, spicy barbecue in Jamaica, and fresh seafood everywhere. Vegetarians can expect a treat, as the fresh fruit and vegetables, both usual and unusual, are plentiful.

Resort breakfasts are frequently lavish buffets that offer tropical fruits and fruit juices, cereal, fresh rolls and pastries, hot dishes, such as codfish, corned beef hash, and potatoes, and prepared-to-order eggs, pancakes, and French toast. Lunch could be at a beachfront café or a picnic at a secluded cove. But dinner is the highlight, often combining the expertise of internationally trained chefs with local know-how and ingredients.

MEALTIMES

Expect breakfast to be served from 7:30 AM to 10 AM; lunch from noon to 2 PM or so; and dinner from 7 PM to about 10 PM—perhaps later on Spanish-heritage islands. Some restaurants have specific mealtimes; others serve continuously all day long. Unless otherwise noted, the restaurants listed in this guide are open daily for lunch and dinner.

PAYING

Major credit cards (Access, American Express, Barclaycard, Carte Blanche, Diners Club, Discover, EnRoute, Eurocard, MasterCard, and/or Visa) are accepted in most restaurants. Exceptions are noted in the reviews.

RESERVATIONS & DRESS

Reservations are always a good idea: we mention them only when they're essential or not accepted. Book as far ahead as you can, and reconfirm as soon as you arrive. We mention dress only when men are required to wear a jacket or a jacket and tie. Beach attire is universally frowned upon in restaurants throughout the Caribbean.

WINE, BEER & SPIRITS

The Caribbean is where "de rum come from," so rum is the base of most cocktails—often fruity, festive ones that really pack a punch. Many islands also have their own breweries, and the local beers are light and refreshing—perfect for hot summer afternoons at the beach.

DISABILITIES & ACCESSIBILITY

In the Caribbean very few attractions and sights are equipped with ramps, elevators, or wheelchair-accessible toilets. Exceptions include places on Puerto Rico and the USVI, which must abide by the Americans with Disabilities Act—although not all facilities are well-equipped.

LODGING

Resorts in hilly or mountainous regions are particularly difficult for travelers with disabilities. Many hotels and resorts have accessible ground-floor guestrooms; others, particularly newer ones, offer some guestrooms with extra-wide doors and bathrooms with grab-bars and easily accessible shower stalls. Some hotels may also help arrange rentals of special equipment. Be sure to **make your special needs known when reserving your room.**

RESERVATIONS

When discussing accessibility with an operator or reservations agent, **ask hard questions.** Are there any stairs, inside *or* out? Are there grab bars next to the toilet *and* in the shower/tub? How wide is the doorway to the room? To the bathroom? Are there many stairs between the guestroom and the restaurant, beach, or other public areas? For the most extensive facilities meeting the latest legal specifications, **opt for newer accommodations.**

TRANSPORTATION

At most Caribbean airports passengers board and disembark aircraft directly from and onto the tarmac, which requires negotiating a steep staircase. Puerto Rico is one exception, although even there some small planes can't use the connected jetways. It can be a rather long walk to immigration, customs, and the airport exit. Be sure to **request wheelchairs or escort assistance when booking your flight.**

➤ COMPLAINTS: **Aviation Consumer Protection Division** (✉ C-75, Room 4107, Washington, DC 20590, ☎ 202/366–2220, WEB www.dot.gov/airconsumer) for airline-related problems. **Civil Rights Office** (✉ U.S. Department of Transportation, Departmental Office of Civil Rights, S-30, 400 7th St. SW, Room 10215, Washington, DC 20590, ☎ 202/366–4648, FAX 202/366–9371, WEB www.dot.gov/ost/docr/index.htm) for problems with surface transportation. **Disability Rights Section** (✉ U.S. Department of Justice, Civil Rights Division, Box 66738, Washington, DC 20035-6738, ☎ 202/514–0301 or 800/514–0301; 202/514–0383 TTY; 800/514–0383 TTY; FAX 202/307–1198, WEB www.usdoj.gov/crt/ada/adahom1.htm) for general complaints.

TRAVEL AGENCIES

In the United States, the Americans with Disabilities Act requires that travel firms serve the needs of all travelers. Some agencies specialize in working with people with disabilities.

➤ TRAVELERS WITH MOBILITY PROBLEMS: **Access Adventures** (✉ 206 Chestnut Ridge Rd., Scottsville, NY 14624, ☎ 716/889–9096, dltravel@prodigy.net), run by a former physical-rehabilitation counselor. **Care-Vacations** (✉ 5-5110 50th Ave., Leduc, Alberta T9E 6V4, Canada, ☎ 780/986–6404 or 877/478–7827, FAX 780/986–8332, WEB www.carevacations.com), for group tours and cruise vacations. **Flying Wheels Travel** (✉ 143 W. Bridge St., Box 382, Owatonna, MN 55060, ☎ 507/451–5005 or 800/535–6790, FAX 507/451–1685, WEB www.flyingwheelstravel.com). **Tomorrow's Level of Care** (✉ Box 470299,

Brooklyn, NY 11247, ☎ 718/756–0794 or 800/932–2012), for nursing services and medical equipment.

➤ TRAVELERS WITH DEVELOPMENTAL DISABILITIES: New Directions (✉ 5276 Hollister Ave., Suite 207, Santa Barbara, CA 93111, ☎ 805/967–2841 or 888/967–2841, FAX 805/964–7344, WEB www.newdirectionstravel.com). Sprout (✉ 893 Amsterdam Ave., New York, NY 10025, ☎ 212/222–9575 or 888/222–9575, FAX 212/222–9768, WEB www.gosprout.org).

DISCOUNTS & DEALS

Visit during the off-season, when prices usually plummet at even the glitziest resorts; you'll realize savings of up to 50% between April 15 and December 15. Moreover, you'll usually find fewer tourists, it's easier to rent a car, the water tends to be calmer and clearer, and you might stumble onto local festivals.

Remember that your budget will go further on some islands (Dominica or Saba, for example) than on others (St. Barths or Anguilla). And more developed islands (St. Thomas, St. Maarten/St. Martin, Aruba, Puerto Rico, Jamaica, Grand Cayman) tend to be more competitive and creative in their package pricing. You'll also find small hotels or those that are a short walk from the beach offer very pleasant accommodations that are priced considerably lower than their larger, beachfront neighbors.

Be a smart shopper and **compare all your options** before making decisions. A plane ticket bought with a promotional coupon from travel clubs, coupon books, and direct-mail offers or on the Internet may not be cheaper than the least-expensive fare from a discount ticket agency. And always keep in mind that what you get is just as important as what you save.

DISCOUNT RESERVATIONS

To save money, **look into discount reservations services** with toll-free numbers, which use their buying power to get a better price on hotels, airline tickets, even car rentals. When booking a room, always **call the hotel's local toll-free number** (if one is available) rather than the central reservations number—you'll often get a better price. Always ask about special packages or corporate rates.

When shopping for the best deal on hotels and car rentals, **look for guaranteed exchange rates,** which protect you against a falling dollar. With your rate locked in, you won't pay more, even if the price goes up in the local currency. (Note, however, that the currency of most Caribbean islands is fixed in value relative to the U.S. dollar, so this is not generally a critical issue for U.S. visitors.)

➤ AIRLINE TICKETS: ☎ 800/FLY–ASAP.

➤ HOTEL ROOMS: Hotel Reservations Network (☎ 800/964–6835, WEB www.hoteldiscount.com). Players Express Vacations (☎ 800/458–6161, WEB www.playersexpress.com). Turbotrip.com (☎ 800/473–7829, WEB www.turbotrip.com).

PACKAGE DEALS

Don't confuse packages and guided tours. When you buy a package, you travel on your own, just as though you had planned the trip yourself. Fly-drive packages, which combine airfare and car rental, are often a good deal. When you join a guided tour, you travel with a group, and everyone follows the same itinerary.

DIVING

The Caribbean offers some of the best scuba diving in the world. The waters around Bonaire's entire coast, for instance, are part of a protected marine park, with scores of dive sites accessible from the beach. The Cayman Islands, the Turks and Caicos Islands, the British Virgin Islands, St. Lucia, Dominica, and St. Vincent and the Grenadines also offer world-class diving experiences. The water throughout the Caribbean is crystal clear, often to 200 ft (61 m), and the quantity and variety of marine life is astounding.

Resorts often offer guests introductory scuba instruction in a pool, followed by a shallow dive; some hotels have on-site dive shops. All shops offer instruction and certification according to the standards set by either the National Association of Underwater Instructors (NAUI) or the

Professional Association of Diving Instructors (PADI). They also have a variety of day and night dives to wrecks, reefs, and underwater walls.

DIVERS ALERT

Don't fly within 24 hours after scuba diving.

➤ ORGANIZATIONS: **NAUI Worldwide** (✉ Box 89789, 1232 Tech Blvd., Tampa, FL 33619; ☎ 800/553–6284 or 813/628–6284, WEB www.naui.org), **PADI** (✉ 30151 Tomas St., Rancho Santa Margarita, CA 92688; ☎ 800/729–7234 or 949/858–7234, WEB www.padi.com; ✉ 3771 Jacombs Rd., Bldg. C, #535, Richmond, British Columbia, Canada, V6V 2L9, ☎ 604/273–0277 or 800/565–8130; ✉ Unit 7, St. Philip's Central, Albert Rd., St. Philip's, Bristol, United Kingdom, BS2 0PD, ☎ 0117/300–7234; ✉ Unit 3, 4 Skyline Pl., French's Forest, New South Wales, Australia 2086, ☎ 2/9451–2300).

ECOTOURISM

Travelers are being lured to the Caribbean as much by the natural beauty of beaches, rain forests, and even desertscapes (as on Aruba or Bonaire) as by the fancy resort life. Island governments are becoming increasingly aware of the value of their unique natural resources and have begun to create national parks, bird sanctuaries, and marine preserves. Bonaire's entire coast is a national marine park, its northern third is a nature preserve, and its southern third a protected salt flat. Two-thirds of St. John, USVI, is national parkland.

Dominica, the Dominican Republic, Grenada, Guadeloupe, Puerto Rico, Saba, St. Vincent, and St. Lucia are other Caribbean leaders in environmental awareness, each with vast forest preserves and hiking trails. Botanical gardens welcome visitors on St. Lucia, St. Vincent, Barbados, and many other islands. Nearly all islands have special programs, hikes, and tours that promote a better understanding of and a deeper appreciation for nature.

ELECTRICITY

On many islands the current is 110 and 120 volts alternating current (AC), and wall outlets take the same two-prong plugs found in the United States. Exceptions include the French islands and those with a British heritage. **Check with your hotel about current** when making reservations. If the current isn't compatible with your appliances, **bring a converter and an adapter.** With dual-voltage items (like many laptops) you'll need only an adapter. Some hotels will lend guests adapter plugs for small dual-voltage appliances. Many establishments also have hair dryers and irons either in their rooms or available for borrowing, so you can leave yours at home. Don't use 110-volt outlets, marked FOR SHAVERS ONLY, for high-wattage appliances such as blow-dryers.

FURTHER READING

Caribbean Style (Crown Publishers) is a coffee-table book with magnificent photographs of the interiors and exteriors of homes and buildings in the Caribbean. Short stories—some dark, some full of laughs—about life in the southern Caribbean made *Easy in the Islands,* by Bob Schacochis, a National Book Award winner. Schacochis has an ear for local patois and an eye for the absurd. In *Coming About: A Family Passage at Sea,* author Susan Tyler Hitchcock details her family's adventures sailing for nine months in the Bahamas and the Caribbean; it's an intimate look at the islands and a wonderful meditation on marriage and family. Thinking of running away and starting a business on a sun-drenched island? *A Trip to the Beach* by Robert and Melinda Blanchard is the ultimate inspiration. This funny, adventurous tale of how the Blanchards moved to Anguilla, started a restaurant, and learned innumerable lessons (including how to liberate fresh ingredients from the customs warehouse) will have you fantasizing about your own escape. To familiarize yourself with the sights, smells, and sounds of the West Indies, pick up Jamaica Kincaid's *Annie John,* a richly textured coming-of-age novel about a girl growing up on Antigua. The short stories in *At the Bottom of the River,* also by Kincaid, depict island mysteries and manners.

Omeros is Nobel Prize–winning St. Lucian poet Derek Walcott's imaginative Caribbean retelling of the *Odyssey.* Anthony C. Winkler's novels, *The Great Yacht Race, The Lunatic,* and *The Painted Canoe,* provide scathingly witty glimpses into Jamaica's class structure. *Wide Sargasso Sea,* by Dominica's Jean Rhys, is a provocative novel set in Jamaica and Dominica that recounts the early life of the first wife of Edward Rochester (pre–Jane Eyre). James Michener depicted the islands' diversity in his novel *Caribbean.* To probe island cultures more deeply, read Trinidad's V. S. Naipaul, particularly his *Guerrillas, The Loss of El Dorado,* and *The Enigma of Arrival;* Eric William's *From Columbus to Castro;* and Michael Paiewonsky's *Conquest of Eden.*

Though it was written decades ago, Herman Wouk's hilarious *Don't Stop the Carnival* remains as fresh as ever in its depiction of the trials and tribulations of running a small Caribbean hotel. Mystery lovers should pick up a copy of Agatha Christie's *A Caribbean Mystery.* And kids might enjoy reading the Hardy Boys mystery *The Caribbean Cruise Caper.* If you're keen on specific subjects, such as history, cuisine, folklore, bird-watching, or diving, you'll find wonderful books by local authors on each island.

GAY & LESBIAN TRAVEL

Some Caribbean islands are more welcoming than others as travel destinations for gays and lesbians. Puerto Rico is the most gay-friendly island in the Caribbean—and the only one with extensive gay-oriented nightlife. San Juan has gay and lesbian guest houses, bars, clubs, and two gay-popular beaches. The USVI are also a good choice. St. Thomas has a couple of gay bars and discos, and the West End of St. Croix has quietly become gay- and lesbian-friendly. In general, the French and Dutch islands are the most tolerant of gay and lesbian travelers. Attitudes are changing, albeit incrementally: the Cayman Islands, which once banned a gay-chartered cruise ship, now makes it a point to emphasize that all visitors are welcome if they respect the islands' conservative sensibilities.

This is good advice to follow throughout the Caribbean, where nearly every island frowns upon same-sex couples strolling hand in hand down a beach or street, where beach attire is welcome only at the beach, and where most public displays of affection (either straight or gay) are frowned upon. Upscale resorts for adults, where privacy and discretion are the norm, are often the most welcoming to gay and lesbian travelers, but individually rented villas, many of which have private pools, are another good option. Couples-only resorts throughout the Caribbean, including the all-inclusive Sandals resorts, do not, as a rule, welcome same-sex couples.

➤ GAY- & LESBIAN-FRIENDLY TRAVEL AGENCIES: **Different Roads Travel** (✉ 8383 Wilshire Blvd., Suite 902, Beverly Hills, CA 90211, ☎ 323/651–5557 or 800/429–8747, FAX 323/651–3678, lgernert@tzell.com). **Kennedy Travel** (✉ 314 Jericho Turnpike, Floral Park, NY 11001, ☎ 516/352–4888 or 800/237–7433, FAX 516/354–8849, WEB www.kennedytravel.com). **Now Voyager** (✉ 4406 18th St., San Francisco, CA 94114, ☎ 415/626–1169 or 800/255–6951, FAX 415/626–8626, WEB www.nowvoyager.com). **Skylink Travel and Tour** (✉ 1006 Mendocino Ave., Santa Rosa, CA 95401, ☎ 707/546–9888 or 800/225–5759, FAX 707/546–9891, WEB www.skylinktravel.com), serving lesbian travelers.

GUIDEBOOKS

Plan well and you won't be sorry. Guidebooks are excellent tools—and you can take them with you. You may want to check out *Fodor's Exploring Caribbean* (full color), *Fodor's Caribbean Ports of Call, Fodor's Bahamas, Fodor's Puerto Rico, Pocket Aruba,* and *Pocket Bermuda.*

HEALTH

Health-care standards vary from island to island. The staff at your hotel can recommend a doctor, dentist, clinic, or hospital should a need arise. Doctor visits, incidentally, can be costly—even on islands where the general cost-of-living would make you think otherwise.

FOOD & DRINK

Traveler's diarrhea, caused by consuming contaminated water, unpasteurized milk and milk products, and unrefrigerated food isn't a big problem in the Caribbean—unless it happens to you. So **watch what you eat,** especially at outdoor buffets in the hot sun. Make sure cooked food is hot and cold food has been properly refrigerated. As a rule, water is pure and food is wholesome in hotels and local restaurants throughout the Caribbean but **be cautious when buying food from street-beach vendors.** And just as you would at home, **wash or peel all fruits and vegetables** before eating them.

Mild cases of diarrhea may respond to Imodium (known generically as loperamide) or Pepto-Bismol (not as strong), both of which can be purchased in local pharmacies. Drink plenty of bottled water, which is readily available, to keep from becoming dehydrated. A salt-sugar solution (½ teaspoon salt and 4 tablespoons sugar) per quart of water is a good remedy for rehydrating yourself.

OVER-THE-COUNTER REMEDIES

Island drug stores and supermarkets carry familiar patent medicines and other health products that you might need. If you don't see precisely what you want, **ask the pharmacist** to recommend an appropriate substitute.

PESTS & OTHER HAZARDS

The major health risk is sunburn or sunstroke. A long-sleeve shirt, a hat, and long pants or a beach wrap are essential on a boat, for midday at the beach, and whenever you go out sightseeing. **Use sunscreen** with an SPF of at least 15—especially if your complexion is fair—and apply it liberally on your nose, ears, and other sensitive and exposed areas. **Make sure the sunscreen is waterproof** if you're engaging in water sports, **limit your sun time** for the first few days, and **drink plenty of liquids,** monitoring intake of caffeine and alcohol, which hasten the dehydration process.

Even experienced swimmers should **exercise caution in waters on the windward (Atlantic Ocean) side of the islands.** The unseen currents, powerful waves, strong undertows, and rocky bottoms can be extremely dangerous—and lifeguards are rare. Even in the calmest water, **watch out for black, spiny sea urchins**; stepping on one is guaranteed to be painful for quite some time.

The small lizards native to the islands are harmless (and actually keep down the bug population), and poisonous snakes are hard to find, although you should exercise caution while bird-watching in Trinidad. **Beware of the manchineel tree,** which grows near the beach and has green applelike fruit that is poisonous and bark and leaves that burn the skin. The worst insect problem may well be the tiny no-see-ums (sand flies) that appear after a rain, near swampy ground, and around sunset; mosquitoes can also be annoying. **Bring along a good repellent.**

SHOTS & MEDICATIONS

No special shots or vaccinations are required for Caribbean destinations.

➤ HEALTH WARNINGS: **National Centers for Disease Control and Prevention** (CDC; National Center for Infectious Diseases, Division of Quarantine, Traveler's Health Section, ✉ 1600 Clifton Rd. NE, M/S E-03, Atlanta, GA 30333, ☎ 888/232–3228 or 800/311–3435, FAX 888/232–3299, WEB www.cdc.gov).

HOLIDAYS

Most islands observe an annual independence or other national day, certain Christian holidays (Easter weekend, various feast days, and Christmas), and New Year's Day. On many islands the biggest holiday of the year is the last day of Carnival (the Tuesday before Ash Wednesday), a festival that's no longer limited to mid-February. Banks, shops, and offices are closed on holidays.

INSURANCE

The most useful travel-insurance plan is a comprehensive policy that includes coverage for trip cancellation and interruption, default, trip delay, and medical expenses (with a waiver for pre-existing conditions).

Without insurance you will lose all or most of your money if you cancel your trip, regardless of the reason. Default insurance covers you if your tour operator, airline, or cruise line goes out of business. Trip-delay covers expenses that arise because of bad weather or mechanical delays. Study the fine print when comparing policies.

If you're traveling internationally, a key component of travel insurance is coverage for medical bills incurred if you get sick on the road. Such expenses are not generally covered by Medicare or private policies. U.K. residents can buy a travel-insurance policy valid for most vacations taken during the year in which it's purchased (but check pre-existing-condition coverage). British and Australian citizens need extra medical coverage when traveling overseas.

Always **buy travel policies directly from the insurance company**; if you buy them from a cruise line, airline, or tour operator that goes out of business you probably will not be covered for the agency or operator's default, a major risk. Before making any purchase, **review your existing health and homeowner's policies** to find what they cover away from home.

➤ TRAVEL INSURERS: In the U.S.: **Access America** (✉ 6600 W. Broad St., Richmond, VA 23230, ☎ 804/285–3300 or 800/284–8300, FAX 804/673–1586, WEB www.previewtravel.com), **Travel Guard International** (✉ 1145 Clark St., Stevens Point, WI 54481, ☎ 715/345–0505 or 800/826–1300, FAX 800/955–8785, WEB www.noelgroup.com).

➤ INSURANCE INFORMATION: In the U.K.: **Association of British Insurers** (✉ 51–55 Gresham St., London EC2V 7HQ, U.K., ☎ 020/7600–3333, FAX 020/7696–8999, WEB www.abi.org.uk). In Canada: **Voyager Insurance** (✉ 44 Peel Center Dr., Brampton, Ontario L6T 4M8, Canada, ☎ 905/791–8700 or 800/668–4342 in Canada). In Australia: **Insurance Council of Australia** (✉ Level 3, 56 Pitt St., Sydney NSW 2000, ☎ 03/9614–1077, FAX 03/9614–7924). In New Zealand: **Insurance Council of New Zealand** (✉ Box 474, Wellington, New Zealand, ☎ 04/472–5230, FAX 04/473–3011, WEB www.icnz.org.nz).

LANGUAGE

It becomes obvious that the Caribbean's history is linked with that of European and African countries when you consider all the languages that are spoken on the islands. As for "official" languages, English is well represented (14 island nations), followed by Dutch (6 islands, though English is widely spoken), French (3 islands), and Spanish (3 islands). St. Maarten/St. Martin is split geographically, culturally, and linguistically—Dutch (as well as English) is spoken on one side, and French on the other.

You'll also find a variety of idiomatic expressions, West Indian lilts and patois, and French Creole dialects that transform the official languages. On both St. Lucia and Dominica, for example, English is the recognized tongue, but most locals also speak a patois that's a mix of English, French, and African words; on French-speaking St. Barths, some people use the Norman dialect of their ancestors; and on the Dutch islands, you'll encounter perhaps the most worldly tongue of all, Papiamento—a mixture of African languages, as well as Dutch, English, French, Portuguese, *and* Spanish. There are also places, such as Barbados, where early Irish and Scottish settlers affected the island accent; and in Trinidad, East Indian and Chinese arrivals have contributed to culture, food, and terminology.

LANGUAGE-STUDY PROGRAMS

The Paris-based Alliance Française is a nonprofit organization, created in 1883 to spread the French language and culture. It has branches throughout the world, including several in the Caribbean. Classes in the French language are taught at levels from beginner to advanced. AmeriSpan and Languages Abroad offer Spanish-language programs on Puerto Rico and the Dominican Republic for students of all skill levels and ages.

➤ PROGRAMS: **Alliance Française** (✉ Box 2086, St. John's, Antigua, ☎ 268/462–3625; ✉ Box 1210,

Oranjestad, Aruba, ☎ 297/829–055; ⊠ Belleville, St. Michael, Barbados, ☎ 246/436–4675; ⊠ Box 15, Bonaire, ☎ 599/7–8228; ⊠ Box 3450, Willemstad, Curaçao, ☎ 5999/865–5183; ⊠ Box 251 Roseau, Dominica, ☎ 767/448–4557; ⊠ Calle Beller 59 Puerto Plata, Dominican Republic, ☎ 809/586–2828; ⊠ Box 515, St. George's, Grenada, ☎ 473/440–0984; ⊠ 3 March Dr., Kingston, Jamaica, ☎ 876/925–8876; ⊠ 1 Orchid St., Basseterre, St. Kitts, ☎ 869/465–9415; ⊠ La Pyramide, Pointe Seraphine [Box 898], Castries, St. Lucia, ☎ 758/452–6602; ⊠ S. River Rd. [Box 560], Kingstown, St. Vincent and the Grenadines, ☎ FAX 784/456–2095); and ⊠ 76 Pembroke St. [Box 1288], Port of Spain, Trinidad, ☎ 868/623–4680). **AmeriSpan** (⊠ Box 40007, Philadelphia, PA 19106, ☎ 215/751–1100 or 800/879–6640, WEB www.amerispan.com). **Languages Abroad** (⊠ 502–99 Avenue Rd., Toronto, Ontario, M5R 2G5, ☎ 416/925–2112 or 800/219–9924, WEB www.languagesabroad.com).

LANGUAGES FOR TRAVELERS

A phrase book and language-tape set can help get you started. *Fodor's French for Travelers* and *Fodor's Spanish for Travelers* (available at bookstores everywhere) are excellent.

LODGING

Decide whether you want a hotel on the leeward side of an island (with calm water, good for snorkeling and swimming) or the windward (with waves, good for surfing, not good for swimming). Decide, too, whether you want to pay the extra price for a room overlooking the ocean. At less expensive properties, location may mean a difference in price of only $10–$20 per room; at luxury resorts on pricey islands, however, it could amount to as much as $100 per room. Also **find out how close the property is to a beach.** At some hotels you can walk barefoot from your room onto the sand; others are across a road or a 10-minute drive away.

If you go to sleep early or are a light sleeper, **ask for a room away from the dance floor.** Air-conditioning isn't a necessity on all islands, many of which are cooled by trade winds, but it can be a plus if you enjoy an afternoon snooze or are bothered by humidity. Breezes are best in second-floor rooms, particularly corner rooms. If you like to sleep without air-conditioning, make sure that windows can be opened and have screens. If you're staying away from the water, you'll want a ceiling fan. You'll likely notice a candle and box of matches in your room. In even the most luxurious resorts, there are times when things simply *don't* work; it's a fact of Caribbean life. No matter how diligent the upkeep, humidity and salt air (and the whims of the electric company) take their toll.

The lodgings we list are the top of the line in each price category. We always list the available facilities—but we don't specify whether they're included in the rates. When pricing accommodations, always ask what's included and what costs extra.

Assume that hotels operate on the **European Plan** (EP, with no meals), unless we specify that they offer the **All-inclusive Plan** (All-inclusive, with three meals per day, snacks, beverages, activities, sports, taxes, and gratuities), **Breakfast Plan** (BP, with full breakfast daily), **Continental Plan** (CP, with a Continental breakfast), the **Full American Plan** (FAP, with all meals), or the **Modified American Plan** (MAP, with breakfast and dinner).

APARTMENT & VILLA RENTALS

If you want a home base that's roomy enough for a family and comes with cooking facilities, **consider a furnished rental.** These can save you money, especially if you're traveling with a group. Home-exchange directories sometimes list rentals as well as exchanges.

➤ INTERNATIONAL AGENTS: **At Home Abroad** (⊠ 405 E. 56th St., Suite 6H, New York, NY 10022, ☎ 212/421–9165, FAX 212/752–1591, WEB http://members.aol.com/athomabrod/index.html). **Hideaways International** (⊠ 767 Islington St., Portsmouth, NH 03801, ☎ 603/430–4433 or 800/843–4433, FAX 603/430–4444, WEB www.hideaways.com; membership $129). **Hometours International** (⊠ Box 11503, Knoxville, TN 37939, ☎ 865/690–8484 or 800/

367–4668, WEB http://thor.he.net/~hometour/). **Vacation Home Rentals Worldwide** (✉ 235 Kensington Ave., Norwood, NJ 07648, ☎ 201/767–9393 or 800/633–3284, FAX 201/767–5510, WEB www.vhrww.com). **Villas and Apartments Abroad** (✉ 1270 Avenue of the Americas, 15th floor, New York, NY 10020, ☎ 212/897–5045 or 800/433–3020, FAX 212/897–5039, WEB www.vaanyc.com). **Villas International** (✉ 950 Northgate Dr., Ste. 206, San Rafael, CA 94903, ☎ 415/499–9490 or 800/221–2260, FAX 415/499–9491, WEB www.villasintl.com).

CAMPING

Camping is a big draw on St. John, in the USVI, and many other islands have facilities if you want to fend for yourself and sleep under the stars. Some islands have no camping facilities at all and, in fact, discourage campers.

HOME EXCHANGES

If you would like to exchange your home for someone else's, **join a home-exchange organization,** which will send you its updated listings of available exchanges for a year and will include your own listing in at least one of them. It's up to you to make specific arrangements.

➤ EXCHANGE CLUBS: **HomeLink International** (✉ Box 47747, Tampa, FL 33647, ☎ 813/975–9825 or 800/638–3841, FAX 813/910–8144, WEB www.homelink.org; $98 per year). **Intervac U.S.** (✉ Box 590504, San Francisco, CA 94159, ☎ 800/756–4663, FAX 415/435–7440, WEB www.intervacus.com; $93 yearly fee includes one catalogue and on-line access).

HOTELS

All hotels listed have private bath unless otherwise noted. Several major hotel chains have properties on one or more of the islands.

➤ TOLL-FREE NUMBERS: **Best Western** (☎ 800/528–1234, WEB www.bestwestern.com). **Choice** (☎ 800/221–2222, WEB www.hotelchoice.com). **Club Med** (☎ 888/932–2582, WEB www.clubmed.com. **Colony** (☎ 800/777–1700, WEB www.colony.com). **Comfort** (☎ 800/228–5150,

WEB www.comfortinn.com). **Divi Resorts** (☎ 888/367–3484, WEB www.diviresorts.com). **Forte** (☎ 800/225–5843, WEB www.forte-hotels.com). **Hilton** (☎ 800/445–8667, WEB www.hilton.com). **Holiday Inn** (☎ 800/465–4329, WEB www.basshotels.com). **Marriott** (☎ 800/228–9290, WEB www.marriott.com). **Le Meridien** (☎ 800/543–4300, WEB www.lemeridien-hotels.com). **Quality Inn** (☎ 800/228–5151, WEB www.qualityinn.com). **Renaissance Hotels & Resorts** (☎ 800/468–3571, WEB www.renaissancehotels.com/). **Ritz-Carlton** (☎ 800/241–3333, WEB www.ritzcarlton.com). **Sandals** (☎ 800/726–3257, WEB www.sandals.com). **Sheraton** (☎ 800/325–3535, WEB www.starwood.com). **Sleep Inn** (☎ 800/753–3746, WEB www.sleepinn.com). **Sol Melia** (☎ 800/336–3542), WEB www.solmelia.com. **Sonesta** (☎ 800/766–3782), WEB www.sonesta.com. **Wyndham Hotels & Resorts** (☎ 800/822-4200, WEB www.wyndham.com).

MAIL & SHIPPING

Airmail between Caribbean islands and cities in the United States or Canada takes 7–14 days; surface mail can take 4–6 weeks. Airmail to the United Kingdom takes 2–3 weeks; to Australia and New Zealand, 3–4 weeks.

OVERNIGHT SERVICES

Courier services (such as Airborne, Federal Express, UPS, and others) operate throughout the Caribbean, although not every company serves each island. "Overnight" service is more likely to take two or more days, because of the limited number of flights on which packages can be shipped.

MONEY MATTERS

Prices throughout this guide are given for adults. Substantially reduced room rates, meal charges, and admission fees are almost always available for children; students and senior citizens often receive reduced admission fees. For island-specific information on banks, currency, service charges, taxes, and tipping in the Caribbean, *see* the A to Z sections *in* individual island chapters.

ATMS

Debit cards aren't widely used in the islands, although you can use bank cards and major credit card to withdraw cash (in local currency) at automatic teller machines (ATMs). ATMs can be found on most islands at airports, cruise ship terminals, bank branches, shopping centers, and other convenient locations. Although ATM transaction fees may be higher abroad, the rates are excellent because they're based on wholesale rates offered only by major banks.

CREDIT CARDS

Major credit cards are widely accepted at hotels, restaurants, shops, car-rental agencies, other service providers, and ATM machines throughout the Caribbean. The only places that might not accept them are open-air markets or tiny shops in out-of-the-way villages.

It's smart to **write down (and keep separate) the number of the credit card(s) you're carrying** and the toll-free number to call in case the card is lost or stolen.

Throughout this guide, the following abbreviations are used: **AE**, American Express; **D**, Discover; **DC**, Diner's Club; **MC**, MasterCard; and **V**, Visa.

CURRENCY EXCHANGE

The U.S. dollar is the official currency on Puerto Rico and the USVI, as well as the British Virgin Islands. On Grand Cayman, you will usually have a choice of Cayman or U.S. dollars when you take money out of an ATM and may even be able to get change in U.S. dollars. On most other islands U.S. paper currency (not coins) is usually accepted. When you pay in dollars, however, you'll almost always get change in local currency; so it's best to carry bills in small denominations. Canadian dollars and British pounds are occasionally accepted, but don't count on this as the norm. If you do need local currency (say, for a trip to one of the French islands), **change money at a local bank** for the best rate.

Travelers to the Caribbean from countries other than the United States might want to purchase a small amount of local currency (or U.S. dollars) before leaving home to pay for incidentals until you can get to a local bank.

➤ EXCHANGE SERVICES: **International Currency Express** (☎ 888/278–6628 for orders, WEB www.foreignmoney.com). **Thomas Cook Currency Services** (☎ 800/287–7362 for telephone orders and retail locations, WEB www.us.thomascook.com).

TRAVELER'S CHECKS

Traveler's checks are a good idea, but get them in small denominations—$20 or $50. Restaurants and most shops will accept them, and your hotel will cash them for you; but you'll get change in local currency. In rural areas and small villages you'll need cash. Lost or stolen checks can usually be replaced within 24 hours. To ensure a speedy refund, buy your own traveler's checks—don't let someone else pay for them: irregularities like this can cause delays. The person who bought the checks should make the call to request a refund.

PACKING

Travel light. Dress on the islands is generally casual. Bring loose-fitting clothing made of natural fabrics to see you through days of heat and humidity. Pack a beach cover-up, both to protect yourself from the sun and as something to wear to and from your hotel room. On all islands, bathing suits and immodest attire are frowned upon off the beach. A sun hat is advisable, but you don't have to pack one—inexpensive straw hats are available everywhere. For shopping and sightseeing, bring walking shorts, jeans, T-shirts, long-sleeve cotton shirts, slacks, and sundresses. Night time dress can range from really informal to casually elegant, depending on the establishment. A tie is practically never required, but a jacket may be appropriate in the fanciest restaurants and casinos. You may need a light sweater or jacket for evenings and at higher altitudes.

Leave camouflage-pattern clothing at home. It's not permitted for civilians, even children, in some Caribbean countries and may be confiscated if worn.

If you're making one or more airline connections, it's smart to pack some toiletries, a change of clothes, and perhaps a bathing suit in your carry-on bag—just in case your checked luggage doesn't make the connection until a later flight (which may be the next day).

In your carry-on luggage, **pack an extra pair of eyeglasses or contact lenses** and **enough of any medication you take** to last the entire trip. You may also ask your doctor to write a spare prescription using the drug's generic name, since brand names may vary from country to country. In luggage to be checked, **never pack prescription drugs or valuables.** To avoid customs delays, carry medications in their original packaging. And don't forget to carry with you the addresses of offices that handle refunds of lost traveler's checks. Check *Fodor's How to Pack* (available in bookstores everywhere) for more tips.

CHECKING LUGGAGE

How many carry-on bags you can bring with you is up to the airline. Most allow two, but not always, so make sure that everything you carry aboard will fit under your seat or in the overhead bin, and get to the gate early. Note that if you have a seat at the back of the plane, you'll probably board first, while the overhead bins are still empty.

If you are flying internationally, note that baggage allowances may be determined not by piece but by weight—generally 88 pounds (40 kilograms) in first class, 66 pounds (30 kilograms) in business class, and 44 pounds (20 kilograms) in economy.

Airline liability for baggage is limited to $1,250 per person on flights within the United States. On international flights it amounts to $9.07 per pound or $20 per kilogram for checked baggage (roughly $640 per 70-pound bag) and $400 per passenger for unchecked baggage. You can buy additional coverage at check-in for about $10 per $1,000 of coverage, but it excludes a rather extensive list of items, shown on your airline ticket.

Before departure, **itemize your bags' contents** and their worth, and label the bags with your name, address, and phone number. (If you use your home address, cover it so potential thieves can't see it readily.) Inside each bag, **pack a copy of your itinerary.** At check-in, **make sure that each bag is correctly tagged** with the destination airport's three-letter code. If your bags arrive damaged or fail to arrive at all, file a written report with the airline before leaving the airport.

PASSPORTS & VISAS

When traveling internationally, **carry your passport** even if you don't need one (it's always the best form of I.D.) and **make two photocopies of the data page** (one for someone at home and another for you, carried separately from your passport). If you lose your passport, promptly call the nearest embassy or consulate and the local police.

ENTERING THE CARIBBEAN

On most Caribbean islands, vacationers who are U.S., Canadian, and British citizens must have either a valid passport or prove citizenship with a birth certificate (with a raised seal) as well as a government-issued photo ID. Visitors from other countries must present a valid passport. All visitors must have a return or ongoing ticket.

PASSPORT OFFICES

The best time to apply for a passport or to renew is in fall and winter. Before any trip, check your passport's expiration date, and, if necessary, renew it as soon as possible. Current U.S. passport holders may renew by mail; forms are available at local post offices or can be printed from the Internet.

➤ AUSTRALIAN CITIZENS: **Australian Passport Office** (☎ 131–232, WEB www.dfat.gov.au/passports).

➤ CANADIAN CITIZENS: **Passport Office** (☎ 819/994–3500 or 800/567–6868 in Canada, WEB www.dfait-maeci.gc.ca/passport).

➤ NEW ZEALAND CITIZENS: **New Zealand Passport Office** (☎ 04/494–0700, WEB www.passports.govt.nz).

➤ U.K. CITIZENS: **London Passport Office** (☎ 0870/521–0410,

WEB www.ukpa.gov.uk) for fees and documentation requirements and to request an emergency passport.

➤ U.S. CITIZENS: **National Passport Information Center** (☎ 900/225–5674; calls are 35¢ per minute for automated service, $1.05 per minute for operator service; WEB www.travel.state.gov/npicinfo.html).

REST ROOMS

Rest rooms in hotels, restaurants, and public buildings are, as a rule, clean and well-equipped. Pay toilets aren't customary nor are staffed rest rooms.

SAFETY

Be as cautious as you would at home in terms of not walking alone in unfamiliar places, locking away valuables, and not flaunting expensive jewelry in public places. **Don't swim alone in unfamiliar waters,** and don't swim too far offshore; most beaches have no lifeguards.

SENIOR-CITIZEN TRAVEL

To qualify for age-related discounts, **mention your senior-citizen status up front** when booking hotel reservations (not when checking out) and before you're seated in restaurants (not when paying the bill). When renting a car, ask about promotional car-rental discounts, which can be cheaper than senior-citizen rates.

➤ EDUCATIONAL PROGRAMS: **Elderhostel** (✉ 11 Ave. de Lafayette, Boston, MA 02111-1746, ☎ 877/426–8056, FAX 877/426–2166, WEB www.elderhostel.org). **Interhostel** (✉ University of New Hampshire, 6 Garrison Ave., Durham, NH 03824, ☎ 603/862–1147 or 800/733–9753, FAX 603/862–1113, WEB www.learn.unh.edu).

SHOPPING

Shopping in the Caribbean can mean duty-free bargains on watches and jewelry, perfume, designer clothing, china and crystal, and other luxury goods from around the world. It can also mean buying locally produced straw items, wood carvings, original art, batik beachwear, clay pottery, spices, coffee, cigars, and rum.

Bargaining isn't expected (it can even be considered insulting) in shops, but at open-air markets and with street vendors it may be acceptable. Keep in mind, however, that selling handicrafts or home-grown produce may be a local person's only livelihood. When bargaining, consider the amount of work or effort involved and the item's value to you. Vendors don't set artificially high prices and then expect to bargain; they bargain so you'll buy from them instead of their neighbor.

KEY DESTINATIONS

On some islands, such as St. Maarten, St. Barths, St. Thomas, and Aruba, all shopping is duty-free. Other islands, like Barbados and St. Lucia, have certain shops or specific areas where you can purchase duty-free items upon presentation of your passport and/or ongoing ticket; still others, such as Puerto Rico, and Grenada, have very limited duty-free opportunities—one or two stores or just shops in the airport departure area.

SMART SOUVENIRS

Bring home a pantry full of spices from Grenada, pottery from Barbados, lace from Saba, woven-grass mats from St. Vincent, cigars from the Dominican Republic and Puerto Rico, fashions made of hand-printed fabric from St. Lucia, Blue Mountain coffee from Jamaica, Carib straw baskets from Dominica, aloe from Aruba, Angostura bitters from Trinidad—and rum from just about everywhere. St. Maarten and St. Thomas offer the best prices for duty-free shopping on a large scale.

WATCH OUT

U.S. citizens returning home must **consume tropical fruits and other produce, smoke those Cuban cigars, and (with rare exceptions) leave the bouquets of flowers behind** before heading home.

STUDENTS IN THE CARIBBEAN

Hiking in the rain forest, scuba diving, boating, and other Caribbean activities and adventures seem made-to-order for students—and the cultural enrichment and historical perspective add depth to all that book learning. The Caribbean isn't as far out of a student's budget as you might expect. Summer, when most students have free time, is the least expensive time to travel to the Caribbean. All but the toniest islands, such as St. Barths, have camping facilities, inexpensive guest houses, or small no-frills hotels. Tourist boards provide listings of these alternative lodgings on request. You're most likely to meet students from other countries in the French and Dutch West Indies, where many go for vacations or sabbaticals. Puerto Rico, Jamaica, Grenada, and Dominica, among others, have large resident international student populations at their universities. In many cases, your student I.D. card may provide access to their facilities, from the library to the cafeteria.

An alternative to individual travel is an educational program or expedition. Colleges and universities often sponsor programs that coincide with spring or summer breaks, as do independent—usually nonprofit—organizations.

➤ I.D.s & SERVICES: **Council Travel** (CIEE; ✉ 205 E. 42nd St., 15th floor, New York, NY 10017, ☎ 212/822–2700 or 888/268–6245, FAX 212/822–2699, WEB www.councilexchanges.org) for mail orders only, in the U.S. **Travel Cuts** (✉ 187 College St., Toronto, Ontario M5T 1P7, Canada, ☎ 416/979–2406 or 800/667–2887 in Canada, FAX 416/979–8167, WEB www.travelcuts.com).

➤ ORGANIZATIONS: **International Education Resource Center** (IERC; ✉ 860 E. 216th St., Bronx, NY 10467; ☎ 718/231–8333 or 718/515–0093, FAX 718/547–9210). **School for Field Studies** (✉ 16 Broadway, Beverly, MA 01915, ☎ 978/927–7777, FAX 978/927–5127).

TELEPHONES

Phone and fax service to and from the Caribbean is up-to-date and efficient. Phone cards are used throughout the islands; you can buy them (in several denominations) at many retail shops and convenience stores. They must be used in special card phones, which are also widely available.

AREA & COUNTRY CODES

For island area and country codes *see* the A to Z sections *in* individual

island chapters. The country code is 1 for the United States and Canada, 61 for Australia, 64 for New Zealand, and 44 for the United Kingdom.

LONG-DISTANCE SERVICES

AT&T, MCI, and Sprint access codes make calling long distance relatively convenient, but you may find the local access number blocked in many hotel rooms. First ask the hotel operator to connect you. If the hotel operator balks, ask for an international operator, or dial the international operator yourself. One way to improve your odds of getting connected to your long-distance carrier is to travel with more than one company's calling card (a hotel may block Sprint, for example, but not MCI). If all else fails, call from a pay phone.

TIME

The Caribbean islands fall into two time zones. The Cayman Islands, Cuba, Haiti, Jamaica, and the Turks and Caicos Islands are all in the Eastern Standard Time zone, which is five hours earlier than Greenwich Mean Time (GMT). All other Caribbean islands are in the Atlantic Standard Time zone, which is one hour later than Eastern Standard or four hours earlier than GMT. During Daylight Savings Time, between April and October, Atlantic Standard is the same time as Eastern Daylight Time.

TOURS & PACKAGES

Because everything is prearranged on a prepackaged tour or independent vacation, you'll spend less time planning—and often get it all at a good price.

BOOKING WITH AN AGENT

Travel agents are excellent resources. But it's a good idea to collect brochures from several agencies as some agents' suggestions may be influenced by relationships with tour and package firms that reward them for volume sales. If you have a special interest, **find an agent with expertise in that area**; ASTA has a database of specialists worldwide.

Make sure your travel agent knows the accommodations and other services of the place they're recommending. Ask about the hotel's location, room size, beds, and whether it has a pool, room service, or programs for children, if you care about these. Has your agent been there in person or sent others whom you can contact?

Do some homework on your own, too: local tourism boards can provide information about lesser-known and small-niche operators, some of which may sell only direct.

BUYER BEWARE

Each year consumers are stranded or lose their money when tour operators—even large ones with excellent reputations—go out of business. So **check out the operator.** Ask several travel agents about its reputation, and try to **book with a company that has a consumer-protection program.** (Look for information in the company's brochure.) In the United States, members of the National Tour Association and the United States Tour Operators Association are required to set aside funds to cover your payments and travel arrangements in the event that the company defaults. It's also a good idea to choose a company that participates in the American Society of Travel Agents' Tour Operator Program (TOP); ASTA will act as mediator in any disputes between you and your tour operator.

Remember that the more your package or tour includes the better you can predict the ultimate cost of your vacation. Make sure you know exactly what is covered, and **beware of hidden costs.** Are taxes, tips, and transfers included? Entertainment and excursions? These can add up.

➤ TOUR-OPERATOR RECOMMENDATIONS: **American Society of Travel Agents** (ASTA; ☎ 800/965–2782 24-hr hot line, ℻ 703/739–7642, 🕸 www.astanet.com). **National Tour Association** (NTA; ✉ 546 E. Main St., Lexington, KY 40508, ☎ 859/226–4444 or 800/682–8886, 🕸 www.ntaonline.com). **United States Tour Operators Association** (USTOA; ✉ 342 Madison Ave., Suite 1522, New York, NY 10173, ☎ 212/599–6599 or 800/468–7862, ℻ 212/599–6744, 🕸 www.ustoa.com).

VOLUNTEER VACATIONS

A volunteer vacation can add an incalculable dimension to your regular "time off." You become a part of other people's lives forever by digging with archaeologists, helping to build an island's infrastructure, improving its health-care facilities, teaching its children, consulting with its local businesses, or saving its environment. Volunteer vacations aren't free but may be tax-deductible. Fees range from a few hundred to several thousand dollars, depending on the program and its duration, and cover most expenses while you're there. Round-trip transportation is often your own responsibility.

Organizations include Earthwatch, which arranges for you to participate in scientific research; Global Volunteers, which offers opportunities in education, construction, and business; and Habitat for Humanity, which puts you to work building homes.

➤ VOLUNTEER ORGANIZATIONS: **Earthwatch** (✉ 3 Clocktower Place, Ste. 100 (Box 75), Maynard, MA 01754, ☎ 800/776–0188). **Global Volunteers** (✉ 375 E. Little Canada Rd., St. Paul, MN 55117, ☎ 800/487–1074). **Habitat for Humanity** (✉ 121 Habitat St., Americus, GA 31709, ☎ 800/HABITAT).

TRAVEL AGENCIES

A good travel agent puts your needs first. Look for an agency that has been in business at least five years, emphasizes customer service, and has someone on staff who specializes in your destination. In addition, **make sure the agency belongs to a professional trade organization.** The American Society of Travel Agents (ASTA), with 27,000 agents in some 170 countries, is the largest and most influential in the field. Operating under the motto "Integrity in Travel," it maintains and enforces a strict code of ethics and will step in to help mediate any agent-client disputes if necessary. ASTA also maintains a Web site that includes a directory of agents.

➤ LOCAL AGENT REFERRALS: **American Society of Travel Agents** (ASTA; ☎ 800/965–2782 24-hr hot line, ℻ 703/739–7642, 🕸 www.astanet.

com). **Association of British Travel Agents** (✉ 68–71 Newman St., London W1T 3AH, U.K., ☎ 020/7637–2444, FAX 020/7637–0713, WEB www.abtanet.com). **Association of Canadian Travel Agents** (✉ 130 Albert St., Ste. 1705, Ottawa, Ontario K1P 5G4, Canada, ☎ 613/237–3657, FAX 613/237–7502, WEB www.acta.net). **Australian Federation of Travel Agents** (✉ Level 3, 309 Pitt St., Sydney NSW 2000, Australia, ☎ 02/9264–3299, FAX 02/9264–1085, WEB www.afta.com.au). **Travel Agents' Association of New Zealand** (✉ Box 1888, Wellington 10033, New Zealand, ☎ 04/499–0104, FAX 04/499–0827, WEB www.taanz.org.nz).

VISITOR INFORMATION

Many islands have tourist board offices in Canada, the United Kingdom, and the United States. Such boards can be good sources of general information; up-to-date calendars of events; and listings of hotels, restaurants, sights, and shops. The Caribbean Tourism Organization (CTO) is another resource, especially for information on the islands that have limited representation overseas.

➤ CARIBBEAN-WIDE INFORMATION: **CTO** (✉ 80 Broad St., New York, NY 10004, ☎ 212/635–9530; ✉ Vigilant House, 120 Wilton Rd., London SW1V 1JZ, ☎ 0171/233–8382, WEB www.caribtourism.com).

➤ U.S. GOVERNMENT ADVISORIES: **U.S. Department of State** (✉ Overseas Citizens Services Office, Room 4811 N.S., 2201 C St. NW, Washington, DC 20520, ☎ 202/647–5225 for interactive hot line, WEB travel.state.gov/travel.html); enclose a self-addressed, stamped, business-size envelope.

WEB SITES

Do check out the World Wide Web when you're planning. You'll find everything from weather forecasts to virtual tours of various islands. Be sure to **visit Fodors.com** (www.fodors.com), a complete travel-planning site. You can research prices, and book plane tickets, hotel rooms, rental cars, vacation packages, and more. In addition, you can post your pressing questions in the Travel Talk section

and, in the site's Rants & Raves section, read comments about some of the restaurants and hotels in this book—and chime in yourself. Other planning tools include a currency converter and weather reports, and there are loads of links to other travel resources.

For information on the Caribbean, visit: www.caribtourism.com (the CTO's official site, with many island-specific links); www.caribbeanchannel.com (with information presented both thematically and by island); www.caribbeantravel.com (the official Caribbean Hotel Association site); www.caribbeancyberspace.com (for general information and good links); www.caribbeannewspapers.com (with links to newspapers published throughout the Caribbean); www.caribinfo.com (with a directory of Web sites based in or related to the Caribbean and links to local phone directories); www.caribbeanaviation.com (with aviation routes and schedules as well as links to all airlines that serve the region); www.cruising.org (the Cruise Lines International Association's site, with many ship profiles); www.cananews.com and www.cweek.com (for Caribbean news). For island-specific sites *see* Visitor Information *in* the A to Z section at the end of each chapter.

WHEN TO GO

The Caribbean high season is traditionally winter—from December 15 to April 14—when northern weather is at its worst. During this season, you're guaranteed the most entertainment at resorts and the most people with whom to enjoy it. It's also the most fashionable, the most expensive, and the most popular time to visit—and most hotels are heavily booked. You must make reservations at least two or three months in advance for the very best places (sometimes a year in advance for the most exclusive spots). Hotel prices drop 20%–50% after April 15; airfares and cruise prices also fall. Saving money isn't the only reason to visit the Caribbean during the off-season. Temperatures are only a few degrees warmer than at other times of the year, and many islands now schedule their carnivals, music festivals, and other events during the off-season. Late August, September, October, and early November are least crowded.

In summer the flamboyant trees are at their peak, as are most of the flowers and shrubs of the West Indies. The water is clearer for snorkeling and smoother for sailing in the Virgin Islands and the Grenadines in May, June, and July. The peak of local excitement on many islands, most notably Trinidad, St. Vincent, Dominica, and the French West Indies, is Carnival—traditionally held in February, the weekend before Ash Wednesday.

CLIMATE

The Caribbean climate is fairly constant. The average year-round temperatures for the region are 78°F–88°F. The temperature extremes are 65°F low, 95°F high; but, as everyone knows, it's the humidity, not the heat, that makes you suffer, especially when the two go hand in hand. You can count on downtown shopping areas being hot at midday any time of the year, but air-conditioning provides some respite. Spend the day near beaches, where water and trade winds can keep you cool, and shop early or late in the day.

As part of the fall rainy season, hurricanes occasionally sweep through the Caribbean. Check the news daily and keep abreast of brewing tropical storms. The rainy season consists mostly of brief showers interspersed with sunshine. You can watch the clouds thicken, feel the rain, then have brilliant sunshine dry you off, all while remaining on your lounge chair. A spell of overcast days or heavy rainfall is unusual, as everyone will tell you.

High altitudes can be cool, particularly when winter winds hit Caribbean peaks (late November through January). Since many Caribbean islands are mountainous or at least hilly (notable exceptions are the Cayman Islands, Anguilla, Antigua, Aruba, Bonaire, and Curaçao), the altitude always offers an escape from the latitude. Kingston (Jamaica), Port-of-Spain (Trinidad), and Fort-de-France (Martinique) swelter in summer; climb 1,000 ft (305 m) or so and everything is cool.

➤ FORECASTS: **Weather Channel Connection** (☎ 900/932–8437), 95¢ per minute from a Touch-Tone phone.

INDEX

Icons and Symbols

★ Our special recommen-
dations

✕ Restaurant

🏠 Lodging establishment

✕🏠 Lodging establishment
whose restaurant war-
rants a special trip

🐤 Good for kids (rubber
duck)

☞ Sends you to another
section of the guide for
more information

✉ Address

☎ Telephone number

🕐 Opening and closing
times

💵 Admission prices

Numbers in white and black
circles ③ ❸ that appear on
the maps, in the margins, and
within the tours correspond
to one another.

A

Acuario Nacional
(aquarium), 321
Addresses, 851
Admiral's House Museum, 75
Admiralty Bay, 685
Aguadilla, Puerto Rico, 500
Airports, 853–854
Ajoupa-Bouillon, Martinique,
458
Alcaldia (City Hall; Puerto
Rico), 496
Alcazar de Colón (castle),
321
Alexander Hamilton
Birthplace, 590
All Saints Anglican Church,
789
Altar de la Patria
(mausoleum), 324
Alto Vista Chapel, 103
Altos de Chavón (16th-
century village and art
colony), 317, 325–326
Amber Coast, Dominican
Republic, 306–308, 312–
313, 326–328, 329–335
American Caribbean
Museum, 789
Amerindian Mini-Museum, 49
Andromeda Gardens, 140
Anegada, British Virgin
Islands, 206–208, 210–
215
Anglican Cathedral, 291
Anglican Cathedral of St.
John the Divine, 76

Anguilla, 33–54
beaches, 45–46
business hours, 51
electricity, 51
emergencies, 51
etiquette and behavior, 51
festivals and seasonal events,
52
holidays, 52
language, 52
lodging, 34–35, 38–41
mail and shipping, 52
money matters, 52
nightlife and the arts, 48
outdoor activities and sports,
46–47
passports and visas, 52–53
price categories, 34, 41
restaurants, 41–45
safety, 53
shopping, 47–48
sightseeing, 49–50
sightseeing tours, 53
taxes, 53
taxis, 53
telephones, 53–54
tipping, 54
transportation, 50, 51
visitor information, 54
Animal Flower Cave, 139
Annaberg Plantation, 829–
830
Annandale Falls and Visitors
Centre, 355
Anse-à-l'Ane, Martinique,
461
Anse Bertrand, Guadeloupe,
386
Anse-d'Arlets, Martinique,
449–450
Anse des Flamands, St.
Barthélemy, 541
Anse du Gouverneur, St.
Barthélemy, 542
Anse-Mitan, Martinique, 461
Antigua, 55–82
beaches, 68–69
business hours, 78
consulates and embassies, 79
electricity, 78
emergencies, 79
etiquette and behavior, 79
festivals and seasonal events,
79
health issues, 79
holidays, 79
language, 79
lodging, 56–57, 60–64
mail and shipping, 80
money matters, 80
nightlife and the arts, 73–74
outdoor activities and sports,
69–70
passports and visas, 80

price categories, 56, 65
restaurants, 65–68
safety, 80
shopping, 70–73
sightseeing, 74–77
sightseeing tours, 80–81
taxes, 81
taxis, 81
telephones, 81–82
tipping, 82
transportation, 77–78, 82
visitor information, 82
Apartment and villa rentals,
867–868
Apothecary Hall, 815
Appleton Rum Factory, 426
Aquarium de la Guadeloupe,
386
Aquariums, 263, 321, 386,
460, 794–795, 812
Archaeology Museum of
Aruba, 104
Arikok National Wildlife
Park, 103
Art galleries. ☞ See
Museums and galleries
Arts. ☞ See Nightlife and
the arts under specific
islands
Aruba, 83–110
beaches, 94–95
business hours, 106
electricity, 107
emergencies, 107
etiquette and behavior, 107
festivals and seasonal events,
107
holidays, 107
language, 107
lodging, 84–85, 88–91
mail and shipping, 107
money matters, 107–108
nightlife and the arts, 100–102
outdoor activities and sports,
95–98
passports and visas, 108
price categories, 84, 92
restaurants, 91–94
safety, 108
shopping, 98–100
sightseeing, 102–105
sightseeing tours, 108–109
taxes, 109
taxis, 109–110
telephones, 110
transportation, 105–107
visitor information, 110
Asa Wright Nature Center,
715
Athenry Gardens, 431–432
ATMs, 869
Australia, tips for travelers
from, 859, 870

B

Bacardi Rum Plant, *500*
Bahía Fosforescente
(Phosphorescent Bay),
500
Balata, Martinique, *458*
Balata Church, *458*
Balfour Town, Turks and
Caicos Islands, *744*
Barahona, Dominican
Republic, *308–309, 329*
Baranca Sunu (cave), *103*
Barbados, *111–148*
beaches, 126–128
business hours, 142
children, attractions for, 137–
138, 139, 140–141
electricity, 144
embassies, 144
emergencies, 144
etiquette and behavior, 144
festivals and seasonal events,
145
health issues, 145
holidays, 145
language, 145
lodging, 112–113, 116–122
mail and shipping, 146
money matters, 146
nightlife and the arts, 134–135
outdoor activities and sports,
128–132
passports and visas, 146
price categories, 112, 123
restaurants, 122–126
safety, 146
shopping, 132–134
sightseeing, 136–141
sightseeing tours, 146–147
taxes, 147
taxis, 148
telephones, 148
tipping, 148
transportation, 141–142, 143–
144
visitor information, 148
Barbados Museum, *137–138*
Barbados National Trust, *136*
Barbados Synagogue, *136*
Barbados Wildlife Reserve,
139
Barbuda, *69, 74*
Barcadera Cave, *167*
Barclays Park, *140*
Barnett Estates, *428–429*
Barre de l'Isle Forest
Reserve, *620*
Barrouallie, St. Vincent, *674*
Bas-du-Fort, Guadeloupe,
386
Baseball, *255, 316, 326,*
493
Basketball, *190*
Basse-Pointe, Martinique,
440–441, 450, 458
Basse-Terre, Guadeloupe,
374–376, 379–380, 388–
391

Basseterre, St. Kitts, *574–*
575
Bath Springs, *589*
The Baths (grotto), *203*
Bay Gardens, *355*
Bayamón, Puerto Rico, *500*
Beaches
Anguilla, 45–46
Antigua, 68–69
Aruba, 94–95
Barbados, 126–128
Bonaire, 159–160
British Virgin Islands, 186–
187, 200–201, 205, 206
Cayman Islands, 226–227,
234, 236
Curaçao, 253–254
Dominica, 282
Dominican Republic, 313–314
Grenada, 349
the Grenadines, 683, 687,
688, 690, 693
Guadeloupe, 381–382
Jamaica, 419–420
Martinique, 453–454
Nevis, 585
Puerto Rico, 489–490
St. Barthélemy, 538
St. Eustatius, 553–554
St. Kitts, 570–571
St. Lucia, 612
St. Maartan/St. Martin, 646–
647
St. Vincent, 671
Tobago, 725–726
Trinidad, 710–711
Turks and Caicos Islands,
741–742, 743, 750, 754,
755
U.S. Virgin Islands, 778–779,
805–806, 814–825
Bed-and-breakfasts, *703,*
717, 774
Belair, Grenada, *359*
Bellefontaine, Martinique,
459
Bequia, the Grenadines, *677,*
680–685
Bethel Methodist Church, *49*
Better Business Bureau, *857*
Betty's Hope (plantation),
74–75
Biblioteca Nacional, *325*
Bibliothèque Schoelcher,
459–460
Bike and moped travel, *854*
Anguilla, 50
Antigua, 69, 78
Aruba, 105–106
Bonaire, 160, 169
Cayman Islands, 237–238
Dominica, 283
Dominican Republic, 314–315
Grenada, 350
Guadeloupe, 382, 393
Jamaica, 433
Martinique, 454, 464
Puerto Rico, 490
St. Barthélemy, 543

St. Maarten/St. Martin, 656
Turks and Caicos Islands, 742,
750, 756
U.S. Virgin Islands, 780, 806
Bird sanctuaries
Barbuda, 74
Bonaire, 167–168, 169
Cayman Islands, 234, 236
Dominica, 288–289
Dominican Republic, 328
Grenada, 356, 357
Puerto Rico, 501
Jamaica, 428
Bird Sanctuary (Mandeville,
Jamaica), *428*
Bird-watching, *74, 167–168,*
169, 234, 236, 288–289,
420, 428, 501, 622, 711,
715, 726, 815
Black Point Tunnel, *674–675*
Black Rocks (lava deposits),
575
Bloody Point, St. Kitts, *575–*
576
Blow Holes, *231*
Blue Lagoon, Jamaica, *431*
Blue Mountains, Jamaica,
426
Boat and ferry travel, *854.*
☞ *Also* Cruises
to Anguilla, 50–51
to Barbados, 142
to British Virgin Islands, 211,
215
to Dominica, 292
to Grenada, 360–361
to the Grenadines, 694–695
to Guadeloupe, 393
to Martinique, 464
to Nevis, 591–592
to Puerto Rico, 506
to Saba, 523
to St. Barthélemy, 543
to St. Kitts, 591–592
to St. Lucia, 625
to St. Maarten/St. Martin, 656
to St. Vincent, 694–695
to Trinidad and Tobago, 730
to Turks and Caicos Islands,
756
to U.S. Virgin Islands, 832–
833, 838–839
Boating. ☞ *Also* Sailing
Anguilla, 46
Antigua, 69
Bonaire, 172
British Virgin Islands, 188,
201
Cayman Islands, 240–241
Curaçao, 254, 267
Dominica, 283
Dominican Republic, 314
Grenada, 349–350
the Grenadines, 683, 688, 693
Guadeloupe, 382
Jamaica, 436–437
Martinique, 454
Nevis, 585
Puerto Rico, 490

St. Barthélemy, 538–539
St. Kitts, 571
St. Lucia, 629
St. Maarten/St. Martin, 648
St. Vincent, 671
Tobago, 726
Turks and Caicos Islands, 750
U.S. Virgin Islands, 779–800, 825
Bob Marley Museum, 428
Boca Chica, Dominican Republic, 302–303, 311, 313
Boca Tabla (grotto), 261–262
Bodden Town, Cayman Islands, 231
Boeri Lake, 289
Boiling Hole, 755
Boiling Lake, 289
Bonaire, 149–173
beaches, 159–160
business hours, 169
children, attractions for, 167, 168–169
electricity, 170
emergencies, 170
festivals and seasonal events, 170
holidays, 170
language, 170–171
lodging, 150–151, 154–157
mail and shipping, 171
money matters, 171
nightlife and the arts, 165–166
outdoor activities and sports, 160–164
passports and visas, 171
price categories, 150, 157
restaurants, 157–159
safety, 171–172
shopping, 164–165
sightseeing, 166–169
sightseeing tours, 172
taxes, 172
taxis, 172
telephones, 172–173
tipping, 173
transportation, 169–170
visitor information, 173
Boquerón, Puerto Rico, 501
Bordeaux Mountain, St. John, 822, 830
Botanical Garden (St. Vincent), 676
Botanical Gardens (Dominica), 291
Botanical Gardens (Guadeloupe), 389
The Bottom, Saba, 521
Bouillante, Guadeloupe, 389
Bowling, 95
Bridgetown, Barbados, 123, 136–137
Brimstone Hill (fortress), 575
British Virgin Islands, 174–215
beaches, 186–187, 200–201, 205, 206
business hours, 211

electricity, 212
emergencies, 212
etiquette and behavior, 212
festivals and seasonal events, 212
health issues, 213
holidays, 213
language, 213
lodging, 178–179, 182–183, 194–195, 198, 204, 205–206, 207, 208–210
mail and shipping, 213
money matters, 213
nightlife and the arts, 192–193, 202
outdoor activities and sports, 188–190, 201
passports and visas, 213
price categories, 178, 183
restaurants, 183–186, 198–200, 204–205, 207, 208–210
safety, 214
shopping, 190–192, 201–202
sightseeing, 193–194, 202–203, 207–208
sightseeing tours, 214
taxes, 214
taxis, 214
telephones, 214–215
tipping, 215
transportation, 210–211, 212, 215
visitor information, 215
Buck Island Reef National Monument, 812
Bus travel, 854
Bushiribana Gold Smelter (ruins), 104
Business hours, 854
Butterfly Farm (Aruba), 103
Butterfly Farm (St. Maarten/St. Martin), 653

C

Cabo Rojo, Puerto Rico, 501
Cabo Rojo Wildlife Refuge, 501
Cabrits National Park, 287
Caicos Conch Farm, 752
Caicos Islands. ☞ See Turks and Caicos Islands
California Lighthouse, 104
Calle Las Damas (Street of the Ladies), 321
Cameras and photography, 854–855
Campgrounds, 868
British Virgin Islands, 183, 204, 207
St. Lucia, 612
U.S. Virgin Islands, 820
Canadian travelers, tips for, 859, 870
Cane Bay, St. Croix, 805
Canouan, the Grenadines, 686–687
Cap Chevalier, Martinique, 461

Caparra Ruins, 500
Capilla de los Remedios, 321, 323
Capilla del Cristo, 496
Car rentals, 855
Car travel, 855–856
Careenage, Barbados, 136
Carenage, Grenada, 357–358
Carib Indian Territory, 287–288
Carib petroglyphs, 577
Carib's Leap, 355
Caroni Bird Sanctuary, 715
Carriacou, Grenada, 344–345, 348–349, 359, 363–368
Casa Armstrong-Poventud (offices), 502
Casa Blanca (historic home), 496
Casa de Bastidas (historic home), 323
Casa de los Jesuitas (library), 321
Casa de Tostado (historic home), 323
Casa del Cordón (historic home), 323
Cascade aux Ecrevisses, 389
Casinos
Antigua, 73–74
Aruba, 101
Bonaire, 165
Curaçao, 258
Dominican Republic, 319
the Grenadines, 687
Guadeloupe, 385
Martinique, 457
Puerto Rico, 495
St. Kitts, 574
St. Maarten/St. Martin, 652–653
St. Vincent, 674
Castillo Serrallés (museum), 503
Castles
Barbados, 139–139
Cayman Islands, 232
Dominican Republic, 321
Martinique, 459
Castries, St. Lucia, 599, 602–606, 609–611, 619–622
Catedral de Nuestra Señora de Guadelupe, 502
Catedral de San Juan, 497
Catedral Santa María la Menor, 323
Cathédrale de St-Pierre et St-Paul, 388
Cathedral of Our Lady of Guadeloupe, 389
Cathedral of St. Peter and St. Paul, 789
Cathedral of the Immaculate Conception, 620
Catherineberg Ruins, 830

Caverns
Aruba, 103
Barbados, 139, 141
Bonaire, 167
Cayman Islands, 231, 234
Curaçao, 261–262, 263
Dominican Republic, 326
Jamaica, 430–431
Puerto Rico, 501–502
Saba, 521
Turks and Caicos Islands, 755
Cayman Brac, Cayman Islands, 232–234, 237–242
Cayman Brac Museum, 234
Cayman Islands, 216–242
beaches, 226–227, 234, 236
business hours, 238
consulates and embassies, 239
electricity, 238
emergencies, 239
etiquette and behavior, 239
festivals and seasonal events, 239
guided tours, 240–241
health issues, 239
holidays, 239
language, 239
lodging, 217, 220–223, 233–234, 235–236
mail and shipping, 239–240
money matters, 240
nightlife, 230
outdoor activities and sports, 227–229, 234, 236–237
passports and visas, 240
price categories, 217, 224
restaurants, 223–226
safety, 240
shopping, 229–230
sightseeing, 230–233, 234
sightseeing tours, 240–241
taxes, 241
taxis, 241
telephones, 241–242
tipping, 242
tours, 240–241
transportation, 237–238, 241, 242
visitor information, 242
Cayman Islands Legislative Assembly Building, 231
Cayman Islands National Museum, 232
Cayman Islands Turtle Farm, 231
Centro Ceremonial Indígena de Tibes (ruins), *503*
Chalky Mount, Barbados, 140
Champ d'Arbaud, *389*
Chapel of Our Lady of Antigua, 323
Chapel of the Holy Virgin, 463
Charlestown, Nevis, 589–590

Charlotte Amalie, St. Thomas, 770–772, 773, 775–776, 788–789, 791–794
Charlotteville, Tobago, 729
Château Murat, *392*
Children, attractions for. ☞ *See under specific islands*
Children, traveling with, 856–857
Christiansted, St. Croix, 797, 803–804, 811–813
Christoffel Park, 262
Church of St. Paul's Conversion, 522
Churches
Anguilla, 49
Antigua, 75, 76
Aruba, 103
Barbados, 137
Cayman Islands, 231
Dominica, 291
Dominican Republic, 321, 323–324, 326, 328
Grenada, 358
Guadeloupe, 388, 389
Jamaica, 432
Martinique, 458, 460, 461, 462, 463
Nevis, 591
Puerto Rico, 496, 497, 502, 503
Saba, 521, 522
St. Eustatius, 556
St. Kitts, 575
St. Lucia, 620
St. Vincent, 676
U.S. Virgin Islands, 789, 791, 793, 812, 814
Chutes du Carbet (Carbet Falls), *389*
Cibao Valley, Dominican Republic, *327–328*
Climate, *875*
Clothing for the trip, *869*
Coastal Islands, British Virgin Islands, *203*
Cockburn Harbour, Turks and Caicos Islands, *756*
Cockburn Town, Turks and Caicos Islands, *742–743*
Cockpit Country, Jamaica, *426*
Codrington Theological College, *138*
Coffee, *426, 428, 503*
Compass Point Marina, *794*
Computers, *857*
Concepción de la Vega, *328*
Conch Bar Caves, *755*
Concord Falls, *355–356*
Condominiums and villas
Anguilla, 40–41
Barbados, 122
British Virgin Islands, 183, 198
Cayman Islands, 222–223, 236
Grenada, 345
the Grenadines, 689–690

Guadeloupe, 377
Martinique, 448
Puerto Rico, 471
Saba, 513
St. Barthélemy, 533–534
St. Maarten/St. Martin, 642
Turks and Caicos Islands, 737
U.S. Virgin Islands, 773–774, 802–803, 820–821
Consumer protection, *857*
Convento de los Dominicos, *497*
Cooper Island, British Virgin Islands, 208, 210–215
Copper Mine Point, 203
Coral Bay, St. John, 822, 830
Coral World Marine Park, 794–795
Corossol, St. Barthélemy, *542*
Country House Museum, 262
Cove Bay, Saba, 521
Coyaba River Garden and Museum, 430
Credit and debit cards, 869
Cricket
Barbados, 132
British Virgin Islands, 190, 201
St. Eustatius, 555
St. Lucia, 615
Cruises, 857–858
Cruz Bay, St. John, 822–824, 830
Culebra, Puerto Rico, *504*
Curaçao, 243–269
beaches, 253–254
business hours, 265
children, attractions for, 263, 264
electricity, 265
embassies, 265
emergencies, 266
etiquette and behavior, 266
festivals and seasonal events, 266
guided tours, 267–268
health issues, 266
holidays, 266
language, 266–267
lodging, 244–245, 248–250
mail and shipping, 267
money matters, 267
nightlife, 257–258
outdoor activities and sports, 254–255
passports and visas, 267
price categories, 244, 251
restaurants, 250–253
safety, 267
shopping, 255–257
sightseeing, 258–264
sightseeing tours, 267–268
taxes, 268
taxis, 269
telephones, 269
tipping, 269
transportation, 264–265
visitor information, 269

Curaçao Museum, 259
Curaçao Seaquarium, 263
Curaçao Underwater Marine
Park, 263
Currency exchange, 869
Customs and duties, 858–
860

D

D. Hamilton Jackson Park,
812
Danish Consulate Building,
789
Danish Customs House, 812
de la Grenade Industries
(spice processing plant),
358
Den Paradera, 264
Devil's Bridge (natural
formation), 75
Devon House, 427
Diamond Botanical Gardens,
622
Diamond Rock, Martinique,
459
Diamond Waterfall, 622
Dining. ☞ See Restaurants
Disabilities and accessibility,
861–862
Discounts and deals, 862
Discovery Bay, Jamaica, 420,
430
Distilleries
Barbados, 138
Curaçao, 264
Dominican Republic, 326
Grenada, 357
Guadeloupe, 390, 392
Jamaica, 426
Martinique, 460, 461, 462
Puerto Rico, 500
Diving. ☞ See Scuba diving
Dog Islands, British Virgin
Islands, 203
Domaine de Valombreuse,
390
Dominica, 270–296
beaches, 282, 290
business hours, 292
electricity, 293
embassies, 293
emergencies, 293
etiquette and behavior, 293
festivals and seasonal events,
293
guided tours, 294–295
health issues, 293
holidays, 294
language, 294
lodging, 271, 274–278
mail and shipping, 294
money matters, 294
nightlife and the arts, 286–287
outdoor activities and sports,
283–284
passports and visas, 294
price categories, 271, 279
restaurants, 279–282
safety, 294

shopping, 284–286
sightseeing, 287–291
sightseeing tours, 294–295
taxes, 295
taxis, 295
telephones, 295
tipping, 295
transportation, 291–293
visitor information, 295–296
Dominica Museum, 291
Dominican Republic, 297–
335
beaches, 313–314
business hours, 329–330
children, attractions for, 321,
322, 326
electricity, 330
embassies, 330–331
emergencies, 331
etiquette and behavior, 331
festivals and seasonal events,
331
health issues, 331
holidays, 331
language, 331
lodging, 298–299, 302–309
mail and shipping, 331–332
money matters, 332
nightlife, 319–320
outdoor activities and sports,
314–316
passports and visas, 332
price categories, 299, 309
restaurants, 309–313
safety, 332
shopping, 316–318
sightseeing, 320–321, 323–
328
sightseeing tours, 332–333
taxes, 333
taxis, 333–334
telephones, 334
tipping, 334
transportation, 328–329, 330,
334–335
visitor information, 335
Dougaldston Spice Estate,
356
Dows Hill Interpretation
Center, 77
Drake's Seat (overlook),
795
Dubuc Castle, 459
Dunn's River Falls, 430
Dutch Reformed Church (St.
Eustatius), 556
Dutch Reformed Church (St.
Thomas), 789

E

East Coast, Dominican
Republic, 325–326
East End, Anguilla, 44–45
Ecomusée de Martinique, 462
Ecotourism, 863
Eden Brown Estate, 590
Edmund Forest Reserve, 623
Educators Park, 791

Edward Wilmoth Blyden
Marine Terminal, 791
El Batey, Dominican Republic,
327
El Bosque Nacional de Caribe
(Caribbean National
Forest), 503–504
El Capitolio, 499
El Faro a Colón (lighthouse),
323
El Malecón, 324
Elaine Ione Sprauve Library
and Museum, 830
Electricity, 863
Elmslie Memorial United
Church, 231
Emancipation Garden, 791
Emancipation Statue, 138
Emerald Pool, 288
Emergencies
Anguilla, 51
Antigua, 79
Aruba, 107
Barbados, 144
Bonaire, 170
British Virgin Islands, 212
Cayman Islands, 239
Curaçao, 266
Dominica, 293
Dominican Republic, 331
Grenada, 362
the Grenadines, 697
Guadeloupe, 394
Jamaica, 434
Martinique, 466
Nevis, 593
Puerto Rico, 507
Saba, 523
St. Barthélemy, 544–545
St. Eustatius, 557–558
St. Kitts, 593
St. Lucia, 626–627
St. Maarten/St. Martin, 657
St. Vincent, 696
Trinidad and Tobago, 732
Turks and Caicos Islands, 757
U.S. Virgin Islands, 835
Emperor Valley Zoo and the
Botanical Gardens, 717
English Harbour, Antigua, 75
Enid M. Baa Public Library,
791
Enighed Estate Great House,
830
Estate Mount Washington
Plantation, 814
Estate St. Peter Greathouse &
Botanical Gardens, 795
Estate Whim Plantation
Museum, 814
Etang Zombi, 389

F

Fajardo, Puerto Rico, 504
Fallen Jerusalem, British
Virgin Islands, 203
Falls of Baleine, 675
Falmouth, Antigua, 75
Farley Hill, 139–140

Fern Gully, *431*
Festivals and seasonal events. ☞ *See under specific islands*
Fig Tree Drive, Antigua, *75*
Fine Arts Centre, *729*
Firefly (historic home), *426*
Fishing
Anguilla, 46
Antigua, 69
Aruba, 95–96
Barbados, 128
Bonaire, 160–161
British Virgin Islands, 188, 201
Cayman Islands, 227, 236
Curaçao, 254
Dominica, 283
Dominican Republic, 315
Grenada, 350
Grenadines, 688
Guadeloupe, 382
Jamaica, 420–421
Martinique, 454
Nevis, 585
Puerto Rico, 490
Saba, 519
St. Barthélemy, 539
St. Eustatius, 554
St. Kitts, 571
St. Lucia, 613
St. Maarten/St. Martin, 648
St. Vincent, 671
Tobago, 726
Trinidad, 711
Turks and Caicos Islands, 750
U.S. Virgin Islands, 780, 806, 825
Flagstaff Hill, *729*
Flamingos, *167–168, 169, 754*
Flat Point, Saba, *521*
Floating Market, *259–260*
Flower Forest, *140*
Folkestone Marine Park & Visitor Centre, *140–141*
Fontein (cave), *103*
Football Fields (dive site), *753*
The Forest, Anguilla, *43–44*
Forêt de Montravail, Martinique, *459*
Ft. Amsterdam, *260*
Ft. Ashby, *590*
Fort Bay, Saba, *521*
Ft. Burt, *193*
Ft. Charles, *432*
Ft. Charlotte (St. Lucia), *620–621*
Ft. Charlotte (St. Vincent), *675*
Ft. Christian, *791*
Ft. Christiansvaern, *811*
Fort-de-France, Martinique, *441, 450, 459*
Ft. Duvernette, *675*
Fort Fleur d'Épée, *386*
Ft. Frederick, *358*
Ft. Frederik, *814*

Ft. George (Antigua), *75*
Ft. George (Grenada), *358*
Ft. King George, *729*
Fort Louis Delgrès, *389*
Fort Napoléon, *391*
Ft. Oranje (Bonaire), *166*
Ft. Oranje (St. Eustatius), *556*
Ft. Recovery, *193*
Fort St-Louis, *459*
Ft. Shirley, *287*
Ft. Zoutman, *104*
Fortaleza de San Felipe, *326*
Forts
Antigua, 75
Aruba, 104
Bonaire, 166
British Virgin Islands, 193
Cayman Islands, 231
Curaçao, 260
Dominica, 287
Dominican Republic, 324, 326
Grenada, 358
the Grenadines, 685
Guadeloupe, 386, 389, 391
Jamaica, 430, 432
Martinique, 459
Nevis, 590
Puerto Rico, 497–498, 500
St. Eustatius, 556
St. Kitts, 575
St. Lucia, 620
St. Vincent, 675
Tobago, 729
U.S. Virgin Islands, 791, 814
Francia Plantation House, *141*
Frederick Lutheran Church, *791*
Frederiksted, St. Croix, *805, 814–815*
Fregate Island Nature Reserve, *622*
French Cul de Sac, St. Maarten/St. Martin, *653*
Frenchman's Cay, *193*
Frenchtown, St. Thomas, *772–773, 777–778, 795*
Freshwater Lake, *289*
Fuerte San Felipe del Morro, *498*

G
Gardens
Barbados, 140
British Virgin Islands, 193
Curaçao, 262, 264
Dominica, 291
Dominican Republic, 324
Grenada, 355, 357
Guadeloupe, 389, 390
Jamaica, 430–432
Martinique, 458, 460
Nevis, 590
Puerto Rico, 499–500
St. Lucia, 622
St. Vincent, 676
Trinidad, 717
U.S. Virgin Islands, 791, 795, 815

Gay and lesbian travelers, tips for, *864*
General Post Office (Cayman Islands), *231*
George Hill, Anguilla, *43–44*
George Town, Cayman Islands, *231–232*
Golf
Antigua, 70
Aruba, 96
Barbados, 128–129
Cayman Islands, 227
Curaçao, 254
Dominican Republic, 315
Grenada, 350
the Grenadines, 687
Guadeloupe, 382
Jamaica, 421
Martinique, 455
Nevis, 585
Puerto Rico, 490–491
St. Kitts, 571
St. Lucia, 613
St. Maarten/St. Martin, 648
Tobago, 726
Trinidad, 711
Turks and Caicos Islands, 750
U.S. Virgin Islands, 780, 806
Gorges de la Falaise, *458*
Gosier, Guadeloupe, *386*
Goto Meer (saltwater lagoon), *167–168*
Gouyave Nutmeg Processing Cooperative, *356*
Government House (St. Croix), *812*
Government House (St. Lucia), *621*
Government House (St. Thomas), *791–792*
Governor Gore Bird Sanctuary, *236*
Grand Anse, Grenada, *356*
Grand Case, St. Maarten/St. Martin, *654*
Grand Cayman, Cayman Islands, *217, 220–232, 237–242*
Grand Étang National Park and Forest Reserve, *356*
Grand Hotel Court, *792*
Grand' Rivière, Martinique, *461*
Grand Turk, the Turks and Caicos Islands, *737, 740–743, 756–760*
Grande Saline, St. Barthélemy, *542*
Grande-Terre, Guadeloupe, *369, 372–374, 377–379, 386–388*
Green Grotto Caves, *430*
Greenwood Great House, *429*
Grenada, *336–367*
beaches, 349
business hours, 361
children, attractions for, 356, 357

electricity, 362
embassies, 362
emergencies, 362
etiquette and behavior, 362–363
festivals and seasonal events, 363–364
health issues, 364
holidays, 364
language, 364
lodging, 337, 340–345
mail and shipping, 364
money matters, 364–365
nightlife and the arts, 354–355
outdoor activities and sports, 349–352
passports and visas, 365
price categories, 337, 346
restaurants, 345–349
safety, 365
shopping, 352–354
sightseeing, 355–359
sightseeing tours, 365–366
taxes, 366
taxis, 366
telephones, 366
tipping, 366
transportation, 360–362
visitor information, 366–367
Grenada National Museum, 358
the Grenadines, 677, 680–693. ☞ Also St. Vincent and the Grenadines
Grenadines Wharf, 675
Grenville, Grenada, 356–357
Grenville Cooperative Nutmeg Association, 356
Guadeloupe, 368–397
beaches, 381–382
business hours, 393
electricity, 394
emergencies, 394
etiquette and behavior, 394
festivals and seasonal events, 394–395
health issues, 395
holidays, 395
language, 395
lodging, 369, 372–377
mail and shipping, 395
money matters, 395
nightlife, 385–386
outdoor activities and sports, 382–383
passports and visas, 395
price categories, 369, 377
restaurants, 377–381
safety, 395–396
shopping, 384–385
sightseeing, 386–392
sightseeing tours, 396
taxes, 396
taxis, 396
telephones, 396
tipping, 396
transportation, 392–393, 394
visitor information, 397

Guadirikiri (cave), 103
Guana Bay Point, St. Maarten/St. Martin, 654
Guana Island, British Virgin Islands, 208, 210–215
Guest houses and lodges
Cayman Islands, 221
U.S. Virgin Islands, 773
Guide books and publications on the Caribbean, 863–864
Gun Hill Signal Station, 141
Gustavia, St. Barthélemy, 542

H

Haagensen House, 792
Habitation Anse Latouche, 460
Habitation Clément, 460
Hacienda Buena Vista (restored coffee plantation), 503
Hamilton Battery, 685
Harmony Hall (art gallery), 75–76
Harrison's Cave, 141
Harry Bayley Observatory, 138
Hassel Island, St. Thomas, 792
Hato Caves, 263
Health issues, 864–865. ☞ Also Emergencies; Safety under specific islands
Hell, Cayman Islands, 232
Hell's Gate, Saba, 521
Heritage Collection, 49
Heritage Quay, Antigua, 76
High Mountain Coffee Plantation, 428
Hiking
Aruba, 96
Barbados, 129
Cayman Islands, 228
Dominica, 283
Dominican Republic, 315
Grenada, 350–351
Guadeloupe, 382–383
Martinique, 455
Nevis, 585–586
Puerto Rico, 491
Saba, 519
St. Eustatius, 554
St. Kitts, 571–572
St. Lucia, 613
St. Vincent, 672
Tobago, 726–727
U.S. Virgin Islands, 806–807, 825–826
Hindu temple, 458
Historic homes
Anguilla, 49–50
Barbados, 136, 138–139, 140, 141
Bonaire, 168
Cayman Islands, 232
Curaçao, 262, 263, 264
Dominica, 291

Dominican Republic, 323
Grenada, 357
Jamaica, 426, 427, 428–429
Martinique, 460
Nevis, 590
Puerto Rico, 496, 503
St. Barthélemy, 542
St. Eustatius, 556
St. Kitts, 576
Trinidad, 716, 717
U.S. Virgin Islands, 792, 793, 795, 813, 815, 830, 831
Historical Museum, 359
Holidays, 865
Holy Rosary Church, 521
Home and apartment rentals
Bonaire, 150
British Virgin Islands, 183, 198
Curaçao, 244
Grenada, 345
Guadeloupe, 377
Puerto Rico, 471
Saba, 513
St. Eustatius, 549
Turks and Caicos Islands, 737
U.S. Virgin Islands, 774, 803
Home exchanges, 868
Honen Dalim (synagogue), 556
Hooiberg (Haystack Hill), 104
Horse racing
Barbados, 132
Dominican Republic, 316
Nevis, 587
Puerto Rico, 493
U.S. Virgin Islands, 782
Horseback riding
Anguilla, 46
Antigua, 70
Aruba, 96–97
Barbados, 129
Bonaire, 161
British Virgin Islands, 188
Cayman Islands, 227
Curaçao, 254
Dominican Republic, 315
the Grenadines, 691
Guadeloupe, 383
Jamaica, 421
Martinique, 455
Nevis, 586
Puerto Rico, 491
St. Barthélemy, 539
St. Kitts, 572
St. Lucia, 613–614
St. Maarten/St. Martin, 648
U.S. Virgin Islands, 780, 807, 826
Hostal Palacio Nicolás de Ovando (historic home), 323
Hot springs
Dominica, 289
Guadeloupe, 389
Nevis, 589
St. Lucia, 623–624
Hotel 1829, 792

Hotels, *868*
Anguilla, 34–35, 38–40
Antigua, 56–57, 60–64
Aruba, 84–85, 88–91
Barbados, 113, 116–122
Bonaire, 150–151, 154–157
*British Virgin Islands, 178–
179, 192–183, 194–195,
198, 204, 205–206, 207,
208–210*
*Cayman Islands, 217, 220–
223*
*children, accommodations for,
857*
Curaçao, 245, 248–259
*disabilities and accessibility,
861*
Dominica, 271, 274–278
*Dominican Republic, 299,
302–309*
Grenada, 340–345
*the Grenadines, 677, 680–
681, 686–687, 688, 689,
691, 692–693*
Guadeloupe, 369, 372–377
Jamaica, 401, 404–415
*Martinique, 440–441, 444–
448*
Nevis, 576–577, 580–582
*Puerto Rico, 473–475, 478–
483*
Saba, 513, 516–517
*St. Barthélemy, 528–529, 532–
533*
St. Eustatius, 549, 552
St. Kitts, 564–567
St. Lucia, 599, 602–608
*St. Maarten/St. Martin, 634–
635, 638–642*
*St. Vincent, 664–665, 668–
669*
Tobago, 720–722
Trinidad, 706–707
*Turks and Caicos Islands, 737,
740, 743, 744–747, 752–
756*
*U.S. Virgin Islands, 770–773,
797, 800–802, 817, 820*

I

Icons and symbols, *876*
Iglesia St. Stanislaus, *326*
Iglesia Santa Bárbara, *324*
Iglesia y Convento Domínico,
323–324
Iles des Saintes, Guadeloupe,
376, 380–381, 391
Ilet de Pigeon, Guadeloupe,
389
**Ilet Pinel, St. Maarten/St.
Martin,** *653*
Indian River, *288*
Institute of Jamaica, *427*
Insurance, *865–866*
car rental, *855*
Inter Oceans Museum, *542*
Isla Saona (park), *326*
Island Harbour, Anguilla, *49*

J

**J. R. O'Neal Botanic
Gardens,** *193*
J. W. Edwards Building, *291*
Jamaica, *398–438*
beaches, 419–420
business hours, 433
electricity, 434
embassies, 434
emergencies, 434
etiquette and behavior, 434
*festivals and seasonal events,
434*
health issues, 435
holidays, 435
language, 435
lodging, 400–401, 404–415
mail and shipping, 435
money matters, 435
nightlife and the arts, 424–425
*outdoor activities and sports,
420–422*
passports and visas, 435–436
price categories, 401, 416
restaurants, 415–419
safety, 436
shopping, 422–424
sightseeing, 425–432
sightseeing tours, 436–437
taxes, 437
taxis, 437
telephones, 437
tipping, 438
transportation, 432–434
visitor information, 438
**Jamaican People's Museum
of Crafts and Technology,**
432
**Jarabacoa, Dominican
Republic,** *327*
Jardin Botánico, *499–500*
**Jardin Botánico Nacional Dr.
Rafael M. Moscoso,** *324*
Jardin de Balata, *458*
Jardin Pichon, *389*
Jewish Cultural Museum,
260–261
JM Distillery, *461*
**Jost Van Dyke, British Virgin
Islands,** *203–205, 210–215*
**Juan Dolio, Dominican
Republic,** *302–303, 311,
313*
Judith's Fancy (historic
home), *813*

K

**Karl and Marie Lawaetz
Museum,** *815*
Kayaking, *97, 161, 781,
807, 826*
**Kew, Turks and Caicos
Islands,** *754*
Kingston, Jamaica, *401,
404, 416, 419, 426–428*
Kingstown, St. Vincent, *664–
665, 669–670, 675–676*
Kingstown Methodist Church,
676

Kralendijk, Bonaire, *166*
Kura Hulanda Museum, *260*

L

La Atarazana (Royal
Mooring Docks), *321*
La Casa del Libro (museum),
497
La Désirade, Guadeloupe,
377, 392
La Fortaleza (executive
mansion), *497–498*
La Maison du Bois
(museum), *390*
La Maison du Cacao
(museum), *390*
La Moule, Guadeloupe, *386–
383*
Le Musée Volcanologique,
390
**La Romana, Dominican
Republic,** *303–304, 312,
314*
La Savane (park), *459*
La Savane des Pétrifications
(Petrified Forest), *462*
La Soufrière (volcano), *677*
**La Soufrière Drive-in
Volcano,** *623–624*
La Trinité, Martinique, *441,
444, 451*
La Vega Vieja, *327*
Ladder Bay, Saba, *521*
Lago Enriquillo, *328*
Laguna Grí-Grí
(swampland), *326*
Lamentin, Martinique, *450–
451, 461*
Landhuis Brievengat (historic
home), *263*
Landhuis Karpata (historic
home), *168*
Landhuis Knip (historic
home), *264*
Language, *866–867.* ☞
*Also under specific
islands*
**Las Terrenas, Dominican
Republic,** *314*
**Laura Herb and Spice
Garden,** *357*
Layou, *676, St. Vincent, 676*
Le Diamant, Martinique, *444,
459*
Le Domaine de Séverin
(distillery), *390*
Le François, Martinique,
444–445, 451–452, 460
Le Manoir, *542*
Le Marin, Martinique, *461*
Le Morne Rouge, Martinique,
461
Le Moule, Guadeloupe, *386–
387*
Le Moulin de Bézard
(windmill), *392*
Le Musée de la Banane
(Banana Museum), *462*

Le Musée Volcanologique, *390*
Le Prêcheur, Martinique, *462*
Le Robert, Martinique, *460*
Le Vauclin, Martinique, *463*
Legislature Building (St. Thomas), *792*
Les Ilets de l'Impératrice, Martinique, *460*
Les Mamelles (mountains), *389*
Les Ombrages (botanical gardens), *458*
Les Trois-Ilets, Martinique, *445–446, 452–453, 463*
L'Escalier Tête Chien (Snakes Staircase), *288*
Levera National Park and Bird Sanctuary, *357*
Leyritz Plantation, *458*
Libraries
Cayman Islands, 231
Dominica, 291
Dominican Republic, 321, 325
Jamaica, 427, 428
Martinique, 459–460
Puerto Rico, 497
U.S. Virgin Islands, 791, 812, 830
Lighthouses
Aruba, 104
Bonaire, 167
Dominican Republic, 323
Jamaica, 429–430
Lilac House, *291*
Little Cayman, Cayman Islands, *234–242*
Little Fort National Park, *203*
Little Princess Estate, *813*
Little Thatch Island, British Virgin Islands, *209, 210–215*
Little Tobago Island, *729*
Little Tokyo, St. Vincent, *676*
Little Water Cay, Turks and Caicos Islands, *752*
Lodging, *867–868.* ☞
Also Apartment and villa rentals; Bed-and-breakfasts; Campgrounds; Condominiums and villas; Guest houses and lodges; Home and apartment rentals; Home exchanges; Hotels; *under specific islands*
Lopinot Complex, *716*
Lorient, St. Barthélemy, *542*
Los Charamicos, Dominican Republic, *327*
Los Haitises National Park, *327*
Loterie Farms, *655*
Lover's Leap, *428*
Lower Town, St. Eustatius, *556*
Luggage, *870*
Luis A. Ferré Science Park, *500*

Lynch Plantation Museum, *555–556*

M
Macorís Rum distillery, *326*
Macouba, Martinique, *453, 461*
Magnificent Seven (historic homes), *717*
Mail and shipping, *868*
Maison de la Canne (sugar farm), *463*
Maison de la Forêt, *390*
Malibu Beach Club, *138*
Mandeville, Jamaica, *415, 428*
Maria Islands Nature Reserve, *622–623*
Marie-Galante, Guadeloupe, *376–377, 381, 391–392*
Marigot, Dominica, *290*
Marigot, Martinique, *447*
Marigot, St. Maarten/St. Martin, *654*
Marigot Bay, St. Lucia, *621*
Marina Cay, British Virgin Islands, *209–215*
Maritime Museum, *260*
Marquis Estate, *621*
Martello Tower, *74*
Martha Brae River, *428*
Martinique, *439–469*
beaches, 453–454
business hours, 464
electricity, 466
emergencies, 466
festivals and seasonal events, 466
health issues, 466
holidays, 466
language, 466–467
lodging, 440–441, 444–449
mail and shipping, 467
money matters, 467
nightlife and the arts, 457–458
outdoor activities and sports, 454–455
passports and visas, 467
price categories, 440, 449
restaurants, 449–453
safety, 467
shopping, 456–457
sightseeing, 458–463
sightseeing tours, 467–468
taxes, 468
taxis, 468
telephones, 468
tipping, 469
transportation, 464, 465–466
visitor information, 469
Mastic Trail, Cayman Islands, *232*
Mavis Bank (coffee plant), *426*
Mayagüez, Puerto Rico, *501*
Mayreau, the Grenadines, *687–688*
Meal plans, *867*

Megaliths of Greencastle Hill, *76*
Memorial Moravian Church, *793*
Mesopatamia Valley, St. Vincent, *676*
Middle Caicos, Turks and Caicos Islands, *754–755*
Middleham Falls, *290*
Mikveh Israel-Emmanuel Synagogue, *260–261*
Mineral Baths, *622*
Molasses Reef, *744*
Mona, Puerto Rico, *501*
Monasterio de San Francisco, *324*
Money matters, *868–869.* ☞ *Also under specific islands*
Mont Pelée (volcano), *461*
Montego Bay, Jamaica, *408–412, 417–418, 420, 428–429*
Montreal Gardens, *676*
Morne-à-l'Eau, Guadeloupe, *386*
Morne Aux Diables, *288*
Morne Coubaril Estate, *623*
Morne-des-Esses, Martinique, *453*
Morne Diablotin National Park, *288–289*
Morne Fortune, St. Lucia, *621*
Morne Trois Pitons National Park, *289–290*
Mt. Brandaris, *169*
Mt. Christoffel, *262*
Mt. Eagle, *813*
Mount Gay Rum Visitors Centre, *138*
Mt. Healthy National Park, *193*
Mt. Isabel de Torres, *326*
Mt. Pleasant, *685*
Mt. Rodney Estate, *357*
Mt. Scenery, *521–522*
Mountain Top, St. Thomas, *795*
Municipal Museum, *542*
Musée de la Pagerie, *463*
Musée de Saint-Martin, *654*
Musée du Rhum (Martinique), *462*
Musée Gauguin, *461*
Musée St-John Perse, *387*
Musée Schoelcher, *387*
Musée Vulcanologique, *463*
Museo de Ambar Dominicano, *326–327*
Museo de Arte de Ponce, *502–503*
Museo de Arte de Puerto Rico, *499*
Museo de Arte Moderno, *325*
Museo de Historia, Antropología y Arte, *499*
Museo de Historia Natural, *325*

Museo de la Conquista y Colonización de Puerto Rico, 500
Museo de la Familia Dominicana, 323
Museo de la Historia de Ponce, 502
Museo de las Casas Reales, 324
Museo del Hombre Dominicano, 325
Museo Pablo Casals, 498
Museum of Antigua and Barbuda, 76
Museum of Nevis History, 590
Museums and galleries
Anguilla, 49
Antigua, 75, 76
Aruba, 104
Barbados, 137, 139, 140
British Virgin Islands, 193–194
Cayman Islands, 229–230, 232
Curaçao, 256, 259, 260–261, 262
Dominica, 285, 291
Dominican Republic, 324, 325, 326–327
Grenada, 355, 358, 359
the Grenadines, 685
Guadeloupe, 387, 390
Jamaica, 427–428, 430, 432
Martinique, 461, 462, 463
Nevis, 590
Puerto Rico, 496, 497, 498, 499, 500, 502–503
Saba, 522
St. Barthélemy, 542
St. Eustatius, 555–556
St. Maarten/St. Martin, 654, 655
St. Lucia, 621
Tobago, 729
Trinidad, 716, 717
Turks and Caicos Islands, 742–743
U.S. Virgin Islands, 789, 791, 793, 794, 795, 812, 814, 815
Mustique, the Grenadines, 688–691

N

National Gallery (Jamaica), 427–428
National Heroes Square (Barbados), 136
National Museum and Art Gallery (Trinidad), 717
Natural Bridge, 104
Nature reserves
Aruba, 103
Barbados, 139
Bonaire, 168–169
British Virgin Islands, 194, 203
Cayman Islands, 232, 234
Curaçao, 262, 263

Dominica, 287, 288–289, 291
Dominican Republic, 324, 326, 327
Grenada, 357
Guadeloupe, 389–390
Martinique, 462
Puerto Rico, 501, 503–504
St. Lucia, 620, 622–623
Tobago, 729
Trinidad, 715
Turks and Caicos Islands, 754
U.S. Virgin Islands, 813–814
Necker Island, British Virgin Islands, 209, 210–215
Negril, Jamaica, 412–415, 418–419, 420
Nelson Museum, 590
Nelson's Dockyard, 75
Nevis, 560–651, 576–577, 580–597
beaches, 585
business hours, 592
electricity, 593
emergencies, 593
etiquette and behavior, 593
festivals and seasonal events, 593–594
health issues, 594
holidays, 594
language, 594
lodging, 576–577, 580–582
money matters, 594
nightlife, 588–589
outdoor activities and sports, 585–587
passports and visas, 594
restaurants, 582–584
safety, 594
shopping, 587–588
sightseeing, 589–591
sightseeing tours, 594–596
taxes, 595
telephones, 596
tipping, 596
transportation, 591–593, 597
visitor information, 597
Nevis Botanical Gardens, 590
Nevis House of Assembly, 590
New Zealand, tips for travelers from, 859, 870
Nightlife and the arts. ☞ See under specific islands
99 Steps (staircase street), 793
North Caicos, Turks and Caicos Islands, 753–754
North Shore Shell Museum, 193–194
Northeast Coast, Dominica, 290
Numismatic Museum, 104

O

Observatorio de Arecibo, 501
Ocho Rios, Jamaica, 405–407, 416–417, 419–420, 430–431

Old Factory, 49
Old Fort, 430
Old Homestead, 232
Old Market (Marche), 261
Old Prison at Crocus Hill, 49
Old Road Town, St. Kitts, 575–576
Old San Juan, Puerto Rico, 473–474, 484–486, 496–500
Old Sulphur Mine Walk, 521
The Oldhegg Turtle Sanctuary, 685
1,000 Steps (limestone staircase), 168
Onima, Bonaire, 168
Oranjestad, Aruba, 104
Oranjestad, St. Eustatius, 556
Orléans, St. Maarten/St. Martin, 654
Ostrich Farm, 264
Outdoor activities and sports. ☞ See specific sports; under specific islands
Owia, St. Vincent, 677
Oyster Pond, St. Maarten/St. Martin, 654

P

Package deals, 862
Packing for the Caribbean, 869–870
Palm Island, the Grenadines, 691
Paradise Point Tramway, 795
Parasailing
Aruba, 97
Barbados, 129
St. Maarten/St. Martin, 648
Turks and Caicos Islands, 750
U.S. Virgin Islands, 780
Parc Archéologique des Roches Gravées, 389
Parc Floral et Culturel, 460
Parc National de la Guadeloupe, 389–390
Parham, Antigua, 76
Parliament Buildings (Barbados), 136
Parque Ceremonial Indigena de Caguana, 502
Parque Colón, 324
Parque de Bombas (museum), 502
Parque de las Cavernas del Río Camuy, 501–502
Parque de los Tres Ojos, 326
Parque Independencia, 324
Parque Luis Muñoz Marin, 499
Parque Zoológico Nacional, 324
Parrot Cay, Turks and Caicos Islands, 752–753
Parrot Preserve, 234
Paseo de la Princesa, 498

Passports and visas, *870–871.* ☞ *Also under specific islands*
Peace Hill, St. John, *830*
Peace Memorial Building, *231*
Pearls Airport, *356–357*
Pedro St. James Castle, *232*
Père Labat (distillery), *392*
Peter Island, British Virgin Islands, *205–206, 210–215*
Petit-Bourg, Guadeloupe, *390*
Petit St. Vincent, the Grenadines, *692*
Petite Martinique, Grenada, *359*
Philipsburg, St. Maarten/St. Martin, *654–655*
Pic du Paradis, *655*
Pigeon Island, St. Lucia, *621*
Pine Cay, Turks and Caicos Islands, *753*
Pissarro Building, *793*
Pitons (mountains), *623*
Plane travel, *851–853*
  to Anguilla, 50
  to Antigua, 77–78
  to Aruba, 105
  to Barbados, 141–142
  to Bonaire, 169
  to British Virgin Islands, 210, 215
  to Cayman Islands, 237
  with children, 856
  to Curaçao, 264–265
  to Dominica, 291–292
  to Dominican Republic, 328–329, 334
  to Grenada, 360
  to the Grenadines, 693–694
  to Guadeloupe, 392–393
  to Jamaica, 432–433
  luggage restrictions, 870
  to Martinique, 464
  to Nevis, 591, 597
  to Puerto Rico, 505–506
  to Saba, 522–523
  to St. Barthélemy, 543
  to St. Eustatius, 557
  to St. Kitts, 591, 597
  to St. Lucia, 624–625
  to St. Maarten/St. Martin, 655–656
  to St. Vincent, 693–694
  to Trinidad and Tobago, 730, 731
  to Turks and Caicos Islands, 756
  to U.S. Virgin Islands, 831–832, 838, 841–842
Plantations
  Anguilla, 49–50
  Antigua, 74–75
  Barbados, 138, 139, 141
  Bonaire, 168
  Curaçao, 264
  Grenada, 355, 356, 357

Guadeloupe, 390, 392
Jamaica, 426, 428, 430–431
Martinique, 458
Puerto Rico, 503
St. Eustatius, 555–556
St. Lucia, 621, 623
U.S. Virgin Islands, 813, 814, 815, 830, 831
Plaza de Armas, *498*
Plaza de la Cultura, *324–325*
Plaza Piar, *261*
Plazuela de la Rogativa, *498*
Point Udall, St. Croix, *813*
Pointe des Châteaux, Guadeloupe, *387*
Pointe du Bout, Martinique, *461–462*
Pointe Figuier, Martinique, *462*
Pointe-à-Pitre, Guadeloupe, *387–388*
Pointe-Noire, Guadeloupe, *390*
Polo
  Barbados, 132
  Dominican Republic, 316
Ponce, Puerto Rico, *502–503*
Port Antonio, Jamaica, *404–405, 419, 431*
Port Elizabeth, *685*
Port Louis, Guadeloupe, *388*
Port-of-Spain, Trinidad, *716–717*
Port Royal, Jamaica, *432*
Porta Coeli (Gates of Heaven church), *503*
Porte d'Enfer (Gate of Hell), *388*
Portsmouth, Dominica, *290*
Post Office Building (St. Croix), *812*
Praslin, St. Lucia, *622*
Presqu'île du Caravelle, Martinique, *459*
Price categories. ☞ *See under specific islands*
Princess Royal Hospital, *359*
Prospect Plantation, *430*
Providenciales, Turks and Caicos Islands, *744–752*
Puerta de la Misericordia (Gate of Mercy), *325*
Puerto Plata, Dominican Republic, *314, 317, 326–327*
Puerto Rico, *471–511*
  beaches, 489
  business hours, 506
  children, attractions for, 498, 499, 503–504
  electricity, 507
  emergencies, 507
  etiquette and behavior, 507
  festivals and seasonal events, 507–508
  health issues, 508
  holidays, 508
  language, 508

  lodging, 471, 473, 475, 478–483
  mail and shipping, 508
  money matters, 508–509
  nightlife and the arts, 494–496
  outdoor activities and sports, 490–493
  passports and visas, 509
  price categories, 473, 484
  restaurants, 483–489
  safety, 509
  shopping, 493–494
  sightseeing, 496–505
  sightseeing tours, 509–510
  taxes, 510
  taxis, 510
  telephones and mail, 510–511
  tipping, 511
  transportation, 505–507, 511
  visitor information, 511
Punta Cana, Dominican Republic, *304–306, 314*

Q

Queen Elizabeth II Botanic Park, *232*
Queen Emma Bridge, *261*
Queen Juliana Bridge, *261*
Queen's Park, *136–137*
Queen's View, *232*
The Quill (volcanic cone), *556–557*

R

Rabacca Dry River (gulch), *677*
Red Hook, St. Thomas, *795*
Redcliffe Quay, Antigua, *77*
Reef Bay Plantation, *831*
Reef Bay Trail, *830–831*
Rendezvous Bay, Anguilla, *42–43*
Rest rooms, *871*
Restaurants, *860–861*
  Anguilla, 41–45
  Antigua, 65–68
  Aruba, 91–94
  Barbados, 122–126
  Bonaire, 157–159
  British Virgin Islands, 183–186, 198–200, 204–205, 206, 208–210
  Cayman Islands, 223–226
  Curaçao, 251–253
  Dominica, 279–282
  Dominican Republic, 309–313
  Grenada, 345–348
  the Grenadines, 681–683, 686–687, 688, 690, 691, 692, 693
  Guadeloupe, 377–381
  Jamaica, 416–419
  Martinique, 449–453
  Nevis, 582–584
  Puerto Rico, 483–488
  Saba, 517–519
  St. Barthélemy, 535–538
  St. Eustatius, 552–553
  St. Kitts, 568–570

St. Lucia, 609–612
St. Maarten/St. Martin, 642–646
St. Vincent, 669–671
Tobago, 722–724
Trinidad, 708–710
Turks and Caicos Islands, 741, 748–750
U.S. Virgin Islands, 774–778, 803–805, 821–824
Rincon, Bonaire, 168
Rincón, Puerto Rico, 503
Rio Grande, Jamaica, 431–432
River Antoine Rum Distillery, 357
Rivière Madame, 460
Road Town, British Virgin Islands, 178–179, 183–185, 194
Rock formations, Aruba, 104–105
Rodney Bay, St. Lucia, 621–622
Romney Manor, 576
Roosevelt Park, 793
Rose Hall (great house), 429
Roseau, Dominica, 290–291
Rum Factory and Heritage Park, 138
Runaway Bay, Jamaica, 407–408
Running
Grenada, 351

S

Saba, 512–525
business hours, 523
electricity, 523
emergencies, 523
festivals and seasonal events, 523–524
holidays, 524
language, 524
lodging, 513, 516–517
mail and shipping, 524
money matters, 524
nightlife, 520
outdoor activities and sports, 519–520
passports and visas, 524
price categories, 513, 517
restaurants, 517–519
safety, 524
shopping, 520
sightseeing, 521–522
sightseeing tours, 524–525
taxes, 525
taxis, 525
telephones, 525
tipping, 525
transportation, 522–523, 525
visitor information, 525
Saba Marine Park, 522
Saba Museum, 522
Safety, 871
Sage Mountain National Park, 194
Sailing. ☞ Also Boating

Anguilla, 46
Bonaire, 161
British Virgin Islands, 188, 201
Curaçao, 254
Dominica, 283
Dominican Republic, 314
Grenada, 349–350
the Grenadines, 683, 688, 693
Guadeloupe, 382
Martinique, 454
Puerto Rico, 490
St. Barthélemy, 538–539
St. Lucia, 612
St. Maarten/St. Martin, 648
St. Vincent, 651
Turks and Caicos Islands, 750
U.S. Virgin Islands, 779–780, 807, 825
St. Andrew's Presbyterian Church, 358
St. Barthélemy, 526–547
beaches, 538
business hours, 543
electricity, 544
emergencies, 544–545
festivals and seasonal events, 545
health issues, 545
holidays, 545
language, 545
lodging, 527–529, 532–534
mail and shipping, 545
money matters, 545–546
nightlife, 541
outdoor activities and sports, 538–539
passports and visas, 546
price categories, 528, 535
restaurants, 534–538
safety, 546
shopping, 539–541
sightseeing, 541–542
sightseeing tours, 546
taxes, 546
taxis, 546
telephones, 546–547
tipping, 547
transportation, 543–545, 547
visitor information, 547
St-Claude, Guadeloupe, 390
St. Croix, 796–797, 800–815, 831–842. ☞ Also U.S. Virgin Islands
St. Croix Aquarium, 812
St. Croix Leap, 815
St. Eustatius, 548–559
beaches, 553–554
business hours, 557
electricity, 557
emergencies, 557–558
etiquette and behavior, 558
festivals and seasonal events, 558
holidays, 558
language, 558
lodging, 549, 552
mail and shipping, 558
money matters, 558

nightlife, 555
outdoor activities and sports, 554–555
passports and visas, 558
price categories, 549, 552
restaurants, 552–553
safety, 558–559
shopping, 555
sightseeing, 555–557
sightseeing tours, 559
taxes, 559
taxis, 559
telephones, 559
tipping, 559
transportation, 557
visitor information, 559
St. Eustatius Historical Foundation Museum, 556
St-François, Guadeloupe, 388
St. George Village Botanical Gardens, 815
St. George's, Grenada, 357–358
St. George's Anglican Church (Grenada), 358
St. George's Anglican Church (St. Kitts), 575
St. George's Cathedral, 676
St. George's Harbour, 357
St. George's Methodist Church, 358
St. George's Roman Catholic Church, 358
St. George's University, 356
St. Giles Island, 729
St. James (cathedral), 432
St-Jean, St. Barthélemy, 542
St. John, 815–818, 820–842. ☞ Also U.S. Virgin Islands
St. John's, Antigua, 76–77
St. John's Church (Nevis), 591
St. Kitts, 560–561, 564–576, 591–597
beaches, 570–571
business hours, 592
electricity, 593
emergencies, 593
eitquette and behavior, 593
festivals and seasonal events, 593
health issues, 594
holidays, 594
language, 594
lodging, 561, 564–567
mail and shipping, 594
money matters, 594
nightlife, 575
outdoor activities and sports, 571–573
passports and visas, 594
price categories, 564, 568
restaurants, 567–570
safety, 594
shopping, 573–574
sightseeing, 574–576
sightseeing tours, 594–596

taxes, 596
taxis, 596
telephones, 596
tipping, 596
transportation, 591–593, 597
visitor information, 597
St-Louis Cathedral, 460
St. Lucia, 598–632
beaches, 612
business hours, 625
children, attractions for, 620,
   621, 622, 623
electricity, 626
embassies, 626
emergencies, 626–627
etiquette and behavior, 627
festivals and seasonal events,
   627
health issues, 627–628
holidays, 628
language, 628
lodging, 599, 602–608
mail and shipping, 628
money matters, 628–629
nightlife and the arts, 618–619
outdoor activities and sports,
   612–615
passports and visas, 629
price categories, 599, 609
restaurants, 608–611
safety, 629
shopping, 615–618
sightseeing, 619–624
sightseeing tours, 629–631
taxes, 631
taxis, 631
telephones, 631
tipping, 631
transportation, 624–626, 631–
   632
visitor information, 632
St. Lucia National Rain
  Forest, 623
St. Maarten/St. Martin, 633–
  661
beaches, 646–647
business hours, 656–657
electricity, 657
emergencies, 657
etiquette and behavior, 657
festivals and seasonal events,
   658
health issues, 658
holidays, 658
language, 658
lodging, 633–635, 638–642
mail and shipping, 658
money matters, 658–659
nightlife, 652–653
outdoor activities and sports,
   648–651
passports and visas, 659
price categories, 634, 642
restaurants, 642–646
safety, 659
shopping, 651–652
sightseeing, 653–655
sightseeing tours, 659
taxes, 659–660

taxis, 660
telephones, 660
tipping, 660
transportation, 655–656, 657,
   660–661
visitor information, 661
St. Mary's Cathedral of the
  Assumption, 676
St. Michael's Cathedral, 137
St. Nicholas Abbey (great
  house), 140
St. Patrick's Roman Catholic
  Church, 814
St. Paul's Anglican Church,
  814
St. Paul's Church, 75
St. Peter's Church, 76
St-Pierre, Martinique, 453,
  462–463
St. Thomas, 766–777, 770–
  789, 791–796, 831–842.
  ☞ Also U.S. Virgin
  Islands
St. Thomas Anglican Church
  (Nevis), 591
St. Vincent and the
  Grenadines, 662–701
beaches, 671, 683, 687, 689,
   690, 693
business hours, 695
electricity, 696
emergencies, 696–697
etiquette and behavior, 697
festivals and seasonal events,
   697
health issues, 697–698
holidays, 698
language, 698
lodging, 664–665, 668–669,
   677, 680–681, 686–687,
   688, 689–690, 691,
   692–693
mail and shipping, 698
money matters, 698–699
nightlife, 673–674, 687
outdoor activities and sports,
   671–673, 683–684, 687,
   688, 690–691, 693
passports and visas, 699
price categories, 664, 669
restaurants, 669–671, 681–
   683, 686–687, 688, 689–
   690, 691, 692
safety, 699
shopping, 673, 684
sightseeing, 674–677, 685
sightseeing tours, 699
taxes, 700
taxis, 700
telephones, 700
tipping, 700
transportation, 693–696
visitor information, 700
Ste-Anne, Guadeloupe, 388
Ste-Anne, Martinique, 448,
  453, 462
Ste-Luce, Martinique, 462
Ste-Marie, Martinique, 462
Ste-Rose, Guadeloupe, 390

Salina Mathijs (salt pad),
  169
Salt Cay, 743–744
Salt flats, 166–167
Salt River Bay National
  Historical Park and
  Ecological Preserve, 813–
  814
Sam Lord's Castle, 138–139
Samaná, Dominican Republic,
  306, 312, 327
San Cristóbal (fortress),
  498
San Germán, Puerto Rico,
  503
San Juan, Puerto Rico, 474–
  475, 478, 486–487, 498–
  500
San Nicolas, Aruba, 105
San Pedro de Macoris,
  Dominican Republic, 326
Sandy Ground, Anguilla, 42–
  43, 49
Sandy Island, Grenada, 359
Santiago de los Caballeros,
  Dominican Republic, 328
Santo Domingo, Dominican
  Republic, 299, 303, 309–
  311, 317, 320–321, 323–
  325
Sari Sari Falls, 290
Saut Babin (waterfall), 458
Savan, St. Thomas, 793
Scale House, 812
Scarborough, Tobago, 729
Scharloo, Curaçao, 261
Schoelcher, Martinique, 463
Scot's Kirk, 676
Scuba diving, 862–863
  Anguilla, 46
  Antigua, 70
  Aruba, 97–98
  Barbados, 129–130
  Bonaire, 161–163
  British Virgin Islands, 188–
   189, 201
  Cayman Islands, 228–229,
   234, 236–237
  Curaçao, 254–255
  Dominica, 283–284
  Dominican Republic, 315–316
  Grenada, 351–352
  the Grenadines, 683–684,
   687, 691, 693
  Guadeloupe, 383
  Jamaica, 421–422
  Martinique, 455
  Nevis, 586
  Puerto Rico, 491–492
  Saba, 519–520
  St. Barthélemy, 539
  St. Eustatius, 554–555
  St. Kitts, 572
  St. Lucia, 614
  St. Maarten/St. Martin, 649
  St. Vincent, 672–673
  Tobago, 727

Turks and Caicos Islands, 742, 743–744, 751
U.S. Virgin Islands, 781, 807–808, 826
Sea excursions
Anguilla, 46–47
Barbados, 130–131
Guadeloupe, 383
St. Lucia, 614
St. Maarten/St. Martin, 649–650
U.S. Virgin Islands, 781
Sea kayaking. ☞ See Kayaking
Sendall Tunnel, 358
Senior citizens, tips for, 821
Senior Curaçao Liqueur Distillery, 264
Seroe Largu, Bonaire, 168
Seven Arches Museum, 793
Shaw Park Botanical Gardens, 430–431
Shirley Heights, Antigua, 77
Shopping, 871
Anguilla, 47–48
Antigua, 70–73
Aruba, 98–100
Barbados, 132–134
Bonaire, 164–165
British Virgin Islands, 190–192, 201–202, 207–208
Cayman Islands, 229–230
Curaçao, 255–257
Dominica, 284–286
Dominican Republic, 316–318
Grenada, 352–354
the Grenadines, 684
Guadeloupe, 384–385
Jamaica, 422–424
Martinique, 456–457
Nevis, 587–588
Puerto Rico, 493–494
Saba, 520
St. Barthélemy, 539–541
St. Eustatius, 555
St. Kitts, 573–574
St. Lucia, 615–617
St. Maarten/St. Martin, 651–652
St. Vincent, 673
Tobago, 728
Trinidad, 711–713
Turks and Caicos Islands, 751–752
U.S. Virgin Islands, 782–788, 808–810, 826–829
Sint Maarten Museum, 655
Skyworld, 194
Slave huts, 167
Snorkeling
Aruba, 97–98
Barbados, 129–130
Bonaire, 163
British Virgin Islands, 188–189, 201
Cayman Islands, 228–229, 234, 236–237
Curaçao, 254–255
Dominica, 283–284

Grenada, 351–352
the Grenadines, 683–684, 687, 691, 693
Jamaica, 421–422
Martinique, 455
Nevis, 586
Puerto Rico, 491–492
Saba, 519–520
St. Eustatius, 554–555
St. Kitts, 572
St. Lucia, 614
St. Maarten/St. Martin, 649
St. Vincent, 672–673
Tobago, 727
Turks and Caicos Islands, 742, 743–744, 751
U.S. Virgin Islands, 781, 807–808, 826
Soccer
Curaçao, 255
St. Eustatius, 555
St. Lucia, 615
Softball, 190
Sosua, Dominican Republic, 327
Soufrière, Dominica, 291
Soufrière, St. Lucia, 606–608, 611, 622–624
South Caicos, Turks and Caicos Islands, 755–756
South Hill, Anguilla, 42–43
Spanish Town, British Virgin Islands, 203
Spanish Town, Jamaica, 432
Spelunking, 234
Speyside, Tobago, 729
Sports. ☞ See Outdoor activities and sports under specific islands
Sports centers, 455
Squash
Antigua, 70
Barbados, 131
Cayman Islands, 229
Martinique, 455
St. Lucia, 615
Stargazing, 781
Station Thermale de Ravine Chaude René Toribio (spa), 390
Steeple Building, 812
Student travel, 871–872
Submarine rides
U.S. Virgin Islands, 782
Sulphur springs
Dominica, 289
St. Lucia, 623–624
Sun Valley (plantation), 430–431
Sunbury Plantation House & Museum, 139
Surfing
Barbados, 131
Puerto Rico, 492
Swimming, 284
Symbols and icons, 876
Synagogue of Beracha Veshalom Vegmiluth Hasidim, 793

Synagogues
Barbados, 136
Curaçao, 260–261
Puerto Rico, 492
St. Eustatius, 556
U.S. Virgin Islands, 793

T

Teatro Nacional, 325
Teatro Tapia, 498
Telephones, 872. ☞ Also under specific islands
Tennis
Anguilla, 47
Antigua, 70
Aruba, 98
Barbados, 131
Bonaire, 163–164
British Virgin Islands, 189
Cayman Islands, 229
Curaçao, 255
Dominican Republic, 316
Grenada, 352
the Grenadines, 684
Guadeloupe, 383
Jamaica, 422
Martinique, 455
Nevis, 586–587
Puerto Rico, 492
St. Barthélemy, 539
St. Kitts, 572
St. Lucia, 615
St. Maarten/St. Martin, 650
Tobago, 727–728
Trinidad, 711
Turks and Caicos Islands, 751
U.S. Virgin Islands, 782, 808, 826
Terre-de-Haut, Guadeloupe, 391
Theater. ☞ See Nightlife and the arts under specific islands
Tillett Gardens, 795
Time zones, 872
Timing the trip, 874–875
TiTrou Gorge, 289–290
Tobago, 702–703, 717–735. ☞ Also Trinidad and Tobago
Tobago Museum, 729
Toiny coast, 542
Tomb of the Carib Indians, 462
Torre del Homenaje (Tower of Homage), 325
Tortola, 178–179, 182–194, 210–215. ☞ Also British Virgin Islands
Tours and packages, 872–873
Trafalgar Falls, 290
Travel agencies, 873–874
disabilities and accessibility, 861–862
for gay and lesbian travelers, 864
Traveler's checks, 869

Trinidad and Tobago, *702–735*
beaches, 710–711, 725–726
business hours, 730–731
electricity, 731
embassies, 731
emergencies, 732
etiquette and behavior, 732
festivals and seasonal events, 732
health issues, 732
holidays, 732
language, 732
lodging, 703, 706–707, 717, 720–722
mail and shipping, 733
money matters, 733
nightlife and the arts, 713–715, 728
outdoor activities and sports, 711, 726–728
passports and visas, 733
price categories, 703, 708
restaurants, 708–710, 722–724
safety, 733
shopping, 711–713, 728
sightseeing, 715–716, 728–729
sightseeing tours, 733–734
taxes, 734
taxis, 734
telephones, 734–735
tipping, 735
transportation, 730, 731
visitor information, 735
Tropical Research Station, *501*
Turks and Caicos Islands, *736–760*
beaches, 741–742, 743, 750, 754, 755
business hours, 757
electricity, 757
emergencies, 757
etiquette and behavior, 758
holidays, 758
language, 758
lodging, 737, 740, 743, 744–748, 752–755
mail and shipping, 758
money matters, 758
nightlife, 742, 752
outdoor activities and sports, 742, 743–744, 750–751
passports and visas, 758
price categories, 737, 741
restaurants, 741, 748–750
safety, 758–759
shopping, 751–752
sightseeing, 742–743, 744, 752, 754, 755–756
sightseeing tours, 759
taxes, 759
taxis, 759
telephones, 759
transportation, 756–757
visitor information, 759–760

Turks & Caicos National Museum, *742–743*
Turtle Farm, *231*
Tyrol Cot Heritage Village, *139*
Tyrrel Bay, Grenada, *359*

U

U.K., tips for travelers from, *859, 870*
U.S. Government travel information, *874*
U.S. Post Office (St. Thomas), *793*
UNESCO World Heritage Site, *289–290*
Union Island, the Grenadines, *692–693*
United States Virgin Islands, *761–842*
beaches, 778–779, 805–806, 824–825
business hours, 833
children, attractions for, 791, 793, 794–795, 814
electricity, 835
emergencies, 835
etiquette and behavior, 835
festivals and seasonal events, 835–836
health issues, 836
holidays, 836–837
language, 837
lodging, 767–774, 796–797, 800–803, 816–817, 820–821
mail and shipping, 837
money matters, 837–838
nightlife and the arts, 788, 810–811, 829
outdoor activities and sports, 779–782, 806–808, 825–826
passports and visas, 838
price categories, 770, 775
restaurants, 774–778, 803–805, 821–824
shopping, 782–788, 808–810, 826–829
sightseeing, 788–790, 791–796, 811–815, 829–831
sightseeing tours, 838–840
taxes, 840
taxis, 840–841
telephones, 841
tipping, 841
transportation, 831–835, 841–842
visitor information, 842
Universidad de Puerto Rico, *499–500*

V

The Valley, Anguilla, *43–44*
Valley of Desolation, *289*
Vernou, Guadeloupe, *390*
Vieques Island, Puerto Rico, *483*

Vieux Fort, Guadeloupe, *391*
Vieux-Habitants, Guadeloupe, *391*
Villa Beach, St. Vincent, *665, 668, 670–671*
Villa rentals. ☞ *See* Apartment and villa rentals; Condominiums and villas
Virgin Gorda, British Virgin Islands, *194–195, 198–203, 210–215*
Virgin Gorda Peak National Park, *203*
Virgin Islands. ☞ *See* British Virgin Islands; U. S. Virgin Islands
Virgin Islands Museum, *791*
Virgin Islands National Park Headquarters, *796*
Visas, *870*
Visitor information, *874.* ☞ *Also under specific islands*
Volcanoes, *390, 461, 541, 556, 623–624, 677*

W

Wallblake House, *49–50*
Wallilabou Bay, St. Vincent, *677*
Warden's Place (plantation), *50*
Washington/Slagbaai National Park, *168–169*
Water Island, St. Thomas, *794*
Waterfalls
Dominica, 289–290
Grenada, 355–356
Guadeloupe, 389, 390
Jamaica, 430
Martinique, 458
St. Lucia, 622
St. Vincent, 675
Waterskiing
Bonaire, 164
St. Eustatius, 555
St. Maarten/St. Martin, 650
Turks and Caicos Islands, 751
Weather information, *875*
Web sites, *874*
Weibel Museum, *794*
Welchman Hall Gully, *141*
West Caicos, Turks and Caicos Islands, *744*
West End Salt Pond, *815*
West End, Anguilla, *41–42*
Whale-watching, *284*
Whaling Museum, *685*
Whaling Station, *685*
Wildlife reserves. ☞ *See* Nature reserves
Willemstad, Curaçao, *258–261*
Willemstoren Lighthouse, *167*

Windsurfing
Antigua, 70
Aruba, 98
Barbados, 131–132
Bonaire, 164
British Virgin Islands, 190, 201
Cayman Islands, 229
Curaçao, 254
Dominica, 284
Dominican Republic, 316

Guadeloupe, 383
Nevis, 587
St. Barthélemy, 539
St. Kitts, 572–573
St. Lucia, 615
St. Maarten/St. Martin, 650–651
Turks and Caicos Islands, 751
U.S. Virgin Islands, 782, 808, 826
Windwardside, Saba, *522*

Y
York House (Parliament and Supreme Court), *358*

Z
Zoos
Dominican Republic, 324
Puerto Rico, 500
Trinidad, 717

NOTES

ABOUT OUR WRITERS

The more you know before you go, the better your trip will be. The island's most fascinating small museum (or its best duty-free shop or most authentic creole restaurant) could be just around the corner from your hotel, but if you don't know it's there, it might as well be on the other side of the globe. "That's where this book comes in. It's a great step toward making sure your next trip lives up to your expectations. As you plan, check out the Web as well. Guidebooks have been helping smart travelers find the special places for years; the Web is one more tool. Whatever reference you consult, be savvy about what you read, and always consider the source. Images and language can be massaged to make places appear better than they are. And one traveler's quaint is another's grimy. Here at Fodor's, and at our on-line arm, Fodors.com, our focus is on providing you with information that's not only useful but accurate and on target. Every day Fodor's editors put enormous effort into getting things right, beginning with the search for the right contributors—people who have objective judgment, broad travel experience, and the writing ability to put their insights into words. There's no substitute for advice from a like-minded friend who has just come back from where you're going, but our writers, having seen all corners of the Caribbean, are the next best thing. They're the kind of people you'd poll for tips yourself if you knew them.

Pamela Acheson spent 18 years in New York City as a publishing executive before heading south to divide her time between Florida and the Caribbean. She writes extensively about both areas and is a regular contributor to *Travel & Leisure, Caribbean Travel & Life, Fodor's Florida, Fodor's Walt Disney World,* and *Fodor's U.S. and British Virgin Islands.* She's the author of *The Best of the British Virgin Islands, The Best of St. Thomas and St. John, The Best of the Bahamas, The Best Romantic Escapes in Florida* (with her husband, Richard Myers), and *More of the Best Romantic Escapes in Florida.*

Carla Armour, a native Dominican, has worked in the island's tourism industry for more than 25 years and has traveled throughout the Caribbean. A natural artist, Carla studied at the Parsons School of Design and is one of Dominica's foremost painters and writers. She runs her own art gallery and is the president of the island's Society for Historic Architectural Preservation and Enhancement and vice president of the Dominica Writers' Guild. She hopes that her work on the Dominica chapter will enable you to have an authentic island experience when you visit the slice of paradise that she calls home.

St. Thomas–based writer and dietitian **Carol M. Bareuther** publishes two weekly columns on food, cooking, and nutrition in the *Virgin Islands Daily News* and serves as the USVI stringer for the Reuters News Service International. She also writes about sports and travel for *Islands' Nautical Scene, All At Sea, Southern Boating, Caribbean Travel & Life,* and other publications. She's the author of two books, *Sports Fishing in the Virgin Islands* and *Virgin Islands Cooking.*

Although a native of the Windy City (Chicago, Illinois), **Kathy Borsuk** now enjoys the much-warmer trade winds of the Turks and Caicos Islands. For the last seven years, she has served as managing editor of *Times of the Islands* magazine, a quarterly publication covering the stunning natural resources, fascinating history, interesting personalities, and varied hotel and restaurant choices in the Turks and Caicos. Kathy wouldn't trade her job for anything.

New York–based **Karen W. Bressler** rolled up her veteran travel writer's sleeves and updated the ABC islands chapters. In addition to having written several books and having coauthored the new *Fodor's Pocket Guide to Aruba,* Karen has contributed to *Condé Nast Traveler, Bridal Guide, Honeymoon,* and *Elegant Bride,* magazines and is the Caribbean correspondent for Condé Nast's on-line travel publication.

Suzanne Gordon followed her bliss and moved to Nevis four years ago, leaving behind a career with the *Philadelphia Inquirer,* to travel and write about the islands. She contributes to *Caribbean Travel & Life,* Reuters News Service, *Latitudes,* the *American Journalism Review,* and other publications. She's also completing a guide to architecture in the Caribbean and is involved in historic preservation projects throughout the islands. Her goal is never to see snow again.

Lynda Lohr is a veteran mainland and USVI photojournalist who has lived in St. John since 1984. She's the St. Croix bureau chief for the St. Thomas–based *V.I. Daily News* and contributes regularly to national, regional, and local magazines, newspapers, and Web sites. She, her significant other, and their two cats recently moved into their new home-with-a-view at Ajax Peak. Although they're still building the house, it's finished enough to provide protection from any hurricanes that blow their way.

Friends of **Elise Meyer,** who updated the St. Barths chapter, often joke that her middle name is "Let's Go." In addition to being an enthusiastic traveler, art historian, independent curator, Internet enterpreneur, event planner, architectural consultant, and cookbook writer, Elise has contributed articles to myriad newspapers, magazines, and Web sites. She lives in Connecticut with her husband and two teenage children who, luckily, share her passion for adventure.

JoAnn Milivojevic is a freelance writer and photographer living in Chicago. A former television producer, she's produced videos in the Cayman Islands and on St. Kitts & Nevis. Her travel articles have appeared in publications nationwide, including *Caribbean Travel & Life, Elegant Bride,* and *American Way.* She recently released a CD of her adventure travel experiences titled, "Confessions of a Caribbean Addict: A Woman's Sexy and Sensual Tales of the Tropics."

After honeymooning in Jamaica a dozen years ago, **Paris Permenter** and **John Bigley** decided to specialize in writing about and photographing the Caribbean region. From their home base in Texas, they've also contributed to *Fodor's The Southwest's Best Bed and Breakfasts* and *Fodor's Europe.* They're authors of *Caribbean with Kids, Adventure Guide to the Cayman Islands, Cayman Islands Alive!,* and *Romantic Weekends in the Caribbean,* and many others. Their work has appeared in publications nationwide, and they also edit Lovetripper.com Romantic Travel Magazine.

Vernon O'Reilly-Ramesar is a Canadian who has been living in Trinidad for the last nine years. A broadcaster and journalist, he's worked in radio and television in both Trinidad and Canada. He has come to love the natural treasures of the twin-island republic, spending much of his time hiking in the mountains and exploring the miracles of the rain forest. Vernon updated the Trinidad and Tobago chapter for this edition.

Elise Rosen—who worked on the ABC islands chapters—has been a reporter for The Associated Press in New York and Los Angeles and a news producer for Time Warner's cable station, New York 1. She began her career at a weekly community newspaper in her native Brooklyn; since then, her articles have appeared in publications throughout the United States and as far away as Saudi Arabia. Ms. Rosen also has been an editorial contributor to several books, including *Career Opportunities in Art* and *America's Elite 1000,* not to mention coauthor of the new *Fodor's Pocket Aruba.*

Jordan Simon began his West Indies love affair as a child when his artist mother took him to Haiti. He has since visited nearly every Caribbean speck of land for Fodor's and such publications as *Caribbean Travel & Life, Town & Country, Modern Bride, Diversion, Interval, USAir* magazine, *American Way, The Sunday Journal* newspaper syndicate, *Caribbean World, Travel & Leisure, Art & Antiques,* and *Travelage.* He also contributes to Fodor's *Colorado* and the *USA Today Ski Atlas,* and is the author of *Astronumerology: Your Key to Empowerment Using Stars and Numbers* (coauthor, Pam Bell), among many others.

In 1995, Hurricane Marilyn blew **Eileen Robinson Smith** out of the Caribbean and back to her lakeside home in Charleston, South Carolina. For the previous two years she lived in St. John and wrote the travel section and chef's column for *The Virgin Island Journal.* Before that she lived in St. Thomas, St. Croix, and Tortola, where she was the features editor of *The Virgin Islander.* As a travel editor, she has visited many other Caribbean islands, and her articles on food and travel have appeared in local, regional, and national publications, including *Caribbean Travel & Life*.

Jane Zarem is a freelance writer from Connecticut who travels frequently to the Caribbean. Among the score of islands she has explored, she finds it difficult to pick a favorite—she loves them all. She's a member of the New York Travel Writers' Association and the International Food, Wine & Travel Writers' Association, is editor of *Air Lines* newsletter, and has contributed to numerous Fodor's guides, among them *New England, USA, Cape Cod, Bahamas,* and *Great American Sports and Adventure Vacations*.

Don't Forget to Write

Your experiences—positive and negative—matter to us. If we have missed or misstated something, we want to hear about it. We follow up on all suggestions. Contact the Caribbean editor at editors@fodors.com or c/o Fodor's, 280 Park Avenue, New York, New York 10017. And have a fabulous trip!

Karen Cure
Editorial Director

FODOR'S CARIBBEAN 2002

EDITORS: Bree Scott, Douglas Stallings

Editorial Contributors: Pamela Acheson, Carla Armour, Carol Bareuther, John Bigley, Kathy Borsuk, Karen W. Bressler, Suzanne Gordon, Delinda Karle, Lynda Lohr, Karl Luntta, Elise Meyer, JoAnn Milivojevic, Paris Permenter, Vernon Ramesar, Elise Rosen, Eileen Robinson Smith, Jordan Simon, Jane E. Zarem

Editorial Production: Kristin Milavec

Maps: David Lindroth, *cartographer;* Rebecca Baer and Robert Blake, *map editors*

Design: Fabrizio La Rocca, *creative director;* Guido Caroti, *art director;* Jolie Novak, *senior picture editor;* Melanie Marin, *photo editor*

Cover Design: Pentagram

Production/Manufacturing: Yexenia Markland

COPYRIGHT

Copyright © 2002 by Fodors LLC

Fodor's is a registered trademark of Random House, Inc.

All rights reserved under International and Pan-American Copyright Conventions. Published in the United States by Fodor's Travel Publications, a unit of Fodors LLC, a subsidiary of Random House, Inc., and simultaneously in Canada by Random House of Canada Limited, Toronto. Distributed by Random House, Inc., New York.

No maps, illustrations, or other portions of this book may be reproduced in any form without written permission from the publisher.

ISBN 0–679–00849–7

ISSN 1524-9174

SPECIAL SALES

Fodor's Travel Publications are available at special discounts for bulk purchases for sales promotions or premiums. Special editions, including personalized covers, excerpts of existing guides, and corporate imprints, can be created in large quantities for special needs. For more information, contact your local bookseller or write to Special Markets, Fodor's Travel Publications, 280 Park Ave., New York, NY 10017. Inquiries from Canada should be directed to your local Canadian bookseller or sent to Random House of Canada, Ltd., Marketing Department, 2775 Matheson Boulevard East, Mississauga, Ontario L4W 4P7. Inquiries from the United Kingdom should be sent to Fodor's Travel Publications, 20 Vauxhall Bridge Road, London SW1V 2SA, England.

PRINTED IN THE UNITED STATES OF AMERICA

10 9 8 7 6 5 4 3 2 1

IMPORTANT TIP

Although all prices, opening times, and other details in this book are based on information supplied to us at press time, changes occur all the time in the travel world, and Fodor's cannot accept responsibility for facts that become outdated or for inadvertent errors or omissions. So **always confirm information when it matters,** especially if you're making a detour to visit a specific place.

PHOTOGRAPHY

Corbis: Stephen Frink, *cover (Virgin Gorda, British Virgin Islands).*

Aruba Tourism Authority, *2 bottom right.*

Barbados Tourism Authority, *8A.*

Beaches Turks & Caicos Resort & Spa, *26 top left.*

British Virgin Islands Tourist Board, *27B.*

Brooks LaTouche Photography Ltd., *8C.*

Cap Juluca, *28A.*

Pierre Courtinard, *17 top.*

Curtain Bluff, *30Q.*

Grand Lido Sans Souci: Len Kaufman, *30N.*

Grenada Tourist Board, *3 bottom right.*

J. Horncastle/Turnkey, *8B.*

Hyatt Regency Grand Cayman, *30O.*

Joan Iaconetti, *20A, 20B, 23B.*

The Image Bank: J. du Boisberran, *15.* Andy Caulfield, *19 top.* Angelo Cavalli, *13A, 13 center left, 13B, 19A, 26A, 28B.* Amanda Clement, *17 bottom left.* Gary Cralle, *16 center.* Paolo Curto, *6 center, 6 bottom.* Steve Dunwell, *22B.* Macduff Everton, *24A, 24 bottom right.* Rubens Neves da Rocha Filho, *28G.* Foto World, *7B.* Larry Dale Gordon, *6A.* David W. Hamilton, *9A, 11B.* Lionel Isy-Schwart, *10.* Tom King, *7 bottom right.* Joe McNally, *22C.* Margarette Mead, *28F.* Michael Melford, *12 top, 12 bottom left, 12 bottom right.* Alexandra Michaels, *27C.* Piecework Productions, *20 top right.* John Ramey, *21A.* Guido Alberto Rossi, *11A, 11 bottom left, 14B, 22A.* Joseph Szodzinski, *7A.*

Catherine Karnow, *21B, 21 bottom, 23 top, 24B.*

Bob Krist, *4–5, 14 top, 14A, 16A, 18, 23A, 26 bottom, 28C, 28E, 28I, 30L.*

Carol Lee, *1, 16B, 32.*

Le Plein Soleil, *30P.*

Joe Petrocik, *17A.*

Puerto Rico Tourism: Bob Krist, *2 top left, 3 top left.*

The Ritz-Carlton, *30S.*

Rosewood Resorts, *28D.*

Saba Tourist Office, *19 bottom left.*

St. Kitts and Nevis Department of Tourism, *2 bottom left.*

St. Vincent & the Grenadines Tourist Office, *30R.*

Sea Eye Diving, *3 bottom left.*

Spice Island Beach Resort, *30M.*

Jim Stephens/TIDCO, *25A, 25 bottom left.*

Tourism Corporation Bonaire, *2 top right, 3 top right, 9 center right, 9B.*

U.S. Virgin Islands Division of Tourism, *2 bottom center, 27A;* Lynn Seldon, *27 center left.*

Veni Mangé Restaurant, *30J.*

Jane Watkins, *25 bottom right.*

Wyndham Palmas del Mar, *28H.*

Young Island Resort, *30K.*